Asset Protection S

2007 Edition

Lewis D. Solomon
Theodore Rinehard Professor of Business Law
The George Washington University Law School
Washington, D.C.

Lewis J. Saret
Moore & Bruce, LLP
Washington, D.C.

CCH
a Wolters Kluwer business

ISBN-10: 0-8080-9069-0
ISBN-13: 978-0-8080-9069-4

About the Authors

Lewis D. Solomon is the Theodore Rinehart Professor of Business Law at The George Washington University Law School. He is a graduate of Cornell University and Yale Law School. He served as law clerk to the Honorable Edwin D. Steel, Jr., U.S. District Court, Wilmington, Delaware, and practiced law in New York. He is the author of *Corporate Acquisitions, Mergers, and Divestitures.* He co-authored *Business Workout Strategies, Tax Planning Strategies,* and *Federal Income Taxation: Problems, Cases and Materials,* as well as *Corporations: Law and Policy: Materials and Problems.* He has written numerous law review articles, authored or co-authored three BNA tax management portfolios, and has spoken at continuing legal education programs, including the University of Miami Institute on Estate Planning and the American Law Institute-American Bar Association's "Estate Planning in Depth."

Lewis J. Saret is of Counsel with the law firm of Moore & Bruce, LLP, in Washington, D.C., where he practices in the area of estate and asset protection planning, business transactions, tax and business succession planning for closely held businesses, tax and business transaction planning for start-up businesses, planning for tax-exempt organizations, and international tax and estate planning. He is the former Chair of the Estate and Gift Tax Committee of the Greater Washington Society of CPAs, and the former Vice-Chair of the Asset Protection Planning Committee of the Real Property, Probate and Trust Section of the American Bar Association. He received his B.B.A. from Lamar University, his M.B.A. and Masters in Accounting from Rice University, and his J.D. from the George Washington University School of Law. Books that he has co-authored include *Valuation of Closely Held Businesses: Tax and Legal Issues, and Business Workout Strategies: Tax and Legal Aspects.*

To my wife, Janet
L.D.S.

To my wife, Sy, and my son, Josh
L.J.S.

Summary of Contents

Contents

Chapter 4

Choice of Business Entity: Tax Aspects

Chapter 5

Use of Domestic Trusts

Chapter 6

Use of Foreign Trusts

Chapter 7

Retitling Assets: Concurrent Ownership of Property

Chapter 8

Exempt Property

Chapter 9

Foreign Bank Accounts

Chapter 10

Overview of the Enforcement of IRS Claims

Chapter 11

Overview of Forms

Chapter 12

Choice of Business Entity

Contents

Chapter 13

Choice of Domestic Trusts

Chapter 14

Foreign Trusts

Chapter 15

Foreign Trusts: Forms Required for U.S. Tax Compliance

Preface

Since the original publication of this book, the field of asset protection has evolved to become more mainstream and has received much more attention. However, the more things change the more some things remain the same. Specifically, the objective of this book remains the same, which is to provide authoritative, yet practical and pragmatic guidance to planners creating asset protection plans. The emphasis is on planning. To this end, the authors have highlighted "planning pointers" throughout each chapter to point out planning opportunities and generally to assist the asset protection planner in creating the asset protection plan. Additionally, possible pitfalls are highlighted as "cautions" throughout each chapter to alert the planner to possible trouble spots that he or she should be aware of. Also, the authors have placed checklists in almost every chapter to provide the asset protection planner a means of ensuring that no critical planning issue is overlooked. Finally, examples are generously used throughout the text to illustrate the various principles in concrete and pragmatic terms.

This book is designed to be of use to all professionals involved in the asset protection plan, including attorneys, accountants, and financial planners, among others.

The subjects covered are those that the planner must consider when properly preparing an asset protection plan. Chapter 2 presents a discussion of the fraudulent conveyance concepts that the planner must ensure do not impact the asset protection plan. Chapters 3 and 4 present a discussion of the applicable rules and strategies concerning the planner's choice of an appropriate business entity for a client's business. Chapter 5 presents a discussion of the applicable rules and strategies concerning the planner's use of domestic trusts as part of the asset protection plan. Chapter 6 presents a discussion of the applicable rules and strategies concerning the planner's use of foreign trusts as part of the asset protection plan. Chapter 7 presents a discussion of the rules and strategies applicable to retitling assets into various forms of concurrent ownership. Chapter 8 presents a discussion of the rules and strategies applicable to exemption planning, where the planner takes advantage of state exemption provisions. Chapter 9 presents a discussion of the compliance rules concerning foreign bank accounts that the planner must be aware of if he or she uses such foreign trusts. Chapter 10 presents an overview of the IRS enforcement of its tax claims.

The objective of Chapters 11-15 is to provide forms that planners may use to effect asset protection plans and to provide planners with authoritative, yet practical and pragmatic guidance concerning the use of such forms. The accompanying disk provides the forms in a readily usable format. Instructions for the disk's installation and the retrieval of the forms can be found at the end of this book.

The authors have designed the forms to provide maximum asset protection with the greatest ease of use for planners. Chapter 12 provides forms that planners will use when creating business entities as part of the asset protection plan. These forms include, among others, forms to create family limited partnerships and limited liability companies. Chapter 13 provides forms that planners will use when creating domestic trusts as part of the asset protection plan. Such forms include, among others, forms to create revocable and irrevocable trusts, irrevocable life insurance trusts, charitable remainder trusts, spendthrift trust clauses, and discretionary trust clauses. Chapter 14 provides forms that planners may use when creating foreign trusts. Chapter 15 includes sample forms required for United States tax compliance when using foreign trusts.

A comprehensive table of contents precedes most of the forms contained in Chapters 11-15 to ensure that the user has included all required clauses. Most chapters also include checklists to ensure that planners properly use such forms. Also, the forms are designed with a minimum of blanks to make them easier to use. Finally, this volume is extensively cross referenced to the earlier chapters, which provide an exhaustive analysis of the legal and tax implications of each asset protection strategy implemented by the forms in this book.

Appendix A provides the entire text of the Cook Islands' International Trusts Act of 1984, as subsequently amended. Appendix B presents the entire text of the Cayman Islands statute, The Confidential Relationships (Preservation) Law (Law 16 of 1976). Appendix C presents the entire text of the Cayman Islands statute, The Confidential Relationships (Preservation) (Amendment) Law, 1979, (Law 26 of 1979). Appendix D presents the entire text of The Mutual Legal Assistance (United States of America) Law, 1986 (Law 16 of 1986). Appendix E presents the Conveyancing Amendment Act, 1993 (Bermuda), and Appendix F presents The Trusts (Special Provisions) Act 1989 (Bermuda) as amended by The Trusts (Special Provisions) Amendment Act 1998. Appendixes G and H present the Alaska Trust Statute and the Delaware Trust Statute, respectively. And finally, Appendix I presents the Trustee Act 1975 (as amended by the Trustee Amendment Act 1999, effective 10 July 1999) (Bermuda).

Washington, D.C.
October 2006

LEWIS D. SOLOMON
LEWIS J. SARET

Short Reference List

Short Reference	Full Reference
BSA	Bank Secrecy Act, Pub. L. No. 91-508, 84 Stat. 1114-1124 (1970) (codified at scattered sections of 12 U.S.C., 18 U.S.C., 31 U.S.C.)
Cayman Island MLAT	Treaty Relating to Mutual Legal Assistance in Criminal Matters, July 3, 1986, United States-United Kingdom (on behalf of the Cayman Islands)
CRAT	charitable remainder annuity trust
CRP (Amendment) Law	Confidential Relationships (Preservation) (Amendment) Law, 1979 (Law 26 of 1979)
CRP Law	Confidential Relationships (Preservation) Law, 1976 (Law 16 of 1976)
CRT	charitable remainder trust
CRU	charitable remainder unitrust
FLP	Family Limited Partnership
GST	generation-skipping transfer
IRC	Internal Revenue Code
LLC	limited liability company
LLP	Limited Liability Partnership
MLAL	Mutual Legal Assistance (United States of America) Law, 1986 (Law 16 of 1986)
MLCA	Money Laundering Control Act of 1986, Pub. L. No. 99-570, 100 Stat. 3207-18
OAPT	offshore asset protection trust
RULPA	Revised Uniform Limited Partnership Act
UFCA	Uniform Fraudulent Conveyances Act
UFTA	Uniform Fraudulent Transfers Act
ULPA	Uniform Limited Partnership Act
UPA	Uniform Partnership Act

1

Introduction

§1.01 OVERVIEW OF ASSET PROTECTION

Financial and legal planners have engaged in asset protection planning for many years. For example, planners have routinely advised clients to use the corporate form of business to take advantage of that form's limited liability. Today, the litigation explosion has given added impetus to asset protection planning. More specifically, plaintiffs and their lawyers not only target the very wealthy but also professionals and others who would not consider themselves very wealthy.

Asset protection planners have several tools they may use to protect their client's assets and, simultaneously, achieve the client's estate planning objectives. The key to the planner's success is fully understanding the key characteristics of different asset protection tools including such tool's limitations and possibilities, and in fully understanding key strategies that can be used in conjunction with various asset protection tools.

One of the first things the planner must examine as part of the proposed asset protection plan is whether any part of the plan will constitute a fraudulent conveyance. If any part of the asset protection plan does constitute a fraudulent conveyance, the client's creditors may reach the transferred property. Consequently, the plan will not protect such assets. Chapter 2 discusses fraudulent conveyance concepts as they apply to asset protection plans and provides planners with the necessary tools to evaluate whether any part of a proposed asset protection plan will constitute a fraudulent conveyance.

A client's business operation merits special attention because it may generate liabilities that may impact both the business operation itself plus other of the client's assets. In contrast, other assets such as furniture and stocks and bonds generally do not generate liabilities that may reach other assets of their owners. Because of this characteristic, the planner must give special attention to the choice of entity the client uses for his/her business operation. Here, the planner's primary objectives will be (1) to limit the reach of liabilities arising out of the business operation, and (2) to protect the assets of the business operation from the reach of the client's nonbusiness creditors. Chapter 3 discusses asset protection aspects of choice of business entity. Specifically, it discusses asset protection aspects of (1) corporations, (2) limited partnerships, including family limited partnerships, and (3) limited liability companies. Also, it provides the planner with tools to analyze choice of entity, including a choice of entity worksheet, a chart comparing asset protection aspects of different entity forms, and a checklist of choice of entity forms.

The planner, when evaluating choice of entity, must also consider the associated tax consequences of different entity forms. More specifically, the planner must balance any limited liability benefits of a particular entity form against the tax consequences that flow from choosing that particular entity form. Chapter 4 discusses the tax consequences that flow from choosing different entity forms for the client's business operations.

§ 1.02 OVERVIEW OF ASSET PROTECTION TOOLS

Trusts constitute another extremely useful asset protection tool. Furthermore, not only may trusts provide asset protection in their own right, they frequently may be used to complement other asset protection tools. For example, a client may incorporate a business to limit the reach of business liabilities to assets of the business and then place the corporate stock into a trust to protect the business from the owner's other creditors. Chapters 5 and 6 discuss trusts and how they may be used as part of an asset protection plan. Chapter 5 discusses (1) the creditor's rights against various trust parties, and (2) the use of revocable trusts, irrevocable trusts, spendthrift trusts, discretionary trusts, support trusts, and charitable remainder trusts as part of the asset protection plan. This chapter also provides strategies for the asset protection plan suggesting ways the planner may best use domestic trusts as part of the asset protection plan. Chapter 6 discusses a special type of trust, namely offshore asset protection trusts. These are trusts that the settlor establishes in foreign jurisdictions that have enacted laws that protect trust assets to a greater extent than United States law does. When properly used, offshore asset protection trusts may provide a greater degree of asset protection than any other type of trust. For example, the jurisdiction chosen often specifically does not recognize foreign judgments. This would prevent the situs jurisdiction from instantly recognizing judgments entered against the client in the United States. However, the "flip side" to this benefit is that offshore asset protection trusts are more expensive to establish and maintain than domestic trusts. Both Chapter 5 and Chapter 6 provide checklists of issues the planner should consider as well as cost-benefit worksheets to assist the planner when analyzing different types of trusts.

The planner may also use certain forms of concurrent ownership as part of the asset protection plan. Chapter 7 discusses three basic forms of concurrent property ownership. These include tenancies by the entirety, tenancies in common, and joint tenancies. Chapter 7 also discusses the estate and gift tax consequences of using concurrent ownership of property as part of the asset protection plan.

Every state, as well as the federal government, both inside and outside the Bankruptcy Code, exempts certain categories of property from the reach of creditors. These exemptions represent a legislative judgment that the benefits of preserving exempt property for the debtor exceed the costs of not allowing creditors to reach such property to satisfy valid debts. These exemptions are valuable tools for the asset protection planner who may protect a substantial portion of client wealth by moving such wealth into exempt assets. Chapter 8 discusses using exemptions as part of the asset protection plan. Specifically, it discusses the homestead exemption, the life insurance exemption, the federal ERISA qualified retirement plan exemption, certain other income exemptions, and the interaction between state law exemptions and federal bankruptcy law exemptions. Finally, it discusses certain limits on exemption planning that the planner must consider.

The planner may want to use foreign bank accounts as part of the asset protection plan. Such bank accounts raise certain asset protection and regulatory compliance issues, which Chapter 9 addresses. Specifically, Chapter 9 provides the planner with the necessary information to determine:

1. Whether the Bank Secrecy Act will apply to the plan, and if so, what the client must do to comply with its requirements;
2. Whether the Money Laundering Control Act will apply to the plan, and if so, what the client must do to comply with its requirements;
3. How much confidentiality foreign laws may provide to United States clients; and
4. What the ability is of United States plaintiffs to pierce foreign bank secrecy laws.

Finally, the planner must understand how the IRS enforces its tax claims to ensure that the asset protection plan adequately protects client property against IRS tax claims. Chapter 10 provides the planner with an overview of enforcement of IRS claims. Specifically, it discusses:

1. How tax liens arise;
2. How long tax liens last;
3. What the scope of tax liens is;
4. What methods the IRS uses to enforce tax liens;
5. How estate and gift tax liens differ from general tax liens;
6. When and how the IRS makes tax levies;
7. What property the IRS may levy against;
8. What limits exist on IRS use of its tax levy power;
9. What happens when taxpayers do not surrender property the IRS levies against; and
10. When the IRS may seize and sell property it has levied against.

§1.03 PRACTICAL APPROACH TO ASSET PROTECTION PLANNING

Asset protection planning involves many complex legal planning and compliance issues. To help the planner avoid missteps, these sections provide a detailed approach to asset protection planning that the planner may use when preparing a client's customized asset protection plan.[1]

---

§1.03 [1] *See generally* Santo (Sandy) Bisignano, Jr., Protecting Assets from Overzealous Creditors or an Estate *Planner's Guide to Preservation Planning*, 1987 Annual Notre Dame Est. Plan. Inst. 3-80 to 3-87; Duncan E. Osborne, *New Age Estate Planning: Offshore Trusts*, 27th Annual University of Miami Philip E. Heckerling Inst. on Est. Plan. ch. 17 (1993); Charles M. Bruce, *Foreign Trusts: Protection of Assets, Pre-Immigration and Other*, in Section of Taxation American Bar Association 1993 Meeting Materials (Aug. 1993).

[A] Initial Meeting

At the initial meeting, the planner's goal is to answer client questions; to provide clients with information about asset protection planning and the steps that the client and planner must take to establish and implement an asset protection plan; and to begin the screening or vetting process. Therefore, at the initial meeting, the planner should, among other things:

1. Explore the client's motivations for asset protection planning, and the client's asset and estate planning objectives;
2. Explore whether there are any facts that would disqualify the client as a suitable client, such as existing litigation problems or present insolvency;
3. Discuss with the client the limitations of various asset protection techniques;
4. Require the client to provide, after the initial meeting, information that will enable the planner to corroborate information obtained during the screening process, including the following:
    a. Client's full name, address, telephone numbers; date and place of birth; citizenship, including any special immigrant status; state of residency; Social Security numbers; state and federal income tax returns for the past five years;
    b. Spouse's full name, address, telephone numbers; date and place of birth; citizenship, including any special immigrant status; state of residency; Social Security numbers; state and federal income tax returns for the past five years;
    c. Each child's full name, address, telephone numbers; date and place of birth; citizenship, including any special immigrant status; state of residency; Social Security numbers; whether the child is a natural child or is legally adopted;
    d. Information about each legal dependent not covered by prior questions;
    e. If the client has been married previously, information about prior marriages, amounts of outstanding or continuing alimony, child support, or other family support obligations;
    f. Any pertinent information about the individuals listed in the prior questions that the planner should be aware of;
    g. Whether the client desires to restrict the rights of any of the individuals listed in the prior questions and, if so, the reasons therefor;
    h. Names of at least three references;
    i. Banker's name, address, and telephone numbers and written permission to talk with such person;
    j. Bank account numbers and balances;
    k. Attorney's name, address, and telephone numbers and written permission to talk with such person;
    l. Accountant's name, address, and telephone numbers and written permission to talk with such person;
    m. A resume or curriculum vitae for the client and the client's spouse;

n. The client's and spouse's medical history;

o. Whether the client, the client's spouse, children, or other dependents, or any corporation or other entity of which the client is an officer, director, or significant shareholder, has ever filed bankruptcy, and, if so, the details thereof;

p. Whether the client, the client's spouse, children, or other dependents, or any corporation or other entity of which the client is an officer, director, or significant shareholder, has ever been convicted of any crime, indicted, or been the subject of criminal investigation or any investigation by any federal or state enforcement or regulatory body, government, or agency, and, if so, the details thereof;

q. Whether the IRS or any state tax authority has ever audited the client, and, if so, details of such audit;

r. Whether any actions are presently filed against the client, and, if so, the details thereof;

s. Whether any actions are threatened against the client, and, if so, the details thereof;

t. Whether the client knows of any facts that lead him or her to fear that an action may be instituted against him or her due to past events, and, if so, the details thereof;

u. Whether the client holds a U.S. passport;

v. A listing of each country that the client has visited within the past three years and the number of visits to each country;

w. Whether any foreign country has ever denied the client entry, and, if so, a detailed description thereof;

x. Whether the client or the client's spouse uses or has used different names than the name given to the planner, and, if so, a detailed description thereof;

y. Whether the client or the client's spouse has any financial interest or signatory power over any bank or other financial account outside the United States, and, if so, a detailed description thereof;

z. Whether the client or the client's spouse is under the care of a physician for any problems related to alcohol or drug abuse, and, if so, a detailed description thereof;

aa. Whether the client believes that the client or spouse has any alcohol or drug abuse problem not covered by the prior question, and, if so, a detailed description thereof;

bb. Any other information the client feels the planner should be aware of;

cc. A complete listing of the client's present insurance policies, copies of the past three years' malpractice insurance applications, and a copy of the current malpractice insurance policy; for each life insurance policy, the face amount of coverage, current cash value, issue date of policy, current and past beneficiary designation, and current owner;

dd. Information about the client's interests in pension and profit-sharing plans, including the current vested value, value attributable to employer contributions, value attributable to client contributions, and a copy of the plan document and summary plan description;

ee. Information about the client's debts, including the unpaid amount, copies of relevant documents, and for what purposes the debt proceeds were used;

ff. Information about contingent liabilities; and

gg. Information about potential inheritances.

[B] Retainer Letter

The planner must have the client sign a retainer letter that describes the relationship in detail. Among other things, the retainer letter should clearly state that the planner will screen or vet the client; that the planner reserves the right to terminate the representation if the client does not pass the screening or vetting process; and that the client will pay for the screening or vetting process even if the planner determines that the client has not passed the screening process and therefore will not assist the client with asset protection planning.

[C] Screen Client

The most important step the planner must take is to vet or screen prospective clients. A "bad" client can expose the planner to civil and criminal penalties. For example, planners may be found guilty of civil conspiracy for assisting clients to defraud creditors, or they may be subjected to disciplinary proceedings by their state bar.[2]

More specifically, the planner should require the client to provide the following, in addition to the information previously requested:

1. Audited personal financial statements;

2. Audited financial statements for all entities in which the client is a significant shareholder (*e.g.*, 10-percent interest or more) or of which the client is an

---

[2] *See, e.g.*, Van Royen v. Lacey, 277 A.2d 13 (Md. 1971); McElhanon v. Hing, 728 P.2d 256 (Ariz. 1985), *aff'd in part, vacated in part*, 728 P.2d 273 (Ariz. 1986), *cert. denied*, 481 U.S. 1030 (1987); Fraidin v. Weitzman, 611 A.2d 1046 (Md. 1992), *cert. denied*, 617 F.2d 1055 (1993); Dalton v. Meister, 239 N.W.2d 9 (Wis. 1976); Wolfrich Corp. v. United Services Automobile Ass'n, 149 Cal. App. 3d 1206, 197 Cal. Rptr. 446 (1983); Allen v. The State Bar, 570 P.2d 1226, 1229 (Cal. 1977); United States v. Noske, 117 F.3d 1053 (8th Cir. 1997) (Eighth Circuit affirmed convictions of tax planners, their clients, and their accomplices for conspiracy to defraud government, conspiracy to evade taxes, and tax evasion); *cf.* United States v. Wilson, 118 F.3d 228 (4th Cir. 1997) (U.S. Court of Appeals for the Fourth Circuit reversed district court decision to set aside a jury verdict convicting defendant/attorney of obstructing the administration of internal revenue laws and willfully attempting to evade and defeat the payment of taxes by concealing his client's assets from the IRS, backdating documents, advising his client how to conceal assets, and placing strawmen in corporate positions on his client's behalf). Charles M. Bruce, *Foreign Trusts: Protection of Assets, Pre-Immigration and Other*, in Section of Taxation American Bar Association 1993 Meeting Materials (Aug. 1993). *See also* Annotation, *Right of creditor to recover damages for conspiracy to defraud him of claim*, 11 A.L.R.4th 345 (1982 & Supp. 1995); Annotation, *Excessiveness or inadequacy of punitive damages in cases not involving personal injury or death*, 14 A.L.R.5th 242; Annotation, *Liability in tort for interference with attorney-client relationship*, 90 A.L.R.4th 621; Annotation, *Liability for interference with invalid or unenforceable contract*, 96 A.L.R.3d 1294.

officer, the past five years' tax returns for such entities, the names of such entities' other equity holders, and any contracts between such entities and the client;

3. Certificate of insurance;
4. Affidavits from the client that:

    a. The client is not presently in financial difficulties;
    b. The client lacks knowledge of facts or circumstances that may render him/her liable to future claims stemming from past actions;
    c. The client's motive for establishing an asset protection plan is not to place his/her assets beyond the reach of any party (i) to whom the client is presently liable; (ii) to whom the client owes an existing obligation; (iii) from whom the client is contemplating divorce proceedings, or (iv) who is contemplating any action related to environmental damage;
    d. No current legal proceedings are being prosecuted or contemplated against the client, or, if there are and the maximum amount of the claim is identifiable, that the client will set aside sufficient reserves outside the proposed asset protection plan to cover this liability;
    e. There are no liabilities or contingent liabilities the client has not disclosed on the financial statements that you are requiring be provided to you; and
    f. That the client is not aware of any currently existing facts that might render the client liable to legal proceedings that would result in a claim against his/her assets.

The planner also should run the client's name and the names of any related entities through several databases to check the information the client has supplied. These should include NEXIS/LEXIS®, a credit bureau, and Dun & Bradstreet. If the client is a professional, the planner should check with the applicable state licensing agency to see whether any complaints have been filed against the client. The planner also should check for UCC or other judgment liens against the client.

The planner must examine all the information received from the client in great detail and should carefully consider all risks, exposures, guarantees, and contingent liabilities. The planner should gather information about the client's historical method of doing business and determine his/her reputation in the community. Additionally, unless the planner possesses an expertise in the area of creditors' rights and fraudulent transfers issues, the planner should seek the advice of co-counsel with such expertise. The planner must ensure that the client does not have present creditors, including creditors with unliquidated claims, who will be disadvantaged by the asset protection plan's establishment. When examining information about the client's assets, the planner should pay particular attention to the asset's fair market value, title, location, marital character, and any associated debts or security interests held by others in such assets.

[D]   Correspondence Stating What Planner Has Done and Not Done

A letter makes clear to the client exactly what the planner has done, will do, and will not do. The purpose of this letter is to minimize the liability exposure of the planner by identifying who is responsible for what. This correspondence should, based on prior agreement with the client, assign responsibility for all important steps to a designated professional. For example, continuing tax return compliance should be set forth in this correspondence.

[E]   Opinion Letter of Special Counsel

There may be various aspects on which the planner determines that he or she needs the opinion of special counsel. As already mentioned, this is especially desirable in the area of creditors' rights and fraudulent conveyances.

[F]   Execution of Documents

The planner's next step is to execute the necessary legal documents to effect the asset protection plan. Planners who are not licensed attorneys must retain competent legal counsel with asset protection planning experience. Planners should take great care to ensure that all necessary legal documents are carefully drafted. Even though this may sound simplistic, the planner should undertake the asset protection plan assuming a worst case scenario (*i.e.*, assuming that the client will become a defendant in litigation); therefore, every document should be carefully reviewed. Also, it is advisable for the planner to draft an instruction book or "road map" for the client, explaining how the asset protection plan will work and what the client must do to maintain it. When drafting this, the planner must keep the client in mind and consequently must write it at such a level of sophistication that the client will clearly understand it while simultaneously ensuring that all of the important points are still covered.[3]

[G]   Follow-Up Correspondence Stating What Planner Has Done and Not Done

Follow-up correspondence makes clear to the client exactly what the planner has done and has not done. This repeats to some degree the information contained in the retainer letter and prior correspondence; the purpose of this letter is to minimize the planner's liability exposure by identifying who is responsible for what. This correspondence should, based on prior agreement with the client, assign final responsibility to a designated professional for all important steps that remain unexecuted at the conclusion of the planner's engagement.

---

[3] *See* Charles M. Bruce, *Foreign Trusts: Protection of Assets, Pre-Immigration and Other*, in Section of Taxation American Bar Association 1993 Meeting Materials (Aug. 1993).

§1.04 CIRCULAR 230[1]

[A] Generally

Circular 230, which is located in 31 CFR Part 10, contains rules governing the recognition of attorneys, CPAs, and others representing taxpayers before the IRS. It also prescribes duties and restrictions relating to practice before the IRS and sanctions for violating such regulations, as well as providing rules applicable to disciplinary proceedings. The practical importance is amplified by the American Jobs Creation Act of 2004, which in addition to sanctions, suspension, and disbarment, authorizes the Treasury Department and the IRS to impose penalties against practitioners who violate any provision of Circular 230 and authorizes injunctions to prevent Circular 230 violations.

On December 20, 2004, the Treasury Department published final amendments to Circular 230 dealing with tax shelter opinions. In response to numerous comments from several professional organizations, the IRS and the Treasury Department issued modifications to the final regulations on May 18, 2005, which became effective on June 21, 2005.

Because asset protection planners frequently provide written advice and documents that involve Federal tax issues, Circular 230 will have a significant impact on such planners. Besides establishing new standards for certain types of tax advice and significant penalties for failure to comply with such standards, Circular 230 may also establish a new standard of care in giving tax advice, which may impact planners' liability exposure for professional malpractice.[2]

[B] Overview of Key Provisions of Circular 230

The key provisions of the revised Circular 230, which planners should be aware of, include the following:

- Covered opinions, which are governed by Circular 230, § 10.35;
- Other written advice, which are governed by Circular 230, § 10.37;

---

§1.04 [1] *See generally* Jonathon G. Blattmachr, et al., *Circular 230 Redux: Questions of Validity and Compliance Strategies*, 107 Tax Notes 1533 (June 20, 2005); Louis A. Mezzullo & Ronald D. Aucutt, *Circular 230: Estate Planning Issues, in Planning Techniques for Large Estates*, 1 ALI-ABA Course of Study Materials Course No. SL0078 (Apr. 2006); Mary Ann Mancini, *Circular 230 & Estate Planners: One Year Developments*, in Vermont Bar Association Teleconference Materials (July 11, 2006); Dan W. Holbrook, *Where There's a Will: Imagine the Worst the U.S. Treasury Could Do To Us – They've Done It: Revenge of the IRS: Circular 230 Change Law Practice*, 41 Tenn. B.J. 28 (Aug. 2005); Meah Rothman Tell, *Circular 230: Beware the Jabberwock!*, 80 Fla. Bar J. 39 (Jan. 2006); Susan T. Edlavitch & Brian S. Masterson, *"Best Practices" and Written Advice Standards*, in Representing the Growing Business: Tax, Corporate, Securities, and Accounting Issues, in ALI-ABA Course of Study Materials, Course No. SL0054 (Nov. 2005); Isaac J. Roang, *Current Development 2005-2006: To Disclaim or Not To Disclaim: IRS Circular 230 Requirements for Written Advice*, 19 Geo. J. Legal Ethics 937 (Summer 2006).

[2] Jonathon G. Blattmachr, et al., *Circular 230 Redux: Questions of Validity and Compliance Strategies*, 107 Tax Notes 1533, 1536 (June 20, 2005).

- Best practices, which are set forth in Circular 230, § 10.33; and
- Asset protection planning techniques likely to be impacted by Circular 230.

[C] *Covered Opinions*

[1] Generally

Planners (including attorneys, accountants and enrolled agents)[3] who render a covered opinion must satisfy specific requirements to avoid being sanctioned, suspended or disbarred from practice before the IRS.

The key issues that planners must understand regarding covered opinions include the following:

- What constitutes a covered opinion?
- What requirements does Circular 230 impose for covered opinions?

For purposes of these rules, the principal purpose of a partnership or other entity, investment plan or arrangement, or other plan or arrangement is the avoidance or evasion of any tax imposed by the IRC if that purpose exceeds any other purpose.[4] The principal purpose of a partnership or other entity, investment plan or arrangement, or other plan or arrangement is not to avoid or evade Federal tax if that partnership, entity, plan or arrangement has as its purpose the claiming of tax benefits in a manner consistent with the statute and Congressional purpose.[5] A partnership, entity, plan or arrangement may have a significant purpose of avoidance or evasion even though it does not have the principal purpose of avoidance or evasion under Circular 230, § 10.35(b)(10).

> **Note.** The provision that the principal purpose of certain arrangements is not to avoid or evade Federal tax if that partnership, entity, plan or arrangement has as its purpose the claiming of tax benefits in a manner consistent with the statute and Congressional purpose has been viewed as a safe harbor of sorts.[6] However, it is clearly problematic as it is unclear exactly what qualifies for this "safe harbor."

---

[3] Circular 230, § 10.35(b)(1).

[4] Circular 230, § 10.35(b)(10).

[5] Circular 230, § 10.35(b)(10).

[6] *See, e.g.,* Jonathon G. Blattmachr, et al., *Circular 230 Redux: Questions of Validity and Compliance Strategies,* 107 Tax Notes 1533, 1540 (June 20, 2005).

[2] Definition of Covered Opinion

[a] Generally

A covered opinion consists of written advice (including electronic communications, such as e-mails) by a practitioner concerning one or more Federal tax issues[7] arising from any of the following:

1. A transaction that is the same as or substantially similar to a transaction that, at the time the advice is rendered, the IRS has determined to be a tax avoidance transaction and identified by published guidance as a listed transaction under 26 CFR 1.6011-4(b)(2), generally referred to as a "listed transaction;"
2. Any partnership or other entity, any investment plan or arrangement, or any other plan or arrangement, whose principal purpose is the avoidance or evasion of any federal tax, which is generally referred to as a "tax avoidance transaction," and written advice concerning such tax avoidance transactions are generally referred to as "tax avoidance opinions;" or
3. Any partnership or other entity, any investment plan or arrangement, or any other plan or arrangement, a significant purpose of which is the avoidance or evasion of any federal tax if the written advice:

    a. Is a reliance opinion;
    b. Is a marketed opinion;
    c. Is subject to conditions of confidentiality; or
    d. Is subject to contractual protection.[8]

Planning Pointer. All written advice dealing with significant federal tax issues should be in the form of a covered opinion (*i.e.*, should satisfy the requirements for a covered opinion).[9]

[b] Excluded Advice

Circular 230 excludes the following types of written advice from the definition of "covered opinion."

---

[7] For purposes of covered opinions, a Federal tax issue is a question concerning the Federal tax treatment of an item of income, gain, loss, deduction, or credit, the existence or absence of a taxable transfer of property, or the value of property for Federal tax purposes. Circular 230, § 10.35(b)(3). For this purpose, a Federal tax issue is significant if the IRS has a reasonable basis for a successful challenge and its resolution could have a significant impact, whether beneficial or adverse and under any reasonably foreseeable circumstance, on the overall Federal tax treatment of the transaction(s) or matter(s) addressed in the opinion. Circular 230, § 10.35(b)(3).

[8] Circular 230, § 10.35(b)(2)(i).

[9] Mary Ann Mancini, *Circular 230 & Estate Planners: One Year Developments*, in Vermont Bar Association Teleconference Materials, page 2 (July 11, 2006).

Preliminary written advice.[10]   Written advice provided to a client during the course of an engagement where the practitioner reasonably expects to provide subsequent written advice to the client that satisfies the requirements of this section does not constitute a covered opinion.

Specific enumerated types of written advice.[11]   Written advice, other than advice relating to listed transactions, described above, or relating to transactions whose principal purpose is tax avoidance or evasion, that: (1) concerns the qualification of a qualified plan; (2) is a State or local bond opinion; or (3) is included in documents required to be filed with the Securities and Exchange Commission.

Certain post tax return filing advice.[12]   Written advice prepared for and provided to a taxpayer, solely for use by that taxpayer, after the taxpayer has filed a tax return reflecting the tax benefits of the transaction. However, this exclusion does not apply if the practitioner knows or has reason to know that the taxpayer will rely on such written advice to take a tax return filing position (including an amended return claiming tax benefits not reported on a previously filed return) filed after the date on which the advice is provided to the taxpayer.

In-house counsel.[13]   Written advice provided to an employer by a practitioner in that practitioner's capacity as an employee of that employer solely for purposes of determining the tax liability of the employer.

Negative written advice.[14]   Written advice that does not resolve a Federal tax issue in the taxpayer's favor, unless the advice reaches a conclusion favorable to the taxpayer at any confidence level (*e.g.,* not frivolous, realistic possibility of success, reasonable basis or substantial authority) with respect to that issue. If written advice concerns more than one Federal tax issue, the advice must comply with the requirements for covered opinions for any Federal tax issue not described in the preceding sentence.

Prominent disclosure.   As discussed below, a prominent disclosure may prevent a written statement from constituting a covered opinion by virtue of such statement constituting either a reliance opinion or a marketed opinion. In other words, such a disclosure will prevent the written statement from constituting either a reliance opinion or a marketed opinion, which are two types of covered opinions. For this purpose, an item is prominently disclosed if it is readily apparent to a reader of the written advice. Whether an item is readily apparent will depend on the facts and circumstances surrounding the written advice including, but not limited to, the sophistication of the taxpayer and the length of the written advice. At a minimum, to be prominently disclosed an item must be set forth in a separate section (and not in a footnote) in a typeface that is

---

[10] Circular 230, § 10.35(b)(2)(ii)(A).
[11] Circular 230, § 10.35(b)(2)(ii)(B).
[12] Circular 230, § 10.35(b)(2)(ii)(C).
[13] Circular 230, § 10.35(b)(2)(ii)(D).
[14] Circular 230, § 10.35(b)(2)(ii)(E).

the same size or larger than the typeface of any discussion of the facts or law in the written advice.[15]

[c] Reliance Opinion

As noted above, a reliance opinion will generally constitute a covered opinion. For this purpose, a reliance opinion is written advice that concludes at a confidence level of at least more likely than not (a greater than 50 percent likelihood) that one or more significant Federal tax issues would be resolved in the taxpayer's favor.[16]

Planning Pointer. Written advice, other than for listed and tax avoidance transactions, will not be treated as a reliance opinion if the practitioner prominently discloses that such written advice was not intended or written by the practitioner to be used, and that it cannot be used by the taxpayer, for the purpose of avoiding penalties that may be imposed on the taxpayer.[17] For this purpose, an item is prominently disclosed if it is readily apparent to a reader of the written advice. Whether an item is readily apparent will depend on the facts and circumstances surrounding the written advice including, but not limited to, the sophistication of the taxpayer and the length of the written advice. At a minimum, to be prominently disclosed an item must be set forth in a separate section (and not in a footnote) in a typeface that is the same size or larger than the typeface of any discussion of the facts or law in the written advice.[18]

[d] Marketed Opinion

As noted above, a marketed opinion will generally constitute a covered opinion. Written advice constitutes a marketed opinion if the practitioner knows or should know that such advice will be used or referenced by someone other than the practitioner (or members or associates of, or employees of the practitioner's firm) in promoting, marketing or recommending a partnership or other entity, investment plan or arrangement to one or more taxpayer(s).[19]

Planning Pointer. Written advice, other than for listed and tax avoidance transactions, will not be treated as a marketed opinion if the practitioner prominently discloses that:

---

[15] Circular 230, § 10.35(b)(8).
[16] Circular 230, § 10.35(b)(4)(i).
[17] Circular 230, § 10.35(b)(4)(ii).
[18] Circular 230, § 10.35(b)(8).
[19] Circular 230, § 10.35(b)(5)(i).

    (a)   Such written advice was not intended or written by the practitioner to be used, and that it cannot be used by the taxpayer, for the purpose of avoiding penalties that may be imposed on the taxpayer;

    (b)   The advice was written to support the promotion or marketing of the transaction(s) or matter(s) addressed by the written advice; and

    (c)   The taxpayer should seek advice based on the taxpayer's particular circumstances from an independent tax advisor.[20]

For this purpose, an item is prominently disclosed if it is readily apparent to a reader of the written advice. Whether an item is readily apparent will depend on the facts and circumstances surrounding the written advice including, but not limited to, the sophistication of the taxpayer and the length of the written advice. At a minimum, to be prominently disclosed an item must be set forth in a separate section (and not in a footnote) in a typeface that is the same size or larger than the typeface of any discussion of the facts or law in the written advice.[21]

[e]   Confidentiality Opinion

As noted above, written advice subject to conditions of confidentiality will constitute a covered opinion. For this purpose, written advice will be covered by these provisions if the practitioner imposes on any recipients of the written advice a limitation on disclosure of the tax treatment or tax structure of the transaction and the limitation on disclosure protects the confidentiality of that practitioner's tax strategies, regardless of whether the limitation on disclosure is legally binding.[22] A claim that a transaction is proprietary or exclusive is not a limitation on disclosure if the practitioner confirms to all recipients of the written advice that there is no limitation on disclosure of the tax treatment or tax structure of the transaction, which is the subject of the written advice.

[f]   Contractual Protection Opinion

Written advice is subject to contractual protection if the taxpayer has the right to a refund of fees paid to the practitioner (or members or associates of, or employees of the practitioner's firm) if any of the intended tax consequences from matters addressed in the written advice are not sustained, or if the fees paid to the practitioner (or members or associates of, or employees of the practitioner's firm) are contingent on the taxpayer's realization of the transaction's tax benefits.[23] All the facts and circumstances relating to the matters addressed in the written advice will be considered when determining whether a fee is refundable or contingent, including the right to reimbursements of amounts that the

---

[20] Circular 230, § 10.35(b)(5)(ii).
[21] Circular 230, § 10.35(b)(8).
[22] Circular 230, § 10.35(b)(6).
[23] Circular 230, § 10.35(b)(7).

parties to a transaction have not designated as fees or any agreement to provide services without reasonable compensation.[24]

[3]   Requirements for Covered Opinions

[a]   *Factual Matters*

[i]   Reasonable efforts to identify and ascertain facts.   Practitioners must use reasonable efforts to identify and ascertain the facts, which may relate to future events if a transaction is prospective or proposed, and to determine which facts are relevant. The opinion must identify and consider all facts that the practitioner determines to be relevant.[25]

[ii]   No unreasonable factual assumptions.   Practitioners must not base their opinion on any unreasonable factual assumptions (including assumptions as to future events). An unreasonable factual assumption includes a factual assumption that the practitioner knows or should know is incorrect or incomplete. To illustrate, according to Circular 230, it is unreasonable to assume, without more, that a transaction has a business purpose or that a transaction is potentially profitable apart from tax benefits.[26]

For this purpose, factual assumptions include reliance on projections, financial forecasts or appraisals. Therefore, it is unreasonable for practitioner to rely on projections, financial forecasts or appraisals if the practitioner knows or should know that such projections, financial forecasts or appraisals are incorrect or incomplete or were prepared by a person lacking the skills or qualifications necessary to prepare such projection, financial forecast or appraisal. The opinion must identify in a separate section all factual assumptions relied upon by the practitioner.[27]

[iii]   No reliance on unreasonable factual representations.   Circular 230 also states that practitioners must not base their opinion on any unreasonable factual representations, statements or findings of the taxpayer or any other person. For this purpose, an unreasonable factual representation includes a factual representation that the practitioner knows or should know is incorrect or incomplete. To illustrate, a practitioner may not rely on a factual representation that a transaction has a business purpose if the representation does not include a specific description of the business purpose or the practitioner knows or should know that the representation is incorrect or incomplete. The opinion must identify in a separate section all factual representations, statements or findings of the taxpayer relied upon by the practitioner.[28]

---

[24] Circular 230, § 10.35(b)(7).
[25] Circular 230, § 10.35(c)(1)(i).
[26] Circular 230, § 10.35(c)(1)(ii).
[27] Circular 230, § 10.35(c)(1)(ii).
[28] Circular 230, § 10.35(c)(1)(iii).

[b] Relate Law to Facts

The opinion must relate the applicable law (including potentially applicable judicial doctrines) to the relevant facts.[29]

The practitioner must not assume the favorable resolution of any significant Federal tax issue except in the case of a limited scope opinion or if the practitioner relies on the opinion of another practitioner.[30]

The opinion must not contain internally inconsistent legal analyses or conclusions.[31]

[c] Evaluation Of Significant Federal Tax Issues

[i] Generally. The opinion must consider all significant Federal tax issues except in the case of a limited scope opinion or if the practitioner relied upon the opinion of another practitioner.[32]

[ii] Conclusion As To Each Significant Federal Tax Issue. The opinion must provide the practitioner's conclusion as to the likelihood that the taxpayer will prevail on the merits with respect to each significant Federal tax issue considered in the opinion. If the practitioner is unable to reach a conclusion with respect to one or more of those issues, the opinion must state that the practitioner is unable to reach a conclusion with respect to those issues. The opinion must describe the reasons for the conclusions, including the facts and analysis supporting the conclusions, or describe the reasons that the practitioner is unable to reach a conclusion as to one or more issues. If the practitioner fails to reach a conclusion at a confidence level of at least more likely than not with respect to one or more significant Federal tax issues considered, the opinion must include the appropriate disclosure(s) required under Circular 230.[33]

[iii] Evaluation based on chances of success on the merits. In evaluating the significant Federal tax issues addressed in the opinion, the practitioner must not take into account the possibility that a tax return will not be audited, that an issue will not be raised on audit, or that an issue will be resolved through settlement if raised.[34]

[iv] Marketed opinions. For marketed opinions, the opinion must provide the practitioner's conclusion that the taxpayer will prevail on the merits at a confidence level of at least more likely than not with respect to each significant Federal tax issue. If the practitioner is unable to reach a more likely than not

---

[29] Circular 230, § 10.35(c)(2)(i).
[30] Circular 230, § 10.35(c)(2)(ii).
[31] Circular 230, § 10.35(c)(2)(iii).
[32] Circular 230, § 10.35(c)(3)(i).
[33] Circular 230, § 10.35(c)(3)(ii).
[34] Circular 230, § 10.35(c)(3)(iii).

conclusion with respect to each significant Federal tax issue, the practitioner must not provide the marketed opinion, but may provide written advice if such advice contains the appropriate disclosures.[35]

[v] Limited scope opinions. Practitioners may provide an opinion that considers less than all of the significant Federal tax issues if all of the following are satisfied:

- The practitioner and the taxpayer agree that the scope of the opinion and the taxpayer's potential reliance on the opinion for purposes of avoiding penalties that may be imposed on the taxpayer are limited to the Federal tax issue(s) addressed in the opinion;
- The opinion is not a listed transaction opinion, a tax avoidance opinion, or a marketed opinion; and
- The opinion includes the appropriate disclosures.[36]

Practitioners may make reasonable assumptions regarding the favorable resolution of a Federal tax issue (an assumed issue) for purposes of providing an opinion on less than all of the significant Federal tax issues as provided in Circular 230 for limited scope opinions. However, the opinion must identify in a separate section all issues for which the practitioner assumed a favorable resolution.[37]

[d] Overall conclusion

The opinion must provide the practitioner's overall conclusion as to the likelihood that the Federal tax treatment of the transaction or matter that is the subject of the opinion is the proper treatment and the reasons for that conclusion. If the practitioner is unable to reach an overall conclusion, the opinion must state that the practitioner is unable to reach an overall conclusion and describe the reasons for the practitioner's inability to reach a conclusion.[38]

For marketed opinions, the opinion must provide the practitioner's overall conclusion that the Federal tax treatment of the transaction or matter that is the subject of the opinion is the proper treatment at a confidence level of at least more likely than not.[39]

[e] Competence to provide opinion; reliance on others

The practitioner must be knowledgeable in all of the aspects of Federal tax law relevant to the opinion being rendered. However, the practitioner may rely on

---

[35] Circular 230, § 10.35(c)(3)(iv).
[36] Circular 230, § 10.35(c)(3)(v)(A).
[37] Circular 230, § 10.35(c)(3)(v)(B).
[38] Circular 230, § 10.35(c)(4)(i).
[39] Circular 230, § 10.35(c)(4)(ii).

the opinion of another practitioner with respect to one or more significant Federal tax issues, unless the practitioner knows or should know that the opinion of the other practitioner should not be relied on. If a practitioner relies on the opinion of another practitioner, the relying practitioner's opinion must identify the other opinion and set forth the conclusions reached in the other opinion.[40]

The practitioner must be satisfied that the combined analysis of the opinions, taken as a whole, and the overall conclusion, if any, satisfy the requirements of this section.[41]

[f] Required Disclosures

Covered opinions must contain all of the following disclosures that apply.

[i] Relationship between promoter and practitioner. An opinion must prominently disclose the existence of:

- Any compensation arrangement (e.g., referral fees or fee-sharing arrangements), between the practitioner (or his/her firm, or any member, associate, or employee of his/her firm) and any person (other than the client for whom the opinion is prepared) with respect to promoting, marketing or recommending the entity, plan, or arrangement (or a substantially similar arrangement) that is the subject of the opinion; or
- Any referral agreement between the practitioner (or his/her firm, or any member, associate, or employee of his/her firm) and a person (other than the client for whom the opinion is prepared) engaged in promoting, marketing or recommending the entity, plan, or arrangement (or a substantially similar arrangement) that is the subject of the opinion.[42]

[ii] Marketed Opinions. Marketed opinions must prominently disclose that:

- The opinion was written to support the promotion or marketing of the transaction(s) or matter(s) addressed in the opinion; and
- The taxpayer should seek advice based on the taxpayer's particular circumstances from an independent tax advisor.[43]

[iii] Limited Scope Opinions. Limited scope opinions must prominently disclose that:

- The opinion is limited to the one or more Federal tax issues addressed in the opinion;

---

[40] Circular 230, § 10.35(d)(1).
[41] Circular 230, § 10.35(d)(2).
[42] Circular 230, § 10.35(e)(1).
[43] Circular 230, § 10.35(e)(2).

- Additional issues may exist that could affect the Federal tax treatment of the transaction or matter that is the subject of the opinion and the opinion does not consider or provide a conclusion with respect to any additional issues; and
- With respect to any significant Federal tax issues outside the limited scope of the opinion, the opinion was not written, and cannot be used by the tax-payer, for the purpose of avoiding penalties that may be imposed on the taxpayer.[44]

[iv] Opinions that fail to reach a more likely than not conclusion. Opinions that fail to reach a conclusion at a confidence level of at least more likely than not with respect to a significant Federal tax issue must prominently disclose that:

- The opinion does not reach a conclusion at a confidence level of at least more likely than not with respect to one or more significant Federal tax issues addressed by the opinion; and
- With respect to those significant Federal tax issues, the opinion was not written, and cannot be used by the taxpayer, for the purpose of avoiding penalties that may be imposed on the taxpayer.[45]

[v] Advice regarding required. For any disclosure required under the disclosure section for covered opinions of Circular 230, the practitioner may not provide advice to any person that is contrary to or inconsistent with the required disclosure.[46]

[g] Effect of Covered Opinion That Satisfies Circular 230 Standards

An opinion that satisfies the standards of Circular 230 satisfies the practitioner's responsibilities under Circular 230, but the persuasiveness of the opinion with regard to the tax issues in question and the taxpayer's good faith reliance on the opinion will be determined separately under applicable provisions of the law and regulations.[47]

[D] Other Written Advice

A practitioner must not give written advice, including electronic communications, such as e-mails and mobile phone text messages, concerning any Federal tax issues where the practitioner does any of the following:

- Bases the written advice on unreasonable factual or legal assumptions (including assumptions as to future events).

---

[44] Circular 230, § 10.35(e)(3).
[45] Circular 230, § 10.35(e)(4).
[46] Circular 230, § 10.35(e)(5).
[47] Circular 230, § 10.35(f)(1).

- Unreasonably relies upon representations, statements, findings or agreements of the taxpayer or any other person.
- Does not consider all relevant facts that the practitioner knows or should know.
- In evaluating a Federal tax issue, takes into account the possibility that a tax return will not be audited, that an issue will not be raised on audit, or that an issue will be resolved through settlement if raised.[48]

In determining whether a practitioner has failed to comply with this section all facts and circumstances, including the scope of the engagement and the type and specificity of the advice sought by the client will be considered.[49]

For opinions that practitioners know or should know will be used or referred to by persons other than the practitioner (or members, associates, or employees of his/her firm) in promoting, marketing or recommending to taxpayers a partnership, other entity, investment plan or arrangement a significant purpose of which is avoidance or evasion of any federal tax, the determination of whether the practitioner has failed to comply with Circular 230 will be made based on a heightened standard of care. The reason for this increased scrutiny is the increased risk perceived to be caused by the practitioner's lack of knowledge of the taxpayer's particular circumstances.[50]

[E]   Best Practices

Circular 230 includes a section that details best practices for tax advisors. Tax practitioners should aspire to these aspirational practices. However, these standards are not mandatory.

Tax advisors should provide clients with the highest quality representation concerning Federal tax issues by adhering to best practices in providing advice and in preparing or assisting in the preparation of a submission to the Internal Revenue Service. In this regard, best practices include the following:

- Communicating clearly with clients regarding the terms of the engagement. For example, the advisor should determine the client's expected purpose for and use of the advice and should have a clear understanding with the client regarding the form and scope of the advice or assistance to be rendered.
- Establishing the facts, determining which facts are relevant, evaluating the reasonableness of any assumptions or representations, relating the applicable law (including potentially applicable judicial doctrines) to the relevant facts, and arriving at a conclusion supported by the law and the facts.
- Advising the client regarding the import of the conclusions reached, including, for example, whether a taxpayer may avoid accuracy-related

---

[48] Circular 230, § 10.37(a).
[49] Circular 230, § 10.37(a).
[50] Circular 230, § 10.37(a).

penalties under the Internal Revenue Code if a taxpayer acts in reliance on the advice.

- Acting fairly and with integrity in practice before the Internal Revenue Service.

[F] Estate and Asset Protection Planning Techniques Likely Covered by Circular 230

Depending on the circumstances, advice regarding any of the following techniques, or portions thereof, commonly used as part of an asset protection or an estate plan may be subject to Circular 230:[51]

- Creation of Crummey life insurance trusts
- Formations of family limited partnerships and limited liability companies
- S elections or check the box status
- Creation of grantor trusts
- Sales to grantor trusts
- Allocation of GST exemption
- GRATs and QPRTs
- Charitable remainder trusts
- Section 529 plans
- Intrafamily sales
- Stock redemptions in family corporations
- Sale of a remainder interst in a charitable lead trust to a GRAT or GST Trust

---

[51] *See generally* Louis A. Mezzullo & Ronald D. Aucutt, *Circular 230: Estate Planning Issues, in Planning Techniques for Large Estates,* 1 ALI-ABA Course of Study Materials Course No. SL0078 (Apr. 2006); Mary Ann Mancini, *Circular 230 & Estate Planners: One Year Developments,* in Vermont Bar Association Teleconference Materials (July 11, 2006).

2

Fraudulent Conveyance Concepts

§2.01 FRAUDULENT CONVEYANCE CONCEPTS IN GENERAL

Fraudulent conveyance law[1] plays an extremely important role in asset protection plans because, if transfers effected as part of an asset protection plan constitute fraudulent conveyances, the client's creditors may reach the transferred property. This undermines the asset protection plan.

Planning Pointer. For planning purposes, the prudent asset protection planner must assume that the client's creditors will bring fraudulent conveyance claims. The planner must structure the asset protection plan to minimize the ability of the client's creditors to bring successful fraudulent conveyance claims.

Fraudulent conveyances are conveyances made (or presumed to be made) with the intent to delay or defraud creditors.[2] Usually, fraudulent conveyances are characterized by a lack of fair and valuable consideration and/or an attempt by debtors to place their property beyond the reach of creditors. Laws voiding such fraudulent transfers date back to the sixteenth century, when the Statute of 13 Elizabeth was passed.[3] Today, the law of fraudulent conveyances in the United States is embodied in three statutory sources:

1. The Bankruptcy Code §§ 548 and 544(b)
2. The Uniform Fraudulent Conveyances Act (UFCA)
3. The Uniform Fraudulent Transfers Act (UFTA)

Because the structure of these three laws is very similar, case law construing one source of law may be influential in construing the others. This is especially true

---

§2.01 [1] *See* Andrea Bloom, Lender Liability: Practice and Prevention 145–65 (1989); Joseph W. Bartlett, Corporate Restructuring, Reorganizations, and Buyouts (1991); Jack F. Williams, *Revisiting the Proper Limits of Fraudulent Transfer Law*, 8 Bankr. Dev. J. 55 (1991); Douglas Baird & Thomas Jackson, *Fraudulent Conveyance Law and Its Proper Domain*, 38 Vand. L. Rev. 829 (1985); Garrard Glenn, Fraudulent Conveyance and Preferences (rev. ed. 1940); 4 Collier on Bankruptcy 1 548.02[3] (15th ed. 1992); Michael L. Cook, *Fraudulent Transfer Liability under the Bankruptcy Code*, 17 Hous. L. Rev. 263 (1980); Michael L. Cook & Richard E. Mendales, *The Uniform Fraudulent Transfer Act: An Introductory Critique*, 62 Am. Bankr. L.J. 87 (1988); Bruce A. Markell, *Toward True and Plain Dealing: A Theory of Fraudulent Transfers Involving Unreasonably Small Capital*, 21 Ind. L. Rev. 469 (1988); Mary Goulet, *The Rights of Debtholders when a Leveraged Corporation Fails*, 15 J. Corp. L. 257 (Winter 1990); Emily L. Sherwin, *Creditor's Rights Against Participants in a Leveraged Buyout*, 72 Minn. L. Rev. 449 (1988); Cieri et al., *An Introduction to Legal and Practical Considerations in the Restructuring of Troubled Leveraged Buyouts*, 45 Bus. Law. 333 (1989); Note, *Fraudulent Conveyance Law and Leveraged Buyouts*, 87 Colum. L. Rev. 1491 (1987); Helen B. Jenkins, *Rights of Unsecured Estate Creditors Under the Uniform Fraudulent Transfer Act in Property Transferred Prior to Death*, 45 Okla. L. Rev. 275 (1992) (examines applicability of UFTA to inter vivos gifts and insurance disclaimers; identifies fraudulent transfers, rights of creditors, and duties of personal representatives); Kenneth C. Kettering, *The Pennsylvania Uniform Fraudulent Transfer Act*, 65 Pa. B. Ass'n Q. 2 (Apr. 1994).

[2] Black's Law Dictionary 596 (5th ed. 1979).

[3] The Statute of 13 Elizabeth, Chapter 5 (1570). *See also* Twyne's Case, 76 Eng. Rep. 809 (Star Ch. 1601).

when there is little or no case law construing one source and, concerning the provision in question, another source is drafted in a very similar manner.

Planning Pointer. When examining fraudulent conveyance risk, the planner should consider the following analysis:

1. Determine the applicable source of law;[4]
2. Analyze fraudulent conveyance claim risk arising out of an actual intent fraudulent conveyance claim;[5]
3. Analyze fraudulent conveyance claim risk arising out of a constructive fraudulent conveyance claim;[6]
4. If, based on the preceding steps, the planner determines that there is a risk of a valid fraudulent conveyance claim, determine whether any affirmative defenses apply;[7] and
5. If the planner determines that there is a risk that a successful fraudulent conveyance claim may be brought, determine the possible remedies a court may apply.[8]

Planning Pointer. To avoid fraudulent conveyance claims:

1. The planner should obtain from the client a personal financial statement audited by a competent accounting firm, as well as audited financial statements of business entities the client controls.
2. The planner should limit the transfer of assets out of the client's estate (for example, to a trust or to children) to a maximum predetermined amount of the client's assets, which the planner must determine by analyzing the applicable law.
3. The planner should obtain from the client a certificate of all liability insurance maintained; furthermore, the planner should note that in some jurisdictions, liability insurance coverage may be considered when conducting an insolvency analysis.
4. The planner should obtain from the client affidavits that (a) there are no current legal proceedings being prosecuted or contemplated against the client, (b) the client is not liable for liabilities or contingent liabilities that the client has not disclosed in its financial statements, and (c) the client does not know of any currently existing facts that

---

[4] *See* § 2.02.
[5] *See* § 2.03.
[6] *See* §§ 2.04[A]–2.04[D].
[7] *See* § 2.07.
[8] *See* §§ 2.08[A]–2.08[E].

would lead to legal proceedings resulting in a claim against the client's assets.

5. The planner should use the above items to conduct an insolvency analysis under applicable law.

Caution. Asset protection planners must be aware that fraudulent conveyances can take a wide variety of forms. For example, in *Sunrise Industrial Joint Venture v. Ditric Optics, Inc.,*[9] the United States District Court for the Eastern District of New York held that a landlord constituted a "creditor," and future rents constituted "debt" for purposes of New York's fraudulent conveyance law.[10]

§ 2.02 CHOICE OF LAW ISSUES

In any fraudulent conveyance analysis, the planner must first determine which law applies. Unsecured creditors bringing fraudulent conveyance claims will generally do so under state law, usually either the UFCA or the UFTA. The planner must apply conflict of law rules to determine which state's law applies unless one state's law clearly applies or all states have identical law on the subject.

Bankruptcy trustees bringing a fraudulent conveyance claim will do so under the Bankruptcy Code, which contains a fraudulent conveyance cause of action provision under § 548.[1] However, the Bankruptcy Code also empowers the bankruptcy trustee to bring a fraudulent conveyance claim under state law under certain circumstances. Specifically, it allows the bankruptcy trustee to bring any fraudulent conveyance claim that any unsecured creditor may bring under state fraudulent conveyance law.[2] In effect, Bankruptcy Code § 544(b) incorporates state fraudulent conveyance law into the Bankruptcy Code. To use this provision, there must be at least one creditor who has standing under state law to challenge the conveyance in question. If Bankruptcy Code § 548 does not yield favorable results for the bankruptcy trustee, state law may be applicable. This is most likely to occur when the conveyance in question occurred more than one year before the bankruptcy petition date. Here, Bankruptcy Code § 548 could not be successfully used, but many state fraudulent conveyance statutes, with statutes of limitation extending beyond one year, could be used.

---

[9] 873 F. Supp. 765 (E.D.N.Y. 1995).

[10] *See, e.g.,* Tavenner v. Smoot, 257 F.3d 401 (4th Cir. 2001), *cert. denied,* 2002 U.S. LEXIS 566 (U.S. Jan. 22, 2002) (Fourth Circuit held that a bankruptcy trustee may avoid a debtor's fraudulent transfer of property that, but for the transfer, would have been exempt from the bankruptcy estate).

§ 2.02 [1] 11 U.S.C. § 548 (1988 & Supp. II 1991).

[2] *See* §§ 2.03, 2.04[A]–2.04[D]; 11 U.S.C. § 544(b) (1988).

> **EXAMPLE 2–1**
>
> Norman operates a manufacturing business, Norman's Nails, which manufactures steel nails. Norman operates this business as a sole proprietorship. Norman's gross assets are worth $7 million, which consists of (1) Norman's Nails, which is worth $3 million, (2) a marketable securities portfolio, which is worth $3 million, and (3) his home, which is worth $1 million. Norman owes Big Bank $2 million, which leaves him with a net worth of $5 million.

In January 1990, as part of an asset protection plan, Norman transfers 100 percent of Norman's Nails, his stock portfolio, and his house into an irrevocable discretionary trust with his daughter, Nancy, as sole beneficiary. Norman becomes an employee of Norman's Nails, which the trust now owns.

In April 1991 Norman negligently drives his car into Ned, who sues Norman and wins a $20 million judgment against him. This forces Norman into bankruptcy. Tom, the bankruptcy trustee, desires to bring a fraudulent conveyance claim against Norman to reach the assets that Norman transferred into the trust. At this time, Norman has not paid off Big Bank, and Big Bank has the right under applicable state law to bring a fraudulent conveyance claim. The applicable state law provides for a five-year statute of limitations, as opposed to the one-year statute of limitations that applies to Bankruptcy Code § 548. Here, Tom may bring a fraudulent conveyance claim under state law.

§ 2.03   ACTUAL INTENT FRAUDULENT CONVEYANCE

Bankruptcy Code § 548(a) (1) allows the bankruptcy trustee to avoid transfers of property or obligations incurred within one year preceding the bankruptcy filing if the debtor voluntarily or involuntarily "made such transfer or incurred such obligation with actual intent to hinder, delay, or defraud any entity to which the debtor was or became, on or after the date that such transfer was made or such obligation was incurred, indebted." However, the government may prosecute transfers that occur more than one year before the bankruptcy petition, under 18 U.S.C. § 152. Section 152 provides penalties for various kinds of bankruptcy fraud, including knowingly and fraudulently transferring and concealing property in contemplation of a bankruptcy case or with intent to defeat the Bankruptcy Code.[1]

---

§ 2.03   [1] *See, e.g.,* United States v. West, 22 F.3d 586 (5th Cir. 1994), *cert. denied,* 513 U.S. 1020 (1994). *See* § 2.05 for a discussion of 18 U.S.C. § 152. *See also* Federal Deposit Ins. Corp. v. Sullivan (*In re* Sullivan), 204 B.R. 919 (Bankr. N.D. Tex. 1997) (U.S. Bankruptcy Court for the Northern District of Texas held that (1) debtor is denied discharge because of his intentionally fraudulent transfer or concealment of assets in gratuitously conveying assets to family members or to trusts while continuing to enjoy beneficial use and control of such assets, (2) debtor was also denied discharge based on his numerous omissions and false representations, which he made on his bankruptcy schedules and statements, and (3) any reliance that debtor may have had upon his attorneys in connection with the preparation of the bankruptcy schedules and statements was unreasonable and not in good faith and, thus, did not provide him with a defense to the discharge complaint).

The UFCA provides that a "conveyance made with actual intent . . . to hinder, delay, or defraud either present or future creditors, is fraudulent as to both present and future creditors."[2] The UFTA provides that a "transfer made or obligation incurred by a debtor is fraudulent as to a creditor, whether the creditor's claim arose before or after the transfer was made or the obligation incurred, if the debtor made the transfer or incurred the obligation . . . with actual intent to hinder, delay, or defraud any creditor."[3] The UFTA also provides that intentional fraudulent conveyance claims must be brought within the later of (1) four years of the conveyance, or (2) one year after the claimant actually discovers, or reasonably could have discovered, the conveyance.[4]

> **Planning Pointer.** The planner should note that, except for their associated statutes of limitation, the fraudulent conveyance provisions contained in the Bankruptcy Code, the UFCA, and the UFTA are substantially the same.

To bring an intentional fraudulent conveyance claim, the plaintiff must prove four elements. Specifically, the plaintiff must prove:

1. The defendant effected a transfer;
2. Of an interest in the debtor's property;
3. Within the applicable statute of limitations; and
4. Did so with the actual intent of the debtor to hinder, delay, or defraud the creditor.

The element generally most difficult to prove is actual fraudulent intent. Only in very rare circumstances is direct evidence of fraudulent intent available to the trustee. However, the trustee may prove fraudulent intent through circumstantial evidence and inferences drawn from course of conduct. More precisely, the courts have developed certain badges of fraud the trustee may use to prove circumstantially an actual intent to defraud, including the following:[5]

1. Lack or inadequacy of consideration;[6]

---

[2] UFCA § 7, 7A U.L.A. § 509 (1918).

[3] UFTA § 4(a)(1), 7A U.L.A. § 652 (1984).

[4] UFTA § 9(a), 7A U.L.A. § 665 (1984).

[5] *See, e.g.,* Boston Trading Group, Inc. v. Burnazos, 835 F.2d 1504 (Ist Cir. 1987); *In re* Clausen, 44 B.R. 41 (Bankr. D. Minn. 1984); United States v. Sheridan, 1997 U.S. App. LEXIS 22,432 (7th Cir. 1997) (U.S. Court of Appeals for the Seventh Circuit affirms a summary judgment in favor of the IRS, holding that the taxpayer's conveyance of his interest in personal residence to his wife for $2 constituted a fraudulent conveyance under applicable state law. The court stated that, under the applicable Illinois state law, a conveyance was presumptively fraudulent if (1) it is made for inadequate consideration; (2) there is an existing or anticipated debt against the transferor; and (3) the transferor did not retain sufficient property to pay his debt). United States v. Engh, 330 F.3d 954 (7th Cir. 2003) (Court held that transfer to a trust was a fraudulent conveyance, based on several badges of fraud).

[6] *In re* May, 12 B.R. 618 (Bankr. N.D. Fla. 1980); Marc Rich & Co. A.G. v. United States (*In re* Grand Jury Subpoena Duces Tecum), 731 F.2d 1032 (2d Cir. 1984); United States v. Leggett, 292 F.2d 423 (6th Cir.),

2. Family, friendship, or other close relationship among the parties;[7]
3. The retention of possession, benefit, or use of the property in question;[8]
4. The financial condition of the defendant both before and after the transfer in question;[9]
5. The existence or cumulative effect of a pattern of transactions or a course of conduct after the onset of financial difficulties;[10]
6. The general chronology of events;[11]
7. The secrecy of the transaction in question.[12]

Generally, the more badges of fraud present, the greater the probability that a court will find actual intent to defraud.[13] However, a court may find actual fraud present with only a single badge of fraud.[14]

---

cert. denied, 368 U.S. 914 (1961); Tipp v. United Bank, 745 S.W.2d 141 (Ark. 1988); Dahnken, Inc. v. Wilmarth, 726 P.2d 420 (Utah 1986); Butcher v. Butcher (*In re* Estate of Reed), 566 P.2d 587 (Wyo. 1977); Lewis v. Estate of Lewis, 725 P.2d 644 (Wash. Ct. App. 1986); Advanced Chapter 11 Bankruptcy Practice Ch. 6 (Thomas J. Salerno & Craig D. Hansen eds., John Wiley & Sons 1987 & Supp. 1990); Jack F. Williams, Revisiting the Proper Limits of Fraudulent Transfer Law, 8 Bankr. Dev. J. 55, 105 (1991). Annotation, *Right of Creditors to Attack as Fraudulent a Conveyance by Third Person to Debtor's Spouse,* 35 A.L.R.2d 8 (1954).

[7] *In re* May, 12 B.R. 618 (Bankr. N.D. Fla. 1980); Marc Rich & Co. A.G. v. United States (*In re* Grand Jury Subpoena Duces Tecum), 731 F.2d 1032 (2d Cir. 1984); Andrews v. Reynolds, 409 N.W.2d 128 (S.D. 1987); Montana Nat'l Bank v. Michels, 631 P.2d 1260 (Mont. 1981); Cardiovascular & Thoracic Surgery, Inc. v. DiMazzio, 524 N.E.2d 915 (Ohio 1987); Advanced Chapter 11 Bankruptcy Practice Ch. 6 (Thomas J. Salerno & Craig D. Hansen eds., John Wiley & Sons 1987 & Supp. 1990); Jack F. Williams, *Revisiting the Proper Limits of Fraudulent Transfer Law,* 8 Bankr. Dev. J. 55, 105 (1991).

[8] 17 *In re* May, 12 B.R. 618 (Bankr. N.D. Fla. 1980); United States v. Leggett, 292 F.2d 423 (6th Cir.), *cert. denied,* 368 U.S. 914 (1961); Tipp v. United Bank, 745 S.W.2d 141 (Ark. 1988); Advanced Chapter 11 Bankruptcy Practice Ch. 6 (Thomas J. Salerno & Craig D. Hansen eds., John Wiley & Sons 1987 & Supp. 1990); Jack F. Williams, *Revisiting the Proper Limits of Fraudulent Transfer Law,* 8 Bankr. Dev. J. 55, 105 (1991).

[9] *In re* May, 12 B.R. 618 (Bankr. N.D. Fla. 1980); Roland v. United States, 838 F.2d 1400 (5th Cir. 1988); Adams v. Wilhite, 636 S.W.2d 851 (Tex. Ct. App.), *rev'd on other grounds,* 640 S.W.2d 875 (Tex. 1982); Advanced Chapter 11 Bankruptcy Practice Ch. 6 (Thomas J. Salerno & Craig D. Hansen eds., John Wiley & Sons 1987 & Supp. 1990); Jack F. Williams, *Revisiting the Proper Limits of Fraudulent Transfer Law,* 8 Bankr. Dev. J. 55, 105 (1991).

[10] *In re* May, 12 B.R. 618 (Bankr. N.D. Fla. 1980); Advanced Chapter 11 Bankruptcy Practice Ch. 6 (Thomas J. Salerno & Craig D. Hansen eds., John Wiley & Sons 1987 & Supp. 1990).

[11] *In re* May, 12 B.R. 618 (Bankr. N.D. Fla. 1980); Tipp v. United Bank, 745 S.W.2d 141 (Ark. 1988); Texas Sand Co. v. Shield, 381 S.W.2d 48 (Tex. 1964); Cardiovascular & Thoracic Surgery, Inc. v. Di-Mazzio, 524 N.E.2d 915 (Ohio 1987); Dahnken, Inc. v. Wilmarth, 726 P.2d 420 (Utah 1986); Montana Nat'l Bank v. Michels, 631 P.2d 1260 (Mont. 1981); Advanced Chapter 11 Bankruptcy Practice Ch. 6 (Thomas J. Salerno & Craig D. Hansen eds., John Wiley & Sons 1987 & Supp. 1990); Jack F. Williams, *Revisiting the Proper Limits of Fraudulent Transfer Law,* 8 Bankr. Dev. J. 105 (1991).

[12] Marc Rich & Co. A.G. v. United States (*In re* Grand Jury Subpoena Duces Tecum), 731 F.2d 1032 (2d Cir. 1984); Tipp v. United Bank, 745 S.W.2d 141 (Ark. 1988); Advanced Chapter 11 Bankruptcy Practice Ch. 6 (Thomas J. Salerno & Craig D. Hansen eds., John Wiley & Sons 1987 & Supp. 1990); Jack F. Williams, *Revisiting the Proper Limits of Fraudulent Transfer Law,* 8 Bankr. Dev. J. 55, 105 (1991).

[13] Butcher v. Butcher (*In re* Estate of Reed), 566 P.2d 587 (Wyo. 1977).

[14] *Id.*

The UFTA provides the following nonexclusive list of factors to consider when determining if actual intent to defraud is present:

1. Was the transfer or obligation to an insider?[15]
2. Did the debtor retain possession or control of the transferred property after the conveyance?[16]
3. Was the transfer or obligation disclosed or concealed?[17]
4. Was the debtor sued or threatened with suit before the conveyance?[18]
5. Did the conveyance consist of substantially all the debtor's assets?[19]
6. Did the debtor abscond?[20]
7. Did the debtor remove or conceal assets?[21]
8. Was the value of the consideration that the debtor received reasonably equivalent to the value of the conveyance?[22]
9. Was the debtor insolvent at the time of the conveyance or did the debtor become insolvent soon after the conveyance?[23]
10. Did the conveyance occur shortly before or after the debtor incurred a substantial debt?[24]
11. Did the debtor convey the essential assets of the business to a lienor who transferred the assets to an insider of the debtor?[25]

Planning Pointer. The planner must minimize the presence of badges of fraud that may be present in the asset protection plan. The planner must do this to minimize the risk of any part of the transaction being categorized as a fraudulent conveyance.

In a leveraged buyout, when an acquirer finances the purchase of the target by borrowing against the target's assets, a court may infer actual intent to defraud if both (1) the transferor and the transferee have knowledge of the claims of the creditors and know that creditors cannot be paid, and (2) there is a lack of consideration present.[26]

---

[15] UFTA § 4(b)(1), 7A U.L.A. § 653 (1984).
[16] UFTA § 4(b)(2), 7A U.L.A. § 653 (1984).
[17] UFTA § 4(b)(3), 7A U.L.A. § 653 (1984).
[18] UFTA § 4(b)(4), 7A U.L.A. § 653 (1984).
[19] UFTA § 4(b)(5), 7A U.L.A. § 653 (1984).
[20] UFTA § 4(b)(6), 7A U.L.A. § 653 (1984).
[21] UFTA § 4(b)(7), 7A U.L.A. § 653 (1984).
[22] UFTA § 4(b)(8), 7A U.L.A. § 653(1984).
[23] UFTA § 4(b)(9), 7A U.L.A. § 653(1984).
[24] UFTA § 4(b)(10), 7A U.L.A. § 653 (1984).
[25] UFTA § 4(b) (11), 7A U.L.A. § 653 (1984).
[26] United States v. Gleneagles Inv. Co., 565 F. Supp. 556 (M.D. Pa. 1983), aff'd sub nom. United States v. Tabor Court Realty Corp., 803 F.2d 1288 (3d Cir. 1986), cert. denied, 483 U.S. 1005 (1987).

The debtor's intent, as opposed to the transferee's intent, at the time of the transfer is the relevant intent.[27] Historically, the courts have used a subjective standard to determine the existence of actual intent.[28] However, the Third Circuit recently affirmed a case applying an objective standard to determine actual intent.[29] In *Gleneagles*, the court found actual intent when the parties could reasonably foresee that a diversion of corporate assets combined with adverse financial conditions would hinder creditors.[30]

The Bankruptcy Code defines transfer as including "every mode, direct or indirect, absolute or conditional, voluntary or involuntary, of disposing of or parting with an interest in property, including retention of title as a security interest and foreclosure of the debtor's equity of redemption.[31] Therefore, the Bankruptcy Code definition of "transfer" is broad and all-encompassing.[32] However, one controversial issue is whether a § 548 transfer occurs when the debtor's[33] property is sold at a foreclosure sale. Specifically, there is a conflict among the courts about whether such a foreclosure sale constitutes a transfer. The Fifth Circuit Court of Appeals was the first court to hold that a foreclosure sale of the debtor's property is a transfer.[34] The Eighth Circuit followed this approach.[35] On the other hand, the Ninth Circuit[36] and the Sixth Circuit[37] have rejected this approach. The Supreme Court resolved this conflict during 1994, in *BFP v. Resolution Trust Corp.*[38] In that case, the Supreme Court held that a reasonably equivalent value for foreclosed property is the price in fact received at the foreclosure sale, as long as all the requirements of the state's foreclosure law were complied with.

[27] Wilson v. Upreach Ministries (*In re* Missionary Baptist Found. of Am., Inc.), 24 B.R. 973 (Bankr. N.D. Tex. 1982).

[28] Jack F. Williams, *Revisiting the Proper Limits of Fraudulent Transfer Law*, 8 Bankr. Dev. J. 55, 107 (1991).

[29] United States v. Gleneagles Inv. Co., 565 F. Supp. 556 (M.D. Pa. 1983), *aff'd sub nom.* United States v. Tabor Court Realty Corp., 803 F.2d 1288 (3d Cir. 1986), *cert. denied*, 483 U.S. 1005 (1987).

[30] *Id.*

[31] 11 U.S.C. § 101(54) (Supp. 11 1991).

[32] *See* Jack F. Williams, *Revisiting the Proper Limits of Fraudulent Transfer Law*, 8 Bankr. Dev. J. 55, 71–79 (1991), for several examples of "transfers."

[33] *See, e.g.,* Jack F. Williams, *Revisiting the Proper Limits of Fraudulent Transfer Law*, 8 Bankr. Dev. J. 55, 71–72 (1991); Advanced Chapter 11 Bankruptcy Practice Ch. 6 (Thomas J. Salerno & Craig D. Hansen eds., John Wiley & Sons 1987 & Supp. 1990).

[34] Durrett v. Washington Nat'l Ins. Co., 621 F.2d 201 (5th Cir. 1980), *overruled by* BFP v. Resolution Trust Corp., 511 U.S. 531 (1994).

[35] First Fed. Sav. & Loan Ass'n of Bismarck v. Hulm (*In re* Hulm), 738 F.2d 323 (8th Cir.), *cert. denied*, 469 U.S. 990, *on remand*, 45 B.R. 523 (1984).

[36] Madrid v. Lawyers Title Ins. Corp. (*In re* Madrid), 725 F.2d 1197 (9th Cir.), *cert. denied*, 469 U.S. 833 (1984).

[37] *In re* Winshall Settlor's Trust, 758 F.2d 1136 (6th Cir. 1985).

[38] 511 U.S. 531 (1994).

EXAMPLE 2-2

D Corp is a financially troubled corporation. It has $8 million of assets and $20 million of outstanding, unsecured debts. Oliver Dee, who owns 60 percent of D Corp, is the majority shareholder. Paul Dee, Oliver's son, is the president of D Corp. Oliver and Paul determine that D Corp will fail and decide to engage in last minute asset protection planning to save what they can for themselves. They form S Corp, a shell corporation to take D Corp private by means of a leveraged buyout. Next, they obtain an $8 million loan for S Corp, secured by all of D Corp's assets, from B Bank. Bob, Oliver's brother-in-law, controls B Bank. Oliver and Paul use the $8 million to purchase all D Corp's outstanding stock through S Corp as part of a leveraged buyout. In this buyout Oliver receives $4.8 million. Two months later, D Corp fails and its creditors force it into bankruptcy. Here, it is highly probable that either an unsecured creditor or the bankruptcy trustee could bring a successful intentional fraudulent conveyance claim against Oliver, Paul, or B Bank. The trustee or unsecured creditor probably could prove:

1. That the defendant effected a transfer;
2. Of an interest in the debtor's property (the security interest transferred to B Bank);
3. Within the applicable statute of limitations; and
4. With actual intent of the debtor to hinder, delay, or defraud the creditor.[39]

§2.04 CONSTRUCTIVE FRAUDULENT CONVEYANCE IN GENERAL

In addition to addressing actual fraud, the Bankruptcy Code, the UFCA, and the UFTA also provide for constructive fraudulent conveyances. Specifically, Bankruptcy Code §548(a)(2) allows the bankruptcy trustee to avoid transfers of property or obligations incurred within the one year preceding the bankruptcy filing if the debtor voluntarily or involuntarily received less than a reasonably equivalent value in exchange for such transfer or obligation, and

1. Was insolvent on the conveyance date or became insolvent because of such conveyance;
2. Was engaged in a business or a transaction, or was about to engage in a business or a transaction, for which any property remaining with the debtor represented an unreasonably small capital; or
3. Intended to incur, or believed that the debtor would incur, debts that would be beyond the debtor's ability to pay as such debts matured.[1]

---

[39] See United States v. Tabor Court Realty Corp., 803 F.2d 1288 (3d Cir. 1986), cert. denied, 483 U.S. 1005 (1987), for a similar, but not identical, fact pattern and a finding of intentional fraudulent conveyance.
§2.04   [1] 11 U.S.C. §548(a)(2) (1988).

The UFCA provides that conveyances made or obligations incurred, other than in unreasonably small capital cases, are fraudulent as to both present and future creditors (except for insolvency, in which case the transfer is fraudulent only as to present creditors) if:

1. The transferee is insolvent on the transfer date or the transfer renders the transferee insolvent;[2]
2. The transferee is engaged or about to engage in a business or transaction for which the property remaining in his hands after the conveyance is an unreasonably small capital;[3] or
3. The transferee intends or believes that he will incur debts beyond his ability to pay as they mature.[4]

Finally, the UFTA provides that conveyances made or obligations incurred without the debtor's receiving a reasonably equivalent value in exchange for the conveyance are fraudulent if:

1. The debtor engages in or is about to engage in a business or transaction for which any remaining assets are unreasonably small in relation to the business or transaction;[5]
2. The debtor intended to incur or believed or reasonably should have believed that he would incur debts beyond his ability to pay as they became due;[6]
3. The debtor was insolvent at the time or became insolvent because of the transfer or obligation;[7] or
4. The transfer was made to an insider for an antecedent debt, the debtor was insolvent at that time, and the insider had reasonable cause to believe that the debtor was insolvent.[8]

To bring a constructive fraudulent conveyance claim, a trustee or unsecured creditor must prove five elements:

1. That there is a transfer to the defendant of;
2. An interest in the debtor's property;
3. Within the applicable statute of limitations;
4. Without reasonably equivalent value in exchange for such transfer for the Bankruptcy Code, fair consideration for the UFCA, or reasonably equivalent value for the UFTA; and

---

[2] UFCA § 4, 7A U.L.A. § 474 (1918).
[3] UFCA § 5, 7A U.L.A. § 504 (1918).
[4] UFCA § 6, 7A U.L.A. § 507 (1918).
[5] UFTA § 4(a)(2)(i), 7A U.L.A. § 653 (1984).
[6] UFTA § 4(a)(2)(ii), 7A U.L.A. § 653 (1984).
[7] UFTA § 5(a), 7A U.L.A. § 657 (1984).
[8] UFTA § 5(b), 7A U.L.A. § 657 (1984).

5.   Where the debtor was either (1) insolvent or left insolvent,[9] (2) left with an unreasonably small amount of capital,[10] or (3) intentionally left unable to pay debts as they matured.[11]

[A]   Less Than Reasonably Equivalent Value

The primary element the claimant must prove in a constructive fraudulent conveyance case is the debtor's failure to transfer reasonably equivalent value (Bankruptcy Code),[12] fair consideration (UFCA),[13] or reasonably equivalent value (UFTA).[14] Under the Bankruptcy Code, the test for failure of reasonably equivalent value is whether the value transferred is disproportionately small compared to the value received by the debtor.[15] For this purpose, the determination of whether reasonably equivalent value is present is a question of fact.[16] Relevant factors include the relative bargaining positions of the parties to the transfer, the relationship of the parties, and the adequacy of the price after considering the prevailing market conditions and the marketability of the assets involved.[17] Generally, the courts look at the consideration received by the debtor as opposed to the value given by the transferee.[18] More specifically, what constitutes reasonably equivalent value must be determined from the creditor's standpoint.[19] In this regard, intangible benefits generally will not constitute reasonably equivalent value.[20]

For the reasonably equivalent value requirement, the Bankruptcy Code defines value as "property, or satisfaction or securing of a present or antecedent debt of

[9] See § 2.04[B].

[10] See § 2.04[C].

[11] See § 2.04[D].

[12] 11 U.S.C. § 548(a)(2) (1988).

[13] UFCA §§ 4–6, 7A U.L.A. §§ 474–507 (1918).

[14] UFTA §§ 4(a)(2), 5, 7A U.L.A. §§ 653–657 (1984).

[15] Jack F. Williams, Revisiting the Proper Limits of Fraudulent Transfer Law, 8 Bankr. Dev. J. 55, 81 (1991).

[16] Advanced Chapter 11 Bankruptcy Practice Ch. 6 (Thomas J. Salerno & Craig D. Hansen eds., John Wiley & Sons 1987 & Supp. 1990); Jack F. Williams, Revisiting the Proper Limits of Fraudulent Transfer Law, 8 Bankr. Dev. J. 55, 79 (1991). See also Consove v. Cohen (In re Roco Corp.), 701 F.2d 978 (1st Cir. 1983); Klein v. Tabatchnick, 610 F.2d 1043 (2d Cir. 1979); Jacoway v. Anderson Cajun's Wharf (In re Ozark Restaurant Equip. Co.), 74 B.R. 139 (Bankr. W.D. Ark.), remanded, 77 B.R. 686 (W.D. Ark.), on remand, 83 Bankr. 591 (Bankr. W.D. Ark. 1987), aff'd in part and rev'd in part, 850 F.2d 342 (8th Cir. 1988), on subsequent remand, 96 B.R. 187 (Bankr. W.D. Ark. 1988); Adwar v. Capgro Leasing Corp. (In re Adwar), 55 B.R. 111 (Bankr. E.D.N.Y. 1985).

[17] Jack F. Williams, Revisiting the Proper Limits of Fraudulent Transfer Law, 8 Bankr. Dev. J. 55, 81 (1991); Jacoway v. Anderson Cajun's Wharf (In re Ozark Restaurant Equip. Co.), 74 B.R. 139 (Bankr. W.D. Ark.), remanded, 77 B.R. 686 (W.D. Ark.), on remand, 83 B.R. 591 (Bankr. W.D. Ark. 1987), aff'd in part and rev'd in part, 850 F.2d 342 (8th Cir. 1988), on subsequent remand, 96 B.R. 187 (Bankr. W.D. Ark. 1988).

[18] See, e.g., Ohio Corrugating Corp. v. Security Pac. Business Credit, Inc. (In re Ohio Corrugating Corp.), 70 B.R. 920 (Bankr. N.D. Ohio 1987).

[19] Jack F. Williams, Revisiting the Proper Limits of Fraudulent Transfer Law, 8 Bankr. Dev. J. 55, 80 (1991); Mancuso v. Champion (In re Dondi Fin. Corp.), 119 B.R. 106 (Bankr. N.D. Tex. 1990); Bowery v. Vines, 156 S.W.2d 395 (Tenn. 1941).

[20] Jack F. Williams, Revisiting the Proper Limits of Fraudulent Transfer Law, 8 Bankr. Dev. J. 55 (1991); Mancuso v. Champion (In re Dondi Fin. Corp.), 119 B.R. 106 (Bankr. N.D. Tex. 1990).

the debtor, but does not include an unperformed promise to furnish support to the debtor or to a relative of the debtor."[21] Generally, value equals the amount that can be realized from the assets within a reasonable time, as opposed to an immediate liquidation.[22] Generally, a court will find lack of reasonably equivalent value if the debtor transfers property for the benefit of a third party.[23]

In foreclosure cases, there is a split among the courts about whether the foreclosure sale bid price is presumed to be a reasonably equivalent value. The Fifth, Seventh, and Eighth Circuits have held that they will not presume a foreclosure sale bid price to be reasonably equivalent in value.[24] In contrast, the Ninth and Sixth Circuits have held that state law should be used to determine reasonable equivalence.[25] In many states, including California and Michigan, there is a presumption that a foreclosure sale bid price provides reasonably equivalent value.[26]

Under the UFCA, the applicable test for failure of fair consideration is whether either (1) in exchange for the debtor's conveyance, "as a fair equivalent therefore, and in good faith, property is conveyed or an antecedent debt is satisfied,"[27] or (2) the debtor's conveyance "is received in good faith to secure a present advance or antecedent debt in amount not disproportionately small as compared with the value of the property, or obligation obtained."[28] As with the Bankruptcy Code provision, the analysis must be conducted from the creditor's standpoint.[29] For example, in *Allard v. Flamingo Hilton (In re Chomakos)*,[30] the Sixth Circuit held gambling losses a debtor paid to a casino were transferred in exchange for the reasonably equivalent value of the opportunity to win more than the debtor lost. Thus, such payments were not fraudulent conveyances.

Planning Pointer. The planner should note that the UFCA test involves a good faith element.[31] This element is not present under either the Bankruptcy Code or the UFTA.

---

[21] 11 U.S.C. § 548(d) (2) (A) (1988).

[22] Jack F. Williams, *Revisiting the Proper Limits of Fraudulent Transfer Law*, 8 Bankr. Dev. J. 55, 80 (1991). *See, e.g.*, Utility Stationery Stores, Inc. v. American Portfolio (*In re* Utility Stationery Stores, Inc.), 12 B.R. 170 (Bankr. N.D. Ill. 1981).

[23] *See, e.g.*, Gill v. Brooklier (*In re* Burbank Generators, Inc.), 48 B.R. 204 (Bankr. C.D. Cal. 1985).

[24] Bundles v. Banker (*In re* Bundles), 856 F.2d 815 (7th Cir. 1988); Durrett v. Washington Nat'l Ins. Co., 621 F.2d 201 (5th Cir. 1980); First Fed. Sav. & Loan Ass'n of Bismarck v. Hulm (*In re* Hulm), 738 F.2d 323 (8th Cir.), *cert. denied*, 469 U.S. 990, *on remand*, 45 B.R. 523 (1984). These cases were all overruled by BFP v. Resolution Trust Corp., 511 U.S. 531 (1994).

[25] Madrid v. Lawyers Title Ins. Corp. (*In re* Madrid), 725 F.2d 1197 (9th Cir.), *cert. denied*, 469 U.S. 833 (1984); In re Winshall Settlor's Trust, 758 F.2d 1136 (6th Cir. 1985).

[26] *Id.*

[27] UFCA § 3(a), 7A U.L.A. § 448 (1918).

[28] UFCA § 3(b), 7A U.L.A. § 449 (1918).

[29] United States v. Gleneagles Inv. Co., 565 F. Supp. 556 (M.D. Pa. 1983), *aff'd sub nom.* United States v. Tabor Court Realty Corp., 803 F.2d 1288 (3d Cir. 1986), *cert. denied*, 483 U.S. 1005 (1987); Larrimer v. Feeney, 192 A.2d 351 (Pa. 1963).

[30] 69 F.3d 769 (6th Cir. 1995).

[31] UFCA § 3, 7A U.L.A. §§ 448–449 (1918); Cohen v. Sutherland, 257 F.2d 737 (2d Cir. 1958); Bullard v. Aluminum Co. of Am., 468 F.2d 11 (7th Cir. 1972).

Under the UFTA, the applicable test for failure of reasonably equivalent value is whether the transferee acquires an interest in the debtor's assets pursuant to a regularly conducted, noncollusive foreclosure sale or execution of a power of sale for the acquisition or disposition of the debtor's interest upon default under a mortgage, deed of trust, or security agreement.[32]

> **Caution.** Asset protection plans involving gratuitous transfers will generally fail the reasonably equivalent value element of the constructive fraudulent conveyance test. This results because such transferors do not receive any consideration in return for the assets they transfer. Consequently, in such cases the planner must ensure that the asset protection plan does not fail the other elements of the constructive fraudulent conveyance test.

[B] *Insolvency*

To prove constructive fraudulent conveyance, the trustee must prove one of three alternative elements in addition to proving failure of reasonably equivalent value. The first of these alternative elements is insolvency. Concerning this element, the Bankruptcy Code uses a balance sheet test and considers a debtor insolvent when the sum of its debts exceeds the fair market value of its property.[33] For purposes of this test, the Bankruptcy Code excludes all fraudulently transferred property and all exempt property from the debtor's assets.[34] These exclusions increase the probability that the debtor will be considered insolvent. On the other hand, rights of subrogation and contribution[35] and guarantees of debtor debts by third parties may be considered assets.[36]

An important factor in applying the Bankruptcy Code balance sheet test is whether the debtor or client is a going concern on the transfer date. For example, in *Gillman v. Scientific Research Prods. (In re Mama D'Angelo),*[37] using liquidation values the Tenth Circuit determined that the debtor was insolvent on the transfer date because the debtor was not a going concern on that date.

> **Planning Pointer.** To avoid insolvency claims, the planner should attempt to quantify the value of the debtor's rights of subrogation and contribution

---

[32] UFTA § 3(b), 7A U.L.A. § 650 (1984).

[33] 11 U.S.C. § 101(32) (Supp. II 1991).

[34] 11 U.S.C. § 101(32) (Supp. II 1991); Coleman v. Home Savs. Ass'n (*In re* Coleman), 21 B.R. 832 (Bankr. S.D. Tex. 1982).

[35] Join-In Int'l (U.S.A.) Ltd. v. New York Wholesale Distribs. Corp. (*In re* Join-In Int'l (U.S.A.) Ltd.), 56 B.R. 555 (Bankr. S.D.N.Y. 1986); Jack F. Williams, *Revisiting the Proper Limits of Fraudulent Transfer Law,* 8 Bankr. Dev. J. 55, 96 (1991).

[36] 11 U.S.C. §§ 101(5), 101(20) (1988 & Supp. II 1991).

[37] 55 F.3d 552 (10th Cir. 1995).

as well as third-party guarantees of its debts. If a substantial asset of the debtor is not easily liquidated, the planner should adjust its value downward.[38]

Generally, goodwill is not considered an asset for purposes of determining insolvency.[39] However, a court may consider goodwill to be an asset for the insolvency test if there is strong evidence of its existence and value.[40] From an evidentiary standpoint, the bankruptcy trustee must prove insolvency by a preponderance of the evidence.[41]

Under the UFCA, a debtor is insolvent when the amount required to pay the probable liability on its existing debts as they become absolute and matured exceeds the present fair salable value of its assets.[42]

The UFTA provides that a debtor is insolvent if the sum of its debts exceeds all its assets at a fair valuation.[43] However, if the debtor is generally not paying its debts as they come due, the UFTA presumes that the debtor is insolvent.[44] For the UFTA insolvency test, the debtor's assets do not include:

1. Property to the extent of any valid encumbrance;
2. Property exempt under nonbankruptcy law; and
3. Interests in property held in tenancy by the entireties to the extent they are not subject to process by a creditor holding a claim against only one tenant.[45]

Planning Pointer. The planner should note that the insolvency test generally denies standing to creditors who become creditors of the debtor after the conveyance in question.[46]

[C] Unreasonably Small Capital

The second method the claimant may use to prove constructive fraudulent conveyance is to prove that the defendant was engaged, or about to engage, in business or a transaction that would leave, or has left, the debtor with an

---

[38] Northern Va. Bank v. Vecco Constr. Indus., Inc. (*In re* Vecco Constr. Indus., Inc.), 9 B.R. 866 (Bankr. E.D. Va. 1981); Jack F. Williams, *Revisiting the Proper Limits of Fraudulent Transfer Law,* 8 Bankr. Dev. J. 55, 96 (1991).

[39] *See, e.g.,* Consove v. Cohen (*In re* Roco Corp.), 701 F.2d 978 (1st Cir. 1983).

[40] *Id.*

[41] Join-In Int'l (U.S.A.) Ltd. v. New York Wholesale Distribs. Corp. (*In re* Join-In Int'l (U.S.A.) Ltd.), 56 B.R. 555 (Bankr. S.D.N.Y. 1986); Jack F. Williams, *Revisiting the Proper Limits of Fraudulent Transfer Law,* 8 Bankr. Dev. J. 55, 103 (1991).

[42] UFCA § 2(1), 7A U.L.A. § 442 (1918).

[43] UFTA § 2(a), 7A U.L.A. § 648 (1984).

[44] UFTA § 2(b), 7A U.L.A. § 648 (1984).

[45] UFTA § 1(2), 7A U.L.A. § 644 (1984).

[46] 11 U.S.C. § 548(a)(2)(B)(i) (1988); UFCA § 4,7A U.L.A. § 474 (1918); UFTA § 5(a), 7A U.L.A. § 657 (1984).

unreasonably small capital.[47] Historically, practitioners have placed less emphasis on this theory than on the insolvency theory. However, as at least two commentators have noted, with the recently renewed interest in fraudulent conveyance law, more emphasis is likely to be placed on this theory in the future,[48] primarily because the unreasonably small capital theory does not require proof of insolvency.[49]

> **Caution.** The insolvency theory generally denies standing to those who became creditors of the debtor after the fraudulent conveyance. However, the unreasonably small capital theory gives standing to such creditors.[50]

Before determining whether a transaction satisfies the unreasonably small capital element, the planner must determine what constitutes "capital." Generally, capital includes both unencumbered assets at the time of the conveyance, plus the reasonably foreseeable cash flow determined at the time of the conveyance.[51] For this purpose, the source of expected capital may be from future operations,[52] future equity capital infusions,[53] residual equity in equipment through purchase money financing,[54] or new and commercially reasonable loans.[55]

There are three elements that the trustee or unsecured creditor must prove to establish the unreasonably small capital element.[56] First, the trustee or unsecured creditor must prove that a party engaged or about to engage in business or is a transaction[57] that requires working capital made the transfer.[58]

---

[47] 11 U.S.C. § 548(a) (2) (B) (ii) (1988); UFCA § 5, 7A U.L.A. § 504 (1918); UFTA § 4(a) (2) (i), 7A U.L.A. § 653 (1984).

[48] Bruce A. Markell, *Toward True and Plain Dealing: A Theory of Fraudulent Transfers Involving Unreasonably Small Capital*, 21 Ind. L. Rev. 469, 494 (1988); Jack F. Williams, *Revisiting the Proper Limits of Fraudulent Transfer Law*, 8 Bankr. Dev. J. 55, 95 (1991).

[49] Bruce A. Markell, *Toward True and Plain Dealing: A Theory of Fraudulent Transfers Involving Unreasonably Small Capital*, 21 Ind. L. Rev. 469, 494 (1988).

[50] Bruce A. Markell, *Toward True and Plain Dealing: A Theory of Fraudulent Transfers Involving Unreasonably Small Capital*, 21 Ind. L. Rev. 469, 493 94 (1988); Schreyer v. Platt, 134 U.S. 405 (1890); Winchester v. Charter, 94 Mass. (12 Allen) 606 (1866).

[51] Bruce A. Markell, *Toward True and Plain Dealing: A Theory of Fraudulent Transfers Involving Unreasonably Small Capital*, 21 Ind. L. Rev. 469, 496 (1988).

[52] Credit Managers Ass'n v. Federal Co., 629 F. Supp. 175 (C.D. Cal. 1985).

[53] Allied Prods. Corp. v. Arrow Freightways, Inc., 724 P.2d 752 (N.M. 1986); Kupetz v. Continental Ill. Nat'l Bank & Trust of Chicago, 77 B.R. 754 (C.D. Cal. 1987), *aff'd sub nom.* Kupetz v. Wolf, 845 F.2d 842 (9th Cir. 1988).

[54] Lackawanna Pants Mfg. Co. v. Wiseman, 133 F.2d 482 (6th Cir. 1943).

[55] Bruce A. Markell, *Toward True and Plain Dealing: A Theory of Fraudulent Transfers Involving Unreasonably Small Capital*, 21 Ind. L. Rev. 469, 496 (1988); Lackawanna Pants Mfg. Co. v. Wiseman, 133 F.2d 482 (6th Cir. 1943); Credit Managers Ass'n v. Federal Co., 629 F. Supp. 175 (C.D. Cal. 1985).

[56] Bruce A. Markell, *Toward True and Plain Dealing: A Theory of Fraudulent Transfers Involving Unreasonably Small Capital*, 21 Ind. L. Rev. 469, 496–506 (1988).

[57] 11 U.S.C. § 548(a)(2)(B)(ii) (1988); UFCA § 5, 7A U.L.A. § 504 (1918); UFTA § 4(a)(2)(i), 7A U.L.A. § 653 (1984).

[58] Iannocone v. Capital City Bank (*In re* Richards), 58 B.R. 233 (Bankr. D. Minn. 1986); Jacobson v. First State Bank of Benson (*In re* Jacobson), 48 B.R. 497 (Bankr. D. Minn. 1985), *aff'd*, No. BKY. 384-1517, 84-359, CIV. 4 85-687, 1986 WL 1789 (D. Minn. 1986).

Second, the trustee or unsecured creditor must prove that the debt's nonpayment was a reasonably foreseeable consequence of the debtor's failure to retain or provide for an adequate amount of resources from and after the transfer to satisfy the unpaid claim in question.[59] Here, the trustee or unsecured creditor must prove the presence of a connection between the transfer in question and the nonpayment of the debt in question. The amount of capital that is reasonable will differ depending on the nature of the business involved and its individual operating needs.[60] For example, if the transferor can show a course of trade justifying the amount of capital retained or can produce cash flow projections from the time of the transfer through the time the plaintiff's cause of action arose, it may show that an amount of capital normally considered small is not unreasonably small.[61]

Planning Pointer. The planner should conduct an analysis of the client's capital needs. The planner should then (1) document carefully this capital requirements analysis, and (2) ensure that the client maintains this amount of capital after the asset protection plan's execution.

Third, the trustee or unsecured creditor must prove "but-for" causation between the transfer in question and the nonpayment of the debt in question.[62] For example, if the debtor could have reasonably conducted the business more efficiently so that the capital retained would have been sufficient, then "but-for" causation does not exist.[63] Also, "losses in trade, or by fire, or by storms" may cut off liability to future creditors.[64]

[D] Intentionally Incurring Debts Beyond Ability to Pay

The third method a claimant may use to prove constructive fraudulent conveyance is to prove that the defendant intended to incur or believed it would

---

[59] Bruce A. Markell, *Toward True and Plain Dealing: A Theory of Fraudulent Transfers Involving Unreasonably Small Capital,* 21 Ind. L. Rev. 469,499 (1988); Sexton v. Wheaton, 21 U.S. (8 Wheat.) 229 (1823); Kearny Plumbing Supply Co. v. Gland, 149 A. 530 (N.J. 1930); Kepler v. Atkinson (*In re* Atkinson), 63 B.R. 266 (Bankr. W.D. Wis. 1986).

[60] *Id.*

[61] Bruce A. Markell, *Toward True and Plain Dealing: A Theory of Fraudulent Transfers Involving Unreasonably Small Capital,* 21 Ind. L. Rev. 469, 503 (1988).

[62] Bruce A. Markell, *Toward True and Plain Dealing: A Theory of Fraudulent Transfers Involving Unreasonably Small Capital,* 21 Ind. L. Rev. 469, 503–4 (1988).

[63] Hunters v. Waite, 44 Va. (3 Gratt.) 26 (1846); Jacobson v. First State Bank of Benson (*In re* Jacobson), 48 B.R. 497 (Bankr. D. Minn. 1985), *aff'd,* No. BKY. 3-84-1517, 84-359, CIV. 4-85687, 1986 WL 1789 (D. Minn. 1986).

[64] Orlando Bump, A Treatise Upon Conveyances Made By Debtors to Defraud Creditors § 262 (J. Gray ed., rev. 4th ed. 1896); Bruce A. Markell, *Toward True and Plain Dealing: A Theory of Fraudulent Transfers Involving Unreasonably Small Capital,* 21 Ind. L. Rev. 469, 505 (1988).

incur debts beyond the debtor's ability to pay as such debts matured.[65] In proving actual intent to incur debts exceeding the debtor's ability to pay,[66] the plaintiff may show that the transaction was contemporaneous with the belief that the debtor's creditors would be injured by the transfer in question.[67]

Caution. The planner should note that like the unreasonably small capital theory, the fraudulent conveyance test based on the debtor's intentionally incurring debts beyond its ability to pay generally grants standing to both creditors at the time of the conveyance and those creditors who became creditors after the conveyance.[68]

§2.05 BANKRUPTCY FRAUD

The Bankruptcy Reform Act of 1994 amended several provisions of the United States Code dealing with bankruptcy fraud. Specifically, it amended 18 U.S.C. §§152–154, and added §§156–157.

As amended, 18 U.S.C. §152, dealing with the concealment of assets, false claims, and bribery, provides that anyone who knowingly and fraudulently engages in any of the following types of conduct will be fined up to $5,000 or imprisoned for up to five years:

1. Conceals bankruptcy estate property from the bankruptcy trustee, other officers of the bankruptcy court, or creditors;
2. Makes a false oath or account relating to any bankruptcy case;
3. Makes a false statement under penalty of perjury relating to any bankruptcy case;
4. Presents any false claim for proof against a bankruptcy estate or uses any such claim in any bankruptcy case;
5. Receives any material amount of property from a debtor after a bankruptcy case has been filed with the intent to defeat the provisions contained within 11 U.S.C.;
6. Gives, offers, receives, or attempts to obtain remuneration for acting or forbearing to act in any bankruptcy case;
7. Transfers or conceals any of his property or the property of another person or corporation, personally or as an agent of another, either in contemplation of a bankruptcy case or with intent to defeat the provisions contained within 11 U.S.C.;
8. Conceals, destroys, mutilates, falsifies, or makes a false entry in any recorded information relating to a debtor's property or financial affairs,

---

[65] 11 U.S.C. §548(a)(2)(B)(iii) (1988); UFCA §6, 7A U.L.A. §507 (1918); UFTA §4(a)(2)(ii), 7A U.L.A. §653 (1984).

[66] *Id.*

[67] 4 Collier on Bankruptcy ¶¶ 548–558 (15th ed. 1992).

[68] 11 U.S.C. §548(a)(2)(B)(iii) (1988); UFCA §6, 7A U.L.A. §507 (1918); UFTA §4(a)(2)(ii), 7A U.L.A. §653 (1984).

either in contemplation of such debtor's bankruptcy proceeding or after such a bankruptcy proceeding has been filed; or

9. Withholds from an officer of the bankruptcy court any recorded information (*e.g.*, books, records, etc.), relating to the financial affairs of a debtor, after the filing of such debtor's bankruptcy case.

As amended, 18 U.S.C. § 153, dealing with the embezzlement of property from the bankruptcy estate, provides that anyone who knowingly and fraudulently appropriates to his or her own use any property of a bankruptcy estate, or secretes or destroys a document of a bankruptcy estate, will be fined up to $5,000 or imprisoned for up to five years.

As amended, 18 U.S.C. § 154, dealing with conflicts of interest of officers of the bankruptcy court, provides that officers of the court who knowingly engage in any of the following activities will be fined up to $5,000 and forfeit their offices:

1. Buy any of the bankruptcy estate's property;
2. Refuse to allow a reasonable opportunity for parties in interest to inspect the documents and accounts relating to the affairs of bankruptcy estates when directed by the bankruptcy court to do so; or
3. Refuse to allow the United States Trustee a reasonable opportunity to inspect documents and accounts of the bankruptcy estate.

Section 156, which the Bankruptcy Reform Act of 1994 added, deals with the knowing disregard of Bankruptcy Code provisions or bankruptcy rules. It provides that bankruptcy petition preparers will be fined or imprisoned for up to one year, or both, if any bankruptcy proceeding is dismissed because such preparer knowingly attempted to obtain such a result or knowingly disregarded any Bankruptcy Code provision or bankruptcy rule.

Finally, 18 U.S.C. § 157, which the Bankruptcy Reform Act of 1994 added, dealing with bankruptcy fraud, provides that individuals will be fined or imprisoned for up to five years for executing, concealing, or attempting to execute or conceal a scheme to defraud, by means of:

1. Filing a bankruptcy petition;
2. Filing a document in a bankruptcy petition; or
3. Making false or fraudulent representations, claims, or promises regarding a bankruptcy proceeding.

§ 2.06   AFFIRMATIVE DEFENSES

The Bankruptcy Code, the UFCA, and the UFTA provide for a defense for good faith transferees who give value. The Bankruptcy Code provides:

> Except to the extent that a transfer or obligation voidable under this section is voidable under section 544, 545, or 547 of this title, a transferee or obligee of such a transfer or obligation that takes for value and in good faith has a lien on or may retain any interest transferred or may enforce any obligation incurred, as the case may be, to the extent

that such transferee or obligee gave value to the debtor in exchange for such transfer or obligation.[1]

Planning Pointer. The planner should note that, concerning initial transferees, this affirmative defense applies only to the extent that the transferee gives value to the debtor in good faith.[2] However, for subsequent transferees, the affirmative defense applies when either the transferee takes for value, in good faith, and without knowledge of the voidability of the transfer,[3] or the transferee is an immediate or mediate transferee of such transferee.[4]

Regarding the good faith requirement, one commentator suggests that the plaintiff must, at a minimum, prove both (1) a lack of actual knowledge of the debtor's insolvency (or inadequate capitalization), and (2) a lack of knowledge that would cause a reasonably prudent person under the circumstances to inquire about the adequacy of the debtor's capitalization.[5] A disparity in the value of property given compared to that received by the creditor constitutes evidence of the transferee's lack of good faith.[6] Also, if the transaction is not an arm's-length transaction, this also constitutes evidence of the transferee's lack of good faith.[7]

The UFCA considers a conveyance made for "fair consideration" when either (1) in exchange for the debtor's conveyance, "as a fair equivalent therefore, and in good faith, property is conveyed or an antecedent debt is satisfied,"[8] or (2) the debtor's conveyance is received in good faith to secure a present advance or antecedent debt in amount not disproportionately small as compared with the value of the property, or obligations obtained.[9]

Planning Pointer. When the nondebtor defendant provides "fair consideration," the trustee or unsecured creditor cannot win a constructive fraudulent conveyance claim under the UFCA. Thus, the planner should strive to structure transactions so that they involve "fair consideration."

---

§2.06 [1] 11 U.S.C. §548(c) (1988).

[2] 11 U.S.C. §548(c) (1988).

[3] 11 U.S.C. §550(a)(2), (b)(1) (1988).

[4] 11 U.S.C. §550(b)(2) (1988).

[5] Jack F. Williams, *Revisiting the Proper Limits of Fraudulent Transfer Law*, 8 Bankr. Dev. J. 55, 109 (1991). *See also* Cieri et al., *An Introduction to Legal and Practical Considerations in the Restructuring of Troubled Leveraged Buyouts*, 45 Bus. Law. 333 (1989); Bernstein, Leveraged Buyouts: Legal Problems and Practical Suggestions, in Leveraged Buyouts 119, 135 (S. Diamon ed. 1985); 4 Collier on Bankruptcy 1 548.07 (15th ed. 1992).

[6] Jack F. Williams, *Revisiting the Proper Limits of Fraudulent Transfer Law*, 8 Bankr. Dev. J. 55, 109 (1991); Garrard Glenn, Fraudulent Conveyances and Preferences §594, at 511 (1940).

[7] Jack F. Williams, *Revisiting the Proper Limits of Fraudulent Transfer Law*, 8 Bankr. Dev. J. 55, 109 (1991); Bullard v. Aluminum Co. of Am., 468 F.2d 11 (7th Cir. 1972).

[8] UFCA §3(a), 7A U.L.A. §448 (1918).

[9] UFCA §3(b), 7A U.L.A. §449 (1918).

Under the UFTA, a defendant may claim an affirmative defense to an actual intent fraudulent conveyance by proving that it took in good faith and for a reasonably equivalent value or is a subsequent transferee or obligee.[10] A defendant may claim an affirmative defense to constructive fraudulent conveyance (other than constructive insider fraudulent conveyance) by proving that the transfer results from a termination of a lease on default by the debtor when the termination is pursuant to the lease and applicable law,[11] or the enforcement of a security interest in compliance with Article 9 of the Uniform Commercial Code.[12] However, even if the transaction is voidable under the UFTA, a good faith transferee or obligee is entitled to:

1. A lien on or a right to retain any interest in the asset transferred;[13]
2. Enforcement of any obligation incurred;[14] or
3. A reduction of the amount of the liability on the judgment.[15]

In the case of constructive insider fraudulent conveyance, the defendant may claim an affirmative defense:

1. To the extent that the insider gave new value to or for the benefit of the debtor after the transfer except when such new value is secured by a valid lien;[16]
2. When the transfer is made in the ordinary course of business or financial affairs of both the debtor and insider;[17] or
3. When the transfer was made pursuant to a good faith effort to rehabilitate the debtor and the transfer secured present value given for that purpose as well as an antecedent debt of the debtor.[18]

Caution. Under the Bankruptcy Code, the § 548(c) affirmative defense applies only to the extent of the value given.[19] Conversely, under the UFTA, if the defendant gives reasonable value in good faith, then it receives an absolute defense against charges of actual intent fraudulent conveyance. Also, the transferee obtains a lien on property recovered by the bankruptcy trustee to the extent of the cost of any improvements made or any value increase attributable to any improvements made.[20]

---

[10] UFTA § 8(a), 7A U.L.A. § 662 (1984).
[11] UFTA § 8(e)(1), 7A U.L.A. § 662 (1984).
[12] UFTA § 8(e)(2), 7A U.L.A. § 662 (1984).
[13] UFTA § 8(d)(1), 7A U.L.A. § 662 (1984).
[14] UFTA § 8(d)(2), 7A U.L.A. § 662 (1984).
[15] UFTA § 8(d)(3), 7A U.L.A. § 662 (1984).
[16] UFTA § 8(f)(1), 7A U.L.A. §§ 662–663 (1984).
[17] UFTA § 8(f)(2), 7A U.L.A. §§ 662–663 (1984).
[18] UFTA § 8(f)(3), 7A U.L.A. §§ 662–663 (1984).
[19] 11 U.S.C. § 548(c) (1988).
[20] 11 U.S.C. § 550(d)(1) (1988).

A second affirmative defense is the mere conduit defense.[21] This defense, which primarily applies to financial institutions, absolves a party from fraudulent conveyance liability when it acted merely as a conduit for payments from a debtor to a third party.[22] The test for application of this defense is whether the defendant/transferee had control over the transferred asset in question so as to be able to use such asset for its own purposes.[23]

§ 2.07 REMEDIES

The Bankruptcy Code gives the bankruptcy trustee the power to avoid a fraudulent conveyance transfer.[1] When this rule applies, it preserves any benefits recovered for the benefit of the estate, but only with regard to the property of the estate.[2] The trustee may recover either the property transferred or the value of the property transferred.[3] Generally, the courts will return the fraudulent transferred property, if possible, to avoid valuation issues.[4] However, when the value of the fraudulently transferred property has depreciated, the courts will often enter a money judgment.[5] If a court issues a money judgment, the appropriate amount would be the fair market value of the transferred property at the time of the transfer.[6] However, some courts have held that the appropriate money judgment amount would be the fair market value at the time of the bankruptcy petition filing date.[7]

In contrast to the Bankruptcy Code remedies, the UFTA provides for a broad array of remedies, including:

1. Avoidance of the transfer or obligation to the extent necessary to satisfy the creditor's claim;[8]

---

[21] Jack F. Williams, *Revisiting the Proper Limits of Fraudulent Transfer Law*, 8 Bankr. Dev. J. 55, 119–21 (1991).

[22] Kaiser Steel Resources, Inc. v. Jacobs (*In re* Kaiser Steel, Inc.), 110 B.R. 514 (D. Colo.), *aff'd*, 913 F.2d 846 (10th Cir. 1990); Lowry v. Security Pac. Business Credit, Inc. (*In re* Columbia Data Prods., Inc.), 892 F.2d 26 (4th Cir. 1989). Annotation, *What Constitutes "Initial Transferee" Under Sec. 550(A) of Bankruptcy Code, which Permits Recovery of Property, or Value Thereof, from Initial Transferee of Property to Extent Transfer Is Avoided*, 92 A.L.R.Fed. 631 (1989 & Supp. 1995).

[23] Kaiser Steel Resources, Inc. v. Jacobs (*In re* Kaiser Steel, Inc.), 110 B.R. 514 (D. Colo.), *aff'd*, 913 F.2d 846 (10th Cir. 1990); Lowry v. Security Pac. Business Credit, Inc. (*In re* Columbia Data Prods., Inc.), 892 F.2d 26 (4th Cir. 1989).

§ 2.07 [1] 11 U.S.C. §§ 544(1), 548 (1988 & Supp. II 1991).

[2] 11 U.S.C. § 551 (1988).

[3] 11 U.S.C. § 550 (1988). Annotation, *What Constitutes "Initial Transferee" Under Sec. 550(A) of Bankruptcy Code, which Permits Recovery of Property, or Value Thereof, from Initial Transferee of Property to Extent Transfer Is Avoided*, 92 A.L.R.Fed. 631 (1989 & Supp. 1995).

[4] Cooper v. Ashley Communications, Inc. (*In re* Morris Communications NC, Inc.), 75 B.R. 619 (Bankr. W.D.N.C. 1987), *rev'd on other grounds*, 914 F.2d 458 (4th Cir. 1990).

[5] *See, e.g.*, Hall v. Arthur Young & Co. (*In re* Computer Universe, Inc.), 58 B.R. 28 (Bankr. M.D. Fla. 1986).

[6] *See, e.g.*, Joing v. O&P Partnership (*In re* Joing), 82 B.R. 495 (D. Minn. 1987).

[7] Hall v. Arthur Young & Co. (*In re* Computer Universe, Inc.), 58 B.R. 28 (Bankr. M.D. Fla. 1986).

[8] UFTA § 7(a)(1), 7A U.L.A. § 660 (1984).

2. An attachment or other provisional remedy against the asset transferred or other property of the transferee;[9]

3. An injunction against further disposition by the debtor or a transferee, or both, of the asset transferred or of other property;[10]

4. Appointment of a receiver to take charge of the transferred asset or of other property of the transferee;[11] or

5. Any other relief the circumstances require.[12]

Finally, the UFCA remedies regarding creditors whose claims have matured (that is, become due and payable) include (1) having the conveyance set aside or the obligation annulled to the extent necessary to satisfy the claim of the defrauded creditor;[13] and (2) attachment or levy of execution upon the property in question.[14] The UFCA remedies regarding creditors whose claims have not matured include:

1. Restraining the defendant from disposing of the property;[15]

2. Appointing a receiver to take charge of the property;[16]

3. Setting aside the conveyance or annulling the obligation;[17] or

4. Any other order the circumstances may require.[18]

Where the trustee uses the UFTA or the UFCA by way of the Bankruptcy Code § 544(b),[19] there is a split among the courts regarding whether the Bankruptcy Code or the applicable state law provides the legal basis for determining the remedies to be applied. Some courts hold that the remedies provided by the Bankruptcy Code must be used even if state law provides the basis for the underlying cause of action.[20] Other courts hold that if state law provides the legal basis for the cause of action, then such law also provides the applicable remedies.[21]

§ 2.08   FRAUDULENT CONVEYANCE ISSUE CHECKLIST

Use of the following checklist will ensure that no critical issue is overlooked in connection with the planner's fraudulent conveyance analysis.

[9] UFTA § 7(a)(2), 7A U.L.A. § 660 (1984).
[10] UFTA § 7(a)(3)(i), 7A U.L.A. § 660 (1984).
[11] UFTA § 7(a)(3)(ii), 7A U.L.A. § 660 (1984).
[12] UFTA § 7(a)(3)(iii), 7A U.L.A. § 660 (1984).
[13] UFCA § 9(1)(a), 7A U.L.A. §§ 577–578 (1918).
[14] UFCA § 9(1)(b), 7A U.L.A. § 578 (1918).
[15] UFCA § 10(a), 7A U.L.A. § 630 (1918).
[16] UFCA § 10(b), 7A U.L.A. § 630 (1918).
[17] UFCA § 10(c), 7A U.L.A. § 630 (1918).
[18] UFCA § 10(d), 7A U.L.A. § 630 (1918).
[19] 11 U.S.C. § 544(b) (1988).
[20] Jack F. Williams, *Revisiting the Proper Limits of Fraudulent Transfer Law*, 8 Bankr. Dev. J. 55, 119 (1991).
[21] *Id.*

[A] Choice of Law[1]

_____ 1. Is the potential plaintiff an unsecured creditor or the bankruptcy trustee?

If an unsecured creditor, state law will be applicable, in which case some version of the UFTA or the UFCA will apply. The planner should consider conflict of law rules to determine which state's laws apply.

If the bankruptcy trustee, the applicable law will be the Bankruptcy Code, but the Bankruptcy Code also allows the bankruptcy trustee to bring a fraudulent conveyance claim under state law under certain circumstances.

[B] Actual Intent Fraudulent Conveyance[2]

_____ 2. Can the potential plaintiff prove that the potential defendant effected a transfer of an interest in the debtor's property within the applicable statute of limitations and did so with actual intent to hinder, delay, or defraud a creditor?

If yes, the planner is faced with a potential actual intent fraudulent conveyance claim.

_____ 3. Are the answers to any of the following questions yes?

(a) Was the transfer or obligation to an insider or family member?

(b) Did the debtor retain possession or control of the transferred property after the conveyance?

(c) Was the transfer or obligation disclosed or concealed?

(d) Was the debtor sued or threatened with suit before the conveyance?

(e) Did the conveyance consist of substantially all the debtor's assets?

(f) Did the debtor abscond?

(g) Did the debtor remove or conceal assets?

(h) Was the value of the consideration that the debtor received less than reasonably equivalent to the value of the conveyance?

(i) Was the debtor insolvent at the time of the conveyance or did the debtor become insolvent soon after the conveyance?

(j) Did the conveyance occur shortly before or after the debtor incurred a substantial debt?

(k) Did the debtor convey the essential assets of the business to a lienor who transferred the assets to an insider of the debtor?

If the answer to any of the above is yes, this constitutes a "badge of fraud" that may indicate that actual fraud exists.

§2.08 [1] _See_ §2.02.
[2] _See_ §2.03.

[C] Constructive Fraudulent Conveyance[3]

____4. Was there (1) a transfer to the potential defendant, (2) of an interest in the debtor's property, (3) within the applicable statute of limitations, (4) without reasonably equivalent value in exchange for such transfer for the Bankruptcy Code, fair consideration for the UFCA, or reasonably equivalent value for the UFTA, (5) when the debtor was either (a) insolvent or left insolvent,[4] (b) left with an unreasonably small amount of capital,[5] or (c) intentionally left unable to pay debts as they matured?[6]

   If yes, the potential defendant probably is liable for constructive fraudulent conveyance.

[D] Affirmative Defenses[7]

____5. Did the potential defendant (1) receive the transferred property in good faith, and (2) give value?

   If yes, such transferee may have an affirmative defense against potential fraudulent conveyance claims in connection with the transfer that may allow retention of the property in question or may provide a lien on the property, among other possible remedies.

____6. Did the potential defendant/transferee actually have control over the transferred asset in question so as to be able to use such asset for its own purposes?

   If no, the "mere conduit" defense may be available to such defendant.

[E] Remedies[8]

____7. Is there a viable fraudulent conveyance claim under the Bankruptcy Code against a potential defendant?

   If yes, the Bankruptcy Code gives the bankruptcy trustee the power to avoid the fraudulent conveyance transfer in question.

____8. Is there a viable fraudulent conveyance claim under the UFTA against a potential defendant?

   If yes, the UFTA provides remedies for the potential plaintiff that include (1) avoidance of the transfer or obligation to the extent necessary to satisfy the creditor's claim; (2) an attachment or other provisional remedy against the asset transferred or other property of the transferee; (3) an injunction against further disposition by the debtor or a transferee, or both, of the asset transferred or of other property; (4) appointment of a receiver to take

----

[3] See § 2.04.
[4] See § 2.04[B].
[5] See § 2.04[C].
[6] See § 2.04[D].
[7] See § 2.06.
[8] See § 2.07.

charge of the transferred asset or of other property of the transferee; or (5) any other relief the circumstances require.

_____9. 9. Is there a viable fraudulent conveyance claim under the UFCA against a potential defendant?

If yes, the UFCA provides remedies for the potential plaintiff that include (1) having the conveyance set aside or the obligation annulled to the extent necessary to satisfy the claim of the defrauded creditor; and (2) attachment or levy of execution upon the property in question. The UFCA remedies regarding creditors whose claims have not matured include (1) restraining the defendant from disposing of the property; (2) appointing a receiver to take charge of the property; (3) setting aside the conveyance or annulling the obligation; or (4) any other order the circumstances may require.

3

Choice of Business Entity: Nontax Aspects

§3.01 IN GENERAL

The client's business operation merits the asset protection planner's special attention. This is because business operations tend to cause liabilities that may affect both the business operation out of which the liability arises as well as other, unrelated assets. In contrast, other assets, such as furniture, stocks, and bank accounts generally do not cause liabilities. Because of this characteristic, choice of entity assumes great importance for the asset protection planner.

> **Planning Pointer.** The planner's primary objective in this area is to limit the reach of liabilities arising out of a business operation to that business operation's assets. An additional objective is to protect the assets of a business operation from nonbusiness creditors of the business's owner.

EXAMPLE 3-1

Adam owns 100 percent of At-Risk Rentals, a sole proprietorship. At-Risk has $1 million of assets. Adam has an additional $10 million of assets entirely invested in U.S. government bonds. Adam has no outstanding liabilities. Edward Employee, an employee of At-Risk, negligently injures Sue Smart, who sues At-Risk. Sue's lawsuit succeeds and Sue wins a $10 million judgment against At-Risk Rentals. Here, because Adam operates At-Risk Rentals as a sole proprietorship, he faces unlimited liability for At-Risk's debts, including Sue's $10 million judgment. Assuming no insurance coverage, Sue may reach up to $10 million of Adam's assets.

EXAMPLE 3-2

Same facts as Example 3–1, except that Adam operates At-Risk Rentals as a corporation. Here, if Sue cannot pierce At-Risk's corporate veil, she can only reach the $1 million of assets owned by At-Risk. She cannot reach Adam's $10 million of U.S. government bonds. By incorporating, Adam limits his exposure from liabilities arising out of At-Risk to At-Risk's assets. He thereby protects his nonbusiness assets from these liabilities.

The planner can place a business operation into one of five basic business operations. These include:

1. Sole proprietorships,
2. General partnerships,
3. Limited partnerships,

    4. Corporations, and

    5. Limited liability companies.

Each of these entity forms has a unique set of liability limitation characteristics. In addition, each of these forms has very different nonliability characteristics. One of these nonliability characteristics is the associated tax implications of each form of entity. Consequently, the planner must balance any limited liability benefits of a particular form of entity against any additional tax and other costs associated with that particular form of entity.

Planning Pointer. When analyzing choice of entity as part of an asset protection plan, the planner should use the following analysis:

1. What are the asset protection benefits of the different entity forms?[1]
2. What are the tax consequences of using the different entity forms?[2]
3. What are the other legal consequences that result from operating the business under the different entity forms?[3]

§ 3.02 SOLE PROPRIETORSHIPS

In the sole proprietorship form of business organization, one individual owns the business assets and is liable for all business debts. The proprietor faces unlimited personal liability subject to protection by insurance or contractual provisions. The business owner may hire employees and enter the relation of master and servant or principal and agent. Proprietorships generally are small businesses with modest capital needs that can be met from the owner's resources and from lenders. Because the sole proprietorship offers no asset protection benefits, this book will not consider further the sole proprietorship as an organization choice.

§ 3.03 CORPORATIONS

Corporations[1] are legal entities that are legally independent from the corporation's owners. The planner may form a corporation by executing and filing articles of incorporation that applicable state law requires. The

---

§ 3.01 [1] *See* §§ 3.02, 3.03[A]–3.03[G], 3.04, 3.05[A]–3.05[E], 3.06[A]–3.06[B].
[2] *See* Chapter 4.
[3] *See* §§ 3.02, 3.03[H], 3.04, 3.05[G], 3.06[C].
§ 3.03 [1] *See generally* Harry G. Henn & John R. Alexander, Law of Corporations (3d ed. 1983); Robert Charles Clark, Corporate Law (1986); Zolman Cavitch, Business Organizations (1991); Edward Brodsky & M. Patricia Adamski, Law of Corporate Officers and Directors (1984 & Supp. 1990); F. Hodge O'Neal &

corporation conducts business, acquires assets, enters contracts, and incurs liabilities in its own name.

Generally, the corporation's liability is limited to the assets it owns. This is generally referred to as limited liability. Limited liability protects the corporation's shareholders from personal liability for the corporation's liabilities. The shareholders' financial exposure generally equals the amount of their investment in the corporation.

From a tax standpoint, a corporation is a taxable entity apart from its owners.[2] Consequently, the Internal Revenue Code (Code) taxes corporate income twice. First, the Code taxes such income at the corporate level when earned. Second, the Code taxes such income at the shareholder level when the corporation distributes such income as an actual or constructive dividend. This is generally referred to as double taxation of distributed corporate income.

The asset protection planner must analyze the limited liability aspects of corporations as part of any asset protection analysis. In particular, the planner must examine exceptions to the general rule of limited liability to ensure that none of these exceptions will apply to the client.[3] Second, the planner must evaluate the tax consequences of incorporating to ensure that any additional taxes that result do not outweigh the corporate limited liability benefits. Finally, the planner must examine how the corporate form compares to other entity forms in terms of (a) management and control, (b) continuity of existence, (c) transferability of entity interests, and (d) expenses and formalities associated with corporations.[4]

[A] Limited Liability Generally

Limited liability is the planner's primary focus. As previously noted, corporate law limits the reach of corporate liabilities to the corporation's assets.[5] This is extremely important for the planner because limited liability protects corporate shareholders from the corporation's liabilities.[6]

The planner must consider various limitations on a corporation's limited liability. These include:

1. The doctrine of piercing the corporate veil;
2. Defective incorporation;
3. Unpaid stock subscriptions;
4. Illegal dividends; and
5. The 100-percent penalty.

Robert B. Thompson, O'Neal's Close Corporations (3d ed. 1987 & Supp. 1991); Edwin T. Hood, Closely Held Corporations in Business and Estate Planning (1992).

[2] IRC § 11(a).

[3] See §§ 3.03[A]–3.03[G].

[4] See § 3.03[H].

[5] See, e.g., Revised Model Business Corp. Act § 6.22 (1984).

[6] See Examples 3-1 and 3-2 for examples of the practical significance of limited liability.

Planning Pointer. The planner who uses the corporate form must structure a plan to ensure that limited liability limitations and exceptions do not
apply to the client. Also, the planner must consider the cost of eliminating
or minimizing these limitations when comparing various entity forms.

[B]   Piercing the Corporate Veil

Piercing the corporate veil is the process of imposing liability for corporate
activity, in disregard of the corporate entity, on a person or entity other than the
corporation in question.[7] The general rule regarding piercing the corporate veil is
that

> a corporation will be looked on as a legal entity as a general rule, and until sufficient
> reason to the contrary appears; but, when the notion of legal entity is used to defeat
> public convenience, justify wrong, protect: fraud, or defend crime, the law will regard
> the corporation as an association of persons.[8]

Planning Pointer. Piercing the corporate veil is a frequently litigated issue in
corporate law.[9] Therefore, the planner must plan to minimize the risk of corporate
veil piercing.

Unfortunately, there is no strict test for finding shareholder liability under the
piercing the corporate veil doctrine. Generally, courts look to the totality of
the circumstances involved, including the following factors, when determining
whether to disregard the corporation and impose liability on its shareholders by
veil piercing.[10]

[1]   Whether the Liability Arises Out of a Contract or Tort Action

Generally, courts are more likely to pierce a corporation's limited liability veil
when the liability in question arises out of a tort case rather than a contract case.
This is especially true when tort actions occur in combination with inadequate
capital.[11]

---

[7] *See generally* Steven Presser, Piercing the Corporate Veil (1990); Harry G. Henn & John R. Alexander,
Law of Corporations (3d ed. 1983); Robert Charles Clark, Corporate Law (1986); Zolman Cavitch, Business Organizations (1991); Edward Brodsky & M. Patricia Adamski, Law of Corporate Officers and
Directors (1984 & Supp. 1990); F. Hodge O'Neal & Robert B. Thompson, O'Neal's Close Corporations
(3d ed. 1987 & Supp. 1991).

[8] United States v. Milwaukee Refrigerator Transit Co., 142 F. 247 (E.D. Wis. 1905). *See* Harry G. Henn
& John R. Alexander, Law of Corporations 344–75 (3d ed. 1983).

[9] Robert B. Thompson, *Piercing the Corporate Veil: An Empirical Study,* 76 Cornell L. Rev. 1036 (1991).

[10] F. Hodge O'Neal & Robert B. Thompson, O'Neal's Close Corporations (3d ed. 1987 & Supp. 1991).

[11] *See* Harry G. Henn & John R. Alexander, Law of Corporations, 348–49 (3d ed. 1983); Zolman
Cavitch, Business Organizations § 120.05 (1991).

[2] Whether the Corporation Is Adequately Capitalized

When the planner does not adequately capitalize the corporation, a court will be more likely to pierce the corporate veil.[12] Inadequate capitalization refers to capitalization that is very small given the nature, magnitude, and risks of the business, or the reasonableness of the cushion for creditors.[13] For this purpose, capital generally refers to net assets or the total contribution made by shareholders, as opposed to total assets, stated or legal capital, or working capital.[14] When the shareholder provides loans or other credit, such credit may be considered in determining if there is adequate capital.[15]

Planning Pointer. Although it may not be possible to determine the exact amount of capital required in a particular case, the planner should consider the following factors when establishing the capitalization of a new corporation:

- The reasonable needs of the corporation, considering its nature, magnitude, and likely risks;[16]

---

[12] Zolman Cavitch, Business Organizations § 120.05[3] (1991); Harry G. Henn & John R. Alexander, Law of Corporations 344–75 (3d ed. 1983); Robert B. Thompson, *Piercing the Corporate Veil: An Empirical Study*, 76 Cornell L. Rev. 1036, 1063–70 (1991); William P. Hackney & Tracey G. Bensen, *Shareholder Liability for Inadequate Capital*, 43 U. Pitt. L. Rev. 837, 849 (1982); Comment, *Limited Limited Liability: A Definitive Judicial Standard for the Inadequate Capitalization Problem*, 47 Temp. L.Q. 321 (1974); Note, *Inadequate Capitalization as a Basis for Shareholder Liability: The California Approach and a Recommendation*, 45 S. Cal. L. Rev. 823 (1972); Note, *Inadequately Capitalized Subsidiaries*, 19 U. Chi. L. Rev. 872 (1952); Annotation, *Inadequate capitalization as factor in disregard of corporate entity*, 63 A.L.R.2d 1051 (1959); *Liability of corporation for contracts of subsidiary*, 38 A.L.R.3d 1102 § § 1, 18; *Liability of corporation for torts of subsidiary*, 7 A.L.R.3d 1343, § 1; *Disregarding corporate entity in settling accounts between close corporation and its stockholder or stockholders*, 100 A.L.R.2d 385. *See, e.g.*, Francis O. Day Co. v. Shapiro, 267 F.2d 669, 673 (D.C. Cir. 1959); Conner v. 1747 Pennsylvania Ave. Assocs., Ltd. Partnership, 669 A.2d 693 (D.C. 1995) (District of Columbia Court of Appeals held that sole shareholder of an insolvent corporation was liable for unpaid rent that corporation owed, to the extent insolvency was due to preference payments the corporation made to him as a shareholder-creditor).

[13] Zolman Cavitch, Business Organizations § 120.05[3] (1991); Harry G. Henn & John R. Alexander, Law of Corporations 344–75 (3d ed. 1983); Robert B. Thompson, *Piercing the Corporate Veil: An Empirical Study*, 76 Cornell L. Rev. 1036, 1063–70(1991); William P. Hackney & Tracey G. Bensen, *Shareholder Liability for Inadequate Capital*, 43 U. Pitt. L. Rev. 837, 849 (1982).

[14] Edward Brodsky & M. Patricia Adamski, Law of Corporate Officers and Directors § 20:07 (1984 & Supp. 1990); William P. Hackney & Tracey G. Bensen, *Shareholder Liability for Inadequate Capital*, 43 U. Pitt. L. Rev. 837, 890 (1982).

[15] Edward Brodsky & M. Patricia Adamski, Law of Corporate Officers and Directors § 20:07 (1984 & Supp. 1990); William P. Hackney & Tracey G. Bensen, *Shareholder Liability for Inadequate Capital*, 43 U. Pitt. L. Rev. 837, 891 (1982).

[16] Edward Brodsky & M. Patricia Adamski, Law of Corporate Officers and Directors § 20:07 (1984 & Supp. 1990); William P. Hackney & Tracey G. Bensen, *Shareholder Liability for Inadequate Capital*, 43 U. Pitt. L. Rev. 837, 892 (1982).

- When a going concern is incorporated, the amount of capital required by the prior business,[17] especially when the business was successfully run for several years;[18]
- The projected future cash flow of the corporation and the ability of this projected cash flow to give the corporation a reasonable chance to pay its obligations as they mature;[19] and
- The debt to equity ratio of the new corporation.[20]

The proper time for determining adequgacy of capitalization is the time of corporate formation. If the planner adequately capitalizes the corporation at inception but because of unavoidable losses, it becomes undercapitalized, the corporate veil will generally not be pierced.[21]

[3] Whether the Corporation Is Formed for an Illegal Purpose

When the shareholder forms the corporation for an illegal purpose, a court will be more likely to pierce the corporate veil.[22]

[4] Whether the Equity and Justice of the Situation Indicates the Corporate Veil Should Be Pierced

When the equity and justice of the situation suggest that the corporate veil should be pierced, a court will be more likely to pierce the corporate veil.[23]

---

[17] Edward Brodsky & M. Patricia Adamski, Law of Corporate Officers and Directors § 20:07 (1984 & Supp. 1990); William P. Hackney & Tracey G. Bensen, *Shareholder Liability for Inadequate Capital*, 43 U. Pitt. L. Rev. 837, 893 (1982). *See, e.g.*, Costello v. Fazio, 256 F.2d 903 (9th Cir. 1958).

[18] Edward Brodsky & M. Patricia Adamski, Law of Corporate Officers and Directors § 20:07 (1984 & Supp. 1990); William P. Hackney & Tracey G. Bensen, *Shareholder Liability for Inadequate Capital*, 43 U. Pitt. L. Rev. 837, 893 (1982); *Stockholder's personal conduct of operations or management of assets as factor justifying disregard of corporate entity*, 46 A.L.R.3D 428, Supp. § 6. *See, e.g., In re* Branding Iron Steak House, 536 F.2d 299 (9th Cir. 1976); Tigrett v. Pointer, 580 S.W.2d 375 (Tex. Civ. App. 1978), *superseded by statute as stated in Plas-Tex, Inc. v. Jones*, 200 Tex. App. LEXIS 3188 (Tex. App. May 18, 2000).

[19] William P. Hackney & Tracey G. Bensen, *Shareholder Liability for Inadequate Capital*, 43 U. Pitt. L. Rev. 837, 896 (1982). *See, e.g.*, Ohio Edison Co. v. Warner Coal Corp., 72 N.E.2d 487 (Ohio Ct. App. 1947).

[20] William P. Hackney & Tracey G. Bensen, *Shareholder Liability for Inadequate Capital*, 43 U. Pitt. L. Rev. 837, 895 (1982). *See, e.g.*, Fourth Nat'l Bank of Montgomery v. Portsmouth Cotton Oil Ref. Corp., 280 F. 879 (M.D. Ala.), *aff'd*, 284 F. 718 (5th Cit. 1922).

[21] *See, e.g.*, Arnold v. Phillips, 117 F.2d 497 (5th Cir.), *cert. denied*, 313 U.S. 583 (1941).

[22] Edward Brodsky & M. Patricia Adamski, Law of Corporate Officers and Directors Ch. 20 (1984 & Supp. 1990); Zolman Cavitch, Business Organizations § 120.05[5] (1991); Harry G. Henn & John R. Alexander, Law of Corporations 344–75 (3d ed. 1983); Robert B. Thompson, *Piercing the Corporate Veil: An Empirical Study*, 76 Cornell L. Rev. 1036, 1063 (1991).

[23] Edward Brodsky & M. Patricia Adamski, Law of Corporate Officers and Directors Ch. 20 (1984 & Supp. 1990); Zolman Cavitch, Business Organizations § 120.05[6] (1991); Harry G. Henn & John R. Alexander, Law of Corporations 344–75 (3d ed. 1983); Robert B. Thompson, *Piercing the Corporate Veil: An Empirical Study*, 76 Cornell L. Rev. 1036, 1063 (1991).

Caution: Although the corporate veil generally will not be pierced if the corporation becomes undercapitalized because of unavoidable losses, if the corporation becomes insolvent, a court may hold that a fiduciary duty on the part of the corporation's officers and directors arises. Moreover, if a liability arises from the breach of such a fiduciary duty, this liability will not be dischargeable in bankruptcy.[24]

[5] Whether the Corporation Follows Corporate Formalities

When the corporation fails to follow corporate formalities, a court will be more likely to pierce the corporate veil.[25]

[6] Whether the Separateness Between the Corporation and the Shareholder Is Maintained

When the shareholder does not maintain the corporation's separateness, a court will be more likely to pierce the corporate veil.[26] Lack of separateness refers to situations where shareholders, especially controlling shareholders or parent corporations, use the corporation merely as a tool for furthering their private business.

Although the fact that the corporation is closely held will not by itself cause veil piercing, courts generally require close corporations to satisfy two requirements to avoid having its corporate veil pierced: (1) the business must be conducted on a corporate, as opposed to a personal basis;[27] and (2) the corporation must be established on an adequate financial basis.[28] Similarly, although sole ownership of a subsidiary will not, by itself, cause the subsidiary's veil to be pierced, "control" carried to the extent of obliterating the subsidiary's separate identity may cause such piercing.[29]

When a court does pierce the corporation's veil of limited liability, generally it will only hold those persons who control the corporation and actively exercise

---

[24] *In re* Reuscher, 169 B.R. 398 (S.D. Ill. 1994).

[25] Edward Brodsky & M. Patricia Adamski, Law of Corporate Officers and Directors Ch. 20 (1984 & Supp. 1990); Zolman Cavitch, Business Organizations § 120.05 (1991); Harry G. Henn & John R. Alexander, Law of Corporations 344–75 (3d ed, 1983); Robert B. Thompson, *Piercing the Corporate Veil: An Empirical Study*, 76 Cornell L. Rev. 1036, 1063 (1991); Annotation, *Failure to issue stock as factor in disregard of corporate entity*, 8 A.L.R.3d 1122 (1966 & Supp. 1995).

[26] Edward Brodsky & M. Patricia Adamski, Law of Corporate Officers and Directors Ch. 20 (1984 & Supp. 1990); Zolman Cavitch, Business Organizations § 120.05[2] (1991); Harry G. Henn & John R. Alexander, Law of Corporations 344–75 (3d ed. 1983); Robert B. Thompson, *Piercing the Corporate Veil: An Empirical Study*, 76 Cornell L. Rev. 1036, 1063 (1991).

[27] Kimbrell v. Commissioner, 371 F.2d 897 (5th Cir. 1967); Britt v. United States, 431 F.2d 227 (5th Cit. 1970); C.E. Dev. Co. v. Kitchens, 264 So. 2d 510 (Ala. 1972); Dietel v. Day, 492 P.2d 455 (Ariz. 1972); Harris v. Wagshal, 343 A.2d 283 (D.C. 1975); Fagan v. La Gloria Oil & Gas Co., 494 S.W.2d 624 (Tex. Civ. App. 1973); Zolman Cavitch, Business Organizations § 120.05[2][a] (1991).

[28] Zolman Cavitch, Business Organizations § 120.05[2][a] (1991).

[29] Zolman Cavitch, Business Organizations § 120.05[2][b] (1991); Harry G. Henn & John R. Alexander, Law of Corporations 355–56 (3d ed. 1983). *See, e.g.,* Lipschutz v. Gordon Jewelry Corp., 373 F. Supp. 375 (S.D. Tex. 1974); United States Nat'l Bank v. Madison Nat'l Bank, 355 F. Supp. 165 (D.D.C. 1973).

such control liable. Conversely, courts will generally not subject passive shareholders to unlimited liability.[30] The asset protection client will generally be a controlling shareholder. Consequently, the planner must plan to minimize the risk of limited liability veil piercing.

EXAMPLE 3-3

Adam operates and owns 100 percent of At-Risk Rentals, a sole proprietorship. At-Risk has $1 million of assets. Adam has an additional $10 million of assets that he has entirely invested in U.S. government bonds. Adam has no outstanding liabilities. Adam, on Paula Planner's recommendation, incorporates At-Risk as part of an asset protection plan. When Adam forms At-Risk, Inc., he retains the $1 million of assets, which he then leases to At-Risk, Inc. After incorporation, Adam drains all capital that At-Risk accumulates. Furthermore, Adam does not follow any corporate formalities and uses At-Risk, Inc. to conduct personal business.

Edward Employee, an employee of At-Risk, Inc., negligently injures Sue Smart, who sues At-Risk. Sue's lawsuit succeeds and she wins a $10 million judgment against At-Risk Rentals. Moreover, the court pierces At-Risk, Inc.'s corporate veil and allows Sue to recover against Adam. Here, Adam is liable to Sue for the $10 million judgment. Assuming no insurance coverage, Sue may reach up to $10 million of Adam's assets. The result is that poor planning has devastated Adam's asset protection plan.

Planning Point. Planners using corporations should, at a minimum, ensure that the asset protection plan incorporates the following steps to minimize the risk of corporate veil piercing:

- Form the corporation with adequate capital and document the methodology of arriving at the amount of adequate capital. The corporation should carry adequate liability insurance.
- Instruct the client not to drain capital from the corporation in an unwarranted manner and periodically monitor client compliance.
- Ensure that the client forms the corporation for a legal purpose.
- Instruct the client to follow corporate formalities, including the following: complete the organization of the corporation and issue stock for consideration before commencing business; hold meetings of shareholders and directors; maintain complete corporate and financial records; and do not commingle corporate property with the shareholder's personal property. The planner should periodically monitor compliance with this directive.

---

[30] Edward Brodsky & M. Patricia Adamski, Law of Corporate Officers and Directors § 20:12 (1984 & Supp. 1990).

- For closely held corporations, ensure that clients (1) conduct corporate business on a corporate, as opposed to a personal, basis, and (2) establish the corporation on an adequate financial basis.
- For parent-subsidiary situations, ensure that (1) the parent and subsidiary are maintained as separate financial units and each are sufficiently financed so as to be able to meet its normal financial burden,[31] (2) the parent and subsidiary segregate and keep segregated the day-to-day business and records,[32] (3) the parent and subsidiary maintain the formal barriers between their management structures,[33] (4) the parent and subsidiary do not represent themselves as one corporation,[34] and (5) the parent gives the subsidiary at least a minimal amount of management self-determination.[35]

[C] Defective Incorporation

When the client fails to comply with the statutory incorporation procedure under applicable state law, some or all shareholders may be subjected to personal liability. The precise impact of defective incorporation depends on the law of the jurisdiction of incorporation. For example, in jurisdictions that have enacted the Revised Model Business Corporation Act, "[a]ll persons purporting to act as or on behalf of a corporation, knowing that there was no incorporation ... are jointly and severally liable for all liabilities created while so acting."[36]

When the corporation does not comply substantially with all mandatory conditions precedent to incorporation, the shareholders may be protected against unlimited liability by the de facto doctrine. Under the de facto doctrine, a

---

[31] Zolman Cavitch, Business Organizations § 120.05[2][b] (1991); William O. Douglas & Carrol M. Shanks, Insulation From Liability Through Subsidiary Corporations, 39 Yale L.J. 193, 206 (1929). *See, e.g.,* Coles v. Humble Oil & Ref. Co., 348 F. Supp. 1240 (S.D. Tex. 1972); Allright Tex., Inc. v. Simons, 501 SW.2d 145 (Tex. Civ. App. 1973).

[32] Zolman Cavitch, Business Organizations § 120.05[2][b] (1991); William O. Douglas and Carrol M. Shanks, Insulation from Liability Through Subsidiary Corporations, 39 Yale L.J. 193, 206 (1929). *See, e.g.,* RE Collier & Son Corp. v. F.T.C., 427 F.2d 261 (6th Cir.), *cert. denied,* 400 U.S. 926 (1970); Washington & Old Dominion Users Ass'n v. Washington & Old Dominion R.R., 155 S.E.2d 322 (Va. 1967).

[33] Zolman Cavitch, Business Organizations § 120.05[2][b] (1991); William O. Douglas and Carrol M. Shanks, Insulation from Liability Through Subsidiary Corporations, 39 Yale L.J. 193, 206 (1929). *See, e.g.,* RE Collier & Son Corp. v. F.T.C., 427 F.2d 261 (6th Cir.), *cert. denied,* 400 U.S. 926 (1970); American Trading & Prod. Corp. v. Fischback & Moore, Inc., 311 F. Supp. 412 (N.D. 111. 1970).

[34] Zolman Cavitch, Business Organizations § 120.05[2][b] (1991); William O. Douglas and Carrol M. Shanks, Insulation from Liability Through Subsidiary Corporations, 39 YaleL.J. 193, 206 (1929). *See, e.g.,* In re Beck Indus., Inc., 479 F.2d 410 (2d Cir.), *cert. denied,* 414 U.S. 858 (1973); Markow v. Alcock, 356 F.2d 194 (5th Cir. 1966).

[35] Zolman Cavitch, Business Organizations § 120.05[2][b] (1991).

[36] Revised Model Business Corp. Act § 2.04 (1984); *See generally* Annotation, *Personal liability of promoter to third person on or with respect to contract made for corporation or in aid of promotion,* 41 A.L.R.2d 477 (1955); Annotation, *Stockholder's personal conduct of operations or management of assets as factor justifying disregard of corporate entity,* 46 A.L.R.3d 428 (1972 & Supp. 1995); Annotation, *Duty to disclose material facts to stock purchaser,* 80 A.L.R.3d 13, § 1; Annotation, *Failure to issue stock as factor in disregard of corporate entity,* 8 A.L.R.3d 1122 § 1.

corporation not complying substantially with mandatory conditions precedent to incorporation will be protected from attack on its corporateness by all parties other than the state of incorporation when:

1. There is a statute under which the shareholder might have incorporated the corporation;
2. There was a colorable attempt to comply with such statute; and
3. There has been some use or exercise of corporate privileges.[37]

When the state of incorporation has enacted statutory provisions to deal with the consequences of defective incorporation, courts have generally construed these provisions as having overturned the de facto doctrine.[38] For example, some jurisdictions have construed the Model Business Corporation Act to have overturned the de facto doctrine.[39]

When the corporation does not substantially comply with the statutory incorporation requirements and the de facto doctrine does not apply, the shareholders of the purported corporation may be protected against unlimited liability by the estoppel doctrine. Under this doctrine, persons who deal with a purported corporation may be estopped from attacking its corporateness. Conversely, associates who hold themselves out as a corporation may be estopped from arguing against their corporateness.[40] As with the de facto doctrine, when the state of incorporation has enacted statutory provisions regarding defective incorporation, some courts have construed such statutes as having overturned the corporation by estoppel doctrine.[41]

Many jurisdictions have enacted statutes to deal with defective incorporation.[42] These statutes vary greatly in how they operate. Some statutes operate by stating when corporate existence begins. Others operate by providing that certain acts (for example, the issuance of the formal certificate of incorporation) constitute conclusive or presumptive evidence that the corporation exists. Still others operate by defining specific sanctions for noncompliance with statutory incorporation procedures.[43]

When the shareholder defectively incorporates and neither the de facto doctrine, the corporation by estoppel doctrine, nor an applicable statute causes the purported corporation to be treated as a corporation, the impact on the purported corporation's limited liability varies in each jurisdiction. Traditionally, courts have held all the associates, regardless of whether they are active members,

---

[37] Harry G. Henn & John R. Alexander, Law of Corporations 329 (3d ed. 1983); Harold Gill Reuschlein & William A. Gregory, The Law of Agency and Partnership 506 (2d ed. 1989).

[38] Harry G. Henn & John R. Alexander, Law of Corporations 329, 335 (3d ed. 1983); Harold Gill Reuschlein & William A. Gregory, The Law of Agency and Partnership 506 (2d ed. 1989).

[39] *Id. See, e.g.,* Timberlane Equip. v. Davenport, 514 P.2d 1109 (Or. 1973); Robertson v. Levy, 197 A.2d 443 (D.C. 1964).

[40] Harry G. Henn & John R. Alexander, Law of Corporations 335 (3d ed. 1983).

[41] Harry G. Henn & John R. Alexander, Law of Corporations 335 (3d ed. 1983). *See, e.g.,* Robertson v. Levy, 197 A.2d 443 (D.C. 1964).

[42] Harry G. Henn & John R. Alexander, Law of Corporations 336 (3d ed. 1983); Harold Gill Reuschlein & William A. Gregory, The Law of Agency and Partnership 507 (2d ed. 1989).

[43] Harry G. Henn & John R. Alexander, Law of Corporations 336 (3d ed. 1983).

liable for the purported corporation's debts on the ground that the purported corporation is a general partnership.[44] The more modern approach is for a court to examine the facts of each case to decide if the entity should be treated as a partnership. Alternatively, active associates may be held liable for breach of implied warranty of authority or principal. Finally, many jurisdictions have statutes that define the consequences of defective incorporation.[45]

> **Planning Pointer.** Because the consequences of defective incorporation are unpredictable and very easy to prevent, the planner should avoid such problems by properly incorporating in the first instance.

[D] *Unpaid Stock Subscriptions and Watered Stock*

Generally, each stockholder is liable to the corporation for the full amount of the subscription or purchase price agreed on for an original issue of stock.[46] When the shareholder pays the full subscription or purchase price this rule does not apply. When the shareholder does not pay the full price or when the corporation issues stock for property or services that it overvalues, this rule will apply. Such stock is called watered stock. The corporation's creditors will have a right of action against those persons who subscribe to or agree to purchase such watered stock.[47] Transferees of such individuals who have knowledge or notice of the unpaid consideration also will be liable for the deficiency.[48] Bona fide transferees without knowledge or notice of the deficiency will generally not be liable for it.[49] The transfer of watered stock will generally not relieve original subscribers or purchasers or their transferees from liability.[50]

When fiduciaries subscribe to or agree to purchase watered stock, they generally are not personally liable for the deficiency. However, the funds in their trust are generally liable.[51]

---

[44] Gazette Publishing Co. v. Brady, 162 S.W.2d 494 (Ark. 1942); Bonfils v. Hayes, 201 P. 677 (Colo. 1921); Harrill v. Davis, 168 F. 187 (8th Cir. 1909); Harry G. Henn & John R. Alexander, Law of Corporations 342–43 (3d ed. 1983).

[45] Harry G. Henn & John R. Alexander, Law of Corporations 343 (3d ed. 1983).

[46] Cal. Corp. Code § 410 (Deering 1977); Rev. Model Business Corp. Act § 6.22 (1984); Hall v. Hall, 506 S.W.2d 42 (Mo. Ct. App. 1974); Blond Lighting Fixture Supply Co. v. Funk, 392 S.W.2d 586 (Tex. Civ. App. 1965); Zolman Cavitch, Business Organizations § 120.01 (1991).

[47] Zolman Cavitch, Business Organizations § 120.01 (1991).

[48] Raleigh Inv. Co. v. Cureton, 232 S.W. 766, 769 (Mo. Ct. App. 1921), *cert. quashed*, 242 S.W. 77 (1922); Blain v. Patterson, 253 N.W. 478 (S.D. 1934); Zolman Cavitch, Business Organizations § 120.01[2][a] (1991).

[49] Zolman Cavitch, Business Organizations § 120.01[2][a] (1991). *See, e.g.,* Gum v. St. Joseph Foods, Inc., 495 S.W.2d 106 (Mo. Ct. App. 1973); Russell v. Tennessee & Ky. Tobacco Co., 65 S.W.2d 256 (Tenn. 1933).

[50] Zolman Cavitch, Business Organizations § 120.01[2][a] (1991).

[51] Del. Code Ann. tit. 8, § 162(d) (1991); Zolman Cavitch, Business Organizations § 120.01[2][b] (1991).

Planning Pointer. To avoid liability for an unpaid stock purchase price, the planner should ensure that the stockholders pay the full amount of the stock price. When the corporation desires to issue stock for goods or services, the planner should ensure that it properly values such goods or services.

[E] Liability for Illegal Dividends

All jurisdictions provide restrictions on the payment of dividends.[52] When the corporation violates these restrictions by paying illegal dividends, shareholders who receive such dividends may be liable for them. The majority rule for solvent corporations provides that shareholders are not liable for illegal dividends they receive while unaware of the illegality.[53] However, some jurisdictions do allow recovery from such shareholders.[54] For insolvent corporations, shareholders are generally held liable for illegal dividends regardless of whether they are aware of the illegality.[55]

Many jurisdictions have enacted statutes that impose direct liability on shareholders who receive illegal dividends.[56] These statutes vary in their exact application, but they generally codify principles similar to the rules discussed previously.[57]

Planning Pointer. Planners should thoroughly instruct clients on the illegal dividend laws of the jurisdiction of incorporation. Also, they should stress to their clients that failure to comply with such rules may cause the unraveling of part or all of such clients' asset protection plan.

[F] 100-Percent Penalty

The Code provides a special rule that allows the IRS to pierce a corporation's veil of limited liability in cases when the corporation does not pay employment taxes. Specifically, Code Section 6672(a) provides:

Any person required to collect, truthfully account for, and pay over any tax imposed by this title who willfully fails to collect such tax, or truthfully account for and pay over

---

[52] *See, e.g.*, Revised Model Business Corporation Act § 6.40(c) (1984); Cal. Corp. Code § 501 (Deering 1977); Del. Code Ann. tit. 8, § 170 (1991).

[53] Zolman Cavitch, Business Organizations § 120.02[2][a] (1991).

[54] King v. Coosa Valley Mineral Prod., 215 So. 2d 275 (Ala. 1968); Gaunce v. Schoder, 261 P. 393 (Wash. 1927); Zolman Cavitch, Business Organizations § 120.02[2][a] (1991).

[55] Zolman Cavitch, Business Organizations § 120.02[4][a] (1991).

[56] *Id.*

[57] Cal. Corp. Code § 506 (Deering 1977 & Supp. 1992); Zolman Cavitch, Business Organizations § 120.02[4][a] (1991).

such tax, or willfully attempts in any manner to evade or defeat any such tax or the payment thereof, shall, in addition to other penalties provided by law, be liable to a penalty equal to the total amount of the tax evaded, or not collected, or not accounted for and paid over. No penalty shall be imposed under section 6653 or part II of sub-chapter A or chapter 68 for any offense to which this section is applicable.

The 100-percent penalty equals 100 percent of the amount of the tax that should[58] have been withheld and remitted to the IRS.

Compared to other debts that may be imposed on shareholders because the corporation's veil of limited liability is pierced, the 100-percent penalty is much more harmful from the shareholder's standpoint for two reasons. First, the 100-percent penalty may not be discharged by bankruptcy proceedings.[59] Second, although other debts may accrue interest, the 100-percent penalty not only accrues interest, it also accrues various statutory penalties. This causes the dollar amount of the 100-percent penalty liability to increase much faster than for other liabilities.

There are two requirements for the 100-percent penalty to be imposed: (1) the shareholder must be a "responsible person," and (2) "willfulness" must be present. A responsible person is a person who is under a duty to collect, account for, and pay over income and FICA taxes from employees.[60] The issue of whether an individual is a responsible person is a question of fact.[61] A responsible person must willfully fail to collect, account for, and pay over the applicable employment taxes to be liable for the 100-percent penalty.[62] The IRS position is that willfulness exists for 100-percent penalty purposes when taxes withheld from employees are knowingly and intentionally used to pay the operating expenses of the business or for purposes other than paying the government.[63] Courts generally require a voluntary, conscious, and intentional decision not to pay employment taxes to the government.[64]

---

[58] For a complete discussion of the 100-percent penalty, *see* Michael I. Saltzman, IRS Practice and Procedure ¶ 17.07 (2d ed. 1991). *See also* Annotation, *Construction, application, and effect, with respect to withholding, Social Security, and unemployment compensation taxes, of statutes imposing penalties for tax evasion or default*, 22 A.L.R.3d 8 (1968 & Supp. 1995); Annotation, *When are persons other than owners, directors, officers, and employees potentially liable for penalties under IRC § 6672 (26 USC § 6672), concerning failure to collect and pay over tax*, 84 A.L.R.Fed. 170 (1987 & Supp. 1995).

[59] 11 U.S.C. § 507(a)(7) (1988).

[60] IRC § 6671(b) (1988).

[61] Michael I. Saltzman, IRS Practice and Procedure ¶ 17.08 (2d ed. 1991). *See, e.g.*, Vinick v. United States, 205 F.3d 1 (1st Cir. 2000) (First Circuit Court of Appeals held that, although numerous nonexclusive factors have been identified by courts to determine whether someone is a responsible person, under IRC § 6672(a), the central question is whether the taxpayer had the power to pay the taxes during the quarters in question); In re Aboody, 250 B.R. 1 (D. Mass. 2000) (U.S. District Court for the District of Massachusetts held that although the taxpayer was a minority shareholder and treasurer of the corporation, was in charge of the corporation's bookkeeping, and signed most of the corporation's checking account checks, she was not a responsible person. The court reasoned that the taxpayer's brother controlled the corporation and had rejected the taxpayer's pleas to pay the outstanding taxes).

[62] IRC § 6672 (1988).

[63] Rev. Rul. 54-158, 1954-1 C.B. 247, 249; Michael I. Saltzman, IRS Practice and Procedure ¶ 17.09 (2d Ed. 1991).

[64] Kalb v. United States, 505 F.2d 506, 511 (2d Cir. 1974), *cert. denied*, 421 U.S. 979 (1975); Bloom v. United States, 272 F.2d 215, 223 (9th Cir. 1959), *cert. denied*, 363 U.S. 803 (1960); Michael I. Saltzman, IRS Practice and Procedure ¶ 17.09 (2d ed. 1991).

Planning Pointer. The 100-percent penalty can do tremendous damage to an asset protection plan. Therefore, the planner should stress to the client the importance of avoiding the 100-percent penalty. The planner should recommend that the client work with a competent accountant to ensure that the corporation timely pays employment taxes. Furthermore, the planner should impress upon the client that if cash flow becomes strained, the corporation should make employment tax payments a top priority, even over operating expenses.

[G]   Other Exceptions and Planning Strategies

The planner must be aware of certain other corporate limited liability aspects not previously discussed. First, although the corporation's limited liability protects shareholders from liabilities arising out of corporate operations, it cannot protect the shareholder from torts the shareholder commits.

Planning Pointer. Dan Doctor incorporates his medical practice as Doctor Dan, Inc., as part of an asset protection plan. Several years later, Dan sends his nurse, Nancy, to drive to the local hospital to retrieve certain medical records. On her way, Nancy negligently drives into Pamela Plaintiff. Pamela sues Doctor Dan, Inc. on the ground of vicarious liability for the tort of its employee. At this time, Dan has a personal net worth of $10 million, excluding the value of his Doctor Dan, Inc. stock. Doctor Dan, Inc. has a net worth and fair market value of $300,000. Pamela obtains a $20 million judgment against Doctor Dan, Inc. Here, Pam can only recover $300,000, which equals Doctor Dan, Inc.'s net worth.

EXAMPLE 3-6

Same facts as Example 3-5, except that Dan Doctor, instead of Nancy, negligently drives into Pamela. Here, Pamela may sue Dan directly. Because Pam may sue Dan directly, the corporation's limited liability does not limit the amount of Pamela's recovery from Dan.

Planning Pointer. To protect against unlimited liability in situations similar to that described in Example 3-6, the planner should recommend two courses of action. First, clients should purchase sufficient insurance to cover liability for their own torts. Second, clients should use various other asset protection techniques (trusts, exemptions, tenancies by the entirety, etc.) to limit the recovery of potential plaintiffs.

Planning Pointer. As Example 3-5 illustrates, all the assets of the corporation are generally exposed to liabilities arising out of corporate operations. One method of minimizing this is to split the business's assets into two or more corporations.

EXAMPLE 3-7

Bud operates an advertising agency. He operates the agency out of a renovated historic townhouse, which has a $1 million fair market value. The other assets of the agency have a total fair market value of $300,000. The agency has no liabilities. Bud forms two corporations. The first corporation, Agency, Inc., holds all the assets of the agency other than the townhouse. Agency, Inc.'s net worth equals $300,000. The second corporation, Leasco, Inc., holds the renovated townhouse, which Leasco, Inc., leases to Agency, Inc. Leasco's net worth equals $1 million. Subsequently, Edward, an employee of Agency, Inc., negligently injures Paul while engaged on Agency business. Paul sues Agency, Inc. and wins a $2 million judgment against it. Here, Paul's maximum recovery equals $300,000, which represents the net worth of Agency, Inc. Bud has protected his ownership of the townhouse through Leasco, Inc.

EXAMPLE 3-8

Same facts as Example 3-7, except that Bud only forms one corporation, Agency, Inc., which holds Agency's operating assets worth $300,000 and the townhouse worth $1 million. Here, Edward may recover up to $1.3 million, the net worth of Agency, Inc. Bud will lose the townhouse.

Often banks and other creditors of small, closely-held corporations will require, as a condition of loans to the corporation, that shareholders guarantee such loans. Consequently, such shareholders become personally liable for the debt they guarantee. This destroys the limited liability nature of the corporation with regard to these particular debts.

Finally, although corporations protect shareholders from liabilities arising out of corporate activities, corporate stock itself is subject to the stockholder's liabilities.

EXAMPLE 3-9

Same facts as Example 3-7, except that as Bud was taking a Sunday drive for recreation he negligently drives his car into Paul. Paul sues Bud and wins a $2 million judgment against Bud. If Bud's Leasco, Inc. stock and Agency, Inc. stock are his only assets, Bud will lose this stock.

Planning Pointer. The planner should consider placing corporate stock into an irrevocable trust or limited partnership. This would protect such stock against claims against the shareholder arising outside the corporation.

[H] Other Nontax Considerations

Although the corporation's limited liability is the primary focus for asset protection planners, the planner also must consider various other corporate aspects to compare it to other entity forms. The planner must balance the limited liability benefits of corporations against any additional costs attributable to this entity form.[65] Nontax aspects of corporations the planner must consider include:

1. Expenses and formalities of corporate formation;
2. Corporate management and control;
3. Corporate continuity of existence; and
4. Transferability of corporate interests.

[1] Expenses and Formalities of Forming the Corporation

The planner must first consider the expenses and formalities of corporate formation.

Caution. Incorporation formalities and expenses, annual franchise taxes, and the cost of qualifying in each state where a corporation intends to do business are generally considered disadvantages of the corporate entity form. The planner who incorporates must prepare and file articles of incorporation, pay filing fees and organizational taxes, and comply with other statutory procedures. Such procedures may include having an organizational meeting of incorporators or directors named in the articles of incorporation. The corporation also must pay various continuing expenses, such as franchise taxes.

---

[65] *See* § 3.08 for a worksheet that will assist the planner with this analysis.

Planning Pointer. The planner should recommend incorporation in the state where the entity plans to do business to minimize expenses and taxes. If the corporation does business in states other than the state of incorporation, it must qualify in, obtain a certificate of authority from, and designate and maintain a registered agent in such other states.[66]

[2] Management and Control of the Corporation

The planner also must consider the method and manner of conducting the everyday business of the enterprise. A corporation generally possesses centralized management. The board of directors, elected by the shareholders, manages the corporation's business. In turn, the directors appoint the corporate officers over whom the shareholders have no direct control. Shareholder approval may be required for fundamental transactions, such as the sale of substantially all a corporation's assets or the amendment of the corporation's articles of incorporation. Additionally, a shareholder's agreement may permit the shareholders in a close corporation to manage corporate affairs traditionally considered within the purview of the directors.[67] Some state statutes do not require a board of directors and, thus, allow the shareholders more control over the management of corporate affairs.[68]

Caution. The corporate form requires many formalities that other entity forms do not require. For example, the corporation must act in accordance with its articles of incorporation and bylaws, hold shareholders' and directors' meetings, keep minutes, and qualify in other states where it intends to do business.[69] Such a structure may be cumbersome for a small business. Moreover, it is important for the corporation to comply with corporation formalities to minimize the risk of veil piercing.[70]

[3] Continuity of Existence of Corporation

The planner also must consider the ability of the business to continue after the death of one of its principals or after an unforeseen event. A corporation has

---

[66] *See, e.g.,* Md. Corps. & Ass'ns Code Ann. §7-205(a) (1993).

[67] F. Hodge O'Neal & Robert B. Thompson, O'Neal's Close Corporations (3d ed. 1987 & Supp. 1991).

[68] *See, e.g.,* Del. Code Ann. tit. 8, §351 (1991); Md. Corps. & Ass'ns Code Ann. §4-301 (1993); Pa. Cons. Stat. tit. 15, §1382 (1993); F. Hodge O'Neal & Robert B. Thompson, O'Neal's Close Corporations (3d ed. 1987 & Supp. 1991).

[69] *See, e.g.,* Md. Corps. & Ass'ns Code Ann. §7-203 (1993); United Merchants & Mfrs., Inc. v. David & Dash, Inc., 439 F. Supp. 1078 (D. Md. 1977); Rigid Component Sys. v. Nebraska Component Sys., Inc., 276 N.W.2d 659 (Neb. 1979); Tiffany Agency of Modeling, Inc. v. Butler, 295 A.2d 47 (R.I. 1972). *See also* Annotation, *What constitutes doing business within state for purposes of state "closed door" statute barring unqualified or unregistered foreign corporation from local courts – modern cases,* 88 A.L.R.4th 466 §§ 3, 4, 6, 8; Annotation, *Application of statute denying access to courts or invalidating contracts where corporation fails to comply with regulatory statute as affected by compliance after commencement of action,* 23 A.L.R.5th 744 § 5.

[70] *See* §3.03[B].

perpetual existence unless its articles of incorporation specify a limited period of existence. Consequently, the withdrawal or death of a shareholder will not cause the termination of the corporation.

> **Caution.** Although a corporation has perpetual existence, the planner should consider the practical impact of a shareholder's death. Specifically, because closely-held corporate stock generally lacks a ready market, the death of a shareholder may cause the decedent shareholder's estate to own shares that cannot be sold on the open market.

> **Planning Pointer.** The planner should recommend a buy-sell agreement that requires the corporation or remaining shareholders to purchase a deceased shareholder's stock.[71] This furnishes liquidity for the decedent shareholder's estate. Consideration must be given to funding a redemption or repurchase agreement, for example with life insurance on each shareholder.[72]

> **Caution.** One disadvantage of the corporation's perpetual existence is that the corporation is not easily dissolved involuntarily. For example, disgruntled minority shareholders cannot dissolve the corporation until they can show that directors or majority shareholders' acts are illegal, oppressive, or fraudulent.

[4] Transferability of Corporate Interests

The planner also must consider the client's ability to sell or transfer entity interests. Generally, corporations offer greater transferability of business interests than other entity forms. Specifically, shareholders may give or sell all or part of their shares absent a stock transfer restriction.

> **Planning Pointer.** Corporate shareholders, subject to buy-sell agreement provisions, may divide their share ownership and spread future income and growth among family members in a lower tax bracket.

Often restrictions imposed by the corporation or the shareholders may limit the ability of shareholders to transfer business interests freely. Shareholders of closely-held corporations frequently enter buy-sell agreements that restrict

---

[71] *See* R. Stephens et al., Federal Estate and Gift Taxation 4-21 (1983); Lewis D. Solomon & Susan Flax Posner, Tax Planning Strategies Ch. 11 (1991); Lewis D. Solomon & Lewis J. Saret, Tax Planning for Closely Held Corporations Under the New Estate Freeze Rules, 16 Rev. of Tax'n of Individuals 3 (Winter 1992).

[72] Jere D. McGaffey, Tax Analysis & Forms Ch. 14 (1987); F. Hodge O'Neal & Robert B. Thompson, O'Neal's Close Corporations § 7.26 (3d ed. 1987 & Supp. 1991).

shareholders' ability to transfer shares freely.[73] These devices limit corporate ownership. Courts tolerate share transfer restrictions that may be adopted to meet the needs of a particular situation and to protect the shareholders and the business.[74]

Judicial limits exist on share transfers when corporate control is at stake. For example, a controlling shareholder may be accountable for the subsequent looting of a corporation by the purchaser of the controlling interest. Controlling shareholders who receive an excessive premium for their shares also may be liable to the remaining shareholders.

[I] Disclosure Requirements for Foreign Corporations

When foreign-owned corporations are used in the United States, certain disclosure requirements apply. This section discusses the disclosure requirements imposed by Code Section 6038A and IRS Form 5472, which must be filed by a U.S. corporation that is more than 25 percent owned by foreign persons.[75] Section 6038A and the regulations thereunder frequently require the disclosure of the ultimate beneficial owners of U.S. subsidiaries of foreign-controlled groups. This section highlights some of the practical problems created by this set of rules. Among other things, it has been found that these regulations often cause significant numbers of non-U.S. groups to restructure their U.S. involvements in ways that have nothing to do with commercial reality but are intended solely to mitigate or avoid the effects of these rules. For many foreign groups, they are unacceptable in that they can require the disclosure of ultimate beneficial owners. This result is due to the workings of the attribution rules in Treas. Reg. Section 1.6038A-1(e), which cross-reference the constructive ownership rules of Code Sections 318 and 267(c), as modified to broaden their application.

[1] In General

Generally, IRC § 6038A and the regulations thereunder require U.S. corporations, and foreign corporations engaged in a U.S. trade or business, to file a Form 5472 if, during the tax year:

1. The corporation is a "reporting corporation," and
2. The corporation engages in any "reportable transaction" with any "related party."[76]

---

[73] F. Hodge O'Neal & Robert B. Thompson, O'Neal's Close Corporations §§ 7.26–7.29 (3d ed. 1987 & Supp. 1991).

[74] Id.

[75] IRC § 6038A(a). IRC § 6038A and the regulations thereunder also impose substantial record retention requirements, which this section only addresses tangentially.

[76] Treas. Reg. § 1.6038A-2(a)(1). During tax year 2000, 33,255 corporations filed 71,352 Forms 5472. *TIGTA Examines IRS Transfer Pricing Administration*, 2003 TNT 185–39 (Sept. 24, 2003).

Therefore, in determining whether a corporation is subject to a Form 5472 reporting obligation, practitioners must examine these two elements.

[2]   Reporting Corporation

The Code Section 6038A/Form 5472 filing requirement only applies to a "reporting corporation." U.S. corporations that are 25 percent foreign-owned, and foreign corporations that are both 25 percent foreign-owned and engaged in a U.S. trade or business, constitute reporting corporations.[77] A corporation is 25 percent foreign-owned if it has at least one direct or indirect 25 percent foreign shareholder (*i.e.*, a foreign person who owns 25 percent or more of either (a) the total voting power of all classes of the corporation's voting stock, or (b) the total value of all of the corporation's stock) during the tax year.[78] Foreign corporations that have no permanent establishment in the United States under an applicable tax treaty will not constitute "reporting corporations" if they comply with the applicable notice provisions of Section 6114, which deals with treaty-based tax return positions.[79] Accordingly, such corporations need not file a Form 5472.

> **Caution.** For purposes of this analysis, Treasury Regulations state that "consideration will be given to all the facts and circumstances of each case using principles similar to those of Regulation Section 1.957-1(b)(2), which requires the consideration of arrangements to shift formal voting power away from a foreign person."[80] Therefore, planners cannot avoid application of the Code Section 6038A/Form 5472 filing requirement by using superficial, non-substantive techniques.

> **Caution.** One of the most important aspects of the Form 5472 filing requirement is the application of the attribution rules of Sections 318 and 267(c), with certain modifications, for purposes of determining what corporations constitute reporting corporations, because of the pervasive impact of these rules. Although a complete discussion of the Sections 318 and 267(c) attribution rules exceeds the scope of this section, because of their importance to the application of the Section 6038A/Form 5472 filing requirement, there is a brief summary below of the application of these rules in this context.

---

[77] Treas. Reg. § 1.6038A-1(c)(1).
[78] Treas. Reg. §§ 1.6038A-1(c)(3), -(c)(2).
[79] Treas. Reg. § 1.6038A-1(c)(5).
[80] Treas. Reg. § 1.6038A-1(c)(3)(ii).

Under Sections 318 and 267(c), an individual is treated as owning the stock owned, directly or indirectly, by or for his or her spouse, lineal descendants, ancestors, and siblings.[81] Stocks attributed from one family member to another cannot be reattributed to another family member.[82] Stock owned, directly or indirectly, by or for a partnership or estate is generally treated as owned proportionately by its partners or beneficiaries.[83] If a person owns 10 percent or more of the value of a corporation, directly or indirectly, that person is treated as owning the stock owned, directly or indirectly, by or for such corporation, in the proportion which the value of that person's stock bears to the value of all of the corporation's stock.[84]

In addition, stock owned, directly or indirectly, by or for a partner or estate beneficiary is treated as owned by the partnership or estate.[85] Trusts are generally treated as owning stock owned, directly or indirectly, by or for a beneficiary (other than remote contingent beneficiaries), and by or for grantors of grantor trusts.[86] Corporations are generally treated as owning stock owned, directly or indirectly, by or for persons who own, directly or indirectly, 50 percent or more of the value of such corporations.[87] However, for purposes of the Section 6038A/Form 5472 filing requirement, the rules set forth in this paragraph are not applicable to the extent that they cause a U.S. person to be treated as owning stock that is owned by a non-U.S. person.[88] Additionally, the rule attributing stock to a corporation by a majority shareholder does not apply to the extent that it would cause a U.S. corporation to become a reporting corporation if, but for the application of that rule, the U.S. corporation would not be foreign-owned.[89]

Finally, persons with stock options are generally treated as owning the stock subject to such option.[90]

The attribution rules that apply in the Section 6038A/Form 5472 context are best understood by applying them to a detailed example. For this purpose, assume the ownership structure set forth in Exhibit 1. In this example, X and Y are publicly traded corporations. FC1 is a publicly traded foreign corporation, of which a husband (H) owns 12.5 percent, and his wife owns another 12.5 percent. In turn, FC1 owns 50 percent of FC2, 51 percent of FC3, 100 percent of FC4, and 100 percent of FC5, each of which is a foreign corporation. FC4 owns 50 percent of FC6 and 50 percent of FC7, each of which is a foreign corporation. And FC5 owns 100 percent of RC, which is a U.S. corporation.

The statute and regulations require the annual filing by the U.S. foreign-owned corporation (RC, in the example) of a Form 5472 reporting to the IRS not only the identity and other information relating to any direct or indirect 25

---

[81] IRC §§318(a)(1), 267(c); Treas. Reg. §1.6038A-1(e)(1).
[82] IRC §§318(a)(5)(B), 267(c)(5).
[83] IRC §318(a)(2); Treas. Reg. §1.6038A-1(e)(1).
[84] IRC §318(a)(2)(C), 267(c); Treas. Reg. §1.6038A-1(e)(1).
[85] IRC §318(a)(3)(A); Treas. Reg. §1.6038A-1(e)(1).
[86] IRC §318(a)(3)(B); Treas. Reg. §1.6038A-1(e)(1).
[87] IRC §318(a)(3)(C); Treas. Reg. §1.6038A-1(e)(1).
[88] Treas. Reg. §1.6038A-1(e)(1).
[89] Treas. Reg. §1.6038A-1(e)(1).
[90] IRC §318(a)(4); Treas. Reg. §1.6038A-1(e)(1).

percent shareholder, but also information about the U.S. foreign-owned corporation and any foreign-related party with which the reporting corporation had a transaction during the taxable year. For instance, any purchase or sale of goods, payment of rents or royalties, payment for the use of intangible property (i.e., royalty), management fee, or interest payment constitutes a reportable transaction. Obviously, the rationale for the annual report is to provide a list of transactions that have tax effects so as to enable the IRS to audit them.[91]

The reporting corporation and foreign-related parties are required to maintain voluminous and detailed records in order to facilitate the IRS's audit of any questionable transactions. The regulations go into great length in describing the type and specificity of records to be maintained.[92]

Both monetary and criminal penalties can apply in the event that the reporting corporation does not comply with these rules.[93]

In order to make it easier for the IRS to obtain audit information from abroad, foreign-related parties must authorize the U.S. reporting corporation (RC) to act as their agent for purposes of information gathering by means of Information Document Requests and summonses.[94]

Failure to furnish information willingly or due to a failure to maintain required records can lead to the imposition of a draconian noncompliance penalty. In effect, the IRS can deny any deduction and ignore any item of cost so as to tax the reporting corporation on gross income.[95]

These rules are bad enough in that they require a reporting of all related party transactions, the maintenance of IRS-mandated records, the authorization of an agent for the service of information-gathering requests and summonses, and the possible imposition of confiscatory penalties. As previously noted, for many foreign groups they are unacceptable in that they can require the disclosure of ultimate beneficial owners.

In the example, the following entities and individuals would have to be reported on the Form 5472 as 25 percent direct or indirect shareholders: FC5 (because it owns 100 percent of RC directly); FC1 (because it owns 100 percent of RC indirectly by attribution from FC5); H and W (because each is treated as owning 25 percent of RC indirectly by attribution from FC1 and FC5 and family attribution one to another); FC2 (because of attribution from FC1 and FC5); FC3 (because of attribution from FC1 and FC5); FC4 (because of attribution from FC1 and FC5); and FCs 6 and 7 (because of attribution from FC1 and FC5 and reattribution from FC4). X apparently escapes disclosure because Section 318(a)(5)(c) cuts off reattribution to it. The same result pertains to Y. The various public shareholders apparently also escape disclosure. (However, any person that has accumulated 25 percent or more of the shares of FC1 would be reportable. Query how RC complies if FC1's shares are in bearer form.)

---

[91] *See, e.g., LMSB Industry Directive Issued on R&E Expense Audits for Biotech, Pharmaceutical Industries,* 2003 TNT 2004-15 (Oct. 22, 2003) (instructs examiners to review Form 5472); FSA 200132003 (Apr. 25, 2001) (taxpayer's interest expense, which was challenged by IRS, apparently showed up on Form 5472).

[92] Treas. Reg. § 1.6038A-3.

[93] Treas. Reg. § 1.6038A-4.

[94] Treas. Reg. § 1.6038A-5.

[95] Treas. Reg. §§ 1.6038A-6, -7.

Interposing an entity, such as a grantor trust settled by FC5, between FC5 and RC does not bar the attribution of ownership by making FC5 the sole 25 percent shareholder.

Interestingly, disbursal of the share ownership of RC sometimes can avoid disclosure at, say, a holding company level; but this result cannot be achieved by simply spreading the share ownership of RC among wholly-owned foreign members of the group.[96]

It should be noted that Section 318(a)(5)(c) cuts off reattribution from entities to which ownership has been attributed by Section 318(a)(3). Section 267(c) does not provide for "downstream" attribution of ownership to entities—only "upstream" attribution to shareholders. Also, it is unlikely that the constructive ownership rules in the Section 6038A regulations permit ownership to be attributed, say, to FC2 under Section 318 and then reattributed to X under Section 267(c).

[3] Reportable Transactions

The Section 6038A/Form 5472 filing requirement only applies to reporting corporations that engage in "reportable transactions" with related parties. Therefore, a corporation must engage in such a transaction in order to trigger this requirement. Reportable transactions fall into two categories. The first category consists of transactions between the reporting corporation and a foreign related party for which the reporting corporation receives or pays only monetary consideration.[97] Such transactions include the following:

- Sales and purchases of stock in trade (inventory);
- Sales and purchases of tangible property other than stock in trade;
- Rents and royalties paid and received;
- Sales, purchases, and amounts paid and received as consideration for the use of all intangible property, including copyrights, designs, formulas, inventions, models, patents, processes, trademarks, and other similar intangible property rights;
- Consideration paid and received for technical, managerial, engineering, construction, scientific, or other services;
- Commissions paid and received;
- Amounts loaned and borrowed;
- Interest paid and received;
- Premiums paid and received for insurance and reinsurance.

For this category, if the related party is a foreign person, the reporting corporation must set forth on Form 5472 the dollar amounts of all reportable transactions for which monetary consideration (including U.S. and foreign currency) was the sole consideration paid or received during the reporting

---

[96] See Example 3, Treas. Reg. § 1.6038A-1(m).
[97] Treas. Reg. §§ 1.6038A-2(b)(2), 1.6038A-2(b)(3).

corporation's taxable year. In addition, the reporting corporation must report the separate amounts for each of the above types of transaction on Form 5472.

The second category consists of transactions between the reporting corporation and the foreign related party involving nonmonetary consideration or less than full consideration.[98] If the related party is a foreign person, the reporting corporation must report on Form 5472 a description of any reportable transaction of the types listed above for monetary transactions, for which any of the consideration paid or received was not monetary, or for which less than full consideration was paid or received. The reporting corporation must include sufficient information to allow the IRS to determine the nature and approximate monetary value of the transaction or group of transactions, and must include the following:

1. A description of all property (including monetary consideration), rights, or obligations transferred from the reporting corporation to the foreign-related party and from the foreign-related party to the reporting corporation;
2. A description of all services performed by the reporting corporation for the foreign-related party and by the foreign-related party for the reporting corporation; and
3. A reasonable estimate of the fair market value of all properties and services exchanged, if possible, or some other reasonable indicator of value.[99]

[4] Related Party

The Section 6038A/Form 5472 filing requirement only applies to reporting corporations that engage in reportable transactions with "related parties." For this purpose, a related party includes:

1. Any direct or indirect 25-percent foreign shareholder of the reporting corporation;
2. Any person who is related within the meaning of Sections 267(b) or 707(b)(1) to the reporting corporation or to a 25-percent foreign shareholder of the reporting corporation; or
3. Any other person who is related to the reporting corporation within the meaning of Section 482 and the regulations thereunder. However, the term "related party" does not include any corporation filing a consolidated federal income tax return with the reporting corporation.[100]

[5] Penalties for Failure to File

A $10,000 penalty is imposed for each taxable year for which the reporting corporation fails to file a required Form 5472 or keep the required

---

[98] Treas. Reg. §§ 1.6038A-2(b)(2), 1.6038A-2(b)(4).

[99] Treas. Reg. §§ 1.6038A-2(b)(2), 1.6038A-2(b)(4).

[100] Treas. Reg. § 1.6038A-1(d). See, *e.g.,* Int'l Tech. Assistance Mem. 200247045 (Aug. 23, 2002) (two domestic corporations were not related parties for IRC § 6038A/Form 5472 purposes); Int'l Tech.

records.[101] If the corporation fails to correct the delinquency within 90 days of an IRS notice giving it notice of such failure, an additional $10,000 penalty is imposed for each 30 days (or portion of a 30-day period) that the corporation remains out of compliance. If the reporting corporation has transactions with more than one related party, the penalties apply separately to the reporting and record-keeping obligations with respect to each related party.[102] If the reporting corporation is a member of an affiliated group filing a consolidated return, then all members of the group are jointly and severally liable for the penalties.[103]

> **Caution.** If a taxpayer fails to comply with the Section 6038A/Form 5472 filing requirement, Section 6501(c)(8) extends the time for assessment by the IRS until three years after the date that the IRS is furnished with the information required to be reported. However, such an extension only applies to the tax consequences that are related to the information required to be reported under Section 6038A on the Form 5472.[104]

[6] Problem Areas

The obvious problem areas are:

- Non-U.S. groups—like their U.S. counterparts—will not wish to "jump start" a tax audit by attaching, in effect, a fairly complete organization chart to the U.S. tax return;
- Non-U.S. groups will be wary of delivering this information to the IRS because the IRS could then exchange it with the tax authorities in other countries;
- Non-U.S. groups will not want to place themselves in a legal "box" where the United States could demand information from the reporting corporation which would violate another jurisdiction's secrecy or commercial privacy laws and such other jurisdiction could restrain the disclosure of this information;
- Non-U.S. groups will worry about lawsuits by private parties, including competitors, in the United States where the plaintiff may obtain information by simply discovering the defendant's (the reporting corporation's) U.S. tax return.[105]

Assistance Mem. 200238044 (Aug. 20, 2002) (one domestic corporation and another foreign corporation were not related parties for IRC § 6038A/Form 5472 purposes).

[101] IRC §§ 6038A(d), 6038C(c); Treas. Reg. § 1.6038A-4(a)(1). *See, e.g.,* FSA 200026005 (Mar. 8, 2000) (subsidiary's failure to report loan guarantee fee, which was equal to one third of the subsidiary's gross receipts, caused the subsidiary's Form 5472 to be "substantially incomplete," thus triggering penalty).

[102] Treas. Reg. §§ 1.6038A-4(a)(3), 1.6038A-4(d)(1).

[103] Treas. Reg. §§ 1.6038A-1(k)(3), 1.6038A-4(a)(1).

[104] Int'l Tech. Assistance Mem. 200024051 (Apr. 20, 2000).

[105] *See* Rule 26, Fed. Rules of Civil Procedure ("It is not ground for objection that the information sought will be inadmissible at the trial if the information sought appears to be reasonably calculated to lead to the discovery of admissible evidence").

Another problem will arise, for example, where one non-U.S. member of the group deals in some fashion with the U.S. reporting corporation, information regarding this dealing is not captured on a current basis, a tax audit arises several years later, and the group must reconstruct its records. This exercise can be very expensive and time consuming. Also, monitoring ownership levels by institutions holding blocks of bearer shares—for themselves and/or for discretionary accounts—will present special problems.

[7] Sequestration Structures

In order to properly avoid these problems, foreign groups may wish to consider various forms of "sequestration structures." "Sequestration structure" is a generic term that describes a variety of structures. They have been used in the past to do business in politically dangerous African and Middle Eastern countries.

For example, the foreign group may wish to "route" all transactions with RC through FC5 so as to capture the information on a current basis and remind all concerned that the U.S. disclosure requirements are being triggered. (A similar effect can be achieved by requiring all group controllers to report transactions to a designated account.) An "in-house" accountant or controller could be given the responsibility of monitoring these transactions and properly reporting them, or this function might be assigned to a sophisticated trust company. This structure does not save U.S. tax dollars or disclosure of the organization chart or any record-keeping requirements. It merely avoids the problem of very costly reconstruction of records.

If an unrelated foreign minority shareholder of FC6 wishes to make sure that his ownership interest is not disclosed as part of RC's filing, his ownership interest might be dropped below the 25 percent level.

In order to avoid the problems of disclosure, being placed in a "box," or revealing information to private parties, it will be necessary in some fashion to avoid the constructive ownership rules. The solutions will very much depend upon the facts and circumstances of each matter. Even where the chain of constructive ownership can be broken, actual transactions with a party which is effectively controlled, but not to any extent owned, by the foreign group would have to be reported.

It should be noted that a Form 5472 is not required where there are no cross-border transactions with related parties; but a single such transaction will cause the filing requirement to spring into existence.

[8] Trading Companies

Ironically, the beneficiaries of these rules may be non-US trading companies. Foreign groups not wishing to grapple with these new rules can trade with related and unrelated parties in the United States through entirely unrelated, uncontrolled trading companies. In this manner they can avoid disclosure. Of course, some part of the profits on the business will have to be ceded to the trading company.

§ 3.04   GENERAL PARTNERSHIPS

The Uniform Partnership Act (UPA)[1] provides that a partnership is an association of two or more persons to carry on a business as co-owners, for profit.[2] Code Section 761(a) provides that the term partnership includes a syndicate, group, pool, joint venture, or other unincorporated organization through or by means of which any business, financial operation, or venture is carried on, and which is not, for federal tax purposes, a corporation, trust, or estate.

Each partner in a general partnership is individually liable for the partnership's debts.[3] Because the general partnership offers no asset protection benefits, the authors will not consider it further as an organization choice.

§ 3.05   LIMITED PARTNERSHIPS

Limited partnerships[1] are partnerships formed by two or more persons[2] under a limited partnership statute,[3] having as members one or more general partners and one or more limited partners.[4] In a limited partnership, the limited partners provide the capital and are liable only to the extent of their investment.[5] General partners run the business and are liable for the partnership debts. Limited partnerships combine limited liability for the limited partners with income tax advantages.

[A]   Limited Liability

The planner must analyze the liability exposure of both the limited partnership's general and limited partners to liabilities arising out of the limited

---

§ 3.04   [1] UPA § 6(1), 6 U.L.A. 22 (1914).

[2] For a complete discussion of general partnerships, *see* Harold Gill Reuschlein & William A. Gregory, The Law of Agency and Partnership (2d ed. 1990); Zolman Cavitch, Business Organizations (1991).

[3] UPA § 15, 6 U.L.A. 174 (1914).

§ 3.05   [1] For a complete discussion of limited partnerships, *see* Harold Gill Reuschlein & William A. Gregory, The Law of Agency and Partnership (2d ed. 1990); Zolman Cavitch, Business Organizations Ch. 39 (1991); Anne E. Bookout, Limited Partnerships: Legal Aspects of Organization, Operation, and Dissolution, Corp. Prac. (BNA) No. 24-4th.

[2] RULPA § 101(11) (1985), 6 U.L.A. 290 (Supp. 1992) defines the term "person" to include corporations for purposes of this rule. Furthermore, modem corporate statutes often specifically empower a corporation to be a partner. Revised Model Business Corp. Act § 3.02(9) (1984).

[3] Most jurisdictions have adopted the Uniform Limited Partnership Act (ULPA) or the Revised Uniform Limited Partnership Act (RULPA). The Uniform Partnership Act applies to limited partnerships except if the ULPA or RULPA is inconsistent therewith.

[4] ULPA § 1, 6 U.L.A. 562 (1916); RULPA § 101(7) (1985), 6 U.L.A. 289 (Supp. 1992).

[5] ULPA § 7, 6 U.L.A. 582 (1916); RULPA § 303(a) (1985), 6 U.L.A. 343 (Supp. 1992).

partnership's operations.[6] The planner also must examine the impact of the rights of judgment and other creditors of the limited partner and general partner upon the limited partnership.

[B] Liability of General Partners

General partners are liable to third parties for limited partnership debts in a manner similar to a general partner's liability for a general partnership's debts.[7] Consequently, general partners are jointly and severally liable for partnership obligations arising out of any wrongful act or omission by any partner acting in the ordinary course of limited partnership business or with the authority of the other partners or arising out of any partner's breach of trust.[8] Conversely, general partners are only jointly liable for all other partnership debts, including contractual debts.[9] In addition, a general partner may enter a separate contract obligation that will be separate as to that individual, but not as to the other partners.[10] This distinction is important for several reasons. To illustrate, creditors with joint and not several liabilities as to the general partners must join all general partners in litigation and obtain a judgment against all of them to obtain full recovery.[11]

> **Caution.** The planner should note that some jurisdictions have amended the rule regarding joint and several liability of partners to provide joint and several liability for all partnership obligations.[12] Also, the planner should note that when a partnership dissolves, a general partner may become liable for more than her proportionate share of partnership liabilities. Specifically, if the partnership dissolves and one or more general partners do not pay their share of partnership liabilities, either because they are insolvent or not subject to process and refuse to contribute, the remaining general partners are proportionately liable for their shares.[13]

---

[6] *See* Harold Gill Reuschlein & William A. Gregory, The Law of Agency and Partnership (2d ed. 1990); Zolman Cavitch, Business Organizations Ch. 39 (1991); Anne E. Bookout, Limited Partnerships: Legal Aspects of Organization, Operation, and Dissolution, Corp. Prac. (BNA) No. 24-4th, at VI.

[7] ULPA § 9(1), 6 U.L.A. 586 (1916); RULPA § 403 (1985), 6 U.L.A. 362 (Supp. 1992).

[8] UPA § 15, 6 U.L.A. 174 (1914).

[9] *Id.*

[10] *Id.*

[11] Anne E. Bookout, Limited Partnerships: Legal Aspects of Organization, Operation, and Dissolution, Corp. Prac. (BNA) No. 24-4th, at VI; Harold Gill Reuschlein & William A. Gregory, The Law of Agency and Partnership 312–13 (2d ed. 1990).

[12] *See* Zolman Cavitch, Business Organizations § 39.07[1]; Anne E. Bookout, Limited Partnerships: Legal Aspects of Organization, Operation, and Dissolution, Corp. Prac. (BNA) No. 24-4th, at VI; Harold Gill Reuschlein & William A. Gregory, The Law of Agency and Partnership 312 (2d ed. 1990).

[13] UPA § 40(d), 6 U.L.A. 469 (1914).

New general partners generally do not become personally liable for limited partnership obligations incurred before their admission.[14] Conversely, withdrawing general partners generally remain liable for limited partnership obligations incurred while they were general partners but not obligations incurred after withdrawal.[15]

Planning Pointer. Withdrawing general partners should obtain an indemnity from the limited partnership and/or the remaining general partners regarding both liabilities incurred before withdrawal and liabilities incurred after withdrawal.[16]

Finally, a limited partnership agreement may sometimes be interpreted to hold a general partner liable to limited partners for unrealized financial profit on their financial investment.[17] Specifically, this may occur when a general partner has a negative balance in her capital account.

Planning Pointer. To prevent such an interpretation, the limited partnership agreement should provide that (1) each partner will look solely to the assets of the partnership for all distributions of cash and repayment of capital contributions and of loans to the partnership, and (2) each partner shall have no recourse, on dissolution, against any general partner.[18]

Planning Pointer. The planner should consider two methods of reducing the exposure of the general partner. The first is to use a corporate general partner. The second is to use nonrecourse debt.[19] First, the planner should consider structuring the limited partnership so that all the general partners are corporations. This would limit the assets at risk to the assets held by the limited partnership and by the corporate general partners. When the planner uses corporate general partners, the planner must work within certain constraints. First, the corporate general partners must not be undercapitalized. Undercapitalization risks piercing of the corporate veil of limited

---

[14] UPA §17, 6 U.L.A. 207 (1914); Anne E. Bookout, Limited Partnerships: Legal Aspects of Organization, Operation, and Dissolution, Corp. Prac. (BNA) No. 24-4th, at VI.

[15] UPA §36(4), 6 U.L.A. 436 (1914); Anne E. Bookout, Limited Partnerships: Legal Aspects of Organization, Operation, and Dissolution, Corp. Prac. (BNA) No. 24-4th, at VI; Lubin v. Lindermere Properties, Inc., 487 N.Y.S.2d 573 (App. Div. 1985).

[16] Anne E. Bookout, Limited Partnerships: Legal Aspects of Organization, Operation, and Dissolution, Corp. Prac. (BNA) No. 24-4th, at VI.

[17] Park Cities Corp. v. Byrd, 534 S.W.2d 668 (Tex. 1976); Anne E. Bookout, Limited Partnerships: Legal Aspects of Organization, Operation, and Dissolution, Corp. Prac. (BNA) No. 24-4th, at VI.

[18] Anne E. Bookout, Limited Partnerships: Legal Aspects of Organization, Operation, and Dissolution, Corp. Prac. (BNA) No. 24-4th, at VI.

[19] Id.

liability.[20] Second, in some jurisdictions there may be a risk that a corporate general partner, controlled by a limited partner, will cause the limited partner in control of the corporate general partner to become liable as a general partner.[21]

EXAMPLE 3-10

Howard owns 100 percent of Hotdog, Inc., a corporation that operates a chain of hot dog stands. Howard has a net worth of $30 million, excluding the value of Hotdog, Inc. Hotdog, Inc. holds net assets of $5 million, which also represents Hotdog, Inc.'s fair market value. Howard starts a new business, Howard's Hamburgers. Howard does this by creating the HH Limited Partnership (HH). Howard becomes a limited partner with a 90-percent profits interest in HH. Hotdog, Inc. becomes the general partner with a 10-percent profits interest in HH. Howard pays $900,000 for his limited partnership interest. Hotdog, Inc. pays $100,000 for its general partnership interest. Assuming Howard does not risk general partner classification for his control of Hotdog, Inc. and indirect control of HH, his financial exposure from HH equals $5.9 million. This $5.9 million amount equals the assets of Hotdog, Inc. plus the amount Howard paid for his limited partnership interest. If Howard were the general partner, his financial exposure from HH would be unlimited.

A second method of reducing the general partner's financial exposure is for the limited partnership to use nonrecourse debt to the maximum extent possible. A nonrecourse debt is debt on which the debtor is not personally liable. With nonrecourse debt, the creditor's only recourse is to foreclose on the property securing the debt. However, nonrecourse debt will not limit the general partner's exposure to tort liability arising out of the limited partnership.

[C] Liability of Limited Partners

Generally, limited partners are not personally liable for limited partnership obligations beyond the amount of their contributions.[22]

---

[20] See § 3.03[B].

[21] Anne E. Bookout, Limited Partnerships: Legal Aspects of Organization, Operation, and Dissolution, Corp. Prac. (BNA) No. 24-4th, at VI.

[22] ULPA § 7, 6 U.L.A. 582 (1916); RULPA § 303 (1985), 6 U.L.A. 343 (Supp. 1992); Zolman Cavitch, Business Organizations § 39.07[2][a]; Anne E. Bookout, Limited Partnerships: Legal Aspects of

---

EXAMPLE 3-11

Same facts as Example 3-10, except that Sarah, an employee of the HH Limited Partnership, negligently injures Peter. Peter sues HH and wins a $100 million judgment. Here, Howard has limited his exposure to $5.9 million. This equals the $5 million value of Hotdog, Inc. plus Howard's $900,000 contribution for his limited partnership interest. Note that, in terms of Howard's limited partnership interest, Peter cannot recover any more than the value of Howard's capital contribution for such limited partnership interest.

Caution. Limited partners may become liable as general partners with unlimited liability for partnership obligations if any of the following occurs:

- The limited partner participates in the control of the limited partnership;
- There is a lack of substantial compliance in good faith with the statutory requirements of forming the limited partnership;
- There is an unlawful use of a limited partner's name in the limited partnership name;
- The certificate contains a false statement, the limited partner knows of such false statement, and a third party relies to her detriment on such false statement; or
- The limited partner has not paid the entire amount of its agreed contribution for its limited partnership interest.

[1] Limited Partner Participation

When a limited partner participates in the "control" of the limited partnership, such partner may become liable as a general partner.[23] Unfortunately, it is not

---

Organization, Operation, and Dissolution, Corp. Prac. (BNA) No. 24-4th, at V; Harold Gill Reuschlein & William A. Gregory, The Law of Agency and Partnership 439-47 (2d ed. 1990).

[23] ULPA § 7, 6 U.L.A. 582 (1916); RULPA § 303(a) (1985), 6 U.L.A. 343 (Supp. 1992); Zolman Cavitch, Business Organizations § 39.07[2][c]; Anne E. Bookout, Limited Partnerships: Legal Aspects of Organization, Operation, and Dissolution, Corp. Prac. (BNA) No. 24-4th, at V.

[24] Zolman Cavitch, Business Organizations § 39.07[2][c]; Anne E. Bookout, Limited Partnerships: Legal Aspects of Organization, Operation, and Dissolution, Corp. Prac. (BNA) No. 24-4th, at V; Joseph J. Basille, *Limited Liability for Limited Partners: An Argument for the Abolition of the Control Rule*, 38 Vand. L. Rev. 1199 (1985); George W. Coleman & David A. Weatherbie, *Special Problems in Limited Partnership*

clear what actions cross the line into impermissible control.[24] It appears that a key factor for determining impermissible control is creditor reliance on such control.[25]

> **Planning Pointer.** When the planner desires to give the client the limited liability benefits of a limited partnership interest plus control over the limited partnership, the planner should consider using a controlled corporation as the limited partnership's general partner.[26] The planner should note that the law in some jurisdictions may hold that a corporation formed to serve as a limited partnership's general partner may cause the controlling limited partner to be subjected to general partner liability.[27] To minimize this risk, the planner should ensure that the client adequately capitalizes the corporation and forms it for a valid business purpose, the limited partnership takes steps to ensure that its creditors do not rely on the limited partners as the managers of the partnership business, and that there is no fraud or inequitable conduct.[28]

> **Planning Pointer.** In jurisdictions that have enacted the Uniform Limited Partnership Act (ULPA), limited partners retain the right to:

> - Examine limited partnership books;[29]
> - Call for an accounting;[30]
> - Demand dissolution;[31]
> - Recover their capital;[32]
> - Receive a share of the profits or other compensation;[33]
> - Lend money to the limited partnership;[34] and
> - Assign their limited partnership interests without losing their limited partner status.[35]

Planning, 30 Sw. L.J. 887, 897–909 (1976); Alan L. Feld, *The Control Test for Limited Partnerships*, 82 Harv. L. Rev. 1471 (1969).

[25] Zolman Cavitch, Business Organizations § 39.07[2][c]; Anne E. Bookout, Limited Partnerships: Legal Aspects of Organization, Operation, and Dissolution, Corp. Prac. (BNA) No. 24-4th, at V; Annotation, *Liability of limited partner arising from taking part in control of business under Uniform Limited Partnership Act*, 79 A.L.R.4th 427 (1990 & Supp. 1995).

[26] Anne E. Bookout, Limited Partnerships: Legal Aspects of Organization, Operation, and Dissolution, Corp. Prac. (BNA) No. 24-4th, at V.

[27] Delaney v. Fidelity Lease Ltd., 526 S.W.2d 543 (Tex. 1975); Anne E. Bookout, Limited Partnerships: Legal Aspects of Organization, Operation, and Dissolution, Corp. Prac. (BNA) No. 24-4th, at V.

[28] Anne E. Bookout, Limited Partnerships: Legal Aspects of Organization, Operation, and Dissolution, Corp. Prac. (BNA) No. 24-4th,at V.

[29] ULPA § 10(1)(a), 6 U.L.A. 590 (1916).

[30] ULPA § 10(1)(b), 6 U.L.A. 590 (1916).

[31] ULPA § 10(1)(c), 6 U.L.A. 590 (1916).

[32] ULPA § 10(2), 6 U.L.A. 590 (1916).

[33] *Id.*

[34] ULPA § 13(1), 6 U.L.A. 597 (1916).

[35] ULPA § 19(1), 6 U.L.A. 603 (1916).

The Revised Uniform Limited Partnership Act (RULPA) provides that if limited partners do participate in the control of the business, they are liable only to persons who transact business with the limited partnership reasonably believing, based on the limited partner's conduct, that the limited partner is a general partner.[36]

Planning Pointer. Planners working in RULPA jurisdictions should instruct clients not to engage in acts that would cause a person doing business with the limited partnership to believe they are general partners. Also, the planner should structure the client's activities so they fall within one or more of the safe harbors of the jurisdiction's RULPA provisions, if applicable. The RULPA's safe harbor provisions include:

- Being a contractor for or an agent or employee of the limited partnership or of a general partner;[37]
- Consulting with and advising a general partner with respect to the business of the limited partnership;[38]
- Acting as a surety for the limited partnership;[39]
- Approving or disapproving an amendment to the limited partnership agreement;[40]
- Voting on one or more of the following matters: (1) the dissolution and winding up of the limited partnership; (2) the sale, exchange, lease, mortgage, pledge, or other transfer of substantially all the assets of the limited partnership other than in the ordinary course of business; (3) incurring indebtedness by the limited partnership other than in the ordinary course of business; (4) changing the nature of the business; (5) removing a general partner;[41]
- Being an officer, director, or shareholder of a corporate general partner[42]
- Requesting or attending a meeting of partners;[43] and
- Bringing a partnership derivative action.[44]

---

[36] RULPA §303(a) (1985), 6 U.L.A. 343 (Supp. 1992).
[37] RULPA §303(b)(1) (1976), 6 U.L.A. 343 (Supp. 1992).
[38] RULPA §303(b)(2) (1976), 6 U.L.A. 343 (Supp. 1992).
[39] RULPA §303(b)(3) (1976), 6 U.L.A. 343 (Supp. 1992).
[40] RULPA §303(b)(4) (1976), 6 U.L.A. 343 (Supp. 1992).
[41] RULPA §303(b)(5) (1976), 6 U.L.A. 343 (Supp. 1992).
[42] RULPA §303(b)(1) (1985), 6 U.L.A. 343 (Supp. 1992).
[43] RULPA §303(b)(5) (1985), 6 U.L.A. 343 (Supp. 1992).
[44] RULPA §303(b)(4) (1985), 6 U.L.A. 343 (Supp. 1992).

EXAMPLE 3-12

Same facts as Example 3-10, except that HH is formed in a RULPA jurisdiction. Here, RULPA Section 303(b)(1) specifically allows Howard to be an officer, director, or shareholder of a corporate general partner.

If a limited partner does exercise an impermissible degree of control, the ULPA holds such limited partner liable to third-party creditors as if such limited partner were a general partner.[45] The limited partner does not, however, become liable for precontrol obligations[46] and does not obtain any of the rights of a general partner.[47]

[2] Compliance with Statutory Requirements

The planner must comply with certain statutory requirements to form a limited partnership.[48] When a failure to comply in good faith with such statutory requirements occurs, the purported limited partners become exposed to unlimited liability as general partners.[49]

Planning Pointer. The consequences of forming a defective limited partnership are unpredictable and potentially catastrophic for the asset protection plan. Therefore, the planner must ensure there is proper compliance with all the statutory requirements for forming the limited partnership within the jurisdiction in question.

In ULPA jurisdictions a person who contributes capital to a business conducted by a person or partnership and who erroneously believes she has thereby become a limited partner in a limited partnership, does not become, because of her exercise of the rights of a limited partner, a general partner with the person or partnership carrying on the business or bound by the obligations of such person or partnership.[50] However, the purported limited partner, on learning of her mistake, must promptly renounce her interest in the business's profits or other compensation by way of income.[51]

In RULPA jurisdictions[52] persons who contribute to businesses and erroneously but in good faith believe they are limited partners in such business do not

---

[45] ULPA §7, 6 U.L.A. 582 (1916).

[46] Garrett v. Koepke, 569 S.W.2d 568 (Tex. Civ. App. 1978); Anne E. Bookout, Limited Partnerships: Legal Aspects of Organization, Operation, and Dissolution, Corp. Prac. (BNA) No. 24-4th, at V.

[47] Roeschlein v. Watkins, 686 P.2d 1347 (Colo. Ct. App. 1983); Anne E. Bookout, Limited Partnerships: Legal Aspects of Organization, Operation, and Dissolution, Corp. Prac. (BNA) No. 24-4th, at V.

[48] ULPA §2, 6 U.L.A. 568 (1916); RULPA §§201–209 (1985), 6 U.L.A. 312–38 (Supp. 1992).

[49] Zolman Cavitch, Business Organizations §39.07[2][a]; Anne E. Bookout, Limited Partnerships: Legal Aspects of Organization, Operation, and Dissolution, Corp. Prac. (BNA) No. 24-4th, at V.

[50] ULPA §11, 6 U.L.A. 594 (1916).

[51] Id.

[52] RULPA §304 (1976), 6 U.L.A. 353 (Supp. 1992).

become general partners bound by the business's obligations because of the contribution, receiving distributions from the entity, or exercising any rights of a limited partner.[53] However, the purported limited partner, on learning of the mistake, must either (1) execute and file an appropriate certificate of limited partnership (or certificate amendment), or (2) withdraw from future equity participation in the business by executing and filing a certificate declaring withdrawal.[54] When the purported limited partner follows this procedure, she may still be liable to third parties who actually believe, in good faith, that she is a general partner at the time of the transaction.[55] However, the transaction out of which the liability arises must have occurred either before (1) the purported limited partner withdraws and files an appropriate certificate showing withdrawal, or (2) the purported limited partner files an appropriate certificate indicating she is not a general partner.[56]

[3] Unlawful Use of Limited Partner's Name

In ULPA jurisdictions the surname of the limited partner must not appear in the limited partnership name.[57] Limited partners who violate this rule become liable as general partners to partnership creditors who extend credit to the partnership without actual knowledge they are not general partners.[58] There are two exceptions to this rule. Specifically, a limited partner will not become liable under this rule if (1) her surname is also the surname of a general partner, or (2) before the limited partner became a limited partner, the business had been carried on under a name in which her surname appeared.[59] The ULPA does not require the limited partnership name to include the words "limited" or "limited partnership."[60]

> **Planning Pointer.** Planners working with a ULPA jurisdiction should include the words "Limited," "Ltd.," or "Limited Partnership" in the limited partnership's name as a precautionary device against creating a mistaken belief by third parties regarding the true nature of the limited partnership.[61]

---

[53] *Id.*

[54] *Id.*

[55] *Id.*

[56] RULPA § 304(b) (1985), 6 U.L.A. 353 (Supp. 1992). In jurisdictions that have enacted the 1976 version of the RULPA, the transaction must have occurred before the purported limited partner files a certificate showing such limited partner's status as a limited partner, and in the case of an amendment, after expiration of the 30-day period for filing an amendment relating to the person as a limited partner.

[57] ULPA § 5(1), 6 U.L.A. 580 (1916).

[58] ULPA § 5(2), 6 U.L.A. 580 (1916).

[59] ULPA § 5(1), 6 U.L.A. 580 (1916).

[60] ULPA § 5, 6 U.L.A. 580 (1916).

[61] Anne E. Bookout, Limited Partnerships: Legal Aspects of Organization, Operation, and Dissolution, Corp. Prac. (BNA) No. 24-4th, at V; Zolman Cavitch, Business Organizations § 39.05[7]; Robert Kratovil & Raymond J. Werner, Fixing Up the Old Jalopy—The Modern Limited Partnership Under the U.L.P.A., 50 St. John's L. Rev. 51, 55 (1975).

EXAMPLE 3-13

Albert Adams has profitably operated Adams & Associates, a lumber company, for several years. Albert asks his friend Bob Black, a pediatrician, to invest $300,000 in a new venture, which will be a general building contractor. Bob and Albert agree that Bob will invest $300,000 in Albert's new venture but will not exercise any control over the business. Bob consults his lawyer, Leon, who advises Bob to use a limited partnership to obtain the tax benefits of the losses expected in the early years, while protecting Bob from any liabilities that may arise out of the new business. Albert and Bob agree to form a limited partnership and they name it Adams & Black, Contractors (A&B). Albert and Bob each invest $300,000 in the new venture. Albert will be the general partner and Bob will be a limited partner.

Travis loans A&B $400,000 to use to buy materials to complete A&B's first project, a building that A&B agrees to build for Ike. Although neither Albert nor Bob has told Travis they are general partners, Travis believes they are general partners based on the general talk around town. A&B completes Ike's home. One week after Ike moves in, the home collapses, injuring Ike and his family. Ike sues A&B for $10 million, causing it to go into bankruptcy. Travis sues Albert and Bob. Here, because Bob's surname appeared in the name of the limited partnership, Bob is exposed to unlimited liability.

EXAMPLE 3-14

Same facts as above, except that Bob's attorney Leon advises Bob not to allow his name to be used in the limited partnership's name. Instead of Adams & Black, Contractors, the new venture is entitled the Adams Limited Partnership. Here, Bob limits his liability exposure to his $300,000 investment.

The RULPA requires the limited partnership to include the words "limited partnership" without abbreviation in its name.[62] However, some jurisdictions have modified this requirement.[63] Like the ULPA, the RULPA imposes on a limited partner who knowingly allows her name to be used in the limited partnership name, liability for the partnership's obligations to creditors who extend credit to the limited partnership without actual knowledge such person was not a general partner.[64] The RULPA provides the same exceptions as does the ULPA except the RULPA also explicitly allows the limited partnership name to include the name of a limited partner if that name

---

[62] RULPA § 102 (1985), 6 U.L.A. 294 (Supp. 1992).

[63] Cal. Corp. Code § 15612(a) (Deering 1979 & Supp. 1986); Del. Code Ann. tit. 6, § 17102(1) (Supp. 1992); Anne E. Bookout, Limited Partnerships: Legal Aspects of Organization, Operation, and Dissolution, Corp. Prac. (BNA) No. 24-4th, at V.

[64] RULPA § 303 (1985), 6 U.L.A. 343 (Supp. 1992).

is also the corporate name of a corporate general partner.[65] The RULPA also requires a limited partnership to submit its name for clearance by the state of formation to avoid duplication of names.[66] Finally, the 1976 version of the RULPA prohibits the limited partnership name from including any word or phrase implying it is organized other than for a purpose stated in its certificate of limited partnership.[67]

[4] Liability for False Statements

The ULPA holds parties to the limited partnership certificate liable to persons who suffer loss by relying on false statements within such certificate when the parties either (1) knew the statement was false when they signed the certificate, or (2) subsequently learned of the false statement and had a sufficient amount of time to cancel or amend the certificate or file a petition for its cancellation or amendment before the reliance.[68]

The RULPA holds persons who execute or cause others to execute on their behalf a certificate that they know contains false statements liable to third parties who rely on such statements.[69] The RULPA does not hold persons, other than general partners, liable for statements that become false only because of events occurring after the execution of the certificate.[70]

> **Planning Pointer.** The planner and the client should carefully review the certificate for inaccuracies before they file it. Furthermore, the planner and client should periodically review the certificate for statements that become false because of events occurring after its execution. If they find any such false statements, they should promptly correct the certificate.

[5] Liability for Contribution

Under the ULPA, limited partners are liable[71] to the limited partnership for the full amount of their contribution as stated in the certificate.[72] Furthermore, the ULPA treats both (1) property that the certificate states the limited partner contributed but which the limited partner did not contribute, or which the

---

[65] RULPA § 102(2) (1985), 6 U.L.A. 294 (Supp. 1992).

[66] RULPA § 103 (1985), 6 U.L.A. 299 (Supp. 1992).

[67] RULPA § 102(3) (1976), 6 U.L.A. 294 (Supp. 1992).

[68] ULPA § 6, 6 U.L.A. 581 (1916); Zolman Cavitch, Business Organizations § 39.07[2][b]; Anne E. Bookout, Limited Partnerships: Legal Aspects of Organization, Operation, and Dissolution, Corp. Prac. (BNA) No. 24-4th, at V; C.C. Marvel, Annotation, *Liability for false information in certificate of limited partnership under Uniform Limited Partnership Act*§ 6, 34 A.L.R.2d 1454 (1954).

[69] RULPA § 207(1) (1985), 6 U.L.A. 335 (Supp. 1992).

[70] RULPA § 207(2) (1985), 6 U.L.A. 335 (Supp. 1992).

[71] Zolman Cavitch, Business Organizations § 39.07[2][e]; Anne E. Bookout, Limited Partnerships: Legal Aspects of Organization, Operation, and Dissolution, Corp. Prac. (BNA) No. 24-4th, at V.

[72] ULPA § 17(1), 6 U.L.A. 601 (1916).

partnership wrongfully returned, and (2) money or other property the partnership wrongfully conveyed to the limited partner because of the contribution, as held in trust for the limited partnership by that limited partner.[73] However, if all partnership members consent to a waiver or compromise of the limited partner's liability for her contribution, such a waiver or compromise becomes valid.[74] Nevertheless, this exception only applies to creditors who extend credit or whose claim arises after a cancellation or amendment of the certificate to reflect the waiver or compromise of the limited partner's contribution.[75]

When the limited partnership rightfully returns the limited partner's contribution in whole or part, the limited partner remains liable under the ULPA for any sum, up to the amount returned plus interest, required to discharge all limited partnership creditors who extended credit or whose claim arose before such return.[76] The RULPA provides that when the limited partnership returns part of the limited partner's contribution without violating the limited partnership agreement, the limited partner remains liable for one year for the amount returned to the extent required to discharge limited partnership liabilities to creditors who extended credit to the limited partnership during the period the limited partnership held the contribution.[77] If the return violates the limited partnership agreement, the limited partner's period of exposure increases from one year to six years.[78] Limited partners receive a RULPA contribution return when a distribution reduces their share of the fair value of net limited partnership assets below the value of their undistributed contribution set forth in the certificate,[79] or below the value set forth in records required to be kept under Section 105 under the 1985 version of the RULPA.[80]

[D]   Rights of Judgment and Other Creditors

In jurisdictions that have enacted the ULPA, a judgment creditor (or in some jurisdictions, a creditor) of the limited partner may obtain a charging order from a court against the limited partner's limited partnership interest. The charging order charges the indebted limited partner's partnership interest with payment of the unsatisfied amount of the debt.[81] Generally, the charging order is the exclusive remedy of a judgment creditor of a limited or general partner.[82] When

---

[73] ULPA § 17(2), 6 U.L.A. 601 (1916).

[74] ULPA § 17(1), 6 U.L.A. 601 (1916).

[75] *Id.*

[76] *Id.*

[77] RULPA § 608(b) (1985), 6 U.L.A. 387 (Supp. 1992).

[78] *Id.*

[79] *Id.*

[80] *Id.*

[81] ULPA § 22(1), 6 U.L.A. 605 (1916); RULPA § 703 (1985), 6 U.L.A. 391 (Supp. 1992). *See, e.g.,* Keeler v. Acad. Of Am. Franciscan History, Inc., 273 B.R. 416 (D. Md. 2002); Green v. Bellerive Condos. Ltd. Pshp., 135 Md. App. 563, 763 A.2d 252 (2000), *cert denied,* 768 A.2d 55 (2001), *cert. denied,* 534 U.S. 824 (2001); Lauer Constr. V. Schrift, 716 A.2d 1096 (Md. Sp. App. 1998), *cert. denied* 721 A.2d 989 (1998); 91st St. Joint Venture v. Goldstein, 691 A.2d 272, Md. Sp. App. 1997); Ainslie v. Inman, 577 S.E.2d 246 (Va. 2003).

[82] Central Petroleum Corp. v. Korman, 177 N.Y.S.2d 761 (App. Div. 1958); Harold Gill Reuschlein & William A. Gregory, The Law of Agency and Partnership 320 (2d ed. 1990).

a creditor obtains a charging order, the limited partner's interest may be redeemed with a general partner's separate property, but may not be redeemed with partnership property.[83] The charging order does not give the creditor title to the limited partner's interest in the business. It merely gives the creditor the limited partner's right to receive limited partnership income and, on dissolution, the limited partner's share of limited partnership assets. The creditor may foreclose on the limited partner's limited partnership interest and call for a foreclosure sale. Generally, such a foreclosure sale will bring little if any proceeds.

Planning Pointer. The charging order makes the limited partnership form of entity very valuable from an asset protection planning perspective. The charging order makes it very difficult for the limited partner's creditors to collect. Some steps the limited partner's judgment creditor must go through to collect using a charging order include:

- Litigating and obtaining a judgment against the limited partner;
- Obtaining a charging order from a court;
- Having a receiver appointed to receive distributions from the limited partnership; and
- Applying for foreclosure on the limited partner's limited partnership interest.

Because of the many procedural hurdles, the charging order aspect of the limited partner's limited partnership interest places the debtor in a very good position to compromise debts.

Caution: See the discussion below regarding *In Movitz v. Fiesta Invs. LLC (In re Ehmann)*,[84] In *In re Ehmann*, the bankruptcy trustee, Louis Movitz, for the bankruptcy estate of the debtor, Gregory Ehmann, filed a lawsuit against defendant Fiesta Investments, LLC ("the LLC"). Ehmann was a member of the LLC when he filed bankruptcy, and in the lawsuit the court held that the plaintiff-trustee, among other things, had the status of a member in the LLC, and ordered the dissolution and liquidation of the LLC or for the appointment of a receiver for the LLC.

EXAMPLE 3-15

Fred owns Family Business, an unincorporated wire hanger manufacturer. Occasionally, Fred becomes involved with various other economic ventures. Family Business has a $5 million fair market value. As part of an asset

---

[83] ULPA § 22(1), 6 U.L.A. 605 (1916).
[84] 334 BR 437 (Bankr. D. Ariz. 2005), op. withdrawn, mot. granted, 337 B.R. 228 (Bankr. D. Ariz. 2006).

protection plan, Fred forms Fred, Inc., a corporation. Fred retains 0 percent of Fred, Inc.'s common stock and gives 50 percent of Fred, Inc.'s common stock to his wife, Wilma, and 50 percent of Fred, Inc.'s common stock to his daughter, Dorothy. Fred becomes Fred, Inc.'s chief executive officer and president.

Fred then forms the FB Limited Partnership (FB) and contributes Family Business to FB. Fred, Inc. becomes the general partner of FB and obtains a 25-percent capital and profits interest in FB. Fred becomes a limited partner in FB and obtains a 25-percent interest in it. Fred also gives Wilma a 25-percent limited partnership interest and daughter Dorothy a 25-percent limited partnership interest.

Five years later, Fred invests $250,000 in Risky Vittles, a new restaurant. Fred receives a general partnership interest in Risky Vittles. There are three other partners. Risky Vittles fails and enters bankruptcy. This causes each of the other partners to enter into bankruptcy. Risky Vittles's bank, Bigg Bank, sues Fred and obtains a $2 million judgment against him. At this time, Fred's only asset is his FB limited partner interest. Here, Bigg Bank's only recourse is to obtain a charging order against Fred's limited partnership interest. After it does this, all Bigg Bank can receive is whatever distributions FB makes to its limited partners. Because Fred controls Fred, Inc., FB's general partner, Fred controls the distributions that FB makes to its limited partners. Consequently, Fred is in an excellent bargaining position to negotiate a settlement with Bigg Bank. Furthermore, Family Business is protected for Fred's family under this plan.

[E] Family Limited Partnerships

Family limited partnerships[85] are limited partnerships that families use to manage family enterprises and other family investments. They are very valuable from an asset protection standpoint because they are very flexible and because they protect the family enterprise from the creditors of individual family members who hold interests in the partnership. Generally, the rules applicable to limited partnerships also apply to family limited partnerships. Therefore, this section will focus on advice that applies specifically to family limited

---

[85] *See generally* Kathryn G. Henkel, How Family Limited Partnerships Can Protect Assets, 20 Est. Plan. 3 (Jan.–Feb. 1993); Neill G. McBryde, *The Esoterica of Family Partnerships*, 1993 U.S.C. L. Center Tax Inst. ch. 10; Alson R. Martin et al., *Protecting the Assets of a Professional or Other Closely Held Business Owner from Creditors*, in Qualified Plans, PCs, and Welfare Benefits, at 639 (ALI-ABA Course of Study No. C796, Feb. 18, 1993); S. Stacy Eastland, *Family Limited Partnerships: Non-Transfer Tax Benefits*, 7 Prob. & Prop. 10 (Mar./Apr. 1993); Larry W. Gibbs, *A Family Limited Partnership as the Centerpiece of an Estate Plan*, 131 Trusts & Est. 45 (Sept. 1992); Larry W. Gibbs, *A Family Limited Partnership as the Centerpiece of an Estate Plan*, 131 Trusts & Est. 45 (Oct. 1992); Barry S. Engel & Ronald L. Rudman, *Family Limited Partnerships: New Meaning for "Limited,"* 131 Trusts & Est. 46 (July 1993); William P. Barrett, *Ozzie & Harriet, L.P.*, Forbes, June 21, 1993, at 196; Susan Scherreik, *How to Share the Wealth and Keep Control*, Bus. Wk., Jan. 17, 1994, at 94; State Limited Partnership Laws (P-H); Limited Partnerships: A Practitioner's Guide Under Delaware Law (P-H); Dennis W. Reilly, *Estate Planning with the Family Limited Partnership*, 8 Prob. & Prop. 28 (Jan./Feb. 1994); Michael D. Mulligan & Angela Fick Braly, *Family Limited Partnerships Can Create Discounts*, 21 Est. Plan. 195 (1994); Howard M. Zaritsky, *Back to Basics for the Family Limited Partnership*, 27 Est. Plan. 240 (2000).

partnerships. Specifically, this section discusses how family limited partnerships (FLPs) may serve as an integral component of an estate and asset protection plan, and considerations in selecting partners for the FLP and structuring their ownership of FLP interests.

EXAMPLE 3-16

Tom and Becky are married and own the farm Missouriacre. Tom and Becky have two children, Sid and Huck, who live with them on Missouriacre. Tom's Aunt Polly also lives with Tom and Becky on Missouriacre. When Tom is not farming on Missouriacre, he practices as an obstetrician. Tom wants to protect Missouriacre from creditors. His asset protection planner, Mark, advises him to place Missouriacre into a family limited partnership. Under this plan, Tom and Becky would create two children's trusts for the benefit of Sid and Huck. These trusts would contain appropriate spendthrift provisions. Tom and Becky would convey Missouriacre into a family limited partnership in exchange for limited partnership interests for themselves and for each of the children's trusts. Aunt Polly would become the general partner of the partnership.

Tom and Becky implement the plan that Mark recommends. Five years later, one of Tom's patients, Amy, has a baby with birth defects. Although Tom is not at fault, Amy sues and wins a $20 million judgment against Tom. Tom's only major asset at this time is his family limited partnership interest. Amy obtains a charging order against Tom's family limited partnership interest. Here, Amy can only receive amounts that Polly, as general partner, decides to distribute to the limited partners. Because Polly is Tom's aunt, she will probably not distribute anything while the charging order is outstanding. This places Tom in an excellent position to compromise the outstanding judgment against him with Amy.

Planning Pointer. FLPs may serve as valuable components of estate and asset protection plans. Specifically, they (1) allow clients to give wealth to the objects of their bounty without giving up control, (2) allow clients to claim minority discounts for transfer tax purposes, and (3) provide valuable asset protection benefits.

First, FLPs allow clients to give away wealth to the objects of their bounty without giving up control. This results from the FLP's separation of ownership from control. Specifically, and as discussed fully in §§ 3.05[C][1] and 3.05[G][2], the general partner retains control of the FLP. The limited partners retain limited or no control of the FLP. Simultaneously, the client may give a substantial percentage of the ownership of the FLP to the limited partners.

Second, properly structured FLPs allow clients to claim a discount for minority interests. Specifically, when properly structured, gifts of FLP limited partnership interests may enjoy significant discounts, for gift and estate tax purposes, to reflect the lack of control of those interests. The amount of discount may be substantial.[86]

Caution. The planner must ensure that gifts of limited partnership interests do not trigger Chapter 14 of the IRC.[87]

Finally, and most important to the asset protection planner, FLPs provide valuable asset protection benefits. Such benefits stem primarily from the limited rights of judgment and other creditors of a limited partner to the limited partner's FLP interest.[88] Briefly, the exclusive remedy of a judgment creditor of a limited partner of an FLP is to obtain a charging order.[89] The charging order does not give the creditor title to the limited partner's interest in the FLP. It merely gives the creditor the limited partner's right to receive FLP income that the FLP distributes and, on dissolution, the limited partner's share of FLP assets. Because the controlling general partner of an FLP will be a family member, the FLP will generally stop making distributions when a creditor obtains a charging order against an FLP limited partner. Consequently, the FLP interest will be of little value to a creditor. Second, creditors who obtain charging orders must recognize the debtor/partner's proportionate share of the FLP's income for income tax purposes.[90] Therefore, such creditors must pay income taxes on phantom income on the debtor's FLP interest without realizing any significant tangible benefits from charging orders.

In *Miller v. Bill & Carolyn Ltd. P'ship (In re Baldwin)*[91], the Tenth Circuit Court of Appeals held that the underlying bankruptcy court had correctly found that the debtor's partnership interests became property of her estate at the time the bankruptcy petition was filed given factually similar judicial precedent. Likewise, the trustee stepped into the shoes of the debtor with respect to partnership interests and was allowed to assert whatever rights the debtor had under the partnership agreement and state law, including the right to seek dissolution. However, the Tenth Circuit held, dissolution pursuant to the partnership agreement was improper as none of the circumstances under which the partnership could be dissolved were applicable to the present situation. The bankruptcy court erred in dissolving the partnership under Okla. Stat. tit. 54, § 346 (2005) on the ground that it no longer served an estate planning purpose: the partnership was still serving the purpose of allowing the general partner to retain complete control of the partnership assets during his lifetime, while at the

---

[86] *See* Neill G. McBryde, *The Esoterica of Family Partnerships*, 1993 U.S.C. L. Center Tax Inst. ¶ 1005.4.

[87] *See* Lewis D. Solomon & Lewis J. Saret, *Tax Planning for Closely Held Corporations under the New Estate Freeze Rules*, 16 Rev. Tax'n Individuals 3 (Winter 1992); Howard M. Zaritsky & Ronald Aucutt, *Structuring Estate Freezes After Chapter 14* (3d ed. 1993).

[88] *See* § 3.05[D] for a complete discussion of the rights of judgment and other creditors.

[89] *See* ULPA § 22(1), 6 U.L.A. 605 (1916); RULPA § 703 (1985), 6 U.L.A. 391 (Supp. 1992).

[90] *See* Rev. Rul. 77-137, 1977-1 C.B. 178.

[91] 2006 Bankr. LEXIS 1700 (BA.P. 10th Cir. July 11, 2006).

same time removing them from his estate for tax purposes. Moreover, there was no evidence that the partnership could not be continued with the trustee holding the debtor's rights. Thus, the trustee had no right to dissolve the partnership.

Caution. The California Court of Appeal has ordered the sale of a partnership interest with the consent of the other partners. It also ordered the sale of a partnership interest in another case without the consent of partners where the sale would not disrupt partnership business.[92] In these decisions, the court noted that the charging order's original purpose was to prevent the unnecessary interruption of partnership business and to avoid adverse impact on innocent nondebtor partners. It also noted that the charging order's original purpose was not to allow partners to avoid debts.[93] Some commentators have predicted that these cases, though currently limited to California, will be followed in other states, with the following implications for asset protection planners. First, planners can no longer safely assume that courts will restrict the remedies for creditors of FLP interest holders to charging orders. Furthermore, for limited partners, whose management participation is inherently limited, courts would be more likely to use non-charging order remedies, as the sale of such interests are unlikely to disrupt FLP business. Second, because the charging order's underlying rationale is to prevent the unnecessary interruption of partnership business and to avoid adverse impact on innocent nondebtor partners, when the FLP holds only investment assets, as opposed to an operating business, courts will be less likely to limit their remedies to charging orders. Finally, courts will probably continue to erode the asset protection capabilities of FLPs.[94]

If the debtor partner is a general partner who enters bankruptcy, the bankruptcy trustee may force the FLP's dissolution or the general partner's withdrawal from the partnership, thus requiring a distribution to the bankruptcy trustee.[95]

Caution. *In Movitz v. Fiesta Invs. LLC (In re Ehmann)*,[96] the bankruptcy trustee, Louis Movitz, for the bankruptcy estate of the debtor, Gregory Ehmann, filed a lawsuit against defendant Fiesta Investments, LLC ("the LLC"). Ehmann was a member of the LLC when he filed bankruptcy, and in the lawsuit plaintiff-trustee asked the court to declare, among other

[92] *See* Crocker Nat'l Bank v. Perroton, 208 Cal. App. 3d 1, 255 Cal. Rptr. 794 (1989); Hellman v. Anderson, 233 Cal. App. 3d 840, 284 Cal. Rptr. 830 (1991).

[93] Crocker Nat'l Bank v. Perroton, 208 Cal. App. 3d 1 (1989).

[94] *See* Barry S. Engel & Ronald L. Rudman, *Family Limited Partnerships: New Meaning for "Limited,"* 131 Trusts & Est. 46 (July 1993).

[95] 11 U.S.C. §541(a)(1) (1988); UPA §§31(1), 31(2), 31(5), 38, 6 U.L.A. 376, 456–57 (1914); RULPA §§402(4), 402(5), 602, 604, 801, 808 (1985), 6 U.L.A. 359–60, 381–83, 395, 399 (Supp. 1992); *In re* Sunset Developers, 69 B.R. 710 (Bankr. D. Idaho 1987); Neill G. McBryde, *The Esoterica of Family Partnerships,* 1993 U.S.C. L. Center Tax Inst. ¶ 1014.2.

[96] 334 BR 437 (Bankr. D. Ariz. 2005), *op. withdrawn, mot. granted,* 337 B.R. 228 (Bankr. D. Ariz. 2006).

things, that the trustee had the status of a member in the LLC, and for the court to order the dissolution and liquidation of the LLC or for the appointment of a receiver for the LLC.

The bankruptcy court found on the LLC's motion to dismiss that the trustee "has all the rights and powers with respect to (the LLC) that the Debtor held as of the commencement of the case." In reaching that conclusion, the court noted that Bankruptcy Code § 365(e)(2) generally "permits the enforcement of state and contract law restrictions on the Trustee's rights and powers, whereas (Bankruptcy Code § 541(c)(1)), if applicable, would render such restrictions and conditions unenforceable as against the Trustee." The court went on to state that "[b]ecause § 541 applies generally to all property and rights that the Trustee acquires, whereas § 365 applies more specifically to executory contract rights, the answer to this question hinges on whether the Trustee is asserting a property right or an executory contract right." The bankruptcy court concluded that "because the operating agreement of a limited liability company imposes no obligations on its members, it is not an executory contract. Consequently when a member who is not the manager files a Chapter 7 case, his trustee acquires all of the member's rights and interests pursuant to Bankruptcy Code §§ 541(a) and (c)(1), and the limitations of §§ 365(c) and (e) do not apply." Based on this reasoning, the *Ehmann* court denied the LLC's motion to dismiss the trustee's action and, again in direct conflict with the language of the Operating Agreement, stated that dissolution could be an appropriate remedy.

Planning Pointer. The FLP's general partners will be solely responsible for managing and controlling its activities. Accordingly, the family members chosen should be familiar with the business contained within the FLP and with the needs of the limited partners. Also, the decision of which family members should serve as general partners will be influenced by the original owners of property transferred into the FLP, who often desire to retain control over that property by retaining general partnership interests.[97]

Planning Pointer. Because the client often desires to retain control over the property or business transferred into the FLP, the planner should consider using a corporate general partner. This arrangement will benefit the client by limiting any liability arising out of the FLP to the value of the general partnership interest and the corporate general partner. However, such an arrangement is disadvantageous in that it is more complex, and requires more time and money to maintain proper formalities. Also, unless the corporation is an S Corporation, the structure will involve double taxation.[98]

Planning Pointer. The at-risk client should generally not hold a general partner interest. Instead, a closely related and trusted family member

---

[97] Neill G. McBryde, *The Esoterica of Family Partnerships*, 1993 U.S.C. L. Center Tax Inst. ¶ 1014.2.
[98] *See* Chapter 4.

should be the general partner.[99] Although creditors of general partners usually can only obtain charging orders against the general partner's partnership interest, as with creditors of limited partners, the law in this area is not entirely settled. Therefore, to ensure maximum security, the planner should structure the family limited partnership so that the at-risk client does not become the general partner.[100] Also, if the at-risk client enters bankruptcy, the bankruptcy trustee may force the dissolution of the partnership or the withdrawal of the general partner from the partnership, thus requiring a distribution to the bankruptcy trustee.[101]

Planning Pointer. When the planner decides to use a corporate general partner, the at-risk client should not own a controlling interest of such corporate general partner. If the at-risk client does own such an interest, her creditors may reach this interest and thus be able to obtain control over the family limited partnership.[102]

Planning Pointer. The planner should not use the at-risk client's spouse as the general partner.[103] If the at-risk client enters bankruptcy and (1) the client and the spouse are jointly liable for any debts, or (2) the spouse's property is liable for any of the at-risk client's debts under state law, the non-at-risk spouse may also be forced into bankruptcy.

Planning Pointer. The family limited partnership should be used for business or investment assets.[104] It should not be used for personal assets because partnerships must generally carry on a business.[105]

Planning Pointer. The planner should consider using an employment contract between the family limited partnership and the at-risk client.[106] Under such an agreement, the partnership would employ the at-risk client to manage the partnership's assets or business. Alternatively, the planner should consider using a corporate general partner whose stock is held by non-at-risk members of the at-risk client's family. The corporation could then employ the at-risk client to manage the corporate general partner.

---

[99] Kathryn G. Henkel, How Family Limited Partnerships Can Protect Assets, 20 Est. Plan. 3 (Jan.–Feb. 1993).

[100] Kathryn G. Henkel, How Family Limited Partnerships Can Protect Assets, 20 Est. Plan. 3 (Jan.–Feb. 1993); Cherkis, Collier Real Estate Transactions and the Bankruptcy Code 4.07[1] (King ed., 1991).

[101] 11 U.S.C. §541(a)(1) (1988); UPA §§31(1), 31(2), 31(5), 38, 6 U.L.A. 376, 456–7 (1914); RULPA §§402(4), 402(5), 602, 604, 801, 808 (1985), 6 U.L.A. 359–60, 381–3, 395, 399 (Supp. 1992); In re Sunset Developers, 69 B.R. 710 (Bankr. D. Idaho 1987).

[102] Kathryn G. Henkel, How Family Limited Partnerships Can Protect Assets, 20 Est. Plan. 3, 4–5 (Jan.–Feb. 1993).

[103] Kathryn G. Henkel, How Family Limited Partnerships Can Protect Assets, 20 Est. Plan. 3, 5 (Jan.–Feb. 1993).

[104] Kathryn G. Henkel, How Family Limited Partnerships Can Protect Assets, 20 Est. Plan. 3, 7 (Jan.–Feb. 1993).

[105] UPA §6, 6 U.L.A. 22 (1914).

[106] Kathryn G. Henkel, How Family Limited Partnerships Can Protect Assets, 20 Est. Plan. 3, 9–10 (Jan.–Feb. 1993).

[F] Limited Liability Partnerships[107]

Some jurisdictions, most prominently Delaware, have modified their partnership statutes to provide for limited liability partnerships (LLPs).[108]

Generally, an LLP partner will not be liable for debts and obligations of the partnership arising from negligence, wrongful acts, or misconduct committed (1) while the partnership constitutes a registered LLP, and (2) in the course of partnership business by another partner or an employee, agent, or representative of the partnership.[109] However, an LLP will not limit an LLP partner's liability for his or her own negligence, wrongful acts, or misconduct, or that of any person under the partner's direct supervision and control.[110] The Delaware LLP provision states that the ability of attorneys licensed in Delaware to practice law in registered LLPs will be determined by the Rules of the Delaware Supreme Court.[111] Also, some LLP statutes explicitly provide that LLP provisions do not affect the liability of the partnership itself for partnership debts, and that LLP partners remain jointly liable for partnership debts and obligations other than those specified under the LLP limited liability provisions.[112]

Generally, a partnership must file an application with the appropriate government office to become a registered LLP.[113] Usually, the partnership must file an application or renewal application stating the partnership's name, the address of its principal office (or, if its principal office is out of state, the address of its registered office and the name and address of its registered agent for service of process), the number of partners, a brief statement of the business in which the partnership engages, and that the partnership is thereby applying for LLP status or renewal.[114] Generally, the application or renewal application must be executed by a majority in interest of the partners or by one or more partners who are authorized to execute such applications.[115]

Typically, registration as an LLP will be effective for one year from the application or renewal application filing date unless the LLP voluntarily withdraws its registration by filing a written withdrawal notice executed by a majority in interest of the partners or by one or more partners who are authorized to execute such withdrawals.[116] The LLP provisions often provide for fees to accompany the application and renewal applications. They also provide for due dates for renewal applications that occur each year, approximately on the anniversary date of the original application.[117]

---

[107] *See generally* Beth Duncan, Choice of Entity: Conversion to Limited Liability Partnerships Is Easy, But the Safety Net They Offer Is Only a Partial One, BNA's Corp. Counsel Weekly, Feb. 8, 1995, at 8.

[108] *See, e.g.,* Del. Code Ann. tit. 6, §§ 1502(6), 1515(b)–(d), 1544, 1545, 1546, 1547 (1993); D.C. Code Ann. §§ 41-101(2)(a), 41-105.1(6a), 41-143 to 43-148 (Supp. 1994).

[109] *See, e.g.,* Del. Code Ann. tit. 6, § 1515(b) (1993); D.C. Code Ann. § 41-146(a) (Supp. 1994).

[110] *See, e.g.,* Del. Code Ann. tit. 6, § 1515(c) (1993); D.C. Code Ann. § 41-146(a) (Supp. 1994).

[111] Del. Code Ann. tit. 6, § 1515(d) (1993).

[112] *See, e.g.,* D.C. Code Ann. § 41-146(a) (Supp. 1994).

[113] *See, e.g.,* Del. Code Ann. tit. 6, § 1544 (1993); D.C. Code Ann. § 41-143 (Supp. 1994).

[114] *See, e.g.,* Del. Code Ann. tit. 6, § 1544(a) (1993); D.C. Code Ann. § 41-143(a) (Supp. 1994).

[115] *See, e.g.,* Del. Code Ann. tit. 6, § 1544(b) (1993); D.C. Code Ann. § 41-143(b) (Supp. 1994).

[116] *See, e.g.,* Del. Code Ann. tit. 6, § 1544(e) (1993); D.C. Code Ann. § 41-143(d) (Supp. 1994).

[117] *See, e.g.,* Del. Code Ann. tit. 6, §§ 1544(c), (e) (1993); D.C. Code Ann. § 41-143(d), (f) (Supp. 1994).

LLP statutes typically require registered LLPs to include the words "Registered Limited Liability Partnership" or "L.L.P." as the last words or letters of its name.[118] More importantly, LLP statutes require registered LLPs to carry a minimum amount of liability insurance. The Delaware statute requires registered LLPs to carry at least $1 million of liability insurance covering the types of liability that are limited by the Delaware LLP provisions.[119] If the LLP's compliance with this requirement is challenged during litigation, the court will resolve the issue, and the partner claiming the benefit of the LLP provision bears the burden of proof of compliance.[120] However, if the registered LLP is in compliance with this insurance requirement, this insurance requirement cannot be made known to the jury when it determines the issue of liability for or the extent of the debt or obligation or damages in question.[121] The LLP may comply with the insurance requirement by providing $1 million of funds, specifically designated and segregated for the satisfaction of judgments against the LLP or its partners based on the kinds of acts for which the LLP provisions limit liability, by deposit in trust or in bank escrow of cash, bank certificates of deposit, or U.S. Treasury obligations, or by bank letter of credit or insurance company bond.[122] The D.C. provision requires registered LLPs to carry liability insurance in the amount of coverage of either (1) at least $100,000 of liability insurance covering the types of liability that are limited by the D.C. LLP provisions, or (2) coverage in a minimum amount of not less than the amount carried by the individual partner carrying the greatest amount of individual liability insurance, whichever is greater.[123] Like its Delaware counterpart, the D.C. LLP statute provides that if the registered LLP is in compliance with this insurance requirement, this insurance requirement cannot be made known to the jury when it determines the issue of liability for or the extent of the debt or obligation or damages in question.[124]

Finally, both the Delaware and the D.C. statutes include provisions that address the applicability of their LLP provisions to foreign and interstate commerce. Specifically, both the Delaware and D.C. LLP statutes allow LLPs organized under their laws to conduct business, carry out operations, and exercise their powers in any jurisdiction.[125] Also, both statutes provide that their laws will govern LLPs operating in other jurisdictions.[126] Finally, D.C. provides that foreign LLPs may conduct business in D.C. upon filing an appropriate application, and that the laws of the state or jurisdiction under which that LLP was organized will control its organization, internal affairs, and the liability of its partners.[127] Furthermore, it provides that foreign registered LLPs cannot be

---

[118] Del. Code Ann. tit. 6, § 1545 (1993); D.C. Code Ann. § 41-144 (Supp. 1994).

[119] Del. Code Ann. tit. 6, § 1545(a) (1993).

[120] Del. Code Ann. tit. 6, § 1545(b) (1993).

[121] Del. Code Ann. tit. 6, § 1545(c) (1993).

[122] Id.

[123] D.C. Code Ann. § 41-145(a) (Supp. 1994).

[124] D.C. Code Ann. § 41-145(b) (Supp. 1994).

[125] Del. Code Ann. tit. 6, § 1547(a) (1993); D.C. Code Ann. § 41-148(a) (Supp. 1994).

[126] Del. Code Ann. tit. 6, § 1547(b) (1993); D.C. Code Ann. §§ 41-148(b)–(c) (Supp. 1994).

[127] D.C. Code Ann. § 41-147 (Supp. 1994).

prohibited from doing business in D.C. because of any difference between the laws of its state of organization and D.C.'s laws.[128]

[G]   Other Nontax Considerations

The planner also must consider various other aspects of limited partnerships to compare it to other entity forms.[129] The planner must balance the limited liability benefits of limited partnerships against any additional costs attributable to this entity form.[130] The nontax aspects of limited partnerships the planner must consider include the (1) expenses and formalities of organization, (2) management and control, (3) continuity of existence, and (4) transferability of limited partnership interests.

[1]   Expenses and Formalities of Organization

To form a limited partnership, the planner must comply with the statute of the jurisdiction in question.[131]

> **Caution.** Failure to follow the statutory requirements for forming a limited partnership may cause the client (purported limited partner) to be subject to the unlimited liability of general partner status.[132] Consequently, the planner must ensure there is substantial compliance with the applicable statutory formation requirements. The planner should note that, although the ULPA does not expressly mention a partnership agreement, the RULPA does recognize that the basic document in any partnership is the partnership agreement.

> **Planning Pointer.** Even if not required by the statute of the jurisdiction in question, the planner should ensure that the partners execute a partnership agreement. The planner should also ensure that the partnership agreement and the limited partnership certificate are consistent with each other.

The ULPA requires that two or more persons who want to form a limited partnership must execute and file a certificate with the appropriate state office,[133]

---

[128] D.C. Code Ann. § 41-147 (Supp. 1994).

[129] *See* Harold Gill Reuschlein & William A. Gregory, The Law of Agency and Partnership (2d ed. 1990); Zolman Cavitch, Business Organizations Ch. 39 (1991); Anne E. Bookout, Limited Partnerships: Legal Aspects of Organization, Operation, and Dissolution, Corp. Prac. (BNA) No. 24-4th.

[130] *See* § 3.08 for a worksheet that will assist the planner with this analysis.

[131] *See generally* Zolman Cavitch, Business Organizations Ch. 39 (1991); Anne E. Bookout, Limited Partnerships: Legal Aspects of Organization, Operation, and Dissolution, Corp. Prac. (BNA) No. 24-4th, at II.

[132] *See* §§ 3.05[A]–3.05[D].

[133] ULPA § 2(1)(b), 6 U.L.A. 568 (1916).

or with the secretary of state, if a RULPA jurisdiction.[134] Such certificate must generally contain the following:

- The partnership's name;[135]
- The business's character;[136]
- The location of the principal place of business;[137]
- Each member's name and place of residence and whether such member is a general or limited partner;[138]
- The term for which the partnership is to exist;[139]
- The amount of cash and a description of and the agreed value of the other property contributed by each limited partner;[140]
- The additional contributions, if any, each limited partner agrees to make and the times they will make such contributions;[141]
- The time, if agreed on, when the contribution of each limited partner will be returned;[142]
- The share of the profits or the other compensation that each limited partner will receive because of their contributions;[143]
- Any right of a limited partner to substitute an assignee as contributor in her place and the terms and conditions thereof;[144]
- The right, if given, of the partners to admit additional limited partners;[145]
- Any right of one or more limited partners to priority over other limited partners regarding contributions or compensation, and the nature thereof;[146]
- The right, if given, of the remaining general partner or partners to continue the business on the death, retirement, or insanity of a general partner;[147] and
- The right, if given, of a limited partner to demand and receive property other than cash in return for her contribution.[148]

The RULPA generally requires the same information as the ULPA, plus the following information:

- The address of the office and the name and address of the agent for service of process required to be maintained by § 104 of the RULPA;[149]

---

[134] RULPA § 201 (a) (1985), 6 U.L.A. 312 (Supp. 1992).
[135] ULPA § 2(1)(a)(I), 6 U.L.A. 568 (1916).
[136] ULPA § 2(1)(a)(II), 6 U.L.A. 568 (1916).
[137] ULPA § 2(1)(a)(III), 6 U.L.A. 568 (1916).
[138] ULPA § 2(1)(a)(IV), 6 U.L.A. 568 (1916).
[139] ULPA § 2(1)(a)(V), 6 U.L.A. 568 (1916).
[140] ULPA § 2(1)(a)(VI), 6 U.L.A. 568 (1916).
[141] ULPA § 2(1)(a)(VII), 6 U.L.A. 568 (1916).
[142] ULPA § 2(1)(a)(VIII), 6 U.L.A. 568 (1916).
[143] ULPA § 2(1)(a)(IX), 6 U.L.A. 568 (1916).
[144] ULPA § 2(1)(a)(X), 6 U.L.A. 568 (1916).
[145] ULPA § 2(1)(a)(XI), 6 U.L.A. 568 (1916).
[146] ULPA § 2(1)(a)(XII), 6 U.L.A. 568 (1916).
[147] ULPA § 2(1)(a)(XIII), 6 U.L.A. 568 (1916).
[148] ULPA § 2(1)(a)(XIV), 6 U.L.A. 568 (1916).
[149] RULPA § 201(3) (1976), 6 U.L.A. 312 (Supp. 1992).

- Any right of a partner to receive distributions of property, including cash from the limited partnership;[150] and
- Any time contingency that will cause the dissolution of the limited partnership.[151]

Planning Pointer. The certificate should be filed as promptly as possible after the formation of the partnership to minimize the risk of failure to comply substantially with statutory requirements. Furthermore, it may be advisable for the limited partnership agreement to state that no legal entity is formed until the certificate is filed.

Under certain circumstances the limited partnership must amend its certificate. Specifically, in ULPA jurisdictions the limited partnership must amend its certificate when the following occurs:

- There is a change in the partnership's name or in the amount or character of any limited partner's contribution;
- A limited partner substitutes another person as limited partner;
- The partnership admits an additional limited partner;
- The partnership admits a person as a general partner;
- A general partner retires, dies, or becomes insane and the business continues under ULPA Section 20;
- There is a change in the character of the partnership's business;
- The certificate contains a false or erroneous statement;
- There is a change in the time stated in the certificate for the partnership's dissolution or for the return of a contribution;
- The partnership fixes a time for its dissolution or a contribution's return, if the certificate did not previously state such times; or
- The members want to change any other statement within the certificate to represent accurately the partnership agreement.[152]

In ULPA jurisdictions the certificate amendment must conform to the requirements of ULPA Section 2(1) (a) to set forth clearly the change in the certificate and be signed and sworn to by all members. An amendment substituting a limited partner or adding a limited or general partner also must be signed by the new member and the assigning limited partner when applicable.[153] If a person that the ULPA requires to sign the amendment refuses to sign, a court may be petitioned to direct an amendment to the certificate.[154] The certificate becomes amended when either (1) the amendment,[155] or (2) a certified copy of

---

[150] RULPA § 201(9) (1976), 6 U.L.A. 312 (Supp. 1992).
[151] RULPA § 201(11) (1976), 6 U.L.A. 312 (Supp. 1992).
[152] ULPA § 24(2), 6 U.L.A. 609 (1916).
[153] ULPA § 25(1), 6 U.L.A. 610 (1916).
[154] ULPA § 25(3), 6 U.L.A. 611 (1916).
[155] ULPA § 25(5)(a), 6 U.L.A. 611 (1916).

the court order is filed[156] for record in the office where the certificate is recorded.[157]

In RULPA jurisdictions the limited partnership must amend its certificate within 30 days of any of the following events:

- A change in the amount or character of the contribution of any partner, or in any partner's obligation to make a contribution;[158]
- The admission of a new partner (general partner for jurisdictions that have adopted the 1985 amendments);[159]
- The withdrawal of a new partner (general partner for jurisdictions that have adopted the 1985 amendments);[160] or
- The continuation of the business under Section 801 of the RULPA after an event of withdrawal of a general partner.[161]

In RULPA jurisdictions the partnership may amend the certificate by filing a certificate of amendment with the office of the secretary of state.[162] The certificate of amendment must state:

- The name of the limited partnership;[163]
- The date of filing the certificate;[164] and
- The amendment to the certificate.[165]

[2] Management and Control of Limited Partnership

Generally, general partners possess the same authority to manage limited partnership business as a general partner of a general partnership.[166] However, the ULPA provides that, unless a general partner obtains the written consent or satisfaction of all limited partners, that partner cannot:

- Perform any act that contravenes the certificate;
- Perform any act that makes it impossible to carry on the partnership's ordinary business;
- Confess judgments against the partnership;

---

[156] ULPA § 25(5)(b), 6 U.L.A. 611 (1916).

[157] ULPA § 25(5), 6 U.L.A. 611 (1916).

[158] RULPA § 202(b)(1) (1976), 6 U.L.A. 318 (Supp. 1992). This provision was deleted by the 1985 amendments to the RULPA.

[159] RULPA § 202(b)(2) (1976); RULPA § 202(b)(1) (1985), 6 U.L.A. 318 (Supp. 1992).

[160] RULPA § 202(b)(3) (1976); RULPA § 202(b)(2) (1985), 6 U.L.A. 318 (Supp. 1992).

[161] RULPA § 202(b)(4) (1976); RULPA § 202(b)(3) (1985), 6 U.L.A. 318 (Supp. 1992).

[162] RULPA § 202(a) (1976), 6 U.L.A. 318 (Supp. 1992).

[163] RULPA § 202(a)(1) (1976), 6 U.L.A. 318 (Supp. 1992).

[164] RULPA § 202(a)(2) (1976), 6 U.L.A. 318 (Supp. 1992).

[165] RULPA § 202(a)(3) (1976), 6 U.L.A. 318 (Supp. 1992).

[166] ULPA § 9(1), 6 U.L.A. 586 (1916); RULPA § 403 (1976), 6 U.L.A. 362 (Supp. 1992); Anne E. Bookout, Limited Partnerships: Legal Aspects of Organization, Operation, and Dissolution, Corp. Prac. (BNA) No. 24-4th, at VI; Zolman Cavitch, Business Organizations § 39.08[2] (1991).

- Possess partnership property or assign rights in specific partnership property for other than a partnership purpose;
- Admit a person as a general partner;
- Admit a person as a limited partner, except where the certificate gives such right; or
- Continue the business with partnership property on the death, retirement, or insanity of a general partner, unless the certificate gives such right.[167]

The RULPA does not impose any such restrictions on the authority of general partners except for admission of new general partners.[168] Specifically, under the 1976 version of the RULPA, a general partner must obtain the specific written consent of each partner to admit additional new general partners.[169] Under the 1985 RULPA, new general partners may be admitted as the written partnership agreement provides or, if it does not so provide, with the consent of all partners.[170] Finally, the planner should note that general partners are accountable to the limited partners as fiduciaries.[171]

[3]   Continuity of Limited Partnership Existence

A limited partnership lacks the theoretical perpetual existence of a corporation.[172] However, a limited partnership may exist for a substantial period because ULPA Section 2(1)(a)(v) provides that the certificate of limited partnership must state the term of the partnership, which may be extensive. The limited partnership dissolves at the expiration of this term.[173]

The planner may also obtain continuity of existence through the limited partnership agreement. The agreement may provide that a limited partner's capital contribution cannot be withdrawn until a specified date. If the agreement does not fix a date for such capital withdrawal, the limited partner under ULPA Section 16(2) may withdraw her capital contribution on six months' notice to the other partners and, thereby, dissolve the limited partnership.[174]

The limited partnership certificate may expressly empower a limited partner to substitute a new limited partner in her place.[175] When the certificate includes this provision and a limited partner dies, her estate may become a limited partner and continue in the business rather than causing dissolution of the partnership. Death or withdrawal of all general partners or the sole general

---

[167] ULPA § 9(1), 6 U.L.A. 586 (1916).

[168] RULPA § 401 (1976), 6 U.L.A. 358 (Supp. 1992).

[169] Id.

[170] Id.

[171] Anne E. Bookout, Limited Partnerships: Legal Aspects of Organization, Operation, and Dissolution, Corp. Prac. (BNA) No. 24-4th, at VI; Zolman Cavitch, Business Organizations § 39.08[2] (1991).

[172] Anne E. Bookout, Limited Partnerships: Legal Aspects of Organization, Operation, and Dissolution, Corp. Prac. (BNA) No. 24-4th, at IX; Zolman Cavitch, Business Organizations § 39.08[2][a] (1991).

[173] See also RULPA § 201 (a) (11) (1985), 6 U.L.A. 312 (Supp. 1992).

[174] See also RULPA § 603 (1985), 6 U.L.A. 381 (Supp. 1992).

[175] ULPA § 2(1)(a), 6 U.L.A. 568 (1916); RULPA § 201(a)(7) (1985), 6 U.L.A. 312 (Supp. 1992).

partner terminates a limited partnership.[176] The death or withdrawal of less than all general partners will not cause partnership dissolution if (1) the business is continued by the remaining general partners under a right to do so stated in the certificate, or (2) all other members consent to continuation.[177]

[4] Transferability of Limited Partnership Interests

A limited partner[178] may freely assign her limited partnership interest.[179] Absent the consent of all other members and provision in the certificate of limited partnership, however, the assignee will only obtain the assignor's right to share in profits and will not be a substitute limited partner.[180]

Planning Pointer. The planner should note that limited partners have an unrestricted right to transfer their interests without causing the dissolution and liquidation of the limited partnership. Simultaneously, management is restricted to a group of general partners.

§3.06 LIMITED LIABILITY COMPANIES

[A] In General

The limited liability company (LLC)[1] is a relatively new entity form that combines the limited liability benefits of corporations with the tax advantages

---

[176] ULPA §20, 6 U.L.A. 604 (1916).

[177] ULPA §21, 6 U.L.A. 605 (1916).

[178] *See* Anne E. Bookout, Limited Partnerships: Legal Aspects of Organization, Operation, and Dissolution, Corp. Prac. (BNA) No. 24-4th, at VIII; Zolman Cavitch, Business Organizations §39.08[2][e] (1991).

[179] ULPA §19,6 U.L.A. 603 (1916); RULPA §702 (1976), 6 U.L.A. 388 (Supp. 1992).

[180] RULPA §704 (1976), 6 U.L.A. 392 (Supp. 1992); ULPA §19,6 U.L.A. 603 (1916).

§3.06 [1] *See* Robert R. Keatinge et al., The Limited Liability Company: A Study of the Emerging Entity, 47 Bus. Law. 375 (1992); Francis I. Wirtz & Kenneth L. Harris, The Emerging Use of the Limited Liability Company, 70 Taxes 377 (1992); Wayne M. Gazur & Neil M. Goff, Assessing the Limited Liability Company, 41 Case W. Res. L. Rev. 387 (1991); Alan S. Lederman, Miami Device: The Florida Limited Liability Company, 67 Taxes 339 (1989); Ronald D. Platner, Limited Liability Companies Are Increasingly Popular, 20 Tax'n for Law. 225 (Jan.–Feb. 1992); Brian L. Schorr & Aileen R. Leventon, Limited Liability Company: An Alternative Business Form, N.Y. Law J., May 30, 1991, at 1; Lee A. Sheppard, News Analysis: The Dark Side of Limited Liability Companies, 55 Tax Notes 1441 (1992); Robert B. Webb III & James J. Wheaton, Using and Operating a Virginia Limited Liability Company, 1992 Va. Conf. on Federal Tax'n 147; Jerald David August & Richard A. Shaw, The Limited Liability Company—A New Tax Refuge? 7 J. Tax'n Investments 179 (1990); Frank M. Burke & John S. Sessions, The Wyoming Limited Liability Company: An Alternative to Sub S and Limited Partnerships? 50 J. Tax'n 232 (1981); Charles R. Glasheen, The Limited Liability Company: A Unique PassThrough Entity, I J. S Corp. Tax'n 129 (1989); Susan Pace Hamill, The Limited Liability Company: A Possible Choice for Doing Business? 41 Fla. L. Rev. 721 (1989); Annotation, *Construction and application of limited liability company acts,* 79 A.L.R.5th 689; Denison H. Hatch, Jr., Limited Liability Companies: Legal Aspects of Organization, Operation, and Dissolution, Corp. Prac. (BNA) No. 67; Miller, *Recent Cases Involving Limited Liability Companies and*

of partnerships. The LLC is a statutory creation. Today, every state provides for LLCs.

Generally, LLC statutes are very similar. Most are based on the Wyoming LLC statute, which was the first such statute. On the other hand, however, there is still a substantial amount of variation among state LLC statutes. In addition, although there is now a Uniform LLC Act (ULLC), it was not adopted until 1996, after most states had already adopted their own individualized LLC acts. Therefore, while the importance of the ULLC may be expected to grow over time, today, only the following nine jurisdictions have enacted the Uniform LLC Act:

1. Alabama
2. Hawaii
3. Illinois
4. Montana
5. South Carolina
6. South Dakota
7. U.S. Virgin Islands
8. Vermont
9. West Virginia

Currently, the National Conference of Commissioners on Uniform States Laws (NCCUSL) is working on a proposed "second generation" Uniform Limited Liability Company Act. More information about this project, which is currently under way, is located at the NCCUSL web site for this project, at http://www.llcproject.org.

Generally, when available and properly used, LLCs offer advantages of both corporations and partnerships. First, they offer the limited liability of corporations. Second, they offer the tax benefits of partnerships. In particular, they do not involve the double taxation aspects of corporations. Third, they are more advantageous than limited partnerships because they do not require a general partner subject to unlimited liability. Additionally, LLC members may participate in the entity's control while receiving the benefits of limited liability.[2] In contrast, limited partners cannot participate in limited partnership control without risking loss of limited liability. Fourth, the LLC offers several advantages over the S Corporation, which has tax restrictions on special allocations of income and loss and the number and type of shareholders, among other things.[3]

Caution. Because there is a lack of uniformity among state LLC statutes, planners must examine the LLC statute of the jurisdiction in question very carefully. More problematic, the cases on LLCs to date are sporadic and do not yet cover many important issues, such as the piercing of the veil of

---

Limited Liability Partnerships, in New Developments in Limited Liability Companies and Limited Liability Partnerships, at 53 (ALI-ABA Course of Study No. VML0316).

[2] *See* § 3.06[B].

[3] *See* Chapter 4.

limited liability, and the extent and scope of fiduciary duties owed to LLC members by the managers.[4]

Caution. Planners should avoid using single member LLCs, because some cases have held that creditors can reach their underlying assets.[5]

[B] Limited Liability

[1] In General

LLC statutes generally provide for limited liability of LLC managers and members.[6] For example, Wyoming's statute provides that "[n]either the members of a limited liability company nor the managers of a limited liability company managed by a manager or managers are liable under a judgment, decree or order of a court, or in any other manner, for a debt, obligation or liability of the limited liability company."[7] Other LLC jurisdictions generally either use identical language or language very similar to the Wyoming statute.[8]

EXAMPLE 3-17

Lewis and Lynn are brothers. Lynn, an asset protection lawyer, has accumulated a great deal of wealth. Lewis desires to start a new business, Risky Royalties, a publishing company. Lewis asks Lynn to join him in this venture. Lynn agrees and together the two establish the Risky Royalties LLC, a Wyoming LLC. Each invests $100,000 in Risky Royalties for a 50-percent Risky Royalties interest. Each spends substantial time in its operations in addition to their other activities.

The first year, Risky Royalties sustains a $100,000 taxable loss. Assuming no passive activity loss problems, Lewis and Lynn each deduct $50,000 against their other income. Here there is no double taxation as with a corporation. In year two, Risky Royalties sustains an $80,000 taxable loss. Also in year two, Risky Royalties goes out of business owing $500,000 to vendors. Here, Lewis and Lynn may each deduct $40,000 against their other income.

---

[4] *See, e.g.*, Thomas R. Hurst, *Fundamental Themes is Business Law Education: Teaching Limited Liability Companies in the Basic Business Associations Course*, 34 Ga. L. Rev. 773 (Winter 2000).

[5] *In re Albright*, 291 B.R. 538 (Bankr. D. Colo. 2003).

[6] *See generally* Denison H. Hatch, Jr., Limited Liability Companies: Legal Aspects of Organization, Operation, and Dissolution, Corp. Prac. (BNA) No. 67, at IV.C.7; See, *e.g.*, Del. Code Ann. tit. 6, § 18-303 (Supp. 1992); Wyo. Stat. § 17-15-113 (1977); Fla. Stat. Ann. § 608.436 (West 1993); Colo. Rev. Stat. Ann. § 7-80-705 (West 1992); Kan. Stat. Ann. § 17-7620 (Supp. 1992).

[7] Wyo. Stat. § 17-15-113 (1977).

[8] *See, e.g.*, Del. Code Ann. tit. 6, § 18-303 (Supp. 1992); Nev. Rev. Stat. Ann. § 86.371 (Michie Supp. 1991); Tex. Rev. Civ. Stat. Ann. art. 1528n, art. 4.03A (West Supp. 1993); Utah Code Ann. § 48-2b-109 (Supp. 1991); Va. Code Ann. § 13.1-1019 (Michie Supp. 1991).

As in year one, there is no double taxation. Furthermore, Lewis and Lynn are protected from the liabilities that arise out of Risky Royalties.

There are three exceptions to member-limited liability. Specifically, limited liability members will be liable (1) for unpaid contributions, (2) when the veil of limited liability is pierced, and (3) when the LLC is not properly formed.

[2] Liability for Unpaid Contributions

First, statutes provide that LLC members are liable for unpaid contributions that they have agreed to make.[9] Furthermore, LLC members are generally liable for property that the articles of organization state the member has contributed but which the LLC wrongfully or erroneously returns to that member.[10] An exception to these rules generally applies when all the other LLC members consent to a waiver of a member's liabilities. However, such a member generally remains liable to creditors who extended credit or whose claim arose after the filing and before a cancellation or amendment of the articles of organization.[11] In some jurisdictions creditors must rely on the member's contribution when extending credit to hold the member liable for contribution.[12]

[3] Piercing the Limited Liability Veil

It is not clear whether an LLC's veil of limited liability can be pierced. There is little law to date on this topic.[13] An example of a jurisdiction that statutorily provides for piercing the LLC veil of limited liability is Colorado.[14] The Colorado provision provides that "[i]n any case in which a party seeks to hold the members of a limited liability company personally responsible for the alleged improper actions of the limited liability company, the court shall apply the case law which interprets the conditions and circumstances under which the corporate veil of a corporation may be pierced under Colorado law."[15]

---

[9] *See, e.g.,* Del. Code Ann. tit. 6, § 18-502 (Supp. 1992); Wyo. Stat. § 17-15-121(a) (1977); Fla. Stat. Ann. § 608.435 (West 1993); Colo. Rev. Stat. Ann. § 7-80-502 (West 1992); Kan. Stat. Ann. § 17-7619(a) (Supp. 1992); Utah Code Ann. § 48-2b-133(1) (Supp. 1991); Va. Code Ann. § 13.1-1027(B) (Michie Supp. 1991).

[10] *See, e.g.,* Nev. Rev. Stat. Ann. § 86.391(4) (Michie Supp. 1991); Tex. Rev. Civ. Stat. Ann. art. 1528n, art. 5.09(B) (West Supp. 1993); Utah Code Ann. § 48-2b-133(4) (Supp. 1991); Va. Code Ann. § 13.1-1036(B) (Michie Supp. 1991).

[11] *See, e.g.,* Del. Code Ann. tit. 6, § 18-502(b) (Supp. 1992); Wyo. Stat. § 17-15-12 I(c) (1977); Fla. Stat. Ann. § 608.435(3) (West 1993); Colo. Rev. Stat. Ann. § 7-80-502(2) (West 1992); Kan. Stat. Ann. § 17-7619(c) (Supp. 1992).

[12] *See, e.g.,* Del. Code Ann. tit. 6, § 18-502(b) (Supp. 1992); Colo. Rev. Stat. Ann. § 7-80502(2) (West 1992); Tex. Rev. Civ. Stat. Ann. art. 1528n, art. 5.02(D) (West Supp. 1993); Va. Code Ann. § 13.1-1027(C) (Michie Supp. 1991).

[13] *See* Robert R. Keatinge et al., *The Limited Liability Company: A Study of the Emerging Entity,* 47 Bus. Law. 375, 445 (1992); Wayne M. Gazur & Neil M. Goff, Assessing the Limited Liability Company, 41 Case W. Res. L. Rev. 387, 403 (1991).

[14] Colo. Rev. Stat. Ann. § 7-80-107 (West 1992).

[15] *Id.*

Some commentators have argued that the piercing the corporate veil doctrine[16] should apply in those jurisdictions that have not statutorily provided for its application.[17]

> **Planning Pointer.** Because the corporate veil piercing doctrine will probably be applied to LLCs in the future, the planner should ensure that client LLCs take steps to avoid application of this doctrine. Such steps would be similar to those discussed earlier for corporations. Specifically, planners intending to use an LLC should, at a minimum, ensure that it takes the following steps to minimize the risk of having the limited liability veil pierced:

1. Form the LLC with adequate capital and document the methodology of arriving at the amount of "adequate" capital. The LLC should also carry "adequate" liability insurance coverage.
2. Instruct the client not to drain capital from the LLC in an unwarranted manner and then periodically monitor client compliance.
3. Ensure that the members form the LLC for a legal purpose.
4. Instruct the client to follow proper LLC formalities under the applicable statute. The planner should periodically monitor compliance.
5. Ensure that the members (a) conduct LLC business on an LLC basis, as opposed to a personal basis, and (b) establish the LLC on an adequate financial basis.

[4] Liability Arising from Defective Formation

Many LLC jurisdictions hold members of a defectively formed LLC jointly and severally liable for all debts and liabilities of the purported LLC.[18] These provisions are generally modeled after Section 146 of the Model Business Corporation Act.[19]

> **Planning Pointer.** Because defective formation generally causes unlimited liability to the LLC members and because formation is relatively easy, the planner should ensure proper LLC formation.

---

[16] *See* § 3.03[B] for a discussion of the piercing the corporate veil doctrine in the corporate context.

[17] *See* Robert R. Keatinge et al., *The Limited Liability Company: A Study of the Emerging Entity*, 47 Bus. Law. 375, 445 (1992); Wayne M. Gazur & Neil M. Goff, Assessing the Limited Liability Company, 41 Case W. Res. L. Rev. 387, 403 (1991).

[18] *See, e.g.,* Wyo. Stat. § 17-15-133 (1977); Fla. Stat. Ann. § 608.437 (West 1993); Colo. Rev. Stat. Ann. § 7-80-105 (West 1992); Kan. Stat. Ann. § 17-7621 (Supp. 1992).

[19] Model Business Corp. Act § 146 (1979).

[C]   Other Nontax Considerations

The planner also must consider various other aspects of LLCs. The planner must balance the limited liability benefits against any additional costs attributable to LLCs.[20] The nontax aspects that the planner must consider include (1) expenses and formalities of organization, (2) management and control, (3) continuity of existence, and (4) transferability of LLC interests.

[1]   Expenses and Formalities of Organization

To form an LLC, the planner must comply with applicable LLC statutes.[21]

Caution. Under most limited liability company statutes, failure to follow the statutory formation requirements causes unlimited liability exposure for the LLC members.[22]

Generally, two or more persons may form an LLC by filing articles of organization with the appropriate state office of the state of formation.[23] These statutes also generally require that the LLC have at least two members at all times.[24] However, in some jurisdictions an LLC may be formed by one person as long as it always has at least two members.[25] For these rules, the term "person" generally includes individuals, general partnerships, limited partnerships, other LLCs, corporations, trusts, business trusts, real estate investment trusts, estates, and other associations.[26] However, some statutes define "person" more restrictively for this purpose and, thus, the planner must examine carefully the statutes[27] in the appropriate jurisdiction.

---

[20] *See* § 3.08 for a worksheet that will assist the planner with this analysis.

[21] *See* Robert R. Keatinge et al., *The Limited Liability Company: A Study of the Emerging Entity*, 47 Bus. Law. 375, 409–12 (1992); Wayne M. Gazur & Neil M. Goff, *Assessing the Limited Liability Company*, 41 Case W. Res. L. Rev. 387, 396–98 (1991); Denison H. Hatch, Jr., Limited Liability Companies: Legal Aspects of Organization, Operation, and Dissolution, Corp. Prac. (BNA) No. 67, at III.

[22] *See, e.g.,* Colo. Rev. Stat. Ann. § 7-80-105 (West 1992); Wyo. Stat. § 17-15-133 (1977); Fla. Stat. Ann. § 608.437 (West 1993); Kan. Stat. Ann. § 17-7621 (Supp. 1992); Nev. Rev. Stat. Ann. § 86.361 (Michie Supp. 1991); Utah Code Ann. § 48-2b-118(3) (Supp. 1991).

[23] *See, e.g.,* Del. Code Ann. tit. 6, § 18-201 (Supp. 1992); Colo. Rev. Stat. Ann. § 7-80-203 (West 1992); Wyo. Stat. § 17-15-106 (1977); Fla. Stat. Ann. § 608.408 (West 1993); Kan. Stat. Ann. § 17-7605 (Supp. 1992); Nev. Rev. Stat. Ann. § 86.191 (Michie Supp. 1991); Utah Code Ann. § 48-2b-117 (Supp. 1991); Tex. Rev. Civ. Stat. Ann. art. 1528n, art. 3.03 (West Supp. 1993); Va. Code Ann. § 13.1-1010 (Michie Supp. 1991).

[24] *See, e.g.,* Del. Code Ann. tit. 6, § 18-203 (Supp. 1992); Wyo. Stat. § 17-15-106 (1977); Fla. Stat. Ann. § 608.405 (West 1993); Nev. Rev. Stat. Ann. § 86.151 (Michie Supp. 1991); Utah Code Ann. § 48-2b-103 (Supp. 1991).

[25] *See, e.g.,* Colo. Rev. Stat. Ann. § 7-80-203 (West 1992); Kan. Stat. Ann. § 17-7605 (Supp. 1992).

[26] *See, e.g.,* Del. Code Ann. tit. 6, § 18-101(11) (Supp. 1992); Wyo. Stat. § 17-15-102(iv) (1977); Kan. Stat. Ann. § 17-7602(d) (Supp. 1992); Tex. Rev. Civ. Stat. Ann. art. 1528n, art. 1.02A(4) (West Supp. 1993).

[27] *See, e.g.,* Colo. Rev. Stat. Ann. § 7-80-203(1) (West 1992).

Each LLC statute requires slightly different information. Among other items, the various statutes generally require the following information:

1. The name of the LLC;[28]
2. The period of the LLC's duration;[29]
3. The name and address of the LLC's registered agent for service of process;[30]
4. The purpose for which the LLC is formed;[31]
5. The address of the principal place of business within the state of the LLC;[32]
6. The description and fair market value of property and cash contributed to the LLC;[33]
7. The terms and conditions of admission of additional LLC members, if provided for;[34]
8. The right, if provided for, of the remaining LLC members to continue the business on the death, retirement, resignation, expulsion, bankruptcy, or dissolution of a member or of any occurrence that terminates the continued membership of an LLC member;[35]
9. Whether the LLC is to be managed by managers, and if so, the names and addresses of such managers, or alternatively, the names of LLC members who will manage the company;[36] and
10. Any other provision that the members elect to set forth in the articles for the regulation of the LLC.[37]

Each LLC statute allows the amendment of the LLC's articles of organization.[38] Under some circumstances these statutes require certain amendments to

---

[28] *See, e.g.,* Del. Code Ann. tit. 6, § 18-201(a)(1) (Supp. 1992); Colo. Rev. Stat. Ann. § 7-80-204(1)(a) (West 1992); Wyo. Stat. § 17-15-107(i) (1977); Fla. Stat. Ann. § 608.407(1)(a) (West 1993); Kan. Stat. Ann. § 17-7607(1) (Supp. 1992).

[29] *See, e.g.,* Del. Code Ann. tit. 6, § 18-201(a)(3) (Supp. 1992); Nev. Rev. Stat. Ann. § 86.161(1)(b) (Michie Supp. 1991); Tex. Rev. Civ. Stat. Ann. art. 1528n, art. 3.02A(2) (West Supp. 1993).

[30] *See, e.g.,* Del. Code Ann. tit. 6, § 18-201(a)(2) (Supp. 1992); Colo. Rev. Stat. Ann. § 7-80-204(1)(c) (West 1992); Wyo. Stat. § 17-15-107(iv) (1977); Fla. Stat. Ann. § 608.407(1)(d) (West 1993); Kan. Stat. Ann. § 17-7607(4) (Supp. 1992).

[31] *See, e.g.,* Nev. Rev. Stat. Ann. § 86.161(1)(c) (Michie Supp. 1991); Tex. Rev. Civ. Stat. Ann. art. 1528n, art. 3.02A(3) (West Supp. 1993).

[32] *See, e.g.,* Fla. Stat. Ann. § 608.407(1)(d) (West 1993); Kan. Stat. Ann. § 17-7607(4) (Supp. 1992); Nev. Rev. Stat. Ann. § 86.161 (i)(d) (Michie Supp. 1991); Tex. Rev. Civ. Stat. Ann. art. 1528n, art. 3.02A(4) (West Supp. 1993).

[33] *See, e.g.,* Wyo. Stat. § 17-15-107(v) (1977); Fla. Stat. Ann. § 608.407(1)(e) (West 1993).

[34] *See, e.g.,* Wyo. Stat. § 17-15-107(vii) (1977); Fla. Stat. Ann. § 608.407(1)(g) (West 1993); Kan. Stat. Ann. § 17-7607(5) (Supp. 1992); Nev. Rev. Stat. Ann. § 86.161(1)(e) (Michie Supp. 1991).

[35] *See, e.g.,* Wyo. Stat. § 17-15-107(viii) (1977); Fla. Stat. Ann. § 608.407(1)(h) (West 1993); Kan. Stat. Ann. § 17-7607(6) (Supp. 1992); Nev. Rev. Stat. Ann. § 86.161(1)(f) (Michie Supp. 1991).

[36] *See, e.g.,* Colo. Rev. Stat. Ann. § 7-80-204(1)(d) (West 1992); Wyo. Stat. § 17-15-107(ix) (1977); Fla. Stat. Ann. § 608.407(1)(i) (West 1993); Kan. Stat. Ann. § 17-7607(7) (Supp. 1992).

[37] *See, e.g.,* Fla. Stat. Ann. § 608.407(1)(j) (West 1993); Kan. Stat. Ann. § 17-7607(8) (West 1993); Nev. Rev. Stat. Ann. § 86.161(1)(g) (Michie Supp. 1991); Tex. Rev. Civ. Stat. Ann. art. 1528n, art. 3.02A(6) (West Supp. 1993).

[38] *See, e.g.,* Del. Code Ann. tit. 6, § 18-202 (Supp. 1992); Kan. Stat. Ann. § 17-7610 (Supp. 1992); Nev. Rev. Stat. Ann. § 86.221 (Michie Supp. 1991); Utah Code Ann. § 48-2b-121 (Supp. 1991); Tex. Rev. Civ. Stat. Ann. art. 1528n, art. 3.05 (West Supp. 1993); Va. Code Ann. § 13.11014 (Michie Supp. 1991).

the articles of organization. For example, most statutes require an amendment for changes in the LLC's name or the character of its business. Such statutes also generally require an amendment when there is a false or erroneous statement in the articles, or if the LLC members decide to provide or alter the stated time or event on which the company will dissolve.[39]

Most jurisdictions allow LLC members to contribute cash, property, services, or promissory notes in exchange for their membership interests.[40] Some jurisdictions, however, only allow members to contribute cash or other property, but not services.[41] Delaware allows a person to be admitted as a member of the LLC and to receive an LLC interest without making a contribution or being obligated to make a contribution to the LLC.[42]

> **Caution.** When members take a membership interest in exchange for services, they may be taxed on the receipt of such membership interest as ordinary income.[43] To avoid such treatment, the planner should attempt to structure the company's formation so that all members contribute cash or property to the LLC.

[2] Management and Control of the LLC

Generally, the basic document in any LLC is the operating agreement. LLC statutes generally refer to the operating agreement or regulations for some jurisdictions.[44] Many jurisdictions do not require that the operating agreement be in writing.[45] However, other jurisdictions do require the operating agreement to be written.[46] The LLC need not disclose the operating agreement to the public.[47]

> **Planning Pointer.** Even when not required, the planner should ensure that the members execute a written operating agreement. The operating

---

[39] *See, e.g.,* Del. Code Ann. tit. 6, § 18-202 (Supp. 1992); Colo. Rev. Stat. Ann. § 7-80-209 (West 1992); Wyo. Stat. § 17-15-129 (1977); Fla. Stat. Ann. § 608.411 (West 1993); Kan. Stat. Ann. § 17-7610 (Supp. 1992); Nev. Rev. Stat. Ann. § 86.221 (Michie Supp. 1991); Utah Code Ann. § 482b-121 (Supp. 1991).

[40] *See, e.g.,* Colo. Rev. Stat. Ann. § 7-80-102(4) (West 1992); Nev. Rev. Stat. Ann. § 86.041 (Michie Supp. 1991); Utah Code Ann. § 48-2b-124 (Supp. 1991); Tex. Rev. Civ. Stat. Ann. art. 1528n, art. 5.01 (West Supp. 1993); Va. Code Ann. § 13.1-1002 (Michie Supp. 1991).

[41] *See, e.g.,* Wyo. Stat. § 17-15-115 (1977); Fla. Stat. Ann. § 608.421 (West 1992).

[42] Del. Code Ann. tit. 6, § 18-301(c) (Supp. 1992).

[43] *See* Robert R. Keatinge et al., *The Limited Liability Company: A Study of the Emerging Entity,* 47 Bus. Law. 375, 432–33 (1992).

[44] *See id.* at 375, 414 (1992); Denison H. Hatch, Jr., Limited Liability Companies: Legal Aspects of Organization, Operation, and Dissolution, Corp. Prac. (BNA) No. 67, at IV.

[45] *Id.*

[46] *See, e.g.,* Colo. Rev. Stat. Ann. § 7-80-102(11) (West 1992); Nev. Rev. Stat. Ann. § 86. 101 (Michie Supp. 1991).

[47] *See* Robert R. Keatinge et al., *The Limited Liability Company: A Study of the Emerging Entity,* 47 Bus. Law. 375, 414 (1992).

agreement may be used to tailor the LLC's management structure to the members' needs. Also, it may be used to fill gaps in the statute's management provisions to minimize the possibility of future disputes or other problems. Finally, because the operating agreement is not a public document, using it as a vehicle for management provisions provides privacy for the members about their management structure.

Planning Pointer. The planner should ensure that the operating agreement and the articles of organization are consistent with each other. Also, the operating agreement should be written, even when not required by the jurisdiction in question.

[a] Structure Without an Operating Agreement

Generally, the operating agreement will control the management of the LLC. However, if there is no operating agreement, or the agreement contains gaps regarding the company's management, all of the LLC acts provide a default management structure.[48] Most jurisdictions provide that the LLC members manage the company.[49] These jurisdictions generally provide that, absent an operating agreement provision to the contrary, the members receive management authority in proportion to their capital contributions.[50] Some jurisdictions give each member equal management authority without regard to their capital contributions, absent a contrary provision in the operating agreement.[51] Generally, these statutes leave details of the firm's management, such as requirements concerning membership meetings and other day-to-day operations, to the operating agreement.[52]

On the other hand, some jurisdictions, such as Colorado and Texas, vest LLC management in the managers. The Texas provision applies absent a contrary provision in the LLC's regulations.[53] The Colorado provision is mandatory;[54] however, Colorado LLC members may serve as managers.[55] The Texas and

---

[48] *See, e.g.,* Colo. Rev. Stat. Ann. §§ 7-80-401 to -411 (West 1992); Wyo. Stat. § 17-15-116 (1977); Fla. Stat. Ann. § 608.422 (West 1993); Kan. Stat. Ann. § 17-7612 (Supp. 1992); Nev. Rev. Stat. Ann. § 86.291 (Michie Supp. 1991).

[49] *See, e.g.,* Del. Code Ann. tit. 6, § 18-402 (Supp. 1992); Wyo. Stat. § 17-15-116 (1977); Fla. Stat. Ann. § 608.422 (West 1993); Kan. Stat. Ann. § 17-7612 (Supp. 1992); Nev. Rev. Stat. Ann. § 86.291 (Michie Supp. 1991); Utah Code Ann. § 48-2b-125 (Supp. 1991); Va. Code Ann. § 13.1-1022 (Michie Supp. 1991).

[50] *See, e.g.,* Del. Code Ann. tit. 6, § 18-402 (Supp. 1992); Wyo. Stat. § 17-15-116 (1977); Fla. Stat. Ann. § 608.422 (West 1993); Nev. Rev. Stat. Ann. § 86.291 (Michie Supp. 1991).

[51] *See, e.g.,* Kan. Stat. Ann. § 17-7612 (Supp. 1992).

[52] *See* Robert R. Keatinge et al., *The Limited Liability Company: A Study of the Emerging Entity,* 47 Bus. Law. 375, 415 (1992); Wayne M. Gazur & Neil M. Goff, *Assessing the Limited Liability Company,* 41 Case W. Res. L. Rev. 387, 405 (1991). *See, e.g.,* Wyo. Stat. § 17-15-116 (1977); Fla. Stat. Ann. § 608.422 (West 1993); Kan. Stat. Ann. § 17-7612 (Supp. 1992).

[53] Tex. Rev. Civ. Stat. Ann. art. 1528n, arts. 2.12 to 2.22 (West Supp. 1993).

[54] Colo. Rev. Stat. Ann. §§ 7-80-401 to -411 (West 1992).

[55] Robert R. Keatinge et al., *The Limited Liability Company: A Study of the Emerging Entity,* 47 Bus. Law. 375, 415 (1992).

Colorado provisions also provide more detailed provisions regarding membership operations and other day-to-day operations than most other LLC statutes. For example, the Colorado statute contains provisions regarding the election and term of managers,[56] classification of managers,[57] manager vacancies,[58] and removal of managers.[59]

When the LLC statute vests firm management in the firm's members, the members generally may provide for firm management by managers. Consequently, statutes generally allow the LLC to be managed by managers.[60] Some jurisdictions, such as Colorado and Virginia, expressly set forth the fiduciary duties of managers.[61] These statutes generally require an LLC manager to follow standards similar to those imposed on corporate managers.[62] On the other hand, many statutes allow the LLC to indemnify its managers for any legal action taken against them as an LLC representative, to the extent that they were acting on the company's behalf.[63]

Planning Pointer. The management provisions of the various LLC statutes leave many unanswered issues.[64] To avoid potential problems, the planner must ensure that the members execute an operating agreement.

[b]   Authority to Bind the LLC

When the LLC uses managers, members generally do not retain any power to bind the firm for debts and liabilities or to acquire and dispose of property.[65] However, many LLC statutes allow the members to retain such power through the operating agreement or articles of organization.[66] Conversely, when the members manage the LLC, they generally do retain the right to bind the firm.[67]

---

[56] Colo. Rev. Stat. Ann. § 7-80-402 (West 1992).

[57] Colo. Rev. Stat. Ann. § 7-80-403 (West 1992).

[58] Colo. Rev. Stat. Ann. § 7-80-404 (West 1992).

[59] Colo. Rev. Stat. Ann. § 7-80-405 (West 1992).

[60] See Del. Code Ann. tit. 6, § 18-402 (Supp. 1992); Nev. Rev. Stat. Ann. § 86.291 (Michie Supp. 1991); Utah Code Ann. § 48-2b-125(2) (Supp. 1991); Tex. Rev. Civ. Stat. Ann. art. 1528n, art. 2.12 (West Supp. 1993); Va. Code Ann. § 13.1-1024 (Michie Supp. 1991).

[61] Colo. Rev. Stat. Ann. § 7-80-406 (West 1992); Va. Code Ann. § 13.1-1024(G)(1) (Michie Supp. 1991).

[62] See Robert R. Keatinge et al., *The Limited Liability Company: A Study of the Emerging Entity,* 47 Bus. Law. 375, 416 (1992).

[63] See, e.g., Colo. Rev. Stat. Ann. § 7-80-104(1)(k) (West 1992); Wyo. Stat. § 17-15-104(a)(xi) (1977); Fla. Stat. Ann. § 608.404(11) (West 1992); Kan. Stat. Ann. § 17-7604(j) (Supp. 1992); Nev. Rev. Stat. Ann. § § 86.411–421 (Michie Supp. 1991); Utah Code Ann. § 482b105(1)(1) (Supp. 1991); Tex. Rev. Civ. Stat. Ann. art. 1528n, art. 2.20 (West Supp. 1993); Va. Code Ann. § 13.1-1009(16) (Michie Supp. 1991).

[64] See Robert R. Keatinge et al., *The Limited Liability Company: A Study of the Emerging Entity,* 47 Bus. Law. 375, 415 (1992); Wayne M. Gazur & Neil M. Goff, *Assessing the Limited Liability Company,* 41 Case W. Res. L. Rev. 387, 405 (1991).

[65] See, e.g., Fla. Stat. Ann. § 608.424–.425 (West 1993); Wyo. Stat. § § 17-15-117 to -118 (1977).

[66] See, e.g., Fla. Stat. Ann. § 608.424(1) (West 1993); Wyo. Stat. § 17-15-117 (1977).

[67] See, e.g., Wyo. Stat. § 17-15-117 (1977); Fla. Stat. Ann. § 608.424(2) (West 1993); Utah Code Ann. § 48-2b-125(1) (Supp. 1991); Tex. Rev. Civ. Stat. Ann. art. 1528n, art. 2.10(2) (West Supp. 1993); Nev. Rev. Stat. Ann. § 86.301 (Michie Supp. 1991); Va. Code Ann. § § 13.1-1022 to 1024 (Michie Supp. 1991).

Caution. It is not clear in some jurisdictions whether the LLC may limit the authority of one or more managers through the operating agreement or articles of organization.[68]

[c] Voting

In most states the LLC member's voting rights will be in proportion to their contribution to the LLC.[69] Some states, such as Colorado,[70] Texas,[71] and Kansas,[72] either do not provide a mandatory or default rule, or provide each member with an equal vote, regardless of the amount of the member's contribution. Also, most jurisdictions allow the LLC to separate its members into different classes or groups with different duties, rights, and privileges.[73]

[d] Powers and Purposes for Formation

Statutes generally give LLCs, among other powers, the power to:

1. Sue and be sued;[74]
2. Purchase, sell, hold, and otherwise deal with real and personal property;[75]
3. Loan and invest money;[76]
4. Purchase, sell, hold, and otherwise deal with interests in corporations, partnerships, other LLCs, and other business entities;[77]

---

[68] *See* Wayne M. Gazur & Neil M. Goff, *Assessing the Limited Liability Company*, 41 Case W. Res. L. Rev. 387, 407 (1991).

[69] *See, e.g.,* Wyo. Stat. § 17-15-116 (1977); Fla. Stat. Ann. § 608.422 (West 1989); Nev. Rev. Stat. Ann. § 86.301 (Michie Supp. 1991); Utah Code Ann. § 48-2b-125 (Supp. 1991); Va. Code Ann. § 13.1-1022(B) (Michie Supp. 1991).

[70] Colo. Rev. Stat. Ann. § 7-80-706 (West 1992).

[71] Tex. Rev. Civ. Stat. Ann. art. 1528n, art. 4.02 (West Supp. 1993).

[72] Kan. Stat. Ann. § 17-7612 (Supp. 1992).

[73] *See* Del. Code Ann. tit. 6, § 18-404 (Supp. 1992); Colo. Rev. Stat. Ann. § 7-80-503 (West 1992); Tex. Rev. Civ. Stat. Ann. art. 1528n, art. 4.02 (West Supp. 1993); Va. Code Ann. §§ 13.1-1029 to 1030 (Michie Supp. 1991); Robert R. Keatinge et al., *The Limited Liability Company: A Study of the Emerging Entity*, 47 Bus. Law. 375, 417 (1992).

[74] *See, e.g.,* Colo. Rev. Stat. Ann. § 7-80-104(1)(a) (West 1992); Wyo. Stat. § 17-15-104(a)(i) (1977); Fla. Stat. Ann. § 608.404(1) (West 1993); Kan. Stat. Ann. § 17-7604(a) (Supp. 1992); Nev. Rev. Stat. Ann. § 86.286 (Michie Supp. 1991); Tex. Rev. Civ. Stat. Ann. art. 1528n, art. 2.02 (West Supp. 1993).

[75] *See, e.g.,* Colo. Rev. Stat. Ann. § 7-80-104(1)(b)–(c) (West 1992); Wyo. Stat. § 17-15-104(a)(ii)–(iii) (1977); Fla. Stat. Ann. § 608.404(2)–(3) (West 1993); Nev. Rev. Stat. Ann. § 86.286 (Michie Supp. 1991); Tex. Rev. Civ. Stat. Ann. art. 1528n, art. 2.02 (West Supp. 1993).

[76] *See, e.g.,* Colo. Rev. Stat. Ann. § 7-80-104(1) (d) (West 1992); Wyo. Stat. § 17-15-104(a) (iv) (1977); Fla. Stat. Ann. § 608.404(6) (West 1993); Kan. Stat. Ann. § 17-7604(f) (Supp. 1992); Tex. Rev. Civ. Stat. Ann. art. 1528n, art. 2.02 (West Supp. 1993).

[77] *See, e.g.,* Colo. Rev. Stat. Ann. § 7-80-104(1)(e) (West 1992); Wyo. Stat. § 17-15-104(a)(v) (1977); Fla. Stat. Ann. § 608.404(4) (West 1993); Kan. Stat. Ann. § 17-7604(d) (Supp. 1992); Nev. Rev. Stat. Ann. § 86.286 (Michie Supp. 1991).

5. Carry on its business and operations;[78]
6. Elect or appoint managers and agents and define their duties and obligations;[79]
7. Make or amend operating agreements that are not inconsistent with the LLC's articles of organization;[80]
8. Indemnify present or former members or managers against expenses actually and reasonably incurred in connection with the defense of a proceeding, civil or criminal, in which such person is a party due to having been a member or manager of the LLC;[81]
9. Cease its activities and surrender its certificate of organization;[82]
10. Execute all powers necessary or convenient to effect any or all purposes for which the LLC is organized;[83] and
11. Become a member of a partnership, joint venture, or other LLC.[84]

Generally, an LLC may be formed for any lawful purpose.[85] However, some states place restrictions on the types of business that the LLC may engage in.[86]

[3] Continuity of LLC Existence

Unlike a corporation, an LLC does not continue indefinitely. Instead, it more closely resembles a partnership. This similarity to partnerships is intentional to ensure that LLCs receive partnership treatment for federal income tax

---

[78] *See, e.g.,* Del. Code Ann. tit. 6, § 18-106 (Supp. 1992); Wyo. Stat. § 17-15-104(a)(xi) (1977); Fla. Stat. Ann. § 608.404(7) (West 1993); Kan. Stat. Ann. § 17-7604(g) (Supp. 1992); Nev. Rev. Stat. Ann. § 86.286 (Michie Supp. 1991); Tex. Rev. Civ. Stat. Ann. art. 1528n, art. 2.02 (West Supp. 1993).

[79] *See, e.g.,* Colo. Rev. Stat. Ann. § 7-80-104(1)(i) (West 1992); Fla. Stat. Ann. § 608.404(8) (West 1993); Kan. Stat. Ann. § 17-7604(h) (Supp. 1992); Nev. Rev. Stat. Ann. § 86.286 (Michie Supp. 1991); Tex. Rev. Civ. Stat. Ann. art. 1528n, art. 2.02 (West Supp. 1993).

[80] *See* Colo. Rev. Stat. Ann. § 7-80-104(1)(j) (West 1992); Wyo. Stat. § 17-15-104(a)(xi) (1977); Fla. Stat. Ann. § 608.404(9) (West 1993); Nev. Rev. Stat. Ann. § 86.286 (Michie Supp. 1991).

[81] *See, e.g.,* Wyo. Stat. § 17-15-104(a) (xi) (1977); Fla. Stat. Ann. § 608.404(11) (West 1993); Kan. Stat. Ann. § 17-7604(j) (Supp. 1992); Nev. Rev. Stat. Ann. § 86.286 (Michie Supp. 1991); Tex. Rev. Civ. Stat. Ann. art. 1528n, art. 2.02 (West Supp. 1993).

[82] *See, e.g.,* Colo. Rev. Stat. Ann. § 7-80-104(1)(1) (West 1992); Fla. Stat. Ann. § 608.404(12) (West 1993); Kan. Stat. Ann. § 17-7604(k) (Supp. 1992); Nev. Rev. Stat. Ann. § 86.286 (Michie Supp. 1991); Tex. Rev. Civ. Stat. Ann. art. 1528n, art. 2.02 (West Supp. 1993).

[83] *See, e.g.,* Colo. Rev. Stat. Ann. § 7-80-104(1)(m) (West 1992); Wyo. Stat. § 17-15104(a)(xi) (1977); Kan. Stat. Ann. § 17-7604(1) (Supp. 1992); Nev. Rev. Stat. Ann. § 86.286 (Michie Supp. 1991); Tex. Rev. Civ. Stat. Ann. art. 1528n, art. 2.02 (West Supp. 1993).

[84] *See, e.g.,* Del. Code Ann. tit. 6, § 18-106(b) (Supp. 1992); Colo. Rev. Stat. Ann. § 7-80-104(1)(n) (West 1992); Fla. Stat. Ann. § 608.404(16) (West 1993); Kan. Stat. Ann. § 17-7604(o) (Supp. 1992); Nev. Rev. Stat. Ann. § 86.286 (Michie Supp. 1991); Tex. Rev. Civ. Stat. Ann. art. 1528n, art. 2.02 (West Supp. 1993).

[85] *See, e.g.,* Del. Code Ann. tit. 6, § 18-106 (Supp. 1992); Colo. Rev. Stat. Ann. § 7-80-103 (West 1992); Wyo. Stat. § 17-15-103 (1977); Fla. Stat. Ann. § 608.403 (West 1993); Kan. Stat. Ann. § 17-7603 (Supp. 1992); Nev. Rev. Stat. Ann. § 86.141 (Michie Supp. 1992); Tex. Rev. Civ. Stat. Ann. art. 1528n, art. 2.01 (West Supp. 1993); Va. Code Ann. § 13.1-1008 (Michie Supp. 1991).

[86] *See, e.g.,* Wyo. Stat. § 17-15-103 (1977); Nev. Rev. Stat. Ann. § 86.141 (Michie Supp. 1991); Va. Code Ann. § 13.1-1008 (Michie Supp. 1991).

purposes.[87] Specifically, an LLC dissolves (1) after a fixed period, (2) by unanimous agreement of the members, (3) on the disassociation of a member, or (4) involuntarily under certain circumstances.

First, LLC statutes generally require the LLC to dissolve after a fixed period.[88] Most jurisdictions limit the LLC's life to 30 years or less.[89]

Second, all the statutes provide that the LLC dissolves on the unanimous written agreement of the LLC members.[90] Some jurisdictions also provide for additional dissolution events. For example, Texas provides that the LLC's articles of organization may provide that the company dissolves on the occurrence of an event that would not otherwise cause dissolution.[91]

Third, many statutes provide that the LLC must dissolve:

> Upon the death, retirement, resignation, expulsion, bankruptcy, or dissolution of a member or occurrence of any other event which terminates the continued membership of a member in the limited liability company, unless the business of the limited liability company is continued by the consent of all the remaining members under a right to continue stated in the articles of organization of the limited liability company.[92]

Therefore, the LLC dissolves on the disassociation of a member. An exception to this rule applies when the articles of organization provide that the LLC may continue if all the remaining members consent and, in fact, all the remaining members do consent.

Some LLC statutes operate slightly differently than those of the other jurisdictions. For example, the Florida and Kansas statutes provide that the exception to dissolution applies if the business of the LLC is continued by the consent of all the remaining members or under a right to continue stated in the articles of

---

[87] See Wayne M. Gazur & Neil M. Goff, Assessing the Limited Liability Company, 41 Case W. Res. L. Rev. 387, 418–26 (1991); Denison H. Hatch, Jr., Limited Liability Companies: Legal Aspects of Organization, Operation, and Dissolution, Corp. Prac. (BNA) No. 67, at VI.

[88] See, e.g., Del. Code Ann. tit. 6, § 18-801(1) (Supp. 1992); Colo. Rev. Stat. Ann. § 7-80-204(1)(b) (West 1992); Wyo. Stat. § 17-15-107(a)(ii) (1977); Fla. Stat. Ann. § 608.407(1)(b) (West 1993); Nev. Rev. Stat. Ann. § 86.161(i)(b) (Michie Supp. 1991); Tex. Rev. Civ. Stat. Ann. art. 1528n, art. 3.02(2) (West Supp. 1993). Cf. Kan. Stat. Ann. § 17-7607(2) (Supp. 1992) (requires articles to state period of duration, which is not defined); Utah Code Ann. § 48-2b116(1)(b) (Supp. 1991); Va. Code Ann. § 13.1-101 I.A.4 (Michie Supp. 1991).

[89] See, e.g., Del. Code Ann. tit. 6, § 18-801(1) (Supp. 1992); Colo. Rev. Stat. Ann. § 7-80-204(1)(b) (West 1992); Wyo. Stat. § 17-15-107(a)(ii) (1977); Fla. Stat. Ann. § 608.407(1)(b) (West 1993); Nev. Rev. Stat. Ann. § 86.161(i)(b) (Michie Supp. 1991); Tex. Rev. Civ. Stat. Ann. art. 1528n, art. 3.02(2) (West Supp. 1993). Cf. Kan. Stat. Ann. § 17-7607(2) (Supp. 1992) (requires articles to state period of duration, which is not defined); Utah Code Ann. § 48-2b116(1)(b) (Supp. 1991); Va. Code Ann. § 13.1-101 I.A.4 (Michie Supp. 1991).

[90] See, e.g., Del. Code Ann. tit. 6, § 18-801(3) (Supp. 1992); Colo. Rev. Stat. Ann. § 7-80-801(1)(b) (West 1992); Wyo. Stat. § 17-15-123(a)(ii) (1977); Kan. Stat. Ann. § 17-7622(a)(2) (Supp. 1992); Nev. Rev. Stat. Ann. § 86.491(i)(b) (Michie Supp. 1991); Utah Code Ann. § 48-2b-137(2) (Supp. 1991); Tex. Rev. Civ. Stat. Ann. art. 1528n, art. 6.01(3) (West Supp. 1993); Va. Code Ann. § 13.1-1046(1) (Michie Supp. 1991).

[91] Tex. Rev. Civ. Stat. Ann. art. 1528n, art. 6.01(2) (West Supp. 1993).

[92] Wyo. Stat. § 17-15-123(a)(iii) (1977). See also Del. Code Ann. tit. 6, § 18-801(4) (Supp. 1992); Colo. Rev. Stat. Ann. § 7-80-801(1)(c) (West 1992); Nev. Rev. Stat. Ann. § 86.491(f)(c) (Michie Supp. 1991); Utah Code Ann. § 48-2b-137(3) (Supp. 1991); Va. Code Ann. § 13.11046(3) (Michie Supp. 1991).

organization.[93] Also, the Texas statute provides that the exception to dissolution applies if there is at least one remaining member and the business of the company is continued by the consent of either (1) the number of members or class thereof stated in the articles or regulations (Texas's version of the operating agreement), or (2) if the articles and regulations do not state such number, by all of the remaining members.[94]

Finally, under some circumstances, the LLC will dissolve involuntarily. Some jurisdictions allow members to ask a court to dissolve the LLC if it is not reasonably practical to carry on the company's business in conformity with its articles of organization.[95] Other jurisdictions will deem an LLC to be dissolved if it fails for 30 days to appoint and maintain an agent for service of process, fails for 30 days to file with the appropriate state office a statement of a change in its registered office or agent for service of process, or fails to pay the requisite fees charged by the state.[96]

Caution. When the members intentionally decide to dissolve the LLC, each jurisdiction requires the LLC to complete certain procedures, which includes filing certain papers with the appropriate state office. Additionally, the LLC must give notice of the intent to dissolve and how the assets will be distributed to creditors and to certain other parties.[97] The planner should advise the members to properly fulfill these obligations to ensure there is no risk of the member liability for LLC obligations.

Planning Pointer. To avoid the possibility of dissolution upon the disassociation of an LLC member, the planner should consider using a tiered ownership[98] structure. Under such a structure, the ultimate owners form limited partnerships or corporations that, in turn, become LLC members. Corporations have perpetual lives; therefore, the LLC will never dissolve due to the disassociation of a corporate member. However, corporations generally involve problems of double taxation.[99] Limited partnerships do not dissolve on the disassociation of limited partners, only of general partners. Therefore, this structure limits the risk of LLC dissolution due to the disassociation of a member to events pertaining to the general

---

[93] Fla. Stat. Ann. § 608.441(i)(c) (West 1993); Kan. Stat. Ann. § 17-7622(a)(3) (Supp. 1992).

[94] Tex. Rev. Civ. Stat. Ann. art. 1528n, art. 6.01(4) (West Supp. 1993).

[95] See, e.g., Del. Code Ann. tit. 6, § 18-802 (Supp. 1992); Colo. Rev. Stat. Ann. § 7-80-808 (West 1992); Fla. Stat. Ann. § 608.448 (West 1993); Kan. Stat. Ann. § 17-7629(b) (Supp. 1992); Utah Code Ann. § 48-2b-142 (Supp. 1991); Tex. Rev. Civ. Stat. Ann. art. 1528n, art. 6.02 (West Supp. 1993); Va. Code Ann. § 13.1-1047 (Michie Supp. 1991).

[96] Wyo. Stat. § 17-15-104(a)(xi) (1977); Nev. Rev. Stat. Ann. §§ 86.411–421 (Michie Supp. 1991).

[97] See Robert R. Keatinge et al., *The Limited Liability Company: A Study of the Emerging Entity*, 47 Bus. Law. 375, 422–23 (1992).

[98] See Wayne M. Gazur & Neil M. Goff, *Assessing the Limited Liability Company*, 41 Case W. Res. L. Rev. 387, 424–26 (1991).

[99] See Chapter 4.

partner of the limited partnership. When the limited partnership uses a corporate general partner, there is no risk of limited partnership dissolution; consequently, here there will be no risk of LLC dissolution due to the disassociation of a member.

[4] Transferability of LLC Interests

Generally, LLC Acts provide that a member's interest in the LLC constitutes personal property.[100] Furthermore, these Acts allow LLC members to assign their membership interests to other parties as provided for in the LLC operating agreement.[101] However, most of these Acts also provide that the member may not transfer the right to participate in the management of the business and affairs of the LLC without the unanimous consent of the other LLC members.[102]

Caution. The planner should note that this rule requires unanimous consent of the other members as opposed to other managers.[103]

The restrictions on transfers of the right to participate in the LLC's management without the unanimous consent of other members may restrict its ability to attract capital. This limitation causes the membership interests to be less marketable. Additionally, these limitations may cause problems for members' estate plans. For example, members may want to leave their membership interests to their children. However, absent unanimous consent of the remaining members, the children will not receive any management rights.

---

[100] *See* generally Denison H. Hatch, Jr., Limited Liability Companies: Legal Aspects of Organization, Operation, and Dissolution, Corp. Prac. (BNA) No. 67, at IV.C.1.a; See, *e.g.,* Del. Code Ann. tit. 6, § 18-701 (Supp. 1992); Colo. Rev. Stat. Ann. § 7-80-702(1) (West 1992); Wyo. Stat. § 17-15-122 (1977); Fla. Stat. Ann. § 608.431 (West 1993); Kan. Stat. Ann. § 17-7617 (Supp. 1992); Utah Code Ann. § 48-2b-103 (Supp. 1991); Tex. Rev. Civ. Stat. Ann. art. 1528n, art. 4.04 (West Supp. 1993); Va. Code Ann. § 13.1-1038 (Michie Supp. 1991).

[101] *See, e.g.,* Del. Code Ann. tit. 6, § 18-702 (Supp. 1992); Colo. Rev. Stat. Ann. § 7-80-702(1) (West 1992); Wyo. Stat. § 17-15-122 (1977); Fla. Stat. Ann. § 608.431 (West 1993); Kan. Stat. Ann. § 17-7617 (Supp. 1992); Nev. Rev. Stat. Ann. § 86.351 (Michie Supp. 1991); Tex. Rev. Civ. Stat. Ann. art. 1528n, art. 4.04 (West Supp. 1993); Va. Code Ann. § 13.1-1038 (Michie Supp. 1991).

[102] *See, e.g.,* Del. Code Ann. tit. 6, § 18-702 (Supp. 1992); Colo. Rev. Stat. Ann. § 7-80-702(1) (West 1992); Wyo. Stat. § 17-15-122 (1977); Nev. Rev. Stat. Ann. § 86.351 (Michie Supp. 1991); Va. Code Ann. § 13.1-1039 (Michie Supp. 1991); Utah Code Ann. § 48-2b-131(1) (Supp. 1991) (member may transfer interest that includes all rights and privileges if nontransferring members holding a majority of the nontransferred profits of the limited liability company consent to the transfer); Tex. Rev. Civ. Stat. Ann. art. 1528n, arts. 4.05–4.07 (West Supp. 1993) (the limited liability company's regulations may provide that the consent of the other members is not required to transfer the rights and privileges of a membership interest).

[103] *See* Wayne M. Gazur & Neil M. Goff, *Assessing the Limited Liability Company,* 41 Case W. Res. L. Rev. 387, 413–16 (1991).

Planning Pointer. One method of mitigating the LLC transfer restrictions is to establish a tiered ownership structure.[104] Specifically, a prospective member may establish a partnership, trust, or corporation to function as the LLC member. The prospective member could then transfer interests in the partnership, trust, or corporation to whomever she chose. Because the partnership, trust, or corporation would not change, management control would remain with such entity. In turn, the holders of the member entity could exercise management control over the LLC. However, such a structure involves the disadvantages of:

1. Greater formation costs;
2. Greater operational and procedural costs;
3. Greater complexity in managing the two entities; and
4. Possible tax costs.

EXAMPLE 3-18

Same facts as Example 3-17, except that Lewis has a wife and two children and that Risky Royalties does not fail but instead becomes profitable in year three. In year four, however, Lewis dies. His will leaves his LLC interest to his wife and two children. Here, the LLC dissolves on Lewis's death.

EXAMPLE 3-19

Same facts as Example 3-18, except that Lewis wants to ensure that his LLC interest will pass to his wife and children and that they will also receive the right to participate in the management of Risky Royalties. To effectuate this desire, Lewis establishes Control Corporation. He retains 70-percent of Control Corporation's common stock and gives the remaining 10-percent interest to his wife and two children. Lewis's will leaves his 70-percent interest in Control Corporation to his wife.

Here, after Lewis dies, the Risky Royalties LLC does not dissolve. Furthermore, Lewis's wife obtains de facto management rights in the Risky Royalties LLC by virtue of her control of Control Corporation.

---

[104] 719 A.2d 73 (Conn. App. 1998).

[D] Rights of Judgment and Other Creditors

Generally, a judgment creditor of an LLC member may only obtain a charging order from a court against the LLC member's LLC interest, similar to the rights of judgment creditors against a limited partner's limited partnership interest. In *PB Real Estate, Inc. v. Dem II Properties*,[105] the Court relied on the interpretation of an identical provision of the Connecticut Uniform Limited Partnership Act to hold that the payment of money from the company to the judgment debtors, who were members of the LLC, should be characterized as a distribution subject to a charging order. The plaintiff had previously obtained a judgment against the individual members of the company. Pursuant to that judgment, the court granted a charging order directing the company pay to the plaintiff any and all distributions, credits, drawings, or payments due to the judgment debtors. The plaintiff relied on a provision of the Connecticut Limited Liability Company Act, Conn. Gen. Stat. Ann. § 34-171, which stated that a judgment creditor's rights were limited only to the member's limited liability company interest. This was a case of first impression with regard to that section of the act. The court relied on the interpretation of an identical provision of the Uniform Limited Partnership Act in holding that the judgment creditor had only the rights of an assignee of a partnership interest. Based on the facts surrounding the distribution of the money to the judgment debtors, the court held that the payment of the money to the judgment debtors had to be characterized as a distribution subject to the charging order. The court further reasoned that a contrary construction would defeat the legislature's intent to shield members of a limited liability company only from liability for the debts of the entity and not from personal liability for the members' personal debts. The court reasoned that the identical provision contained in the limited liability company act had to be consistently interpreted in accordance with the analogous provisions of the Uniform Partnership Act.

§3.07 BUSINESS ENTITIES COMPARED

A comparison of corporations, limited partnerships, Subchapter S corporations, and limited liability companies appears in Table 3-1.

---

[105] *Id.*

Table 3-1 Comparing Business Entities

Characteristic	Entity	
(1) Limited Liability	Corporation	Yes
	Limited Partnership	Yes
	Subchapter S Corporation	Yes
	Limited Liability Company	Yes
(2) Continuity of Existence	Corporation	Yes
	Limited Partnership	Problematic
	Subchapter S Corporation	Yes
	Limited Liability Company	Varies
(3) Transferability of Interests	Corporation	Yes, but may be restricted by a shareholder's agreement
	Limited Partnership	Probematic
	Subchapter S Corporation	Yes, but may be restricted by a shareholder's agreement or by requirements for Subchapter S Corporation
	Limited Liability Company	Problematic
(4) Cost of Operations	Corporation	More costly
	Limited Partnership	Less costly
	Subchapter S Corporation	More costly
	Limited Liability Company	Less costly
(5) Formation, Organization	Corporation	Generally tax free
	Limited Partnership	Generally tax free
	Subchapter S Corporation	Generally tax free
	Limited Liability Company	Generally tax free

§3.08 CHOICE OF ENTITY WORKSHEET

The planner should use the worksheet in Table 3-2 to analyze the benefits and costs of using various entity forms in monetary terms.

Table 3-2 Worksheet

Corporation	(A) S Corporation	(B) Limited Partnership	(C) Limited Liability Company	(D)
+ 1. limited liability protection provided by the entity form chosen				
− 2. expenses of forming the entity and complying with required formalities				
− 3. costs unique to the entity form's management and control structure				
− 4. costs associated with dissolution of entity if the entity lacks continuity of existence				
− 5. costs associated with transfers of entity interests (e.g., loss of marketability of entity interests due to inability to transfer management powers without consent of other entity holders, etc.)				
− 6. tax burden associated with using the entity form= Net benefit/cost of using the entity form				

§3.09 CHECKLIST OF CHOICE OF ENTITY ISSUES

The planner should use the following checklist to ensure no critical issue is overlooked in connection with the planner's choice of entity analysis.

[A]   Sole Proprietorships[1]

____1. Does the asset protection client operate any businesses as sole proprietor-ships?

       If yes, the planner should advise the client to change the entity form for such interests to the corporate, limited partnership, or limited liability company forms because the sole proprietorship offers no asset protection benefits and exposes the client to unlimited liability.

[B]   Corporations[2]

____2. Is the asset protection planner considering using the corporate entity form as part of the asset protection plan?

       If yes, the planner must analyze the following issues:

(1) What limited liability benefits accrue to the client from the corporate entity form?[3]

(2) How do the following exceptions apply to the client's asset protection plan?

    (a) The piercing the corporate veil doctrine;
    (b) The defective incorporation doctrine;
    (c) The exception to limited liability for unpaid stock subscriptions and stock not fully paid for;
    (d) The exception to limited liability for illegal dividends; and
    (e) The 100-percent penalty.[4]

(3) How does the corporate entity form compare to other entity forms in terms of (a) management and control, (b) continuity of existence, (c) transferability of entity interests, and (d) expenses and formalities associated with corporations?[5]

[C]   General Partnerships[6]

____3. Does the asset protection client own any general partnership interests?

       If yes, such interests expose the client to unlimited liability. The plan-ner should advise the client to (a) change the entity form for such interests

---

§ 3.09 [1] *See* § 3.02.
[2] *See* § 3.03.
[2] *See* § 3.03.
[3] *See* § 3.03[A].
[4] *See* §§ 3.03[A]–3.03[G].
[5] *See* § 3.03[H].
[6] *See* § 3.04.

to the corporate, limited partnership, or limited liability company forms, or (b) alternatively, place such interests into a trust, limited partnership, or other asset protection device that will limit the liability exposure stemming from such interests.

[D] Limited Partnerships[7]

____4. Is the asset protection planner considering using one or more limited partnerships as part of the asset protection plan?

If yes, the planner must analyze the following issues:

1. What limited liability benefits accrue to the client from the limited partnership entity form?[8]
2. What is the liability exposure of general partners of the limited partnership?[9]
3. What is the liability exposure of limited partners of the limited partnership, and what is the impact of the following on such exposure?

   (a) Limited partner participation in the control of the limited partnership;
   (b) Lack of substantial compliance in good faith with the statutory requirements for forming the limited partnership;
   (c) Unlawful use of a limited partner's name in the limited partnership name;
   (d) False statements contained within the certificate when a limited partner knows of such false statements, and when a third party relies to her detriment on such false statements; and
   (e) Unpaid amounts of the contribution that a limited partner[10] agrees to pay to the limited partnership.

4. What rights do judgment and other creditors of a limited partner have against the limited partnership?[11]
5. How may the planner use family limited partnerships to the client's advantage?[12]
6. How do limited partnerships compare to other entity forms in terms of (a) management and control, (b) continuity of existence, (c) transferability of entity interests, and (d) expenses and formalities?[13]

---

[6] *See* § 3.04.
[7] *See* § 3.05.
[8] *See* §§ 3.05[A]–3.05[D].
[9] *See* § 3.05[B].
[10] *See* §§ 3.05[B]–3.05[D].
[11] *See* § 3.05[D].
[12] *See* § 3.05[E].
[13] *See* § 3.05[G].

[E] *Limited Liability Companies*[14]

____5. Is the asset protection planner considering using one or more limited lia-
bility companies as part of the asset protection plan?

If yes, the planner must analyze the following issues:

1. What limited liability benefits accrue to the client from the limited
liability company form?[15]
2. What is the liability exposure of members of limited liability companies, both for intrastate and interstate transactions?[16]
3. How do limited liability companies compare to other entity forms in
terms of (a) management and control, (b) continuity of existence, (c)
transferability of entity interests, and (d) expenses and formalities?[17]

[14] *See* § 3.06.
[14] *See* § 3.06.
[15] *See* § 3.06[A].
[16] *See* § 3.06[B].
[17] *See* § 3.05[C].

4

CHOICE OF BUSINESS ENTITY: TAX ASPECTS

§4.01 IN GENERAL

The client's business operation merits the asset protection planner's special attention. This is because business operations tend to cause liabilities that may impact both the business operation out of which the liability arises as well as other unrelated assets. In contrast, other assets, such as furniture, stocks, and bank accounts, generally do not cause liabilities. Because of this characteristic, choice of entity assumes great importance for the asset protection planner.

The planner's primary objective in this area is to limit the reach of liabilities arising out of a business operation to that business operation's assets. An additional objective is to protect the assets of the business operation from other creditors of the business owners. Chapter 3 discusses these issues.

The planner, when evaluating choice of entity, must also consider the associated tax consequences of different entity forms. The planner must balance any limited liability benefits of a particular entity form against any additional tax costs associated with that particular form.

As Chapter 3 discusses, the planner may choose one of five different entity forms. These include (1) sole proprietorships, (2) general partnerships, (3) limited partnerships, (4) corporations, and (5) limited liability companies. Because sole proprietorships and general partnerships offer no asset protection benefits, they will not be discussed further here. However, the asset protection planner must determine the tax implications of choosing corporate, limited partnership, or limited liability company entity forms.

§4.02 CORPORATIONS

[A] Types of Corporations

The planner must carefully examine the tax consequences of incorporating. Planners must balance the limited liability benefits arising from using the corporate entity form against any resulting tax disadvantages.[1]

For federal tax purposes, there are two types of corporations: C corporations, so called because such corporations are organized under Subchapter C of the IRC, and S corporations, so called because such corporations are organized under Subchapter S of the IRC. A C corporation is any entity that is a corporation for federal income tax purposes, which does not elect to be an S corporation or subject to some other pass-through taxation scheme. The planner must consider the following aspects of C and S corporations:

- Taxation of corporate income and dividends;
- Taxation of corporate losses;
- Choice of fiscal year for tax purposes;

---

§4.02 [1] *See* Chapter 3 for a worksheet that will assist the planner with this analysis.

- Taxation of corporate formation;
- Tax treatment of transfers of corporate interests by shareholders;
- Taxation of corporate liquidations;
- Tax consequences of the death or retirement of a shareholder; and
- The consequences of the termination of the S election.

[B] Taxation of C Corporation Income

Planners must first consider how the entity's income would be taxed if incorporated.[2] Generally, the IRC treats C corporations as separate taxpayers by taxing the corporation's earnings and profits at the corporate level. The IRC imposes an additional tax on corporate dividends at the shareholder level.

> **Caution.** Planners should note that C corporations have several disadvantages from a tax standpoint. First, an individual's marginal tax bracket is generally lower than a C corporation's marginal tax bracket. Second, the IRC taxes corporate earnings paid to shareholders twice. Third, the IRS may levy double penalty taxes, such as the accumulated earnings tax and the personal holding company tax, on the corporation.[3]

The IRC taxes C corporations on their taxable income at the rates of 15 percent on the first $25,000 of taxable income, 25 percent on the next $50,000, 34 percent on taxable income up to $15,000,000, and 35 percent on taxable income in excess of $15,000,000. In addition, shareholders are taxable on dividends distributed by a C corporation.

[1] Alternative Minimum Tax

Corporations, other than small business corporations after 1997, are also subject to an alternative minimum tax.[4] Specifically, each year, corporations must compute their regular tax and their alternative minimum tax and pay whichever tax is higher.

---

[2] *See generally* Boris I. Bittker & James S. Eustice, Federal Income Taxation of Corporations and Shareholders (5th ed. 1987); Daniel Posin, Corporate Tax Planning (1990); Michael D. Rose & John C. Chommie, Federal Income Taxation Ch. 10; Joseph W. Bartlett, Corporate Restructurings, Reorganizations, and Buyouts Ch. 4 (1991).

[3] Jere D. McGaffey, Tax Analysis and Forms Ch. 4 (1987); Bittker & Eustice, Federal Income Taxation of Corporations and Shareholders Ch. 8; Posin, Corporate Tax Planning; Rose & Chommie, Federal Income Taxation § 10.25.

[4] IRC §§ 55–59.

Planning Pointer. The corporate alternative minimum tax was repealed for small business corporations for tax years beginning after December 31, 1997. Corporations that had average gross receipts of $5 million or less for the three-year period beginning after December 31, 1994, are a small business corporation for any tax year beginning after December 31, 1997. A corporation that meets the $5 million gross receipts test will continue to be treated as a small business corporation exempt from the alternative minimum tax as long as its average gross receipts do not exceed $7.5 million.[5]

The IRC imposes the alternative minimum tax on regular taxable income, increased by preference items and subject to certain other adjustments.[6] The IRC imposes the alternative minimum tax at a 20-percent rate[7] on the corporation's alternative minimum taxable income that exceeds $40,000,[8] but only if the tentative minimum tax is more than the regular corporate income tax.[9] The $40,000 exemption amount is reduced by 25 cents for each dollar that minimum taxable income exceeds $150,000 and, thus, is not available when minimum taxable income exceeds $310,000.[10] The foreign tax credit reduces the amount of the corporation's alternative minimum tax. However, the credit cannot reduce the liability by more than 90 percent of the tentative alternative minimum tax liability.[11]

For corporations, the five major tax preference items are the following:[12]

1. The amount of tax-exempt interest on private activity bonds issued after August 7, 1986 (interest on "qualified" bonds issued for the benefit of a charitable organization, and on certain refundings, is exempt from this preference).
2. The percentage depletion deduction over the property's adjusted basis at year end.[13]
3. Certain adjustments for intangible drilling costs.[14]
4. Certain adjustments for the excess of accelerated depreciation.
5. Certain adjustments for accelerated amortization of certified pollution control facilities.

[5] IRC § 55(e).
[6] IRC §§ 55–59.
[7] Id.
[8] IRC § 55(d)(2).
[9] IRC § 55(a).
[10] IRC § 55(d)(3).
[11] IRC §§ 55(b), 59(a).
[12] See generally Business Organizations With Tax Planning § 68.04.
[13] IRC § 57(a)(1).
[14] IRC § 57(a)(2).

[2]   Taxation of C Corporation Dividends

[a] *In General*

The treatment of C corporation dividends[15] to the recipient shareholder hinges on whether the shareholder is a corporation itself. When the shareholder is a corporation, it may generally deduct from gross income 70 percent of dividends received in any year from the distributing corporation.[16] Consequently, the corporate shareholder includes only 30 percent of the distribution in its taxable income. Conversely, noncorporate shareholders do not receive the 70-percent dividends-received deduction and, therefore, must include the full amount of the dividend received in their income.[17]

Property distributions made out of the corporation's earnings and profits are characterized as dividends.[18] Earnings and profits generally include all income received by a corporation even if otherwise excluded from taxation. When a corporation with no current or accumulated earnings and profits makes a property[19] distribution, the shareholder does not receive a taxable dividend. Instead, the recipient shareholder reduces its adjusted basis in its stock by the distribution[20] amount. To the extent the distribution exceeds the adjusted basis of the stock, the shareholder receives gain from the sale or exchange of property.[21]

The distributing corporation generally recognizes gain (as if the corporation sold such property for its fair market value) but not loss on nonliquidating distributions of appreciated property.[22] If the corporation distributes property subject to a liability or a shareholder assumes a liability in connection with a distribution, the property value is reduced, but not below zero, by the amount of the liability.[23]

> **Planning Pointer.** Dividends are generally disadvantageous to shareholders because of their double taxation aspect. In addition, the IRC treats certain transactions between the corporation and its shareholders as constructive dividends. A constructive dividend is a direct or indirect dividend to a stockholder, in his capacity as such, that is treated for tax purposes as a taxable dividend even though the corporation has not formally declared a dividend. The planner should structure transactions between the corporation and its shareholders so that they will not risk constructive dividend treatment.

---

[15] *See generally* Bittker & Eustice, Federal Income Taxation of Corporations and Shareholders; Posin, Corporate Tax Planning; Rose & Chommie, Federal Income Taxation §§ 10.08–10.12; Bartlett, Corporate Restructurings, Reorganizations, and Buyouts § 4.2(a).

[16] IRC § 243(a)(1).

[17] IRC § 301(c).

[18] IRC § 316(a); Treas. Reg. § 1.316-2(a).

[19] IRC §§ 301(c)(1), 316.

[20] *Id.*

[21] IRC § 301(c)(3).

[22] IRC § 311 (b)(1); Rev. Proc. 86-18, 1986-1 C.B. 551.

[23] IRC §§ 301(b)(2), 336(b).

[b] Constructive Dividends

The following items may constitute constructive dividends:

1. Corporate payments on shareholder obligations to third parties and payments for the shareholder's benefit constitute constructive dividends.[24] However, if the corporation pays an obligation on which both the corporation and the shareholder are concurrently liable and the payor corporation is a primary obligor, this payment does not constitute a constructive dividend.[25]
2. Corporate loans to shareholders that lack a bona fide intent to repay constitute constructive dividends.[26]
3. If the corporation sells or rents property to the shareholder for less than fair market value, the IRC treats the difference between the amount paid and the property's fair market value as a constructive dividend.[27] Conversely, if the shareholder sells or loans property to the corporation for more than fair market value, the IRC treats the difference between the amount paid and the property's fair market value as a constructive dividend.[28]
4. If the corporation allows the shareholder or the shareholder's family to use corporate property for private purposes at a discount from fair market value, the IRC generally treats the discount as a constructive dividend.[29]

Planning Pointer. To prevent constructive dividend treatment, the planner should recommend that the client take the following steps:

1. Ensure that the corporation does not pay shareholder obligations to third parties unless the corporation and shareholder are joint obligors and the corporation is a primary obligor on such obligation.
2. Ensure that corporate loans to shareholders are evidenced by interest-bearing notes and that the shareholder repays the corporation periodically.
3. Transactions between the corporation and the shareholder should be made at fair market value, with the methodology of fair market value determination being well documented. If the transaction is material, the corporation should obtain an appraisal.
4. Neither the shareholder nor the shareholder's family should use corporate property for private use without paying the fair rental value to the corporation.

---

[24] Silverstein v. Comm'r, 36 T.C. 438 (1961).
[25] Fischer v. Comm'r, 6 T.C.M. (CCH) 520 (1947).
[26] Regensburg v. Comm'r, 144 F.2d 41 (2d Cir.), *cert. denied*, 323 U.S. 783 (1944); IRC §7872.
[27] Treas. Reg. §1.301-1(j).
[28] Goldstein v. Comm'r, 298 F.2d 562 (9th Cir. 1962).
[29] Robert R. Walker, Inc. v. Comm'r, 362 F.2d 140 (7th Cir.), *cert. denied*, 385 U.S. 865 (1966).

[c]   Double Taxation

> **Planning Pointer.** Planners choosing incorporation should recommend that the corporation strive to reduce corporate double taxation.

There are at least three different ways to reduce corporate double taxation. First, the corporation may make deductible payments to the shareholder/employees for reasonable compensation.[30] If the compensation is unreasonably high, the excess is treated as nondeductible dividends to the shareholders.[31] The general test of reasonableness is that the compensation must be paid pursuant to a free bargain between the corporate employer and the shareholder/employee before the shareholder/employee renders services, and that reasonable compensation is what would ordinarily be paid for like services under similar circumstances.[32] The circumstances existing at the time of the contract execution are the critical ones.[33] Important factors include what similar corporations pay their executives; the business's success and size; the shareholder's contribution and whether the corporation's success can be traced to it; the shareholder's education, business contacts, and prior earning capacity or compensation; and general economic conditions.[34]

> **Planning Pointer.** The shareholder/employees and the corporation should develop a record to support the compensation. This record should include documentation of:
>
> 1. Salaries paid to persons in similar positions elsewhere in the industry or statistical data from the industry's trade association;
> 2. The individual's worth to the corporation at least equaling the level of compensation paid;
> 3. Special qualifications required for the job;
> 4. The relationship of the level of compensation to the corporation's income or sales;
> 5. Special sacrifices made by the shareholder/employee to build the corporation;
> 6. The size and complexity of the corporation; and
> 7. Any formula used to set compensation.

---

[30] IRC § 162(a)(1).

[31] IRC § 301.

[32] Treas. Reg. § 1.162-7(b)(2).

[33] Treas. Reg. § 1.162-7(b)(3).

[34] Charles Schneider & Co. v. Comm'r, 500 F.2d 148 (8th Cir. 1974), *cert. denied,* 420 U.S. 908 (1975); Catalano, Inc. v. Comm'r, 38 T.C.M. (CCH) 763 (1979).

A second technique the planner should consider to mitigate double taxation is to recommend payments of other deductible expenses to shareholders. For example, these payments could be structured as:

1. Interest on shareholder loans to the corporation,
2. Rent on property leased to the corporation, or
3. Royalties for patents or licenses owned by the shareholder.

All transactions between the corporation and shareholder should be bona fide and at arm's length.

A third method the planner should consider is to have the corporation retain its earnings instead of paying them to shareholders. This defers taxation at the shareholder level until subsequent transactions, such as shareholder stock sales, corporate stock redemptions, or corporate liquidation.

> **Caution.** The planner should note that the third method is subject to two limits, the accumulated earnings tax and the personal holding company tax.

The first limitation is the accumulated earnings tax. Specifically, under IRC Section 531, corporations are subject to an additional tax on any improper earnings accumulation. The IRC generally imposes this tax only on amounts accumulated that exceed $250,000 ($150,000 for certain service corporations).[35] The accumulated earnings tax equals 39.6 percent of accumulated taxable income.[36] Accumulated taxable income is computed by making certain adjustments to taxable income under IRC Section 535.

The second limitation is the personal holding company tax. Specifically, if five or fewer individuals own 50 percent or more of the value of the corporation's outstanding stock during the last half of the taxable year, and at least 60 percent of the corporation's adjusted ordinary gross income is personal holding company income as defined in IRC Section 543(a), the personal holding company tax may be imposed.[37] For this purpose, personal holding company income consists of passive investment income such as dividends, interest, rents, and royalties.[38] Under IRC Section 541, the personal holding company tax equals 39.6 percent of the corporation's undistributed personal holding company income.

---

[35] IRC § 535(c)(2).
[36] IRC § 531.
[37] IRC § 542.
[38] IRC § 543.

[3]   C Corporation Losses and IRC Section 1244 Stock

C corporation shareholders[39] cannot deduct corporate losses against their other income. However, the corporation may carry over net operating losses (NOLs) to other non-loss years. Specifically, IRC Section 172 allows an NOL to be carried back to each of the two years preceding the loss year and to the 20 years following the loss year.[40]

Shareholders having losses on stock sales realize and recognize a capital loss. The amount of such loss equals the difference between the stock's adjusted basis and its selling price.[41] If the shareholder's securities become worthless, the shareholder recognizes a capital loss on the last day of the taxable year in which the securities become worthless.[42]

Losses on shareholder loans to the corporation, which do not constitute securities, are treated as short-term capital losses[43] unless the debt constitutes a business bad debt, in which case it results in an ordinary loss deduction.[44] A business debt is a debt created or acquired in connection with the taxpayer's trade or business, or a debt that became worthless while being used in the taxpayer's trade or business.[45]

Planning Pointer. The shareholder may establish that a debt is a business bad debt if the debt arises:

1. In the taxpayer's business of loaning money;
2. In the taxpayer's business of financing or promoting corporate enterprises; or
3. In an effort to protect or advance the taxpayer's business of working as an employee of the debtor.[46]

Planning Pointer. The planner should consider recommending that newly formed corporations issue IRC Section 1244 stock when possible. Generally, shareholders may obtain favorable ordinary loss treatment on IRC Section 1244 small business stock, as opposed to capital loss under IRC Section 165(g) on non-IRC Section 1244 stock. The maximum amount that may be treated as an ordinary loss on IRC Section 1244 stock in any taxable year

---

[39] *See generally* Bittker & Eustice, Federal Income Taxation of Corporations and Shareholders (5th ed. 1987); Posin, Corporate Tax Planning (1990); Rose & Chommie, Federal Income Taxation.

[40] IRC § 172(b)(1)(A).

[41] IRC § 1001(a).

[42] IRC § 165(g).

[43] IRC § 166(d)(1)(B).

[44] IRC § 166(a).

[45] IRC § 166(d)(2).

[46] Whipple v. Comm'r, 373 U.S. 193 (1963).

equals $50,000, or $100,000 for spouses filing a joint return.[47] However, only the corporation's original investors may use IRC Section 1244.[48]

The corporation must satisfy certain requirements to issue IRC Section 1244 stock. First, it must not receive more than $1 million of money and other property as a contribution to capital and as paid-in surplus for its issued stock.[49] Second, the stock must be issued for money or other property as opposed to stock or securities.[50] Third, the corporation must have derived over 50 percent of its aggregate gross receipts for the five taxable years before worthlessness from sources other than investment activities.[51] Finally, the planner should note that IRC Section 1244 stock may be used with a Subchapter S election.

[4] C Corporation Choice of Fiscal Year

A corporation may generally select a taxable year[52] that can be any 12-month period, usually ending on the last day of the same month each year.[53] Selection of a fiscal year enables the C corporation to time the making of deductions and thus defer the realization and recognition of income. The accounting period should be selected so the business cycle best matches income and expenses. Therefore, the year should end at the completion of the cycle when inventories are low and liquidity is high.

Personal service corporations must adopt a calendar year unless they obtain IRS consent to use a different year.[54] The IRS does not consider the deferral of income to shareholders to be a business purpose for obtaining IRS consent.[55] Personal service corporations are corporations, other than S corporations, whose principal activity is the performance of personal services where the services are substantially performed by the employee/owners and whose employee/owners are employees who own outstanding stock at least one day during the tax year.[56]

[5] C Corporation Corporate Formation

A C corporation may be organized in either a taxable or nontaxable transaction.[57] A person transferring assets to a corporation generally does not trigger

---

[47] IRC § 1244(b).

[48] Treas. Reg. § 1.1244(a)-1(b).

[49] IRC § 1244(c)(3).

[50] IRC § 1244(c)(1)(B).

[51] IRC § 1244(c)(1)(C).

[52] *See generally* Bittker & Eustice, Federal Income Taxation of Corporations and Shareholders 1 5.07; Posin, Corporate Tax Planning.

[53] Temp. Treas. Reg. § 1.441-IT.

[54] IRC § 441(i)(1).

[55] *Id.*

[56] IRC §§ 269A(b), 441(i)(2).

[57] *See generally* Bittker & Eustice, Federal Income Taxation of Corporations and Shareholders Ch. 3; Posin, Corporate Tax Planning; Rose & Chommie, Federal Income Taxation §§ 10.04–10.07; Bartlett, Corporate Restructurings, Reorganizations, and Buyouts § 4.2(c).

any tax consequences if such person satisfies the requirements of IRC Section 351. Section 351 requirements include (1) transfer to a corporation of (2) property by (3) one or more persons, (4) solely in exchange for, (5) stock or securities in such corporation, (6) where the transferors control the corporation immediately after the transfer. If IRC Section 351 applies, it causes the following consequences:

1. The transferors of property recognize no gain or loss on the exchange, except for depreciation and investment tax credit recapture;[58]
2. The corporation succeeds to the transferors' adjusted basis for transferred property;[59] and
3. The transferors' basis for stock or securities received is the same as the adjusted basis of the property they transferred to the corporation.[60]

Planning Pointer. Sometimes a taxable incorporation may produce more favorable tax consequences than a tax-free incorporation. One method of structuring the incorporation so it becomes taxable is to structure the transaction as a sale of assets to the corporation.[61]

This structure is advantageous in at least three situations. First, if the shareholder wants to transfer depreciable property with a low basis to the corporation and wants the corporation to obtain a fair market value basis in such property, this structure is advantageous. Second, if the transferor has expiring loss carryforwards, the recognition of income from a sale to the corporation offsets such losses and eliminates or lessens tax consequences. Finally, if the transferor's property has declined in value so its basis exceeds its fair market value, a loss may be recognized if the transferor sells the property to the corporation.

Corporate organizational expenses and the legal fees associated with drafting the corporate charter, bylaws, minutes of organizational meetings, accounting services, and state incorporation fees may be amortized over a period of at least five years if the corporation so elects.[62] If the electing corporation dissolves before the amortization period ends, the unamortized expenditures may be deducted as an ordinary and necessary business expense.[63] However, not all expenses can qualify as an organizational expenditure for this purpose.[64] For example, the corporation can never deduct fees, commissions, and other costs associated with issuing or selling stock.[65]

---

[58] IRC § 351(a).
[59] IRC § 362(a).
[60] IRC § 358(a).
[61] Bittker & Eustice, Federal Income Taxation of Corporations and Shareholders Ch. 3.
[62] IRC § 248; Treas. Reg. § 1.248-1(b)(2).
[63] IRC § 162(a).
[64] IRC § 248(b); Treas. Reg. § 1.248-1(b).
[65] Treas. Reg. § 1.2481(b)(3)(i).

[6] Transfer of Corporate Interests

Shareholders generally recognize capital gain or loss on the sale of their stock.[66] However, two exceptions to this rule exist. First, this rule does not apply if the shareholder is a securities dealer. Second, this rule does not apply if the corporation is a collapsible corporation.

If the shareholders are securities dealers, the shares are considered property held principally for sale to customers in the ordinary course of business.[67] The sale of such shares results in the realization and recognition of ordinary income. IRC Section 1236 provides special rules allowing capital gain treatment for securities dealers who segregate and clearly identify their portfolios of securities held for investment.

A collapsible corporation is a corporation designed to convert ordinary income to capital gains through liquidation or early sale of stock. Such corporations are formed or availed of principally to either (1) manufacture, construction, or production property, or (2) purchase IRC Section 341 assets, with the intent to sell, liquidate, or distribute such property before (a) the corporation has realized two-thirds of the taxable income to be derived from such property, and (b) the shareholders have realized the gain attributable to the property.[68] A shareholder who disposes of stock in a collapsible corporation realizes and recognizes ordinary income.

[7] Death or Retirement of Shareholder

On a shareholder's death or retirement,[69] the corporation may redeem the shareholder's stock, or the remaining shareholders may purchase the shares. There usually is no market for closely-held corporate stock.[70] An agreement should be executed among the shareholders or between the shareholders and the corporation. Such agreement should provide that remaining or surviving shareholders will purchase the departing shareholder's stock, or alternatively, the corporation[71] will redeem his shares. A shareholders' agreement providing for the purchase of the decedent's shares, combined with an adequate funding plan such as life insurance, provides liquidity for the decedent's estate and prevents unwanted changes in the control of the corporation.[72] Additionally, the buy-sell agreement may help in establishing the stock's value for estate tax

---

[66] *See generally* Bittker & Eustice, Federal Income Taxation of Corporations and Shareholders Ch. 4; Posin, Corporate Tax Planning; Rose & Chommie, Federal Income Taxation.

[67] IRC § 1221(1).

[68] IRC § 341.

[69] *See generally* Bittker & Eustice, Federal Income Taxation of Corporations and Shareholders; Posin, Corporate Tax Planning; Rose & Chommie, Federal Income Taxation; Lewis D. Solomon & Lewis J. Saret, *Tax Planning for Closely Held Corporations under the New Estate Freeze Rules,* 16 Rev. Tax'n Individuals 3 (Winter 1992).

[70] *See* F. Hodge O'Neal & Robert B. Thompson, O'Neal's Close Corporations (3d ed. 1987 & Supp. 1991).

[71] *See* Jere D. McGaffey, Tax Analysis & Forms Ch. 15 (1987).

[72] *See* O'Neal & Thompson, O'Neal's Close Corporations; McGaffey, Tax Analysis & Forms Ch. 15.

purposes.[73] A buy-out provision also allows shareholders to diversify the assets of their estates.[74] This is particularly desirable in close corporations because the corporation's success may depend largely on the abilities and efforts of one or two shareholders. Here, it would be imprudent for the estate to retain a large investment in the corporation after the death of such a shareholder.

If a corporate repurchase qualifies as a redemption, it is treated as a capital transaction by the redeemed shareholder or his estate.[75] This eliminates most, if not all, of the tax impact because there generally is little post-death appreciation to tax as gain.[76] If the transaction is not a redemption, the proceeds may be taxed as a dividend.[77]

[8]   C Corporation Liquidation

Liquidating corporations[78] must recognize gains and losses on property distributions.[79] If the corporation distributes property subject to a liability or the shareholder assumes a liability in connection therewith, the IRC deems the fair market value of the property equal to or greater than the amount of the liability.[80]

Special limits exist with regard to loss recognition. Specifically, losses cannot be recognized on a property distribution to a related person (*i.e.*, a more than 50-percent shareholder, directly or indirectly) unless the corporation distributes the property pro rata to all shareholders.[81] Also, the distributing corporation cannot recognize losses on distributions that consist of property acquired by the liquidating corporation in certain types of tax-free transfers from the shareholders during the five-year period preceding the distribution.[82] If the liquidating corporation acquires loss property from shareholders in such tax-free transfers when a principal purpose of the transfer is to permit the corporation to recognize a loss, the IRC reduces the basis of such property by the difference between its basis and its fair market value at the time of the transfer.[83] Finally, no loss can be recognized on distributions of property in connection with the complete liquidation of controlled subsidiaries.[84]

---

[73] Solomon & Saret, *Tax Planning for Closely Held Corporations under the New Estate Freeze Rules*, 16 Rev. Tax'n Individuals 3 (Winter 1992).

[74] *See* O'Neal & Thompson, O'Neal's Close Corporations.

[75] IRC §§ 302, 303.

[76] IRC §§ 302(a), 1014.

[77] IRC § 306.

[78] *See generally* Bittker & Eustice, Federal Income Taxation of Corporations and Shareholders Ch. 1; Posin, Corporate Tax Planning; Rose & Chornmie, Federal Income Taxation § 10.18; Bartlett, Corporate Restructurings, Reorganizations, and Buyouts.

[79] IRC § 336(a).

[80] IRC § 336(b).

[81] IRC § 336(d)(1).

[82] IRC § 336(d)(2).

[83] *Id.*

[84] IRC § 336(d)(3).

There are two major exceptions to the rule of gain or loss recognition. First, nonrecognition applies for liquidating distributions to controlling corporate shareholders. For this purpose, a controlling corporate shareholder is a corporation that satisfies the 80-percent ownership requirement for tax-free liquidations of subsidiaries under IRC Section 332.[85] Second, nonrecognition applies to distributions of property to the extent there is nonrecognition of gain or loss to the distributee with regard to such property pursuant to a tax-free reorganization.[86]

[C] S Corporations

[1] In General

The Subchapter S[87] election provides for a pass-through of profits and losses to the shareholders, similar to partnership pass-throughs. The IRC taxes S corporations and their shareholders under rules similar to the partnership taxation rules. Specifically, there is generally no corporate income tax, accumulated earnings tax, or personal holding company tax.

> **Planning Pointer.** The S corporation election allows shareholders to obtain the corporate form's limited liability protection without being subjected to corporate double taxation.

Generally, the S corporation election allows S corporation shareholders who materially participate in the corporation's business on a regular, continuous, and substantial basis to use corporate losses, deductions, and credits to offset other personal income, including earned income and portfolio income. Furthermore, under this election the corporation's tax attributes retain their original character when passed through to the shareholders. An S corporate shareholder who does not materially participate can only offset such passive activity losses and credits against passive activity income.[88]

A corporation may elect S corporation status if it meets all the following requirements:

1. It is a domestic corporation.
2. It has no more than 75 shareholders.[89]
3. Its shareholders are individuals, with the exception of estates, trusts described in IRC Section 1361(c)(2).[90]

---

[85] IRC § 337.

[86] IRC § 336(c).

[87] *See generally* Bittker & Eustice, Federal Income Taxation of Corporations and Shareholders Ch. 6; Posin, Corporate Tax Planning; Rose & Chommie, Federal Income Taxation § 10.39; Bartlett, Corporate Restructurings, Reorganizations, and Buyouts § 4.5(b)(iii)(1).

[88] IRC § 469(a).

[89] IRC § 1361(b)(1)(A).

[90] IRC § 1361(b)(1)(B).

4. No shareholder is a nonresident alien.[91]
5. It has only one class of stock.[92] For purposes of this rule, differences in voting rights of common stock do not violate the one class of stock requirement.[93] Also, a "straight debt" instrument is not treated as a second class of stock. A straight debt instrument is a corporate, written, unconditional promise to pay on demand or on a specified date, a sum certain in money, where the interest rate is fixed, the debt is not convertible into stock, and the lender is either (a) eligible to be an S corporation stockholder, or (b) regularly engaged in the business of lending money.[94]

[2] Taxation of S Corporation Income at Corporate Level

As previously noted, S corporations are generally not taxed at the corporate level on corporate income.[95] However, there are three exceptions to this rule. First, for an S corporation, which formerly was a C corporation that elected S corporation status, the IRC taxes any gain recognized on the sale or distribution of property by the S corporation during the ten-year period after the S corporation election. It taxes such S corporation at the maximum corporate rate then applicable to that type of income.[96] This rule also applies if the corporation transfers such property to a shareholder. The IRC assumes that all such gains accrued while the corporation was a C corporation unless otherwise established.[97]

Second, the IRC imposes a special tax on S corporations whose passive income exceeded 25 percent of gross receipts for the year and accumulated earnings and profits from its C corporation years. Specifically, the IRC subjects such a corporation to a tax computed by multiplying the excess net passive income by the highest rate of tax specified in IRC Section 11(b).[98] The IRS may waive this tax if the corporation determines, in good faith, that it has no Subchapter C earnings and profits and the earnings are distributed after their discovery.[99]

Finally, an S corporation must pay taxes that result from the recapture of any investment credits claimed while it was a C corporation because of the early disposition of property on which the credits were claimed.[100]

---

[91] IRC § 1361(b)(1)(C).

[92] IRC § 1361(b)(1)(D).

[93] IRC § 1361(c)(4).

[94] IRC § 1361(c)(5).

[95] *See generally* Bittker & Eustice, Federal Income Taxation of Corporations and Shareholders Ch. 6; Posin, Corporate Tax Planning; Rose & Chommie, Federal Income Taxation § 10.39; Bartlett, Corporate Restructurings, Reorganizations, and Buyouts § 4.5(b)(iii)(1).

[96] IRC § 1374.

[97] IRC § 1374(c).

[98] IRC § 1375(b)(2).

[99] IRC § 1375(d).

[100] IRC § 1371(d)(2).

[3] Taxation of S Corporation Income at Shareholder Level

An S corporation shareholder computes his taxable income in essentially the same manner as a partner's income.[101] Specifically, a shareholder must consider separately items of income, loss, deduction, and credit if an item can affect the computation of the shareholder's tax liability.[102] The corporation passes these separately stated items directly through to the shareholders on a pro rata basis.[103] These items do not impact the computation of the corporation's non-separately computed income or loss.[104]

A shareholder's share of an S corporation's non-separately computed income and separately computed items depends on his stock ownership percentage on each day of the corporation's taxable year.[105] The daily portion of each item equals the corporation's total amount of each item divided by the number of days in the taxable year.[106] Separately computed S corporation items that the S corporation passes through to its shareholders retain their character in the shareholder's hands.[107] The following items also pass through to shareholders and are added to the shareholders' items of like character: capital gains and capital losses, IRC Section 1231 gains and losses, charitable deductions, tax-exempt interest, foreign taxes paid, dividends and interest, investment credit, depletion allowances, and foreign income and loss.[108] However, the IRC applies certain limits on the availability of pass-through items at both the corporate and shareholder levels. For example, limits on currently expensing the cost of certain depreciable business assets apply at both the corporate and shareholder levels.[109]

S corporations calculate depreciation deductions the same way C corporations do. Depreciation is not a pass-through item. The S corporation deducts depreciation in its tax return by arriving at the taxable income or loss it passes through to shareholders. The corporation, not the shareholders, makes depreciation elections.

The IRC prohibits S corporation shareholders who do not "materially participate" in the corporation's business on a "regular, continuous, and substantial" basis from deducting such passive activity losses and passive activity credits.[110] Such shareholders cannot use S corporation losses and credits to shelter earned income and portfolio income.[111] Losses and credits disallowed because of the passive loss rules may then be carried forward indefinitely and used to offset

---

[101] *See generally* Bittker & Eustice, Federal Income Taxation of Corporations and Shareholders Ch. 6; Posin, Corporate Tax Planning; Rose & Chommie, Federal Income Taxation § 10.39; Bartlett, Corporate Restructurings, Reorganizations, and Buyouts § 4.5(b)(iii)(1).

[102] IRC § 1366(a)(1)(A).

[103] IRC § 1366(a)(1).

[104] IRC § 1366(a).

[105] IRC § 1377(a)(1).

[106] *Id.*

[107] IRC § 1366(b).

[108] IRC § 1366(a).

[109] IRC § 179.

[110] IRC § 469(c)(1), (h)(1).

[111] IRC § 469(a).

passive income in future years.[112] Such losses are allowed in full when the shareholder disposes of his entire S corporation interest.[113]

Taxable and nontaxable income and deductible and nondeductible expenses serve, respectively, to increase and decrease the shareholder's S corporation stock basis.[114] The rules for adjusting a shareholder's basis for stock for S corporate income and loss parallel the basis adjustments that partners make in similar situations.[115] The shareholder's stock basis is first adjusted by corporate income and loss for the year.[116] After this, stock basis is decreased, but not below zero, by corporate distributions for the year that the shareholder did not include in income.[117] To the extent the shareholder's stock basis would otherwise be reduced below zero, the reduction lowers the basis of S corporation debt held by the shareholders.[118] An S shareholder's basis includes any loans by that shareholder to the S corporation. Thus, a shareholder's loans to an S corporation create basis and enable the shareholder to deduct his share of losses.[119]

[4] Taxation of S Corporation Dividends

If an S corporation without accumulated earnings and profits distributes cash to its shareholders,[120] there is no tax at the corporate level. At the shareholder level, the distribution is tax-exempt up to the amount of a shareholder's basis for the stock and reduces his basis in the stock.[121] If the distribution exceeds the shareholder's basis, the shareholder recognizes gain.[122] Generally, this gain is taxed at the shareholder's top marginal tax rate.[123]

The IRC treats distributions by S corporations with accumulated earnings and profits as if made by an S corporation with no earnings and profits up to the amount of the corporation's accumulated adjustments account.[124] The IRC treats amounts exceeding the accumulated adjustments account first as a taxable distribution to the extent of accumulated earnings and profits, next against the shareholder's basis in the stock, and then as capital gains.[125] S corporations formed before 1983 may have accumulated earnings and profits attributable to (1) tax years for which an election was not in effect, (2) tax years before 1983 for

---

[112] IRC § 469(b).

[113] IRC § 469(g).

[114] IRC § 1367(a).

[115] *See, e.g.,* IRC § 705(a).

[116] IRC § 1367(a)(1)(A), (B).

[117] IRC § 1367(a)(2)(A).

[118] IRC § 1367(b)(2).

[119] IRC § 1366(d)(1)(B).

[120] *See generally* Bittker & Eustice, Federal Income Taxation of Corporations and Shareholders Ch. 6; Posin, Corporate Tax Planning; Rose & Chommie, Federal Income Taxation § 10.39; Bartlett, Corporate Restructurings, Reorganizations, and Buyouts § 4.5(b)(iii)(1).

[121] IRC § 1368(b).

[122] *Id.*

[123] IRC § 1(a), (g).

[124] IRC § 1368(c).

[125] *Id.*

which an election was in effect, and (3) a corporate acquisition that results in a carryover of earnings and profits.[126] A distribution from an S corporation with no accumulated earnings and profits is tax-exempt and reduces the shareholder's basis in his stock.[127]

[5] Taxation of S Corporation Losses

Net operating losses,[128] like all items, pass through on a per-share, per-day basis to S corporation shareholders.[129] However, the IRC restricts the use of passive losses by S corporation shareholders who do not "materially participate" in the corporation on a "regular, continuous, and substantial" basis.[130] An S corporation shareholder's passive losses can be offset only against passive activity income, not against earned income and portfolio income.[131] Even if the shareholder overcomes the passive loss limitation, the IRC limits the shareholder's deduction for such losses to the sum of his adjusted basis in the S corporate stock and his loans to the corporation.[132] Loss pass-throughs that exceed the currently deductible amount are carried forward indefinitely.[133]

An S corporation cannot deduct a carryforward or carryback loss arising in a year that it was a C corporation.[134] Consequently, it may be unwise for a C corporation with unexpired net operating losses to elect S corporation status. The prohibition against carryovers of net operating losses between a C corporation and its S corporation years also extends to carryovers of other tax attributes. If the corporation expects future losses, an S corporation election may still be desirable, despite the loss of the C corporation's carryforward.

If S corporation stock becomes worthless, each shareholder may claim a short-term or long-term capital loss deduction.[135] Before computing a shareholder's worthless stock deduction, the S corporation's separately computed items and its non-separately computed income or loss for that year must be taken into account and the required basis adjustments made to each shareholder's stock.[136]

---

[126] Rose & Chommie, Federal Income Taxation § 10.39.

[127] IRC § 1368(b)(1).

[128] *See generally* Bittker & Eustice, Federal Income Taxation of Corporations and Shareholders Ch. 6; Posin, Corporate Tax Planning; Rose & Chommie, Federal Income Taxation § 10.39; Bartlett, Corporate Restructurings, Reorganizations, and Buyouts § 4.5(b)(iii)(1); Grant W. Newton & Gilbert D. Bloom, Bankruptcy & Insolvency Taxation Ch. 6 (John Wiley & Sons 1991); Lewis D. Solomon & Lewis J. Saret, Business Workout Strategies: Tax and Legal Aspects Ch. 7 (John Wiley & Sons 1992).

[129] IRC § 1366(a)(1)(A).

[130] IRC § 469(b)(1), (c)(1).

[131] IRC § 469(a).

[132] IRC § 1366(d).

[133] IRC § 1366(d)(2).

[134] IRC § 1371(b)(1).

[135] IRC §§ 165, 1367(b)(3).

[136] *Id.*

Planning Pointer. S corporations always should attempt to qualify their stock under IRC Section 1244. There is no price for the Section 1244 tax benefit and no penalty for failing to qualify. If the S corporation can use Section 1244, the tax savings will be substantial. Unlike C corporation shareholders, S corporation shareholders may deduct corporate losses currently as ordinary losses, subject to the passive activity loss rules.[137] IRC Section 1244 also allows S corporation shareholders to deduct losses sustained on sales or exchanges of their stock as ordinary loss if such stock becomes worthless. Additionally, IRC Section 1244 qualification entitles the S corporation shareholders to take an ordinary loss if the stock becomes worthless due to S election termination or revocation. The maximum amount that may be treated as ordinary loss on IRC Section 1244 stock in any taxable year is $50,000 or $100,000 for spouses filing a joint return.[138]

Unlike partners, S corporation shareholders do not include their share of corporate liabilities in their basis for determining the amount of deductible losses.[139] The shareholder may include shareholder loans to the S corporation in his basis.[140]

Each S corporation shareholder's pro rata share of income passed through to him increases his basis for stock in the corporation.[141] Conversely, if the corporation has a loss, each shareholder deducts his pro rata share of such loss.[142] This, in turn, reduces each shareholder's basis for his stock and debt, to the extent that the loss does not exceed such basis.[143] A shareholder reduces his stock basis by items of deduction that were treated separately by the corporation.[144] Distributions to S corporation shareholders also reduce such shareholders's corporate stock basis.[145]

S corporation losses cannot be retroactively allocated. Each shareholder of an S corporation deducts his pro rata share of loss based on his percentage of stock ownership on each day of the corporation's taxable year.[146] Consequently, S corporation losses are allocated on a per-share, per-day basis without regard to who owns the stock at year end.

---

[137] IRC § 1366(b).
[138] IRC § 1244(b).
[139] IRC §§ 752(a), 1367(a)(1).
[140] IRC § 1366(d)(1)(B).
[141] IRC § 1367(a)(1).
[142] IRC § 1366.
[143] IRC § 1367(a)(2).
[144] *Id.*
[145] *Id.*
[146] IRC § 1377(a).

[6] S Corporation Choice of Fiscal Year

An S corporation must adopt a "permitted" taxable year,[147] regardless of when the corporation elected to be taxed as an S corporation.[148] A permitted year is either (1) a taxable year ending December 31 (a calendar year), or (2) any other accounting period for which the corporation establishes a business purpose. S corporations desiring to use other tax years must obtain IRS approval. Deferral of income to shareholders will not constitute a business purpose for purposes of these rules.[149]

[7] Death or Retirement of S Corporation Shareholder

The IRC treats transactions by an S corporation with respect to its own stock as if the S corporation were a C corporation.[150] The Subchapter C rules do not apply when the result would be inconsistent with the purpose of the Subchapter S rules, which is to treat the S corporation as a pass-through entity.[151] For redemptions, an adjustment to the corporation's accumulated earnings and profits account must be made.[152]

[8] S Corporation Liquidation

S corporations and their shareholders receive the same tax treatment as a liquidating C corporation,[153] except when Subchapter S provides otherwise or when such treatment would be inconsistent with Subchapter S.[154] However, because every item of gain or loss passes directly to S corporation shareholders, generally no tax at the corporate level exists. Nevertheless, the IRC taxes any gain recognized on the sale or distribution of property by an S corporation that was formerly a C corporation within 10 years of the S election at the maximum corporate rate then applicable to that type of income.[155] Unexpired C corporation attributes, such as net operating loss carryforwards, may be used to offset this income at the corporate level.[156] Gains, reduced by the tax paid by one corporation, are then passed through to the shareholders and taxed to them.

---

[147] *See generally* Bittker & Eustice, Federal Income Taxation of Corporations and Shareholders Ch. 6; Posin, Corporate Tax Planning; Rose & Chommie, Federal Income Taxation § 10.39; Bartlett, Corporate Restructurings, Reorganizations, and Buyouts § 4.5(b)(iii)(1).

[148] IRC § 1378(a).

[149] IRC § 1378(b).

[150] *See generally* Bittker & Eustice, Federal Income Taxation of Corporations and Shareholders Ch. 6; Posin, Corporate Tax Planning; Rose & Chommie, Federal Income Taxation § 10.39; Bartlett, Corporate Restructurings, Reorganizations, and Buyouts § 4.5(b)(iii)(1).

[151] IRC § 1371(a).

[152] IRC § 1371(c)(2).

[153] *See generally* Bittker & Eustice, Federal Income Taxation of Corporations and Shareholders Ch. 6; Posin, Corporate Tax Planning; Rose & Chommie, Federal Income Taxation § 10.39; Bartlett, Corporate Restructurings, Reorganizations, and Buyouts § 4.5(b)(iii)(1).

[154] IRC § 1371(a).

[155] IRC § 1374.

[156] IRC § 1374(b)(2).

[9] Termination of S Corporation Election

Certain events may occur during the tax year that cause a corporation to fail to meet the definition of an S corporation. Such events cause the termination of the S corporation election[157] as of the date the event occurs.[158] These events include:

1. Exceeding the 75-shareholder limit;
2. Transferring stock to a foreign trust, nonresident alien, corporation, or partnership;[159]
3. Creating more than one class of stock;[160]
4. Receiving more than 25 percent of the corporation's gross receipts for three successive tax years from passive income sources;[161] and
5. Voluntary revocation by the consent of shareholders holding more than 50 percent of the S corporation's stock.[162]

Planning Pointer. To avoid an inadvertent S corporation termination due to the transfer to disqualifying shareholders, the planner should draft a shareholder's agreement requiring shareholders to give the corporation or other shareholders the right of first refusal before the shareholder sells or transfers any of the stock.

An election can be revoked only by shareholders holding more than one-half of the corporation's voting stock on the revocation date.[163] A revocation made on or before the 15th day of the third month of the taxable year is effective for the entire taxable year, unless the revocation specifies a prospective effective date. Revocations made after the 15th day of the third month of the taxable year become effective on the first day of the following taxable year.[164] However, when the revocation states another prospective date, the revocation is effective on the specified date.[165]

After termination or revocation of an election, a new election may not be made until the fifth year beginning after the revocation or termination.[166] This rule also applies to successor corporations that acquire a substantial portion of the terminating corporation's assets when the persons who own the successor

---

[157] *See generally* Bittker & Eustice, Federal Income Taxation of Corporations and Shareholders Ch. 6; Posin, Corporate Tax Planning; Rose & Chommie, Federal Income Taxation § 10.39; Bartlett, Corporate Restructurings, Reorganizations, and Buyouts § 4.5(b)(iii)(1).

[158] IRC § 1362(d)(2).

[159] IRC § 1361(b)(1)(B).

[160] IRC §§ 1361(b)(1)(D), 1361(c)(4).

[161] IRC § 1362(d)(3).

[162] IRC § 1362(d)(1)(B).

[163] *Id.*

[164] IRC § 1362(d)(1)(C).

[165] IRC § 1362(d)(1)(D).

[166] IRC § 1362(g).

corporation also substantially owned (at least 50-percent ownership) the terminating corporation. When the termination was not reasonably within the corporation's control and was not planned, the IRS may consent to an earlier reelection.[167]

Planning Pointer. An S corporation that lacks C corporation accumulated earnings and profits need not concern itself with the passive income rule.[168] S corporations with C corporation accumulated earnings and profits and sufficient passive income for two years may avoid S corporation termination when they pass the test in the third year. Normal sales that result in nonpassive income may be accelerated or the receipt or accrual of passive income may be deferred.

S corporation shareholders cannot terminate the initial election unless they own more than one-half the S corporation's voting stock.[169] However, a successor current income beneficiary of a qualified Subchapter S trust may terminate the trust's qualified status by affirmatively refusing to elect such status.[170]

Planning Pointer. To transfer assets with growth potential to children above age 14 in lower tax brackets, the planner should consider terminating the S election. If the shareholders terminate the S election, a C corporation would result. Limited liability would be preserved and a recapitalization would be an option available to the tax planner. Recapitalizations, involving exchanges of common stock for preferred stock, are not available to S corporations because of the prohibition against more than one class of stock.[171] When recapitalizing the new C corporation, the planner should select the termination date carefully to avoid a bunching of income problem.

If the IRS determines that an S corporation has inadvertently terminated its election, it can waive the termination for any period if (1) the corporation makes a timely correction, and (2) the corporation and shareholders agree to be treated as if the election had been in effect for such period.[172]

---

[167] *See, e.g.,* Rev. Rul. 78-274, 1978-2 C.B. 220; Rev. Rul. 78-333, 1978-2 C.B. 224; Rev. Rul. 78-332, 1978-2 C.B. 223.

[168] IRC § 1362(d)(3)(A)(i).

[169] IRC § 1362(d)(1)(B).

[170] IRC § 1361(d)(2)(B)(ii).

[171] IRC § 1361(b)(1)(D). *See* Solomon & Saret, *Tax Planning for Closely Held Corporations under the New Estate Freeze Rules,* 16 Rev. Tax'n Individuals 3 (Winter 1992), for a discussion of estate freeze recapitalizations.

[172] IRC § 1362(f).

§ 4.03 PARTNERSHIPS

The planner must also examine the tax consequences of choosing the limited partnership as an entity form.[1] Specifically, the planner must consider the following tax aspects of limited partnerships:

1. The taxation of limited partnership income and distributions;
2. The tax treatment of limited partnership losses;
3. Choice of fiscal year;
4. Tax treatment of limited partnership formation;
5. Tax treatment of limited partnership interest transfers;
6. Tax treatment of the retirement or death of a partner; and
7. The tax treatment of partnership liquidation.

[A] Taxation of Partnership Income

The IRC treats partnerships as tax conduits instead of as separate taxable entities.[2] A partnership files only an information return that reports the partnership's income, loss, credits, deductions, and the apportionment of each category to individual partners for inclusion in their income tax return.[3] The IRC then taxes each partner on his share of partnership income, gain, loss, deduction, or credit without regard to the amount actually distributed to him.[4] However, the passive activity loss rules provide that passive activity losses generally can be offset only against passive activity income, not against earned income and portfolio income (dividends, interest, and gains on sale of investments).[5]

The passive activity loss rules provide that disallowed passive loss is carried forward and allowed in subsequent years to the extent of the taxpayer's net passive income in such year. If not so used, such disallowed losses may be used to offset any gain on the sale of the passive activity generating the loss; if any passive loss remains, it may be used to offset other income in the year of sale.[6]

Concerning the computation of partnership income or loss, which passes through to the partners, several items must be separately stated in determining the partner's tax[7] even though they are excluded from computation of partnership income.[8] The tax character of each separately stated item within the partner's distributive share is the same as the character of the item at the partnership level. For example, tax-exempt income realized by a partnership

---

§ 4.03   [1] *See generally* William S. McKee, et al., Federal Taxation of Partnerships and Partners (2d ed. 1990); Harold Gill Reuschlein & William A. Gregory, The Law of Agency and Partnership Ch. 21 (2d ed. 1990); Rose & Chommie, Federal Income Taxation Ch. 9.

[2] IRC § 701; Treas. Reg. § 1.701-1.
[3] IRC § 6031.
[4] IRC § 702(a).
[5] IRC § 469(a).
[6] IRC § 469(g)(1)(A).
[7] IRC §§ 702(a), 703.
[8] IRC §§ 702(b), 703.

and distributed to the partners retains its tax-exempt status in the hands of each partner. In a corporation, tax-exempt income retains its tax-free character only at the corporate level and results in an increase of the corporation's earnings and profits.[9] Dividends paid from the tax-exempt income produce ordinary income for noncorporate shareholders.[10]

Partners may allocate among themselves their share of the various partnership items. This affords great flexibility to the partnership. For example, an individual may invest a substantial amount of the capital and want to receive most of the tax write-offs, such as depreciation.

[B] Allocation of Tax Consequences

The partnership agreement generally determines each partner's allocation of income, loss, deduction, or credit.[11] However, limits exist on the partners' ability to allocate tax consequences freely. Specifically, if the partnership agreement is silent or if the partnership agreement's allocation does not have "substantial economic effect," then each partner's share of items is determined according to the partner's partnership interest by considering all the facts and circumstances.[12]

Treasury Regulations use a two-part test to determine whether an allocation has substantial economic effect.[13] Under the first part of the test, the allocation must have economic effect. Specifically, if an economic benefit or burden corresponds to the allocation, the partner receiving such allocation must receive such benefit or bear such burden.[14] The allocation must be consistent with the partner's underlying economic arrangement. An allocation does not have economic effect unless the partnership:

1. Maintains the partner's capital accounts properly;
2. Distributes liquidation proceeds in accordance with the partners' capital account balances; and
3. Following the distribution of such proceeds, requires the partners to restore any deficits in their capital accounts to the partnership.[15]

Detailed provisions exist concerning the determination and maintenance of a partner's capital account. The partnership must increase a partner's capital account by the amount of his contributions and income allocations. Also the partnership must decrease the partner's capital account by the amount of

---

[9] IRC § 312(f)(2).
[10] IRC § 301(b)(1).
[11] IRC § 704(a).
[12] IRC § 704(b).
[13] Treas. Reg. § 1.704-1(b)(2)(i) (1991).
[14] Treas. Reg. § 1.704-1(b)(2)(ii)(a) (1991).
[15] Treas. Reg.§ 1.704-1(b)(2)(ii)(b). Rules are provided concerning the sufficiency of a partner's obligation to restore the deficit balance in his capital account to the partnership; however, the obligation to restore need not be unlimited. Treas. Reg. § 1.704-1(b)(2)(ii)(c).

distributions to such partner and by the amount of losses, deductions, and expenditures allocated to the partner under § 705(a)(2)(B). The regulations provide that the partnership must increase a partner's capital account by the fair market value of contributed property and must decrease the capital account by the fair market value of the property distributed to the partner.[16] The IRS accepts fair market values assigned to partnership assets by partners when partners with sufficiently adverse interests reasonably agree to those values in arm's-length negotiations.

Capital accounts may be adjusted, upon the occurrence of certain events, to reflect unrealized appreciation (or depreciation) in the value of distributed property.[17] Capital accounts may also be adjusted to reflect unrealized appreciation (or depreciation) in partnership property in connection with acquisitions and dispositions of partnership interests and certain other events.[18]

If a partnership does not comply with the capital account test, the regulations provide an alternative economic effect test.[19] This test establishes the validity of an allocation to a partner if (1) the allocation does not cause or increase a deficit balance in such partner's capital account, considering any distributions "reasonably" expected to occur in future years, and (2) the agreement contains a "qualified income offset" designed to restore any negative balance in such partner's capital account resulting from unanticipated losses or distributions. In short, under the alternative economic effect test, limited partners may take deductions against the full amount of their capital contribution provided the partnership does not purposely defer anticipated distributions until the partners exhaust their capital accounts.

Under the second part of the two-part substantial economic effect test, the allocation's economic effect must be substantial. The allocation must have a reasonable possibility of affecting the dollar amounts to be received by the partners from the partnership, independent of tax consequences.[20] The allocation is not substantial if because of it (1) the after-tax economic consequences of at least one partner, in present value terms, may be enhanced compared to such consequences without the allocation, and (2) a strong likelihood exists that the after-tax economic consequences of no partner will, in present value terms, be substantially diminished compared to such consequences without the allocation.[21] Allocations made between (or among) interests that assist one partner while not adversely affecting others generally lack substantiality. Allocations are not substantial if they merely shift tax attributes and cause little or no change in the partners' respective capital accounts without the special allocation.

The economic effect of one or more allocations is not substantial if, at the time the allocations become part of the partnership agreement, (1) a strong likelihood exists that net increases (and decreases) to the partners' respective capital

---

[16] Treas. Reg. § 1.704-1(b)(2)(iv)(b).
[17] Treas. Reg. § 1.704-1(b)(2)(iv)(g).
[18] Treas. Reg. § 1.704-1(b)(2)(iv)(1).
[19] Treas. Reg. § 1.704-1(b)(2)(ii)(d).
[20] Treas. Reg. § 1.704-1(b)(2)(iii)(a).
[21] *Id.*

accounts for the taxable years resulting from the allocations will not differ substantially from the net increases (and decreases) that would have been recorded without the allocations in the partnership agreement, and (2) the total tax liability of the partners is less than if the allocations were not contained in the agreement.[22] The IRS presumes that if these two conditions occur in any taxable year, there is a strong likelihood that these results would occur at the time the allocation became part of the partnership agreement. The partnership may overcome this presumption by facts and circumstances proving otherwise.

If an allocation fails to meet the substantial economic effect test, the IRS reallocates the affected tax attributes with reference to the partner's partnership interests. The IRS bases the reallocation on the underlying economic arrangement of the partners relating to the particular allocation in question. If that economic arrangement cannot be determined, the IRS presumes each partner's interest is equal.[23]

The regulations also set forth requirements for losses and deductions attributable to nonrecourse debt to be deemed made in accordance with the partners' interest in the partnership. In brief, the allocation of losses and deductions must be made in accordance with the partners' interests in the partnership.[24]

[C] Nonallowable Allocations

The planner should note that computation of certain income items may not be allocated to each partner. The partnership may allocate only items of income, gain, loss, deduction, or credit.[25] This excludes gross receipts and basis. The partners and limited partnership must treat depreciation recapture, percentage depletion allowance, IRC Section 179 depreciation allowance, guaranteed payments, and partnership distributions differently than other items.

The IRC requires recapture of depreciation deductions on the disposition of depreciable property placed in service before 1981, property subject to accelerated cost recovery placed in service before 1987, and depreciable personal property placed in service after 1986 and used in the transferor's trade or business. Each partner's distributive share of depreciation recapture is allocated in the same ratio as the gain would be allocated from disposition of the property in question.[26]

The percentage depletion allowance was designed to encourage the development of natural resources and to compensate prospectors and miners for the financial risks involved in these endeavors. The allowance permits taxpayers to deduct a flat percentage of "gross income from the property" provided the deduction does not exceed 50 percent of the taxpayer's "taxable income from the property."[27] The percentage depletion allowance cannot be specifically

---

[22] Treas. Reg. § 1.704-1(b)(2)(iii)(b).

[23] Treas. Reg. § 1.704-1(b)(3).

[24] Id.

[25] IRC § 702(a).

[26] Treas. Reg. § 1.1245-1(e), (f).

[27] Treas. Reg. §§ 1.1245-1(e), 1.1250-1(f).

allocated but is related to the income by which it is measured. Each partner's allowance is limited to the percentage of his distributive shares of gross income generated by the property. For oil and gas wells, the percentage depletion is calculated separately by the partners rather than the partnership and the opportunity to allocate the allowance specially is precluded.[28]

IRC Section 179 allows taxpayers to deduct, up to a specified dollar amount, the cost of property acquired for use in a trade or business.[29] After the partnership selects the property for which the expense is allowable, the partnership passes the deduction through to the partners up to the annual dollar limitation. A partner's share of Section 179 depreciation is based solely on his distributive share of the partnership's depreciation allowance and cannot be allocated as a separate item.[30] The deduction of an expense item is limited, pursuant to the Tax Reform Act of 1986, to income derived from any active trade or business.[31]

If a partner, acting in a capacity other than as a partner, engages in a business transaction with the partnership, payments to the partner for services rendered or for the use of capital constitute guaranteed payments.[32] If the partnership determines these payments without regard to the partnership's income, the partnership may deduct such expenses.[33] For a guaranteed payment to be deductible to the partnership, it must be an ordinary and necessary business expense.[34] Otherwise the payments must be capitalized.[35]

To determine whether a partner acts in his capacity as a partner, the IRS looks at the following factors: whether the partner provides similar services to others in his regular trade or business; whether the partner can be relieved of his duties by a majority vote of the partners; whether the partner pays his own expenses; and whether the partner is personally liable for any losses incurred in the work completed for the partnership.[36]

To establish that the partnership makes the guaranteed payment without regard to the partnership's income, the payment should resemble compensation rather than a share of partnership profits. The IRS looks at whether the payments are reasonable for the services provided and whether the calculation methodology would have been used to pay a nonpartner for identical services.[37]

The IRC treats partnership guaranteed payments for interest on capital and investment income on the working capital of a passive activity as portfolio, not passive, income.[38] The IRC treats partnership guaranteed payments for services as active income. Neither portfolio nor active income is subject to the limitations imposed on passive activity losses and income.

---

[28] IRC § 613A(c)(7)(D).

[29] IRC § 179(b)(1), (d)(8).

[30] Treas. Reg. § 1.179-2(d)(1).

[31] IRC § 179(b)(3)(A).

[32] IRC § 707(a).

[33] IRC § 707(c).

[34] IRC § 162(a). Cagle v. Comm'r, 63 T.C. 86 (1974), aff'd, 539 F.2d 409 (5th Cir. 1976).

[35] IRC § 263 (1988 & Supp. 1990); Rev. Rul. 75-214, 1975-1 C.B. 185.

[36] Rev. Rul. 81-301, 1981-2 C.B. 145; Pratt v. Comm'r, 550 F.2d 1023 (5th Cir. 1977).

[37] Rev. Rul. 81-300, 1981-2 C.B. 143.

[38] IRC § 469(e)(1)(B).

A partnership usually can make a tax-free distribution of money or property to a partner.[39] However, if a partnership distributes cash that exceeds the partner's adjusted basis for his partnership interest, the partner recognizes capital gain in the amount of that excess.[40] A partner may recognize a tax loss on a distribution in complete liquidation of his interest only if the property distributed consists of money, unrealized receivables, and substantially appreciated inventory.[41] The loss is recognized only to the extent of the excess of the adjusted basis of such partner's interest in the partnership over the sum of (1) any money distributed, and (2) his basis as determined in Section 732 of any unrealized receivables and substantially appreciated property.[42]

[D] Treatment of Partnership Losses

Partnership losses pass through to each partner to the extent of his distributive share of such losses.[43] The IRC restricts the use of passive activity losses and credits by partners who do not materially participate in the partnership's business on a regular, continuous, and substantial basis.[44] Furthermore, a partner may only use partnership losses to the extent of his adjusted basis in the partnership interest at the end of the partnership loss year.[45] A partner's basis includes a pro rata share of partnership liabilities or debt.[46]

A partner's basis in his partnership interest equals the amount of money and the adjusted basis of property contributed to the partnership, plus the amount of gain recognized by the partner on the contribution.[47] If a partner acquires the interest in a taxable purchase from another partner, the basis is determined by the general rules regarding the purchase of assets. The basis usually is equal to the partnership interest's purchase price.[48]

The partner's initial basis in the partnership interest is adjusted to reflect partnership operations. Specifically, the partner increases his basis by his share of partnership income and the excess of any deductions for depletion over the

---

[39] IRC §731(b). Note that recognized gain or loss may result to the partnership from distributions of IRC §751 property that will be treated as a sale or exchange of property between the distributee partner and the partnership. If the distribution of property is not made in complete liquidation of the partner's interest, the basis of each item of property distributed (other than money) is the same as its adjusted basis to the partnership immediately before the distribution. IRC §732(a)(1). However, the partner's basis in the property may not exceed the partner's adjusted basis of the partner's interest in the partnership, reduced by any cash distributed to him in that transaction. IRC §732(a)(2). If more than one item of property is distributed, basis allocations are made in accordance with IRC §732(c).

[40] IRC §731(a)(2).
[41] IRC §§731(a)(2), 751.
[42] IRC §731(a)(2).
[43] IRC §702.
[44] IRC §469(a), (c)(1), (h)(1).
[45] IRC §704(d).
[46] IRC §§705, 752.
[47] IRC §§705, 722, 742.
[48] IRC §§742, 1012.

basis of property subject to depletion.[49] The partner decreases his basis, but not below zero, by the following:

1. His share of partnership losses;
2. Distributions;
3. Expenditures that are neither deductible by the partnership in computing taxable income nor properly capitalized;
4. The partner's deduction for depletion with respect to oil and gas wells.[50]

Disallowed passive losses do not affect the partner's basis. Such suspended losses and credits are suspended and carried forward indefinitely and are allowed against passive activity income or on complete liquidation.[51]

Caution. The passive activity loss rules conclusively presume that a limited partner does not materially participate in partnership activities.[52] Consequently, a limited partner's loss will be passive.

Any increase or decrease in partnership liabilities increases or decreases each partner's basis in his partnership interest.[53] The IRC treats partnership liability increases and decreases as contributions or distributions of money.[54] Partners share recourse liabilities in proportion to their loss-sharing ratios under the partnership agreement. However, a limited partner's share of partnership liabilities cannot exceed the difference between such partner's contribution and the amount he must contribute under the partnership agreement.[55]

Planning Pointer. When a partner expects a loss but lacks sufficient basis to use it, he may do one of two things. First, the partner can do nothing if he does not have any other income against which to apply the loss. Here, the loss can be carried over to future years by subsequently increasing the partner's basis in the partnership interest.[56] Second, the partner can increase his basis in the partnership interest before year end. A basis increase may be achieved by agreeing to contribute an amount on call or making an additional capital contribution.

---

[49] IRC § 705(a)(1).
[50] IRC § 705(a)(2).
[51] IRC § 469(b)(1988).
[52] IRC § 469(h)(2).
[53] IRC § 752.
[54] IRC § 752(a), (b).
[55] Treas. Reg. § 1.752-1(e) (1991).
[56] Treas. Reg. § 1.704-1(d)(1) (1991).

Sometimes a partner joins a partnership late in the tax year and seeks tax benefits (for example, losses) shifted to him at year end. When this occurs, the incoming partner can claim his ratable share of loss only for the period during which he is a partner.[57] An incoming partner determines his distributive share of tax benefits by taking into account his varying interest in the partnership during the taxable year.[58] Partnerships cannot retroactively allocate to incoming partners distributive shares of profits, income, gain, loss, deduction, or credit that the partnership sustained before such individual's admittance.

A partner cannot avoid these rules by delaying the payment of certain deductible cash basis items until the first day of the year following a change in partnership interest. If such items are properly attributable to a period before the year of a partnership interest change, such portion must be allocated to the persons who were partners on the days to which such portion is attributable in proportion to their varying interests in the partnership.[59]

IRC Section 706(d) (2) defines cash basis items as interest, taxes, payments for services or the use of property, and any other payments the IRS designates as a cash basis item.

[E] Choice of Fiscal Year

A partnership may not have a taxable year except the taxable year of its partners owning a majority interest in participating profits and capital, unless the partnership establishes to IRS satisfaction a business purpose for having a different taxable[60] year. If all partners owning a majority of partnership profits and capital do not have the same taxable year, the partnership must adopt the taxable year of its principal partners.[61] If the principal partners do not have the same taxable year and a majority of partnership partners do not have the same taxable year, the partnership must adopt a calendar tax year.[62] A partnership need not adopt the taxable year of the partners owning a majority interest in its profits and capital unless partners with the same taxable year have owned a majority interest in partnership profits and capital for the three preceding taxable years of the partnership.[63]

[F] Partnership Formation

A partnership may be formed in either a taxable or nontaxable manner. If a tax-free formation occurs, neither the partners nor the partnership incur any tax

---

[57] IRC § 706(d).
[58] IRC § 706(d)(1).
[59] IRC § 706(d)(2).
[60] IRC § 706(b)(1988).
[61] IRC § 706(b)(1)(B)(i), (ii).
[62] IRC § 706(b)(1)(B)(iii).
[63] IRC § 706(b)(4).

liability. Specifically, the partnership and its partners recognize no gain or loss when a partner contributes property having unrealized appreciation to the partnership in exchange for a partnership interest.[64] The contributing partner's partnership interest basis equals the sum of:

1. The money contributed;
2. The adjusted basis of property contributed; and
3. The amount of any gain the partner recognizes on the contribution.[65]

The determination of a partner's basis is critical because the partner's basis limits the amount of partnership losses the partner may deduct.[66] The partnership's basis in contributed property equals the contributing partner's adjusted basis at contribution, increased by any gain recognized on contribution.[67] The partnership values contributed property at the time of contribution and credits the amount of the contribution to the partner's capital account. For limited partnerships, the certificate of limited partnership must state the amount of cash and property contributed to the partnership and its agreed value.[68]

> **Planning Pointer.** Some prospective partners may prefer a taxable formation. For example, a potential partner may have high-value assets with low basis due to prior depreciation deductions. When the partner contributes the property in a tax-free transaction, the partnership will receive the low basis for its depreciation.[69] The partner may make the transaction taxable by structuring the transaction as a sale.[70] The partner could then contribute other property or money to form the partnership. Here, the partnership takes a basis in the property that equals the purchase price. This yields a greater depreciation deduction for the partnership than if the partner had contributed the property in a tax-free transaction.[71] Partners with low-value assets and a high basis also may want to structure the transaction as a sale. Here, a sale of such property to the partnership will generate a loss for the partner.[72]

> **Caution.** Partners holding greater than a 50-percent partnership interest cannot deduct losses from transactions with the partnership.[73]

---

[64] IRC § 721(a).
[65] IRC § 722(1988).
[66] IRC § 704(d).
[67] IRC § 723.
[68] ULPA § 2, 6 U.L.A. 568 (1916); RULPA § 201(5) (1976), 6 U.L.A. 312 (Supp. 1992).
[69] IRC § 723; Treas. Reg. § 1.723-1 (1956).
[70] IRC § 707 (1988).
[71] IRC § 723.
[72] IRC § 707 (1988).
[73] IRC § 707(b).

Amounts paid or incurred to organize a partnership or promote the sale of partnership interests are not deductible by the partnership or any partner.[74] However, the partnership may elect to amortize organization expenses over a period of five years or more.[75] When the partnership liquidates before the end of the amortization period, it deducts the unamortized expenses as a business loss.[76]

[G] Transfer of Partnership Interests and Death or Retirement of a Partner

Generally, if a partner sells or exchanges his partnership interest, he recognizes capital gain or loss.[77] The amount of such capital gain or loss equals the difference between the amount realized and the adjusted basis of the partnership interest. However, when part of the partner's interest is attributable to unrealized receivables or substantially appreciated inventory, this portion will be treated as ordinary income.[78]

The partner's death or retirement may be structured as (1) a sale or exchange so that the above rules apply, or (2) as a liquidation of a partnership interest. When the planner uses a liquidation, the partnership makes payments to the departing partner in liquidation of his entire partnership interest.[79] A liquidation of a partner's interest requires the termination of his entire partnership interest because of a distribution from the partnership to the partner.[80]

Payments made in liquidation of a partner's interest fall into two categories: (1) payments made in exchange for the partner's interest in partnership property,[81] and (2) all other payments.[82] If the partnership makes such distribution in exchange for the withdrawing partner's interest in partnership property, such partner will generally realize capital gain or loss and the remaining partners cannot claim a deduction.[83] If the payments do not fall into this category, the withdrawing partner will realize ordinary income and the remaining partners may deduct the expense.[84] Payments falling into this second category include payments made for the departing partner's share of unrealized receivables, goodwill, and any other payments not made in exchange for the partner's interest in partnership assets.[85] However, payments will fall into this second category only if (1) capital is not a material income-producing factor for the

---

[74] IRC § 709(a).
[75] IRC § 709(b).
[76] IRC § 709(b)(1).
[77] IRC § 741.
[78] IRC § 751.
[79] IRC § 736.
[80] Treas. Reg. § 1.761-1(d) (1972).
[81] IRC § 736(b).
[82] IRC § 736(a).
[83] IRC § 736(b).
[84] IRC § 736(a).
[85] IRC § 736(b)(2).

partnership, and (2) the retiring or deceased partner was a general partner in the partnership.[86]

[H] Partnership Liquidation

A partnership recognizes no gain or loss on a distribution in complete liquidation of a partner's interest.[87] A partner will recognize gain or loss on a liquidating distribution only to the extent the cash distributed exceeds his adjusted basis in the partnership interest immediately before the distribution.[88] A partner will recognize a loss only if the partnership distributes cash, unrealized receivables, or inventory and no other property.[89] A partner's gain or loss, unless attributable to unrealized receivables or substantially appreciated inventory, will be capital gain or loss.[90]

The partnership will terminate for tax purposes if (1) no part of any business, financial operation, or venture of the partnership continues to be carried on by any of its partners,[91] or (2) within a 12-month period, there is a sale or exchange of 50 percent or more of the total interest in partnership capital or profits.[92]

> **Caution.** The inadvertent termination of a partnership may cause a closing of the partnership's taxable year, which could cause a bunching of income, the loss of certain elections, the recognition of gain or loss on a hypothetical distribution of assets, or possible basis adjustments.

§ 4.04 LIMITED LIABILITY COMPANIES IN GENERAL

The planner also must carefully examine the tax consequences of choosing an LLC as an entity form. More specifically, the planner must consider whether the LLC will be taxed as a corporation or as a partnership.

> **Planning Pointer.** The main attraction of LLCs is that, when properly structured, the IRC treats them as partnerships for tax purposes. Therefore, the issue of how a particular LLC will be classified for tax purposes constitutes a critical issue.[1]

---

[86] IRC § 736(b)(3).
[87] IRC § 731(b).
[88] IRC § 731(a)(1).
[89] IRC § 731(a).
[90] IRC § 751.
[91] IRC § 708(b)(1)(A).
[92] IRC § 708(b)(1)(B).
§ 4.04   [1] See § 4.04[A].

[A] Tax Treatment of Limited Liability Companies

[1] In General

On April 3, 1995, the IRS published Notice 95-14, in which it announced that it was considering simplifying the classification regulations to allow taxpayers to treat unincorporated businesses as partnerships or as corporations on an elective basis.[2] Commentators called this proposal the "check the box" proposal because it allowed taxpayers to check a box on their tax form as to whether they would like the IRS to tax their unincorporated business (*e.g.,* limited liability company) as a corporation or as a partnership. On May 9, 1996, the IRS issued the long-awaited "check the box" proposed regulations. On December 18, 1996, the IRS released the final "check the box" regulations, which were effective beginning January 1, 1997. These regulations dramatically simplify the tax treatment of limited liability entities.

Under prior law, IRC Sections 7701(a)(2)–(3) and the existing regulations issued thereunder controlled the classification of entities as either partnerships or corporations. Section 7701(a)(3) defined a *corporation* as including associations, joint stock companies, and insurance companies. IRC Section 7701(a)(2) defined a *partnership* as including a syndicate, group, pool, joint venture, or other unincorporated venture. Consequently, the IRC defined partnerships principally as entities other than corporations.

The prior regulations set forth six major characteristics that distinguish corporations from other organizations:

1. Associates;
2. An objective to carry on a business and divide the gains therefrom;
3. Continuity of life;
4. Centralization of management;
5. Liability for corporate debts limited to corporate property; and
6. Free transferability of interests.

In determining whether an entity constituted a corporation or a partnership, the existing regulations ignored characteristics common to both. Thus, they ignored the factors of (1) associates, and (2) an objective to carry on a business and divide the gains therefrom. They also provided that an entity was not taxable as a corporation unless it possessed more corporate than noncorporate characteristics.[3] Consequently, the existing regulations treated entities that failed to possess at least two of the last four factors as partnerships.

The preamble to the proposed regulations notes that, although the existing regulations are based on historical differences between partnerships and corporations under state law, today those differences have all but disappeared with the arrival of new forms of entities, such as limited liability companies

---

[2] 1995-1 C.B. 297.
[3] Treas. Reg. § 301.7701-2(a).

(LLCs).[4] However, changes in entity forms under state law have required both taxpayers and the IRS to expend ever-greater resources on classifying entities for tax purposes. For example, the IRS has issued at least 17 revenue rulings analyzing individual state limited liability company statutes. It has also issued numerous revenue procedures and private letter rulings relating to classification of various business organizations.[5] An additional problem is that many small businesses lack the resources and expertise to achieve the tax classification they want under the current classification regulations. For all these reasons, both the IRS and commentators have concluded that a simpler classification scheme would be beneficial.

[2] The Final Regulations

[a] *Step 1—Is There a Separate Entity for Tax Purposes?*

Under the final regulations, the first step in classifying an entity is to determine whether a separate entity exists for federal tax purposes. The final regulations explain that certain joint undertakings, which do not constitute entities under state law, may constitute separate entities for federal tax purposes and vice versa.[6] Also, they retain the current rule that qualified cost-sharing arrangements described in Treas. Reg. § 1.482-7 are not partnerships for federal tax purposes.[7]

Generally, the regulations provide that joint ventures or other arrangements constitute separate entities for tax purposes if their participants carry on a trade, business, financial operation, or venture and divide the profits therefrom. However, as under existing law, joint undertakings merely to share expenses do not create separate entities for tax purposes.[8]

EXAMPLE 4-1

Richard and Ada, who are brother and sister, own Bleak House as tenants in common. They use Bleak House as their principal residence and live together merely as a cost-sharing arrangement. Here, under the proposed regulations, no separate entity exists.

EXAMPLE 4-2

Same facts as Example 4-1, except that Richard and Ada operate Bleak House as a bed and breakfast and divide the profits therefrom. Here, the proposed

---

[4] "Preamble to Proposed Treasury Regulations," 61 Fed. Reg. 21,989 (1996).
[5] *Id.*
[6] Treas. Reg. §§ 301.7701-1(a)(2), (3).
[7] Treas. Reg. § 301.7701-1(c).
[8] Treas. Reg. § 301.7701-1(a)(2).

regulations may treat Richard and Ada as operating a separate entity, even though they have not actually formed a separate entity. This results because they are carrying on a trade, business, or venture and dividing the profits therefrom.[9]

Caution. Although most entities formed by asset protection planners will constitute separate entities for tax purposes, this step is not entirely an academic exercise. This results because some asset protection planners recommended that all types of assets, including purely personal property, be placed into partnerships to protect those assets. In such cases, if the partnership holds only personal property, the purported entity may not constitute an entity under the proposed regulations.

The proposed regulations allow one-person entities to elect to be recognized or disregarded as entities separate from their owners.[10]

[b] Step 2—If There Is a Separate Entity for Tax Purposes, Is It a Business Entity or a Trust?

Under the final regulations, the second step that planners must follow is to determine whether they should classify the entity as a trust or business entity.[11] Although entities will generally be treated as either a business entity or trust for tax purposes, some types of entities will be treated differently. For example, Real Estate Mortgage Investment Conduits are treated differently under IRC Section 860A(a). The final regulations provide that trusts generally do not have associates or an objective to carry on business for profit. The preamble to the proposed regulations states that the determination of whether organizations are classified as trusts for federal tax purposes is intended to remain the same as under current law. Thus, the final regulations treat all entities recognized for tax purposes under the final regulations that do not constitute trusts as "business entities."

In turn, the final regulations treat business entities with two or more members as either corporations or partnerships. They either treat single-member business entities as corporations, or they disregard such entities as separate entities for tax purposes. If the regulations disregard the entity, the single-member owner will treat the business as a sole proprietorship. The reason for this treatment is that a fundamental characteristic of partnerships is the presence of associates. The preamble to the proposed regulations states that the lack of associates precludes classification of single-member entities as partnerships.

---

[9] *Id.*
[10] Treas. Reg. § 301.7701-1(a)(4).
[11] Treas. Reg. §§ 301.7701-2, -3, and -4, unless an IRC section provides otherwise (*e.g.*, IRC § 860A(a)).

EXAMPLE 4-3

Esther and Mr. Jarndyce form the E&J LLC, in which they are the sole members, and elect partnership treatment under the proposed regulations. At the end of the year, the E&J LLC files a Form 1065 and gives K-1 forms to Esther and to Mr. Jarndyce. Esther and Mr. Jarndyce each report items from their K-1 forms on their individual income tax returns.

EXAMPLE 4-4

Same facts as Example 4-3, except that Esther forms a single-member LLC in a state that allows such LLCs. Here, if Esther elects non-corporation treatment, she will treat the LLC as a sole proprietorship and report its income on her Form 1040, on Schedule C.

---

[c]   Step 3—Is the Entity a Corporation?

[i]   Mandatory Corporate Classification

The third step planners must take is to determine whether the final regulations require the entity to be treated as a corporation. If the entity falls into any of the following categories, the regulations require the entity be treated as a corporation for tax purposes:

1. Business entities organized under federal or state statutes as corporations.
2. Business entities organized under state statutes, where such statutes describe or refer to the entity as a joint-stock company or joint-stock association.
3. Insurance companies.
4. State-chartered banks, where any of their deposits are insured under the Federal Deposit Insurance Act or similar federal statute.
5. Business entities wholly owned by a state or any political subdivision thereof.
6. Business entities taxable as corporations under any IRC provision other than IRC Section 7701(a)(3).
7. Any of the enumerated foreign entities listed in Table 4-1, *infra,* unless the foreign entity satisfies each of the following requirements, in which case it will be treated as a partnership: (1) the entity was in existence and claimed to be a partnership on May 8, 1996, and for all prior periods; (2) that classification was relevant on May 8, 1996; (3) no person, including the entity itself, treated the entity as a corporation for federal income tax purposes for the tax year that included May 8, 1996; (4) the entity had a reasonable basis (within the meaning of Section 6662) for claiming partnership classification; and (5) neither the entity nor any member has been notified in writing on or before May 8, 1996, that the classification of the entity is under examination (in which case the entity's classification will be determined in the examination).

When the entity does fall into any of these categories, treatment as a corporation is mandatory and the entity cannot elect partnership treatment.

EXAMPLE 4-5

Dana and Fox form X Corp in the District of Columbia by filing articles of incorporation with the District of Columbia government. Here, classification of X Corp as a corporation for tax purposes is mandatory.

Table 4-1 Foreign Entity Names

Country	Entity Name
American Samoa	Corporation
Argentina	Sociedad Anonima
Australia	Public Limited Company
Austria	Aktiengesellschaft
Barbados	Limited Company
Belgium	Societe Anonyme
Belize	Public Limited Company
Bolivia	Sociedad Anonima
Brazil	Sociedade Anonima
Canada	Corporation and Company
Chile	Sociedad Anonima
People's Republic of China	Gufen Youxian Gongsi
Republic of China (Taiwan)	Ku-fen Yu-hsien Kung-szu
Colombia	Sociedad Anonima
Costa Rica	Sociedad Anonima
Cyprus	Public Limited Company
Czech Republic	Akciova Spolecnost
Denmark	Aktieselskab
Ecuador	Sociedad Anonima or Compania Anonima
Egypt	Sharikat Al-Mossahamah
El Salvador	Sociedad Anonima
Finland	Julkinen Osakeyhtio/Publikt Aktiebolag
France	Societe Anonyme
Germany	Aktiengesellschaft
Greece	Anonymos Etairia
Guam	Corporation
Guatemala	Sociedad Anonima
Guyana	Public Limited Company
Honduras	Sociedad Anonima
Hong Kong	Public Limited Company
Hungary	Reszvenytarsasag
Iceland	Hlutafelag
India	Public Limited Company

Indonesia	Perseroan Terbuka
Ireland	Public Limited Company
Israel	Public Limited Company
Italy	Societa per Azioni
Jamaica	Public Limited Company
Japan	Kabushiki Kaisha
Kazakstan	Ashyk Aktsionerlik Kogham
Republic of Korea	Chusik Hoesa
Liberia	Corporation
Luxembourg	Societe Anonyme
Malaysia	Berhad
Malta	Public Limited Company
Mexico	Sociedad Anonima
Morocco	Societe Anonyme
Netherlands	Naamloze Vennootschap
New Zealand	Limited Company
Nicaragua	Compania Anonima
Nigeria	Public Limited Company
Northern Mariana Islands	Corporation
Norway	Aliment Aksjeselskap
Pakistan	Public Limited Company
Panama	Sociedad Anonima
Paraguay	Sociedad Anonima
Peru	Sociedad Anonima
Philippines	Stock Corporation
Poland	Spolka Akcyjna
Portugal	Sociedade Anonima
Puerto Rico	Corporation
Romania	Societe pe Actiuni
Russia	Otkrytoye Aktsionemoy Obshchestvo
Saudi Arabia	Sharikat Al-Mossahamah
Singapore	Public Limited Company
Slovak Republic	Akciova Spolocnost
South Africa	Public Limited Company
Spain	Sociedad Anonima
Surinam	Naamloze Vennootschap
Sweden	Publika Aktiebolag
Switzerland	Aktiengesellschaft
Thailand	Borisat Chamkad (Mahachon)
Trinidad and Tobago	Limited Company
Tunisia	Societe Anonyme
Turkey	Anonim Sirket
Ukraine	Aktsionerne Tovaristvo Vidkritogo Tipu
United Kingdom	Public Limited Company
United States Virgin Islands	Corporation
Uruguay	Sociedad Anonima
Venezuela	Sociedad Anonima or Compania Anonima

[ii] Election Available for All Other Entities

Generally, all other business entities, which the proposed regulations do not require to be classified as corporations, may elect classification as either corporations or partnerships for tax purposes. However, as discussed earlier, single-member entities may only elect to be classified as corporations or to be disregarded for tax purposes.[12]

[iii] Default Provisions—Domestic Business Entities

The final regulations provide two default provisions for entities not required to be classified as corporations when the entity does not make an election. First, the regulations classify entities created after the regulations' effective date that fail to make an election as partnerships. However, if they have only one member, such entities are disregarded as separate entities for tax purposes.[13] Second, entities created before the regulations' effective date will retain the classification that such entities claimed under the existing regulations before the final regulations' effective date. However, single-member entities that claim partnership treatment before the regulations' effective date are disregarded for tax purposes after the effective date of the regulations.[14]

EXAMPLE 4-6

Same facts as Example 4-5, except that Dana and Fox form the X LLC, a limited liability company, rather than a corporation. Also, the X LLC fails to make a classification election. Here, the proposed regulations' default provisions will classify the X LLC as a partnership.

[iv] Default Provisions—Foreign Business Entities

When the regulations do not require foreign business entities be classified as corporations and such entities do not make an election, the regulations provide three default provisions. First, the regulations classify foreign entities as partnerships if they have two or more members and any member has unlimited liability. Second, the regulations classify foreign entities as corporations if all members have limited liability. Third, the regulations disregard foreign entities as entities separate from their owners if they have a single owner that has unlimited liability.[15]

Foreign entity members have limited liability, for purposes of the final regulations, if they have no personal liability for the entity's debts because of the fact they are members. This determination is based solely on the statute or law pursuant to which the entity is organized. However, if such underlying statute

---

[12] Treas. Reg. § 301.7701-3(a).
[13] Treas. Reg. § 301.7701-3(b)(1).
[14] Treas. Reg. § 301.7701-3(b)(3).
[15] Treas. Reg. § 301.7701-3(b)(2).

or law allows the entity to specify in its organizational documents whether the members will have limited liability, the organizational documents may also be relevant. Members also have personal liability for this purpose if the entity's creditors may seek satisfaction of any of their debts against the entity from the member as such. Finally, members have personal liability even if they make an agreement under which another person (without regard to whether such person is a member of the entity) assumes such liability or agrees to indemnify that member for any such liability.

[d] Method of Making Election

The final regulations provide that an eligible entity may elect to be classified as a type of entity other than as provided under the default rules under Treas. Reg. § 301.7701-3(b) by filing Form 8832, Entity Classification Election, with the IRS service center indicated on Form 8832. In addition, entities that must file federal tax or information returns for the tax year of the election must attach a copy of their Form 8832 to such return for that year. If they do not have to file returns for that year, a copy of their Form 8832 must be attached to the federal income tax or information return or any direct or indirect owner of the entity for the tax year of the owner that includes the election's effective date. Indirect owners of entities do not have to attach a copy of Form 8832 to their returns if the entity is already filing such a copy with its return.

If an entity, or one of its direct or indirect owners, fails to attach a copy of Form 8832 to its return, this does not invalidate an otherwise valid election. However, such failure may subject the non-filing party to penalties. Such penalties may include any applicable penalties if the federal tax or information returns are inconsistent with the entity's election.

Elections under the regulations become effective on the date the entity specifies on Form 8832. If it does not specify any date on the election form, the election becomes effective on the date the entity files Form 8832. However, the specified effective date cannot be more than (1) 75 days before, or (2) 12 months after the date the entity files the election. If the entity erroneously specifies a date outside these periods, the election becomes effective either 75 days before or 12 months after the filing date, whichever is applicable. Finally, if the entity's election form specifies an effective date before January 1, 1997, the election becomes effective as of January 1, 1997.

After electing to change its classification, an entity generally cannot make another election within 60 months after the election's effective date. However, the IRS may permit a new election within this 60-month period if, on the new election date, persons that did not own any interests in the entity on the first election's filing date or effective date, own more than 50 percent of the entity's ownership interests at the effective date of new election.

Under certain circumstances, the regulations treat entities as having made an election. First, the regulations treat entities the IRS has determined were, or claim to be, exempt from taxation under IRC Section 501(a) as having elected association classification. The regulations treat such deemed election as being effective as of the first day for which exemption is claimed or determined to apply. This is true regardless of when the claim or determination is made. Such deemed election remains in effect, unless an election is made after the date the claim for exempt status is withdrawn or rejected or the date the determination of exempt status is revoked. Second, entities that file an election under IRC Section 856(c)(1) to be treated as a real estate investment trust are treated as electing association classification. Such elections become effective as of the first day the entity is treated as a real estate investment trust.

EXAMPLE 4-7

In July 1, 2000, Dickens Corp., a domestic corporation, buys a 10 percent interest in Austin Entity, an entity formed under foreign law in 1990. Austin's classification was not relevant to any person for federal tax purposes before Dickens bought an interest in Austin. Thus, Austin is not considered to be in existence on the effective date of the proposed regulations. Under the applicable foreign law, no member of Austin has unlimited liability as defined in the proposed regulations. Accordingly, Austin is classified as a corporation unless it elects to be treated as a partnership. Here, to be classified as a partnership as of July 1, 2000, Austin must file an election by September 13, 2000. Because an election cannot be effective more than 75 days prior to the date on which it is filed, if Austin files its election after September 13, 2000, it will be classified as a corporation from July 1, 2000, until the effective date of the election. In that case, it could not change its classification by election under paragraph (c) of this section during the 60 months succeeding the effective date of the election.[16]

---

§4.05 COMPARISON BY TAX ASPECTS

A comparison of corporations, limited partnerships, Subchapter S corporations, and limited liability companies appears in Table 4-2.

Table 4-2
Comparison of Tax Aspects

Characteristic	*Entity*	
Tax on income	Corporation	Tax on income at corporate level and second tax on dividends at shareholder level. Dividends result in ordinary income to individual shareholders. However,

---

[16] Treas. Reg. § 301.7701-3(c)(1)(iv), Example 1.

		shareholders do not pay tax until dividends are paid. Corporation must address accumulated earnings tax.
	Limited Partnership	Income taxed directly to partners whether or not distributed. Avoids double taxation. Specifically treated income items pass through to partners without loss of items' character. No accumulated earnings tax.
	Subchapter S Corporation	Income taxed directly to shareholders. Avoids double taxation. Specifically treated income items pass through to partners without loss of items' character. No accumulated earnings tax.
	Limited Liability Company	If properly structured, entity is treated as partnership for all tax purposes.
Deductibility of losses	Corporation	Losses of corporation do not pass through to shareholders.
	Limited Partnership	Partnership losses may be used by the partners, subject to at-risk and passive activity loss rules.
	Subchapter S Corporation	Losses may be used by shareholders, subject to at-risk and passive activity loss rules.
	Limited Liability Company	If properly structured, entity is treated as partnership for all tax purposes. This allows losses to be used by members.
Possibility of allocating different types of income and deductions among owners by agreement	Corporation	No.

	Limited Partnership	Yes, if there is substantial economic effect.
	Subchapter S Corporation	No.
	Limited Liability Company	If properly structured, entity is treated as partnership for all tax purposes. Therefore, there may be special allocations.
Choice of fiscal year	Corporation	No restriction.
	Limited Partnership	Must be the same as principal partners unless IRS consents.
	Subchapter S Corporation	Must use a calendar year.
	Limited Liability Company	If properly structured, entity is treated as partnership for all tax purposes. Therefore, must be the same as principal partners unless IRS consents
Sale of ownership interest	Corporation	Generally all capital gain, unless corporation is collapsible.
	Limited Partnership	May be part capital gain and part ordinary income.
	Subchapter S Corporation	Generally all capital gain, unless corporation is collapsible.
	Limited Liability Company	If properly structured, entity is treated as partnership for all tax purposes. Therefore, may be part capital gain and part ordinary income.
Distribution/redemption by entity on death or withdrawal of owner	Corporation	Capital gain on redemption, unless taxed as a dividend.
	Limited Partnership	Generally, no tax.
	Subchapter S Corporation	Capital gain on redemption, unless taxed as a dividend.
	Limited Liability Company	If properly structured, entity is treated as partnership for all tax purposes. Therefore, generally no tax.

Liquidation of business	Corporation	Generally, taxable either as capital gains or, if a collapsible corporation, as ordinary income.
	Limited Partnership	Generally, no tax.
	Subchapter S Corporation	Generally, taxable either as capital gains or, if a collapsible corporation, as ordinary income.
	Limited Liability Company	If properly structured, entity is treated as partnership for all tax purposes. Therefore, generally no tax.

5

Use of Domestic Trusts

---

§5.01 IN GENERAL

Trusts are among the most useful and widely used asset protection tools. Where properly structured, they provide excellent asset protection. Also, trusts may complement other asset protection tools. For example, a client may incorporate her business to limit business liabilities to corporate assets, and then place the corporate stock into a trust to protect the business from her other creditors. A properly planned trust also provides the added benefit of furthering the settlor's estate planning goals.

Planning Pointer. When considering using trusts as part of an asset protection plan, planners should consider the following issues:

1. What rights will creditors have against the various trust parties?[1]
2. What are the income tax consequences of using different types of trusts as part of an asset protection plan?[2]
3. What are the gift tax consequences of using trusts as part of an asset protection plan?[3]
4. What are the estate tax consequences of using trusts as part of an asset protection plan?[4]
5. What are the generation-skipping transfer tax consequences of using trusts as part of an asset protection plan?[5]

Planning Pointer. Asset protection planners should be familiar with the following types of trusts:

1. Revocable trusts[6]
2. Irrevocable trusts[7]
3. Spendthrift trusts[8]
4. Discretionary trusts[9]
5. Support trusts[10]
6. Charitable remainder trusts[11]

§5.01 [1] *See* §5.02.
[2] *See* §5.03.
[3] *See* §5.04.
[4] *See* §5.05.
[5] *See* §5.06.
[6] *See* §5.07.
[7] *See* §5.08.
[8] *See* §5.09.
[9] *See* §5.10.
[10] *See* §5.11.
[11] *See* §5.12.

7. Qualified personal residence trusts[12]
8. Alaska- and Delaware-type asset protection trusts[13]
9. Foreign asset protection trusts[14]

§ 5.02   CREDITORS' RIGHTS AGAINST TRUST PARTIES

When evaluating trusts, asset protection planners must evaluate the liability exposure of the trustee, settlor, and trust beneficiaries. Generally, planners must consider the type of claimant involved, the different bases of liability that claimants might assert, and the terms of the trust. Most important, planners must examine local law.

[A]   Trustee Liability

Generally, trustees hold trust property for the benefit of the trust beneficiaries and not for their own advantage. Consequently, the trustee's creditors cannot reach the trust corpus. Furthermore, the trust corpus is not subject to the elective share, dower, or curtesy rights of the trustee's spouse.[1]

On the other hand, the trustee must exercise due care, diligence, and skill in the trust's administration.[2] Trustees who fail to meet this standard become liable for all losses resulting therefrom to the trust estate.[3] To illustrate, if the trustee conveys trust assets to beneficiaries and, subsequently, it is determined that certain claims attach to the trust assets, or conversely, the trustee pays creditors' claims from trust assets without adequate legal authority, the trustee may become liable to injured creditors or beneficiaries.[4] Trustees are generally not personally liable for postmortem distributions the trustee makes before a creditor takes appropriate action against the trust's assets. However, this rule does not apply to death taxes.[5]

---

[12] *See* § 5.13.

[13] *See* § 5.14.

[14] *See* Chapter 6.

§ 5.02   [1] George T. Bogert, Trusts § 32 (6th ed. 1987).

[2] *Probate & Trust Division Committee D-3 on Special Problems of Fiduciaries, Creditors' Rights Against Trust Assets,* 22 Real Prop. Prob. & Tr. J. 735 (1987).

[3] *Probate & Trust Division Committee D-3 on Special Problems of Fiduciaries, Creditors' Rights Against Trust Assets,* 22 Real Prop. Prob. & Tr. J. 735 (1987); 76 Am. Jur. 2d Trusts § 325 (1975). *See, e.g.,* Hartlove v. The Maryland School for the Blind, 681 A.2d 584 (Md. Ct. Spec. App. 1996), in which the Maryland Court of Special Appeals, in a case of first impression, held that Maryland recognized an independent cause of action for breach of fiduciary duty. In so holding, it noted that the Maryland Court of Appeals has not yet decided whether a cause of action exists for breach of fiduciary duty, but has instead assumed, without deciding, the viability of such causes of action. In support of this proposition, the court cited Adams v. Coates, 626 A.2d 36 (1993) (involving a dispute between partners), and Alleco, Inc. v. The Harry & Jeanette Weinberg Foundation, Inc., 665 A.2d 1038 (1995).

[4] *Probate & Trust Division Committee D-3 on Special Problems of Fiduciaries, Creditors' Rights Against Trust Assets,* 22 Real Prop. Prob. & Tr. J. 735, 736 (1987).

[5] Frank S. Berall et al., Revocable Inter Vivos Trusts, Tax Mgmt. (BNA) No. 468-2d, at A-20 (1975).

Planning Pointer. When potential claims exist against trust property, the trustee should obtain a court order.[6] This protects the trustee against liability for conveying trust property to the wrong person through a mistake of law or an erroneous interpretation of the trust instrument.[7]

Planning Pointer. The planner's client is generally the settlor. Therefore, the planner's goal is to ensure that the trustee is precluded from paying out trust assets to the settlor's creditors to avoid personal liability, as this would be contrary to the asset protection plan's objectives. To do this, the planner must ensure that property placed into the trust will not be subjected to the reach of the settlor's creditors. For example, the planner may conclude that by placing property into an irrevocable trust, the property is placed outside the reach of future creditors of the settlor. Conversely, the planner may conclude such future creditors could reach the property if placed into a revocable trust. Under such circumstances, the planner should use an irrevocable trust.

[B] Settlor Liability

Because the settlor is generally the asset protection planner's client, planners should be most concerned with the settlor's liability exposure. The first step of the planner's analysis involves determining whether the transfer to the trust constitutes a fraudulent conveyance.[8] If the transfer constitutes a fraudulent conveyance, creditors generally can reach the transferred property even if the settlor is not a beneficiary. For example, if the settlor conveys property to the trust without receiving any consideration and was insolvent at the time of the conveyance or because of the conveyance, the transfer generally constitutes a fraudulent conveyance.[9] Here, creditors may sue to have the trust set aside and the trust assets made available to satisfy their judgments,[10] to have trust

---

[6] *Probate & Trust Division Committee D-3 on Special Problems of Fiduciaries, Creditors' Rights Against Trust Assets*, 22 Real Prop. Prob. & Tr. J. 735, 736 (1987); James R. Wade, *Surcharge Litigation-Miscellaneous Aspects*, 16 Real Prop. Prob. & Tr. J. 760, 764 (1981).

[7] *Probate & Trust Division Committee D-3 on Special Problems of Fiduciaries, Creditors' Rights Against Trust Assets*, 22 Real Prop. Prob. & Tr. J. 735, 736 (1987).

[8] *See* Chapter 2.

[9] Austin Wakeman Scott & William Franklin Fratcher, The Law of Trusts § 330.12 (4th ed. 1987). *See, e.g.,* United States v. Sherlock, 1996 U.S. Dist. LEXIS 1087, 96-2 U.S. Tax. Cas. (CCH) ¶ 50,462 (E.D. La. 1996) (the U.S. District Court held that an individual's transfer of his residence to a domestic "family preservation trust" while he had substantial tax liabilities outstanding was in fraud of the IRS's rights, and consequently, the IRS could foreclose on such property).

[10] George Gleason Bogert & George Taylor Bogert, The Law of Trusts and Trustees § 211 (rev. 2d ed. 1992); Harper v. Atlanta Mill Co., 48 S.E.2d 89 (Ga. 1948).

property made available to satisfy their judgments without setting aside the trust,[11] or asserting a constructive trust with regard to the property.[12]

Planning Pointer. Planners should refer to Chapter 2, Fraudulent Conveyance Concepts, to ensure that transfers do not constitute fraudulent conveyances.

All states have enacted fraudulent conveyance statutes. Generally, these statutes void the following transfers:

1. Transfers made with actual intent to hinder, delay, or defraud either present or future creditors;[13]
2. Transfers that occur when transferors are insolvent on the transfer date or that cause transferors to become insolvent;[14]
3. Transfers that occur when transferors engage in or are about to engage in a business or transaction for which the property remaining in their hands after the conveyance constitutes an unreasonably small amount of capital;[15] or
4. Transfers that occur when transferors intend or believe that they will incur debts beyond their ability to pay such debts as they mature.[16]

Planning Pointer. Planners must ensure that transfers do not constitute fraudulent conveyances.[17] Not only would this entail litigation for the client, but it could entail litigation for the planner as well.[18]

---

[11] George Gleason Bogert & George Taylor Bogert, The Law of Trusts and Trustees § 211 (rev. 2d ed. 1992). *See, e.g.*, Sackin v. Kersting, 466 P.2d 758 (Ariz.), *reh'g denied*, 468 P.2d 925 (Ariz. 1970).

[12] Mesa Petroleum Co. v. Coniglio, 629 F.2d 1022 (5th Cir. 1980); George Gleason Bogert & George Taylor Bogert, The Law of Trusts and Trustees § 211 (rev. 2d ed. 1992).

[13] *See, e.g.*, UFCA § 7, 7A U.L.A. 113 (1918).

[14] *See, e.g.*, UFCA § 4, 7A U.L.A. 67 (1918).

[15] *See, e.g.*, UFCA § 5, 7A U.L.A. 105 (1918).

[16] *See, e.g.*, UFCA § 6, 7A U.L.A. 110 (1918).

[17] The case of United States v. Sherlock, 1996 U.S. Dist. LEXIS 1087, 96-2 U.S. Tax. Cas. (CCH) ¶ 50,462 (E.D. La. 1996), illustrates what can happen when the asset protection client's funding of an irrevocable domestic asset protection trust constitutes a fraudulent conveyance. In *Sherlock*, the U.S. District Court held that an individual's transfer of his residence to a domestic "family preservation trust" while he had substantial tax liabilities outstanding was in fraud of the IRS's rights, and consequently, the IRS could foreclose on such property. Specifically, in *Sherlock*, Richard was a self-employed salesman of industrial products. Beginning in 1982, Richard was continuously involved in substantial tax litigation with the IRS. This litigation involved, among other things, his failure to file income tax returns for 1975 through 1984, and his failure to report commission and interest income.

[18] The planner should refer to Chapter 2, which discusses fraudulent conveyances in greater detail.

Planning Pointer. To ensure that transfers to a trust do not constitute fraudulent conveyances, planners should take the following steps:

1. The planner should ensure that the transferor is solvent when the transfer occurs and does not become insolvent because of the transfer. The planner must examine local law for the applicable definition of insolvency and ideally should obtain a recent audited personal financial statement from the client, which the planner should analyze under local law. For example, local law may define insolvency so that, if the transaction leaves the transferor with insufficient funds to pay his or her debts as they come due, it falls within the local law definition of insolvency. Here, the planner should consider including a provision in the trust instrument that would require the trust to distribute funds to the settlor in the event that judgments against the settlor, stemming from obligations outstanding at the time of the transfer to the trust, exceed the settlor's remaining net worth after the transfer.
2. The planner should structure the transfer so that it includes as few badges of fraud as possible.[19] This minimizes the risk that the transfer will be deemed to be in pursuit of a plan to hinder, delay, or defraud creditors (*i.e.*, actual intent fraud).
3. The planner should obtain assurance that the client does not have the intent, at the time of the transfer to the trust, to engage in a new transaction or business for which its remaining capital will constitute an unreasonably small capital. The planner should thoroughly interview the client about this issue and should obtain an affidavit from the client to this effect.
4. The planner should ensure that the client does not intend or believe that she will incur debts beyond her ability to pay. Here again, the planner should thoroughly interview the client about this issue and should obtain an affidavit to this effect.

EXAMPLE 5-1

Alice Accountant is a solo practitioner C.P.A. On May 31, 2000, Alice's largest audit client, F Co, Inc., discloses that it has been the subject of massive fraud and will be going out of business. On August 15, 2000, Wilma Widow, F Co, Inc.'s largest shareholder, sues Alice for malpractice concerning the F Co, Inc. audit. Wilma wins a $20 million judgment against Alice on December 31, 2000. On January 5, 2001, Alice establishes an irrevocable trust, the Accountant Trust, and transfers $12 million of assets into the Accountant Trust. The trust beneficiary is Alice's son, Sam. Immediately before the transfer, Alice owns

---

[19] *See* Chapter 2 for a detailed discussion of the badges of fraud.

assets of $12 million and has outstanding liabilities of $2 million, for a net worth of $10 million. Immediately after the transfer, Alice has a negative net worth of $2 million. Here, Alice's transfer of property to the trust constitutes a fraudulent conveyance. Therefore, Wilma can successfully attack Alice's transfer to the trust as a fraudulent conveyance and, thus, she can collect on her judgment.

When settlors are also beneficiaries of the trust, their creditors can generally reach their beneficial interests.[20] Therefore, the settlor's beneficial interest will generally not be protected. When settlors retain beneficial interests in trusts that include spendthrift provisions[21] such spendthrift clauses are generally not valid against the settlor's present and future creditors.[22]

EXAMPLE 5-2

Same facts as Example 5-1, except that Alice establishes the Accountant Trust in 1985 and contributes regularly into it as part of an estate administration plan. Furthermore, Alice retains a life interest in the trust, by which she receives all the trust income each year. The Accountant Trust always earns $1 million of income each year. At December 31, 2000, the trust corpus equals $50 million. Here, Wilma may reach Alice's life interest in the trust. Therefore, this amount is not protected.

EXAMPLE 5-3

Same facts as Example 5-2, except that the Accountant Trust is a spendthrift trust. Here the result is the same as in Example 5-2.

Planning Pointer. The planner must balance the client's need to receive trust income or to use trust property against the loss of asset protection that results from a retained beneficial interest in the trust.

---

[20] Austin Wakeman Scott & William Franklin Fratcher, The Law of Trusts §§ 147, 330.12 (4th ed. 1987); George T. Bogert, Trusts § 39 (6th ed. 1987). However, *see* the discussion of Alaska- and Delaware-type asset protection trusts, discussed in § 5.14.

[21] *See* § 5.09.

[22] Harrison v. City Nat'l Bank, 210 F. Supp. 362 (S.D. Iowa 1962); Wilmington Trust Co. v. Carpenter, 75 A.2d 815 (Del. Ch. 1950); Glass v. Carpenter, 330 S.W.2d 530 (Tex. Civ. App. 1959); Procter v. Woodhouse, 241 A.2d 785 (Vt. 1968); Austin Wakeman Scott & William Franklin Fratcher, The Law of Trusts § 156 (4th ed. 1987); George T. Bogert, Trusts § 40 (6th ed. 1987); Restatement (Second) of Trusts § 156 (1957).

Planning Pointer. Alaska, Delaware, and a few other states have enacted statutes that protect assets from the claims of the settlor's creditors under certain circumstances, where those assets are held by Alaska or Delaware asset protection trusts.[23]

If the settlor not only retains a beneficial interest, but also retains a general power of appointment, creditors can generally reach all trust property.[24]

EXAMPLE 5-4

Same facts as Example 5-2, except Alice also retains a general power of appointment over the trust corpus, which if Alice does not exercise goes to her heirs by default under the trust instrument. Here, Wilma may recover her $20 million judgment out of the Accountant Trust corpus.

Planning Pointer. The planner must ensure that the client never retains both a beneficial interest plus a general power of appointment over the trust corpus. Failure to follow this advice destroys the asset protection benefits of a revocable trust.

When the settlor merely retains the right to revoke the trust, but does not retain any beneficial interest or general power of appointment, the majority rule is that her creditors cannot reach the trust corpus.[25] In other words, the settlor's creditors cannot compel her to revoke the trust for their benefit.[26] On the other hand, many courts hold that the settlor's creditors may reach the trust corpus when the settlor retains the power to revoke the

---

[23] *See* § 5.14.

[24] Ward v. Marie, 68 A. 1084 (N.J. Ch. 1907); Benedict v. Benedict, 104 A. 581 (Pa. 1918); Morton v. Morton, 147 A.2d 150 (Pa. 1959); Austin Wakeman Scott & William

Franklin Fratcher, The Law of Trusts §§ 147.3, 156 (4th ed. 1987); Restatement (Second) of Trusts § 156 cmt. c (1957).

[25] Austin Wakeman Scott & William Franklin Fratcher, The Law of Trusts § 330.12 (4th ed. 1987); George Gleason Bogert & George Taylor Bogert, The Law of Trusts and Trustees § 233 (rev. 2d ed. 1992); L. Henry Gissel, Jr. & Karen R. Schiller, *Trusts Made Easy: A Simplified Overview of the Reasons for Creating, Modifying, and Terminating Express Trusts*, 10 Prob. L. J. 241 (1991); *Probate & Trust Division Committee D-3 on Special Problems of Fiduciaries, Creditors' Rights Against Trust Assets*, 22 Real Prop. Prob. & Tr. J. 735, 739 (1987); Lawrence Berger, *The General Power of Appointment as an Interest in Property*, 40 Neb. L. Rev. 104 (1960); Note, *Creditor's Ability to Reach Assets under a General Power of Appointment*, 24 Vand. L. Rev. 367 (1971). *See, e.g.,* Jones v. Clifton, 101 U.S. 225 (1879); Guthrie v. Canty, 53 N.E.2d 1009 (Mass. 1944); Abruzzese v. Oestrich, 47 A.2d 883 (N.J. Ch. 1946).

[26] Austin Wakeman Scott & William Franklin Fratcher, The Law of Trusts § 330.12 (4th ed. 1987); Restatement (Second) of Trusts § 330 cmt. o (1959); Richard W. Effland, *Rights of Creditors in Nonprobate Assets*, 48 Mo. L. Rev. 431 (1983); Notes and Comments, *Rights of a Creditor of a Settlor to Reach the Corpus of a Revocable Trust*, 39 Ky. L.J. 131 (1950).

trust.[27] Additionally, some jurisdictions have enacted statutes providing that settlors retaining absolute or unqualified powers to revoke trusts are deemed the absolute owner of the trust property to satisfy creditor claims.[28] Where such statutes exist, the settlor's creditors can reach the trust corpus.

Planning Pointer. Many commentators believe that revocable trusts provide little or no asset protection benefits.[29] They base this belief on the theory that a court would force the settlor to revoke such a trust in favor of creditors. However, some commentators do believe that revocable trusts constitute a valuable asset protection tool.[30] Although the amount of asset protection that revocable trusts provide is not clear, it does appear that irrevocable trusts provide substantially more asset protection than revocable trusts. Therefore, to obtain the maximum amount of asset protection, the planner should use irrevocable trusts.

[1] Spousal Rights

Planners also must consider possible claims of the settlor's surviving spouse or of a spouse who is divorced from the settlor. Specifically, spouses may assert the following claims against the trust:

1. That the transfer of property into the trust constituted a fraudulent conveyance;
2. That the transfer of property to the trust was illusory;
3. An election to claim a surviving spouse's elective share of the settlor's estate, which may include certain inter vivos trust property; or
4. Fraud in the inducement of marriage.[31]

---

[27] State St. Bank & Trust Co. v. Reiser, 389 N.E.2d 768 (Mass. 1979); Johnson v. Commercial Bank, 588 P.2d 1096, 1099 (Or. 1978); *In re* Kovalyshyn's Estate, 343 A.2d 852 (N.J. Super. Ct. 1975); Restatement of Property § 328 (1940); Austin Wakeman Scott & William Franklin Fratcher, The Law of Trusts § 330.12 (4th ed. 1987); George Gleason Bogert & George Taylor Bogert, The Law of Trusts and Trustees § 233 (rev. 2d ed. 1992); L. Henry Gissel, Jr. & Karen R. Schiller, *Trusts Made Easy: A Simplified Overview of the Reasons for Creating, Modifying, and Terminating Express Trusts*, 10 Prob. L.J. 241 (1991).

[28] Ala. Code § 35-4-290 (1975); Cal. Prob. Code § 18200 (Deering 1991); N.Y. Est. Powers & Trusts Law § 10-10.6 (McKinney 1981 & Supp. 1993). *See* George Gleason Bogert & George Taylor Bogert, The Law of Trusts and Trustees § 233 (rev. 2d ed. 1992).

[29] *See, e.g.,* Santo (Sandy) Bisignano, Jr., Protecting Assets from Overzealous Creditors or an Estate Planner's Guide to Preservation Planning, 1987 Annual Notre Dame Est. Plan. Inst. 3–40.

[30] *See, e.g.,* L. Henry Gissel, Jr. & Karen R. Schiller, *Trusts Made Easy: A Simplified Overview of the Reasons for Creating, Modifying, and Terminating Express Trusts*, 10 Prob. L.J. 241 (1991); James F. Farr & Jackson W. Wright, Jr., An Estate Planner's Handbook § 18 (1979 & Supp.1989).

[31] *Probate & Trust Division Committee D-3 on Special Problems of Fiduciaries, Creditors' Rights Against Trust Assets,* 22 Real Prop. Prob. & Tr. J. 735, 743 (1987); E. LeFevre, Annotation, *Gift or other voluntary*

First, if the transfer constitutes a fraudulent conveyance as to a spouse, then the defrauded spouse can reach the transferred trust corpus under the fraudulent conveyance doctrine.[32] Factors that courts frequently focus on in marital rights cases include the portion of the settlor's property transferred, the proximity of the transfer to the death or divorce date, any provisions made by the settlor for the spouse, the settlor's relationship to the trust beneficiaries, and participation by the trust beneficiaries in the transfer.[33]

Second, if the settlor retains excessive control, a court may find that the transfer of property to the trust was "illusory." A court may find a transfer to the trust illusory when the settlor retains excessive control over the trust property.[34]

EXAMPLE 5-5

Bronte, an oil wildcatter, marries Charlotte. The day after their marriage, Bronte hits oil, which provides him with approximately $6 million of after-tax cash flow annually. Before the marriage, Bronte has a net worth of $1 million and Charlotte has a net worth of $15,000. After their marriage, Bronte begins transferring $6 million each year into the Bronte Trust, a newly created trust. Bronte retains the right to alter or amend the trust, the right to receive all trust income for life, and a general power of appointment over the remainder interest. Five years later, Charlotte learns that Bronte has been committing adultery throughout the course of their marriage, and she begins divorce proceedings. At this time the Bronte Trust holds $36,630,000 of assets, and Bronte personally holds $1 million of assets. Bronte argues that only the $1 million of assets he personally holds is available for an equitable distribution between the spouses. Consequently, he argues that the $36 million trust corpus is not available for equitable distribution. Here Charlotte may argue that Bronte's transfer of assets to the trust was illusory because of the powers he retains. Consequently, the trust corpus should be made available for

---

transfer by husband as fraud on wife, 49 A.L.R.2d 521 (1963); Annotation, *Validity of inter vivos trust established by one spouse which impairs the other spouse's distributive share or other statutory rights in property*, 39 A.L.R.3d 14(1971 & Supp. 1995); Annotation, *Gift or other voluntary transfer by husband as fraud on wife*, 49 A.L.R.2d 521 (1956); Annotation, *Inclusion of funds in savings bank trust (Totten trust) in determining surviving spouse's interest in decedent's estate*, 64 A.L.R.3d 187 (1975 & Supp. 1995); Annotation, *Surviving spouse's right to marital share as affected by valid contract to convey by will*, 85 A.L.R.4th 418 (1991 & Supp. 1995); Annotation, *Validity of trust created by nontestamentary instrument reserving benefit to settlor for life with power of revocation*, 32 A.L.R.2d 1270 (1953).

[32] *See* Chapter 2; Kasinski v. Questel, 472 N.Y.S.2d 807 (N.Y. App. Div. 1984).

[33] Hanke v. Hanke, 459 A.2d 246 (N.H. 1983); Norris v. Barbour, 51 S.E.2d 334 (Va. 1949); *Probate & Trust Division Committee D-3 on Special Problems of Fiduciaries, Creditors' Rights Against Trust Assets*, 22 Real Prop. Prob. & Tr. J. 735, 743 (1987); W.D. MacDonald, Fraud on the Widow's Share (1960); 37 Am. Jur. 2d Fraudulent Conveyances § 10 (1987).

[34] *Probate & Trust Division Committee D-3 on Special Problems of Fiduciaries, Creditors' Rights Against Trust Assets*, 22 Real Prop. Prob. 4 Tr. J. 735, 743 (1987); W.D. MacDonald, Fraud on the Widow's Share (1960).

equitable distribution between the spouses. The planner should note that Charlotte could alternatively argue that the trust corpus should be made available for equitable distribution because Bronte retains the power to revoke the trust in conjunction with a general power of appointment over the trust corpus.

Third, concerning surviving spouses, the planner must consider whether trust assets should be included in the settlor's estate for purposes of determining the surviving spouse's statutory share of the settlor's estate.[35] The law concerning this issue varies greatly from state to state. Many states have enacted § 2-202 of the Uniform Probate Code. This provision provides that the augmented estate includes assets in trusts in which the settlor retains the power of revocation for purposes of determining the amount of the surviving spouse's elective or statutory share.[36] Therefore, in these states, property contained within revocable trusts will be reachable by the settlor's surviving spouse. Other states have enacted statutes that have the same general effect as § 2-202 of the Uniform Probate Code.[37]

In jurisdictions that have not enacted statutory provisions, the courts have reached differing results. One view holds that property conveyed into a revocable trust is not considered when determining the spouse's statutory or elective share of the estate.[38] Many other courts, however, hold that the settlor's transfer of assets to a revocable trust either constitutes a fraud on the surviving spouse's marital rights, or that the transfer is illusory. Therefore, these courts include such property in the surviving spouses statutory election calculation.[39]

---

[35] See J.R. Kemper, Annotation, *Validity of inter vivos trust established by one spouse which impairs the other spouse's distributive share or other statutory rights in property*, 39 A.L.R.3d 14 (1971); J.R. Kemper, Annotation, *Inclusion of funds in savings bank trust (Totten trust) in determining surviving spouse's interest in decedent's estate*, 64 A.L.R.3d 187(1985); Patricia J. Roberts, *The 1990 Uniform Probate Code's Elective Share Provisions—West Virginia's Enactment Paves the Way*, 95 W. Va. L. Rev. 55 (1992); Margaret V. Turano, *UPC Section 2-201: Equal Treatment of Spouses?* 55 Alb. L. Rev. 983 (1992); Lawrence W. Waggoner, *Spousal Rights in Our Multiple-Marriage Society: The Revised Uniform Probate Code*, 26 Real Prop. Prob. & Tr. J. 683 (1992); James F. Walsh, Note, *The Effect of Divorce on the Beneficiary Rights to a Nonprobate Asset*, 7 Conn. Prob. L.J. 163 (1992) (analyzes impact of divorce on nonprobate assets naming a former spouse); Ira M. Bloom, *The Treatment of Trust and Other Partial Interests of the Surviving Spouse Under the Redesigned Elective-Share System: Some Concerns and Suggestions*, 55 Alb. L. Rev. 941 (1992) (focuses on spouse's rights as income beneficiary for life and addresses valuation problems, disclaimed property, and separate property).

[36] U.P.C. § 2-202, 8 U.L.A. 75–77 (1969); R.U.P.C. § 2-202 (1990), 8 U.L.A. 90–92 (Supp. 1992).

[37] See George T. Bogert, Trusts § 48 (6th ed. 1987). See, e.g., N.Y. Est. Powers & Trusts Law § 51.1(b)(1) (McKinney 1981 & Supp. 1993); Pa. Cons. Stat. Ann. § 2203 (1992).

[38] See George Gleason Bogert & George Taylor Bogert, The Law of Trusts and Trustees §§ 211, 233 (rev. 2d ed. 1992); George T. Bogert, Trusts § 48 (6th ed. 1987); Restatement (Second) of Trusts § 57 cmt. e (1957). See, e.g., Windsor v. Leonard, 475 F.2d 932 (D.C. Cir. 1973); Theodore v. Theodore, 249 N.E.2d 3 (Mass. 1969); Johnson v. LaGrange State Bank, 383 N.E.2d 185 (Ill. 1978); Leazenby v. Clinton County Bank & Trust Co., 355 N.E.2d 861 (Ind. Ct. App. 1976).

[39] See George Gleason Bogert & George Taylor Bogert, The Law of Trusts and Trustees §§ 211, 233 (rev. 2d ed. 1992); George T. Bogert, Trusts § 48 (6th ed. 1987); Restatement (Second) of Property (Donative Transfers) § 13.7, reporter's note (1982). See, e.g., Sullivan v. Burkin, 460 N.E.2d 572 (Mass. 1984);

Fourth, if the settlor enters an antenuptial or postnuptial agreement before a conveyance to a trust that was made in contemplation of marriage and that violates a promise or representation made within the antenuptial or postnuptial agreement, the conveyance may be fraudulent. Alternatively, a court may consider such a conveyance to be contrary to public policy or illusory due to the nature of the control retained by the settlor.[40]

Caution. If the planner or client fails to follow proper formalities, a court may disregard a trust as constituting a sham transaction.[41]

EXAMPLE 5-6

William and Harriet are engaged to be married on April 1, 2000. On March 1, Harriet has a net worth of $100 million. On March 15, Harriet creates a revocable trust with herself as life beneficiary and conveys property worth $95 million into the trust. Harriet retains the power to direct the trustee to pay all or any portion of the principal as Harriet might direct and the power to change beneficiaries. Harriet also reserves the power to manage, pay taxes on, borrow against, direct the sale and investment of, and use the trust corpus. Here, if Harriet lacks actual intent to defraud William of his marital rights, the transfer is valid and William lacks rights in the trust corpus.[42]

EXAMPLE 5-7

Same facts as Example 5-6, except that William and Harriet enter a prenuptial agreement on March 1 by which Harriet represents to William that (1) she has a net worth of $100 million, and (2) she will leave $$$25 percent of her estate to William under her will. Here, Harriet runs the risk that her conveyance of property to the trust will be considered fraudulent.[43]

Ackers v. First Nat'l Bank of Topeka, 387 P.2d 840 (Kan. 1963), *reh'g denied*, 389 P.2d 1 (Kan. 1964); Sherrill v. Mallicote, 417 S.W.2d 798 (Tenn. Ct. App. 1967).

[40] *See* George Gleason Bogert & George Taylor Bogert, The Law of Trusts and Trustees § 211 (rev. 2d ed. 1992).

[41] *See, e.g., In re* Gillespie, 269 B.R. 383 (Bankr. E.D. Ark. 2001) (U.S. Bankruptcy Court for the Eastern District of Arkansas held that an irrevocable trust into which debtor placed all her assets and most of her husband's assets, and in which she commingled the assets of several corporations held by the trust without regard for trust or corporate formalities, constituted a sham and must be disregarded).

[42] Rose v. Rose, 1 N.W.2d 458 (Mich. 1942).

[43] Dublin v. Wise, 354 N.E.2d 403 (Ill. App. Ct. 1976).

Concerning divorce, courts may treat transfers made to third parties before a divorce as part of the marital estate. Consequently, such property would then be subject to equitable division between the spouses.[44]

EXAMPLE 5-8

Same facts as Example 5-6, except that Harriet establishes the trust on August 1, 2002, and Harriet begins divorce proceedings against William on August 20, 2002. Here, Harriet runs the risk that her conveyance of property to the trust will be considered fraudulent.[45]

[2] Bankruptcy

Generally, when a settlor enters bankruptcy,[46] the bankruptcy estate acquires all of the settlor's legal and equitable interests in property at the time that the bankruptcy proceeding commences.[47] The bankruptcy estate acquires such interests regardless of any provisions in agreements, transfer instruments, or any applicable nonbankruptcy law that restricts or conditions the transfer of such property interest by the debtor.[48] Any beneficial interests in trusts that the settlor retains constitute equitable interests for purposes of the Bankruptcy Code.[49] This rule also applies if the settlor creates a spendthrift trust for her own benefit.[50]

EXAMPLE 5-9

Sam Settlor establishes a revocable trust, the SS Trust, in 2000 as part of an estate and asset protection plan. He retains a life interest and gives the re-

---

[44] Shannon v. Shannon, 680 S.W.2d 367 (Mo. Ct. App. 1984); Rosenberg v. Rosenberg, 497 A.2d 485 (Md. Ct. Spec. App.), *cert. denied*, 501 A.2d 845 (Md. 1985); Kessel v. Kessel, 370 N.W.2d 889 (Minn. Ct. App. 1985); see George Gleason Bogert & George Taylor Bogert, The Law of Trusts and Trustees § 211 (rev. 2d ed. 1992).

[45] *In re* Marriage of Frederick, 578 N.E.2d 612 (Ill. App. Ct. 1991).

[46] For a detailed discussion of the Bankruptcy Code, *see* J. Pearson et al., Drafting Bankruptcy Reorganization Plans (John Wiley & Sons, 2d ed. 1993); Advanced Chapter 11 Bankruptcy Practice (Thomas J. Salerno & Craig D. Hansen eds., John Wiley & Sons 1987 & Supp. 1990); Grant W. Newton & Gilbert D. Bloom, Bankruptcy & Insolvency Taxation (John Wiley & Sons 1991); Lewis D. Solomon & Lewis J. Saret, Business Workout Planning Strategies Ch. 2 (John Wiley & Sons 1992).

[47] 11 U.S.C. § 541(a)(1).

[48] 11 U.S.C. § 541(c)(1)(A).

[49] 11 U.S.C. § 541(a); *Probate & Trust Division Committee D-3 on Special Problems of Fiduciaries, Creditors' Rights Against Trust Assets,* 22 Real Prop. Prob. & Tr. J. 735, 746 (1987).

[50] 11 U.S.C. § 541(c)(1)(A), (B); *Probate & Trust Division Committee D-3 on Special Problems of Fiduciaries, Creditors' Rights Against Trust Assets,* 22 Real Prop. Prob. & Tr. J. 735, 746 (1987). *See, e.g., In re* Dias, 37 B.R. 584 (Bankr. D. Idaho 1984).

mainder interest to his daughter, Dolly. He contributes $1 million of marketable securities in 2000. Sam receives approximately $100,000 from the trust each year. In 2005 Sam becomes a partner in the Aggressive Accounting Firm. In 2010 the Aggressive Accounting Firm becomes the subject of several lawsuits stemming from audits of bankrupt savings and loan associations. Sam's liability exposure from these lawsuits equals approximately $100 million, which greatly exceeds his net worth. Consequently, Sam files for bankruptcy protection in 2010. Here, Sam's life interest in the SS Trust inures to the benefit of the bankruptcy estate.

The bankruptcy trustee acquires the bankrupt settlor's ability to exercise her power of revocation.[51] Therefore, if this power is a general power of revocation, the bankruptcy trustee may revoke the trust. This would cause the trust corpus to revert to the settlor's bankruptcy estate. If the settlor also retains a power of appointment, the bankruptcy trustee also acquires this power.[52]

EXAMPLE 5-10

Same facts as Example 5-9, except that the trust is a revocable trust and the bankruptcy trustee exercises the right to revoke the trust. This causes the $1 million trust corpus to revert to the bankruptcy estate. Consequently, this devastates Sam's estate and asset protection plan.

Planning Pointer. Planners must note that retaining an unqualified power of revocation opens the door for creditors to reach the corpus of a revocable trust. For this reason, planners should generally avoid revocable trusts. When using a revocable trust, planners should limit the settlor's power of revocation by making it exercisable only when exercised by the settlor in conjunction with an independent person or under certain circumstances. When the trust instrument provides that the power of revocation may be exercised in a specific manner or subject to certain conditions precedent, these limitations generally control.[53] Furthermore, the Bankruptcy Code

---

[51] *See Probate & Trust Division Committee D-3 on Special Problems of Fiduciaries, Creditors' Rights Against Trust Assets,* 22 Real Prop. Prob. & Tr. J. 735, 746 (1987); Restatement (Second) of Trusts § 330 cmt. o (1939); George T. Bogert, Trusts § 48 (6th ed. 1987). *See, e.g.,* Jones v. Clifton, 101 U.S. 225 (1879); Murphey v. C.I.T. Corp., 33 A.2d 16 (Pa. 1943); Chase Nat'l Bank v. Ginnel, 50 N.Y.S.2d 345 (Sup. Ct. 1944).

[52] *See Probate & Trust Division Committee D-3 on Special Problems of Fiduciaries, Creditors' Rights Against Trust Assets,* 22 Real Prop. Prob. & Tr. J. 735, 746 (1987); Restatement (Second) of Trusts § 330 cmt. o (1939).

[53] George T. Bogert, Trusts § 48 (6th ed. 1987); Worthington v. Rich, 26 A. 403 (Md. 1893); Kelley v. Snow, 70 N.E. 89 (Mass. 1904).

provides that the bankruptcy estate does not include any power (*e.g.,* power of revocation or appointment) the settlor/debtor may exercise entirely for the benefit of other persons.[54]

Planners should note that, for the bankruptcy trustee to access the trust corpus, the trustee must begin such an action during the settlor's life. Otherwise, the bankruptcy trustee cannot access the trust corpus.[55]

[3] Effect of Illegal Purpose Trust

If a court finds that the settlor established a trust for an illegal purpose (to defraud creditors or a spouse), the claimant can ask the court to set aside the trust. When this occurs, the purported trust's property reverts to the settlor, and her creditors or spouse can then reach the property.[56] If the trust is not attached, then innocent beneficiaries may request a court to grant them performance of the trust as long as the trust's performance does not enable the innocent parties to profit from the illegality.[57] Conversely, if the trust's performance would advance the accomplishment of the illegal objectives, then courts generally do not grant performance of the trust.[58] When the trust serves several purposes, only one of which is illegal, then if the different objectives can be separated and the valid purpose can be effected without effecting the illegal purpose, the trust will be so enforced.[59]

[C] *Beneficiary Liability*

Generally, absent a valid spendthrift trust provision[60] or a controlling statute to the contrary, creditors of trust beneficiaries may reach a beneficiary's trust interest to satisfy their claims.[61] If the debtor is the sole trust beneficiary and is entitled to an immediate conveyance of the corpus, creditors may request a court to order a sale of the corpus. The court then pays the creditor's claims out of the proceeds.[62] If the beneficiary/debtor is not the sole beneficiary, the creditor cannot reach the trust corpus unless this can be done without interfering with

---

[54] 11 U.S.C. § 541(b).

[55] *See Probate & Trust Division Committee D-3 on Special Problems of Fiduciaries, Creditors' Rights Against Trust Assets,* 22 Real Prop. Prob. & Tr. J. 735, 747 (1987); Richard W. Effland, *Rights of Creditors in Nonprobate Assets,* 48 Mo. L. Rev. 331, 441 (1983).

[56] George T. Bogert, Trusts § 48 (6th ed. 1987); Brundage v. Cheneworth, 70 N.W. 211 (Iowa 1897).

[57] George T. Bogert, Trusts § 48 (6th ed. 1987).

[58] Pace v. Wainwright, 10 So. 2d 755 (Ala. 1942); Murphy v. Murphy, 213 S.W.2d 601 (Ky. 1948); George T. Bogert, Trusts § 48 (6th ed. 1987).

[59] Younger v. Moore, 103 P. 221 (Cal. 1909); Culross v. Gibbons, 29 N.E. 839 (N.Y. 1892); George T. Bogert, Trusts § 48 (6th ed. 1987).

[60] *See* § 5.09.

[61] George T. Bogert, Trusts § 39 (6th Ed. 1987); Austin Wakeman Scott & William Franklin Fratcher, The Law of Trusts § 147–147.3 (4th ed. 1987).

[62] George T. Bogert, Trusts § 39 (6th ed. 1987); Austin Wakeman Scott & William Franklin Fratcher, The Law of Trusts § 147.2 (4th ed. 1987).

the other beneficiaries' rights. If this cannot be done without interfering with the rights of other beneficiaries, the creditor can only reach the beneficiary's equitable interest in the trust.[63]

If the beneficiary has a life estate only, the creditor may request a court to order the sale of the life interest. However, courts generally do not order such a sale when it would cause a hardship on the beneficiary and the life interest is sufficient to satisfy the debt within a reasonable amount of time.[64]

If the beneficiary has a future interest only, courts generally order a sale of the future interest unless it is so indefinite or contingent that it cannot be sold with fairness to creditors.[65] However, in rare cases a court may give the creditor only a charge or mortgage on the future interest.[66]

When the beneficiary enters bankruptcy, the bankruptcy estate acquires the beneficiary's trust interest.[67] However, the bankruptcy estate does not acquire any power that the debtor may exercise solely for the benefit of another person.[68] Also, restrictions on transfers of beneficial interests of a nonsettlor beneficiary/debtor in a trust that are enforceable under applicable nonbankruptcy law are enforceable for purposes of the Bankruptcy Code.[69] Therefore, spendthrift provisions are generally effective for nonsettlor beneficiaries.

[1] Donees of Powers of Appointment

When settlors grant a special power to appoint among a group of individuals, that power is not considered beneficial to the donee. Thus, such a power cannot be reached by the donee's creditors.[70]

EXAMPLE 5-11

Daphne and Rebecca are sisters. Daphne, as part of an asset protection plan, contributes one-half of her entire estate, worth $50 million, to an irrevocable

---

[63] Austin Wakeman Scott & William Franklin Fratcher, The Law of Trusts § 147.2 (4th ed. 1987).

[64] Id.

[65] George T. Bogert, Trusts § 39 (6th ed. 1987); Austin Wakeman Scott & William Franklin Fratcher, The Law of Trusts § 147.2 (4th ed. 1987).

[66] Austin Wakeman Scott & William Franklin Fratcher, The Law of Trusts § 147.2 (4th ed. 1987).

[67] 11 U.S.C. § 541; George T. Bogert, Trusts § 39 (6th ed. 1987); Austin Wakeman Scott & William Franklin Fratcher, The Law of Trusts § 147.1 (4th ed. 1987). *See, e.g.,* Horton v. Moore, 110 F.2d 189 (6th Cir.), *cert. denied,* 311 U.S. 692, *reh'g denied,* 311 U.S. 728 (1940); *In re* Dolard, 275 F. Supp. 1001 (C.D. Cal. 1967).

[68] 11 U.S.C. § 541(b)(1).

[69] 11 U.S.C. § 541(c)(2); Austin Wakeman Scott & William Franklin Fratcher, The Law of Trusts § 147.1 (4th ed. 1987).

[70] Restatement of Property § 326 (1940); Charles C. Callahan & W. Barton Leach, Powers of Appointment, in American Law of Property § 23.15 (A. James Casner ed., 1952); Restatement (Second) of Property (Donative Transfers) § 13.1 (1982); Austin Wakeman Scott & William Franklin Fratcher, The Law of Trusts § 147.3 (4th ed. 1987); *see generally* Sheldon F. Kurtz, *Powers of Appointment Under the 1990 Uniform Probate Code: What Was Done—What Remains to Be Done,* 55 Alb. L. Rev. 1151 (1992) (discusses Uniform Probate Code provisions regarding powers of appointment and impact of certain events, such as divorce, on creation of powers of appointment).

trust, the Family Trust. Daphne retains a life interest in the Family Trust and gives a special power of appointment over the trust corpus to Rebecca. Under the special power of appointment, Rebecca can appoint the trust corpus among Daphne's three sons, Benjamin, Thomas, and George.

Ten years later, Chaucer sues Rebecca and wins a $100 million judgment against her. Rebecca has no assets at this time. Therefore, Chaucer tries to reach the Family Trust corpus on the grounds that Rebecca has a power of appointment over the Family Trust corpus. Here, Chaucer will not be able reach the Family Trust corpus because Rebecca's power is limited to appointing the corpus among Daphne's three sons. Consequently, Rebecca's power is not beneficial to her and her creditors, including Chaucer, cannot reach the trust corpus.

When the power is a general power, including the power to appoint to the holder of the power, the power will be considered beneficial to the donee.[71] Several states have enacted statutes providing that creditors of such holders of general powers of appointment may reach the trust corpus that is the subject of such power.[72] However, in some states, when holders of such a general power of appointment do not exercise that power, their creditors generally cannot reach the trust corpus.[73] Of course, even in these states, if holders exercise the power in their own favor, their creditors may then reach the property. If the holder of the general power of appointment is also the settlor, his or her creditors generally may always reach the trust corpus.[74]

EXAMPLE 5-12

Same facts as Example 5-11, except that Rebecca is the settlor of the Family Trust, and she retains a general power of appointment, including the power to appoint to herself. Here, Chaucer can reach the Family Trust's corpus.

---

[71] Restatement of Property §§ 329, 330 (1940); Austin Wakeman Scott & William Franklin Fratcher, The Law of Trusts § 147.3 (4th ed. 1987); Charles C. Callahan & W. Barton Leach, Powers of Appointment, in American Law of Property § 23.16 (A. James Casner ed., 1952); Restatement (Second) of Property (Donative Transfers) § 13.4 (1982); Erwin N. Griswold, Spendthrift Trusts §§ 94–97 (2d ed. 1947).

[72] Austin Wakeman Scott & William Franklin Fratcher, The Law of Trusts § 147.3 (4th ed. 1987).

[73] Restatement of Property § 327 (1940); Restatement (Second) of Property (Donative Transfers) § 13.2 (1982); Note, *Creditors' Ability to Reach Assets under a General Power of Appointment*, 24 Vand. L. Rev. 367 (1971); Charles C. Callahan & W. Barton Leach, Powers of Appointment, in American Law of Property § 23.17 (A. James Casner ed., 1952); Austin Wakeman Scott & William Franklin Fratcher, The Law of Trusts § 147.3 (4th ed. 1987).

[74] Austin Wakeman Scott & William Franklin Fratcher, The Law of Trusts §§ 147.3, 156 (4th ed. 1987); Restatement (Second) of Trusts § 156 cmt. c (1957). *See, e.g.,* Ward v. Marie, 68 A. 1084 (N.J. Ch. 1907); Benedict v. Benedict, 104 A. 5 81 (Pa. 1918); Morton v. Morton, 147 A.2d 150 (Pa. 1959).

§5.03 INCOME TAXATION OF TRUSTS[1]

Planners must evaluate the income tax consequences of using trusts as part of an asset protection plan. Trusts other than grantor trusts[2] are generally treated as separate entities for income tax purposes. Notwithstanding this general principal however, because a trust may deduct any amount properly distributed or required to be distributed to its beneficiaries, and because such beneficiaries must include such distributions in their taxable income, a trust may effectively be taxed as a conduit.[3]

From a procedural standpoint, trusts must generally:

- File their own income tax return, (*i.e.,* a Form 1041);[4]
- Have their own taxpayer identification number;
- Use the calendar year as their taxable year, with the exception of charitable trusts.[5]

Caution. The Internal Revenue Code highly compresses the income tax rates for trusts. Specifically, the income tax rate schedule for trust income, for calendar years beginning in the year 2000 reaches the maximum rate of 39.6 percent when the trust's taxable income exceeds $8,650. This contrasts with the income tax rate schedule for individuals, for calendar years beginning in the year 2000, which reach the maximum rate of 39.6 percent when a single individual's taxable income exceeds $91,857.

As noted above, trusts may deduct amounts that they distribute, or are required to distribute, to their beneficiaries.[6] In this regard, Treasury Regulations distinguish between "simple" trusts and "complex" trusts. Simple trusts are those:

(a) Whose terms require them to distribute all of their income currently, and do not provide that any amounts may be paid, permanently set aside, or used in the taxable year for charitable purposes, and

(b) That do not make any distribution other than of current income.[7]

Trusts that can accumulate income, can make charitable distributions, and can distribute principal are called complex trusts.[8] Generally, for simple trusts, the

---

§5.03 [1] *See generally* Howard M. Zaritsky & Norman H. Lane, Federal Income Taxation of Estates and Trusts (2d ed.) for a complete discussion of the income taxation of domestic trusts.

[2] *See* §5.03[A].

[3] IRC §§651, 661.

[4] IRC §6012(a)(4).

[5] IRC §644.

[6] IRC §§651, 661.

[7] Treas. Reg. §1.651(a).

[8] Treas. Reg. §1.662(a)-1.

beneficiaries who receive the trust's income pay tax on the income the trust pays to them. In contrast, complex trusts pay income tax on all income not distributed to beneficiaries.

For beneficiaries who pay tax on trust distributions, the character of income that the trust realizes is preserved for the beneficiary, by means of the provisions in the Internal Revenue Code for Distributable Net Income (DNI).[9]

> **Planning Pointer.** Planners may reduce the income tax burden of trusts by investing their corpus in assets that do not generate taxable income, such as tax-exempt bonds.

[A] Grantor Trust Rules

Internal Revenue Code Sections 671 through 679 set forth the grantor trust rules. The grantor trust rules provide that under certain circumstances, the IRC will ignore a trust for income tax purposes and will treat all or part of its income, deductions, and credits as being included directly in the grantor's personal tax calculations.[10]

The grantor rules apply in the following six situations:

1. Where the grantor retains a reversionary interest in either the trust's corpus or income, if at the inception of that part of the trust, the value of that interest exceeds 5 percent of the value of such portion.[11]
2. Where the grantor retains the power to control the beneficial enjoyment of the trust without the consent of a nonadverse party.[12]
3. Where the grantor, the grantor's spouse, or any other nonadverse person holds certain administrative powers.[13]
4. Where the grantor, the grantor's spouse, or any other nonadverse party holds the power, exercisable without an adverse party's consent, to revoke the trust.[14]
5. Where the trust's income is or may be distributed (or held for future distribution) to the grantor or grantor's spouse, or may be used to pay the premiums on life insurance policies on the grantor or the grantor's spouse, without an adverse party's consent.[15]
6. Where the trust is a foreign trust, which has, or could have, directly or indirectly, a beneficiary who is a U.S. citizen or resident alien.[16]

---

[9] IRC § 643(a); Treas. Reg. §§ 1.643(a)-0 through 1.643(a)-7.
[10] IRC § 671.
[11] See § 5.03[A][1].
[12] See § 5.03[A][2].
[13] See § 5.03[A][3].
[14] See § 5.03[A][4].
[15] See § 5.04[A][5].
[16] See § 5.05[A][6].

[1] Reversionary and Remainder Interests

Under IRC Section 673, the grantor trust rules apply to any part of a trust to which the grantor retains a reversionary interest in either the trust's corpus or income, where, at the creation of that part of the trust, the value of that reversionary interest exceeds 5 percent of the value of such part. For this rule, the grantor is also treated as owning any part of the trust in which his spouse has a remainder interest that exceeds 5 percent of the value of the trust fund on the creation date.[17]

Although the Internal Revenue Code itself does not provide guidance on the valuation of reversionary or remainder interests for IRC Section 673 purposes, at least one commentator has stated that the same 5-percent valuation method the IRS applies under IRC Section 2037, which relates to the inclusion of certain retained reversionary interests in a grantor's gross estate, should apply here.[18]

Caution. IRS actuarial tables do not apply to terminally ill beneficiaries.[19] For this purpose, the IRS considers individuals who are known to have an incurable illness or other deteriorating physical condition to be terminally ill if there is at least a 50-percent probability they will die within one year. However, if such a person lives for 18 months or more, then the IRS presumes that he was not terminally ill on the valuation date.[20]

[2] Power to Control Beneficial Enjoyment

IRC Section 674 treats a grantor as the owner of any part of a trust over which the grantor, the grantor's spouse, or any nonadverse party holds a power to control the beneficial enjoyment of such part, without the consent of a nonadverse party.[21] However, IRC Section 674(b) provides for eight exceptions to the foregoing rule. Specifically, IRC Section 674 will not treat the grantor as owning part of a trust merely because the grantor or a nonadverse party holds any of the following, with respect to a trust:

1. A power to apply income to the support of the grantor's legal dependents, except to the extent income is actually so applied;[22]
2. A power that can only affect the beneficial enjoyment of the income for a period that begins after the occurrence of an event, such that a grantor would not be treated as the owner under IRC Section 673 if the power constituted a reversionary interest;[23]

---

[17] IRC § 672(e).
[18] *See* Howard M. Zaritsky, Tax Planning for Family Wealth Transfers (3d ed. 1997) ¶ 3.02[4][a].
[19] Treas. Reg. § 20.7520-3(b)(3)(i).
[20] *Id.*
[21] IRC § 674(a).
[22] IRC § 674(b)(1).
[23] IRC § 674(b)(2).

3. A power that is exercisable solely by will, other than a power of the grantor to appoint by will the trust income where the income is accumulated for such disposition by the grantor (or may be so accumulated in the grantor or a nonadverse party's discretion without the approval or consent of any adverse party);[24]

4. A power to allocate income or principal among charitable beneficiaries;[25]

5. A power to distribute corpus to or for (a) a beneficiary or class of beneficiaries if such power is limited by a reasonably definite standard; or (b) a current income beneficiary if such corpus distribution must be charged against the proportionate share of corpus held for the payment of income to that beneficiary as if the corpus constituted a separate trust.[26] However, this exception does not apply if any person has a power to add to the beneficiaries or class of beneficiaries designated to receive the income or corpus, except where such action is to provide for after-born or after-adopted children;[27]

6. A power to withhold income distributions temporarily if the accumulated income ultimately must be distributed to either the beneficiary or its estate, or must be distributed under a broad limited power of appointment held by the beneficiary, or must be distributed in designated shares to the trust's income beneficiaries at the trust's termination;[28]

7. A power to withhold income during the beneficiary's disability, including the beneficiary's minority;[29]

8. A power to allocate receipts and disbursements between income and principal.[30]

In addition to the foregoing, IRC Section 674 does not treat the grantor as the owner of any portion of a trust as a result of an independent trustee holding a power to distribute, apportion, or accumulate income to or among the beneficiaries, even if the trustee is a nonadverse party.[31] In addition, IRC Section 674 will not treat the grantor as the owner of any part of the trust solely as a result of the trustee holding the power to allocate income among the beneficiaries subject to a reasonably definite external standard contained in the trust instrument, if neither the grantor nor his spouse is a trustee.[32]

[3] Administrative Powers

IRC Section 675 taxes the grantor as the owner of any part of a trust over which the grantor, the grantor's spouse, or any other nonadverse person holds

---

[24] IRC § 674(b)(3).
[25] IRC § 674(b)(4).
[26] IRC § 674(b)(5).
[27] Id.
[28] IRC § 674(b)(6).
[29] IRC § 674(b)(7).
[30] IRC § 674(b)(8).
[31] IRC § 674(c).
[32] IRC § 674(d).

certain administrative powers, or if certain events have occurred or may occur.[33] The powers that will cause the grantor trust rules to apply under IRC Section 675 include the following:

1. The power to purchase, exchange, or otherwise deal with the trust assets for less than adequate and full consideration;[34]
2. The power to lend trust funds to the grantor without adequate interest and security, unless the loan is permissible under a power held by an independent trustee to make such loans to anyone;[35]
3. The grantor has directly or indirectly borrowed corpus or income and has not completely repaid the loan, including any interest, before the beginning of the taxable year. However, this rule does not apply to loans made by an independent trustee, which provide for adequate interest and adequate security;[36] and
4. Any person may exercise a power of administration in a non-fiduciary capacity without the consent of any person in a fiduciary capacity. For this purpose, a "power of administration" includes any one or more of the following:

    a. A power to vote or direct the voting of stock or other securities of a corporation in which the holdings of the grantor and the trust are significant from the viewpoint of voting control;
    b. A power to control the investment of the trust funds either by directing investments or reinvestments, or by vetoing proposed investments or reinvestments, to the extent that the trust funds consist of stocks or securities of corporations in which the holdings of the grantor and the trust are significant from the viewpoint of voting control; or
    c. A power to reacquire the trust corpus by substituting other property of an equivalent value.[37]

[4] Power to Revoke

IRC Section 676 treats the grantor as owning any part of a trust over which the grantor, the grantor's spouse, or any other nonadverse party holds a power, exercisable without an adverse party's consent, to revoke the trust.[38] A power to revoke that does not become effective until the expiration of a term which, had the power been a reversionary interest, would not have been worth more than 5 percent of the trust fund, does not trigger the grantor trust rules under IRC Section 676 until the term expires and the power becomes effective.[39]

---

[33] IRC § 675.
[34] IRC § 675(1).
[35] Id.
[36] Id.
[37] Id.
[38] IRC § 676(a).
[39] IRC § 676(b).

[5] Possibility of Income Paid to Grantor or Grantor's Spouse

IRC Section 677 treats the grantor as owning any part of a trust whose income is or may be either (1) distributed (or held for future distribution) to the grantor or grantor's spouse, or (2) used to pay the premiums on life insurance policies on the grantor or the grantor's spouse, without an adverse party's consent. However, this rule does not apply to powers whose exercise can only affect the beneficial enjoyment of the income for a period beginning after an event occurs, such that the grantor would not be treated as the owner under IRC Section 673 if the power were a reversionary interest. On the other hand, in such circumstances, the grantor may be treated as the owner after the event actually occurs unless the grantor relinquishes the power.[40]

IRC Section 677 also treats the grantor as owning any income actually used to discharge legal support obligations of the grantor or his spouse, without an adverse party's consent.[41] However, IRC Section 677 does not treat the grantor as owning part of a trust merely because income, in the discretion of another person, the trustee, or the grantor acting as trustee or co-trustee, may be applied or distributed for the support or maintenance of a beneficiary (other than the grantor's spouse) whom the grantor is legally obligated to support.[42]

[6] Foreign Trusts

IRC Section 679 treats the grantor of a foreign trust as the owner of the trust for any year in which the trust has, or could have, either directly or indirectly, a beneficiary who is a U.S. citizen or resident alien.[43] However, this rule does not apply to persons who transfer property to foreign trusts in a transfer for value.[44]

[7] Trusts Owned by Someone Other Than the Grantor

Planners must be aware that the grantor trust rules may treat persons other than the grantor as owning part of the trust. Specifically, IRC Section 678 applies if a person holds a power, exercisable alone, to demand distribution of the corpus or income of the trust.[45] IRC Section 678 also treats such a third party as owning any part of a trust over which he previously held such a prohibited power, where he released a part of the power, but retained a power such that, had the grantor held such power, it would have triggered the grantor trust rules under IRC Sections 671 through 677.[46] If both the grantor and a third person hold powers over trust income, the grantor trust rules only apply to the grantor.[47]

---

[40] IRC § 677(a).
[41] IRC § 677(b).
[42] Id.
[43] IRC § 679(a)(1).
[44] IRC § 679(a)(2).
[45] IRC § 678(a)(1).
[46] IRC § 678(a)(2).
[47] IRC § 678(b).

§5.04   GIFT TAXATION OF TRANSFERS TO TRUSTS[1]

Typically, using a trust as part of an asset protection plan involves a transfer of property to that trust. Such transfers may involve gift tax consequences, which planners must analyze.

Planning Pointer. Planners should note that, contrary to what one might think, a completed gift is not necessarily a bad thing. This results because, by effecting a completed gift for gift tax purposes, the planner will generally move the transferred asset out of the transferor's estate, for estate tax purposes. Therefore, when the transferor dies, any appreciation in the value of the transferred asset, which occurs after the date of the gift, will escape estate taxation.

Planning Pointer. Planners should analyze the following gift tax issues in connection with asset protection plans involving domestic trusts:

- When will a transfer constitute a completed gift for gift tax purposes?
- If a transfer constitutes a completed gift for gift tax purposes, what is the value of such gift?
- In computing a gift's value, does Chapter 14 apply, and if so, what is its impact on the gift's value?
- How does the gift tax annual exclusion interact with the foregoing?

Generally, when a settlor transfers property for less than adequate and full consideration, the value of the property transferred, less consideration received by the donor, constitutes a taxable gift.[2] For this purpose, the Internal Revenue Code only imposes a gift tax on completed transfers in which the donor completely terminates dominion and control over the property.[3] Therefore, if the donor retains any interest or power (exercisable alone or in conjunction with someone who lacks a substantial adverse interest) permitting him to change the gift's disposition, the transfer will not constitute a completed taxable gift. To illustrate, the transfer of property to a revocable trust does not constitute a completed gift because the transferor retains the power to revoke the trust.[4] The issue of whether a transfer constitutes a completed gift or not is generally a fact issue.

---

§5.04   [1] *See generally* Stephens, Maxfield, Lind & Calfee, Federal Estate and Gift Taxation (6th ed. 1990) for a complete discussion of the estate and gift tax aspects of transfers to trusts.

[2] IRC §2512(b); Treas. Reg. §25.2512-8.

[3] Treas. Reg. §25.2511-2.

[4] *Id.*

Generally, the following features of a transfer to a trust will cause the transfer to constitute an incomplete gift for gift tax purposes:

- The donor retains the power to revoke the transfer.[5]
- The donor retains the power to change the beneficiaries or their respective interests.[6]
- The trustee is given the power to distribute trust principal to the donor and applicable state law gives the donor or his creditors an enforceable right to compel the trustee to make such distributions.[7]

Generally, the IRS will not consider a gift to be incomplete merely because the donor reserves the power to change the manner or time of enjoyment. Thus, the creation of a trust with income payable annually to a donee for a fixed period, with corpus payable to the donee at the end of the period, constitutes a completed gift even though the donor retains the power to accumulate trust income so that it is paid to the donee at the end of the period.[8]

§ 5.05   ESTATE TAXATION OF INTERESTS IN TRUSTS[1]

Planners must evaluate the estate tax consequences of using trusts as part of an asset protection plan. Specifically, they must evaluate whether any powers or interests that the settlor retains in the trust will cause the corpus to be included in his or her estate for estate tax purposes.

Planning Pointer. Generally, a settlor's estate will include the value of property transferred to a domestic asset protection trust where any of the following occur:

- The settlor retains a life estate;[2]
- Possession and enjoyment of the property can, through ownership of such property, be obtained only by surviving the settlor, and the settlor retains a reversionary interest in the property whose value, immediately before the settlor's death, exceeds 5 percent of the value of the property;[3] or
- The settlor retains the power to alter, amend, revoke, or terminate the transfer.[4]

---

[5] Treas. Reg. § 25.2511-2(c).
[6] *Id.*
[7] Rev. Rul. 77-378, 1977-2 C.B. 347.
[8] Treas. Reg. § 25.2511-2(d).
§ 5.05   [1] *See generally* Stephens, Maxfield, Lind & Calfee, Federal Estate and Gift Taxation (6th ed. 1990) for a complete discussion of the estate and gift tax aspects of transfers to trusts.
[2] IRC § 2036.
[3] IRC § 2037.
[4] IRC § 2038.

Notwithstanding the foregoing, however, a transfer for full and adequate consideration will generally cause the transferred property to be excluded from the deceased settlor's estate.[5]

[A] Retained Life Estate

Under IRC Section 2036(a), a decedent's gross estate includes the value of property the decedent transfers, including by trust, where he retains one of the following interests for his life, a period unascertainable without reference to his death, or a period that does not, in fact, end before he dies:

1. The right to possess or enjoy the property, or the right to the income from the property, and
2. The right (alone or with others) to designate persons who will enjoy the property or the income therefrom.

For purposes of the foregoing rule, the Internal Revenue Code deems the right to vote the stock of a controlled corporation as retaining the enjoyment of the transferred stock.[6]

If a trust requires the trustee to pay expenses of the settlor or if it gives the settlor the power to use trust funds to satisfy his or her personal obligations, then the settlor's estate must include the value of the property transferred to the trust.[7]

Caution. If the settlor serves as a trustee and the trust agreement gives the trustee the right to direct who will benefit from the trust (*e.g.*, the ability to sprinkle the trust benefits among several beneficiaries), this provision will cause the property transferred to the trust to be includable in his gross estate.[8] However, where such a retained power is subject to an ascertainable standard, it will not trigger inclusion of the transferred property in the settlor's gross estate. For purposes of this rule, the Internal Revenue Code will deem the settlor to possess any power of the trustee if the settlor has the power to become trustee or to remove or replace the trustee at his death, even if such power is subject to a contingency, which has not occurred.[9]

[B] Retained Reversionary Interests and Transfers Taking Effect at Death

IRC Section 2037 provides that a donor's gross estate includes the value of any lifetime gift if "possession or enjoyment of the property can, through ownership

---

[5] *See, e.g.,* Estate of Brown v. Comm'r, T.C. Memo 1997-195.
[6] IRC § 2036(b)(1).
[7] Treas. Reg. § 20.2036-1(b)(2).
[8] Treas. Reg. § 20.2036-1(b)(3).
[9] *Id.*

of such interest, be obtained only by surviving the decedent" and if "the decedent has retained a reversionary interest in the property" worth more than five percent of the value of the property in question immediately before the decedent's death. Section 2037 applies only if both the "possession or enjoyment" and the "five percent" requirements are met.

EXAMPLE 5-13

Frank Eustace transfers a diamond necklace in trust with the income payable to his wife, Lizzie, for life and, at her death, remainder to his then surviving children, or if none, to himself or his estate. Here, because each beneficiary can possess or enjoy the property without surviving Frank, no part of the property is includible in Frank's gross estate under IRC Section 2037, regardless of the value of his reversionary interest.[10]

EXAMPLE 5-14

Lucy transfers property in trust with the income to be accumulated for Lucy's life, and at her death, principal and accumulated income to be paid to her then surviving issue, or, if none, to Lizzie or Lizzie's surviving issue. Since Lucy retains no reversionary interest in the property, no part of the property is includible in her gross estate. This is true even though her issue can obtain possession or enjoyment of the property only by surviving Lucy.[11]

EXAMPLE 5-15

Frank transfers property in trust with the income payable to his wife, Lizzie, for life and with the remainder payable to Frank, or if he is not living at Lizzie's death, to his daughter or her estate. Here, the daughter cannot obtain possession or enjoyment of the property without surviving the decedent. Therefore, if Frank's reversionary interest immediately before his death exceeds five percent of the value of the property, the value of the property, less the value of Lizzie's outstanding life estate, is includible in Frank's gross estate.[12]

---

[10] Treas. Reg. § 20.2037-1(e), Example 1.
[11] Treas. Reg. § 20.2037-1(e), Example 2.
[12] Treas. Reg. § 20.2037-1(e), Example 3.

[C] Gift with Power to Alter, Amend, Revoke, or Terminate

IRC Section 2038 provides that a donor's gross estate includes the value of any lifetime gift if, on the date of the donor's death, the donor held a power to alter, amend, revoke, or terminate the transfer. Section 2038 applies to a donor's power regardless of (1) its source, or (2) whether the power is exercisable alone or in conjunction with someone else.

Section 2038 requires gross estate inclusion for the following interests, among others:

1.   Revocable transfers,
2.   A power to change a trust's beneficiaries,[13]
3.   A power to change the relative shares of interest of fixed beneficiaries of a trust,[14] and
4.   A power to affect the timing of the beneficiary's interest.[15]

Planning Pointer. If a donor retains a power to alter, amend, revoke, or terminate, which is subject to an ascertainable standard, then such power will not be includible in the transferor's gross estate under Section 2038.[16]

Caution. Notwithstanding the foregoing, a power to alter, amend, revoke, or terminate will cause inclusion in the transferor's gross estate under IRC Section 2038 regardless of the following:

- What capacity the power was exercisable in;
- Whether the power was exercisable alone or only in conjunction with one or more other persons, regardless of whether they have an adverse interest to the transferor;
- At what time or from what source the transferor acquired his power.[17]

---

[13] Porter v. Comm'r, 288 U.S. 436 (1933).

[14] Hurd v. Comm'r, 160 F.2d 610 (1st Cir. 1947); Rev. Rul. 73-143, 1973-1 C.B. 407.

[15] Lober v. United States, 346 U.S. 335 (1953); Estate of Alexander v. Comm'r, 81 T.C. 767 (1983).

[16] See, e.g., Leopold v. United States, 510 F.2d 617 (9th Cir. 1975); United States v. Powell, 307 F.2d 821 (10th Cir. 1962). See also Tech. Adv. Mem. 9722001 (IRS ruled that a decedent did not have a general power of appointment over a trust's corpus and, thus, the trust was not included in her estate, where (1) the trust directed the trustee to pay income to the decedent's niece for life, (2) the trust gave the niece a testamentary power to appoint the corpus among a specified class of beneficiaries, and (3) the trust instrument's language stated that the settlor intended the corpus to be used to give the niece a comfortable living and for her investment or business purposes).

[17] Treas. Reg. § 20.2038-1(a). See, e.g., William R. Powers v. United States, 79 A.F.T.R.2d ¶ 97-818 (Fed. Cl. 1997) (Court of Federal Claims, granting summary judgment to the IRS, held that a decedent's power of appointment, which her will exercised, constituted a general power of appointment under state law and, consequently, her estate must include such power for estate tax purposes, pursuant to IRC § 2041(b)(1)).

Planning Pointer. A power to alter, amend, revoke, or terminate will not cause the inclusion of the gift subject to the power where such power is exercisable only upon the occurrence of some event or contingency beyond the transferor's control, which has not yet occurred.[18]

[D] Reciprocal Trust Doctrine

In the *Estate of Grace v. United States*,[19] the Supreme Court held that interests in or control over property traced to interrelated reciprocal transfers would be imputed to the individual donors to prevent avoidance of the operation of IRC Sections 2036 and 2038. This is commonly referred to as the reciprocal trust doctrine.[20]

More specifically, the reciprocal trust doctrine imputes to one donor the interest that a second donor retains if:

1. Each makes transfers that are substantially identical;
2. Such transfers are made under a common plan; and
3. The retained powers are reciprocal.[21]

[E] Certain Transfers within Three Years of Death

IRC Section 2035(a) provides that a deceased transferor's gross estate includes the value of property subject to a power or interest described in IRC Sections 2036, 2037, 2038, or 2042 if the donor released or gave away such power within three years of the date of death.

Caution. One of the most common applications of this rule is the transfer of a life insurance policy (or powers over such a policy that would cause estate tax inclusion of the policy if such powers had been retained) to an irrevocable life insurance trust within three years of the transferor's death.

§ 5.06 GENERATION-SKIPPING TRANSFER (GST) TAX

[A] Generation-Skipping Transfers

The GST tax is imposed on "generation-skipping transfers," which are defined as taxable distributions, taxable terminations, and direct skips.[1] Generally a

---

[18] Treas. Reg. § 20.2038-1(b).
[19] 395 U.S. 316 (1969).
[20] *See generally* Howard M. Zaritsky, Family Wealth Transfers ¶ 3.04[5].
[21] *Id.*
§ 5.06   [1] IRC § 2611.

generation-skipping transfer is a transfer of income or principal to a beneficiary who is at least two generations below the transferor's generation.[2] Thus, in general, only transfers to grandchildren (or persons similarly removed from the transferor) would be taxable.

[B]   55 Percent GST Tax Rate

The GST tax is applied at a flat 55 percent rate (the highest estate and gift tax rate).[3] The Internal Revenue Code defines "generation-skipping transfer" to exclude certain lifetime transfers such as transfers that qualify for the gift tax exclusions for educational and medical expenses and, in some cases, for the $10,000 annual exclusion.[4]

[C] $1 Million GST Exemption

Each transferor is allowed a $1,000,000 exemption from the generation-skipping tax.[5] In general, the exemption is allocated by the transferor, or his personal representative, and is generally irrevocable once allocated. If no allocation is chosen, then the Internal Revenue Code provides for a deemed allocation of the exemption.

§5.07   REVOCABLE TRUSTS

Revocable trusts are trusts that allow the settlor to revoke the trust during his or her life.[1] They may be funded or unfunded. In a funded revocable trust, the settlor transfers substantial assets to the trust.[2]

Caution. An unfunded revocable trust provides absolutely no asset protection benefits. Therefore, the planner should not use this type of trust for asset protection purposes.

Revocable trusts are beneficial for four nonasset protection reasons:

1.   They allow the settlor to control the trust property during life and determine who receives the trust's benefits after her death.

---

[2] IRC § 2613.
[3] IRC § 2641.
[4] IRC § 2611.
[5] IRC § 2631.
    §5.07   [1] L. Henry Gissel, Jr. & Karen R. Schiller, *Trusts Made Easy: A Simplified Overview of the Reasons for Creating, Modifying, and Terminating Express Trusts,* 10 Prob. L.J. 241 (1991); Gordon Williamson, *Your Living Trust: How to Protect Your Estate from Probate Taxes & Lawyers* (1992); Clifton B. Kruse, *Twenty-Six Reasons for Caution in Using Revocable Trusts,* 21 Colo. Law. 1131 (1992); Robert A. Esperti & Renno L. Peterson, *Proper Drafting and Planning for the Use of Revocable Trusts,* 21 Colo. Law. 2565 (1992).

2. They provide for the orderly transfer of the settlor's property at death, outside probate.

3. They may provide for the management of the settlor's financial assets during periods of the settlor's incapacity, by providing for a successor trustee during the settlor's life for periods that the settlor is subject to incapacity.

4. Revocable trusts are particularly useful at reducing the administrative burdens and costs of probate when the settlor owns real property in several different states. In such cases, if the settlor owns such property outright, his estate must initiate an ancillary probate proceeding in each jurisdiction where the settlor owns real property. If the settlor places such property in revocable trusts, this generally eliminates the need for such ancillary probate proceedings.

Caution. Revocable trusts offer virtually no asset protection benefits. Therefore, planners should not use them for asset protection purposes.

For income tax purposes, revocable trust income will be taxed to the settlor under the grantor trust rules.[3] At the settlor's death, the trust property will be included in the settlor's estate.

Caution. In most jurisdictions, the trust instrument must provide the settlor with the power of revocation.[4] These jurisdictions generally provide that the trust is irrevocable unless the trust instrument provides otherwise. However, some jurisdictions provide otherwise.[5]

Planning Pointer. The planner should ensure that all trusts, intended to be revocable trusts, provide for the settlor's power to revoke in the trust instrument.

[A] Asset Protection Aspects

Generally, revocable trusts provide little or no asset protection. The following factors cause this result:

1. In many jurisdictions, the settlor's creditors may reach the corpus of a revocable trust;[6] and

---

[2] *See* Lewis D. Solomon & Susan Flax Posner, Tax Planning Strategies § 15.17 (1992).
[3] IRC § 676.
[4] George T. Bogert, Trusts § 148 (6th ed. 1987); Gray v. Union Trust Co. of S.F., 154 P. 306 (Cal. 1915).
[5] George T. Bogert, Trusts § 148 (6th ed. 1987).

2. If the settlor enters bankruptcy, the bankruptcy trustee acquires the settlor's right to revoke the trust.[7]

However, under certain circumstances revocable trusts provide some degree of asset protection while allowing the settlor to retain more control over the trust corpus than for an irrevocable trust.

The primary use of the revocable trust for asset protection occurs for married couples with stable marriages when one spouse is more at risk than the other. Generally, this strategy involves the spouses dividing their property, setting up two revocable trusts, and placing their property into these trusts.[8] Specifically, this strategy would be executed as follows:

1. **Asset inventory.** The planner should cause the spouses to take an inventory of their assets. As part of this inventory, the planner must determine the value of each asset and the risk of litigation claims arising out of such asset. For example, furniture generally does not give rise to litigation claims. In contrast, a professional practice is more likely to give rise to litigation claims in the form of malpractice suits.

2. **Partition or division of property between spouses.** The planner should cause the spouses to divide or partition their property between themselves. For community property jurisdictions, the spouses should enter transmutation agreements to change the statutory impact of the applicable state's community property laws. Generally, the asset protection plan should give the at-risk spouse exempt assets,[9] and the spouse who is less at risk, non-exempt assets. Generally, the planner should attempt to divide the property equally between the spouses.

3. **Trust transfers.** The planner establishes a revocable trust for each spouse. Each spouse becomes the (1) grantor, (2) initial beneficiary, and (3) trustee of his/her trust. The trust should provide that the other spouse becomes the beneficiary of the trust if the grantor/beneficiary spouse dies or disclaims his/her interest. The trust should give a remainder interest to the couple's children.

---

[6] Restatement of Property § 328 (1940); Austin Wakeman Scott & William Franklin Fratcher, The Law of Trusts § 330.12 (4th ed. 1987); George Gleason Bogert & George Taylor Bogert, The Law of Trusts and Trustees § 233 (rev. 2d ed. 1992); L. Henry Gissel, Jr. & Karen R. Schiller, *Trusts Made Easy: A Simplified Overview of the Reasons for Creating, Modifying, and Terminating Express Trusts,* 10 Prob. L.J. 241 (1991). *See, e.g.,* State St. Bank & Trust Co. v. Reiser, 389 N.E.2d 768, 770 (Mass. 1979); Johnson v. Commercial Bank, 588 P.2d 1096, 1099 (Or. 1978); *In re* Kovalyshyn's Estate, 343 A.2d 852 (N.J. Super. Ct. 1975); *In re* Estate of Fischer, 901 S.W.2d 239 (Mo. Ct. App. 1995) (Missouri Court of Appeals held that where decedent-grantor transfers all his assets into a revocable trust, his creditor may bring action opening a no-asset estate to reach the trust corpus).

[7] *See* Jones v. Clifton, 101 U.S. 225 (1879); Murphey v. C.I.T. Corp., 33 A.2d 16 (Pa. 1943); Chase Nat'l Bank v. Ginnel, 50 N.Y.S.2d 345 (Sup. Ct. 1944); *Probate & Trust Division Committee D-3 on Special Problems of Fiduciaries, Creditors' Rights Against Trust Assets,* 22 Real Prop. Prob. & Tr. J. 735, 746 (1987); Restatement (Second) of Trusts § 330 cmt. o (1939); George T. Bogert, Trusts § 48 (6th ed. 1987).

[8] *See* John Dedon, *Protecting Personal Assets,* 7-91 J. Acct. 60 (July 1990); Alfred J. Olsen & Susan K. Smith, 1990 Family Business and Professional Corporate Tax Strategies, in Qualified Plans, PCs, and Welfare Benefits (ALI-ABA Course of Study, 1990); Peter J. Parenti, Typical Asset Protection Game Plans (1991); How to Protect Assets From the IRS, Bender's Federal Tax Service, Tax Practice Guide No. 4 (Dec. 1991, Rel. No. 46, pt. 3).

This strategy has the following asset protection impact: (1) the non-at-risk spouse's trust becomes protected from the at-risk spouse's creditors, and (2) the revocable trust places a barrier between the at-risk spouse's creditors and the assets in the at-risk spouse's trust. The at-risk spouse's creditors' ability to reach that spouse's trust corpus depends on the law of the jurisdiction involved and the types of issues concerning revocable trusts that were previously discussed.

EXAMPLE 5-16

Harold and Winnie are married. Winnie is a plastic surgeon and Harold does not work but instead stays home with their three children. Harold and Winnie own a house worth $1 million, a portfolio of publicly traded securities worth $4 million, Winnie's medical practice (Winnie, L.L.P.), a limited liability company worth $5 million, and other miscellaneous personal assets (autos, etc.) worth another $1 million. Their assets' fair market values total $11 million.

Harold and Winnie, on the recommendation of their respective attorneys, Hugo and William, decide to partition their property between themselves and transfer their individual property into two revocable trusts. Under the partition, Harold receives ownership of the house, the portfolio of publicly traded securities, and one-half of the personal property. The fair market value of the property that Harold receives equals $5.5 million. Winnie receives her medical practice, Winnie, L.L.P., and one-half of the personal property. The fair market value of the property that Winnie receives equals $5.5 million.

Harold creates the H Trust, a revocable trust, and contributes all his property into this trust. Similarly, Winnie creates the W Trust, a revocable trust, and contributes all her property into this trust. Both the H Trust and the W Trust provide a lifetime income interest to the grantor. Each trust also provides a remainder interest to Winnie and Harold's three children.

Three years later, one of Winnie's employees, while driving on company business, negligently drives into Pauline Plaintiff. Pauline sues Winnie, L.L.P. and wins a $20 million judgment against Winnie, L.L.P. If Pauline cannot successfully pierce Winnie, L.L.P.'s veil of limited liability, the most that Pauline can reach equals the assets of Winnie, L.L.P., which are worth $5 million. If Pauline successfully pierces Winnie, L.L.P.'s veil of limited liability, the most that Pauline can reach equals $5.5 million, which equals the assets within the W Trust. This results for two reasons. First, the W Trust is the owner of Winnie, L.L.P.; therefore, any liability imposed would be imposed on it, and its assets equal only $5.5 million. Second, even if liability is imposed on Winnie, no more could be reached because Winnie owns no assets outright. Finally, the planner should note that this plan completely protects Harold's assets. In no event can Pauline reach the assets contained within the H Trust.

Planning Pointer. The planner may use a tenancy by the entirety instead of the above trust arrangement to achieve similar results. Alternatively, the planner may use other trusts, such as irrevocable trusts for the benefit of the client couple's children, that can obtain both asset protection benefits plus additional income and estate tax benefits.

Caution. The planner must consider the possibility that the spouses will divorce and the impact of a divorce on the asset protection plan. For example, the planner must use care when the at-risk spouse has much greater wealth than the non-at-risk spouse.

[B] Tax Aspects

Planners must consider the tax implications of a revocable trust, vis-a-vis other asset protection plans, to evaluate fully such an asset protection vehicle. Specifically, the planner must analyze the gift, estate, generation-skipping, and income tax implications of revocable trusts.[10]

[1] Gift Tax Implications

When the settlor retains the power to revoke a trust, the transfer of property into that trust is not complete for gift tax purposes.[11] Consequently, the IRC does not impose a gift tax on this transaction. On the other hand, when the trust makes a distribution to the beneficiary, the IRC treats this event as a completed gift on which it imposes a gift tax. Specifically, the receipt of income by revocable trust beneficiaries constitutes a taxable gift by the settlor to the beneficiary. The gift occurs in the calendar year the nonsettlor beneficiary receives such income. The annual per donee exclusion applies to the gift by the settlor for the income received by the beneficiary.[12] When the settlor relinquishes control over the trust, the settlor makes a completed gift for federal gift tax purposes.[13] For example, a settlor relinquishes control over the trust when giving up the power of revocation or the power to change beneficiaries.

[2] Estate Tax Consequences

The estate tax applies to interests gratuitously transferred by decedents during their lives when they possessed powers to alter, amend, revoke, or terminate the

---

[9] *See* Chapter 8.

[10] *See generally* Richard B. Stephens, et al., Federal Estate and Gift Taxation (5th ed. 1983); Lewis D. Solomon, et al., Federal Taxation of Estates, Trusts and Gifts (1989).

[11] Treas. Reg. § 25.2511-2.

[12] IRC § 2503(b).

interest at death.[14] The decedent's possession at her death of a discretionary power over an interest in property that she gratuitously transferred during her lifetime constitutes the equivalent of the retention of the interest itself. Federal estate tax cannot be avoided by a gratuitous lifetime transfer over which the transferor retains control or strings, specifically, in the case of revocable trusts, the power of revocation. The amount included in the decedent's gross estate equals the fair market value of the trust property subject to the taxable power that the decedent possessed at death.[15]

If the settlor retains the unrestricted power (1) to discharge a third-party trustee who has the power to revoke or alter the trust, and (2) to appoint herself as trustee, her gross estate will include the trust corpus.[16] However, if the settlor could have named herself trustee on a contingency that has not occurred at the settlor's death, such as an independent trustee's voluntary resignation, the settlor's gross estate does not include the property unless the original trustee resigned or ceased to act before the settlor's death.[17] If a settlor/trustee retains powers limited by an ascertainable standard, the decedent's gross estate does not include the value of the property subject to the power.[18]

> **Planning Pointer.** The planner must be aware of several factors when drafting the trust instrument that includes an ascertainable standard limiting the powers of a settlor/trustee. Federal courts decide the sufficiency of the ascertainable standard. On the other hand, the standard must be enforceable in a state court that would either compel or restrain compliance by the trustee when the specified contingency either occurs or fails to occur.[19] For example, an ascertainable standard exists if the settlor/trustee retains the power to revoke the trust property for support, maintenance, and education of the beneficiary.[20]

> **Planning Pointer.** The ascertainable standard should be expressed in the instrument itself and should be specific. The standard must place reasonable limits on the settlor/trustee's powers and must be objectively determinable. The limits on the settlor/trustee's discretion must be

---

[13] Treas. Reg. § 25.2511-2(f).

[14] IRC § 2038(a)(1). *See generally* Jay D. Waxenberg & Henry J. Leibowitz, *Comparing the Advantages of Estates and Revocable Trusts,* 22 Est. Plan. 265 (Oct. 1995).

[15] Treas. Reg. § 20.2038-1(a).

[16] *See, e.g.,* Estate of Edmonds v. Comm'r, 72 T.C. 970 (1979), *acq.,* 1980-2 C.B. 1; United States v. Winchell, 289 F.2d 212 (9th Cir. 1961).

[17] *See, e.g.,* Estate of Cutter v. Comm'r, 62 T.C. 351 (1974).

[18] *See, e.g.,* Jennings v. Smith, 161 F.2d 74 (2d Cir. 1947).

[19] *See, e.g.,* Estate of Budd v. Comm'r, 49 T.C. 468 (1968), *acq.,* 1973-2 C.B. 1; Estate of Kasch v. Comm'r, 30 T.C. 102 (1958), *acq.,* 1958-2 C.B. 6; Estate of Frew v. Comm'r, 8 T.C. 1240 (1947), *acq.,* 1947-2 C.B. 2; Jere D. McGaffey, Legal Forms with Tax Analysis Ch. 15A (1987).

defined, and a state court must be able to determine whether the settlor/trustee's power is enforceable by a trust beneficiary.

In Tech. Adv. Mem. 9722001, the IRS ruled that a decedent did not have a general power of appointment over a trust's corpus and, thus, the trust was not included in her estate, where (1) the trust directed the trustee to pay income to the decedent's niece for life, (2) the trust gave the niece a testamentary power to appoint the corpus among a specified class of beneficiaries, and (3) the trust instrument's language stated that the settlor intended the corpus to be used to give the niece a comfortable living and for her investment or business purposes. Thus, the niece's estate did not include the trust corpus.

[3] Income Tax Consequences

The IRC treats the grantor as the owner of a trust if the grantor (or spouse) retains the power to revoke the trust.[21] As a grantor trust, the IRC taxes the income to the grantor at her top marginal income tax rate.

In *Buckmaster v. Commissioner*,[22] the Tax Court sustained the IRS's determination that a floor installer's gross income includes his personal service income paid to a trust, ruling that the trust was a sham.

[4] GST Tax Consequences

Retaining a power of revocation can delay imposition of the generation-skipping transfer tax, just as it does the imposition of the gift tax. If the transaction would constitute a direct skip without regard to the power, the fact that the power would negate the gift tax also would negate the generation-skipping transfer tax.[23] However, the IRC does not define the retention of a power as retention of an interest, so a retained power would not keep the trust from being a skip person if it had only skip persons as beneficiaries.[24] Still, the inclusion ratio cannot be established until the transferor's power terminates.[25]

On the termination of power to revoke, the transaction is complete for generation-skipping tax purposes. The transaction might then constitute a taxable transfer as a direct skip. It would not, however, constitute a taxable termination because the power holder would not be defined as having an interest. If a distribution resulted from the termination of the power to revoke, such as a payment of income to a skip person, the distribution could constitute a direct skip.

---

[20] *See* Jere D. McGaffey, Legal Forms with Tax Analysis Ch. 15A (1987).

[21] IRC §§ 672(e), 676.

[22] T.C. Memo 1997-236.

[23] IRC § 2612(c)(1).

[24] IRC § 2613(a)(2).

[25] IRC § 2642(f).

§ 5.08 IRREVOCABLE TRUSTS

Irrevocable trusts do not allow the settlor to revoke or modify the trust after the settlor establishes the trust. Irrevocable trusts are very effective asset protection tools. This results because, by transferring property into an irrevocable trust, the settlor completely transfers ownership of the property to another. Consequently, the settlor's creditors cannot subsequently reach the transferred property because the settlor no longer owns this property. Generally, irrevocable trusts provide the greatest benefit when the settlor does not need to retain control over the transferred property. Conversely, irrevocable trusts provide the least benefit when the settlor either needs or strongly desires to retain an interest in or control over the conveyed property.[1]

Planning Pointer. The asset protection planner should utilize the following analysis for examining irrevocable trusts:

1. What are the asset protection benefits of using irrevocable trusts?[2]
2. What are the tax consequences of using irrevocable trusts?[3]
3. Do the net asset protection advantages of using irrevocable trusts outweigh the loss of control to the settlor over the conveyed property?

[A] Asset Protection Benefits

Irrevocable trusts generally provide greater asset protection than revocable trusts. This results because the transferor completely transfers ownership of that property to the trust. In contrast, in many jurisdictions the creditors of a settlor of a revocable trust may force the settlor to revoke the trust, thus giving the creditors access to the trust corpus.[4] Additionally, if the settlor enters bankruptcy, the bankruptcy trustee acquires any right that the settlor possesses to revoke the trust.[5]

---

§ 5.08 [1] When the settlor desires to retain control over or an interest in property to be conveyed to a trust, the planner should consider using an offshore asset protection trust. For a discussion of offshore asset protection trusts, *see* Chapter 6.

[2] *See* § 5.08[A] for a discussion of the asset protection aspects of irrevocable trusts.

[3] *See* § 5.08[B] for a discussion of the tax aspects of irrevocable trusts.

[4] Austin Wakeman Scott & William Franklin Fratcher, The Law of Trusts § 330.12 (4th ed. 1987); George Gleason Bogert & George Taylor Bogert, The Law of Trusts and Trustees § 233 (rev. 2d ed. 1992); L. Henry Gissel, Jr. & Karen R. Schiller, *Trusts Made Easy: A Simplified Overview of the Reasons for Creating, Modifying, and Terminating Express Trusts*, 10 Prob. L.J. 241 (1991); Restatement of Property § 328 (1940). *See, e.g.,* State St. Bank & Trust Co. v. Reiser, 389 N.E.2d 768 (Mass. 1979); Johnson v. Commercial Bank, 588 P.2d 1096, 1099 (Or. 1978); *In re* Kovalyshyn's Estate, 343 A.2d 852 (N.J. Super. Ct. 1975).

[5] *See Probate & Trust Division Committee D-3 on Special Problems of Fiduciaries, Creditors' Rights Against Trust Assets,* 22 Real Prop. Prob. & Tr. J. 735, 746 (1987); Restatement (Second) of Trusts § 330 cmt. o (1939); George T. Bogert, Trusts § 48 (6th ed. 1987) (*citing* Jones v. Clifton, 101 U.S. 225 (1879)). *See, e.g.,* Murphey v. C.I.T. Corp., 33 A.2d 16 (Pa. 1943); Chase Nat'l Bank v. Ginnel, 50 N.Y.S.2d 345 (Sup. Ct. 1944).

Caution. On the other hand, transfers of property to an irrevocable trust require the settlor to give up a greater degree of control over the trust corpus than the settlor would be required to give up for a revocable trust.

EXAMPLE 5-17

Sam Settlor establishes the SS trust, an irrevocable trust, in 1985 as part of an asset protection plan. Sam transfers $3 million into this trust. At this time, his net worth equals $7 million. Ten years later, after a severe recession, Sam's business fails. Sam's business failure leaves him with no income and no assets. Here, Sam cannot revoke the trust to gain access to trust corpus. However, if the trust was revocable, Sam could revoke the trust and gain access to trust corpus.

Planning Pointer. To account for the possibility of the settlor's impoverishment, the planner should include a provision in the trust instrument allowing the trustee to distribute to the settlor at the trustee's discretion or pursuant to an ascertainable standard.

When analyzing irrevocable trusts, the planner must first ensure that transfers into such a trust do not constitute fraudulent conveyances.[6] If the proposed transfer would constitute a fraudulent conveyance, creditors generally can reach the transferred property.[7]

Planning Pointer. The planner should refer to Chapter 2, Fraudulent Conveyance Concepts, to ensure that the transfer does not constitute a fraudulent conveyance.

If the settlor also retains a beneficial interest in the trust, her creditors can generally reach the beneficial interest.[8] Therefore, the settlor's beneficial interest is not protected. When the settlor retains a beneficial interest in the trust that includes a spendthrift provision,[9] the spendthrift clause will not protect against the settlor/beneficiary's present and future creditors.[10]

---

[6] *See* Chapter 2.

[7] Austin Wakeman Scott & William Franklin Fratcher, The Law of Trusts § 330.12 (4th ed. 1987).

[8] Austin Wakeman Scott & William Franklin Fratcher, The Law of Trusts §§ 330.12, 147 (4th ed. 1987); George T. Bogert, Trusts § 39 (6th ed. 1987).

[9] *See* § 5.09.

[10] Restatement (Second) of Trusts § 156 (1957); Austin Wakeman Scott & William Franklin Fratcher, The Law of Trusts § 156 (4th ed. 1987); George T. Bogert, Trusts § 40 (6th ed. 1987). *See, e.g.,* Harrison v.

This rule generally holds true even when the settlor is only one of several permissible beneficiaries.[11] If the settlor not only retains a beneficial interest, but also retains a general power of appointment, creditors can generally reach all trust property.[12]

Planning Pointer. One strategy the planner should consider would be to establish an irrevocable trust that:

1. Gives the settlor an income interest in the irrevocable trust.
2. Gives the settlor a special power of appointment over the trust corpus, only in favor of the objects of the settlor's bounty (*e.g.*, the settlor's spouse or children).
3. Gives the trustee the discretionary power to distribute trust corpus among the objects of the settlor's bounty, but prohibits the trustee from using this discretionary power to distribute to discharge any of the settlor's legal obligations to the objects of the settlor's bounty. This prevents the settlor from becoming a deemed beneficiary of the trust.
4. Includes a spendthrift provision in the trust instrument.[13]

This strategy has the following asset protection impact:

1. The settlor's retained income interest is exposed to the claims of creditors.
2. The settlor's creditors cannot reach the trust corpus.
3. Because the trust instrument prohibits the trustee from using trust assets to discharge any of the settlor's legal obligations to support beneficiaries who are the objects of her bounty, this plan protects the settlor from creditor claims based on the argument that she is an indirect beneficiary of the trust and thus can reach funds for the support and maintenance of her beneficiaries.[14]
4. This arrangement gives the client almost complete control over the trust corpus, except for allowing the client to access the corpus herself and for allowing the client to appoint those persons who do not fall within the special class set forth in the special power of appointment.

City Nat'l Bank, 210 F. Supp. 362 (S.D. Iowa 1962); Wilmington Trust Co. v. Carpenter, 75 A.2d 815 (Del. Ch. 1950); Glass v. Carpenter, 330 S.W.2d 530 (Tex. Civ. App. 1959); Procter v. Woodhouse, 241 A.2d 785 (Vt. 1968).

[11] Santo (Sandy) Bisignano, Jr., Protecting Assets from Overzealous Creditors or an Estate Planner's Guide to Preservation Planning, 1987 Annual Notre Dame Est. Plan. Inst. 3-36.

[12] Austin Wakeman Scott & William Franklin Fratcher, The Law of Trusts §§ 147.3, 156 (4th ed. 1987); Restatement (Second) of Trusts § 156 cmt. c (1957). *See, e.g.,* Ward v. Marie, 68 A. 1084 (N.J. Ch. 1907); Benedict v. Benedict, 104 A. 581 (Pa. 1918); Morton v. Morton, 147 A.2d 150 (Pa. 1959).

[13] Santo (Sandy) Bisignano, Jr., Protecting Assets from Overzealous Creditors or an Estate Planner's Guide to Preservation Planning, 1987 Annual Notre Dame Est. Plan. Inst. 3-38 to 3-39.

[14] *Id.*

The planner should consider using language such as the following to give the client a special power of appointment:

> The Trustee shall distribute any part or all of the income and principal of the Trust Property to or for the benefit of any one or more of such Charitable and Political Organizations (defined in Paragraph X below) and such Relatives (defined in Paragraph X below) in such proportions and subject to such trusts, powers (including the granting of general and special powers), and conditions as the Settlor at any time and from time to time may provide and appoint by written instrument signed by the Settlor and filed with the Trustee during his/her lifetime. Without limiting the generality of the foregoing, the Settlor shall have the power to create so called grantor retained income and annuity trusts, charitable lead trusts, charitable remainder trusts, and other similar types of split interests trusts where the grantor shall, in effect, be this Trust as opposed to the Settlor individually.

The planner may want to consider using the following definition of "relatives," in the definitional section of the trust instrument, that will give the client maximum flexibility:

> The term Relatives shall mean the descendants at any level of the Settlor's mother and the ancestors of those descendants; and such descendants and ancestors in each case shall include such persons whether now living or born or adopted in the future. Children adopted by any Relative and the descendants by blood or adoption of such children shall be considered to be the descendants of such Relative and of the ancestors of such Relative, but only if adopted prior to attaining the age eighteen (18). Despite the above provisions, the Settlor shall not be a Relative.

EXAMPLE 5-18[15]

Victoria is an obstetrician. Pursuant to an asset protection plan, she establishes an irrevocable trust in 1980. Victoria retains an income interest for life and a special power of appointment of the trust corpus only among her children, Albert and Frederick. She gives the trustee, Winston, a discretionary power to distribute trust corpus among Albert and Frederick, but the trust prohibits Winston from distributing to discharge Victoria's legal obligations to support Albert or Frederick. In 1980 Victoria contributes 75 percent of her net estate, worth $10 million, to the trust. Each year after that, Victoria contributes 50 percent of her net income after taxes to the trust. Victoria spends all her remaining income and all trust distributions she receives each year in

---

[15] *See, e.g..* United States v. Baldwin, 391 A.2d 844 (Md. 1978); Trust Co. v. Bergdorf, 173 A.31 (Md. 1934).

their entirety. In 1990 when the trust corpus is worth $15 million, Victoria accidentally injures a child during childbirth, permanently injuring his arm. The child, Wilhelm, sues Victoria. Wilhelm wins a $20 million judgment against Victoria. At this time, Victoria carries $5 million in liability insurance. Wilhelm's judgment exceeds Victoria's liability insurance by $15 million. Here, Wilhelm may reach Victoria's right to income distributions from the trust. However, Wilhelm cannot reach the trust corpus itself because Victoria retains no right to revoke the trust and retains no general power of appointment over the trust corpus.

Planning Pointer. A second strategy the planner should consider would be to establish an irrevocable trust for the settlor and the settlor's children or spouse that:

1. Is a wholly discretionary trust.[16]
2. Permits distributions to the settlor (a) only for the settlor's health, support, and maintenance, when (b) such distribution would not jeopardize distributions for the children's or spouse's health, support, maintenance, and education.
3. Gives the settlor a special power of appointment over the trust corpus, only in favor of the objects of the settlor's bounty (*e.g.,* the settlor's spouse or children).
4. Prohibits the trustee from using the discretionary power to distribute to discharge any of the settlor's legal obligations to the objects of the settlor's bounty. This prevents the settlor from becoming a deemed beneficiary of the trust.
5. Includes a spendthrift provision in the trust instrument.[17]

This strategy would have the following asset protection impact:

1. The settlor retains no income interest that would be exposed to a creditor's claims.
2. The settlor receives protection from the possibility of impoverishment by the trustee's power to distribute to the settlor, which is limited by both the trustee's discretion and an ascertainable standard.
3. The settlor's creditors cannot reach the trust corpus.
4. Because the trust instrument prohibits the trustee from using trust assets to discharge any of the settlor's legal obligations to support beneficiaries who are the objects of her bounty, this plan protects the settlor from creditor claims based on the argument that she is an

[16] *See* § 5.10 for a discussion of discretionary trusts.
[17] Santo (Sandy) Bisignano, Jr., Protecting Assets from Overzealous Creditors or an Estate Planner's Guide to Preservation Planning, 1987 Annual Notre Dame Est. Plan. Inst. 3-38 to 3-39.

indirect beneficiary of the trust and thus can reach funds for the support and maintenance of her beneficiaries.

5. However, if the trust corpus becomes too large in relation to the needs of the settlor's spouse and children, the settlor's creditors may be able to reach the trust corpus.[18]

[B] Tax Aspects

The planner must consider the tax consequences[19] of using an irrevocable trust to fully evaluate its benefits and detriments. Specifically, the planner must consider the gift, estate, and income tax consequences of the contemplated transaction.

[1] Gift Tax Implications

Generally, when a settlor transfers property for less than adequate and full consideration, the value of the property transferred, less consideration received by the donor, constitutes a gift.[20] Transfers to irrevocable trusts may be subject to tax on a net basis, so the $10,000 annual gift tax exclusion[21] may reduce the taxable gift.

> **Planning Pointer.** The settlor may choose to use the trust's unified credit amount to minimize or eliminate the gift tax.[22] The planner should note that the annual gift tax exclusion only applies to present interest gifts and does not apply to gifts of future interests.[23] Present interests are interests in which the donee's use, possession, or enjoyment is immediate, unfettered, and ascertainable at the time of the gift.[24] Future interests are interests in which the donee's use, possession, or enjoyment will not commence until a future date or time.[25]
>
> Transfers of property to the trust may involve both present and future interests. For example, transfers to trusts that pay income to income beneficiaries for life and then the remainder to a remainderman involve two gifts. The first gift is the present interest to the income beneficiary. The second gift is the future interest given to the remainderman.

---

[18] *Id.*

[19] *See generally* Richard B. Stephens, et al., Federal Estate and Gift Taxation (5th ed. 1983); Lewis D. Solomon, et al., Federal Taxation of Estates, Trusts and Gifts (1989).

[20] IRC § 2512(b); Treas. Reg. § 25.2512-8.

[21] IRC §§ 2503(b), 2513.

[22] IRC § 2505.

[23] IRC § 2503(b).

[24] Treas. Reg. § 25.2503-3(b).

[25] Treas. Reg. § 25.2503-3(a).

[2] Estate Tax Consequences

A transfer in trust that is irrevocable for income tax purposes may be includible in the grantor's gross estate. IRC Sections 2036, 2037, and 2038 generally control the inclusion in the settlor's gross estate of property the settlor transfers to an irrevocable trust.

Pursuant to IRC Section 2036, a decedent's gross estate will include the value of all property transferred during the decedent's lifetime in which the decedent retains or reserves:

(a) The right to use, possess, or enjoy the property or the right to receive the income from the property for the decedent's life or for a period that either is not ascertainable without reference to the decedent's death or does not in fact end before the decedent's death;

(b) The right, either alone or with any other person, to designate the persons who should possess or enjoy the property or the income from the property.[26]

The grantor's estate also must include trust property to the extent that the use, possession, right to the income, or other enjoyment discharges the grantor's legal obligations.[27] For this purpose, a "legal obligation" includes a legal obligation to support a dependent during the grantor's lifetime. However, the grantor's gross estate will not include the corpus when the trust's terms do not require that income or principal be used for the beneficiary's support[28] or when the trust contains no restriction about the use of trust income for the obligation to support a dependent.[29]

The grantor's gross estate may include a trust created entirely for the benefit of another if a reciprocal trust arrangement exists. A reciprocal trust arrangement involves a course of conduct from which can be drawn the inference of a mutual agreement to provide income from the use of two trusts. For example, when a husband and wife each names the other as a life beneficiary of their trust, a reciprocal trust arrangement probably exists.

---

[26] IRC § 2036(a). *See, e.g.,* Priv. Ltr. Rul. 199903025. In Priv. Ltr. Rul. 199903025, a married couple (H and W) created four irrevocable trusts, one for each of their four children and each child's descendants. H and W were the trustees, and each trustee had a power to distribute income and principal to the beneficiaries for "the general welfare, education and the maintenance in health and reasonable comfort of the members of the class, considering the needs, circumstances and the usual standard of living of each, using the guidelines set out in the following paragraphs." The trustees also had discretion to add undistributed income to principal. Each child was a co-trustee of the trust for his benefit. However, co-trustees were required to act by unanimous agreement. The trusts were funded in part with minority stock interests. In Priv. Ltr. Rul. 199903025, H, W, and the trust beneficiaries proposed petitioning a court to modify the trust to prohibit W from participating, as trustee, in voting the shares of the corporation. The IRS ruled that the trust fund was not part of either H or W's estate under IRC §§ 2036(a)(2) or 2038 because of their fiduciary power to distribute income and principal. Citing Rev. Rul. 73-143, 1973-1 C.B. 407, the IRS reasoned that such power was limited by a definite ascertainable standard. The IRS also ruled that if W lived for at least three years after the trust modification, her gross estate would not include the stock held by the trusts under IRC §§ 2035(a) or 2036(b).

[27] Treas. Reg. § 20.2036-1(b) (2) (1960); Helvering v. Mercantile Commerce Bank & Trust Co., 111 F.2d 224 (8th Cir.), *cert. denied,* 310 U.S. 654 (1940); Estate of McKeon v. Commissioner, 25 T.C. 697 (1956).

[28] Estate of Mitchell v. Comm'r, 55 T.C. 576 (1970).

[29] Colonial-Am. Nat'l Bank of Roanoke v. United States, 243 F.2d 312 (4th Cir. 1957).

The grantor's gross estate must include corpus when, by prearrangement, an irrevocable, discretionary trust distributes all of its income to the settlor.[30]

Planning Pointer. If the asset protection plan gives an independent trustee the uncontrolled discretion to pay the income from the trust to the settlor, the IRC does not consider the settlor to have retained the right to the income absent an understanding between the trustee and the settlor that the income would be so distributed.[31] Here, the settlor's estate would not include the trust corpus. However, if under local law the trustee must use the income from the discretionary trust to discharge the settlor's debts, the IRC considers the settlor to have retained the right to the income from the trust.[32] Under such circumstances, the settlor's estate must include the trust corpus.

Pursuant to IRC Section 2037, a grantor's gross estate must include property transferred to an irrevocable trust when the beneficiary can only possess or enjoy the corpus if the beneficiary survives the settlor. The gross estate also must include the corpus when the grantor retains a reversionary interest worth more that five percent of the value of the property immediately before the grantor's death.[33] The grantor's estate will not include the value of trust corpus unless the beneficiary could only obtain possession or enjoyment of the property by surviving the decedent.[34] Trust property will be included in the grantor's estate if a beneficiary could only have obtained possession or enjoyment of the property by surviving the grantor or through the occurrence of some other event such as the expiration of a term of years.[35] If the beneficiary could obtain possession or enjoyment of the property during the grantor's life through the exercise of a general power of appointment exercisable immediately before the grantor's death, the interest in the transferred property will not be includible in the grantor's gross estate.[36]

Reversionary interests include the possibility the trust corpus may be returned to the grantor and the possibility the transferred property may become subject to the grantor's power of disposition. Thus, a reversionary interest includes interests arising under the trust's terms or by operation of law.[37] Reversionary interests do not include rights to income only. Reversionary interests also do

---

[30] Estate of Skinner v. United States, 316 F.2d 517 (3d Cir. 1963).

[31] Estate of Green v. Comm'r, 64 T.C. 1049 (1975), *acq.*, 1976-2 C.B. 2; Estate of Skinner v. United States, 316 F.2d 517 (3d Cir. 1963); Lewis D. Solomon & Susan Flax Posner, Tax Planning Strategies §15.21 (1992).

[32] Treas. Reg. §20.2036-1(b) (1) (i); Lewis D. Solomon & Susan Flax Posner, Tax Planning Strategies §15.21 (1992).

[33] IRC §2037(a).

[34] IRC §2037.

[35] *Id.*

[36] Treas. Reg. §20.2037-1(b).

[37] Treas. Reg. §20.2037-1(c)(2).

not include (1) the possibility the grantor might receive back the trust corpus through the estate of another, or (2) the statutory right of a spouse to receive a portion of whatever estate the grantor may leave at death.[38]

To be includible in the grantor's estate, the value of the property subject to the reversionary interest must be greater than five percent of the transferred property's value immediately before the grantor's death.[39] The estate determines the value according to the valuation principle for determining the value of future or conditional interests in property for estate tax purposes as illustrated in the Treasury Regulations.[40] To determine whether the grantor retained the reversionary interest of a value exceeding five percent, the estate compares the value of the reversionary interest with the value of the transferred property, including interests not dependent upon survivorship of the grantor.[41]

Generally, pursuant to IRC Section 2038, a grantor's gross estate also includes trust corpus when the enjoyment of the beneficial interest in the property was subject at the date of the grantor's death to the exercise of power to alter, amend, revoke, or terminate or effect beneficial enjoyment, either by the grantor alone or with any other person, or if the grantor relinquishes such a power in contemplation of death. This rule will not apply if the transfer was for full and adequate consideration,[42] if the grantor's power could be exercised only with the consent of all parties having an interest in the transferred property, if the power added nothing to the rights of the parties under local law,[43] or if the power was held by a person other than the grantor.[44]

Planning Pointer. Irrevocable trusts may assist planners in achieving valuation discounts for estate tax purposes.[45]

[3]   Income Tax Consequences

The planner also must consider the income tax consequences of the proposed transaction. Generally, the planner's primary concern will be whether the trust

---

[38] *Id.*

[39] Treas. Reg. § 20.2037-1(c)(3).

[40] Treas. Reg. § 20.2031-1, -7, -9.

[41] Treas. Reg. § 20.2037-1(c)(4).

[42] Treas. Reg. § 20.2038-1(a)(1).

[43] Treas. Reg. § 20.2038-1(a)(2).

[44] Treas. Reg. § 20.2038-1(a)(3).

[45] *See, e.g.,* Estate of Bonner v. United States, 84 F.3d 196 (5th Cir. 1996) (the Fifth Circuit allowed valuation discounts for the decedent's undivided interests where decedent's spouse's qualified terminable interest property (QTIP) trust held remaining interests); Estate of Mellinger. v. Comm'r, 112 T.C. 24, *acq.,* 1999-35 I.R.B. 314 (1999) (Tax Court held that stock held in a QTIP trust is not aggregated with other property held by the decedent at his or her death for purposes of determining valuation discounts for estate tax purposes); *c.f.* TAM 9550002. *See also* Estate of Nowell v. Comm'r, T.C. Memo 1999-015 (1999).

will be taxed to the settlor or separately to the trust or its beneficiaries. The grantor trust rules under IRC Sections 671 through 679 control this issue. Specifically, when the trust constitutes a grantor trust, the trust's income will be taxed to the settlor as if she earned that income. This rule holds true without regard to whether the settlor has a right to such income. Specifically, when a trust constitutes a grantor trust, the grantor must consider, when computing taxable income and credits, those items of income, deduction, and credit against the trust's tax, to the extent such items would be taken into account in computing the taxable income or credits of the trust, if it were not a grantor trust.[46]

A trust will constitute a grantor trust under the following circumstances:

1. When either the grantor or grantor's spouse possesses a reversionary interest in either the corpus or income therefrom, whose value, at the trust's inception, exceeds five percent of the value of the trust, the trust will constitute a grantor trust.[47] However, if the return of the trust corpus to the settlor takes place only on the death of a lineal descendant beneficiary before such beneficiary's attaining age 21, as long as the minor holds all of the present interest in any portion of the trust, the trust will not constitute a grantor trust.[48]

2. When either the grantor or a nonadverse party has the power to dispose of the trust income or corpus without the consent of an adverse party, the trust will constitute a grantor trust.[49] An adverse party is a person who has a substantial beneficial interest in the trust that would be adversely affected by the exercise or nonexercise of the power the grantor possesses.[50] However, the trust will not be a grantor trust merely because the grantor retains a power:

   a. To apply income to the support of a dependent;[51]
   b. Affecting beneficial enjoyment only after the occurrence of an event, which would not cause the trust to be a grantor trust because of a reversionary interest retained by the grantor;[52]
   c. Exercisable only by will, other than the power to appoint income accumulated by the grantor or at the discretion of the grantor without the approval of a nonadverse party;[53]
   d. To allocate among charitable beneficiaries;[54]
   e. To distribute corpus to or for beneficiaries when a reasonably definite standard set forth in the trust instrument limits the power, or to or for current income beneficiaries when the distribution must be chargeable

---

[46] IRC § 671.
[47] IRC § 673(a).
[48] IRC § 673(b).
[49] IRC § 674(a).
[50] IRC § 672(a).
[51] IRC § 674(b)(1).
[52] IRC § 674(b)(2).
[53] IRC § 674(b)(3).
[54] IRC § 674(b)(4).

against the proportionate share of corpus held in trust for the payment of income to that beneficiary as if the corpus constituted a separate trust;[55]

f.   To withhold income temporarily under certain circumstances;[56]

g.   To withhold income during a beneficiary's disability, under certain circumstances;[57] or

h.   To allocate between corpus and income.[58]

3.   When the grantor retains or possesses certain administrative powers the trust will constitute a grantor trust.[59] Such powers include:

a.   The power to deal with trust corpus or income for less than adequate and full consideration without the consent of an adverse party;[60]

b.   The power to borrow without adequate interest or security, unless a trustee other than the grantor is authorized under a general lending power to make loans without regard to interest or security;[61]

c.   The grantor has actually borrowed corpus or income and has not re-paid such loan, including interest, before the beginning of the tax year, except when an adequately secured loan that draws adequate interest was made by a trustee other than the grantor or a related or subservient party;[62] and

d.   A general power of administration exercisable in a nonfiduciary capac-ity by any person without the approval or consent of any person in a nonfiduciary capacity.[63]

4.   When the grantor retains the power to revoke the trust, the trust will con-stitute a grantor trust.[64] However, when the grantor cannot exercise such a power until after an event, the trust will not be treated as a grantor trust until such event.[65]

5.   When, in the grantor's or a nonadverse party's discretion, without the ap-proval of an adverse party, trust income may be distributed to the grantor or the grantor's spouse,[66] held or accumulated for future distribution to the grantor or the grantor's spouse,[67] or applied to the payment of life insurance premiums on the grantor's or the grantor's spouse's life, the trust will con-stitute a grantor trust.[68] However, when the grantor cannot exercise such a

---

[55] IRC § 674(b)(5).
[56] IRC § 674(b)(6).
[57] IRC § 674(b)(7).
[58] IRC § 674(b)(8).
[59] IRC § 675.
[60] IRC § 675(1).
[61] IRC § 675(2).
[62] IRC § 675(3).
[63] IRC § 675(4).
[64] IRC § 676(a).
[65] IRC § 676(b).
[66] IRC § 677(a)(1).
[67] IRC § 677(a)(2).
[68] IRC § 677(a)(3).

power until after an event occurs, the trust will not be treated as a grantor trust until such event occurs.[69] When the trust income may be applied to satisfy the grantor's legal support obligation, the income will be taxed to the grantor to the extent so used.[70]

6. When the grantor is a United States person who directly or indirectly transfers property to a foreign trust that has a United States beneficiary, that trust will constitute a grantor trust.[71] However, this rule will not apply when that transfer resulted from the death of the transferor[72] or the transfer was a sale or exchange at fair market value in which the transferor recognized gain at the time of the transfer.[73] For purposes of this rule, the trust will be treated as having a United States beneficiary unless both (a) under the trust instrument, no part of the trust's income or corpus may be paid or accumulated to or for the benefit of a United States person, and (b) if the trust were terminated at any time, no part of the trust's income or corpus could be paid to or for the benefit of a United States person.[74] For purposes of this rule, an amount will be treated as paid or accumulated to or for the benefit of a United States person if such amount is paid to or accumulated for a foreign corporation, partnership, trust, or estate, and

   a. For a corporation, United States shareholders own or are deemed to own more than 50 percent of the total combined voting power of all classes of voting stock;

   b. For a partnership, a United States person is a partner of the partnership; or

   c. For a trust or estate, the trust or estate has a United States beneficiary.[75]

Caution. The planner also should be aware that under certain circumstances, the trust may be treated as a grantor trust with the trust income attributable to an individual other than the grantor. This will generally occur when a power described previously in items 1 through 5 is conveyed to someone other than the grantor.[76]

Planners should ensure that clients establishing irrevocable trusts are advised properly on limiting beneficiary involvement with the trust. Failure to follow such advice may cause the Internal Revenue Service to tax the trust as a corporation instead of as either a trust or a grantor trust.[77]

---

[69] IRC § 677(a).
[70] IRC § 677(b).
[71] IRC § 677(a).
[72] IRC § 677(a)(2)(A).
[73] IRC § 677(a)(2)(B).
[74] IRC § 677(c).
[75] IRC § 677(c)(2).
[76] IRC § 678.
[77] *See* Carl Radom & Michael A. Yuhus, *Excess Beneficiary Involvement Can Cost Trust Its Tax Status*, 21 Tax'n for Law. 17 (1992).

§ 5.09   SPENDTHRIFT TRUSTS

Spendthrift trusts are trusts that prevent beneficiaries from transferring or assigning their rights to future payments of income or principal. Spendthrift trusts also prevent the beneficiaries' creditors from subjecting the beneficiaries' interests to the payment of the creditors' claims.[1] The following discusses asset protection planning strategies the planner should consider, the general spendthrift trust rules, and drafting considerations the planner should consider when using spendthrift trusts. The tax treatment of the spendthrift trust will depend on whether it is irrevocable or revocable.[2]

> **Planning Pointer.** Planners traditionally have used spendthrift trusts when the settlor believed the beneficiary was a spendthrift. Today, however, as many professional baby boomers begin to inherit wealth from their parents, spendthrift trusts provide a great planning tool. Specifically, the older generation can transfer their estates to their heirs via spendthrift trusts that will protect their estates from their heirs' creditors. The astute planner will note that the heirs do not need to be spendthrifts for spendthrift trusts to be beneficial. For example, when a parent desires to leave her estate to a professional child who is subject to the risk of malpractice, a spendthrift trust may be advisable.

EXAMPLE 5-19

Gertrude establishes a trust for her son, Bob, an obstetrician. The trust provides that the income goes to Bob for his life, and the remainder interest goes to Bob's daughter, Dana. At Bob's request, because of the risk of his being sued, Gertrude includes in the trust a valid spendthrift provision. Each year, the trust distributes approximately $150,000 to Bob. Five years after the trust's establishment, Pam sues Bob and wins a $1 million judgment against him. Here, Pam cannot reach the trust's corpus. However, each year after the trust makes a distribution to Bob, Pam can reach the amount distributed to him.

---

§ 5.09   [1] George T. Bogert, Trusts § 40 (6th ed. 1987); Austin Wakeman Scott & William Franklin Fratcher, The Law of Trusts §§ 149–163 (4th ed. 1987); George Gleason Bogert & George Taylor Bogert, The Law of Trusts and Trustees §§ 221–227 (rev. 2d ed. 1992); Erwin N. Griswold, Spendthrift Trusts (2d ed. 1947); Frank J. Rief III, Current and Future Family Asset Protection, in Sophisticated Estate Planning Techniques (ALI-ABA Course of Study, 1991); Santo (Sandy) Bisignano, Jr., Protecting Assets from Overzealous Creditors or an Estate Planner's Guide to Preservation Planning, 1987 Annual Notre Dame Est. Plan. Inst. 3-31 to 3-34; Nancy Smith Roush & Robert K. Kirkland, Spendthrift Trusts Not Limited to Protection of Immature Dependents, 18 Est. Plan. 16 (1991).

[2] See § 5.07[B] for a discussion of the tax treatment of revocable trusts. See § 5.08[B] for a discussion of the tax treatment of irrevocable trusts.

The majority rule in the United States concerning spendthrift trusts is that spendthrift trust provisions are valid.[3] However, some states subject spendthrift trusts to certain restrictions and others do not allow spendthrift trusts at all.[4] Where allowed, spendthrift trusts prevent a beneficiary's creditors from reaching that beneficiary's trust interest. In other words, the spendthrift provision prevents the beneficiary's creditors from reaching the beneficiary's future income stream from the trust.[5] On the other hand, the spendthrift provision does not protect funds the trust distributes to the beneficiary. Consequently, the creditor can reach these amounts.

Planning Pointer. To avoid creditors reaching distributed amounts, the trust instrument should provide that the trustee may either (1) distribute funds to the beneficiary, or (2) distribute funds on behalf of the beneficiary.[6]

EXAMPLE 5-20

Same facts as Example 5-19, except that the trust instrument provides that the trustee may distribute the trust income either (1) directly to Bob, or (2) on Bob's behalf. After Pam successfully sues Bob, the trustee begins paying income to various individuals on Bob's behalf, instead of to Bob directly. For example, the trustee directly pays off Bob's grocery store account balance and his credit card balances each month without paying funds to Bob directly. Here, Bob's creditors cannot reach the amounts the trust pays on Bob's behalf. Conversely, if the trustee paid these amounts directly to Bob, Pam could reach these amounts.

---

[3] Austin Wakeman Scott & William Franklin Fratcher, The Law of Trusts §§ 149–163 (4th ed. 1987); George Gleason Bogert & George Taylor Bogert, The Law of Trusts and Trustees § 222 (rev. 2d ed. 1992); Annotation, Validity of spendthrift trusts, 34 A.L.R.2d 1135 (1954); Invalidity of spendthrift provisions as affecting other provisions of trust, 9 A.L.R.2d 1361 (1950). *See, e.g.,* Duvall v. McGee, 826 A.2d 416 (Md. 2003) (Maryland discretionary spendthrift trust protected trust corpus from tort judgment, which resulted from beneficiary's battery and murder of another individual); Doksansky v. Norwest Bank Neb., N.A., 615 N.W.2d 104 (Neb. 2000) (spendthrift trust protected trust assets from claim for past due child support against interest of beneficiary); Scheffel v. Krueger, 782 A.2d 410 (N.H. 2001) (spendthrift trust protected trust assets from tort judgment against beneficiary relating to the beneficiary's sexual assault of the claimant).

[4] George T. Bogert, Trusts § 40 (6th ed. 1987).

[5] Nancy Smith Roush & Robert K. Kirkland, Spendthrift Trusts Not Limited to Protection of Immature Dependents, 18 Est. Plan. 16 (1991).

[6] Nancy Smith Roush & Robert K. Kirkland, Spendthrift Trusts Not Limited to Protection of Immature Dependents, 18 Est. Plan. 16, 17 (1991).

Planning Pointer. The planner should consider using language similar to the following to provide spendthrift protection for the trust beneficiaries:

> No beneficiary of this trust, including but not limited to the Settlor, shall have the power to anticipate, transfer, sell, assign, or encumber any payment or distribution of either principal or income to be made under the provisions of this trust, and any anticipation, transfer, sale, assignment, or encumbrance by any such beneficiary, either of principal or income, whether by voluntary act or by operation of law, shall be void and of no effect whatsoever, and no distribution or payment shall be made by the Trustee to any creditor, assignee, receiver, or trustee in bankruptcy of any such beneficiary. If, notwithstanding the above, it shall be held that the interest, whether of principal or income, of any beneficiary under this trust has vested in any third party, whether by voluntary transfer or by operation of law, then, to the extent of such vestment, such interest shall cease and the Trustee shall thereupon apply any payment or distribution, whether of income or principal, thus attempted to be sold, transferred, assigned, levied upon, or taken, to the use of the beneficiary who would have been entitled thereto in the absence of such sale, transfer, assignment, levy or taking.

Planning Pointer. In jurisdictions that do not allow spendthrift trusts, the planner has three options:

1. The planner may establish the spendthrift trust in a jurisdiction that allows such trusts. For this purpose, the trust's situs, the location of its assets and trustee, and the statements contained within the trust instrument will generally control which jurisdiction's law will apply.[7] Consequently, with proper planning, the planner may utilize the laws of a state other than the one the settlor lives in, by establishing a trust in another jurisdiction, transferring assets to that jurisdiction, and providing in the trust instrument that the law of that jurisdiction controls.[8]
2. The planner may use a discretionary trust, which will have essentially the same desired effect as a spendthrift trust. Namely, the creditors of the beneficiary will not be able to attach the beneficiary's interest for payment of their claims.[9] Under a discretionary trust, the trustee has complete discretion whether to pay or apply to or for the benefit of a beneficiary any, all, or none of the trust income or principal as the trustee deems appropriate.[10] Because a beneficiary of a discretionary trust lacks any legally enforceable right to a distribution of any income

---

[7] Austin Wakeman Scott & William Franklin Frateher, The Law of Trusts § 611 (4th ed. 1987).
[8] Austin Wakeman Scott & William Franklin Fratcher, The Law of Trusts § 611 (4th ed. 1987).
[9] *See* § 5.10 for a discussion of discretionary trusts.
[10] George T. Bogert, Trusts § 41 (6th ed. 1987).

or principal of the trust, the beneficiary's interest is not assignable or reachable by creditors.[11]

3. In some circumstances planners should consider mandatory support trusts. Mandatory support trusts require the trustee to provide so much of the income or principal of the trust as is necessary for the education and support of a beneficiary.[12] Some jurisdictions provide that the beneficiary of such a trust cannot assign her trust interest and that her creditors cannot reach her trust interest.[13] Mandatory support trusts provide the settlor with assurance that the beneficiary will be provided for. This is an advantage over discretionary trusts, which do not provide such assurance.

EXAMPLE 5-21

Same facts as Example 5-19, except that the state Gertrude lives in does not recognize spendthrift trusts. Therefore, instead of a spendthrift provision, Gertrude sets up a discretionary trust. Here, Pam cannot reach the trust corpus although the trust does not include a spendthrift provision and although spendthrift provisions are not allowed in the jurisdiction in question.

Planning Pointer. The planner should ensure that the spendthrift provision includes both a prohibition against (1) the beneficiary assigning her interest, and (2) the beneficiary's creditors attaching the beneficiary's trust interest for payment of their claims.[14]

Even in jurisdictions that allow spendthrift trusts, there are certain exceptions when a spendthrift trust provision will have no effect. The first exception occurs when the settlor is also the beneficiary. When the settlor establishes such a trust, the trust will generally be valid. However, the trust's spendthrift provision (1) will not prevent the settlor/beneficiary's creditors from reaching her interest, and (2) will not prevent the settlor/beneficiary from transferring her interest.[15]

---

[11] *Id.*

[12] Nancy Smith Roush & Robert K. Kirkland, *Spendthrift Trusts Not Limited to Protection of Immature Dependents*, 18 Est. Plan. 16, 18 (1991).

[13] *Id.*

[14] Nancy Smith Roush & Robert K. Kirkland, *Spendthrift Trusts Not Limited to Protection of Immature Dependents*, 18 Est. Plan. 16, 17 (1991).

[15] George T. Bogert, Trusts § 40 (6th ed. 1987); *but cf.* Sylvester v. Sylvester, 557 So. 2d 599 (Fla. Dist. Ct. App. 1990) (Florida District Court of Appeal held that trial court could not have jurisdiction over corpus of trust benefiting settlor/beneficiary unless it obtained jurisdiction over trustee and settlor's children who were contingent beneficiaries); *see, e.g.,* Shurley v. Texas Commerce Bank—Austin, N.A. (*In re*

The second exception is when a federal tax claim is involved the IRS can generally reach a beneficiary's interest in a spendthrift trust.[16] However, the IRS cannot reach more than the beneficiary's interest in the trust.[17]

> **Planning Pointer.** A discretionary trust may prevent the IRS from reaching the trust corpus. Therefore, when the planner desires to protect against federal tax claims, the planner should consider a discretionary trust.

Third, when a beneficiary enters bankruptcy, the bankruptcy estate acquires the beneficiary's trust interest.[18] However, the bankruptcy estate does not acquire any power that the debtor may exercise solely for the benefit of an entity other than the debtor.[19] Also, restrictions on transfers of beneficial interests of the beneficiary/debtor in a trust that are enforceable under applicable nonbankruptcy law are enforceable for purposes of the Bankruptcy Code.[20] Therefore, spendthrift provisions are generally effective for nonsettlor beneficiaries.[21]

Fourth, when a beneficiary receives a nondiscretionary income interest in a trust, the trust interest will generally be subject to claims of alimony and child support. However, when the trust is a discretionary trust, the trust interest will generally not be subject to claims of alimony or child support.[22]

Shurley), 115 F.3d 333 (5th Cir. 1997) (Fifth Circuit holds that property that a Chapter 7 debtor contributed to a spendthrift trust that she established with her parents and sister was not protected from creditors' claims under the Texas self-settlor rule and, thus, was includable in her bankruptcy estate. However, the court held, all other trust assets were excludable from the estate). *See also* Tri-State Equip. v. United States, 97-1 U.S. Tax Cas. (CCH) ¶ 50,437 (E.D. Cal. 1997) (U.S. District Court for the Eastern District of California holds that domestic trust was the taxpayer's nominee and alter ego in favor of the United States); Walker v. United States by & Through the IRS, 1997 U.S. Dist. LEXIS 10271 (D. Or. 1997) (U.S. District Court for the District of Oregon dismisses a couple's suit challenging an IRS levy on a trust, which the IRS determined was the couple's alter ego or nominee. The court stated that, because the Walkers failed to identify any basis upon which the United States had waived its sovereign immunity, it lacked jurisdiction over the action).

[16] *See, e.g.,* First Northwestern Trust Co. of S.D. v. IRS, 622 F.2d 387 (8th Cir. 1980).

[17] Nancy Smith Roush & Robert K. Kirkland, Spendthrift Trusts Not Limited to Protection of Immature Dependents, 18 Est. Plan. 16, 20 (1991).

[18] 11 U.S.C. § 541 (1988 & Supp. 1991); George T. Bogert, Trusts § 39 (6th ed. 1987); Austin Wakeman Scott & William Franklin Fratcher, The Law of Trusts § 147.1 (4th ed. 1987). See, e.g., Horton v. Moore, 110 F.2d 189 (6th Cir.), cert. denied, 311 U.S. 692, reh'g denied, 311 U.S. 728 (1940); In re Dolard, 275 F. Supp. 1001 (C.D. Cal. 1967).

[19] 11 U.S.C. § 541(b)(1) (1988 & Supp. 1991).

[20] 11 U.S.C. § 541(c)(2); Austin Wakeman Scott & William Franklin Fratcher, The Law of Trusts, § 147.1 (4th ed. 1987).

[21] *See* § 5.09 for a detailed discussion of spendthrift trusts.

[22] Nancy Smith Roush & Robert K, Kirkland, Spendthrift Trusts Not Limited to Protection of Immature Dependents, 18 Est. Plan 16, 20 (1991); Annotation, Trust income or assets as subject to claim against beneficiary for alimony, maintenance, or child support, 91 A.L.R.2d 262 (1963).

EXAMPLE 5-22

Same facts as Example 5-19, except that at the time of the trust creation Bob is engaged to Carol and Gertrude establishes the trust as a discretionary trust with a spendthrift provision. Gertrude's sister, Sally, is trustee. Five years later, Bob and Carol divorce. Here, if Bob should be delinquent on his alimony payments to Carol, Carol cannot recover against Bob's interest in the trust. However, if instead of a discretionary trust, Gertrude set the trust up to provide all income to Bob during his life, Carol could reach Bob's trust interest under the majority rule.

Fifth, in some jurisdictions, a spendthrift provision does not protect a beneficiary's interest from tort claims.[23]

Finally, a creditor whose claim is based on necessary services or goods the creditor has provided to the beneficiary may generally reach the beneficiary's trust interest.[24] This is especially true when the goods or services are of the type the trust instrument specifies the trust is to provide for. For example, when the trust requires the trustee to pay out income for the beneficiary's health, education, and welfare, then claims of a doctor or of a university would generally be able to be satisfied from the beneficiary's interest in the trust.

§5.10 DISCRETIONARY TRUSTS

Discretionary trusts[1] give the trustee the discretion to pay or apply to or for the beneficiary's benefit, any, all, or no trust income or principal as the trustee deems appropriate.[2] Because the trust beneficiary has no right to any trust income or principal before a trustee elects to pay or apply income or principal to or for the beneficiary's benefit and because creditors can only reach the interest that a beneficiary has a legal right to, the beneficiary cannot assign her interest to creditors and her creditors cannot reach the beneficiary's trust interest. Following is a discussion of planning strategies the planner should consider for discretionary trusts, the general discretionary trust rules, and certain drafting considerations.

---

[23] George T. Bogert, Trusts §40 (6th ed. 1987).

[24] Id.

§5.10   [1] See generally Austin Wakeman Scott & William Franklin Fratcher, The Law of Trusts H 155-155.1 (4th ed. 1987); George Gleason Bogert & George Taylor Bogert, The Law of Trusts and Trustees §228 (rev. 2d ed. 1992); Frank J. Rief, III, Current and Future Family Asset Protection, in Sophisticated Estate Planning Techniques (ALI-ABA Course of Study, 1991); George T. Bogert, Trusts §41 (6th ed. 1987); Evelyn Ginsberg Abravanel, Discretionary Support Trusts, 68 Iowa L. Rev. 273 (1983); Annotation, *Trust provisions for payment, in the trustee's discretion or for a designated purpose, of part or all of the principal to a beneficiary*, 2 A.L.R.2d 1383 (1948); Annotation, *Propriety of considering beneficiary's other means under trust provision authorizing invasion of principal for beneficiary's support*, 41 A.L.R.3d 255 (1972 & Supp. 1995).

[2] George T. Bogert, Trusts §41 (6th ed. 1987).

Generally, beneficiaries of true discretionary trusts (*i.e.*, a trust whose terms entitle the beneficiary only to the amount of trust income or principal the trustee, in her uncontrolled discretion, decides to give to the beneficiary) cannot force the trustee to pay any amount from the trust. The only exception to this rule occurs when the beneficiary can show that the trustee abused her discretion.[3] Consequently, the beneficiary's creditors cannot reach the beneficiary's trust interest because the creditor cannot reach any greater interest than the beneficiary can reach. This results even in jurisdictions that do not allow spendthrift trusts.[4]

Planning Pointer. In jurisdictions that do not recognize spendthrift trusts, the planner should consider using a discretionary trust (1) to prevent creditors from reaching a beneficiary's interest, or (2) to prevent a beneficiary from assigning her interest to creditors.

EXAMPLE 5-23

Same facts as Example 5-19, except that the state Gertrude resides in does not recognize spendthrift trusts. Here, Gertrude and Bob can accomplish the same results by establishing a discretionary trust.

Caution. Discretionary trusts are disadvantageous in the sense that, because they give the trustee complete discretion, they give the grantor no assurance the beneficiary will be provided for.

Planning Pointer. To ensure the trust provides for the beneficiary's needs and effects the grantor's intention, the planner must use extreme care in selecting the trustee.

---

[3] Austin Wakeman Scott & William Franklin Fratcher, The Law of Trusts § 155 (4th ed. 1987). *See, e.g., In re* Larkins Will, 51 N.W.2d 396 (Iowa 1952); Damon v. Damon, 44 N.E.2d 657 (Mass. 1942); Scully v. Scully, 76 N.W.2d 239 (Neb. 1956); *But cf.* State *ex rel.* Secretary of Social & Rehabilitative Servs. v. Jackson, 822 P.2d 1033 (Kan. 1991) (court held that trust that used language from § 155 of Restatement (Second) of Trusts, which state had previously followed, was not discretionary trust; trust language construed narrowly when beneficiaries became recipients of public assistance).

[4] Austin Wakeman Scott & William Franklin Fratcher, The Law of Trusts § 155 (4th ed. 1987).

EXAMPLE 5-24

Same facts as Example 5-23, except that Gertrude makes her sister, Gwen, the trustee of the trust. Gertrude, Gwen, and Bob are a very close family unit. Here, although Gwen has complete discretion over the timing and amounts of trust principal and income payments to Bob, because of the existing family ties, Gertrude receives assurance that her intent and Bob's needs will be met.

When the trust is not purely discretionary, the beneficiary's creditors may be able to reach the beneficiary's interest when the trust is not a spend-thrift trust.[5] A trust will be purely discretionary when the trustee may with-hold the income and principal altogether from the beneficiary. A trust will not be purely discretionary when the trustee only has discretion concerning the time or method of making payments to, or for the benefit of, a beneficiary.[6]

EXAMPLE 5-25

Same facts as Example 5-24, except that the trust instrument provides that Gwen has complete discretion regarding when and how much any one pay-ment to Bob will be from the trust, as long as she pays out all trust income completely every five years. Here, the trust is not purely discretionary. Con-sequently, absent a valid spendthrift trust provision, Pam can reach Bob's trust interest.

Planning Pointer. The asset protection planner who uses a discretionary trust must ensure that the trust is a purely discretionary trust.

Caution. If the trust uses language stating or implying the use of an ascertainable standard concerning the trustee's distribution decisions, such language may give the beneficiary and, thus, her creditors some right to distributions. If this occurs, the beneficiary's creditors may be able to reach the beneficiary's trust interest.

Even for purely discretionary trusts, once the trustee elects to pay trust income to or for the benefit of a beneficiary, creditors may reach that amount.[7] Furthermore, once the beneficiary's creditors serve the trustee

---

[5] Austin Wakeman Scott & William Franklin Fratcher, The Law of Trusts § 155 (4th ed. 1987). *See, e.g.,* Bank of Union v. Heath, 121 S.E. 24 (N.C. 1924); *In re* Smith, 129 A. 657 (R.I. 1927).
[6] Austin Wakeman Scott & William Franklin Fratcher, The Law of Trusts § 155 (4th ed. 1987).

with process, the trustee will be liable to those creditors for any amounts subsequently paid to or for the benefit of the beneficiary.[8] However, if the trust includes a valid spendthrift provision, then the beneficiary's creditors cannot reach amounts the trustee elects to pay to or for the benefit of the beneficiary.[9]

EXAMPLE 5-26

Same facts as Example 5-24, except that Pam serves Gwen with process, notifying Gwen of her $1 million judgment against Bob. One week later, Gwen pays to Bob $500,000 of trust income. Here, absent a valid spendthrift trust provision, Gwen is personally liable to Pam for $500,000.

Planning Pointer. When valid, the planner should include a spendthrift trust provision in the discretionary trust's trust instrument. Furthermore, the trust instrument should clearly state that the beneficiary does not have any right to any amount before its actual distribution.[10]

Alternatively, the planner may provide that the trust will be discretionary but that if a creditor seeks to reach any trust interest, the trust becomes a spendthrift trust.[11] Also, the planner may provide that the trust becomes a trust for the beneficiary's family if any creditor of the beneficiary attempts to reach any trust interest.[12]

Caution. A discretionary trust established for the grantor's benefit will not provide asset protection from the grantor's creditors.[13]

---

[7] George T. Bogert, Trusts § 41 (6th ed. 1987).

[8] George T. Bogert, Trusts § 41 (6th ed. 1987); Austin Wakeman Scott & William Franklin Fratcher, The Law of Trusts § 155.1 (4th ed. 1987). *See, e.g.,* Todd's Executor v. Todd, 86 S.W.2d 168 (Ky. 1935); Calloway v. Smith, 186 S.W.2d 642 (Ky. Ct. App. 1945).

[9] George T. Bogert, Trusts § 41 (6th ed. 1987).

[10] Frank J. Rief III, Current and Future Family Asset Protection, in Sophisticated Estate Planning Techniques (ALI-ABA Course of Study, 1991).

[11] George T. Bogert, Trusts § 41 (6th ed. 1987). *See, e.g.,* Canfield v. Security-First Nat'l Bank, 87 P.2d 830 (Cal. 1939).

[12] George T. Bogert, Trusts § 41 (6th ed. 1987).

[13] George T. Bogert, Trusts § 41 (6th ed. 1987). *See, e.g.,* Greenwich Trust Co. v. Tyson, 27 A.2d 166 (Conn. 1942).

§5.11 SUPPORT TRUSTS

Support trusts[1] provide that the trustee must pay or apply trust income or principal for the benefit of the beneficiary, but only to the extent required to educate and support that beneficiary, and then only to the extent trust distributions can accomplish the goals of educating and supporting the trust beneficiary.[2] Because the trustee may only make trust distributions that will accomplish the education and support of the beneficiary, creditors and the beneficiary's assignees cannot reach the beneficiary's interest because such distributions would not accomplish the trust's objectives.[3] This is true even when the trust is not a spendthrift trust or in jurisdictions where spendthrift trusts are not valid.[4]

Planning Pointer. The planner should consider using support trusts as an alternative to discretionary trusts when the settlor desires to provide for the support and education of the beneficiary, for example, the settlor's children. Such trusts will be less attractive when the settlor desires the trust to make distributions to beneficiaries that will not be for the beneficiaries' support or education.

EXAMPLE 5-27

Charles and his wife Barbara live in a jurisdiction that does not recognize spendthrift trust provisions. They desire to establish a trust for their son, Ebenezer. Ebenezer is an entrepreneur who frequently invests in risky ventures, some of which are very successful and some of which are losers. Charles and Barbara want the trust to ensure that Ebenezer will not become homeless should one or more of his ventures wipe him out. They are especially concerned about this occurring after their deaths. On the other hand, they do not want Ebenezer's creditors to reach his trust interest, as this would not be in accord with their intent in establishing the trust. Finally, they want the remainder interest to go to Ebenezer's daughter, Nancy. Here a support trust would work well for Charles and Barbara. Specifically, such a trust

---

§5.11   [1] *See generally* Austin Wakeman Scott & William Franklin Fratcher, The Law of Trusts §154 (4th ed. 1987); George Gleason Bogert & George Taylor Bogert, The Law of Trusts and Trustees §229 (rev. 2d ed. 1992); George T. Bogert, Trusts §42 (6th ed. 1987); Evelyn Ginsberg Abravanel, *Discretionary Support Trusts*, 68 Iowa L. Rev. 273 (1983); Annotation, *Surplus income of trust, in excess of amount required for support and education of beneficiary, as subject to claims of creditors*, 36 A.L.R.2d 1215 (1954).

[2] George T. Bogert, Trusts §42 (6th ed. 1987).

[3] George T. Bogert, Trusts §42 (6th ed. 1987). *See, e.g., In re* McLoughlin, 507 F.2d 177 (5th Cir. 1975); Jones v. Coon, 295 N.W. 162 (Iowa 1940); First Nat'l Bank v. Department of Health & Mental Hygiene, 399 A.2d 891 (Md. 1979).

[4] Austin Wakeman Scott & William Franklin Fratcher, The Law of Trusts §154 (4th ed. 1987). *See, e.g.,* Thurber v. Thurber, 112 A. 209 (R.I. 1921).

would (1) provide for Ebenezer's support, (2) protect the trust corpus from Ebenezer's creditors, and (3) provide any remainder to Nancy.

EXAMPLE 5-28

Same facts as Example 5-27, except that Charles and Barbara have previously established a support trust for Ebenezer and would like the new trust to provide funds for Ebenezer to start a new venture should he be completely wiped out financially. Here, a support trust would not effect Charles and Barbara's intentions. In this instance, a discretionary trust with a carefully chosen trustee would better serve their needs.

Caution. If the trust instrument provides that the trust is to distribute a fixed amount or percentage of funds for the beneficiary's education and support, it will not be considered a true support trust.[5] Consequently, the beneficiary's creditors can reach the beneficiary's interest in such a trust, absent a valid spendthrift trust provision.[6]

§ 5.12 CHARITABLE REMAINDER TRUSTS

[A] Introduction

Charitable remainder trusts (CRTS)[1] provide for specified distributions at least annually to one or more beneficiaries, at least one of which is not a charity, for life or for a term of years not exceeding 20 years, with an irrevocable remainder interest to be held for the benefit of or paid over to a charity.[2] CRTs may be inter vivos trusts or testamentary trusts.

EXAMPLE 5-29

Lew creates a charitable remainder trust (CRT) on January 1, 2002, and he transfers $1 million of appreciated stock, with a $0 basis to it. Lew is the

---

[5] George T. Bogert, Trusts § 42 (6th ed. 1987).

[6] George T. Bogert, Trusts § 42 (6th ed. 1987). *See, e.g.,* Meade v. Rowe's Executor, 182 S.W.2d 30 (Ky. 1944); Young v. Easley, 26 S.E. 401 (Va. 1897).

§ 5.12 [1] *See generally* Lewis D. Solomon & Lewis J. Saret, Asset Protection Strategies: Forms and Commentary § 3.08 (2001); Conrad Teitell, *Charitable Remainder Trust Gift Planning . . . Including the Full-Monty CRUT,* in *II Estate Planning In Depth* (ALI-ABA Course of Study Materials, Course No. SF93, 2001); Howard M. Zaritsky, Tax Planning for Family Wealth Transfers ¶ 5.02 (3d ed. 1997 & Supp. 2002).

[2] Treas. Reg. § 1.664-1(a)(1)(i).

beneficiary for 20 years and will receive a payment equal to 5 percent of the trust corpus, or $50,000 each year. At the end of 20 years, the remainder interest goes to a qualified charity, such as the World Wildlife Fund, the Kennedy Center, or the Phillips Museum.

The tax consequences are:

Income Tax Charitable Contribution Deduction:
$413,773.41

Gift Tax: None

Estate Tax: None

A qualified CRT is exempt from income tax. The grantor may claim a charitable income and estate and/or gift tax deduction based on the present value of the remainder interest passing to the charity. Generally, CRTs are very valuable from financial planning and wealth preservation planning standpoints. They are particularly valuable for high-income individuals who want to dispose of highly appreciated property and who are charitably inclined.

There are two types of CRTs: charitable remainder annuity trusts (CRATs) and charitable remainder unitrusts (CRUTs). A CRAT must pay a sum certain annually to one or more beneficiaries, at least one of which must be a noncharitable beneficiary (*i.e.,* the annuity payment). The annuity payment must be at least 5 percent but not more than 50 percent of the fair market value of the trust assets valued on the date that such assets are transferred to the CRAT.[3] In addition, the value of the remainder interest that passes to the charitable beneficiary must be at least 10 percent of the value of the property transferred to the CRAT.[4]

A CRUT must pay a fixed percentage of its net fair market value at least annually to one or more beneficiaries, at least one of which must be a noncharitable beneficiary (*i.e.,* the unitrust payment). The fixed percentage must be at least 5 percent but not more than 50 percent of the net fair market value of the trust assets as valued annually. In addition, the value of the remainder interest that passes to the charitable beneficiary must be at least 10 percent of the value of the property transferred to the CRUT.[5] Therefore, unlike a CRAT, which must pay a fixed dollar amount each year, a CRUT pays an amount that fluctuates each year with the value of the CRUT assets.

A CRUT (but not a CRAT) may also provide for the payment of the lesser of the fixed percentage or the trust accounting income (*i.e.,* a "net income only" unitrust). Net income only unitrusts may also provide that any amount by which the trust accounting income falls short of the fixed unitrust percentage must be paid out in later years, to the extent the CRUT's accounting income exceeds the unitrust percentage (*i.e.,* a "makeup" provision). Such CRUTs are commonly referred to as "NIMCRUTs."[6] Finally, CRUTs may contain a provision allowing

---

[3] IRC § 664(d)(1)(A).
[4] IRC § 664(d)(1)(D).
[5] IRC § 664(d)(2)(D).
[6] Treas. Reg. § 1.664-3(a)(1)(i)(c).

them to begin as net income only unitrusts but to convert (*i.e.*, flip) to a regular unitrust. Such CRUTs are commonly referred to as "flip unitrusts."

> **Planning Pointer.** A CRT may:
>
> 1. Provide the grantor with a charitable contribution deduction for income tax purposes for the year of the transfer of property to the CRT;
> 2. Provide the grantor with a gift or estate tax charitable contribution deduction;
> 3. Provide a noncharitable beneficiary with a stream of income for a fixed period not to exceed 20 years or the beneficiary's life;
> 4. Allow the grantor to avoid the direct realization of taxable gain on the sale of appreciated property;[7] and
> 5. Reduce federal estate taxes without lowering the amount of assets that the grantor transfers to her family when used with an irrevocable life insurance trust.

On the other hand, to obtain such benefits, planners must ensure that a CRT complies with applicable rules.

EXAMPLE 5-30

George owns stock in White Corporation, which he founded and which has a fair market value of $2.5 million and a basis of $0. Having watched friends at Enron lose their entire savings through lack of diversification, George decides to sell his stock and purchase a diversified investment portfolio. He sells his stock in 2002 and recognizes a $2.5 million long term capital gain. Here, he pays capital gains tax of $500,000 (*i.e.*, $2.5 million 20 percent), and is left with a diversified portfolio worth $2 million.

EXAMPLE 5-31

Same facts as Example 5-30, except that George donates his White Corporation stock to a CRAT, retaining a 5 percent payout for 20 years with the remainder interest to go to a qualified charity. The CRT sells the stock and invests in a diversified portfolio of stock. Here, because the CRT is tax exempt,

---

[7] However, taxable gain on the sale of appreciated property by a CRT may flow out to the noncharitable beneficiary of the CRT.

it pays $0 tax on the sale of the White Corporation stock and is able to acquire a diversified portfolio worth $2.5 million rather than $2.0 million, as in Example 5-30. In addition, George receives an income tax charitable contribution deduction in the year that he funds the CRT. The amount of the charitable income tax deduction is $1,034,433.53. This yields a tax savings, at George's combined federal and state marginal income tax rate of 40 percent, of $413,773.41. In addition, George receives an annuity of $125,000 per year. If the CRAT had no other income, this would be taxable as capital gains.

[B] Charitable Remainder Trust Rules

IRC Section 664 and Treasury Regulations thereunder constitute the primary source for the applicable rules for qualified CRTs. Failure to satisfy the CRT requirements set forth by IRC Section 664 may cause trust income to be attributed to the grantor and disallowance of the grantor's income tax charitable deduction. In addition, the CRT must constitute a valid irrevocable trust under applicable local law.[8]

[1] CRATs and CRUTs

Section 664 provides for two types of charitable remainder trusts: CRATs and CRUTs.[9] A CRT must be either a CRAT or a CRUT. A CRT cannot combine the payment arrangements of a CRAT and a CRUT into one CRT.[10] To illustrate, a CRT cannot provide for an annual payment to a noncharitable beneficiary of the greater of a sum certain or a fixed percentage of the annually determined value of the trust assets.

[a] CRATs

CRATs provide for fixed amount payments that must be made at least annually to one or more noncharitable beneficiaries (*i.e.*, the annuity amount)[11] for either a fixed number of years, not longer than 20 years, or for the life of the beneficiary.[12] These payments are the annuity payments, and they must be no less than 5 percent and no more than 50 percent of the initial fair market value of all property placed into the trust.[13] In addition, the present value of the remainder interest must be at least 10 percent of the fair market value of the assets contributed to the CRAT.[14]

---

[8] Treas. Reg. § 1.664-1(a)(1)(i); Rev. Proc. 89-20, 1989-1 C.B. 841.
[9] IRC § 664(d).
[10] *See, e.g.,* Priv. Ltr. Rul. 7848075.
[11] Treas. Reg. § 1.6641(a)(1)(iii).
[12] IRC § 664(d)(1).
[13] IRC § 664(d)(1).
[14] IRC § 664(d)(1)(D).

Planning Pointer. The annuity payment may be stated in the CRT instrument as either an absolute dollar amount or as a fraction or percentage of the initial fair market value of the property placed into the trust.[15] It is generally advantageous to draft the CRAT instrument to provide for annuity payments as a percentage or fraction of the initial net fair market value of assets transferred to the trust as opposed to a fixed dollar amount. This ensures that the annuity payment will meet the percentage requirements (*i.e.*, the requirement that the annuity payments be no less than 5 percent and no more than 50 percent of the initial fair market value of all property placed into the trust).

Caution. The CRAT must prohibit any additional contributions by any party, including the grantor, after its initial funding.[16] However, for this purpose, Treasury Regulations treat all property passing to a CRAT because of the death of the grantor as one contribution. Also, when the CRAT income is insufficient to pay the annual annuity amount, the CRAT must use its corpus to pay such amount. However, no other payment may be made out of the trust corpus to any noncharitable recipient.[17] To illustrate, the grantor cannot give a power to invade, alter, amend, or revoke a CRAT for the beneficial use of a person other than a qualified charity under IRC Section 170(c).

At the annuity period's end, the trust's remainder interest must be transferred to or for the use of a charitable organization described in IRC Section 170(c) or retained by the CRAT for such a use.[18] Other than the annuity payments, no other payments may be paid from the CRAT to or for the use of any person other than an IRC Section 170(c) organization.[19]

[b] CRUTs

There are four types of CRUTs: standard CRUTs, net income unitrusts, NIM-CRUTs, and flip unitrusts.

[i] Standard CRUTs

Standard CRUTs are similar to CRATs, except that instead of fixed amount annuity payments, CRUTs provide for the payment of an amount of money equivalent to a fixed percentage that is not less than 5 percent or more than 50

---

[15] Treas. Reg. § 1.664-2(a)(1)(ii), (iii).
[16] Treas. Reg. § 1.664-2(b); Rev. Rul. 72-95, 1972-2 C.B. 395.
[17] Treas. Reg. § 1.664-2(a)(4).
[18] IRC § 664(d)(1).
[19] IRC § 664(d)(1).

percent of the fair market value of the trust assets, initially and redetermined annually, for a fixed number of years that equals 20 years or less or for the beneficiary's life.[20] The CRUT instrument may express the fixed percentage as either a fraction or as a percentage.[21] In addition, the present value of the remainder interest must be at least 10 percent of the fair market value of the assets contributed to the CRUT.[22] As with a CRAT, the annuity payments must be made at least annually. For purposes of the CRT rules, a percentage is considered fixed if the percentage is the same as to each recipient or as to the total percentage payable each year.[23] As with CRATs, when the CRUT's income is not sufficient to pay the annual annuity amount, the CRUT must use its corpus to make the payment.[24] As with CRATs, no other payments may be made out of the trust corpus to any noncharitable organization.[25]

> **Planning Pointer.** Unlike a CRAT, which cannot allow any additional contributions after the initial funding of the trust, a CRUT may allow such additional contributions. However, when the CRUT includes such a provision, it must also include provisions for the valuation of additional contributions and for the adjustment of the unitrust payout amount for the remainder of the year in which the additional contributions are made.[26]
>
> One advantage of using a CRUT instead of a CRAT is that CRUT payments are better able to keep pace with inflation than CRAT payments, which are fixed in amount.[27]
>
> One disadvantage associated with CRUTs is that they involve the cost of obtaining an appraisal of trust assets each year. Specifically, the CRUT must value its assets annually, either (1) as of a specified date during the year, selected either by the trust instrument or by the trustee when the trust is silent, or (2) by computing an average of the values of the trust assets determined on various dates throughout the year.[28] The method and date(s) chosen in the first year must generally be used in each subsequent year.[29]

EXAMPLE 5-32

Same facts as Example 5-29, except that the CRT is a CRUT. Here the CRUT instrument provides that it will make a unitrust payment each year of 5

---

[20] IRC § 664(d)(2).
[21] Treas. Reg. § 1.664-3(a)(1)(ii).
[22] IRC § 664(d)(2)(D).
[23] Treas. Reg. § 1.664-3(a)(1)(ii).
[24] Treas. Reg. § 1.664-3(a)(1)(i)(a).
[25] Treas. Reg. § 1.664-3(a)(4).
[26] Treas. Reg. § 1.664-3(b); Rev. Rul. 74-481, 1974-2 C.B. 190; Rev. Rul. 74-149, 1974-1 C.B. 157.
[27] William L. Hoisington, *The Truth about Charitable Remainder Trusts*, 45 Tax Law. 293, 305 (1992).
[28] Treas. Reg § 1.664-3(a)(1)(iv).
[29] Treas. Reg. § 1.664-3(a)(1)(iv).

percent of the value of the CRUT assets, and in 2003 the CRUT's assets are worth $1,100,000. Here, the CRUT payment would be $55,000. Conversely, if the value of the CRUT's assets equaled $700,000, the unitrust payment would be $35,000.

[ii] Net Income Unitrusts

The CRUT may, as an alternative to a fixed percentage of trust assets, provide that the annual annuity amounts will equal the lesser of (1) the designated unitrust amount or (2) all of the unitrust income.[30] Such CRUTs are generally referred to as "net income only" unitrusts (NICRUTs).

EXAMPLE 5-33

Same facts as Example 5-29, except that the CRUT is a Net Income CRUT (NICRUT) and has no income in 2003. Here, the unitrust payment for 2003 would be $0. If the CRUT were a standard CRUT, it would have to make a distribution of corpus to Lew.

[iii] NIMCRUTs

When a net income unitrust is used, the trust may include a "makeup" provision that provides that any amount by which the trust accounting income falls short of the fixed unitrust percentage must be paid out in later years, to the extent the NIMCRUT's accounting income exceeds the unitrust percentage. The 5-percent minimum payout requirement is not violated merely because the trust provides for a reduction in the fixed unitrust payout percentage either on the death of a noncharitable recipient or a term of years if (1) a distribution is made to an IRC Section 170(c) organization at the death of such recipient or the expiration of such term of years and (2) the distribution percentage payable after the reduction is not less than 5 percent.[31]

EXAMPLE 5-34

Same facts as Example 5-33, except the CRUT is a NIMCRUT. The value of the NIMCRUT assets remains at $1,000,000, and the NIMCRUT has income of $50,000 in 2002, $0 in 2003, and $150,000 in 2004. Here, the NIMCRUT would make unitrust payments of $50,000 in 2002, $0 in 2003, and $100,000 in 2004.

[iv] Flip Unitrusts

A flip unitrust is a CRUT that begins as either a net income unitrust or a NIMCRUT but subsequently changes to a standard CRUT. Flip unitrusts are

---

[30] IRC § 664(d)(3)(A); Treas. Reg. § 1.664-3(a)(1)(i)(b)(1).
[31] Treas. Reg. § 1.664-3(a)(2)(ii).

allowed under Treasury Regulation Section 1.664-3(a)(1)(i)(c). They can be very useful in certain circumstances. For example, flip unitrusts are valuable where the grantor contributes an appreciated non-income producing asset, such as undeveloped land, to a CRUT. Here, a flip unitrust can pay income only until the property is sold and after the sale "flip" into a standard CRUT, giving the grantor greater assurance that he or she will receive the unitrust payment, regardless of how the funds are invested.

To qualify as a CRT, the flip unitrust instrument must provide each of the following:[32]

- The change to a standard CRUT must be triggered on a specific date or by a single event whose occurrence is not discretionary with, or within the control of, the trustees or any other persons. For purposes of this rule, a triggering event based on the sale of unmarketable assets (as defined in Treasury Regulation Section 1.664-1(a)(7)(ii)) or the marriage, divorce, death, or birth of a child with respect to any individual will not be considered discretionary with, or within the control of, the trustees or any other persons.[33]
- The change to standard CRUT occurs at the beginning of the taxable year that immediately follows the taxable year during which the triggering event occurs.
- Following the conversion to a standard CRUT, the trust will pay at least annually to the noncharitable beneficiaries the standard CRUT amount, and not a net income unitrust amount or a NIMCRUT unitrust amount.

[2] Income Beneficiaries

CRTs must provide for the payment of a sum certain (*i.e.*, annuity payment) or a fixed percentage (*i.e.*, unitrust amount) to one or more named persons, at least one of whom must be a noncharitable beneficiary.[34] However, a CRT may pay part of the annuity or unitrust payment to a charitable organization as well, as long as there is always a noncharitable income beneficiary. In such a case, however, the grantor generally cannot claim an additional charitable contribution deduction for income tax purposes for the annuity or unitrust payment.[35]

The Internal Revenue Code generally defines the term "person" to include individuals, trusts, estates, partnerships, associations, companies, and corporations.[36] Notwithstanding the fore going, in order for the annuity payments to extend for the life of the beneficiary, the beneficiary must be an individual.[37] Otherwise, the annuity period must be a fixed period that does not exceed

---

[32] Treas. Reg. § 1.664-3(a)(1)(i)(c).
[33] Treas. Reg. § 1.664-3(a)(1)(i)(d).
[34] IRC § 664(d)(1)(A), (2)(A).
[35] Treas. Reg. §§ 1.664-2(d), -3(d).
[36] IRC § 7701(a)(1). *See, e.g.,* Priv. Ltr. Rul. 9419021 (limited partnership constituted permissible unitrust beneficiary).
[37] Treas. Reg. § 1.664-2(a)(5).

20 years.[38] When a beneficiary does receive annuity payments for life, the annuity payments must be based on the beneficiary's life, instead of another individual's life.[39] The annuity or unitrust amount must begin with the first year of the CRT.[40]

> **Caution.** No amount other than the annuity or unitrust payment can be paid to any person other than the charitable beneficiary.[41] Among other things, this rule prohibits the testamentary trust from bearing the cost of any of the estate administration expenses and costs, including estate tax.[42]

> **Caution.** Pets are not permissible noncharitable beneficiaries.[43] However, on May 10, 2001, Rep. Earl Blumenauer, D-Or., did introduce H.R. 1796, which, if enacted, would have amended IRC Section 664 to permit the creation of "charitable remainder pet trusts." Such trusts would operate in a manner similar to normal charitable remainder trusts with income payable for the exclusive benefit of one or more pets for a term of up to 20 years or for the life or lives of such pet or pets.

[3] Charitable Remainder Beneficiary

On the termination of the annuity period, the entire trust corpus must be (1) irrevocably transferred, in whole or in part, to or for the use of one or more IRC Section 170(c) organizations or (2) retained for such a use.[44] However, the CRT may include a provision that allows the grantor to appoint other qualified organizations as the trust remainderman instead of the original charitable remainderman.[45] The CRT must provide for the selection of an alternative charitable remainderman if the designated charitable beneficiary does not qualify as an organization described in IRC Section 170(c) at the expiration of the last noncharitable interest.[46]

> **Planning Pointer.** Although the IRC Section 664 rules require the charitable remainderman to be a qualified charitable organization as defined by IRC Section 170(c), the definitions of "qualified charitable organizations" for the estate and gift tax charitable deductions differ slightly. To ensure that the CRT will qualify for both the income and transfer tax charitable deductions,

---

[38] Treas. Reg. § 1.664-2(a)(5).
[39] IRC § 664(d)(1)(A); Treas. Reg. § 1.664-2(a)(5).
[40] Treas. Reg. §§ 1.664-2(a)(5), -3(a)(5).
[41] IRC § 664(d)(1)(B), (2)(B); Treas. Reg. § 1.664-2(a)(4).
[42] Treas. Reg. § 1.664-1(a)(6), Examples (3), (4), and (5); Priv. Ltr. Rul. 7724055.
[43] Rev. Rul. 78-105, 1978-1 C.B. 295.
[44] Treas. Reg. § 1.664-2(a)(6).
[45] *See, e.g.,* Rev. Rul. 76-8, 1976-1 C.B. 179.
[46] Treas. Reg. §§ 1.664-2(a)(6)(iv), -3(a)(6)(iv).

the planner should include a provision in the trust instrument that the designated charitable remainderman, and any alternative charitable remainderman, must qualify as an organization under both IRC Section 170(c) and Sections 2055(c) and 2522(a).[47]

As noted above, the value of the interest given to the charitable remainder beneficiary must be at least equal to 10 percent of the value of the property transferred to the trust, determined using the applicable IRC Section 7520 rate.[48] As a practical matter, this limits the use of CRTs with young life beneficiaries or with multiple life beneficiaries.

[4] Contributions and Investments

[a] Contributions

IRC Section 664 and Treasury Regulations there under contain no explicit limits on the types of assets that grantors may contribute to a CRT. On the other hand, contributions of certain types of assets will cause serious ancillary problems, resulting from a variety of rules, including the private foundation rules, the unrelated business income tax, and so on. In addition, as discussed more fully below, grantors frequently contribute appreciated property to CRTs because no gain will be recognized on the contribution of such appreciated property to the CRT and the CRT can then sell the property without paying any tax on the gain.

One problem asset for CRTs is encumbered property. Specifically, the IRS takes the position that encumbered property cannot be transferred to a CRT when the grantor remains personally liable on the debt.[49] It also takes the same position with respect to transfers to CRTs of options to purchase encumbered property.[50] The IRS's rationale is that because the CRT could potentially be forced to pay the debt, the CRT's income could be used to discharge the grantor's legal liability, within the meaning of Treasury Regulation Section 1.677(a)-1(d), thereby making the trust a grantor trust, which cannot qualify as a CRT.[51] In addition, the transfer of encumbered property to a CRT raises other qualification issues, including IRC Section 4941 self-dealing and IRC Section 514 debt-financed income.

> **Caution.** When considering what assets to contribute to a CRT, planners should analyze the impact of such asset upon the following rules, which interact with the IRC Section 664 CRT requirements:
>
> - **The grantor trust rules.** A grantor trust cannot qualify as a CRT.

---

[47] *See, e.g.,* Rev. Rul. 76-307, 1976-2 C.B. 56, Rev. Rul. 77-385, 1977-2 C.B. 331.
[48] IRC § 664(d)(1)(D), (2)(D).
[49] *See, e.g.,* Priv. Ltr. Rul. 9015049.
[50] *See* Priv. Ltr. Rul. 9501004.
[51] Treas. Reg. § 1.664-1(a)(4).

- **The unrelated business income tax (UBIT).** If a CRT has any UBIT, it will be taxed as a complex trust rather than be exempt from tax.[52]
- **The private foundation rules.** Some of the private foundation rules, which provide for various sanctions including a variety of excise taxes, apply to CRTs. Therefore, planners must ensure that contributed property does not violate the applicable private foundation rules.
- The Code treats CRATs and CRUTs differently with respect to additional contributions. Specifically, the IRC prohibits additional contributions to a CRAT after its initial funding.[53] However, for this purpose, Treasury Regulations treat all property passing to a CRAT because of the death of the grantor as one contribution. Conversely, the IRC allows additional contributions to a CRUT after its initial funding.[54]

[b]   Restrictions on Investments

A trust will not qualify as a CRT if the trust instrument restricts the trustee from investing the trust assets in a manner that could result in the annual realization of a reasonable amount of income or gain from the sale or disposition of trust assets.[55] Although the regulations do not require that a CRT instrument include a provision providing that the trustee is not restricted in his or her investments, each of the sample CRT instruments, which the IRS has published in Revenue Procedures 89-20,[56] 89-21,[57] 90-31,[58] and 90-32,[59] contains such a provision.

Generally, the IRS has looked at whether CRT instrument provisions, or other aspects of the CRT arrangement, have legally restricted the trustee's investment options. To illustrate:

- Provisions suggesting or recommending certain courses of investment action are generally allowed.[60]
- Provisions mandating certain courses of investment action generally disallow CRT qualification.[61]
- Contribution of assets, in which a life estate is retained, will generally disqualify the CRT because the IRS takes the position that this violates the requirement that the trustee must be free to invest the assets in a manner that will permit the assets to realize a reasonable rate of return.[62]

---

[52] IRC § 664(c).

[53] Treas. Reg. § 1.664-2(b).

[54] Treas. Reg. § 1.664-3(b).

[55] Treas. Reg. § 1.664-1(a)(3).

[56] 1989 -1 C.B. 841.

[57] 1989 -1 C.B. 842.

[58] 1990 -1 C.B. 539.

[59] 1990 -1 C.B. 546.

[60] *See, e.g.,* Priv. Ltr. Rul. 7803029 (provision expressing grantor's belief that mutual funds were best investment, without requiring such an investment strategy, did not disqualify CRT).

[61] *See, e.g.,* Priv. Ltr. Rul. 7802037 (provision requiring trustee to invest in tax-exempt securities disallowed CRT).

[62] Rev. Rul. 73-601, 1973-2 C.B. 213.

[5] Restrictions on Powers of Invasion or Reversion

A trust will not qualify as a CRT if it is subject to a power to invade, alter, amend, or revoke for the benefit of a person other than the charitable beneficiary. The sole exception to this rule is that the grantor of the CRT may retain a testamentary power to revoke or terminate the life interest of a noncharitable beneficiary.[63]

Caution. Sometimes drafters of CRTs have included provisions requiring the trust to return assets to the grantor where the grantor fails to receive the desired tax results. The IRS has ruled that such provisions will disqualify a CRT.[64] However, planners can, as a practical matter, do an end run around this prohibition by including a provision in the trust instrument granting the trustee a limited power to amend the trust in any manner required for the sole purpose of ensuring that the trust qualifies and continues to qualify as a CRT under IRC Section 664. Such a provision is included in the sample CRT trust instruments that the IRS has issued.[65]

Caution. Because a CRT is a trust that is governed by local state law, in some states drafters may have to affirmatively include language in the CRT instrument to negate a power that state law otherwise would give to the trustee to invade the CRT for the grantor or a noncharitable beneficiary's benefit.[66]

[6] Who May Be Trustee?

[a] Grantor as Trustee

The grantor may serve as the trustee of his or her own CRT.[67] However, where the grantor does serve as the CRT's trustee, the grantor must not retain any powers that would cause the trust to be treated as a grantor trust. Grantor trust treatment would disqualify the CRT. To illustrate, a grantor/trustee cannot retain the ability to "sprinkle" income unless there is a co-trustee with an adverse interest in the CRT.[68] For this purpose, any power exercisable by a

---

[63] Treas. Reg. §§ 1.664-2(a)(4), -3(a)(4).

[64] Rev. Rul. 76-309, 1976-2 C.B. 196.

[65] See Rev. Proc. 89-20, 1989-1 C.B. 841, § 10; Rev. Proc. 89-21, 1989-1 C.B. 842, § 10.

[66] See Rev. Rul. 77-58, 1977-1 C.B. 175 (trust did not qualify as CRT because of failure to negate applicable state trust law giving trustee the power, under certain circumstances, to invade the trust for the grantor or income beneficiary's benefit).

[67] See, e.g., Priv. Ltr. Rul. 7730015.

[68] IRC § 674(a).

trustee is imputed to the grantor if the grantor retains the power to remove, substitute, or add trustees.[69]

Where the grantor serves as the trustee of a CRT that holds difficult to value assets, the CRT must obtain a qualified appraisal from a qualified appraiser, as defined in Treasury Regulation Sections 1.170A-13(c)(3) and -13(c)(5), respectively.[70]

Where the grantor serves as trustee, the grantor may receive commissions for his or her services as trustee, as long as the commissions do not exceed the statutory rate allowed by applicable state law.[71]

[b] Charitable Beneficiary as Trustee

The charitable beneficiary can also serve as the CRT trustee, as long as applicable state law does not prohibit this and the organization is allowed to do so by its governing charter. As with a grantor/trustee, if the CRT holds difficult to value assets, the CRT must obtain a qualified appraisal from a qualified appraiser, as defined in Treasury Regulation Sections 1.170A-13(c)(3) and -13(c)(5), respectively.[72]

In addition to the foregoing, where the charitable beneficiary serves as the CRT trustee, it may invest the trust assets with its general endowment fund or with the assets of other CRTs.[73] However, the Philanthropy Protection Act of 1995 requires a charity acting as trustee of a CRT to provide written disclosure to the donor concerning commingling of funds. If the charity is acting as trustee of a CRT in which the remainder is irrevocably dedicated to any charitable organization and if the assets of the CRT are not segregated but instead are commingled with other charitable assets in a collective investment vehicle, the trustee must disclose enough information about the operation of the charity income fund in which the gift may be pooled to permit the donor to make informed decisions about whether to make a gift and whether to permit a gift to be pooled in such a fund.[74]

[c] Institutional Trustee as Trustee

An institutional trustee may serve as trustee, as long as the CRT instrument authorizes it to do so and state law does not prohibit the institutional trustee from serving as the CRT's trustee. Institutional trustees may invest CRT assets in their own common trust funds.[75]

---

[69] Treas. Reg. § 1.674(d)-2(a).

[70] Treas. Reg. § 1.664-1(a)(7).

[71] *See* Priv. Ltr. Ruls. 8033026, 8035078.

[72] Treas. Reg. § 1.664-1(a)(7).

[73] Rev. Rul. 83-19, 1983-1 C.B. 115; Priv. Ltr. Ruls. 8212067, 8220120, 8903019.

[74] P.L. 104-62, Dec. 8, 1995, 109 Stat. 682.

[75] Rev. Rul. 73-571, 1973-2 C.B. 213.

[C] Income Taxation of CRT's Income Beneficiary

Generally, IRC Section 664(b) and the regulations thereunder determine the tax character of annuity or unitrust payments to the noncharitable beneficiary. For this purpose, these provisions supersede all other provisions of the IRC.[76] These rules are commonly referred to as the "tier" rules. The tier rules apply to each tax year of the CRT, regardless of whether the CRT becomes subject to taxation due to the presence of unrelated business income tax.[77] If the CRT becomes taxable because of unrelated business taxable income, any resulting tax is ignored in determining the character of distributions.[78] Consequently, the noncharitable income beneficiary does not receive any credit for taxes paid by the CRT.

Regardless of the actual CRT trust income for a particular year, all annuity or unitrust payments are deemed to be made first from ordinary income, second from capital gains, third from "other income" (*e.g.*, tax-exempt income), and last from trust corpus.[79] Current and previously undistributed income of each tier must be exhausted in the order set forth above before income earned in the next year is deemed distributed.

[1] Tiers of Income

Distributions of income from a CRT to the noncharitable income beneficiary are treated as follows.

[a] Ordinary Income

First, distributions are treated as ordinary income to the extent of the CRT's ordinary income for the taxable year in question and its undistributed ordinary income for prior years. An ordinary loss (*i.e.*, any loss from the sale or exchange of any property that is not a capital asset) for the current year will reduce undistributed ordinary income for prior years and any excess will be carried forward indefinitely to reduce ordinary income for future years. For purposes of this rule, the amount of current and prior years' income must be computed without regard to the deduction for net operating losses provided by IRC Sections 172 or 642(d).[80]

[b] Capital Gains

Second, distributions are treated as capital gains to the extent of the CRT's undistributed capital gains. Undistributed capital gains are determined on a

---

[76] IRC § 664(b); Treas. Reg. § 1.664-1(d)(1).

[77] Treas. Reg. § 1.664-1(c).

[78] Treas. Reg. § 1.664-1(c).

[79] IRC § 664(b).

[80] Treas. Reg. § 1.664-1(d)(1)(i)(a).

cumulative net basis under the rules of IRC Section 664 without regard to the normal capital gain provisions of IRC Section 1212. With respect to capital gains, the following rules apply:[81]

- **Long- and short-term capital gains.** If, in any tax year of the CRT, the CRT has both undistributed short-term capital gain and undistributed long-term capital gain, then the short-term capital gain must be deemed distributed before any long-term capital gain.
- **Capital losses in excess of capital gains.** If the CRT has, for any tax year, capital losses in excess of capital gains, any excess of the net short-term capital loss over the net long-term capital gain for such year must be a short-term capital loss in the succeeding tax year and any excess of the net long-term capital loss over the net short-term capital gain for such year must be a long-term capital loss in the succeeding tax year.
- **Capital gains in excess of capital losses.** If the CRT has for any tax year capital gains in excess of capital losses, any excess of the net short-term capital gain over the net long-term capital loss for such year shall be, to the extent not deemed distributed, a short-term capital gain in the succeeding tax year, and any excess of the net long-term capital gain over the net short-term capital loss for such year must be, to the extent not deemed distributed, a long-term capital gain in the succeeding tax year.

[c]   Other Income

Third, distributions are treated as other income (including tax exempt income) to the extent of the sum of the CRT's other income for the taxable year and its undistributed other income for prior years. A loss in this category for the current year is used to reduce undistributed other income for prior years and any excess is carried forward indefinitely to reduce such income for future years.[82]

[d]   Corpus

Finally, CRT distributions are treated as a distribution of trust corpus. For purposes of this rule, the term "corpus" means the net fair market value of the trust assets less the total undistributed income (but not loss) in each of the above categories.[83]

[2]   Allocation of Deductions

CRTs are allowed certain deductions in calculating the annual amount of income and corpus in each tier. However, such permissible deductions do not

---

[81] Treas. Reg. § 1.664-1(d)(1)(i)(b).
[82] Treas. Reg. § 1.664-1(d)(1)(i)(c).
[83] Treas. Reg. § 1.664-1(d)(1)(i)(d).

include several deductions ordinarily available to trusts. Specifically, the non-allowable deductions include the following:

- Personal exemption (IRC Section 642(b));
- Charitable deduction (IRC Section 642(c));
- Distributions deduction (IRC Section 661).[84]

On the other hand, a CRT is not subject to the 2 percent floor for certain ordinary income "miscellaneous deductions."[85]

Deductions directly attributable to one or more classes of items within a tier are allocated to those items.[86] All other deductions are allocated among the items in a particular tier in the proportion that the gross income of each class of items included in the tier, reduced by deductions attributed to that class under the first allocation, bears to all income in the tier.[87] However, the allocation cannot create or increase a net loss within a class. Any deductions not allocable under either of the first two provisions can be allocated in any manner.[88] All taxes imposed due to any unrelated business income tax, along with any expense not deductible in determining taxable income and not allocable to any class of items in the "other income" tier, are allocated to corpus.[89]

[D] CRT Taxation and Administration

[1] CRT Taxation

A CRT is exempt from income tax except for any year that it has unrelated business taxable income or debt-financed income.[90] If a CRT has either unrelated business taxable income or debt-financed income, it will be taxed as a complex trust under IRC Sections 641-644 and 661-664. Accordingly, the trust is subject to all the taxes imposed on complex trusts, including, for example, the alternative minimum tax and depreciation recapture.

In addition to such complex trust tax treatment, the tier rules discussed above will continue to apply.[91] Therefore, the CRT distributions to beneficiaries would continue to be taxed under the tier rules, without credit for any taxes paid by the CRT.

[2] Calendar Year

CRTs must use a calendar year for tax purposes.[92]

---

[84] Treas. Reg. § 1.664-1(d)(2).
[85] IRC § 67(a), (b).
[86] Treas. Reg. § 1.664-1(d)(2).
[87] Treas. Reg. § 1.664-1(d)(2).
[88] Treas. Reg. § 1.664-1(d)(2).
[89] Treas. Reg. § 1.664-1(d)(2).
[90] IRC § 664(c); Treas. Reg. § 1.664-1(a)(1)(i).
[91] Treas. Reg. § 1.664-1(d)(1)(i).
[92] IRC § 644.

[3]   Recordkeeping Requirements

It is critical that the CRT maintain detailed records. Such records should include information about the following types of items:

- All income items as adjusted for carryovers and carrybacks, and all deductions and the allocations thereof. This information is required for purposes of computing the character of current and undistributed income for the tier rules, discussed above.
- All sales of property and certain deemed sales, noted and characterized.
- All items of tax preference for alternative minimum tax purposes.
- Documentation regarding the basis and holding period of all trust assets.

[4]   Tax Reporting Requirements

CRTs must file certain tax returns annually, on or before the 15th day of the fourth month following the close of the trust's taxable year, or April 15.[93] Specifically, CRTs must file, on an annual basis, a Form 1041-A, U.S. Information Return—Trust Accumulation of Charitable Amount (with the exception of any year in which all of the net income for the year is required to be distributed currently to the beneficiaries), and a Form 5227, Split-Interest Trust Information Return. In addition, for the CRT's first tax year, it must file a copy of the governing instrument, certified by the fiduciary under penalties of perjury to be true and correct, and attached to Form 5227. The CRT must also distribute Form 1041, Schedule K-1, to the recipient of the unitrust or annuity trust amount reporting the income and deductions reflected on Form 5227. Finally, if the CRT has unrelated business taxable income, it must file Form 1041, and it may be required to make estimated payments with Form 1041-ES.

[E]   Charitable Deduction for Income, Gift, and Estate Tax Purposes

[1]   In General

Grantors may claim a charitable income tax deduction and a charitable gift or estate tax deduction for the gift of the remainder interest in a CRT. To claim the charitable deduction for a gift of a remainder interest in trust, the taxpayer must attach a statement to the appropriate return that sets forth the computation of the present value of the remainder interest, which must include the information normally required to support a charitable income tax, and charitable gift or estate tax deduction.[94]

---

[93] Treas. Reg. § 1.6034-1(c).
[94] Treas. Reg. §§ 1.664-2(d), 1.664-4(c), 1.170A-13, 20.2055-1(c), 25.2522(a)-1(c).

[2]   Valuation of Remainder Interest

[a]   CRAT

The present value of a remainder interest in an annuity trust is the net fair market value of the property placed in trust less the present value of the annuity.[95] Generally, the appropriate valuation date is the date on which the property is transferred to the trust by the grantor. For federal estate tax purposes, it is the date of death, unless the alternate valuation date is elected pursuant to Section 2032.

The valuation of a CRT charitable remainder interest is determined under Treasury Regulation Section 1.664-2(c), which provides that the remainder interest value equals the fair market value of the property placed into the CRT, less the present value of the annuity. It then provides that tables contained in Treasury Regulation Section 20.2031-7(d) must be used to value the annuity interest. For annuities for a term of years, Table B in Treasury Regulation Section 20.2031-7(d)(6) must be used. To convert a remainder factor to an annuity factor, it is necessary to subtract the Table B remainder factor from 1.000000 and then divide the result by the applicable Section 7520 rate. This annuity factor is then multiplied by the amount of the annual annuity payment to arrive at the present value of the annuity. This amount is then subtracted from the value of the property placed in trust to arrive at the value of the charitable remainder interest.

Note that Table B assumes that the annuity will be paid annually at the end of each period. If the annuity is instead to be paid at the beginning of the period, it is necessary to make an adjustment using Table J in Treasury Regulation Section 20.2031-7(d)(6), which also allows for the use of semiannual, quarterly, monthly, and weekly payments at the beginning of each interval. If the payment is made at the end of the interval, but is made more frequently than annually, adjustment factors are found in Table K of Treasury Regulation Section 20.2031-7(d)(6).

If the noncharitable income interest in the CRT uses a measuring life, rather than a term of years, it is necessary to use the Table S factors in Treasury Regulation Section 20.2031-7(d)(7) to determine the value of the charitable remainder. Once the proper Table S remainder factor has been determined, the value of the charitable remainder is calculated in the manner described above. If the payment is made more frequently than annually, or is made at the beginning of the period, it will be necessary to make adjustments to the value using Table J or Table K in Treasury Regulation Section 20.2031-7(d)(6).

[b]   CRUT

Valuing the remainder interest in a CRUT is more complex. Specifically, the present value of a CRUT remainder interest is determined by computing an "adjusted payout rate" and following the procedures outlined in Treasury Regulation Section 1.664-4(e)(3) or (4), depending on whether the unitrust amount is to be paid for a term of years or for the life of an individual.

---

[95] Treas. Reg. § 1.664-2(c).

[i] Adjusted Payout Rate

The adjusted payout rate is determined by multiplying the fixed unitrust percentage provided in the CRUT instrument by a "payout factor" contained in Table F under Treasury Regulation Section 1.664-4(e)(6). The purpose of Table F is to adjust the basic fixed percentage for the fact that the payout sequence of the unitrust affects the amount of trust corpus that ultimately will go to the charitable remainder-man. The more frequently unitrust payments are made to the noncharitable beneficiary, the smaller the value of the charitable remainder interest the charitable beneficiary will receive. Table F contains subtables, each of which corresponds to an IRC Section 7520 rate from 4.2 percent to 14.0 percent. It is necessary to use the subtable for the Section 7520 rate that applies to the valuation.

It is important that the unitrust instrument specifically state the date or dates on which the unitrust amount is to be paid. If the instrument does not so state, it will be assumed that the distribution of the unitrust amount or a portion thereof will be payable on the first day of the period for which the payment is made.[96]

[ii] Valuation Factor

After the adjusted payout rate is determined from Table F, refer to either Table D (for unitrust payments that are payable for a term of years) or Table U(1) (for unitrust payments that are payable for the life of an individual). A valuation factor is obtained from these tables by matching the adjusted payout rate with the appropriate term of years or the appropriate age of the measuring life. The appropriate age of the measuring life is the individual's age at his or her birthday nearest to the date of the transfer to the unitrust.[97] If the precise adjusted payout rate determined from Table F cannot be found in either Table D or Table U(1), it is necessary to interpolate the appropriate factor.

[iii] Computing the Value of the Remainder Interest

After the appropriate valuation factor is obtained from either Table D or Table U(1), the present value of the remainder interest is determined simply by multiplying the factor by the net fair market value of the assets placed in trust.

> **Caution.** The present value of the remainder interest of the charitable trust must be at least 10 percent of the fair market value of the property transferred to the trust.[98]

[F] Tax Consequences to Grantor

[1] Income Tax Consequences of Gift

The grantor of the CRT receives an income tax charitable deduction for the year of the contribution to the CRT. The amount of the deduction equals the

---

[96] Treas. Reg. § 1.664-4(a)(3).
[97] Treas. Reg. § 1.664-4(e)(5).
[98] IRC § 664(d)(2)(D).

value of the remainder interest transferred to a charitable organization as limited by IRC Section 170 deductibility ceilings, which are determined by the type of property contributed and the type of charitable organization that receives the remainder interest.[99] For example, the amount of the deduction would be limited if the recipient charitable organization were a private foundation.

More specifically, the deductibility ceilings limit the charitable contribution deduction based on a percentage of an individual's "contribution base" in the taxable year of the gift. The contribution base for a given year is the donor's adjusted gross income without regard to any NOL carry-backs. Relevant factors include the type of charitable donee and property contributed and the terms of the gift. For individuals, the deductibility ceilings are as follows:

- 50 percent of the donor's contribution base for gifts (other than qualified long-term capital gain property) to 50 percent charities;
- 30 percent for gifts (other than gifts of certain appreciated securities) to charities other than 50 percent charities or "for the use of" 50 percent charities or for gifts of qualified long-term capital gain property to 50 percent charities;
- 20 percent for gifts of certain appreciated marketable securities to charities other than 50 percent charities.

If a donor is unable to use the full amount of a charitable contribution in the year of the gift, he or she may carry over any unused portion for a period of five years. In addition to the ceiling rules, certain charitable deduction reduction rules operate to reduce the amount of the contribution depending on the character of the donee and the type of property donated.

[2] Gift Tax Consequences of Gift

If the CRT only gives an income interest to the grantor, either for life or for a term of years, and the only other CRT interests transferred are remainder interests conveyed to qualified charitable organizations, the CRT results in no gift tax consequences.[100] If the grantor gives the sole CRT income interest to a spouse for the spouse's life or for a term of years, the gift of the income interest to the spouse qualifies for the gift tax marital deduction under a special rule applicable to CRTs.[101] The gift of the remainder interest to a charitable organization qualifies for the gift tax charitable deduction.[102] Consequently, such a transfer results in no transfer tax consequences.

If the grantor gives an income interest to someone other than a spouse and the remainder interest to a qualified charitable organization, the Code imposes a gift tax on the gift of the income interest.[103] However, this gift qualifies for the

---

[99] IRC § 170.
[100] IRC § 2522(c)(2)(A).
[101] IRC § 2523(g)(1).
[102] *See generally* IRC § 2522; Treas. Reg. § 25.2522.
[103] IRC § 2511.

annual gift tax exclusion because it constitutes a gift of a present interest.[104] The gift of the remainder interest to a charitable organization qualifies for the gift tax charitable deduction.[105]

The CRT may provide for income interests for two individuals, the first of which the grantor retains and the second of which the grantor gives to her spouse. Here, transfer tax consequences are avoided because:

1. The grantor retains an income interest;
2. The gift of an income interest is to the spouse (the gift tax marital deduction);[106] and
3. The gift of the remainder interest is to a qualified charitable organization (the gift tax charitable deduction).[107]

The CRT may also provide for income interests for two individuals, the first of which the grantor retains for life and the second of which the grantor gives to a nonspouse individual. Here the gift of the income interest to the nonspouse constitutes a taxable gift if it is irrevocable.[108] Furthermore, because this gift is a gift of a future interest, it will not qualify for the annual gift tax exclusion of $10,000 per year.[109]

Finally, the planner may structure the CRT so that the grantor gives two or more income interests to other, nonspouse individuals. Here, both gifts constitute taxable gifts.[110] The gift to the first beneficiary constitutes a gift of a present interest, which qualifies for the annual gift tax exclusion of $10,000 per year.[111] Subsequent income interests will not qualify for the annual gift tax exclusion of $10,000 per year because they will constitute future interests.[112]

When the grantor transfers an income interest to the spouse along with another interest to another individual other than herself or a qualified charitable organization, the transfer to the spouse will not qualify for the gift tax marital deduction.

[3] Estate Tax Consequences of Gift

If the CRT's grantor retains the sole noncharitable annuity interest with the remainder passing to a qualified charitable organization, the grantor includes the full value of the trust corpus in her estate[113] and takes a deduction for the full value of the remainder interest that passes to the charitable beneficiary.[114] If the

---

[104] IRC § 2503(b).
[105] *See generally* IRC § 2522; Treas. Reg. § 25.2522.
[106] IRC § 2523(g)(1).
[107] IRC § 2522; Treas. Reg. § 25.2522.
[108] IRC § 2511(a); Treas. Reg. § 25.2511-2(b).
[109] IRC § 2503(b).
[110] IRC § 2511(a).
[111] IRC § 2503(b).
[112] IRC § 2503(b).
[113] IRC § 2036(a).
[114] § 2055(e)(2)(A); Treas. Reg. § 1.664-4.

grantor retains no interest in the CRT, the grantor will not include any portion of the trust corpus in her estate.

When the grantor retains the initial annuity interest in the CRT, which is followed by one or more other noncharitable annuity interests, the grantor's estate includes the full value of the trust corpus.[115] If no other noncharitable annuitant survives the grantor so that at the end of the grantor's annuity the trust remainder passes to a qualified charitable organization, the grantor's estate may deduct the full value of the trust corpus as the estate tax charitable organization.[116]

If the only noncharitable annuitant who survives the grantor's interest is the grantor's spouse, the estate may deduct the value of the spouse's interest as the estate tax marital deduction and may deduct the remainder interest as the estate tax charitable deduction.[117] Consequently, the estate will pay no estate tax on the CRT's corpus in this instance.

If another noncharitable, nonspouse annuitant survives the grantor's annuity interest so that such person receives an annuity interest in the CRT, then only the value of the charitable remainder interest of the CRT, determined at the time of the grantor's death, will qualify for the estate tax charitable deduction.[118] Here, the grantor's estate must pay estate tax on the value of the interests that pass to noncharitable, nonspouse annuitants. However, the estate may claim a credit for gift taxes previously paid on such amounts.[119]

If the grantor creates a CRT at her death, the estate may claim an estate tax charitable deduction for the remainder interest that passes to a qualified charitable organization,[120] and it may claim an estate tax marital deduction for interests passing to the grantor's spouse.[121] Consequently, the grantor's estate will pay estate tax only on the noncharitable interests that pass to nonspouses.

[4] Generation-Skipping Transfer Tax Consequences of Gift

If the planner structures the CRT so that no beneficiary constitutes a skip person, the generation-skipping transfer (GST) tax will not apply. A skip person generally is a person who is two or more generations younger than the transferor.[122] If the grantor names a skip person as a potential beneficiary of the CRT, this will trigger application of the GST tax. When a skip person is named as an annuity recipient of the CRT, the CRT will be assigned to the generation level of the grantor. Consequently, the CRT itself will not be a skip person and the GST tax will not apply to the transfer to the trust.[123] However, when the

---

[115] IRC § 2036(a).
[116] IRC § 2055(e)(2)(A); Treas. Reg. § 20.2031-7.
[117] IRC § 2056(b)(8).
[118] IRC § 2055(e)(2)(A); Treas. Reg. § 20.2031-7.
[119] IRC § 2012.
[120] IRC § 2055(e)(2)(A); Treas. Reg. § 20.2031-7.
[121] IRC § 2056(b)(8).
[122] IRC § 2613.
[123] IRC §§ 2612, 2613, 2651(e)(3).

CRT distributes to the skip person, the GST tax will be imposed on this distribution.[124]

[G] Planning and Strategic Issues

[1] Choosing Between CRAT and CRUT

Relevant factors to consider when choosing between a CRAT and a CRUT include the following:

- Composition of the trust corpus;
- The desired terms of the trust;
- The grantor's financial situation; and
- Other miscellaneous factors.

The key differences between CRATs and CRUTs, for planning purposes, are discussed below.

[a] Distribution to Noncharitable Income Beneficiary

With a CRAT, the noncharitable beneficiary will receive a fixed distribution amount each year. In contrast, with a CRUT, the noncharitable beneficiary will receive an amount equal to a fixed percentage of the current fair market value of the trust's net assets. Therefore, CRUTs are advantageous where the trust corpus is expected to increase in value. In contrast, if greater security were desired, in the sense that the grantor desires to give the noncharitable income beneficiary a fixed dollar amount annuity payment, this would tend to weigh in favor of a CRAT.

[b] Recordkeeping and Administrative Duties

CRUTs impose greater recordkeeping and administrative duties on the trustee than CRATs do. To illustrate, use of a CRUT requires the determination of the fair market value of the trust assets on the CRUT's creation and at least annually thereafter. For hard to value assets, such annual valuations may be difficult and costly.

[c] Additional Contributions

CRUTs can receive additional future contributions, but CRATs cannot. However, this difference can be dealt with by creating a new CRAT.

---

[124] IRC § 2612.

[d] Additional Payout Options

With CRUTs, grantors have additional payout options, which are not available for CRATs. Specifically, with a CRUT, the grantor can select a standard percentage payout, a net income unitrust, a net income unitrust with make-up provisions, or a flip unitrust.

[2] Using CRTs for Investment Diversification

CRTs are frequently used to dispose of highly appreciated stock or other assets in order to facilitate the diversification of the donor's investment portfolio. Specifically, CRTs can be used to convert appreciated property into an annual payout based on the donated property's entire value, without diminution for federal or state income taxes.[125]

[3] Using CRTs in Conjunction with Wealth Replacement Life Insurance

Frequently, donors combine a CRT with the acquisition of life insurance, as a means of replacing the wealth transferred to charity.

§5.13 QUALIFIED PERSONAL RESIDENCE TRUSTS

Qualified personal residence trusts (QPRTs) are irrevocable trusts to which clients transfer their residence, retaining the right personally to use the residence for a specified term of years and in which the grantor has designated one or more beneficiaries to receive the residence after the trust term ends. QPRTs provide asset protection for a client's personal residence, where alternative forms of asset protection (*e.g.*, tenancy by the entirety, homestead exemptions, etc.) are unavailable.

Planning Pointer. Planners should use the following analysis when considering using QPRTs as part of an asset protection plan:

1. What are the estate planning aspects of QPRTs?[1]
2. What requirements must asset protection planners satisfy to form a QPRT?[2]
3. What are the asset protection aspects of QPRTs?[3]
4. What factors should asset protection planners consider when structuring QPRTs?[4]

---

[125] Rev. Rul. 78-197, 1978-1 C.B. 83.
§5.13 [1] *See* §5.13[A].
[2] *See* §5.13[B].
[3] *See* §5.13[C].
[4] *See* §5.13[D].

[A] Estate Planning Aspects of QPRTs

QPRTs take advantage of assumptions the IRS makes about the valuation of partial interests in property, such as life estate, term, and remainder interests. The value of a gift to a QPRT equals the value of the transferred property less the value of the grantor's retained income interest. This treatment allows grantors to discount the values of gifts of personal residences to a fraction of their full values, which in turn results in substantial transfer tax savings. Moreover, if the grantor survives the income term, all appreciation of the residence, beginning with the transfer to the QPRT, accrues to the remainder beneficiaries. Thus, the QPRT excludes such appreciation from the client's estate at death for estate tax purposes.

> **Caution.** If the grantor dies during the income term, his or her estate must include the property at its full value at her date of death. However, in such a case the grantor is generally no worse off than if she had not created the QPRT. This results because the grantor gets a credit for any gift tax the IRC previously imposed on her.

EXAMPLE 5-35

Diana, age 50, is a widow and mother of one child, Cynthia. She is a physician who plans to continue her practice indefinitely, and consults with Catherine Claire, an asset protection planner. Diana owns a home worth $1 million, in a jurisdiction whose homestead exemption is limited to $1,000. Catherine Claire advises Diana to place her residence into a QPRT. The QPRT would hold the residence for five years or until Diana's earlier death. The QPRT would then terminate in favor of Cynthia. Upon the transfer of the home to the trust, Diana makes a gift whose fair market value equals $599,361. Diana does not pay any gift tax on this transfer because the unified credit covers it. Five years later, the residence passes to Cynthia. At this time, the residence's fair market value, which has increased in value at a 10-percent annual rate, equals $1,610,510.

EXAMPLE 5-36

Same facts as Example 5-35, except that Diana leases the home from Cynthia after Cynthia takes ownership of it, and Diana dies one year later. At this time, the fair market value of the residence equals $1,771,561. However, Diana does not include any amount for the residence in her estate. She dies owning $10 million of property. Her estate pays estate tax of $5,140,800.

EXAMPLE 5-37

Same facts as Example 5-36, except that Diana does not transfer her residence to a QPRT. At her death, Diana's estate includes property with a fair market value of $11,771,561, which includes her personal residence. Her estate tax equals $6,010,936.70. Consequently, Diana's total transfer tax is $870,136.70 greater than if she had used a QPRT.

Caution. Planners should be aware of the following aspects of QPRTs:

- The QPRT must be a grantor trust; thus the grantor must pay income tax on trust income during the trust term.
- If the grantor dies during the retained term for years, the grantor's estate must include the trust assets pursuant to IRC Section 2036(a) and, therefore, no benefits accrue.
- No part of the gift of the personal residence to the QPRT qualifies for the annual gift tax exclusion, because it is a gift of a future interest.

[B] *Requirements for Forming QPRT*

Generally, to form a QPRT, clients must satisfy the following requirements:

1. The QPRT instrument must allow the QPRT to hold only one of the following:
   a. The term holder's principal residence;
   b. Another residence that the term holder owns, which must satisfy IRC Section 280A(d)(1) but without regard to Section 280A(d)(2); or
   c. An undivided fractional interest in either of the foregoing.[5]
2. The primary use of the residence must be as the term holder's residence, when she occupies it.[6]
3. The QPRT instrument must require it to distribute, at least annually, any trust income to the term holder.[7]
4. The QPRT instrument must prohibit corpus distributions to any beneficiary other than the transferor before the retained term interest expires.[8]
5. The QPRT instrument must prohibit it from holding cash greater than certain limitations.[9]

---

[5] Treas. Reg. § 25.2702-5(c)(2)(i).
[6] Treas. Reg. § 25.2702-5(c)(2)(iii).
[7] Treas. Reg. § 25.2702-5(c)(3).
[8] Treas. Reg. § 25.2702-5(c)(4).
[9] Treas. Reg. § 25.2702-5(c)(5).

6. The QPRT instrument must prohibit commutation (prepayment) of the term holder's interest.[10]

7. The QPRT instrument must terminate the trust if and when the grantor stops using the residence as her personal residence.[11]

8. The QPRT instrument must require the QPRT to dispose of trust assets in a specified manner when the grantor stops using the residence as her personal residence.[12]

9. The QPRT must prohibit the resale of the personal residence owned by the QPRT to the settlor or his or her spouse.[13]

Some of these requirements require additional explanation. First, the primary use of the residence must be as the term holder's residence when she occupies it. The QPRT will not fail this requirement merely because the grantor uses part of the residence in an activity described by IRC Section 280A(c)(1) or (4) (*i.e.*, the taxpayer's trade or business; place of business used by patients, clients, etc.; meetings with the taxpayer; or as a day care facility), if such use is secondary to the residence's use as a residence. However, the residence will not qualify if it is used to provide transient lodging and substantial services are provided in connection therewith (*e.g.*, a hotel or a bed and breakfast). The residence will also not qualify as a personal residence if, during any period the term holder does not occupy it, its primary use is not as a residence.[14]

EXAMPLE 5-38

Same facts as Example 5-35, except that during the QPRT term Diana occasionally sees patients in her home. Here, the QPRT satisfies the requirement that the residence's primary use be as Diana's personal residence.

EXAMPLE 5-39

Same facts as Example 5-38, except that during the QPRT term Diana converts the residence into a bed and breakfast. Here, it violates the requirement that the residence's primary use be as Diana's personal residence. Consequently, the QPRT terminates.

---

[10] Treas. Reg. § 25.2702-5(c)(6).
[11] Treas. Reg. § 25.2702-5(c)(7).
[12] Treas. Reg. § 25.2702-5(c)(8).
[13] Treas. Reg. § 25.2702-5(b)(1).
[14] Treas. Reg. § 25.2702-5(c)(2)(iii).

Second, the QPRT instrument must generally prohibit the trust from holding, for its entire term, any assets other than one personal residence and cash for certain restricted purposes.[15] More specifically, the QPRT instrument may allow (1) cash to be added to the trust, and (2) the trust to hold such additions in a separate account. However, cash held must not exceed amounts required:

- To pay trust expenses (including mortgage payments) the trust has either already incurred or reasonably expects to pay within six months from the addition date.
- To improve the residence, which the trust will pay for within six months from the addition.
- To buy the initial residence within three months of the QPRT's creation. However, no addition may be made for this purpose, and the QPRT may not hold such additions, unless the trustee enters a contract to buy that residence before such addition.
- To buy a replacement residence within three months of the addition date. However, no addition may be made for this purpose, and the trust may not hold any such addition, unless the trustee previously enters a contract to buy such residence before such addition.

EXAMPLE 5-40

Same facts as Example 5-35, except that when Diana executes the QPRT she also executes a document titled "Agreement by Tenant for Years to Pay Expenses" providing that she will pay to the QPRT trustee all property taxes; costs for maintenance, repairs, and remodeling; homeowner's insurance; and mortgage payments during the QPRT's term. As long as the QPRT's and the agreement's applicable provisions conform to the requirements of Treas. Reg. § 25.2702-5(c)(5)(ii)(A)(1)(i), they do not adversely affect the QPRT's status as a qualified personal residence trust.[16]

Caution. If the QPRT instrument allows cash contributions, it must also require the trustee to determine, at least quarterly, the amount of cash it may retain to pay the above-enumerated expenses. The QPRT instrument must require the trustee to distribute, immediately after such determination, any excess cash amounts to the term holder. Finally, the QPRT instrument must require that the trustee distribute outright to the term holder, within 30 days of the term interest's termination, any cash amounts the trust holds for such allowable purposes that it has not used to pay trust

---

[15] Treas. Reg. § 25.2702-5(c)(5).
[16] Priv. Ltr. Rul. 9315010.

expenses due and payable on the termination date (including expenses directly related to termination).

Third, the trust must absolutely prohibit any commutation of the interest of the term holder. Treas. Reg. § 25.2702-5(c)(6). Commutation would otherwise occur when, under either applicable state law or the governing instrument, the parties decide to terminate the trust early and distribute a fractional share of the real estate to the term owner and a fractional share to the remainder owner, based on the actuarial value of their respective interests.

EXAMPLE 5-41

Same facts as Example 5-35, except that three years after effecting the QPRT, Diana is diagnosed with cancer and learns she has only one year to live. Here, if Diana does die four years after she effects the QPRT, her estate must include the full value of the personal residence at its date-of-death value. Diana wants to effect a commutation of her term interest to ensure that her estate does not have to include the residence's full value on her date of death. However, Treas. Reg. § 25.2702-5(c)(6) precludes Diana from doing this.

Fourth, the QPRT instrument must require the trust to terminate if the residence it holds ceases to be a personal residence of the term owner.[17] For this purpose, the regulations consider the residence to be held for the term holder's use as a personal residence as long as no other person occupies the residence (other than the term holder's spouse or dependent) and it is always available for the term holder's use as a personal residence.

Finally, the QPRT instrument must require the QPRT to dispose of trust assets in a specified manner if the personal residence ceases to be used as a personal residence.[18] More specifically, the QPRT instrument must provide that, within 30 days after the date it stops qualifying as a QPRT, it either:

1. Distributes its assets outright to the term holder;
2. Converts its assets to hold them for the term holder's remaining term in a separate share of the trust meeting the requirements of a qualified annuity interest; or
3. In the trustee's sole discretion, elects to comply with either of the foregoing.

[C] Asset Protection Aspects of QPRTs

The QPRT settlor will also be the term holder. Generally, when settlors are also the trust beneficiaries, their creditors can reach their beneficial

---

[17] Treas. Reg. § 25.2702-5(c)(7).
[18] Treas. Reg. § 25.2702-5(c)(8).

interests.[19] Therefore, the QPRT will not, by itself, protect the settlor/term holder's interest from creditors. Consequently, it appears that the settlor's creditors may be able to obtain the term holder's ability to use the property. However, Treas. Reg. §25.2702-5(c)(8) requires the QPRT trustee to dispose of the residence when the QPRT ceases to qualify as a QPRT. This would occur if the term holder stopped using the personal residence held by the QPRT as a personal residence. Here, the trustee must either distribute the trust assets outright to the term holder or convert the assets into a qualified annuity interest. The QPRT instrument may mandate which option the trustee must choose, or it may leave the decision to the trustee's sole discretion.

> **Planning Pointer.** Planners using QPRTs for asset protection purposes should generally require the QPRT to convert the assets into a qualified annuity rather than distribute them to the term holder. Otherwise, absent a homestead exemption that protects the residence, the term holder's creditors can reach the personal residence. If the trustee converts the QPRT to a qualified annuity, then (1) the remainder interest remains protected from creditors, and (2) the annuity interest will be subject to the reach of creditors, unless the applicable jurisdiction exempts such annuities from the reach of creditors. In either event, however, the QPRT will protect at least part of the value of the residence from creditors.

EXAMPLE 5-42

Same facts as Example 5-35, except that one year after Diana effects the QPRT, one of her patients, Lewis, sues her for malpractice and obtains a judgment against her. Assuming the transfer of the residence to the trust was not a fraudulent conveyance, Lewis can only reach Diana's interest in the residence. More specifically, the most Lewis could possibly reach is Diana's ability to use the home for the remainder of the QPRT term. However, the QPRT must, to comply with Treasury Regulations, provide that it will liquidate the residence and convert it into a qualified annuity. Here, the trustee could sell the home to Cynthia and make annuity payments to Diana for her remaining four-year term interest. Lewis's ability to reach the annuity payments depends on local law. In any event, after Diana's five-year term ends, the remaining assets in the trust pass to Cynthia free of Lewis's claims.

After the term interests ends, the residence passes to the remainder beneficiary. At this point, the QPRT has entirely protected the residence from the reach of the settlor's creditors.

---

[19] *See* Restatement (Second) of Property (Donative Transfers) §13.3 and cms. a, b (1986); Austin Wakeman Scott & William Franklin Fratcher, The Law of Trusts §§147, 330.12 (4th ed. 1987); George T. Bogert, Trusts §39 (6th ed. 1987).

EXAMPLE 5-43

Same facts as Example 5-42, except that Lewis sues and wins a judgment against Diana six years after she creates and funds the QPRT. At this time she is leasing the residence from Cynthia at fair market value. Lewis cannot reach the personal residence at all. Here, Diana has completely removed the residence from Lewis's reach.

Note. In *United States v. Murray*,[20] the First Circuit held that the IRS's tax lien attached to the taxpayer's interest in a trust consisting of a marital home, even if the taxpayer's wife and her stepbrother, as trustees, could have divested the taxpayer's interest. Although, apparently not involving a QPRT, the analysis of the First Circuit in this case seems to be consistent with the foregoing asset protection analysis.

[D] *Structuring the QPRT*

Within the limits set by the IRC and Treasury Regulations, planners may customize QPRTs to their clients' individual needs. More specifically, planners must consider the following issues concerning the QPRT structure:

- QPRT term
- QPRT remainder interest
- Selection of QPRT trustee
- Continued possession of the residence after the QPRT's initial term

[1] QPRT Term

Planners must consider several factors when determining the duration of the grantor's term interest. First, the grantor's term must be short enough so the grantor is likely to survive it. If the grantor does not survive her QPRT term, her estate must include the full value of the personal residence at date of death for estate tax purposes. It will receive a credit for gift taxes previously paid. Consequently, the opportunity for transfer tax savings will be lost and the grantor's estate will be out of pocket the transaction costs of effecting the QPRT.

Second, clients generally do not want to pay any actual gift tax on the QPRT's creation. Consequently, planners should determine the term with the grantor's unused unified credit in mind. If the unified credit exceeds the gift of the remainder interest, the grantor will not have to pay any gift tax on the QPRT's creation. Generally, the amount of the gift tax imposed on the gift of the remainder interest will decrease as the duration of the trust term increases.

---

[20] 217 F.3d 59 (1st Cir. 2000).

Third, the shorter the trust term, the less the residence will be exposed to creditors' claims. The sooner the term ends, the sooner the residence passes to the remainder beneficiary and outside the reach of the client's creditors. Also, the shorter the term interest, the less valuable the term interest to creditors. Consequently, creditors will be less inclined to try to reach such an interest.

Factors for Planners to Consider	*Implications for Settlor's Term*
Grantor's anticipated remaining life span	**SHORTER:** Trust term must be shorter than grantor's anticipated remaining life span
Gift taxation on creation of QPRT	**LONGER:** The longer the trust term, the less the amount of gift taxation on the QPRT's creation
Exposure of grantor's term interest to creditors	**SHORTER:** The shorter the grantor's interest, the smaller the exposure of the residence to the claims of the grantor's creditors

[2] QPRT Remainder Interest

The QPRT may distribute the residence at the end of the grantor's term either directly to the remainderman or in trust for the benefit of the remainderman. Planners should consider retaining the residence in the trust after the term ends, especially where the remainderman may be subject to creditors. Such a situation could arise where the remainderman is the grantor's child, who is a professional subject to potential malpractice suits.

[3] Selection of QPRT Trustee

Anybody can serve as the QPRT's trustee. The grantor could serve as the trustee without any particular income, gift, or estate tax problems because the trust will constitute a grantor trust under IRC Sections 673 and 677. Consequently, the IRS treats the grantor as the owner of the trust assets for tax purposes. Also, if the grantor dies during the trust term, IRC Section 2036 causes inclusion of the trust property in the grantor's estate. On the other hand, however, from an asset protection standpoint, the planner should not use the grantor as the QPRT trustee. This is because creditors, especially a trustee in bankruptcy, will step into the grantor's shoes. Instead, a trusted individual should serve as the trustee.

[4] Continued Possession of Residence After QPRT's Initial Term

Clients often want the right to continue living in their home after their term ends. In the asset protection context, planners have two options for dealing with this. First, planners may make the spouse a beneficiary of the trust after the income term. At the end of the term, the residence is retained in a trust under which the spouse is permitted to use it rent-free. Only after the spouse's death does the property pass to the descendants or other remaindermen. This strategy provides a way for married couples to continue occupying the residence after the income term without adverse transfer tax consequences.[21]

> **Planning Pointer.** Planners using this method should name as beneficiary "the person to whom the grantor is married at the end of the income term."[22] This will prevent problems if the client remarries.
>
> Another method to ensure the grantor retains the right to live in the residence after the trust term is to have the grantor lease the residence from the remainder beneficiaries after the grantor's term ends. The planner can enter an advance lease with the beneficiaries.[23]

> **Caution.** Planners must be careful when creating advance rental agreements with QPRT remainder beneficiaries. More specifically, they must ensure that such leases require the grantor to pay fair market value for any lease. Otherwise, the client risks inclusion in its gross estate of a retained interest in the residence under IRC Section 2036.

> **Planning Pointer.** The planner should structure the QPRT so that, after the grantor's term ends, the trust retains the residence for the benefit of objects of the grantor's bounty. The grantor or her spouse could then enter a rental agreement with the trustee, rather than with the trust's remainder beneficiaries. This protects the property from the reach of the remainder beneficiaries' creditors.

§ 5.14   ALASKA- AND DELAWARE-TYPE ASSET PROTECTION TRUSTS

Generally, when a person who creates and transfers assets to a spendthrift trust is also a beneficiary of that trust, the trust's spendthrift provision (1) will not prevent the settlor/beneficiary's creditors from reaching his interest in the trust, and (2) will not prevent the settlor/beneficiary from transferring his

---

[21] Treas. Reg. § 25.2702-5. *See, e.g.,* Priv. Ltr. Rul. 9448035.

[22] C.D. Fox IV, D.R. Hodgman, & K. Van Meter, *Qualified Personal Residence Trusts Yield Tax Savings,* 22 Est. Plan. 206, 210 (July–Aug. 1995).

[23] *See, e.g.,* Priv. Ltr. Rul. 9425028.

interest.[1] In contrast, as Chapter 6 discusses in detail, the law of many foreign jurisdictions provides that when a person who creates and transfers assets to a foreign asset protection trust is also a beneficiary of that trust, he may include a provision that precludes his creditors from reaching his trust interest.

In 1997, Alaska statutorily modified its laws to reverse the general rule in the United States concerning self-settled spendthrift trusts, and shortly thereafter Delaware similarly modified its laws.[2] Alaska and Delaware also repealed the rule against perpetuities. Subsequently, Nevada and Rhode Island enacted similar laws.[3] (For purposes of convenience, these types of trusts will be sometimes collectively referred to as Alaska-and Delaware-type asset protection trusts). Because of these amendments, Alaska and Delaware trusts provide asset protection planners with an extremely valuable tool for asset protection purposes. Moreover, even ignoring the asset protection benefits, these trusts provide outstanding estate planning opportunities. However, as with all asset protection tools, asset protection planners must evaluate the relevant risks presented by Alaska and Delaware asset protection trusts.[4]

Planning Pointer. Asset protection planners should use the following analysis when evaluating Alaska and Delaware asset protection trusts:

1. What are the provisions of the Alaska trust statute?[5]
2. What are the provisions of the Delaware trust statute?[6]

---

§5.14 [1] *See generally* §5.09. Also, note that some courts have held that creditors of a settlor who is also a trust beneficiary cannot demand payment of any part of the trust assets where the settlor is merely eligible and not entitled to receive trust distributions. *See, e.g.,* Herzog v. Comm'r, 116 F.2d 591 (2d Cir. 1941); Uhl v. United States, 241 F.2d 867 (7th Cir. 1957); German v. United States, 85-1 U.S. Tax Cas. (CCH) ¶ 13,610 (Ct. Cl. 1985). *See also* Richard W. Hompesch 11, et al., *Does the New Alaska Trusts Act Provide an Alternative to the Foreign Trust,* 2 J. Asset Protection 9 (July/August 1997).

[2] Appendix G provides the full text of the Alaska trust legislation, and Appendix H provides the full text of the Delaware trust legislation.

[3] *See* Nev. Rev. Stat. §166.040(1)(b) (1999); R.I. Gen. Laws §§18-9.2-1 to 18-9.2-5 (1999).

[4] *See generally* Leslie G. Giordani & Duncan E. Osborne, *Will the Alaska Trusts Work?* 3 J. Asset Protection 7 (Sept./Oct. 1997); Michael P. Franzmann & Alan R. Jahde, *Onshore vs. Offshore Asset Protection Trusts: Which One is Right for Your Client?* 3 J. Asset Protection 9 (Nov./Dec. 1997); Jonathan G. Blattmachr et al., *New Alaska Trust Act Provides Many Estate Planning Opportunities,* 24 Est. Plan. 347 (Oct. 1997); David G. Shafterl, *Newest Developments in Alaska Law Encourage Use of Alaska Trusts,* 26 Est. Plan. 51 (Feb. 1999); Richard W. Nenno, *Delaware Law Offers Asset Protection and Estate Planning Benefits,* 26 Est. Plan. 3 (Jan. 1999); Stephen E. Greer & David G. Shaftel, *Alaska Enacts Additional Estate Planning Legislation,* 27 Est. Plan. 376 (2000); Robert L. Manley, *Estate Planning With Self-Settled Spendthrift Trusts: Steering Clear of Debts and Taxes,* in Estate Planning Techniques (ALI-ABA 1999); Karen E. Boxx, *Gray's Ghost—A Conversation About the Onshore Trust,* 85 Iowa L. Rev. 1195 (May 2000); Thomas L. Flynn & Matthew T. Cronin, *Self-settled Spendthrift Trusts Move Close to Home,* 2000 ABI Jnl. LEXIS 70 (Sept. 2000); John K. Eason, *Home From the Islands: Domestic Asset Protection Trust Alternatives Impact Traditional Estate and Gift Tax Planning Considerations,* 52 Fla. L. Rev. 41 (Jan. 2000); Steward E. Sterk, *Asset Protection Trusts: Trust Law's Race to the Bottom?* 85 Cornell L. Rev. 1035 (May 2000).

[5] *See* §§5.14[A][1]–5.14[A][5].

[6] *See* §§5.14[B][1]–5.14[B][2].

3. What estate planning benefits do Alaska and Delaware asset protection trusts provide?

4. What are the risks of using Alaska and Delaware asset protection trusts?

[A] Alaska Trusts

[1] Requirements for Alaska Trust Statute

If a trust governed by the Alaska trust statute contains a choice of law provision providing that Alaska law governs that trust's validity, construction, and administration, and providing that the trust is subject to the jurisdiction of Alaska, that provision will be valid, effective, and conclusive for the trust if it satisfies the following four requirements:[7]

[a] Some Assets Must Be Deposited in Alaska and Administered by a Qualified Person[8]

At least "some" assets must be "deposited" in Alaska, and a "qualified person" must administer such assets. For this purpose, the Alaska statute defines "deposited" in Alaska as including being held in a checking account, time deposit, certificate of deposit, brokerage account, trust company fiduciary account, or other similar account or deposit located in Alaska.[9]

The Alaska statute defines a "qualified person" as including the following:

- *Alaskan Individuals.* Individuals who, except for brief intervals, military service, attendance at an educational or training institution, or for absences for good cause shown, (1) reside in Alaska, (2) whose true and permanent home is in Alaska, and (3) who do not have a present intent of moving from Alaska, and who have the intention of returning to Alaska while they are away from Alaska.[10]
- *Alaskan Trust Companies.* Trust Companies organized under Alaska Stat. § 06.25, and having their principal place of business in Alaska.[11]
- *Alaskan Banks.* A bank organized under Alaska Stat. § 06.05, or a national banking association organized under 12 U.S.C. §§ 21-216d, if such bank or national banking association possesses and exercises trust powers and has its principal place of business in Alaska.[12]

---

[7] Alaska Stat. § 13.36.035(c) (2000).
[8] Alaska Stat. § 13.36.035(c)(1) (2000).
[9] *Id.*
[10] Alaska Stat. § 13.36.390(2)(A) (2000).
[11] Alaska Stat. § 13.36.390(2)(B) (2000).
[12] Alaska Stat. § 13.36.390(2)(c) (2000).

The Alaska statute does not define the term "some" for purposes of determining the amount of assets that must be deposited in Alaska. This results in some uncertainty as to what a trust must do to satisfy this requirement. Some commentators have stated that if a trust owns $10,000, which it holds in the form of a certificate of deposit or a brokerage account located in Alaska, this should satisfy this requirement.[13]

> **Planning Pointer.** One way to satisfy the requirement to deposit some assets in Alaska is to transfer the assets the client wishes to convey into the Alaska trust to an Alaska family limited partnership (FLP) or Alaska limited liability company (LLC), and then subsequently use the interests in such Alaskan limited partnership or Alaskan limited liability company to fund the Alaska trust.

[b] Trust Instrument or Court Must Designate a Qualified Person (i.e., Alaskan Person) as a Trustee[14]

Either the trust instrument or a court that has jurisdiction over the trust must designate a qualified person as a trustee of the trust.[15] The definition of "qualified person" for this purpose is the same as that discussed above. From a practical standpoint, this means that at least one trustee must be Alaskan to ensure that the trust qualifies as an Alaska trust.[16]

[c] Trust Provides Trustee with Required Powers[17]

The Alaska trust statute states that the powers given to the trustee who is a qualified person must include or be limited to the following:

- Maintaining records for the trust on an exclusive basis or a nonexclusive basis; and
- Preparing or arranging for the preparation of, on an exclusive basis or a nonexclusive basis, an income tax return that the trust must file.

[d] Alaska Administration[18]

At least part of the trust's administration must occur in Alaska, including maintaining trust records in Alaska. Some commentators have stated that hold-

---

[13] Jonathan G. Blattmachr & Douglas J. Blattmachr, An Overview of the Alaska Trust Act (1997).
[14] Alaska Stat. § 13.36.035(c)(2) (2000).
[15] Id.
[16] Jonathan G. Blattmachr & Douglas J. Blattmachr, An Overview of the Alaska Trust Act (1997).
[17] Alaska Stat. § 13.36.035(c)(3) (2000).
[18] Alaska Stat. § 13.36.035(c)(4) (2000).

ing trustee meetings in Alaska, holding meetings in Alaska with trust beneficiaries, maintaining accounts in Alaska, or initiating "trades" in Alaska should
satisfy this requirement.[19]

[2] Effect of Application of Alaska Law

Where a trust includes a valid choice of law provision causing Alaska law to
govern such trust (*i.e.,* an Alaskan trust), then Alaskan law determines the
validity, construction, and administration of that trust.[20] The statute explicitly
provides that Alaska law determines (1) the settlor's[21] capacity; (2) the trustees'
powers, obligations, liabilities, and rights; (3) the appointment and removal of
the trustees; and (4) the existence and extent of powers, conferred or retained,
including (a) a trustee's discretionary powers, (b) the powers retained by a trust
beneficiary, and (c) the validity of the exercise of the power.[22]

The Alaska trust statute also provides that trusts governed by Alaska law
cannot be set aside on the ground that they or any transfer to them avoids or
defeats any right, claim, or interest conferred by law on a person because of any
business or personal relationship with the settlor or because of a marital or
similar right.[23] This provision precludes Alaskan trusts from being set aside as
void, voidable, defective in any fashion, or questionable as to the settlor's
capacity.[24]

[3] Alaska Spendthrift Trust Provisions

The Alaska statute explicitly provides for spendthrift trust provisions. Specifically, it provides that persons who in writing transfer property in trust may
provide that interests of trust beneficiaries cannot be voluntarily or involuntarily
transferred before the trustee pays or delivers that interest to the beneficiary.[25]
For this purpose, the Alaska statute defines "property" as including real property, personal property, and interests in real or personal property.[26] The statute
defines "transfer" as including any form of transfer, including deed, conveyance,
or assignment.[27]

The Alaska statute goes on to provide that if an Alaskan trust contains
a spendthrift trust provision provided for by the Alaska statute (Transfer

---

[19] Jonathan G. Blattmachr & Douglas J. Blattmachr, An Overview of the Alaska Trust Act (1997).

[20] Alaska Stat. § 13.36.035(d) (2000).

[21] For this purpose, the Alaska statute defines "settlor" as "a person who transfers property in trust;
'settlor' includes a person who furnishes the property transferred to a trust even if the trust is created by
another person." Alaska Stat. § 13.36.390(3) (2000).

[22] Alaska Stat. § 13.36.035(d) (2000).

[23] Alaska Stat. § 13.36.310 (2000).

[24] *Id.*

[25] Alaska Stat. § 34.40.110(a) (2000).

[26] Alaska Stat. § 34.40.110(a)(1) (2000).

[27] Alaska Stat. § 34.40.110(a)(2) (2000).

Restriction), that Transfer Restriction prevents the following creditors from satisfying their claims out of the beneficiary's trust interest:

- Persons who are creditors of the beneficiary when the trust is created;
- Persons who become creditors of the beneficiary after the trust is created; and
- Any other persons.[28]

This spendthrift trust applies to all trust beneficiaries, even those beneficiaries who are also the settlor of the spendthrift trust.[29]

However, there are four exceptions, under which a Transfer Restriction will not prevent creditors from reaching a beneficiary's trust interest. These are the following:

1. **Intentional fraudulent conveyances.** Transfer Restrictions will not be valid as to transfers that were intended, wholly or partially, to hinder, delay, or defraud creditors or other persons under Alaska law.[30]

2. **Settlor retains the unrestricted right to revoke trust.** Transfer Restrictions will be invalid to the extent that the trust provides that the settlor may revoke or terminate any part of the trust without an adverse party's consent. For this purpose, an adverse party is a person who has a substantial beneficial interest in the trust, where the exercise of the settlor's power to revoke or terminate any part the trust would adversely affect that interest.[31] Also, for this purpose, the statute specifically provides that the term "revoke or terminate" does not include any of the following:

   a. Power to veto a trust distribution;
   b. A testamentary special power of appointment or similar power; or
   c. The right to receive a distribution of income, corpus, or both in the discretion of a person, including a trustee, other than the settlor.[32]

3. **Trust instrument mandates distribution to settlor.** Transfer Restrictions will be invalid as to that part of the trust's income or principal that the trust must distribute to the settlor.[33]

---

[28] Alaska Stat. § 34.40.110(b) (2000).

[29] Jonathan G. Blattmachr & Douglas J. Blattmachr, An Overview of the Alaska Trust Act (1997).

[30] Alaska Stat. § 34.40.110(b)(2) (2000). Alaska Statute § 34.40.010 provides that:
except as provided in as § 34.40.110 a conveyance or assignment, in writing or otherwise, of an estate or interest in land, or in goods, or things in action, or of rents or profits issuing from them or a charge upon land, goods, or things in action, or upon the rents or profits from them, made with the intent to hinder, delay, or defraud creditors or other persons of their lawful suits, damages, forfeitures, debts, or demands, or a bond or other evidence of debt given, action commenced, decree or judgment suffered, with the like intent, as against the persons so hindered, delayed, or defrauded is void.

[31] Alaska Stat. § 34.40.010(b)(2) (2000).

[32] Id.

[33] Alaska Stat. § 34.40.010(b)(3) (2000).

4. **Child support payments.** Transfer Restrictions are invalid to the extent that, when the settlor transfers assets to the trust, he is in default by 30 or more days of making a payment due under a child support judgment or order.[34]

The Alaska statute explicitly states that if one or more of the foregoing four exceptions to a valid Transfer Restriction applies, that exception is limited to that part of the trust to which that exception applies.[35]

Planning Pointer. Asset protection planners must, at a minimum, take the following steps to ensure that none of the foregoing exceptions to a valid spendthrift clause applies to Alaska trusts they establish for their clients:

- The planner must properly vet the client to ensure that (1) by establishing the Alaska trust he or she does not assist the client in effectuating a fraudulent conveyance, and (2) the settlor is not in default on his or her child support payments.[36]
- The planner must ensure that the trust is irrevocable.
- The planner must ensure that the trust instrument does not provide for any mandatory distributions to the settlor. However, the trust instrument may allow for discretionary payments to the settlor.

[4]   Alaska Fraudulent Conveyance Provisions

The Alaska trust statute provides that Transfer Restrictions will not be valid as to transfers that constitute intentional fraudulent conveyances under Alaska Stat. § 34.40.010.[37] Thus, as with all trusts, Alaska trusts will not protect assets if the transfer of such assets to the trust constitutes a fraudulent conveyance. However, for a creditor to attack a transfer of assets into an Alaska trust as constituting a fraudulent conveyance, that creditor must bring any such fraudulent conveyance claim within the statute of limitations period, for which the Alaska trust statute provides. Specifically, persons who were creditors when the settlor created the Alaska trust must bring any fraudulent conveyance claims with respect to such trust within four years of the transfer or within one year after the creditor discovered the transfer in question or reasonably could have discovered such

---

[34] Alaska Stat. § 34.40.010(b)(4) (2000).

[35] Alaska Stat. § 34.40.010(c) (2000).

[36] *See generally* Chapter 1.

[37] Alaska Stat. § 34.40.010(b)(1) (2000). Alaska Statute § 34.40.0100 provides that:

except as provided in as § 34.40.110 a conveyance or assignment, in writing or otherwise, of an estate or interest in land, or in goods, or things in action, or of rents or profits issuing from them or a charge upon land, goods, or things in action, or upon the rents or profits from them, made with the transfer.[38] Persons who become creditors after the transfer in question cannot bring such fraudulent conveyance claims unless they bring such actions within four years of the transfer.[39] For purposes of this fraudulent conveyance statute of limitations, the Alaska statute defines a "settlor" as a person who transfers real property, personal property, or an interest in real or personal property, in trust.[40]

[5] Other Alaska Provisions

In addition to the Alaska trust statute, Alaska has enacted two other provisions that asset protection planners should familiarize themselves with when considering Alaska asset protection trusts. First, Alaska has effectively repealed the rule against perpetuities for certain interests in trusts. Specifically, Alaska's new provision expressly states that the common law rule against perpetuities does not apply to Alaska. It then adopts a two-pronged approach designed to avoid the so-called Delaware Tax Trap.[41]

Second, Alaska has amended its limited partnership and limited liability company statutes in ways that are advantageous for asset protection and estate planning purposes. These changes generally facilitate valuation discounts for intrafamily transfers of Alaskan limited partnership or LLC interests. To illustrate, the changes that Alaska has made to its LLC and limited partnership statutes include the following:

- **LLC—unanimous consent required for amendment of articles of organization or operating agreement.** The written consent of *all* of the members of an Alaskan LLC is required to (1) amend the articles of organization; (2) amend the LLC's operating agreement; or (3) authorize a manager or member to perform an act on behalf of the LLC that contravenes the LLC's operating agreement, including an act that contravenes a provision of the operating agreement that expressly limits the purposes, affairs, or conduct of the affairs of the LLC.[42] This virtually eliminates the possibility a creditor could modify the LLC's articles or operating agreement, even if it could get more than a charging order against the LLC.
- **LLC—resignation of members prohibited.** Alaska law prohibits an LLC member from resigning from an Alaskan LLC except at the time or upon the happening of events specified in the LLC's operating agreement and in accordance with its operating agreement.[43] Also, unless the LLC's operating

---

intent to hinder, delay, or defraud creditors or other persons of their lawful suits, damages, forfeitures, debts, or demands, or a bond or other evidence of debt given, action commenced, decree or judgment suffered, with the like intent, as against the persons so hindered, delayed, or defrauded is void.

[38] Alaska Stat. § 34.40.010(d)(1) (2000).

[39] Alaska Stat. § 34.40.010(d)(2) (2000).

[40] Alaska Stat. § 34.40.010(d) (2000).

[41] Alaska Stat. §§ 34.27.051, 34.27.053, 34.27.070, 34.27.075, 34.27.100.

[42] Alaska Stat. § 10.50.150(c) (2000).

[43] Alaska Stat. § 10.50.185(a) (2000).

agreement provides otherwise, a member cannot resign from an Alaskan LLC before it dissolves and winds up.[44] The amended statute also provides that if a member resigns and that resignation violates the LLC's operating agreement, then besides any remedy otherwise available under applicable law, the LLC may recover from the resigning member damages for breach of the operating agreement and may offset those damages against the amount otherwise distributable to the resigning member.[45] Finally, the amended statute provides that, unless otherwise provided in the LLC's operating agreement, after a member resigns from the LLC, his rights become merely those of an assignee.[46]

- **LLC—dissolution.** The amended statute provides that Alaskan LLCs are dissolved and their affairs must be wound up when the first of the following occurs: (1) at the time or on the happening of events specified for dissolution in the LLC's operating agreement; (2) all of the members of the LLC consent in writing; or (3) the superior court enters a decree for judicial dissolution of the company under Alaska Stat. § 10.50.405. For this purpose, Alaska Stat. § 10.50.405 has been amended to provide that the superior court may order an LLC to be dissolved, on application by or for an LLC member if the court determines that it is impossible for the company to carry on its purposes.

- **Limited Partnership—withdrawal of limited partner.** Alaska's amended limited partnership statute provides that limited partners *cannot* withdraw from a limited partnership except at the time or upon the happening of events specified in the partnership agreement. Moreover, unless the partnership agreement provides otherwise, a limited partner may not withdraw from a limited partnership before the dissolution and winding up of the limited partnership.[47]

- **Limited Partnership—amendment of partnership agreement.** Alaska's amended limited partnership statute requires the unanimous consent of all partners to amend the partnership agreement.[48]

[B] *Delaware Asset Protection Trusts*

Delaware enacted the Delaware Trust Statute[49] (the Delaware statute) to facilitate the establishment in Delaware of irrevocable trusts that would allow trust settlors to transfer their assets to reduce their federal estate taxes and, presumably, to facilitate asset protection planning. Delaware specifically intended its legislation to resemble the Alaska trust legislation.[50]

---

[44] Alaska Stat. § 10.50.185(b) (2000).
[45] Alaska Stat. § 10.50.185(c) (2000).
[46] Alaska Stat. § 10.50.185(d) (2000).
[47] Alaska Stat. § 32.11.260 (2000).
[48] Alaska Stat. § 32.11.835 (2000).
[49] *See* full text of Delaware Trust Statute at Appendix H.
[50] *See* §§ 5.14[A][1]–5.14[A][4].

[1]   Requirements for Delaware Trust Statute

The Delaware statute generally protects "qualified dispositions" of "property" in trust from certain claims of creditors.[51] For this purpose, a "qualified disposition" is a disposition by or from a transferor to a qualified trustee or qualified trustees, with or without consideration, by means of a trust instrument.[52] "Property" for this purpose includes real property, personal property, and interests in real or personal property.[53]

For the Delaware statute to apply, the trustee must constitute a "Qualified Trustee." The Delaware statute defines a Qualified Trustee as including the following:

1. **Natural Persons.** A natural person must be both (1) a Delaware resident, and (2) someone other than the transferor in order to constitute a Qualified Trustee.
2. **All Other Trustees.** For all other trustees, the trustee must be authorized by Delaware law to act as a trustee and such persons' activities must be subject to supervision by the Delaware Bank Commissioner, the Federal Deposit Insurance Corporation, the Comptroller of the Currency, or the Office of Thrift Supervision or any successor thereto.

In addition to the foregoing requirements, the Delaware statute requires the trustee to maintain or arrange one or more of the following:

1. Custody in Delaware of at least some of the trust corpus that is the subject of the "qualified disposition";
2. Maintain records for the trust on an exclusive or nonexclusive basis;
3. Prepare or arrange for the preparation of fiduciary income tax returns for the trust; or
4. Otherwise materially participates in the administration of the trust.[54]

Planning Pointer. Although the Delaware statute prohibits settlor and certain other persons (*e.g.,* nonresidents of Delaware) from serving as a "Qualified Trustee," the settlor may appoint one or more advisors, including but not limited to:

1. Advisors who have authority under the terms of the trust instrument to remove and appoint qualified trustees or trust advisors; and
2. Advisors who have authority under the terms of the trust instrument to direct, consent to, or disapprove distributions from the trust.

---

[51] Del. Code Ann. tit. 35, § 3572(a) (2000).
[52] Del. Code Ann. tit. 35, § 3570(6) (2000).
[53] Del. Code Ann. tit. 35, § 3570(5) (2000).
[54] Del. Code Ann. tit. 35, § 3570(9) (2000).

3. A trust "protector" or any other person who, in addition to a qualified trustee, holds one or more trust powers.[55]

Caution. The settlor generally cannot serve as an advisor of a Delaware trust, except as an investment advisor described in Del. Code Ann. tit. 35, § 3313. However, the settlor can retain the right to veto a distribution from a Delaware trust.[56]

Note. The Delaware Code provides that, for a Qualified Disposition that is made to more than one trustee, such a disposition that is otherwise a "Qualified Disposition" will not fail to qualify as such solely because not all of the trustees are qualified trustees.[57]

The trust instrument must also meet certain requirements before the Delaware statute will protect a Delaware trust. Specifically, the trust instrument must do the following:[58]

1. **Appoint trustee.** Appoint one or more qualified trustees;
2. **Incorporate Delaware law.** Expressly incorporate Delaware law to govern the validity, construction, and administration of the trust;
3. **Irrevocable.** Provide that the trust is irrevocable; however, for this purpose, a trust instrument will not be deemed revocable because of the inclusion of any of the following provisions:

   a. A transferor's power to veto a distribution from the trust;
   b. A special power of appointment exercisable by will or other written instrument of the transferor effective upon the transferor's death;
   c. The transferor's potential or actual receipt of income, including rights to such income retained in the trust instrument;
   d. The transferor's potential or actual receipt of income or principal from a charitable remainder unitrust or charitable remainder annuity trust as such terms are defined in Section 664 of the Internal Revenue Code of 1986 and any successor provision thereto;
   e. The transferor's receipt each year of a percentage (up to five percent) specified in the trust instrument of the value of the trust determined from time to time pursuant to the trust instrument; or

---

[55] Id.
[56] Del. Code Ann. tit. 35, § 3570(9)(d) (2000).
[57] Del. Code Ann. tit. 35, § 3570(9)(f) (2000).
[58] Del. Code Ann. tit. 35, § 3570(10)(f) (2000).

f. The transferor's potential or actual receipt of principal if such potential or actual receipt of principal is either in the sole discretion of the qualified trustee or is pursuant to an ascertainable standard contained in the trust instrument.

4. **Spendthrift provision.** Provide that the tranferor or other beneficiary's interest in the trust property or the income therefrom cannot be transferred, assigned, pledged, or mortgaged, whether voluntarily or involuntarily, before the qualified trustee or qualified trustees actually distribute the property or income therefrom to the beneficiary, and such provision of the trust instrument shall be deemed a restriction on the transfer of the transferor's beneficial interest in the trust that is enforceable under applicable nonbankruptcy law within the meaning of Section 541(c)(2) of the Bankruptcy Code[59] or any successor provision thereto.

For purposes of the foregoing, the Delaware statute provides that a disposition by a trustee that is not a qualified trustee to a trustee that is a qualified trustee shall not be treated as other than a qualified disposition solely because the trust instrument fails to meet the requirements of subparagraph a. of this paragraph.

[2] Effect of Application of Delaware Law

[a] In General

The Delaware statute provides that no action of any kind, including, without limit, an action to enforce a judgment entered by a court or other body having adjudicative authority, may be brought for attachment or other remedy against property that is the subject of a "qualified disposition" or for avoidance of a "qualified disposition."[60] The sole exception under the Delaware statute is for fraudulent conveyance actions brought pursuant to Del. Code Ann. tit. 6, §§ 1304 and 1305, which are discussed below.[61] Moreover, the Delaware statute provides that the Delaware Court of Chancery has exclusive jurisdiction over any action brought with respect to a "qualified disposition."[62]

[b] Statute of Limitations

In addition to the foregoing provision, the Delaware statute provides that if a creditor brings a claim against a "Qualified Disposition," that claim is barred unless:

1. **Claim arose before transfer; actual intent fraudulent conveyance.** The creditor alleges actual intent fraudulent conveyance, that his claim arose

---

[59] 11 U.S.C. §541(c)(2).
[60] Del. Code Ann. tit. 35, §3572(a) (2000).
[61] *Id.*
[62] *Id.*

before the transfer, and the creditor brings his action within four years of the transfer or, if later, within one year after the creditor could have reasonably discovered the transfer;[63]

2. **Claim arose before transfer; constructive fraudulent conveyance.** The creditor alleges constructive fraudulent conveyance, that his claim arose before the transfer, and the creditor brings his action within four years of the transfer;[64]

3. **Claim arose before transfer; fraudulent conveyance transfers to insiders for antecedent debt.** The creditor alleges the tranferor was insolvent at the time of the transfer, the transfer was made to an insider for an antecedent debt, the insider had reasonable cause to believe the transferor was insolvent, and the creditor brings his action within one year after the transfer occurred, and that his claim arose before the transfer.[65]

4. **Claim did not arise before transfer.** The creditor alleges that his claim arose simultaneously with or after the transfer, and the creditor brings his action within four years of the transfer.[66]

[c]   Burden of Proof

The Delaware statute provides that in any fraudulent conveyance action described brought against a Qualified Disposition, the creditor must prove such fraudulent conveyance by clear and convincing evidence.[67]

[d]   Protection for Trustees and Advisors

The Delaware statute provides that no person, including a creditor, has any claim or cause of action against the following parties who might be involved with the Qualified Disposition, and that no action of any kind may be brought against such parties:[68]

1. The trustee;
2. Any advisor described in Del. Code. Ann. tit. 35, § 3570(9)c;
3. Any person involved in the counseling, drafting, preparation, execution, or funding of a trust that is the subject of a qualified disposition.

[e]   Exceptions to Asset Protection

The Delaware statute provides for two exceptions to the asset protection it gives to Delaware asset protection trusts. First, the Delaware statute does not

---

[63] Del. Code Ann. tit. 35, § 3572(b) (2000); Del. Code Ann. tit. 6, § 1309(1) (2000).
[64] Del. Code Ann. tit. 35, § 3572(b) (2000); Del. Code Ann. tit. 6, § 1309(2) (2000).
[65] Del. Code Ann. tit. 35, § 3572(b) (2000); Del. Code Ann. tit. 6, § 1309(3) (2000).
[66] Del. Code Ann. tit. 35 § 3572(b) (2000).
[67] Id.
[68] Del. Code Ann. tit. 35 § 3572(d)-(e) (2000).

protect any assets from certain domestic relations obligations of the transferor. Specifically, it does not protect assets from any claims that exist as to any person to whom the transferor owes money because of an agreement or court order for the payment of support or alimony in favor of such transferor's spouse, former spouse, or children, or for a division of distribution of property in favor of such transferor's spouse or former spouse.[69] However, this exception does not apply to any claim for forced heirship or legitime.[70]

Second, the Delaware statute does not protect assets from the claims of a person who suffers death, personal injury, or property damage on or before the date of a qualified disposition by a transferor, which death, personal injury, or property damage is at any time determined to have been caused in whole or in part by the act or omission of either such transferor or by another person for whom such transferor is or was vicariously liable.[71]

If an exception to the asset protection of a Delaware asset protection trust applies, the Delaware statute provides that a qualified disposition can only be avoided to the extent required to satisfy the transferor's debt to the creditor at whose instance the disposition had been avoided, along with such costs, including attorney's fees, as the court may allow.[72] If a qualified disposition is avoided, and the court is satisfied that the trustee has not acted in bad faith in accepting or administering the property that is the subject of the qualified disposition, this results in the following consequences:

- **Trustee's lien.** The Delaware statute gives the trustee a first and paramount lien against the property that constitutes the qualified disposition. The amount of this lien equals the entire cost, including attorney's fees, that the trustee properly incurred defending the action or proceedings to avoid the qualified disposition.[73]
- **Avoidance of qualified disposition subject to trustee fees.** The Delaware statute avoids the qualified disposition, but subject to the proper fees, costs, preexisting rights, claims, and interests of the trustee, including those of any predecessor trustee that has not acted in bad faith.[74]
- **No presumed bad faith.** For purpose of the foregoing two provisions, the Delaware statute presumes that the trustee did not act in bad faith merely by accepting such property.[75]

If a qualified disposition is avoided and the court is satisfied that a trust beneficiary has not acted in bad faith, then the avoidance of the qualified disposition is subject to the right of that beneficiary to retain any distribution made upon the exercise of a trust power or discretion vested in the trustee, if that

---

[69] Del. Code Ann. tit. 35, § 3573(1) (2000).
[70] Del. Code Ann. tit. 35, § 3573 (2000).
[71] Del. Code Ann. tit. 35, § 3573(2) (2000).
[72] Del. Code Ann. tit. 35, § 3574(a) (2000).
[73] Del. Code Ann. tit. 35, § 3574(b)(1)(a) (2000).
[74] Del. Code Ann. tit. 35, § 3574(b)(1)(b) (2000).
[75] Del. Code Ann. it. 35, § 3574(b)(1)(c) (2000).

power or discretion was properly exercised before the creditor commenced the action to avoid the qualified disposition.[76]

[f] Termination of Trustee

On June 30, 2003, Delaware signed into law an amendment to Del. Code Ann. Tit. 12, § 3572, which added the following paragraph (g):

> (g) If, any *action brought against a trustee* of a trust that is the result of a qualified disposition, a court takes any action whereby such court declines to apply the law of this State in determining the validity, construction or administration of such trust, or the effect of a spendthrift provision thereof, such trustee shall immediately upon such court's action and without the further order of any court, cease in all respects to be trustee of such trust and a successor trustee shall thereupon succeed as trustee in accordance with the terms of the trust instrument or, if the trust instrument does not provide for a successor trustee and the trust would otherwise be without a trustee, the Court of Chancery, upon the application of any beneficiary of such trust, shall appoint a successor trustee upon such terms and conditions as it determines to be consistent with the purposes of such trust and this statute. Upon such trustee's ceasing to be trustee, such trustee shall have no power or authority other than to convey the trust property to the successor trustee named in the trust instrument in accordance with this section.

Generally, this modification provides that a trustee's authority is terminated upon the occurrence of another state court's attempt to exercise jurisdiction over a trustee if such other court does not apply Delaware law with respect to the validity, construction, or administration of the trust. If the trust instrument does not provide for a successor trustee, this provision provides that the Delaware Court of Chancery would appoint a successor trustee.

[C] Tax Consequences of Alaska- and Delaware-Type Trusts

In Priv. Ltr. Rul. 9837007 (Sept. 11, 1998), the IRS ruled, for the first time, that a transfer of property to an irrevocable self-settled spendthrift trust, widely believed to be an Alaska trust, which was for the benefit of both the settlor and her living descendants, constituted a completed gift for federal gift tax purposes. In Priv. Ltr. Rul. 9837007, the donor planned to create an irrevocable trust that benefited herself and her descendants. The trustee would pay, during the donor's lifetime, any or all of the income and/or principal in such amounts and at such times as the trustee, in its sole and absolute discretion, determined among one or more of the class consisting of the donor and the donor's living descendants. Any income not distributed would be added to the corpus. Upon the donor's death, the corpus would be divided into separate trusts for each then living child of the donor, and a separate trust for each child who died leaving

---

[76] Del. Code Ann. tit. 35, § 3574(b)(2) (2000).

issue. The trustee would distribute the income and principal, in its discretion, among the beneficiaries. If no descendant of the donor was living at the time of the donor's death, the income and principal of the trust was to be distributed to one or more organizations described in Sections 170(c), 2055(a), and 2522(a) of the Internal Revenue Code, as the trustee may determine.

The trust instrument precluded the donor, her descendants, or any person related or subordinate to these persons (within the meaning of IRC Section 672(c)) from serving as trustee. It also precluded the donor from having the power to remove or replace the trustee or to appoint a successor trustee. The donor was not a shareholder, director, officer, or employee of the trustee. The trust instrument provided that if the trustee ceased to serve as trustee, the donor's authorized representative would name a successor trustee.

The ruling stated that there was no agreement, express or implied, between the donor and the trustee as to how the trustee would exercise its sole and absolute discretion to pay income and principal among the beneficiaries. The ruling also stated that the donor would fund the trust with cash, securities, and/or undeveloped land, and that the donor had no known or anticipated debts other than a home mortgage loan and that the donor was not under any obligation or order of child support.

The trust instrument also provided the following:

- That the interest of a beneficiary (including the grantor) of the trust could not be either voluntarily or involuntarily transferred before payment or delivery of the interest to the beneficiary by the trustee.
- That the validity, construction, and effect of the trust was to be governed by the law of the "State," which, as noted, was widely presumed to be Alaska.
- That the situs of the trust would be "State."

The ruling noted that the law of "State" provides that a person who in writing transfers property in trust may provide that the interest of a beneficiary of the trust may not be either voluntarily or involuntarily transferred before the payment or delivery of the interest to the beneficiary by the trustee. If a trust contains this transfer restriction, the restriction prevents a creditor existing when the trust is created, a person who subsequently becomes a creditor, or any other person from satisfying a claim out of the beneficiary's interest in the trust unless:

1. The transfer was intended in whole or in part to hinder, delay, or defraud creditors or other persons;
2. The trust provides that the settlor may revoke or terminate all or part of the trust without the consent of a person who has a substantial beneficial interest in the trust and the interest would be adversely affected by the exercise of the power held by the settlor to revoke or terminate all or part of the trust;
3. The trust requires that all or a part of the trust's income or principal, or both, must be distributed to the settlor; or
4. At the time of the transfer, the settlor is in default by 30 or more days of making a payment due under a child support order.

The IRS ruled that the transfer by the donor of property to the trustee to be held under the trust agreement would constitute a completed gift for federal gift tax purposes. It expressly based its ruling on the donor's representation that there was no express or implied agreement between the donor and the trustee as to how the trustee would exercise its sole and absolute discretion to pay income and principal among the beneficiaries. In addition, the IRS expressly did not rule on whether the assets held under the trust agreement at the time of the donor's death would be includible in the donor's gross estate for federal estate tax purposes.

[D]   The Bankruptcy Abuse Prevention and Consumer Protection Act of 2005

The Bankruptcy Abuse Prevention and Consumer Protection Act of 2005 (the "2005 Bankruptcy Act") became law on April 20, 2005. It contains provisions designed to target Alaska and Delaware type asset protection trusts. Specifically, it added Section 548(e) to the Bankruptcy Code.

Section 548(e)(1) provides as follows:

> (e)(1) In addition to any transfer that the trustee may otherwise avoid, the trustee may avoid any transfer of an interest of the debtor in property that was made on or within 10 years before the date of the filing of the petition, if –
>
> (A)   such transfer was made to a self-settled trust or similar device;
> (B)   such transfer was by the debtor;
> (C)   the debtor is a beneficiary of such trust or similar device; and
> (D)   the debtor made such transfer with actual intent to hinder delay, or defraud any entity to which the debtor was or became, on or after the date that such transfer was made, indebted.

In addition, the 2005 Bankruptcy Act clarifies, in Bankruptcy Code Section 548(e)(2), that a "transfer" includes a transfer made in anticipation of any money judgment, settlement, civil penalty, equitable order, or criminal fine incurred by, or which the debtor believed would be incurred by:

> (A)   any violation of state or federal securities laws and regulations; or
> (B)   fraud, deceit, or manipulation in a fiduciary capacity or in connection with the purchase or sale of any registered security.

Therefore, it is clear that this modification of the Bankruptcy Code in the 2005 Bankruptcy Act applies to future creditors, not just creditors existing at the time of the transfer to the Alaska or Delaware type asset protection trust.

Caution. The ten-year look back period applies from the date of the filing of a bankruptcy petition. In addition, existing Alaska and Delaware type asset protection trusts are not grandfathered in. Therefore, this change severely damages the usefulness of Alaska and Delaware asset protection trusts.

6

Use of Foreign Trusts

§6.01   IN GENERAL

Foreign asset protection trusts (FAPTs) are trusts that settlors establish in foreign jurisdictions that have enacted laws protecting the trust assets to a greater extent than United States law does.[1] When properly used, FAPTs provide a greater amount of asset protection than any other type of trust. However, they are more expensive than other trusts, and they require more competent advisors due to the increased complexity involved.

Generally, when properly selected, the foreign jurisdiction provides such greater protection for, among others, the following reasons:

1. The foreign jurisdiction does not recognize foreign (*e.g.*, United States) judgments. This forces potential claimants to litigate their claims in the foreign jurisdiction, usually for a second time after having previously litigated the claim in the United States.
2. The foreign jurisdiction generally requires plaintiffs to use attorneys licensed in that jurisdiction, thus increasing the plaintiffs' costs and risks of prosecuting their cases.
3. The foreign jurisdiction generally prohibits contingency fee arrangements. This forces the plaintiff to finance the litigation himself instead of having a law firm finance the litigation through a contingency fee arrangement.
4. The foreign jurisdiction's substantive law is generally much more favorable to defendants (*e.g.*, asset protection clients). For example, some foreign jurisdictions impose a higher standard of proof upon civil litigation plaintiffs, such as the "beyond a reasonable doubt" standard. This contrasts with the "preponderance of the evidence" standard for civil cases in the United States.

Caution. Before using an FAPT, planners must decide whether such a vehicle is appropriate for the client involved. FAPTs are normally appropriate only for clients with substantial wealth. Also, clients must feel comfortable with transmitting a substantial amount of their wealth to a foreign jurisdiction.

EXAMPLE 6-1

Bronte embarks on a career as a plastic surgeon. He opens his practice in 2000. In 2001, Bronte becomes concerned about protecting his estate from frivolous lawsuits after he sees several friends become the subjects of such lawsuits.

---

§6.01   [1] *See generally* Charles M. Bruce, United States Taxation of Foreign Trusts (2000); Foreign Protection of Assets Trusts for U.S. Persons: What Are They? How Do They Work? (1992 Conf. by Kluwer Law & Tax'n Publishers); Charles M. Bruce & Stephen Gray, Offshore Protection-of-Assets Trusts, U.S. Tax'n of Int'l Operations (WGL) ¶ 13,510 (1988); Charles M. Bruce et al., *Protection of Assets Trusts: Fallout from Litigation Explosion*, 206 N.Y. L.J. 1 (Sept. 13, 1991); Cyrn H. Lowell, International Estate Planning Considerations, in Sophisticated Estate Planning Techniques 63 (1989); Barry S. Engel, Asset Protection Planning: A Critical Part of Any Estate Plan, 145 Fin. & Est. Planning Ideas & Trends (CCH) ¶ 30,001 (Jan. 27, 1992); Jeffrey Schoenblum, Multistate & Multinational Estate Planning (1992).

> Bronte consults an asset protection attorney, Charlotte. Bronte and Charlotte design an asset protection strategy that involves an FAPT, which will be established in the Cook Islands. At this time, Bronte's net worth equals $11 million, which is composed of (1) his home and other real property worth $5 million, (2) other liquid assets, such as publicly traded stocks and bonds, worth $5 million, and (3) his medical practice worth $1 million.

Bronte establishes a trust in the Cook Islands in January 2002. The trust instrument provides that the law of the Cook Islands controls the trust's administration, the rights of all persons beneficially entitled under the trust, and the interpretation of the trust. Bronte then transfers all his liquid assets to the FAPT. The trust's beneficiary is Susan, Bronte's mother. Bronte designs the trust to be a grantor trust for United States income tax purposes. Consequently, each year, Bronte must recognize the trust's income.

In 2009 Ingrid, a patient of Bronte, successfully sues Bronte for malpractice. Ingrid wins a $20 million judgment against Bronte. At this time, Bronte's assets consist of $10 million in his FAPT, his home, worth $1 million and protected by a homestead exemption,[2] and real estate worth $1 million. Bronte turns over the real property to Ingrid, which leaves him obligated to Ingrid for $19 million. Ingrid takes her judgment to the Cook Islands. Here, however, she discovers that the Cook Islands will not recognize her judgment. She must litigate her claim a second time in the Cook Islands. Furthermore, under the Cook Islands' fraudulent conveyance provisions, Ingrid cannot reach the assets in the trust. Finally, even if Ingrid could reach the trust assets, the trust instrument includes a flight provision. This provision causes the removal of the trust to another non-United States jurisdiction if any event occurs that threatens the trust or its assets. Consequently, Ingrid cannot reach the FAPT's corpus.

Planning Pointer. FAPTs may also serve purposes other than asset protection. Specifically, they may assist the client in achieving traditional estate planning goals, such as the orderly transfer of wealth between generations, and may serve a client's need for economic diversification. For example, a settlor can effect a completed gift for estate and gift tax purposes to an FAPT, while continuing to remain a beneficiary of that FAPT. Also, FAPTs may be used to manage foreign assets, foreign businesses, or foreign real estate. Finally, FAPTs may be used as a unilateral method for premarital planning. In other words, they may be used as a surrogate for, or as a complement to, prenuptial agreements.[3]

The planner should consider the following issues when analyzing an FAPT:

1. How should the FAPT plan be structured?[4]

---

[2] *See* Chapter 8, Exempt Property.
[3] *See* Duncan E. Osborne, *The Offshore Trust: A Friendly Alien*, 18 ACTEC Notes 19 (1992).
[4] *See* §§ 6.04–6.05.

2. What is the ability of United States creditors to reach the FAPT's assets?[5]
3. What are the tax consequences of the FAPT on the settlor?[6]
4. What reports must the planner ensure are properly filed?[7]

§ 6.02 CREDITOR'S RIGHTS UNDER UNITED STATES LAW

The planner must analyze the rights of United States creditors under state law and under the law of the foreign situs of the FAPT. First, the planner must analyze a creditor's rights under state law and under bankruptcy laws. The settlor's creditors will ordinarily bring any actions against the settlor first in a state or bankruptcy court.[1] Generally, if the creditor fails here, it will not pursue the case further. However, there always is the possibility that the creditor will pursue the case in the trust's situs. In this event, the planner should note that a properly chosen situs will have a legal structure favorable to defendant settlors in creditor's rights cases.

When evaluating trusts, the asset protection planner must evaluate the liability exposure of the settlor and trust beneficiaries. Generally, the planner must consider the type of claimant involved, the different bases of liability the claimant might assert, and the terms of the trust. Most important, the planner must examine local law.

[A] Settlor Liability In General

The first step of the planner's analysis involves determining whether the transfer to the trust constitutes a fraudulent conveyance.[2] If the transfer constitutes a fraudulent conveyance, creditors generally can reach the transferred property even if the settlor is not a beneficiary.[3] For example, if the settlor conveys property to the trust without receiving any consideration and was insolvent at the time of the conveyance or because of the conveyance, the transfer generally constitutes a fraudulent conveyance.[4] Here, the creditor may sue (1) to have the trust set aside and the trust assets made available to satisfy his judgment,[5] (2) to have trust property made available to satisfy his judgment without

---

[5] See §§ 6.02–6.03.

[6] See § 6.06.

[7] See § 6.06.

§ 6.02   [1] See, e.g., In re Marriage of Dick, 15 Cal. App. 4th 136 (1993).

[2] See Chapter 2, Fraudulent Conveyance Concepts.

[3] Austin Wakeman Scott & William Franklin Fratcher, The Law of Trusts § 330.12 (4th ed. 1987).

[4] Scott & Fratcher, The Law of Trusts § 330.12.

[5] George Gleason Bogert & George Taylor Bogert, The Law of Trusts and Trustees § 211 (rev. 2d ed. 1992); Harper v. Atlanta Milling Co., 48 S.E.2d 89 (Ga. 1948).

setting aside the trust,[6] or (3) asserting a constructive trust with regard to the property.[7]

> **Planning Pointer.** The planner should refer to Chapter 2, Fraudulent Conveyance Concepts, to ensure that the transfer does not constitute a fraudulent conveyance.

All states have enacted fraudulent conveyance statutes. Generally, these statutes void the following transfers:

1. Transfers made with actual intent to hinder, delay, or defraud either present or future creditors;[8]
2. Transfers when the transferor is insolvent on the transfer date or becomes insolvent because of the transfer;[9]
3. Transfers when the transferor engages in or is about to engage in a business or transaction for which the property remaining in his hands after the conveyance is an unreasonably small capital;[10] or
4. Transfers when the transferor intends or believes he will incur debts beyond his ability to pay as they mature.[11]

> **Planning Pointer.** The planner must ensure the transfer does not constitute a fraudulent conveyance. Not only would this entail litigation for the client, but it could entail litigation for the planner as well.[12]

> **Planning Pointer.** To ensure the transfer to the trust does not constitute a fraudulent conveyance, the planner should take the following steps:

1. The planner should ensure the transferor is solvent at the time of the transfer and does not become insolvent because of the transfer. The planner must examine local law for the applicable definition of insolvency. He should require the client to submit an audited personal financial statement, which the planner should analyze under local law. For example, local law may define insolvency so that, if the

---

[6] Bogert & Bogert, The Law of Trusts and Trustees § 211. *See, e.g.,* Sackin v. Kersting, 466 P.2d 758 (Ariz.), *reh'g denied,* 468 P.2d 925 (Ariz. 1970).

[7] Mesa Petroleum Co. v. Coniglio, 629 F.2d 1022 (5th Cir. 1980); Bogert & Bogert, The Law of Trusts and Trustees § 211.

[8] *See, e.g.,* UFCA § 7, 7A U.L.A. § 509 (1918).

[9] *See, e.g.,* UFCA § 4, 7A U.L.A. § 474 (1918).

[10] *See, e.g.,* UFCA § 5, 7A U.L.A. § 504 (1918).

[11] *See, e.g.,* UFCA § 6, 7A U.L.A. § 507 (1918).

[12] The planner should refer to Chapter 2, which discusses fraudulent conveyances in greater detail.

transaction leaves the transferor with insufficient solvency to pay his debts as they come due, it falls within the local law definition of insolvency. Here, the planner should consider including a provision in the trust document that would require the trust to distribute funds to the settlor in the event that judgments against the settlor, stemming from obligations outstanding at the time of the transfer to the trust, exceed the settlor's remaining net worth after the transfer.

2. The planner should structure the transfer so it includes as few badges of fraud as possible.[13] This minimizes the risk that the transfer will be deemed in pursuit of a plan to hinder, delay, or defraud creditors (that is, actual intent fraud).

3. The planner should ensure the client will not engage in a new transaction or business for which his remaining capital will constitute an unreasonably small capital. The planner should thoroughly interview the client about this issue and should obtain an affidavit from the client to this effect.

4. The planner should ensure the client does not intend or believe he will incur debts beyond his ability to pay. Here again, the planner should thoroughly interview the client about this issue and should obtain an affidavit to this effect.

When settlors are also beneficiaries of the trust, their creditors can generally reach their beneficial interests.[14] Therefore, the settlor's beneficial interest is not protected. When settlors retain beneficial interests in trusts that include spendthrift provisions, such spendthrift clauses are not valid against the settlor's present and future creditors.[15]

Planning Pointer. The planner must balance the client's need to receive trust income or to use trust property against the loss of asset protection that results from a retained beneficial interest in the trust.

If the settlor not only retains a beneficial interest, but also retains a general power of appointment, creditors can generally reach all trust property.[16]

---

[13] *See* Chapter 2 for a detailed discussion of the badges of fraud.

[14] Scott & Fratcher, The Law of Trusts §§ 147, 330.12; George T. Bogert, Trusts § 39 (6th ed. 1987).

[15] Harrison v. City Nat'l Bank, 210 F. Supp. 362 (S.D. Iowa 1962); Wilmington Trust Co. v. Carpenter, 75 A.2d 815 (Del. Ch. 1950); Glass v. Carpenter, 330 S.W.2d 530 (Tex. Civ. App. 1959); Procter v. Woodhouse, 241 A.2d 785 (Vt. 1968); Scott & Fratcher, The Law of Trusts § 156; Bogert, Trusts § 40; Restatement (Second) of Trusts § 156 (1957).

[16] Ward v. Marie, 68 A. 1084 (N.J. Ch. 1907); Benedict v. Benedict, 104 A. 581 (Pa. 1918); Morton v. Morton, 147 A.2d 150 (Pa. 1959); Scott & Fratcher, The Law of Trusts §§ 147.3, 156; Restatement (Second) of Trusts § 156 cmt. c (1957).

Planning Pointer. The planner must ensure the client never retains both a beneficial interest plus a general power of appointment over the trust corpus. Failure to follow this advice destroys the asset protection benefits of a revocable trust.

When the settlor merely retains the right to revoke the trust, but does not retain any beneficial interest or general power of appointment, the majority rule is that his creditors cannot reach the trust corpus.[17] In other words, the settlor's creditors cannot compel him to revoke the trust for their benefit.[18]

Caution. If the settlor does revoke the trust, the trust corpus reverts to the settlor and, thus, becomes available to the settlor's creditors.

On the other hand, many courts hold that the settlor's creditors may reach the trust corpus when the settlor retains the power to revoke the trust.[19] Additionally, some jurisdictions have enacted statutes providing that settlors retaining absolute or unqualified powers to revoke trusts are deemed the absolute owner of the trust property to satisfy creditor claims.[20] Where such statutes exist, the settlor's creditors can reach the trust corpus. Finally, if the settlor enters bankruptcy, the bankruptcy trustee acquires the settlor's right to revoke the trust, which pulls the trust corpus into the bankruptcy estate. This devastates the asset protection plan.

---

[17] Scott & Fratcher, The Law of Trusts § 330.12; Bogert & Bogert, The Law of Trusts and Trustees § 233; L. Henry Gissel, Jr. & Karen R. Schiller, *Trusts Made Easy: A Simplified Overview of the Reasons for Creating, Modifying, and Terminating Express Trusts*, 10 Prob. L.J. 241 (1991); *Probate & Trust Division Committee D-3 on Special Problems of Fiduciaries, Creditors' Rights Against Trust Assets*, 22 Real Prop. Prob. & Tr. J. 735, 739 (1987); Lawrence Berger, *The General Power of Appointment as an Interest in Property*, 40 Neb. L. Rev. 104 (1960); Note, *Creditor's Ability to Reach Assets under a General Power of Appointment*, 24 Vand. L. Rev. 367 (1971). *See, e.g.,* Jones v. Clifton, 101 U.S. 225 (1879); Guthrie v. Canty, 53 N.E.2d 1009 (Mass. 1944); Abruzzese v. Oestrich, 47 A.2d 883 (N.J. Ch. 1946).

[18] Scott & Fratcher, The Law of Trusts § 330.12; Restatement (Second) of Trusts § 330 cmt. o (1959); Richard W. Effland, *Rights of Creditors in Nonprobate Assets*, 48 Mo. L. Rev. 431 (1983); Notes and Comments, *Rights of a Creditor of a Settlor to Reach the Corpus of a Revocable Trust*, 39 Ky. L.J. 131 (1950).

[19] State St. Bank & Trust Co. v. Reiser, 389 N.E.2d 768, 770 (Mass. 1979); Johnson v. Commercial Bank, 588 P.2d 1096, 1099 (Or. 1978); *In re* Kovalyshyn's Estate, 343 A.2d 852 (N.J. Super. 1975); Restatement of Property § 328 (1940); Scott & Fratcher, The Law of Trusts § 330.12; Bogert & Bogert, The Law of Trusts and Trustees § 233; L. Gissel. & Schiller, *Trusts Made Easy: A Simplified Overview of the Reasons for Creating, Modifying, and Terminating Express Trusts*, 10 Prob. L.J. 241.

[20] *See* Bogert & Bogert, The Law of Trusts and Trustees § 233. *See, e.g.,* Ala. Code § 35-4-290 (1975); Cal. Prob. Code § 18200 (Deering 1991); N.Y. Est. Powers & Trusts Law § 10-10.6 (McKinney 1981 & Supp. 1993).

Planning Pointer. Many commentators believe that revocable trusts provide no asset protection benefits.[21] They base this belief on the theory that a court would force the settlor to revoke the trust in favor of creditors. However, other commentators believe that revocable trusts constitute a valuable asset protection tool.[22] Although the amount of asset protection that revocable trusts provide is not clear, it does appear that irrevocable trusts provide substantially more asset protection than revocable trusts. Therefore, to obtain the maximum amount of asset protection, the planner should use irrevocable trusts.

[B]   Settlor Liability: Spousal Rights

The planner also must consider possible claims of the settlor's surviving spouse or of a spouse who is divorcing the settlor. Specifically, spouses may assert the following claims against the trust:

1.   That the transfer of property into the trust constituted a fraudulent conveyance;
2.   That the transfer of property to the trust was illusory;
3.   An election to claim a surviving spouse's elective share of the settlor's estate which may include certain inter vivos trust property; or
4.   Fraud in the inducement of marriage.[23]

First, if the transfer constitutes a fraudulent conveyance as to a spouse, then the defrauded spouse can reach the transferred trust corpus under the fraudulent conveyance doctrine.[24] Unique factors that courts consider in marital rights cases include the portion of the settlor's property transferred, the proximity of the transfer to the death or divorce date, any provisions made by the settlor for the spouse, the settlor's relationship to the trust beneficiaries, and participation by the trust beneficiaries in the transfers.[25]

Second, a spouse may assert that the transfer of property into the trust was illusory. If the settlor retains excessive control, a court may find that the transfer

---

[21] *See, e.g.,* Santo (Sandy) Bisignano, Jr., *Protecting Assets from Overzealous Creditors or an Estate Planner's Guide to Preservation Planning,* 1987 Annual Notre Dame Est. Plan. Inst. 3-40.

[22] *See, e.g.,* Gissel & Schiller, 10 Prob. L.J. 241; James F. Farr & Jackson W. Wright, Jr., An Estate Planner's Handbook §18 (1979 & Supp. 1989).

[23] Probate & Trust Division Committee D-3 on Special Problems of Fiduciaries, *Creditors' Rights Against Trust Assets,* 22 Real Prop. Prob. & Tr. J. 735, 743 (1987); E. LeFevre, Annotation, *Gift or other voluntary transfer by husband as fraud on wife,* 49 A.L.R.2d 521 (1963).

[24] *See* Chapter 2. *See also* Kasinski v. Questel, 472 N.Y.S.2d 807 (App. Div. 1984).

[25] Hanke v. Hanke, 459 A.2d 246 (N.H. 1983); Norris v. Barbour, 51 S.E.2d 334 (Va. 1949). Probate & Trust Division Committee D-3 on Special Problems of Fiduciaries, *Creditors' Rights Against Trust Assets,* 22 Real Prop. Prob. & Tr. J. 735, 743 (1987); W.D. MacDonald, Fraud on the Widow's Share (1960); 37 Am. Jur. 2d, Fraudulent Conveyances §10 (1987).

of property to the trust was "illusory."[26] For example, the settlor's retention of the power to revoke a trust in conjunction with a retained right to income for life, and substantial control over the trust's administration may constitute an illusory trust.[27]

Third, concerning surviving spouses, the planner must consider whether trust assets will be included in the settlor's estate for purposes of determining the surviving spouse's statutory share of the settlor's estate.[28] The law concerning this issue varies greatly from state to state. Many states have enacted Section 2-202 of the Uniform Probate Code. This provision provides that the augmented estate includes assets in trusts in which the settlor retains the power of revocation for purposes of determining the amount of the surviving spouse's elective or statutory share.[29] Therefore, in these states property contained within revocable trusts will be reachable by the settlor's surviving spouse. Other states have enacted statutes that have the same general effect as Section 2-202 of the Uniform Probate Code.[30] Because the FAPT should always be irrevocable, it will generally not be reachable by the settlor's surviving spouse.

Fourth, if the settlor enters an antenuptial or postnuptial agreement before a conveyance to a trust made in contemplation of marriage and that violates a promise or representation made within the antenuptial or postnuptial agreement, the conveyance may be fraudulent.[31] Alternatively, a court may consider such a conveyance to be contrary to public policy or illusory due to the nature of the control retained by the settlor.[32]

Concerning divorce, courts may treat transfers made to third parties before a divorce as part of the marital estate. Consequently, such property would then be subject to equitable division between the spouses.[33]

[C] Settlor Liability: Bankruptcy

Generally, when a settlor enters bankruptcy,[34] the bankruptcy estate acquires all of the settlor's legal and equitable interests in property as of the bankruptcy

---

[26] Probate & Trust Division Committee D-3 on Special Problems of Fiduciaries, *Creditors' Rights Against Trust Assets*, 22 Real Prop. Prob. & Tr. J. 735, 743 (1987); W.D. MacDonald, Fraud on the Widow's Share.

[27] Probate & Trust Division Committee D-3 on Special Problems of Fiduciaries, *Creditors' Rights Against Trust Assets*, 22 Real Prop. Prob. & Tr. J. 735, 743-44 (1987).

[28] *See* J.R. Kemper, Annotation, *Validity of inter vivos trust established by one spouse which impairs the other spouse's distributive share or other statutory rights in property*, 39 A.L.R.3d 14 (1971); J.R. Kemper, Annotation, *Inclusion of funds in savings bank trust (Totten trust) in determining surviving spouse's interest in decedent's estate*, 64 A.L.R.3d 187 (1985).

[29] U.P.C. § 2-202, 8 U.L.A. 75-77 (1969); R.U.P.C. § 2-202 (1990), 8 U.L.A. 90-92 (Supp. 1992).

[30] *See* Bogert, Trusts § 48. *See, e.g.*, N.Y. Est. Powers & Trusts Law § 51.1(b)(1) (McKinney 1981 & Supp. 1993); Pa. Cons. Stat. Ann. § 2203 (1990).

[31] *See* Bogert & Bogert, The Law of Trusts and Trustees § 211.

[32] *Id.*

[33] *See* Bogert & Bogert, The Law of Trusts and Trustees § 211. *See, e.g.*, Shannon v. Shannon, 680 S.W.2d 367 (Mo. Ct. App. 1984); Rosenberg v. Rosenberg, 497 A.2d 485 (Md.), *cert. denied*, 501 A.2d 845 (Md. 1985); Kessel v. Kessel, 370 N.W.2d 889 (Minn. Ct. App. 1985).

[34] For a detailed discussion of the Bankruptcy Code, *see* J. Pearson et al., Drafting Bankruptcy Reorganization Plans (2d ed., John Wiley & Sons 1993); Advanced Chapter 11 Bankruptcy Practice (Thomas J.

proceeding commencement.[35] The bankruptcy estate acquires such interests regardless of any provisions in agreements, transfer instruments, or applicable nonbankruptcy law that restricts or conditions the transfer of such property interest by the debtor.[36] Any beneficial interests in trusts that the settlor retains constitute equitable interests for purposes of the Bankruptcy Code.[37] This rule also applies if the settlor creates a spendthrift trust for his own benefit.[38]

The bankruptcy trustee also acquires the bankrupt settlor's ability to exercise his power of revocation.[39] Therefore, if this power is a general power of revocation, the bankruptcy trustee may revoke the trust. This would cause the trust corpus to revert to the settlor's bankruptcy estate. If the settlor also retains a power of appointment, the bankruptcy trustee also acquires this power.[40]

> **Planning Pointer.** The planner must note that retaining an unqualified power of revocation opens the door for creditors to reach the corpus of the revocable trust. For this reason, the planner should avoid revocable trusts. Furthermore, the Bankruptcy Code provides that the bankruptcy estate does not include any power (for example, power of revocation or appointment) the settlor/debtor may exercise entirely for the benefit of other persons.[41] Finally, the planner should note that, for the bankruptcy trustee to access the trust corpus, the trustee must begin such an action during the settlor's life.[42] Otherwise, the bankruptcy trustee cannot access the trust corpus.[43]

[D] Settlor Liability: Effect of Illegal Purpose Trust

If a court finds that the settlor established a trust for an illegal purpose (to defraud creditors or a spouse), the claimant can ask the court to set aside the

---

Salerno & Craig D. Hansen eds., John Wiley & Sons 1987 & Supp. 1990); Grant W. Newton & Gilbert D. Bloom, Bankruptcy & Insolvency Taxation (John Wiley & Sons 1991); Lewis D. Solomon & Lewis J. Saret, Business Workout Planning Strategies Ch. 2 (John Wiley & Sons 1992).

[35] 11 U.S.C. §541(a)(1) (1988).

[36] 11 U.S.C. §541(c)(1)(A) (1988).

[37] 11 U.S.C. §541(a) (1988); Probate & Trust Division Committee D-3 on Special Problems of Fiduciaries, *Creditors' Rights Against Trust Assets*, 22 Real Prop. Prob. & Tr. J. 735, 746 (1987).

[38] 11 U.S.C. §541(c)(1)(A), (B) (1988); Probate & Trust Division D-3 on Special Problems of Fiduciaries, *Creditors' Rights Against Trust Assets*, 22 Real Prop. Prob. & Tr. J. 735, 746 (1987).

[39] *See* Probate & Trust Division Committee D-3 on Special Problems of Fiduciaries, *Creditors' Rights Against Trust Assets*, 22 Real Prop. Prob. & Tr. J. 735, 746 (1987); Restatement (Second) of Trusts § 330 cmt. o (1939); Bogert, Trusts § 48. *See, e.g.*, Jones v. Clifton, 101 U.S. 225 (1879); Murphey v. C.I.T. Corp., 33 A.2d 16 (Pa. 1943); Chase Nat'l Bank v. Ginnel, 50 N.Y.S.2d 345 (Sup. Ct. 1944).

[40] *See* Probate & Trust Division Committee D-3 on Special Problems of Fiduciaries, *Creditors' Rights Against Trust Assets*, 22 Real Prop. Prob. & Tr. J. 735, 746 (1987); Restatement (Second) of Trusts § 330 cmt. o (1939).

[41] 11 U.S.C. §541(b) (1988 & Supp. 1991).

[42] *See* Probate & Trust Division Committee D-3 on Special Problems of Fiduciaries, *Creditors' Rights Against Trust Assets*, 22 Real Prop. Prob. & Tr. J. 735, 747 (1987); Effland, 48 Mo. L. Rev. at 441.

[43] *See* Probate & Trust Division Committee D-3 on Special Problems of Fiduciaries, *Creditors' Rights Against Trust Assets*, 22 Real Prop. Prob. & Tr. J. 735, 747 (1987); Effland, 48 Mo. L. Rev. at 441.

trust. When this occurs, the purported trust's property reverts to the settlor, and his creditors or spouse can then reach the property.[44] If the trust is not attached, then innocent beneficiaries may request a court to grant them performance of the trust as long as the trust's performance does not enable the innocent parties to profit from the illegality.[45] Conversely, if the trust's performance would advance the accomplishment of the illegal objectives, then courts generally do not grant performance of the trust.[46] When the trust serves several purposes, only one of which is illegal, if the different objectives can be separated and the valid purpose can be effected without effecting the illegal purpose, the trust is so enforced.[47]

[E] Beneficiaries Generally

Generally, absent a valid trust provision or a controlling statute to the contrary, creditors of trust beneficiaries may reach the beneficiaries' trust interest to satisfy their claims.[48] If the debtor is the sole trust beneficiary and is entitled to an immediate conveyance of the corpus, creditors may request a court to order a sale of the corpus. The court then pays the creditor's claims out of the proceeds.[49]

If the beneficiary/debtor is not the sole beneficiary, the creditor cannot reach the trust corpus unless this can be done without interfering with the other beneficiaries' rights. If this cannot be done without interfering with the rights of other beneficiaries, the creditor can only reach the beneficiary's equitable interest in the trust.[50] If the beneficiary has a life estate only, the creditor may request a court to order the sale of the life interest. However, courts generally do not order such a sale when it would cause a hardship on the beneficiary and the life interest is sufficient to satisfy the debt within a reasonable amount of time.[51]

If the beneficiary has a future interest only, courts generally order a sale of the future interest unless it is so indefinite or contingent that it cannot be sold with fairness to creditors.[52] In rare cases, however, a court may only give the creditor a charge or mortgage on the future interest.[53]

When the beneficiary enters bankruptcy, the bankruptcy estate acquires the beneficiary's trust interest.[54] However, the bankruptcy estate does not acquire any power the debtor may exercise solely for the benefit of an entity other than

---

[44] Bogert, Trusts § 48; Brundage v. Cheneworth, 70 N.W. 211 (Iowa 1897).

[45] Bogert, Trusts § 48.

[46] Bogert, Trusts § 48. See, e.g., Pace v. Wainwright, 10 So. 2d 755 (Ala. 1942); Murphy v. Murphy, 213 S.W.2d 601 (Ky. 1948).

[47] Younger v. Moore, 103 P. 221 (Cal. 1909); Culross v. Gibbons, 29 N.E. 839 (N.Y. 1892); Bogert, Trusts § 48.

[48] Bogert, Trusts § 39; Scott & Fratcher, The Law of Trusts § 147-147.3.

[49] Bogert, Trusts § 39; Scott & Fratcher, The Law of Trusts § 147.2.

[50] Scott & Fratcher, The Law of Trusts 58 § 147.2.

[51] Id.

[52] Bogert, Trusts § 39; Scott & Fratcher, The Law of Trusts § 147.2.

[53] Scott & Fratcher, The Law of Trusts § 147.2.

[54] 11 U.S.C. § 541 (1988 & Supp. 1991); Bogert, Trusts § 39; Scott & Fratcher, The Law of Trusts § 147.1. See, e.g., Horton v. Moore, 110 F.2d 189 (6th Cir.), cert. denied, 311 U.S. 692, reh'g denied, 311 U.S. 728 (1940); In re Dolard, 275 F. Supp. 1001 (C.D. Cal. 1967).

the debtor.[55] Also, restrictions on transfers of beneficial interests of the beneficiary/debtor in a trust that are enforceable under applicable nonbankruptcy law are enforceable for purposes of the Bankruptcy Code.[56] Therefore, spendthrift provisions are generally effective for nonsettlor beneficiaries.

[F] Donees of Powers of Appointment

When settlors grant a special power to appoint among a group of individuals, that power is not considered beneficial to the donee. Thus, such a power cannot be reached by the donee's creditors.[57]

When the power is a general power, including the power to appoint to the holder himself, the power will be considered beneficial to the donee.[58] However, when a holder of a general power of appointment, created by a third person, does not exercise that power, the holder's creditors generally cannot reach the trust corpus.[59] Of course, if the holder exercises the power in his own favor, then his creditors may reach the property. On the other hand, if the holder of the general power of appointment is also the settlor, his creditors may reach the trust corpus.[60]

> **Caution.** Several states have enacted statutes that control this issue. Such statutes provide that creditors of holders of general powers of appointment created by other persons may reach the corpus of the trust that is the subject of that power.[61]

§6.03 CREDITOR'S RIGHTS UNDER FOREIGN LAW

The planner also must analyze the FAPT under the law of the FAPT's situs. If the creditor succeeds in a U.S. court, the creditor will then attempt to enforce his judgment in the FAPT's situs. The issue then becomes whether the foreign situs

---

[55] 11 U.S.C. §541(b)(1) (1988 & Supp. 1991).

[56] 11 U.S.C. §541(c)(2) (1988); Scott & Fratcher, The Law of Trusts §147.1.

[57] Scott & Fratcher, The Law of Trusts §147.3; Restatement of Property §326 (1988); Charles C. Callahan & W. Barton Leach, Powers of Appointment, in 5 American Law of Property §23.15 (A. James Casner ed., 1952); Restatement (Second) of Property (Donative Transfers) §13.1 (1982).

[58] Scott & Fratcher, The Law of Trusts §147.3; Restatement of Property §§329, 330 (1988); Callahan & Leach, Powers of Appointment, in 5 American Law of Property §23.16; Restatement (Second) of Property (Donative Transfers) §13.4 (1982); Erwin N. Griswold, Spendthrift Trusts §§94-97 (2d ed. 1947).

[59] Scott & Fratcher, The Law of Trusts §147.3; Restatement of Property §327 (1988); Callahan & Leach, Powers of Appointment, in 5 American Law of Property §23.17; Restatement (Second) of Property (Donative Transfers) §13.2 (1982); Note, *Creditors' Ability to Reach Assets under a General Power of Appointment*, 24 Vand. L. Rev. 367 (1971).

[60] Scott & Fratcher, The Law of Trusts §§147.3, 156; Restatement (Second) of Trusts §156 cmt. c (1957). *See, e.g.,* Ward v. Marie, 68 A. 1084 (N.J. Ch. 1907); Benedict v. Benedict, 104 A. 581 (Pa. 1918); Morton v. Morton, 147 A.2d 150 (Pa. 1959).

[61] Scott & Fratcher, The Law of Trusts §147.3.

will enforce the U.S. judgment. At this juncture, the planner must analyze the situs jurisdiction's law regarding the enforcement of foreign judgments.

If the trust holds property within the United States, the creditor may try to seize such property in disregard of the trust. Whether the creditor is successful will depend on law of the jurisdiction in question.

> **Planning Pointer.** To protect against creditors trying to seize property located in the United States, the trust should only hold liquid assets such as bank accounts, stocks, and bonds, which can be liquidated easily with the proceeds transferred by wire instantaneously to other jurisdictions. Furthermore, the trust should contain anti-duress provisions that trigger changes in the FAPT's management structure so that no person who is subject to the jurisdiction of a U.S. court will have any control over the FAPT or its assets.[1]

Sections 6.10 through 6.12 will discuss the applicable provisions of the laws of the Cook Islands, the Cayman Islands, and the Bahamas to provide a sampling of how FAPT jurisdiction laws operate.

[A]   Cook Islands

Under the International Trusts Act 1984, Section 13I (Cook Islands),[2] as amended by Section 6 of the International Trusts Amendment Act 1989 (Cook Islands), the Cook Islands will give no effect to foreign laws that void or set aside an international trust governed by Cook Islands law on the grounds that:

1. The laws of the foreign jurisdiction prohibit or do not recognize trusts in general;
2. The FAPT or the transfer thereto (a) avoids or defeats rights, claims, or interests conferred by the foreign jurisdiction's laws on the claimant or creditor, or (b) contravenes a foreign law or order intended to recognize, protect, enforce, or give effect to such rights, claims, or interests; or
3. The laws of the Cook Islands are inconsistent with the foreign law in question.[3]

Furthermore, when a foreign judgment is based on any law that is inconsistent with the International Trusts Act 1984 or if the judgment relates to a matter governed by the law of the Cook Islands, the Cook Islands do not recognize or enforce that foreign judgment against:

1. An international trust;

---

§ 6.03   [1] *See* § 6.05[D] for a discussion of anti-duress provisions.
[2] *See* Appendix A for the full text of the International Trusts Act 1984 (Cook Islands).
[3] International Trusts Act 1984, § 13I (Cook Islands).

2. An international trust's (a) settlor, (b) trustee, (c) protector, (d) beneficiary, (e) person appointed or instructed to exercise a function or undertake any act, matter, or thing in connection with an international trust; or

3. Property of an international trust, trustee, or beneficiary.[4]

For a claimant to successfully bring a fraudulent conveyance claim against an international trust in the Cook Islands, the claimant must prove beyond a reasonable doubt (as opposed to merely by a preponderance of the evidence) that the international trust was established, or property was transferred to such a trust (1) with the principal intent to defraud that creditor, and (2) such transaction did in fact, at the time of that transaction, render the settlor insolvent or without sufficient property to satisfy the creditor's claim. When a claimant succeeds on a fraudulent conveyance claim, then under Cook Islands law (1) that transaction is not void or voidable, but (2) the international trust will be liable to satisfy the creditor's claim out of the property that, but for the transfer, would have been available to satisfy the creditor's claim. However, the liability only extends to the extent of the settlor's interest in the property before the transaction and any accumulation thereto.[5]

Planning Pointer. Cook Islands law provides that the establishment of an international trust and transfers thereto will not be fraudulent against the settlor's creditors when (1) the creditor's cause of action accrues more than two years before the settlor established the trust or made the transfer in question, or (2) the creditor's cause of action accrued less than two years before the settlor established the trust or made the transfer in question, but the creditor failed to commence his action before the expiration of one year from the date that such establishment or transfer in question took place.[6] Furthermore, Cook Islands law provides that the establishment of an international trust and transfers of property to such trust will not be fraudulent against creditors of the settlor when the transfers occur before the creditor's cause of action against the settlor arises or accrues.[7]

Cook Islands law also provides that it will not impute an intent to defraud to a settlor solely by reason of the fact that the settlor (1) established an international trust or transferred property to such a trust, (2) is a beneficiary of such trust, or (3) retains, possesses, or acquires any of the following powers, which Cook Islands law expressly allows the settlor to possess:[8]

1. Power to revoke the trust;

---

[4] International Trusts Act 1984, § 13D (Cook Islands).
[5] International Trusts Act 1984, § 13B (Cook Islands).
[6] International Trusts Act 1984, § 13B(3) (Cook Islands).
[7] International Trusts Act 1984, § 13B(4) (Cook Islands).
[8] International Trusts Act 1984, § 13C (Cook Islands).

2. Power of disposition over the property of the trust or the subject of the instrument;

3. Power to amend the trust;

4. Any benefit interest or property retained or acquired from the trust, or pursuant to the trust;

5. Power to remove or appoint a trustee or protector; or

6. Power to direct a trustee or protector on any matter.[9]

Also, the planner should note that Cook Islands law provides that international trusts and transfers thereto cannot be found defective or void in any fashion because such trust defeats the rights, claims, or interests that a claimant asserts because of a personal relationship to the settlor or because of heirship rights.[10] Furthermore, the planner should note that, generally, no action may be brought to challenge an international trust or transfers thereto after two years of the transaction in question.[11]

[B] Cayman Islands

The Trusts Law (No. 6 of 1987) (Revised) (Cayman Islands) and the Trust (Foreign Element) Law 1987 (Cayman Islands) control trusts in the Cayman Islands. Under Cayman Islands law, if a trust instrument provides that it is to be governed by Cayman Islands law, then the Cayman Islands recognize this provision as being valid.[12] When the trust instrument provides that (1) Cayman Islands law governs a particular aspect of the trust, or (2) that the Cayman Islands or its courts are the forum for the trust or any of its provisions, then subject to contrary terms within the trust instrument, the Cayman Islands recognize that its law governs such trust or provision.[13] Finally, when the trust instrument so provides, the Cayman Islands allow the governing law of the trust to be changed to or from Cayman Islands law if (1) for changes to the law of the Cayman Islands, the law of the prior jurisdiction recognizes the change,[14] or (2) for changes from the law of the Cayman Islands, the law of the new jurisdiction recognizes both the validity of the trust and the respective interests of the beneficiaries.[15]

When a trust is governed by Cayman Islands law, then that law governs any questions as to the following:

1. The capacity of the settlor;[16]

---

[9] International Trusts Act 1984, § 13B(3)(b) (Cook Islands).

[10] International Trusts Act 1984, § 13E (Cook Islands).

[11] International Trusts Act 1984, § 13K (Cook Islands).

[12] Trust (Foreign Element) Law 1987, § 4(1)-(2) (Cayman Islands).

[13] Trust (Foreign Element) Law 1987, § 4(3) (Cayman Islands).

[14] Trust (Foreign Element) Law 1987, § 4(4)(i) (Cayman Islands).

[15] Trust (Foreign Element) Law 1987, § 4(4)(ii) (Cayman Islands).

[16] Trust (Foreign Element) Law 1987, § 5(i) (Cayman Islands).

2. Any aspect of the validity of the trust or its disposition, or the interpretation or effect thereof;[17]
3. The administration of the trust, regardless of whether the trust is administered in the Cayman Islands or elsewhere, including questions regarding the powers, obligations, liabilities, and rights of trustees and their appointment and removal;[18] or
4. The existence and extent of powers that are conferred or retained, including any powers of variation or appointment, and the validity of the exercise of any such powers."[19]

However, although Cayman Islands law governs the preceding questions, it does so with the following caveats:

1. Cayman Islands law does not validate a property disposition that is neither owned by the settlor nor the subject of a power vested in him.[20] For purposes of this rule, this section does not affect the recognition of foreign laws when determining whether the settlor owns the property or holds a pertinent power;[21]
2. Cayman Islands law applies to the FAPT subject to any trust instrument provisions to the contrary;[22]
3. When there is a question as to the capacity of a corporation, the laws of the place of incorporation control;[23]
4. The preceding rules do not impact the recognition of foreign laws generally concerning the formalities for the disposition of property, other than with reference to the existence or terms of the trust;[24]
5. Cayman Islands law does not validate any trust or disposition of real property that is located outside of the Cayman Islands that is not valid according to the laws of such jurisdiction;[25]
6. Cayman Islands law does not validate a testamentary trust or disposition that is not valid according to the laws of the testator's domicile.[26]

Cayman Islands law also provides that a settlor's capacity will not be questioned, and no trust or disposition of property that the Cayman Islands law governs will be declared void, voidable, set aside, or defective in any way because (1) the laws of any foreign jurisdiction prohibit or do not recognize the trust concept,[27] or (2) the trust or disposition (a) defeats or avoids the rights,

---

[17] Trust (Foreign Element) Law 1987, § 5(ii) (Cayman Islands).
[18] Trust (Foreign Element) Law 1987, § 5(iii) (Cayman Islands)
[19] Trust (Foreign Element) Law 1987, § 5(iv) (Cayman Islands)
[20] Trust (Foreign Element) Law 1987, § 5(a) (Cayman Islands).
[21] Id.
[22] Trust (Foreign Element) Law 1987, § 5(b) (Cayman Islands).
[23] Trust (Foreign Element) Law 1987, § 5(c) (Cayman Islands).
[24] Trust (Foreign Element) Law 1987, § 5(d) (Cayman Islands).
[25] Trust (Foreign Element) Law 1987, § 5(e) (Cayman Islands).
[26] Trust (Foreign Element) Law 1987, § 5(f) (Cayman Islands).
[27] Trust (Foreign Element) Law 1987, § 6(a) (Cayman Islands).

claims, or interests conferred by foreign law on any person because of a personal relationship between such person and the settlor or heirship rights, or (b) contravenes any rule of foreign law or foreign judicial or administrative order or action that is intended to recognize, protect, enforce, or give effect to any such rights, claims, or interests.[28]

[C] The Bahamas

The Trusts (Choice of Governing Law) Act, 1989[29] and the Fraudulent Dispositions Act, 1991[30] are the two main pieces of Bahamas legislation the planner should consider.

Under Bahamas law, if a trust instrument provides that it is to be governed by Bahamas law, then the Bahamas recognize this provision as being valid.[31] When the trust instrument provides that (1) Bahamas law governs a particular aspect of the trust, or (2) that the Bahamas or its courts are the forum for the trust or any of its provisions, then subject to contrary terms within the trust instrument, the Bahamas recognize that Bahamas law governs such trust or provision.[32] Finally, when the trust instrument so provides, the Bahamas allow the governing law of the trust to be changed to or from Bahamas law if (1) for changes to the law of the Bahamas, the law of the prior jurisdiction recognizes the change,[33] or (2) for changes from the law of the Bahamas, the law of the new jurisdiction recognizes both the validity of the trust and the respective interests of the beneficiaries.[34]

When a trust is governed by Bahamas law, then Bahamas law governs all questions arising with regard to the trust, including the following:

1. The capacity of the settlor;[35]
2. Any aspect of the validity of the trust or its disposition, or the interpretation or effect thereof;[36]
3. The administration of the trust, regardless of whether the trust is administered in the Bahamas or elsewhere, including questions regarding the powers, obligations, liabilities, and rights of trustees and their appointment and removal;[37] or
4. The existence and extent of powers that are conferred or retained, including any powers of variation or appointment, and the validity of the exercise of any such powers.[38]

---

[28] Trust (Foreign Element) Law 1987, § 6(b) (Cayman Islands).

[29] Trusts (Choice of Governing Law) Act, 1989 (Bahamas).

[30] Fraudulent Dispositions Act, 1991 (Bahamas).

[31] Trusts (Choice of Governing Law) Act, 1989 § 4(2) (Bahamas).

[32] Trusts (Choice of Governing Law) Act, 1989 § 4(3) (Bahamas).

[33] Trusts (Choice of Governing Law) Act, 1989 § 5(1)(a) (Bahamas).

[34] Trusts (Choice of Governing Law) Act, 1989 § 5(1)(b) (Bahamas).

[35] Trusts (Choice of Governing Law) Act, 1989 § 7(1)(a) (Bahamas).

[36] Trusts (Choice of Governing Law) Act, 1989 § 7(1)(b) (Bahamas).

[37] Trusts (Choice of Governing Law) Act, 1989 § 7(1)(c) (Bahamas).

[38] Trusts (Choice of Governing Law) Act, 1989 § 7(1)(d) (Bahamas).

However, although Bahamas law governs the preceding questions, it does so with the following caveats:

1. Bahamas law does not validate a property disposition neither owned by the settlor nor the subject of a power vested in him.[39] For purposes of this rule, this section does not affect the recognition of foreign laws when determining whether the settlor owns the property or holds a pertinent power;[40]
2. Bahamas law is subject to any trust instrument provisions to the contrary;[41]
3. When there is a question as to the capacity of a corporation, the laws of the place of incorporation control;[42]
4. The preceding rules do not impact the recognition of foreign laws generally concerning the formalities for the disposition of property, other than with reference to the existence or terms of the trust;[43]
5. Bahamas law does not validate any trust or disposition of real property that is located outside of the Bahamas that is not valid according to the laws of such jurisdiction;[44]
6. Bahamas law does not validate a testamentary trust or disposition that is not valid according to the laws of the testator's domicile.[45]

Bahamas law also provides that a settlor's capacity will not be questioned, and no trust or disposition of property that the Bahamas law governs will be declared void, voidable, set aside, or defective in any way because (1) the laws of any foreign jurisdiction prohibit or do not recognize the trust concept,[46] or (2) the trust or disposition (a) defeats or avoids the rights, claims, or interests conferred by foreign law on any person because of a personal relationship between such person and the settlor or heirship rights, or (b) contravenes any rule of foreign law or foreign judicial or administrative order or action that is intended to recognize, protect, enforce, or give effect to any such rights, claims, or interests.[47]

Concerning fraudulent conveyances, Bahamas law generally provides that every property disposition that the transferor makes (1) with the intent to defraud, and (2) with no or significantly less consideration than the value of the property in question, will be voidable at the instance of the creditor that is prejudiced by such transfer.[48] However, the creditor has the burden of establishing the intent to defraud.[49] Furthermore, the Bahamas law precludes any creditor from bringing a fraudulent conveyance claim unless the creditor brings that claim within two years of the disposition in question.[50]

[39] Trusts (Choice of Governing Law) Act, 1989 § 7(2)(a)(i) (Bahamas).
[40] Trusts (Choice of Governing Law) Act, 1989 § 7(2)(b) (Bahamas).
[41] Trusts (Choice of Governing Law) Act, 1989 § 7(2)(c) (Bahamas).
[42] Trusts (Choice of Governing Law) Act, 1989 § 7(2)(d) (Bahamas).
[43] Trusts (Choice of Governing Law) Act, 1989 § 7(2)(e) (Bahamas).
[44] Trusts (Choice of Governing Law) Act, 1989 § 7(2)(a)(ii) (Bahamas).
[45] Trusts (Choice of Governing Law) Act, 1989 § 7(2)(a)(iii) (Bahamas).
[46] Trusts (Choice of Governing Law) Act, 1989 § 8(a) (Bahamas).
[47] Trusts (Choice of Governing Law) Act, 1989 § 8(b) (Bahamas).
[48] Fraudulent Dispositions Act, 1991 § 4(1) (Bahamas).
[49] Fraudulent Dispositions Act, 1991 § 4(2) (Bahamas).
[50] Fraudulent Dispositions Act, 1991 § 4(3) (Bahamas).

Planning Pointer. The planner should note that this provision completely bars fraudulent conveyance claims that the creditor brings two years after the actual transfer. Therefore, when the creditor does not discover the transaction until more than two years after the transfer, Bahamas law completely bars the creditor from proceeding with his claim.

When a transfer is to be set aside as a fraudulent conveyance under Bahamas law, unless the court finds that the transferee acts in bad faith, (1) the transferee will have a first and paramount charge over the property in question in the amount of the entire costs properly incurred by the trustee to defend the fraudulent conveyance question (as opposed to merely the costs that the court might otherwise allow),[51] and (2) the disposition in question must be set aside, subject to the proper fees, costs, preexisting rights, claims, and interests of the transferee (and any predecessor transferees not acting in bad faith).[52] Furthermore, Bahamas law specifically provides that, unless the court determines that a trust beneficiary acts in bad faith, the disposition can only be set aside subject to the right of such beneficiary to retain any distribution made consequent on the prior exercise of a trust power or discretion that is vested in the trustee or any other person, which is properly exercised.[53] The creditor bears the burden of proving that the transferee or beneficiary acts in bad faith.[54] Additionally, Bahamas law provides that transfers that are set aside as fraudulent conveyances are only set aside to the extent necessary to satisfy the obligation to the creditor at issue, plus the creditor's costs.[55]

On the other hand, Bahamas law does not (1) validate any disposition of property that the transferor neither owned nor controlled by way of power vested in such transferor,[56] or (2) affect the recognition of foreign law for purposes of determining whether the transferor is the owner of the property in question or the holder of a relevant power over the property.[57]

§ 6.04   SITUS OF TRUST

The planner must give careful consideration to the FAPT transaction and various general matters, such as the situs of the FAPT. The planner must choose the appropriate jurisdiction in which to establish the trust. In choosing the FAPT's situs, the planner should consider:

---

[51] Fraudulent Dispositions Act, 1991 § 5(1)(a)(i) (Bahamas).
[52] Fraudulent Dispositions Act, 1991 § 5(1)(a)(ii) (Bahamas).
[53] Fraudulent Dispositions Act, 1991 § 5(1)(b) (Bahamas).
[54] Fraudulent Dispositions Act, 1991 § 5(2) (Bahamas).
[55] Fraudulent Dispositions Act, 1991 § 6 (Bahamas).
[56] Fraudulent Dispositions Act, 1991 § 7(a) (Bahamas).
[57] Fraudulent Dispositions Act, 1991 § 7(b) (Bahamas).

1. The applicable law of the situs;
2. The communications facilities of the situs;
3. The standard of the judiciary and the effectiveness of the court system;
4. The financial and political stability of the situs;
5. Availability of a professional trustee at reasonable fees; and
6. The accessibility of the situs to the settlor.[1]

Planning Pointer. Generally, the Bahamas, Barbados, Bermuda, the Cayman Islands, the Cook Islands, Gibraltar, and the Isle of Man, among other locations, provide suitable locations for establishing an FAPT.

§6.05 TRUST FEATURES

The well-planned FAPT should contain certain features. Specifically, the planner should make the FAPT irrevocable for a period of years. Generally, the settlor should not be a trust beneficiary, and the planner must choose the FAPT trustees with extreme caution. Further, the planner must ensure that the FAPT trust instrument contains anti-duress provisions. Finally, the trust instrument should require the trustee to follow detailed guidelines regarding investments and distributions. The trust should allow the trustee to make discretionary payments from corpus or income to tax authorities to cover tax liabilities of the settlor that result from income attributed to him from the trust.

[A] Irrevocable for Term of Years

The planner must ensure that the FAPT is irrevocable.[1] As previously discussed, many courts hold that the settlor's creditors may reach the trust corpus when the settlor retains the power to revoke the trust.[2]

Also, some jurisdictions have enacted statutes providing that when the settlor retains an absolute or unqualified power to revoke the trust, he is deemed the absolute owner of the trust property for purposes of satisfying creditor claims.[3] Where such statutes exist, the settlor's creditors can reach the trust corpus. Consequently, the planner must ensure that the FAPT is irrevocable.

---

§6.04 [1] *See generally* Barbara Wall, *The Offshore Trust: Notorious but Useful,* Int'l Herald Trib., Feb. 22, 1992 (Money Report).

§6.05 [1] *See generally* Foreign Protection of Assets Trusts for U.S. Persons: What Are They? How Do They Work? (1992 Conf. by Kluwer Law & Tax'n Publishers).

[2] Scott & Fratcher, The Law of Trusts §330.12; Bogert & Bogert, The Law of Trusts and Trustees §233; Gissel & Schiller, 10 Prob. L.J. 241; Restatement of Property §328 (1940). *See, e.g.,* State St. Bank & Trust Co. v. Reiser, 389 N.E.2d 768, 770 (Mass. 1979); Johnson v. Commercial Bank, 588 P.2d 1096, 1099 (Or. 1978); *In re* Kovalyshyn's Estate, 343 A.2d 852 (N.J. Super. Ct. 1975).

[3] *See* Bogert & Bogert, The Law of Trusts and Trustees §233. *See, e.g.,* Ala. Code §35-4-290 (1975); Cal. Prob. Code §18200 (Deering 1991); N.Y. Est. Powers & Trusts Law §10-10.6 (McKinney 1981 & Supp. 1993).

Planning Pointer. The planner should consider using language similar to the following to ensure that the trust is irrevocable:

> The Settlor expressly waives all right, power and authority to alter, amend, modify, revoke or terminate this Trust, except as otherwise provided within this Trust Agreement.

Second, the trust should be for a period of years, which the client should select. The planner, however, must ensure that the trust period does not violate the rule against perpetuities.

Planning Pointer. The trust instrument should include an anti-duress provision that extends the trust term in cases of duress. This will protect the settlor from creditors who raise claims near the end of the trust's term. Alternatively, the planner may use an extensive trust term and give the trustees the ability to shorten this period, absent an event of duress. Planners choosing this option may want to consider using the following language:

> Trust Period means the period commencing with the date of the execution of this Trust Agreement and ending on the first to occur of the following dates, namely:
>
> (a) The date of the one hundredth anniversary of the date of this Settlement;
> (b) the period commencing on the execution hereof and continuing until such day as the Trustees with the consent of the Protector may by deed or written declaration at any time and at their discretion declare to be the date of the expiration of the Trust Period. Notwithstanding the foregoing, the Trustees shall have no authority to shorten the duration of the Trust Period if such act is the result of any compulsion or Event of Duress.

[B] Beneficiaries

Generally, the FAPT should provide for either mandatory or discretionary distributions to a class of beneficiaries that does not include the settlor during the trust term, and for a final distribution of the trust principal and accumulated income to the settlor at the termination of the trust.[4] Alternatively, the trust may provide for no income interests in the trust.

---

[4] *See generally* Foreign Protection of Assets Trusts for U.S. Persons: What Are They? How Do They Work? (1992 Conf. by Kluwer Law & Tax'n Publishers).

Planning Pointer. The planner should generally ensure that the settlor is not an income beneficiary of the trust. If the settlor retains an income interest, his creditors can reach that interest. Furthermore, the planner must ensure that all beneficial interests are protected by a spendthrift provision. When the client strongly desires to retain a beneficial income interest, the planner may allow this. However, the planner must advise the client that this interest will be at risk because creditors are generally able to reach beneficial interests retained by the client.

Planning Pointer. Under one optional structure, the planner may establish a U.S.-based corporation to hold the assets that would otherwise be held directly by the trust.[5] The settlor would then transfer all of the stock of the corporation to the FAPT. The settlor would serve as the sole director and officer of the corporation. When the requirements are satisfied, the corporation elects S corporation status.[6] This structure allows the settlor to maintain direct control over the assets contained within the trust. The trust instrument would provide that during duress, the trust would liquidate or encumber all the corporation's assets and send the cash proceeds to the foreign trustee, which would then invest those proceeds in financial institutions that would be located outside the United States. This also allows the corporation to pay a salary to the settlor, thus providing income to the settlor during the trust term. However, this structure is disadvantageous in that the settlor remains subject to U.S. court orders. Consequently, a U.S. court may prevent him from liquidating the corporate assets and transferring them to the FAPT trustee.

Alternatively, the settlor may establish a family limited partnership.[7] This would work much like the corporation structure, except that the settlor would retain a 1-percent general partnership interest and would transfer a 99-percent limited partnership interest to the FAPT.[8]

Planning Pointer. The trust should be a discretionary trust for added asset protection.

---

[5] Bruce & Gray, Offshore Protection-of-Assets Trusts, U.S. Tax'n of Int'l Operations (WGL) ¶ 13,510.1.

[6] *See* Chapter 4.

[7] *See* Chapter 4.

[8] Barry S. Engel, *Asset Protection Planning: A Critical Part of Any Estate Plan,* 145 Fin. & Est. Planning Ideas & Trends (CCH) ¶ 30,001 (Jan. 27, 1992).

[C]   Trustees

The planner must carefully select the FAPT's trustees.[9] He should consider using three trustees: a U.S. trust company, a U.S. individual, and a foreign trustee.[10] The U.S. trust company should be an experienced trust company that has had an ongoing relationship with the settlor. The U.S. individual should be somebody who is familiar with the settlor and his personal and business needs. Finally, the foreign trustee should be an independent trust company or bank that has had experience managing FAPTs.

Planning Pointer. In some jurisdictions the settlor may establish a corporation or company that will become the trustee of the trust. This allows the settlor to retain control over the trust.[11]

The planner should also include a trust instrument provision that establishes a committee of trust protectors or advisors. The settlor would generally be the chairman of this committee, which may have the power to remove trustees and appoint a successor trustee. Also, the committee of protectors or advisors may provide nonbinding advice to the trustee concerning the investments that the trustee makes. Generally, the trust instrument suspends these powers during times of duress. This allows the settlor to retain control over the trust until a judgment creditor attempts to reach the settlor's assets.

Planning Pointer. Beneficiaries of the FAPT or individuals with interests adverse to the settlor's interests should also sit on the committee of protectors or advisors. This will minimize the risk that the settlor will be deemed a de facto trustee of the FAPT.[12]

The trust should include a provision that provides for an emergency trustee. Such a provision provides that if an event of duress occurs in the trust situs jurisdiction, the trustee is deemed to transfer the trust fund and its income to the emergency trustee and to change the forum of management, control, and administration of the trust fund from its original location to the location where the emergency trustee resides. Generally, the emergency trustee resides in a second foreign location. For example, the original trustee may be located in the Cook Islands, and the emergency

---

[9] See generally Foreign Protection of Assets Trusts for U.S. Persons: What Are They? How Do They Work? (1992 Conf. by Kluwer Law & Tax'n Publishers).

[10] Bruce & Gray, Offshore Protection-of-Assets Trusts, U.S. Tax'n of Int'l Operations (WGL) ¶ 13,510.1.

[11] See, e.g., International Trusts Act 1984 (Cook Islands); International Companies Act 198182 (Cook Islands).

[12] See generally Foreign Protection of Assets Trusts for U.S. Persons: What Are They? How Do They Work? (1992 Conf. by Kluwer Law & Tax'n Publishers).

trustee may be located in the Cayman Islands. The trust also should provide for successor emergency trustees to protect the trust in the event that an event of duress occurs in the jurisdiction of the emergency trustee. The trust instrument must provide that the trustee must execute all necessary documents and do everything necessary to perfect the emergency trustee's title. The trust instrument should include a schedule of emergency trustees that sets out the hierarchy of the emergency foreign trustees.

Planning Pointer. The planner should consider using language similar to the following in the trust instrument:

(a) Notwithstanding any other provision contained in this Trust Agreement, the Trustees upon the happening of an Event of Duress in the jurisdiction where any Trustees or part of the Trust Fund are located, shall transfer the Trust Fund and income therefrom to the remaining Trustee (if any) located in a jurisdiction not having the Event of Duress, and shall change the forum of any management, control, and administration of the Trust Fund from the jurisdiction having the Event of Duress to the place in which the remaining Trustee shall for the time being reside.

(b) Should there be no remaining Trustee in a jurisdiction not having the Event of Duress or should a further Event of Duress occur in the jurisdiction of the remaining Trustee then such Trustee or remaining Trustee (as the case may be) shall be deemed to have transferred the Trust Fund and income therefrom to the Emergency Trustee and to have changed the forum of management, control, and administration of the Trust Fund from its then existing location to the place in which the Emergency Trustee shall for the time being reside.

(c) Should a further Event of Duress in the jurisdiction of any Emergency Trustee occur, then the Emergency Trustee shall be deemed to have transferred the Trust Fund and income thereon to a successor or another successor Emergency Trustee and to have changed the forum of management, control, and administration of the Trust Fund from its then existing location to the place in which the successor Emergency Trustee may for the time being reside.

(d) The Trust Fund so transferred shall be held in Trust and shall be subject to the same provisions declared and contained in this Trust Agreement except for any changes the Trustees in their discretion deem necessary pursuant to the powers to amend contained in this Trust Agreement herein.

(e) Any Trustee, when called upon to do so by a remaining Trustee or the Emergency Trustee, shall execute all documents, deeds, and contracts and do all things as shall be necessary in order to perfect the title of the Emergency Trustee to the Trust Fund.

(f) The Emergency Trustee, on the transfer to the Emergency Trustee of the Trust Fund or any part thereof, shall for the purposes of this Trust Agreement constitute the Trustee for the time being of this Trust Agreement. Upon the occurrence of any transfer or deemed transfer of the Trust Fund, the Trustee then in office shall give notice to the Protector of such transfer or deemed transfer.

Planning Pointer. The safest strategy is for the settlor to transfer all control over liquid assets to the foreign trustee. Title to real property should not be transferred to the foreign trustee because U.S. courts would generally retain control over such property. Instead such property should either be (1) sold, or (2) encumbered, with the sale or loan proceeds sent to the foreign trustee for foreign investment.

[D] Duress Provision

Because the settlor or a close relative will often be a protector or advisor to the FAPT and because such settlor or relative will generally be a U.S. citizen subject to the personal jurisdiction of U.S. courts, the planner must include anti-duress provisions in the trust instrument.[13] Specifically, the trust should provide that, in the event of duress, the following should occur. If the duress occurs in the trust's situs jurisdiction, the duress provision should provide that the trustee will be deemed to transfer the trust fund and income therefrom to an emergency trustee in a different jurisdiction and to have changed the forum of the management, control, and administration of the trust from the original jurisdiction (or prior jurisdiction in the event of a prior transfer) to the jurisdiction that the emergency trustee resides in. If the duress occurs in the United States, the duress provision should:

1. Require the foreign trustee to discharge the U.S. co-trustees;
2. Require the foreign trustee to ignore advice given by the committee of trust protectors or advisors when a U.S. court or trustee in bankruptcy compels such advice;
3. Require the foreign trustee to ignore committee of trust protectors decisions to discharge or replace trustees when such decisions result from court orders or other compulsion;
4. When the planner structures the trust as the sole owner of a corporation of which the settlor is the sole director and officer, require the foreign trustee to liquidate the corporation immediately.

[13] Bruce & Gray, Offshore Protection-of-Assets Trusts, U.S. Tax'n of Int'l Operations (WGL) ¶ 13,510.1.

Planning Pointer. The planner should consider using the following language to provide a flight provision that would change the governing law of the trust in the event of duress:

(a) This Trust Agreement is established under the laws of the (Situs Jurisdiction) and shall be considered and take effect according to the laws of the (Situs Jurisdiction) which shall be the forum for the administration hereof and whose law shall be the Proper Law of this Trust Agreement, and that the rights of all persons beneficially entitled hereunder and the construction of each and every provision hereof shall (subject as is hereunder provided) be governed exclusively by such law.

(b) Notwithstanding the provisions of Subclause (a), but subject to Subclause (d), the Trustees, with the consent of the Protector, may by deed declare that this Trust Agreement shall from the date of such Agreement take effect in accordance with the law of some other place in any part of the world which shall be the forum for the administration hereof (but subject to the power conferred by this Subclause and until any further declaration is made hereunder).

(c) For the purposes for subclause (b) hereof the Trustees may by deed make such consequential alterations in the trust's powers and provision of this Trust Agreement as the Trustees, with the consent of the Protector, shall consider necessary or desirable to secure that so far as may be possible such trust's powers and provisions shall be as valid and effective under the law of the place named in such declaration as they are under the law of the (Situs Jurisdiction).

(d) Notwithstanding anything contained in this Clause, the Trustees shall not have the power to take any action under this clause which:

  (i) Might directly or indirectly result in this Trust Agreement becoming revocable or unenforceable.

  (ii) Might in any way make any alteration in the beneficial trusts and the dispositive powers hereof which could not then have been made by the Trustees in exercise of any one or more of the other powers conferred on them by the other provisions of this Trust Agreement.

  (iii) Would or might directly or indirectly result in any of the following obtaining a benefit:

    a. Any and all courts, administrative or judicial bodies, except for the court, administrative or judicial bodies organized and empowered under the laws of (The Situs Jurisdiction).

    b. Any and all creditors, claimants, judgment creditors, etc. of any Settlor, of any Trustee, or any Beneficiary under the Trust Agreement.

(e)   The happening of any of the following events or circumstances shall forthwith and without further action on the part of any person, terminate the tenure of the then-trustees of this Trust, and they shall thereupon cease to be Trustees of this Trust and shall thereby be divested of the property and the title to the Trust Fund:

    (i)   The declaration by the Government of (The Situs Jurisdiction) or the existence of a state of war between the Government of the (The Situs Jurisdiction) with any jurisdiction in which any property which forms part of the Trust Fund is located.

    (ii) The invasion of the (The Situs Jurisdiction) by military force.

    (iii) The enactment of any law, or any action by any governmental authority, agency, court or officer, the aim, purpose or effect of which is:

        a.   The acquisition, expropriation or confiscation of any of the assets comprising the Trust Fund.

        b.   The restriction, suspension or abrogation, in whole or in part, of this Trust Agreement or of any contract in relation to the Trust Fund to which the Trustee is a party.

        c.   The compulsory conversion of the assets comprising the Trust Fund into the currency of the (The Situs Jurisdiction).

        d.   To compel the Trustee to sell, transfer, assign, convey or otherwise dispose of the assets comprising the Trust Fund or any part thereof for the benefit of any of the following:

            (i)   Any and all courts, administrative or judicial bodies, except for the court, administrative or judicial bodies organized and empowered under the laws of (The Situs Jurisdiction).

            (ii) Any and all creditors, claimants, judgment creditors, etc. of any Settlor, of any Trustee, or any Beneficiary under the Trust Agreement.

The planner should consider using language similar to the following to define event of duress:

Event of Duress means the occurrence of any one of the following:

(a) War or civil disturbance which will or may endanger, whether directly or indirectly, the safety of any money, investments or property which may from time to time be included in or form a part of the Trust Fund;

(b) Political action in any part of the world whether instigated by any government, political organization or individual, whether constitution or otherwise, which will or may endanger, whether directly or indirectly, the safety of any money, investments or property which may from time to time be included in or form a part of the Trust Fund;

(c) The enactment in any part of the world of any law, regulation, decree or measure which will or may directly or indirectly, expropriate, sequestrate or in any way control, restrict or prevent the free disposal by the Trustees of any money, investments or property which may from time to time be included in or form a part of the Trust Fund;

(d) Action or threat of action by any government, department or agency in any part of the world or by any official purporting to act on the instructions and with authority of such government, department or agency which will or may directly or indirectly, expropriate, sequestrate, levy, lien or in any way control, restrict or prevent the free disposal by the Trustee of any money, investments or property which may from time to time be included in or form a part of the Trust Fund;

(e) Any order, decree or judgment of any court or tribunal in any part of the world which will or may directly or indirectly, expropriate, sequestrate, levy, lien or in any way control, restrict or prevent the free disposal by the Trustees of any money, investments or property which may from time to time be included in or form a part of the Trust Fund and any distribution therefrom.

[E] Blind Trust Feature

An optional feature that the planner should consider is a blind trust feature. Under the blind trust feature, the trust must provide the settlor with general information about the composition of the FAPT's corpus each year. This information must be sufficiently general so that the settlor cannot learn what the corpus has specifically invested in. With this type of trust, the trust specifically prohibits the trustees from supplying the settlor with information concerning particular trust assets. The benefits of this type of trust are that it:

1. Limits the amount of information available to future creditors desiring to attach the trust assets (for example, where the FAPT has invested in U.S. securities);
2. Protects the settlor from insider trading violations; and
3. Protects the settlor from conflicts of interest.[14]

§ 6.06 TAX IMPACT

[A] Introduction

Historically, foreign trusts have been very useful tools for sophisticated estate planners. However, they have also been the focus of great suspicion and scrutiny by the IRS.

Before 1976, properly designed foreign trusts created in low tax jurisdictions provided significant income tax deferral and, in some cases, complete income tax avoidance, even where both the grantor and current trust beneficiaries were U.S. persons.

---

[14] Foreign Protection of Assets Trusts for U.S. Persons: What Are They? How Do They Work? (1992 Conf. by Kluwer Law and Tax'n Publishers).

Over the years, Congress has repeatedly attempted to discourage the use of foreign trusts by U.S. individuals by passing legislation that has gradually reduced the tax benefits accruing from such trusts. Such legislation has included the following

Revenue Act of 1962[1]
Tax Reform Act of 1976[2]
Revenue Reconciliation Act of 1990[3]
The Small Business Job Protection Act of 1996[4]
Taxpayer Relief Act of 1997

As a result of the aforementioned legislative changes, the tax and other benefits flowing from foreign trusts to U.S. persons have been greatly eroded. Notwithstanding this, foreign trusts continue to be very useful in certain circumstances.

[B] What Constitutes a Foreign Trust?[5]

[1] Importance of Classification of Trust as "Foreign" or "Domestic"

Classification of a trust as "foreign" or "domestic" has significant tax consequences. Domestic trusts are both: (1) treated as U.S. persons, and (2) subject to tax on worldwide income. In contrast, foreign trusts are both: (1) treated as nonresident aliens ("NRAs"), and (2) subject to tax only on U.S. source income or income effectively connected with a U.S. trade or business.[6]
Classification of trust also impacts the following:

1. Whether a grantor will be treated as the owner of the trust for income tax purposes under the grantor trust rules;
2. Whether gain must be recognized upon transfers to the trust;
3. The application of certain withholding provisions.

[2] What Makes a Trust a "Foreign Trust?"

[a] In General

A different set of rules applies to determine whether a trust constitutes a foreign trust, as opposed to a domestic trust, depending on whether the

---

§ 6.06 [1] P.L. 87-834, § 7, 87th Cong. 2d Sess. (1962).
[2] P.L. 94-455, 94th Cong., 2d Sess., 90 Stat. 1928 (1976).
[3] P.L. 101-508, § 11343.
[4] P. L. 104-188, 110 Stat. 1755 (1996).
[5] Classification of an entity as a foreign trust requires that it first be classified as a "trust" and, then, that it be treated as a "foreign" entity. This outline only addresses the second issue. *See* Howard Zaritsky, *U.S. Tax'n of Foreign Estates, Trusts and Beneficiaries*, 854-2d Tax Mgmt. Portfolio III.A-B (2002), for a discussion of what characteristics an entity must possess to be treated as a "trust" for tax purposes.
[6] IRC § 641(b); Treas. Reg. § 301.7701-7(a)(3).

amendments enacted as part of the Small Business Job Creation Act of 1996 (the "1996 Act") apply to the trust. The 1996 Act generally applies to tax years beginning after December 31, 1996, and at the trustee's election to tax years ending after August 20, 1996.

Before the enactment of the 1996 Act, a subjective analysis was required to determine whether the United States treated a trust as domestic or foreign for U.S. tax purposes. The 1996 Act changed the classification scheme to one that determines a trust's nationality based on a set of objective criteria.

Note. The situs of a trust for tax years beginning before January 1, 1997 may be relevant, among other things, because that situs may determine the character of accumulated trust income that will be taxed when ultimately distributed to a U.S. beneficiary.

[b] Definition of Foreign Trust Before the 1996 Act

For tax years beginning before January 1, 1997, Internal Revenue Code (IRC or "the Code") Section 7701(a)(31) provided that a foreign trust was one "the income of which, from sources without the United States which is not effectively connected with the conduct of a trade or business within the United States, is not includible in gross income under subtitle A."

Essentially, the pre-1996 Act version of IRC Section 7701(a)(31) provided for a subjective analysis of whether the trust was more comparable to a resident or a nonresident alien individual.[7] Generally, the pre-1996 Act version of IRC Section 7701(a)(31), by itself, provided no guidance as to how to determine whether a trust would be classified as domestic or foreign.

Judicial and administrative authority partially filled the void left by the pre-1996 Act version of IRC Section 7701(a)(31) by providing for a test that required a weighing of a trust's foreign contacts against its U.S. contacts.[8] The cases and rulings provided that the following six major factors in were to be considered determining the situs and nationality of a trust:

1. The country under whose laws the trust was created;
2. The situs of the trust's corpus;
3. The nationality and residence of the trustee;
4. The situs of the trust administration;
5. The nationality and residence of the grantor; and
6. The nationality and residence of the beneficiaries.

Where the various indicia were inconsistent, this test was extremely difficult to apply. The courts and the IRS tended to place more weight on the following factors:

---

[7] Rev. Rul. 60-181, 1960-1 C.B. 257, *citing* B.W. Jones Trust v. Comm'r, 46 B.T.A. 531 (1942), *aff'd,* 132 F.2d 914 (4th Cir. 1943).

[8] *See, e.g.,* Maximov v. United States, 373 U.S. 49 (1963); B. W. Jones Trust v. Comm'r, 132 F.2d 914 (4th Cir., 1943); First National City Bank v. Internal Revenue Service, 271 F.2d 616 (2d Cir. 1959), *cert. denied,* 361 U.S. 948 (1960); Rev. Rul. 60-181, 1960-1 C.B. 257.

- The situs of the trust's corpus;
- The nationality and residence of the trustee; and
- The situs of the trust administration.[9]

[c]   Current (i.e., Post-1996 Act) Definition of Foreign Trust

[i]   In General

For tax years beginning after December 31, 1996, a trust is a U.S. trust if both: (1) a court within the United States is able to exercise primary supervision over the trust's administration ("Court Test"); and (2) one or more U.S. persons have authority to control all substantial decisions of the trust ("Control Test").[10]

Note. A trust that does not satisfy both of these tests will constitute a foreign trust.[11]

Note 2. For purposes of the foreign trust definition:

1. A trust is a U.S. person on any day that the trust meets both the court test and the control test;
2. A domestic trust means a trust that constitutes a U.S. person;
3. A foreign trust means any trust other than a domestic trust;[12]
4. Treasury Regulations apply the terms of the trust instrument and applicable law to determine whether the court test and the control test are met.[13]

[ii]   Background—Rationale for Enactment of the Post-1996 Act Rule

Congress's primary objective was clearly to provide an objective test, rather than the prior subjective test.[14] In addition, it appears that one of the principal objectives for the post-1996 definition of foreign trusts was to level the competitive playing field for trust administration business between U.S. and foreign institutions. The pre-1997 rule effectively acted as an incentive for a foreign person to avoid using a U.S. financial institution as trustee because of the significant risk that this would cause the trust to be taxed as a U.S. domestic trust. Under the post-1996 Act rule, a foreign person can easily use a U.S. financial institution without creating a domestic trust.[15]

---

[9] *See, e.g.,* Maximov v. United States, 373 U.S. 49 (1963) (Supreme Court held that trust created under Connecticut law, which was administered in the United States by a U.S. trustee for the benefit of foreign beneficiaries was a domestic trust); B. W. Jones Trust v. Comm'r, 132 F.2d 914 (4th Cir., 1943) (Fourth Circuit held that trust created by a foreign grantor for the benefit of foreign beneficiaries, which was governed by foreign law, but whose corpus consisted primarily of U.S. securities held in a safe deposit box in New York, where three trustees were foreign and one was U.S., was a U.S. trust); Rev. Rul. 60-181, 1960-1 C.B. 257 (IRS ruled that testamentary trust created under laws of a foreign country, with corpus consisting primarily of U.S. securities, with a U.S. trustee, was a domestic trust)

[10] IRC § 7701(a)(30)(E), (31)(B); Reg. § 301.7701-7(a)(1).

[11] IRC § 7701(a)(31).

[12] Reg. § 301.7701-7(a)(2).

[13] Reg. § 301.7701-7(b).

[14] Treasury Dept., *General Explanation of the Administration's Revenue Proposals* 25 (Feb. 7, 1995). *See also* IRS Notice 96-65, 1996 C.B. 232.

[15] Treasury Dept., *General Explanation of the Administration's Revenue Proposals* 25 (Feb. 7, 1995). *See also* IRS Notice 96-65, 1996 C.B. 232.

[iii] Effective Date

The post-1996 Act rule applies to tax years beginning after December 31, 1996, and at the lection of the trustee, to tax years ending after August 20, 1996.

EXAMPLE 6-2

Ms. Havisham, a U.S. citizen who resides in Maryland, creates a trust for her children, all of whom are U.S. citizens. She names the Dickens Trust Company, a Delaware corporation, and her brother, Pip, a Bermuda citizen and resident, as co-trustees. The trust instrument (a) gives Pip the right to determine the ages at which each child receives its share of the trust fund, and (b) directs that the trust funds be maintained in the United States in the custody of the Dickens Trust Company, and that Maryland law governs the trust's administration. Here, the trust will be treated as a foreign trust because a foreign person will possess control over a substantial trust decision.

[iv] Court Test

The court test is one of the two tests that a trust must satisfy in order to be classified as a domestic trust. To satisfy the court test, a court within the United States must be able to exercise primary supervision over the trust's administration.[16]

Planning Pointer. Treasury regulations provide a safe harbor for the court test. Specifically, a trust satisfies the court test if:

1. The trust instrument does not direct that the trust be administered outside of the United States;
2. The trust in fact is administered exclusively in the United States; and
3. The trust is not subject to an automatic migration provision described in Treas. Reg. § 301.7701-7(c)(4)(ii).

EXAMPLE 6-3[17]

Charles creates a trust for the equal benefit of his two children, Biddy and Pip, called the Dickens Trust. The trust instrument provides that DC, a Virginia corporation, is the trustee of the Dickens Trust. DC administers the trust exclusively in Virginia and the trust instrument is silent as to where the Dickens Trust is to be administered. In addition, the Dickens Trust is not subject to an automatic migration provision. Here, the Dickens Trust satisfies the court test.

---

[16] IRC § 7701(a)(30)(E), (31)(B).
[17] Reg. § 301.7701-7(c)(2).

The following definitions apply for purposes of the court test:

Court. "Court" means any federal, state, or local court;[18]

The United States. "United States" is used in a geographical sense. Thus, for court test purposes, the United States includes only the States and the District of Columbia. Note that a court within a territory or possession of the United States (*e.g.,* Puerto Rico) or within a foreign country is not a court within the United States;[19]

Is able to exercise. "Is able to exercise" means that a court has or would have the authority under applicable law to render orders or judgments resolving issues concerning administration of the trust;[20]

Primary supervision. "Primary supervision" means that a court has or would have the authority to determine substantially all issues regarding the administration of the entire trust. Note that a court may have primary supervision under this definition notwithstanding the fact that another court has jurisdiction over a trustee, a beneficiary, or trust property;[21]

Administration. "Administration" of the trust means the carrying out of the duties imposed by the terms of the trust instrument and applicable law, including maintaining the books and records of the trust, filing tax returns, managing and investing the assets of the trust, defending the trust from suits by creditors, and determining the amount and timing of distributions.[22]

> **Planning Pointer—Bright line rules for satisfying or failing the Court Test.** Treasury regulations provide the following bright line rules for determining when a trust will satisfy or fail the court test, which are not intended to be an exclusive list:[23]
>
> > **Uniform Probate Code.** A trust satisfies the court test if an authorized fiduciary registers the trust in a court within the United States pursuant to a state statute containing provisions substantially similar to Uniform Probate Code, Article VII, Trust Administration;[24]
> >
> > **Testamentary trust.** A testamentary trust created by a will probated within the United States (other than ancillary probate) will satisfy the court test if all fiduciaries of the trust have been qualified as trustees by a court within the United States;[25]
> >
> > **Inter vivos trust.** For inter vivos trusts, if the fiduciaries and/or beneficiaries take steps with a court within the United States that cause the

---

[18] Reg. § 301.7701 7(c)(3)(i).
[19] Reg. § 301.7701-7(c)(3)(ii).
[20] Reg. § 301.7701-7(c)(3)(iii).
[21] Reg. § 301.7701-7(c)(3)(iv).
[22] Reg. § 301.7701-7(c)(3)(v).
[23] Reg. § 301.7701-7(c)(4)(i).
[24] Reg. § 301.7701-7(c)(4)(i)(A).
[25] Reg. § 301.7701-7(c)(4)(i)(B).

trust's administration to be subject to the primary supervision of such court, the trust will satisfy the court test;[26]

- **A U.S. court and a foreign court are able to exercise primary supervision over the administration of the trust.** If both a U.S. court and a foreign court can exercise primary supervision over the trust's administration, the trust satisfies the court test.[27]

A court within the United States is not considered to have primary supervision over a trust's administration if the trust instrument provides that a U.S. court's attempt to assert jurisdiction or otherwise supervise the trust's administration, directly or indirectly, will cause the trust to migrate from the United States. Such provisions are commonly referred to as "flight provisions," "migration provisions," and "duress provisions." This rule will not apply, however, if the trust instrument provides that the trust will migrate from the United States only in the case of foreign invasion of the United States or widespread confiscation or nationalization of property in the United States.[28]

EXAMPLE 6-4

Oliver, a U.S. citizen, creates a trust for the equal benefit of his two children, both of whom are U.S. citizens. The trust instrument provides that the Dickens Trust Company, a U.S. corporation will serve as trustee and the trust shall be administered in Bermuda. The Dickens Trust Company maintains a branch office in Bermuda with personnel authorized to act as trustees there. The trust instrument provides that Maryland law governs the trust. Assume that under Bermuda law, a Bermuda court may exercise primary supervision over the trust's administration. Pursuant to the trust instrument, a Bermuda court applies the Maryland law to the trust. However, under the terms of the trust instrument, the trust is administered in Bermuda, and no court within the United States is able to exercise primary supervision over its administration. Here, the trust fails to satisfy the court test. Therefore, it constitutes a foreign trust.[29]

EXAMPLE 6-5

Estelle, a U.S. citizen, creates a trust for her own benefit and the benefit of her spouse, Pip, a U.S. citizen. The trust instrument provides that the trust is to be

[26] Reg. § 301.7701-7(c)(4)(i)(C).
[27] Reg. § 301.7701-7(c)(4)(i)(D).
[28] Reg. § 301.7701-7(c)(4)(ii).
[29] Reg. § 301.7701-7(c)(5), Ex. 1.

administered in Maryland, by Copperfield Corporation, a Maryland corpo-ration. The trust instrument further provides that if a creditor sues the trustee in a U.S. court, the trust will automatically migrate from Maryland to Gibral-tar, a foreign country, so that no U.S. court will have jurisdiction over the trust. Here, a court within the U.S. is unable to exercise primary supervision over the trust's administration because of the flight provisions. Therefore, the trust fails to satisfy the court test from the time of its creation and constitutes a foreign trust.[30]

[v] Control Test

The control test is one of the two tests that a trust must satisfy in order to be classified as a domestic trust. To satisfy the control test: (i) one or more U.S. persons (ii) must have authority to control (iii) all substantial decisions of the trust.[31]

For purposes of the control test, the term "United States person" means a U.S. person within the meaning of IRC Section 7701(a)(30).[32] For example, a domestic corporation is a U.S. person, regardless of whether its shareholders are U.S. persons.[33]

Note. The control test, as originally enacted in the Small Business Job Protec-tion Act of 1996, required that one or more "U.S. fiduciaries" have the authority to control all substantial decisions of the trust in order for the trust to be treated as a domestic trust.[34] Treasury regulations use the term "persons" as defined in IRC Section 7701(a)(30), which includes U.S. citizens and residents, and domestic corporations and partnerships.[35] As a technical correction to the Small Business Job Protection Act of 1996, the Taxpayer Relief Act of 1997 substituted the term "U.S. persons" for "U.S. fiduciaries."[36]

Treasury regulations define "substantial decisions" as non-ministerial deci-sions that persons are authorized or required to make under the terms of the trust instrument and applicable law.[37] For this purpose, ministerial decisions, which do not constitute "substantial decisions," include decisions regarding

---

[30] Reg. § 301.7701-7(c)(5), Ex. 2.

[31] IRC § 7701(a)(30)(E), (31)(B); Reg. § 301.7701-7(a)(1).

[32] IRC § 7701(a)(30) provides "that the term "United States person" means –

(A) a citizen or resident of the United States

(B) a domestic partnership,

(C) a domestic corporation,

(D) any estate (other than a foreign estate, within the meaning of paragraph (31), and

(E) any trust if –

(i)   a court within the United States is able to exercise primary supervision over the administration of the trust, and

(ii) one or more United States persons have the authority to control all substantial decisions of the trust.

[33] Reg. § 301.7701-7(d)(1)(i).

[34] Small Business Job Protection Act of 1996, Pub. L. No. 104-188, § 1907(a)(1).

[35] Reg. § 301.7701-7(d)(1)(i).

[36] Taxpayer Relief Act of 1997, Pub. L. No. 105-34, § 1601(i)(3)(A).

[37] Reg. § 301.7701-7(d)(1)(ii).

details such as the bookkeeping, the collection of rents, and the execution of investment decisions.[38]

Treasury regulations provide the following non-exclusive list of substantial decisions:[39]

1. Whether and when to distribute income or corpus;
2. The amount of any distributions;
3. The selection of a beneficiary;
4. Whether a receipt is allocable to income or principal;
5. Whether to terminate the trust;
6. Whether to compromise, arbitrate, or abandon claims of the trust;
7. Whether to sue on behalf of the trust or to defend suits against the trust;
8. Whether to remove, add, or replace a trustee;
9. Whether to appoint a successor trustee to succeed a trustee who has died, resigned, or otherwise ceased to act as a trustee, even if the power to make such a decision is not accompanied by an unrestricted power to remove a trustee, unless the power to make such a decision is limited such that it cannot be exercised in a manner that would change the trust's residency from foreign to domestic, or vice versa; and
10. Investment decisions.

Note. With respect to investment decisions, if a U.S. person hires an investment advisor for the trust, investment decisions made by the investment advisor will be considered substantial decisions controlled by the U.S. person if the U.S. person can terminate the investment advisor's power to make investment decisions at will.

Treasury regulations define "control" as having the power, by vote or otherwise, to make all of the substantial decisions of the trust, with no other person having the power to veto any substantial decisions.[40] In order to determine if U.S. persons have control, it is necessary to consider *all* persons who have authority to make substantial decisions of the trust, not only the trust fiduciaries.

Note. A trust can have a foreign fiduciary and still be a domestic trust, if the foreign fiduciary can be outvoted by domestic fiduciaries. For example, if the trust has one foreign trustee, two domestic trustees, and the trust instrument provides for a majority vote for trustee decisions, the trust satisfies the control test as a domestic trust.[41]

Planning Pointer—Safe Harbor for Certain Employee Benefit Trusts and Investment Trusts. Certain employee benefit trusts will be deemed to satisfy the control test as long as U.S. fiduciaries control all of the substantial decisions to be made by trust fiduciaries.[42]

---

[38] Reg. § 301.7701-7(d)(1)(ii).
[39] Reg. § 301.7701-7(d)(1)(ii).
[40] Reg. § 301.7701-7(d)(1)(iii).
[41] Reg. § 301.7701-7(d)(1)(v), Ex. 2.
[42] Reg. § 301.7701-7(d)(1)(iv).

EXAMPLE 6-6[43]

The Sherlock Trust is a testamentary trust with three fiduciaries, Holmes, Watson, and Doyle. Holmes and Watson are U.S. citizens, and Doyle is an NRA. No persons except the fiduciaries have authority to make any trust decisions (*e.g.,* no Protector, Trust Advisor, etc.). The trust instrument provides that no substantial decisions of the trust can be made unless there is unanimity among the fiduciaries. Here, the control test is not satisfied because U.S. persons lack control over all of the substantial decisions of the trust because no substantial decisions can be made without Doyle's agreement.

EXAMPLE 6-7[44]

The same facts as Example 6-6, except that the Sherlock Trust instrument provides that all substantial decisions of the trust are decided by majority vote among the fiduciaries. Here, the trust satisfies the control test because a majority of the fiduciaries are U.S. persons and, therefore, U.S. persons control all the substantial decisions of the trust.

EXAMPLE 6-8[45]

The same facts as Example 6-7, except that the Sherlock Trust instrument directs that Doyle makes all of the investment decisions, but that Holmes and Watson may veto Doyle 's investment decisions. Holmes and Watson cannot act to make the investment decisions on their own. Here, the control test is not satisfied because the U.S. persons, (*i.e.,* Holmes and Watson), do not have the power to make all of the substantial decisions of the trust.

---

[43] Reg. § 301.7701-7(d)(1)(v), Ex. 1.
[44] Reg. § 301.7701-7(d)(1)(v), Ex. 2.
[45] Reg. § 301.7701-7(d)(1)(v), Ex. 3.

EXAMPLE 6-9[46]

The same facts as in Example 6-8, except Holmes and Watson may accept or veto Doyle's investment decisions and can make investments that Doyle has not recommended. Here, the control test is satisfied because the U.S. persons control all substantial decisions of the trust.

Note: Reversing an unintended change in trust status. If an inadvertent change occurs with respect to any person possessing the power to make substantial trust decisions, which causes the trust's residency to change (*i.e.,* from domestic to foreign residency, or vice versa), Treasury regulations give the trust a grace period for making the required changes to avoid such residency change.[47] Specifically, Treasury regulations allow the trust 12 months from the date of the change to make necessary changes either with respect to the persons who control the substantial decisions or with respect to the residence of such persons to avoid a change in the trust's residency.

For purposes of the 12 month grace period, an inadvertent change includes the death, incapacity, resignation, change in residency or other change with respect to a person with a power to make substantial trust decisions, which would cause a change to the trust's residency, which was not intended to change the trust's residency.[48]

If the necessary change is made within 12 months, the trust is treated as retaining its pre-change residency during the 12-month period. If the necessary change is not made within 12 months, the trust's residency changes *as of the date of the inadvertent change.*[49]

If reasonable actions are taken to make necessary changes to prevent a change in trust residency, but due to circumstances beyond the trust's control the trust is unable to make such the modification within 12 months, the trust may request an extension of time to make the required change.[50] The decision about whether to grant an extension is in the sole discretion of the IRS District Director. If granted, the extension may contain such terms with respect to assessment as may be necessary to ensure that the correct amount of tax will be collected from the trust, its owners, and its beneficiaries. If the district director does not grant an extension, the trust's residency changes as of the date of the inadvertent change.

---

[46] Reg. § 301.7701-7(d)(1)(v), Ex. 4.
[47] Reg. § 301.7701-7(d)(2)(i).
[48] Reg. § 301.7701-7(d)(2)(i).
[49] Reg. § 301.7701-7(d)(2)(i).
[50] Reg. § 301.7701-7(d)(2)(ii).

Caution. Automatic migration provisions (*i.e.*, flight clauses) will cause a trust to fail the control test. Specifically, under Treasury regulations U.S. persons will not be considered to control all substantial trust decisions, and thus the trust will fail the control test, if an attempt by any governmental agency or creditor to collect information from or assert a claim against the trust causes one or more substantial decisions of the trust to no longer be controlled by U.S. persons.[51]

Planning Pointer. The Taxpayer Relief Act of 1997 permitted nongrantor trusts in existence on August 20, 1996, which were treated as domestic trusts on August 19, 1996 to elect to continue to be treated as U.S. trusts notwithstanding the new criteria for qualification as a U.S. trust.[52] For this purpose, a trust is considered to have been treated as a domestic trust on August 19, 1996 if:

1. The trustee filed on behalf of the trust a Form 1041 (U.S. income tax return for estates and trusts), and not a Form 1040NR (U.S. nonresident alien income tax return), for the period that includes August 19, 1996; and

2. The trust had a reasonable basis (within the meaning of IRC Section 6662) under IRC Section 7701(a)(3), before amendment by the 1996 Act, for reporting as a domestic trust for that period.[53]

Trusts that were treated as wholly owned grantor trusts on August 20, 1996 could not make this election. However, a trust could make this election if only a part of the trust was treated as owned by the grantor on August 20, 1996, in which case the election would be effective for the entire trust.[54]

Trusts that were not required to file either the Form 1041 or the Form 1040NR were treated as domestic trusts on August 19, 1996 if they satisfied the second criteria and if they had a reasonable basis for filing neither form.

Treas. Reg. Section 301.7701-7(f)(3) details the procedure that was required to make the election to remain a domestic trust. Once the election was made, it could only be revoked with IRS consent. However, an election will terminate if changes are made to the trust after the effective date of the election that cause the trust to no longer have a reasonable basis for being treated as a domestic trust under old IRC Section 7701(a)(30).

---

[51] Reg. § 301.7701-7(d)(3).

[52] P.L. No. 105-34, 111 Stat. 788 (1997) § 1161.

[53] The final regulations supersede Notice 98-25, 1998-18 I.R.B. 11, which provided guidance as to the application of § 1161 of the Taxpayer Relief Act of 1997.

[54] Reg. § 301.7701-7(f).

[3] Creation of and Transfer of Property to a Foreign Trust by a U.S. Person

[a] Tax Consequences of Creation and Transfer

[i] Creation of Foreign Trust

Generally, the United States does not impose any tax upon the creation of a foreign trust by a U.S. person. However, IRC Section 6048 requires that a U.S. person report his/her creation of a foreign trust. This requirement applies regardless of whether or not the trust has U.S. beneficiaries.[55] A U.S. person who creates a foreign trust or who transfer property to a foreign trust (other than a transfer for full value) must report the creation or transfer on Form 3520, Annual Return to Report Transfer With Foreign Trusts and Receipt of Certain Foreign Gifts. Form 3520 is due at the same time that the U.S. person's income tax return is due for the year in which the creation of the foreign trust occurs.[56]

[ii] Transfer of Property to Foreign Trust

Any transfer of property by a U.S. person[57] to a foreign trust is treated as a sale or exchange for an amount equal to the property's fair market value, and the transferor must recognize as gain the excess of that fair market value over the transferor's adjusted basis.[58] The amount of gain recognized is determined on an asset-by-asset basis.[59]

Note. See exception for transfers to grantor trusts, discussed below.

No loss recognition. The taxpayer may not recognize any loss on the transfer.[60]

Caution/Planning Pointer. A U.S. person may not offset gain realized on the transfer of an appreciated asset to a foreign trust or foreign estate by a loss realized on the transfer of a depreciated asset to the foreign trust or foreign estate.[61] To avoid harsh implications of this rule, planners who desire to transfer a mixed portfolio of assets to a foreign trust, which includes both property with built in gains and built in losses, should sell the assets with built in losses rather than transferring them in kind to the foreign trust. This would allow the losses recognized on such sales to be offset against the gains recognized on the transfer in kind of the assets with built in gains to the trust.

---

[55] IRC § 6048(a)(3)(A)(i).

[56] IRC § 6677(a)

[57] For this purpose, the term "U.S. person" means a United States person as defined in IRC § 7701(a)(30), and includes an NRA individual who elects under IRC § 6013(g) to be treated as a U.S. resident. Treas. Reg. § 1.684-1(b)(1).

[58] Reg. § 1.684-1(a)(1).

[59] Reg. § 1.684-1(a)(1).

[60] Reg. § 1.684-1(a)(2).

[61] Reg. § 1.684-1(a)(2).

EXAMPLE 6-10

Lestrade transfers Blackacre, with a fair market value of $1,000,000, and Whiteacre, with a fair market value of $2,000,000, to the Doyle Trust, a foreign trust. At the time of the transfer, Lestrade's adjusted basis in Blackacre is $700,000, and his adjusted basis in Whiteacre is $2,200,000. Here, Lestrade recognizes the $300,000 of gain attributable to Blackacre, but he does not recognize the $200,000 loss attributable to Whiteacre. Therefore, Lestrade may not offset that loss against the gain attributable to Blackacre.

EXAMPLE 6-11

Same facts as Example 6-10, except that Lestrade sells Whiteacre for $2,000,000, and transfers the $2 million sales proceeds to the Doyle Trust. Here, Lestrade may offset the $200,000 capital loss realized on the sale of Whiteacre against the $300,000 gain recognized upon the transfer of Blackacre to the Doyle Trust. Assuming a 15 percent capital gains tax rate, this saves Lestrade $30,000.

For purposes of the IRC Section 648 gain recognition rules, treasury regulations take the position that direct, indirect, and constructive transfers will all trigger the IRC Section 648 gain recognition.[62] If a trust (or part of a trust), for which a U.S. person is treated as the owner under the grantor trust rules, transfers property to a foreign trust, that transfer is treated as a transfer from the US owner for purposes of the IRC Section 648 gain recognition rules.[63] For example, if a domestic revocable trust of a U.S. individual transfers property to a foreign trust, this transfer triggers IRC Section 648 gain recognition.

Planning Pointer—Exceptions to Immediate Income Recognition by U.S. Transferor upon Transfer

   Transfers to grantor trusts. IRC Section 684 gain recognition does not apply to property transfers by U.S. persons to foreign trusts to the extent that such trust is treated as a grantor trust.[64] However, IRC Section 684 gain recognition occurs when a grantor trust ceases to be a grantor trust whose income is taxable to a U.S. grantor. If this occurs during the grantor's lifetime, a capital gains tax will arise.[65]

- **Transfers to charitable trusts.** IRC Section 684 gain recognition does not apply to property transfers by U.S. charitable trusts.[66]

[62] Reg. § 1.684-2.
[63] Reg. § 1.684-2(d).
[64] Reg. § 1.684-3(a).
[65] Reg. § 1.684-2(e).
[66] Reg. § 1.684-3(b).

- **Certain transfers at death.** IRC Section 684 gain recognition does not apply to testamentary property transfers of U.S. transferors if the property is property's basis in the hands of the foreign trust is determined under IRC Section 1014(a).[67]

EXAMPLE 6-12

In 2001, Adam transfers property with a $1 million fair market value and an adjusted basis of $400,000 to Foreign Trust. Adam dies on July 1, 2004. The fair market value at his death of all property transferred to Foreign Trust by Adam is $1,500,000. The basis in the property is $400,000. Adam retained the power to revoke Foreign Trust, thus, the value of all property owned by Foreign Trust at Adam' s death is includible in his gross estate for US estate tax purposes. Here, Adam is not required to recognize gain under IRC Section 684 because the basis of the property in the hands of the foreign trust is determined under IRC Section 1014(a).[68]

EXAMPLE 6-13

Same facts as Example 6-12 except Adam retains no power over Foreign Trust, and Foreign Trust's basis in the property transferred is not determined under IRC Section 1014(a). Here, Adam is treated as having transferred the property to Foreign Trust immediately before his death, and must recognize $1,100,000 of gain at that time.[69]

- **Transfers for fair market value to unrelated trusts.** IRC Section 684 gain recognition does not apply to any property transfer at fair market value to a foreign trust that is not a related foreign trust as defined in Regulations Section 1.679-1(c)(5).[70]
- **Transfers to which section 1032 applies.** IRC Section 684 gain recognition does not apply to any stock transfer by domestic corporations to a foreign trust if the domestic corporation is not required to recognize gain on the transfer under IRC Section 1032. IRC Section 1032 generally provides that a corporation does not recognize gain/loss on receiving money or property in exchange for its stock.

---

[67] Reg. § 1.684-3(c).
[68] Reg. § 1.684-3(g), Ex. 2.
[69] Reg. § 1.684-3(g), Ex. 3.
[70] Reg. § 1.684-3(d).

If a U.S. trust becomes a foreign trust, that trust is treated as having transferred, immediately before becoming a foreign trust, all of its assets to a foreign trust. IRC Section 684 gain recognition is then triggered at that time.[71] Treasury regulations provide relief provisions for inadvertent outbound migrations.[72]

[b]   Tax Treatment During Life of U.S. Creator/Transferor

[i]   Grantor Trust Rules—Overview of Grantor Trust Rules

IRC Sections 671-679 set forth the grantor trust rules. The grantor trust rules provide that under certain circumstances, the Code will ignore a trust for income tax purposes and will treat all or part of its income, deductions and credits as being included directly in the grantor's personal tax calculations.[73]

The grantor trust rules generally treat a grantor that retains certain interests in or powers over the trust income or corpus as the owner of the trust's assets, and taxes the grantor directly on the trust's income to the extent of such ownership. If the grantor is a U.S. citizen/resident grantor, the grantor trust rules tax him/her on worldwide trust income. If the grantor is an NRA, the grantor trust rules tax him/her only on trust income either derived from U.S. sources or effectively connected with a U.S. trade or business.

As a general matter (*i.e.,* not limited to the foreign trust context), the grantor rules generally apply in the following situations:

- Where the grantor retains a reversionary interest in either the trust's corpus or income, if at the inception of that part of the trust, the value of that interest exceeds 5 percent of the value of such portion;[74]
- Where the grantor retains the power to control the beneficial enjoyment of the trust without the consent of a nonadverse party;[75]
- Where the grantor, the grantor's spouse, or any other nonadverse person holds certain administrative powers;[76]
- Where the grantor, the grantor's spouse, or any other nonadverse party holds the power, exercisable without an adverse party's consent, to revoke the trust;[77]
- Where the trust's income is or may be distributed (or held for future distribution) to the grantor or grantor's spouse, or may be used to pay the premiums on life insurance policies on the grantor or the grantor's spouse, without an adverse party's consent;[78]

---

[71] Reg. § 1.684-4.
[72] Reg. § 1.684-4(c).
[73] IRC § 671.
[74] IRC § 673.
[75] IRC § 674.
[76] IRC § 675.
[77] IRC § 676.
[78] IRC § 677.

- Where the trust is a foreign trust, which has, or could have, directly or indirectly, a beneficiary who is a U.S. citizen or resident alien.[79]

Before the 1996 Act, the grantor trust rules applied without regard to whether the grantor was a U.S. or foreign person. Therefore, when a foreign person was treated as owner of a trust under the grantor trust rules, U.S. beneficiaries were not subject to U.S. tax on distributions from the trust. Rather, the distributions were treated as non-taxable gifts.[80] Further, if the trust income was not U.S. source income or connected with a U.S. trade or business, the income would not be subject to U.S. income tax in the hands of the foreign grantor. The 1996 Act amended the grantor trust rules to significantly limit the circumstances in which a foreign person may be treated as the owner of trust property for U.S. income tax purposes.

[ii]   IRC Section 679—Grantor Trust Treatment for U.S. Creator/Transferor to Foreign Trust with U.S. Beneficiaries

In General. If a U.S. person[81] transfers property to a foreign trust, he is treated as the owner of the portion of the trust attributable to the property transferred if there is a U.S. beneficiary of any portion of the trust.[82]

Interaction with Other Grantor Trust Rules (*i.e.*, IRC Sections 673-678). IRC Section 679 applies without regard to whether the U.S. transferor retains any power or interest described in IRC Sections 673 through 677.[83] If a U.S. transferor would be treated as the owner of part of a foreign trust under IRC Section 679 and another person would be treated as the owner of the same portion under IRC Section 678 (*i.e.*, person other than grantor treated as substantial owner), then the U.S. transferor is treated as the owner and the other person is not treated as the owner.[84] In other words, IRC Section 679 will override the other grantor trusts rules where there is a conflict.

Trusts with U.S. Beneficiaries. A foreign trust is treated as having a U.S. beneficiary unless during the U.S. transferor's tax year:

1. No part of the trust's income or corpus may, directly or indirectly, be paid or accumulated to/for the benefit of a U.S. person; and
2. If the trust is terminated at any time during the tax year, no part of the income or corpus of the trust could, directly or indirectly, be paid to/for the benefit of a U.S. person.[85]

The determination of whether a foreign trust has a U.S. beneficiary is made annually.

---

[79] IRC § 679.

[80] Rev. Rul. 69-70, 1969-1 C.B.182.

[81] The term U.S. person means a U.S. person as defined in IRC § 7701(a)(30), an NRA individual who elects under IRC § 6013(g) to be treated as a U.S. resident, and an individual who is a dual resident taxpayer within the meaning of Reg. § 301.7701(b)-7(a).

[82] Reg. § 1.679-1(a).

[83] Reg. § 1.679-1(b).

[84] Reg. § 1.679-1(b).

[85] Reg. § 1.679-2(a)(1).

For purposes of this test, income or corpus may be paid or accumulated to/for a U.S. person's benefit during a U.S. transferor's tax year if during that year, directly or indirectly:

1. Income may be distributed to, or accumulated for a U.S. person's benefit; or
2. Corpus may be distributed to, or held for the future benefit of, a U.S. person.[86]

This determination is made without regard to whether: (i) income or corpus is actually distributed to a U.S. person during that year, and (ii) a U.S. person's interest in the trust income or corpus is contingent on a future event.[87]

Treasury regulations provide that for purposes of this determination, persons who are not named as beneficiaries and are not members of a class of beneficiaries as defined under the trust instrument are not considered if the U.S. transferor demonstrates to IRS satisfaction that the person's contingent interest in the trust is so remote as to be negligible. To illustrate, a class of beneficiaries generally does not include heirs who will benefit from the trust under intestacy if the named beneficiaries have all passed away. This exception, however, does not apply to persons to whom distributions could be made pursuant to a grant of discretion to the trustee or any other person.

The possibility that a non-U.S. beneficiary could become a U.S. beneficiary does not cause that person to be treated as a U.S. beneficiary for IRC Section 679 purposes until that person actually becomes a U.S. person.[88]

If a non-U.S. beneficiary becomes a U.S. beneficiary for the first time more than five years after a transfer to a foreign trust by a U.S. transferor, that beneficiary is not treated as a U.S. beneficiary for IRC Section 679 purposes with respect to that transfer.[89]

EXAMPLE 6-13

In 2001, Adam, a resident alien, transfers property to a foreign trust. The trust instrument provides that all income shall be distributed currently to Adam's daughter, Charlotte, an NRA, and that, upon the trust's termination, all corpus will be distributed to Charlotte. Here, the foreign trust is not treated as having a U.S. beneficiary during the years that Charlotte remains an NRA. If Charlotte first becomes a resident alien in 2004, the trust is treated as having a U.S. beneficiary beginning in 2004.

---

[86] Reg. § 1.679-2(a)(2).
[87] Reg. § 1.679-2(a)(2).
[88] Reg. § 1.679-2(a)(3).
[89] Reg. § 1.679-2(a)(3).

EXAMPLE 6-14

Same facts as Example 6-13, except that Charlotte first becomes a resident alien in 2007. Here the foreign trust is not treated as having a U.S. beneficiary with respect to the property transferred by Adam, even after Charlotte becomes a U.S. beneficiary.

EXAMPLE 6-15

Same facts as Example 6-14, except that Charlotte had previously been a U.S. person during a prior period. Here, the five-year exception does not apply, and the trust is treated as having a U.S. beneficiary in 2007.

Treasury regulations provide that, even if, based on the trust instrument, a foreign trust is not treated as having a U.S. beneficiary under the foregoing analysis, the IRS may nevertheless reclassify the trust as having a U.S. beneficiary based on the following:

- All written and oral agreements and understandings relating to the trust;
- Memoranda or letters of wishes;
- All records that relate to the actual distribution of income and corpus;
- All other documents that relate to the trust, whether or not of any purported legal effect.
- The following factors:

  - If the trust instrument allows the trust to be amended to benefit a U.S. person, all potential benefits that could be provided to a U.S. person pursuant to such an amendment must be considered;
  - If the trust instrument does not allow the trust to be amended to benefit a U.S. person, but the law applicable to the trust may require payments or accumulations of income or corpus to/for the benefit of a U.S. person (by judicial reformation or otherwise), all potential benefits that could be provided to a U.S. person pursuant to the law must be taken into account, unless the U.S. transferor demonstrates to IRS satisfaction that the law is not reasonably expected to be applied or invoked under the facts and circumstances; and
  - If the parties to the trust ignore the trust instrument's terms, or if it is reasonably expected that they will do so, all benefits that have been, or are reasonably expected to be, provided to a U.S. person must be considered.

For IRC Section 679 purposes, an amount is treated as paid or accumulated to or for the benefit of a U.S. person if the amount is paid to or accumulated for the benefit of:

- A controlled foreign corporation;
- A foreign partnership, if a U.S. person is a partner of such partnership;
- A foreign trust or estate, if such trust or estate has a U.S. beneficiary.[90]

An amount is also treated as paid or accumulated to or for the benefit of a U.S. person if the amount is paid to or accumulated for the benefit of a U.S. person through an intermediary, such as an agent or nominee, or by any other means where a U.S. person may obtain an actual or constructive benefit.[91]

If a foreign trust to which a U.S. person has transferred property is treated as not having a U.S. beneficiary for a tax year of the transferor, but then it is treated as having a U.S. beneficiary in any subsequent year, the U.S. transferor is treated as having additional income in his/her first such tax year in which the trust is treated as having a U.S. beneficiary.[92]

The amount of additional income equals the trust's undistributed net income[93] at the end of the U.S. transferor's immediately preceding tax year.[94]

Such additional income is subject to IRC Section 668, which provides for an interest charge on accumulation distributions from foreign trusts.[95]

If a foreign trust that received property from a U.S. transferor ceases to be treated as having a U.S. beneficiary, the U.S. transferor ceases to be treated as the owner of that part of the trust attributable to the transfer beginning in the first tax year that follows the U.S. transferor's last tax year during which the trust is treated as having a U.S. beneficiary (unless the U.S. transferor is treated as an owner thereof pursuant to the IRC Sections 673-677 grantor trust rules).

The U.S. transferor is treated as making a property transfer to the foreign trust on the first day of the first tax year that follows the U.S. transferor's last tax year during which the trust was treated as having a U.S. beneficiary. The amount of the deemed property transfer to the trust is the portion of the trust attributable to the prior transfer for which the U.S. transferor was treated as having a U.S. beneficiary. In addition, the grantor must recognize gain on the deemed transfer of appreciated property to the foreign trust under IRC Section 684, which is discussed above.

EXAMPLE 6-16

In 2001, Adam, a resident alien, transfers stock with a fair market value of $100,000 to a foreign trust. The stock has an adjusted basis of $50,000 at this time. The trust instrument provides that income may be paid currently to, or

---

[90] Reg. § 1.679-2(b)(1).
[91] Reg. § 1.679-2(b)(2).
[92] Reg. § 1.679-2(c)(1).
[93] *See* IRC § 665(a).
[94] Reg. § 1.679-2(c)(1).
[95] Reg. § 1.679-2(c)(1).

accumulated for the benefit of Adam's son, Bob, and that, on the trust's termination, all income and corpus must be distributed to Bob. At the time of this transfer, Bob is an NRA and Adam is not treated as the owner of any portion of the foreign trust under IRC Section 673-677. The trust accumulates $30,000 of income during the 2001 through 2003. In 2004, Bob moves to the United States and becomes a resident alien. Here, Adam is treated as receiving an accumulation distribution in the amount of $30,000 in 2004 and immediately transferring that amount back to the trust. This accumulation distribution is subject to the IRC Section 668 rules providing for interest charges on accumulation distribution. In addition, beginning in 2005, Adam is treated as the owner of the portion of the foreign trust attributable to the stock Adam transferred to the foreign trust in 2001, including the portion attributable to the accumulated income deemed to be retransferred in 2004.

EXAMPLE 6-17

Assume the same facts as in Example 6-16 In 2008, Bob becomes an NRA. When Bob becomes an NRA, the stock transferred by Adam to the foreign trust in 2001 has a fair market value of $125,000 and an adjusted basis of $50,000. Here, beginning in 2009, the foreign trust is not treated as having a U.S. beneficiary, and Adam is not treated as the owner of the portion of the trust attributable to the prior transfer of stock.

Transfers. For IRC Section 679 purposes, a transfer means a direct, indirect, or constructive transfer.[96]

If a U.S. person is treated as owning part of a grantor trust (e.g., a revocable trust),[97] then transfers of property from that part of the grantor trust to a foreign trust are treated as transfers from the U.S. grantor to the foreign trust.[98]

Treasury regulations broadly define indirect transfers to include transfers made by a U.S. person through an intermediary if the U.S. person is related to a trust beneficiary (or has another relationship with a beneficiary that establishes a reasonable basis for the transferor making a gratuitous transfer to the foreign trust) and the U.S. person cannot demonstrate that:

- The intermediary had a relationship with a beneficiary that establishes a reasonable basis for the intermediary making a gratuitous transfer to the trust;
- The intermediary acted independently of the U.S. person;
- The intermediary is not an agent of the U.S. person; and
- The intermediary timely complied with the foreign trust information reporting requirements of IRC Section 6048.[99]

---

[96] Reg. § 1.679-3(a).
[97] Reg. § 1.679-3(b)(2).
[98] Reg. § 1.679-3(b)(1).
[99] Reg. § 1.679-3(c).

IRC Section 679 also applies if a U.S. person makes a constructive transfer to a foreign trust.[100] To illustrate, for this purpose, a constructive transfer includes an assumption or satisfaction of a foreign trust's obligation to a third party. A U.S. person who is related to a beneficiary of a foreign trust and who guarantees a loan to the trust is treated as making a transfer to the foreign trust equal to the portion of the obligation guaranteed.[101] For this purpose, a guarantee includes any arrangement under which a person, directly or indirectly, assures on a conditional or unconditional basis, the payment of another person's obligation. A commitment to contribute capital to the debtor, or otherwise maintain its financial viability, is a guarantee even if the arrangement is not a legally binding obligation or is subject to a contingency that has not yet occurred.[102]

Transfers by U.S. persons to entities owned by a foreign trust are treated as transfers to the foreign trust followed by a transfer by the trust to the entity unless the U.S. person is not related to a trust beneficiary or the U.S. person demonstrates that the transfer is attributable to the U.S. person's ownership interest in the entity.[103] For example, if a foreign trust and a U.S. person jointly fund a corporation, each taking back stock proportionate to their transfers, IRC Section 679 does not apply.

[c] Exceptions to IRC Section 679 Grantor Trust Treatment

[i] In General.

IRC Section 679 does not apply to the following:

- Transfer of property to a foreign trust because of the transferor's death;[104]
- Transfers to certain compensatory foreign trusts;[105]
- Transfers to certain charitable foreign trusts;[106]
- Transfers of property to a foreign trust to the extent the transfer is for fair market value.[107]

[ii] Transfers for Fair Market Value

A transfer is not a gratuitous transfer if it was made for full fair market value.[108] For purposes of determining whether full fair market value has been received, if the transferor is the grantor or a trust beneficiary (or a person related within the meaning of IRC Section 643(i)(2)(B) to any grantor or trust

---

[100] Reg. § 1.679-3(d).
[101] Reg. § 1.679-3(e).
[102] Reg. § 1.679-3(e).
[103] Reg. § 1.679-3(f).
[104] IRC § 679(a)(2)(A); Reg. § 1.679-4(a)(1).
[105] Reg. § 1.679-4(a)(2).
[106] Reg. § 1.679-4(a)(3).
[107] IRC § 679(a)(2)(B); Reg. § 1.679-4(a)(4).
[108] Reg. § 1.679-4(b).

beneficiary), any obligation issued by the trust (or by certain related persons) is disregarded, except as provided in regulations.[109]

Treasury regulations provide that certain "qualified obligations" will be recognized as consideration.[110] An obligation is a qualified obligation only if:

1. The obligation is reduced to writing by an express written agreement;
2. The term of the obligation does not exceed five years (for purposes of determining the term of an obligation, the obligation's maturity date is the last possible date that the obligation can be outstanding under the terms of the obligation);
3. All payments on the obligation are denominated in U.S. dollars;
4. The yield to maturity of the obligation is not less than 100 percent of the applicable Federal rate and not greater than 130 percent of the applicable Federal rate (the applicable Federal rate for an obligation is the applicable Federal rate in effect under IRC Section 1274(d) for the day on which the obligation is issued, as published in the Internal Revenue Bulletin);
5. The U.S. transferor extends the period for assessment of any income tax attributable to the loan and any consequential income tax changes for each year that the obligation is outstanding, to a date not earlier than three years after the maturity date of the obligation issued in consideration for the loan (this extension is not necessary if the maturity date of the obligation does not extend beyond the end of the U.S. person's taxable year and is paid within such period); when properly executed and filed, such an agreement will be deemed to be consented to by the Service Center Director or the Assistant Commissioner (International) for purposes of Treas. Reg. Section 301.6501(c)-1(d); and
6. The U.S. transferor reports the status of the obligation, including principal and interest payments, on Form 3520 for each year that the obligation is outstanding.[111]

[d] Tax Treatment at Death of U.S. Owner of Foreign Trust

[i] General Rule – No Gain Recognition at Death of U.S. Transferor

At one time there was concern among commentators that IRC Section 684 (which requires that any transfer of property by a U.S. person to a foreign trust be treated as a sale or exchange for an amount equal to the property's fair market value, thus requiring recognition of unrealized gains) triggered gain recognition upon the death of a U.S. transferor to a foreign trust.[112] The issuance of final treasury regulations under IRC Section 684 disposed of this concern for the most, with the exception noted below.

---

[109] IRC § 679(a)(3)(A)(i).
[110] Reg. § 1.679-4(d).
[111] Reg. § 1.679-4(d).
[112] *See* Henry Christensen, III, *International Estate Planning* § 4.04[1] (2002).

IRC Section 684 gain recognition does not apply to testamentary property transfers of U.S. transferors if the property's basis in the hands of the foreign trust is determined under IRC Section 1014(a).[113] Therefore, transfers by will of U.S. decedents to a foreign nongrantor trust will generally not trigger gain recognition under IRC Section 684 because the foreign nongrantor trust will take a stepped up basis under IRC Section 1014.

[ii] Exception to General Rule

Some commentators argue that there may be IRC Section 684 gain recognition upon deaths of U.S. transferors to foreign trusts, which occur in 2010. The argument in favor of this result is as follows:[114]

- Until the U.S. person's death, such person is treated as the owner of the property for U.S. income tax purposes under IRC Section 671;
- The U.S. grantor's death terminates the trust's grantor trust status;
- Treas. Reg. Section 1.1001-2(c), Example 5, treats the termination of grantor trust status as a transfer of the trust property by the grantor.[115] If this rule applies to IRC Section 684, and if it applies to terminations caused by death, the deceased U.S. person will be treated as making a transfer to a foreign trust at death;
- Treasury regulations under IRC Section 684 confirm this tax treatment for U.S. owners, except that that they provide that transfers to the foreign trust are treated as occurring immediately before the U.S. owner's death;[116]
- Treas. Reg. Section 1.684-3(c) provides an exception to this gain recognition rule where the basis of the assets of the property in the hands of the foreign trust is determined under IRC Section 1014(a);
- The Economic Growth and Tax Relief Reconciliation Act repeals or suspends IRC Section 1014 in 2010 when the federal estate tax is not in effect;
- Therefore, if the grantor of a foreign trust dies in 2010, this exception will not apply.

Planning Pointer. Planners can avoid the risk that gain will be recognized upon the U.S. transferor's death by giving a U.S. person, the right to withdraw the foreign trust's property immediately before the death of the U.S. person. The withdrawal power would give the deceased U.S. person the protection of IRC Section 684(b). IRC Section 684(b) excepts transfers to trusts to the extent such trusts are owned by any person (other than a foreign nongrantor trust) under IRC Section 871.[117]

---

[113] Reg. § 1.684-3(c).

[114] *See* Ellen K. Harrison, et al., *US Tax'n of Foreign Trusts, Trusts With Non-U.S. Grantors and Their U.S. Beneficiaries, in* Sophisticated Estate Planning Techniques (ALI-ABA Course No. SJ016 Sept. 2003).

[115] *See also* Madorin v. Comm'r, 84 T.C. 667 (1985); Rev Rul. 77-402, 1977-2 C.B. 222.

[116] Reg. § 1.684-2(e), Ex. 2.

[117] *See* Ellen K. Harrison, et al., *U.S. Tax'n of Foreign Trusts, Trusts With Non-U.S. Grantors and Their U.S. Beneficiaries, in* Sophisticated Estate Planning Techniques (ALI-ABA Course No. SJ016 Sept. 2003).

[e] Tax Treatment After Death of U.S. Person

After the death of the U.S. person who has made transfers to a foreign trust, the trust will no longer be subject to IRC Section 679. Thereafter, the foreign trust will be treated as a foreign nongrantor trust.

[f] Treatment of Trusts that Become Foreign Trusts – Outbound Migrations

[i] Impact under IRC Section 679 Grantor Trust Rules

A U.S. person, who transfers property to a domestic trust that thereafter becomes a foreign trust while the U.S. transferor is still alive, is treated as U.S. transferor to a foreign trust and is deemed to transfer the property to the foreign trust on the date the domestic trust becomes a foreign trust.[118]

The property deemed transferred to the trust when it becomes a foreign trust includes both the original transfer and the undistributed net income, as defined by IRC Section 665(a), attributable to the property previously transferred. Undistributed net income for periods before the migration is taken into account only for purposes of determining the portion of the trust that is attributable to the property transferred by the U.S. person.

EXAMPLE 6-18

On January 1, 2002, Alex, a resident alien, transfers property to a domestic trust, for the benefit of Ben, Alex's son, who is also a resident alien. On January 1, 2003, the domestic trust acquires a foreign trustee who has the power to determine whether and when distributions will be made to Ben. Here, the trust becomes a foreign trust on January 1, 2003. In addition, Alex is treated as transferring property to a foreign trust on January 1, 2003. The property deemed transferred to the trust when it becomes a foreign trust includes undistributed net income, as defined in IRC Section 665(a), attributable to the property deemed transferred.[119]

[ii] Impact under IRC Section 684 Gain Recognition Rules

If a U.S. trust becomes a foreign trust, that trust is treated as having transferred, immediately before becoming a foreign trust, all of its assets to a foreign trust, and subject to IRC Section 684 gain recognition at that time.[120] Treasury regulations provide relief provisions for inadvertent outbound migrations.[121]

---

[118] Reg. § 1.679-6(a).
[119] Reg. § 1.679-6(c).
[120] Reg. § 1.684-4.
[121] Reg. § 1.684-4(c).

[4]   Creation of Foreign Trust by Non-U.S. Person

Neither IRC Section 684(a) nor IRC Section 679 applies to transfers to a foreign trust by a non-U.S. person. Consequently, no U.S. income tax is imposed on such transfers.

The trust's income will be treated for U.S. income tax purposes as if earned by a foreign nongrantor trust (unless IRC Sections 672(f) applies to the trust).

Prior to the 1996 Act, trusts created by non-U.S. persons were subject to the "grantor trust" rules to the same extent as trusts created by U.S. persons. As a result, this application of the grantor trust rules shifted the trust's income, for virtually all U.S. income tax purposes, from the trust to its non-U.S. grantor. As discussed below, IRC Section 672(f) denies grantor trust status to trusts with non-U.S. grantors unless:

- The grantor retains the right, exercisable either unilaterally or with the consent of another person who is a related or subordinate party who is subservient to the grantor, to revoke the trust; or
- The only amounts permitted to be distributed from the trust during the grantor's life are amounts distributable to the grantor or her spouse.[122]

[C]   *Tax Treatment of Foreign Nongrantor Trust ("FNGT")*

[1]   In General

[a]   *Overview*

The income tax rules governing FNGTs are a combination of the income tax rules governing domestic trusts and NRAs. Trust income may be entirely taxable to the FNGT, the FNGT's beneficiaries, or partly to each. Under IRC Sections 651 and 661, trusts may deduct amounts properly paid or credited to beneficiaries. Therefore, trusts are treated as conduits to the extent of distributed income, and as separate taxable entities to the extent of undistributed income.

Note. Foreign grantor trusts, as noted elsewhere in this outline, are treated as owned entirely by the trust's grantor and deemed not to exist for income tax purposes. Therefore, the rules discussed in this section (*i.e.*, the rules governing the taxation of FNGTs) do not apply to foreign grantor trusts.

In very general terms, the steps required to analyze the taxation of FNGTs may be thought of as follows:

1. FNGT pays tax (at FNGT level) on the FNGT's gross income from within the United States *less* DNI distribution deduction, in a manner similar to that in which NRA individuals are taxed (without the DNI distribution deduction). In addition, there is typically withholding on FDAP income (*i.e.*, fixed or

---

[122] IRC § 672(f).

determinable annual or periodic gains, profits, and income from U.S. sources) that is paid to the FNGT;

2. U.S. beneficiaries are taxed on income distributed to them, to the extent of DNI, which reflect the FNGT's worldwide income;

3. NRA beneficiaries are taxed on income distributed to them, to the extent of DNI, which reflects the FNGT's U.S. source income.

[b] Income Taxed to Trust, Beneficiaries, or Partly to Each – DNI

[i] In General

Income of FNGTs are taxed to the trust, the beneficiaries, or partly to each. The concept of DNI, along with its limitation on the trust's distribution deduction, is the mechanism through which the IRC allocates income between the FNGT and its beneficiaries. The concept of DNI is discussed in below.

[ii] Simple Versus Complex Trusts

By means of different DNI calculations, the IRC and treasury regulations thereunder divide nongrantor trusts (both foreign and domestic) into two basic types, simple and complex, which the IRC taxes differently.

A FNGT constitutes a "simple" trust if it satisfies *all* of the following requirements:

1. All income must be distributed currently;
2. No amounts may be paid, permanently set aside for, or used for a charitable beneficiary;
3. No distributions are made other than of current income (*i.e.*, no distributions of accumulated income or corpus).[123]

All of a simple FNGT's income is taxed to the beneficiaries. In turn the FNGT receives a deduction for its current income, which it must pay to the beneficiaries, regardless of whether it actually distributes such income.[124] The amounts that the beneficiaries must include in their gross income, along with the trust's deduction, are limited by the trust's DNI.[125]

A FNGT constitutes a "complex" trust if *any* of the following are true:

1. It is not required to distribute all income currently;
2. It distributes accumulated income or principal; or
3. It has a charitable beneficiary.[126]

---

[123] IRC § 651(a); Reg. § 1.651(a)-1.
[124] IRC §§ 651(a), 652.
[125] IRC §§ 651(b), 652(a).
[126] IRC § 661(a); Reg. § 1.661(a)-1.

A complex FNGT receives a deduction for that portion of its current income that it must distribute, plus that portion of its current income that the trustee actually distributes to the beneficiaries pursuant to the trust instrument.[127] The trust's deduction is limited to the amount of its DNI.[128]

Beneficiaries of a complex FNGT must include in their gross income all income that the trust is required to distribute and all income actually distributed to the beneficiaries pursuant to the trust instrument.[129] Each beneficiary must include in his gross income an amount equal to his pro rata share of the trust's DNI.[130] Distributions that exceed the FNGT's DNI are treated either as nontaxable distributions of principal or as distributions of accumulated income from prior years, which are taxable under the throwback rule (discussed below).[131]

[c]   Tax at the FNGT Level

[i]   In General

Unlike the gross income of domestic trusts, which includes the domestic trust's worldwide gross income, the gross income of an FNGT, for purposes of taxation imposed on the trust (as opposed to tax imposed on the trust beneficiaries), consists only of:

1. **Non-trade/business U.S. source gross income.** Gross income derived from sources within the United States that is not effectively connected with the conduct of a trade or business within the United States; and
2. **Trade/business within the United States.** Gross income that is effectively connected with the conduct of a trade or business within the United States.[132]

Note. FNGTs generally are not subject to U.S. income taxation on undistributed foreign source income because of a lack of a nexus between the United States and the FNGT for income tax purposes. However, foreign source income of an FNGT that is distributed to U.S. beneficiaries may be taxed to such beneficiaries.[133]

[ii]   Imposition of U.S. Income Tax—In General

Income earned by a foreign nongrantor trust ("FNGT"), which as mentioned above is taxed as an NRA, will generally fall into one of two taxing regimes. For FNGTs "engaged in a trade or business" in the United States, the U.S. taxes the net income that is "effectively connected" with the conduct of such trade or business in the same manner as net income earned by a U.S. resident.[134] In

---

[127] IRC § 661(a); Reg. § 1.661(a)-1.

[128] IRC § 661(a).

[129] IRC § 662(a).

[130] IRC § 662(a)(2).

[131] IRC §§ 662(a)(2), 665-668.

[132] IRC §§ 641(b), 872(a).

[133] Howard Zaritsky, *US Tax'n of Foreign Estates, Trusts and Beneficiaries*, 854-2d Tax Mgmt. Portfolio V.C.2. (2002),

[134] IRC § 871(b).

contrast, fixed or determinable annual or periodical gains, profits, and income from U.S. sources (commonly referred to as "FDAP" income), which an FNGT earns is typically taxed on a gross basis at a flat 30 percent rate.[135] In other words, the IRC taxes trade or business income on a *net* basis at *graduated* rates. In contrast, the IRC taxes non-business income on a *gross* basis, without the benefit of deductions, at a *flat rate of 30 percent.*

From an analytical standpoint, planners must first determine whether an FNGT in question is engaged in a U.S. trade or business at anytime within the tax year. If yes, then the planner must determine whether the FNGT has any income that is "effectively connected" with such U.S. trade or business. After conducting the foregoing analysis, the planner must determine if the FNGT has any U.S. source income that is not effectively connected with a U.S. trade or business, but which the United States subjects to taxation, typically at the 30 percent flat rate.

[iii]   Is FNGT Engaged in a Trade or Business within the United States?

In General. A FNGT engaged in a business within the United States is treated as an NRA engaged in a U.S. trade or business. In other words, the trust's worldwide effectively connected income is subject to U.S. income tax.[136]

> **Caution.** It may be dangerous for a foreign trust to engage in business in the United States because: (i) this may impact its characterization as a trust; and (ii) this may impact its status as a foreign as opposed to a domestic trust.[137]

Note. As a practical matter, most well advised FNGT's that engage in U.S. business activities, will do so through a corporation, rather than directly. They will do this both in order to limit the FNGT's liability exposure and to avoid any inference that the trust or its beneficiaries are engaging directly in a U.S. business activity. Typically, the FNGT will own a U.S. corporation, which in turn may be owned by a foreign corporation that is directly owned by the trust.

Facts and Circumstances Test.   The IRC applies a facts and circumstances test to determine if an FNGT is engaged in a trade or business within the United States. The only guidance to planners with respect to this determination is case law, of which there is a substantial amount, and which far exceeds the scope of this outline.[138] However, the following discussion provides a brief summary of the issues presented.

---

[135] IRC § 871(a).

[136] IRC § 871(b).

[137] Christensen, *International Estate Planning,* § 4.06 (2002).

[138] For a detailed discussion of court decisions and rulings regarding whether an NRA is engaged in a trade or business within the United States, *see* 156 TM, *Foreign Corporations – U.S. Income Taxation. See also* Garelik, *What Constitutes Doing Business Within the United States by a Non-Resident Alien Individual or a Foreign Corporation,* 18 Tax L. Rev. 423 (1963).

Generally, the facts and circumstances test examines the nature and extent of an FNGT's economic activities and contacts within the United States.[139] A U.S. trade or business does not include isolated and nonrecurring transactions by an FNGT in the United States absent a profit motive.[140] The FNGT taxpayer must, during some substantial part of the tax year, have been regularly and continuously transacting a substantial portion of its ordinary business in the United States.[141]

Owning real property in the United States does not constitute a U.S. trade or business unless other activities are present in addition to ownership.[142] To illustrate, if an FNGT taxpayer leases and manages property through rental agents, he will engage in a U.S. trade or business.[143] Having said this, special FIRPTA rules apply in the real estate context, which are discussed in more detail below.

Personal Services. A U.S. trade of business includes performing personal services at any time during the tax year.[144]

Investors. Generally, the IRC treats a foreign individual, corporation or trust that trades in stocks, securities or commodities in the United States as not conducting a U.S. trade or business if that person does not have an office in the United States through which, or under the direction of which, the securities transactions are effected.[145] Under the IRC Section 864(b)(2)(A)(ii) safe harbor, a foreign individual, corporation or trust is not treated as conducting a U.S. trade or business provided the transactions are for the taxpayer's own account, even if:

- The trading is conducted by the foreign taxpayer or its agent or employee;
- Such agent or employee has discretionary authority to make decisions in effecting the transactions.

Planning Pointer. An FNGT can generally substantiate trading for its own account by trading through an independent stockbroker, commission agent or custodian. This holds true regardless of whether the agent had discretionary authority.[146]

---

[139] U.S. v. Balanovski, 236 F.2d 298 (2d Cir. 1956), *cert. denied*, 352 U.S. 968 (1957), *reh'g denied*, 352 U.S. 1019 (1957); Spermacet Whaling & Shipping Co. v. Comm'r, 30 T.C. 618 (1958), *aff'd*, 281 F.2d 646 (6th Cir. 1960).

[140] Continental Trading, Inc. v. Comm'r, T.C. Memo. 1957-164, *aff'd*, 265 F.2d 40 (9th Cir. 1959), *cert. denied*, 361 U.S. 827 (1959).

[141] Spermacet Whaling & Shipping Co. v. Comm'r, 30 T.C. 618 (1958), *aff'd*, 281 F.2d 646 (6th Cir. 1960); Consolidated Premium Iron Ores, Ltd. v. Comm'r, 28 T.C. 127 (1957); Continental Trading, Inc. v. Comm'r, T.C. Memo. 1957-164, *aff'd*, 265 F.2d 40 (9th Cir. 1959), *cert. denied*, 361 U.S. 827 (1959); Lewenhaupt v. Comm'r, 20 T.C. 151 (1953), *aff'd*, 221 F.2d 227 (9th Cir. 1955).

[142] De Amodio v. Comm'r, 34 T.C. 894 (1960), *aff'd*, 299 F.2d 623 (3c Cir. 1962).

[143] Lewenhaupt v. Comm'r, 20 T.C. 151 (1953), *aff'd*, 221 F.2d 227 (9th Cir. 1955); De Amodio v. Comm'r, 34 T.C. 894 (1960), *aff'd*, 299 F.2d 623 (3d Cir. 1962); Reiner v. U.S., 222 F.2d 770 (7th Cir. 1955).

[144] IRC § 864(b); Reg. § 1.864-2(a).

[145] IRC § 864(b)(2)(A)(i).

[146] Reg. § 1.864-2(c)(2)(i)(C).

Partnerships.[147]   If an FNGT is a partner in a partnership engaged in a trade or business within the United States, the IRC treats an FNGT partner of that partnership as engaged in a trade or business within the United States.[148] Generally, the fact that the partnership is organized under U.S. or foreign law will be irrelevant for this analysis.

If the partnership is engaged in a trade or business within the United States, the partner will be taxed on this distributive share of the partnership's effectively connected income, after reduction for the partnership's allocable deductions and the FNGT's allowable deductions under IRC Section 873. The test to determine if a partnership is engaged in a U.S. trade or business is the same as for an NRA individual.[149]

Caution. In partnership cases, IRC Section 1446 requires that the partnership withhold and deposit tax on each foreign partner's distributive share of partnership income, whether that income is actually distributed to foreign partners or not. The FNGT then credits the withholding tax at the end of the year against its actual tax for the year. Special withholding tax rules apply if a partnership makes a distribution to an FNGT of items of fixed or determinable annual or periodical gains, profits, and income.

Deemed Status of Engaging in U.S. Trade or Business.   Under some circumstances, the IRC will deem an FNGT as engaging a U.S. trade or business. These situations are discussed below.

- **FIRPTA Rules for Gain on Sales of U.S. Real Property.** Gains and losses realized by FNGTs from the disposition of U.S. real property interests are treated as effectively connected with a U.S. trade or business.[150] Transferees are required to withhold tax on such transfers.[151] These provisions are generally known as FIRPTA, which is the acronym for the Foreign Investment in Real Property Tax Act.[152]
- **Payments Deferred into a Year that FNGT Is Not Engaged in a U.S. Trade or Business.** If payments that the IRC would treat as effectively connected with a U.S. trade or business in one year are deferred to another year in which the FNGT is not engaged in a U.S. trade or business, the IRC taxes such payments as if they are effectively connected with a U.S. trade or business in the year received.[153]

---

[147] For a detailed discussion of foreign partners and partnerships, *see* 910 T.M., *Foreign Partnerships and Partners.*

[148] IRC § 875(a); Reg. § 1.875-1.

[149] Reg. § 1.875-1.

[150] IRC § 897.

[151] IRC § 1445.

[152] Pub. L.No. 96-499, 96th Cong. 2d Sess. (Dec. 5, 1980).

[153] IRC § 864(c)(6).

- **Sale of Assets from a U.S. Trade or Business in Subsequent Year.** If a foreign person has property that it uses in a U.S. trade or business, which that person sells within ten years after it ceases to be used in the business, the United States may tax any gain on such sale as being effectively connected with a US trade or business.[154]
- **Real Property Net Election Under IRC Section 871(d).** IRC Section 871(d) allows an FNGT to elect to treat rental income from his/her U.S. real property rental activities as effectively connected with a U.S. trade or business. This allows the FNGT to avoid the uncertainty of the facts and circumstances test as to whether its activity constitutes engaging in a U.S. trade or business. This would allow the FNGT to be able to deduct expenses associated with its U.S. real property rental activity, rather than to pay a flat 30 percent tax on a gross basis.

[iv] Taxation of FNGT Not Engaged in U.S. Trade or Business – FDAP Income

In General. IRC Sections 871 and 881 tax NRAs, and therefore, FNGTs, at a flat 30 percent tax on several types of nonbusiness income. The tax is imposed at a flat 30 percent rate without any deductions or other allowances for costs incurred in producing the income and is typically collected through withholding.[155] This tax applies to interest, dividends, rents, royalties and other "fixed or determinable annual or periodical" income ("FDAP" income) if such income is: (1) includible in income; (2) from U.S. sources; and (3) not effectively connected in the conduct of a U.S. trade or business.

FDAP income from sources outside the United States is generally not taxable when received by an FNGT. FDAP income from sources within the United States that is effectively connected with the conduct of a U.S. trade or business is taxed in the manner described above.

Generally, FDAP income includes interest (other than OID interest), dividends, rent, salaries, wages, premiums (other than insurance premiums),[156] annuities, compensation, remunerations, and royalties,[157] and may include certain commission[158] and alimony payments.[159]

Interest. OID is the difference between the issue price and the stated redemption price at maturity (as defined in IRC Section 1273) of a bond or other evidence of indebtedness ("OID Obligation"). Generally, the IRC treats OID as if interest payments were actually paid by the borrower to the lender, and then are loaned back to the borrower. In the FNGT context, however, OID accrued by an FNGT lender is not subject to the 30 percent tax on investment income until the

---

[154] IRC § 864(c)(7).

[155] For a complete discussion of the withholding rules, *see* Charles M. Bruce, New US Withholding Tax Rules: A Practical Guide (2002).

[156] Rev. Rul. 80-222, 1980-2 C.B. 211.

[157] IRC § 871(a)(1)(A); Reg. § 1.871-7(b).

[158] Reg. § 1.1441-2(a)(2).

[159] Trust of Welsh v. Comm'r, 16 T.C. 1398 (1951), *aff'd*, 194 F.2d 708 (3d Cir. 1952), *cert. denied*, 344 U.S. 821 (1952).

debt instrument is sold, exchanged or retired.[160] For this purpose, only OID accruing during the time the FNGT holds the OID Obligation is subject to tax.[161] In addition, the tax cannot exceed the amount of the payment less any part of the payment that represents expressly stated interest.[162]

OID taxed on a payment is not taxed subsequently on the sale or exchange of the OID obligation.[163] Upon disposition of an OID obligation, all untaxed OID accruing during the time the obligation was held by the FNGT is taxed, even if the accrued amount exceeds the gain on disposition.

Portfolio interest on certain types of obligations, which is paid to an FNGT, is not subject to the 30 percent tax.[164]

Interest received by FNGTs or foreign corporations on deposits with banks, savings institutions or insurance companies are exempt from tax if they are not effectively connected with the recipient's U.S. trade or business.[165]

Gain on Sale of Capital Asset. If an FNGT is not engaged in the conduct of a U.S. trade or business, then the FNGT's U.S. source non-real estate capital gains will not be subject to U.S. federal income tax. This results because (1) FNGTs are taxed as NRAs not present in the United States at any time,[166] and (2) in order for the capital gains of an NRA (which an FNGT is treated as) to be subject to U.S. federal income tax, the NRA must be physically present in the United States for at least 183 days.[167]

Note. An FNGT's U.S. capital gains will be subject to U.S. income tax at the beneficiary level if the FNGT distributes them to a U.S. beneficiary.

Source Rules.

In General. An FNGT is subject to income tax on income from U.S. sources, including both U.S. source passive income (*i.e.*, FDAP)[168] and income that is effectively connected with the conduct of a trade or business in the United States.[169] Because FNGTs are taxed only on income from U.S. sources, it is critical to know the source of the FNGT's income.

In very general terms, the IRC statutorily provides the following source rules:

Interest. Interest is generally sourced by reference to the payer's residence. Therefore, interest from U.S. borrowers; except for interest from U.S. bank

---

[160] IRC § 871(a)(1)(C).
[161] IRC § 871(a)(1)(C).
[162] IRC §§ 871(a)(1), 881(a)(3)(B).
[163] IRC §§ 871(a)(1)(C)(ii), 881(a)(3)(B).
[164] IRC § 871(h)(1).
[165] IRC §§ 871(i), 881(d).
[166] IRC § 641(b).
[167] IRC § 871(a)(2); Reg. § 1.871-7(c).
[168] IRC § 871(a)(1).
[169] IRC §§ 871-872. For a detailed discussion of the source of income rules, *see* 905 TM, *Source of Income Rules*.

deposits (unless effectively connected with a U.S. trade or business) and portfolio interest, is treated as U.S. source income;[170]

Dividends. Dividends paid by a U.S. corporation are U.S. source income. If a foreign corporation is engaged in a U.S. trade or business, a portion of any dividend payment may be treated as U.S. source income. Specifically, if 25 percent or more of the foreign corporation's gross income for the three preceding years is U.S. business income, the portion of the dividend attributable to the corporation's U.S. business income will be treated as U.S. source income;[171]

Personal service income. Income from the performance of personal services in the United States is U.S. source income, subject to the de minimis exception, discussed above;[172]

Rental income. Rental income from property located in the United States is U.S. source income;[173]

Royalty income. Royalty income generated in the United States is U.S. source income;[174]

Real property sales. Income from the sale of real property located in the United States is U.S. source income.[175]

Income from personal property dispositions. In the NRA context, income from the disposition of personal property generally follows the seller's residence. Therefore, sales by a U.S. resident are generally sourced in the United States, and sales by an NRA are generally sourced outside the United States.[176] However, income from the disposition of personal property by an FNGT will be treated as U.S. source income under any of the following circumstances:

- The personal property is inventory to be sold in the United States;
- The disposition is attributable to a U.S. office;
- The personal property is U.S. timber.[177]

Miscellaneous rules.

- **Depreciable tangible property.** Gain from the disposition of depreciable tangible property by an FNGT may have a U.S. source if depreciation was allowable as a deduction for U.S. tax purposes.[178]
- **Intangible property.** Gain from the sale of intangible property such as a patent, trademark, goodwill or franchise may have a U.S. source if the gain is contingent on use or productivity in the United States.

---

[170] IRC §§ 861(a)(1), 871(h)-(i).
[171] IRC § 861(a)(2)(A)-(B).
[172] IRC § 861(a)(3).
[173] IRC § 861(a)(4).
[174] IRC § 861(a)(4).
[175] IRC §§ 861(a)(5), 897(c).
[176] IRC § 865(a).
[177] IRC § 865(a), (b), (e).
[178] IRC § 865(c)(1)(A).

Deductions and credits.

Deductions related to income effectively connected with U.S. trade or business.

In General. In computing an FNGT's taxable income that is effectively connected with the conduct of a trade or business within the United States, the FNGT is entitled to reduce its gross income so connected (or treated as so connected) by the deductions that are "connected" with such income.[179] The proper apportionment and allocation of deductions for this purpose is determined in accordance with Regulations Section 1.873-1. In addition, the FNGT is also entitled to deduct against its effectively connected income the following:

- The deduction for losses allowed by IRC Sections 165(c)(3) if the loss occurred with respect to property located in the United States;
- The deduction for charitable contributions allowed by IRC Section 170; and
- The deduction for personal exemptions allowed by IRC Section 151.[180]

Distributions to beneficiaries. In addition to the foregoing, distributions to beneficiaries made by either a simple trust[181] or a complex trust[182] are deductible. However, this merely shifts the taxability for such amounts from the trust to the beneficiaries.

Deductions related to other income. No deductions are permitted against U.S. source fixed or determinable annual or periodic income, except to the extent such income is effectively connected to a U.S. trade or business.

Foreign Tax Credit. A FNGT engaged in a trade or business within the United States that pays foreign income, war profits or excess profits taxes on income that is effectively connected with such trade or business may, subject to certain limitations, credit the foreign tax against its U.S. income tax liability.[183] Alternatively, it may deduct such taxes.[184]

Applicable tax rates.

Income effectively connected with a U.S. trade or business. For FNGTs "engaged in a trade or business" in the United States, the U.S. taxes the net income that is "effectively connected" with the conduct of such trade or business

---

[179] IRC § 873(a).
[180] IRC § 873(b).
[181] IRC § 651.
[182] IRC § 661.
[183] IRC § 901(b)(4), 906(a).
[184] IRC § 164(a)(3).

in the same manner as net income earned by a U.S. resident.[185] In other words, this type of income is subject to the normal tax rates applicable to trusts under IRC Section 1(e).[186]

FDAP income. In contrast to income effectively connected with a trade or business, fixed or determinable annual or periodical gains, profits, and income from U.S. sources, which an FNGT earns is typically taxed on a gross basis at a flat 30 percent rate.[187] In other words, the IRC taxes trade or business income on a *net* basis at *graduated* rates. In contrast, the IRC taxes non-business income on a *gross* basis, without the benefit of deductions, at a *flat rate of 30 percent.*

> **Caution.** The 15 percent maximum tax rate applicable to dividend income does not apply to income received by FNGTs.

Withholding.[188] FNGTs are subject to withholding, which are set forth in very detailed and extensive treasury regulations, and which are too extensive to cover in detail in this outline. However, it is important for practitioners to be aware that these rules exist.

[D] Tax Treatment of Beneficiaries of FNGTs

[1] In General

As noted above, FNGT income may be entirely taxable to the FNGT, the FNGT's beneficiaries, or partly to each. Under IRC Sections 651 and 661, trusts may deduct amounts properly paid or credited to beneficiaries. Therefore, trusts are treated as conduits to the extent of distributed income, and as separate taxable entities to the extent of undistributed income. Because DNI is so critical to the tax consequences of distributions to FNGT beneficiaries, this outline next discusses DNI.

[2] Distributable Net Income ("DNI")

[a] Simple Versus Complex Trusts

[i] Simple Trust

A FNGT will constitute a "simple" trust if it satisfies *all* of the following requirements:

1. All income must be distributed currently;

---

[185] IRC § 871(b).
[186] IRC § 871(b).
[187] IRC § 871(a).
[188] For a complete discussion of the withholding rules, *see* Charles M. Bruce, New US Withholding Tax Rules: A Practical Guide (2002).

2. No amounts may be paid, permanently set aside for, or used for a charitable beneficiary;
3. No distributions are made other than of current income (*i.e.,* no distributions of accumulated income or corpus).[189]

All of a simple FNGT's income will be taxed to the beneficiaries. In turn the FNGT will receive a deduction for its current income, which it must pay to the beneficiaries, regardless of whether such income is actually distributed or not.[190] The amounts that the beneficiaries must include in their gross income, along with the trust's deduction, are both limited by the trust's DNI.[191]

[ii]   Complex Trust

A FNGT will constitute a "complex" trust if *any* of the following are true:

1. It is not required to distribute all of its income currently;
2. It distributes accumulated income or principal; or
3. It has a charitable beneficiary.[192]

A complex FNGT receives a deduction for that portion of its current income that it must distribute plus that portion of its current income that the trustee actually distributes to the beneficiaries pursuant to the trust instrument.[193] The trust's deduction is limited to the amount of its DNI.[194]

Beneficiaries of a complex FNGT must include in their gross income all income that the trust is required to distribute plus all income actually distributed to the beneficiaries pursuant to the trust instrument.[195] Each beneficiary must include in its gross income an amount equal to his pro rata share of the trust's DNI.[196] Distributions that exceed the FNGT's DNI are treated either as nontaxable distributions of principal or as distributions of income accumulated from prior years, which are taxable under the throwback rule, which is discussed later in this outline.[197]

[b]   Computation of DNI

[i]   In General

A trust's DNI generally equals its taxable income computed with the following modifications:

1. There is no deduction for distributions to beneficiaries;

---

[189] IRC § 651(a); Reg. § 1.651(a)-1.
[190] IRC §§ 651(a), 652.
[191] IRC §§ 651(b), 652(a).
[192] IRC § 661(a); Reg. § 1.661(a)-1.
[193] IRC § 661(a); Reg. § 1.661(a)-1.
[194] IRC § 661(a).
[195] IRC § 662(a).
[196] IRC § 662(a)(2).
[197] IRC §§ 662(a)(2), 665-668.

2. There is no personal exemption deduction;
3. The trust's taxable income is increased by any tax-exempt income (net of allocable expenses).[198]

[ii]   Modifications to DNI for FNGT

The DNI of a FNGT is calculated in the same manner as for a domestic trust, with the modifications discussed below.

Worldwide Income. A FNGT's DNI begins with its worldwide taxable income, including both U.S. and foreign source income, without any distribution deduction or personal exemption, and increased by net tax-exempt income, as with a domestic trust.[199]

The FNGT's DNI specifically includes gross income from sources outside the United States, reduced by disbursements allocable to such income that would have been deductible were it not for the IRC Section 265(a)(1) limitation, which disallows certain deductions with respect to tax-exempt income.[200]

The FNGT's DNI also includes U.S. source gross income, determined without regard to IRC Section 894, which otherwise extends to taxpayers the benefits of U.S. income tax treaties.[201] In other words, income that is exempt from tax by treaty must nevertheless be taken into account in computing the FNGT's DNI.[202]

The two foregoing adjustments are reduced proportionately to the extent that the FNGT is allowed a deduction for charitable distributions or set asides.[203]

Capital Gains. Unlike domestic trusts, for which DNI generally does not include capital gains, the DNI of FNGTs includes capital gains, regardless of whether they are allocated to income or to corpus under either the governing law or instrument, and regardless of whether they are currently distributed.[204] Capital losses reduce such capital gains to the extent that they do not exceed capital gains.[205] If a FNGT recognizes both capital gains and ordinary income in one tax year, then distributions to U.S. beneficiaries will include a proportionate share of both ordinary income and capital gains, based on the relative inclusion of both in the FNGT's DNI.

---

[198] IRC § 643(a).
[199] IRC § 643(a)(6), (a)(5).
[200] IRC § 643(a)(6)(A).
[201] IRC § 643(a)(6)(B).
[202] Reg. § 1.643(a)-6(a).(3)(i).
[203] Reg. § 1.643(a)-5(b).
[204] IRC § 643(a)(6)(C); Reg. § 1.643(a)-6(a)(3)(iii).
[205] Reg. § 1.643(a)-6(a)(3)(ii).

[3]   Taxation of Current Distributions

[a]   *In General*

FNGT beneficiaries are taxed on the trust's income to the extent such income is either distributed or required to be distributed.[206] However, the exact U.S. income tax treatment of income distributed to FNGT beneficiaries depends on the following:

- Whether the distribution is of current income (*i.e.,*. DNI) or accumulated income (*i.e.*, UNI);
- Whether the beneficiary is a U.S. or foreign person; and
- Whether the FNGT's income is from within or outside the United States.

[b]   *Distributions to U.S. Beneficiaries*

[i]   In General

U.S. beneficiaries of FNGTs must include the following in their gross income:
From simple trusts U.S. beneficiaries of FNGTs must include in their gross income the amount of any trust income required to be distributed to such beneficiary in the year in question, regardless of whether such income is actually distributed, but limited to the extent of that beneficiary's share of the trust's DNI for that year.[207]
From complex trusts U.S beneficiaries of FNGTs must include both of the following in their gross income:

1. The amount of any trust income required to be distributed to such beneficiary in the year in question, regardless of whether such income is actually distributed, but limited to the extent of that beneficiary's share of the trust's DNI for the year;[208] and
2. Any other amount (1) required to be distributed to such beneficiary, regardless of whether such amount is actually distribute, or (2) that is properly and actually distributed to such beneficiary, to the extent of such beneficiary's share of the trust's DNI for the year in question.[209]

[ii]   Determining the Beneficiaries' Share of DNI

Simple Trusts   If the amount of income required to be distributed currently to beneficiaries exceeds the FNGT's DNI, each beneficiary includes in his gross income his proportionate share of such DNI.

---

[206] IRC §§ 652(a), 662(a); Reg. § 1.652(a)-1.
[207] IRC § 651.
[208] IRC § 662(a)(1).
[209] IRC § 662(a)(2).

EXAMPLE 6-19

Adam, a beneficiary of Simple FNGT, a simple trust, is to receive two-thirds of the trust income. Bob is to receive one-third. The income required to be distributed currently is $99,000. Here, Adam will receive $66,000 and Bob will receive $33,000. However, if the DNI is only $90,000, Adam will include two-thirds ($60,000) of the DNI in his gross income, and Bob will include one-third ($30,000) in his gross income.

Complex Trusts.[210]   Th⌐ IRC breaks income from complex trusts into two (2) groups (or tiers) of income. However, the amount of income that can be taxed to a beneficiary is limited to the trust's DNI.

DNI > Tier 1 income. If the entire amount of income in tier 1 (*i.e.,* income required to be distributed currently) is less than the trust's DNI, then the entire amount of the trust's income is taxable to the trust's beneficiaries.

DNI < Tier 1 income. If the entire amount of income in tier 1 is more than DNI, then each beneficiary is taxable only to the extent of his proportionate share of DNI.

Tier 2 distributions. Tier 2 distributions (*i.e.,* other amounts properly paid, credited or required to be distributed to beneficiaries for the tax year) are taxed to beneficiaries only if the trust's DNI exceeds distributions falling into tier 1. If DNI exceeds distributions falling into tier 1, distributions are taxable to a beneficiary to the extent that they do not exceed his proportionate share of the trust's DNI after reduction for amounts required to be distributed currently.

[iii]   Tax Character of Income

The tax character of distributions that a beneficiary receives in a year proportionately reflects the character of the trust's income for that year.[211] If the trust agreement or local law requires the trust to allocate particular types of trust income to particular beneficiaries, then the character of distributions to such beneficiaries will reflect that allocation if it has economic significance independent of the tax consequences.[212]

[iv]   Credit for U.S. Income Tax Withheld at Source

FNGT beneficiaries may claim a credit against their U.S. income tax for U.S. income taxes withheld at the source on U.S. source income paid to the FNGT (*e.g.,* withholding on FDAP income or FIRPTA withholding).[213] The withholding

---

[210] IRC § 662.
[211] IRC §§ 652(b), 662(b).
[212] IRC §§ 652(b), 662(b); Reg. § 1.652(b)-2(a); Reg. § 1.662(b)-1.
[213] Reg. § 1.1462-1(b).

tax is treated as if it were paid by the beneficiary. To claim the credit, however, the beneficiary must report as his income from the trust the sum of the tax withheld in addition to the amount actually distributed to him.[214]

[v] Credit for Foreign Taxes Paid by FNGT

Although most FNGTs are established in a low/no tax jurisdictions, the FNGT may nevertheless incur foreign taxes or it may be established in a foreign country that does impose taxes upon the trust. If an FNGT pays foreign taxes, its U.S. beneficiaries who receive income distributions on which such taxes have been paid may elect to take a credit for the share of foreign taxes attributable to their share of the income.[215] Alternatively, such beneficiaries may deduct such taxes as an itemized deduction.[216] To claim the credit, however, it appears that the beneficiary must report as his income from the trust the sum of the foreign taxes paid in addition to the amount actually distributed to him.[217]

[c] Distributions to NRA Beneficiaries

[i] Foreign Source Income

NRA beneficiaries of FNGTs are generally not subject to U.S. income tax on an FNGT's foreign source income. This results because there is no U.S. nexus on which to tax such income to the foreign beneficiary.

[ii] U.S. Source Income

NRA beneficiaries of FNGTs are subject to U.S. income tax on such FNGT's U.S. source income. Generally, such beneficiaries are liable for U.S. income taxes on the lesser of (1) the income the FNGT actually distributes or is required to distribute, or (2) the FNGT's DNI.

The character of the FNGT's U.S. income (*i.e.*, as either effectively connected with a US trade or business, or as FDAP income) establishes the beneficiary's U.S. tax liability in the same manner that it establishes the FNGT's tax liability on undistributed income.[218]

[iii] Withholding

As a practical matter, most of an NRA's U.S. tax liability stemming from an FNGT with U.S. source income may be paid in the form of withholding.[219]

---

[214] IRC § 1462; Reg. §§ 1.1441-3(f), 1.1462-1(b).

[215] IRC §§ 901, 666, 667.

[216] IRC § 164(a)(3).

[217] *See* Howard Zaritsky, *U.S. Tax'n of Foreign Estates, Trusts and Beneficiaries*, 854-2d Tax Mgmt. Portfolio V.D.1. (2002).

[218] *See* Isidro Martin-Montis Trust v. Comm'r, 75 TC 381 (1980), *acq.* 1981-2 C.B. 21, *acq.* 1981-2 C.B. 21; Rev Rul. 81-244, 1981-2 C.B. 151, *amplified by* Rev. Rul. 86-76, 1986-1 C.B. 284).

[219] For a complete discussion of the withholding rules, *see* Charles M. Bruce, New US Withholding Tax Rules: A Practical Guide (2002).

[4]   Taxation of Accumulation Distributions

[a]   In General

If an FNGT makes distributions that exceed its DNI in any particular year, the U.S. beneficiaries receiving such distributions must apply the throwback rule, which may subject such distributions to both taxation and an interest charge. Generally, the IRC allocates a foreign trust's income for income tax purposes each year between the trust and the trust beneficiaries by means of its DNI.[220] To the extent that DNI is either actually distributed or required to be distributed, (a) the trust deducts such DNI from its taxable income,[221] and (b) the beneficiaries are taxed on such DNI.[222]

If a trust does not distribute all of its DNI in any year, the amount of its DNI that it does not distribute becomes "undistributed net income" ("UNI"),[223] to which the throwback rule may apply in a future year. (In other words, UNI is the excess of the amount available from DNI for distribution to trust beneficiaries over the amount that the trust actually distributes to such beneficiaries.) In any year that the trust makes a distribution to its beneficiaries that exceeds its DNI for such year, if it has UNI from prior year(s), the IRC will treat the trust as making an "accumulation distribution." As noted above, the IRC then applies the throwback rule, which may subject such distributions to both taxation and an interest charge.

The throwback rule is designed to impose on trust beneficiaries approximately the same income taxes that would have been imposed had the trust distributed all of its income on a current basis. Application of the throwback rule involves the following concepts:

- The mechanics of the throwback rule;
- Definition of "accumulation distribution;"
- Definition of "undistributed net income" ("UNI");
- Computation of the interest charge imposed on accumulation distributions from foreign trusts;
- Application of the character rule.

[b]   Throwback Rule Mechanics

Step 1 – Determine number of preceding tax years of trust to which distribution attributable. Determine the number of preceding taxable years of the trust to which the distribution is attributable. The years to which the distribution is attributed are the earliest years of the trust in which the trust had UNI.[224]

---

[220] IRC § 643.
[221] IRC §§ 651, 661.
[222] IRC §§ 652, 662.
[223] IRC § 665.
[224] IRC § 666(a).

These are the actual years in which the income was accumulated based on the trust records.

> **Caution.** If the trust's records are insufficient to establish which years have UNI, the accumulation distribution will be allocated to the earliest year that the trust was in existence.[225]

If the amount of the trust's UNI in one of the accumulation years is less than 25 percent of the average annual accumulation, (*i.e.,* the total accumulation distribution divided by the number of years of accumulation) that year is disregarded in determining the number of years in which the distribution has been accumulated. However, amounts accumulated in any such disregarded year still are considered part of the total accumulation distribution.[226]

EXAMPLE 6-20A

Chandler creates the Chandler trust, an FNGT, in 2000. In 2004, the Chandler trust distributes $35,000 to its beneficiary, Marlowe, when it has DNI of $10,000. The Chandler trust had the following amounts of UNI: 2000—$8,000; 2001—$10,000; 2002 - $7,000, and 2003—$18,000. Here, the accumulation distribution would be attributed to three years (*i.e.,* 2000, 2001, and 2002).

Step 2 – Determine beneficiary's average years. Determine the beneficiary's average years. This is determined by examining the beneficiary's taxable income for the five immediately preceding tax years and then ignoring the high and low years.

EXAMPLE 6-20B

Marlowe has the following amounts of taxable income in the five years preceding the 2004 accumulation distribution:

2003	$100,000
2002	$10,000
2001	$75,000
2000	$75,000
1999	$65,000

Here, Marlowe's average years are 2001, 2000, and 1999.

---

[225] IRC § 666(d).
[226] IRC § 667(b)(3).

Step 3 – Determine the average annual accumulation. Determine the average annual accumulation, which is calculated by dividing the total accumulation distribution (including any taxes that the trust paid on the such amounts) by the number of years in which such accumulation distribution was accumulated.

Note. The number of years in which the accumulation distribution was accumulated was determined in Step 1.

EXAMPLE 6-20C

Here, the average annual accumulation equals $8,333.33. This amount is calculated by dividing the total accumulation distribution of $25,000 by the number of years in which that accumulation distribution was accumulated, which was three.

Step 4 – Add average annual accumulation to beneficiary's average years. The average annual accumulation, calculated in Step 3, is added to each of the beneficiary's (three) average years, determined in Step 2.

EXAMPLE 6-20D

Here, this step would yield the following adjusted amounts of taxable income for Marlowe:

2001	$83,333
2000	$83,333
1999	$73,333

Step 5 – Compute the average additional tax. Compute and average the increase in the beneficiary's tax caused by the addition of the average annual accumulation in each of the beneficiary's average years.[227] If the beneficiary is an NRA during some or all of the applicable years, this should be reflected by a change in the additional tax in such years.

EXAMPLE 6-20E

Assume that this step yields the following increase in Marlowe's tax for each of his average years:

---

[227] IRC § 667(b)(1)(D).

2001	$2,531
2000	$2,573
1999	$2,573

This yields an average increase in tax of $2,559.

Step 6 – Calculate the partial tax on the accumulation distribution. Determine the partial tax on the accumulation distribution by multiplying the average additional tax (computed in Step 5) by the number of years of accumulation.[228]

EXAMPLE 6-20F

Here, ignoring the credit for taxes paid on the distribution, the partial tax would be $7,677, which equals $2,559 (average additional tax) multiplied by 3 (number of years of accumulation).

Step 7 – Subtract credit for the taxes paid on the UNI being distributed. Subtract from the partial tax, determined in Step 6, a credit for the taxes paid on the UNI by the trust.[229]

Note. Because the beneficiary is given a credit for the taxes paid by the FNGT, the accumulation distribution must be grossed up to reflect such taxes. In other words, such taxes must be added to the accumulation distribution.

Note. If a beneficiary receives accumulation distributions from more than two trusts, he/she can only subtract a credit for the taxes paid by the first two trusts. Taxes by any additional trusts are ignored for purposes of this step.[230]

EXAMPLE 6-20G

Assume that the Chandler Trust paid $2,000 of tax on the UNI that it distributes to Marlowe as part of the accumulation distribution. Here, the partial tax is reduced by $2,000.

[c] *Character Rule*

[i] **In General**

Under IRC Section 667, the IRC taxes accumulation distributions that FNGT beneficiaries receive as ordinary income, regardless of the character of the income that the trust itself receives, with certain exceptions.[231]

---

[228] IRC § 667(b)(1).
[229] IRC §§ 666, 667.
[230] IRC § 667(c)(1).
[231] IRC §§ 667(a), 662(a)(2).

[ii] Exceptions

Tax-exempt Income. This rule does not apply to tax-exempt income, which does retain its character in the hands of the beneficiary in the form of an accumulation distribution.[232]

NRAs. Accumulation distributions that an FNGT makes to NRA beneficiaries retain the character of such income as recognized by the trust.[233]

[iii] Capital Gains

Since capital gains are included in DNI, if they are not distributed currently, but instead are distributed to a U.S. beneficiary as part of an accumulation distribution, such capital gains will be taxed at ordinary income tax rates when the U.S. beneficiary receives them.

[iv] Elimination of Character Rule is not Limited as to Types of Character of Income to which it Applies

The elimination of character rule does not limit the character of income to which it applies. Therefore, among other things, it results in the following types of implications:

Foreign tax credit.   Because a U.S. beneficiary of an FNGT cannot treat any part of the foreign income included in an accumulation as foreign income, such beneficiary loses the benefits of the foreign tax credit.

Passive activity income.   If passive activity income is included in an accumulation distribution, the beneficiary cannot use such income to offset passive activity losses.

Tax preference items.   If tax preference items are included in an accumulation distribution, the beneficiary does not have to take such items into account for alternative minimum tax purposes.

[d] Interest Charge

[i] In General

IRC Section 668 imposes a nondeductible "interest" charge on an FNGT beneficiary's tax, which the IRC imposes on accumulation distributions from the FNGT.[234] The IRC imposes the interest charge in addition to any other tax liabilities of the beneficiary of such FNGT. The interest charge is imposed on the amount of additional tax imposed on the beneficiary because of the accumulation distribution, but after reduction for any credit for any taxes that the FNGT paid on such distributed income.

---

[232] IRC §§ 667(a), 662(b).
[233] IRC § 667(e).
[234] IRC § 668.

[ii] Pre-1996 Interest Charge

Under pre-1996 law, the interest rate was a simple 6 percent per year rate.

[iii] Post-1995 Interest Charge

The 1996 Act changed the interest rule. Under rules enacted by the 1996 Act, the following rules apply. First, simple interest accrues at the rate of 6 percent through December 31, 1995.[235] Second, compound interest accrues, beginning January 1, 1996, using the monthly underpayment rate.[236] This compound rate also applies to the total simple interest that accrues for pre-1996 periods. Third, the accumulation distribution is allocated proportionately to prior trust years in which the trust has UNI (as opposed to the earliest of such years), and is treated as reducing UNI from prior years proportionately from each year.[237]

[iv] Limit on Interest Charge

IRC Section 668(b) provides that the interest charge, when added to the federal tax imposed on the accumulation distribution (*i.e.,* under the throwback rules described above), cannot exceed the amount of the accumulation distribution itself. To illustrate, if you arrived at an additional tax of $70 and an interest charge of $50 on an accumulated distribution of $100, the interest charge would be limited to $30, and after taxes and the interest charge, you would be left with $0 (*i.e.,* rather than being worse off by $20).

[v] Not Deductible

The IRC Section 668 interest charge is not deductible.[238]

[e] *Planning to Avoid Throwback Rule and Interest Charge*

Commentators have suggested the following methods of avoiding taxation of accumulation distributions under the throwback rules.

[i] Specific Gifts[239]

Distributions in satisfaction of a gift of a specific sum of money or of specific property described in IRC Section 663(a)(1) do not constitute an accumulation distribution. Therefore, such distributions will not trigger the throwback rules. For this purpose, a specific sum of money or of specific property described in IRC Section 663(a)(1) is an amount that the trust instrument requires to be paid to a beneficiary as a gift of a specific sum of money or of specific property and which is actually paid to such beneficiary all at once or in no more than three installments.[240]

---

[235] IRC § 668(a)(6).

[236] IRC § 668(a).

[237] IRC § 668(a)(5).

[238] IRC § 668(c).

[239] Howard Zaritsky, *U.S. Tax'n of Foreign Estates, Trusts and Beneficiaries,* 854-2d Tax Mgmt. Portfolio V.E.2.e. (2002); Ellen K. Harrison, et al., *U.S. Tax'n of Foreign Trusts, Trusts With Non-U.S. Grantors and Their U.S. Beneficiaries, in* Sophisticated Estate Planning Techniques (ALI-ABA Course No. SJ016 Sept. 2003).

[240] IRC § 663(a)(1).

[ii] Distributions in Kind[241]

FNGT trustees can distribute appreciated securities in kind, but not claim a distribution deduction for the value distributed that exceeds the FNGT's adjusted basis.[242] This defers the tax until the U.S. beneficiary recognizes the capital gain and, therefore, will distribute greater value to the beneficiary without exceeding DNI.

[iii] Use of Holding Company[243]

If an FNGT holds investments through a holding company, the trust will have not DNI (and therefore no UNI) until the holding company pays dividends to the FNGT. This allows the trust to accumulate income at the holding company level and ensure that all distributions to FNGT beneficiaries constitute current distributions.

Caution. This strategy runs the risk of running afoul of the following tax regimes, each of which has negative tax consequences:

1. Passive foreign investment company, which subjects U.S. beneficiaries to the PFIC tax;[244]
2. Foreign personal holding company;[245]
3. Controlled foreign corporation.[246]

[iv] Investment in High Yield Securities[247]

Because the throwback rules only apply to accumulation distributions after the current year's DNI is exhausted, one effective way to avoid the throwback rule is to change the FNGT's investment mix in years that distributions are desired to increase DNI. If DNI equals or exceeds the contemplated distribution, there should be no accumulation distribution.

[5] Loans to U.S. Beneficiaries Treated as Distributions

[a] In General

IRC Section 643(i) provides that, if a foreign trust loans cash or marketable securities directly or indirectly to any U.S. grantor or beneficiary, or any U.S. person who is related to such grantor or beneficiary, then the amount of such loan is treated as a distribution by that trust to such grantor or beneficiary.

---

[241] *See* Henry Christensen, III, *International Estate Planning* § 4.09[5][b] (2002).
[242] IRC § 643(e).
[243] *See* Henry Christensen, III, *International Estate Planning* § 4.09[5][a] (2002).
[244] IRC §§ 1291-1298.
[245] IRC §§ 551-558.
[246] IRC §§ 951-964.
[247] *See* Henry Christensen, III, *International Estate Planning* § 4.09[5][b] (2002).

[b] Definitions and Special Rules

For purposes of this rule, the following definitions and special rules apply.

[i] Cash

Cash includes foreign currencies and cash equivalents.[248]

[ii] Related Person

For purposes of this rule, a person is related to another person if the relationship between them would cause a loss disallowance under IRC Section 267 (but applying IRC Section 267(c)(4) as if the family of an individual includes the spouses of the members of the family) or IRC Section 707(b).[249]

[iii] Trust not Treated as Simple Trust

A trust that is treated as making a distribution under this rule is treated as a complex trust.[250]

[iv] Subsequent Transactions Regarding Loan Principal

IRC Section 643(i)(3) provides that this rule applies, then "any subsequent transaction between the trust and the original borrower regarding the principal of the loan (by way of complete or partial repayment, satisfaction, cancellation, discharge, or otherwise) shall be disregarded for purposes of this title."

[c] Loans of Marketable Securities

As noted above, under IRC Section 643(e), unless the trustee elects otherwise, the amount of a distribution other than cash is the lesser of (a) the trust's basis in the distributed property or (b) its fair market value. Therefore, it appears that if an FNGT trust lends marketable securities with a fair market value that exceeds its basis, the deemed distribution under this rule will be the amount of the basis unless the trustee elects to recognize gain on the distribution.

[6] Intermediary Rule—Distributions Through Intermediaries

[a] General Rule

The IRC treats a U.S. person (*i.e.*, recipient) who receives property from another person (*i.e.*, an intermediary) who received such property from a foreign trust as having received the property directly from such trust if the property the recipient receives was derived directly/indirectly from such foreign trust.[251]

---

[248] IRC § 643(i)2)(A).
[249] IRC § 643(i)(2)(B).
[250] IRC § 643(i)(2)(C).
[251] IRC § 643(h).

[b] Exception for Grantors

This rule does not apply if the person from whom the recipient receives the property is the grantor of the foreign trust.

[c] Treasury Regulations—Limit Rule to Tax Avoidance Transactions

Treasury regulations only apply this intermediary rule if the transaction in question has a principal purpose of avoiding U.S. tax. (Note that the IRC itself does not make tax avoidance a prerequisite to application of the intermediary rule).[252]

[d] Tax Avoidance Purpose

Treasury regulations deem tax avoidance motivation to exist for purposes of the intermediary rule if *all* the following requirements are satisfied:[253]

[i] Relationship

The U.S. recipient is related[254] to a grantor of the foreign trust, or has another relationship with a grantor that establishes a reasonable basis to or conclude that the grantor would make a gratuitous transfer to such recipient;

[i] Time Frame

The U.S. recipient receives from the intermediary, within the period beginning 24 months before and ending 24 months after the intermediary receives the property from the foreign trust, either:

- The property the intermediary received from the foreign trust;
- Proceeds from such property; or
- Property in substitution for such property; and

[i] Lack of Alternate Explanation

The U.S. recipient cannot prove to IRS satisfaction that:

a. The intermediary has a relationship with the U.S. recipient that establishes a reasonable basis to conclude that the intermediary would make a gratuitous transfer to such recipient;
b. The intermediary acted independently of the grantor and the trustee of the foreign trust;
c. The intermediary is not an agent of the U.S. recipient under generally applicable U.S. agency principles; and
d. The U.S. recipient timely complied with the reporting requirements of IRC Section 6039F (notice of large gifts from foreign persons, which is filed on Form 3520), if applicable, if the intermediary is a foreign person.

---

[252] Reg. § 1.643(h)-1(a)(1).
[253] Reg. § 1.643(h)-1(a)(2).
[254] For this purpose, "related" means related within the meaning of Reg. § 1.643(h)-1(e).

[e] Exceptions

The intermediary rule does not apply in the following cases.

[i] Non-Gratuitous Transfers

The intermediary rule does not apply to the extent that either the transfer from the foreign trust to the intermediary or the transfer from the intermediary to the U.S. recipient does not constitute a gratuitous transfer within the meaning of Section 1.671-2(e)(2).[255]

[ii] Grantor as Intermediary

The intermediary rule does not apply if the intermediary is the grantor of the portion of the trust from which the transferred property that is derived.[256]

[f] *Effect of Application of Intermediary Rule*

[i] General Rule

If the intermediary rule applies, then the intermediary is treated as an agent of the foreign trust. In addition, the property is treated as transferred to the U.S. recipient in the year the property is transferred, or made available, by the intermediary to the U.S. recipient (as opposed to when the trust transfers the property to the intermediary). Also, the fair market value of the property transferred is determined as of the date of the transfer by the intermediary to the U.S. recipient.

[ii] Alternative Treatment

If the IRS determines, or if the taxpayer can prove to IRS satisfaction, that the intermediary is the U.S. recipient's agent (rather than the foreign trust's agent), then the IRS will treat the property as transferred to the U.S. recipient in the year the foreign trust transfers the property to the intermediary. In addition, the fair market value of the property transferred will be determined on the transfer date from the foreign trust to the intermediary.[257]

[iii] Intermediary's Taxation

If the intermediary rule applies to cause the property to be treated as transferred directly by the foreign trust to a U.S. recipient, the intermediary does not take into account such property's fair market value in computing his/her gross income.[258]

[g] *De Minimis Rule*

The intermediary rule does not apply if, during the U.S. recipient's tax year, the aggregate fair market value of all property transferred to such person from all foreign trusts either directly or through one or more intermediaries does not exceed $10,000.

---

[255] Reg. § 1.643(h)-1(b)(1).
[256] IRC § 643(h); Reg. § 1.643(h)-1(b)(1).
[257] Reg. § 1.643(h)-1(c)(2).
[258] Reg. § 1.643(h)-1(c)(3).

[h] Related Parties

For purposes of the intermediary rule, a U.S. recipient is treated as related to a foreign trust grantor trust if the U.S. recipient and the grantor are related for purposes of IRC Section 643(i)(2)(B), with the following modifications. First, for purposes of applying IRC Section 267 (other than IRC Section 267(f)) and IRC Section 707(b)(1), "at least 10 percent" is used instead of "more than 50 percent" each place it appears. Second, the principles of IRC Section 267(b)(10), using "at least 10 percent" instead of "more than 50 percent," apply to determine whether two corporations are related.

[E] Tax Treatment of U.S. Beneficiaries of Foreign Grantor Trusts ("FGTs")

[1] Background

Prior to the 1996 Act, trusts created by non-U.S. persons were subject to the "grantor trust" rules to the same extent as trusts created by U.S. persons. As a result, the grantor trust rules shifted such a trust's income, for virtually all U.S. income tax purposes, from the trust to its non-U.S. grantor.

Where a foreign person was treated as the owner of the income because of the grantor trust rule, then (i) the foreign grantor-owner was taxed on such income only under the limited rules for taxing NRA individuals and foreign corporations; and (ii) distributions from the trust to U.S. beneficiaries were treated as gifts from the foreign grantor-owner. Such gifts generally were not taxable to the U.S. beneficiary as income.[259] Gift tax would frequently not be imposed (*e.g.*, where the subject matter of the gift was situated outside the United States).

Today, IRC Section 672(f) generally denies grantor trust status to trusts with non-U.S. grantors.

[2] General Rule—No Grantor Status for Foreign Grantors

IRC Section 672(f)(1) provides that the grantor trust rules apply only to the extent that they cause an amount to be currently taken into account (directly or through one or more entities) in computing the income of a U.S. citizen/resident or a domestic corporation. Accordingly, they apply to the extent that any part of a trust, upon application of the grantor trust rules without regard to IRC Section 672(f), is treated as owned by a U.S. citizen or resident, or domestic corporation.

The grantor trust rules specifically do not apply to any part of a trust to the extent that, upon application of the grantor trust rules without regard to IRC Section 672(f), that part would be treated as owned by a non-U.S. citizen or resident, or a foreign corporation.

Any portion of the trust that is not treated as owned by a grantor or another person is treated as a nongrantor trust.

For purposes of this rule, the determination of the part of a trust treated as owned by the grantor or other person is made based on the trust terms,

---

[259] Rev. Rul. 69-70, 1969-1 C.B. 182.

application of the grantor trust rules, and IRC Section 671 and the regulations thereunder.[260]

EXAMPLE 6-21

Chandler, an NRA, funds an irrevocable domestic trust, DTrust, for the benefit of his son, Marlowe, a U.S. citizen, with X Corporation stock. Chandler's brother, Raymond, also a U.S. citizen, contributes Y Corporation stock to the Dtrust for Marlowe's benefit. Chandler has a reversionary interest within the meaning of IRC Section 673 in the X stock, which would cause him to be treated as the owner of the X stock upon application of the grantor trust rules without regard to IRC Section 672(f). Raymond has a reversionary interest within the meaning of IRC Section 673 in the Y stock that would cause Raymond to be treated as the owner of the Y stock upon application of the grantor trust rules without regard to IRC Section 672(f). The trustee has discretion to accumulate or currently distribute income of DTrust to Marlowe. Here, because Chandler is an NRA, the grantor trust rules (ignoring IRC Section 672(f)) would not cause the portion of the trust consisting of the X stock to be treated as owned by a U.S. citizen/resident. Therefore, Chandler is not treated as an owner of the portion of the trust consisting of the X stock under the grantor trust rules. However, because Raymond is a U.S. citizen, the foregoing rule does not apply to him, and he is treated as the owner of the portion of the trust consisting of the Y stock under the grantor trust rules.[261]

---

[3] Exceptions to the General Rule

[a] Certain Revocable Trusts

The IRC Section 672(f) foreign nongrantor trust rule does not apply to any part of a trust if the grantor retains the power to revest[262] absolutely in him/herself title to such part, and such power is exercisable solely by the grantor without the approval or consent of any other person.[263] This exception is satisfied if, in the event of the grantor's incapacity, this power is exercisable by a guardian or other person who has unrestricted authority to exercise such power on the grantor's behalf.[264] This exception is also satisfied if the grantor can exercise such power

---

[260] Reg. § 1.672(f)-1(a)(2).

[261] Reg. § 1.672(f)-1(b).

[262] For purposes of this rule, the grantor is treated as having a power to revest for a taxable year of the trust only if the grantor has such power for a total of 183 or more days during the taxable year of the trust. If the first or last taxable year of the trust (including the year of the grantor's death) is less than 183 days, the grantor is treated as having a power to revest for purposes of paragraph (a)(1) of this section if the grantor has such power for each day of the first or last taxable year, as the case may be. Reg. § 1.672(f)-3(a)(2).

[263] Reg. § 1.672(f)-3(a)(1).

[264] Reg. § 1.672(f)-3(a)(1).

only with the approval of a related or subordinate party who is subservient to the grantor.[265]

The IRC Section 672(f) foreign nongrantor trust rule does not apply to any part of a trust that was treated as owned by the grantor under IRC Section 676 (revocable trusts) on September 19, 1995, if it would continue to be so treated thereafter. However, this exception does not apply to any portion of the trust attributable to gratuitous transfers to the trust after September 19, 1995. This exception also is subject to certain rules relating to separate accounting for gratuitous transfers to the trust after September 19, 1995, under Treas. Reg. Section 1.672(f)-3(d).[266]

EXAMPLE 6-22[267]

Dashiell, a foreign person, creates and funds a revocable trust, Hammett Trust, for the benefit of his children, who are resident aliens. The trustee is a foreign bank, Maltese Bank, which is owned and controlled by Dashiell and Nick, who is Dashiell's brother. The power to revoke the Hammett Trust and revest absolutely in Dashiell title to the trust property is exercisable by Dashiell, but only with the approval or consent of Maltese Bank. The trust instrument contains no standard that Maltese Bank must apply in determining whether to approve or consent to the revocation of the Hammett Trust. There are no facts that would suggest that Maltese Bank is not subservient to Dashiell. Therefore, the revocable trust exception applies to the Hammett Trust.

EXAMPLE 6-23[268]

Assume the same facts as in Example 21, except that Dashiell dies. After Dashiell's death, Nick has the power to withdraw the assets of the Hammett Trust, but only with the approval of Maltese Bank. There are no facts that would suggest that Maltese Bank is not subservient to Nick. However, the revocable trust exception is no longer applicable, because Nick is not a grantor of Hammett Trust.

EXAMPLE 6-24[269]

Assume the same facts as in Example 21, except that neither Dashiell nor any member of Dashiell's family has any substantial ownership interest or other

---

[265] Reg. § 1.672(f)-3(a)(1).
[266] Reg. § 1.672(f)-3(a)(3).
[267] Reg. § 1.672(f)-3(a)(4), Ex. 1.
[268] Reg. § 1.672(f)-3(a)(4), Ex. 2.
[269] Reg. § 1.672(f)-3(a)(4), Ex. 3.

connection with Maltese Bank. Dashiell can remove and replace Maltese Bank at any time for any reason. Although Dashiell can replace Maltese Bank with a related or subordinate party if Maltese Bank refuses to approve or consent to Dashiell's decision to revest the trust property in himself, Maltese Bank is not a related or subordinate party. Therefore, the revocable trust exception does not apply.

[b] Trusts That Can Distribute Only to the Grantor or Grantor's Spouse

[i] In General

The IRC Section 672(f) foreign nongrantor trust rule does not apply to a trust of which, at all times during the grantor's lifetime the only amounts distributable from such trust are amounts distributable to the grantor or the grantor's spouse.[270] For purposes of this exception, payments of amounts that are not gratuitous transfers do not constitute amounts that are distributable.

Note. This exception may also apply to only part of a trust.[271]

[ii] Amounts Distributable in Discharge of Legal Obligations

A trust will not fail this exception solely because amounts are distributable from the trust to discharge a legal obligation of the grantor or the grantor's spouse. For this purpose, an obligation is considered a "legal obligation" if it is enforceable under the local law of the jurisdiction where the grantor or his/her spouse resides.[272]

For purposes of this exception, obligations to related persons do not constitute legal obligations unless they are either:

- Contracted bona fide and for adequate and full consideration in money or money's worth; or
- The related person is legally separated from the grantor under a decree of divorce or separate maintenance; or
- The obligation is to support an individual who both: (a) would be treated as the grantor's (or his spouse's) dependent under IRC Section 152(a)(1)-(9) (without regard to the requirement that over half of the individual's support be received from the grantor or the spouse of the grantor); and (b) is either permanently and totally disabled, or less than 19 years old.[273]

[c] Compensatory Trusts

The IRC Section 672(f) foreign nongrantor trust rule does not apply to a certain compensatory trusts. Specifically, treasury regulations provide that it does not apply to any part of (1) a nonexempt employees' trust described in IRC Section 402(b), including a trust created on behalf of a self-employed individual; (2) a trust, including a trust created on behalf of a self-employed individual, that

---

[270] Reg. § 1.672(f)-3(b).
[271] Reg. § 1.672(f)-3(b).
[272] Reg. § 1.672(f)-3(b)(2)(i).
[273] Reg. § 1.672(f)-3(b)(2).

would be a nonexempt employees' trust described in IRC Section 402(b) but for the fact that the trust's assets are not set aside from the claims of creditors of the actual or deemed transferor within the meaning of Treas. Reg. Section 1.83-3(e); and (3) any additional category of trust that the Commissioner may designate in revenue procedures, notices, or other guidance published in the Internal Revenue Bulletin.

[4] Recharacterization of Certain Purported Gifts

IRC Section 672(f)(4) provides that direct or indirect transfers from a partnership or foreign corporation that are treated as gifts by the transferee may be recharacterized in the manner that the Treasury Department deems appropriate to prevent the avoidance of the IRC Section 672(f) rules. The preamble to the proposed regulations under IRC Section 672(f)(4) indicated that this provision was intended as a backstop to IRC Section 672(f) and was intended to "prevent taxpayers from avoiding the general rule of section 672(f) by using a partnership or foreign corporation as a substitute for a trust."[274]

[5] Trusts Created by Certain Foreign Corporations

IRC Section 672(f)(3) and the regulations thereunder provide that the IRC Section 672(f) foreign nongrantor trust rule does not apply to controlled foreign corporations ("CFC"), passive foreign investment companies ("PFICs"), or foreign personal holding companies ("FPHCs"). This prevents CFCs, PFICs, and FPHCs from using foreign trusts to avoid U.S. tax.

Although IRC Section 672(f)(3) treats CFCs, PFICs and FPHCs as domestic corporations for grantor trust rule purposes, IRC Section 674(f)(4) (discussed above) gives the IRS authority to recharacterize purported gifts to U.S. persons that are made directly or indirectly from foreign corporations. The regulations treat gifts to U.S. persons that are made from a trust funded by a foreign corporation as if made indirectly by such corporation if that incurs more U.S. tax.

[6] Recharacterizing Beneficiary as Grantor of Inbound Trust

[a] In General

If a foreign person is treated as owning part of a trust, any U.S. beneficiary of such trust is treated as grantor to the extent he directly/indirectly transferred property[275] to such foreign person in excess of transfers to the U.S. beneficiary

---

[274] Preamble to Prop. Reg. § 1.672(f)-4, 62 Fed. Reg. 30,785, 30.788 (June 5, 1997), referring to Staff of the Joint Committee on Taxation, 104th Cong., 2d Sess., "General Explanation of the Tax Legislation Enacted in the 104th Congress," at 271 (1996) (Committee Print).

[275] For purposes of this rule, the term property includes cash, and a transfer of property does not include a transfer that is not a gratuitous transfer (within the meaning of Reg. § 1.671-2(e)(2)). In addition, a gift is not taken into account to the extent such gift would not be characterized as a taxable gift under IRC § 2503(b). Reg. § 1.672(f)-5.

from the foreign person.[276] This rule applies without regard to whether such beneficiary was a U.S. beneficiary at the time of any transfer.[277]

[b] Exception

This recharacterization rule does not apply to the extent the U.S. beneficiary can prove to IRS satisfaction that his/her transfer to the foreign person was wholly unrelated to any transaction involving the trust.

EXAMPLE 6-25

Dashiell, an NRA, contributes property to the Maltese Corporation, a foreign corporation that is wholly owned by Dashiell. Maltese Corporation creates a foreign trust, Maltese Trust, for the benefit of Dashiell and his children. Maltese Trust is revocable by Maltese Corporation without the approval or consent of any other person. Maltese Corporation funds Maltese Trust with the property received from Dashiell. Dashiell and his family move to the United States. Under the recharacterization rule of IRC Section 672(f)(5), Dashiell is treated as a grantor of Maltese Trust.

Note. Dashiell may also be treated as an owner of Maltese Trust under IRC Section 679(a)(4).

EXAMPLE 6-26

Nick, a U.S. citizen, makes a gratuitous transfer of $1 million to his aunt, Nora, an NRA. Nora creates a foreign trust, the Charles Trust, for the benefit of Nick and his children. Charles Trust is revocable by Nora without the approval or consent of any other person. Nora funds the Charles Trust with the property that she received from Nick. Under the recharacterization rule of IRC Section 672(f)(5), Nick is treated as a grantor of the Charles Trust.

Note. Nick also would be treated as an owner of the Charles trust as a result of IRC Section 679.

---

[276] Reg. § 1.672(f)-5.
[277] Reg. § 1.672(f)-5.

[7] Pre-immigration Trusts

[a] In General

If an NRA becomes a U.S. person and has a residency starting date within five years after transferring property to a foreign trust (the "Original Transfer"), the IRC treats him as having transferred to the trust on the residency starting date an amount equal to the portion of the trust attributable to the property he transferred in the Original Transfer.[278]

[b] Cessation of Application of Grantor Trust Rules

If an NRA who is treated as owning any part of a trust under the grantor trust rules, subsequently ceases to be so treated, he/she is treated as making the original transfer to the foreign trust immediately before the trust ceases to be treated as owned by him/her.

[c] Treatment of Undistributed Income

For purposes of the pre-immigration trust rules, the property deemed transferred to the foreign trust on the residency starting date includes undistributed net income, as defined in IRC Section 665(a), attributable to the property deemed transferred. However, undistributed net income for periods before the individual's residency starting date is taken into account only for purposes of determining the amount of the property deemed transferred. In other words, an NRA who immigrates to the United States within five years of creating a foreign trust is deemed to have transferred to the trust both (a) the amounts previously transferred, plus (b) the undistributed income and appreciation in the assets held by the trust and attributable to the original transfers, on the date that the NRA becomes a U.S. resident.

[F] Reporting Requirements

The following forms may need to be filed in connection with a foreign trust.

- Form 3520: Annual return to report transactions with foreign trusts and receipt of certain foreign gifts.
- Form 3520-A: Annual information return of foreign trust with U.S. owner.
- Form 1040 NR: U.S. nonresident alien income tax return.
- Form 4970: Tax on accumulation distributions of trusts.
- Form TD F 90-22.1: Report of foreign bank and financial accounts.
- FIRPTA reports.

---

[278] IRC § 679(a)(4); Reg. § 1.679-5(a).

§ 6.07 CHECKLIST OF FAPT ISSUES

The planner should use the following checklist to ensure that no critical issue is overlooked in connection with his analysis:

[A] In General[1]

____1. Is the planner considering the use of FAPTs in the asset protection plan? If yes, the planner should analyze the following issues:

   (a) How should the FAPT plan be structured?[2]
   (b) What is the ability of U.S. creditors to reach the FAPT's assets?[3]
   (c) What are the tax consequences, both in the United States and in the foreign jurisdiction selected, of the FAPT settlor?[4]
   (d) What reports must the planner ensure are properly filed?[5]

[B] Creditor's Rights Against Trust Parties[6]

____2. Has the planner conducted an analysis of the rights of creditors against various trust parties?
   If not, the planner should analyze the following issues:

   (a) Would the proposed transfer of assets into the irrevocable trust constitute a fraudulent conveyance?
   If yes, the trust corpus will be exposed to the claims of the settlor's creditors.[7]
   (b) Under the proposed arrangement, does the settlor retain a beneficial interest in the trust?
   If yes, the settlor's creditors can reach assets available to the settlor through that beneficial interest.
   (c) Under the proposed arrangement, does the settlor retain both a beneficial interest and a general power of appointment?
   If yes, the settlor's creditors can reach all of the trust corpus that is subject to the general power of appointment.
   (d) Under the proposed arrangement, does the settlor retain a special power of appointment that is not in the settlor's favor, and no other interest in the trust?
   If yes, the settlor's creditors generally cannot reach the trust corpus.

---

§ 6.07   [1] See § 6.01.
[2] See §§ 6.04–6.05.
[3] See §§ 6.02–6.03.
[4] See § 6.06.
[5] See § 6.06.
[6] See §§ 6.02–6.03.
[7] See Chapter 2.

(e) Does the proposed arrangement violate any spousal right of the settlor's spouse?

If yes, the settlor's spouse may be able to reach the trust corpus.[8]

(f) If the settlor entered bankruptcy, what impact would this have on the
trust?

Generally, when a settlor enters bankruptcy, the bankruptcy estate acquires all
of the settlor's legal and equitable interests in property as of the bankruptcy
proceeding commencement.

(g) What does the applicable law in the FAPT jurisdictions under consideration provide regarding the enforcement of foreign judgments
and fraudulent conveyances?

Most FAPT jurisdictions do not recognize foreign judgments, do require
plaintiffs to use attorneys licensed in that jurisdiction, do prohibit contingent
fee arrangements, and do provide a body of substantive law that is much more
favorable to the FAPT client than United States law is.

[C] Structure of the FAPT Transaction[9]

___3. Has the planner properly designed the FAPT transaction?
The planner should ensure that the FAPT incorporates the following features:

(a) The trust should be irrevocable for a term of years.

(b) The trust beneficiaries, ideally, should not include the settlor, and the
trust should be designed as a discretionary trust.

(c) The planner should consider using three trustees, (1) a U.S. trust
company, (2) a U.S. individual, and (3) a foreign trustee.

(d) The trust should include a duress provision that provides that, in the
event of duress, the following will occur. If the duress occurs in the
trust's situs jurisdiction, the duress provision should provide that the
trustee is deemed to transfer the trust fund and income therefrom to
an emergency trustee in a different jurisdiction and to have changed
the forum of the management, control, and administration of the
trust from the original jurisdiction (or prior jurisdiction in the
event of a prior transfer) to the jurisdiction that the emergency trustee resides in. If the duress occurs in the United States, the duress
provision should:

(i) Require the foreign trustee to discharge the United States co-
trustees;

(ii) Require the foreign trustee to ignore advice given by the committee of trust protectors or advisors when a U.S. court or trustee
in bankruptcy compels such advice;

---

[8] *See* Chapter 5 for a discussion of spousal rights.
[9] *See* §§ 6.04–6.05.

(iii) Require the foreign trustee to ignore committee of trust protectors decisions to discharge or replace trustees when such decisions result from court orders or other compulsion; and

(iv) When the planner structures the trust as the sole owner of a corporation of which the settlor is the sole director and officer, require the foreign trustee to liquidate the corporation immediately.

[D] FAPT Taxation[10]

____ 4. Has the planner analyzed the tax issues raised by the FAPT? If not, the planner should address the following issues:

(a) What must the planner do to ensure that the FAPT constitutes a grantor trust for United States federal income taxation purposes?

(b) Once the FAPT is properly structured so that it constitutes a grantor trust, how will the FAPT and the various FAPT parties be taxed for United States federal income taxation purposes?

(c) How will the FAPT be taxed in the situs jurisdiction?

(d) What governmental reports must the planner ensure are filed in connection with the FAPT transaction?

§6.08 FAPT COST-BENEFIT WORKSHEET

The planner should use the following worksheet to analyze the benefits and costs of using FAPTs in monetary terms.

(1) __+ asset protection provided by the FAPT
(2) __− expenses of forming the FAPT and complying with required formalities
(3) __− costs unique to the FAPT
(4) __− tax burden associated with using the FAPT
(5) __+ tax benefits associated with using the FAPT

_____

= net benefit/cost of using the FAPT

[10] *See* §6.06.

7

Retitling Assets: Concurrent Ownership of Property

§7.01 GENERALLY

The planner may use certain forms of concurrent ownership as part of the asset protection plan.[1] The planner will want to consider three basic forms of property. These include tenancies by the entirety, tenancies in common, and joint tenancies. When clients convey solely owned property into tenancies in common or joint tenancies with others (for example, their children, spouses, or parents), this transfer greatly reduces the value of the property to creditors. When clients convey solely owned property into tenancies by the entirety with their spouses, this may completely protect the subject property from the client's sole creditors.

Planning Pointer.   The planner should analyze the following:

1. What are the asset protection benefits of the tenancy by the entirety form of property ownership?[2]
2. What are the asset protection benefits of the tenancy in common form of property ownership?[3]
3. What are the asset protection benefits of the joint tenancy form of property ownership?[4]
4. What are the estate and gift tax consequences of concurrent ownership of property?[5]

Planning Pointer.   As with all forms of asset protection, the planner must conduct a fraudulent conveyance analysis as part of the asset protection analysis. Specifically, the planner must ensure that the conveyance of property into a different form of entity does not constitute a fraudulent conveyance.[6]

---

§7.01 [1] *See generally* Russell D. Niles & William F. Walsh, Concurrent Estates and Their Characteristics, in 2 American Law of Property §6.6 (A. James Casner ed., 1952 & Supp. 1977); 4A Richard R. Powell, The Law of Real Property Ch. 52 (Patrick J. Rohan rev. ed., 1993); Committee on Death Taxation of Estates and Trusts, Probate and Trust Division, *Property Owned with Spouse: Joint Tenancy, Tenancy by the Entireties and Community Property*, II Real Prop. Prob. & Tr. J. 405 (1976); Michael F. Beausang, Jointly Owned Property (1992); Susan L. Repetti et al., When Is Joint Ownership Appropriate (1992); George P. Levendis, *Asset Protection and the Owners of Investment Real Estate*, 8 Tax Mgmt. Real Est. J. 23 (1992).

[2] *See* §7.02.
[3] *See* §7.03.
[4] *See* §7.04.
[5] *See* §§7.05–7.06.
[6] *See* Chapter 2.

§ 7.02   TENANCY BY THE ENTIRETY

A tenancy by the entirety is a form of concurrent ownership that can be held only by a husband and wife. A tenancy by the entirety is created and exists only if the required unities of time, title, interest, possession, and a valid marriage are present. It resembles a joint tenancy in that it possesses similar unities and because the surviving tenant, after the other's death, takes the whole property. However, it differs from joint tenancies in that only spouses to valid marriages may participate in it, that neither tenant can force the partition of the tenancy by themselves, and that the tenancy ends on the marriage's termination.[1]

Today many states recognize tenancies by the entirety.[2] In such states, planners may use the tenancy by the entirety as part of an asset protection plan. They may do this because the tenancy by the entirety is generally immune to the claims of an individual spouse's creditors.[3] Therefore, when a couple is likely to be subjected to the claims of one spouse or the other, but not of both spouses combined, the planner may protect property by placing it into a tenancy by the entirety. On the other hand, tenancies by the entirety do not protect property from the claims of both spouses combined. Therefore, when the planner anticipates such claims, she should not use a tenancy by the entirety.

Planning Pointer. The planner must consider the following issues when considering tenancies by the entirety:

1. What rights do the client's creditors have against property held in a tenancy by the entirety?[4]
2. How does the planner create a tenancy by the entirety for the client?[5]
3. What key characteristics, which the planner should be aware of, do tenancies by the entirety possess?[6]
4. What are the gift and estate tax consequences of using a tenancy by the entirety?[7]
5. What events terminate a tenancy by the entirety?[8]
6. How do tenancies by the entirety compare to tenancies in common and joint tenancies?

---

§ 7.02   [1] 4A Richard R. Powell, The Law of Real Property ¶ 620[1] <$>trick J. Rohan rev. ed., 1993). *See, e.g.,* Estate of Reigle, 652 A.2d 853 (Pa. Super. Ct. 1995).

[2] *See* 4A Richard R. Powell, The Law of Real Property ¶ 620[4] (Patrick J. Rohan rev. ed., 1993) for an analysis of the status of the tenancy by the entirety in each of the 50 states plus the District of Columbia; Annotation, *Estate by entireties as affected by statute declaring nature of tenancy under grant or devise to two or more persons,* 32 A.L.R.3d 570 (1970 & Supp. 1995); Annotation, *Estates by entirety in personal property,* 64 A.L.R.2d 8 (1959); Annotation, *Proceeds or derivatives of real property held by entirety as themselves held by entirety,* 22 A.L.R.4th 459 (1983 & Supp. 1995); Annotation, *Retrospective operation of legislation affecting estates by the entireties,* 27 A.L.R.2d 868 (1953).

[3] *See* § 7.02[B].

[4] *See* § 7.02[B].

[5] *See* § 7.02[C].

[6] *See* § 7.02[A].

[7] *See* § 7.02[C], [D].

[8] *See* § 7.02[D].

Planning Pointer. In some jurisdictions, clients against whom judgments have been entered may be able to reconvey property they own in joint tenancies with their spouses into tenancies by the entirety without such transfers constituting fraudulent conveyances.[9]

[A] Characteristics of Tenancy by the Entirety

To evaluate a tenancy by the entirety, the planner must understand its key characteristics. Specifically, the planner must evaluate:

1. The ability of the tenants to partition the tenancy by the entirety;
2. The amount of control the husband obtains over property held in the tenancy by the entirety;
3. Each spouse's right to possess the property held in the tenancy by the entirety;
4. The treatment of property held in the tenancy by the entirety if one or both spouses file for bankruptcy.

[1] No Unilateral Partition

The tenancy by the entirety's primary characteristic is that neither spouse may solely defeat the other's right of survivorship by mortgage, conveyance, partition, or any other means.[10]

EXAMPLE 7-1

Jack and Jill own Hillacre in a tenancy by the entirety. In 1990 Jack wants to sell Hillacre to Martha. However, Jill refuses to agree to a sale of Hillacre. Here, the most that Jack could possibly convey to Jill would be a present interest in Hillacre, subject to Jill's right of survivorship. Also, in many jurisdictions, Jack cannot convey any interest in Hillacre.

EXAMPLE 7-2

The same facts as Example 7-1, except that the jurisdiction involved allows Jack to convey a present interest in Hillacre, and Jack sells a present interest in

---

[9] *See, e.g.,* E.J. McKernan Co. v. Gregory, 643 N.E.2d 1370 (Ill. App. Ct. 1994).

[10] Committee on Death Taxation of Estates and Trusts, Probate and Trust Division, *Property Owned with Spouse: Joint Tenancy, Tenancy by the Entireties and Community Property,* II Real Prop. Prob. & Tr. J. 409 (1976).

Hillacre to Martha. In 1992 Jack dies. Here, Martha loses any interest that she holds in Hillacre and Jill obtains full and complete title to Hillacre.

[2] Husband's Control over Property

At common law, the husband possesses exclusive control over the property held in a tenancy by the entirety.[11] Some states still recognize this rule.[12] Where this rule still applies, the husband may lease, mortgage, or convey good title and possession to the property during his life without his wife's consent.[13] When the husband conveys the property under this rule, the transferee takes her interest subject to the wife's contingent right of survivorship.[14]

EXAMPLE 7-3

The same facts as Example 7-1, except that Jack, Jill, and Hillacre are located in a jurisdiction that follows the common law rule. Here, Martha takes a valid interest in Hillacre. However, if Jack predeceases Jill, Martha loses her interest in Hillacre to Jill.

In states that follow the common law rule, the husband also may encumber the property.[15] More importantly, in these jurisdictions the hus-

---

[11] Committee on Death Taxation of Estates and Trusts, Probate and Trust Division, *Property Owned with Spouse: Joint Tenancy, Tenancy by the Entireties and Community Property*, II Real Prop. Prob. & Tr. J. 409 (1976); Russell D. Niles & William F. Walsh, Concurrent Estates and Their Characteristics, in 2 American Law of Property § 6.6(b) (A. James Casner ed., 1952 & Supp. 1977); 4A Richard R. Powell, The Law of Real Property ¶ 622[21] (Patrick J. Rohan rev. ed., 1993). *See, e.g.*, Pray v. Stebbins, 4 N.E. 824 (Mass. 1886).

[12] Forbes v. United States, 472 F. Supp. 840 (D. Mass. 1979); Arbesman v. Winer, 468 A.2d 633 (Md. 1983); Committee on Death Taxation of Estates and Trusts, Probate and Trust Division, *Property Owned with Spouse: Joint Tenancy, Tenancy by the Entireties and Community Property*, II Real Prop. Prob. & Tr. J. 409 (1976); Russell D. Niles & William F. Walsh, Concurrent Estates and Their Characteristics, in 2 American Law of Property § 6.6(b) (A. James Casner ed., 1952 & Supp. 1977); 4A Richard R. Powell, The Law of Real Property ¶ 622[21] (Patrick J. Rohan rev. ed., 1993).

[13] Krokyn v. Krokyn, 390 N.E.2d 733 (Mass. 1979); Porth v. Porth, 165 S.E.2d 508 (N.C. Ct. App. 1969); Committee on Death Taxation of Estates and Trusts, Probate and Trust Division, *Property Owned with Spouse: Joint Tenancy, Tenancy by the Entireties and Community Property*, II Real Prop. Prob. & Tr. J. 409 (1976); Russell D. Niles & William F. Walsh, Concurrent Estates and Their Characteristics, in 2 American Law of Property § 6.6(b) (A. James Casner ed., 1952 & Supp. 1977); 4A Richard R. Powell, The Law of Real Property ¶ 622[21] (Patrick J. Rohan rev. ed., 1993).

[14] Committee on Death Taxation of Estates and Trusts, Probate and Trust Division, *Property Owned with Spouse: Joint Tenancy, Tenancy by the Entireties and Community Property*, II Real Prop. Prob. & Tr. J. 409 (1976); Russell D. Niles & William F. Walsh, Concurrent Estates and Their Characteristics, in 2 American Law of Property § 6.6(b) (A. James Casner ed., 1952 & Supp. 1977); 4A Richard R. Powell, The Law of Real Property ¶ 622[2] (Patrick J. Rohan rev. ed., 1993).

[15] Russell D. Niles & William F. Walsh, Concurrent Estates and Their Characteristics, in 2 American Law of Property § 6.6(b) (A. James Casner ed., 1952 & Supp. 1977).

band's creditors may reach the entire property held in the tenancy by the entirety, subject to the wife's right of survivorship.[16]

Many states have enacted married women's property acts. These jurisdictions have followed different approaches in determining the impact of these statutes on tenancies by the entirety. For example, Massachusetts still follows the common law rule, holding that such statutes have not changed the husband's common law rights in the tenancy by the entirety.[17]

Other jurisdictions, such as New York and New Jersey, hold that the married women's property acts changed the common law rule regarding the tenancy by the entirety. In these jurisdictions, each spouse now holds a one-half interest in the property that he or she may convey or encumber.[18] In these jurisdictions, each individual spouse's creditors may reach their one-half interest to satisfy the spouse's debt, subject to the other spouse's right to possession and contingent right of survivorship.[19]

Still other jurisdictions hold that the married women's property acts have modified the common law rule regarding tenancies by the entirety so that neither spouse holds any interest that he or she may solely convey or encumber. In these jurisdictions, creditors of one spouse, but not of both spouses, cannot reach property held in a tenancy by the entirety to satisfy their debts.[20] Furthermore, the majority rule in these jurisdictions holds that purported transfers or creditors of one spouse cannot reach the property held in the tenancy by the entirety if that spouse survives the other spouse.[21]

EXAMPLE 7-4

Same facts as in Example 7-3, except that Jack, Jill, and Hillacre are located in Massachusetts. Here the result is the same as in Example 7-3.

---

[16] King v. Greene, 153 A.2d 49 (N.J. 1959); Russell D. Niles & William F. Walsh, Concurrent Estates and Their Characteristics, in 2 American Law of Property § 6.6(b) (A. James Casner ed., 1952 & Supp. 1977); H.D. Warren, Annotation, *Interest of spouse in estate by entireties as subject to satisfaction of his or her individual debt*, 166 A.L.R. 969, 971-74 (1947).

[17] Raptes v. Pappas, 155 N.E. 787 (Mass. 1927); Russell D. Niles & William F. Walsh, Concurrent Estates and Their Characteristics, in 2 American Law of Property § 6.6(b) (A. James Casner ed., 1952 & Supp. 1977).

[18] Russell D. Niles & William F. Walsh, Concurrent Estates and Their Characteristics, in 2 American Law of Property § 6.6(b) (A. James Casner ed., 1952 & Supp. 1977).

[19] Russell D. Niles & William F. Walsh, Concurrent Estates and Their Characteristics, in 2 American Law of Property § 6.6(b) (A. James Casner ed., 1952 & Supp. 1977); H.D. Warren, Annotation, *Interest of spouse in estate by entireties as subject to satisfaction of his or her individual debt*, 166 A.L.R. 969 (1947).

[20] Russell D. Niles & William F. Walsh, Concurrent Estates and Their Characteristics, in 2 American Law of Property § 6.6(b) (A. James Casner ed., 1952 & Supp. 1977).

[21] United States v. Nathanson, 60 F. Supp. 193 (E.D. Mich. 1945); Bloomfield v. Brown, 25 A.2d 354 (R.I. 1942); Russell D. Niles & William F. Walsh, Concurrent Estates and Their Characteristics, in 2 American Law of Property § 6.6(b) (A. James Casner ed., 1952 & Supp. 1977).

EXAMPLE 7-5

Same facts as Example 7-3, except that the jurisdiction involved is one that holds that the married women's property acts modify the common law rule to provide that neither spouse holds an interest that it may solely convey or encumber. Here, Jack's conveyance to Martha will not be valid.

[3] Right of Possession

Generally, when a husband and wife hold property in a tenancy by the entirety, each spouse receives the right to possess the entire property.[22] Each spouse also receives the right to protect the property from outsiders[23] and from waste by the other spouse.[24]

[4] Tenancy by the Entirety as an Asset in Bankruptcy

Generally, the bankruptcy trustee of one spouse cannot reach property held in a tenancy by the entirety.[25] However, when the bankrupt spouse receives the power to transfer the property alone within six months of a bankruptcy adjudication, the bankruptcy trustee may acquire the property as of the date of the bankruptcy.[26]

Caution. If both spouses enter individual bankruptcy proceedings, the bankruptcy trustee may consolidate the two proceedings.[27] This allows the bankruptcy trustee to reach property held in a tenancy by the entirety. To avoid this, the planner should advise clients to structure any future bankruptcy proceedings so that both spouses are not in bankruptcy simultaneously.

---

[22] Lewis v. United States, 485 F.2d 606 (Ct. Cl. 1973); Connolly v. Connolly, 448 So. 2d 641 (Fla. Dist. Ct. App. 1984); 4A Richard R. Powell, The Law of Real Property ¶ 622[3] (Patrick J. Rohan rev. ed., 1993).

[23] MacFarland v. State, 29 N.Y.S.2d 996 (Ct. Cl. 1941); 4A Richard R. Powell, The Law of Real Property ¶ 622[3] (Patrick J. Rohan rev. ed., 1993).

[24] Tannis v. Tannis, 213 N.Y.S.2d 320 (Sup. Ct. 1961); 4A Richard R. Powell, The Law of Real Property ¶ 622[3] (Patrick J. Rohan rev. ed., 1993).

[25] Blodgett v. United States, 161 F.2d 47 (8th Cir. 1947); 4A Richard R. Powell, The Law of Real Property ¶ 622[4] (Patrick J. Rohan rev. ed., 1993); Andrew J. Heaton, *Administration of Entireties Property in Bankruptcy*, 50 Ind. L.J. 305 (1985).

[26] 11 U.S.C. § 110 (1988); 4A Richard R. Powell, The Law of Real Property ¶ 622[4] (Patrick J. Rohan rev. ed., 1993). *See, e.g.,* Williams v. Peyton (*In re* Williams), 1997 U.S. App. LEXIS 832 (4th Cir. 1997) (Fourth Circuit held that Chapter 7 bankruptcy trustee could sell property that debtor owned with her husband as tenancy by the entirety property to pay off the claims of the couple's joint creditors).

[27] *In re* Hawks, 471 F.2d 305 (4th Cir. 1973); Reid v. Richardson, 304 F.2d 351 (4th Cir. 1962); 4A Richard R. Powell, The Law of Real Property ¶ 622[4] (Patrick J. Rohan rev. ed., 1993).

[B] Asset Protection Aspects

The planner's primary concern is with the asset protection benefits that tenancies by the entirety yield for clients. The precise asset protection benefits hinge on the clients' ability to convey their interest in the tenancy by the entirety under applicable state law.[28] In states retaining the common law rule giving the husband exclusive control over the property held in the tenancy by the entirety, the husband's creditors generally may reach the property, subject to the wife's right of survivorship.[29]

> **Planning Pointer.** In states retaining the common law rule giving the husband exclusive control over property held in the tenancy by the entirety, planners should not use tenancies by the entirety as an asset protection planning device on a husband's behalf. Second, the planner should be very cautious about using a tenancy by the entirety for a wife in such a jurisdiction because this device deprives her of control over the property during her husband's life.

EXAMPLE 7-6

George, an accountant, is married to Nancy, a housewife. George and Nancy live in a state that recognizes the common law rule by which the husband receives the power to convey all tenancy by the entirety interests, subject to the wife's right of survivorship. George asks Bill, an asset protection planner, to advise George about whether he should transfer Homeacre, separate property that George acquired before marrying Nancy, into a tenancy by the entirety with Nancy. Bill's analysis shows that if George transfers Homeacre into a tenancy by the entirety, this plan will have the following consequences:

1. George loses an interest in Homeacre to Nancy. Specifically, this interest equals Nancy's right to take full ownership of Homeacre if she survives George.
2. George's ability to dispose of Homeacre on his own is restricted, from a practical standpoint, by Nancy's right of survivorship. Specifically,

---

[28] *See* § 7.02[A]. Annotation, *Interest of spouse in estate by entireties as subject to satisfaction of his or her individual debt*, 75 A.L.R.2d 1172 (1961); Annotation, *Estate by entireties as affected by statute declaring nature of tenancy under grant or devise to two or more persons*, 32 A.L.R.3d 570 (1970 & Supp. 1995).

[29] Committee on Death Taxation of Estates and Trusts, Probate and Trust Division, *Property Owned with Spouse: Joint Tenancy, Tenancy by the Entireties and Community Property*, II Real Prop. Prob. & Tr. 1409 (1976); Russell D. Niles & William F. Walsh, Concurrent Estates and Their Characteristics, in 2 American Law of Property § 6.6(b) (A. James Casner ed., 1952 & Supp. 1977); 4A Richard R. Powell, The Law of Real Property ¶ 622[2] (Patrick J. Rohan rev. ed., 1993).

Homeacre will be worth substantially less to potential buyers because of Nancy's right of survivorship in Homeacre.

3. George's creditors may reach Homeacre after George transfers it into the tenancy by the entirety. However, Homeacre will be less valuable to them than it would be if they obtained full and complete title because of Nancy's right of survivorship.

Therefore, the tenancy by the entirety provides George with only marginal asset protection. The benefit comes to George in the loss of value to potential creditors because of Nancy's right of survivorship. On the other hand, George loses a significant amount of control over the property as the cost of this marginal asset protection. Consequently, Bill should recommend that George not transfer Homeacre into a tenancy by the entirety with Nancy.

EXAMPLE 7-7

Same facts as Example 7-6, except that Nancy owns Homeacre as separate property and she requests advice from Bill. Here, Bill's analysis shows that if Nancy transfers Homeacre into a tenancy by the entirety with George, this plan will have the following consequences:

1. Nancy's individual creditors cannot reach Homeacre after she transfers it into the tenancy by the entirety.
2. Nancy loses the ability to convey any interest by herself in Homeacre to other parties. Furthermore, George acquires this ability. Therefore, Nancy becomes exposed to the risk that George could convey Homeacre, subject to Nancy's right of survivorship.

Therefore, although the tenancy by the entirety provides Nancy with substantial asset protection benefits, it does so with a substantial cost.

Some jurisdictions hold that each spouse maintains a one-half interest in property held in a tenancy by the entirety that each spouse may convey or encumber.[30] In such jurisdictions, each spouse's individual creditors may reach that one-half interest to satisfy their claim, subject to the other spouse's right of survivorship.[31]

---

[30] Russell D. Niles & William F. Walsh, Concurrent Estates and Their Characteristics, in 2 American Law of Property § 6.6(b) (A. James Casner Ed., 1952 & Supp. 1977).

[31] Russell D. Niles & William F. Walsh, Concurrent Estates and Their Characteristics, in 2 American Law of Property § 6.6(b) (A. James Casner ed., 1952 & Supp. 1977); H.D. Warren, Annotation, *Interest of spouse in estate by entireties as subject to satisfaction of his or her individual debt*, 166 A.L.R. 969 (1947).

Planning Pointer. In jurisdictions holding that each spouse holds a one-half interest in tenancy by the entirety property, the planner may obtain the following benefits with a tenancy by the entirety:

1. The tenancy by the entirety completely protects half of that property from the individual debts of one spouse.
2. The tenancy by the entirety provides some protection for the other one-half interest that the spouse retains. The property is less valuable to that spouse's creditors because (a) any interest the creditors take, they take subject to the other spouse's right of survivorship, and (b) they can only take a one-half interest in the property instead of a whole interest.
3. Because property held in the tenancy by the entirety is less valuable to the vulnerable spouse's creditors than it would otherwise be, that spouse is placed into a much better bargaining position to compromise debts.

EXAMPLE 7-8

Louis and Marie are married. They hold Frenchacre in a tenancy in common. It is their only asset of substance, and it is worth $10 million. Marie is a physician. Both Louis and Marie are concerned about the possibility of litigation. However, they procrastinate and do nothing. In 1990 Robespierre sues Marie for malpractice and wins a $20 million judgment against her. Here, Robespierre may reach Marie's interest in Frenchacre.

EXAMPLE 7-9

Same facts as Example 7-8, except that Louis and Marie consult an asset protection planner, Talleyrand. Talleyrand advises Louis and Marie to convert their ownership of Frenchacre to a tenancy by the entirety. They follow Talleyrand's advice and do this. Here, although Robespierre may reach Marie's one-half interest in Frenchacre, he may only take an interest that is subject to Louis's right of survivorship. This makes Frenchacre much less valuable to him. Consequently, this places Marie in a much improved bargaining position to compromise her debt to Robespierre.

Most states hold that neither spouse maintains any interest that can be separately conveyed, encumbered, or reached by the individual creditors of either spouse.[32] In these states neither spouse's individual creditors can reach the property contained in the tenancy by the entirety.

Planning Pointer. In states holding that neither spouse maintains any interest that can be separately conveyed or encumbered, the tenancy by the entirety becomes an extremely valuable asset protection tool. In these jurisdictions, planners may protect property held by one or both spouses from each spouse's creditors by transferring such property into a tenancy by the entirety.

EXAMPLE 7-10

Same facts as in Example 7-9, except that Louis, Marie, and Frenchacre are located in a jurisdiction where neither spouse can separately convey or encumber any interest in a tenancy by the entirety. Here, Robespierre cannot reach any interest in Frenchacre.

Caution. As with all tenancies by the entirety, creditors of both spouses may reach property held in a tenancy by the entirety.

EXAMPLE 7-11

Same facts as Example 7-10, except that Louis and Marie file a joint United States federal income tax return. In 1992 the IRS audits Louis and Marie. The IRS determines that Louis substantially underreported his income for 1990 and 1991 from his construction company, Versailles Builders. The IRS

---

[32] Elko v. Elko, 49 A.2d 441 (Md. 1946); Sawada v. Endo, 561 P.2d 1291 (Haw. 1977); Roger A. Cunningham et al , The Law of Property § 5.5 (1984); Committee on Death Taxation of Estates and Trusts, Probate and Trust Division, *Property Owned with Spouse: Joint Tenancy, Tenancy by the Entireties and Community Property,* II Real Prop. Prob. & Tr. J. 409 (1976); Russell D. Niles & William F. Walsh, Concurrent Estates and Their Characteristics, in 2 American Law of Property § 6.6(b) (A. James Casner ed., 1952 & Supp. 1977); 4A Richard R. Powell, The Law of Real Property ¶ 622[2] (Patrick J. Rohan rev. ed., 1993). *See, e.g.,* Massie v. Yamrose, 169 B.R. 585 (W.D. Va. 1994) (court held that, under Virginia law, property held by tenants by the entirety is completely immune from claims of creditors of either spouse alone, and creditor may not enforce judgment against such property until and unless debtor spouse acquires an interest other than as tenant by the entirety).

assesses Louis and Marie with $20 million of additional taxes. Marie was aware of this substantial understatement of Louis's income; therefore, she does not qualify for innocent spouse relief. Here, the IRS may ultimately reach Frenchacre because the federal tax liability is a joint liability of both spouses.[33]

[C] Creation of Tenancy by the Entirety

The planner must consider the requirements for creating a tenancy by the entirety as part of the analysis. Generally, the planner must satisfy the four unities of time, title, interest, and possession to create a tenancy by the entirety.[34] Additionally, the planner must satisfy the unity of person requirement to create a valid tenancy by the entirety.[35]

Generally, the unity of time requirement refers to the requirement that the interests of all the tenants in the tenancy by the entirety vest at the same time. The unity of title requirement refers to the requirement that both tenants acquire their interests under the same title or deed. The unity of interest requirement refers to the requirement that the ownership shares of the tenants in the tenancy by the entirety be equal. The unity of possession requirement refers to the requirement that each tenant must possess an equal right to use and possess the whole property that is the subject of the tenancy by the entirety.[36] The planner must also ensure that the transaction satisfies the unity of person (valid marriage) requirement to create a valid tenancy by the entirety. Specifically, two persons can only become co-tenants in a tenancy by the entirety if they are legally married to each other.[37]

Planning Pointer. As a precautionary measure, the planner should request the client to provide the planner with a copy of the client's certificate of marriage. At a minimum, this will protect the planner in the event of misunderstanding on the client's behalf. This also will provide documentation should a creditor attack the tenancy by the entirety.

---

[33] *See* Chapter 10. *See also* Tony Thornton Auction Serv., Inc. v. United States, 791 F.2d 635 (8th Cir. 1986); Michael I. Saltzman, IRS Practice and Procedure ¶ 14.07[2][b] (2d ed. 1991).

[34] Roger A. Cunningham et al., The Law of Property § 5.5 (1984); 4A Richard R. Powell, The Law of Real Property ¶ 621 (Patrick J. Rohan rev. ed., 1993); Russell D. Niles & William F. Walsh, Concurrent Estates and Their Characteristics, in 2 American Law of Property § 6.6(a) (A. James Casner ed., 1952 & Supp. 1977).

[35] *Id.*

[36] Cornelius J. Moynihan, Introduction to the Law of Real Property Ch. 10 (2d ed. 1988).

[37] *In re* Estate of Suggs, 405 So. 2d 1360 (Fla. Dist. Ct. App. 1981); Roger A. Cunningham et al., The Law of Property § 5.5 (1984); 4A Richard R. Powell, The Law of Real Property ¶ 621 (Patrick J. Rohan rev. ed., 1993); Russell D. Niles & William F. Walsh, Concurrent Estates and Their Characteristics, in 2 American Law of Property § 6.6(a) (A. James Casner ed., 1952 & Supp. 1977); Annotation, *Character and incidents of estate created by a deed to persons as husband and wife who are not legally married*, 83 A.L.R.2d 1051 (1962).

EXAMPLE 7-12

Peter and Catherine, a doctor and accountant, respectively, live together in a jurisdiction that does not recognize common law marriages. Peter and Catherine, however, mistakenly believe that they have a valid common law marriage. They consult with Alexis, an asset protection planner. Alexis advises them to place Blackacre, a parcel of property that they want to purchase, into a tenancy by the entirety. Alexis informs Peter and Catherine that this will protect Blackacre from their individual creditors. They follow Alexis's advice and place Blackacre into a purported tenancy by the entirety. Subsequently, Charles sues Peter and wins a $5 million judgment against him. Charles then tries to reach Peter's interest in Blackacre. Peter argues that Charles cannot reach Blackacre because he and Catherine hold it in a tenancy by the entirety. Here, Charles may successfully attack the tenancy by the entirety because Peter and Catherine are not legally married. Consequently, a court probably will find that Peter and Catherine hold Blackacre in a joint tenancy or a tenancy in common. Thus, Charles can reach Peter's interest in Blackacre.

In rare cases, the grantees of a purported tenancy by the entirety may preserve the tenancy by the entirety by marrying before title vests.[38] In other cases, a tenancy by the entirety may be recognized when there is no marriage at all or when there is a voidable marriage if the party challenging the tenancy by the entirety is estopped for some reason,[39] or if the deed includes a recital of marriage, that is deemed conclusive.[40]

Planning Pointer. The general rule is that no tenancy by the entirety arises when no valid marriage exists at the time of the creation of the purported tenancy by the entirety.[41] Therefore, the planner should not rely on any exceptions to the marriage requirement when planning a transaction.

---

[38] 4A Richard R. Powell, The Law of Real Property ¶ 621[1] (Patrick J. Rohan rev. ed., 1993). *See, e.g.,* Chichester's Executor v. Vass, 15 Va. (I Munf.) 98 (1810).

[39] Kerivan v. Fogel, 22 So. 2d 584 (Fla. 1945); Franklin v. Franklin, 93 N.W.2d 321 (Mich. 1958); Estate of Whiteman v. Whiteman, 353 A.2d 386 (Pa. 1976); 4A Richard R. Powell, The Law of Real Property ¶ 621[1] (Patrick J. Rohan rev. ed., 1993).

[40] 4A Richard R. Powell, The Law of Real Property ¶ 621 [1] (Patrick J. Rohan rev. ed., 1993); Donald Kepner, *The Effect of an Attempted Creation of an Estate by the Entirety in Unmarried Grantees,* 6 Rutgers L. Rev. 550 (1952). *See, e.g.,* Orthwein v. Thomas, 21 N.E. 430 (111. 1889).

[41] Emmons v. Sanders, 342 P.2d 125 (Or. 1959); Lopez v. Lopez, 243 A.2d 588 (Md. 1968); Knight v. Knight, 458 S.W.2d 803 (Tenn. Ct. App. 1970); Russell D. Niles & William R Walsh, Concurrent Estates and Their Characteristics, in 2 American Law of Property § 6.6(a) (A. James Casner ed., 1952 & Supp. 1977); Annotation, *Estate created by deed to persons described as husband and wife but not legally married,* 9 A.L.R.4th 1189 (1981 & Supp. 1995); Annotation, *Rights of party to void marriage in respect of transfers or gifts to other in mistaken belief marriage was valid,* 14 A.L.R.2d 918 (1950).

Under the common law rule, any conveyance to a husband and wife creates a tenancy by the entirety.[42] Today, many jurisdictions presume that a conveyance to a husband and wife constitutes a tenancy by the entirety.[43]

Other jurisdictions hold that conveyances to a husband and wife, not clearly expressing an intent for the husband and wife to hold as co-tenants in a tenancy by the entirety, cause the married couple to hold a tenancy in common.[44]

Planning Pointer. The planner should ensure that the conveyance to a married couple expressly states that it intends to create a tenancy by the entirety.

Conveyances to a married couple and a third person cause the husband and wife to take fractional interests as tenants by the entirety and the third person to become a joint tenant or tenant in common with the married couple.[45]

EXAMPLE 7-13

Charles conveys Blackacre to Oliver, Oliver's wife Olivia, and Oliver's brother, Orson. Charles, Oliver, Olivia, Orson, and Blackacre are located in a jurisdiction that presumes that conveyances to a husband and wife results in a tenancy by the entirety. Here, Oliver and Olivia hold a fractional interest in Blackacre, probably a one-half interest. They hold this interest as tenants by the entirety. Oliver and Olivia hold this interest as either tenants in common or as joint tenants with Orson.

Conveyances to two or more married couples transfer to each couple a fractional interest in the property as tenants by the entirety, and each couple holds as tenants in common or as joint tenants with the other couples.[46]

---

[42] 2 William Blackstone, Commentaries *181; Cornelius J. Moynihan, Introduction to the Law of Real Property (2d ed. 1988); 4A Richard R. Powell, The Law of Real Property ¶ 621[21] (Patrick J. Rohan rev. ed., 1993); Roger A. Cunningham et al., The Law of Property § 5.5 (1984).

[43] Cornelius J. Moynihan, Introduction to the Law of Real Property 220 (2d ed. 1988); 4A Richard R. Powell, The Law of Real Property ¶ 621[21] (Patrick J. Rohan rev. ed., 1993); Roger A. Cunningham et al., The Law of Property § 5.5 (1984). *See, e.g.,* Carrick v. Carrick, 679 S.W.2d 800 (Ark. Ct. App. 1984); Butler v. Butler, 322 N.W.2d 488 (Mich. Ct. App. 1983); Madden v. Madden, 486 A.2d 401 (Pa. Super. Ct. 1984).

[44] D.C. Code Ann. § 45-816 (1961); Mass. Ann. Laws ch. 184, § 7 (Law. Co-op. 1987); Cornelius J. Moynihan, Introduction to the Law of Real Property 220 (2d ed. 1988); 4A Richard R. Powell, The Law of Real Property ¶ 621[2] (Patrick J. Rohan rev. ed., 1993); Roger A. Cunningham et al., The Law of Property § 5.5 (1984); David E. Hollowell, *Resulting Trusts in Entireties Property when Wife Furnishes Purchase Money,* 17 Wake Forest L. Rev. 415 (1981).

[45] Fulton v. Katsowney, 174 N.E.2d 366 (Mass. 1961); Cornelius J. Moynihan, Introduction to the Law of Real Property 220-21 (2d ed. 1988); 4A Richard R. Powell, The Law of Real Property ¶ 621[4] (Patrick J. Rohan rev. ed., 1993).

[46] Burt v. Edmonds, 456 S.W.2d 342 (Tenn. 1970); 4A Richard R. Powell, The Law of Real Property ¶ 621[4] (Patrick J. Rohan rev. ed., 1993); Roger A. Cunningham et al., The Law of Property § 5.5 (1984).

EXAMPLE 7-14

Same facts as in Example 7-13, except that Orson is married to Pauline and that Charles's conveyance is also to Pauline. Here, Oliver and Olivia hold a fractional interest in Blackacre as tenants by the entirety. Orson and Pauline also hold a fractional interest in Blackacre as tenants by the entirety. Each couple holds its interest as a joint tenant or as a tenant in common with the other couple, depending on local law.

At common law, one spouse who solely owns property cannot convey that property into a valid tenancy by the entirety for both spouses. The unities of time and title are lacking under such an arrangement.[47] Consequently, common law requires the grantor to transfer property to a straw man who then conveys the property back to the spouses. Today, most jurisdictions allow one spouse who solely owns property to convey such property to both spouses as a valid tenancy by the entirety.[48]

Caution. Some states still preclude one spouse who solely owns property from directly conveying that property into a valid tenancy by the entirety for both spouses. The planner must carefully check local law.

At common law, married couples cannot hold personal property in a tenancy by the entirety because the husband acquires absolute ownership of his wife's personal property.[49] Some jurisdictions still follow this rule regarding the ability of a couple to hold personal property in a tenancy by the entirety.[50] Many others allow married couples to hold personal property in tenancies by the entirety when they indicate their intent to create a tenancy by the entirety.[51]

---

[47] Cornelius J. Moynihan, Introduction to the Law of Real Property 221 (2d ed. 1988); 4A Richard R. Powell, The Law of Real Property ¶ 621[5] (Patrick J. Rohan rev. ed., 1993); Roger A. Cunningham et al., The Law of Property § 5.5 (1984).

[48] Mass. Ann. Laws ch. 184, § 8 (Law. Co-op. 1987); N.J. Rev. Stat. § 37:2 18 (1968); Nicholson v. Shipp, 486 S.W.2d 691 (Ark. 1972); Kluck v. Metsger, 349 S.W.2d 919 (Mo. 1961); Cornelius J. Moynihan, Introduction to the Law of Real Property 221 (2d ed. 1988); 4A Richard R. Powell, The Law of Real Property ¶ 621[5] (Patrick J. Rohan rev. ed., 1993); Roger A. Cunningham et al., The Law of Property § 5.5 (1984); W.W. Allen, Annotation, *Character of tenancy created by owner's conveyance to himself and another, or to another alone, of an undivided interest,* 44 A.L.R.2d 595 (1955).

[49] 4A Richard R. Powell, The Law of Real Property ¶ 621[5] (Patrick J. Rohan rev. ed., 1993); Roger A. Cunningham et al., The Law of Property § 5.5 (1984); Annotation, *Proceeds or derivatives of real property held by entirety as themselves held by entirety,* 22 A.L.R.2d 459 (1952); Annotation, *Estates by entirety in personal property,* 64 A.L.R.2d 8 (1959).

[50] 4A Richard R. Powell, The Law of Real Property ¶ 621[5] (Patrick J. Rohan rev. ed., 1993); Roger A. Cunningham et al., The Law of Property § 5.5 (1984). *See, e.g., In re* Blumenthal's Estate, 141 N.E. 911 (N.Y. 1923); Hawthorne v. Hawthorne, 192 N.E.2d 20 (N.Y. 1963).

[51] Carlisle v. Parker, 188 A. 67 (Del. Super. Ct. 1936); Dodson v. National Title Ins. Co., 31 So. 2d 402 (Fla. 1947); 4A Richard R. Powell, The Law of Real Property ¶ 621[4] (Patrick J. Rohan rev. ed., 1993); Roger A. Cunningham et al., The Law of Property § 5.5 (1984).

Caution. The planner may have difficulty creating a tenancy by the entirety in a bank account where either co-tenant may withdraw funds. The ability to withdraw funds unilaterally amounts to a right to unilaterally terminate the tenancy by the entirety. This makes the bank account inconsistent with the basic nature of a tenancy by the entirety.[52]

The fact that one spouse pays all the consideration for the property does not preclude both spouses from holding the property as a tenancy by the entirety.[53] However, if the property is conveyed to the husband in violation of the wife's rights (for example, when the husband fraudulently procures the deed in both spouses' names, but the wife is emitled to a deed in her name alone), equity will prevent the husband from receiving benefits to his wife's disadvantage or from taking the property by survivorship, by impressing a trust on the property for the wife's protection.

[D] Termination of Tenancy by the Entirety

A tenancy by the entirety may be terminated in four different ways. Specifically, it may be terminated by a sale of the property by both spouses, by a release from one spouse to the other, by the death of one spouse, and by the divorce of the spouses.

First, a tenancy by the entirety may be terminated by the sale of the property by both spouses to a third party.[54] However, in some jurisdictions, sale proceeds of tenancy by the entirety property are also held as entireties property. For example, in *Fairfield v. United States (In re Ballard)*,[55] the Fourth Circuit, in a case of first impression, held that sales proceeds of tenancy by the entirety property were also held as entireties property. Consequently, in that case, on the wife's subsequent death, the husband became the property's sole owner and, thus, proceeds became subject to tax debt without regard to whether such debt was sole or joint tax debt.

EXAMPLE 7-15

Paul and Jane, who are husband and wife, own Blackacre in a tenancy by the entirety. Paul and Jane sell Blackacre to Connie. This sale terminates Paul and Jane's tenancy by the entirety.

---

[52] Roger A. Cunningham et al., The Law of Property §5.5 (1984); Annotation, *Estate by entireties in personal property*, 117 A.L.R. 915 (1938); Annotation, *Estates by entirety in personal property*, 8 A.L.R. 1017 (1920); Committee on Death Taxation of Estates and Trusts, Probate and Trust Division, *Property Owned with Spouse: Joint Tenancy, Tenancy by the Entireties and Community Property*, II Real Prop. Prob. & Tr. J. 405, 408 (1976).

[53] Russell D. Niles & William F. Walsh, Concurrent Estates and Their Characteristics, in 2 American Law of Property §6.6(a) (A. James Casner ed., 1952 & Supp. 1977). *See, e.g.*, Hargett v. Hargett, 24 So. 2d 305 (Fla. 1946); Sutorius v. Mayor, 170 S.W.2d 387 (Mo. 1943).

[54] 4A Richard R. Powell, The Law of Real Property ¶ 624[1] (Patrick J. Rohan rev. ed., 1993). *See, e.g.*, Pace v. Woods, 177 So. 2d 779 (Fla. Dist. Ct. App. 1965).

[55] 65 F.3d 367 (4th Cir. 1995).

Second, a married couple may terminate a tenancy by the entirety by one spouse releasing his or her interest in the tenancy by the entirety to the other spouse.[56]

EXAMPLE 7-16

Same facts as Example 7-15, except that instead of selling Blackacre to Connie, Paul releases his tenancy by the entirety interest in Blackacre to Jane. This terminates the tenancy by the entirety.

Third, the death of one spouse causes the termination of the tenancy by the entirety.[57] Specifically, after one spouse's death, the tenancy by the entirety terminates. The other spouse then takes a fee simple, absolute interest in the property that he or she previously held in the tenancy by the entirety. However, if one spouse murders the other, the survivor/murderer often does not take possession of the whole property. In such cases, courts often impose a constructive trust on the murderer's estate or declare the victim's estate vested with a half-interest in the property.[58]

The planner should note that property held in a tenancy by the entirety generally is not included in the decedent spouse's probate estate. Consequently, such property is not subject to the surviving spouse's right of election.[59] However, in Uniform Probate Code jurisdictions, the decedent's probate estate includes tenancy by the entirety property to the extent that the decedent provided the consideration for such property and such property is subject to the surviving spouse's elective share of the decedent's estate.[60]

EXAMPLE 7-17

Sam and Sheila live in a jurisdiction not bound by the Uniform Probate Code. They hold Greenacre in a tenancy by the entirety. Sam dies. Here, the tenancy by the entirety terminates, and Sheila takes a fee simple interest in Greenacre. Greenacre will not be included in Sam's probate estate.

---

[56] 4A Richard R. Powell, The Law of Real Property ¶ 624[1] (Patrick J. Rohan rev. ed., 1993). *See, e.g.,* Backus v. Backus, 346 A.2d 790 (Pa. 1975).

[57] Beall v. Beall, 434 A.2d 1015 (Md. 1981); Kahn v. Kahn, 371 N.E.2d 809 (N.Y. 1977), 4A Richard R. Powell, The Law of Real Property ¶ 624[1] (Patrick J. Rohan rev. ed., 1993).

[58] 4A Richard R. Powell, The Law of Real Property ¶ 624[1] (Patrick J. Rohan rev. ed., 1993).

[59] *Id.*

[60] U.P.C. § 2-202(3), 8 U.L.A. 75-77 (1969); RUPC § 2-202 (1990), 8 U.L.A. 90-92 (Supp. 1992); 4A Richard R. Powell, The Law of Real Property ¶ 624[1] (Patrick J. Rohan rev. ed., 1993); Elias Clark, *The Recapture of Testamentary Substitute to Preserve the Spouse's Elective Share: An Appraisal of Recent Statutory Reforms,* 2 Conn. L. Rev. 513 (1970).

Finally, if the spouses divorce, the tenancy by the entirety terminates.[61] The divorce converts the tenancy by the entirety into a tenancy in common with each spouse receiving a fractional interest in the property, usually a one-half interest.[62] Generally, the husband and wife continue to hold the property as a tenancy by the entirety until their divorce becomes final.[63]

EXAMPLE 7-18

Chuck and Di own Blueacre in a tenancy by the entirety. They divorce, with their divorce becoming final on July 1, 1993. Here, their tenancy by the entirety terminates on July 1, 1993. After this date, each holds a one-half interest in a tenancy in common. Their individual creditors may reach Blueacre on or after July 1, 1993, because they no longer hold Blueacre in a tenancy by the entirety.

---

§7.03 TENANCY IN COMMON

The following summary of the law applicable to tenancies in common will enable the planner to compare a tenancy by the entirety with a tenancy in common. Generally, a tenancy in common is a form of concurrent ownership by which the co-tenants each hold (1) a distinct and separate interest in the property, plus (2) a common right to enjoy and possess the property with all the other co-tenants.[1]

Unlike the tenancy by the entirety, which requires five unities for its creation, the tenancy in common only requires one unity. Specifically, the tenancy in common only requires the unity of possession. The unity of possession requirement refers to the requirement that each co-tenant must be entitled to possess and enjoy the whole property and every part thereof, subject to the same right of possession held by the other co-tenants.[2] Consequently, unlike the tenancy by the entirety, the tenancy in common does not require co-tenants to be married.

---

[61] Sebold v. Sebold, 444 F.2d 864 (D.C. Cir. 1971); Travis v. Benson, 360 A.2d 506 (D.C. 1976); Dobbyn v. Dobbyn, 471 A.2d 1068 (Md. Ct. Spec. App. 1984); 4A Richard R. Powell, The Law of Real Property ¶ 624[3] (Patrick J. Rohan rev. ed., 1993); Roger A. Cunningham et al., The Law of Property §5.5 (1984); *See, e.g.,* Cordova v. Mayer (*In re* Cordova), 177 B.R. 527 (E.D. Va. 1995), *aff'd,* 73 F.3d 38 (4th Cir. 1996) (when the debtor was awarded tenancy by the entirety property in divorce, her property interest became converted into a fee simple interest, which did not possess the asset protection benefits of tenancy by the entirety property).

[62] Sebold v. Sebold, 444 F.2d 864 (D.C. Cir. 1971); Travis v. Benson, 360 A.2d 506 (D.C. 1976); Dobbyn v. Dobbyn, 471 A.2d 1068 (Md. Ct. Spec. App. 1984); 4A Richard R. Powell, The Law of Real Property ¶ 624[3] (Patrick J. Rohan rev. ed., 1993); Roger A. Cunningham et al., The Law of Property §5.5 (1984).

[63] *In re* Ikuta's Estate, 639 P.2d 400 (Haw. 1981); 4A Richard R. Powell, The Law of Real Property ¶ 624[3] (Patrick J. Rohan rev. ed., 1993).

§7.03 [1] Cornelius J. Moynihan, Introduction to the Law of Real Property 213-14 (2d ed. 1988); Roger A. Cunningham et al., The Law of Property §5.2 (1984).

[2] *Id.*

Also, unlike both the tenancy by the entirety and the joint tenancy, the co-tenants do not need to satisfy the unities of time, title, or interest. Specifically, the co-tenants may acquire their interests at different times because they do not need to satisfy the unity of time. The co-tenants also may acquire the interest from a different conveyance than any or all other co-tenants due to the lack of the unity of title requirement. Finally, a co-tenant may hold a different interest from any or all other co-tenants because there is no unity of interest requirement.

The right of survivorship is not an incident of the tenancy in common. Therefore, the tenant may devise her interest in the tenancy in common through her will. Furthermore, tenancy in common interests are generally freely alienable.[3] Thus, tenants in common may generally transfer their interests without the consent of co-tenants.[4]

> **Planning Pointer.** Because a tenant's tenancy in common interest is freely alienable, the tenant's creditors may generally reach the tenancy in common interest.[5] Therefore, the tenancy in common offers very little asset protection compared to the tenancy by the entirety. The tenancy in common's primary asset protection benefit is the decrease in value of the property held in the tenancy in common compared to the value of such property if it were solely held by the creditor.

EXAMPLE 7-19

Ted owns Blackacre. In 1990 Ted converts his fee simple interest in Blackacre into a tenancy in common with Sam and Dora, Ted's two children. This transaction effectively cuts the financial exposure of Blackacre to Ted's creditors to one-third of what it was before the conversion into the tenancy in common. On the other hand, this transaction exposes Blackacre to the creditors of Sam and Dora.

> **Planning Pointer.** Once a creditor does reach a tenant's tenancy in common interest, that creditor may then begin an action to partition the

---

[3] Roger A. Cunningham et al., The Law of Property § 5.2 (1984); Russell D. Niles & William F. Walsh, Concurrent Estates and Their Characteristics, in 2 American Law of Property § 6.10 (A. James Casner ed., 1952 & Supp. 1977).

[4] Moore v. Foshee, 38 So. 2d 10 (Ala. 1948); Wilk v. Vencill, 180 P.2d 351 (Cal. 1947); Sun Oil Co. v. Oswell, 62 So. 2d 783 (Ala. 1953); Schank v. North Am. Royalties, Inc., 201 N.W.2d 419 (N.D. 1972); Roger A. Cunningham et al., The Law of Property § 5.2 (1984); Russell D. Niles & William F. Walsh, Concurrent Estates and Their Characteristics, in 2 American Law of Property § 6.10 (A. James Casner ed., 1952 & Supp. 1977).

[5] See, e.g., Cal. Civ. Proc. Code § 701.640 (Deering 1983).

property.[6] Planners using tenancies in common should consider using an agreement between the co-tenants imposing a restraint on alienation that prohibits judicial partition of a concurrent estate in fee simple. Such a restraint will generally be sustained if it is for a reasonable period of time.[7]

§7.04   JOINT TENANCY

The following summary of the law applicable to joint tenancies will enable the planner to compare tenancies by the entirety to joint tenancies. Generally, joint tenancies are estates in real or personal property owned by two or more persons under one conveyance, where all tenants hold an equal right to share in the possession and enjoyment of the property during their lives, and where right of survivorship is given to the tenants. The planner must ensure that the four unities of time, title, interest, and possession are present to create a joint tenancy.[1]

Planning Pointer. Planners selecting a joint tenancy should ensure that the conveyance expressly states that it intends to create a joint tenancy.

At common law, a grantor who solely owns property cannot convey that property to herself and other individuals as joint tenants. The unities of time and title are lacking under such an arrangement. Consequently, common law requires the grantor to transfer property to a straw man who then conveys the property back to the tenants.[2] Today, some jurisdictions allow a grantor who solely owns property to convey such property to herself and other individuals as joint tenants.[3] However, many other states still preclude the grantor who solely owns property from directly conveying that property into a valid joint tenancy for herself and other individuals. The planner must carefully check local law.

The primary characteristic of the joint tenancy is the right of survivorship. Specifically, on the death of a joint tenant, her interest passes to the other joint tenants. Joint tenants cannot pass their interests to their heirs by will or under intestacy statutes.[4]

Joint tenancy interests are generally freely alienable. Therefore, joint tenants generally may freely transfer their interests without the consent of

---

[6] Roger A. Cunningham et al., The Law of Property §§ 5.11-5.13 (1984); Russell D. Niles & William F. Walsh, Concurrent Estates and Their Characteristics, in 2 American Law of Property §§ 6.19-6.26 (A. James Casner ed., 1952 & Supp. 1977).

[7] Roger A. Cunningham et al., The Law of Property § 5.11 (1984).

§7.04   [1] Cornelius J. Moynihan, Introduction to the Law of Real Property 207-08 (2d ed. 1988); Roger A. Cunningham et al., The Law of Property § 5.3 (1984). *See, e.g.,* Hoover v. Smith, 444 S.E.2d 546 (Va. 1994).

[2] Cornelius J. Moynihan, Introduction to the Law of Real Property 209-11 (2d ed. 1988); Roger A. Cunningham et al., The Law of Property § 5.3 (1984).

[3] *Id.*

[4] *Id.*

other joint tenants.[5] When a joint tenant does transfer an interest to a third party (1) the remaining original joint tenants continue to hold their interests with each other as joint tenants, and (2) the remaining joint tenants hold their interests as tenants in common with the new tenant.[6]

EXAMPLE 7-20

Moe, Larry, and Joe own Blackacre as joint tenants. Moe transfers his interest in Blackacre to one of his creditors, Curly, in satisfaction of Moe's debt to Curly. After the transfer, Larry and Joe continue to hold their interests as joint tenants between themselves. However, they hold their interests as tenants in common with Curly.

Planning Pointer. Because a joint tenant's interest is freely alienable, the tenant's creditors may generally reach the joint tenancy interest.[7] Therefore, the joint tenancy offers much less asset protection than the tenancy by the entirety. The joint tenancy's primary asset protection benefit is the decrease in the joint tenancy property's value compared to the value of such property if it were solely held by the creditor.

EXAMPLE 7-21

Bob owns Blackacre. In 1989 Bob converts his fee simple interest in Blackacre into a joint tenancy with his two children Laura and Harry. In 1992 Jerry, one of Bob's creditors, wants to reach Bob's interest in Blackacre to satisfy his debt. Here, the most that Jerry could possibly reach would be Ted's joint tenancy interest in Blackacre, which is subject to Laura and Harry's right of possession. Because of this right of possession, this interest is much less valuable than if Bob owned a fee simple interest in Blackacre.

Planning Pointer. The planner should be aware that a creditor who reaches the joint tenancy interest may begin an action to partition the joint tenancy.[8]

---

[5] *Id.*

[6] *See* § 7.03.

[7] Cal. Civ. Proc. Code § 701.640 (Deering 1983).

[8] Roger A. Cunningham et al., The Law of Property §§ 5.11-5.13 (1984); Russell D. Niles & William F. Walsh, Concurrent Estates and Their Characteristics, in 2 American Law of Property §§ 6.19-6.26 (A. James Casner ed., 1952 & Supp. 1977). *See, e.g.,* Estate of Phillips v. Nyhus, 874 P.2d 154 (Wash. 1994).

The planner should consider using an agreement between the co-tenants imposing a restraint on alienation that prohibits judicial partition of a concurrent estate in fee simple. Such a restraint will generally be sustained if it is for a reasonable period of time.[9]

§7.05 TAX CONSEQUENCES OF NONSPOUSAL CONCURRENT OWNERSHIP

The planner must evaluate the transfer tax consequences of using concurrent ownership of property as part of an asset protection plan.[1] The creation of concurrent ownership interests in property may trigger the federal gift tax. Generally, the gratuitous creation of a tenancy in common interest will constitute a taxable gift. This rule generally holds true regardless of whether the donor is a co-tenant after the conveyance of the interest in the tenancy in common. This rule also generally holds true for conveyances of joint tenancy interests in property.[2] However, the planner must look carefully at the rights of the donee/tenant under local law to determine whether the donor retains the right to reverse or modify the donee's rights.[3] Where this occurs, the gift will not be taxable. For example, when the grantor creates a joint tenancy with another person in a bank account, this generally does not constitute a completed gift.[4]

For purposes of valuation, the planner should value the gift made at the amount that the recipient tenant could at will convert her interest into. The planner may use both the annual $10,000 gift tax exclusion and the unified credit to reduce the gift tax on the gift of a concurrent ownership interest.[5]

EXAMPLE 7-22

Alfred buys 100 shares of Gotham stock in the names of Alfred and Robert as joint tenants. Here, Alfred makes a completed gift of one-half the Gotham stock at the time of its acquisition. The rationale is that Robert receives the right to sever or partition the joint tenancy any time after the gift and take his one-half interest. Therefore, for gift tax purposes, Alfred values the gift at one-half of the fair market value of the Gotham stock at the time of the joint tenancy's creation.[6]

---

[9] Roger A. Cunningham et al., The Law of Property §5.11 (1984).
§7.05 [1] *See generally* Lewis D. Solomon & Susan Flax Posner, Tax Planning Strategies Ch. 16 (1992); Lewis D. Solomon et al., Federal Taxation of Estates, Trusts and Gifts Ch. 13 (1989); Richard B. Stephens et al., Federal Estate and Gift Taxation (5th ed. 1983 & Supp. 1992).
[2] Reg. §25.2511-1(h) (5) (1986).
[3] Lewis D. Solomon et al., Federal Taxation of Estates, Trusts and Gifts 566 (1989).
[4] *See* U.P.C. §6-103(a) (1969); Treas. Reg. §25.2511-1(h)(4) (1986).
[5] IRC §§2503(b), 2505 (1988).
[6] IRC §§2501(a)(1), 2511(a) (1988); Treas. Reg. §25.2511-1(h)(5) (1986).

Caution. When two or more persons jointly purchase property and one or more persons contribute more than their proportionate share of the purchase price, such person(s) make a taxable gift of the excess amount.[7] When joint tenants pay more than their share of mortgage payments on joint tenancy property without expectation of repayment, the excess constitutes a gift from that donor/tenant to the other tenants.[8]

When joint tenants enter a contractual agreement preventing alienation of their interests, a taxable gift may still occur but the valuation will be different. Specifically, the value of the interest conveyed must be determined actuarially because the joint tenants can only own the property if they survive all of the other joint tenants.[9]

At a tenant in common's death, the tenant only includes the fractional interest that tenant owned at death in her gross estate as property owned at death under IRC Section 2033.[10] However, at a joint tenant's death, when the joint tenancy was created by a gift of the property by someone other than any of the joint tenants, the decedent's gross estate includes that tenant's aliquot share of the joint tenancy. If a joint tenant created the joint tenancy, IRC Section 2040(a) requires that the decedent tenant's gross estate include the entire property, except to the extent that surviving tenants can show that they contributed to the property's acquisition.[11] For example, if the other tenants can show that they provided 100 percent of the consideration for the property, then no portion of the property would be included in the decedent tenant's gross estate.

Generally, in order for the decedent tenant's estate to determine what percent of the consideration was furnished by the survivors, the executor must bring forward sufficient facts to prove that the property was not bought entirely with the decedent tenant's funds.[12] Further, the consideration furnished by the surviving tenants for the property must never have been provided by the decedent tenant.[13]

Planning Pointer. The planner should use the following formula for determining the value of the decedent joint tenant's joint tenancy interest to be included in the decedent's gross estate:

---

[7] Lewis D. Solomon et al., Federal Taxation of Estates, Trusts and Gifts 567 (1989).

[8] Rev. Rul. 78-362, 1978-2 C.B. 248; Lewis D. Solomon et al., Federal Taxation of Estates, Trusts and Gifts 567 (1989)

[9] Lewis D. Solomon et al., Federal Taxation of Estates, Trusts and Gifts 567 (1989).

[10] IRC § 2033 (1988); Lewis D. Solomon et al., Federal Taxation of Estates, Trusts and Gifts 567 (1989).

[11] IRC § 2040(a) (1988); Lewis D. Solomon et al., Federal Taxation of Estates, Trusts and Gifts 570 (1989).

[12] Reg. § 20.2040-1 (a) (1958).

[13] Reg. § 20.2040-1(c)(5) (1958); Lewis D. Solomon et al., Federal Taxation of Estates, Trusts and Gifts 570 (1989).

+	original purchase price of property that decedent furnished
÷	total original purchase price of property
×	total fair market of property at date of decedent's death
=	amount that decedent's gross estate must include as the value of decedent's interest in the property

EXAMPLE 7-23[14]

Frank Father owns a fee simple interest in Blackacre. As part of an asset protection plan, Frank gives Blackacre to his three children, Albert, Betty, and Charles, as joint tenants with the right of survivorship. One year later, Betty dies. At this time Blackacre's fair market value equals $90,000. Here, Betty's estate includes $30,000, determined by dividing Blackacre's value by the number of joint tenants.

EXAMPLE 7-24

Frank Father and Charles also jointly purchased Purpleacre for $80,000 as joint tenants with the right of survivorship. Frank paid $60,000 for his interest, and Charles paid $20,000 for his interest. Frank dies when Purpleacre's fair market value equals $100,000. Here, Frank's gross estate must include $75,000 as the value of his interest in Purpleacre. Frank's executor calculates this value as follows:

+	$60,000 original purchase price of Purpleacre that Frank furnished
÷	$80,000 total original purchase price of Purpleacre
×	$100,000 total fair market of Purpleacre at date of Frank's death
=	$75,000 amount that Frank's gross estate must include as the value of Frank's interest in Purpleacre

To determine the consideration furnished by the surviving tenants, any consideration furnished by the decedent tenant to the surviving tenants for purposes of enabling those surviving tenants to enter the joint tenancy must be excluded from the survivor's contribution for purposes of the consideration furnished test. However, any income, which the survivor has recognized on the joint tenancy property from the time of the survivor's receipt of the decedent's consideration, is not excluded from the survivor's contribution for purposes of the consideration furnished test.[15]

[14] Lewis D. Solomon et al., Federal Taxation of Estates, Trusts and Gifts 570 (1989).
[15] Estate of Goldsborough v. Commissioner, 70 T.C. 1077 (1978), aff'd, 673 F.2d 1305, 1310 (4th Cir. 1982); Lewis D. Solomon et al., Federal Taxation of Estates, Trusts and Gifts 570-75 (1989).

Planning Pointer. Numerous judicial opinions have held that taxpayers may claim significant discounts for partial interests in real estate based on comparable sales of partial interests, the fact that most buyers do not want to sue for partition, and the fact that many properties are difficult, if not impossible, to partition. In such cases, the buyer of a partial interest really acquires only the right to force a sale to a third party and a right to a share of the proceeds.[16]

On the other hand, the IRS has historically objected to valuation discounts for partial interests in real estate. For example, in Letter Ruling 9336002, the IRS stated that if a buyer could sue to partition the property with relative ease, any discount must be limited to the estimated costs of partition. However, the Tax Court specifically rejected the IRS approach in *Williams v. Commissioner.*[17] There, the taxpayer made gifts of undivided one-half interests in certain real estate and later died owning the other one-half interest. The Tax Court upheld a total discount of 44 percent for the minority interests (30 percent for lack of control and a sequential 20 percent for lack of marketability). It expressly rejected the IRS argument that such discounts should be limited to costs of partitioning the property, finding that this approach did "not give adequate weight to other reasons for discounting a fractional interest in real property, such as lack of control and the historic difficulty of selling an undivided fractional interest in real property."[18]

§ 7.06   TAX CONSEQUENCES OF SPOUSAL CONCURRENT OWNERSHIP

Generally, the gift tax implications of one spouse creating a gratuitous tenancy in common or joint tenancy are the same as for nonspouses. However, unlike for nonspouses, these transfers generally qualify for the gift tax marital deduction.[1] This is true even for gratuitous transfers of a joint tenancy with a right of survivorship.[2] This rule results because the joint tenancy may be converted into a tenancy in common. Finally, the planner should note that IRC Section 6019 exempts interspousal transfers from the gift tax filing requirement. Therefore, no gift tax return is due for such transfers.[3]

For estate tax purposes, the IRC generally treats tenancies in common the same as for nonspousal situations. However, the IRC treats joint tenancies differently

---

[16] *See* Lefrak v. Commissioner, T.C. Memo 1993-526 (30-percent discount for lack of marketability and control in partial interests in certain apartment buildings); Estate of Cervin v. Commissioner, T.C. Memo 1994-550 (20-percent discount for undivided fractional interest in farm).

[17] T.C. Memo 1998-59.

[18] *See also* TAM 199943003.

§ 7.06   [1] Lewis D. Solomon et al., Federal Taxation of Estates, Trusts and Gifts 581 (1989).

[2] IRC § 2523(d) (1988); Lewis D. Solomon et al., Federal Taxation of Estates, Trusts and Gifts 581 (1989).

[3] IRC § 6019 (1988).

for spousal situations than for nonspousal situations.[4] Specifically, for any qualified joint tenancy or tenancy by the entirety, the value included in the decedent spouse's gross estate under IRC Section 2040(b) equals one-half the value of the interest held by both the husband and wife. IRC Section 2040(b) only applies to qualified joint interest property.[5] For this purpose, IRC Section 2040(b) defines qualified joint interest property as any interest in property held by the decedent and the decedent's spouse as (1) tenants by the entirety, or (2) joint tenants with the right of survivorship, but only if the decedent and the spouse of the decedent are the only joint tenants.[6]

EXAMPLE 7-25[7]

Harold buys stock with $80,000 of his own money, and he holds the stock with his wife Wilma, as tenants by the entirety. Harold subsequently dies when the stock's fair market value equals $100,000. Here, the result is that Harold's gross estate includes $50,000 as Harold's share of the stock, which equals one-half the fair market value of the stock at Harold's date of death. This amount qualifies for the marital deduction under IRC Section 2065(c)(5) because it passes to Wilma.

EXAMPLE 7-26[8]

Same facts as Example 7-25, except that two days after Harold dies, Wilma dies. Here, Wilma's gross estate includes $100,000 as her share of the stock at the date of her death under IRC Section 2033.

When a husband and wife hold property as joint tenants with a third person, any amount that is deemed contributed by the decedent and that passes to the spouse would qualify under the preceding IRC rules.[9]

EXAMPLE 7-27[10]

Same facts as Example 7-25, except that Harold and Wilma hold as joint tenants and they hold as joint tenants with a third person, Thelma.

---

[4] Lewis D. Solomon et al., Federal Taxation of Estates, Trusts and Gifts 581 (1989).

[5] IRC § 2040(b) (1988).

[6] IRC § 2040(b)(2) (1988).

[7] Lewis D. Solomon et al., Federal Taxation of Estates, Trusts and Gifts 582 (1989).

[8] Id.

[9] IRC § 2040(b)(2)(B) (1988); Lewis D. Solomon et al., Federal Taxation of Estates, Trusts and Gifts 583 (1989).

[10] Lewis D. Solomon et al., Federal Taxation of Estates, Trusts and Gifts 583 (1989).

Furthermore, Harold furnished 80 percent of the original consideration for the property and Thelma contributed 20 percent of the consideration for the property. Harold dies. Here, Harold's estate includes $80,000, which represents 80 percent of the property. Fifty percent of the joint tenancy property would be deemed to pass to Wilma and 30 percent would be deemed to pass to Thelma.

Planning Pointer. When tenants sever a joint tenancy or tenancy by the entirety, each nonspousal tenant must receive an interest in the property equal to the value of her interest before the severing transaction. Otherwise a gift to the co-tenant occurs in the amount of an excess value over that tenant's interest.[11] On the other hand, a spousal tenancy may be severed without gift tax liability, even if consideration for the property's purchase came from only one spouse, because of the impact of the marital transfer tax deduction.

Planning Pointer. Planners may also obtain valuation discounts by using joint property. To illustrate, in *Estate of Young v. Commissioner*,[12] the Tax Court held that a marketability discount may be appropriate where the decedent and the surviving spouse own property as community property or as tenants in common. However, it held, such a discount is not appropriate where the spouses own property jointly with right of survivorship, or as tenants by the entirety.

§ 7.07   CHECKLIST OF CONCURRENT OWNERSHIP ISSUES

The planner should use the following checklist to ensure that no critical issue is overlooked in connection with the concurrent ownership analysis.

[A]   *In General*[1]

____1.   1. Is the planner considering using concurrent ownership as part of the asset protection plan?
If yes, the planner must consider the following issues:

(a)   What are the asset protection benefits of the tenancy by the entirety form of property ownership?[2]

---

[11] Lewis D. Solomon et al., Federal Taxation of Estates, Trusts and Gifts 585 (1989).
[12] 110 T.C. 297 (1998).
§ 7.07   [1] *See* § 7.01.
[2] *See* § 7.02[B].

    (b)   What are the asset protection benefits of the tenancy in common form of property ownership?[3]

    (c)   What are the asset protection benefits of the joint tenancy form of property ownership?[4]

    (d)   What are the estate and gift tax consequences of concurrent ownership of property?[5]

[B] *Tenancy by the Entirety*[6]

____2.   Is the planner considering using a tenancy by the entirety as part of the asset protection plan?

    If yes, the planner should be aware of the following key characteristics of tenancies by the entirety:

    (a)   Each spouse receives the right of survivorship. Furthermore, neither spouse may solely defeat the other's right of survivorship by mortgage, conveyance, partition, or any other means.

    (b)   In some states, the husband may solely lease, mortgage, or convey good title and possession of the tenancy by entirety property during his life without the wife's consent, but subject to her contingent right of survivorship. Here, the husband's creditors may reach the entire property, subject to the wife's contingent right of survivorship. In another group of states, each spouse may solely convey or encumber a one-half interest in the tenancy by entirety property, subject to the other spouse's right of survivorship. Here, each spouse's creditors may reach a one-half interest in the property, subject to the other spouse's contingent right of survivorship. In a third group of states, neither spouse may solely convey or encumber any interest in the property. Here, creditors of one spouse, but not both spouses, cannot reach the property.

    (c)   Each spouse receives the right to possess the entire property and to protect it from outsiders or the other's waste.

    (d)   When only one spouse enters bankruptcy, the bankruptcy trustee cannot reach property held in a tenancy by the entirety, but the bankruptcy trustee may reach such property when both spouses enter bankruptcy and the bankruptcy trustee consolidates the two proceedings.

    (e)   The tenancy by the entirety will be terminated by any of the following:

        (i) The sale of the property by both spouses to a third party;

        (ii) By one spouse releasing his or her interest to the other spouse;

---

[3] *See* § 7.03.
[4] *See* § 7.04.
[5] *See* §§ 7.05–7.06.
[6] *See* § 7.02.

           (iii) By the death of one spouse; or

           (iv) By the divorce of the spouses.

   (f) The tenancy by the entirety yields the following asset protection benefits:

       (i) In jurisdictions where neither spouse may convey any interest in the property, the tenancy by the entirety completely protects the property from the creditors of only one spouse.

       (ii) In other cases, the tenancy by the entirety protects the property by reducing its value by subjecting the property to the other spouse's contingent right of survivorship and right to use the property.

       (iii) For creditors of both spouses, the tenancy by the entirety provides no asset protection.

___3. If the planner has decided to use the tenancy by the entirety form of property ownership as part of the asset protection plan, does the plan ensure that (a) the interests of all the tenants in the tenancy by the entirety vest at the same time (unity of time), (b) both tenants acquire their interests under the same title or deed (unity of title), (c) the ownership shares of the tenants in the tenancy by the entirety are equal (unity of interest), (d) each tenant possesses an equal right to use and possess the whole property that is the subject of the tenancy by the entirety (unity of possession), and (e) the two prospective co-tenants are legally married to each other (unity of person)? If not, the plan will not result in the creation of a tenancy by the entirety.

___4. Does the plan involve the conveyance of the property to more than just the two married co-tenants (that is, to three or more co-tenants)? If yes, only the two married co-tenants will hold as tenants by the entirety. The other tenants will hold as tenants in common or joint tenants with the married couple.

[C] *Tenancy in Common*[7]

___5. Is the planner considering using a tenancy in common as part of the asset protection plan?

If yes, the planner should be aware of the following key characteristics of tenancies in common:

   (a) No tenant obtains the right of survivorship.

   (b) Each tenant's tenancy in common interest is freely alienable. Consequently, the tenant's creditors may reach the tenant's interest in the tenancy in common.

   (c) Each tenant receives the right to possess and enjoy the whole property and every part thereof, subject to the same right of possession held by the other co-tenants.

[7] *See* § 7.03.

   (d) The only asset protection benefit that the tenancy yields is that it (a) reduces the client's amount at risk by the portion of the property that is gifted to members of her bounty, and (b) it reduces the value of the property to creditors because (i) the client owns a smaller portion of the property and (ii) the portion that the client retains is subject to the right of possession by the other co-tenants.

___6. If the planner has decided to use the tenancy in common form of property ownership as part of the asset protection plan, does the plan ensure that each tenant must possess an equal right to use and possess the whole property that is the subject of the tenancy in common (unity of possession)?

     If not, the plan will not result in the creation of a tenancy in common.

[D] Joint Tenancy[8]

___7. Is the planner considering using a joint tenancy as part of the asset protection plan?

     If yes, the planner should be aware of the following key characteristics of joint tenancies:

   (a) Each tenant receives the right of survivorship.

   (b) Each tenant's interest in the joint tenancy is freely alienable. Therefore, each tenant's creditors may generally reach that tenant's joint tenancy interest.

   (c) Each tenant receives the right to possess and enjoy the whole property and every part thereof, subject to the same right of possession held by the other co-tenants.

   (d) The only asset protection benefit that the tenancy yields is that it (a) reduces the client's amount at risk by the portion of the property that is gifted to members of her bounty, and (b) it reduces the value of the property to creditors because (i) the client owns a smaller portion of the property and (ii) the portion that the client retains is subject to the right of possession by the other co-tenants.

___8. If the planner has decided to use the joint tenancy form of property ownership as part of the asset protection plan, does the plan ensure that (a) the interests of all the tenants in the joint tenancy vest at the same time (unity of time), (b) each tenant acquires its interest under the same title or deed (unity of title), (c) the ownership shares of the tenants in the joint tenancy are equal (unity of interest), and (d) each tenant possesses an equal right to use and possess the whole property that is the subject of the joint tenancy (unity of possession)?

     If not, the plan will not result in the creation of a joint tenancy.

---

[8] *See* § 7.04.

[E] *Estate and Gift Tax Consequences*[9]

____9. Does the asset protection plan involve the gratuitous creation of tenancy in common or joint tenancy interests on the behalf of nonspouses?
If yes, the plan may trigger federal gift and estate taxation.

____10. Does the asset protection plan involve the gratuitous creation of tenancy in common, joint tenancy, or tenancy by the entirety interests on the behalf of spouses?
If yes, the plan may trigger federal gift and estate taxation. However, the client generally will be able to use the estate and gift tax marital deductions to reduce the consequences of such taxation.

§ 7.08 CONCURRENT OWNERSHIP COST-BENEFIT WORKSHEET

The planner should use the following worksheet to analyze the benefits and costs of using concurrent ownership in monetary terms.

(1) ____+ asset protection provided by concurrent ownership
(2) ____– expenses of using concurrent ownership and complying with required formalities
(3) ____– costs unique to concurrent ownership
(4) ____– tax burden associated with using concurrent ownership
(5) ____+ tax benefits associated with using the concurrent ownership

_____

= net benefit/cost of using concurrent ownership

---

[9] *See* §§ 7.05–7.06.

8

Exempt Property

---

§8.01   IN GENERAL

Every state, as well as the federal government, both inside and outside the Bankruptcy Code, exempts certain categories of property from the reach of creditors.[1] These exemptions represent a legislative judgment that the benefits of preserving exempt property for the debtor exceed the costs of not allowing creditors to reach such property to satisfy valid debts.[2] Exemptions are valuable tools for the asset protection planner because he may protect a substantial portion of client wealth by moving such wealth into exempt assets.

EXAMPLE 8-1

Harry, an attorney, lives in a jurisdiction whose homestead exemption exempts from creditors' reach the entire value of the debtor's home plus all fixtures attached to that home. As part of an asset protection plan, Harry buys a home for $1 million cash. Each year after that Harry spends a substantial sum improving his home. For example, in 1997 Harry replaces all his fixtures with new fixtures made of solid gold. In 2000 one of Harry's client's, Bess, sues Harry and wins a $10 million judgment against him. Harry files for bankruptcy. In bankruptcy, Harry elects to use his state exemption system instead of the bankruptcy exemption system. This allows Harry to retain his home. After the bankruptcy court discharges Harry, he no longer remains liable for the judgment against Bess or for most other debts that he previously was liable for.[3]

Planning Pointer. The planner should use the following analysis when engaging in exemption planning:

1. How does the homestead exemption apply to the client?[4]
2. How does the life insurance exemption apply to the client?[5]

---

§8.01   [1] *See generally* Santo (Sandy) Bisignano, Jr., Protecting Assets from Overzealous Creditors or an Estate Planner's Guide to Preservation Planning, 1987 Annual Notre Dame Est. Plan. Inst.; Rhonda H. Brink, Planning Perspectives for Creditor Conscious Clients ¶ 704, in 22d Annual University of Miami Philip E. Heckerling Inst. on Est. Plan. (John T. Gaubatz ed., 1988); William J. Woodward, Jr., Enforcements of Money Judgments: Objectives and Restrictions, in 9 Debtor-Creditor Law ¶ 37.03[B] (Theodore Eisenberg ed., 1992); 2A Richard R. Powell, The Law of Real Property ¶ 263 (Patrick J. Rohan rev. ed., 1993); David G. Epstein et al., Debtors and Creditors 127-45 (1987).

[2] William J. Woodward, Jr., Enforcements of Money Judgments: Objectives and Restrictions ¶ 37.03[B] at 37-58, in 9 Debtor-Creditor Law (Theodore Eisenberg ed., 1992).

[3] *See* Advanced Chapter 11 Bankruptcy Practice (Thomas J. Salerno & Craig D. Hansen eds., John Wiley & Sons 1987 & Supp. 1990) for a general discussion of Chapter 11 bankruptcy.

[4] *See* §8.02.

[5] *See* §8.03.

3. How does the ERISA qualified retirement plan exemption apply to the client?[6]
4. How do other income exemptions apply to the client?[7]
5. How do state law exemptions interact with federal bankruptcy law exemptions?[8]
6. What limitations must the planner consider when advising a client to move assets into exemption assets?[9]

§ 8.02   HOMESTEAD EXEMPTION

Almost all states have enacted homestead exemption statutes, which protect an individual's home from the reach of creditors under certain circumstances.[1] The homestead exemption offers an excellent opportunity to asset protection planners to protect the client's wealth.

Planning Pointer. When considering the homestead exemption, the planner should analyze:

1. What consequences result from the client placing wealth into homestead property;

---

[6] *See* § 8.04.

[7] *See* § 8.05.

[8] *See* § 8.06.

[9] *See* § 8.07.

§ 8.02   [1] *See generally* Santo (Sandy) Bisignano, Jr., Protecting Assets from Overzealous Creditors or an Estate Planner's Guide to Preservation Planning, 1987 Annual Notre Dame Est. Plan. Inst. 3-65 to 3-68; William J. Woodward, Jr., Enforcements of Money Judgments: Objectives and Restrictions, in 9 Debtor-Creditor Law ¶ 37.03[B][2] (Theodore Eisenberg ed., 1992); George L. Haskins, Estates Arising from the Marriage Relationship and Their Characteristics, in 1 American Law of Property Ch. IV (A. James Casner ed., 1952 & Supp. 1977); 2A Richard R. Powell, The Law of Real Property ¶ 263 (Patrick J. Rohan rev. ed., 1993); David G. Epstein et al., Debtors and Creditors 127-45 (1987). *See, e.g.,* Howard v. American Credit Co. (*In re* Howard), 169 B.R. 71 (D. Colo. 1994) (holding that judicial lien on debtor's homestead could be avoided under § 522(f) to extent that reasonable market value of property exceeded consensual liens against it, up to maximum amount of debtor's homestead exemption, and that unavoided portion of lien survives bankruptcy and attaches to debtor's equity in property above homestead exemption); Wilson Sporting Goods v. Pederson, 886 P.2d 203 (Wash. Ct. App. 1994) (judgment lien did not attach to debtor's homestead); Graziade v. Graziade (*In re* Graziade), 32 F.3d 1408 (9th Cir. 1994) (court held that debtor was not barred from using Nevada homestead exemption as defense to obligation to make payments from sale proceeds of homestead property to former wife's attorney in divorce proceeding, noting that payments were not for former wife's support but for attorney's fees); *In re* Pladson, 35 F.3d 462 (9th Cir. 1994) (court held that bankruptcy debtors in California can claim California homestead exemption); *In re* Sanders, 39 F.3d 258 (10th Cir. 1994) (Tenth Circuit held that Bankruptcy Code § 522(f) only protects homestead property from judicial liens to amount of debtor's homestead exemption); *In re* Galvin, 158 B.R. 806 (Bankr. W.D. Mo. 1993) (purchaser under contract for deed entitled to homestead exemption under Missouri law); Dietz v. Becker (*In re* Becker), 215 B.R. 585, 1998 Bankr. LEXIS 15 (B.A.P. 8th Cir. 1998) (finding that debtors may claim a rural homestead exemption for rural-use property under Minnesota law, even where such property is located in an area zoned for suburban residential homes); *In re* Lewis, 1998 Bankr. LEXIS 30 (Bankr. N.D. Okla. Jan. 12, 1998) (holding that property division money judgment secured by a lien constitutes "proceeds" of homestead, and thus constitutes exempt property under Oklahoma law).

2. What requirements must the client satisfy for the homestead protection to arise;
3. What exceptions exist to homestead protection;
4. What events cause the loss of homestead protection.

[A] Consequences of Homestead Protection

When the planner causes the client to place wealth into property protected by the homestead exemption (homestead property), this causes the following consequences: the exemption protects homestead property from the reach of the client's creditors, to the extent of the homestead exemption under applicable law; married clients cannot convey the property without their spouse's consent; and when debtors predecease spouses, the homestead exemption gives the surviving spouse an interest resembling a life estate in the land free of the same claims from which it was exempt while the debtor spouse was alive.

[1] Protects Property from Creditor's Reach

First, the homestead exemption protects the homestead property from the reach of the client's creditors. The exact amount of homestead protection, however, varies greatly from state to state. Originally, homestead laws only protected real estate and traditional houses affixed to such real estate.[2] Today, many jurisdictions have extended their homestead exemptions to mobile homes, condominiums, cooperative apartments, and other forms of property that serve as dwellings.[3]

EXAMPLE 8-2

Hillary, a partner in the ABC law partnership, lives in a jurisdiction whose homestead exemption applies to condominiums. As part of an asset protection plan, Hillary buys a condominium for $300,000 cash in 1995. In 2000 Claire, a former client of the ABC law partnership, sues the ABC

---

[2] George L. Haskins, Estates Arising from the Marriage Relationship and Their Characteristics, in 1 American Law of Property §5.75 (A. James Casner ed., 1952 & Supp. 1977); David G. Epstein et al., Debtors and Creditors 128 (1987). *See, e.g.,* Havoco of Am., Ltd. v. Hill, No. SC99-98, 790 So. 2d 1018 (Fla. 2001) (Florida Supreme Court held that debtors seeking to keep otherwise nonexempt funds away from creditors need only buy a house in Florida to do so); Abernathy v. LaBarge (In re Abernathy), 259 B.R. 330 (B.A.P. 8th Cir., *aff'd,* 2001 U.S. App. LEXIS 20644 (8th Cir. Sept. 20, 2001) (U.S. Bankruptcy Appellate Panel for the Eighth Circuit held that debtor, who was one of three joint-tenant owners of real estate, was not restricted to claiming only one-third of the homestead exemption under Missouri law).

[3] Cal. Civ. Proc. Code §704.710(a) (Deering 1983 & Supp. 1993); Ohio Rev. Code Ann. §2329.66 (Anderson 1991 & Supp. 1992); David G. Epstein et al., Debtors and Creditors 129 (1987).

partnership and wins a $100 million judgment against it. Because Hillary is a general partner in the ABC law partnership and jointly and severally liable for its debts, Claire tries to collect from Hillary, among others. Here, the homestead exemption protects Hillary's condominium from Claire's reach.

EXAMPLE 8-3

Same facts as Example 8-2, except Hillary and her condominium are located in a jurisdiction whose homestead exemption only applies to traditional houses located on real property. Therefore, the homestead exemption does not cover condominiums. Here, Claire may reach Hillary's condominium to satisfy her claim.

Caution. Although some states do not impose any dollar limitation on their homestead exemptions,[4] most states do impose such dollar limitations.[5]

Planning Pointer. The planner should ensure that the client's investment in homestead property does not materially exceed the applicable exemption's dollar limitation. Any such excess will be exposed to creditors' claims, absent other protective measures.

Caution. Jurisdiction methods vary in determining the homestead property values for purposes of determining the extent of homestead exemption protection.[6] For example, some jurisdictions do not consider the estate or interest of the owner in the homestead property. These jurisdictions look at the value of a fee simple interest in that property. Other jurisdictions do consider the owner's estate.[7]

---

[4] *See, e.g.,* Minn. Stat. Ann. § 510.02 (West 1990 & Supp. 1992).

[5] *See, e.g.,* Ind. Code Ann. § 34-2-28-1 (West 1983 & Supp. 1992); N.D. Cent. Code § 47-1801 (1983 & Supp. 1991); Mass. Ann. Laws ch. 188, § I (Law. Co-op. 1981 & Supp. 1993).

[6] George L. Haskins, Estates Arising from the Marriage Relationship and Their Characteristics, in 1 American Law of Property § 5.82 (A. James Casner ed., 1952 & Supp. 1977).

[7] *See, e.g.,* Wilson v. Devasher, 264 S.W. 1057 (Ky. 1924).

EXAMPLE 8-4

Same facts as Example 8-2, except that (1) the applicable law limits the exemption to $100,000 of property, (2) when Hillary buys the condominium, she gives a remainder interest to her daughter, Barbara, and only retains a life estate, and (3) the value of Hillary's life estate equals $100,000. Here, if the applicable law looks at only the value of Hillary's interest or estate in the property, the homestead exemption will protect all of the condominium. However, if the applicable law looks at the full value of a fee simple interest in the condominium, Hillary will be considered to hold an excessive homestead.

Most states hold that the homestead's value includes the value of existing improvements at the time of its establishment.[8] Also when calculating value, most states deduct encumbrances existing at the homestead's establishment.[9] Most states determine the homestead value at the homestead's establishment or acquisition. However, some states hold that if the homestead falls within the value limits at establishment, but the owners increase the value by substantial improvements so that the value exceeds the limits when a creditor attempts to reach such property, creditors may reach the excess. Some states limit the homestead exemption by acreage or size, either instead of or besides value limitations.[10] Usually, such statutes provide for a greater allowable size for rural homesteads than for urban homesteads.[11]

When the dollar value of homestead property exceeds the homestead value limitation, most states provide for one or both of two alternative procedures. First, if feasible, the property may be partitioned so that a portion approximating the maximum exemption is set aside as exempt, and the remainder is subjected to the creditor's execution. When partition is not feasible, the entire property may be sold and an amount equal to the maximum exemption paid to the owner. However, the specific procedures involved vary from jurisdiction to jurisdiction.[12]

Generally, the homestead property owner will not lose homestead protection merely because he leases a portion of the property.[13] Furthermore, in

---

[8] George L. Haskins, Estates Arising from the Marriage Relationship and Their Characteristics, in 1 American Law of Property § 5.82 (A. James Casner ed., 1952 & Supp. 1977). *See, e.g.,* Lubbock v. McMann, 22 P. 1145 (Cal. 1889).

[9] George L. Haskins, Estates Arising from the Marriage Relationship and Their Characteristics, in 1 American Law of Property § 5.82 (A. James Casner ed., 1952 & Supp. 1977). *See, e.g.,* John Hancock Mut. Life Ins. Co. v. Wagner, 24 P.2d 420 (Wash. 1933).

[10] George L. Haskins, Estates Arising from the Marriage Relationship and Their Characteristics, in 1 American Law of Property § 5.82 (A. James Casner ed., 1952 & Supp. 1977).

[11] David G. Epstein et al., Debtors and Creditors 130 (1987). *See, e.g.,* Tex. Const. art. 16, § 51.

[12] George L. Haskins, Estates Arising from the Marriage Relationship and Their Characteristics, in 1 American Law of Property § 5.98 (A. James Casner ed., 1952 & Supp. 1977).

[13] George L. Haskins, Estates Arising from the Marriage Relationship and Their Characteristics, in 1 American Law of Property § 5.97 (A. James Casner ed., 1952 & Supp. 1977); Phelps v. Loop, 148 P.2d 674 (Cal. Ct. App. 1944).

some jurisdictions the homestead exemption also extends to the rental income itself.[14]

When a casualty destroys the homestead, the homestead exemption generally extends to casualty insurance proceeds.[15] However, this protection may be conditioned on an intent to repair the homestead or apply the insurance proceeds to a replacement.[16] The homestead exemption also generally extends to sale proceeds of the homestead property for a reasonable period to allow the debtor to invest in a new homestead.[17]

Planning Pointer. Under some circumstances, the homestead exemption also may protect the homestead property against prebankruptcy liens.[18]

Caution. The Bankruptcy Abuse Prevention and Consumer Protection Act of 2005 (the "2005 Bankruptcy Act") has significantly limited the asset protection benefits of the homestead exemption. Specifically, the 2005 Bankruptcy Act has modified Bankruptcy Code § 522 so that it limits any state homestead exemption in a bankruptcy proceeding to $125,000 regardless of whether the applicable state's homestead law provides for a

---

[14] David G. Epstein et al., Debtors and Creditors 130 (1987).

[15] Idaho Code § 55-1008 (1988 & Supp. 1992); Tenn. Code Ann. § 26-2 304 (1980 & Supp. 1992); George L. Haskins, Estates Arising from the Marriage Relationship and Their Characteristics, in 1 American Law of Property § 5.97 (A. James Casner ed., 1952 & Supp. 1977).

[16] David G. Epstein et al., Debtors and Creditors 130 (1987).

[17] Idaho Code § 55-1008 (1988 & Supp. 1992); George L. Haskins, Estates Arising from the Marriage Relationship and Their Characteristics, in 1 American Law of Property § 5.97 (A. James Casner ed., 1952 & Supp. 1977).

[18] See 11 U.S.C. § 522(f) (1988); In re Mayer, 156 B.R. 54 (Bankr. S.D. Cal. 1993), aff'd in part, vacated in part & remanded, 167 B.R. 186 (Bankr. 9th Cir. 1994); David Dorsey Distributing Inc. v. Sanders (In re Sanders), 156 B.R. 667 (Bankr. D. Utah 1993), aff'd, 39 F.3d 258 (10th Cir. 1994). See also Annotation, Estate or interest in real property to which a homestead claim may attach, 74 A.L.R.2d 1355 (1960); Hastings v. Holmes (In re Hastings), 185 B.R. 811 (Bankr. 9th Cir. 1995) (the Ninth Circuit Bankruptcy Appellate Panel held that the debtors may avoid a judicial lien on the home they moved into after the lien arises and they previously held as rental property); Burrus v. Oklahoma Tax Commission, 59 F.3d 147 (10th Cir. 1995) (the Tenth Circuit held that (1) the Oklahoma homestead exemption precluding state foreclosure of homestead property does not preclude state lien priority over IRS lien, and (2) the homestead exemption, precluding foreclosure of homestead property, does not preclude attachment of a lien against homestead property); Scott v. United States Trustee (In re Allen), 203 B.R. 928 (W.D. Va. 1997) (the United States District Court for Western District of Virginia held that a bankruptcy trustee was not permitted to invade the debtor's homestead exemption to realize the trustee's fees and costs arising from the sale of the debtor's property; Kretzinger v. First State Bank of Waynoka (In re Kretzinger), 103 F.3d 943 (10th Cir. 1996) (the Tenth Circuit held that a lease of 78 acres of an 80-acre parcel of rural home for agricultural activities, which if conducted by resident owners themselves would be consistent with homestead status, did not preclude homestead protection); Davis v. Davis (In re Davis), 105 F.3d 1017 (5th Cir. 1997) (Fifth Circuit held that creditors may seize exempt homestead property to collect nondischargeable debts that debtor owed to former spouse for alimony, maintenance, and child support).

larger or unlimited homestead exemption. This limitation applies to residences acquired within 1,215 days before the filing of a bankruptcy petition. However, the homestead exemption is limited to $125,000 without regard to when the residence was acquired, if any of the following occurs:

- The court determines, after notice and a hearing, that the debtor has been convicted of a felony, which under the circumstances, demonstrates that the filing of the case was an abuse of the provision of this title.
- The asset protection client/debtor owes a debt arising from any violation of federal or state securities laws or regulations.
- The asset protection client/debtor owes a debt arising from fraud, deceit, or manipulation in a fiduciary capacity or in connection with the purchase or sale of any registered security.
- The asset protection client/debtor owes a debt arising from any RICO civil remedy.
- The asset protection client/debtor owes a debt arising from any criminal act, intentional tort, or willful or reckless misconduct that caused serious physical injury or death to another individual in the preceding five years.

In addition, if an asset protection client moves from one state in which his/her homestead is completely protected from creditors' claims (*e.g.*, Florida) to another state in which state law provides for an unlimited homestead exemption, the 1,215 holding period begins upon the acquisition of the new home. In other words, the fact that the asset protection client's prior residence was completely protected from claims of creditors is irrelevant to the application of this limitation.

[2] Spousal Consent for Conveyance of Property

Generally, married clients cannot convey homestead property without their spouse's consent.[19] Conveyances or mortgages that violate this rule are generally void.[20] This prohibition against homestead property conveyances without spousal consent applies to (1) conveyances of the homestead property itself, (2) contracts to convey the homestead property, (3) conveyances of leases that interfere with the use of the property as a home (and in some jurisdictions, all leases), (4) conveyances of oil and gas leases on the property, (5) the granting of

---

[19] George L. Haskins, Estates Arising from the Marriage Relationship and Their Characteristics, in 1 American Law of Property §5.101 (A. James Casner ed., 1952 & Supp. 1977); David G. Epstein et al., Debtors and Creditors 128 (1987).

[20] George L. Haskins, Estates Arising from the Marriage Relationship and Their Characteristics, in 1 American Law of Property §5.101 (A. James Casner ed., 1952 & Supp. 1977). *See, e.g.*, Cleveland v. Milner, 170 S.W.2d 472 (Tex. Ct. App. 1943).

easements on the homestead property, and (6) the granting of encumbrances on the property.[21]

Caution. When clients want to protect against spousal claims, homestead property should not be used as part of the asset protection plan.

The prohibition against homestead property conveyances without spousal consent does not apply to:

1. Mortgages given to secure the homestead's purchase price;
2. Deeds given by one spouse when the other spouse is insane, a non-resident, or guilty of certain kinds of misconduct; or
3. Conveyances from one spouse to the other.[22]

EXAMPLE 8-5

Bess, an accountant, consults with Franklin, an asset protection planner. Franklin recommends that Bess and her husband, Harry, purchase a homestead for $500,000 cash in 1995. Bess and Harry follow this advice. Bess provides $400,000 of the cash used to purchase the house. Under applicable law, homestead protection arises at the time of purchase without limit to value or acreage. In 2000 Bess wants to sell the home. Here, Bess must obtain Harry's consent to sell the house because of the homestead protection that arises on the purchase of the home.

EXAMPLE 8-6

Same facts as in Example 8-5, except that in 2001 Harry is declared legally insane. Here, Bess can now convey the home without Harry's consent.

Planning Pointer. The planner should note that the termination of the marriage or the homestead protection generally terminates the prohibition against conveying homestead interests without spousal concurrence.[23]

---

[21] George L. Haskins, Estates Arising from the Marriage Relationship and Their Characteristics, in 1 American Law of Property §§ 5.102-106 (A. James Casner ed., 1952 & Supp. 1977).

[22] George L. Haskins, Estates Arising from the Marriage Relationship and Their Characteristics, in 1 American Law of Property §§ 5.101-102 (A. James Casner ed., 1952 & Supp. 1977).

[23] George L. Haskins, Estates Arising from the Marriage Relationship and Their Characteristics, in 1 American Law of Property § 5.101 (A. James Casner ed., 1952 & Supp. 1977).

[3] Homestead Rights of Surviving Spouse

Most states provide that surviving spouses are entitled to a decedent spouse's homestead and that such homestead is exempt from the same debts from which it was exempt during the decedent spouse's lifetime. Many states also afford this protection to children of the marriage. Such a homestead is generally referred to as the probate homestead.[24]

The probate homestead gives the surviving spouse two types of protection. First, it assures the surviving spouse a property interest in the homestead property. Second, it exempts this homestead property from certain claims of creditors. The types of claims that the probate homestead provides protection against, as well as the requirements for the probate homestead to arise, may differ from that of normal homesteads.[25] When the applicable law entitles the surviving spouse to dower, courtesy, or a distributive share of the deceased spouse's property, such law often requires the surviving spouse to elect between such interest and homestead rights. A failure to elect generally results in a deemed waiver of homestead rights. However, some states do not require the surviving spouse to elect between such distributive share rights and homestead rights.[26]

Caution. The probate homestead cannot last any longer than the decedent spouse's estate entitled him to occupy the homestead property.[27]

EXAMPLE 8-7

In 1995 Alice, as part of an asset protection plan, conveys a life estate in Homewood, a house that she previously leased out, to her son, Jack. Alice gives the remainder interest in Homewood to George, her nephew. In 1997 Jack marries Jill. Jack dies in 2001. Here, Jill cannot claim a probate homestead in Homewood because the probate homestead cannot last any longer than Jack's estate in Homewood, which ended on Jack's death.

The duration of the probate homestead varies from jurisdiction to jurisdiction. Some jurisdictions provide that the probate homestead gives the surviving spouse a fee simple interest. Others however, only give the surviving spouse a life estate. Finally, others make the probate homestead contingent on children of the marriage or other factors.[28]

[24] George L. Haskins, Estates Arising from the Marriage Relationship and Their Characteristics, in 1 American Law of Property § 5.114 (A. James Casner ed., 1952 & Supp. 1977).

[25] Id.

[26] George L. Haskins, Estates Arising from the Marriage Relationship and Their Characteristics, in 1 American Law of Property § 5.115 (A. James Casner ed., 1952 & Supp. 1977).

[27] George L. Haskins, Estates Arising from the Marriage Relationship and Their Characteristics, in 1 American Law of Property § 5.116 (A. James Casner ed., 1952 & Supp. 1977).

[28] George L. Haskins, Estates Arising from the Marriage Relationship and Their Characteristics, in 1 American Law of Property § 5.117 (A. James Casner ed., 1952 & Supp. 1977).

The surviving spouse's ability to convey or encumber the property depends on the nature of the probate homestead under the applicable law. For example, when the survivor's interest is a fee simple absolute, the surviving spouse generally may freely convey or encumber the property. Conversely, when the survivor's interest equals merely a right to occupy the homestead property, the surviving spouse generally may not convey or encumber any interest.[29]

The applicable law sets forth the events that will cause the termination of the probate homestead. These events vary in different jurisdictions. Events that cause termination of the probate homestead in several jurisdictions include remarriage, failure to occupy the homestead property, and death of the surviving spouse.[30]

[B] Requirements for Homestead Protection

Each jurisdiction has different requirements for homestead protection to arise. However, these different requirements may be broken down into the following six categories, one or more of which each state generally requires the owner to satisfy to claim homestead protection: family, property that qualifies for homestead protection, property interest in the property that qualifies for homestead protection, size and value limitations on homestead property, occupancy and use of the homestead property, and formal declaration of homestead protection.

[1] Family

Some states provide homestead exemption protection to any individual who owns a home. Most states, however, only provide homestead protection to individuals who head a household or family.[31] Although states define "family" or "household" differently, many jurisdictions define a family as existing when two or more persons reside together under one head, with a legal or moral obligation of the head of the family to support one or more of the other members, with at least a partial state of dependence by the recipient of such support. Furthermore, the family relationship must be of a permanent and domestic character, as opposed to merely a temporary expedient.[32]

---

[29] George L. Haskins, Estates Arising from the Marriage Relationship and Their Characteristics, in 1 American Law of Property § 5.119 (A. James Casner ed., 1952 & Supp. 1977).

[30] George L. Haskins, Estates Arising from the Marriage Relationship and Their Characteristics, in 1 American Law of Property § 5.120 (A. James Casner ed., 1952 & Supp. 1977).

[31] George L. Haskins, Estates Arising from the Marriage Relationship and Their Characteristics, in 1 American Law of Property § 5.79 (A. James Casner ed., 1952 & Supp. 1977); David G. Epstein et al., Debtors and Creditors 128 (1987).

[32] George L. Haskins, Estates Arising from the Marriage Relationship and Their Characteristics, in 1 American Law of Property § 5.79 (A. James Casner ed., 1952 & Supp. 1977); David G. Epstein et al., Debtors and Creditors 128 (1987). *See, e.g.,* State v. Haney, 277 SW.2d 632 (Mo. 1955). *See also* In re Dawson, 266 B.R. 355 (Bankr. N.D. Tex. 2001) (U.S. Bankruptcy Court for the Northern District of

[2] Property That Qualifies for Homestead Protection

There is substantial diversity among jurisdictions about types of property that qualify as homestead property.[33] Originally, only real estate and traditional houses and service buildings constructed on land and affixed permanently thereto qualified as homestead property.[34] Although some states retain this rule[35] most states have expanded their homestead exemptions. Today, many states' homestead exemptions include mobile homes, condominiums, cooperative apartments, and other forms of property that serve as dwellings.[36]

[3] Property Interests for Homestead Protection

Not all interests in property allow individuals to claim homestead protection in property.[37] Most jurisdictions hold that any interest that gives an individual against another a right to possess the property, enables the holder to claim homestead protection.[38] For example, some courts hold that leases[39] and title by adverse possession,[40] under certain circumstances, qualify the holder for homestead protection.

[4] Size and Value Limitations on Property

Most jurisdictions place value or size limitations, or both, on homestead property.[41] These limitations vary greatly between jurisdictions. However, of

Texas held that, under Texas law, a debtor is not entitled to claim a separate homestead exemption from his wife because of a pending divorce, based on the rationale that because a family is entitled to one homestead, a debtor cannot claim a homestead separate from that established by the family until a final and enforceable divorce decree is rendered and the familial relationship is terminated).

[33] William J. Woodward, Jr., Enforcements of Money Judgments: Objectives and Restrictions ¶ 37.03[B][2], in 9 Debtor-Creditor Law ¶ 37.03[B][2] (Theodore Eisenberg ed., 1992); Annotation, *Estate or interest in real property to which a homestead claim may attach,* 74 A.L.R.2d 1355 (1960).

[34] David G. Epstein et al., Debtors and Creditors 129 (1987).

[35] George L. Haskins, Estates Arising from the Marriage Relationship and Their Characteristics, in 1 American Law of Property §5.80 (A. James Casner ed., 1952 & Supp. 1977).

[36] Cal. Civ. Proc. Code §704.710(a) (Deering 1983 & Supp. 1993); Ohio Rev. Code Ann. §2329.66 (Anderson 1991 & Supp. 1992); David G. Epstein et al., Debtors and Creditors 129 (1987); *In re* Mangano, 158 B.R. 532 (Bankr. S.D. Fla. 1993) (homestead exemption protection applied to motor home).

[37] George L. Haskins, Estates Arising from the Marriage Relationship and Their Characteristics, in 1 American Law of Property §5.81 (A. James Casner ed., 1952 & Supp. 1977); C.S. Wheatley, Jr., Annotation, *Estate or interest in real property to which a homestead claim may attach,* 89 A.L.R. 511 (1934).

[38] David G. Epstein et al., Debtors and Creditors 129-30 (1987); George L. Haskins, Estates Arising from the Marriage Relationship and Their Characteristics, in 1 American Law of Property §5.81 (A. James Casner ed., 1952 & Supp. 1977).

[39] *See, e.g.,* Wright v. Flatterick, 281 N.W. 221 (Iowa 1938).

[40] *See, e.g.,* Ferguson v. Roberts, 170 P.2d 855 (Ariz. 1946); Howard v. Mitchell, 105 S.W.2d 128 (Ky. 1936).

[41] Ind. Code Ann. §34-2-28-1 (West 1983 & Supp. 1992); N.D. Cent. Code §47-18-01 (1983 & Supp. 1991); Mass. Ann. Laws ch. 188, §1 (Law. Co-op. 1981 & Supp. 1993); George L. Haskins, Estates Arising from the Marriage Relationship and Their Characteristics, in 1 American Law of Property §5.82 (A. James Casner ed., 1952 & Supp. 1977).

the states imposing size restrictions, generally large size limitations apply to rural homesteads more than to urban homesteads.[42] The methodology for determining the homestead property value for homestead exemption purposes also varies a great deal.[43] For example, some jurisdictions do not consider the owner's estate or interest in the homestead property. These jurisdictions generally look at the value of a fee simple interest in that property. Other jurisdictions do consider the owner's estate.[44]

Most states include the value of existing improvements at the homestead's establishment in the homestead value.[45] Also, most states deduct encumbrances existing at the homestead's establishment when calculating value for homestead exemption purposes.[46] Most states determine the homestead value at its establishment or acquisition. However, some states hold that if the homestead falls within the value limits at establishment, but the owners increase the value by substantial improvements so that the value exceeds the homestead value limits when a creditor attempts to reach such property, creditors may reach the excess.[47]

When the dollar value of the homestead property exceeds the homestead value limitation, most states provide for one or both of two alternative procedures. First, if feasible, the property may be partitioned so that a portion approximating the maximum exemption is set aside as exempt, and the remainder is subjected to the creditor's execution. When partition is not feasible, the entire property may be sold and an amount equal to the maximum exemption paid to the owner. However, the specific procedures vary from jurisdiction to jurisdiction.[48]

[5] Occupancy and Use of Property

Most states require individuals to occupy property before claiming homestead protection.[49] However, homestead protection may generally be obtained before actual occupancy when the individual clearly manifests an intent to occupy the

---

[42] *See, e.g.,* Minn. Stat. Ann. § 510.02 (West 1990 & Supp. 1992).

[43] George L. Haskins, Estates Arising from the Marriage Relationship and Their Characteristics, in 1 American Law of Property § 5.82 (A. James Casner ed., 1952 & Supp. 1977).

[44] *See, e.g.,* Wilson v. Devasher, 264 S.W. 1057 (Ky. 1924).

[45] George L. Haskins, Estates Arising from the Marriage Relationship and Their Characteristics, in 1 American Law of Property § 5.82 (A. James Casner ed., 1952 & Supp. 1977). *See, e.g.,* Lubboch v. McMann, 22 P. 1145 (Cal. 1889).

[46] George L. Haskins, Estates Arising from the Marriage Relationship and Their Characteristics, in 1 American Law of Property § 5.82 (A. James Casner ed., 1952 & Supp. 1977). *See, e.g.,* John Hancock Mut. Life Ins. Co. v. Wagner, 24 P.2d 420 (Wash. 1933).

[47] George L. Haskins, Estates Arising from the Marriage Relationship and Their Characteristics, in 1 American Law of Property § 5.82 (A. James Casner ed., 1952 & Supp. 1977).

[48] George L. Haskins, Estates Arising from the Marriage Relationship and Their Characteristics, in 1 American Law of Property § 5.98 (A. James Casner ed., 1952 & Supp. 1977); Annotation, *Lien of judgment on excess value of homestead,* 41 A.L.R.4th 292 (1985 & Supp. 1995).

[49] David G. Epstein et al., Debtors and Creditors 128 (1987); George L. Haskins, Estates Arising from the Marriage Relationship and Their Characteristics, in 1 American Law of Property § 5.83 (A. James Casner ed., 1952 & Supp. 1977).

property as a home by overt acts of preparation and, in fact, carries out that intent within a reasonable period.[50]

EXAMPLE 8-8

John and Gina, who are married, agree to build and occupy a home on Black-acre, undeveloped land previously held by John and Gina. They begin construction on January 1, 2003. Here, many courts will find that John and Gina have satisfied the occupancy requirement if they occupy the new home within a reasonable period.

Generally, the owners or their family must occupy the property as a residence to satisfy the occupancy requirement.[51] However, if the owners primarily occupy the property as a residence, the fact that they use the remainder of the property incidentally for other purposes will generally not preclude homestead protection.[52]

[6] Formal Declaration

Most states do not require a formal declaration of any type in order for homestead protection to arise; however, some states do require such a formal declaration.[53] The exact formalities differ for each state. Usually such formalities include entries on the recorded deed's margin[54] or declarations of homestead that must be executed, recorded, and acknowledged as the applicable statute requires.[55]

---

[50] George L. Haskins, Estates Arising from the Marriage Relationship and Their Characteristics, in 1 American Law of Property § 5.83 (A. James Casner ed., 1952 & Supp. 1977). *See, e.g.,* Haight v. Reynolds, 239 N.W. 880 (Mich. 1932).

[51] George L. Haskins, Estates Arising from the Marriage Relationship and Their Characteristics, in 1 American Law of Property § 5.83 (A. James Casner ed., 1952 & Supp. 1977); Ariz. Rev. Stat. Ann. § 33-1101 (1990).

[52] George L. Haskins, Estates Arising from the Marriage Relationship and Their Characteristics, in 1 American Law of Property § 5.83 (A. James Casner ed., 1952 & Supp. 1977). *See, e.g.,* McKay v. Gesford, 124 P. 1016 (Cal. 1912).

[53] David G. Epstein et al., Debtors and Creditors 131 (1987); George L. Haskins, Estates Arising from the Marriage Relationship and Their Characteristics, in 1 American Law of Property § 5.84 (A. James Casner ed., 1952 & Supp. 1977); *In re* Dudeney, 159 B.R. 1003 (Bankr. S.D. Fla. 1993).

[54] George L. Haskins, Estates Arising from the Marriage Relationship and Their Characteristics, in 1 American Law of Property § 5.84 (A. James Casner ed., 1952 & Supp. 1977); *In re* McKinney-Jones, 219 B.R. 619 (W.D. Okla. 1998) (holding that Chapter 7 bankruptcy debtor can avoid lien attaching to his homestead under Bankruptcy Code § 522(f)(1)(A) only if he proves that lien impairs homestead exemption). Here, the court stated, Oklahoma law precludes the forced sale of the debtor's homestead as long as he lives on the property. Therefore, the court concluded that the lien in question could not have impaired his exemption).

[55] Ariz. Rev. Stat. Ann. § 33-1101 (1990); Colo. Rev. Stat. Ann. § 38-41 202 (West 1990); Idaho Code § 55-1004 (1988 & Supp. 1992); George L. Haskins, Estates Arising from the Marriage Relationship and Their Characteristics, in 1 American Law of Property § 5.84 (A. James Casner ed., 1952 & Supp. 1977).

Caution. Many jurisdictions hold that their statutory formal declaration procedures must be strictly complied with before homestead protection arises.[56] These jurisdictions generally find that owners not complying with the statutory requirements are not entitled to homestead protection.[57]

Caution. Some jurisdictions hold that homestead protection is not effective against claims arising before the owner properly files the formal declaration of homestead.[58]

Planning Pointer. In jurisdictions requiring the owner to make a formal declaration, the planner should ensure that the client fully complies with the applicable requirements at the earliest possible time.

[7]   Title of Property

Some cases indicate that the way a personal residence is technically titled impacts the availability of homestead protection. Specifically, in *Crews v. Bosonetto (In re Bosonetto)*,[59] the Bankruptcy Court for the Middle District of Florida held that a Florida real property held by the trustee of a revocable trust used as the primary residence of the trust's grantor did not qualify for the Florida homestead exemption.[60]

[C]   Exceptions to Homestead Protection

There are nine exceptions to homestead exemption protection that the planner must consider. These include exceptions for liabilities arising before the owner establishes the homestead, liabilities incurred before the owner acquires the

---

[56] George L. Haskins, Estates Arising from the Marriage Relationship and Their Characteristics, in 1 American Law of Property § 5.84 (A. James Casner ed., 1952 & Supp. 1977); Farmers' Nat'l Bank of Seymore v. Coffman, 79 S.W.2d 905 (Tex. Ct. App. 1935).

[57] George L. Haskins, Estates Arising from the Marriage Relationship and Their Characteristics, in 1 American Law of Property § 5.84 (A. James Casner ed., 1952 & Supp. 1977).

[58] Mass. Ann. Laws ch. 188, § I (Law. Co-op. 1981 & Supp. 1993); George L. Haskins, Estates Arising from the Marriage Relationship and Their Characteristics, in 1 American Law of Property § 5.84 (A. James Casner ed., 1952 & Supp. 1977).

[59] 271 B.R. 403 (Bankr. M.D. Fla. 2001).

[60] *C.f. Callava v. Feinberg*, 2003 Fla. App. LEXIS 15467 (Fla. Dist. Ct. App. 3d Dist. 2003) (Court held that property held in trust that was used by grantor-beneficiary as primary residence qualifies for the Florida homestead exemption).

homestead property, liabilities incurred to purchase the homestead property, liabilities incurred to improve the homestead property, criminal penalties, tax liabilities, tort liabilities, alimony, and superior title in the homestead property.

[1] Liabilities Arising Before Homestead Establishment

Most jurisdictions hold that once homestead protection arises, such protection protects the homestead from liabilities arising before the establishment of the property as a homestead.[61] However, some jurisdictions hold that homestead exemption protection does not apply to liabilities incurred before homestead establishment.[62]

EXAMPLE 8-9

Macbeth, a plastic surgeon, purchases a new home, Castlerock, for $500,000 cash on December 10, 2002. Macbeth and Castlerock are located in a jurisdiction that requires owners to file a formal declaration of homestead before homestead protection arises. Macbeth files such a formal declaration on January 1, 2003, and this is the last requirement that he must fulfill under local law before homestead protection arises. Consequently, Macbeth's homestead protection becomes effective on January 1, 2003. At January 30, 2003, Macbeth has two liabilities outstanding against him. Liability number 1 is a judgment entered against Macbeth in a malpractice suit brought by Otto for $1 million on December 20, 2002. Liability number 2 is a judgment entered against Macbeth in a malpractice suit brought by Tootsie for $2 million on January 10, 2003. If the jurisdiction that Macbeth lives in follows the majority rule, Macbeth's homestead protection protects Castlerock against the claims of both Otto and Tootsie. However, if the applicable law follows the minority rule, Macbeth's homestead protection only protects Castlerock against Tootsie's claim.

Caution. When creditors reduce their claims against owners to judgments that constitute liens on the debtors' realty before the owners establish the homestead, many jurisdictions' homestead protection does not protect against such claims.[63]

---

[61] George L. Haskins, Estates Arising from the Marriage Relationship and Their Characteristics, in 1 American Law of Property § 5.86 (A. James Casner ed., 1952 & Supp. 1977). *See, e.g.,* Snelling v. Butler, 119 P. 3 (Wash. 1911); Barnett v. Knight, 3 P. 747 (Colo. 1884).

[62] Me. Rev. Stat. Ann. tit. 14, § 4422(1) (West 1980 & Supp. 1992); George L. Haskins, Estates Arising from the Marriage Relationship and Their Characteristics, in 1 American Law of Property § 5.86 (A. James Casner ed., 1952 & Supp. 1977).

[63] George L. Haskins, Estates Arising from the Marriage Relationship and Their Characteristics, in 1 American Law of Property § 5.86 (A. James Casner ed., 1952 & Supp. 1977); P.V. Smith, Annotation, *Creation of homestead right in real estate as affecting existing judgment lien,* 110 A.L.R. 883 (1937).

[2] Liabilities Arising Before Homestead Acquisition

Another minority group of jurisdictions holds that homestead protection does not protect against claims arising before the owner acquires the homestead property.[64] Most jurisdictions, however, hold that liabilities incurred by the owner before the owner acquires the homestead property may not be enforced against the homestead.[65] However, when a creditor reduces his claim to a judgment that has become a lien on the property before it is acquired, the homestead exemption generally does not protect against such a lien.[66]

[3] Liabilities Incurred to Mortgage or Purchase Homestead Property

Most states provide that their homestead exemption does not protect the homestead from the claims of creditors holding a valid mortgage on the property that both spouses execute.[67]

EXAMPLE 8-10

Marie, a doctor, and Louis, a lawyer, buy a home, Versailles, for $ 1 million cash in 1995 as part of an asset protection plan. Louis, Marie, and Versailles are located in a jurisdiction in which tort claims cannot reach property protected by the homestead exemption. In 2002 Marie and Louis take out a $400,000 mortgage on Versailles from French-Banc and use the proceeds to pay off their credit card bills. In 2003 Marie and Louis, while playing with a loaded gun in their backyard, accidentally shoot Ben, their neighbor. Ben sues Marie and Louis for tort damages and wins a $20 million judgment against them, for which they are jointly and severally liable. Because the applicable law does not allow tort claimants to reach property protected by the homestead exemption, Ben cannot reach Versailles. However, Ben's $20 million claim forces Marie and Louis into bankruptcy. This causes Marie and Louis into default on their mortgage to FrenchBanc. The result is that FrenchBanc may now reach Versailles to satisfy its claim because the homestead exemption will not apply to it.

---

[64] Ky. Rev. Stat. Ann. § 427.060 (Baldwin 1992); George L. Haskins, Estates Arising from the Marriage Relationship and Their Characteristics, in 1 American Law of Property § 5.87 (A. James Casner ed., 1952 & Supp. 1977).

[65] George L. Haskins, Estates Arising from the Marriage Relationship and Their Characteristics, in 1 American Law of Property § 5.87 (A. James Casner ed., 1952 & Supp. 1977). See, e.g., Kelly v. Connell, Green & Co., 18 So. 9 (Ala. 1895); Milton v. Milton, 58 So. 718 (Fla. 1912).

[66] George L. Haskins, Estates Arising from the Marriage Relationship and Their Characteristics, in 1 American Law of Property § 5.87 (A. James Casner ed., 1952 & Supp. 1977).

[67] Ala. Code § 6-10-2 (1977 & Supp. 1992); George L. Haskins, Estates Arising from the Marriage Relationship and Their Characteristics, in 1 American Law of Property § 5.89 (A. James Casner ed., 1952 & Supp. 1977).

Planning Pointer. The planner should advise clients using homestead property as part of an asset protection plan not to mortgage the homestead property.

A related exception is the purchase money obligation exception. Specifically, most states' homestead exemption does not protect the homestead property from creditors holding purchase money obligations whose proceeds were used to purchase the homestead property.[68]

Planning Pointer. The planner should recommend to clients using the homestead exemption that they completely pay off existing loans that they previously used to acquire the homestead property. Alternatively, if they acquire new property, clients should not use new loans.

Caution. The planner should note that courts often construe the purchase money obligation exception liberally.[69] Consequently, any liability whose proceeds the owner uses to purchase the homestead property may potentially reach such property.

[4] Liabilities Incurred to Improve Homestead Property

Many states also exempt from homestead protection liabilities whose proceeds the owner uses to pay for improvements on the homestead property or for crops raised on such property. This exception to homestead protection extends to mechanics' and materialmen's liens and the claims of laborers or servants whose work involved the improvement of the homestead property.[70]

Planning Pointer. The planner should advise the client not to borrow funds for improving the homestead property in jurisdictions where this exception exists. Instead, in such jurisdictions when the client desires to improve the homestead property, the client should use his own funds.

---

[68] Kan. Stat. Ann. § 60-2301 (Supp. 1992); George L. Haskins, Estates Arising from the Marriage Relationship and Their Characteristics, in 1 American Law of Property § 5.90 (A. James Casner ed., 1952 & Supp. 1977).

[69] George L. Haskins, Estates Arising from the Marriage Relationship and Their Characteristics, in 1 American Law of Property § 5.90 (A. James Casner ed., 1952 & Supp. 1977).

[70] George L. Haskins, Estates Arising from the Marriage Relationship and Their Characteristics, in 1 American Law of Property § 5.91 (A. James Casner ed., 1952 & Supp. 1977).

[5] Criminal Penalties

Some states exempt criminal penalties from homestead protection. Such penalties may include forfeited bail bonds or fines for carrying deadly weapons contrary to applicable law.[71]

[6] Taxes

Most states exempt the owner's liability for taxes from homestead protection. In most states the homestead is subject to execution and sale for taxes.[72] However, in some jurisdictions this exception only applies to taxes levied on the homestead itself.[73] Also, United States federal tax claims constitute liens on taxpayers realty, which are not subject to the homestead exemption.[74]

Planning Pointer. The planner should ensure that the client pays all applicable taxes.

[7] Tort Liability

Many jurisdictions do not extend homestead exemption protection to tort liabilities.[75]

Planning Pointer. If the applicable law does not extend homestead protection to tort claims, the planner should consider either (1) using tools other than the homestead as part of the asset protection plan, or (2) shifting ownership of the homestead property to a nonvulnerable spouse or other party.

EXAMPLE 8-11

Same facts as Example 8-10, except that the applicable law does not extend homestead exemption protection to tort claims and that Marie and Louis's

---

[71] George L. Haskins, Estates Arising from the Marriage Relationship and Their Characteristics, in 1 American Law of Property § 5.92 (A. James Casner ed., 1952 & Supp. 1977).

[72] George L. Haskins, Estates Arising from the Marriage Relationship and Their Characteristics, in 1 American Law of Property § 5.93 (A. James Casner ed., 1952 & Supp. 1977).

[73] Utah Code Ann. § 78-23-3 (1992); George L. Haskins, Estates Arising from the Marriage Relationship and Their Characteristics, in 1 American Law of Property § 5.93 (A. James Casner ed., 1952 & Supp. 1977).

[74] See Chapter 10; George L. Haskins, Estates Arising from the Marriage Relationship and Their Characteristics, in 1 American Law of Property § 5.93 (A. James Casner ed., 1952 & Supp. 1977).

[75] Me. Rev. Stat. Ann. tit. 14, § 4422(1) (West Supp. 1992); George L. Haskins, Estates Arising from the Marriage Relationship and Their Characteristics, in 1 American Law of Property § 5.94 (A. James Casner ed., 1952 & Supp. 1977).

asset protection advisor convinces them to transfer ownership of Versailles to their child, Charles. Here, Ben cannot reach Versailles, even though the applicable law does not extend homestead protection against tort claims.

[8] Alimony

Many jurisdictions provide that their homestead exemptions do not protect against alimony claims.[76] Many other jurisdictions, however, do extend homestead protection against alimony claims.[77] When the owner remarries, courts generally do extend homestead protection against the alimony claims of the first spouse.[78]

[9] Claims Based on Superior Title

Homestead protection does not protect the homestead against others who hold a superior title in the homestead or who hold a right that constitutes a defect in the homestead owner's interest.[79]

EXAMPLE 8-12

Tammy Tenant, who lives in a jurisdiction that gives lessees a homestead right, leases an apartment from Laura Landlord. Tammy's lease runs out on December 31, 2000. Tammy continues to live in the apartment in 2001 but does not pay rent. Here, Laura may reclaim the apartment, absent applicable law to the contrary.

[D] Loss of Homestead Protection

Under certain circumstances, the owner loses the protection of the applicable homestead exemption. This may occur due to the dissolution of the family, changed use of the homestead, or abandonment of the homestead.

---

[76] George L. Haskins, Estates Arising from the Marriage Relationship and Their Characteristics, in 1 American Law of Property § 5.95 (A. James Casner ed., 1952 & Supp. 1977). *See, e.g.,* Ayers v. Ayers, 288 N.W. 679 (Iowa 1939); Davis v. Davis (*In re* Davis), 105 F.3d 1017 (5th Cir. 1997); Annotation, *Enforcement of claim for alimony or support, or for attorneys 'fees and costs incurred in connection therewith, against exemptions,* 54 A.L.R.2d 1422 (1957).

[77] George L. Haskins, Estates Arising from the Marriage Relationship and Their Characteristics, in 1 American Law of Property § 5.95 (A. James Casner ed., 1952 & Supp. 1977). *See, e.g.,* Stafford v. Stafford, 140 P.2d 545 (Wash. 1943).

[78] George L. Haskins, Estates Arising from the Marriage Relationship and Their Characteristics, in 1 American Law of Property § 5.95 (A. James Casner ed., 1952 & Supp. 1977). *See, e.g.,* Anderson v. Anderson, 123 P.2d 315 (Kan. 1942).

[79] George L. Haskins, Estates Arising from the Marriage Relationship and Their Characteristics, in 1 American Law of Property § 5.96 (A. James Casner ed., 1952 & Supp. 1977). *See, e.g.,* King v. Welburn, 47 N.W. 106 (Mich. 1890).

First, in jurisdictions requiring owners to be the head of a household or family, the family's dissolution may terminate the homestead exemption protection. However, in most jurisdictions once homestead protection arises, it continues for the benefit of a single individual after the breakup of a marriage.[80]

Second, many jurisdictions hold that if the owner subsequently devotes the homestead entirely to nonresidential (business) uses, the homestead protection stops. However, some jurisdictions hold that once homestead protection arises, the fact that the owner subsequently uses the property principally for business does not terminate the homestead protection.[81]

Finally, the owner may lose homestead protection by abandoning the property. Abandonment results when the debtor voluntarily leaves the homestead with the present, or later developed, definite intention never to occupy the homestead property again as a homestead. The key factor courts use to decide whether the owner abandoned the homestead is the owner's intent. This is a question of fact, and courts look at such factors as prolonged absence, renting the homestead, and admissions or declarations against interest. However, courts have held that owners did not abandon property when they rented it out, moved away from it, or purchased new homes.[82]

§ 8.03   LIFE INSURANCE

[A]   In General

Life insurance contracts generally provide that the contract holder pays a series of payments to the life insurance company.[1] In exchange, the life insurance company promises to pay a lump sum payment (or series of payments) to a beneficiary on the happening of a contingency (usually the insured's death) set forth in the contract.[2] The life insurance policy "matures" when such a contingency occurs.

---

[80] David G. Epstein et al., Debtors and Creditors 132 (1987); George L. Haskins, Estates Arising from the Marriage Relationship and Their Characteristics, in 1 American Law of Property §§ 5.107 to 5.111 (A. James Casner ed., 1952 & Supp. 1977).

[81] George L. Haskins, Estates Arising from the Marriage Relationship and Their Characteristics, in 1 American Law of Property § 5.112 (A. James Casner ed., 1952 & Supp. 1977).

[82] David G. Epstein et al., Debtors and Creditors 132 (1987); George L. Haskins, Estates Arising from the Marriage Relationship and Their Characteristics, in 1 American Law of Property § 5.113 (A. James Casner ed., 1952 & Supp. 1977).

§ 8.03   [1] See generally Santo (Sandy) Bisignano, Jr., Protecting Assets from Overzealous Creditors or an Estate Planner's Guide to Preservation Planning, 1987 Annual Notre Dame Est. Plan. Inst. 3-40 to 349; Rhonda H. Brink, Planning Perspectives for Creditor Conscious Clients 1 704.3, in 22d Annual University of Miami Philip E. Heckerling Inst. on Est. Plan. (John T. Gaubatz ed., 1988); William J. Woodward, Jr., Enforcements of Money Judgments: Objectives and Restrictions, in 9 Debtor-Creditor Law ¶ 37.03[B][4] (Theodore Eisenberg ed., 1992); Steven G. Margolin, Exemption Planning, in California Asset Protection Planning (1992).

[2] William J. Woodward, Jr., Enforcements of Money Judgments: Objectives and Restrictions, in 9 Debtor-Creditor Law ¶ 37.03[B][4] at 37-73 (Theodore Eisenberg ed., 1992).

Life insurance constitutes an important component of an estate plan.[3] This is primarily because, besides providing risk-shifting benefits for clients, the IRC provides special tax rules for life insurance that make it more advantageous than other comparable investments.[4] More importantly, from the planner's viewpoint many states exempt life insurance from the reach of creditors.[5]

Planning Pointer. The planner should analyze:

1. How the exemption statute applies to protect the insurance policy proceeds and cash value from the insured's creditors,
2. How the exemption statute applies to protect the insurance policy proceeds from the beneficiary's creditors, and
3. The tax consequences of using insurance as part of the asset protection plan.[6]

United States Bankruptcy Code Section 522(d)(7) and (8) exempts certain interests in life insurance policies from the reach of the bankruptcy trustee.[7] Specifically, these provisions exempt: (1) any unmatured life insurance contract owned by the debtor other than a credit life insurance contract;[8] and (2) the debtor's aggregate interest, not to exceed in value $4,000, less any amount of property of the estate transferred in any manner specified in Section 542(d) (that is, dealing with insurance companies taking the policy to pay premiums or carry out a nonforfeiture option, if such option is automatic under the contract), in any accrued dividend or interest under, or loan value of, any unmatured life insurance contract owned by the debtor under which the insured is the debtor or an individual of whom the debtor is a dependent.[9] Also, most states provide exemption statutes that protect life insurance policies from the insured's creditors.[10]

---

[3] *See, e.g.,* Lewis D. Solomon & Susan Flax Posner, Tax Planning Strategies (1992); Lee F. Holdmann, *Income and Estate Planning Advantages of Life Insurance Enhanced by TRA 86 Changes*, 14 Est. Plan. 130 (1987).

[4] *See* §§ 8.03[D]–8.03[F].

[5] Annotation, *Right of creditors of life insured as to options or other benefits available to him during his lifetime*, 37 A.L.R.2d 268 (1954).

[6] *See* §§ 8.03[D]–8.03[F].

[7] 11 U.S.C. § 522(d) (7), (8) (1988).

[8] 11 U.S.C. § 522(d)(7) (1988).

[9] 11 U.S.C. § 522(d)(8) (1988).

[10] Cal. Civ. Proc. Code § 704.100 (Deering 1983); Ind. Code Ann. § 27-1-12-14 (West 1993); Kan. Stat. Ann. § 40-414 (Supp. 1992); Rhonda H. Brink, Planning Perspectives for Creditor Conscious Clients ¶ 704.3 at 7-19, in 22d Annual University of Miami Philip E. Heckerling Inst. on Est. Plan. (John T. Gaubatz ed., 1988); Santo (Sandy) Bisignano, Jr., Protecting Assets from Overzealous Creditors or an Estate Planner's Guide to Preservation Planning, 1987 Annual Notre Dame Est. Plan. Inst. 3-43.

EXAMPLE 8-13

Ike Insured lives in a jurisdiction that completely exempts life insurance policies from the claims of the insured's creditors. In 1995 Ike purchases a $1 million life insurance policy as part of an asset protection plan. Ike designates Sam, Ike's son, as the policy's beneficiary. Ike dies in 2002. At this time, Ike has a negative net worth of $2 million. Ike's creditors want to reach Ike's life insurance policy proceeds. Here, Ike's creditors cannot reach such proceeds because of the state exemption statute.

Caution. Although most states exempt life insurance policies from the insured's creditors, there are certain exceptions to this rule. The planner also must ensure that the product purchased as part of the asset protection plan falls within the applicable exemption's definition of life insurance.[11]

[B] *Exceptions to Life Insurance Exemptions*

First, many states restrict their exemptions to life insurance policies whose beneficiaries fall within a prescribed class of relationship to the insured.[12] For example, Illinois limits its exemption to policies whose proceeds are payable to the insured's spouse, children, or dependent relatives,[13] and Ohio limits its exemption to policies whose proceeds are payable to the insured's spouse, children, dependent relatives, creditors, or trustee of any of the foregoing.[14]

Caution. If the beneficiary falls originally within the applicable statute's parameters but either the state amends the statute or the beneficiary's relationship to the insured changes, the exemption protection may cease.[15]

Planning Pointer. When the planner uses life insurance as part of the asset protection plan, he should review the client's plan periodically for changes causing beneficiaries to fall outside the applicable statute's parameters.

---

[11] *See, e.g.,* Kennedy v. Pikush (*In re* Pikush), 157 B.R. 155 (Bankr. 9th Cir. 1993), *aff'd*, 27 F.3d 386 (9th Cir. 1994).

[12] Santo (Sandy) Bisignano, Jr., Protecting Assets from Overzealous Creditors or an Estate Planner's Guide to Preservation Planning, 1987 Annual Notre Dame Est. Plan. Inst. 3-41.

[13] Ill. Rev. Stat. ch. 73, para. 850 (1965 & Supp. 1992).

[14] *Id.*

[15] Santo (Sandy) Bisignano, Jr., Protecting Assets from Overzealous Creditors or an Estate Planner's Guide to Preservation Planning, 1987 Annual Notre Dame Est. Plan. Inst. 3-41. *See, e.g.,* Hoffman v. Weiland, 29 N.E.2d 33 (Ohio Ct. App. 1940).

Second, if the insured validly assigns the insurance policy to a creditor as collateral for debt, that creditor may generally reach the insurance policy and its proceeds.[16]

Planning Pointer. The planner should advise clients who use life insurance as part of an asset protection plan not to assign their policies to creditors.

Third, if the insured commits fraud in the formation of the insurance contract and the beneficiary and insurance company are aware of such fraud, the insured's creditors may reach the insurance policy and its proceeds.[17]

Planning Pointer. The planner should conduct a fraudulent conveyance analysis to ensure that the transaction does not constitute a fraudulent conveyance.[18]

Fourth, if the insured is insolvent when he designates the beneficiary, the insured's creditors may reach the policy.[19]

Planning Pointer. The planner should obtain reliable financial statements from the client. He should use these to conduct a solvency analysis under applicable law as part of the fraudulent conveyance analysis.[20] This step should alert the planner to any solvency problems.

Finally, if the insured makes premium payments with fraudulent intent or while insolvent, the insured's creditors may be able to reach the insurance policy to the extent of premiums.[21]

---

[16] Santo (Sandy) Bisignano, Jr., Protecting Assets from Overzealous Creditors or an Estate Planner's Guide to Preservation Planning, 1987 Annual Notre Dame Est. Plan. Inst. 3-43. *See, e.g.,* Parker Square State Bank v. Huttash, 484 S.W.2d 429 (Tex. Civ. App. 1972); *In re* Hardings Estate, 16 N.W.2d 585 (Iowa 1944).

[17] Santo (Sandy) Bisignano, Jr., Protecting Assets from Overzealous Creditors or an Estate Planner's Guide to Preservation Planning, 1987 Annual Notre Dame Est. Plan. Inst. 3-44. *See, e.g.,* San Jacinto Bldg. v. Brown, 79 S.W.2d 164 (Tex. Civ. App. 1935).

[18] *See* Chapter 2.

[19] *See* Chapter 2. *See also* Santo (Sandy) Bisignano, Jr., Protecting Assets from Overzealous Creditors or an Estate Planner's Guide to Preservation Planning, 1987 Annual Notre Dame Est. Plan. Inst. 3-44. *See, e.g.,* Pope Photo Record, Inc. v. Malone, 539 S.W.2d 224 (Tex. Civ. App. 1976).

[20] *See* Chapter 2.

[21] Mich. Stat. Ann. §24-12207 (Callaghan 1987); Ohio Rev. Code Ann. §3911. 10 (Anderson 1989 & Supp. 1992); Santo (Sandy) Bisignano, Jr., Protecting Assets from Overzealous Creditors or an Estate Planner's Guide to Preservation Planning, 1987 Annual Notre Dame Est. Plan. Inst. 3-44 to 3-45.

Planning Pointer. The planner must examine the applicable law to determine how it applies to (1) the claims of the insured's creditors, and (2) the beneficiary's creditors. Some states' exemption provisions vary depending on whether they apply to the claims of the insured's or the beneficiary's creditors.[22]

EXAMPLE 8-14

Ike Insured dies in 2001. Ike's death triggers payment of a $1 million life insurance policy to his son, Bob. Both Ike and Bob have outstanding judgments against them. The applicable law exempts life insurance proceeds from the claims of the insured's creditors but not the claims of the beneficiary's creditors. Here, Ike's creditors cannot reach the insurance policy, but Bob's creditors can reach the insurance policy.

[C] Extension of Life Insurance Exemptions

Many states extend life insurance exemption protection to the life insurance policy's cash surrender value. Many states also provide that the insured's retention of the power to change beneficiaries will not, by itself, impact their exemption's application. Finally, some states have extended their exemption to include property purchased with life insurance proceeds.[23] On the other hand, many states limit their life insurance protection to a fixed dollar amount.[24]

Planning Pointer. Some state exemption statutes expressly recognize spendthrift (that is, anti-alienation) provisions included in insurance contracts.[25] Where such provisions exist, the planner should advise the client to use life insurance policies that include such a provision.

---

[22] Santo (Sandy) Bisignano, Jr., Protecting Assets from Overzealous Creditors or an Estate Planner's Guide to Preservation Planning, 1987 Annual Notre Dame Est. Plan. Inst. 3-43.

[23] Santo (Sandy) Bisignano, Jr., Protecting Assets from Overzealous Creditors or an Estate Planner's Guide to Preservation Planning, 1987 Annual Notre Dame Est. Plan. Inst. 3-41 to 3-42.

[24] Tex. Prop. Code Ann. § 42.002(7) (West 1984 & Supp. 1992); Santo (Sandy) Bisignano, Jr., Protecting Assets from Overzealous Creditors or an Estate Planner's Guide to Preservation Planning, 1987 Annual Notre Dame Est. Plan. Inst. 3-43.

[25] Ind. Code Ann. § 27-2-5-1 (West 1993); Kan. Stat. Ann. § 40-414a (1986); Tex. Ins. Code Ann. art. 21.22 (West 1984 & Supp. 1992); Santo (Sandy) Bisignano, Jr., Protecting Assets from Overzealous Creditors or an Estate Planner's Guide to Preservation Planning, 1987 Annual Notre Dame Est. Plan. Inst. 3-43.

Planning Pointer. The planner must analyze the law of the applicable jurisdiction to determine whether the exemption provided under the life insurance exemption is added to the personal property exemption that such jurisdiction provides under its general exemption statute, or is merely a subset of that personal property exemption.[26] Generally, exemption provisions providing that the life insurance exemption is in addition to the general personal property provision offer greater asset protection potential than when the life insurance is merely a subset of the general personal property exemption. In any event, the planner must determine the exact amount of protection afforded by the exemption to determine the overall asset protection plan to recommend.

Planning Pointer. The planner should consider using an irrevocable life insurance trust. Such a vehicle offers both additional asset protection and tax savings for the client. An irrevocable insurance trust involves the following:

1. The settlor establishes an irrevocable life insurance trust for beneficiaries that he designates.
2. Either (a) the settlor gives an existing life insurance policy on his life to the trust, or (b) gives money to the trust, that the trust uses to purchase a life insurance policy on his life.
3. The settlor gives cash to the trust periodically to enable the trust to make premium payments on the life insurance policy.
4. The settlor gives Crummey powers to the beneficiaries.[27] Briefly, Crummey powers are powers that enable the beneficiary to withdraw his portion of the gift to the trust within a designated period following the gift. If the beneficiary does not withdraw his portion of the gift within the designated period, the beneficiary's withdrawal right lapses. Such powers qualify the gift for the annual gift tax exclusion.

The irrevocable life insurance trust adds the asset protection provided by a trust to that provided by the applicable exemption statute.[28] Moreover, the irrevocable life insurance trust adds significant tax advantages over the settlor owning the life insurance policy outright.[29]

---

[26] Santo (Sandy) Bisignano, Jr., Protecting Assets from Overzealous Creditors or an Estate Planner's Guide to Preservation Planning, 1987 Annual Notre Dame Est. Plan. Inst. 3-45; *In re* Bowes, 160 B.R. 290 (Bankr. N.D. Tex. 1993) (debtors allowed, under Texas Insurance Code, to exempt full $77,000 of their life insurance policies, but in so doing they exhausted the $60,000 personal property exemption provided under Texas Property Code).

[27] *See* §§ 8.03[D]–8.03[F].

[28] *See* Chapters 5–6.

[29] *See* Jonathan G. Blattmachr & Georgiana J. Slade, *Life Insurance Trusts: How to Avoid Estate and GST Taxes*, 22 Est. Plan. 259 (Oct. 1995).

[D]   Gift Tax on Life Insurance

The planner must evaluate the transfer tax consequences of using life insurance as part of an asset protection plan.[30] First, he should determine the gift tax implications of the proposed life insurance. A policy owner makes a taxable gift when terminating ownership by transferring the policy to the donee and when such transfer is absolute. Conversely, when the policy owner merely designates a policy beneficiary or transfers policy ownership while retaining the right to name or change beneficiaries, no taxable gift occurs.[31]

When the policy owner transfers the policy to an irrevocable trust, the owner generally makes a completed taxable gift. However, if the recipient trust is a revocable trust, the owner does not make a taxable gift.[32]

When a nonowner pays life insurance premiums, such payments generally constitute taxable gifts.[33] Also, when one party who is not the insured owns a policy and names a different party as the beneficiary, the insured's death completes a contingent gift and, thus, constitutes a taxable gift.[34]

> **Planning Pointer.** The gift tax value of most life insurance policies is low relative to the face value of such policies. Consequently, the client can transfer great amounts of wealth to his beneficiaries with a minimum of transfer tax consequences by gifting life insurance policies. Furthermore, because such wealth no longer constitutes part of the client's property, this plan protects such wealth from his creditors.
>
> Generally, the gift tax value of life insurance depends on the type of policy involved and when the gift occurs. For example, if the client purchases life insurance and gifts such life insurance at the time of purchase, the value will generally equal the policy's cost.[35] When the client gifts a paid-up policy, the Treasury Regulations determine the value by looking at

---

[30] *See generally* Lewis D. Solomon & Susan Flax Posner, Tax Planning Strategies Ch. 16 (1992); Lewis D. Solomon et al., Federal Taxation of Estates, Trusts and Gifts Ch. 12 (1989); Richard B. Stephens et al., Federal Estate and Gift Taxation 1 4.14 (1983 & Supp. 1992); Michael D. Rose & John C. Chommie, Federal Income Taxation (3d ed. 1988). Mark A. Segal, *Crummey Trusts: Multiple Exclusions and Remote Contingent Beneficiaries,* 16 Rev. Tax'n Individuals 359 (1992); James C. Cavanaugh & Robert J. Preston, *When Will Crummey Transfers to Contingent Beneficiaries Be Excludable Present Interests?* 76 J. Tax'n 68 (1992); Nicholas A.J. Vliestra, Note, *Estate of Cristofani v. Commissioner: The Expanded Potential of Crummey Powers for Transfer Tax Avoidance,* 45 Tax Law. 583 (1992); Charlotte M. Wilson, Note, *The Crummey Power and Inter Vivos Trusts: An Analysis of Estate, Gift, and Income Tax Consequences to the Trust Beneficiary,* 22 Mem. St. U. L. Rev. 297 (1992); David N. Barhkhausen, *When to Trust in a Trust: A Sure-Footed Guide to Using Irrevocable Life-Insurance Trusts,* Compleat Law. 26 (Fall 1992).

[31] Reg. § 25.2511-1(h)(8) (1986).

[32] *See* Lewis D. Solomon et al., Federal Taxation of Estates, Trusts and Gifts 517 (1989).

[33] Reg. § 25.2511-1(h)(8) (1986).

[34] *See* Goodman v. Commissioner, 156 F.2d 218 (2d Cir. 1946); Rev. Rul. 77-48,1977-1 C.B. 292; Lewis D. Solomon et al., Federal Taxation of Estates, Trusts and Gifts 517 (1989).

[35] Reg. § 25.2512-6(a), Ex. (1) (1974); Guggenhiem v. Rasquin, 312 U.S. 254 (1941); Phipps v. Commissioner, 43 B.T.A. 790 (1941).

the value of comparable contracts sold by the insurer.[36] If the client gifts a policy that has been in force for some time and that requires further premiums to be made, the Treasury Regulations determine the value by looking at the interpolated terminal reserve.[37] The interpolated terminal reserve is the reserve (1) that the insurer maintains to cover its liability under the policy and the insured portion of the last premium paid before the gift, and (2) that covers the period after the date of the gift.[38]

Planning Pointer. The planner should strive to structure the transaction so that taxable transfers qualify for the annual $10,000 per donee gift tax exclusion.

When the client transfers all the incidents of ownership to a single donee, this constitutes a gift of a present interest, which qualifies for the $10,000 annual gift tax exclusion.[39] However, if the transfer is subject to restrictions, the IRS may consider it to be a gift of a future interest, which would not qualify for the annual exclusion.[40]

EXAMPLE 8-15[41]

Mark gives a life insurance policy to his three children, Tom, Huck, and Becky. Here, this transfer will not qualify for the annual exclusion because no one child can exercise all the ownership rights without the consent of the other co-owners.

If the life insurance policy's donee receives a present interest in such policy, then premiums paid by another person will constitute a present interest. Such payments will qualify for the annual exclusion.[42]

Gifts of life insurance policies to trusts generally constitute gifts of future interests, which do not qualify for the annual gift tax exclusion.[43] Furthermore, gifts of or payments of premiums of life insurance policies held by trusts constitute gifts of future interests that do not qualify for the annual exclusion.[44]

---

[36] Reg. § 25.2512-6(a), Ex. (3) (1974).
[37] Reg. § 25.2512-6(a), Ex. (4) (1974).
[38] Lewis D. Solomon et al., Federal Taxation of Estates, Trusts and Gifts 518 (1989).
[39] Reg. § 25.2503-3(a) (1983).
[40] Rev. Rul. 55408, 1955-1 C.B. 113.
[41] See Skouras v. Commissioner, 14 T.C. 523 (1950), aff'd, 188 F.2d 831 (2d Cir. 1951).
[42] Reg. § 25.2503-3(c), Ex. (6) (1983).
[43] Reg. § 25.2503-3(c), Ex. (2) (1983); Rev. Rul. 79-47, 1979-1 C.B. 312.
[44] Rev. Rul. 76-490, 1976-2 C.B. 300.

Planning Pointer. The planner should use Crummey powers in connection with life insurance trusts. Such Crummey powers allow life insurance premium payments to qualify for the annual gift tax exclusion. Crummey powers are powers given to the trust's beneficiaries. They allow the beneficiaries to make effective outright demand for property held in trust, usually for a defined period following the gift of such property to the trust.[45] This right constitutes a present right to possession, which is deemed to be equal to actual present possession for annual gift tax exclusion purposes.

EXAMPLE 8-16

David gives five life insurance policies to an irrevocable trust as part of an asset protection plan. David's wife and child are the beneficiaries. The trust instrument provides that for 30 days after the time of any contribution or gift by David to the trust, the wife and child may demand the lesser of (1) that beneficiary's fractional share of the trust, or (2) $10,000, the amount of the annual exclusion. This structure allows the contributions of cash that David makes to enable the trust to pay the life insurance premiums to constitute gifts of present interests. Consequently, such gifts qualify for the annual exclusion.

EXAMPLE 8-17

Same facts as Example 8-16, except that the trust does not provide Crummey powers to the beneficiaries. Here, each time David makes a cash gift to the trust to enable it to pay the life insurance premiums, this transfer constitutes a taxable gift not qualifying for the annual gift tax exclusion. Consequently, David must pay gift tax each time he makes such a transfer.

[E]   Estate Tax on Life Insurance

In evaluating the transfer tax consequences of using life insurance as part of an asset protection plan, the planner must determine the estate tax implications.

---

[45] Lewis D. Solomon et al., Federal Taxation of Estates, Trusts and Gifts 519-21 (1989). Crummey v. Commissioner, 397 F.2d 82 (9th Cir. 1968); Estate of Cristofani v. Commissioner, 97 T.C. 74 (1991).

Estate tax treatment of life insurance policies depends on whether the life insurance policy:

1. Is one that the decedent owns but that insures another person's life;
2. Is one that the decedent owns and that is payable to the decedent's estate; or
3. Is one that the decedent owns and that is payable to others.

Generally, when decedents own life insurance policies insuring the life of another, the IRC treats such policies like any other contractual right. Consequently, the IRC includes such property in the decedent's gross estate.[46] If the decedent did not own the policy but merely had rights to cash in the policy for its cash value, to borrow against the policy, or similar such powers, the IRC also includes the policy in the decedent's gross estate as property over which the decedent possessed a general power of appointment.[47] Such policies are taxed at their value at death instead of at their face value, using the principles that were previously discussed for gift tax purposes.[48]

EXAMPLE 8-18

Harry owns a life insurance policy on the life of John, his father, which he obtained as part of John's asset protection plan. The life insurance policy has a $1 million face value. It is a completely paid-up policy, and comparable policies would be sold by the insurance company for $35,000, which also constitutes the policy's value for gift tax purposes. Harry dies. Here, Harry's gross estate includes the life insurance policy at the $35,000 value.

When the decedent owns a life insurance policy that is payable to his estate, IRC Section 2042(1) requires the decedent to include the amount of the life insurance proceeds in his estate.

EXAMPLE 8-19

Same facts as Example 8-18, except that John owns the life insurance policy, the policy is payable to his estate, and John dies. Here, John's gross estate must include the $1 million in life insurance proceeds.

When the decedent possesses any of the incidents of ownership in a life insurance policy that insures his life but that is payable to others, IRC Section 2042(2) requires the decedent to include the life insurance proceeds in his gross

---

[46] IRC § 2033 (1988).
[47] IRC § 2042 (1988).
[48] Reg. § 20.2031-8 (1974).

estate. This rule only requires one or more incidents of ownership over the property, instead of full ownership. For purposes of this rule, incidents of ownership include, among others, the economic benefits of the insurance, the power to change beneficiaries, the power to surrender or cancel the policy, the power to assign the policy, the power to revoke an assignment of the policy, the power to pledge the policy for a loan, the power to obtain from the insurer a loan against the surrender value of the policy, and the power to affect the time and manner of the life insurance proceeds.[49]

Planning Pointer. The planner should ensure that the asset protection plan does not give any incidents of ownership to the insured. Failure to follow this rule causes a great increase in transfer taxes that could otherwise be avoided.

EXAMPLE 8-20

Same facts as Example 8-19, except that the policy is payable to Harry. Here, John's gross estate must include the $1 million in life insurance proceeds.

A contingent right over a life insurance policy also may be sufficient to constitute an incident of ownership that triggers IRC Section 2042(2) inclusion in the decedent's gross estate. Specifically, IRC Section 2042(2) provides that if a right, which includes the possibility that the policy or its proceeds may return to the insured or become subject to a power of disposition by him, is valued at more than 5 percent of the value of the policy immediately before the insured's death, then such right constitutes an incident of ownership. However, the mere possibility that the decedent may receive the policy or proceeds through the estate of another is not sufficient to constitute an incident of ownership.[50]

Planning Pointer. If the assignee possesses an unqualified right to cash in the policy immediately before the decedent's death, this prevents the reversionary interest from attaining a value that exceeds 5 percent of the policy's value or proceeds.[51]

The IRC applies enterprise attribution rules to determine whether the decedent possesses any incident of ownership in a policy or its proceeds. Specifically, if the decedent owns a controlling interest in a corporation

---

[49] Estate of Lumpkin v. Commissioner, 474 F.2d 1092 (5th Cir. 1973).
[50] Reg. § 20.2042-1(c)(3) (1979).
[51] Reg. § 20.2042-1(c)(3) (1979).

(that is, 50 percent or greater interest) that owns a life insurance policy on the insured's life that is payable to someone other than the corporation, the IRC requires the decedent's gross estate to include such policy or proceeds. However, if the policy's proceeds are payable to the corporation, the policy will not be included in the decedent's gross estate.[52]

Concerning life insurance trusts, the IRC treats decedents as possessing incidents of ownership in policies held in trust if, under the terms of the policy, the decedent, either alone or with another party, has the power as trustee or otherwise to change (1) the beneficial ownership of the policy or its proceeds, or (2) the time and manner of its enjoyment, even when the decedent lacks any beneficial interest in the trust.[53] However, the IRS does not deem the decedent to have any incidents of ownership of policies held in trust when (1) the decedent's powers are (a) held in a fiduciary capacity (b) that are not exercisable for the decedent's personal benefit, and (2) the decedent did not transfer the policy or any of the consideration or funds used for buying or maintaining the policy as part of a prearranged plan involving the participation of the decedent.[54]

In community property states, the estate taxation of life insurance depends on the applicable law's contours. For example, if the applicable law entitles the surviving spouse to half the proceeds of policies purchased before the marriage where the premiums were paid for with community funds, then the decedent's gross estate does not include proceeds to which the spouse is entitled.[55] If the surviving spouse is entitled to only a return of half the premiums paid with community funds on a policy purchased before the marriage, then the decedent's gross estate must include all the proceeds less the premiums the estate is obligated to return to the other spouse.[56] Generally, when the asset protection plan calls for the decedent to own the policy and for the proceeds to go to the decedent's spouse, the decedent's gross estate includes the proceeds, and the estate may claim the marital deduction for amounts going to the spouse.[57]

Caution. The terminable interest rule applies here. Therefore, the planner must carefully analyze the various payout options available under the policy to ensure that the payout qualifies for the marital deduction. For example, if the proceeds are left with the insurance company and interest paid to the spouse with the principal sum paid at the spouse's death to the decedent's children, the terminable interest rule would bar the marital deduction.[58]

---

[52] Reg. §§ 20.2031-2(f) (1992), 20.2042-1(c)(6) (1979).
[53] Reg. § 20.2042-1(c)(4) (1979).
[54] Rev. Rul. 84-179, 1984-2 C.B. 195.
[55] Reg. § 20.2042-1(c)(5) (1979).
[56] Rev. Rul. 80-242, 1980-2 C.B. 276.
[57] IRC § 2056(b)(7) (1988).
[58] Lewis D. Solomon et al., Federal Taxation of Estates, Trusts and Gifts 538 (1989).

Planning Pointer. IRC Section 2056(b) provides that the decedent may claim the marital deduction for a life insurance settlement arrangement in which the proceeds of a life insurance policy are held by an insurance company under a contract pursuant to which the surviving spouse is to receive the proceeds in installments or the interest on the proceeds if he has a power to appoint all interests.[59]

Caution. The planner should note that the IRC requires the decedent's gross estate to include policies transferred within three years of the decedent's death as if the decedent had retained the policy.[60]

EXAMPLE 8-21

Mark has a $1 million life insurance policy on his life, which he acquired several years ago as part of an asset protection plan. In 2003 Mark learns that he has less than one year to live. He consults with his asset protection planner, Sam, who advises him to give the policy to his son, Tom. Sam tells Mark that this plan will result in excluding the proceeds from Mark's estate. Mark follows this advice and gives absolute ownership of the policy to Tom on February 1, 2003. On May 1, 2003, Mark dies. Here, Sam's advice was erroneous. Because the transfer was within three years of Mark's death, Mark's gross estate includes the life insurance proceeds.

Planning Pointer. When the asset protection plan calls for gifting the policy out of the insured's hands, the plan should be executed as early as possible to minimize the risk of IRC Section 2035 pulling the proceeds back into the insured's gross estate.

Caution. When the planner uses term life insurance with a one-year term and the decedent purchases a new policy each year and then gifts this policy to another, the IRC Section 2035 three-year rule will be triggered.[61]

---

[59] IRC § 2056(b) (1988).
[60] IRC § 2035 (1988).
[61] Bel v. United States, 452 F.2d 683 (5th Cir. 1971), *cert. denied*, 406 U.S. 919 (1972).

However, if the term policy gives the insured the right of renewal without regard to the insured's insurable status, this will not trigger the IRC Section 2035 three-year rule.[62]

When the transferee of the insurance policy makes premium payments after a policy's transfer, that occurs within three years of the decedent's death, the amount includible in the decedent's gross estate is calculated as follows:[63]

+ premiums paid by transferor/insured before the transfer
÷ total premiums paid before and after the transfer
_____
= amount includible in the decedent/insured's gross estate

Caution. When the decedent transfers funds within three years of death to a transferee, who then purchases a life insurance policy on the decedent with such funds, the IRC Section 2035 three-year rule will apply.[64]

EXAMPLE 8-22

Same facts as Example 8-21, except that instead of owning the life insurance directly, Mark gives Tom the money to buy a life insurance policy. Here the result is the same; namely, the proceeds are included in Mark's gross estate.

Planning Pointer. A prerequisite for the IRC Section 2035 three-year rule to apply is that the decedent must transfer an interest in property included in the decedent's gross estate or an interest that would have been included if the decedent had retained such an interest.[65] Consequently, when the planner has a client who may die within three years, the planner may avoid the IRC Section 2035 three-year rule by structuring the plan so that the decedent does not transfer property that would be included in his estate. For example, the decedent may make a valid loan to the beneficiary to allow the beneficiary to purchase the life insurance.

---

[62] Rev. Rul. 82-13, 1982-1 C.B. 132.
[63] Estate of Silverman v. Commissioner, 61 T.C. 338 (1973), aff'd, 521 F.2d 574 (2d Cir. 1975).
[64] Bel v. United States, 452 F.2d 683 (5th Cir. 1971), cert. denied, 406 U.S. 919 (1972).
[65] Estate of Leder v. Commissioner, 89 T.C. 235 (1987), aff'd, 893 F2d 237 (10th Cir. 1989).

EXAMPLE 8-23

Same facts as Example 8-22, except that Mark owns 100 percent of Twain Corp, and Twain Corp loans funds to Tom that Tom uses to purchase the life insurance policy. Mark never possesses any interest in the policy, and Twain Corp never possesses any interest in the policy. Here, because Mark never possesses any interest in the policy, his estate would not include the policy under IRC Section 2042. Consequently, the policy will not be included in Mark's estate under the IRC Section 2035 three-year rule.

[F] Income Tax on Life Insurance

In evaluating the transfer tax consequences of using life insurance as part of an asset protection plan, the planner must determine the income tax implications. Generally, the IRC exempts life insurance proceeds from income taxation.[66] However, the IRC does not exempt income produced by life insurance proceeds from taxation.

EXAMPLE 8-24

Abe gives a $2 million face value life insurance policy on his life to his son, George, as part of an asset protection plan in 1995. Abe, having exhausted his unified credit, pays gift tax on the value of the policy at this time, which equals $50,000. Abe dies in 2003. The $2 million in life insurance proceeds that George receives at Abe's death is not subject to income taxation. However, any interest that is earned on the insurance proceeds is subject to taxation.

If an insurance policy is transferred for value, the IRC limits the owner's income tax exclusion to the amount of consideration paid by the recipient plus any subsequent payments.[67]

[G] Offshore Private Placement Life Insurance

[1] In General

Offshore private placement life insurance (OPPLI) has become a hot topic among planners because of the significant benefits that it confers.[68] Among others, these benefits include:

- Lower life insurance premiums and internal overhead costs

---

[66] IRC § 101(a)(1) (1988).

[67] IRC § 101(a)(2) (1988).

[68] *See, e.g.,* Russ Alan Prince, *Private Placement Variable Life Strikes Chord with the Wealthy,* 105 Nat'l Underwriter Life & Health Fin. Services Ed. 14 (May 7, 2001); Norse N. Blazzard & Judith A. Hasenauer, *Private Placement VL is Getting Attention,* 101 Nat'l Underwriter Life & Health Fin. Services Ed. 12 (Dec.

- Greater investment choices
- Increased confidentiality
- Increased asset protection
- Advantageous tax treatment for assets contained within the OPPLI policy.

However, because OPPLI policies are relatively new, they entail significant risks, which planners must guard against.

Planning Pointer. Planners should consider the following benefits, risks, and issues associated with OPPLI:

- The tax and asset protection advantages of OPPLI and the manner in which OPPLI is typically used.
- OPPLI design issues, focusing primarily on features that OPPLI policies must possess to constitute "life insurance" for federal tax purposes.
- Other practical considerations, including the structure used to hold OPPLI policies and the tax consequences of such structures.

[2] Preliminary Considerations: Advantages and the Manner in Which OPPLI Is Typically Used

[a] OPPLI as Investment Vehicle for Wealth Accumulation

As a preliminary matter, planners must understand that OPPLI policies, which are typically variable universal life insurance policies,[69] serve primarily as investment vehicles for the OPPLI policy owner's lifetime wealth accumulation. This contrasts with the typical purpose of most life insurance, which is usually to create wealth, or to replace wealth used to pay estate and inheritance taxes.

Planning Pointer. Because of the tax benefits of life insurance, OPPLI policies work particularly well for assets that would otherwise constitute inefficient components of the client's investment portfolio.

[b] Tax Benefits of Life Insurance

Life insurance receives special tax treatment,[70] which makes it ideal for holding passive investments for wealth accumulation. It is critical to note that such tax

---

15, 1997); Russ Alan Prince, *Private Placement VL Is Next Big Thing,* 104 Nat'l Underwriter Life & Health Fin. Services Ed. 15 (May 29, 2000); Ron Panko, *A Quiet Hurricane; Insurers Capitalizing on Private Placement Markets,* 98 Best's Review—Life-Health Ins. Ed. 93 (Nov. 1997).

[69] Variable universal life insurance policies are policies that provide the policy owner with the flexibility to adjust the premium payments and death benefits while the cash value accumulates, and that give the policy owner the opportunity to invest in any of several non-public stock, bond, or other mutual funds offered by the insurer.

[70] *See generally* The National Underwriter Co., Tax Facts 2001; Howard M. Zaritsky & Stephen R. Leimberg, Tax Planning with Life Insurance: Analysis with Forms (2002).

benefits are the driving force behind OPPLI's popularity. When properly structured, life insurance provides tax-deferred growth of the cash value, tax-free access to cash value, and tax-free death benefits. Traditional life insurance products, however, limit the types of investments that may be made with the cash value. In contrast, as described in this section, an OPPLI policy greatly expands the range of investments that may be made with the cash value and increases the control that the policy owner may effectively exercise over the investments made with the cash value.

Planning Pointer. OPPLI imparts the following tax benefits to policy owners:

- *Cash deferral.* Earnings on variable life insurance policy cash values, including interest, dividends, and capital gains, are tax-deferred as long as such earnings remain in the policy.[71] Consequently, the cash value grows much more rapidly than a taxable investment portfolio.
- *Tax-free withdrawals and loans.* During the insured's life, the policy owner may withdraw cash and obtain policy loans against cash value on an income-tax-free basis, assuming the policy is not a modified endowment contract (MEC, discussed more fully later in this section).
- *Tax-free death benefits.* Section 101 excludes death benefit proceeds payable at the insured's death from the insured's gross income.[72] In addition, with proper planning the death benefits may also be excluded from the insured's taxable estate.[73]

EXAMPLE 8-25

Harry, a successful author, invests $10 million in the Magical Hedge Fund (MH Fund) on January 1, 2000. The MH Fund generates a 20 percent annual return, all of which is taxable to Harry at his marginal combined federal and state tax rate of 45 percent. Harry's sister, Gwyneth, an actress who also has a marginal combined federal and state tax rate of 45 percent, also invests $10 million in the MH Fund on January 1, 2000. However, Gwyneth invests in the fund by means of a Bermuda OPPLI policy.

Between 2000 and 2020, Harry's investment in the MH Fund grows from $10 million to more than $80 million. However, during this same period Gwyneth's investment in the MH Fund grows from $10 million to more than $383 million. This difference results from the income tax deferral on Gwyneth's investment, ignoring the cost of death benefit insurance for the time being. This difference can be seen in Table 8-1 and, graphically, in Figure 8-1.

---

[71] IRC §§ 72, 7702(g)(1)(A).
[72] IRC § 101(a)(1).
[73] IRC § 2042.

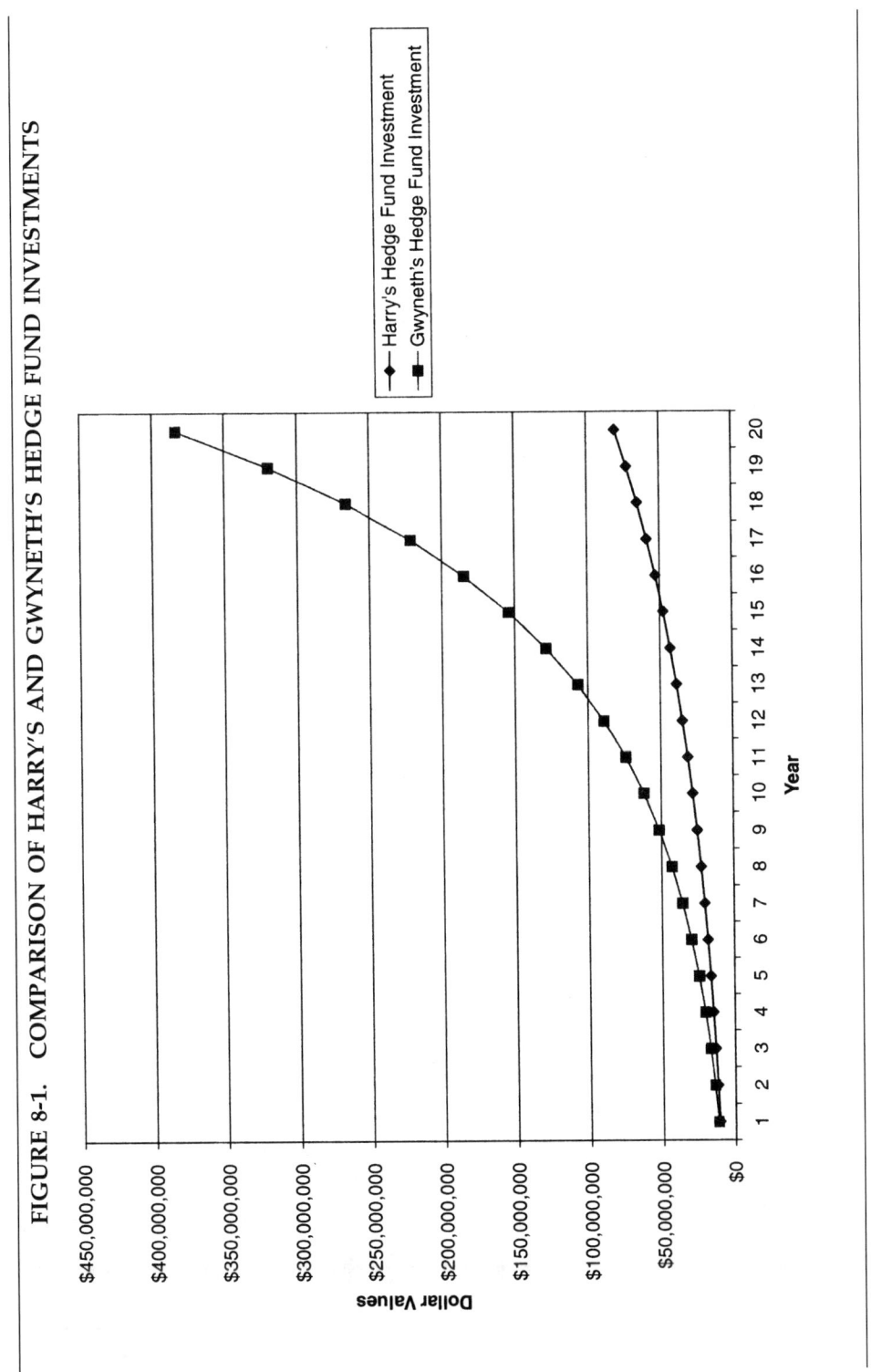

FIGURE 8-1.   COMPARISON OF HARRY'S AND GWYNETH'S HEDGE FUND INVESTMENTS

TABLE 8-1
Investment Growth

Harry's Hedge Fund

Year	Beginning of Year Hedge Fund Investment	Income Generated on Fund	Taxes on Income Generated	End of Year Hedge Fund Investment
2000	$10,100,000	$2,000,000	$900,000	$11,100,000
2001	$11,100,000	$2,220,000	$999,000	$12,321,000
2002	$12,321,000	$2,464,200	$1,108,890	$13,676,310
2003	$13,676,310	$2,735,262	$1,230,868	$15,180,704
2004	$15,180,704	$3,036,141	$1,366,263	$16,850,582
2005	$16,850,582	$3,370,116	$1,516,552	$18,704,146
2006	$18,704,146	$3,740,829	$1,683,373	$20,761,602
2007	$20,761,602	$4,152,320	$1,868,544	$23,045,378
2008	$23,045,378	$4,609,076	$2,074,084	$25,580,369
2009	$25,580,369	$5,116,074	$2,302,233	$28,394,210
2010	$28,394,210	$5,678,842	$2,555,479	$31,517,573
2011	$31,517,573	$6,303,515	$2,836,582	$34,984,506
2012	$34,984,506	$6,996,901	$3,148,606	$38,832,802
2013	$38,832,802	$7,766,560	$3,494,952	$43,104,410
2014	$43,104,410	$8,620,882	$3,879,397	$47,845,895
2015	$47,845,895	$9,569,179	$4,306,131	$53,108,943
2016	$53,108,943	$10,621,789	$4,779,805	$58,950,927
2017	$58,950,927	$11,790,185	$5,305,583	$65,435,529
2018	$65,435,529	$13,087,106	$5,889,198	$72,633,437

Gwyneth's Hedge Fund

Year	Beginning of Year Hedge Fund Investment	Income Generated on Fund	Taxes on Income Generated	End of Year Hedge Fund Investment
2000	$10,000,000	$2,000,000	$0	$12,000,000
2001	$12,000,000	$2,400,000	$0	$14,400,000
2002	$14,400,000	$2,880,000	$0	$17,280,000
2003	$17,280,000	$3,456,000	$0	$20,736,000
2004	$20,736,000	$4,147,200	$0	$24,883,200
2005	$24,883,200	$4,976,640	$0	$29,859,840
2006	$29,859,840	$5,971,968	$0	$35,831,808
2007	$35,831,808	$7,166,362	$0	$42,998,170
2008	$42,998,170	$8,599,634	$0	$51,597,804
2009	$51,597,804	$10,319,561	$0	$61,917,364
2010	$61,917,364	$12,383,473	$0	$74,300,837
2011	$74,300,837	$14,860,167	$0	$89,161,004
2012	$89,161,004	$17,832,201	$0	$106,993,205
2013	$106,993,205	$21,398,641	$0	$128,391,846
2014	$128,391,846	$25,678,369	$0	$154,070,216
2015	$154,070,216	$30,814,043	$0	$184,884,259
2016	$184,884,259	$36,976,852	$0	$221,861,111
2017	$221,861,111	$44,372,222	$0	$266,233,333
2018	$266,233,333	$53,246,667	$0	$319,479,999

EXAMPLE 8-26

Same facts as Example A, except that Gwyneth's OP PLI policy is held by a foreign irrevocable life insurance trust (foreign ILIT) and Gwyneth dies in 2020. Here, the full OPPLI death benefit is excluded from Gwyneth's taxable estate for federal estate tax purposes and the tax deferral on the inside cash buildup becomes permanent.

Planning Pointer. One technique that planners have used in conjunction with OPPLI arrangements is to form a company wholly owned by the OPPLI arrangement. The company would purchase a highly appreciated asset (*e.g.*, low basis, pre-IPO stock) from the client in exchange for a deferred private annuity. The company would subsequently sell the highly appreciated asset. This technique allows the client to defer the gain on the sale of his or her asset to the OPPLI over the life of the private annuity. Moreover, the wholly

FIGURE 8-2. ASSET SALE GAIN DEFERRAL

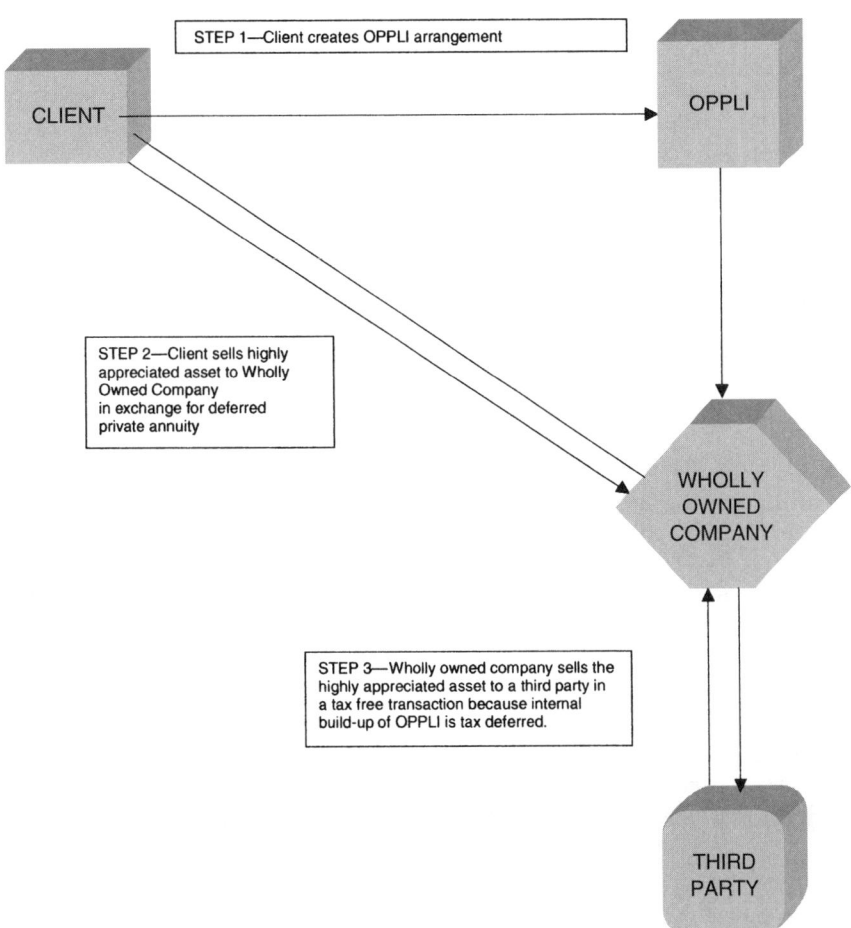

owned company can sell the asset that it owns without any gain recognition. This arrangement is graphically represented in Figure 8-2.

[c] Product Pricing

The costs of life insurance may be less expensive for OPPLI than for domestic insurance. This generally results from lower overhead costs for offshore life insurance and the absence of a state premium tax. For example, many foreign insurance companies operate in no-tax or low-tax jurisdictions, and are therefore subject to a much lower tax rate than U.S.-based life insurance companies. The savings from absence of a state premium tax typically approximates 2 to $3\frac{1}{2}$; percent of the premium.[74] In addition, for foreign issuers that have not made an IRC section 953(d) election to be taxed as a domestic corporation, the OPPLI policy may avoid the federal deferred acquisition cost (DAC) tax that might other wise apply.

[d] Confidentiality

OPPLI may offer greater confidentiality than other foreign asset protection techniques because offshore insurance companies are not subject to the same reporting and compliance requirements as domestic insurance carriers. In addition, at least one commentator has stated that offshore life insurance products do not constitute foreign bank accounts, securities accounts, or other financial accounts for Bank Secrecy Act reporting purposes.[75]

[e] Asset Protection

A substantial benefit of OPPLI is that it protects the assets of the insured, which are contained within the OPPLI policy, while allowing the insured to access and use such assets. This is a substantial advantage, compared to other asset protection techniques, which generally limit the asset protection client's ability to access the protected asset.

Planning Pointer. When considering the asset protection benefits of OPPLI, planners should consider the following issues.

- *Asset protection from creditors of the life insurance company or its policyholders.* Funds in all variable annuity life insurance policies, including OPPLI,

---

[74] *See* Leslie C. Giordani, *Offshore Life Insurance Planning* (ALI-ABA Course of Study Materials; International Trust and Estate Planning, Aug. 2000).

[75] *See* Charles L. Ratner, *Private Placement Life Products: Domestic, Offshore or Atoll? The Reality Check Please; Variable Universal Life Insurance,* 140 Tr. & Est. 48 (July 1, 2001). In addition, a staff member of the Financial Crimes Enforcement Network of the U.S. Treasury Department, sometimes referred to as FinCEN, has expressed the view to one of the authors that payment of life insurance premiums to foreign life insurance companies generally does not trigger Bank Secrecy Act reporting requirements, assuming that such payments do not involve the transfer of more than $10,000 of currency out of the United States.

are held separately from the insurer's general account.[76] Consequently, funds held in such a separate account are not subject to the insurer's creditors. This contrasts with traditional cash value policies, which are subject to the creditors of the insured. Therefore, the cash value invested in an OPPLI policy is protected from the insurer's creditors. However, the death benefit amount would be exposed to the insurer's creditors in the sense that the insurer may be practically precluded from being able to pay the death benefit by a lack of funds, bankruptcy, and so on.

- *Exemption for life insurance under U.S. law.* Many states exempt life insurance from the claims of creditors.[77] These exemptions may protect the death benefit and any cash value from the insured's creditors, the beneficiary's creditors, or both of the foregoing. Some states have also extended the exemption to include property purchased with life insurance proceeds. For OPPLI, the laws of many foreign jurisdictions often provide even greater asset protection to life insurance contracts governed by such laws than do exemptions under U.S. state law.

- *Foreign ILIT.* Frequently, planners place OPPLI policies into foreign irrevocable life insurance trusts (foreign ILITs). Generally such foreign ILITs will include one or more of the asset protection features typically found in foreign asset protection trusts, such as anti-duress flight provisions and the nonrecognition of U.S. court judgments by courts in the situs jurisdiction of the foreign ILIT, which enhances the asset protection accorded to the OPPLI cash value.

[3]   OPPLI Design Issues: Ensuring Life Insurance Treatment

The primary issue in designing OPPLI policies in ensuring that such policies qualify as life insurance for U.S. federal tax purposes. An OPPLI policy must constitute life insurance for U.S. federal tax purposes if it is to obtain the favorable tax treatment that U.S. federal tax law confers upon life insurance—which, as discussed earlier, is the driving force behind OPPLI.

Planning Pointer. Because most clients are primarily motivated by the tax and asset protection benefits of OPPLI policies, planners will generally want to minimize the death benefit and maximize the cash value of the OPPLI policy.

Planning Pointer. The key issues that planners must examine when designing OPPLI arrangements include:

- What parameters must the OPPLI contract satisfy to constitute life insurance under IRC Section 7702?

---

[76] *See* IRC § 817.

[77] *See generally* Annotation, *Right of creditors of life insured as to options or other benefits available to him during his lifetime,* 37 A.L.R.2d 268 (1954 & 2000 Supp.).

- What parameters must the OPPLI contract meet to satisfy the IRC Section 817 diversification requirements?
- What are the consequences of modified endowment contract (MEC) status, and what parameters must the OPPLI contract fall within to avoid MEC status?

What other product design issues should planners consider?

[a] In General

IRC Section 7702(a) defines a *life insurance contract* as a life insurance contract under the applicable law, but only if such contract either:

1. Satisfies the cash value accumulation (CVA) test; or
2. Satisfies both (a) the guideline premium test (GPT) and (b) the cash value corridor test (CVCT).

Generally, the Code allows taxpayers to select which of these two tests will apply. However, once elected, the life insurance contract must continue to satisfy the requirements of that policy throughout the policy term.

> **Planning Pointer.** The planner should obtain a representation from the OPPLI issuer that the policy satisfies the Code's definition of life insurance, as determined by its actuaries. Also, although these tests generally require an actuary's services, planners must understand their basic operation.

[b] CVA Test

A policy satisfies the CVA test if, by the contract's terms, the policy's cash surrender value (*i.e.*, cash value) cannot, at any time during the contract term, exceed the net single premium that would have to be paid at that time to fund future benefits under the contract, making certain statutorily mandated assumptions. Generally, the CVA test is used less frequently for OPPLI than the GPT/CVCT tests.

The net single premium is determined by using (1) the greater of a 4 percent interest rate or the interest rate guaranteed in the OPPLI contract; (2) the mortality charge set forth in the contract, or, if more is set forth, the mortality charge used to calculate the statutory reserves for the policy; and (3) any other charges set forth in the contract. As the insured ages, the CVAT generally requires a higher minimum death benefit than the GPT/CVCT, which is why the latter test is more common in OPPLI policies.

EXAMPLE 8-27

Dick Chewy, the 25-year-old founder of Chewy Candy Bars, buys an OPPLI policy with a $10 million face value. The net single premium for a person his age is $1.5 million. Here, as long as the OPPLI contract's cash value is less than $1.5 million at this time, it will pass the CVA test.

---

[c] GPT/CVCT

To satisfy the second test, the policy must satisfy both (1) the GPT and the (2) CVCT. To satisfy the GPT, the sum of the premiums paid under the contract must not, at any time, exceed the greater of (1) the guideline single premium at such time, or (2) the sum of the guideline level premiums to such date.[78] Essentially, the GPT requires a minimum death benefit relative to the premiums paid under the contract. For this purpose, *premiums paid* means premiums paid under the contract less amounts to which IRC section 72(e) applies (*i.e.*, amounts not received as annuities).[79] The *guideline single premium* is the premium required to fund future benefits under the OPPLI contract, determined at the time the contract is issued, using the same factors as for the net single premium but using a 6 percent interest rate rather than a 4 percent rate.[80] The guideline level premium is the level annual amount payable over a period that does not end before the insured becomes 95, calculated in the same manner as for the single guideline premium, except the annual effective rate remains at 4 percent.[81]

EXAMPLE 8-28

Billy Bob, a 25-year-old technology entrepreneur, buys a $10 million face value OPPLI policy with a scheduled annual premium of $50,000 and a guaranteed interest rate of 4.5 percent. Based on actuarial assumptions, the guideline single premium equals $1,110,000, and the guideline level premium equals $9,000. Billy Bob wants to contribute an additional $700,000 during the first contract year. Here, the guideline single premium is calculated with the statutory rate of 6 percent and the guideline level premium is computed using the guaranteed minimum interest rate of 4.5 percent. Therefore, Billy Bob may not contribute the additional $700,000 without violating the GPT. This is because in years 9 through 17, the premiums that Billy Bob would actually pay would exceed the greater of (a) the guideline single premium (*i.e.*, $1,110,000), or (b) the sum of the guideline level premiums. Table 8-2 and Figure 8-3 reflect this analysis.

---

[78] IRC § 7702(c).
[79] IRC § 7702(f)(1).
[80] IRC § 7702(c)(3).
[81] IRC § 7702(c)(4).

Table 8-2
Application of GPT/CVCT

Year	Cumulative Annual Premium	Special Premium	Amount Actually Paid: Cumulative Special and Annual Premium	Guideline Single Premium	Cumulative Guideline Level Premiums
1	$50,000	$700,000	$750,000	$1,100,000	$90,000
2	$100,000	0	$800,000	$1,100,000	$180,000
3	$150,000	0	$850,000	$1,100,000	$270,000
4	$200,000	0	$900,000	$1,100,000	$360,000
5	$250,000	0	$950,000	$1,100,000	$450,000
6	$300,000	0	$1,000,000	$1,100,000	$540,000
7	$350,000	0	$1,050,000	$1,100,000	$630,000
8	$400,000	0	$1,100,000	$1,100,000	$720,000
9	$450,000	0	$1,150,000	$1,100,000	$810,000
10	$500,000	0	$1,200,000	$1,100,000	$900,000
11	$550,000	0	$1,250,000	$1,100,000	$990,000
12	$600,000	0	$1,300,000	$1,100,000	$1,080,000
13	$650,000	0	$1,350,000	$1,100,000	$1,170,000
14	$700,000	0	$1,400,000	$1,100,000	$1,260,000
15	$750,000	0	$1,450,000	$1,100,000	$1,350,000
16	$800,000	0	$1,500,000	$1,100,000	$1,440,000
17	$850,000	0	$1,550,000	$1,100,000	$1,530,000
18	$900,000	0	$1,600,000	$1,100,000	$1,620,000
19	$950,000	0	$1,650,000	$1,100,000	$1,710,000
20	$1,000,000	0	$1,700,000	$1,100,000	$1,800,000
	$10,500,000	$700,000	$24,500,000	$22,000,000	$18,900,000

FIGURE 8-3.   GUIDELINE PREMIUM TEST ANALYSIS

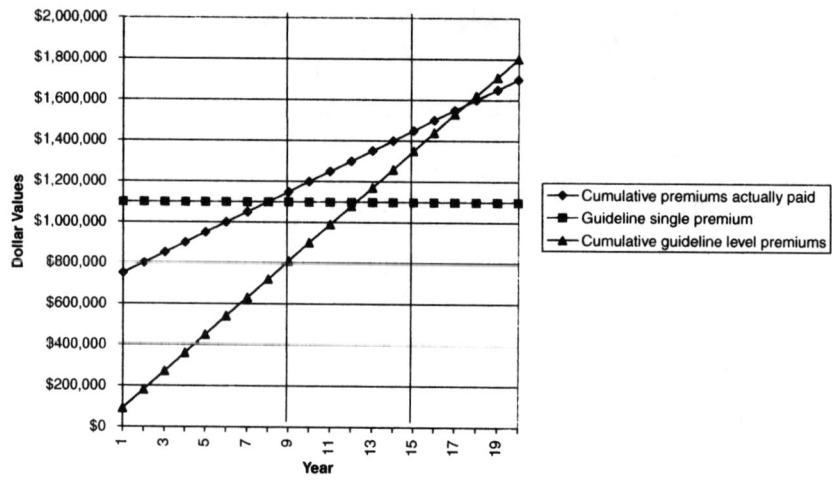

EXAMPLE 8-29

Assume the same facts as Example D, except that Billy Bob wants to contribute an additional $500,000 in year one, rather than $700,000. Here, as Table 8-3 and Figure 8-4 illustrate, Billy Bob may do this without violating the GPT.

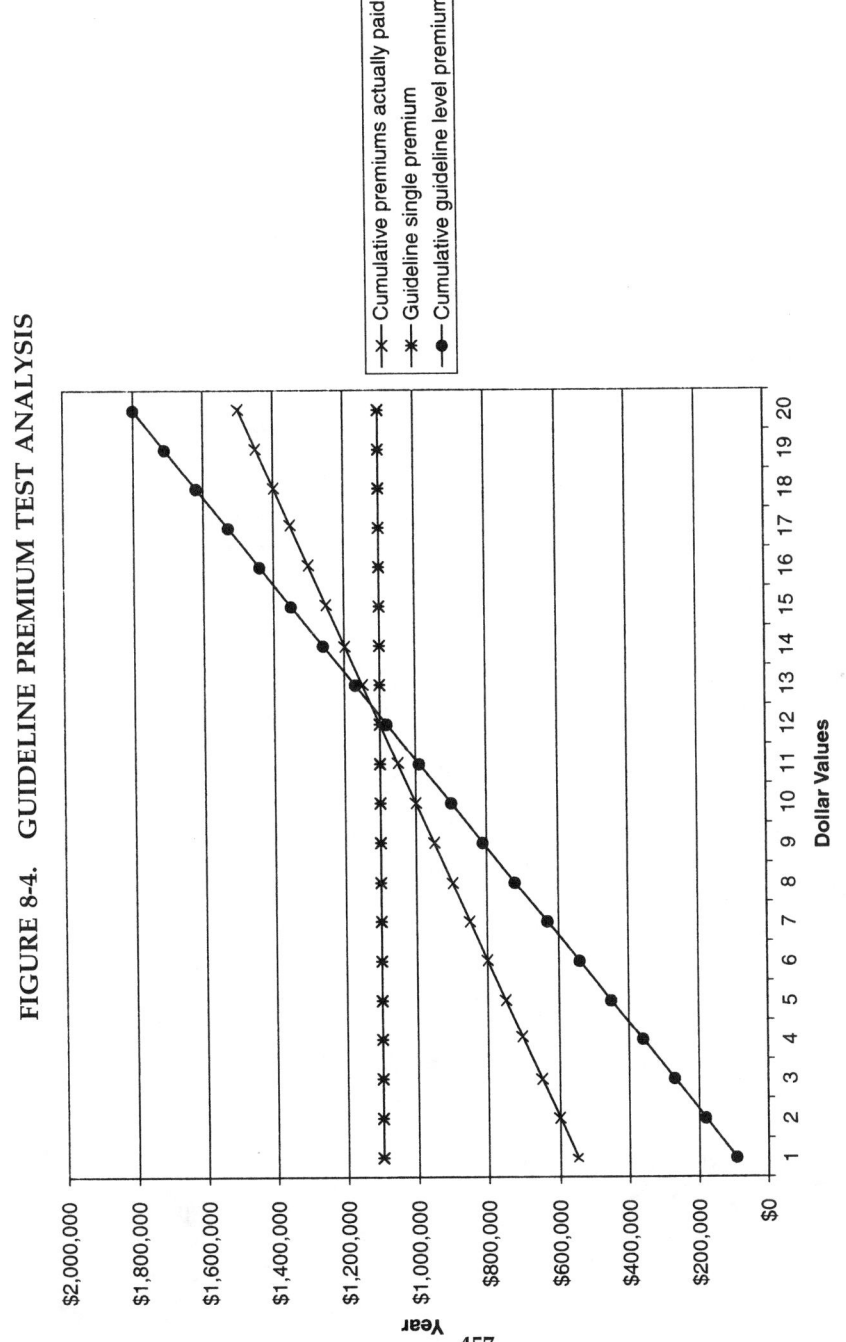

FIGURE 8-4. GUIDELINE PREMIUM TEST ANALYSIS

Table 8-3
Application of GPT

Year	Cumulative Annual Premium	Special Premium	Amount Actually Paid: Cumulative Special and Annual Premium	Guideline Single Premium	Cumulative Guideline Level Premiums
1	$50,000	$500,000	$550,000	$1,100,000	$90,000
2	$100,000	0	$600,000	$1,100,000	$180,000
3	$150,000	0	$650,000	$1,100,000	$270,000
4	$200,000	0	$700,000	$1,100,000	$360,000
5	$250,000	0	$750,000	$1,100,000	$450,000
6	$300,000	0	$800,000	$1,100,000	$540,000
7	$350,000	0	$850,000	$1,100,000	$630,000
8	$400,000	0	$900,000	$1,100,000	$720,000
9	$450,000	0	$950,000	$1,100,000	$810,000
10	$500,000	0	$1,000,000	$1,100,000	$900,000
11	$550,000	0	$1,050,000	$1,100,000	$990,000
12	$600,000	0	$1,100,000	$1,100,000	$1,080,000
13	$650,000	0	$1,150,000	$1,100,000	$1,170,000
14	$700,000	0	$1,200,000	$1,100,000	$1,260,000
15	$750,000	0	$1,250,000	$1,100,000	$1,350,000
16	$800,000	0	$1,300,000	$1,100,000	$1,440,000
17	$850,000	0	$1,350,000	$1,100,000	$1,530,000
18	$900,000	0	$1,400,000	$1,100,000	$1,620,000
19	$950,000	0	$1,450,000	$1,100,000	$1,710,000
20	$1,000,000	0	$1,500,000	$1,100,000	$1,800,000
	$10,500,000	$500,000	$20,500,000	$22,000,000	$18,900,000

An OPPLI policy will satisfy the CVCT if the death benefit payable under the OPPLI contract equals or exceeds the applicable percentage of the cash surrender value, which is set forth in Table 8-4.

TABLE 8-4
Applicable Percentage for CVCT

For an Insured with an Attained Age as of the Beginning of the Contract Year, of:		The Applicable Percentage Decreases by a Ratable Portion for Each Full Year:	
More Than:	But Not More Than:	From:	To:
0	40	250	250
40	45	250	215
45	50	215	185

50	55	185	150
55	60	150	130
60	65	130	120
65	70	120	115
70	75	115	105
75	90	105	105
90	95	105	100

For variable life insurance policies, such as OPPLI policies, the determination of whether the policy satisfies either of the two IRC section 7702 tests must be made whenever the death benefit under the policy changes, and at least once every 12 months.[82]

EXAMPLE 8-30

Ben Sillier, a 40-year-old actor, has an OPPLI policy with a cash value of $10 million. Here the death benefit must be at least $25 million to satisfy the CVCT. This results because the CVCT requires a life insurance policy's death benefit to equal or exceed 250 percent of the policy's cash value for a 40-year-old individual.

EXAMPLE 8-31

Assume the same facts as Example F, except that Ben is now 60 years old and his OPPLI policy now has a cash value of $30 million.

Here, the OPPLI policy's death benefit must be at least $39 million. This results because the CVCT requires the OPPLI policy's death benefit to equal or exceed 130 percent of the policy's cash value for a 60-year-old.

[d] IRC Section 817 Requirements

IRC Section 817 sets forth certain diversification requirements that variable life insurance, such as OPPLI, must satisfy to constitute life insurance for tax purposes. There are two relevant IRC Section 817 issues: (1) diversification requirements and (2) owner control issues.

First, IRC Section 817 provides that a variable life insurance contract will not be treated as a life insurance policy for tax purposes for any calendar quarter for which investments made by such account are not adequately diversified.[83]

---

[82] IRC § 7702(f)(9).
[83] Treas. Reg. § 1.817-5(a)(1).

Caution. If an OPPLI contract fails the IRC Section 817 diversification requirement for any period during which such requirement applies, it will not be treated as a variable life insurance contract for any future period, regardless of whether the contract subsequently satisfies the diversification requirement.[84] Such a failure would cause the contract holder to become subject to current taxation under the contract.[85] Therefore, the consequences of such a failure would likely be severe.

The IRS will consider a variable contract to be adequately diversified if it satisfies the following conditions:

1. No one investment constitutes more than 55 percent of the value of the total assets of the account;
2. No two investments constitute more than 70 percent of the value of the total assets of the account;
3. No three investments constitute more than 80 percent of the value of the total assets of the account; and
4. No four assets constitute more than 90 percent of the value of the total assets of the account.[86]

A segregated asset account that satisfies the diversification requirements at the end of any calendar quarter will not be treated as nondiversified in a subsequent quarter because of a discrepancy between the value of its assets and the diversification requirements unless that discrepancy exists immediately after an asset acquisition and such discrepancy results from such acquisition.[87]

The diversification requirement generally does not apply until the first anniversary of the account. However, in the case of a real property account, the diversification requirements are presumed to be satisfied until the earlier of the fifth anniversary of the account or the date that the account ceases to be a real property account.[88] For this purpose, an account constitutes a real property account if, on the anniversary date or date a plan of liquidation is adopted, not less than the applicable percentage of the account's total assets is represented by interests in real property. The applicable percentage for this purpose equals 40 percent for the period ending on the first anniversary date on which premium income is received, 50 percent for the year ending on the second anniversary, 60 percent for the year ending on the third anniversary, 70 percent for the year ending on the fourth anniversary, and 80 percent thereafter. Alternatively, an account will constitute a real property account on its first anniversary if, (1) on or

---

[84] Treas. Reg. § 1.817-5(a)(1).
[85] Treas. Reg. § 1.817-5(a)(1).
[86] Treas. Reg. § 1.817-5(b)(1)(i).
[87] Treas. Reg. § 1.817-5(d).
[88] Treas. Reg. § 1.817-5(c)(2)(ii).

before such date, the issuer has stated in the contract, prospectus, or a regulatory submission that it intends to invest the account assets primarily in real estate, and (2) at least 40 percent of the total assets are so invested within six months of the first anniversary.[89]

Although a complete discussion of the IRC Section 817 diversification requirement is beyond the scope of this book, planners should be aware of the following:

1. The IRS provides relief from inadvertent failures to satisfy the diversification requirements under certain circumstances.[90]
2. A regulatory safe harbor is provided for accounts that satisfy certain rules that apply to regulated investment companies.[91]
3. Treasury regulations provided look-through rules in certain cases.[92]

Some commentators take the position that the IRC Section 817 diversification requirements may not apply to OPPLI. IRC Section 817(d)(1) defines a *variable contract* as a contract "which provides for the allocation of all or part of the amounts received under the contract to an account, which pursuant to *State* law or regulation, is segregated from the general asset accounts of the company" (emphasis added); IRC Section 7701(a)(9) and (10) define the term *State* as referring to the District of Columbia and the States of the United States. These commentators reason, therefore, that technically an OPPLI policy cannot constitute a variable contract under IRC Section 817.[93] However, the more prudent course of action is to assume that IRC Section 817 does apply to OPPLI policies.

The second significant IRC Section 817 issue involves investor control. If income generated by OPPLI assets is to qualify for tax deferral, those assets must be treated as owned by the insurer rather than by the policy owner. The IRS takes the position that, for variable contracts, if the owner retains certain incidents of ownership, this may cause the policy owner to be treated as directly owning the underlying segregated account assets for U.S. tax purposes.[94] Some commentators opine that the enactment of IRC Section 817 effectively rendered the IRS's position on investor control obsolete.[95]

Planning Pointer. To avoid the harsh consequences that would result from attribution of underlying account assets to OPPLI policy owners, planners

---

[89] Treas. Reg. § 1.817-5(h)(4).

[90] *See* Treas. Reg. § 1.817-5(a)(2); Rev. Proc. 92-25, 1992-1 C.B. 741.

[91] IRC § 817(h)(2); Treas. Reg. § 1.817-5(b)(2).

[92] Treas. Reg. § 1.817-5(f).

[93] Gordon O. Pehrson et al., *Annuities, Life Insurance, and Long Term Care Insurance Products,* 546 Tax Mgmt. (BNA) A-51 (2001).

[94] *See* Rev. Rul. 77-85, 1977-1 C.B. 12; Rev. Rul. 80-274, 1980-2 C.B. 27; Rev. Rul. 81-225, 1981-2 C.B. 13; Christopherson v. Commissioner, 749 F.2d 513 (8th Cir. 1984).

[95] *See e.g.,* ABA Section of Taxation, Committee of Insurance Companies, *A Roadmap to the Federal Income Taxation of Non-Qualified Annuity Contracts,* 45 Tax Law. 123 (1991); Joint Committee on Taxation, General Explanation of the Deficit Reduction Act of 1984 at 608.

should structure OPPLI policies to satisfy the following, which are representations the IRS has previously required before it would issue private letter rulings stating that owners did not retain an impermissible degree of control over variable contracts:[96]

- Policyholders should not possess a legally binding right to require the insurance company or separate account to acquire any particular investment item with premiums or other amounts paid to or earned by the insurance company or separate account, or to invest any premiums or other amounts in any particular investment item.
- Policyholders may be informed of the general investment strategy to be followed.
- Policyholders may choose among broad investment strategies. To illustrate, policyholders could choose between stocks, bonds, money market instruments, instruments of financial institutions, instruments of governmental bodies, U.S. government securities, state government securities, foreign government securities, real property, and commodities.
- No policyholder can possess any legal, equitable, direct, indirect, or other interest in any specific investment item held by the insurance company and/ or the separate account.
- Policyholders should have only a contractual claim against the insurance company and/ or the separate account for cash as a result of purchasing the life insurance contract.

[e] Modified Endowment Contract Status

As discussed earlier, a primary objective for planners using OPPLI policies is to maximize the growth of the OPPLI policy's cash value, while simultaneously (1) preserving the policy owner's ability to access such cash value on a tax-free basis, and (2) providing asset protection for the accumulated cash value. However, if the OPPLI owner overfunds the policy, it will constitute a modified endowment contract (MEC). If this happens, MEC status will cause the IRS to tax the policy owner at ordinary income tax rates on certain distributions from the policy, *including loans from the policy*. Specifically, when a policy constitutes a MEC, the IRS treat distributions as ordinary income when received, to the extent that the cash value in the OPPLI contract immediately before the payment exceeds the investment in the contract.[97] In other words, MEC distributions are taxed on an "income first basis last" basis. The investment in the contract is increased by the amount of such recognized income. This eliminates one of the

---

[96] *See, e.g.,* Priv. Ltr. Rul. 8427085; Priv. Ltr. Rul. 8427091; Priv. Ltr. Rul. 8335124.
[97] IRC § 72(e).

key advantages of OPPLI, namely, the ability to access cash placed into an asset protection vehicle on a tax-free basis.

In addition to ordinary income taxation, IRC Section 72(v) imposes a 10-percent penalty tax on amounts the policy owner receives from a MEC that are includable in the owner's gross income. However, the penalty does not apply to distributions made:

- After the owner becomes disabled;
- After the owner attains the age of 59½ or
- When the distribution is part of a series of substantially equal periodic payments made for the taxpayer's life or life expectancy or the joint lives or joint life expectancies of the owner and his or her beneficiary.

For purposes of determining the amount of income recognized, the IRS treats all MECs issued by the same company to the same policyholder within one calendar year as one MEC.[98]

An OPPLI policy will constitute a MEC if it satisfies the IRC Section 7702 definition of life insurance, but either (1) fails to satisfy the seven-pay test, or (2) is received in exchange for a policy that constitutes a MEC. An OPPLI contract will fail the seven-pay test if the cumulative amount paid under the contract at any time during the first seven contract years or after a material change exceeds the sum of the net level premiums that would have been paid on or before that time, if the contract had provided for paid-up future benefits after the payment of seven level annual premiums.[99] Essentially, the seven-pay test requires a minimum level of insurance per premium dollar for the OPPLI contract's first seven years.

> **Caution.** If the benefits or other terms of a contract that was previously determined to not constitute a MEC materially change, the IRC treats the contract as a new contract issued on the date of such material change. A material change includes a material increase in the contract's future benefits. However, such an increase will not constitute a material change when either: (1) the increase is attributable to premiums required to fund the lowest death benefit during the first seven years of the contract, or interest or other earnings on the premium; or (2) certain cost-of-living benefits to the extent provided by Treasury Regulations.

EXAMPLE 8-32

George wants to buy an OPPLI policy with $10 million of initial death benefits. He also wants to invest additional funds in the policy to build cash value

---

[98] IRC § 72(b)(11).
[99] IRC § 7702A(b).

on a tax-free basis. However, the seven-pay test limits the premium George can pay in each of the first seven years. The reasonable mortality charge under the prevailing commissioners' standard tables for a male the same age as George is $28.36 per $1,000 of death benefit.

Here, the maximum first-year premium George can pay equals $283,600, which equals [$10,000,000/$1,000] × 28.36. Therefore, George could invest up to $283,600 in the first year without exceeding the seven-pay test limitation. George may calculate the cumulative premium limit for years two through seven by multiplying the maximum first-year premium by the number of years expired under the contract. To illustrate, the maximum total premium George could pay after two years of the contract expires without failing the seven-pay test equals $562,672, which equals 2 multiplied by $283,600.

Planning Pointer. If the purpose of the OPPLI policy is to pass wealth to the next generation without having access to such wealth, MEC status is irrelevant. Moreover, in such circumstances, MEC status may be more advantageous because it would allow the funding of the OPPLI policy with a single, up-front premium payment, which could then grow more rapidly because of tax-free compounding.

Planning Pointer. Other product design features that planners should consider include:

- *Single life or joint and survivor annuity.* Planners must decide whether to establish a single life or joint and survivor annuity policies.
- *Policy loans.* Planners must evaluate the OPPLI contract's policy loan provisions. Among other things, planners should examine the owner's ability to access cash value through policy loans and the charges associated with such loans. In addition, as discussed previously, policy MEC status will affect the tax consequences of any such policy loans actually made.
- *Extended maturity options.* Planners should find out whether extended maturity options are available. If so, planners should seriously consider such provisions. The issue here arises when the insured attains the contract maturity age, resulting in the forced return of cash value. This would cause the policy owner to be faced with a harsh tax situation.
- *The cost of the insurance.* Planners must, of course, examine the cost of the insurance, as this will affect the financial projections of the OPPLI policy.
- *Split-dollar capability.* If the planners will be using the OPPLI policy as part of a split-dollar arrangement, the planner should examine whether the insurer offers competitive alternate term rates. Competitive

alternate term rates will minimize the economic benefit component of split-dollar premium payments. The absence of such alternate rates will require the planners to use the PS58 tables, which in turn will typically result in an increased economic benefit amount.

- *"Force-outs."* Planners should seek a guarantee from the insurer that will not "force out" cash value if the policy cash value increases more rapidly than expected, thereby increasing the required net amount at risk. If the insurer mandates such a force-out, the IRS taxes the policy owner on the forced-out amount. In addition, such amounts become immediately subject to the claims of creditors of the policy owner. Consequently, it is much more advantageous to have the insurer guarantee that the at-risk portion of the OPPLI policy will always remain sufficiently ahead of the cash value without forcing out cash value.

[4] Other Considerations: Holding Structure and Practical Considerations

[a] Holding Structure

As with all other life insurance, planners must plan for the structure that will hold the policy. As a general matter, the OPPLI holding structure will be the point where the insured or policy owner most closely interfaces with the OPPLI arrangement and will require the planner to focus more closely on personal family and transfer tax issues than will other elements of the arrangement.

As with other life insurance, the most popular holding structure for OPPLI is an irrevocable life insurance trust (ILIT). ILITs are popular because they offer significant tax and asset protection advantages.[100] To illustrate, transfer of an OPPLI policy into a properly structured ILIT avoids income tax when the policy matures, estate tax on the death of the insured, and gift tax upon the creation and funding of the ILIT.[101] In addition, by placing the OPPLI policy into an ILIT, the planner gains the asset protection advantages of an irrevocable trust.[102]

Typically, planners prefer ILITs that are treated as domestic trusts for tax purposes, but which are foreign trusts for all other legal purposes, for use with OPPLI policies. Planners can ensure that the IRS treats the ILIT as a domestic trust for tax purposes by structuring it to satisfy the following requirements, set forth in IRC section 7701(a)(30)–(31):

- A court within the United States must be able to exercise primary supervision over administration of the ILIT;

---

[100] Because of the plethora of commentary about ILITs, the authors have kept this discussion of ILITs to a minimum. To read more about this subject, the reader is referred to Howard M. Zaritsky & Stephan R. Leimberg, Tax Planning with Life Insurance (2d ed. 2000 & Supp. 2001).

[101] *See generally* Lewis D. Solomon & Lewis J. Saret, Asset Protection Strategies, § 8.03[D]-[F] (2006); Among other things, the broker must determine that the insurer will be able to fulfill its performance obligations under the contract.

[102] *See generally* Lewis D. Solomon & Lewis J. Saret, Asset Protection Strategies, chs. 5–6 (2006).

- One or more U.S. persons must have the authority to control all substantial decisions of the ILIT.

This structure will avoid many of the reporting requirements associated with foreign trusts.[103]

> **Planning Pointer.** Planners may also use the OPPLI policy as part of a split-dollar arrangement to leverage gift tax payments and GST tax exemptions, while excluding the policy owner's share of the death benefit from the insured's estate.[104]

[b] Practical Considerations

There are several practical, nontax aspects that planners must also consider when establishing OPPLI arrangements.[105] In particular, planners must consider issues related to the solicitation and underwriting of the OPPLI policy, the servicing of the OPPLI policy, the selection of the foreign jurisdiction, and the appropriate involvement of various professionals.

1. *Solicitation of the OPPLI policy.* Generally, the foreign insurer should not solicit the OPPLI policy in the United States from the client. Such solicitation raises the risk that the state in which the insured is domiciled will assert a claim that such state's state premium tax applies.

> **Planning Pointer.** The insured should travel to the situs jurisdiction of the OPPLI arrangement for personal communications regarding the OP PLI arrangement including a physical examination, signing the OPPLI contract application, and so forth.

2. *Underwriting.* Although the primary motivation for entering into an OPPLI arrangement is to defer, permanently if possible, income taxation of the inside buildup of the OPPLI policy, all the parties to the arrangement must treat it as they would any other significant life insurance policy. Therefore, the parties must ensure that the insurer assumes the risk associated with the death benefit and that the appropriate underwriting steps, including a physical examination of the person to be insured, are undertaken.

---

[103] *See generally* Lewis D. Solomon & Lewis J. Saret, Asset Protection Strategies, chs. 14–15 (2006).

[104] *See* Anthony M. Sardis & Jeffrey J. Jenei, *Creating a Life Insurance Private Pension via Split-Dollar*, 25 Est. Plan. 51 (Feb. 1998); Robert J. Adler, *Private Split-Dollar Provides Transfer Tax Savings*, 61 Tax'n for Acct. 196 (Sept./Oct. 1998); Gerald R. Nowotny, *The Use of Private Placement Life Insurance and Split Dollar to Transfer Post-Mortem Appreciation*, 140 Tr. & Est. 62 (Feb. 1, 2001).

[105] *See* Leslie C. Giordani & Derry W. Swanger, *Offshore Life Insurance Planning for U.S. Clients*, 26 ACTEC Notes 70, 78 (2000).

Planning Pointer. Planners should ensure that, as part of the underwriting process, the insured has a physical examination (conducted outside the United States), and that the parties establish that the policy owner will have an insurable interest in the insured.

3. *Selection of jurisdiction and insurance carrier.* Planners must guide the client in selecting the jurisdiction and insurer to use for the OPPLI policy. Factors that planners should consider include:
   —The applicable law of the situs, regarding both insurance and asset protection
   —The communications facilities of the situs
   —The standard of the judiciary and the effectiveness of the court system
   —The financial and political stability of the situs
   —The availability of a professional at reasonable fees
   —The accessibility of the situs to the client.

4. *Involvement of professionals.* Because OPPLI is subject to less regulation than domestic life insurance, the involvement of reputable and knowledgeable professionals is critical to minimize the client's risk exposure. At a minimum, OPPLI arrangements require the involvement of a knowledgeable attorney and insurance broker. However, other professionals, such as accountants and financial planners, may also be involved.

An experienced attorney will generally assist the client in integrating an OPPLI arrangement into the client's overall tax, estate, and asset protection plan. Among other things, an attorney should:

- Conduct due diligence on the client to confirm financial solvency before making any transfers to an OPPLI arrangement. Among other things, this is required to avoid effecting a fraudulent conveyance.
- Provide the client with an analysis of the tax and other legal consequences of the OPPLI arrangement for the client. Typically, this will take the form of a memorandum or letter from counsel.
- Provide the client with recommendations for estate and tax planning to leverage the benefits of the OPPLI arrangement. For example, the attorney may recommend the use of an ILIT or of a private split-dollar arrangement with respect to the OPPLI policy.
- Facilitate communications between the client and insurance professionals. An experienced insurance broker will assist the client by interfacing between the client and insurer. Among other things, the insurance broker should:
- Assist the client by making recommendations regarding the appropriate offshore insurer and the terms of the OPPLI contract, and by negotiating the OPPLI contract and associated fees.
- Conduct due diligence on the insurance carriers under consideration.

- Analyze reinsurance agreements between insurance carriers being considered and their reinsurers.
- Facilitate the underwriting process.
- Analyze the insurance carrier's mortality costs and other fees associated with the OPPLI arrangement.
- Monitor the OPPLI arrangement by reviewing the arrangement on a periodic basis, no less frequently than annually, and ensure that the OPPLI arrangement continues to be tax compliant for U.S. tax purposes.

§ 8.04   ERISA QUALIFIED RETIREMENT PLANS

[A]   In General

Generally, retirement plans, and especially ERISA (Employee Retirement Income Security Act) qualified retirement plans (qualified plans), constitute an important part of a client's financial and estate plan. When properly used, qualified plans also offer a great amount of asset protection.[1] Consequently, such plans also constitute an important part of a client's asset protection plan. Because of the extreme complexity of the law applicable to qualified plans, a discussion of the requirements for ERISA qualification is beyond the scope of this text.

Planning Pointer. The planner should consult a competent ERISA attorney when considering or using qualified plans as part of the asset protection plan.

Planning Pointer. The planner should analyze:

- The ability of the client's creditors to reach the client's interest in the qualified plan in a bankruptcy context;
- The ability of the client's creditors to reach the client's interest in the qualified plan outside of a bankruptcy context;
- The tax consequences of using a qualified plan as part of the asset protection plan.[2]

---

§ 8.04 [1] *See generally* Annotation, *Employee retirement pension benefits as exempt from garnishment, attachment, levy, execution, or similar proceedings,* 93 A.L.R.3d 711 (1979 & Supp. 1995); Annotation, *Retirement fund benefits or refund of retirement fund contributions as 'Property' of debtor passing, under section 70(a)(5) of Bankruptcy Act (11 U.S.C.S. § 110(a)(5)) to trustee, in bankruptcy,* 34 A.L.R. Fed. 316 (1977 & Supp. 1995). Annotation, *Effect of antialienation provisions of Employee Retirement Income Security Act (29 U.S.C.S. § 1056(d)) (ERISA) on rights of judgment creditors,* 131 A.L.R. Fed. 427; Annotation, *Individual retirement accounts as exempt property in bankruptcy,* 133 A.L.R. Fed. 1.

[2] *See* § 8.04[D].

[B] Bankruptcy Context

Under the Bankruptcy Code,[3] the bankruptcy estate acquires all legal and equitable interests of the debtor.[4] However, restrictions on transfers of beneficial interests of the beneficiary/debtor in a trust that are enforceable under applicable nonbankruptcy law are enforceable for Bankruptcy Code purposes.[5] Qualified plans are generally established as trusts. Furthermore, both ERISA and the IRC require such plans to contain anti-alienation (spendthrift) provisions.[6] The Supreme Court, in a unanimous decision, finally resolved a split among the circuit courts by holding that the ERISA and IRC mandated anti-alienation provision in qualified plans constitutes a valid restriction on the transfer of beneficial interests of the beneficiary/debtor in a trust that is enforceable under applicable nonbankruptcy law. Consequently, the Court held that a debtor's interest in an ERISA qualified plan is excluded from the property of the bankruptcy estate.[7] Thus, the bankrupt debtor's creditors cannot reach plan assets in a bankruptcy proceeding.

EXAMPLE 8-33

Franklin is an accountant. He is a shareholder in Accounting Corp. As part of an asset protection plan, Franklin places $10,000 per year into Accounting Corp's qualified plan, beginning in 1990. In 2000 Franklin's interest in his qualified plan equals $250,000. In 2003, Sally, a shareholder of one of Franklin's clients, sues Franklin and Accounting Corp jointly. Sally wins a $20 million judgment against both Accounting Corp and against Franklin. Franklin files for bankruptcy protection. Here, when the bankruptcy court discharges Franklin from bankruptcy, he will retain his interest in the Accounting Corp qualified plan.

Caution. Although a plan participant's bankruptcy estate will not include his interest in qualified plans, due to the ERISA mandated anti-alienation provision, a different result historically occured for nonqualified plans and for Individual Retirement Accounts (IRAs). Specifically, such plans could

---

[3] For a detailed discussion of the Bankruptcy Code, *see* J. Pearson et al., Drafting Bankruptcy Reorganization Plans (2d ed., John Wiley & Sons 1993); Advanced Chapter 11 Bankruptcy Practice (Thomas J. Salerno & Craig D. Hansen eds., John Wiley & Sons 1987 & Supp. 1990); Grant W. Newton & Gilbert D. Bloom, Bankruptcy & Insolvency Taxation (John Wiley & Sons 1991); Lewis D. Solomon & Lewis J. Saret, Business Workout Planning Strategies, Ch. 2 (John Wiley & Sons 1992).

[4] 11 U.S.C. § 541(a)(1) (1988).

[5] 11 U.S.C. § 541(c)(2) (1988).

[6] 29 U.S.C. § 1056(d)(1) (1988); IRC § 401(a)(13) (1988); Treas. Reg. § 1.403(a) 13(b)(1) (1992).

[7] Patterson v. Shumate, 112 S. Ct. 2242 (1992). *See also* Sidney M. Weaver & Robin J. Baikovitz, *The Status of ERISA Plan Benefits in Bankruptcy after Patterson v. Shumate,* 17 Nova L. Rev. I (Fall 1992).

become a part of the bankruptcy estate because they do not contain an ERISA mandated anti-alienation provision.[8] The planner should note that small plans in which only the client and his spouse participate may be considered to be nonqualified plans.[9] Although the ERISA-mandated anti-alienation provision historically did not protect IRAs by excluding them from the bankruptcy estate under 11 U.S.C. § 542(c), many states have enacted exemption statutes that exempt such IRAs.[10] However, planners must examine each state's law to determine whether it exempts IRAs.[11]

In addition, under bankruptcy law prior to the 2005 Bankruptcy Act, under the federal exemption list, the right to receive "a payment under a stock bonus, pension, profit-sharing, annuity, or similar plan or contract on account of illness, disability, death, age, or length of service"[12] was considered an exempt asset "to the extent reasonably necessary for support of the debtor and his/her dependents."[13] Unfortunately, courts differed in their interpretations of whether IRAs were eligible for exemption under these provisions. In *Rousey v. Jacoway*, 125 S. Ct. 1561, 161 L. Ed. 2d 563 (2005), the Supreme Court resolved differences of

---

[8] Rhonda H. Brink, *Planning Perspectives for Creditor Conscious Clients* ¶ 704.4, in 22d Annual University of Miami Philip E. Heckerling Inst. on Est. Plan. (John T. Gaubatz ed., 1988).

[9] *See, e.g., In re* Fred Lane, Jr., 1993 Bankr. LEXIS 103 (Bankr. E.D.N.Y. 1993).

[10] *See, e.g.,* Md. Code Ann., Cts. & Jud. Proc. § 11-504(h) (1989); In re Solomon, 166 B.R. 832 (Bankr. D. Md. 1994), *aff'd & remanded,* 173 B.R. 325 (D. Md. 1995), *rev'd & remanded,* 67 F.3d 1128 (4th Cir. 1995) (court held that qualified plan benefits rolled over into IRA were exempt under Maryland exemption provision); In re Youngblood, 29 F.3d 225 (5th Cir. 1994) (court held that IRA was exempt under Texas exemption provision); Orr v. Yuhas (In re Yuhas), 104 F.3d 612 (3d Cir. 1997) (Third Circuit held that a New Jersey statute protecting a debtor's IRA from creditors' claims constituted a restriction on the transfer of a beneficial interest of the debtor in trust, within the meaning of Bankruptcy Code § 541 (c)(7), and thus caused the exclusion of the IRA from the bankruptcy estate); Meehan v. Wallace (In re Meehan), 102 F.3d 1209 (11th Cir. 1997) (Eleventh Circuit held that debtor's IRA was excluded from the estate under Bankruptcy Code § 541(c)(2) because it was protected by Georgia state law); Seltzer v. Cochrane (In re Seltzer), 104 F.3d 234 (9th Cir. 1997) (Ninth Circuit held that the retroactive application of a Nevada statute allowing debtors to exempt IRAs from bankruptcy did not violate the Contract Clause of the United States Constitution); Dubroff v. First Nat'l Bank (In re Dubroff), 119 F.3d 75 (2d Cir. 1997) (U.S. Court of Appeals for the Second Circuit holds that a Chapter 7 Bankruptcy debtor's IRA is exempt from his bankruptcy estate under N.Y. Debt. & Cred. Law § 282(2)(e) as in effect before a September 1994 amendment that specifically provided for a bankruptcy exemption for IRAs). In re Pepmeyer, 2002 U.S. Dist. LEXIS 305 (N.D. Iowa Jan. 7, 2002) (U.S. District Court for the Northern District of Iowa held that an IRA is an exempt asset under Iowa law); Premier Capital Inc. v. DeCarolis (In re DeCarolis), 259 B.R. 467 (B.A.P. 1st Cir. 2001) (U.S. Bankruptcy Appellate Panel for the First Circuit held that under New Hampshire law, a debtor is entitled to fully exempt the proceeds of an individual retirement account).

[11] *See, e.g.,* Steelstone Indus. Inc. v. McCrum, 785 A.2d 1256 (Me. 2001) (Maine Supreme Judicial Court held that a debtor's IRA was not exempt from collection under a creditor's money judgment because debtor did not make prima facie showing that his IRA was necessary for support of dependents); Anderson v. Seaver (In re Anderson), 260 B.R. 27 (B.A.P. 8th Cir. 2001) (U.S. Bankruptcy Appellate Panel for the Eighth Circuit held that a bankruptcy debtor whose interest in his ex-spouse's individual retirement account arose through a marriage dissolution decree could not make use of Minnesota's exemption for IRA amounts).

[12] 11 U.S.C. § 522(d)(10)(E).

[13] 11 U.S.C. § 522(d)(10)(E).

interpretation in the lower courts by definitively confirming that IRAs constitute a "similar plan," and that the age-related penalty restrictions applicable to IRAs means that the right to receive payments from IRAs are "on account of age." Consequently, the court ruled that IRAs should be protected from creditors, subject to the limitation that they would be exempted only to the extent of the "reasonably necessary" provisions. This ruling meant that debtors' IRAs would be protected from creditors, to the extent reasonably necessary for support, for any debtor subject to the federal exemptions (*i.e.*, debtors in states that granted the choice between state or federal where the debtor chose the federal exemptions, or debtors in states that had not opted out of the federal exemptions). But those debtors subject to state-plus-add-on exemptions would still need to look to the state-specific treatment of IRAs because the Supreme Court interpretation affects only the application of federal exemptions and those debtors subject to them.

In addition to the foregoing, the 2005 Bankruptcy Act substantially modifies the bankruptcy provisions as they apply to retirement plans. Under the 2005 Bankruptcy Act's provisions, virtually all types of retirement accounts are now exempt assets in bankruptcy proceedings. The 2005 Bankruptcy Act effectuates this change by adding a provision creating a new exemption for "retirement funds to the extent that those funds are in a fund or account that is exempt from taxation under Sections 401, 403, 408, 408A, 414, 457, or 501(a) of the Internal Revenue Code."[14] This exhaustive list of sections applicable to tax-deferred retirement plans that will now be exempt covers 401(k) plans, 403(b) plans, profit-sharing and money purchase plans, IRAs (including SEP and SIMPLE plans), as well as defined-benefit plans.

> **Caution.** Nonqualified annuities, although tax-deferred and ostensibly for retirement, will not be protected under these provisions since the applicable IRC §72 is not listed (although qualified annuities will still be protected under the applicable IRA or qualified plan section, and nonqualified annuities may still otherwise be protected under state law).

Unfortunately, although the 2005 Bankruptcy Act has created an exemption for all types of retirement plans, that exemption is limited in some cases. Specifically, for Roth and traditional IRAs, the maximum exemption is limited to an aggregate IRA account value of $1 million[15] (adjusted every three years for inflation[16]). SEP and SIMPLE IRAs, along with all other types of non-IRA retirement accounts such as 401(k)s and 403(b)s, are not included in determining the $1 million limit, which applies only to traditional and Roth IRAs. In addition, the $1 million limit does not include any amounts held in an IRA attributable to eligible rollover contributions (and subsequent rollover growth). Eligible rollover

---

[14] 11 U.S.C. §522(b)(3)(C), (d)(10)(E).
[15] 11 U.S.C. §522(n).
[16] 11 U.S.C. §104(b).

contributions are those that occur under a series of explicitly listed Internal Revenue Code rollover provisions; the end result is that rollovers from any qualified employer retirement plan will qualify, but IRA-to-IRA rollovers will not.[17]

> **Caution.** Planners should note that rollovers from other protected IRAs that are not subject to the $1 million limitation (*e.g.*, SEP and SIMPLE IRAs) appear not to be eligible rollovers (because such rollovers are completed under a code section that is not listed as a "protected" eligible rollover). Consequently, a rollover from a SEP or SIMPLE IRA to a traditional IRA would appear to forfeit unlimited protection and potentially subject the assets to the $1 million aggregate traditional and Roth IRA protection cap.

> **Caution.** In addition, the 2005 Bankruptcy Act's changes allow for the courts to increase the $1 million IRA exemption limit in cases where it is in the "interests of justice" to do so.

[C] *Nonbankruptcy Context*

While ERISA qualification no longer has the same impact it did prior to the 2005 Bankruptcy Act, it is still relevant in the nonbankruptcy context. Specifically, in the nonbankruptcy context, it appears that ERISA preempts state law.[18] Consequently, the asset protection client's interest in a qualified plan is generally protected from his creditor's reach.

EXAMPLE 8-34

Same facts as in Example 8-33, except that Franklin does not enter bankruptcy. Here, Sally still cannot reach Franklin's interest in the Accounting Corp's qualified plan.

---

[17] 11 U.S.C. § 522(n).

[18] Tenneco, Inc. v. First Va. Bank of Tidewater, 698 F.2d 688 (4th Cir. 1983); General Motors Corp. v. Buha, 623 F.2d 455 (6th Cir. 1980); Santo (Sandy) Bisignano, Jr., Protecting Assets from Overzealous Creditors or an Estate Planner's Guide to Preservation Planning, 1987 Annual Notre Dame Est. Plan. Inst. 3-63; William J. Woodward, Jr., Enforcements of Money Judgments: Objectives and Restrictions, in 9 Debtor-Creditor Law ¶ 37.03[B][4][b][i] (Theodore Eisenberg ed., 1992); Annotation, *Employee retirement pension benefits as exempt from garnishment, attachment, levy, execution, or similar proceedings,* 93 A.L.R.3d 711 (1979).

Caution. The client's spouse, child, or other dependent may reach his interest in the qualified plan by using a Qualified Domestic Relations Order (QDRO).[19] A QDRO is issued under state domestic relations law that provides for child support, alimony, or transfer of marital rights to spouses, children, or other dependents. It creates or recognizes the existence of an alternate payee's right, or assigns to the alternate payee the right to a benefit payable to the plan participants.

Planning Pointer. When the client desires to protect assets from future spousal claims, the planner should use other asset protection tools (such as trusts) rather than qualified retirement plans.

EXAMPLE 8-35

Harry is courting Bess and plans to propose to Bess that they become engaged to be married. Harry consults with Dwight, an asset protection planner. Harry's goal is to protect his separate property, which he has acquired primarily through inheritance, from any spousal claims of Bess in the event the marriage fails. Although Harry's inherited property is his separate property in the jurisdiction in which he and Bess live in, Harry is concerned about the possibility of this property being commingled in the future or otherwise being attacked in the event of divorce. Harry's paramount concern is with a spousal attack, rather than any fear of tort or other litigation. Furthermore, Harry is not concerned about providing for his retirement. Here, Dwight should not focus on retirement plans because such plans would not provide protection from any claims that Bess might bring against Harry.

In *Peacock v. Thomas*,[20] the Supreme Court held that ERISA plan beneficiaries cannot pierce a corporate veil of limited liability in federal district court to impose liability for a prior ERISA judgment on a shareholder/director who diverted corporate funds, because the beneficiary lacked both ERISA and ancillary jurisdiction.

In *Boggs v. Boggs*,[21] the United States Supreme Court held that ERISA preempts state community property law that would have allowed a nonparticipant

---

[19] ERISA § 206, 29 U.S.C. § 1056 (1988); IRC § 414(p) (1988). *See also* Stacy L. Anderson, Comment, *The Right to Pension Benefits Under ERISA When a Nonemployee Spouse Predeceases the Employee Spouse*, 67 Wash. L. Rev. 625 (1992); *see, e.g.,* Gallant v. Gallant, 876 P.2d 1084 (Alaska 1994).

[20] 516 U.S. 349 (1996).

[21] 520 U.S. 833 (1997).

spouse to transfer by testamentary instrument an interest in undistributed pension plan benefits.

In *In re Baker*,[22] the Seventh Circuit held that a debtor's irregular transactions involving his ERISA qualified pension plan did not affect the plan's status as property excepted from the bankruptcy estate under Section 541(c)(2) of the U.S. Bankruptcy Code. The court indicated that violations of the Employee Retirement Income Security Act do not make that act inapplicable because under *Patterson v. Shumate*,[23] "what matters is application of ERISA's subchapter I, rather than the observance of its rules."

For IRAs and other non-ERISA qualified retirement plans, the federal bankruptcy exemptions discussed above will not apply outside of bankruptcy. Therefore, to protect non-ERISA retirement plans, planners must rely on state exemptions.

[D] Taxes on Retirement Plans

The planner must evaluate the tax consequences of using qualified retirement plans as part of an asset protection plan. He should determine the gift tax implications, the estate tax implications, and the income tax implications of the proposed qualified retirement plan.

[1] Gift Taxation

Generally, there are no gift tax implications that are unique to qualified plans.[24] If a plan participant irrevocably designates another person to take a survivor annuity or a lump-sum payment, he makes a taxable gift. This gift generally does not qualify for the annual $10,000 gift tax exclusion.[25]

EXAMPLE 8-36

George, as part of an asset protection plan, begins to put $10,000 per year into a defined contribution qualified plan. In 2003, after participating in the plan

---

[22] 114 F.3d 636 (7th Cir. 1997).

[23] 504 U.S. 753 (1992).

[24] Lewis D. Solomon et al., Federal Taxation of Estates, Trusts and Gifts 694 (1989); Louis A. Mezzullo, An Estate Planner's Guide to Qualified Retirement Plan Benefits (1992); Carol V. Berger & Kathleen A. Odle, *Spousal Estate Planning Considerations for Qualified Plan Distributions*, 21 Colo. Law. 725 (1992); Kenneth G. Frantz, *Estate Planning for Large Balance IRAs*, 20 Tax Mgmt. Compensation Plan. J. 55 (1992); Gair B. Petrie, *Adding Qualified Retirement Plan and IRA Benefits to the Estate Planning Mix*, 16 Rev. Tax'n Individuals 211 (1992); Gair B. Petrie, *Adding Qualified Retirement Plan and IRA Benefits to the Estate Planning Mix—Part 2*, 16 Rev. Tax'n Individuals 305 (1992); Richard S. Rothberg & Paul M. Ritter, *Estate Planning: Planning for Retirement Plan Benefits*, 10 J. Tax'n Investments 74 (1992); Robert B. Wolf, *Estate Planning with Retirement Accounts: Top Tax Tips and Traps for the Estate Planner*, 63 Pa. B. Ass'n Q. 87 (1992); Deborah Walker & Sallie Olson, *Maximizing the Benefits of Deferred Compensation Plans Funded Through Secular Trusts*, 77 J. Tax'n 90 (1992).

[25] IRC § 2523(f) (6) (1988); Lewis D. Solomon et al., Federal Taxation of Estates, Trusts and Gifts 694 (1989).

for 15 years, when George's vested interest in the plan is worth $320,000, George irrevocably designates his son, Bill, to receive a lump-sum payment out of the plan when George retires. Here, George makes a taxable gift to Bill, which does not qualify for the $10,000 annual exclusion. However, if George's designation of Bill as beneficiary was not irrevocable, then there would not be a completed gift for gift tax purposes.

[2]   Estate Taxation

IRC Section 2039 controls the estate taxation of qualified plans. It requires the decedent's gross estate to include the value of any annuity or other payment receivable by any beneficiary if, under the decedent's contract, the decedent possessed the right to receive an annuity or other payment payable to him, either alone or with another, for his life.[26] However, any estate taxes attributable to the inclusion of qualified plan benefits in an employee's gross estate qualify as an income deduction for the recipient of the distribution.[27]

In community property states, if the participant spouse dies first, his gross estate includes only one half the benefits.[28] Conversely, if the nonparticipant spouse dies first, her gross estate includes the value of her community property interest in the qualified plan.[29]

Caution. In addition to IRC Section 2039 inclusion in the decedent's gross estate, IRC Section 4980A subjects excess retirement accumulations to a 15-percent added penalty estate tax.[30] For this rule, the IRC defines excess accumulations as the value of the decedent's interests in the plan at death, less the present value of a single life annuity with annual payments equal to the greater of (1) $150,000 or (2) $112,500, adjusted for inflation, for the decedent, assuming for purposes of this rule that the decedent had not died.[31] The planner should note that the penalty excise tax is not subject to the unified and other estate tax credits.[32] Furthermore, the penalty excise tax cannot be avoided by leaving the retirement benefits to charity or to a surviving spouse.[33] However, the decedent can defer the excise tax by leaving the retirement benefits to a surviving spouse.[34]

---

[26] IRC § 2039(a) (1988 & Supp. 1990).
[27] IRC § 691 (1988).
[28] Lewis D. Solomon et al., Federal Taxation of Estates, Trusts and Gifts 695 (1989).
[29] Id.
[30] IRC § 4980A(d) (1988).
[31] IRC § 4980A(d)(3) (1988).
[32] IRC § 4980A(d)(2) (1988).
[33] Lewis D. Solomon et al., Federal Taxation of Estates, Trusts and Gifts 697 (1989).
[34] IRC § 4980A(d)(5) (1988).

Planning Pointer. The planner should structure an asset protection plan involving retirement benefits so that the IRC Section 4980A excise tax does not apply to the transaction.

Caution. Without careful planning, the taxes imposed on the retirement benefit plans at death may cause severe problems. Such taxes can consume nearly all of the retirement plan benefits.[35] This results because, although generally assets passing at death receive a stepped-up basis, this rule does not apply to ERISA qualified retirement benefit plans and IRAs. In turn, this results because the receipt of such assets after the decedent's death constitutes *income in respect of a decedent* (IRD). IRD is income owed to a decedent at death, or income that would have been paid to the decedent if the decedent had survived. For estate tax purposes, the decedent's gross estate includes IRD, but such IRD does not receive a stepped-up basis. Consequently, such IRD proceeds (*i.e.*, the retirement benefit plan or IRA proceeds), are subjected to federal income taxation when the beneficiaries receive it. Moreover, often, the 10-percent excise applies. Consequently, the combined federal and state taxes applicable to retirement plan benefits and IRAs may approach 100 percent of such asset's value.

Planning Pointer. Several commentators have recommended avoiding the severe tax burden applicable to retirement plan benefits by using such assets to fund charitable bequests.[36] This allows for an estate tax charitable deduction and precludes the recognition of income tax upon IRD by noncharitable beneficiaries. However, charitable bequests of qualified plans and IRAs cannot escape the 10-percent excise tax if the plan is subject to such tax.[37]

Caution. Presently, taxpayers who want to fund charitable bequests with qualified plans or IRAs at death cannot make an assignment of such assets

---

[35] *See generally* Frank M. Burke, *Why Not Allow Lifetime Charitable Assignments of Qualified Plans and IRAs?* 76 Tax Notes 121 (July 7, 1997); Saunders, *The Donated IRA*, Forbes 182 (Mar. 24, 1997); Fenster, *Naming the IRA Beneficiaries That Cut Taxes*, J. Acct. 85 (May 1996).

[36] *See generally* Frank M. Burke, *Why Not Allow Lifetime Charitable Assignments of Qualified Plans and IRAs?* 76 Tax Notes 121 (July 7, 1997); Saunders, *The Donated IRA*, Forbes 182 (Mar. 24, 1997); Fenster, *Naming the IRA Beneficiaries That Cut Taxes*, J. Acct. 85 (May 1996).

[37] *See, e.g.*, Ltr. Rul. 9723038 (IRS ruled that IRA distribution to charitable organization qualified for the estate tax charitable deduction under IRC § 2053).

during their lives. This results because (1) ERISA qualified retirement plans are not assignable (except in divorce and for tax liens), and (2) although IRAs are assignable, their assignment to any assignee other than a 100-percent grantor trust causes the IRS to tax the assignor immediately on the full value of the IRA assigned.

[3] Income Taxation

Qualified plans offer several income tax advantages. First, employer (or self-employed participant) contributions are not taxed as income to the employee when made.[38] Second, the IRC exempts income generated by a qualified plan from income taxation until withdrawal.[39] Finally, distributions from qualified plans to the participant can often be deferred, thus deferring further the imposition of the income tax.

IRC Section 4980A imposes an additional 15-percent penalty excise tax on distributions from a qualified plan that exceed the greater of $150,000 or $112,500, adjusted for inflation, per year.[40]

§8.05 OTHER INCOME EXEMPTIONS

Every state exempts certain types of income from the reach of creditors. However, every state also restricts its exemptions to certain types of income. Often, earned income is exempt in the form of wages, salary, etc., and Social Security and welfare payments. However, the parameters of any individual state's exemption protection depends heavily on the wording of the statute.[1]

> **Planning Pointer.** The planner should determine which types of income the applicable law exempts and try to structure the client's financial affairs so that his income falls within the exempt categories.

Wages are also partially exempt by the Consumer Credit Protection Act.[2] The federal limit looks at the employee's disposable income, which generally equals the employee's gross pay less federal and state income tax withholding and less certain other payments.[3]

---

[38] *See* Reg. §§ 1.402(a)-I(a), 1.403(a)-I(a) (1992).

[39] IRC § 501(a) (1988).

[40] IRC § 4980A(c) (1988).

§ 8.05 [1] David G. Epstein et al., Debtors and Creditors 135-36 (1987). *See, e.g., In re* Williams, 171 B.R. 451 (D.N.H. 1994) (holding that automobile, purchased with workers' compensation benefits that were exempt under state law, was exempt); King v. Webb (*In re* Webb), 1997 U.S. Dist. LEXIS 17,836 (E.D. Va. 1997) (holding that settlement proceeds of gender discrimination suit under 1964 Civil Rights Act constitute exempt personal injury action proceeds under Virginia law).

[2] 15 U.S.C. §§ 1601-1693r (1988).

[3] *Id.*

§ 8.06   INTERACTION BETWEEN STATE AND BANKRUPTCY EXEMPTIONS

To fully understand the applicable exemptions, the planner must understand the interaction between state and bankruptcy exemptions.[1] The planner must always consider the possibility of bankruptcy in the context of asset protection planning and the ability of creditors to reach the client's property both inside and outside the bankruptcy context.

The U.S. Bankruptcy Code has its own set of exemptions. The Bankruptcy Code allows a debtor in bankruptcy to choose between the federal Bankruptcy Code exemptions or the exemptions provided by the debtor's state of domicile.[2] However, the Bankruptcy Code allows any state to prevent its citizens from electing the Bankruptcy Code exemptions by passing legislation precluding resident debtors from so electing.[3] Such legislation is commonly referred to as opt-out legislation.

> **Planning Pointer.** In jurisdictions that have not enacted opt-out legislation, the planner should carefully examine the applicable bankruptcy exemptions as well as the applicable state law exemptions. The planner also should note that the client cannot pick and choose between different exemptions from the state and Bankruptcy Code. Instead, the client must choose either all the state exemptions or all the Bankruptcy Code exemptions.[4]

In joint bankruptcy cases, filed by both the husband and wife, or in jointly administered cases involving separate petitions filed by or against spouses, each spouse is entitled to his and her exemptions.[5] However, both spouses must elect the same exemption system.[6] When the spouses are unable to agree, the Bankruptcy Code deems the spouses to elect the federal bankruptcy exemptions, except when the applicable state has enacted opt-out legislation.[7]

§ 8.07   LIMITS ON EXEMPTION PLANNING

As with all asset protection planning, the planner must conduct a fraudulent conveyance analysis to ensure that transactions involved in the asset protection plan do not constitute fraudulent conveyances.[1]

---

§ 8.06   [1] *See generally* Benjamin Weintraub & Alan N. Resnick, Bankruptcy Law Manual ¶ 4.07 (3d ed. 1992); Richard 1. Aaron, Bankruptcy Law Fundamentals Ch. 7 (1991); Norton Bankruptcy Law and Practice pt. 26 (William L. Norton, Jr., ed., 1987).

[2] 11 U.S.C. § 522(b), (d) (1988).

[3] 11 U.S.C. § 522(b)(1) (1988).

[4] Benjamin Weintraub & Alan N. Resnick, Bankruptcy Law Manual ¶ 4.07 (3d ed. 1992).

[5] 11 U.S.C. § 522(m) (1988).

[6] 11 U.S.C. § 522(b), (m) (1988).

[7] *Id.*

§ 8.07   [1] *See* Chapter 2.

Planning Pointer. Exemption planning differs from most asset protection planning in that it involves the client moving wealth from one type of asset owned by the client to another exempt asset also owned by the client. Most other asset protection tools involve the client moving assets owned by the client to others, such as relatives or trusts. Fraudulent conveyance law primarily focuses on transfers by a debtor to others. Consequently, creditors have a more difficult time making a good fraudulent conveyance claim against debtors involved in exemption planning.[2]

Caution. Although creditors have a more difficult time making a fraudulent conveyance claim against debtors involved in exemption planning, such planning may prevent a debtor in bankruptcy from receiving a discharge from bankruptcy.[3] Also, when a court finds that the purchase of exempt assets in contemplation of bankruptcy is accompanied by actual fraud, the court may deny the exemption to the debtor.[4] Unfortunately, it is difficult to predict with any degree of certainty what a court's reaction to exemption planning will be.[5] Furthermore, some cases cite factors that are reminiscent of badges of fraud used in fraudulent conveyance cases.[6]

Planning Pointer. The planner should conduct a fraudulent conveyance analysis in connection with asset protection plans involving exemption planning, even though it is more difficult for creditors to make fraudulent conveyance claims against debtors. This should help the planner ensure that the exemptions will hold up in court. Furthermore, some courts have held that the fact that the exemption planning was done long before the creditor's claim arose may be a factor in the debtor's favor.[7]

---

[2] *See generally* H.R. Rep. No. 595, 95th Cong., 2d Sess. 361 (1977), reprinted in 1978 U.S.C.C.A.N. 5963 ("as under current law, the debtor will be permitted to convert non-exempt property before filing a bankruptcy petition. The practice is not fraudulent as to creditors, and permits the debtor to make full use of the exemptions to which he is entitled under the law."); Panuska v. Johnson (*In re* Johnson), 80 BR. 953 (Bankr. D. Minn. 1987); Benjamin Weintraub & Alan N. Resnick, Bankruptcy Law Manual ¶ 4.09 (3d ed. 1992); Norton Bankruptcy Law and Practice pt. 27 (William L. Norton, Jr., ed., 1987).

[3] 11 U.S.C. § 727(a)(2) (1988); Norton Bankruptcy Law and Practice § 27.27 (William L. Norton, Jr., ed., 1987).

[4] Benjamin Weintraub & Alan N. Resnick, Bankruptcy Law Manual ¶ 4.09 (3d ed. 1992).

[5] *See, e.g.,* McCormick v. Security State Bank, 822 F.2d 806 (8th Cit. 1987); Ford v. Poston, 773 F.2d 52 (4th Cir. 1985). Benjamin Weintraub & Alan N. Resnick, Bankruptcy Law Manual ¶ 4.09 (3d ed. 1992).

[6] *See, e.g., In re* Mehrer, 2 B.R. 309 (E.D. Wash. 1980).

[7] *See, e.g.,* Oberst v. Oberst (*In re* Oberst), 91 B.R. 97 (Bankr. C.D. Cal. 1988).

Caution. As with all asset protection plans, the planner should use extreme care. Poor planning may expose both the client and the planner to criminal liability.[8]

Some courts have explicitly held that when individuals engage in a systematic conversion of their assets into exempt assets for the specific purpose of placing them out of creditors' reach, they forfeit the right to the exemption for such assets.[9]

EXAMPLE 8-37[10]

MacBeth opens a hardware store in his home town in Wisconsin. Wisconsin has a $40,000 homestead exemption. MacBeth guarantees a note payable to Bigg Bank for $1 million. After one year, the business begins to deteriorate rapidly. MacBeth interviews for jobs in Wisconsin and receives job offers, but refuses these offers. Instead, MacBeth sells his house in Wisconsin for $250,000. The next day he buys a home for $248,000 in Florida, which has an unlimited homestead exemption, using the cash proceeds for his Wisconsin house to pay for his Florida home. MacBeth closes his hardware store and moves to Florida the following month, without any outstanding job offer. He then spends several months looking for work before accepting a job with MacDuff. One year and one week after moving to Florida, MacBeth files for bankruptcy and attempts to use the unlimited Florida homestead exemption. Here, MacBeth's homestead exemption will be limited to the $40,000 exemption that he could have claimed if he had remained in Wisconsin.

§ 8.08   EXEMPTION PLANNING CHECKLIST

The planner should use the following checklist to ensure that no critical issue is overlooked while developing the asset protection plan.

[A]   In General[1]

_____ 1.   Is the planner considering using exemption provisions as part of the asset protection plan?

---

[8] *See* 18 U.S.C. §§ 152, 3284 (1988).

[9] *See, e.g., In re* Schwarb, 150 B.R. 470 (Bankr. M.D. Fla. 1992); *In re* Coplan, 156 B.R. 88 (Bankr. M.D. Fla. 1993).

[10] *See In re* Coplan, 156 B.R. 88 (Bankr. M.D. Fla. 1993).

§ 8.08   [1] *See* § 8.01.

If yes, the planner should consider the following issues:

(a) How the homestead exemption applies to the client;
(b) How the life insurance exemption applies to the client;
(c) How the ERISA qualified retirement plan exemption applies to the client;
(d) How other income exemptions apply to the client;
(e) How state exemptions interact with federal bankruptcy law exemptions;
(f) What limitations exist on exemption planning.

[B] Homestead Exemption[2]

____2. Is the planner considering using the homestead exemption as part of the asset protection plan?
If yes, the following consequences will generally result from such a plan:

(a) The homestead property is protected from the reach of the client's creditors;
(b) Married clients cannot convey the property without spousal consent after homestead protection arises;
(c) If the client predeceases his or her spouse, the homestead survives in the spouse's favor and gives the spouse an interest that resembles a life estate in the land free of the same claims from which it was exempt while the debtor spouse was alive.

If yes, the client must satisfy one or more of the following requirements, with the exact requirements contingent on the applicable law:

(a) The client must be the head of a family or household;
(b) The property must be of the type covered by the applicable law;
(c) The client's interest in the property must be of the type covered by the applicable law;
(d) The proposed homestead property must fall within the applicable size and value limitations set forth by applicable law;
(e) The client must occupy and use the property as a residence;
(f) The client must make a formal declaration of homestead.

____3. If the planner is considering using the homestead exemption as part of the asset protection plan, does the client have or does the planner reasonably expect the client to develop any of the following types of liabilities:

(a) Liabilities incurred before the homestead's establishment?
(b) Liabilities incurred before the homestead's acquisition?
(c) Liabilities incurred to improve the homestead property?
(d) Criminal penalty liabilities?

[2] See § 8.02.

(e) Tax liabilities?

(f) Tort liabilities?

(g) Superior title in the homestead property held by another party?

If yes to any of the above, the homestead exemption protection may not apply to such liabilities.

____4. If the planner is considering using the homestead exemption as part of the asset protection plan, does the planner reasonably expect any of the following to occur:

(a) The client's family to dissolve?

(b) The homestead's use to change from primarily residential use to some other type of use?

(c) The client to abandon the homestead property?

If yes to any of the above, the homestead exemption protection may be lost due to such circumstances.

[C] Life Insurance[3]

____5. Is the planner considering using life insurance as part of the asset protection plan?

If yes, the following consequences will generally result from such a plan:

(a) The life insurance policy, its cash value, and its proceeds may be protected from the reach of the client's creditors;

(b) A taxable gift will occur if the policy owner irrevocably transfers absolute ownership of the policy to another;

(c) If a noninsured party owns the policy at his death, such party will include the policy in his gross estate for estate tax purposes;

(d) If the insured owns the policy and it is payable to his estate, such estate must include the life insurance proceeds for estate tax purposes;

(e) If the insured possesses any of the incidents of ownership in a life insurance policy that is payable to another, his estate must include the life insurance proceeds, but if the insured possesses no incidents of ownership, his estate does not include the life insurance proceeds;

(f) Generally, the life insurance proceeds will be exempt from income taxation unless the insurance policy is transferred for value, in which case, the owner's income tax exclusion applies only to the consideration paid for the policy.

____6. If the planner is considering using life insurance as part of the asset protection plan, does the planner reasonably expect any of the following circumstances to occur:

---

[3] See § 8.03.

   (a)   The client will desire to name a beneficiary who falls outside of the prescribed class of protected beneficiaries under the exemption statute?

   (b)   The client will desire to assign the insurance policy to a creditor as collateral for a loan?

   (c)   The client will commit fraud in the formation of the insurance contract with the beneficiary and insurance company aware of such fraud?

   (d)   The client will be insolvent at the time that he designates the policy beneficiary or pays insurance premiums?

   If yes to any of the above, the life insurance exemption protection may be lost.

____ 7.   Is the planner considering using an irrevocable life insurance trust as part of the asset protection plan?

   If yes, the following consequences will generally result from such a plan:

   (a)   The life insurance policy, its cash value, and its proceeds may be protected from the reach of the client's creditors;

   (b)   The transfer of the policy to the trust will constitute a taxable gift of a future interest, which will not qualify for the annual gift tax exclusion;

   (c)   Future gifts of money to the trust, to enable the trust to make insurance premium payments, will not qualify for the annual gift tax exclusion unless the trust includes Crummey powers;

   (d)   The policy will not be included in the insured's gross estate if he divests himself of all of the incidents of ownership in the policies transferred to the trust;

   (e)   The trust will not recognize taxable income when the decedent dies and the insurance company pays the insurance proceeds to the trust because the IRC exempts the proceeds from income taxation.

[D]   ERISA Qualified Retirement Plans[4]

____ 8.   Is the planner considering using an ERISA qualified retirement plan as part of the asset protection plan?

   If yes, the following consequences will generally result from such a plan:

   (a)   The client's interest in the plan may be protected from the reach of the client's creditors, but not the client's spouse or dependents who obtain a Qualified Domestic Relations Order;

   (b)   A taxable gift will occur if the policy owner irrevocably designates another person to take a survivor annuity or lump-sum payment from the plan;

---

[4] *See* §8.04.

    (c) The client's gross estate must include any interest receivable by any beneficiary if, under the decedent's contract, the decedent possessed the right to receive an annuity or other payment payable to him for his life;

    (d) If the client's interest in the plan contains "excess accumulations," the IRC will subject such "excess accumulations" to a 15-percent added penalty tax;

    (e) Client contributions to the plan will not be taxed as income to the employee when made, and income generated by the plan will be exempt from income taxation until distributed to the client, when all distributions will be taxable.

[E] Other Income Exemptions[5]

____9. Is the planner considering using a state income exemption as part of the asset protection plan?

    If yes, the following consequence will generally result from such a plan:

    Such income, to the extent that it falls within the protective limits of the applicable exemptions statute, will be protected from the reach of creditors.

[F] Interaction Between State and Bankruptcy Exemptions[6]

____10. Has the applicable jurisdiction enacted legislation that precludes resident debtors from electing to use Bankruptcy Code exemptions instead of such jurisdiction's in bankruptcy cases?

    If yes, the planner should limit its analysis of exemption provisions to only those of the jurisdiction in question.

    If no, the planner should consider both the exemption provisions of the jurisdiction in question and the federal bankruptcy code.

[G] Limits on Exemption Planning[7]

____11. Has the planner conducted a fraudulent conveyance analysis as part of his analysis?

    If not, the planner runs the risk that a bankruptcy court may preclude the client from receiving a discharge of his liabilities in bankruptcy, and the planner may be exposing himself and his client to criminal liability.

---

[5] See § 8.05.
[6] See § 8.06.
[7] See § 8.07.

§8.09 EXEMPTION PLANNING COST-BENEFIT WORKSHEET

The planner should use the following worksheet to analyze the benefits and costs of using exemption provisions in monetary terms.

(1) __+ asset protection provided by exemption provision

(2) __– expenses of using exemption provision and complying with required formalities

(3) __– costs unique to exemption planning

(4) __– tax burden associated with exemption planning

(5) __+ tax benefits associated with using exemption planning

= net benefit/cost of using exemption planning

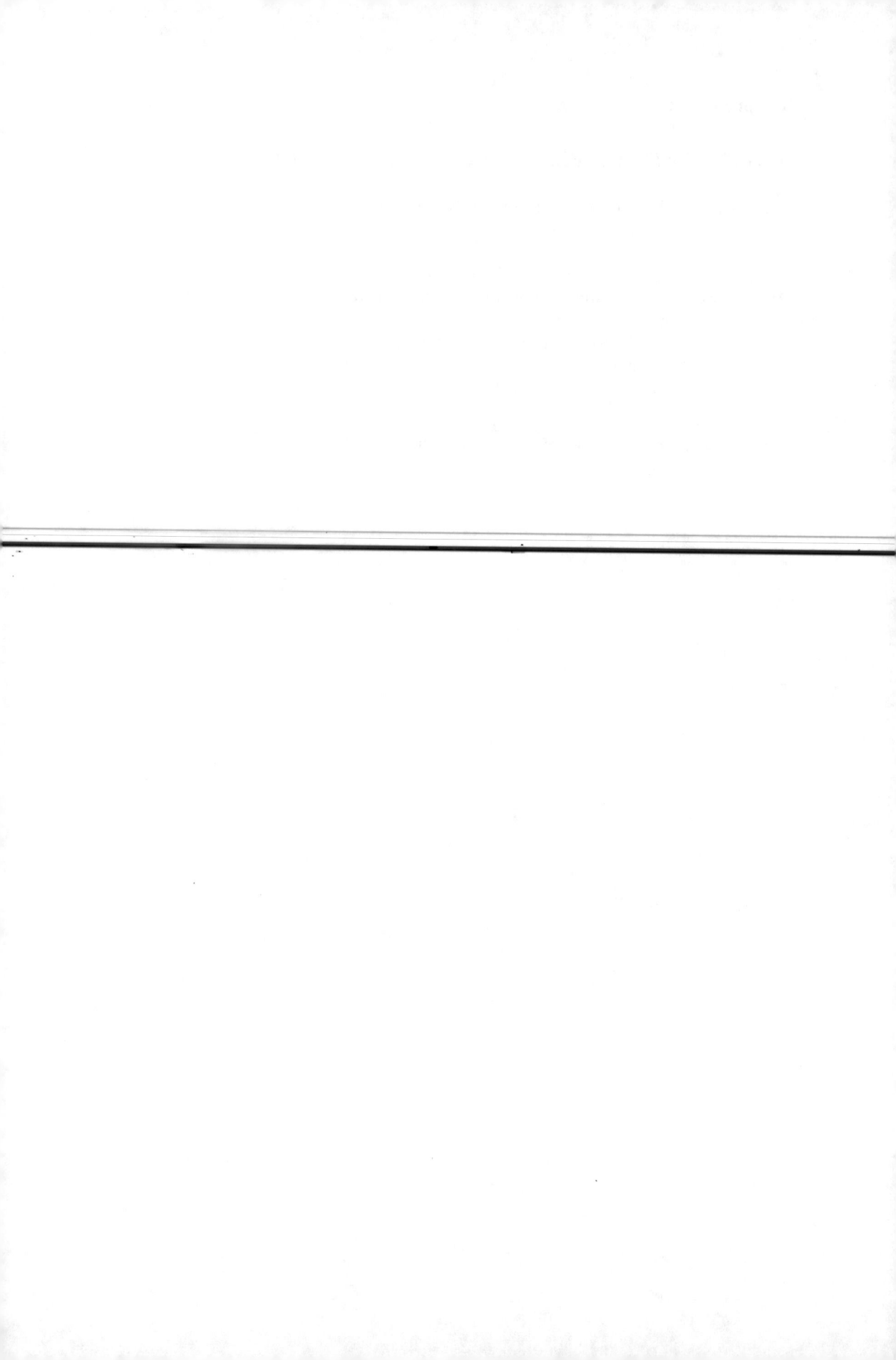

9

Foreign Bank Accounts

[F] Rules Prohibiting Correspondent Accounts with Foreign Shell Banks
[G] Cooperation among Financial Institutions, Regulatory Authorities, and Law Enforcement Authorities
[H] Inclusion of Foreign Corruption Offenses as Money Laundering Crimes
[I] Long-Arm Jurisdiction
[J] Forfeiture of Funds from U.S. Interbank Account
[K] Bank Records Related to Anti-Money Laundering Programs
[L] "Financial Institutions" under the Bank Secrecy Act
[M] Concentration Accounts
[N] Verification of Identification
[O] Anti-Money Laundering Programs

§9.01 IN GENERAL

The planner may want to use foreign bank accounts as part of the asset protection plan. Such bank accounts raise certain asset protection and regulatory compliance issues. Specifically, the planner should analyze the following issues when considering foreign bank accounts:

1. Will the Bank Secrecy Act apply to the plan, and if so, what must the client do to comply with its requirements?[1]
2. Will the Money Laundering Control Act apply to the plan, and if so, what must the client do to comply with its requirements?[2]
3. How much confidentiality does foreign law provide to U.S. clients?[3]
4. What is the ability of U.S. plaintiffs to pierce foreign bank secrecy laws?[4]

Caution. The planner should not consider foreign bank accounts by themselves to constitute valid asset protection tools. Individuals who own foreign bank accounts generally must disclose such accounts to the federal government.[5] This limits their asset protection usefulness. However, planners may use foreign bank accounts with other asset protection tools, such as foreign situs asset protection trusts.[6]

§9.02 BANK SECRECY ACT

Congress enacted the Bank Secrecy Act (BSA)[1] in 1970 to enable the United States to counteract strict foreign bank secrecy laws and to detect and prosecute tax evasion and other criminal cases.[2]

Planning Pointer. The planner should analyze the following when considering the impact of the BSA on asset protection plans:

1. What BSA reporting requirements must the client satisfy for foreign bank accounts?

§9.01 [1] *See* §9.02.
[2] *See* §9.03.
[3] *See* §9.04.
[4] *See* §9.05.
[5] *See* §§9.02–9.04.
[6] *See* Chapter 6.

§9.02 [1] *See generally* L. Richard Fischer, The Law of Financial Privacy Ch. 4 (3rd ed. 1998); James E. Eldridge, *The Bank Secrecy Act; Privacy, Comity, and the Politics of Contraband*, 11 N.C. J. Int'l L. & Com. Reg. 667 (1986); U.S. Dep't of Treas. & U.S. Customs Serv., Fines, Penalties & Forfeitures Handbook (Apr. 1986 rev.); William C. Caccamise, Jr., U.S. *Coutermeasures Against Tax Haven Countries*, 26 Colum. J. Transnat'l L. 553 (1988); Fletcher N. Baldwin, Jr. & Robert J. Munro, Money Laundering, Asset Forfeiture & International Financial Crimes (1993).

[2] Pub. L. No. 91-508, 84 Stat. 1114-24 (1970) (codified as amended in scattered sections of 12 U.S.C., 18 U.S.C., 31 U.S.C.).

2. What BSA reporting requirements must the client satisfy for imports and exports of currency and monetary instruments?

3. What BSA reporting requirements imposed on financial institutions should the planner be aware of?

4. What penalties may be imposed on the client for failure to comply with BSA requirements?

[A] BSA Reporting Requirements for Foreign Bank Accounts

Generally, every person subject to U.S. jurisdiction must report foreign bank accounts on U.S. Treasury Form 90–22.1, Report of Foreign Bank and Financial Accounts.[3] More specifically, every person subject to U.S. jurisdiction must generally file Form 90–22.1 every year that such person possesses a financial interest in, or signature or other authority over any bank, securities, or other financial account in any foreign country.[4] Additionally, the BSA requires individuals who possess such foreign accounts to retain certain financial records. These records include the name the person maintains the account under, the account number, the type of account, and the account's maximum value during the reporting period. The account owner must retain such records for five years. However, if the IRS charges the owner with filing a false or fraudulent federal income tax return or with failing to file a federal income tax return, the BSA extends the five-year period.[5]

The Treasury Department may require selected domestic financial institutions to report transactions with selected foreign financial agencies. Specifically, the Treasury Department may require this when it considers it necessary to combat money laundering, drug trafficking, and tax evasion.[6] Foreign financial agencies are persons acting outside the United States for a person as a financial institution, a bailee, depository trustee, or agent or acting in a similar way related to money, credit, securities, gold, or a transaction in money, credit, securities, or gold.[7] Procedurally, when the Treasury Department deems it appropriate, it notifies a selected financial institution, by publication in the Federal Register or personal service, to begin filing reports for transactions with designated foreign financial agencies.[8] The Treasury Department may require domestic financial institutions to report information about the following types of transactions:

1. Checks, drafts, and traveler's checks received by the institution for collection or credit to the account of foreign financial agencies, sent by the institution to foreign countries for collection or payment, drawn by the institution on

---

[3] Richard Fischer, The Law of Financial Privacy ¶ 4.03[1], F4.1 (3rd ed. 1998).

[4] 31 C.F.R. § 103.24 (1992); L. Richard Fischer, The Law of Financial Privacy ¶ 4.03[1] (3rd ed. 1998).

[5] 31 C.F.R. § 103.32 (1992); L. Richard Fischer, The Law of Financial Privacy ¶ 4.03[1] (3rd ed. 1998).

[6] 50 Fed. Reg. 27,821, 27,822 (1985); L. Richard Fischer, The Law of Financial Privacy ¶ 4.03[2] (3rd ed. 1998).

[7] 31 C.F.R. § 103.1 I(i) (1992); L. Richard Fischer, The Law of Financial Privacy ¶ 4.03[2] (3rd ed. 1998).

[8] 31 C.F.R. § 103.25(a) (1992); L. Richard Fischer, The Law of Financial Privacy ¶ 4.03[2] (3rd ed. 1998).

foreign financial agencies, or drawn by foreign financial agencies on the institution;

2. Wire or electronic funds transfers received or sent by the institution to or from foreign financial agencies;

3. Loans made by the institution to or through foreign financial agencies;

4. Commercial paper received or shipped by the domestic financial institution to or from foreign financial agencies;

5. Stocks received or shipped by the institution from or to foreign financial agencies;

6. Bonds received or shipped by the institution from or to foreign financial agencies; and

7. Certificates of deposit received or shipped by the institution from or to foreign financial agencies.[9]

[B] BSA Reporting Requirements for Imports and Exports of Currency and Monetary Instruments

The BSA requires each person importing or exporting $10,000 or more of currency or other monetary instruments on any one occasion to report such transactions. Such persons should use Form 4790, Report of International Transportation of Currency or Monetary Instruments for this purpose.[10] They must state on Form 4790 the amount of currency and instruments sent or received, the date of transmission or receipt, the form of any monetary instruments, and the person to whom they were transmitted or from whom they were received.[11] For this purpose, monetary instruments include any country's coin or currency, and they also include bank checks, traveler's checks, money orders, investment securities, and negotiable instruments, other than warehouse receipts or bills of lading, that are in bearer form or otherwise in a form allowing title to pass to the bearer on delivery.[12]

Whenever any person physically transports, mails, or ships currency or monetary instruments to or from the United States, the currency import-export reporting requirements are triggered. These requirements are also triggered whenever a person causes currency or monetary instruments to be physically transported, mailed, or shipped into or out of the United States. The BSA deems persons to cause the transportation, mailing, or shipping of currency if they aid, abet, counsel, command, procure, or request a financial institution or other person to effect such transportation.[13] However, transfers of funds pursuant to normal banking procedures not involving the physical transportation of currency or monetary instruments do not require any person to file a report.[14]

---

[9] 31 C.F.R. § 103.25(b) (1992); L. Richard Fischer, The Law of Financial Privacy ¶ 4.03[2] (3rd ed. 1998).

[10] 31 C.F.R. § 103.25(e)(2) (1992); L. Richard Fischer, The Law of Financial Privacy ¶ 4.04 (3rd ed. 1998).

[11] 31 C.F.R. § 103.23(b) (1992); L. Richard Fischer, The Law of Financial Privacy ¶ 4.04 (3rd ed. 1998).

[12] 31 C.F.R. § 103.11(k) (1992); L. Richard Fischer, The Law of Financial Privacy ¶ 4.04 (3rd ed. 1998).

[13] 31 C.F.R. § 103.23(a) (1992); L. Richard Fischer, The Law of Financial Privacy ¶ 4.04 (3rd ed. 1998).

[14] 31 C.F.R. § 103.23(d) (1992); L. Richard Fischer, The Law of Financial Privacy ¶ 4.04 (3rd ed. 1998).

Caution. Fund transfers pursuant to normal banking procedures not involving the physical transportation of currency or monetary instruments do not trigger the Form 4790 filing requirement. However, such transfers generally must be reported by the financial institutions involved on Form 4789, Currency Transaction Report.[15] This requirement is discussed later in this section.

Planning Pointer. The planner should note that the BSA does not preclude persons from transporting currency or monetary instruments into or out of the United States, but merely requires such persons to file a Form 4790.

Caution. The Bank Secrecy Act (BSA) as amended by the Annunzio-Wylie Anti-Money Laundering Act, prohibits persons from attempting to structure, or assisting in structuring, any importation or exportation of monetary instruments for purposes of evading the BSA reporting requirements.[16] Furthermore, the BSA provides for the seizure and forfeiture of any property involved in a transaction or attempted transaction that violates this prohibition on structuring.[17]

The BSA exempts certain senders or recipients of currency or monetary instruments from filing Form 4790. Specifically, the BSA does not require:

1. Federal Reserve Banks to satisfy the reporting requirements;
2. Banks, foreign banks, and securities brokers and dealers to satisfy the reporting requirements for items mailed or shipped through the postal service or by common carrier;
3. State or federal commercial banks and trust companies to satisfy the reporting requirements for items sent to or received from established customers who maintain a deposit relationship with the bank when the bank may conclude that the amounts of the items do not exceed those commensurate with the customary conduct of the business, industry, or profession of the customer concerned;
4. Nonresident noncitizens of the United States to satisfy the reporting requirements for items mailed or shipped from foreign countries to banks or securities brokers or dealers through the postal service or by common carriers;

---

[15] 31 C.F.R. § 103.22(a) (1992); L. Richard Fischer, The Law of Financial Privacy ¶ 4.06 (3rd ed. 1998).
[16] 31 U.S.C. § 5324(b)(3) (1988 & Supp. 1993).
[17] 31 U.S.C. § 5317(c) (1988 & Supp. 1993).

5. Common carriers of passengers to report items in its passengers' possession or common carriers of goods to report shipments of items not declared as currency or monetary instruments by the shipper;

6. Issuers of traveler's checks to report the transportation of traveler's checks before their delivery to selling agents for sale to the public; or

7. Persons engaged in the business of transporting currency or monetary instruments over land between foreign persons and established offices of banks or securities brokers or dealers to report such transportation.[18]

[C] BSA Reporting Requirements Imposed on Financial Institutions

The BSA imposes certain requirements on financial institutions with which clients deal. Although clients need not worry about complying with such requirements, the planner should be aware of them. Generally, these requirements fall into three categories: (1) transaction recordkeeping requirements, (2) currency transaction reporting requirements, and (3) bank and security broker and dealer recordkeeping requirements.

[1] Transaction Recordkeeping Requirements

Financial institutions must retain copies of records of two types of transactions. First, they must retain records of each credit extension that exceeds $10,000 and is not secured by real estate interests. Such records must include the customer's name and address, the amount of credit extended, the nature or purpose of the transaction, and the date.[19]

Second, financial institutions must maintain records of transactions that result in the transfer of more than $10,000 in money or credit to persons, accounts, or places outside the United States.[20] For purposes of this rule, the BSA deems transfers to U.S. accounts when the financial institution knows the account holder's address is outside the United States, to be transfers to foreign countries. However, this rule does not apply when the financial institution knows the account holder is "temporarily" outside the United States. This rule also does not apply when the account holder's address is within 50 miles of the institution's location.[21] The BSA deems account holders to be temporarily outside the United States when they are on vacation or on business assignments expected to last less than six months.[22]

The planner should also note that financial institutions may also maintain records concerning electronic funds transfers. Such information may include

---

[18] 31 C.F.R. § 103.23(c) (1992); L. Richard Fischer, The Law of Financial Privacy ¶ 4.04 (3rd ed. 1998).

[19] 31 C.F.R. § 103.33(a) (1992); L. Richard Fischer, The Law of Financial Privacy ¶ 4.05 (3rd ed. 1998).

[20] 31 C.F.R. § 103.33(b), (c) (1992); L. Richard Fischer, The Law of Financial Privacy ¶ 4.05 (3rd ed. 1998).

[21] 31 C.F.R. § 103.39 (1992); L. Richard Fischer, The Law of Financial Privacy ¶ 4.05 (3rd ed. 1998).

[22] L. Richard Fischer, The Law of Financial Privacy ¶ 4.05 (3rd ed. 1998).

the name, address, and account number of the person initiating a payment order in a funds transfer; the beneficiary's name and address; and the account number, among other information.[23]

[2]   Currency Transaction Reporting Requirements

The BSA requires financial institutions to report all transactions involving currency in amounts greater than $10,000.[24] Generally, financial institutions must use FINCEN Form 104, Currency Transaction Report, to satisfy this reporting requirement.

> **Caution.** The Treasury Department may require individual financial institutions to report currency transactions of less than $10,000 for limited periods of time or transactions falling within certain other specifications.[25]

The BSA requires financial institutions to treat multiple currency transactions as one transaction if it knows the transactions are by or for one person and result in cash in or out of more than $10,000 on any one business day.[26] Treasury Department regulations require financial institutions to aggregate all deposits and all withdrawals during each business day to determine if the account owner has reached a reportable deposit or withdrawal limit. For this rule, it does not matter whether one person with one account, several persons with the same account, or one person with several accounts completes the transactions.[27]

The BSA also imposes special reporting requirements on casinos and on the postal service, generally requiring these organizations to report currency transactions exceeding $10,000.[28]

The BSA generally applies to any person who is engaged in a trade or business and who in the course of such trade or business receives more than $10,000 in cash in one transaction or in more than one related transaction.[29] This rule also applies to attorneys.[30]

The planner should note that the BSA provides several exceptions from its currency transaction reporting requirements. Specifically, the BSA does not require:

---

[23] *See* FDIC Release FIL-16-93; L. Richard Fischer, The Law of Financial Privacy ¶ 4.05 (2d ed. 1991 & Supp. 1993).

[24] 31 C.F.R. § 103.22(a) (1992); L. Richard Fischer, The Law of Financial Privacy ¶ 4.06 (3rd ed. 1998).

[25] 31 C.F.R. § 103.26 (1992); L. Richard Fischer, The Law of Financial Privacy ¶ 4.06 (3rd ed. 1998).

[26] 31 C.F.R. § 103.22(a)(1) (1992); L. Richard Fischer, The Law of Financial Privacy ¶ 4.06 (3rd ed. 1998).

[27] 52 Fed. Reg. 11,438 (1987); L. Richard Fischer, The Law of Financial Privacy ¶ 4.06 (3rd ed. 1998).

[28] 31 C.F.R. § 103.36 (1992); 54 Fed Reg. 1165 (1989); L. Richard Fischer, The Law of Financial Privacy ¶ 4.06 (3rd ed. 1998).

[29] IRC § 60501(a) (1988 & Supp. 1990).

[30] *See, e.g.,* United States v. Goldberger & Dubin, P.C., 935 F.2d 501 (2d Cir. 1991).

1. Financial institutions to report transactions with federal reserve banks or federal home loan banks;[31]
2. Domestic banks to report transactions between domestic banks;[32]
3. Nonbank financial institutions to report transactions with commercial banks unless otherwise instructed by the assistant secretary of the Treasury for Enforcement or by the IRS.[33]

Also, the planner should note that financial institutions may exempt certain transactions from their reporting requirements under certain circumstances. A discussion of exempt transactions is beyond the scope of this text.[34]

[3] Bank and Security Broker and Dealer Recordkeeping Requirements

The BSA requires financial institutions and securities brokers and dealers to maintain certain records. These recordkeeping requirements may be broken down into two groups. The first group generally requires financial institutions and securities dealers and brokers to record their customer's taxpayer identification number and certain other information concerning each account opened.[35] The second group requires financial institutions and securities dealers and brokers to retain copies of several specified items and documents that relate to their accounts.[36]

[D] Failure to Comply with Bank Secrecy Act

Failure to comply with BSA requirements results in one or more of three types of penalties: (1) civil penalties, (2) forfeiture, or (3) criminal penalties. Financial institution regulators carry out BSA enforcement concerning financial institutions.[37] The SEC carries out BSA enforcement concerning securities brokers and dealers.[38] The Commissioner of Customs carries out BSA enforcement concerning the transportation of currency or monetary instruments to or from foreign

---

[31] 31 C.F.R. § 103.22(b)(1)(i) (1992); L. Richard Fischer, The Law of Financial Privacy ¶ 4.06[1] (3rd ed. 1998).

[32] 31 C.F.R. § 103.22(b)(1)(ii) (1992); L. Richard Fischer, The Law of Financial Privacy ¶ 4.06[1] (3rd ed. 1998).

[33] 31 C.F.R. § 103.22(b)(2) (1992); L. Richard Fischer, The Law of Financial Privacy ¶ 4.06[1] (3rd ed. 1998).

[34] *See* L. Richard Fischer, The Law of Financial Privacy ¶ 4.06[1]-[3] (3rd ed. 1998) for a complete discussion of exempt transactions.

[35] 31 C.F.R. §§ 103.34(a)(1), 103.35(a)(1) (1992); L. Richard Fischer, The Law of Financial Privacy ¶ 4.08[1] (3rd ed. 1998).

[36] L. Richard Fischer, The Law of Financial Privacy ¶¶ 4.07[2], 4.08[2] (3rd ed. 1998).

[37] 31 C.F.R. § 103.46(b) (1992); L. Richard Fischer, The Law of Financial Privacy ¶ 4.09 (3rd ed. 1998).

[38] 31 C.F.R. § 103.46(b)(6) (1992); L. Richard Fischer, The Law of Financial Privacy ¶ 4.09 (3rd ed. 1998).

countries.[39] The IRS carries out BSA enforcement when specific administrative authority is not otherwise provided, and the assistant secretary of the Treasury for Enforcement has overall responsibility for interagency cooperation.[40]

[1] Civil Penalties

The Treasury Department may assess civil penalties on domestic financial institutions and on any of their partners, directors, officers, or employees who willfully participate in a BSA violation.[41] The maximum civil penalty the Treasury Department may impose for reporting requirement violations equals the greater of $25,000 or the amount involved in the transaction, if any, up to $100,000.[42] The maximum penalty the Treasury Department may impose for willful BSA recordkeeping requirement violations equals $10,000.[43]

The Treasury Department also may impose a special civil penalty for failure to file reports concerning imports and exports of currency or monetary instruments. The Treasury Department may also impose this penalty for material omissions or misstatements in such reports. The maximum penalty amount equals the amount of the currency or monetary instruments transported, less any amounts forfeited due to failure to satisfy the normal reporting requirements.[44]

The Treasury Department may also impose civil penalties of up to $500 on any financial institution that negligently violates the BSA.[45] However, the Treasury Department may impose additional civil penalties of up to $50,000 on financial institutions that engage in a pattern of negligent violations of the BSA.[46]

[2] Forfeiture

The Commissioner of Customs may seize currency or monetary instruments that persons transport into or out of the United States either (1) without filing the appropriate reports, or (2) by filing the appropriate reports but with material omissions or misstatements.[47] However, the Commissioner of Customs may

---

[39] 31 C.F.R. § 103.46(b)(7) (1992); L. Richard Fischer, The Law of Financial Privacy ¶ 4.09 (3rd ed. 1998).

[40] 31 C.F.R. §§ 103.46(b)(8), 103.46(a) (1992); L. Richard Fischer, The Law of Financial Privacy ¶ 4.09 (3rd ed. 1998).

[41] 31 C.F.R. § 103.47(a) (1992); L. Richard Fischer, The Law of Financial Privacy ¶ 4.09[1] (3rd ed. 1998).

[42] 31 C.F.R. § 103.47(g) (1992); L. Richard Fischer, The Law of Financial Privacy ¶ 4.09[1] (3rd ed. 1998).

[43] 12 U.S.C. § 1955(a) (1988); 31 C.F.R. § 103.47(b) (1992); L. Richard Fischer, The Law of Financial Privacy ¶ 4.09[1] (3rd ed. 1998).

[44] 31 U.S.C. § 5321(a)(2) (1988); L. Richard Fischer, The Law of Financial Privacy ¶ 4.09[1] (3rd ed. 1998).

[45] 31 U.S.C. § 5321(a)(6)(A) (1988 & Supp. 1993).

[46] Id.

[47] 31 U.S.C. § 5317 (1988); 31 C.F.R. § 103.48 (1992); L. Richard Fischer, The Law of Financial Privacy ¶ 4.09[2] (3rd ed. 1998).

remit or mitigate any forfeiture in whole or part on whatever terms and conditions it deems reasonable.[48] Moreover, the Commissioner of Customs may seize any property involved in a series of money-laundering transactions, structured transactions, or transactions in property derived from certain specified unlawful activities.[49] Persons guilty of violating these rules also may be subject to fines and imprisonment for up to 20 years.[50] The only exception applies to reporting violations of financial institutions that a federal agency examines.[51]

The BSA provides that if property subject to forfeiture under United States law is located in a foreign country, or has been detained or seized pursuant to legal process of a foreign government, the United States may bring an action for forfeiture in the District Court for the District of Columbia or under any other district court authorized under that statute.[52] Furthermore, the BSA provides that the property's removal does not deprive the court of jurisdiction and that courts possessing jurisdiction over such a forfeiture action can serve in any other district the necessary process required to bring the property before such court.[53] Finally, the BSA provides procedures for subpoenaing bank records in connection with such a forfeiture action.[54]

[3] Criminal Penalties

The BSA also authorizes criminal penalties for BSA violations. The BSA provides for punishment by fines of up to $1,000, imprisonment of up to one year, or both, for willful recordkeeping requirement violations.[55] However, when violations are in the furtherance of other crimes, the criminal penalties may be more severe. Specifically, when defendants violate the recordkeeping requirements in the furtherance of any major violation of federal law (that is, crimes punishable by imprisonment for more than one year), the BSA provides for punishment by fines of up to $5,000, imprisonment of up to five years, or both.[56] Furthermore, the BSA subjects any person conspiring to violate the recordkeeping requirements to the same penalties as the offense that is the subject of the conspiracy.[57]

When persons violate the BSA reporting provisions relating to foreign transactions and accounts or domestic currency transactions, in the furtherance of

---

[48] 31 U.S.C. § 5321 (1988); 31 C.F.R. § 103.48 (1992); L. Richard Fischer, The Law of Financial Privacy ¶ 4.09[2] (3rd ed. 1998).

[49] Anti Drug Abuse Act of 1988, 18 U.S.C. § 981(a)(1) (1988); L. Richard Fischer, The Law of Financial Privacy ¶ 4.09[2] (3rd ed. 1998).

[50] Anti Drug Abuse Act of 1988, 18 U.S.C. § 1956(a)(3) (1988); L. Richard Fischer, The Law of Financial Privacy ¶ 4.09[2] (3rd ed. 1998).

[51] Anti Drug Abuse Act of 1988, 18 U.S.C. § 982(a) (1988); L. Richard Fischer, The Law of Financial Privacy ¶ 4.09[2] (3rd ed. 1998).

[52] 28 U.S.C. § 1355(b)(2) (1988 & Supp. 1993).

[53] Id.

[54] 18 U.S.C. § 986 (1988 & Supp. 1993).

[55] 12 U.S.C. § 1956 (1988); 31 C.F.R. § 103.49(a) (1992); L. Richard Fischer, The Law of Financial Privacy ¶ 4.09[3] (3rd ed. 1998).

[56] Id.

[57] 18 U.S.C. §§ 1956, 1957 (1988 & Supp. 1993).

other federal law violations or as part of a pattern of illegal activity involving transactions exceeding $100,000 over any 12-month period, the BSA provides for fines of up to $500,000, imprisonment of up to 10 years, or both.[58] When persons knowingly make false, fictitious, or fraudulent statements or representations in BSA-mandated reports, the BSA provides for fines of up to $10,000, imprisonment of up to five years, or both.[59]

[4] Administrative Penalties

The BSA gives the Attorney General the authority to appoint a conservator for financial institutions that he or she finds guilty of violating certain BSA provisions by notifying the appropriate federal banking agency in writing of this fact.[60] Furthermore, the BSA requires the Attorney General to notify the Comptroller of the Currency of the conviction of a national bank, federal branch, or federal agency of violations of the BSA and to provide a certified copy of the court's conviction order to the Comptroller of the Currency. The Comptroller of the Currency either may or must, depending on the BSA provisions violated, then issue a notice of intent to terminate all rights, privileges, and franchises of the institution's charter and must or may schedule a pretermination hearing concerning the charter revocation.[61]

[E] Offshore Voluntary Compliance Initiative

At the beginning of 2003, the IRS initiated a program, effective January 14, 2003 and ending three months later, on April 15, 2003, permitting U.S. taxpayers, who have used offshore accounts and other financial arrangements to avoid reporting or to underreport taxable income, to come forward, report the income, and avoid many of the otherwise applicable civil and criminal penalties and related costs.

According to published reports, Pamela Olson, Treasury Assistant Secretary for Tax Policy, has stated that the voluntary compliance initiative will constitute an important source of information for the Treasury Department, which is continuing its efforts to improve and expand the U.S.'s broad network of bilateral tax treaties and tax information exchange agreements. Also, according to Ms. Olson, better tax information exchange relationships will permit the IRS to obtain the information it needs from other countries so it can pursue taxpayers attempting to hide income offshore to avoid their tax obligations.

The United States recently expanded its network of tax information exchange agreements with offshore financial jurisdictions, and now has agreements with

---

[58] 31 U.S.C. § 5322(b) (1988); 31 C.F.R. § 103.49(c) (1992); L. Richard Fischer, The Law of Financial Privacy ¶ 4.09[3] (3rd ed. 1998).

[59] 18 U.S.C. § 1001 (1988); 31 C.F.R. § 103.49(d) (1992); L. Richard Fischer, The Law of Financial Privacy ¶ 4.09[3] (3rd ed. 1998).

[60] 12 U.S.C. §§ 1786(h)(1)(C), 1821(c)(5)(M) (1988 & Supp. 1993).

[61] 12 U.S.C. § 93(c)(1)(A) (1988 & Supp. 1993).

Antigua, Bahamas, BVI, Cayman Islands, Guernsey, Jersey, Isle of Man, and the Netherlands Antilles. It can be assumed that the IRS will exchange information with these countries, as well as others within its extensive network of tax treaties, including the United Kingdom, France, and Germany.

Acting IRS Commissioner, Robert Wenzel, in testimony before a Senate appropriations subcommittee, has indicated that the IRS has received a good response to the initiative, and has received several promising leads on promoters of offshore arrangements.

[1] The Voluntary Compliance Initiative

The program was aimed at taxable years 1999 to 2002. Years prior to 1999, in certain circumstances, may not be subject to scrutiny, but taxpayers nonetheless will have to provide information about their involvement in offshore financial arrangements during these years.

The interest and penalties imposed depended on the amount of the unpaid tax liability, the years involved, whether a return was inaccurate or if a return should have been filed and was not.

By way of example, a taxpayer who understated his income to avoid $100,000 in taxes in 1999 would wind up paying $149,319. This includes the tax liability plus $29,319 in interest and an additional accuracy-related penalty of $20,000.

If a taxpayer did not step forward, his tax liability generally would include the civil fraud penalty of $75,000, and therefore higher interest of $42,758. The total amount due would be $217,758, without considering probable additional civil penalties for failure to file certain information returns. Also, without coming forward, the taxpayer must worry about possible criminal penalties.

Not an amnesty: Although loosely referred to as an offer of tax amnesty, this was a misnomer, as taxes were not wholly or partially forgiven. Instead, if the taxpayer met the requirements of the program, the IRS agreed not to impose a number of civil and criminal penalties. The taxpayer will have to pay the tax and, in appropriate circumstances, certain delinquency and accuracy-related penalties. If the Foreign Bank and Financial Accounts Report (Treasury Form 90-22.1) also was not filed, the civil and criminal penalties associated with this failure would also be dropped.

Those who participated in the program were required to give complete information about how they were introduced to the account or arrangement, information about any promoter or other person involved, etc.

There are really two groups of persons affected by the Offshore Voluntary Compliance Initiative (the "Initiative"), the term the IRS uses for this program: U.S. taxpayers that have used offshore arrangements and, therefore, have some exposure, and non-U.S. persons-advisors, banks, trust companies, investment management firms, and other persons that might be characterized by the IRS as "promoters."

Individual taxpayers: In regard to individuals, they were required to assess the "opportunity" rapidly. Were they eligible? What was the possibility of being drawn into the program but learning later that there are hidden detriments?

What happens if the individual is not able to make full payment of taxes and penalties due?

The taxpayer must fully pay the tax liabilities and interest or make "other financial arrangements" that are acceptable to the IRS. What these arrangements are and the negotiation of the details will now be very important. If some type of workout is called for, it will be necessary to carefully prepare the necessary financial statements. In this regard, the IRS has stated that, although the Initiative requires taxpayers to fully pay their tax liabilities, including applicable penalties and interest for all years involved, as well all other unpaid, previously assessed liabilities, it is possible to request other payment arrangements acceptable to the IRS. However, the IRS also indicates that the burden will be on the taxpayer to establish inability to pay, based on full disclosure of all assets and income sources, domestic and offshore under the taxpayer's control.

For those who made the initial filing, called a written request to participate, they have approximately five months (150 calendar days) within which to submit a number of items including:

- Copies of previously filed original and amended federal income tax returns for tax periods ending after December 31, 1998;
- Copies of any powers of attorney granted by the taxpayer with respect to the subject tax years;
- Descriptions of offshore payment cards and foreign and domestic accounts of any kind (including the name and address of the bank or financial institution, the account number, and the date the account was opened), and descriptions of foreign assets in which the taxpayer has or had any ownership or beneficial interest, or that are or were controlled by the taxpayer (*i.e.*, the taxpayer has or had the practical ability to direct or influence the financial transactions or affairs of an account or entity, or the use or disposition of an asset, whether this ability was exercised directly or indirectly through a nominee, agent, power of attorney, letter of directions, letter of wishes, or any other device whatsoever) at any time after December 31, 1998;
- Descriptions of entities of any kind (including corporations, partnerships, trusts, and estates) and any nominees through which the taxpayer exercised control over foreign funds, assets, or investments at any time after December 31, 1998;
- Descriptions of the source of any foreign funds, assets, or investments owned or controlled by the taxpayer at any time after December 31, 1998;
- All related promotional materials, transactional materials, and other related correspondence and documentation received subsequent to the date the taxpayer submits the request to participate in the Program (such materials received prior to submitting a request will have been supplied with the request);
- Complete and accurate amended or delinquent original federal income tax returns of the taxpayer for all tax years ending after December 31, 1998, which are supported by an explanation of previously unreported income or incorrectly claimed deductions or credits (whether or not related to offshore payment cards or offshore financial arrangements);

- Complete and accurate amended or delinquent original information returns required by sections 6035, 6038, 6038A, 6038B, 6038C, 6039F, 6046, 6046A, and 6048 for which the taxpayer requests relief from penalties; and
- Complete and accurate Foreign Bank Account Reports for tax years ending after December 31, 1998.

Taxpayers and their advisors will be hard pressed to pull together these materials in this short period. It remains be seen whether requests for extensions of time will be granted.

Also, as with all exercises involving the filing of late returns, there will be a large number of "judgment calls" including how to handle the section 911 earned income exclusion and foreign tax credit issues.

There will be issues as to what to do with respect to non-U.S. tax authorities, and State tax authorities, which may be owed returns and taxes as well. Obviously, information provided to the United States can be exchanged by the United States with State and other countries' tax authorities. In the case of States, the IRS has announced that ten states have indicated they will grant special consideration to individuals who apply to the Initiative. According to the IRS, if individuals amend their state returns and pay all tax, penalties, and interest by October 15, they can avoid prosecution by these states. The states participating are California, Idaho, Louisiana, Maryland, Nebraska, New Jersey, New York, North Carolina, Utah, and Vermont. The IRS has indicated that additional states are expected to announce they will offer similar treatment to applicants of the Initiative.

An additional issue is whether, where taxpayers are denied eligibility for participation in the Initiative, the IRS will use admissions made in requests to participate in the program to prosecute them. Here, the IRS has stated that information about a taxpayer requesting participation in the Initiative is legally admissible in subsequent criminal proceedings.

At the end of the process, the taxpayer and the IRS will enter into a closing agreement, which like all such agreements entails a number of legal issues. The exact wording of that agreement should be constructed with great care. There will be issues that arise in connection with joint returns, especially where one spouse was not aware of the activities of the other spouse. There will be special issues where the taxpayer is a trust or an estate.

Unusual issues can arise where the foreign trustee bears obligations to other beneficiaries. For example, to what degree should a trustee cooperate where one U.S. beneficiary wishes to participate but this has implications for other U.S. and non-U.S. beneficiaries? Also, the trust, acting through the trustee, may be required to join in the filings. What indemnifications should the trustee obtain?

Offshore promoters: While at first blush it seems this program was aimed at taxpayers who used offshore accounts, credit cards paid against those accounts, foreign corporations, foreign trusts, and the like, to avoid U.S. taxes, in no small measure the program is designed to enable the IRS to proceed "with a vengeance" against promoters and facilitators of these schemes. The wording of various announcements and explanations makes clear that the IRS intends to use every means available to it to attack these persons.

For the advisors, banks, trust companies, investment management firms, and the like who may be thrown into the category—rightly or wrongly—of "promoters," they will want to anticipate the IRS's next steps. They probably should not wait until they receive, for example, a request for information or writ issued by their "home country" tax authority at the behest of the IRS pursuant to an applicable tax information exchange agreement.

[2] Filing Amended Returns Versus Filing Under the Initiative

The IRS has clearly tried to steer taxpayers to use the Initiative, rather than quietly file amended tax returns, reflecting offshore accounts and other arrangements. In this regard, the IRS is currently screening all amended returns against newly developed criteria to identify taxpayers who tried to circumvent the Initiative, and it has stated that it will audit amended returns identified during this screening process.

[3] What's Next?

What is the IRS's next step? We believe that the next step will be for the IRS to pursue U.S. taxpayers who had these arrangements and did not come forward, as well as promoters, wherever they are located. We think that the IRS will be looking to make examples of some people. Concerning non-U.S. firms, such firms run the risk of aiding and abetting a tax fraud, among other possible things.

[F] Foreign Bank Account Report (TD F 90-22.1): Tricky Turns Dangerous

[1] In General

The form for reporting foreign bank and similar accounts has always been a little tricky, but because of a little known implication of the new Patriot Act and greatly increased enforcement attention, this form has become dangerous.

[2] Background

The requirement for filing this form arises from the Bank Secrecy Act (BSA), first enacted in 1970, amended, in order to add a number of anti-money laundering provisions, in 1992, and amended most recently in October 2001 by the Patriot Act.[62] The BSA, in general, authorizes the Secretary of the Treasury to promulgate regulations requiring financial institutions and other persons to keep

---

[62] 1 Titles 1 and II of Public Law 91-508, as amended, codified at 12 U.S.C. § 1829b, 12 U.S.C. § 1951-1959, and 31 U.S.C. § 5311-5330.

records and file reports that he determines will have a high degree of usefulness in criminal, tax, regulatory, intelligence, and counter-terrorism matters, and to implement counter-money laundering programs and compliance procedures. Section 5314 of the BSA specifically authorizes the Secretary to require residents or citizens of the United States, or a person in and doing business in the United States, to keep records and/or file reports concerning transactions with a foreign financial agency. "This provision reflected congressional concern that foreign financial institutions located in jurisdictions with strict bank secrecy laws were being used to violate or evade domestic criminal, tax, and regulatory requirements."[63]

> Pursuant to this provision, the Treasury Department promulgated regulations[64] stating: Each person subject to the jurisdiction of the United States (except a foreign subsidiary of a U.S. person) having a financial interest in, or signature or other authority over, a bank, securities or other financial account in a foreign country shall report such relationship to the Commissioner of the Internal Revenue for each year in which such relationship exists, and shall provide such information as shall be specified in a reporting form. . . . [65]

The form referenced is TD F 90-22.1 (Report of Foreign Bank and Financial Accounts, sometimes referred to as the Foreign Bank Accounts Report or FBAR). (The most recent version of this form, dated July 2000) is available in the Internal Revenue Service website.)

The Secretary of the Treasury delegated the authority to administer this requirement to the Director of the Financial Crimes Enforcement Network (FinCEN). FinCEN is a bureau of the Treasury Department, alongside other bureaus and services, such as the IRS. FinCEN is responsible for the U.S. government's domestic and international anti-money laundering efforts. Among other things, it engages in information collection, data analysis, dissemination of analytical products, and technological assistance. This bureau is overseen by the Under Secretary of Enforcement, who reports to the Secretary of the Treasury through the Deputy Secretary.

Both FinCEN and its sister organization, the IRS, have responsibilities and roles with respect to the FBAR. The FBAR is an information return or report that is filed with the IRS Detroit Computing Center and input into the BSA financial database, which is jointly administered by Detroit Computing Center and FinCEN. After FBARs are posted—presumably by hand—to the BSA financial database, the forms are available to FinCEN analysts, law enforcement, and appropriate regulatory authorities for use, among other things, in tracking flows of money.[66] For example, with proper authorization from supervisors, a revenue agent or international examiner can obtain access to this information.

---

[63] U.S. Treasury Department, Report to Congress in Accordance with § 361(B) of the USA Patriot Act Submitted by the Secretary of the Treasury April 26, 2002, p. 3 [hereinafter "Treasury Report"]. This report is required to be made each year, but the one due April 26, 2003 has not been filed as of January 23 1, 2004.

[64] 31 C.F.R. Part 103 (2002).

[65] 31 C.F.R. 103.24 (2002).

[66] In the last several years it has become more common, it appears, for the IRS Detroit Computing Center to send requests for missing information to individuals who have filed a FBAR.

Pursuant to Treasury Directive 15-41 (12/1/92), the Secretary of the Treasury delegated to the IRS the authority to investigate possible violations of 31 U.S.C. § 5314 and federal regulation § 103.24. The IRS examines for compliance with the FBAR requirements. The IRS/Criminal Investigation Division (CI) reviews failures to file identified by the IRS examination staff (revenue agents and international examiners, for example) for possible criminal investigation. CI forwards cases that it recommends for prosecution through the IRS Office of Chief Counsel (which conducts its own independent review) to the Department of Justice, which has the final say on whether to initiate a criminal prosecution.

More recently, FinCEN delegated its enforcement authority for the FBAR to the IRS, to increase enforcement with respect to FBARs. Such authority includes the authority to collect civil penalties, to investigate possible civil violations of these provisions, to employ the summons power of subpart F of part 103, and to take any other action reasonably necessary for the enforcement of such provisions, including the pursuit of injunctions.[67]

It will be noted that the FBAR is not a tax return, as such, and is not attached to a taxpayer's Individual Federal Income Tax Return (Form 1040). It follows that the information appearing on a FBAR is not subject to the stringent disclosure restrictions of Section 6103 (relating to confidentiality and disclosure of returns and return information). Thus, information contained in this form can be shared with other agencies of the federal government. In addition, "[t]he information collected may also be provided to appropriate state, local, and foreign law enforcement and regulatory personnel in the performance of their official duties."[68] What is not widely appreciated is that a private litigant may request and may well be given access to this information in a lawsuit. For example, a spouse might seek discovery of this information in the course of an action for divorce or separate maintenance. If the form has been filed, the information, one can anticipate, will be made available pursuant to a court order. If it has not been filed, but should have been, the other spouse can be liable for all the very serious penalties described herein. If the other spouse says that he or she has not filed the form because there are no foreign bank accounts, and the requesting spouse doubts this is true, a court presumably could order the other spouse to request a copy of any and all filings with the IRS Detroit Computing Center.

Cases that CI declines to investigate as a criminal matter may be reviewed further by the IRS for possible civil enforcement action. If a taxpayer refuses to pay the penalty, the matter can be referred to the Department of Justice to institute a penalty action in which both liability and the amount of penalty must be litigated.

Complying with the statutory and regulatory requirement to report foreign financial accounts is a two-part process. Form 1040 Schedule B, Part III, instructs

---

[67] Financial Crimes Enforcement Network; Delegation of Enforcement Authority Regarding the Foreign Bank Account Report Requirements, 68 Fed. Reg. 26,489 (May 16, 2003) (to be codified at 31 C.F.R. § 103.56(g)).

[68] Privacy Act Notification on the face of TD F Form 90-22.1 (Rev. 7/00).

a taxpayer to indicate an interest in a financial account in a foreign country by checking "Yes" or "No" in the appropriate box. Form 1040 then refers the taxpayer to Form 90-22.1, which provides that it should be used to report a financial interest in, or authority over, bank accounts, securities accounts, or other financial accounts in a foreign country. The instructions for Form 1040, Schedule B, provide that the taxpayer must check "Yes" if he or she owns more that 50 percent of the stock of any corporation (U.S. or foreign) that owns one or more foreign bank accounts or at any time during the year the taxpayer had any interest in, or signature or other authority over, a financial account in a foreign country (such as a bank account, securities account, or other financial account). Among the exceptions noted in these instructions, the only one of general application is the one stating that if the combined value of the accounts was $10,0000 or less during the whole year, the "Yes" box need not be checked. If the account is denominated in a foreign currency, the value of the foreign currency is converted into U.S. dollars using the "official" exchange rate at the end of the year; "official" in the case of freely traded currencies probably means interbank or market rate of exchange.[69]

The deadline for filing a FBAR is June 30 of the year following the calendar year during which the threshold requirements are met (*see* discussion below).

While the number of FBAR filings has been steadily increasing—from 116,600 in 1991 to 177,151 in 2001, the Treasury Department believes that many persons that should file are failing to do so.

> It is difficult to determine with any accuracy how many taxpayers are failing to file required FBARs in any calendar year. Extrapolating from the limited information available concerning the number of foreign bank and credit card accounts held by United States citizens, the IRS estimates that there may be as many as 1 million U.S. taxpayers who have signature authority or control over a foreign bank account and may be required to file FBARs. Thus, the approximate rate of compliance with the FBAR filing requirements based on this information could be less than 20 percent.[70]

In the past, criminal and civil prosecutions under these provisions have been few and far between. Between 1996 and 1998, only nine indictments were filed charging failure to comply with section 5314. In the following two years, no one appears to have been charged. The Customs Service reports only three convictions since 1995.[71] This picture may be slightly distorted since it is the case that IRS agents will sometimes raise the issue with taxpayers and use a failure to file a FBAR as a means of obtaining a favorable settlement of the tax case. Also, the issue might be raised in a different form, for example, as a charge of willfully subscribing false tax returns in violation of Internal Revenue Code § 7206(1) for failing to "check the box" on Schedule B of Form 1040.

---

[69] With the precipitous rise in the value of the Euro, many Euro-denominated accounts, which were opened with an initial deposit of say 8,000-9,000 dollars that were then converted into Euros, will have drifted above the reporting threshold.

[70] Treasury Report at p. 6.

[71] Treasury Report at p. 8.

[3]   Important Developments

While in the past the FBAR has had a relatively low profile, it is receiving and undoubtedly will continue to receive much greater attention.

The government's focus on foreign bank accounts is clear. The past year and a half alone has witnessed the following developments:

- *Enactment of the Patriot Act,* which makes it easier for the Treasury Department to obtain foreign bank account information and puts the foreign bank somewhat at risk of losing its ability to maintain a correspondent account with a U.S. bank.[72] See discussion at "Caution—Danger Ahead," below.
- *The Treasury Department Report to Congress concerning FBAR reporting,* as mandated by the Patriot Act, which stated among other things that the only way to improve FBAR filing compliance among those individuals who are aware of the FBAR involves "a series of highly publicized criminal actions against intentional violators to raise the cost of being an FBAR scofflaw. Ideally, such cases would be brought not only as adjuncts to other types of criminal conduct, such as tax evasion and bankruptcy fraud, but also as stand-alone cases."[73]
- *The implementation of the IRS Voluntary Compliance Initiative Program,* which offered taxpayers with unreported foreign bank accounts an opportunity to avoid many otherwise applicable penalties.[74]
- *The ongoing IRS John Doe summons investigations,* where the IRS has issued a series of summonses to obtain information about U.S. citizens holding payment cards tied to foreign bank accounts. This investigation has produced numerous cases being referred to the Criminal Investigation Division of the IRS.[75]

On the other hand, the FBAR, which is a short, two-page form, is deceptively simple. Its concise format hides several latent issues. More critically, the FBAR filing requirements' broad applicability combined with the association in the minds of most practitioners and lay people of the FBAR with so-called "tax cheats," who use unreported foreign bank accounts to commit tax fraud, causes many people to fail to understand that they must file an FBAR.

[4]   Who Must File an FBAR?

Each U.S. person with a financial interest in, or signature or other authority over, any financial account in a foreign country must file an FBAR if the

---

[72] Almost all foreign banks that need to receive or make payments in dollars maintain a correspondent account with a U.S. bank, typically a large bank located in New York. Today, dollars are dealt with electronically through the DTC system, and access to this system is through the large banks that have usually one DTC account.

[73] Treasury Report at p. 11.

[74] Rev. Proc. 2003-11, 2003-4 I.R.B. 311.

[75] *See Early Information Reveals Strong Response to Offshore Initiative, IRS Says,* 2003 TNT 85-17 (May 1, 2003).

aggregate value of all such accounts exceeds $10,000 at any time during the calendar year. The FBAR must be filed on or before the June 30 after the calendar year in which the relationship existed. The FBAR is required in addition to the reporting obligations with respect to foreign accounts on Form 1040, Schedule B.[76]

Certain people do not have to file an FBAR. These include officers or employees of certain banks and large publicly-traded corporations with signature/other authority over foreign financial accounts maintained by that bank or large corporation, where they have no personal financial interest in the account, and they have been advised in writing by the corporation's chief financial officer that the corporation has filed a current FBAR, which includes such account. To illustrate, *E*, a General Motors executive based in London, with signature authority over a GM bank account in London in which *E* has no personal financial interest, and who otherwise satisfies the requirements of the exception, does not have to file an FBAR. In contrast, *F*, an executive in London under exactly the same circumstances but employed by a non-publicly traded company, must file an FBAR.

[5] Key Definitions

For FBAR purposes, a person has a "financial interest" in a foreign financial account if he is the owner of record or has legal title, regardless of whether that account is maintained for his own benefit or for the benefit of others, including non-U.S. persons. For joint accounts, each owner has a financial interest in that account. In addition, a U.S. person has a financial interest in a foreign financial account where the owner of record is any of the following:

- Another person who acts on such person's behalf (*e.g.*, agent, nominee, attorney);
- A corporation in which such person owns more than 50 percent of the value of the shares;
- A partnership in which such person owns an interest in more than 50 percent of the profits;
- A trust in which such person either has a present interest in more than 50 percent of the assets or from which such person receives more than 50 percent of the current income.[77]

A "financial account" includes any bank, securities, securities derivatives or other financial instruments accounts. Such accounts generally also "encompass any accounts in which the assets are held in a commingled fund, and the account

---

[76] There is not a great deal of authority bearing on the "backfiling" of FBARs voluntarily or even after notice from the IRS or FinCEN. In the case of nonfilers who are "catching up" with their filing of income tax returns, the authors recommend that they also "backfile" FBARs. The recent Voluntary Compliance Initiative Program requires, among other things, the backfiling of FBARs.

[77] Tying reporting requirements to a percentage of profits or current income can cause difficulties, as the individual concerned may not know the total amount of profits or current income. In some cases another filing might help him or her, as is the case with beneficiaries of foreign trusts that may receive statements from the foreign trust showing the necessary figures.

holder holds an equity interest in the fund." But there are many gray areas. To illustrate, if a U.S. person places $1 million cash into a safe deposit box in Switzerland, does this constitute a financial interest in a foreign account, which triggers the FBAR filing requirements? As with many other FBAR issues, no authoritative guidance answers this issue. However, it appears that in the safe deposit box context, application of the FBAR requirements depends on the precise nature of the arrangement between the bank and the safe deposit box holder. For example, if the holder gives the bank the right to access more than $10,000 of cash in a safe deposit box in order to secure a credit card issued by that bank, then it appears that the holder may be required to file an FBAR. The rationale for this is that this arrangement is substantively no different than if the holder deposited such cash into a checking or other financial account with the bank, which would trigger the FBAR filing requirements. To illustrate a different situation, if a U.S. person creates a grantor trust, which in turn owns a foreign financial account valued at more than of $10,000, does the U.S. person need to file an FBAR? Here, it appears that the U.S. person must file an FBAR if he is treated as the grantor of the trust under the grantor trust rules.[78]

To determine whether the $10,000 filing threshold has been surpassed, "account valuation" is defined as "the largest amount of currency and nonmonetary assets that appear on any quarterly or more frequent account statements issued for the applicable year." If periodic account statements are not issued, the maximum account asset value is the largest amount of currency and non-monetary assets in the account at any time during the year. For this purpose, filers must convert foreign currency by using the year-end official exchange or conversion rate. The value of stock, securities, or other non-monetary assets is the fair market value at year-end, or at withdrawal from the account, if earlier. Each account must be valued separately in accordance with the foregoing rules. The $10,000 filing threshold is an aggregate threshold; that is, it applies if the aggregate value of all foreign financial accounts held by the person in question exceeds $10,000 at any time during the calendar year.

A person has "signature authority" over an account if he can control the disposition of money or other property in that account by delivery of a document containing his signature, or his signature along with that of one or more other persons, to the bank or other person with whom the account is maintained. A person has "other authority" if that person can exercise comparable power over an account by direct communication to the bank or other person with whom the account is maintained, either orally or by some other means. This definition occasionally has counter-intuitive results. For example, it is clear that an individual who establishes a foreign bank account and receives a credit card secured by that account has the requisite signature authority to trigger the FBAR filing requirements. On the other hand, if a German entrepreneur gives his U.S. resident daughter a credit card issued to his German closely held company by a German bank, does the daughter now have to file an FBAR? If the credit card is secured by the German bank account, the answer is yes. This results even though

---

[78] This point can be argued either way. The argument for the proposition that filing is required is based not on section 671 of the Internal Revenue Code but on the BSA provisions.

the daughter is certainly not the type of person the FBAR is directed at. On the other hand, if the credit card is unsecured, similar to most credit cards issued in the United States, then it appears the daughter need not file an FBAR.

A U.S. person, for FBAR purposes, includes U.S. citizens and residents, domestic partnerships, domestic corporations, and domestic estates or trusts. This definition catches several types of people unawares. To illustrate, each of the following individuals must file an FBAR, even though they may not realize this:

- A U.S. citizen studying overseas who opens up a bank account at a foreign bank for convenience, which had over $10,000 at any time during the year.
- A child of a foreign entrepreneur who attends college in the United States, who has a foreign bank account from childhood on, worth more than $10,000, will become subject to the FBAR requirements if that child ultimately becomes a U.S. resident or if it obtains an immigrant visa permitting him/her to reside in the United States on a permanent basis (*i.e.*, a "green card").
- A U.S. citizen marries a Dutch citizen who is temporarily stationed in the United States. If the U.S. citizen, along with his new spouse, returns to Denmark, retains U.S. citizenship, and opens a financial account (e.g., a brokerage account) in Denmark, he or she must file an FBAR if the account value exceeds $10,000 at any time during the year.
- A U.S. citizen or resident is temporarily stationed in Mexico by his employer. The individual opens a bank account in Mexico, and maintains a nominal amount in that account throughout the year. At yearend, the employer gives the individual a $15,000 bonus, which he deposits in his bank account in Mexico.
- A so-called "accidental American" has an account outside the United States. An "accidental American" is someone who was born in the United States of foreign parents. For example, a couple give birth to a daughter while studying in the United States. The daughter is a U.S. citizen, even though she, together with her parents, lives in Switzerland, and she has never returned to the United States after leaving at a very early age. This individual should file an FBAR for all foreign accounts.

Each of the foregoing situations is common. In each situation, frequently, the individuals do not realize that they must file an FBAR, and that they are subject to both civil and criminal penalties for failing to do so. Moreover, often the accountants, attorneys, financial planners, and other professionals who advise such individuals do not think about the FBAR, thus exposing them to malpractice liability.

[6] What Information Is Required?

What about the FBAR itself? Is it difficult to complete? No, the FBAR itself is very easy to complete. It requires taxpayers to provide the following information:

- Filer's name, address, taxpayer identification number, date of birth, and country.

- Whether the accounts are jointly owned, and if so, the number of joint owners. If the filer owns the account jointly with only one other party, and all accounts listed are held jointly with that party, then the filer must provide the name of that party, and its taxpayer identification number, if known.
- The number of foreign financial accounts in which the filer holds an interest.
- The type of account.
- The maximum value of the account during the year.
- The account number and the name of the financial institution with which the account is held.
- The name, address, and taxpayer identification number of the account holder.

If the filer has a "financial interest" in more than 25 foreign bank accounts, information for the accounts need not be provided but must be made available to the Treasury Department upon request. If the filer has an interest in fewer than 25 accounts, the information listed above must be provided for each account.

[7] Criminal and Civil Penalty Exposure

What happens if someone fails to file an FBAR? What is his or her liability exposure? Failure to file a FBAR or filing a false FBAR may trigger criminal penalties. The base penalty is a maximum fine of $250,000, a maximum term of imprisonment of five years, or both. The alternative penalty, which is a fine of not more than $500,000, or imprisonment of not more than ten years, or both, applies if the defendant violates any other U.S. law or if the violation was part of a pattern of any illegal activity involving more than $100,000 in a twelve-month period. In addition, the false-statement statute, 18 U.S.C. § 1001, may be violated if a false form is filed. For this purpose, a separate criminal violation will occur for each FBAR not filed or falsely filed. Because Form 1040, Schedule B outlines the FBAR reporting requirement, willfulness may not be exceptionally difficult for the government to prove.

In addition to criminal penalties, failure to file a FBAR or filing of a false FBAR may also trigger civil penalties. To illustrate, an individual who willfully violates the FBAR reporting requirement can be fined either $25,000 or an amount equal to the balance in the account at the time of violation (not to exceed $100,000), whichever is greater. Although not entirely clear, it appears that if multiple accounts exist, the fine would be a minimum of $25,000 per account, even if multiple accounts should have been reported on the same form.

[8] Caution—Danger Ahead

The requirement to file an FBAR falls within the anti-money laundering programs instituted by the U.S. government; section 5314, in fact, sits in the U.S. Code just a few sections away from a number of new provisions added by the Patriot Act. Under section 5318 of Title 31 (Compliance, Exemptions, and

Summons Authority) of Section II (Records and Reports on Monetary Instruments Transactions), of Chapter 53 (Monetary Transactions, which Chapter also deals with money laundering and related crimes), the Secretary of the Treasury or the Attorney General[79] may issue a summons or subpoena to any foreign bank that maintains a correspondent account in the United States and request records related to such correspondent account, including records maintained outside of the United States relating to the deposit of funds into the foreign bank. "Correspondent account" is defined in new section 5318A (Special Measures for Jurisdictions, Financial Institutions, or International Transactions of Primary Money Laundering Concern) as "an account established to receive deposits from, make payments on behalf of a foreign financial institution, or handle other financial transactions related to such institution." Service and acceptance of service are streamlined by new provisions that, in effect, require the foreign bank to appoint an authorized agent for receipt of legal process for records regarding the correspondent account. (The U.S. bank that is operating the account will require this. The U.S. bank is referred to by the statute as a "covered financial institution.") If a foreign bank fails to comply with a summons or subpoena issued under these new provisions, the covered financial institution, upon notification by the Secretary of the Treasury or the Attorney General, can be forced to terminate (shut down) the correspondent account or itself face severe penalties.

While a FBAR is clearly not the only "predicate" to institution of these summons or subpoena procedures, it is one, and the requirement to file an accurate report is an easy one to point to. Foreign banks will want to take note of the connection between Patriot Act summons and subpoenas and FBARs. They may wish to provide reminders to customers that the rules of countries, such as the United States, may require them, the customers, to report "foreign" accounts, and that information regarding the account may become the subject of a summons or subpoena directed at the bank. The bank may wish to notify its customers that it will comply with such formal requests and to obtain the customers' consent in advance. So far as summons and subpoenas based on a FBAR or failure to file a correct and complete FBAR, these thoughts are, in general, only relevant to U.S. persons, that is, U.S. citizens, U.S. residents, U.S. partnerships, U.S. corporations, U.S. trusts, and U.S. estates.[80] Affected individuals

---

[79] Apparently this authority does not run to a grand jury. This is a technical problem that may be fixed by legislation or otherwise.

[80] The regulations promulgated under 31 U.S.C. 5314 speak in terms of "[e]ach person subject to the jurisdiction of the United States (except a foreign subsidiary of a U.S. person) having a financial interest in, or signature or other authority over, a bank, securities or other financial account in a foreign country...." The instructions to the FBAR form, however, refer to "United States person" and define that term as a citizen or resident of the U.S., a domestic partnership, a domestic corporation, or a domestic estate or trust. The Internal Revenue Code contains a definition of "United States person" that is similar but not identical to the FBAR-related definitions, and clearly the FBAR rules are not simply cross-referencing the tax law definition. For example, a Delaware trust that "flunks" the test in IRC § 7701(a)(30)(E) is not a United States person for tax purposes but may be for FBAR reporting purposes. Also, there is no clarity as to the definition of a "domestic estate." Is the estate of a U.S. citizen who lived the last 40 years of his life in Europe, which estate is administered outside the United States., a domestic estate? What if the decedent was not a U.S. citizen or resident but the estate owns commercial real estate

should know that these new mechanisms make it much easier for the U.S. government to look at foreign accounts.

The Patriot Act and newer generation mutual legal assistance treaties are obviously designed to make it easier for the U.S. government to obtain admissible evidence of undisclosed foreign accounts. Prosecutors, it is believed, will be urged to take a second look when deciding whether to charge a FBAR failure to file.

Also, it should be noted that the Senate version of the Jobs and Growth Tax Relief Reconciliation Act of 2003 (P.L. 108-27) would have added an additional $5,000 civil penalty that, if enacted, would have allowed the IRS to impose such penalty on any person who failed to properly file an FBAR, *without regard to willfulness*.[81] This change would make it considerably easier for a prosecutor to charge the violation. Although this provision did not make it into the final version of the Act, such proposals have a way of recurring until they are enacted.

The FBAR form almost certainly will be changed in many important respects in the very near future. In its Report to Congress dated April 26, 2002, the Treasury Department stated that FinCEN would take responsibility for updating this form and the accompanying instructions. The target date for doing so was set at December 31, 2002. One suspects that the delay is due in part to work on Patriot Act and other regulations, the contents of which will bear on this form.

[9] Conclusion

The Foreign Bank Accounts Form has never been something to sneeze at, as it is a crime to violate the underlying rules. It is undoubtedly true, however, that individuals and their advisers have too often not given this form the attention it deserves. In light of the Treasury Department's and IRS's new focus on these provisions, born in large measure from the events of "9/11" and the drive to prevent money-laundering, and the new Patriot Act provisions, TD F 90-22.1 must be treated with a great deal more respect. If in doubt, the answer should be to file the forms; there is no indication that the fact that one files triggers an audit. To do otherwise is dangerous.

§ 9.03 MONEY LAUNDERING CONTROL ACT

The Money Laundering Control Act of 1986 (MLCA)[1] (1) outlaws certain components of money laundering, (2) outlaws dealings in monetary transactions with property derived from certain specified crimes, and (3) adds penalties for structuring transactions to avoid currency reporting requirements.[2]

---

in the United States? This last estate probably is a "foreign estate" under the income tax rules in IRC § 7701(a)(31). It is this type of confusion that needs to be dispelled.

[81] *See* Ratzlaff v. United States, 510 U.S. 135 (1994), involving a different part of the BSA.

§ 9.03 [1] *See generally* L. Richard Fischer, The Law of Financial Privacy ¶ 4.09[4] (3rd ed. 1998); U.S. Dep't of Treas. & U.S. Customs Serv., Fines, Penalties & Forfeitures Handbook (Apr. 1986 rev.).

[2] Money Laundering Control Act of 1986, Pub. L. No. 99-570, 100 Stat. 3207-18 to 3207-39 (1986) (codified as amended in scattered sections of 12 U.S.C., 18 U.S.C., 31 U.S.C.); L. Richard Fischer, The Law of Financial Privacy ¶ 4.09[4] (3rd ed. 1998).

First, the MLCA outlaws certain components of money laundering. Specifically, the MLCA makes dealing with proceeds of certain unlawful activities a criminal act when such dealings are aimed at furthering the unlawful activities or at concealing or disguising the source, ownership, location, or nature of the proceeds.[3] The specified unlawful activities generally include crimes commonly associated with organized crime, drug trafficking, and financial misconduct.[4] The MLCA provides a maximum jail sentence of 20 years plus a maximum fine of the greater of $500,000 or double the value of the monetary instruments or currency involved, for each offense.[5] The MLCA also provides a civil penalty for such offenses. The maximum civil penalty amount equals the greater of the property's value or the funds involved, or $10,000.[6] Finally, the United States may seize any property representing the receipts obtained, directly or indirectly, because of this rule's violation or that may be traced to its violation.[7]

Second, the MLCA makes it a criminal offense for individuals to knowingly engage in or attempt to engage in monetary transactions involving $10,000 or more of criminally derived property when such property derives from certain forms of unlawful activity.[8] The defendant need not know the specific type of criminal activity involved, only that the property derives from some type of criminal activity.[9] The MLCA provides a maximum jail sentence of 10 years for such violations.[10] Furthermore, the MLCA provides a maximum fine of the greater of $250,000, or twice the amount of the criminally derived property involved in the transaction.[11]

Finally, the MLCA outlaws activities for purposes of evading BSA reporting requirements by persons who:

1. Cause or attempt to cause domestic financial institutions not to file a currency transaction report;
2. Cause or attempt to cause domestic financial institutions to file a currency transaction report containing material omissions or misstatements of fact; or
3. Structure or assist in structuring any transaction with one or more domestic financial institutions.[12]

---

[3] 18 U.S.C. § 1956(a) (1988); L. Richard Fischer, The Law of Financial Privacy ¶ 4.09[4] (3rd ed. 1998).
[4] 18 U.S.C. § 1956(c)(7) (1988); L. Richard Fischer, The Law of Financial Privacy ¶ 4.09[4] (3rd ed. 1998).
[5] 18 U.S.C. § 1956(a) (1988); L. Richard Fischer, The Law of Financial Privacy ¶ 4.09[4] (3rd ed. 1998).
[6] 18 U.S.C. § 1956(b) (1988); L. Richard Fischer, The Law of Financial Privacy ¶ 4.09[4] (3rd ed. 1998).
[7] 18 U.S.C. § 981(a)(1)(A) (1988); L. Richard Fischer, The Law of Financial Privacy ¶ 4.09[4] (3rd ed. 1998).
[8] 18 U.S.C. § 1957 (1988); L. Richard Fischer, The Law of Financial Privacy ¶ 4.09[4] (3rd ed. 1998).
[9] 18 U.S.C. § 1957(c) (1988); L. Richard Fischer, The Law of Financial Privacy ¶ 4.09[4] (3rd ed. 1998).
[10] 18 U.S.C. § 1957(b)(1) (1988); L. Richard Fischer, The Law of Financial Privacy ¶ 4.09[4] (3rd ed. 1998).
[11] 18 U.S.C. § 1957(b)(1), (2) (1988); L. Richard Fischer, The Law of Financial Privacy ¶ 4.09[4] (3rd ed. 1998).
[12] 31 U.S.C. § 5324 (1988); 31 C.F.R. § 103.53 (1992); L. Richard Fischer, The Law of Financial Privacy ¶ 4.09[4] (3rd ed. 1998).

The BSA subjects persons willfully violating this rule to a maximum civil penalty of up to the amount of the monetary instruments involved, less any forfeiture to the United States imposed in connection with the transaction; a maximum fine of $250,000; a maximum jail sentence of up to five years; or any combination of these.[13] Moreover, the BSA subjects persons willfully violating this rule while violating another federal law, or as a pattern of any illegal activity involving more than $100,000 during any 12-month period, to a maximum $500,000 fine, a maximum 10-year jail sentence, or both.[14]

The Supreme Court has held that in order for a person to structure or assist in structuring any transaction with one or more domestic financial institutions with the required degree of "willfulness," that individual must possess "knowledge that his conduct was unlawful."[15] In another recent case, *United States v. Trapilo*,[16] the United States Court of Appeals for the Second Circuit held that a scheme to defraud a foreign government of tax revenue is recognizable under the federal wire fraud statute.[17]

Comment. A recent case shows that banks that assist the government by providing certain information about their depositors' accounts may be held liable to them. In *Lopez v. First Union National Bank*,[18] the Eleventh Circuit held that banks that cooperated with the United States by providing information about bank account holders' accounts may be liable to such account holders.

§ 9.04 CAYMAN ISLANDS LAW: EXAMPLE OF BANK SECRECY LAW

Asset protection planners may advise a client to transfer funds to countries having a bank secrecy law. Foreign bank secrecy laws vary from country to country. This section summarizes the Cayman Islands bank secrecy law to provide planners with an example of how such laws operate.

---

[13] 31 U.S.C. § 5322 (1988); 31 C.F.R. §§ 103.47(e), 103.49(b) (1992); L. Richard Fischer, The Law of Financial Privacy ¶ 4.09[4] (3rd ed. 1998).

[14] 31 U.S.C. § 5322(b) (1988); 31 C.F.R. § 103.49(c) (1992); L. Richard Fischer, The Law of Financial Privacy ¶ 4.09[4] (3rd ed. 1998).

[15] Ratzlaf v. United States, 510 U.S. 135 (1994). *See also* Annotation, *Validity, construction, and effect of domestic currency transaction reporting requirement based upon 31 USC § 5313(a)*, 89 A.L.R. Fed. 770 (1988 & Supp. 1995). *See also* United States v. London, 66 F.3d 1227 (1st Cir. 1995), *reh'g en banc denied*, 1995 U.S. App. LEXIS 29722 (1st Cir. Oct. 20, 1995), wherein the First Circuit held that jury instructions on willfulness, in a prosecution for failure to file currency transaction reports, framed in terms of "reckless disregard" of the law, fell within the concept of "knowledge" that the Supreme Court articulated in United States v. Ratzlaf.

[16] 130 F.3d 547 (2d Cir. 1997).

[17] 18 U.S.C. § 1343.

[18] 129 F.3d 1186 (11 th Cir. 1997).

Planning Pointer. The law controlling bank secrecy in the Cayman Islands derives from three statutory sources. The planner working with Cayman Islands law must understand each of these statutory provisions to understand its bank secrecy law. These three sources are as follows:

1. Confidential Relationships (Preservation) Law, 1976 (Law 16 of 1976);
2. Confidential Relationships (Preservation) (Amendment) Law, 1979 (Law 26 of 1979); and
3. Mutual Legal Assistance (United States of America) Law, 1986 (Law 16 of 1986).

Planning Pointer. The planner should refer to Appendix B for the text of the Confidential Relationships (Preservation) Law, 1976 (Law 16 of 1976); to Appendix C for the text of the Confidential Relationships (Preservation) (Amendment) Law, 1979 (Law 26 of 1979); and to Appendix D for the text of the Mutual Legal Assistance (United States of America) Law, 1986 (Law 16 of 1986).

[A] Confidential Relationships (Preservation) Law, 1976

The primary Cayman Islands legislation dealing with bank secrecy is the Confidential Relationships (Preservation) Law, 1976 (Law 16 of 1976) (CRP Law). It applies to all confidential information concerning businesses of a professional nature arising in or brought into the Cayman Islands and to all persons possessing such information. Furthermore, this law applies regardless of whether the persons involved are located inside or outside the Cayman Islands.[1] The CRP Law defines confidential information as including any "information concerning any property which the recipient thereof is not, otherwise than in the normal course of business, authorized by the principal to divulge."[2]

The CRP Law provides that whoever possesses confidential information, regardless of how obtained, who either (1) divulges, or attempts, offers, or threatens to divulge information to someone not entitled to possess such information, or (2) willfully obtains or attempts to obtain confidential information to which she is not entitled, will be held guilty of an offense. Such person will be liable on summary conviction to a fine not exceeding $5,000, to imprisonment for up to two years, or both.[3]

The CRP Law increases the penalties for violations under three circumstances. First, if someone violates the CRP Law and receives or solicits any reward for

---

§ 9.04 [1] CRP Law § 3(1) (1976).
[2] CRP Law § 2 (1976).
[3] CRP Law § 4(1) (1976).

such violation, the CRP Law (1) holds that person guilty of an offense and liable on summary conviction to a fine not exceeding $10,000, to imprisonment for up to four years, or both, (2) adds a fine equal to the amount of the reward, and (3) requires forfeiture of the reward.[4]

Second, if someone who possesses confidential information, clandestinely, or without the principal's consent, uses such information for her or another's benefit, the CRP Law (1) holds that person guilty of an offense and liable on summary conviction to a fine not exceeding $10,000, to imprisonment for up to four years, or both, (2) adds a fine equal to the amount of the profit accruing to any person out of any relevant transaction, and (3) requires forfeiture of such profit.[5]

Third, if a professional person, entrusted as such with confidential information, violates any of the above rules concerning such confidential information, the CRP Law doubles the penalty.[6] The CRP Law defines a professional person as including public or government officials, banks, trust companies, attorneys, accountants, estate agents, insurers, brokers, and every kind of commercial agent and advisor, whether or not answering the foregoing descriptions and whether or not licensed or authorized to act in such a capacity, plus every person subordinate to or in the employ or control of such person for the purpose of her professional activities.[7]

For purposes of the CRP Law, when a bank gives a credit reference concerning a customer without first obtaining that customer's authorization, the CRP Law considers the bank to have violated the CRP Law.[8]

[B] Confidential Relationships (Preservation) (Amendment) Law, 1979

In 1979 the Cayman Islands amended the CRP Law by the Confidential Relationships (Preservation) (Amendment) Law, 1979 (Law 26 of 1979) CRP (Amendment) Law. The CRP (Amendment) Law modifies the CRP Law[9] by changing the exceptions to its application so that it now does not apply to the seeking, divulging, or obtaining of confidential information:

1. In compliance with the directions of the Grand Court of the Cayman Islands pursuant to CRP (Amendment) Law § 3A
2. By or to
    (a) Any professional person acting in the normal course of business or with the consent of the relevant principal
    (b) A constable of the rank of inspector or above who is investigating an offense committed or alleged to have been committed within the jurisdiction

---

[4] CRP Law § 4(2) (1976).
[5] CRP Law § 4(3) (1976).
[6] CRP Law § 4(4) (1976).
[7] CRP Law § 2 (1976).
[8] CRP Law § 4(5) (1976).
[9] *See* CRP Law § 2(a)-(d) (1976) in App. B.

(c) A constable of the rank of inspector or above, specifically authorized by the governor of the Cayman Islands in that behalf, investigating an offense committed or alleged to have been committed outside the Cayman Islands which offense, if committed within the Cayman Islands, would be an offense against its laws

(d) The financial secretary, the inspector or, in relation to particular information specified by the governor, such other person as the governor may authorize

(e) A bank in any proceedings, cause or matter when and to the extent to which it is reasonably necessary for the protection of the bank's interests, either as against its customers or as against third parties concerning transactions of the bank for, or with, its customer, or

(f) The relevant professional person with the approval of the financial secretary when necessary for the protection of herself or any other person against crime or

3. In accordance with the provisions of any other Cayman Islands law.[10]

The CRP (Amendment) Law also added a new §3A to the CRP Law. Section 3A(1) provides that whenever a person intends or must give confidential information as evidence in or in connection with proceedings in a court, tribunal, or other authority, either inside or outside of the Cayman Islands, such person must apply for directions before doing so.[11]

Section 3A(2) provides that applications for directions must be made to, heard, and determined by a judge of the Grand Court of the Cayman Islands sitting alone and in camera.[12] Section 3A(2) allows the attorney general to appear at the hearing as amicus curiae. Furthermore, it allows any party who receives notice of the proceeding to be heard, either personally or through counsel.[13]

Section 3A(4) provides that to protect the confidentiality of statements, answers, or testimony ordered to be given, judges may order (1) statements, answers, or testimony be only divulged to certain named persons, (2) evidence be taken in camera, and (3) reference to the names, addresses, and descriptions of any particular persons be by alphabetical letters, numbers, or symbols representing such persons, the key to which will be restricted.[14]

Section 3A(5) holds every person receiving confidential information under Section 3A(2) bound by the provisions of the CRP Law, as amended, as if a principal had entrusted such information to her in confidence.[15]

Section 3A(6) instructs the judge to consider the following when determining what order to make under Section 3A:

1. Whether such order would operate as a denial of the rights of any person in the enforcement of a just claim;

---

[10] CRP (Amendment) Law §3 (1979).
[11] *Id.*
[12] *Id.*
[13] *Id.*
[14] *Id.*
[15] *Id.*

2. Any offer of compensation or indemnity made to any person desiring to enforce a claim by any person having an interest in the preservation of secrecy under the CRP Law, as amended; and
3. In criminal cases, the requirements of the interests of justice.[16]

[C] Mutual Legal Assistance (United States of America) Law, 1986

The United States has Mutual Legal Assistance Treaties (MLATs) with several countries including Switzerland,[17] the Cayman Islands,[18] and the Bahamas[19] among others. MLATs offer a broad range of assistance for the prosecution of criminal offenses that fall within their scope. Generally, such assistance includes the exchange of witness testimony, the production of documents, the location of persons, the service of subpoenas and other documents, the execution of requests for search and seizure, the voluntary appearance of witnesses for testimony, the transportation of prisoners in custody for testimony abroad, and the seizure and forfeiture of criminally obtained assets.[20]

The Mutual Legal Assistance (United States of America) Law, 1986 (Law 16 of 1986) (MLAL) gives effect to the MLAT between the United States and the Cayman Islands.[21] The text of the MLAL, which includes the text of the Treaty Relating to Mutual Legal Assistance in Criminal Matters, July 3, 1986, United States-United Kingdom (on behalf of the Cayman Islands) (hereinafter Cayman Islands MLAT) is set forth in Appendix D.

Under the Cayman Islands MLAT, the Cayman Islands and the United States agree to provide mutual assistance for the investigation, prosecution, and suppression of criminal offenses set forth in the MLAT.[22] Such assistance generally includes the following:

1. Taking the testimony or statement of persons;
2. Providing documents, records, and articles of evidence;
3. Serving documents;
4. Locating persons;
5. Transferring persons in custody for testimony;
6. Executing requests for searches and seizures;
7. Immobilizing criminally obtained assets;

---

[16] Id.

[17] Treaty on Mutual Assistance in Criminal Matters, May 25, 1973, U.S.-Switz., 27 U.S.T. 2019, T.I.A.S. No. 8302.

[18] Treaty Relating to Mutual Legal Assistance in Criminal Matters, July 3, 1986, U.S.-U.K. (on behalf of the Cayman Islands), S. Treaty Doc. No. 8, 100th Cong., 1st Sess. (1987), 26 I.L.M. 537.

[19] Treaty on Mutual Assistance in Criminal Matters, Aug. 18, 1987, U.S.-Bah., S. Treaty Doc. No. 17, 100th Cong., 2d Sess. (1988).

[20] James P. Springer, *An Overview of International Evidence and Asset Gathering in Civil and Criminal Tax Cases*, 22 Geo. Wash. J. Int'l L. & Econ. 277, 304 (1988).

[21] MLAL § 3 (1986).

[22] Cayman Islands MLAT art. 1, § 1 (1986).

8. Assisting in proceedings related to forfeiture, restitution, and collection of fines; and
9. Any other steps deemed appropriate by both Central Authorities.[23]

The Cayman Islands MLAT requires each party to establish a central authority.[24] The attorney general or her designate serves as the U.S. central authority.[25] The chief justice serves as the Cayman Islands central authority.[26] Cayman Islands MLAT requests for assistance must be made to the other party's central authority.[27]

The Cayman Islands MLAT explicitly restricts the use of evidence obtained under the Cayman Islands MLAT to proceedings regarding offenses covered under the MLAT.[28] Specifically, the Cayman Islands MLAT states that it is "intended solely for mutual legal assistance between the Parties," and that the MLAT's provisions "shall not create any right on the part of any private person to obtain, suppress, or exclude any evidence, or to impede the execution of a request."[29] Furthermore, Article 7 of the Cayman Islands MLAT specifically limits the use of information or evidence provided under its provisions. First, Article 7 provides that the requesting party must not use information or evidence provided under the Cayman Islands MLAT for any purposes other than the investigation, prosecution, or suppression of the criminal offenses stated in the request in the requesting party's territory, unless the requested party gives its prior consent.[30] Second, Article 7 requires both central authorities to keep information or evidence furnished under the Cayman Islands MLAT confidential, except to the extent when such evidence or information is needed for investigations or prosecutions of offenses stated in the request.[31] Third, the requesting central authority may request that the request's contents, related documents, and grant of assistance be kept confidential.[32] When this cannot be accommodated, the requested central authority must so inform the requesting central authority, who then may decide whether to proceed.[33] Except when otherwise permitted, information or evidence obtained under the Cayman Islands MLAT that has been made public in the requesting party's territory in a proceeding forming part of the prosecution of a criminal offense described in the request may only be used for the following additional purposes:

1. When the trial results in a conviction for a criminal offense falling within the Cayman Islands MLAT's scope, for any purpose against the person convicted;

---

[23] Cayman Islands MLAT art. 1, § 2 (1986).
[24] Cayman Islands MLAT art. 2, § 1 (1986).
[25] Cayman Islands MLAT art. 2, § 2 (1986).
[26] Cayman Islands MLAT art. 2, § 2; MLAL § 4 (1986).
[27] Cayman Islands MLAT art. 2, § 3 (1986).
[28] James P. Springer, *An Overview of International Evidence and Asset Gathering in Civil and Criminal Tax Cases*, 22 Geo. Wash. J. Int'l L. & Econ. 277, 306 (1988).
[29] 97 Cayman Islands MLAT art. 1, § 3 (1986).
[30] Cayman Islands MLAT art. 7, § 1 (1986).
[31] Cayman Islands MLAT art. 7, § 2 (1986).
[32] Cayman Islands MLAT art. 7, § 3 (1986).
[33] *Id.*

2. Whether or not a trial results in the conviction of any person, in the prosecution of any person for any criminal offense within the Cayman Islands MLAT's scope; and

3. In civil or administrative proceedings, only if and to the extent that such proceedings relate to:

   a) The recovery of the unlawful proceeds of criminal offenses within the treaty's scope from persons who knowingly receive such proceeds;

   b) The collection of tax or the enforcement of tax penalties resulting from the knowing receipt of the unlawful proceeds of criminal offenses within the treaty's scope;

   c) The recovery in rem of the unlawful proceeds or instrumentalities of criminal offenses within the treaty's scope.[34]

Article 3 of the Cayman Islands MLAT limits the assistance provided under the treaty. First, Article 3 provides that the treaty's assistance does not include (1) assistance concerning offenses relating to tax laws other than tax matters arising from unlawful activities otherwise covered by the treaty, and (2) any conduct not punishable for more than one year of imprisonment.[35] Second, Article 2 provides that the requested central authority may deny assistance when:

1. The request is not made in conformity with the Cayman Islands MLAT;

2. The request relates to political offenses or offenses under military law which would not be an offense under ordinary criminal law; or

3. The request does not establish reasonable grounds for believing (a) that the criminal offense specified in the request was committed, and (b) that the information sought relates to the offense and is located in the territory of the requested party.[36]

Consequently, this provision limits fishing expeditions. Third, Article 2 requires the central authority to deny assistance when the requested party's attorney general issues a certificate that the request's execution will be contrary to the requested party's public interest.[37] However, the Cayman Islands MLAT requires the requested central authority to consult with the requesting central authority before denying assistance. Here the two central authorities must consider whether assistance can be given subject to such conditions that the requested central authority deems necessary.[38]

The Cayman Islands MLAT defines criminal offense as including, among others, the following:

1. Any conduct punishable by more than one year's imprisonment under the laws of both the Cayman Islands and the United States;

---

[34] Cayman Islands MLAT art. 7, §4 (1986).
[35] Cayman Islands MLAT art. 3, §1 (1986).
[36] Cayman Islands MLAT art. 3, §2 (1986).
[37] Cayman Islands MLAT art. 3, §3 (1986).
[38] Cayman Islands MLAT art. 3, §4 (1986).

2. Racketeering;
3. Narcotics trafficking;
4. Willfully or dishonestly obtaining money, property, or valuable securities from others by false or fraudulent pretenses regarding or affecting benefits available in connection with the laws and regulations relating to income or other taxes;
5. Willfully or dishonestly making false statements to government tax authorities concerning tax matters arising from the unlawful proceeds of any criminal offense covered by any other provision of the definition of "criminal offense," other than Cayman Islands MLAT Article 19, § 3(f) (dealing with willful or dishonest failures to report currency transactions), or willfully or dishonestly failing to make a report to government tax authorities as required by law concerning taxes due on any such unlawful proceeds;
6. Willfully or dishonestly failing to file government reports concerning international currency transfers or other financial transactions connected with, arising from, or related to unlawful proceeds of criminal offense falling within the Cayman Islands MLAT's definition of "criminal offense," other than Cayman Islands MLAT Article 19, § 3(e) (dealing with the willful or dishonest making of false statements or failure to make statements to government tax authorities);
7. Insider trading;
8. Fraudulent securities practices; and
9. Foreign corrupt practices.[39]

The MLAL gives effect to the Cayman Islands MLAT.[40] It requires the Cayman authority to notify the attorney general immediately on a request's receipt. Furthermore, it requires the Cayman authority to provide the attorney general with the request's particulars and copies of applicable documents. The attorney general then becomes entitled, in a manner analogous to amicus curiae, to appear or take part in Cayman Islands proceedings arising directly or indirectly from the request.[41]

The MLAL provides that persons who divulge confidential information or give testimony in conformity with requests will not violate the CRP Law or any other Cayman Islands law because of such disclosure or testimony.[42] Furthermore, the MLAL provides that such disclosures will not breach any confidential relationship between the disclosing person and any other person. Furthermore, no civil claim or action may lie against such person or such person's principal or employer for making such disclosures.[43]

The MLAL provides that when instructed by the Cayman authority, all matters relating to a request must be treated as confidential. Consequently, persons notified of requests or required to take action pursuant to requests must not

---

[39] Cayman Islands MLAT art. 19, § 3 (1986).
[40] MLAL § 3 (1986).
[41] MLAL § 5 (1986).
[42] MLAL § 10 (1986).
[43] *Id.*

disclose the receipt or particulars of such requests. However, this proscription does not apply to the person's attorney or to other persons authorized by the Cayman authority. This proscription applies for 90 days, or for whatever period the Cayman authority otherwise indicates.[44]

The MLAL holds persons not producing documents in their possession or control within the applicable time guilty of an offense and liable to fines of up to $10,000, imprisonment of up to two years, or both.[45] The MLAL holds persons who inform others, other than their attorneys, of information regarding Cayman Islands MLAT requests, contrary to the MLAL requirement that such person must keep such information confidential, guilty of an offense and liable for fines of up to $1,000, imprisonment of up to six months, or both.[46] The MLAL holds persons refusing to attend or provide testimony according to Cayman authority requests or subpoenas served on them, guilty of an offense and liable to fines of up to $5,000, imprisonment for up to one year, or both.[47]

§ 9.05   UNITED STATES ABILITY TO PIERCE FOREIGN BANK SECRECY

Because foreign bank secrecy laws attract persons desiring to use such secrecy for illegal purposes, they have attracted much attention.[1] As part of the U.S. effort to fight drugs, racketeering, and other criminal activities, the United States has attempted to pierce such bank secrecy laws. The United States has used several different methods to try to pierce such foreign bank secrecy laws including, among others:

1. Subpoenas or summonses to obtain foreign information directly;
2. Subpoenas or summonses to obtain testimony of nonresidents who are temporarily in the United States;
3. Compelled directives to obtain disclosure of financial matters covered by foreign bank secrecy laws;
4. Court orders directing parties to not take blocking measures in foreign courts;

[44] MLAL § 13 (1986).
[45] MLAL § 16(1) (1986).
[46] MLAL § 16(2) (1986).
[47] MLAL § 16(5) (1986).
§ 9.05   [1] *See generally* Ellen C. Auwarter, *Compelled Waiver of Bank Secrecy in the Cayman Islands: Solution to International Tax Evasion or Threat to Sovereignty of Nations,* 9 Fordham Int'l L.J. 680 (1986); William C. Caccamise, Jr., *U.S. Countermeasures Against Tax Haven Countries,* 26 Colum. J. Transnat'l L. 553 (1988); John L. O'Donnell, Jr., *The Secrets of Foreign Bankers and the Federal Investigation: Tottering Balances,* 20 Case W. Res. J. Int'l L. 509 (1988); Harvey M. Silets & Susan W. Brenner, *"Compelled Consent": An Oxymoron with Sinister Consequences for Citizens Who Patronize Foreign Banking Institutions,* 20 Case W. Res. J. Int'l L. 435 (1988); James P. Springer, *An Overview of International Evidence and Asset Gathering in Civil and Criminal Tax Cases,* 22 Geo. Wash. J. Int'l L. & Econ. 277 (1988); L. Richard Fischer, The Law of Financial Privacy (2d ed. 1991); John J. Tigue Jr. & Bryan C. Skarlatos, *Obtaining Evidence Abroad,* N.Y.L.J. 3 (Jan. 20, 1994); Annotation, *Discovery of, or compelled access to, records of foreign bank accounts, in federal criminal proceeding or investigation,* 93 A.L.R.3d 711 (1979 & Supp. 1995).

5. Equitable measures to reach assets located in foreign countries;
6. U.S. Tax Court orders requiring foreign parties to produce evidence located in foreign countries; and
7. IRC Section 982 formal document requests.[2]

[A] Subpoenas or Summonses to Obtain Foreign Information Directly

When a client places funds into foreign bank accounts subject to foreign bank secrecy laws and when the bank has a U.S. branch, the United States may obtain evidence about the foreign account through the U.S. branch. Specifically, the United States may serve subpoenas or summonses on the U.S.-based branches, and generally, those branches must produce evidence possessed by their related foreign branches or entities.[3] This rule holds true even if the person whose account is the subject of the subpoena or summons has no connection with the U.S. branch and all pertinent documents are located in the foreign branch.[4]

[B] Subpoenas or Summonses to Obtain Testimony of Nonresidents Who Are Temporarily in the United States

The United States may also obtain information from nonresidents who temporarily visit the United States. Specifically, it may serve notice of a subpoena or summons on nonresidents who possess information about foreign bank accounts or other information while such nonresidents temporarily visit the

---

[2] James P. Springer, *An Overview of International Evidence and Asset Gathering in Civil and Criminal Tax Cases*, 22 Geo. Wash. J. Int'l L. & Econ. 277, 318-26 (1988).

[3] James P. Springer, *An Overview of International Evidence and Asset Gathering in Civil and Criminal Tax Cases*, 22 Geo. Wash. J. Int'l L. & Econ. 277,319 (1988); L. Richard Fischer, The Law of Financial Privacy ¶ 2.09[1] (2d ed. 1991). *See, e.g.*, United States v. Bank of Nova Scotia, 691 F.2d 1384 (11th Cir. 1982), *cert. denied*, 462 U.S. 1119 (1983); Marc Rich & Co., A.G. v. United States, 707 F.2d 663 (2d Cir.), *cert. denied*, 463 U.S. 1215 (1983). *In re* Does, 86 A.F.T.R.2d 6727 (S.D. Fla. 2000) (court granted government's ex parte petition under IRC §7609 to serve American Express and MasterCard with "John Doe" summonses seeking information about credit and debit card accounts held by customers with offshore bank accounts); Ip v. United States, 205 F.3d 1168 (9th Cir. 2000) (IRC §7609(a) required IRS to give notice when it issued a summons for a third-party recordkeeper for the financial records of a party that had no outstanding tax liability and no legal relationship to any party against whom an assessment had been made); LoBello v. United States, 2001-1 U.S. Tax Cas. (CCH) ¶ 50,120 (D.N.J. 2000) (court denied a couple's petition to quash a third-party recordkeeper summons, finding that, although they may not have received it, the summons was properly sent to their last known address and they suffered no prejudice as a result); Urtuzuastegui v. United States, 2001-1 U.S. Tax Cas. (CCH) ¶ 50,179 (D. Ariz. 2000) (court ordered enforcement of an IRS summons issued to taxpayer's investment broker at the request of the Mexican taxing authority under the U.S.-Mexican tax treaty, and denied taxpayer's motion to quash, after concluding that the summons satisfied the four-step analysis set forth in United States v. Stuart, 489 U.S. 353 (1989)).

[4] Garpeg, Ltd. v. United States, 583 F. Supp. 789 (S.D.N.Y.), *motion to vacate denied*, 583 F. Supp. 1240 (S.D.N.Y. 1984); L. Richard Fischer, The Law of Financial Privacy ¶ 2.09[1] (2d ed. 1991).

United States.[5] This rule applies even when the nonresident's testimony causes her to violate foreign laws.[6] The nonresident may be compelled to produce documentary evidence besides her testimony.[7]

[C] Compelled Directives to Obtain Disclosure of Financial Matters Covered by Foreign Bank Secrecy Laws

The United States may also obtain court orders compelling U.S. citizens owning foreign bank accounts to direct the foreign bank or institution to disclose matters that otherwise would be protected by foreign bank secrecy laws.[8] Such court orders are generally referred to as compelled consents. Foreign countries vary in their response to compelled consents. Some jurisdictions allow their bankers to comply with compelled consents, but others do not.[9]

[D] Court Orders Directing Parties Not to Take Blocking Measures in Foreign Courts

Sometimes when the United States attempts to obtain evidence located in foreign countries, the impacted parties may institute actions in the foreign country to block the U.S. effort.[10] To preclude such actions, the United States may seek orders directing such parties to refrain from instituting or maintaining such actions.[11]

[E] Equitable Measures to Reach Assets Located in Foreign Countries

After criminal proceedings have reached their termination, or during their pendency in jeopardy or termination assessment situations, the IRS may seek

---

[5] United States v. Bowe, 694 F.2d 1256 (1st Cir. 1982); United States v. Field, 532 F.2d 404 (5th Cir.), *cert. denied*, 429 U.S. 940 (1976); James P. Springer, *An Overview of International Evidence and Asset Gathering in Civil and Criminal Tax Cases*, 22 Geo. Wash. J. Int'l L. & Econ. 277, 320 (1988); L. Richard Fischer, The Law of Financial Privacy ¶ 2.09[1] (2d ed. 1991).

[6] United States v. Field, 532 F.2d 404 (5th Cir.), *cert. denied*, 429 U.S. 940 (1976).

[7] United States v. Bowe, 694 F.2d 1256 (1st Cir. 1982).

[8] United States v. Ghidoni, 732 F.2d 814 (1st Cir.), *cert. denied*, 469 U.S. 932 (1984); James P. Springer, *An Overview of International Evidence and Asset Gathering in Civil and Criminal Tax Cases*, 22 Geo. Wash. J. Int'l L. & Econ. 277, 320 (1988); L. Richard Fischer, The Law of Financial Privacy ¶ 3.09[3] (2d ed. 1991).

[9] James P. Springer, *An Overview of International Evidence and Asset Gathering in Civil and Criminal Tax Cases*, 22 Geo. Wash. J. Int'l L. & Econ. 277, 321 (1988).

[10] James P. Springer, *An Overview of International Evidence and Asset Gathering in Civil and Criminal Tax Cases*, 22 Geo. Wash. J. Int'l L. & Econ. 277, 321 (1988); Annotation, *Propriety of federal court injunction against suit in foreign country*, 78 A.L.R. Fed. 831 (1986).

[11] United States v. Davis, 767 F.2d 1025 (2d Cir. 1985); Laker Airways v. Sabena, Belgian World Airlines, 731 F.2d 909 (D.C. Cir. 1984); James P. Springer, *An Overview of International Evidence and*

to reach foreign assets.[12] Specifically, the IRS may take one of the following actions to try to reach assets in foreign bank accounts:

1. Actions to freeze bank account proceeds in foreign branches of banks having a U.S. branch;[13]
2. Actions for the appointment of a receiver to step into the taxpayer's shoes and exercise equity powers to reach the taxpayer's foreign assets;[14]
3. Actions seeking injunctions enjoining taxpayers from taking actions that would jeopardize the ultimate collection of taxes;[15]
4. Actions for writs of ne exeat republica, restraining the taxpayer's freedom to leave the jurisdiction pending the satisfactory resolution of the tax liability;[16]
5. Actions seeking orders directing taxpayers to repatriate assets located in foreign countries to satisfy their tax liabilities;[17] or
6. Actions to enforce levies served within the United States concerning deposits held in foreign banks.[18]

Generally, foreign countries do not enforce the revenue laws of other countries, due to the rule of Comity.[19] Consequently, the IRS generally has a difficult time reaching assets located in foreign countries.

[F] U.S. Tax Court Orders Requiring Foreign Parties to Produce Evidence Located in Foreign Countries

The IRS may request the U.S. Tax Court to order any foreign corporation, trust, estate, or nonresident alien that seeks relief from the Tax Court to produce foreign-based evidence or prove the inability to produce such evidence.

Asset Gathering in Civil and Criminal Tax Cases, 22 Geo. Wash. J. Int'l L. & Econ. 277, 321 (1988); Annotation, *Propriety of federal court injunction against suit in foreign country,* 78 A.L.R. Fed. 831 (1986).

[12] James P. Springer, *An Overview of International Evidence and Asset Gathering in Civil and Criminal Tax Cases,* 22 Geo. Wash. J. Int'l L. & Econ. 277, 322 (1988).

[13] IRC § 7402(a) (1988); United States v. First Nat'l City Bank, 379 U.S. 378 (1965); James P. Springer, *An Overview of International Evidence and Asset Gathering in Civil and Criminal Tax Cases,* 22 Geo. Wash. J. Int'l L. & Econ. 277, 322 (1988).

[14] IRC § 7403(d) (1988); United States v. Ross, 302 F.2d 831 (2d Cir. 1962); James P. Springer, *An Overview of International Evidence and Asset Gathering in Civil and Criminal Tax Cases,* 22 Geo. Wash. J. Int'l L. & Econ. 277, 322 (1988).

[15] *Id.*

[16] IRC § 7402(a) (1988); United States v. Ross, 302 F.2d 831 (2d Cir. 1962); James P. Springer, *An Overview of International Evidence and Asset Gathering in Civil and Criminal Tax Cases,* 22 Geo. Wash. J. Int'l L. & Econ. 277, 323 (1988).

[17] IRC § 7402(a) (1988); United States v. McNulty, 446 F. Supp. 90 (N.D. Cal. 1978); James P. Springer, *An Overview of International Evidence and Asset Gathering in Civil and Criminal Tax Cases,* 22 Geo. Wash. J. Int'l L. & Econ. 277, 323 (1988).

[18] IRC § 6332 (1988 & Supp. 1990); Treas. Reg. § 301.6332-1(2) (1992); James P. Springer, *An Overview of International Evidence and Asset Gathering in Civil and Criminal Tax Cases,* 22 Geo. Wash. J. Int'l L. & Econ. 277, 323 (1988).

[19] *See* James P. Springer, *An Overview of International Evidence and Asset Gathering in Civil and Criminal Tax Cases,* 22 Geo. Wash. J. Int'l L. & Econ. 277, 317-18 (1988).

The Tax Court may issue a default judgment, dismiss a party's requests for relief in whole or part, or strike its pleadings in whole or part when such party fails to comply with such an order.[20]

[G]   IRC Section 982 Formal Document Requests

The IRS can serve formal requests on taxpayers to produce foreign-based documentation as part of an investigation. If the taxpayer fails without reasonable cause to comply with such a request within the applicable time period, then IRC Section 982 requires any U.S. court having jurisdiction over a tax case in which the requested item is at issue to preclude the introduction of any evidence covered by the order. This rule holds true even when such evidence would cause a ruling in the taxpayer's favor.[21]

> **Comment.** In an important case, *United States v. Gertner*,[22] the First Circuit denied enforcement of IRS summonses to obtain the identity of the attorneys' client who paid fees in cash, but the court avoided the issue whether the attorney-client privilege protects such information.

§ 9.06   FOREIGN BANK ACCOUNT CHECKLIST

The planner should use the following checklist to ensure that no critical issue is overlooked when developing the asset protection plan or when using foreign bank accounts.

[A]   Bank Secrecy Act[1]

____1.   Does the asset protection plan involve the client possessing a financial interest in or signature or other authority over any bank, securities, or other financial account in any foreign country?
   If yes, the planner must ensure that the client takes the following actions:

   a.   File U.S. Treasury Form 90-22.1, Report of Foreign Bank and Financial Accounts, with the IRS on or before June 30 for each calendar year the client possesses such an interest; and
   b.   Retain for at least five years financial records about the account, which must include the name in which the account is maintained, the number or other designation of the account, the name and address of the

---

[20] IRC § 7456(b) (1988); *see* James P. Springer, *An Overview of International Evidence and Asset Gathering in Civil and Criminal Tax Cases*, 22 Geo. Wash. J. Int'l L. & Econ. 277, 324 (1988).

[21] IRC § 982 (1988); *see* James P. Springer, *An Overview of International Evidence and Asset Gathering in Civil and Criminal Tax Cases*, 22 Geo. Wash. J. Int'l L. & Econ. 277, 325 (1988).

[22] 65 F.3d 963 (1st Cir. 1995).

§ 9.06   [1] *See* § 9.02.

foreign bank or other person with whom the account is maintained, the type of account, and the maximum value of the account during the reporting period.

_____2. Does the asset protection plan involve any of the following:

    a. The client physically transporting, mailing, or shipping $10,000 or more of currency or monetary instruments to or from the United States from or to any foreign country;

    b. The client causing $ 10,000 or more of currency or monetary instruments to be physically transported, mailed, or shipped into or out of the United States from or to a foreign country; or

    c. The client aiding, abetting, counseling, commanding, procuring, or requesting that a financial institution or other person physically transport, mail, or ship $10,000 or more of currency or monetary instruments to or from the United States from or to any foreign country?
    If yes, the planner generally must ensure that the client files U.S. Treasury Form 4790, Report of International Transportation of Currency or Monetary Instruments.

_____3. Does the asset protection plan involve either (1) a financial institution extending credit to the client of more than $10,000, which is not secured by real estate, or (2) transfers of more than $10,000 in money or credit to persons, accounts, or places outside the United States?
If yes, the planner should be aware that the financial institution will generally maintain records of such transactions to comply with BSA requirements.

_____4. Does the asset protection plan involve transactions involving currency of more than $10,000 with a financial institution, casino, or the postal service?
If yes, the planner should be aware that the financial institution will generally report such transactions on Form 4789, Currency Transaction Report, to the United States to comply with BSA requirements.

_____5. Does the asset protection plan involve transactions with a financial institution or securities broker or dealer?
If yes, the planner should be aware that the financial institution or securities broker or dealer will generally maintain records of (1) the client's taxpayer identification number plus certain other information concerning the account, and (2) certain specified items and documents that relate to its accounts with the client.

_____6. Does the asset protection plan trigger BSA reporting or record-keeping requirements?
If yes, the planner should be aware that the BSA imposes severe civil and criminal penalties for BSA violations. Furthermore, under some circumstances the BSA provides for forfeiture of currency or monetary instruments transported into or out of the United States without filing the appropriate reports or filing such reports with material omissions or misstatements.

[B]   Money Laundering Control Act[2]

____ 7.   Does the asset protection plan involve the client dealing with proceeds of unlawful activities when such dealings are aimed at furthering the unlawful activities or at concealing or disguising the source, ownership, location, or nature of the proceeds?
If yes, the plan probably violates the Money Laundering Control Act of 1986 and may expose the client or the planner to criminal sanctions.

____ 8.   Does the asset protection plan involve the client knowingly engaging in or attempting to engage in monetary transactions involving criminally derived property whose value exceeds $10,000?
If yes, the plan probably violates the Money Laundering Control Act of 1986 and may expose the client or the planner to criminal sanctions.

____ 9.   Does the asset protection plan involve the client, for the purpose of evading the BSA reporting requirements, willfully (1) causing or attempting to cause domestic financial institutions to fail to file a currency transaction report, (2) causing or attempting to cause domestic financial institutions to file a currency transaction report that contains material omissions or misstatements of fact, or (3) structuring or assisting in structuring any transaction with one or more domestic financial institutions?
If yes, the plan probably violates the Money Laundering Control Act of 1986 and may expose the client or the planner to criminal sanctions.

[C]   Foreign Bank Secrecy and U.S. Ability to Pierce It[3]

____ 10.   Does the asset protection plan involve the use of foreign bank accounts to take advantage of foreign bank secrecy laws?
If yes, the planner should:

   a.   Review § 9.05, which provides a discussion of Cayman Islands bank secrecy laws as an example of foreign bank secrecy laws, and
   b.   Be aware that the United States may use the following methods to attempt to pierce foreign bank secrecy laws:

      i.   Subpoenas or summonses to obtain foreign information directly,
      ii.   Subpoenas or summonses to obtain testimony of nonresidents who are temporarily in the United States,
      iii.   Compelled directives to obtain disclosure of financial matters covered by foreign bank secrecy laws,
      iv.   Court orders directing parties to not take blocking measures in foreign courts,
      v.   Equitable measures to reach assets located in foreign countries,

----

[2] See § 9.03.
[3] See §§ 9.04–9.05.

vi. U.S. Tax Court orders requiring foreign parties to produce evidence located in foreign countries, and

vii. IRC Section 982 formal document requests.

§ 9.07 PATRIOT ACT—INTERNATIONAL MONEY LAUNDERING ABATEMENT AND ANTI-TERRORISM FINANCING ACT OF 2001 (IMLAFA)

[A] In General

On October 26, 2001, President Bush signed into law Public Law Number 107-56, commonly referred to as the USA Patriot Act.[1] Title III of the Patriot Act constitutes the International Money Laundering Abatement and Anti-Terrorism Financing Act of 2001 (IMLAFA). IMLAFA substantially changes the legal rules that apply to foreign bank accounts. These changes can be divided into the following six categories:

1. *Special rules dealing with primary money laundering concerns.* These rules authorize the Secretary of the Treasury (Secretary) to designate non-U.S. jurisdictions, classes of transactions, financial institutions, or types of accounts as of "primary money laundering concern." Under these rules, the Secretary may also require domestic financial institutions and domestic financial agencies to take any of five types of special measures designed to detect and prevent money laundering.

2. *Rules regarding general due diligence for correspondent and private banking accounts.* These rules require financial institutions to establish "appropriate, specific, and, where necessary, enhanced, due diligence policies, procedures, and controls" relating to money laundering for correspondent accounts and private banking accounts in the United States for non-U.S. persons.

3. *Rules imposing additional due diligence requirements for certain foreign banks with correspondent accounts.* These rules impose additional due diligence standards on foreign banks with correspondent accounts that have "offshore banking licenses" or are licensed by countries designated as "non co-operative" by certain intergovernmental organizations. Among others, these standards require that affected financial institutions ascertain (a) the identity of each owner of the foreign bank, if it is not publicly traded, and (b) the identities of foreign banks that maintain correspondent accounts with the respondent foreign bank and related due diligence information.

---

§ 9.07 [1] *See generally Money Laundering: Summary of Selected Sections of H.R. 3162, The International Money Laundering Abatement and Anti-Terrorist Financing Act of 2001 (Title III, USA Patriot Act)*, Banking Daily, Nov. 5, 2001; Audrey Strauss, *New Law Requires Updating Anti-Money Laundering Programs*, N.Y.L.J. 5 (Nov. 1, 2001); Financial Institutions Group of Sullivan & Cromwell, *Money Laundering: Anti-Terrorism Law Changes, Expands Responsibilities for Financial Institutions*, Banking Daily, Nov. 20, 2001; Emilio W. Cividanes et al., *Summary and Analysis of Key Sections of the USA Patriot Act of 2001*, 6 Cyberspace L. 2 (Nov. 2001).

4. *Rules imposing additional due diligence standards for private banking accounts.* These rules impose special due diligence requirements for "private banking accounts." Among other things, these standards require that affected organizations ascertain the nominal and beneficial owners of, and the source of funds deposited in, private banking accounts. These standards also mandate enhanced scrutiny of accounts maintained by senior political figures, their immediate families, and their close associates.

5. *Rules prohibiting correspondent accounts with foreign shell banks.* These rules prohibit "covered financial institutions" from maintaining correspondent accounts for shell banks (*i.e.,* banks with no physical presence in any country), and require that such institutions take reasonable steps to ensure that correspondent accounts of foreign banks are not used to provide banking services to shell banks.

6. *Rules regarding maintenance of records regarding foreign banks with correspondent accounts.* These rules require that "covered financial institutions" that maintain correspondent accounts in the United States for foreign banks must maintain records in the United States identifying such foreign banks' owners. These rules also require such records to include the name and address of a U.S. resident who is authorized to accept service of legal process from the Secretary and the Attorney General for records regarding each such correspondent account.

[B] Special Rules to Deal with Primary Money Laundering Concerns

[1] In General

IMLAFA section 311 added 31 U.S.C. § 5318A, which contains special rules dealing with primary money laundering concerns. Under this provision, if the Secretary finds that reasonable grounds exist for concluding that certain "primary money laundering concerns" exist, the Secretary may take certain special measures.

[2] Primary Money Laundering Concern Finding

The primary money laundering concern rules are triggered only when the Secretary makes a finding that reasonable grounds exist to conclude that any of the following constitutes a primary money laundering concern:

- A jurisdiction outside the United States
- One or more financial institutions operating outside of the United States
- One or more classes of transactions within, or involving, a foreign jurisdiction
- One or more types of accounts.[2]

---

[2] 31 U.S.C. § 5318A(a).

31 U.S.C. §5318A(c) provides that, in finding reasonable grounds for concluding that a primary money laundering concern exists, the Secretary must consult with the Secretary of State and the Attorney General.[3] In addition, the Secretary may consider any other information it considers relevant. Section 5318A(c) sets forth the following list of "jurisdictional" factors that the Secretary may consider in the case of a particular jurisdiction:

- Evidence that organized criminal groups, international terrorists, or both have transacted business in that jurisdiction
- The extent to which that jurisdiction or financial institutions operating in that jurisdiction offer bank secrecy or special regulatory advantages to nonresidents or nondomiciliaries of that jurisdiction.
- The substance and quality of administration of the bank supervisory and counter-money laundering laws of that jurisdiction.
- The relationship between the volume of financial transactions occur ring in that jurisdiction and the size of its economy.
- The extent to which that jurisdiction is characterized as an offshore banking or secrecy haven by credible international organizations or multilateral expert groups.
- Whether the United States has a mutual legal assistance treaty with that jurisdiction, and the experience of U.S. law enforcement officials and regulatory officials in obtaining information about transactions originating in or routed through or to such jurisdiction.
- The extent to which high levels of official or institutional corruption characterize that jurisdiction.[4]

Section 5318A(c) also sets forth the following "institutional" factors that the Secretary may consider when deciding to apply any of the primary money laundering concern rules only to a financial institution or institutions, or to a transaction or class of transactions, or to a type of account, or to all three, within or involving a particular jurisdiction:

- The extent to which such financial institutions, transactions, or types of accounts are used to facilitate or promote money laundering in or through the jurisdiction.
- The extent to which such institutions, transactions, or types of accounts are used for legitimate business purposes in the jurisdiction.
- The extent to which such action is sufficient to ensure, for transactions involving the jurisdiction and institutions operating in it, that the purposes of these rules continue to be fulfilled, and to guard against international money laundering and other financial crimes.[5]

---

[3] 31 U.S.C. §5318A(c).
[4] 31 U.S.C. §5318A(c)(2)(A).
[5] 31 U.S.C. §5318A(c)(2)(B).

[3] Special Measures

If the Secretary finds reasonable grounds to conclude that a primary money laundering concern exists, then the special measures[6] discussed in this subsection will apply. These measures include provisions dealing with the following:

- Recordkeeping and reporting
- Beneficial ownership of financial accounts
- Payable-through accounts
- Correspondent accounts
- Prohibitions or conditions on opening or maintaining certain correspondent or payable-through accounts.

[a] Recordkeeping and Reporting

The Secretary may require domestic financial institutions or domestic financial agencies to maintain records, file reports, or both, concerning the aggregate amount of transactions or concerning individual transactions. Among others, the Secretary may require reports or records concerning:

- The identity and address of participants in a transaction or relation ship, including the identity of the originator of any funds transfer
- The legal capacity in which a participant in any transaction is acting
- The identity of the beneficial owner of funds involved in any transaction
- A description of any transaction.[7]

[b] Beneficial Ownership

The Secretary may require domestic financial institutions or domestic financial agencies to take such steps as the Secretary determines to be reasonable and practicable to obtain and retain information concerning the beneficial ownership of any U.S. account opened or maintained by foreign persons or their representatives. However, such measures do not apply to foreign entities whose shares are either publicly traded or subject to public reporting requirements.[8]

[c] Payable-Through Accounts

The Secretary may require any domestic financial institution or domestic financial agency that opens or maintains a U.S. payable-through account for a foreign financial institution, to obtain or report certain information. This information may include:

---

[6] 31 U.S.C. § 5318A.
[7] 31 U.S.C. § 5318A(b)(1).
[8] 31 U.S.C. § 5318A(b)(2).

- The identity of each customer (and its representative) of the financial institution who is permitted to use, or whose transactions are routed through, such payable-through account
- For each such customer (and its representative), information substantially comparable to that which the depository institution obtains in the ordinary course of business for its U.S. resident customers.[9]

[d] Correspondent Accounts

The Secretary may require any domestic financial institution or domestic financial agency that opens or maintains a U.S. correspondent account to obtain certain information. This information may include:

- The identity of each customer (and its representative) of the financial institution permitted to use, or whose transactions are routed through, such correspondent account; and
- For each such customer (and its representative), information that is substantially comparable to that which the depository institution obtains in the ordinary course of business for its U.S. resident customers.[10]

[e] Prohibitions or Conditions on Opening or Maintaining Certain Correspondent or Payable-Through Accounts

The Secretary may prohibit or impose conditions on opening or maintaining correspondent accounts or payable-through accounts in the United States by domestic financial institutions or domestic financial agencies for or on behalf of foreign banking institutions. However, to use this measure, the Secretary must first consult with the Secretary of State, the Attorney General, and the Federal Reserve Board Chairman.[11]

[f] Procedural and Other Issues

The Secretary may impose the special rules dealing with primary money laundering concerns in any sequence or combination. In addition, it may implement any of these measures either (1) by regulation or, (2) except for prohibiting or conditioning the opening of certain correspondent or payable-through accounts (*i.e.,* discussed in subsection [e]) by order or any other manner allowed by law.[12] If the Secretary implements a measure by order, such order must be issued along with a notice of proposed rulemaking relating to the imposition of such special measure. In addition, such an order may not remain in effect for

---

[9] 31 U.S.C. §5318A(b)(3).
[10] 31 U.S.C. §5318A(b)(4).
[11] 31 U.S.C. §5318A(b)(5).
[12] 31 U.S.C. §5318A(a)(2).

more than 120 days, except pursuant to a rule promulgated before the 120-day period ends.[13]

The IMLAFA also provides that, without limiting any other authority granted to the Secretary, in selecting which special measure or measures to take, the Secretary must:

- Consult with the Federal Reserve Board Chairman, any other appropriate federal banking agency, as defined by Federal Deposit Insurance Act Section 3, the Secretary of State, the Securities and Exchange Commission, the Commodity Futures Trading Commission, the National Credit Union Administration Board, and in the Secretary's sole discretion, such other agencies and interested parties as it may deem appropriate.
- Consider (1) whether similar action has been or is being taken by other nations or multilateral groups; (2) whether imposing any particular special measure would create a significant competitive disadvantage, including any undue cost or burden associated with compliance, for financial institutions organized or licensed in the United States; (3) the extent to which the action or the timing of the action would cause a significant adverse systemic impact on the international payment, clearance, and settlement system, or on legitimate business activities involving the particular jurisdiction, institution, or class of transactions; and (4) the effect of the action on U.S. national security and foreign policy.

[4] Definitions

[a] Account

For banks, the IMLAFA defines an *account* as a formal banking or business relationship established to provide regular services, dealings, and other financial transactions. This definition specifically includes demand deposits, savings deposits, other transaction or asset accounts, credit accounts, and other extensions of credit.[14]

For nonbank institutions, the Secretary must, after consulting with the appropriate Federal functional regulators (as defined in Gramm-Leach-Bliley Act section 509), define by regulation the term *account*, and must include within the meaning of that term, to the extent, if any, that the Secretary deems appropriate, arrangements similar to payable-through and correspondent accounts.[15]

[b] Correspondent Account

For banks, a *correspondent account* means an account established to receive deposits from a foreign financial institution, to make payments on behalf of

---

[13] 31 U.S.C. § 5318A(a)(3).
[14] 31 U.S.C. § 5318A(e)(1)(A).
[15] 31 U.S.C. § 5318A(e)(2).

a foreign financial institution, or to handle other financial transactions related to such an institution.[16]

For nonbank institutions, the Secretary must include within the definition of account arrangements similar to correspondent accounts, to the extent it deems appropriate, after consulting with the appropriate federal function regulators.[17]

[c] Payable-Through Account

A *payable-through account* is an account opened at a depository institution by a foreign financial institution and through which the foreign institution permits its customers to engage, directly or through a sub-account, in normal U.S. banking activities. Such accounts may include transaction accounts (as defined in Federal Reserve Act section 19(b)(1)(C)).

For nonbank institutions, the Secretary must include within the definition of *account* arrangements similar to payable-through accounts, to the extent it deems appropriate, after consulting with the appropriate federal function regulators.[18]

[d] Beneficial Ownership

IMLAFA directs the Secretary to promulgate regulations defining beneficial ownership of an account for purposes of 31 U.S.C. §§ 5318A and 5318(i) and (j). Such regulations must address:

- Issues related to an individual's authority to fund, direct, or manage the account (including, without limitation, the power to direct payments into or out of the account).
- An individual's material interest in the income or corpus of the account.

The IMLAFA also directs the Secretary to ensure that such regulations do not require the identification of individuals whose beneficial interest in the income or corpus of an account is immaterial.[19]

[C] *Rules Regarding General Due Diligence for Correspondent and Private Banking Accounts*

IMLAFA imposed a general due diligence requirement for correspondent and private banking accounts, by adding 31 U.S.C. § 5318(i).[20] This provision requires

---

[16] 31 U.S.C. § 5318A(e)(1)(B).
[17] 31 U.S.C. § 5318A(e)(2).
[18] 31 U.S.C. § 5318A(e)(2).
[19] 31 U.S.C. § 5318A(e)(3).
[20] 31 U.S.C. § 5318(i)(1). For this purpose, 31 U.S.C. § 5318(i)(4) defines a *private banking account* as an account (or any combination of accounts) that (1) requires minimum aggregate deposits of funds or other assets of not less than $1,000,000; (2) is established on behalf of one or more individuals who have a direct

financial institutions that establish, maintain, administer, or manage private banking or correspondent accounts in the United States, for non-U.S. persons, institute appropriate, specific, and, if necessary, enhanced due diligence policies, procedures, and controls that are reasonably designed to detect and report money laundering through those accounts.[21] For this purpose, non-U.S. persons include foreign individuals visiting the United States and representatives of non-U.S. persons.

The effective date for the general due diligence provisions for correspondent and private banking accounts is 270 days after IMLAFA's date of enactment (i.e., July 23, 2002). In addition, IMLAFA requires the Secretary to issue regulations, elaborating on the general due diligence provisions for correspondent and private banking accounts, within 180 days after IMLAFA's enactment (i.e., April 24, 2002). In this regard, the effective dates of these provisions are not contingent upon the issuance of regulations. The requirement also applies to accounts covered by these provisions which are opened before, on, or after the date of enactment of IMLAFA.[22]

[D] Rules Imposing Additional Due Diligence Requirements for Certain Foreign Banks with Correspondent Accounts

IMLAFA also imposes additional due diligence requirements for certain foreign banks with foreign correspondent accounts.[23] Specifically, these requirements apply with respect to correspondent accounts that are requested or maintained by, or on behalf of, a foreign bank operating:

1. Under an offshore banking license;[24] or
2. Under a banking license issued by a foreign country that has been designated as noncooperative with international anti-money laundering principles or procedures by an intergovernmental group or organization of which the United States is a member, with which designation the U.S. representative to the group or organization concurs; or
3. Under a banking license issued by a foreign country that has been designated by the Secretary as warranting special measures due to money laundering concerns.[25]

Presently, the only intergovernmental group or organization that has designated countries as noncooperative is the Financial Action Task Force on Money Laundering (FATF). The additional due diligence requirements would apply to

---

or beneficial ownership interest in the account; and (3) is assigned to, or is administered or managed by, in whole or in part, an officer, employee, or agent of a financial institution acting as a liaison between the financial institution and the direct or beneficial owner of the account.

[21] 31 U.S.C. § 5318(i)(1).

[22] IMLAFA § 312(b).

[23] 31 U.S.C. § 5318(i)(2).

[24] 31 U.S.C. § 5318(i)(4)(A) defines an *offshore banking license* as a license to conduct banking activities which, as a condition of the license, prohibits the licensed entity from conducting banking activities with the citizens of, or with the local currency of, the country that issued the license.

[25] 31 U.S.C. § 5318(i)(2)(A).

banks from countries on the FATF list because the U.S. representative to FATF concurred with the FATF designations and has not withdrawn that concurrence.[26] The FATF list of noncooperative countries currently includes the following 19 countries: Cook Islands, Dominica, Egypt, Grenada, Guatemala, Hungary, Indonesia, Israel, Lebanon, Marshall Islands, Myanmar, Nauru, Nigeria, Niue, Philippines, Russia, St. Kitts and Nevis, St. Vincent and the Grenadines, and Ukraine.

When the enhanced due diligence requirements for foreign banks with foreign correspondent accounts are triggered, the U.S. financial institution must, at a minimum, take reasonable steps to:

- Ascertain for any such foreign bank, if the foreign bank is not publicly traded, the identity of each of such bank's owners, and the nature and extent of each such owner's ownership interest.
- Conduct enhanced scrutiny of such account to guard against money laundering and report any suspicious transactions.
- Ascertain whether such foreign bank provides correspondent accounts to other foreign banks and, if so, the identity of those foreign banks and related due diligence information, as appropriate under the general due diligence requirements for correspondent banking accounts (discussed in § 9.07[C]).[27]

The effective date for these provisions for correspondent banking accounts is 270 days after IMLAFA's date of enactment (*i.e.*, July 23, 2002).[28]

[E] Rules Imposing Additional Due Diligence Standards for Private Banking Accounts

IMLAFA also imposes enhanced due diligence standards for private banking accounts. Specifically, if a non-U.S. person requests or maintains a U.S. private banking account, then at a minimum the financial institution must take reasonable steps to identify the account's nominal and beneficial owners, and the source of funds deposited in it.[29] In addition, the financial institution must conduct enhanced scrutiny of any private banking account requested or maintained by or for a senior foreign political figure, or any of his or her immediate family members or close associates. Such scrutiny must be reasonably designed to detect and report transactions that may involve the proceeds of foreign corruption.[30]

The effective date for these provisions for private banking accounts is 270 days after IMLAFA's date of enactment (*i.e.*, July 23, 2002).[31]

---

[26] Financial Institutions Group of Sullivan & Cromwell, *Money Laundering: Anti-Terrorism Law Changes, Expands Responsibilities for Financial Institutions*, Banking Daily, Nov. 20, 2001.

[27] 31 U.S.C. § 5318(i)(2)(B).

[28] IMLAFA § 312(b).

[29] 31 U.S.C. § 5318(i)(3)(A).

[30] 31 U.S.C. § 5318(i)(3)(B).

[31] IMLAFA § 312(b).

[F]   *Rules Prohibiting Correspondent Accounts with Foreign Shell Banks*

IMLAFA prohibits certain "covered financial institutions" from opening correspondent accounts for foreign shell banks.[32] Specifically, IMLAFA prohibits a covered financial institution from establishing, maintaining, administering, or managing correspondent accounts in the United States for foreign banks that lack a physical presence in any country.[33]

For purposes of this provision, *covered financial institutions* include:[34]

- Insured banks (as defined in Section 3(h) of the Federal Deposit Insurance Act)
- Commercial banks and trust companies
- Private bankers
- Agencies or branches of foreign banks in the United States
- Insured institutions (as defined in Section 401(a) of the National Housing Act)
- Thrift institutions
- Registered brokers or dealers under the Securities Exchange Act of 1934.

Physical presence means a place of business that (1) a foreign bank maintains; (2) located at a fixed address (other than solely an electronic address) in a country where the foreign bank is authorized to conduct banking activities, and where it both employs individuals on a full-time basis, and maintains operating records related to its banking activities; and (3) is subject to inspection by the banking authority that licensed it to conduct banking activities.[35]

Covered financial institutions must also take reasonable steps to ensure that any correspondent account that covered financial institutions establish, maintain, administer, or manage in the United States for a foreign bank is not being used by such foreign bank to indirectly provide banking services to another foreign bank, that does not have a physical presence in any country.[36] IMLAFA requires the Secretary to issue regulations delineating the reasonable steps required to comply with this provision.

Notwithstanding the foregoing, a covered financial institution may provide a correspondent account to a foreign bank, if the foreign bank is an affiliate[37] of a depository institution, credit union, or foreign bank that does maintain a physical presence in the United States or a foreign country, and the affiliate is subject to supervision by a banking authority in such country.[38]

---

[32] 31 U.S.C. § 5318(j)(1).

[33] 31 U.S.C. § 5318(j)(1).

[34] 31 U.S.C. § 5312(a)(2)(A)–(G).

[35] 31 U.S.C. § 5318(J)(4)(B).

[36] 31 U.S.C. § 5318(j)(2).

[37] For this purpose, the term *affiliate* means a foreign bank that is controlled by or is under common control with a depository institution, credit union, or foreign bank. 31 U.S.C. § 5318(j).

[38] 31 U.S.C. § 5318(j)(3).

These rules with respect to correspondent accounts with foreign shell banks take effect 60 days after IMLAFA's enactment (*i.e.*, December 25, 2001).[39]

[G] Cooperation among Financial Institutions, Regulatory Authorities, and Law Enforcement Authorities

IMLAFA requires the Secretary to issue regulations encouraging cooperation among financial institutions, regulatory authorities, and law enforcement authorities.[40] Specifically, within 120 days after IMLAFA's enactment (*i.e.*, February 23, 2002), the Secretary must adopt regulations encouraging regulatory authorities and law enforcement authorities to share with financial institutions information regarding parties engaged in or suspected of engaging in terrorist acts or money laundering activities. IMLAFA prohibits financial institutions from using any information that it receives under such regulations for any purpose other than identifying and reporting on activities that may involve terrorist acts or money laundering activities.[41] In addition, IMLAFA provides that the receipt of information under these regulations will not relieve or modify the obligations of a financial institution concerning any other person or account.[42]

IMLAFA also allows financial institutions and associations of financial institutions to share information, after notifying the Secretary, regarding parties suspected of possible terrorist or money laundering activities, including individuals, organizations, and countries.[43] IMLAFA provides immunity from liability to any person under U.S. or state law (including the financial privacy provisions contained in Title V of the Gramm-Leach-Bliley Act) or under any contract for either making a disclosure or failing to notify any person identified in such a disclosure related to information sharing under this provision.[44]

Finally, IMLAFA requires the Secretary, at least semiannually, to publish and distribute to financial institutions a report containing a detailed analysis identifying patterns of suspicious activity and other investigative insights derived from suspicious activity reports and investigations conducted by law enforcement agencies, to the extent appropriate.[45]

[H] Inclusion of Foreign Corruption Offenses as Money Laundering Crimes

IMLAFA adds the following to the activities that constitute "specified unlawful activities," which are required to trigger a crime of money laundering under

---

[39] IMLAFA § 313(b).
[40] IMLAFA § 314(a).
[41] IMLAFA § 314(a)(5).
[42] IMLAFA § 314(a)(4).
[43] IMLAFA § 314(b).
[44] IMLAFA § 314(b).
[45] IMLAFA § 314(d).

18 U.S.C. § 1956:

- Bribery of a public official
- Misappropriation, theft, or embezzlement of public funds
- Smuggling and export control violations
- Offenses for which the United States would be obligated, under a multilateral treaty, to extradite the offender or to submit the case to prosecution if the offender were found within the United States.[46]

[I] Long-Arm Jurisdiction

IMLAFA Section 317 grants federal courts long-arm jurisdiction over foreign persons, including foreign financial institutions, under certain circumstances. Specifically, courts may exercise such jurisdiction when the foreign person in question has been served with process pursuant to the Federal Rules of Civil Procedure or the laws of the country where the foreign person is located, and at least one of the following occurs:

- The foreign person commits a money laundering offense involving a transaction that occurs wholly or partially in the United States.
- The foreign person converts property in which the United States has an ownership interest by virtue of a civil or criminal forfeiture judgment.
- The foreign person is a financial institution that maintains a correspondent account at a U.S. financial institution.

IMLAFA also authorizes courts, given long-arm jurisdiction under this provision, to issue a pretrial restraining order or take other action required to ensure that any bank account or other property that a defendant holds in the United States is available to satisfy a judgment under this provision.

[J] Forfeiture of Funds from U.S. Interbank Account

IMLAFA amends 18 U.S.C. § 981 to provide that funds deposited into an account of a foreign bank, which in turn has a U.S. interbank account[47] with a covered financial institution, will be deemed as being deposited into the U.S. interbank account.[48] This allows a restraining order, seizure warrant, or arrest warrant in rem regarding such funds to be served on the covered financial institution, and funds in the interbank account, up to the value of the funds deposited into the account at the foreign bank, to be restrained, seized, or arrested.[49] However, the Attorney General may suspend or terminate a forfeiture

---

[46] IMLAFA § 315.

[47] The term *interbank account* has the same meaning as in 18 U.S.C. § 984(c)(2)(B).

[48] U.S.C. § 981(k)(1)(A).

[49] 18 U.S.C. § 981(k)(1)(A).

when, after consulting the Secretary, he or she determines that a conflict of law exists between the foreign bank jurisdiction and U.S. laws regarding the liabilities arising from the seizure of such funds, and such suspension or termination is in the interest of justice and will not harm U.S. interests.[50]

> **Caution.** This allows the United States to seek funds in the foreign bank's interbank account, rather than being required to commence a forfeiture action in the foreign bank's home country jurisdiction. Planners should also note that this forfeiture provision does not require the United States to prove that the funds seized are directly traceable to the funds deposited into the foreign bank. Moreover, the foreign bank can challenge the seizure only if the basis for the forfeiture is the bank's own alleged wrongdoing or if the bank can prove, by a preponderance of the evidence, that before the seizure, the bank had discharged its obligation to the prior owner of the funds.[51]

[K] *Bank Records Related to Anti-Money Laundering Programs*

IMLAFA requires covered financial institutions to provide, to the appropriate federal banking agency, information and account documentation for any account that it opens, maintains, administers, or manages in the United States. This information shall be provided no later than 120 hours after receiving a request for information related to either its own or its customer's anti-money laundering compliance.[52]

IMLAFA further provides that the Secretary or Attorney General may issue a summons or subpoena to any foreign bank that maintains a U.S. correspondent account, requesting records related to such correspondent account, including records maintained outside of the United States relating to the deposit of funds into the foreign bank. Such a summons or subpoena may be served on the foreign bank in the United States if such foreign bank has a U.S. representative, or in a foreign country pursuant to any mutual legal assistance treaty, multilateral agreement, or other request for international law enforcement assistance.[53] To facilitate this provision, IMLAFA requires covered financial institutions that maintain U.S. correspondent accounts for foreign banks to maintain records in the United States identifying the owners of such foreign banks and the names and addresses of persons who reside in the United States who are authorized to accept service of legal process for records regarding such correspondent accounts.[54] If a federal law enforcement officer requests such information, a covered financial institution must respond within seven days of the request.[55]

---

[50] 18 U.S.C. § 981(k)(1)(B).
[51] 18 U.S.C. § 981(k)(2)–(3).
[52] 31 U.S.C. § 5318(k)(2).
[53] 31 U.S.C. § 5318(k)(3)(A).
[54] 31 U.S.C. § 5318(k)(3)(B).
[55] 31 U.S.C. § 5318(k)(3)(B)(2).

IMLAFA also requires covered financial institutions to terminate any such correspondent relationship within 10 business days of receiving a written notice from the Secretary or Attorney General that the foreign bank has failed to (1) comply with such a summons or subpoena, or (2) initiate proceedings in a U.S. court contesting such summons or subpoena.[56]

IMLAFA limits the liability of covered financial institutions to any other persons in any court or arbitration proceeding resulting from the termination of a correspondent relationship under the foregoing provisions.[57] However, if such an institution fails to terminate such a correspondent relationship pursuant to these provisions, it will be subjected to a civil penalty of up to $10,000 per day until the correspondent relationship is terminated.[58]

[L] "Financial Institutions" under the Bank Secrecy Act

IMLAFA adds the following entities to the definition of *financial institution* in the Bank Secrecy Act: (1) credit unions; (2) futures commission merchants; (3) commodity trading advisors; and (4) commodity pool operators required to register under the Commodity Exchange Act.[59]

[M] Concentration Accounts

IMLAFA authorizes the Secretary to prescribe regulations governing the maintenance of "concentration accounts" at financial institutions, to ensure that such accounts are not used to prevent association of the identity of an individual customer with the movement of funds of which the customer is the direct or beneficial owner.[60] If the Secretary does prescribe these regulations, they must, at a minimum, provide as follows:

- Prohibit financial institutions from allowing clients to direct transactions that move their funds into, out of, or through concentration accounts.
- Prohibit financial institutions and their employees from informing customers of the existence of, or the means of identifying, the concentration accounts of the institution.
- Require each financial institution to establish written procedures governing documentation of all transactions involving concentration accounts, including the identity of any customer whose funds are commingled in a concentration account and the specific amount belonging to each such customer.[61]

---

[56] 31 U.S.C. § 5318(k)(3)(C).
[57] 31 U.S.C. § 5318(k)(3)(C)(ii).
[58] 31 U.S.C. § 5318(k)(3)(C)(iii).
[59] IMLAFA § 321.
[60] 31 U.S.C. § 5318(h)(3).
[61] 31 U.S.C. § 5318(h)(3).

[N] Verification of Identification

IMLAFA provides that, within one year of its enactment (*i.e.*, October 26, 2002), the Secretary, in consultation with the appropriate federal functional regulators, must promulgate final regulations setting forth minimum standards for financial institutions and their customers regarding customer identity.[62] At a minimum, these regulations must require financial institutions to implement, and their customers (after being given adequate notice) to comply with, reasonable procedures for:

- Verifying the identity of any person seeking to open an account, to the extent reasonable and practicable.
- Maintaining records of the information used to verify a person's identity, including name, address, and other identifying information.
- Consulting lists of known or suspected terrorists and terrorist organizations provided to the financial institution by governmental agencies.

In prescribing these regulations, the Secretary is required to consider the various types of financial institutions, the various methods of opening accounts, and the various types of identifying information available.[63] The Secretary may, by regulation or order, exempt any financial institution or type of account from these provisions.[64]

IMLAFA also provides that the Secretary must, within six months of IMLAFA's enactment, submit a report to Congress with recommendations relating to verification of the identity of foreign nationals seeking to open accounts and development of an identification number, similar to a Social Security number, as a condition of opening an account.[65]

[O] Anti-Money Laundering Programs

IMLAFA requires financial institutions to establish anti-money laundering programs which, at a minimum, must address:[66]

- The development of internal policies, procedures, and controls
- The designation of a compliance officer
- An ongoing employee training program
- An independent audit function to test this program.

The Secretary may prescribe minimum standards for these anti-money laundering programs. This provision becomes effective 180 days after enactment (*i.e.*, on April 24, 2002).

[62] 31 U.S.C. § 5318(l) (1), (6).
[63] 31 U.S.C. § 5318(l)(2).
[64] 31 U.S.C. § 5318(l)(5).
[65] IMLAFA § 326(b).
[66] 31 U.S.C. § 5318(h).

10

Overview of the Enforcement of IRS Claims

§ 10.01   IN GENERAL

The planner must understand how the IRS enforces its tax claims[1] to ensure that the asset protection plan adequately protects client property against IRS tax claims.

Planning Pointer. The planner should understand the following:

1. How tax liens arise;[2]
2. How long tax liens last;[3]
3. What the scope of tax liens is;[4]
4. What methods the IRS uses to enforce tax liens;[5]
5. How estate and gift tax liens differ from general tax liens;[6]
6. When and how the IRS may make tax levies;[7]
7. What property the IRS may levy against;[8]
8. What limits exist on IRS use of its tax levy power;[9]
9. What happens when taxpayers do not surrender property the IRS levies against;[10]
10. When the IRS may seize and sell property it has levied against.[11]

§ 10.02   TAX LIEN

Tax liens represent an IRS claim or charge against the taxpayer's property for the payment of tax debts.[1] Generally, the IRS makes reasonable efforts to contact and give the delinquent taxpayer opportunities to pay taxes before it files and makes public tax liens.[2] Thirty days after a tax lien begins, the IRS may levy on, seize, and sell all the taxpayer's property and rights to the property.[3]

---

§ 10.02   [1] *See generally* Michael I. Saltzman, IRS Practice and Procedure (2d ed. 1991); Robert McKenzie, Representation Before the Collection Division of the IRS (1989); Laurence F. Casey, Casey Federal Tax Practice (1989).

[2] *See* § 10.03.
[3] *See* § 10.04.
[4] *See* § 10.05.
[5] *See* § 10.06.
[6] *See* §§ 10.07–10.08.
[7] *See* § 10.10.
[8] *See* § 10.11.
[9] *See* § 10.11[D].
[10] *See* § 10.11[E].
[11] *See* § 10.12.

§ 10.02   [1] Michael I. Saltzman, IRS Practice and Procedure ¶ 14.04 (2d ed. 1991).
[2] Saltzman, IRS Practice and Procedure ¶ 14.04; Internal Revenue Manual, Policies of the I.R.S. Handbook, P-5-57 (approved June 13, 1983).
[3] IRC § 6331(d).

Caution. If taxpayers attempt to avoid tax liens by gratuitously transferring property after tax liens begin, (1) the tax lien encumbers the transferred property, (2) the transfer may be set aside as fraudulent, and (3) if the transfer leaves taxpayers judgment proof, the IRC may subject such taxpayers to criminal liability.[4]

The IRC protects some persons who deal with the taxpayer from the tax lien before the IRS files a notice of the tax lien, which makes the lien public.[5] However, persons who know of the tax lien before the IRS files such notice take property from the taxpayer subject to the tax lien.[6] After the IRS files a notice of the tax lien, generally all persons, with certain exceptions, take property from the taxpayer subject to the tax lien. Furthermore, any claim such persons have is subordinate to the tax lien.[7]

Planning Pointer. The planner should consider the following issues when considering IRS liens:

1. How does the general tax lien originate?[8]
2. How long does the general tax lien last?[9]
3. What is the scope of the general tax lien?[10]
4. What methods does the IRS use to enforce the general tax lien?[11]
5. What is the estate tax lien, and how does it differ from the general tax lien?[12]
6. What is the gift tax lien, and how does it differ from the general tax lien?[13]

§ 10.03   ORIGINATION OF TAX LIEN

Tax liens[1] arise after (1) the IRS makes a tax assessment, (2) it gives notice of the assessment to the taxpayer stating the assessment amount and demanding

---

[4] United States v. Bess, 357 U.S. 51 (1958); United States v. Livingstone, 381 F. Supp. 607 (D. Mass. 1974); Saltzman, IRS Practice and Procedure ¶ 14.04.

[5] IRC § 6323(a); Saltzman, IRS Practice and Procedure ¶ 14.04.

[6] IRC § 6323(b); Saltzman, IRS Practice and Procedure ¶ 14.04.

[7] Saltzman, IRS Practice and Procedure ¶ 14.04.

[8] *See* § 10.03.

[9] *See* § 10.04.

[10] *See* § 10.05.

[11] *See* § 10.06.

[12] *See* § 10.07.

[13] *See* § 10.08.

§ 10.03   [1] *See generally* Saltzman, IRS Practice and Procedure ¶¶ 14.05, 16.03.

payment, and (3) the taxpayer fails to pay the assessment amount.[2] After these events occur, the tax lien arises by operation of law.[3] However, before the tax lien becomes effective, the IRS must satisfy the filing requirement.[4]

First, before tax liens arise, the IRS must make an assessment. An assessment occurs when the IRS officially records the taxpayer's liability.[5] The IRS must make the assessment within the applicable statute of limitations. In this regard, in *Bilski v. Commissioner*,[6] the Fifth Circuit held that Form 872-A, Consent to Extend Time for Assessment, constituted a waiver of the statute of limitations, rather than an executory contract that terminated automatically 60 days after the taxpayer's filing for bankruptcy.

Second, the IRS must give notice of the assessment to the taxpayer. This notice must state the assessment amount and demand payment as soon as practicable and within 60 days after the assessment.[7] The IRS must leave this notice at the taxpayer's dwelling or usual place of business, or send it by mail to the taxpayer's last known address.[8] If the IRS does not give notice and demand payment, no lien arises and, thus, no IRS levy can be effective.[9]

Caution. The relevant issue is whether the IRS mails the notice of assessment to the taxpayer, not whether the taxpayer receives the notice.[10]

Third, taxpayers must fail to pay the assessment amount before tax liens arise. Specifically, when taxpayers neglect or refuse to pay taxes after demand, the amount demanded plus costs becomes a lien on all their property and rights to property.[11] This lien continues from the assessment until the debtor pays the debt or the debt becomes unenforceable due to the lapse of time.[12]

Before tax liens become effective or gain priority over certain of the taxpayer's other creditors, the IRS must satisfy the filing requirement.[13] When applicable state law provides for the filing of liens in one office, the IRS must file the federal tax lien in this office.[14] When applicable state law provides for the filing of liens in several offices, the IRS must file the federal tax lien with the clerk of the U.S. district court for the judicial district where the property is situated.[15] For real

---

[2] IRC § 6321; Saltzman, IRS Practice and Procedure ¶ 14.05.
[3] Saltzman, IRS Practice and Procedure ¶ 14.05.
[4] IRC § 6323(f); Saltzman, IRS Practice and Procedure ¶ 6.03.
[5] IRC § 6303.
[6] 69 F.3d 64 (5th Cir. 1995).
[7] IRC § 6303(a).
[8] IRC § 6303(a).
[9] Mrizek v. Long, 187 F. Supp. 830 (N.D. Ill. 1959); Saltzman, IRS Practice and Procedure ¶ 14.05.
[10] *See* United States v. Zollar, 724 F.2d 808, 810 (9th Cir. 1984); Pursifull v. United States, 849 F. Supp. 597, 601 (S.D. Ohio 1993).
[11] IRC § 6321.
[12] IRC § 6322.
[13] IRC § 6323(a); Saltzman, IRS Practice and Procedure ¶ 16.03.
[14] IRC § 6323(f)(1)(A).
[15] IRC § 6323(f)(1)(B).

property, the notice of tax lien also must be entered and recorded in a public[16] index maintained by the state. The IRC considers real property to be situated at its physical location and personal property to be situated at the taxpayer's residence when the IRS files the tax lien.[17]

§ 10.04   DURATION OF TAX LIEN

After tax liens begin,[1] they continue until (1) the taxpayer satisfies the tax liability, or (2) the tax liability becomes unenforceable because the statute of limitations expires.[2] Generally, the IRS must collect assessed taxes by levy or distraint or begin court action to collect such taxes within 10 years of assessment.[3] However, the taxpayer and the IRS may agree to extend the statute of limitations beyond the 10-year limit. If the IRS does not collect the tax or institute court action to do so within the period prescribed by the statute of limitations, the lien ends at the statute of limitations' termination.[4]

> **Note.** After December 31, 1999, the 10-year statute of limitations on collection cannot be extended by agreement and the 10-year period after assessment applies absolutely, subject only to the following two exceptions:
>
> 1. Where the taxpayer and the IRS enter into an installment payment agreement that provides for an agreed upon period of collection, the IRS may collect during the 90 days after that agreed upon period expires; or
> 2. If the taxpayer and the IRS agree upon a release of levy after the 10-year collection period expires, the IRS may collect within any time period that the taxpayer and the IRS agree to.[5]

The planner should note that under some circumstances the statute of limitations extends beyond 10 years. In these circumstances, the tax lien continues until the statute of limitations ends. Specifically, the IRC extends the statute of limitations on collections under the following circumstances:

1. The IRC suspends the statute of limitations during the period beginning when the IRS sends the statutory notice of deficiency to the taxpayer, during which the IRC prohibits the IRS from making assessments, plus 60 days after the IRC prohibition on assessments ends.[6]

---

[16] IRC § 6323(f)(4).

[17] IRC § 6323(f)(2).

§ 10.04   [1] *See generally* Saltzman, IRS Practice and Procedure ¶ 14.06.

[2] IRC § 6322.

[3] IRC § 6502(a). *See* New England Acceptance Corp. v. United States, 80 A.F.T.R.2d ¶ 97-5419 (D.N.H. 1997) (special gift tax lien expired after 10 years because the government failed to fully enforce such lien).

[4] IRC § 6502(a)(2).

[5] IRC § 6502(a).

[6] IRC § 6503(a)(1).

2. The IRC suspends the statute of limitations while the taxpayer's assets are in the custody of a court and, thus, not subject to administrative collection procedures. The IRC also extends the statute of limitations for six months after the court releases control over such assets.[7]

3. The IRC suspends the statue of limitations during periods when taxpayers are outside the United States for continuous periods of six months or more. The IRC also extends the statute of limitations for six months after taxpayers return to the United States.[8]

4. When the IRS wrongfully seizes a third party's property, the IRC extends the statute of limitations beginning with the wrongful seizure and ending with the property's return or the date on which a judgment secured pursuant to IRC Section 7426 becomes final, and for 30 days after that. However, this extension only applies to an amount equal to the value of the property wrongfully seized.[9] For assessments for which the IRS made a lien on property, the IRC extends the statute of limitations for a period equal to the period beginning on the date any person becomes entitled to a certificate under IRC Section 6325(b)(4) (*i.e.*, certificate of discharge of property where the person deposits an amount of money equal to the value of the property subject to the lien, or the person furnishes a bond with the IRS in such amount), and ending 30 days after the earlier of the following dates:

    a. The earliest date that the IRS no longer holds any amount as a deposit or bond under IRC Section 6325(b)(4), which results from the fact that such deposit or bond is used to satisfy the unpaid tax or such deposit or bond is refunded or released; or

    b. The date that the judgment secured under IRC Section 7426(b)(5) (*i.e.*, judgment refunding or releasing property or bond under IRC Section 6325(b)(4) that exceeds the IRS interest) becomes final.

5. When taxpayers enter bankruptcy proceedings, the IRC suspends the statute of limitations during the period that the bankruptcy proceedings prohibit the IRS from assessing or collecting the taxes involved and for (a) 60 days thereafter for assessments, and (b) six months thereafter for collection.[10]

6. The IRC suspends the statute of limitations against corporations (or persons to whom such corporations have transferred records) regarding any tax return by such corporation with respect to which the corporation is being examined under the coordinated examination program. In such cases, the statute of limitations is extended as follows:

    a. During any judicial enforcement period with respect to such summons or any other summons;

    b. If the court in any proceeding with respect to such summons requires any compliance with such a summons, then during the 120-day period

---

[7] IRC § 6503(b).
[8] IRC § 6503(c).
[9] IRC § 6503(f).
[10] IRC § 6503(h).

beginning with the first day after the close of the suspension that occurs during a judicial enforcement period.[11]

A designated summons is a summons issued by the IRS to determine any tax imposed by the IRC where (a) before the IRS issues the summons, the applicable regional counsel of the Office of Chief Counsel reviews such issuance, (b) the IRS issues the summons at least 60 days before the assessment period's expiration, including extensions, and (c) the IRS clearly denominates the summons as a "designated summons."[12]

When the IRS obtains a judgment against a taxpayer in U.S. district court, IRC Section 6322 extends the assessment lien until the taxpayer satisfies the liability or the lien becomes unenforceable because of the lapse of time.[13] This allows the IRS to maintain its priority against competing creditors and to enforce its lien without having to pursue the process of foreclosing its judgment.[14]

When the IRS begins a court proceeding and reduces a tax lien to judgment, the judgment entered by the applicable U.S. district court constitutes a lien on property located within the state in which that court sits in the same manner, to the same extent, and under the same conditions as a judgment of a court of general jurisdiction in that state. Consequently, such a judgment ceases to be a lien in the same manner and time.[15] Generally, after the IRS obtains a judgment, it may no longer collect the tax by administrative action after the statute of limitations would have run but for the court action.[16] When the judgment becomes unenforceable because of the end of the state law statute of limitations, the extended assessment lien also expires.[17]

§ 10.05   SCOPE OF TAX LIEN

Asset protection planners should be aware of certain general characteristics of tax liens.[1] Furthermore, they should pay particular attention to the interaction between tax liens and certain types of property commonly used in asset protection plans.

[A]   General Characteristics of Tax Lien

First, although tax liens attach to all the taxpayer's property and rights to property, they generally extend only to the taxpayer's interest in property.[2]

---

[11] IRC § 6503(j)(1).

[12] IRC § 6503(j)(2).

[13] IRC § 6322.

[14] Saltzman, IRS Practice and Procedure ¶ 14.06.

[15] 28 U.S.C. § 1962; Saltzman, IRS Practice and Procedure ¶ 14.06.

[16] Moyer v. Mathas, 332 F. Supp. 357 (M.D. Fla. 1971), aff'd, 458 F.2d 431 (5th Cir. 1972); Saltzman, IRS Practice and Procedure ¶ 14.06.

[17] Saltzman, IRS Practice and Procedure ¶ 14.06.

§ 10.05   [1] See generally Saltzman, IRS Practice and Procedure ¶ 14.07.

[2] Rev. Rul. 54-154, 1954-1 C.B. 277; Saltzman, IRS Practice and Procedure ¶ 14.07.

Thus, when the taxpayer's interest in property lapses, the IRS lien generally does not attach to such property.

Second, tax liens encumber both property acquired on the assessment date, plus property acquired after that date until the taxpayer pays the liability or the statute of limitations expires.[3]

Third, tax liens do not attach property that taxpayers transfer before the assessment date.[4] However, the planner should be aware of fraudulent conveyances.[5]

Fourth, the IRC does not provide for any exceptions to the tax lien.[6] Therefore, tax liens also extend to property exempted from collection under state exemption provisions.[7] However, the IRC exempts certain property, which is not exempt for tax lien purposes, from IRS levy. Federal law provides the only exemptions to the general tax lien.[8]

Finally, although tax liens affect all the taxpayer's property and rights to property, state law controls the issues of (1) whether taxpayers own property or rights to property, and (2) when taxpayers do own property or rights to property, the extent of such ownership.[9]

[B] Application of Tax Lien to Certain Types of Commonly Used Asset Protection Property

[1] Homestead Property[10]

When taxpayers own fee simple absolute interests in homestead property, the tax lien attaches to such property.[11] Because exemption statutes generally do not protect property from tax liens, the homestead exemption also does not protect property from tax liens. This rule generally holds true for both delinquent and nondelinquent spouses.[12] However, the IRC entitles nondelinquent spouses to a distribution of so much of the proceeds as represents complete compensation for the loss of his homestead interest.[13] Also, IRC Section 7403 gives courts limited discretion not to order sales of homestead property after engaging in an individualized equitable balancing of the interests of the government and the nondelinquent spouse.[14]

---

[3] Glass City Bank v. United States, 326 U.S. 265 (1945); Saltzman, IRS Practice and Procedure ¶ 14.07.

[4] United States v. Mentelos, 81-1 U.S. Tax Cas. (CCH) ¶ 9257 (S.D.Fla. 1980); Midland Ins. Co. v. Friedgood, 577 F. Supp. 1407 (S.D.N.Y. 1984); Saltzman, IRS Practice and Procedure ¶ 14.07.

[5] *See, e.g.,* Continental Oil Co. v. United States, 326 F. Supp. 266 (S.D.N.Y. 1971).

[6] Saltzman, IRS Practice and Procedure ¶ 14.07.

[7] *See* Chapter 8. *See also* Saltzman, IRS Practice and Procedure ¶ 14.07.

[8] Saltzman, IRS Practice and Procedure ¶ 14.07.

[9] Aquilino v. United States, 363 U.S. 509 (1960); Morgan v. Commissioner, 309 U.S. 78 (1940); United States v. Bess, 357 U.S. 51 (1958); Saltzman, IRS Practice and Procedure ¶ 14.07.

[10] Saltzman, IRS Practice and Procedure ¶ 14.07.

[11] United States v. Rodgers, 461 U.S. 677 (1983); Saltzman, IRS Practice and Procedure ¶ 14.07.

[12] *Id.*

[13] Saltzman, IRS Practice and Procedure ¶ 14.07.

[14] United States v. Rodgers, 461 U.S. 677 (1983); Saltzman, IRS Practice and Procedure ¶ 14.07.

[2] Concurrent Interests[15]

Generally, creditors may reach the interests of tenants in a tenancy in common. Consequently, the general tax lien also extends to such interests.[16] Most courts also hold that general tax liens also reach joint tenancy interests.[17] State law determines whether general tax liens reach a spouse's interest in tenancies by the entirety. Many states hold that neither spouse may transfer individual interests in a tenancy by the entirety. In these states, tax liens generally do not extend to interests in tenancies by the entirety.[18] Finally, state law also determines whether general tax liens reach a spouse's interest in community property.[19]

[3] Life Insurance[20]

Generally, tax liens may attach only to the cash value of life insurance policies owned by the taxpayer.[21] Therefore, if a tax lien attaches to the insured's property, when the insured does not own the life insurance policy, the tax lien does not attach to the cash value of the policy. Conversely, when a tax lien attaches to the property of a noninsured who does own the policy, the tax lien does attach to the cash value of the policy.

When a tax lien attaches to an insured's property before his death, the lien attaches to insurance proceeds that would otherwise be paid to beneficiaries, to the extent of premiums paid by the insured.[22] However, if the assessment does not occur until after the insured's death, the lien does not attach to any of the life insurance proceeds.[23]

[4] Trusts[24]

Generally, tax liens attach to the corpus of revocable, but not irrevocable, trusts[25] and to trusts in which the grantor retains a life interest and reserves

---

[15] *See* Chapters 7 and 8.

[16] Rev. Rul. 79-55, 1979-1 C.B. 400; Saltzman, IRS Practice and Procedure ¶ 14.07.

[17] Shaw v. United States, 331 F.2d 493 (9th Cir. 1964); United States v. Kocher, 468 F.2d 503 (2d Cir. 1972), *cert. denied*, 411 U.S. 931 (1973); Saltzman, IRS Practice and Procedure ¶ 14.07.

[18] American Nat'l Bank of Jacksonville v. United States, 255 F.2d 504 (5th Cir.), *cert. denied*, 358 U.S. 835 (1958); Saltzman, IRS Practice and Procedure ¶ 14.07. *See, e.g.,* Fairfield v. United States (*In re* Ballard), 65 F.3d 367 (4th Cir. 1995) (Fourth Circuit, in a case of first impression, held that sales proceeds of joint debtors' tenancy by the entirety property was also entireties property; consequently, on wife's subsequent death, the husband became property's sole owner and, thus, proceeds became subject to tax debt without regard to whether such debt was sole or joint tax debt.).

[19] Saltzman, IRS Practice and Procedure ¶ 14.07.

[20] *See* Chapter 8.

[21] United States v. Burgo, 175 F.2d 196 (3d Cir. 1949); Saltzman, IRS Practice and Procedure ¶ 14.07.

[22] United States v. Bess, 357 U.S. 51 (1958); Saltzman, IRS Practice and Procedure ¶ 14.07.

[23] Saltzman, IRS Practice and Procedure ¶ 14.07.

[24] *See* Chapters 5 and 6.

[25] United States v. Peelle, 159 F. Supp. 45 (E.D.N.Y. 1958); Saltzman, IRS Practice and Procedure ¶ 14.07.

a general power of appointment.[26] Tax liens also generally attach to a beneficiary's beneficial interest in a trust. Conversely, tax liens do not attach to a beneficiary's beneficial interest in a discretionary trust.[27] However, when the trustee exercises his discretion to pay income or principal to beneficiaries, the tax lien attaches to such payments.[28] Finally, the tax lien generally attaches to beneficial interests in spendthrift trusts.[29] However, there is a conflict among districts concerning whether tax liens attach to beneficial interests in spendthrift trusts.[30]

> **Caution.** The Sixth Circuit has held that where (1) a spendthrift trust has a forfeiture provision providing that the beneficiary/taxpayer's beneficial interest in the trust terminates and vests in another person if a creditor attaches the beneficiary/taxpayer's interest in the trust, and (2) the IRS serves a levy to seize the beneficiary/taxpayer's interest, the levy does not retroactively defeat the tax lien that had attached to the taxpayer's beneficial interest before the levy. Therefore, while the levy may have been sufficient under the forfeiture provision to terminate the taxpayer's previously nondiscretionary interest in the trust, "any such termination came too late to defeat the government's right to the money."[31]

§10.06 METHODS OF ENFORCING TAX LIEN

The IRS may enforce tax liens within the United States in one of three ways.[1] First, it may enforce tax liens by administrative levy.[2] Second, it may enforce tax liens by bringing actions to reduce the tax assessment to judgment. Third, it may enforce tax liens by lien foreclosure suits. Also, the IRS may try to enforce tax liens in foreign countries. As a preliminary matter, planners should note that the IRS must follow prescribed procedures for beginning civil actions.[3] When it does not follow such procedures, taxpayers may successfully move to have the action dismissed.[4]

---

[26] United States v. Ritter, 558 F.2d 1165 (4th Cir. 1977); Saltzman, IRS Practice and Procedure ¶ 14.07.

[27] Saltzman, IRS Practice and Procedure ¶ 14.07; *see* Chapter 5.

[28] Hamilton v. Drogo, 150 N.E. 496 (N.Y. 1926); Saltzman, IRS Practice and Procedure ¶ 14.07.

[29] United States v. Grimm, 865 F. Supp. 1303 (N.D. Ind. 1994); Lasalle Nat'l Bank v. United States, 636 F. Supp. 874 (N.D. 111. 1986); Saltzman, IRS Practice and Procedure ¶ 14.07.

[30] *See* United States v. Cohn, 855 F. Supp. 572 (D. Conn. 1994); Bank One Ohio Trust Co., N.A. v. United States, 857 F. Supp. 592 (S.D. Ohio 1994), *rev'd & remanded*, 80 F.3d 173 (6th Cir. 1996).

[31] Bank One Ohio Trust Co. NA v. United States, 80 F.3d 173 (6th Cir. 1996).

§10.06 [1] *See generally* Saltzman, IRS Practice and Procedure ¶¶ 14.08, 14.10, 14.21.

[2] *See* §§ 10.11–10.12.

[3] IRC §§ 7401, 7403; Saltzman, IRS Practice and Procedure ¶ 14.08.

[4] Saltzman, IRS Practice and Procedure ¶ 14.08.

[A]   Suit to Reduce Tax Assessment to Judgment

Generally, suits to reduce tax assessments to judgments occur when the IRS cannot collect by administrative levy and sale within the normal 10-year statute of limitations, the amounts involved are significant, or the taxpayer is arrogant, evasive, or concealing property.[5] To reduce tax assessments to judgment, the government must prove that it made a timely assessment and that it timely began the collection suit.[6] Once the United States makes a prima facie case by proving that the IRS made a timely assessment, the burden of proof shifts to the taxpayer to prove by a preponderance of the evidence that the assessment was erroneous.[7]

[B]   Lien Foreclosure Suit

When taxpayers refuse or neglect to pay taxes, regardless of whether the IRS has levied on the taxpayer's property, the IRS may request the attorney general to commence a civil action in U.S. district court to foreclose the tax lien against any taxpayer property or any property in which the taxpayer possesses any right, title, or interest.[8] In lien foreclosure suits, the IRS must join as parties to the action, all persons having liens in or claiming any interest in the property involved.[9] After the IRS notifies such parties of the action, the court must adjudicate all matters involved and finally determine the merits of all claims to and liens on the property involved. After the government establishes its claim or interest in the property involved, the IRC allows the court to order the property to be sold and the sale proceeds distributed according to the court's findings.[10]

The U.S. Supreme Court holds that IRC Section 7403, which provides for lien foreclosure suits, contemplates not merely the sale of the delinquent taxpayer's interest, but the sale of the entire property and the recognition of third-party interests through the mechanism of judicial valuation.[11] However, when courts order sales of property in which nondelinquent third parties hold interests, such courts must distribute enough proceeds to completely compensate the third parties for their loss.[12]

---

[5] *Id.*

[6] United States v. Besase, 623 F.2d 463 (6th Cir.), *cert. denied*, 449 U.S. 1062 (1980); Saltzman, IRS Practice and Procedure ¶ 14.08.

[7] Saltzman, IRS Practice and Procedure ¶ 14.08.

[8] IRC § 7403(a).

[9] IRC § 7403(b).

[10] IRC § 7403(c).

[11] United States v. Rodgers, 461 U.S. 677 (1983).

[12] United States v. Rodgers, 461 U.S. 677 (1983); Harris v. United States, 764 F.2d 1126 (5th Cir. 1985); Saltzman, IRS Practice and Procedure ¶ 14.08.

EXAMPLE 10-1[13]

Tom Taxpayer is married to Wilma. Tom owes the IRS $1 million. Tom and Wilma own Homeacre, which their state's homestead exemption protects. Tom dies and the state homestead provision entitles Wilma to live in the home until death. Before his death, Tom and Wilma owned the home as tenants in common. Here, a court could order the sale of the entire home, though Wilma, who is not liable for the tax liability involved, holds an interest in the home. However, the court must pay to Wilma a portion of the sale proceeds that represents complete compensation for the loss of her interest.

The U.S. Supreme Court suggests that federal district courts possess a limited degree of discretion not to order forced sales of property in which taxpayers own interests with other nondelinquent persons. However, district courts must first engage in an individualized equitable balancing of the interests of the government and the nondelinquent owners before exercising this discretion.[14] The Supreme Court indicates that the trial court should consider the following factors:

1. What extent would the government's interest be prejudiced by a forced sale of the partial interest, as opposed to the whole property?
2. Do innocent third parties have legally recognized expectations that the property will not be subjected to forced sale by the delinquent taxpayer or his creditors?
3. What is the likely prejudice to the nondelinquent person, both in personal dislocation costs and in practical undercompensation?
4. What are the relative characteristics and value of the interests in the property held by the delinquent taxpayer, as compared to the interests held by the other interest holders?[15]

[C] Foreign Enforcement of Tax Liens

Because the tax lien attaches to all the taxpayer's property and rights in property, it also attaches to the taxpayer's foreign property.[16] However, the IRS often encounters trouble enforcing the tax lien in foreign countries.[17]

---

[13] United States v. Rodgers, 461 U.S. 677 (1983); Harris v. United States, 764 F.2d 1126 (5th Cir. 1985); Michael I. Saltzman, IRS Practice and Procedure ¶ 14.08 (2d ed. 1991).

[14] United States v. Rodgers, 461 U.S. 677 (1983).

[15] United States v. Rodgers, 461 U.S. 677 (1983).

[16] Saltzman, IRS Practice and Procedure ¶ 14.08.

[17] Her Majesty the Queen ex rel. British Columbia v. Gilbertson, 433 F. Supp. 410 (D. Or. 1977), aff'd, 597 F.2d 230 (9th Cir. 1979); Saltzman, IRS Practice and Procedure ¶ 14.08; Alan R. Johnson et al., Reciprocal Enforcement of Tax Claims Through Tax Treaties, 33 Tax Law, 469 (1980).

§ 10.07   ESTATE TAX LIEN

When estate taxes are involved,[1] the IRC provides for a special estate tax lien in addition to the general tax lien.[2] The special estate tax lien arises on the date of the decedent's death.[3] It attaches to all property included in the decedent's gross estate, other than property used to pay charges against the estate and estate administrative expenses. Moreover, the estate tax lien remains attached to estate property even after such property is sold to an innocent third party.[4] However, in such cases the transferee's liability for unpaid estate taxes is limited to the actual value of the property he or she receives at the time of the transfer.[5]

The estate tax lien runs for 10 years from the decedent's death, unless the estate tax is paid in full or becomes unenforceable due to the expiration of the statute of limitations.[6]

> **Caution.** Because the estate tax lien attaches to all property included in the gross estate, it may encompass more property than the general tax lien. For example, when decedents retain general powers of appointment over trust property so that their gross estates include the trust corpus, the estate tax lien attaches to such trust corpus. The same rule holds true for gifts made within three years of death.[7]

Probate property becomes divested of the special estate tax lien when courts having jurisdiction over the estate allow such property to be used to pay charges against the estate and estate administration expenses.[8] For both probate and nonprobate property, when estate tax lien property is transferred to purchasers or security interest holders, the estate tax lien shifts from the property transferred to the consideration furnished to the transferor.[9] Finally, the IRS may issue certificates of discharge from the special estate tax lien when it finds that the estate tax liability is fully satisfied or provided for.[10]

When the estate tax is not paid when due, the (1) spouse, (2) transferee, (3) trustee, (4) surviving tenant, (5) persons in possession of the property because of the exercise, nonexercise, or release of powers of appointment, or (6) beneficiary, who receives or possesses on the decedent's death property included in the decedent's gross estate, becomes personally liable for the estate tax, to the extent

---

§ 10.07   [1] *See generally* Saltzman, IRS Practice and Procedure ¶¶ 14.18, 14.19.
[2] IRC § 6324(a).
[3] IRC § 6324(a)(1); Saltzman, IRS Practice and Procedure ¶ 14.18.
[4] Evelpis Properties v. United States, 79 A.F.T.R.2d 97-831 (S.D. Ohio Apr. 15, 1997).
[5] Baptiste v. Commissioner, 29 F.3d 433 (8th Cir. 1994), *cert. denied*, 513 U.S. 1190 (1995).
[6] IRC § 6324(a)(1); *see, e.g.*, United States v. Schneider, 91-1 U.S. Tax Cas. (CCH) ¶ 60,068 (D.N.D. 1991) (court held that 10-year estate tax lien on property in decedent's estate expires 10 years after decedent's death, even if IRS files foreclosure action before 10-year period expires).
[7] Saltzman, IRS Practice and Procedure ¶ 14.19.
[8] IRC § 6324(a)(1).
[9] Saltzman, IRS Practice and Procedure ¶ 14.19; IRC § 6324(a)(3).
[10] IRC § 6325(c).

of such property's value. Any such property becomes divested of the estate tax lien, and the estate tax lien then attaches to all such party's property except property transferred to purchasers or holders of security interests.[11]

> **Caution.** In *United States v. Estate of Kime*,[12] the U.S. District Court for the District of Nebraska held that personal representatives of the decedent's estate (1) were personally liable for the estate's federal estate tax liabilities, and (2) had made various transfers that constituted fraudulent conveyances as to the IRS, which were thus void.

§10.08 GIFT TAX LIEN

When gift taxes are involved,[1] the IRC provides for a special gift tax lien in addition to the general tax lien.[2] The special gift tax lien attaches to all gifts made during the period for which a gift tax return is filed. 1It continues for 10 years from the date of the gift unless the gift tax is paid sooner or becomes unenforceable due to the lapse of the statute of limitations. Furthermore, if donors do not pay gift taxes when due, the donees become personally liable for the gift tax to the extent of their gifts' value. When donees transfer gifted property to purchasers or holders of security interests, the gift tax lien shifts from the gifted property to all the donee's property, including after-acquired property.[3]

§10.09 TAX LEVY

The IRS levy[1] constitutes a summary nonjudicial process that the IRS uses as a self-help method, authorized by the IRC, to promptly and conveniently satisfy delinquent tax claims.[2] When the IRS levies property, it seizes property. Generally, when the IRS assesses a tax, gives notice, and makes demand and the taxpayer does not pay that tax, the IRS may levy against all the taxpayer's property and rights to property.[3] Persons possessing the property must surrender it when the IRS demands such property.[4] If they do not surrender such property, they become personally liable and subject to penalty.[5] Conversely, the

---

[11] IRC §6324(a)(2).

[12] 97-1 U.S. Tax Cas. (CCH) ¶ 60,256 (D. Neb. 1996).

§10.08 [1] *See generally* Saltzman, IRS Practice and Procedure ¶ 14.20; Michael S. Paul & Alan L. Frank, *A Gift from a Tax Debtor May Have a Price Tag*, 20 Tax'n for Law. 265 (1992).

[2] IRC §6324(b).

[3] *Id.*

§10.09 [1] *See generally* Saltzman, IRS Practice and Procedure ¶ 14.10.

[2] United States v. Sullivan, 333 F.2d 100 (3d Cir. 1964); Michael I. Saltzman, IRS Practice and Procedure ¶ 14.12 (2d ed. 1991).

[3] IRC §6331; Saltzman, IRS Practice and Procedure ¶ 14.10.

[4] IRC §6332 (1988 & Supp. 1990); Saltzman, IRS Practice and Procedure ¶ 14.10.

[5] IRC §6332(d); Saltzman, IRS Practice and Procedure ¶ 14.10.

IRC discharges persons who do honor IRS levies from all liability that arises from such surrender or payment.[6]

The IRC establishes time limits and other conditions within which the IRS must sell property that it obtains by levy.[7] The IRS must give buyers of seized property certificates for personal property and deeds for real property that constitute prima facie evidence that such buyers obtained the property in a valid sale and obtained all the taxpayer's rights in such property in that sale.[8] The delinquent taxpayer possesses certain rights to redeem the property before the sale and, for real property, within 180 days after the sale.[9] Under certain conditions, the IRS may release the levy to facilitate tax collection from the taxpayer or, when third parties are involved, to relieve a wrongful levy.[10]

Planning Pointer. The planner should consider the following issues when considering IRS levies:

1. When and how the IRS may make a levy;[11]
2. What limitations exist on IRS levy authority;[12]
3. What property the IRS may levy upon;[13]
4. What occurs when the property holder surrenders or fails to surrender the property levied on;[14]
5. What procedures the IRS must follow concerning the sale of property that it has levied on.[15]

§ 10.10 WHEN AND HOW IRS MAY MAKE TAX LEVY

Generally,[1] if the IRS makes notice and demand to a taxpayer to pay a delinquent tax and the taxpayer neglects or refuses to pay such tax within 10 days, the IRS may collect the tax by levying on any or all the taxpayer's property and rights to property.[2] The IRS must provide two notices to taxpayers before seizing their property.[3] First, it must give notice of the assessment to taxpayers. This notice must state the assessment amount and demand payment as soon as practicable and within 60 days after the assessment. The IRS must leave this

---

[6] IRC § 6332(e).

[7] IRC § 6335; Saltzman, IRS Practice and Procedure ¶ 14.10.

[8] IRC §§ 6338–6339; Saltzman, IRS Practice and Procedure ¶ 14.10.

[9] IRC § 6337; Saltzman, IRS Practice and Procedure ¶ 14.10.

[10] IRC § 6343; Saltzman, IRS Practice and Procedure ¶ 14.10.

[11] See § 10.10.

[12] See § 10.11[D].

[13] See § 10.11.

[14] See § 10.11[E].

[15] See § 10.12.

§ 10.10 [1] See generally Saltzman, IRS Practice and Procedure ¶ 14.12.

[2] IRC § 6331(a).

[3] Saltzman, IRS Practice and Procedure ¶¶ 14.12, 14.15.

notice at the taxpayer's dwelling or usual place of business, or send it by mail to the taxpayer's last known address.[4]

Second, IRC Section 6331(d) requires the IRS to give pre-levy notice to taxpayers.[5] The IRS must give this notice at least 30 days before the levy date.[6] It must provide this notice to the taxpayer by giving it to the taxpayer in person;[7] leaving it at the taxpayer's dwelling or usual place of business;[8] or sending it by certified or registered mail to such person's last known address.[9]

The pre-levy notice must set forth a brief, nontechnical statement in simple and nontechnical terms that includes the following:

1. The IRC provisions and procedures concerning levy and sale of property;[10]
2. The administrative appeal rights and procedures available to the taxpayer concerning the levy and sale;[11]
3. The alternatives available to the taxpayer that could prevent the levy, including IRC Section 6159 installment agreements;[12]
4. The IRC provisions and procedures relating to redemptions of property and releases of liens.[13]

If the IRS levies before following these procedures, the levy will be void.[14] Furthermore, the IRS must not levy within 10 days of making notice and demand on the taxpayer to pay the tax. When the IRS levies within this 10-day period, the levy will be void.[15] The IRS also must wait at least 30 days after the second notice before levying on property.[16]

§10.11 SCOPE OF TAX LEVY

The asset protection planner should be aware of certain general characteristics of tax levies.[1] The planner also should be aware of property that the IRC exempts from IRS levy. Furthermore, the asset protection planner should pay particular attention to the interaction between tax levies and property commonly used as part of asset protection plans.

---

[4] IRC § 6303(a).
[5] IRC § 6331(d).
[6] IRC § 6331(d)(2).
[7] IRC § 6331(d)(2)(A).
[8] IRC § 6331(d)(2)(B).
[9] IRC § 6331(d)(2)(C).
[10] IRC § 6331(d)(4)(A)-(B).
[11] IRC § 6331(d)(4)(C).
[12] IRC § 6331(d)(4)(D).
[13] IRC § 6331(d) (4) (E)-(F).
[14] L.O.C. Indus., Inc. v. United States, 423 F. Supp. 265 (M.D. Tenn. 1976); Saltzman, IRS Practice and Procedure ¶ 14.12.
[15] IRC § 6331(a); Saltzman, IRS Practice and Procedure ¶ 14.12.
[16] IRC § 6331(d).
§ 10.11 [1] See generally Saltzman, IRS Practice and Procedure ¶ 14.12.

[A] General Characteristics of Tax Levies

First, planners should note that the IRS may levy on delinquent taxpayer property by any means.[2] Consequently, the IRS uses different methods for different types of property. For example, it may physically seize tangible personal property such as automobiles.[3] For intangible property, the IRS generally levies on such property by serving notice of levy.[4]

Second, the levy only seizes the taxpayer's interest in property.[5] Thus, when the taxpayer holds a partial interest in property, the levy does not impact the rights of others holding interests in such property.

Third, the U.S. Supreme Court holds that levies transfer legal custody of the property levied on to the IRS. When the IRS sells this property, the sale divests the taxpayer of title to the property.[6]

Fourth, IRS levies generally do not seize after-acquired property.[7] Consequently, the IRS must use a subsequent levy to reach property that the taxpayer receives after a prior levy. For example, when the IRS levies on the taxpayer's bank account, the levy does not reach deposits made after the levy.[8] However, one exception does exist to this rule. Specifically, when the IRS levies on salary and wages, the levy runs continuously from the levy date until either the taxpayer satisfies the liability, or the levy becomes unenforceable because of the statute of limitations.[9]

> **Caution.** Although levies do not reach after-acquired property, they do reach the taxpayer's right to future income, which represents a fixed or present right to property.[10] For example, when the taxpayer possesses a right to future payments from a trust that is fixed and determinable, the IRS may levy on this right.[11]

Finally, the IRS may demand the production of any books or records containing evidence or statements relating to the property or rights in property subject to levy.[12] The IRS generally uses this power to identify property that it may levy on.[13]

---

[2] IRC § 6331(b).

[3] Saltzman, IRS Practice and Procedure ¶ 14.12.

[4] IRC § 6331(b).

[5] Id.

[6] Phelps v. United States, 421 U.S. 330 (1975); Saltzman, IRS Practice and Procedure ¶ 14.12.

[7] IRC § 6331(b); Saltzman, IRS Practice and Procedure ¶ 14.14.

[8] Reg. § 301.6331-1(a)(1) (1983).

[9] IRC § 6331(e).

[10] Dallas Nat'l Bank v. United States, 167 F.2d 468 (5th Cir. 1948); Saltzman, IRS Practice and Procedure ¶ 14.14.

[11] Saltzman, IRS Practice and Procedure ¶ 14.14.

[12] IRC § 6333.

[13] Saltzman, IRS Practice and Procedure ¶ 14.12.

[B] Property Exempt from IRS Levy

The IRC exempts the following types of property from IRS levy:

1. Items of wearing apparel and schoolbooks necessary for the taxpayer and his family.[14]
2. If the taxpayer is the head of a family, so much of the fuel, provisions, furniture, and personal effects in the household and of the arms for personal use, livestock, and poultry of the taxpayer, up to $1,650 of value.[15]
3. Books and tools necessary for the taxpayer's trade, business, or profession, up to $1,100 of value.[16]
4. Any unemployment benefits payable to an individual.[17]
5. Mail addressed to any person that has not been delivered to the addressee.[18]
6. Annuity or pension payments under the Railroad Retirement Act, benefits under the Railroad Unemployment Insurance Act, special pension payments received by persons whose name has been entered on the Army, Navy, Air Force, and Coast Guard Medal of Honor roll, and annuities based on retired or retainer pay.[19]
7. Any workmen's compensation benefits payable to an individual.[20]
8. When a judgment of a court order entered before the levy date requires the taxpayer to pay child support, so much of the taxpayer's income as is necessary to comply with this order.[21]
9. Amounts payable to the individual taxpayer as wages or salary for personal services or as income from other sources, during any period, to the extent that the total of such amounts payable to or received by the taxpayer during the period do not exceed the applicable "exempt amount."[22] IRC Section 6334(d) defines the weekly exempt amount as the standard deduction plus the aggregate amount of deductions for personal exemptions under IRC Section 151, divided by 52.[23] The IRC states that individuals who receive payments on a nonweekly basis determine their exemption amount under Treasury Regulations, which set forth an exemption amount that is equivalent to the weekly exemption amount.[24]
10. Amounts payable to the taxpayer as service-connected disability payments.[25]
11. Certain public assistance payments.[26]

---

[14] IRC § 6334(a)(1).
[15] IRC § 6334(a)(2).
[16] IRC § 6334(a)(3).
[17] IRC § 6334(a)(4).
[18] IRC § 6334(a)(5).
[19] IRC § 6334(a)(6).
[20] IRC § 6334(a)(7).
[21] IRC § 6334(a)(8).
[22] IRC § 6334(a)(9).
[23] IRC § 6334(d).
[24] IRC § 6334(d)(3).
[25] IRC § 6334(a)(10).
[26] IRC § 6334(a)(11).

12. Amounts payable to taxpayers as participants under the Job Training Partnership Act from funds appropriated pursuant to such Act.[27]
13. The taxpayer's principal residence, unless the district director or assistant
district director gives his approval, or unless there is a finding that collection
of the tax is in jeopardy.[28]

[C] Application of Tax Levies to Certain Types of Commonly Used Asset Protection Property

[1] Salary and Wages[29]

The IRS levy runs continuously from the levy date until the taxpayer satisfies
the liability or the levy becomes unenforceable because of the statute of limitations.[30]

[2] Insurance Policies[31]

The IRC provides a special levy procedure for life insurance policies. Specifically, after the IRS serves a levy on the insurer, the IRC gives taxpayers 90 days
to pay the delinquent tax or work out an arrangement with the IRS.[32] For
example, taxpayers may transfer policies to beneficiaries during this period
who may then discharge the tax lien by paying the cash loan value to the
IRS.[33] After the 90-day period expires, the insurer must honor the levy by paying
to the IRS the amount of the cash loan value on the 90th day, plus any improper
cash advances made after the insurer became aware of the tax lien.[34] This
procedure allows the policy to continue to protect the taxpayer's family but
requires the cash value be paid to the IRS.[35]

[3] Bank Accounts[36]

Generally, banks must comply with IRS levies. However, for certificates of
deposit, the IRS must actually seize the certificate to obtain payment from

---

[27] IRC § 6334(a)(12).

[28] IRC § 6334(a)(13).

[29] See generally Saltzman, IRS Practice and Procedure ¶ 14.14.

[30] IRC § 6331(e).

[31] See generally Saltzman, IRS Practice and Procedure ¶ 14.14.

[32] Saltzman, IRS Practice and Procedure ¶ 14.14.

[33] Saltzman, IRS Practice and Procedure ¶ 14.14; S. Rep. No. 1708, 89th Cong., 2d Sess. (1966), reprinted in 1966-2 C.B. 876, 888-89.

[34] IRC § 6322(b)(2).

[35] Saltzman, IRS Practice and Procedure ¶ 14.14.

[36] See generally Saltzman, IRS Practice and Procedure ¶ 14.14. See also United States v. Borock (In re
Ruggeri Elec. Contractors), 214 B.R. 481 (E.D. Mich. 1997) (holding that IRS levy on funds of debtor's
bank account before debtor's bankruptcy petition filing date constitutes avoidable preference under
Bankruptcy Code § 547(b)).

a bank.[37] For joint checking or savings accounts, the IRS may levy the entire account even though only one owner is liable for a delinquent tax.[38] When nonliable account owners own some or all of the funds seized, such owners may apply to the IRS for return of their funds.[39] The IRS takes the position that notice of levy served on a main branch of a bank reaches accounts held by other branch banks.[40]

[D] Limitations on IRS Use of Tax Levy

The IRS may not use its levy authority without limit.[41] Specifically, two limits constrain IRS use of levies. First, the IRS must levy on property (1) within 10 years after it assesses the applicable tax, or (2) before the end of any agreement to extend the collection period, which the taxpayer and the IRS enter before the original 10-year limit expires.[42] If the taxpayer and the IRS enter into an agreement to extend the 10-year period, they may also enter into subsequent extension agreements. Also, if the IRS commences a timely court proceeding to collect the tax, the 10-year statute of limitations extends and does not expire until the tax liability is satisfied or becomes unenforceable.[43]

Second, the IRS must not violate the Fourth Amendment of the U.S. Constitution when exercising its levy authority.[44] Levies violating the Fourth Amendment are not valid.[45]

[E] Surrender of Property Subject to Tax Levy

Taxpayers must comply with IRS levies and surrender property levied upon to the IRS.[46] The IRC imposes both criminal and civil penalties on persons who interfere with IRS levies.

First, the IRC imposes various criminal penalties for failing to cooperate with the IRS in levying on property. The IRC provides that persons who corruptly or by force, or threats of force, try to intimidate or impede IRS collection will be fined up to $5,000, imprisoned for up to three years, or both.[47] However, the IRC provides that persons who use only threats of force to try to intimidate or impede IRS collection will be fined up to $3,000, imprisoned for up to one

---

[37] Rev. Rul. 75-355, 1975-2 C.B. 478; Saltzman, IRS Practice and Procedure ¶ 14.14.

[38] United States v. National Bank of Commerce, 472 U.S. 713 (1985); Saltzman, IRS Practice and Procedure ¶ 14.14.

[39] Saltzman, IRS Practice and Procedure ¶ 14.14.

[40] Reg. § 301.6332-1(a)(2) (1993); Saltzman, IRS Practice and Procedure ¶ 14.14.

[41] See generally Saltzman, IRS Practice and Procedure ¶ 14.13.

[42] IRC § 6502(a) (1988 & Supp. 1990).

[43] IRC § 6502(a) (1988 & Supp. 1990).

[44] Saltzman, IRS Practice and Procedure ¶ 14.13.

[45] G.M. Leasing Corp. v. United States, 429 U.S. 338 (1977); Saltzman, IRS Practice and Procedure ¶ 14.13.

[46] See generally Saltzman, IRS Practice and Procedure ¶ 14.16.

[47] IRC § 7212(a).

year, or both.[48] Furthermore, the IRC provides that persons who forcibly try to rescue or cause to be rescued any property after the IRS seizes such property will be fined up to the greater of $500 or double the value of the property, or imprisoned for up to two years.[49] Also, the IRC provides that persons removing, depositing, or concealing property subject to levy with intent to evade or defeat tax collection will be guilty of a felony. The IRC imposes fines of up to $100,000 ($500,000 for corporations), imprisonment of up to three years, or both, plus the costs of prosecution on such persons.[50]

Second, the IRC imposes various civil penalties for failing to cooperate with the IRS in levying on property. When persons fail or refuse to surrender levy property on demand to the IRS, IRC Section 6332(d)(1) imposes a civil penalty equal to the value of the property or rights not surrendered, but not exceeding the taxes involved plus the costs and interests from the date of levy. However, amounts recovered from the taxpayer for this penalty must be credited against the underlying tax liability.[51] Essentially, this penalty serves as a collection device for the IRS. Furthermore, when persons fail or refuse to surrender property without reasonable cause, IRC Section 6332(d)(2) imposes a civil penalty equal to 50 percent of the IRC Section 6332(d)(1) penalty. Unlike the IRC Section 6332(d)(1) penalty, the IRC Section 6332(d)(2) penalty that the taxpayer pays cannot be credited against the underlying tax liability.[52]

The IRC provides two defenses to noncompliance with levy requests. First, the IRC will not penalize parties who do not possess the property. Second, the IRC will not penalize parties when the property is subject to prior judicial attachment or execution.[53]

Finally, when persons surrender the levied upon property, the IRC discharges such persons from any liability to the taxpayer.[54]

§ 10.12 SEIZURE AND SALE

After levying on the delinquent taxpayer's property, the IRS may sell the property to satisfy the tax liability.[1] However, it must follow procedures that the IRC sets forth. Specifically, the IRS must follow certain presale procedures, certain sale procedures, and certain procedures concerning the taxpayer's ability to redeem the property after the sale.

---

[48] *Id.*
[49] IRC § 7212(b).
[50] IRC § 7206(4).
[51] IRC § 6332(d)(1).
[52] IRC § 6332(d)(2).
[53] IRC § 6332(a) (1988 & Supp. 1990); Saltzman, IRS Practice and Procedure ¶ 14.16.
[54] IRC § 6332(e).
§ 10.12   [1] *See generally* Saltzman, IRS Practice and Procedure ¶ 14.17.

[A] Presale Procedures

First, as soon as practicable after the IRS seizes property, it must provide written notice to the owners of the property or, for personal property, to the possessor of such property.[2] The IRS must deliver this notice personally or leave it at the person's usual place of abode or business if such place is within the IRS district where the seizure took place. When the person cannot be readily located or has no dwelling or business within the IRS district where the seizure took place, the IRS must mail the notice to the person's last known address. This notice must include:

1. The sum demanded;
2. For personal property, an account of the property seized; and
3. For real property, a description with reasonable certainty of the property seized.

Failure to provide this notice renders the sale voidable.[3]

Second, the IRS must provide a notice of sale, in the same manner as for the notice of seizure.[4] The IRS also must publish this notice in a newspaper published or generally circulated within the county where it made the seizure. If no newspaper is published or generally circulated within the county where IRS made the seizure, the IRS must post this notice at the post office nearest to the location where it made the seizure, plus in at least two other public places. This notice must specify the property to be sold and the time, place, manner, and conditions of the sale. Failure to provide this notice renders the sale voidable.[5]

Third, the IRS must hold the sale no less than 10 days after, and no more than 40 days after the date it gives public notice of the sale.[6] If the IRS holds the sale outside these parameters, the sale will not be valid.[7] However, the IRS may sell perishables less than 10 days after the date it gives public notice of the sale under some circumstances. Specifically, it may do this when it gives taxpayers notice of the appraised value of the property and the opportunity to pay or post bonds equal to the property's appraised value.[8]

[B] Sale Procedures

First, the IRS must determine (1) the minimum price at which it will sell the property, and (2) whether, on the basis of IRS determined criteria, it would be in the best interests of the United States to buy such property at such minimum

---

[2] IRC § 6335(a).
[3] Saltzman, IRS Practice and Procedure ¶ 14.17.
[4] IRC § 6335(b).
[5] Saltzman, IRS Practice and Procedure ¶ 14.17.
[6] IRC § 6335(d).
[7] Saltzman, IRS Practice and Procedure ¶ 14.17.
[8] IRC § 6336.

price.[9] If no person offers to buy the property at the minimum price and the IRS determines that the purchase of such property is in the best interests of the United States at the minimum price, the IRS declares the property sold to the United States at the minimum price and credits the taxpayer's account with the minimum price less the cost of the levy and sale. If the IRS does not sell the property under the above rules, it returns the property to the taxpayer and increases the taxpayer's amount due by the costs of the levy and sale.[10]

Second, because levies seize only the taxpayer's rights in property, the IRS obtains only such rights and nothing more.[11] If it is determined that the taxpayer did not have any rights in the property that the IRS sells, the buyer suffers the loss. The IRS does not make any warranties concerning the validity of the title to the property that it sells.

Third, the IRS must conduct the sale by either (1) public auction, or (2) public sale under sealed bids.[12] Bids must be transmitted to the IRS before it opens the bidding.[13] The IRS does not announce the minimum price if the highest bid exceeds that price. However, the IRS announces the minimum price when it declares the property purchased for the government at the minimum price.[14] The IRS retains possession of the property after the sale until the purchaser fully pays for it. However, the risk of loss and the responsibility for the property's preservation shifts to the purchaser when the IRS accepts his bid.[15] If the IRS requires full payment at the time of acceptance and the purchaser does not tender such payment, the IRS may immediately resell the property.[16] When the payment of a portion of the price is deferred but the purchaser does not pay this amount within the prescribed period, the IRS may sue the purchaser for the unpaid purchase price or may resell the property free and clear of any claim of the defaulting purchaser.[17]

Fourth, the IRS gives certificates of sale to purchasers after they pay the full purchase price.[18] It gives deeds to purchasers of real property after the redemption period expires and the purchaser surrenders its certificate of sale to the IRS.[19] For personal property, the certificate of sale transfers all the delinquent taxpayer's right, title, and interest in the property to the purchaser.[20] Deeds to real property constitute prima facie evidence of the facts stated therein and operate as conveyances of all the taxpayer's right, title, and interest in the property sold at the time that the tax lien attached to such property.[21]

---

[9] IRC § 6335(e)(1).

[10] IRC § 6335(e)(1)(D).

[11] Saltzman, IRS Practice and Procedure ¶ 14.17.

[12] IRC § 6335(e)(2)(A).

[13] Reg. § 301.6335-1(c)(5) (1992); Saltzman, IRS Practice and Procedure ¶ 14.17.

[14] Internal Revenue Manual 56(14)4.2(3), Manual Transmittal 5600-10 (Jan. 15, 1987) (Consideration of Bids and Sale of Property); Saltzman, IRS Practice and Procedure ¶ 14.17.

[15] Saltzman, IRS Practice and Procedure ¶ 14.17.

[16] Reg. § 301.6335-1(c)(8) (1992); Saltzman, IRS Practice and Procedure ¶ 14.17.

[17] Reg. § 301.6335-1(c)(6) (1992); Saltzman, IRS Practice and Procedure ¶ 14.17.

[18] IRC § 6338(a).

[19] IRC § 6338(b).

[20] IRC § 6339(a)(2).

[21] IRC § 6339(b).

Fifth, certificates of sale of personal property and deeds to real property discharge the property from all liens, encumbrances, and titles subordinate to the tax lien.[22]

Sixth, the levied property's sale proceeds must be applied in the following order:

1. Against the expenses of the levy proceedings;[23]
2. When the property sold is subject to a tax imposed by the IRC (for example, alcohol taxes), against such tax;[24]
3. Against the tax liability for which the levy was made;[25]
4. Any remaining surplus must be credited or refunded to the person legally entitled to such surplus, which generally is the taxpayer.[26]

[C] Redemption Procedures

At any time before the levy sale, the person whose property the IRS has seized may redeem the property.[27] To do this, the owner must pay the tax liability due plus the expenses of the levy proceeding. After the owner redeems the property, the IRS must return the property to the owner and must not levy on that property again.

After the levy sale, the owner of personal property loses the right to redeem such property.[28] However, the owner of real property retains certain redemption rights. Specifically, the IRC allows real property owners, their heirs, executors, administrators, or any other persons having interests in the property or liens thereon to redeem the property within 180 days of its sale.[29] The redemption price equals the purchase price plus interest at the annual rate of 20 percent.[30] The redemption occurs when the owner pays the redemption price to the purchaser. However, when owners cannot locate the purchaser within the county where the redeemed property is located, the owner may pay the IRS.

---

[22] IRC § 6339(c).
[23] IRC § 6342(a)(1).
[24] IRC § 6342(a)(2); Saltzman, IRS Practice and Procedure ¶ 14.17.
[25] IRC § 6342(a)(2).
[26] IRC § 6342(a); Saltzman, IRS Practice and Procedure ¶ 14.17.
[27] IRC § 6337(a).
[28] IRC § 6337; Saltzman, IRS Practice and Procedure ¶ 14.17.
[29] IRC § 6337(b)(1).
[30] IRC § 6337(b)(2).

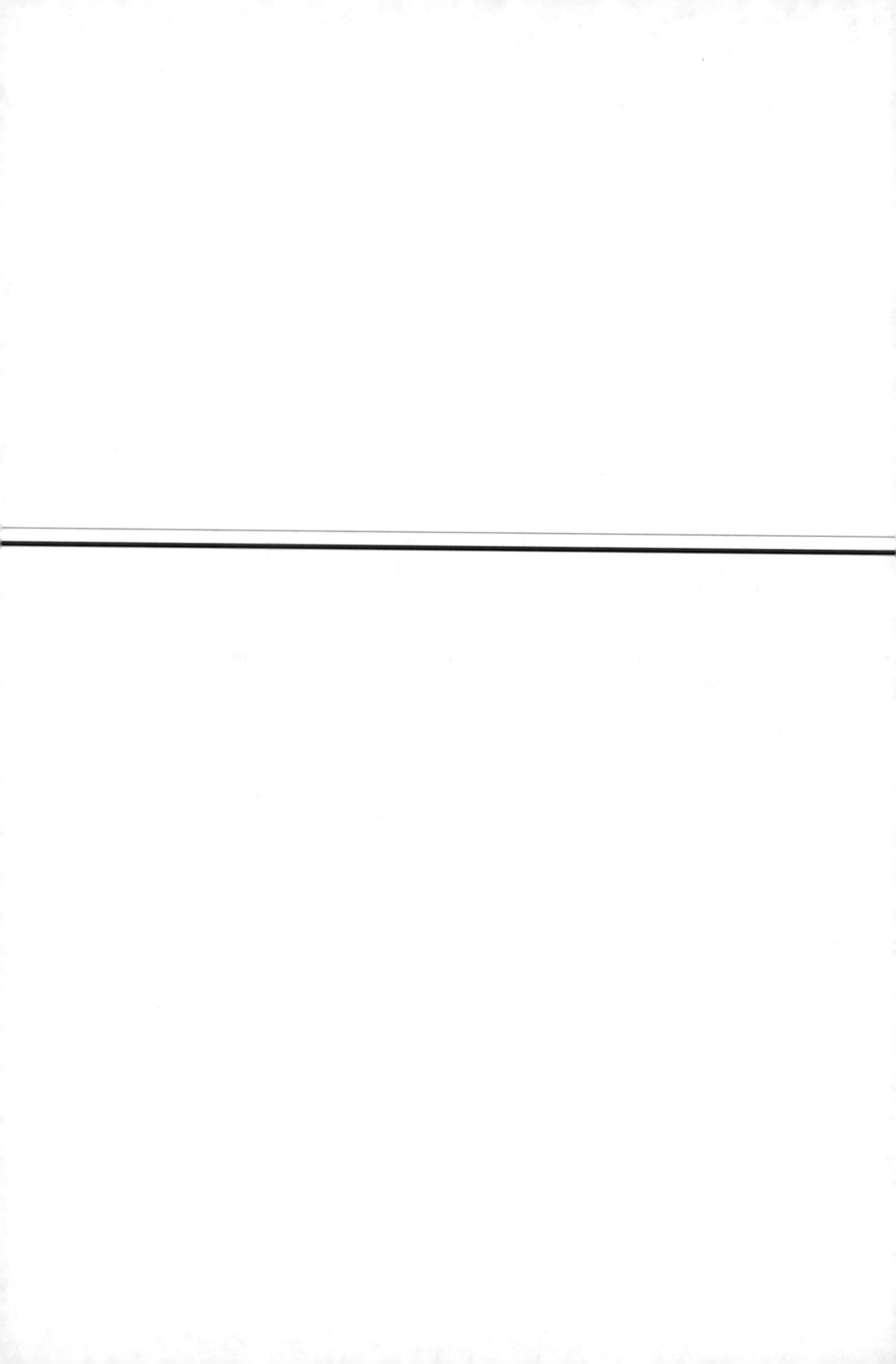

11

OVERVIEW OF FORMS

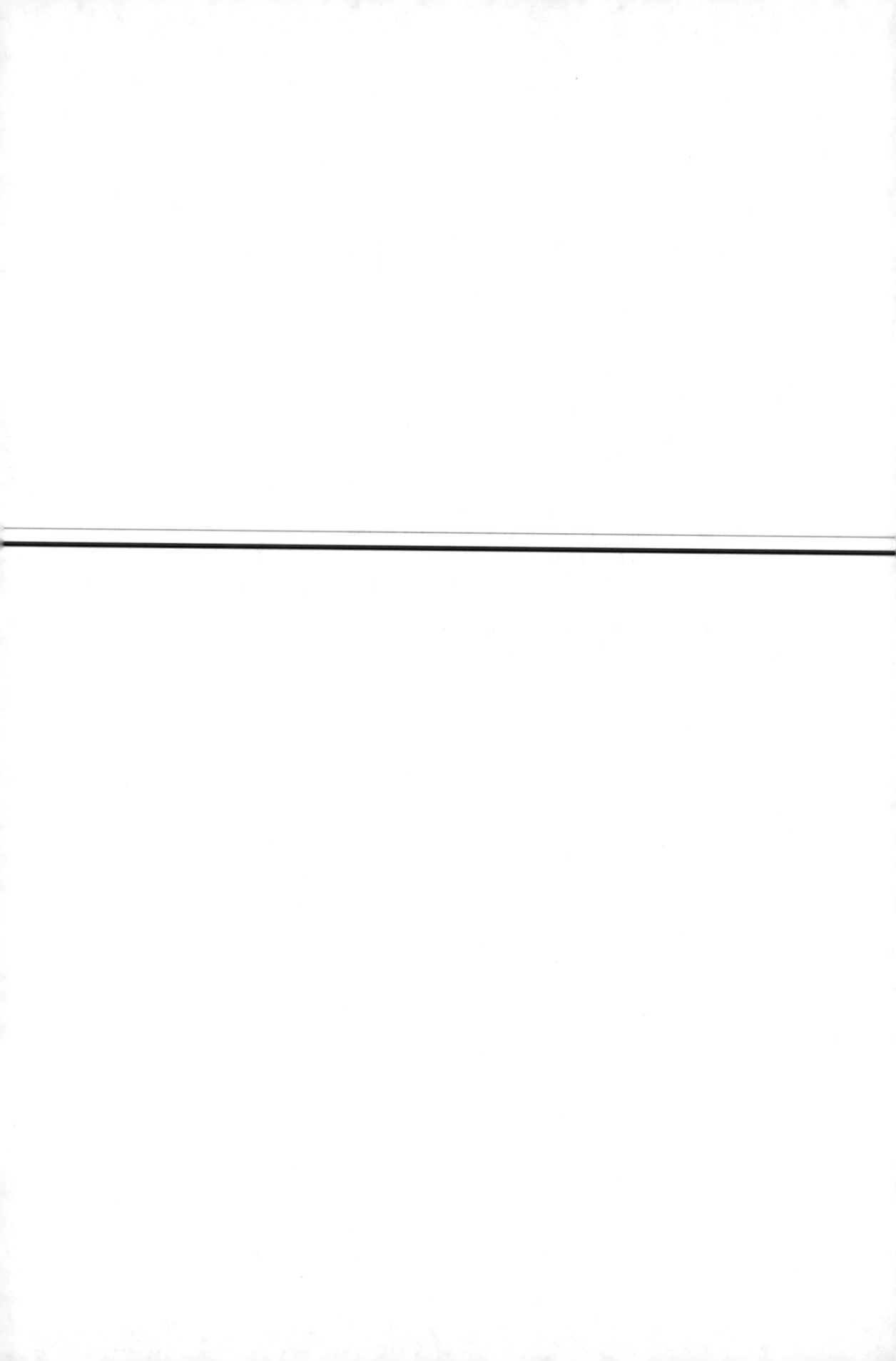

§11.01 OVERVIEW OF ASSET PROTECTION

Financial and legal planners have engaged in asset protection planning for many years. For example, planners have routinely advised clients to use the corporate form of business to take advantage of that form's limited liability. Today the litigation explosion has given added impetus to asset protection planning. More specifically, plaintiffs and their attorneys target not only the very wealthy but also professionals and others who would not consider themselves to be very wealthy.

Asset protection planners have several tools that they may use to protect their client's assets and, simultaneously, achieve the client's estate planning objectives. The first steps to the planner's success in the field of asset protection planning are fully understanding the key characteristics of different asset protection tools, including such tools' limitations and possibilities, and fully understanding key strategies that can be used in conjunction with various asset protection tools.

After gaining a full understanding of key strategies that are available, the planner is prepared to use such strategies. This treatise gives the planner the tools needed to execute asset protection plans. It provides forms for using the following tools as part of an asset protection plan:

- Corporations[1]
- Family limited partnerships[2]
- Limited liability partnerships[3]
- Limited liability companies[4]
- Domestic revocable trusts[5]
- Domestic irrevocable trusts[6]
- Spendthrift trusts[7]
- Discretionary trusts[8]
- Support trusts[9]
- Charitable remainder trusts[10]
- Irrevocable life insurance trusts[11]
- Supplemental needs trusts[12]
- Offshore trusts organized under the laws of the Bahamas, the Cayman Islands, and the Cook Islands.[13]

---

§11.01 [1] *See* Chapter 12.
[2] *See* Chapter 12.
[3] *See* Chapter 12.
[4] *See* Chapter 12.
[5] *See* Chapter 13.
[6] *See* Chapter 13.
[7] *See* Chapter 13.
[8] *See* Chapter 13.
[9] *See* Chapter 13.
[10] *See* Chapter 13.
[11] *See* Chapter 13.
[12] *See* Chapter 13.
[13] *See* Chapter 14.

In addition to the forms required for using the various asset protection tools, Chapter 5 provides United States tax forms that planners must be familiar with in order to ensure that the foreign trusts comply with U.S. tax-reporting requirements.

§ 11.02   INITIAL INFORMATION

Before using the tools contained in this book, the planner should obtain basic client information to screen out unsuitable clients. The following recommendations should help the planner get this information.

[A]   *Initial Meeting*

At the initial meeting, the planner's goals are to answer client questions, to provide clients with information about asset protection planning and the steps that the client and planner must take to establish and implement the asset protection plan, and to begin the screening or vetting process. To accomplish these goals, at the initial meeting the planner should

1. Explore the client's motivations for asset protection planning and the client's asset and estate planning objectives
2. Explore whether there are any facts that would disqualify the client as a suitable client, such as existing litigation problems or insolvency
3. Discuss with the client the limitations of various asset protection techniques
4. Require the client to provide, after the initial meeting, information that will enable the planner to corroborate information obtained during the screening process, including the following:

   - Client's full name, address, telephone numbers, date and place of birth, citizenship including any special immigrant status, state of residency, social security numbers, state and federal income tax returns for the past five years
   - Spouse's full name, address, telephone numbers, date and place of birth, citizenship including any special immigrant status, state of residency, social security numbers, state and federal income tax returns for the past five years
   - Each child's full name, address, telephone numbers, date and place of birth, citizenship including any special immigrant status, state of residency, social security numbers, whether the child is a natural child or is legally adopted
   - Information about each legal dependent not covered by prior questions
   - Information about prior marriages, amounts of outstanding or continuing alimony, child or other family support obligations
   - Any pertinent information about the individuals listed in the prior questions of which the planner should be aware

- Whether the client desires to restrict the rights of any of the individuals listed in the prior questions and if so the reasons therefore
- Names of at least three references
- Banker's name, address, and telephone number and written permission to talk with such person
- Bank account numbers and balances
- Attorney's name, address, and telephone number and written permission to talk with such person
- Accountant's name, address, and telephone number and written permission to talk with such person
- A resume or curriculum vitae for the client and client's spouse
- The client's and spouse's medical history
- Whether the client, the client's spouse, children, or other dependents, or any corporation or other entity of which the client is an officer, director, or significant shareholder, has ever filed bankruptcy, and if so the details thereof
- Whether the client, the client's spouse, children, or other dependents, or any corporation or other entity of which the client is an officer, director, or significant shareholder, has ever been convicted of any crime, indicted, or been the subject of criminal investigation or any investigation by any federal or state enforcement or regulatory body, government, or agency, and if so the details thereof
- Whether the IRS or any state tax authority has ever audited the client, and if so details of such audit
- Whether there are any actions presently filed against the client, and if so the details thereof
- Whether there are any actions threatened against the client, and if so the details thereof
- Whether the client knows of any facts that lead him to fear that an action may be instituted against him due to past actions, and if so the details thereof
- Whether the client holds a U.S. passport
- A listing of each country that the client has visited within the past three years and the number of visits to each country
- Whether any foreign country has ever denied the client entry, and if so a detailed description thereof
- Whether the client or spouse uses or has used different names than the name given to the planner, and if so a detailed description thereof
- Whether the client or spouse has any financial interest or signatory power over any bank or other financial account outside the United States, and if so a detailed description thereof
- Whether the client or spouse is under the care of a physician for any problems related to alcohol or drug abuse, and if so a detailed description thereof
- Whether the client believes that he or his spouse has any alcohol or drug abuse problem not covered by the prior question, and if so a detailed description thereof

- Any other information of which the client feels the planner should be aware
- A complete listing of the client's present insurance policies, copies of the past three years' malpractice insurance applications, and a copy of the current malpractice insurance policy. For each life insurance policy, the face amount of coverage, current cash value, issue date of policy, current and past beneficiary designation, and current owner
- Information about the client's interests in pension and profit-sharing plans, including the current vested value, value attributable to employer contributions, value attributable to client contributions, and a copy of the plan's plan document and summary plan description
- Information about the client's debts, including the unpaid amount, copies of relevant documents, and for what purposes the debt proceeds were used
- Information about contingent liabilities
- Information about potential inheritances.

[B] Retainer Letter

The planner must have the client sign a retainer letter that describes their relationship in detail. Among other things, the retainer letter should clearly state that the planner will screen or vet the client, that the planner reserves the right to terminate the representation if the client does not pass the screening or vetting process, and that the client will pay for the screening or vetting process even if the planner determines that the client has not passed the screening process and therefore will not assist the client with asset protection planning.

[C] Screen Client

The most important step the planner must take is to vet or screen prospective clients. A "bad" client can expose the planner to civil and criminal penalties. For example, planners may be found guilty of civil conspiracy for assisting clients to defraud creditors or they may be subjected to disciplinary proceedings by their state bar.[1]

More specifically, the planner should require the client to provide the following, in addition to the information previously requested:

1. Audited personal financial statements

---

§ 11.02 [1] *See, e.g.,* McElhanan v. Hing, 728 P.2d 256 (Ariz. 1985), *aff'd in part and vacated in part,* 728 P.2d 273 (Ariz. 1986), *cert. denied,* 481 U.S. 1030 (1987); Durant Software v. Herman, 257 Cal. Rptr. 200, 208 (Ct. App. 1989), *appeal dismissed,* 272 Cal. Rptr. 612 (Ct. App. 1990); Wolfrich Corp. v. United Servs. Auto. Ass'n, 197 Cal. Rptr. 446 (Ct. App. 1983); Allen v. State Bar, 570 P.2d 1226, 1229 (Cal. 1977); Fraidin v. Weitzman, 611 A.2d 1046 (Md. 1992); Van Royen v. Lacey, 277 A.2d 12 (Md. 1971); Dalton v. Meister, 239 NW.2d 9 (Wis. 1976); Charles M. Bruce, Foreign Trusts: Protection of Assets, Pre-Immigration and Other, in 1993 A.B.A. Sec. of Tax'n.

2. Audited financial statements for all entities in which the client is a significant shareholder (for example, 10 percent interest or more) or in which the client is an officer, the past five years' tax returns for such entities, the names of such entities' other equity holders, and any contracts between such entities and the client

3. Certificate of insurance

4. Affidavits from the client that:

   - The client is not presently in financial difficulties
   - The client lacks knowledge of facts or circumstances that may render him liable to future claims stemming from past actions
   - The client's motive for establishing an asset protection plan is not to place his assets beyond the reach of any party to whom the client (1) is presently liable, (2) owes an existing obligation, (3) is contemplating divorce proceedings, or (4) is seeking shelter from any contemplated action related to environmental damage
   - There are no current legal proceedings being prosecuted or contemplated against the client, or if there are and the maximum amount of the claim is identifiable, that he will set aside sufficient reserves outside the proposed asset protection plan to cover this liability
   - There are no liabilities or contingent liabilities that the client has not disclosed on the financial statements that you are requiring to be provided to you, and
   - The client is not aware of any currently existing facts that might render him liable to legal proceedings that would result in a claim against his assets.

The planner also should run the client's name and any of his related entities through several databases to check the information that the client has supplied. These should include Nexis/Lexis®, a credit bureau, and Dun & Bradstreet. If the client is a professional, the planner should check with the applicable state licensing agency to see whether any complaints have been filed against the client. The planner also should do a check for Uniform Commercial Code (U.C.C.) or other judgment liens against the client.

The planner must examine all the information received from the client in great detail and should consider carefully all risks, exposures, guarantees, and contingent liabilities. The planner should gather information about the client's past method of doing business and determine his reputation in the community. Additionally, unless the planner possesses an expertise in the area of creditor's rights and fraudulent transfers issues, the planner should seek the advice of cocounsel with such expertise. The planner must ensure that the client does not have present creditors, including creditors with unliquidated claims, who will be disadvantaged by the asset protection plan's establishment. When examining information about the client's assets, the planner should pay particular attention to the asset's fair market value, title, location, marital character, and any associated debts or security interests held by others in such assets.

[D]　Correspondence Stating What Planner Has Done and Not Done

This makes clear to the client exactly what the planner has done, will do, and will not do. The purpose of this letter is to minimize the liability exposure of the planner by identifying who is responsible for what. This correspondence should, based on prior agreement with the client, assign responsibility for all important steps to a designated professional. For example, continuing tax return compliance should be set forth in this correspondence.

[E]　Opinion Letter of U.S. Special Counsel

There may be various reasons the planner determines that he needs the opinion of special counsel. As already mentioned, one area in which this is especially desirable is creditors' rights and fraudulent conveyances.

[F]　Execution of Documents

The client must execute the requisite legal documents to effect the asset protection plan. The appropriate formalities that the planner must follow will depend on the tools that the planner uses and the law of the applicable jurisdiction.

[G]　Follow-Up Correspondence Stating What Planner Has Done and Not Done

This makes clear to the client exactly what the planner has done and has not done. This repeats to some degree the information contained in the retainer letter and prior correspondence stating what the planner has done and has not done. The purpose of this letter is to minimize the liability exposure of the planner by identifying who is responsible for what. This correspondence should, based on prior agreement with the client, assign final responsibility to a designated professional for all important steps that remain unexecuted at the conclusion of the planner's engagement.

§ 11.03　ESTATE PLANNING QUESTIONNAIRE

Please see Form 11-1 on the accompanying CD for the Estate Planning Questionnaire.

12

Choice of Business Entity

§12.01   IN GENERAL

The client's business operation merits the asset protection planner's special attention. This is because business operations tend to cause liabilities that may impact both the business operation out of which the liability arises plus other, unrelated assets. In contrast, other assets, such as furniture, stocks, and bank accounts, generally do not cause liabilities. Because of this characteristic, choice of entity assumes great importance for the asset protection planner.

This chapter discusses the requirements that planners must satisfy to organize a business into one of four types of business entities, which will assist the client in limiting the reach of liabilities arising out of those businesses. Specifically, this chapter will assist planners in setting up the following types of entities:

- Corporations[1]
- Family Limited Partnerships[2]
- Limited Liability Partnerships[3]
- Limited Liability Companies.[4]

§12.02   CORPORATIONS

Corporations[1] are legal entities that are legally independent from the corporation's owners. Planners may form a corporation by executing and filing articles of incorporation that satisfy applicable state law. Then the corporation conducts business, acquires assets, enters contracts, and incurs liabilities in its own name.

Generally, the corporation's liability is limited to the assets that it owns. This is generally referred to as limited liability. Limited liability protects the corporation's shareholders from personal liability for the corporation's liabilities. The shareholders' financial exposure generally equals the amount of their investment in the corporation.

From a tax standpoint, a corporation is a taxable entity apart from its owners.[2] Consequently, the Internal Revenue Code (IRC) taxes corporate income twice. First, the IRC taxes such income at the corporate level when earned. Second, the IRC taxes such income at the shareholder level when the corporation distributes such income as an actual or constructive dividend. This is generally referred to as double taxation of distributed corporate income.

---

§12.01   [1] See §2.02.
[2] See §2.03.
[3] See §2.04.
[4] See §2.05.

§12.02   [1] For a complete discussion of corporations and their use in the asset protection context, see Lewis D. Solomon & Lewis J. Saret, Asset Protection Strategies, §§3.03 and 4.02.
[2] I.R.C. §11(a) (1988).

EXAMPLE 12-1

Hamlet is a computer programmer. Hamlet develops a new software package that accurately picks stocks whose price will double within one year. He wants to exploit this package and consults with his attorney and asset protection planner, Ophelia. Ophelia helps Hamlet form a corporation, H Corp. Hamlet capitalizes H Corp with $1 million cash.

H Corp begins selling Hamlet's software package, which it labels "Laertes." Unfortunately, Laertes is defective, causing all computers on which it is loaded to erase their hard drives within six months of being installed. Polonius purchases Laertes and loses valuable data on his hard drive. He sues H Corp and wins a $10 million judgment against it. Here, Hamlet's financial exposure is limited to his $1 million investment in H Corp.

EXAMPLE 12-2

Same facts as Example 12-1, except that H Corp has $1 million of net income in year one and it pays a $500,000 dividend to Hamlet. Here, H Corp must pay corporate income tax on its $1 million of income, and Hamlet must pay individual income tax on the $500,000 dividend that he receives from H Corp.

The planner should consider the following issues when organizing a corporation:

1. The jurisdiction where the business will be incorporated
2. Formalities required to incorporate the business[3]
3. Optional formalities at time of incorporation.

[A] Jurisdiction of Incorporation

Before incorporating a business, planners must decide where they will incorporate that business. A corporation doing business in more than one jurisdiction can only incorporate in one jurisdiction. It must then qualify to do business as a "foreign corporation" in the others.

EXAMPLE 12-3

Napoleon, a retired general, owns a business that manufactures tanks for the military. It does business as a sole proprietorship under the name Napoleon's

---

[3] This chapter discusses only business and professional corporations and will not discuss other types of corporations, such as nonprofit corporations, banks, and insurance companies.

Tank Works (NTW). NTW has two tank factories, one in California and the other in Virginia. Napoleon's attorney recommends that he incorporate to minimize his liability exposure. Here, Napoleon must incorporate in either California or Virginia. He cannot incorporate in both unless he forms two separate corporations.

If a corporation may be conducting business in more than one jurisdiction, the decision about where to incorporate is significant. The law of the jurisdiction of incorporation generally governs the corporation's "internal affairs," including such issues as the substantive rights of the corporation's stockholders.

Planning Pointer. Factors that planners should consider when determining which jurisdiction to incorporate a business include:

1. The location of the business's headquarters
2. The jurisdiction in which the business is doing business
3. Each relevant jurisdiction's substantive corporate law and the judicial decisions construing such law. Examples of substantive law that planners should consider include the law concerning corporate obligations; the rights and responsibilities of stockholders, officers, and directors; the protection afforded minority stockholders and directors; the indemnification of directors; and the flexibility granted to the board of directors concerning corporate governance.

[B] Required Incorporation Formalities

Generally, to incorporate a business, the planner must do the following:

1. Select a corporate name
2. File articles of incorporation
3. Execute corporate bylaws
4. Hold an organizational meeting of directors
5. Qualify the corporation to do business in other jurisdictions that it operates in besides the jurisdiction of incorporation
6. Obtain a tax identification number
7. Obtain applicable licenses, permits, and so forth.

[1] Select Corporate Name

First, the planner must select a corporate name for the business. Most jurisdictions require the corporate name include the word "corporation," "company," "incorporated," "limited," or an abbreviation of one of such words. Typically, jurisdictions also preclude corporate names from containing any words or phrases suggesting that they were organized for any purpose other than those specified in their articles of incorporation. Also, most jurisdictions provide that the corporate name cannot be identical or similar to the name of any other corporation incorporated or doing business in that jurisdiction.

> **Planning Pointer.** Planners should choose several possible corporate names. Then they should make a preliminary informal check by contacting the incorporation jurisdiction and each jurisdiction the corporation will do business in to see whether the chosen names are available. Many jurisdictions allow incorporating businesses to reserve a corporate name for a limited time; therefore, once planners select a corporate name and ensure its availability in the applicable jurisdictions, they should immediately take steps to protect the name in those jurisdictions.

> **Caution.** The planner should also check the proposed corporate name against registered federal trademarks, trade or fictitious names, or common-law rights to a particular business name. Such names may receive protection from other law sources (for example, patent law) that the corporate name may infringe upon, thus resulting in corporate liability. Planners should also consider obtaining a trademark for the corporation's name if they believe that it possesses value.

[2]   File Articles of Incorporation

Next, the planner should prepare and file articles of incorporation. Typically one or more incorporators will form the corporation. Such incorporators need not have any financial or other interest in the corporation. Instead, they may act solely to form the corporation. The planner will probably draft the articles of incorporation that the incorporators will sign to form the corporation. Articles of incorporation for states under the Revised Model Business Corporation Act are found at § 12.06.

> **Caution.** The information planners must include in the articles of incorporation varies for each state. Therefore, planners should carefully review the law of the state of incorporation to ensure that they include all required information in the articles of incorporation. Typically, the articles of incorporation must include the following:
>
> 1. The corporation's name
> 2. The corporation's duration, which incorporators often show to be perpetual
> 3. The corporation's purpose, which incorporators often draft in broad terms

4. Aggregate number of shares that the articles of incorporation will authorize the corporation to issue
5. The corporation's minimum capital requirements. The planner should note that most jurisdictions set forth a minimum capital requirement that the corporation must satisfy
6. The corporation's registered agent and office
7. The corporation's initial directors
8. The corporation's incorporators.

Each jurisdiction will have different filing procedures and fees. The planner should contact the appropriate state office to learn what the applicable filing procedures are. If the corporation will be qualifying to transact business in another jurisdiction, it must order certified copies of the articles of incorporation, or a certificate of good standing, to accompany the subsequent filing of the qualification application in that jurisdiction. Planners should obtain these documents when they file the articles of incorporation.

[3] Execute Bylaws

Third, planners must prepare bylaws. These provide the administrative guide for the corporation's regulation and the management of its affairs. Generally, planners should include provisions that the applicable statute requires, plus provisions that apply to the corporation's internal management and operations. Conversely, planners should not include any provision inconsistent with the applicable law or the corporation's articles of incorporation. The corporation's directors will adopt the bylaws at the organizational meeting.

> **Drafting Pointer.** Planners should consider drafting the bylaws to cover gaps in the applicable statute. For example, if the applicable statute does not deal with officer and director indemnifications, planners may want to include provisions dealing with these issues in the bylaws.

[4] Organizational Meeting of Directors

Fourth, planners must hold an organizational meeting of directors. Typically, at the organizational meeting the directors will adopt bylaws, elect officers, adopt a fiscal or calendar year for tax and accounting purposes, authorize the opening of one or more bank accounts, and authorize the corporation to qualify for business in foreign jurisdictions.

> **Planning Pointer.** Some jurisdictions allow directors to take actions, normally taken at board of directors meetings, without such a meeting. Generally, they require that each director sign a consent to waive the board of directors meeting and that the corporation file such consents

with the board of directors meeting minutes. In such jurisdictions, planners should consider using such procedures instead of holding an organizational meeting. This avoids the cost and inconvenience of holding the meeting.

[5] Qualify in Foreign Jurisdiction

Fifth, planners must qualify the corporation to do business in foreign jurisdictions in which it does business. The exact procedures for effecting such a qualification differ for each state. Typically, the planner must submit a certificate of good standing from the jurisdiction of incorporation along with a filing fee and an application to the applicable jurisdiction. Planners should generally send such applications by certified mail, return receipt requested. Upon acceptance of such form for filing, the applicable state will generally issue a certificate of qualification to do business in that state. When planners receive such certificates, they should insert them in the corporation's minutes book. Generally, a corporation qualifying to do business in a foreign state must maintain a registered agent and registered office in that jurisdiction. Moreover, by qualifying in a foreign state, the corporation may subject itself to additional burdens, such as taxation by the foreign state.

> **Caution.** If the planner fails to qualify a corporation doing business in a foreign jurisdiction, this may expose the corporation to liability for penalties and fines. Moreover, this may also preclude the corporation from being able to sue in such jurisdiction's courts.[4]

[6] Obtain Tax Identification Number

Sixth, planners must obtain employer identification numbers (EINs) from the IRS. The corporation will use the EIN in all correspondence with and remittances to the IRS. Planners may obtain EINs in either of two ways. First, they may submit a Form SS-4, Application for Employer Identification Number, to the IRS.[5] Second, they may submit the information that goes on a Form SS-4 over the telephone, by telephoning one of the Tele-TIN numbers listed on the instructions to Form SS-4, and obtain an EIN immediately.

[7] Obtain Applicable Licenses

Finally, planners must determine which licenses and permits the corporation must obtain before it commences business. Typically, the corporate client or its accountant obtains these licenses, permits, and registrations. However, the

---

[4] *See* Va. Code Ann. § 13.1-758 (Michie 1985 & Supp. 1992); Md. Code Ann., Corps. & Ass'ns §§ 7-301, 7-302 (1985).

[5] *See* Form 5-1 in Chapter 5.

planner must verify that they comply with this because, as noted elsewhere, if the corporation fails to follow corporate formalities, a creditor may be able to pierce the corporate veil of limited liability.

[C] Optional Incorporation Formalities

Besides the required incorporation formalities previously discussed, the planner should consider the following nonrequired incorporation formalities:

1. Preparing and executing a shareholders agreement
2. Subchapter S election
3. Employment agreements
4. Informing the client about corporate formalities.

[1] Preparing and Executing a Shareholders Agreement

First, planners should recommend that corporate shareholders enter a shareholders agreement. A Shareholders Agreement is located at § 12.02[F]. Such agreements serve several purposes, including the following:

1. Avoiding stockholder disputes by addressing areas of potential dispute and setting up mechanisms to resolve conflicts
2. Establishing a means for stock sales by providing mechanisms through which shares can be purchased from the stockholder (for example, so-called buyback provisions)
3. Keeping out "unwanted outsiders" by preventing stockholders from selling, or defining the circumstances under which stockholders can sell their stock to third parties
4. Valuing the stock by setting up a mechanism or formula by which the stock may be valued
5. Defining the relationships between the stockholders and the corporation in their capacities as stockholders, officers, or directors.

Shareholders agreements generally contain a buy-sell element in which one owner's corporate interest will be sold or offered for sale to other owners or to the corporation itself upon a stated event (for example, the owner's death) at a stated price or according to a valuation method contained within the agreement. Such an agreement can be structured as a corporate cross-purchase agreement in which one shareholder agrees to sell all or part of his stock to another shareholder, or as a corporate entity purchase in which a shareholder agrees to sell all or part of his stock to the corporation. The tax treatment of the selling shareholder varies depending on the structure of the buy-sell agreement.[6]

---

[6] For a detailed discussion of the income tax treatment of buy-sell agreements, see Lewis D. Solomon & Susan Flax Posner, Tax Planning Strategies 18-17 (1991); Jones & Fisher, Income Tax Considerations of

The planner's primary objectives when drafting buy-sell agreements are (1) to enable the shareholder to offset his basis in the stock against the amount realized so as to reduce or eliminate any gain, and (2) to have the transaction treated as a sale or exchange to the selling shareholder equal to the difference between his basis in the stock sold and the amount received under the agreement for such stock.

A shareholder who sells all or part of his shares to another shareholder under a cross-purchase buy-sell agreement realizes capital gain or loss as long as the corporation is not collapsible. The gain realized equals the difference between the amount realized on the sale and the shareholder's basis in the stock.[7] The purchasing shareholder takes a basis in the stock purchased under the buy-sell agreement equal to the purchase price paid.[8] If the corporation is a collapsible corporation, under I.R.C. § 341 (1988) the gain is ordinary income and not capital gain.

If the corporation purchases the shareholder's shares under the buy-sell agreement, the general rule is that, unless one of the tests discussed below is met, the entire distribution to such shareholder will be treated as a redemption, which in turn is treated as a dividend to the extent of the corporation's earnings and profits. This "dividend" is taxable as ordinary income instead of as capital gain.[9] If the distribution exceeds the corporation's earnings and profits, the excess is treated as a return of capital that reduces the recipient's basis in the stock.[10] It must be emphasized that under this rule, the shareholder can reduce his recognized income on the sale by his basis only if the amount he receives exceeds the corporation's earnings and profits. Generally, if the distribution is treated as a redemption, the shareholder has no basis offset.

In order for a corporate entity purchase arrangement to be treated as a sale or exchange, resulting in capital gain equal to the difference between the amount realized on the sale and the shareholder's basis in such stock, one of the following tests must be met:[11]

1. The redemption must not be essentially equivalent to a dividend.[12]
2. There must be a substantially disproportionate redemption of stock.[13]
3. The redemption must result in a complete termination of all of the stock owned by the shareholder, after application of the Code Section 318

Buy-Sell Agreements, 19 Tax'n for Law. 164 (1990); Lewis D. Solomon & Lewis J. Saret, Tax Planning for Closely Held Corporations under the New Estate Freeze Rules, 16 Rev. Tax'n of Individuals 3; James D. Fife, Structuring Buy-Sell Agreements to Fix Estate Tax Value, 22 Est. Plan. 67 (1995).

[7] I.R.C. §§ 1001(a), 1011. If a party to the buy-sell agreement dies, his beneficiary or his estate will obtain a stepped-up basis to fair market value at death.

[8] I.R.C. § 1012.

[9] I.R.C. § 301(a).

[10] I.R.C. § 301(c)(2).

[11] If the sale takes place after the death of one of the parties to the buy-sell agreement, the estate or its beneficiaries obtain the benefit of a stepped-up basis to fair market value at the death of the party to the agreement.

[12] I.R.C. § 302(b)(1). This is an amorphous standard that, because of its lack of clarity, the planner should avoid.

[13] I.R.C. § 302(b)(2).

attribution rules. The IRC provides that the family attribution rules may be waived if certain requirements are met.[14]

4.   The distribution must be in partial liquidation of stock held by a noncorporate shareholder.[15]

The basis that the remaining shareholders have in their stock remains the same. The redemption may, however, reduce the corporation's earnings and profits, thus limiting the distribution of taxable dividends to the remaining shareholders. A redemption of one shareholder's stock will usually not cause income to be attributed to the remaining shareholders even if they receive an increased percentage interest in the corporation because of the redemption.[16]

If the buy-sell agreement assigns the primary and unconditional obligation to buy the stock to one or more of the remaining shareholders and the corporation finances the purchase of such stock, however, the corporation's payments may be considered a constructive dividend to the shareholder whose obligation has been relieved by such corporate payments.[17] To avoid such a constructive dividend, the buy-sell agreement should be structured so that the remaining shareholders are not obligated to purchase stock that is redeemed by the corporation and the stock redeemed is transferred directly to the corporation and does not end up in the remaining shareholders' hands.

The distribution of cash by the corporation does not result in gain or loss when the distribution is in redemption of its stock. Gain but not loss is recognized, however, on nonliquidating distributions of appreciated property, other than obligations of the corporation, to which Code Sections 301 through 307 would apply if the corporation sold such property at fair market value.[18]

When a corporation distributes money or its obligation to pay money, its earnings and profits are decreased by the amount of the distribution. When property is distributed, the corporation's earnings and profits are decreased by the adjusted basis for the distributed property. If inventory or unrealized receivables are distributed and their fair market value exceeds their adjusted bases, however, the corporation's earnings and profits are increased by the amount of the excess.[19]

[2]   Subchapter S Election

Next, planners should consider whether the corporation should elect Subchapter S status for federal income tax purposes.[20] The Subchapter S election provides

---

[14] 18 I.R.C. § 302(b)(3).

[15] I.R.C. § 302(b)(4).

[16] Rev. Rul. 58-614, 1958-2 C.B. 920.

[17] *See* Wall v. United States, 164 F.2d 462 (4th Cir. 1947); Sullivan v. United States, 363 F.2d 724 (8th Cir. 1966), *cert. denied*, 387 U.S. 905, *reh'g denied*, 388 U.S. 924 (1967); Deutsch v. Commissioner, 38 T.C. 118 (1962); Miles v. Commissioner, 25 T.C.M. (CCH) 1278 (1966); Lacefield v. Commissioner, 32 T.C.M. (CCH) 151 (1973); Rev. Rul. 69-608, 1969-2 C.B. 42.

[18] I.R.C. § 311(d)(1).

[19] I.R.C. § 312(b)(2).

[20] *See* § 4.02[C] for a complete discussion of the taxation of S corporations.

for a pass-through of profits and losses to the shareholders, similar to partnership pass-throughs. The Code taxes S corporations and their shareholders under rules similar to the partnership taxation rules. Specifically, there is generally no corporate income tax, accumulated earnings tax, or personal holding company tax.

> **Planning Pointer.** The S corporation election allows shareholders to obtain the corporate form's limited liability protection without being subjected to corporate double taxation.

Generally, the S corporation election allows S corporation shareholders who materially participate in the corporation's business on a regular, continuous, and substantial basis to use corporate losses, deductions, and credits to offset other personal income, including earned income and portfolio income. Furthermore, under this election the corporation's tax attributes retain their original character when passed through to the shareholders. An S corporate shareholder who does not materially participate can only offset such passive activity losses and credits against passive activity income.

A corporation may elect S corporation status if it meets all the following requirements:

1. It has no more than 75 shareholders[21]
2. It has no shareholders other than individuals who are United States citizens. The Code treats shareholder estates or trusts, voting trusts, testamentary trusts, and qualified S corporation trusts as meeting this requirement[22]
3. It is not a member of an affiliated group of corporations[23]
4. It has only one class of stock. For purposes of this rule, differences in voting rights of common stock do not violate the one class of stock requirement. Also, a "straight debt" instrument is not treated as a second class of stock. A straight debt instrument is a corporate, written, unconditional promise to pay on demand, or on a specified date, a certain sum of money, where the interest rate is fixed, the debt is not convertible into stock, and the lender is eligible to be an S corporation stockholder.[24]

[3] Employment Agreement

Planners should also consider executing appropriate agreements between the corporation and its key employees. This also holds true if such key employees are stockholders. For example, planners may design the employment contract to benefit the employee.

[21] I.R.C. § 1361(b)(1).
[22] I.R.C. § 1361(b)(1), (c).
[23] I.R.C. § 1361(b)(2).
[24] I.R.C. § 1361(b)(1)(D).

[4]   Informing Client about Formalities

Finally, planners should instruct clients about the corporate formalities they should follow after the business is incorporated. Examples of these formalities are the following:

1. Issue stock for legal consideration
2. Do not commingle personal funds with corporate funds
3. Use the corporation's full and correct name and address on all stationery, business cards, announcements, contracts, and so forth
4. Include all significant corporate action in appropriate minutes authorizing the action
5. Hold annual meetings of the stockholders
6. Hold annual meetings of the board of directors
7. File all required annual reports
8. Record all stock transactions in the stock certificate book and stock transfer ledger.

Caution. Planners should note that failure to follow corporate formalities is one of the most important reasons why courts allow creditors to pierce the corporate veil of limited liability.[25] Consequently, planners must stress the importance of such formalities to clients and the consequences that may stem from their failure to follow through with such corporate formalities. At this stage planners should work with clients to assign responsibility for follow-up corporate formalities, such as annual meetings.

Planning Pointer. Planners should remind clients about corporate formalities with correspondence to the client repeating the importance of such formalities and what such formalities entail. Moreover, planners should put dates on their calendars to check with clients periodically to ensure that they are following through with corporate formalities.

[D]   Articles of Incorporation

Please see Form 12-1, Articles of Incorporation, on the accompanying CD.

[E]   Model Bylaws

Please see Form 12-2, Proposed Form of Bylaws for Use Under the Revised Model Business Corporation Act, on the accompanying CD.

---

[25] *See* § 3.03[B] for a complete discussion of piercing the corporate veil doctrin.

[F] *Shareholders Buy-Sell Agreement*

Please see Form 12-3, Shareholders Agreement, on the accompanying CD.

§ 12.03   FAMILY LIMITED PARTNERSHIPS

Family limited partnerships (FLPs) are limited partnerships that families use to manage family enterprises and other family investments. They are valuable from an asset protection standpoint because they are very flexible and because they protect the family enterprise from the creditors of individual family members who hold partnership interests.[1] More specifically, such benefits stem primarily from the limited rights of judgment and other creditors of a limited partner to the limited partner's FLP interest. Briefly, the exclusive remedy of a judgment creditor of a limited partner of an FLP is to obtain a charging order.[2] The charging order does not give the creditor title to the limited partner's interest in the FLP. It merely gives the creditor the limited partner's right to receive FLP income that the FLP distributes and, on dissolution, the limited partner's share of FLP assets. Because the controlling general partner of an FLP is a family member, the FLP will generally stop making distributions when a creditor obtains a charging order against an FLP limited partner. Consequently, the FLP interest will be of little value to a creditor. Second, creditors who obtain charging orders must recognize the debtor-partner's proportionate share of the FLP's income for income tax purposes.[3] Therefore, such creditors must pay income taxes on phantom income on the debtor's FLP interest without realizing any significant tangible benefits from charging orders.

EXAMPLE 12-4

George and Eliot are brothers. Each is a plastic surgeon. In 1990 they inherit a mill from their father. They are concerned about losing this mill because of a frivolous lawsuit, so they consult with Mr. Brooke, an asset protection planner. Mr. Brooke recommends that George and Eliot form an FLP to hold and operate the mill. He structures the FLP to give George and Eliot limited partnership interests in the FLP. He gives George and Eliot's mother, Dorothea, the general partnership interest in the FLP. Mr. Brooke gives George and Eliot each a 40 percent interest in the FLP. Mr. Brooke gives Dorothea a 20 percent interest in the FLP.

From 1990 through 1994, the FLP earns $1 million each year of net income. This $1 million is divided among the three partners as follows, for both cash

---

§ 12.03   [1] *See* § 3.05[E].
[2] *See* ULPA § 220), 6 U.L.A. 605 (1916); RULPA § 703 (1985), 6 U.L.A. 391 (Supp. 1992).
[3] *See* Rev. Rul. 77-137, 1977-1 C.B. 178.

distributions and income taxation purposes:

$400,000	George[4]
$400,000	Eliot[5]
$200,000	Dorothea[6]
$1,000,000	Total FLP income

In 1995 one of Eliot's patients, Celia, is unhappy with her nose job and sues Eliot. Celia wins a $10 million judgment against Eliot. She obtains a charging order against the FLP, which is her exclusive remedy against the FLP. Dorothea, as the FLP's general partner, immediately stops making cash distributions to the partners. The FLP continues to earn $1 million each year. Here, Celia does not receive any cash from the FLP. However, she must include $400,000 of income on her federal and state income tax return.

Planning Pointer. The at-risk client should generally not hold a general partner interest. Instead, a closely related and trusted family member should be the general partner. Although creditors of general partners usually can obtain charging orders only against the general partner's partnership interest, as with creditors of limited partners, the law in this area is not entirely settled. Therefore, to ensure maximum security, the planner should structure the family limited partnership so that the at-risk client does not become the general partner. Also, if the at-risk client enters bankruptcy, the bankruptcy trustee may force the dissolution of the partnership or the withdrawal of the general partner from the partnership, thus requiring a distribution to the bankruptcy trustee.

Planning Pointer. When the planner decides to use a corporate general partner, the at-risk client should not own a controlling interest of such corporate general partner. If the at-risk client does own such an interest, her creditors may reach this interest and thus be able to obtain control over the family limited partnership.

---

[4] This amount is calculated as follows: $1,000,000 net income × 40% profits interest = $400,000 income allocation.

[5] This amount is calculated as follows: $ 1,000,000 net income × 40% profits interest = $400,000 income allocation.

[6] This amount is calculated as follows: $1,000,000 net income × 20% profits interest = $200,000 income allocation.

EXAMPLE 12-5

Same facts as Example 12-4 except that instead of making Dorothea the general partner, Mr. Brooke forms a corporation, M Corp, which Eliot owns entirely and which serves as the FLP's general partner. Here Celia may reach Eliot's M Corp stock, take control of M Corp, and cause the FLP to make distributions to satisfy her charging order.

Planning Pointer. The planner should not use the at-risk client's spouse as the general partner. If the at-risk client enters bankruptcy and (1) the client and the spouse are jointly liable for any debts or (2) the spouse's property is liable for any of the at-risk client's debts under state law, the non-at-risk spouse may also be forced into bankruptcy.

Planning Pointer. The family limited partnership should be used for business or investment assets. It should not be used for personal assets because partnerships must generally carry on a business.

Planning Pointer. The planner should consider using an employment contract between the family limited partnership and the at-risk client. Under such an agreement, the partnership would employ the at-risk client to manage the partnership's assets or business. Alternatively, the planner should consider using a corporate general partner whose stock is held by non-at-risk members of the at-risk client's family. The corporation could then employ the at-risk client to manage the corporate general partner.

The FLP's general partners will be solely responsible for managing and controlling its activities. Accordingly, the family members chosen should be familiar with the business contained within the FLP and with the needs of the limited partners. Also, the decision of which family members should serve as general partners will be influenced by the original owners of property transferred into the FLP, who often desire to retain control over that property by retaining general partnership interests.

Planning Pointer. Planners should consider the following issues when organizing an FLP:

1. The jurisdiction in which the FLP will be organized[7]

---

[7] *See* § 12.03[A].

2. Formalities required to properly form the FLP[8]
3. Tax provisions that should be included in the FLP operating agreement.[9]

[A] Jurisdiction of Organization

Before forming an FLP, planners must decide in which jurisdiction they will form the FLP. If the FLP will contain an operating business, then the location where that business does business will be a relevant factor. A business doing business in more than one jurisdiction cannot form an FLP in more than one jurisdiction. It must form as a limited partnership in one jurisdiction and qualify to do business as a foreign FLP in the others.

If an FLP may be conducting business in more than one jurisdiction, the decision about where to organize is significant. The law of the jurisdiction of organization generally will govern its internal affairs, including such issues as the substantive rights of the FLP's partners.

Planning Pointer. Among other items, factors the planner should consider when determining which jurisdiction to organize a business include:

1. The location of the business's headquarters
2. Jurisdiction in which the business is doing business
3. Each relevant jurisdiction's substantive partnership law, and the judicial decisions construing such law.

[B] Required Formation Formalities

Generally, to form an FLP, the planner must do the following:

1. Select an FLP name
2. Select a principal office and registered agent
3. File certificate of limited partnership
4. Qualify the business to do business in other jurisdictions that the business operates in besides the jurisdiction of organization
5. Obtain a tax identification number
6. Obtain applicable licenses, permits, and so forth.

---

[8] See § 12.03[B].
[9] See § 12.03[C].

Caution. Failure to follow the statutory requirements for forming a limited partnership may cause the client (purported limited partner) to be subject to the unlimited liability of general partner status. Consequently, the planner must ensure that there is substantial compliance with the applicable statutory formation requirements. The planner should note that, although the Uniform Limited Partnership Act (ULPA) does not expressly mention a partnership agreement, the Revised Uniform Limited Partnership Act (RULPA) does recognize that the basic document in any partnership is the partnership agreement.

First, the planner must select a name for the FLP. Most jurisdictions require that the FLP's name include the words "limited partnership" or the abbreviation "L.P." Also, the FLP's name generally cannot contain any limited partner's name unless that name is also a general partner's name or the FLP's business had been carried on under that name before the limited partner's admission as a limited partner. Finally, the FLP's name cannot be identical to or deceptively similar to the name of any corporation or limited partnership organized or doing business in the jurisdiction in question.

Planning Pointer. Planners should choose several possible FLP names. Then they should make a preliminary informal check by contacting the jurisdiction where the FLP will be organized and each jurisdiction that it will do business in to see whether the chosen names are available. Many jurisdictions allow a business that will be forming as an FLP to reserve a name for a limited time. Therefore, once planners select a name and ensure its availability in the applicable jurisdictions, they should immediately take steps to protect the name in those jurisdictions.

Caution. The planner should also check the proposed name against registered federal trademarks, trade or fictitious names, or common-law rights to a particular business name. Such names may receive protection from other law sources (for example, patent law) that the name may infringe upon, thus resulting in liability. The planner should also consider obtaining a trademark for the partnership's name if she believes that it possesses value.

Second, most jurisdictions require planners to select a principal office and registered agent for service of process. Generally, the registered agent must be either an individual resident of the jurisdiction in question, a domestic corporation, or a foreign corporation authorized to do business in that jurisdiction.

Caution. Some jurisdictions require FLPs to obtain their registered agent's consent to serve as registered agent of the partnership. In such jurisdictions, the planner must submit a consent form signed by the registered agent with the certificate of limited partnership.

The ULPA requires that two or more persons who want to form a limited partnership must execute and file a certificate with the appropriate state office, or with the secretary of state, if a RULPA jurisdiction.[10] Such certificate must generally contain the following:

1. The partnership's name[11]
2. The business's character[12]
3. The location of the principal place of business[13]
4. Each member's name and place of residence and whether such member is a general or limited partner[14]
5. The term for which the partnership is to exist[15]
6. The amount of cash and a description of and the agreed value of the other property contributed by each limited partner[16]
7. The additional contributions, if any, each limited partner agrees to make and the times they will make such contributions[17]
8. The time, if agreed on, when the contribution of each limited partner will be returned[18]
9. The share of the profits or the other compensation that each limited partner will receive because of their contributions[19]
10. Any right of a limited partner to substitute an assignee as contributor in her place and the terms and conditions thereof[20]
11. The right, if given, of the partners to admit additional limited partners[21]
12. Any right of one or more limited partners to priority over other limited partners regarding contributions or compensation, and the nature thereof[22]
13. The right, if given, of the remaining general partner or partners to continue the business on the death, retirement, or insanity of a general partner[23]

---

[10] RULPA § 201(a) (1985), 6 U.L.A. 312 (Supp. 1992).
[11] ULPA § 2(l)(a)(1), 6 U.L.A. 568 (1916).
[12] ULPA § 2(l)(a)(11), 6 U.L.A. 568 (1916).
[13] ULPA § 2(l)(a)(111), 6 U.L.A. 568 (1916).
[14] ULPA § 2(l)(a)(IV), 6 U.L.A. 568 (1916).
[15] ULPA § 2(l)(a)(V), 6 U.L.A. 568 (1916).
[16] ULPA § 2(l)(a)(VI), 6 U.L.A. 568 (1916).
[17] ULPA § 2(l)(a)(VII), 6 U.L.A. 568 (1916).
[18] ULPA § 2(l)(a)(VIII), 6 U.L.A. 568 (1916).
[19] ULPA § 2(l)(a)(IX), 6 U.L.A. 568 (1916).
[20] ULPA § 2(l)(a)(X), 6 U.L.A. 568 (1916).
[21] ULPA § 2(l)(a)(XI), 6 U.L.A. 568 (1916).
[22] ULPA § 2(l)(a)(XII), 6 U.L.A. 568 (1916).
[23] ULPA § 2(l)(a)(XIII), 6 U.L.A. 568 (1916).

14. The right, if given, of a limited partner to demand and receive property other than cash in return for her contribution.[24]

The RULPA generally requires the same information as the ULPA, plus the following information:

1. The address of the office and the name and address of the agent for service of process required to be maintained by § 104 of the RULPA[25]
2. Any right of a partner to receive distributions of property, including cash from the limited partnership[26]
3. Any time contingency that will cause the dissolution of the limited partnerships.[27]

Planning Pointer. The certificate should be filed as promptly as possible after the formation of the partnership to minimize the risk of failure to comply substantially with statutory requirements. Furthermore, it may be advisable for the limited partnership agreement to state that no legal entity is formed until the certificate is filed.

Planning Pointer. Even if not required by the statute of the jurisdiction in question, the planner should ensure that the partners execute a partnership agreement. The planner should also ensure that the partnership agreement and the limited partnership certificate are consistent with each other. A limited partnership agreement is located at § 12.03[E]. Generally, from a practical standpoint, the partnership agreement is the most important document the planner will prepare in connection with the FLP's organization.

Fourth, planners must qualify the FLP to do business in foreign jurisdictions in which it does business. The exact procedures for effecting such a qualification differ for each state. Typically, the planner must obtain a certificate of authority from the foreign jurisdiction. Failure to qualify in the foreign jurisdiction can result in various penalties. Consequently, the planner should ensure that the FLP qualifies in each jurisdiction in which it does business.

Fifth, planners must obtain employer identification numbers (EINs) from the IRS. The FLP will use the EIN number in all correspondence with and remittances to the IRS. Planners may obtain EINs in either of two ways. First, they may submit a Form SS-4, Application for Employer Identification Number, to

---

[24] ULPA § 2(l)(a)(XIV), 6 U.L.A. 568 (1916).
[25] RULPA § 201(3) (1976), 6 U.L.A. 312 (Supp. 1992).
[26] RULPA § 201(9) (1976), 6 U.L.A. 312 (Supp. 1992).
[27] RULPA § 201(11) (1976), 6 U.L.A. 312 (Supp. 1992).

the IRS.[28] Second, they may submit the information that goes on a Form SS-4 form over the telephone, by telephoning one of the Tele-TIN numbers listed on the instructions to Form SS-4, and obtain an EIN immediately.

Finally, planners must determine which licenses and permits the FLP must obtain before it commences business. Typically, the FLP or its accountant obtains these licenses, permits, and registrations. However, the planner must verify that they comply with this.

[C] Requisite Tax Provisions for FLP Operating Agreement

When drafting the FLP operating agreement, planners must include certain tax provisions in the agreement. Failure to include such provisions may cause horrible unanticipated consequences.

Drafting Pointer. Planners must include the following tax provisions in their FLP operating agreements:

1. Partnership minimum gain chargeback provision for partnership non-recourse liabilities
2. Partner minimum gain chargeback provision for partner nonrecourse debt
3. Qualified income offset provision
4. Special allocation provision.

[1] Partnership Minimum Gain

Partnership agreements must contain a partnership minimum gain chargeback provision in order for their nonrecourse allocations to fall within the Treas. Reg. Section 1.704-1(b) regulatory safe harbor. Form 12-5 in § 12.03[E] contains a minimum gain chargeback provision in Article VII, Section 3. It provides the following:

3. MINIMUM GAIN CHARGEBACK:

   a. If the Partnership experiences a net decrease in Partnership Minimum Gain for a fiscal year of the Partnership, then it shall allocate items of income and gain for such year (and if necessary for subsequent years) in accordance with Reg. § 1.704-2 (f) to each Partner.
   b. Partnership Minimum Gain shall be determined in accordance with and have the meaning ascribed to the term "Partnership Minimum Gain" by Reg. § 1.704-2(d).

---

[28] *See* Chapter 15, Form 15-1.

    c. A Partner's share of Partnership Minimum Gain shall be determined in accordance with and have the meaning ascribed to the term "Share of Partnership Minimum Gain" by Reg. § 1.704-2(g).

To understand the partnership minimum gain chargeback provision, planners must first understand what partnership nonrecourse liabilities are. Generally, partnership nonrecourse liabilities are either partnership nonrecourse debts that partners do not guarantee or loans that partners do not make to the partnership. For this purpose, partnership nonrecourse debt is debt for which no partner bears the economic risk of loss.[29]

Partnership minimum gain occurs whenever a partnership asset secures a nonrecourse liability that exceeds the partnership's adjusted basis in that asset. Partnership minimum gain is important because it will either (1) determine the partnership nonrecourse deductions and distributions of nonrecourse liability proceeds, or (2) be instrumental when calculating the partnership minimum gain chargeback amount.

Each year the partnership calculates its partnership minimum gain by assuming that it disposes of the asset solely for the cancellation of the nonrecourse debt that it secures. The partnership then calculates gain by comparing the amount realized on the deemed sale to the asset's adjusted tax basis.

Caution. Assets may produce partnership minimum gain increases, thus adding to the partnership's nonrecourse deductions, although such assets do not produce any deductions.[30]

If one asset secures more than one liability, the partnership first allocates the basis of such assets to the debt of highest priority in an amount equal to the principal amount of such debt. The partnership then allocates the remaining basis to the junior liability.[31]

EXAMPLE 12-6

Clausewitz and Brooke form a partnership, the CB Partnership, to build military helicopters. It purchases Blackacre, with the intent to build a helicopter factory on Blackacre. The CB Partnership's basis in Blackacre equals $1,100,000 which secures a nonrecourse liability of $1,000,000 and a recourse of obligation of $ 200,000. If the nonrecourse debt is superior to the recourse debt, there is no minimum gain with respect to the asset. If the CB partnerships sells Blackacre for $1,000,000, it would recognize a loss of $100,000 on the sale.

---

[29] Treas. Reg. §§ 1.704-2(b)(3), 1.752-1(a)(2).
[30] Treas. Reg. § 1.704-2(m), Ex. 4 (partnership minimum gain attributable to raw land).
[31] Treas. Reg. § 1.704-2(d)(2).

EXAMPLE 12-7

Same facts as Example 12-6, except that the recourse obligation is superior to the nonrecourse debt. Here the partnership has minimum gain that equals $100,000. This results because the recourse obligation absorbs the first $200,000 of basis. This leaves only $900,000 of basis to allocate to $1,000,000 of gain on the nonrecourse debt. Here, if the CB Partnership sold Blackacre for $1,000,000, this sale would generate $100,000 of minimum gain.

If an asset secures more than one liability of equal rank, Treas. Reg. Section 1.704-2(d)(2) requires the partnership to allocate the basis among the liabilities in proportion to their outstanding principal balances. If the book value and the adjusted tax basis of an asset subject to nonrecourse debt are not equal, the partnership must use the book value to calculate partnership minimum gain.[32]

Planning Pointer. Planners must pay attention to the partners' shares of partnership minimum gain for the following reasons:

1. A partner's share of decreases in partnership minimum gain constitutes an important component of the minimum gain chargeback provision.
2. Partners must add their shares of partnership minimum gain to any amounts that they are obligated to contribute to satisfy their deficit capital accounts for purposes of the Treas. Reg. Section 1.7041(b)(2)(ii)(d) alternate substantial economic effect test.

Partners calculate their shares of partnership minimum gain as follows:

+ the cumulative nonrecourse deductions allocated to the partner and its predecessors in interest up to that time
+ the aggregate distributions to the partner and its predecessors in interest of nonrecourse liability proceeds up to that time
− the partner's aggregate share and the shares of its predecessors in interest of any decreases in minimum gain up to that time.[33]

---

[32] *See* Treas. Reg. § 1.704-2(m), Ex. 3(iv).

[33] The partner's share equals the net decrease in partnership minimum gain multiplied by a fraction, the numerator of which is its partnership minimum gain as of the close of the prior year, and the denominator of which is the total partnership minimum gain as of the close of such year. If the decrease in partnership minimum gain is attributable to a revaluation of partnership assets, its share of the decrease equals the increase in its capital account attributable to the revaluation. Treas. Reg. § 1.7042(g)(2).

  — the partner's and its predecessor in interest's shares of any decreases in minimum gain resulting from a revaluation of the partnership's assets, notwithstanding that such decreases were added back in determining the net increase or decrease in minimum gain for the year of revaluation.[34]

  = the partner's share of partnership minimum gain

Minimum gain chargeback provisions provide that whenever partnership minimum gain for the year decreases, the partnership must allocate items of income or gain among the partners. The partnership must make such allocation before it allocates other items for the year. Also, this allocation must equal each partner's share of the net decrease in partnership minimum gain during the year.[35]

Finally, Treas. Reg. Section 1.704-2(f)(2) provides two primary exceptions to the chargeback requirement. First, it does not subject partners to chargeback to the extent that a guarantee, refinancing, or other change in a debt instrument that causes such debt instrument to become partially or wholly recourse debt or partner nonrecourse debt, when such partners bear the economic risk of loss for the changed liability, causes their share of the net decrease in partnership minimum gain.[36] Second, Treas. Reg. Section 1.704-2(f)(3) does not subject partners to chargeback to the extent that their share of the decrease in partnership minimum gain is attributable to a contribution of capital by such partners that is used to repay the nonrecourse liability or to improve the property.[37]

[2] Partner Minimum Gain

Partnership agreements must also contain a minimum gain chargeback provision for partner nonrecourse debt in order for nonrecourse allocations to come within the Treas. Reg. Section 1.7041(b) regulatory safe harbor. Form 12-5 in § 12.03[E] contains a partner minimum gain provision in Article VII, Section 4. It provides the following:

 4. NONRECOURSE DEBT OF THE PARTNERSHIP WHERE A PARTNER BEARS THE ECONOMIC RISK OF LOSS:

  a. The Partnership shall allocate its losses, deductions, or I.R.C. § 705(a)(2)(b) expenditures (expenditures that are not deductible and are not added to capital accounts) that are attributable to a particular Partner's Nonrecourse Liability (hereinafter called "Partner Nonrecourse Deductions") to the Partner that bears the economic risk of loss of the liability.

---

[34] Treas. Reg. § 1.704-2(g)(1).
[35] Treas. Reg. § 1.704-2(f)(1).
[36] Treas. Reg. § 1.704-2(f)(2).
[37] Treas. Reg. § 1.704-2(f)(3).

b. The amount of Partner Nonrecourse Deductions with respect to Partner Nonrecourse Debt for any year equals (1) the net increase during the year in Minimum Gain attributable to the Partner Nonrecourse Debt (hereinafter referred to as "Partner Nonrecourse Debt Minimum Gain"), (2) reduced (but not below zero) by proceeds of the liability distributed during the year to the Partner bearing the economic risk of loss for the liability that are both attributable to the liability and allocable to an increase in the Partner Nonrecourse Debt Minimum Gain.

c. If during a Partnership taxable year a net decrease in Partner Nonrecourse Debt Minimum Gain occurs, then the Partnership must allocate items of income and gain for the year (and, if necessary, for succeeding years) to any Partner with a share of that Partner Nonrecourse Debt Minimum Gain as of the beginning of the year in an amount that equals that Partner's share of the net decrease in the Partner Nonrecourse Debt Minimum Gain. Notwithstanding the foregoing, a Partner shall not be subject to the Minimum Gain Chargeback in this Section 4.c in the following circumstances:

  i. To the extent the net decrease in Partner Nonrecourse Debt Minimum Gain arises because the liability ceases to be Partner Nonrecourse Debt due to a conversion, refinancing, or other change in the debt instrument that causes it to become partially or wholly a Nonrecourse Liability.

     The Partnership shall add to the Partner's share of Partnership Minimum Gain the amount that would otherwise be subject to the Partner Nonrecourse Debt Minimum Gain Chargeback.

  ii. To the extent the Partner's share of the net decrease in Partner Nonrecourse Debt Minimum Gain is caused by a guarantee, refinancing, or other change in the debt instrument causing it to become partially or wholly recourse debt and the Partner bears the economic risk of loss for the newly guaranteed, refinanced, or otherwise changed liability.

  iii. To the extent the Partner contributes capital to the Partnership that the Partnership uses to repay the Partner Nonrecourse Liability or to increase the basis of the property subject to the Partner Nonrecourse Liability, and the Partner's share of the net decrease in Partner Nonrecourse Debt Minimum Gain results from the repayment or the increase to the property's basis.

d. Partner Nonrecourse Liability means any nonrecourse liability for which a Partner or related person (within the meaning of Reg. § 1.752-4(b)) bears the economic risk of loss. For this purpose, a Partner bears the economic risk except as otherwise provided in Reg. § 1.752-2, to the extent that, if the Partnership is constructively liquidated, the Partner or related person would be obligated to make a payment to any person (or a contribution to the Partnership) because that liability becomes due and payable and the Partner or related person would not be entitled to reimbursement from another Partner or person that is a related person to another Partner. For this purpose, all of the following events shall be deemed to occur simultaneously upon such a constructive liquidation:

   i.   All of the Partnership's liabilities become payable in full;

   ii.   With the exception of property contributed to secure a Partnership liability, all of the Partnership's assets, including cash, have a value of zero;

   iii.   The Partnership disposes of all of its property in a fully taxable transaction for no consideration (except relief from liabilities for which the creditor's right to repayment is limited solely to one or more assets of the Partnership);

   iv.   All items of income, gain, loss, or deduction are allocated among the Partners; and

   v.   The Partnership liquidates.

      All interpretations of the foregoing shall be in accordance with Reg. § 1.752-2.

e. Determinations under this section shall be made in a manner consistent with Section 3:

   i.   The Partnership shall determine what Partnership items constitute the Partner nonrecourse deductions with respect to a Partner Nonrecourse Debt in a manner consistent with the determination of Nonrecourse Deductions.

   ii.   The Partnership shall determine Partner Nonrecourse Debt Minimum Gain and the net increase or decrease in Partner Nonrecourse Debt Minimum Gain in a manner consistent with the determination of Partnership Minimum Gain and net increase or decrease in Partnership Minimum Gain.

   iii.   The Partnership shall determine the Partner's share of the net decrease in Partner Nonrecourse Debt Minimum Gain in a manner consistent with the determination of a Partner's share of net decrease in Partnership Minimum Gain.

   iv.   The Partnership shall determine a Partner's share of Partner Nonrecourse Debt Minimum Gain at the end of any year in a manner consistent with the determination of a Partner's share of Partner Minimum Gain. The Partnership shall determine distributions of the proceeds of Partner Nonrecourse Debt consistently with it determination of distribution of proceeds of Partnership Nonrecourse Debt.

f.   It is intended that the provisions of this section are consistent with Reg. § 1.704-2(i), and to the extent inconsistent, the Regulations should apply.

To understand the partner minimum gain provision, planners must first understand what constitutes partner nonrecourse debt. Generally, partner nonrecourse debt is debt that is nonrecourse as to the partnership and the partners in general, but for which a partner or related person bears the economic risk of loss under Treas. Reg. Section 1.752-2.[38] Such a situation could occur because the partner or related person is the creditor or a guarantor of the debt.[39]

Treasury Regulations require the partnership to allocate deductions attributable to partner nonrecourse debt to the partner who bears the economic risk of loss with respect to the debt.[40] Consequently, the partnership must allocate the related minimum gain chargeback to the partner who bears the economic risk of loss with respect to a particular debt.

Partner nonrecourse debt is not nonrecourse debt for purposes of the general nonrecourse rules discussed. Consequently, each partner nonrecourse debt generates its own increase in minimum gain ("partner nonrecourse debt minimum gain"). This, in turn, determines partner nonrecourse deductions and distributions of nonrecourse liability proceeds allocable to the partner nonrecourse debt.[41] Treas. Reg. Section 1.704-2(i)(4) provides a mirror minimum gain chargeback rule to the rule for partnership nonrecourse debt for partner nonrecourse debt. A reduction in minimum gain with respect to partner nonrecourse debt triggers this rule. However, unlike the general minimum gain chargeback rule, the partner nonrecourse debt minimum gain chargeback with respect to each partner nonrecourse debt is triggered only by a reduction in the minimum gain attributable to that particular partner nonrecourse debt, rather than by a reduction in aggregate minimum gain.[42]

Treas. Reg. Section 1.704-2(j) controls the interaction between the two minimum gain chargeback rules. It provides that partnership minimum gain chargeback consists first of gain from the disposition of property subject to nonrecourse liabilities and then of a pro rata portion of the partnership's other items of income and gain for the year. This second category of items includes gain from dispositions of property subject to partner nonrecourse debt only to the extent the gain is not used to satisfy a partner nonrecourse debt minimum gain chargeback. A mirror rule applies for gain from the disposition of property subject to nonrecourse liabilities for a partner nonrecourse debt minimum gain chargeback.

[3] Qualified Income Offset

Allocations of partnership items of income, gains, losses, deductions, and credits may have economic effect according to Code Section 704(b) absent a deficit restoration obligation (or if the partner is obligated to restore only a limited dollar amount of her deficit capital account balance), if the partnership agreement contains a "qualified income offset" provision. Form 12-5 in § 12.03[E]

---

[38] Treas. Reg. § 1.704-2(b)(4).
[39] Treas. Reg. § 1.704-2(b)(4).
[40] Treas. Reg. § 1.704-2(i).
[41] Treas. Reg. § 1.704-2(i)(2), (6).
[42] Treas. Reg. § 1.704-2(i)(4).

contains a qualified income offset provision in Article VII, Section 2. It provides the following:

> 2. QUALIFIED INCOME OFFSET: If a Partner unexpectedly receives an adjustment, allocation, or distribution described in Regulation § 1.704-1(b)(2)(ii)(d)(4), (5), or (6), then the Partnership shall allocate items of income and gain to any Partner with a deficit capital account in an amount and manner sufficient to eliminate such deficit balance as quickly as possible.

The qualified income offset must require that, in the event of any unexpected distribution (or adjustment or allocation to capital accounts in certain circumstances), there must be an allocation of income and gain to eliminate the resulting capital account deficit "as quickly as possible."[43]

[4] Special Allocation Provisions

Planners must include a provision that will cause the partnership agreement to adhere to Code Section 704(c) and eliminate any book-tax differences with respect to contributed properties. Form 12-5 in § 12.03[E] contains such a provision that provides for tax allocations with respect to property contributions in Article VII, Section 5. It provides the following:

> 5. TAX ALLOCATIONS WITH RESPECT TO PROPERTY CONTRIBUTIONS:
>
>   a. The Partnership shall allocate income, gain, loss, and deductions with respect to any property contributed to the Partnership's capital, solely for tax purposes, among the Partners so as to take account of any variation between the adjusted basis of such property to the Partnership for federal income tax purposes and its fair market value at time of contribution in accordance with Section 704(c) of the Code and the Treasury Regulations thereunder. Any property contributed to the Partnership when its fair market value differs from its tax basis shall be known as "Section 704(c) Property."
>
>   b. When the Partnership disposes of Section 704(c) Property, it shall allocate any built-in gain or loss at the time of contribution to the contributing Partner. If the Partnership only disposes of part of Section 704(c) Property, it shall allocate a proportionate part of any built-in gain or loss to the contributing Partner.
>
>   c. If Section 704(c) Property is subject to amortization, depletion, depreciation, or other cost recovery, the Partnership shall first allocate such deduction to the noncontributing Partners to the extent of the allocation they would have received if the property's basis equaled its fair market value upon contribution. If the Section 704(c) Property does not produce enough amortization, depletion, depreciation, or other cost recovery

---

[43] Treas. Reg. § 1.704-1(b)(2)(ii)(d).

deduction to satisfy the requirement of the preceding sentence, the Partnership shall allocate additional deductions to the noncontributing Partners to result in such deduction. To the extent the Partnership does not have sufficient deductions to result in such an allocation, it shall allocate items of income from the noncontributing Partners to the contributing Partner. If the Partnership has neither sufficient items of deductions nor items of income to result in such an allocation, it shall make an allocation in the next succeeding taxable year to accomplish such allocation. Only any remaining deduction may then be allocated to the contributing Partner.

d. If the Partnership disposes of Section 704(c) Property in a transaction in which it does not recognize gain or loss, then it shall treat any substituted basis property as Section 704(c) Property.

e. All references to contributing Partner in this section shall include any contributing Partner's donee.

[D] Limited Partnership Certificate

Please see Form 12-4, Family Limited Partnership Certificate, on the accompanying CD.

[E] Family Limited Partnership Agreement

Please see Form 12-5, Limited Partnership Agreement, on the accompanying CD.

§12.04 LIMITED LIABILITY PARTNERSHIPS

Some jurisdictions have modified their partnership statutes to provide for limited liability partnerships (LLPs).[1] Generally, LLP partners are not liable for the partnership's debts and obligations arising from negligence, wrongful acts, or misconduct committed (1) while the partnership constitutes a registered LLP, and (2) in the course of partnership business by another partner or an employee, agent, or representative of the partnership.[2] However, an LLP will not limit an LLP partner's liability for his own negligence, wrongful acts, or misconduct, or that of any person under the partner's direct supervision and control.[3] Also, some LLP statutes explicitly provide that LLP provisions do not affect the liability of the partnership itself for partnership debts, and that LLP partners

§12.04 [1] See, e.g., Del. Code Ann. tit. 6, §§1502(6), 1515(b)-(d), 1544-1547 (1993); D.C. Code Ann. §§41-101(a), 41-105, 41-143 to 43-148 (Supp. 1994).

[2] See, e.g., Del. Code Ann. tit, 6, §1515(b) (1993); D.C. Code Ann. §41-146(a) (Supp. 1994).

[3] See, e.g., Del. Code Ann. tit. 6, §1515(c) (1993); D.C. Code Ann. §41-146(a) (Supp. 1994).

remain jointly liable for partnership debts and obligations other than those specified under the LLP limited liability provisions.[4]

Generally, a partnership must file an application with the appropriate government office to become a registered LLP.[5] An example of such an application is located at § 12.04[A]. Usually, the partnership must file an application or renewal application stating the partnership's name, the address of its principal office (or, if its principal office is out of state, the address of its registered office and the name and address of its registered agent for service of process), the number of partners, a brief statement of the business in which the partnership engages, and that the partnership is thereby applying for LLP status or renewal." Generally, the application or renewal application must be executed by a majority in interest of the partners or by one or more partners who are authorized to execute such applications.[6]

Typically, registration as an LLP will be effective for one year from the application or renewal application filing date unless the LLP voluntarily withdraws its registration by filing a written withdrawal notice executed by a majority in interest of the partners or by one or more partners who are authorized to execute such withdrawals.[7] The LLP provisions often provide for fees to accompany the application and renewal applications. They also provide for due dates for renewal applications that occur each year, approximately on the anniversary date of the original application.[8]

Limited liability partnership statutes typically require registered LLPs to include the words "Registered Limited Liability Partnership[9] or "LLP" as the last words or letters of its name.[10] More importantly, LLP statutes require registered LLPs to carry a minimum amount of liability insurance. The Delaware statute requires registered LLPs to carry at least $1 million of liability insurance covering the types of liability that are limited by the Delaware LLP provisions.[11] If the LLP's compliance with this requirement is challenged during litigation, the court will resolve the issue, and the partner claiming the benefit of the LLP provision bears the burden of proof of compliance.[12] However, if the registered LLP is in compliance with this insurance requirement, this insurance requirement cannot be made known to the jury when it determines the issue of liability for or the extent of the debt or obligation or damages in question.[13] The LLP may comply with the insurance requirement by providing $1 million of funds, specifically designated and segregated for the satisfaction of judgments against the LLP or its partners based on the kinds of acts for which the LLP provisions limit liability, by deposit in trust or in bank escrow of cash, bank certificates of

---

[4] See, e.g., D.C. Code Ann. § 41-146(a) (Supp. 1994).

[5] See, e.g., Del. Code Ann. tit. 6, § 1544 (1993); D.C. Code Ann. § 41-143 (Supp. 1994).

[6] See, e.g., Del. Code Ann. tit. 6, § 1544(a) (1993); D.C. Code Ann. § 41-143(a) (Supp. 1994).

[7] See, e.g., Del. Code Ann. tit. 6, § 1544(b) (1993); D.C. Code Ann. § 41-143(b) (Supp. 1994).

[8] See, e.g., Del. Code Ann. tit. 6, § 1544(e) (1993); D.C. Code Ann. § 41-143(d) (Supp. 1994).

[9] See e.g., Del. Code Ann. tit. 6, § 1544(c), (e) (1993); D.C. Code Ann. § 41-143(d), (f) (Supp. 1994).

[10] Del. Code Ann. tit. 69 § 1545 (1993); D.C. Code Ann. § 41-144 (Supp. 1994).

[11] Del. Code Ann. tit. 6, § 1545(a) (1993).

[12] Del. Code Ann. tit. 6, § 1545(b) (1993).

[13] Del. Code Ann. tit. 6, § 1545(c) (1993).

deposit, or U.S. Treasury obligations, or by bank letter of credit or insurance company bond.[14] The District of Columbia provision requires registered LLPs to carry liability insurance in the amount of coverage of either (1) at least $100,000 of liability insurance covering the types of liability that are limited by the D.C. LLP provisions, or (2) coverage in a minimum amount of not less than the amount carried by the individual partner carrying the greatest amount of individual liability insurance, whichever is greater.[15] Like its Delaware counterpart, the D.C. LLP statute provides that if the registered LLP is in compliance with this insurance requirement, this insurance requirement cannot be made known to the jury when it determines the issue of liability for or the extent of the debt or obligation or damages in question.[16]

Finally, both the Delaware and the D.C. statutes include provisions that address the applicability of their LLP provisions to foreign and interstate commerce. Specifically, both the Delaware and D.C. LLP statutes allow LLPs organized under their laws to conduct business, carry out operations, and exercise their powers in any jurisdiction.[17] Also, both statutes provide that their laws will govern LLPs operating in other jurisdictions.[18] Finally, the District of Columbia provides that foreign LLPs may conduct business in D.C. upon filing an appropriate application, and that the laws of the state or jurisdiction under which that LLP was organized will control its organization, internal affairs, and the liability of its partners.[19] Furthermore, it provides that foreign registered LLPs cannot be prohibited from doing business in the District of Columbia because of any difference between the laws of its state of organization and D.C.'s laws.[20]

[A] *LIMITED LIABILITY PARTNERSHIP APPLICATION*

Please see Form 12-6, Sample Application of Limited Liability Partnership, on the accompanying CD.

§ 12.05 LIMITED LIABILITY COMPANIES

Generally, when available and properly used, limited liability companies (LLCs) offer advantages of both corporations and partnerships.[1] First, they offer the limited liability of corporations. Second, they offer the tax benefits of

---

[14] Del. Code Ann. tit. 6, § 1545(c) (1993).

[15] D.C. Code Ann. § 41-145(a) (Supp. 1994).

[16] D.C. Code Ann. § 41-145(b) (Supp. 1994).

[17] Del. Code Ann. tit. 6, § 1547(a) (1993); D.C. Code Ann. § 41-148(a) (Supp. 1994).

[18] Del. Code Ann. tit. 6, § 1547(b) (1993); D.C. Code Ann. § 41-148(b)-(c) (Supp. 1994).

[19] D.C. Code Ann. § 41-147 (Supp. 1994).

[20] D.C. Code Ann. § 41-147 (Supp. 1994).

§ 12.05 [1] The planner should refer to Chapters 3 and 4, which discuss the substantive law and planning uses of LLCs in greater detail.

partnerships. In particular, they do not involve the double taxation aspects of corporations. Third, they are more advantageous than limited partnerships because they do not require a general partner subject to unlimited liability. Additionally, LLC members may participate in the entity's control while receiving the benefits of limited liability. In contrast, limited partners cannot participate in limited partnership control without risking loss of limited liability. Fourth, LLCs offer several advantages over S corporations, which have tax restrictions on special allocations of income and loss and the number and type of shareholders, among other things.

> **Caution.** Because limited liability company statutes do not exist in all states and are not uniform, the planner must analyze limited liability separately for intrastate and interstate transactions.

> **Planning Pointer.** The planner should consider the following issues when organizing and creating an LLC (discussed in the following sections):
>
> 1. Formalities that applicable state law requires for the LLC's formation[2]
> 2. Preparation of an LLC operating agreement[3]
> 3. Use of an LLC by professionals[4]
> 4. Requirements that the planner must ensure the LLC satisfies to qualify as a partnership for federal income tax purposes[5]
> 5. Various other tax issues and elections[6]

[A]   LLC Formation Formalities

The formalities that applicable state law requires for the LLC's formation will vary from state to state. Consequently, the planner must carefully check the applicable state statute.

> **Caution.** The planner's failure to properly form the LLC will cause its members to be jointly and severally liable for its debts and liabilities under many state statutes. Consequently, the planner must carefully form the LLC.

---

[2] *See* § 12.05[A].
[3] *See* § 12.05[D].
[4] *See* § 12.05[E].
[5] *See* § 12.05[F].
[6] *See* § 12.05[G].

Typically, the primary formalities that the planner must fulfill to form an LLC include the following:

1. File articles of organization with the proper state office[7]
2. Give the newly formed LLC a proper name
3. Ensure that the LLC's business falls within those types of businesses the state statute allows to form as an LLC
4. Execute an operating agreement.

[B] LLC Articles of Organization

First, the planner must prepare articles of organization and ensure that the LLC organizer executes and files the articles with the appropriate state office.[8] Most states require at least two organizers. Also, states typically require the articles of organization to include at least some of the following information:

1. The LLC's name
2. The LLC's term or duration
3. The name and address of the LLC's registered agent for service of process, and the registered agent's consent to being named as such
4. The purpose for which the organizers are forming the LLC
5. The LLC's principal place of business
6. A description of the property and cash contributed to the LLC, along with the fair market value of such property and cash
7. The terms and conditions of the admission of additional LLC members
8. The right, if the LLC provides for it, for the remaining LLC members to continue the LLC's business on any member's death, retirement, resignation, expulsion, bankruptcy, or dissolution, or on the occurrence of any other event that terminates the continued membership of an LLC member
9. Whether managers will manage the LLC, and if so, their names and addresses. Alternatively, if the members will manage the LLC, the names and addresses of LLC members who will manage the company.

The exact time the LLC becomes formed varies depending on the applicable state statute. For example, in Colorado an LLC is formed upon the filing of the LLC's articles of organization with the applicable state office.[9] Conversely, in other states, such as Florida, the state does not consider the LLC formed until it issues a certificate of formation.[10]

---

[7] See § 12.05[B].
[8] See § 3.05[G][1].
[9] See, e.g., Colo. Rev. Stat. § 7-80-207 (1990).
[10] See, e.g., Fla. Stat. Ann. § 608.409 (West 1986).

[C] LLC Name

Second, the planner must give the LLC a proper name. Most statutes require the LLC to include in its name the words, "Limited Liability Company," "LLC," "L.L.C.," or some similar words that indicate the entity operates as an LLC. Also, similar to corporations, LLC statutes generally preclude LLCs from using a name that is identical or confusingly similar to another LLC's name. In some jurisdictions, if the LLC is a professional LLC, it must contain the words "Professional Limited Liability Company," "P.L.L.C.," or a similar term.[11] Also, many jurisdictions allow the LLC's organizers to reserve a name before they file the LLC's articles of organization.[12]

The LLC's organizers must also ensure that the LLC's business falls within those types of businesses that the applicable state statute allows to form as an LLC. Types of businesses that LLC statutes may preclude LLCs forming to do business as, include the following:

1. Unlawful activities
2. Professional practices, such as law or accounting practices
3. Banking
4. Insurance.

[D] LLC Operating Agreement

While generally not required for the LLC's formation, the planner should always ensure that the LLC's members execute an operating agreement. This will constitute the LLC's primary governing document. Limited liability company operating agreements should generally provide, among other things, the amount and timing of member contributions, member distribution rights, procedures for admission of new members, provisions concerning the LLC's management structure, and LLC members' dissolution rights.

> **Planning Pointer.** The planner should always ensure that LLC members execute a written operating agreement. The LLC members may use such an agreement to tailor the LLC's management structure to their needs. Also, they may use it to fill gaps in the statute's management provisions to reduce the possibility of future disputes or other problems. Finally, because the operating agreement is not a public document, using it as a vehicle for management provisions provides privacy for the members about their management structure.

---

[11] *See, e.g.,* D.C. Code Ann. § 29-1304(a).
[12] *See, e.g.,* D.C. Code Ann. § 29-1305.

Drafting Pointer. The planner must ensure that the LLC's operating agreement and its articles of organization are consistent with each other. Also, the planner must ensure the operating agreement is written, even when not required by the applicable state statute.

Drafting Pointer. The planner should generally err on the side of greater detail when drafting an LLC operating agreement. This stems from the fact that law surrounding LLCs is relatively new and the planner should provide for gaps the applicable law does not cover to avoid uncertainty.

Caution. The planner must tailor the LLC operating agreement to the applicable state statute. The planner must ensure that the operating agreement satisfies the applicable state statute. He should carefully review the applicable statute and use it as a drafting checklist to ensure that the LLC operating agreement covers all of the applicable statutory requirements. Among other things, the planner's LLC operating agreement should deal with the following:

1. The LLC's name, business purposes, term of existence, place of business, and its registered agent and office for service of process
2. Who will manage the LLC (its members or managers), how the managing members or managers will be selected, what their rights and powers will be, what their duties or obligations will be, what standard of care will be applied to them, and how the LLC will compensate them. If the LLC will indemnify them, the agreement should detail in what amount and under what circumstances
3. Who the members will be and what their addresses are, what their rights will be, and provisions relating to conflicts of interest
4. The registration of LLC interests under federal and state securities laws or the qualification of such interests under exemptions from such registration requirements
5. Initial member contributions, additional member contributions, and a member's failure to honor his obligations to the LLC
6. Allocations of profits and losses among members, LLC distributions, the maintenance of LLC capital accounts, and the accounting method the LLC may use
7. Transfers and assignments of member interests, and the rights of assignees and transferees
8. The LLC's termination and dissolution, including what events cause such a dissolution, what the effect of such a dissolution will be, and how the LLC will distribute its assets on dissolution

9. The operating agreement's amendment
10. Various tax issues, including who the tax matters partner will be and who will be authorized to make various tax elections
11. Partnership tax provisions.[13]

[E] Professional LLCs

Professionals organizing to do business as an LLC will have special concerns. First, the planner should determine whether the applicable state statute contains separate provisions for professionals. Some jurisdictions, such as Virginia, provide separate statutory provisions for professional LLCs. Alternatively, other jurisdictions do not contain separate statutory provisions, but still have special provisions that apply to professional LLCs. In any event, the planner must determine whether any special provisions apply to a professional LLC, and if so, what their requirements are, and what their impact will be.

Second, the planner must determine whether the applicable state statute allows the profession in question to organize as an LLC. For example, Oregon and California prohibit law firms from operating as LLCs. Conversely, the District of Columbia LLC statute expressly allows professionals to organize as LLCs.[14]

Also, the planner must examine whether the particular profession in question's applicable professional regulatory authority allows its members to use the LLC form. In this regard, accountants generally may use LLCs. Specifically, the AICPA Code of Professional Conduct allows accounting firms to practice in any organizational form permitted under state law, including LLCs.[15] On the other hand, the legal profession has not fully resolved this issue. The American Bar Association has not considered whether law firms may organize as LLCs. Although some state bar associations have considered this issue, they have reached different conclusions.

[F] Tax Classification

[1] In General

On April 3, 1995, the IRS published Notice 95-14,[16] in which it announced that it was considering simplifying the classification regulations to allow taxpayers to treat unincorporated businesses as partnerships or as corporations on an elective basis. Commentators have called this proposal the "check the box" proposal

---

[13] See § 12.03[C] for a discussion of partnership tax provisions.
[14] D.C. Code Ann. § 29-1301(24) (1994).
[15] See AICPA Code of Professional Conduct, Rule 505.
[16] 1995-1 C.B. 297.

because it would allow taxpayers to check a box on their tax form as to whether they would like the IRS to tax their unincorporated business (e.g., limited liability company) as a corporation or as a partnership. On May 9, 1996, the IRS issued the long-awaited "check the box" proposed regulations. On December 18, 1996, the IRS released the final "check the box" regulations, which were effective beginning January 1, 1997. These regulations dramatically simplify the tax treatment of limited liability entities.

Under prior law, Code Sections 7701(a)(2)-(3) and the existing regulations issued thereunder controlled the classification of entities as either partnerships or corporations. Section 7701(a)(3) defined a *corporation* as including associations, joint stock companies, and insurance companies. Code Section 7701(a)(2) defined a *partnership* as including a syndicate, group, pool, joint venture, or other unincorporated venture. Consequently, the I.R.C. defined partnerships principally as entities other than corporations.

The prior regulations set forth six major characteristics that distinguish corporations from other organizations:

1. Associates
2. An objective to carry on a business and divide the gains therefrom
3. Continuity of life
4. Centralization of management
5. Liability for corporate debts limited to corporate property
6. Free transferability of interests.

In determining whether an entity constituted a corporation or a partnership, the existing regulations ignored characteristics common to both. Thus, they ignore the factors of (1) associates, and (2) an objective to carry on a business and divide the gains therefrom. They also provided that an entity was not taxable as a corporation unless it possessed more corporate than noncorporate characteristics.[17] Consequently, the existing regulations treated entities that failed to possess at least two of the last four factors as partnerships.

The preamble to the proposed regulations notes that, although the existing regulations are based on historical differences between partnerships and corporations under state law, today those differences have all but disappeared with the arrival of new forms of entities, such as limited liability companies.[18] However, changes in entity forms under state law have required both taxpayers and the IRS to expend ever-greater resources on classifying entities for tax purposes. For example, the IRS has issued at least 17 revenue rulings analyzing individual state limited liability company statutes. It has also issued numerous revenue procedures and private letter rulings relating to classification of various business organizations.[19] An additional problem is that many small businesses lack the resources and expertise to achieve the tax classification they want under the current classification regulations. For all these reasons, both the IRS and

---

[17] Treas. Reg. § 301.7701-2(a).

[18] "Preamble to Proposed Treasury Regulations," 61 Fed. Reg. 21,989 (1996).

[19] "Preamble to Proposed Treasury Regulations," 61 Fed. Reg. 21,989 (1996).

commentators have concluded that a simpler classification scheme would be beneficial.

[2] The Final Regulations

[a] Step 1—Is There a Separate Entity for Tax Purposes?

Under the final regulations, the first step in classifying an entity is to determine whether a separate entity exists for federal tax purposes. The final regulations explain that certain joint undertakings, which do not constitute entities under state law, may constitute separate entities for federal tax purposes and vice versa.[20] Also, they retain the current rule that qualified cost-sharing arrangements described in Treas. Reg. Section 1.482-7 are not partnerships for federal tax purposes.[21]

Generally, the regulations provide that joint ventures or other arrangements constitute separate entities for tax purposes if their participants carry on a trade, business, financial operation, or venture and divide the profits therefrom. However, as under existing law, joint undertakings merely to share expenses do not create separate entities for tax purposes.[22]

> **Caution.** Although most entities formed by asset protection planners will constitute separate entities for tax purposes, this step is not entirely an academic exercise. This results because some asset protection planners recommended that all types of assets, including purely personal property, be placed into partnerships to protect those assets. In such cases, if the partnership holds only personal property, the purported entity may not constitute an entity under the proposed regulations.

The proposed regulations allow one-person entities to elect to be recognized or disregarded as entities separate from their owners.[23]

[b] Step 2—If There Is a Separate Entity for Tax Purposes, Is It a Business Entity or a Trust?

Under the final regulations, the second step that planners must follow is to determine whether they should classify the entity as a trust or business entity.[24] Although entities will generally be treated as either a business entity or trust for

---

[20] Treas. Reg. §§ 301.7701-1(a)(2), (3).

[21] Treas. Reg. § 301.7701-1(c).

[22] Treas. Reg. § 301.7701-1(a)(2).

[23] Treas. Reg. § 301.7701-1(a)(4).

[24] Treas. Reg. §§ 301.7701-2, -3, and -4, unless an I.R.C. section provides otherwise (*e.g.*, I.R.C. § 860A(a)).

tax purposes, some types of entities will be treated differently. For example, Real Estate Mortgage Investment Conduits are treated differently under Code Section 860A(a). The final regulations provide that trusts generally do not have associates or an objective to carry on business for profit. The preamble to the proposed regulations states that the determination of whether organizations are classified as trusts for federal tax purposes is intended to remain the same as under current law. Thus, the final regulations treat all entities recognized for tax purposes under the final regulations that do not constitute trusts as "business entities."

In turn, the final regulations treat business entities with two or more members as either corporations or partnerships. They either treat single-member business entities as corporations, or they disregard such entities as separate entities for tax purposes. If the regulations disregard the entity, the single-member owner will treat the business as a sole proprietorship. The reason for this treatment is that a fundamental characteristic of partnerships is the presence of associates. The preamble to the proposed regulations states that the lack of associates precludes classification of single-member entities as partnerships.

[c] Step 3—Is the Entity a Corporation?

[i] Mandatory Corporate Classification

The third step planners must take is to determine whether the final regulations require the entity to be treated as a corporation. If the entity falls into any of the following categories, the regulations require the entity be treated as a corporation for tax purposes:

1. Business entities organized under Federal or State statutes as corporations
2. Business entities organized under State statutes, where such statutes describe or refer to the entity as a joint-stock company or joint-stock association
3. Insurance companies
4. State-chartered banks, where any of their deposits are insured under the Federal Deposit Insurance Act or similar federal statute
5. Business entities that are wholly owned by a State or any political subdivision thereof
6. Business entities taxable as corporations under any I.R.C. provision other than I.R.C. §7701(a)(3)
7. Any of the enumerated foreign entities listed in Exhibit 4-1, unless the foreign entity satisfies each of the following requirements, in which case it will be treated as a partnership: (1) the entity was in existence and claimed to be a partnership on May 8, 1996, and for all prior periods; (2) that classification was relevant on May 8, 1996; (3) no person, including the entity itself, treated the entity as a corporation for federal income tax purposes for the tax year that included May 8, 1996; (4) the entity had a reasonable basis (within the meaning of section 6662) for claiming partnership classification; and (5) neither the entity nor any member has been notified in writing on or before May 8, 1996, that the classification of the entity is under examination (in which case the entity's classification will be determined in the examination).

When the entity does fall into any of these categories, treatment as a corporation is mandatory and the entity cannot elect partnership treatment.

[ii]   Election Available for All Other Entities

Generally, all other business entities, which the proposed regulations do not require to be classified as corporations, may elect classification as either corporations or partnerships for tax purposes. However, as discussed earlier, single-member entities may only elect to be classified as corporations or to be disregarded for tax purposes.[25]

[iii]   Default Provisions—Domestic Business Entities

The final regulations provide two default provisions for entities not required to be classified as corporations when the entity does not make an election. First, the regulations classify entities created after the regulations' effective date that fail to make an election as partnerships. However, if they have only one member, such entities are disregarded as separate entities for tax purposes.[26] Second, entities created before the regulations' effective date will retain the classification that such entities claimed under the existing regulations before the final regulations' effective date. However, single-member entities that claim partnership treatment before the regulations' effective date are disregarded for tax purposes after the effective date of the regulations.[27]

[iv]   Default Provisions—Foreign Business Entities

When the regulations do not require foreign business entities be classified as corporations and such entities do not make an election, the regulations provide three default provisions. First, the regulations classify foreign entities as partnerships if they have two or more members and any member has unlimited liability. Second, the regulations classify foreign entities as corporations if all members have limited liability. Third, the regulations disregard foreign entities as entities separate from their owners if they have a single owner that has unlimited liability.[28]

Foreign entity members have limited liability, for purposes of the final regulations, if they have no personal liability for the entity's debts because of the fact that they are members. This determination is based solely on the statute or law pursuant to which the entity is organized. However, if such underlying statute or law allows the entity to specify in its organizational documents whether the members will have limited liability, the organizational documents may also be relevant. Members also have personal liability for this purpose if the entity's creditors may seek satisfaction of any of their debts against the entity from the member as such. Finally, members have personal liability even if they make an agreement under which another person (without regard to whether such person is a member of the entity) assumes such liability or agrees to indemnify that member for any such liability.

---

[25] Treas. Reg. § 301.7701-3(a).
[26] Treas. Reg. § 301.7701-3(b)(1).
[27] Treas. Reg. § 301.7701-3(b)(3).
[28] Treas. Reg. § 301.7701-3(b)(2).

[d] Method of Making Election

The final regulations provide that an eligible entity may elect to be classified as a type of entity other than as provided under the default rules under Treas. Reg. Section 301.7701-3(b) by filing Form 8832, Entity Classification Election, with the IRS service center indicated on Form 8832. In addition, entities that must file federal tax or information returns for the tax year of the election must attach a copy of their Form 8832 to such return for that year. If they do not have to file returns for that year, a copy of their Form 8832 must be attached to the federal income tax or information return or any direct or indirect owner of the entity for the tax year of the owner that includes the election's effective date. Indirect owners of entities do not have to attach a copy of Form 8832 to their returns if the entity is already filing such a copy with its return.

If an entity, or one of its direct or indirect owners, fails to attach a copy of Form 8832 to its return, this does not invalidate an otherwise valid election. However, such failure may subject the non-filing party to penalties. Such penalties may include any applicable penalties if the federal tax or information returns are inconsistent with the entity's election.

Elections under the regulations become effective on the date that the entity specifies on Form 8832. If it does not specify any date on the election form, the election becomes effective on the date that the entity files Form 8832. However, the specified effective date cannot be more than (a) 75 days before or (b) 12 months after the date that the entity files the election. If the entity erroneously specifies a date outside these periods, the election becomes effective either 75 days before or 12 months after the filing date, whichever is applicable. Finally, if the entity's election form specifies an effective date before January 1, 1997, the election becomes effective as of January 1, 1997.

After electing to change its classification, an entity generally cannot make another election within 60 months after the election's effective date. However, the IRS may permit a new election within this 60-month period if, on the new election date, persons that did not own any interests in the entity on the first election's filing date or effective date, own more than 50 percent of the entity's ownership interests at the effective date of new election.

Under certain circumstances, the regulations treat entities as having made an election. First, the regulations treat entities that the IRS has determined were, or claim to be, exempt from taxation under Code Section 501(a) as having elected association classification. The regulations treat such deemed election as being effective as of the first day for which exemption is claimed or determined to apply. This is true regardless of when the claim or determination is made. Such deemed election remains in effect, unless an election is made after the date the claim for exempt status is withdrawn or rejected or the date the determination of exempt status is revoked. Second, entities that file an election under Code Section 856(c)(1) to be treated as a real estate investment trust are treated as electing association classification. Such elections become effective as of the first day the entity is treated as a real estate investment trust.

EXHIBIT 2-1

Country	Entity Name
Argentina	Sociedad Anonima
Australia	Public Limited Company
Austria	Aktiengesellschaft
Barbados	Limited Company
Belgium	Societe Anonyme
Belize	Public Limited Company
Bolivia	Sociedad Anonima
Brazil	Sociedade Anonima
Canada	Corporation and Company
Chile	Sociedad Anonima
People's Republic of China	Gufen Youxian Gongsi
Republic of China (Taiwan)	Ku-fen Yu-hsien Kung-szu
Colombia	Sociedad Anonima
Costa Rica	Sociedad Anonima
Cyprus	Public Limited Company
Czech Republic	Akciova Spolecnost
Denmark	Aktieselskab
Ecuador	Sociedad Anonima or Compania Anonima
Egypt	Sharikat Al-Mossahamah
El Salvador	Sociedad Anonima
Finland	Julkinen Osakeyhtio/Publikt Aktiebolag
France	Societe Anonyme
Germany	Aktiengesellschaft
Greece	Anonymos Etairia
Guam	Corporation
Guatemala	Sociedad Anonima
Guyana	Public Limited Company
Honduras	Sociedad Anonima
Hong Kong	Public Limited Company
Hungary	Reszvenytarsasag
Iceland	Hlutafelag
India	Public Limited Company
Indonesia	Perseroan Terbuka
Ireland	Public Limited Company
Israel	Public Limited Company
Italy	Societa per Azioni
Jamaica	Public Limited Company
Japan	Kabushiki Kaisha
Kazakstan	Ashyk Aktsionerlik Kogham
Republic of Korea	Chusik Hoesa
Liberia	Corporation
Luxembourg	Societe Anonyme
Malaysia	Berhad
Malta	Public Limited Company

Mexico	Sociedad Anonima
Morocco	Societe Anonyme
Netherlands	Naamloze Vennootschap
New Zealand	Limited Company
Nicaragua	Compania Anonima
Nigeria	Public Limited Company
Northern Mariana Islands	Corporation
Norway	Allment Aksjeselskap
Pakistan	Public Limited Company
Panama	Sociedad Anonima
Paraguay	Sociedad Anonima
Peru	Sociedad Anonima
Philippines	Stock Corporation
Poland	Spolka Akcyjna
Portugal	Sociedade Anonima
Puerto Rico	Corporation
Romania	Societe pe Actiuni
Russia	Otkrytoye Aktsionernoy Obshchestvo
Saudi Arabia	Sharikat Al-Mossahamah
Singapore	Public Limited Company
Slovak Republic	Akciova Spolocnost
South Africa	Public Limited Company
Spain	Sociedad Anonima
Surinam	Naamloze Vennootschap
Sweden	Publika Aktiebolag
Switzerland	Aktiengesellschaft
Thailand	Borisat Chamkad (Mahachon)
Trinidad and Tobago	Limited Company
Tunisia	Societe Anonyme
Turkey	Anonim Sirket
Ukraine	Aktsionerne Tovaristvo Vidkritogo Tipu
United Kingdom	Public Limited Company
United States Virgin Islands	Corporation
Uruguay	Sociedad Anonima
Venezuela	Sociedad Anonima or Compania Anonima

[G] Miscellaneous Tax Issues

[1] Private Letter Ruling Requests

Planning Pointer. Planners should consider obtaining a private letter ruling regarding the taxation of the LLC and its organization. Revenue
Procedure 95-10[29] sets forth the requirements that planners must satisfy

---

[29] 1995-3 I.R.B. 20.

before the IRS will issue a private letter ruling. Among other things, the planner must submit the following information with such a private letter ruling:

1. The LLC's name and taxpayer identification number (if any)
2. The LLC's business
3. Where and when the LLC's articles of organization will be filed
4. The jurisdiction whose law controls the formation and LLC's operation
5. A representation that the LLC has been, and will always be, in conformance with the controlling laws of the domestic or foreign jurisdiction
6. The nature, amount, and timing of capital contributions the LLC members have and will make to the LLC
7. The extent that the LLC's members and managers will participate in its profits and losses, including any possible shift in the profit- and loss-sharing ratios over time
8. A description of the relationships, direct and indirect, between the members and the managers that would suggest that the managers, individually or taken together, may not always act independently of the members (because of individual or aggregate influence or control by the members in their capacity as such over the managers). These relationships include (a) ownership by nonmanager members of 5 percent or more of the stock or other beneficial interests in a manager; (b) control by nonmanager members of 5 percent or more of the voting power in a manager; (c) ownership of 5 percent or more of the stock or other beneficial interests in any manager and in any nonmanager members by the same person or persons acting as a group; and (d) control of 5 percent or more of the voting power in any manager and in any nonmanager members by the same person or persons acting as a group. A person will be considered to own any beneficial interest owned by a related person and is considered to control any voting power controlled by a related person. The IRS will treat persons as related if they bear a relationship to each other specified in Code Section 267(b) or Code Section 707(b)(1)
9. If the planner asserts that the LLC lacks the corporate characteristic of limited liability: (a) a description of the legal arrangements supporting this assertion; (b) a representation of the net worth (based on assets at current fair market value) of the member or members assuming personal liability for all obligations of the LLC ("assuming member"), excluding interests in the LLC held by such members; (c) a description of the assuming members' assets and liabilities arising from transactions with the LLC or with a person related to any member or members under Code Section 267(b) or Code Section 707(b)(1); and (d) a description of all other organizations in which the member or members have an interest
10. If the Internal Revenue Service has issued a revenue ruling on the applicable domestic or foreign law, a discussion of how the revenue ruling applies to the taxpayer's ruling request.

Planners should note that the IRS will respond only to private letter ruling requests for LLCs that have at least two members.[30]

[2] Partnership Allocations

One major advantage of an LLC is that LLC members can specially allocate items of income, loss, deduction, and credits however they choose, if such allocations have substantial economic effect.[31] Generally, the Code will treat allocations as having substantial economic effect if all of the following occur:

1. The LLC maintains capital accounts in the appropriate fashion
2. The LLC operating agreement requires the LLC to make liquidating distributions according to the members' positive capital accounts
3. Either

   a. The LLC operating agreement requires members with negative capital accounts after liquidation to timely restore such deficit account balances to the LLC, or
   b. The LLC agreement contains a "qualified income offset" provision.

Special rules govern allocations when nonrecourse debt is involved. Generally, these rules require that LLCs allocate nonrecourse deductions similarly to allocations attributable to property securing nonrecourse debt, which has substantial economic effect, and that the agreement contains a minimum gain chargeback provision.

> **Drafting Pointer.** When the planner wants to allow for special allocations among the LLC members, the planner should not use a deficit restoration requirement when organizing the LLC. This would expose LLC members to liability to the LLC. Instead, the planner should design the LLC operating agreement to use a "qualified income offset" provision.

[3] Tax Matters Partners

Assuming the LLC is properly structured and classified as a partnership for tax purposes, it will be subject to the unified audit procedures. Consequently, the LLC must have a tax matters partner (TMP). Code Section 6231(a)(7) generally provides that the TMP is the general partner that the partnership properly so designates. If the partnership fails to make such a designation, it provides that the TMP will be the general partner with the largest profits interest. It further

---

[30] Rev. Proc. 95-10, 1995-3 I.R.B. 20.

[31] *See* § 12.03[C] for a discussion of tax provisions planners must include in their LLC operating agreements to take advantage of special allocations for tax purposes.

provides that, if neither of the foregoing rules applies, the IRS will select the TMP.

In the case of an LLC, technically, the IRS will select the TMP. This follows because there are no general partners in an LLC. Consequently, the first two selection rules set forth under Code Section 6231(a)(7) would not appear to apply. The IRS has not indicated whether, in making such a selection, it will follow a designation made for that purpose in the LLC's operating agreement.

Drafting Pointer. The LLC operating agreement should set forth provisions governing the selection of the TMP.

[H]   Articles of Organization

Please see Form 12-7, L.L.C. Articles of Organization, on the accompanying CD.

[I]   Operating Agreement

Please see Form 12-8, L.L.C. Operating Agreement, on the accompanying CD.

[J]   Single Member LLC Operating Agreement

Please see Form 12-9, Single Member LLC Operating Agreement, on the accompanying CD.

§ 12.06   CHECKLIST OF BUSINESS ENTITY FORMATION ISSUES

The planner should use the following checklist to ensure that no critical issue is overlooked in connection with the planner's business entity formation.

Corporations

_____1.   Is the planner forming a corporation?
If yes, the planner must analyze the following issues:

   _____(a)   In what jurisdiction will the business be incorporated?[32] Factors that planners should consider include:

      _____ (i)   The location of the business's headquarters
      _____ (ii) The jurisdiction in which the business is doing business

---

[32] See § 1 2.02[A].

___(iii)   Each relevant jurisdiction's substantive corporate law, and the judicial decisions construing such law.

___(b)   Has the planner completed all of the formalities required to incorporate the business?[33] Such formalities include the following:

    ___ (i)   Select a proper corporate name
    ___ (ii)   File articles of incorporation
    ___(iii) Execute corporate bylaws
    ___(iv) Hold an organizational meeting of directors
    ___ (v)   Qualify the corporation to do business in other jurisdictions that it operates in besides the jurisdiction of incorporation
    ___(vi) Obtain a tax identification number
    ___(vii) Obtain applicable licenses, permits, and so forth.

___(c)   Has the planner considered appropriate optional incorporation formalities, including the following:[34]

    ___ (i)   Preparing and executing a shareholders agreement
    ___ (ii)   Making a Subchapter S election
    ___(iii) Preparing and executing employment agreements with key employees
    ___(iv) Informing the client about corporate formalities.

FLPs

___2.   Is the planner forming a FLP? If yes, the planner must analyze the following issues:

___(a)   In what jurisdiction will the business be organized?[35] Factors that the planner should consider include the following:

    ___ (i)   The location of the business's headquarters
    ___ (ii)   The jurisdiction in which the business is doing business
    ___(iii) Each relevant jurisdiction's substantive corporate law, and the judicial decisions construing such law.

___(b)   Has the planner completed all of the formalities required to organize the FLP?[36] Such formalities include the following:

    ___ (i)   Select an FLP name
    ___ (ii)   Select a principal office and registered agent
    ___(iii) File a certificate of limited partnership

---

[33] *See* § 12.02[B].
[34] *See* § 12.02[C].
[35] *See* § 12.03[A].
[36] *See* § 12.03[B].

    ____(iv) Qualify the business to do business in other jurisdictions that the business operates in besides the jurisdiction of incorporation

    ____(v) Obtain a tax identification number

    ____(vi) Obtain applicable licenses, permits, and so forth.

___(c) Has the planner included the requisite tax provisions in the FLP operating agreement?[37] Such provisions include the following:

    ____ (i) Partnership minimum gain chargeback provisions

    ____ (ii) Partner minimum gain chargeback provisions

    ____(iii) Qualified income offset provision

    ____(iv) Special allocation provisions.

Limited Liability Partnerships

____3. Is the planner forming a limited liability partnership? If yes, the planner must file an application with the appropriate government office.[38]

LLCs

____4. Is the planner forming a limited liability company (LLC)? If yes, the planner must ensure that he has considered the following:

___(a) Has the planner completed all of the formalities required to properly form the LLC?[39] Such formalities include the following:

    ____ (i) File articles of organization with the proper state office

    ____ (ii) Give the newly formed LLC a proper name

    ____(iii) Ensure that the LLC's business falls within those types of businesses that the state allows to form as an LLC

    ____(iv) Execute an operating agreement.

___(b) Has the planner ensured that the LLC's members have executed an operating agreement?[40] Such an agreement typically contains provisions dealing with the following:

    ____ (i) The LLC's name, business purposes, term of existence, place of business, and its registered agent and office for service of process

    ____ (ii) Who will manage the LLC (that is, its members or managers); how the managing members or managers will be selected, what their rights and powers will be, what their duties or obligations will be, what standard of

---

[37] See § 12.03[C].
[38] See § 12.04.
[39] See § 12.05[A].
[40] See § 12.05[D].

care will be applied to them, how the LLC will compensate them; and whether the LLC will indemnify them, and if so, in what amount and under what circumstances

___(iii) Who the members will be and what their addresses are; what their rights will be, and provisions relating to conflicts of interest

___(iv) The registration of LLC interests under federal and state securities laws or the qualification of such interests under exemptions from such registration requirements

___ (v) Initial member contributions, additional member contributions, and a member's failure to honor his or her obligations to the LLC

___(vi) Allocations of profits and losses among members, LLC distributions, the maintenance of LLC capital accounts, and the accounting method the LLC may use

___(vii) Transfers and assignments of member interests, and rights of assignees and transferees

___(viii) The LLC's termination and dissolution, including what events cause such a dissolution, what the effect of such a dissolution will be, and how the LLC will distribute its assets on dissolution

___(ix) The operating agreement's amendment

___ (x) Various tax issues, including who the tax matters partner will be and who will be authorized to make various tax elections

___(xi) Partnership tax provisions.

___(c) Will the LLC be used for a professional practice?[41] If yes, the planner should consider the following issues:

___ (i) Does the applicable jurisdiction have any special provisions that apply to professional LLCs?

___ (ii) Does the applicable state statute allow the profession in question to organize as an LLC?

___(iii) Does the particular profession in question's applicable regulatory authority allow its members to use the LLC form of entity?

___(d) Has the planner considered obtaining a private letter ruling concerning the LLC's tax treatment?[42]

___ (i) This could minimize the planner's liability exposure due to errors causing corporate taxation of the LLC.

[41] *See* § 12.05[E].
[42] *See* § 12.05[G].

      ___(e)   Does the LLC operating agreement include appropriate tax allo-
cation provisions?[43]

      ___(f)   Does the LLC operating agreement set forth provisions governing
the selection of a tax management partner?[44]

---

[43] *See* §§ 12.03[C], 12.05[G].
[44] *See* § 12.05[G].

13

Choice of Domestic Trusts

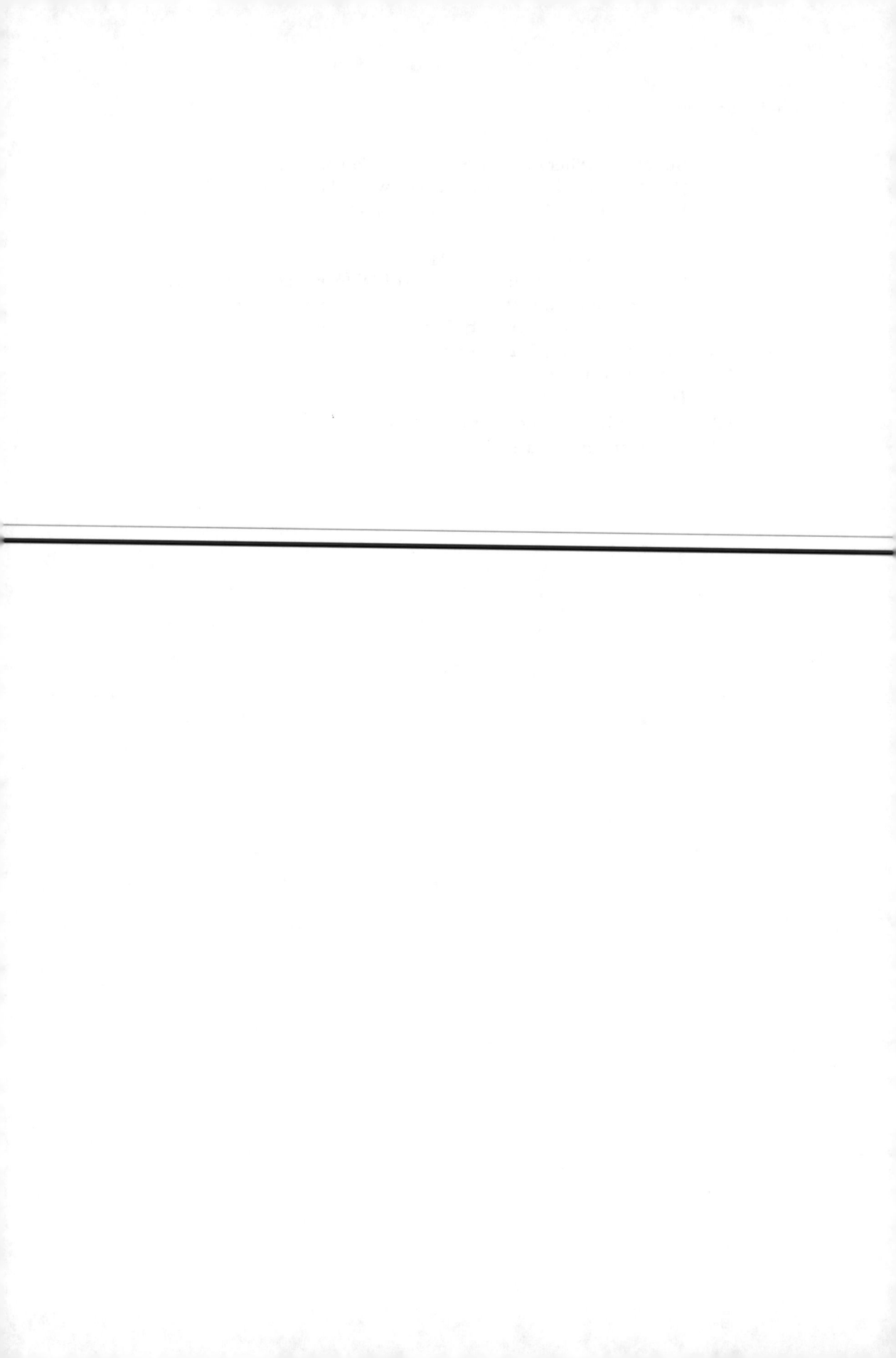

§ 13.01 IN GENERAL

Trusts are among the most useful asset protection tools. If properly structured, they may provide better protection than any other technique. Also, trusts may complement other asset protection tools. For example, a client may incorporate her business to limit business liabilities to corporate assets and then place the corporate stock into a trust to protect the business from her other creditors. A properly planned trust also provides the added benefit of furthering the settlor's estate planning goals.

This chapter discusses the requirements that planners must satisfy to establish the following types of trusts:

- Revocable trusts[1]
- Irrevocable trusts[2]
- Spendthrift trusts[3]
- Discretionary trusts[4]
- Support trusts[5]
- Charitable remainder trusts[6]
- Irrevocable life insurance trusts.[7]

§ 13.02 REVOCABLE AND IRREVOCABLE TRUSTS

Domestic trusts may be classified as either revocable or irrevocable trusts. Revocable trusts allow the settlor (that is, the person who intentionally causes the trust to come into existence) to revoke the trust during the settlor's life.[1] Irrevocable trusts do not allow the settlor to revoke the trust after the settlor establishes the trust.[2]

> **Caution.** Revocable trusts offer little or no asset protection benefits. Therefore, planners must use extreme care with revocable trusts. The following factors cause this result: (1) in many jurisdictions, the settlor's creditors may reach the corpus of a revocable trust; and (2) if the settlor enters bankruptcy, the bankruptcy trustee acquires the settlor's right to revoke the trust. However, under certain circumstances revocable trusts provide

---

§ 13.01 [1] *See* § 13.03 infra.
[2] *See* § 1 3.04 infra.
[3] *See* § 13.05 infra.
[4] *See* § 13.06 infra.
[5] *See* § 13.07 infra.
[6] *See* § 13.08 infra.
[7] *See* § 13.09 infra.

§ 13.02 [1] For a complete discussion of revocable trusts and their use in the asset protection context, see L.D. Solomon & L.J. Saret, Asset Protection Strategies, § 5.07 (2006).

[2] For a complete discussion of irrevocable trusts and their use in the asset protection context, *see* § 5.08.

the required degree of asset protection while allowing the settlor to retain more control over the trust corpus than for an irrevocable trust.

On the other hand, irrevocable trusts provide much greater asset protection than revocable trusts provide. This results because, by transferring property into an irrevocable trust, the settlor completely transfers such property to another. Consequently, the settlor's creditors cannot subsequently reach the transferred property because the settlor no longer owns this property.

Planning Pointer. Planners should always recommend and use irrevocable trusts for asset protection planning purposes unless absolutely precluded from doing so. When clients refuse to transfer assets without retaining the power to revoke the trust, planners should require such clients to provide them with an acknowledgment that the planner has recommended the use of an irrevocable trust, which the client has declined.

§ 13.03   REVOCABLE TRUST

Asset protection planners may use revocable trusts for married couples with stable marriages when one spouse is more at risk than the other. Generally, this strategy involves the spouses dividing their property, setting up two revocable trusts, and placing their property into these trusts. Planners should use the following steps to execute this strategy:

[A]   Step 1: Inventory Assets

First, planners should cause the spouses to inventory their assets. As part of this inventory, the planner must determine each asset's value, the risk of litigation claims arising out of such assets, and how the spouses have titled such assets.

[B]   Step 2: Partition Spouses' Property

Second, planners should cause the spouses to divide or partition their property. For community property jurisdictions, the spouses should enter transmutation agreements to change the statutory impact of the applicable state's community property laws. Generally, the asset protection plan should give exempt assets to the at-risk spouse. Conversely, the plan should generally give nonexempt assets to the spouse who is less at risk. The planner should attempt to divide the property equally between the spouses.

To partition the property effectively, the spouses may enter an agreement under which they agree:

1. That they jointly desire to sever their jointly held tenancy
2. On the property division of their property in aliquot shares, and
3. On the assignment of such shares to the individual owners.[1]

Next, the spouses will exchange mutual deeds in which (1) both spouses join in as grantors to one spouse who will be the grantee for one of the two properties, and (2) both spouses join in as grantors to the other spouse who will be the grantee for the other property. Such a transaction will cause each spouse to become sole owner of one parcel of property, formerly held jointly by both spouses.

Caution. The spouses must agree about both (1) the fact that they desire to sever their joint ownership, and (2) the allocation of the divided property interests.[2]

Planning Pointer. If the spouses do not agree about the division of the property, the planner may use a neutral third party to allocate the shares.[3] However, this assumes the spouses will agree to the use of such a neutral third party.

Planning Pointer. Planners must also use a written partition conveyance instrument to ensure that the partition is effective.[4]

[C] Step 3: Establish Trusts

Third, planners establish revocable trusts for each spouse. Each spouse becomes the (1) grantor, (2) initial beneficiary, and (3) trustee of his or her trust. The trusts should provide that the other spouse becomes the beneficiary of the

---

§ 13.03 [1] *See generally* Patricia Reyhan, Partition, in 4 Thompson On Real Property § 38.02(a) (Thomas ed., 1994); Russell D. Niles & William F. Walsh, Concurrent Estates and Their Characteristics, in 2 American Law of Property § 6.19 (A. James Casner ed., 1952 & Supp. 1977). *See, e.g.,* Moore v. Hill, 79 A.2d 840 (N.H. 1951); O'Brien v. O'Brien, 391 N.Y.S.2 502 (Sup. Ct. 1976); Houston Oil Co. v. Kirkindall, 145 S.W.2d 1074 (Tex. 1941).

[2] *See* Patricia Reyhan, Partition, in 4 Thompson On Real Property § 38.d 502 (Sup. Ct. 1976); Houston Oil Co. v. Kirkindall, 145 SW.2d 1074 (Tex. 1941). 02(a) (Thomas ed., 1994); Swindle v. Curry, 129 S.E.2d 144 (Ga. 1962).

[3] Hemphill v. Hemphill, 7 S.E.2d 762 (Ga. Ct. App. 1940); Glovier v. Dingus, 4 S.E.2d 551 (Va. 1939); Frankfurth v. Steinmeyer, 89 N.W. 148 (Wis. 1902).

[4] *See* Patricia Reyhan, Partition, in 4 Thompson On Real Property § 38.02(a) (Thomas ed., 1994). *See, e.g.,* Tex. Fam. Code Ann. § 5.54 (West).

trust if the grantor/beneficiary spouse dies or disclaims his or her interest. The trusts should give a remainder interest to the couple's children.

This strategy has the following asset protection impact. First, the non-at-risk spouse's trust becomes protected from the at-risk spouse's creditors. Second, the revocable trusts place a barrier between the at-risk spouse's creditors and the assets in the at-risk spouse's trust. The at-risk spouse's creditors' ability to reach that spouse's trust corpus depends on the law of the jurisdiction involved.

Once the trusts are established, planners transfer the property of each spouse into a trust for that spouse. Planners may use the revocable trust form located at § 3.04[A] for this purpose.

> **Planning Pointer.** Planners should advise clients to follow proper formalities in the trusts' operations to ensure that the trusts' existence is not questioned. For example, for both trusts such formalities should include the following:
>
> 1. The trust instrument should require that any instructions to be provided to the trustee (such as powers of appointment) be in writing.
> 2. The planner should advise the client in actual practice to provide any instructions to the trustee in writing.
> 3. Income from trust assets should flow through the trust's bank accounts and not through any individuals' bank accounts (for example, the grantor's).
> 4. The grantor should not list any assets transferred to the trust on his or her personal financial statements or on any applications to any lending organizations.
> 5. Proper tax returns should be prepared and filed by the trust.
> 6. The trust should maintain separate accounting records.

EXAMPLE 13-1

Harold and Wilma Nimitz are husband and wife. Wilma is a mergers and acquisitions attorney, and Harold is a freelance fiction writer. The Nimitzes are concerned about their liability exposure from Wilma's practice. They believe that there is little or no liability exposure from Harold's freelance writing. They jointly own the following assets:

Value	Asset
1. $2 million	Stock portfolio
2. $1 million	Home
3. $1 million	Qualified retirement benefits
$4 million	Total assets

The home is subject to an unlimited homestead exemption and the retirement benefits are entirely protected under *Patterson v. Shumate*[5] and its progeny.

In 1990 the Nimitzes consult with an asset protection planner, Gerald Khan. Khan helps the Nimitzes execute the following steps as part of an asset protection plan:

1. Wilma and Harold divide their property so that Wilma takes sole ownership of the home and the qualified retirement plan, and Harold takes sole ownership of the stock portfolio.
2. Wilma and Harold each establish a revocable trust.
3. Wilma transfers her home into her revocable trust, which benefits her for her life, and then benefits Harold.
4. Harold transfers the stock portfolio into his revocable trust.

In 1995 Bob Bondholder, who holds $10 million of bonds issued by LBO Corp, a corporation that Wilma assisted with a leveraged buyout, sues Wilma for LBO Corp's default of Bob's bonds. Bob asserts several theories for recovery and wins a $5 million judgment against Wilma. Here, Bob cannot recover against either Wilma's home or her retirement benefits, even if he can get through her trust, because these assets are exempt assets.[6] More importantly, Bob cannot reach the stock portfolio held by Harold's trust because Wilma has no ownership interest in this asset, other than her contingent remainder interest.

[D] Revocable Trust Instrument

Please see Form 13-1, Single Grantor Revocable Trust, and Form 13-2, Marital Revocable Trust, on the accompanying CD.

§13.04 IRREVOCABLE TRUST

Irrevocable trusts[1] do not allow settlors to revoke or modify them after their establishment by the settlor. Irrevocable trusts are very effective asset protection tools. This results because, by transferring property into an irrevocable trust, the settlor completely transfers ownership of the property to another. The settlor's creditors cannot subsequently reach the transferred property because the settlor no longer owns this property. Generally, irrevocable trusts provide the greatest benefit when the settlor does not need to retain control over the transferred property. Conversely, irrevocable trusts provide the least benefit when the settlor either needs or strongly desires to retain an interest in or control over the conveyed property.

---

[5] 504 U.S. 753 (1992).
[6] *See generally* Chapter 8.
§13.04   [1] *See* §5.08.

Planning Pointer. The asset protection planner should follow the following analysis for examining irrevocable trusts:[2]

1. What are the asset protection benefits of using irrevocable trusts?
2. What are the tax consequences of using irrevocable trusts?
3. Do the net asset protection advantages of using irrevocable trusts outweigh the loss of control to the settlor over the conveyed property?

Planning Pointer. One strategy the planner should consider would be to establish an irrevocable trust that:

1. Gives the settlor an income interest in the irrevocable trust
2. Gives the settlor a special power of appointment over the trust corpus, which is limited to benefiting only the objects of the settlor's bounty (for example, the settlor's spouse or children)
3. Gives the trustee the discretionary power to distribute trust corpus among the objects of the settlor's bounty, but prohibits the trustee from using this discretionary power to distribute to discharge any of the settlor's legal obligations to the objects of the settlor's bounty. This prevents the settlor from becoming a deemed beneficiary of the trust
4. Includes a spendthrift provision in the trust instrument
5. Includes an In Terrorem provision that causes any person who sues or contests any trust provision to forfeit all of his or her interest in the trust.

This strategy has the following asset protection impact:

1. The settlor's retained income interest is exposed to the claims of creditors.
2. The settlor's creditors cannot reach the trust corpus.
3. Because the trust instrument prohibits the trustee from using trust assets to discharge any of the settlor's legal obligations to support beneficiaries who are the objects of her bounty, this plan protects the settlor from creditor claims that are based on the argument that she is an indirect beneficiary of the trust and thus can reach funds for the support and maintenance of her beneficiaries.
4. This arrangement gives the client almost complete control over the trust corpus, except for allowing the client to access the corpus herself and for allowing the client to appoint those persons who do not fall within the special class set forth in the special power of appointment.

[2] *Id.*

Planning Pointer. The planner may use the trust instrument at § 13.6 to achieve the above asset protection results.

[A]   Irrevocable Trust Instrument

Please see Form 13-3, Irrevocable Trust Instrument, on the accompanying CD.

§ 13.05   SPENDTHRIFT TRUST

Spendthrift trusts[1] are trusts that prevent beneficiaries from transferring or assigning their rights to future payments of income or principal. Spendthrift trusts also prevent the beneficiaries' creditors from subjecting the beneficiaries' interests to the payment of the creditors' claims.[2] Subsection [A] provides a spendthrift trust clause that planners should consider using.

Caution. Planners must check the applicable jurisdiction's law to ensure that the provisions contained in subsection [A] will satisfy the law's requirements.

[A]   Spendthrift Trust Provisions

Please see Form 13-4, Spendthrift Trust Clause, on the accompanying CD.
Please see Form 13-5, Spendthrift Trust Clause Number 2, on the accompanying CD.
Please see Form 13-6, Spendthrift Trust Clause Number 3, on the accompanying CD.

§ 13.06   DISCRETIONARY TRUST

Discretionary trusts[1] give the trustee the discretion to pay or apply to or for the beneficiary's benefit, any, all, or no trust income or principal as the trustee deems

§ 13.05   [1] See § 5.09.
[2] See George T. Bogert, Trusts § 40 (6th ed. 1987); Austin Wakeman Scott & William Franklin Fratcher, The Law of Trusts §§ 149-163 (4th ed. 1987); George Gleason Bogert & George Taylor Bogert, The Law of Trusts and Trustees §§ 221-227 (rev. 2d ed. 1992); Erwin N. Griswold, Spendthrift Trusts (2d ed. 1947); Frank J. Rief III, Current and Future Family Asset Protection, in Sophisticated Estate Planning Techniques (ALI-ABA Course of Study, 1991); Santo (Sandy) Bisignano, Jr., Protecting Assets from Overzealous Creditors or an Estate Planner's Guide to Preservation Planning, 1987 Ann. Notre Dame Est. Plan. Inst. 3-31 to 3-34; Nancy Smith Roush & Robert K. Kirkland, Spendthrift Trusts Not Limited to Protection of Immature Dependents, 18 Est. Plan. 16 (1991).
§ 13.06   [1] For a discussion of discretionary trusts in the asset protection context, see § 5.10. See generally Austin Wakeman Scott & William Franklin Fratcher, The Law of Trusts §§ 155-155.1 (4th ed. 1987);

appropriate. Because the trust beneficiary has no right to any trust income or principal before a trustee elects to pay or apply income or principal to or for the beneficiary's benefit, and because creditors can only reach the interest that a beneficiary has a legal right to, the beneficiary cannot assign her interest to creditors and her creditors cannot reach the beneficiary's trust interest.

Planning Pointer. Subsection [A] provides a discretionary trust provision that planners may use as part of their asset protection plans.

[A] *Discretionary Trust Clause*

Please see Form 13-7, Discretionary Trust Clause, on the accompanying CD.

§ 13.07 SUPPORT TRUST

Support trusts provide that the trustee must pay or apply trust income or principal for the benefit of the beneficiary, but only to the extent required to educate and support that beneficiary, and then only to the extent that trust distributions can accomplish the goals of educating and supporting the trust beneficiary. Because the trustee may make only trust distributions that will accomplish the education and support of the beneficiary, creditors and the beneficiary's assignees cannot reach the beneficiary's interest because such distributions would not accomplish the trust's objectives. This is true even when the trust is not a spendthrift trust or in jurisdictions where spendthrift trusts are not valid.

Planning Pointer. The planner should consider using support trusts as an alternative to discretionary trusts when the settlor desires to provide for the support and education of the beneficiary, for example, the settlor's children. Such trusts will be less attractive when the settlor desires the trust to make distributions to beneficiaries that will not be for the beneficiary's support or education.

[A] *Support Trust Clause*

Please see Form 13-8, Support Trust Clause, on the accompanying CD.

George Gleason Bogert & George Taylor Bogert, The Law of Trusts and Trustees § 228 (rev. 2d ed. 1992); Frank J. Rief III, Current and Future Family Asset Protection, in Sophisticated Estate Planning Techniques (ALIABA Course of Study, 1991); George T. Bogert, Trusts § 41 (6th ed. 1987); Evelyn Ginsberg Abravanel, Discretionary Support Trusts, 68 Iowa L. Rev. 273 (1983).

§13.08 CHARITABLE REMAINDER TRUST

Charitable remainder trusts (CRTs)[1] provide for specified distributions at least annually to one or more beneficiaries, at least one of which is not a charity, for life or for a term of years with an irrevocable remainder interest to be held for the benefit of or paid over to a charity.[2] They may be inter vivos trusts or testamentary trusts. They are very valuable from both an asset protection planning standpoint and an estate planning standpoint.

> **Planning Pointer.** CRTs are best used when high-income clients possess highly appreciated property that they want to dispose of. The planner should note that CRTs may be valuable even when grantors do not possess a donative intent. When properly used, they are more advantageous than standard irrevocable trusts because of the great tax savings that they yield.

A qualified charitable remainder trust may:

1. Give the grantor an immediate charitable contribution deduction on the transfer of property to the CRT
2. Give the grantor a gift or estate tax charitable contribution deduction
3. Give a noncharitable beneficiary a stream of income for a fixed period not to exceed 20 years or the beneficiary's life
4. Allow the grantor to avoid the realization of income tax on the sale of appreciated property
5. Reduce federal estate taxes without lowering the amount of assets that the grantor transfers to her family when used with an irrevocable life insurance trust.

On the other hand, however, to obtain such benefits the planner must ensure that the trust complies with applicable rules. Qualified CRTs must be irrevocable trusts; therefore, they generally possess the same asset protection benefits that irrevocable trusts generally possess. Specifically, CRTs protect their corpus from creditors if transfers to the CRT are not fraudulent conveyances and do not impinge on spousal rights. On the other hand, however, any interest the grantor/beneficiary retains will be reachable by creditors.[3]

---

§ 13.08 [1] *See* § 5.12 for a complete discussion of charitable remainder trusts in the asset protection planning context. See generally William L. Hoisington, The Truth about Charitable Remainder Trusts, 45 Tax Law. 293 (1992); William A. Raabe & Karen J. Boucher, Using Charitable Remainder Trusts in the Estate Plan, 13 Rev. Tax'n Individuals 3 (Winter 1989); Burton W. Kanter, AARP Asset Accumulation, Retention and Protection: Prelude to Transmission, 69 Taxes 717 (1991); A. James Casner, Estate Planning §§ 14.9-14.22.6 (5th ed. 1988); Jeffrey S. Taylor, The Charitable Remainder Trust: A Unique Estate Planning Technique, 69 Taxes 106 (1991); L. Henry Gissel, Jr. & Karen R. Schiller, Trusts Made Easy: A Simplified Overview of the Reasons for Creating, Modifying, and Terminating Express Trusts, 10 Prob. L.J. 241 (1991).

[2] Reg. § 1.664-1(a)(1)(i).

[3] Section 5.12 discusses the requirements for establishing a qualified CRT; the valuation of remainder interests for purposes of claiming charitable income and transfer tax deductions; the income, gift, estate,

Planning Pointer. Planners establishing asset protection plans involving CRTs must consider the following issues:

1. The requirements that the planner must satisfy when drafting CRT instruments
2. The factors the planner must consider when choosing a trustee for the CRT
3. Whether to use an annuity trust or unitrust CRT
4. The payout rate to use for the CRT
5. The impact of prearranged sales upon the CRT
6. The impact of transferring S corporation interests into the CRT, and
7. Whether to use the CRT as a substitute for or supplement for the client's retirement benefits.

[A]   Drafting Requirements

This section reviews some of the more important requirements that planners must satisfy when completing their CRT instruments. First, the planner must decide whether to use an annuity trust or a unitrust. Under the applicable rules, every CRT must be either an annuity trust or unitrust, but not both.[4] Annuity trusts pay noncharitable beneficiaries a fixed percentage, not less than 5 percent, of the initial fair market value of the trust assets for life or a period of years.[5] These payments are fixed and cannot vary from year to year. This holds true even if the trust investment income falls below the payout amount. If necessary, the trustee must invade trust principal to pay the annuity.

On the other hand, unitrusts pay to noncharitable beneficiaries for life or a period of years a specific percentage, not less than 5 percent, of their annually revalued trust assets.[6] Therefore, the income beneficiary's payments will vary depending on the CRT's investment performance. If the CRT earns a greater return than the income payments, it recapitalizes its excess earnings. The income beneficiary receives a percentage of the increase in value when the trust revalues its assets. Conversely, if the CRT earns a lesser return than the income payments, the trust principal may decrease in value. This, in turn, will result in smaller income payments.

Second, the planner must be careful about including any investment restrictions in the CRT instrument. More specifically, the trust must not include any provision that restricts the trustee from investing the trust assets in a way that could result in the annual realization of a reasonable amount of income or gain from the sale or disposition of trust assets.[7]

---

and generation-skipping transfer tax consequences of the transaction to the settlor; and the income taxation of the CRT and its beneficiary.

[4] Reg. § 1.664-1(a)(2).
[5] Reg. § 1.664-2(a)(1)(ii).
[6] Reg. § 1.664-3(a)(1)(i)(a).
[7] Reg. § 1.664-1(a)(3).

Caution. Clients sometimes want the trust to hold the asset that they contribute to the CRT. Such clauses violate the prohibition against provisions restricting trustees from investing CRT assets to result in the annual realization of a reasonable amount of income or gain. On the other hand, the CRT may authorize the trustee to continue to hold the property that the client originally contributed to the trust, without mandating that it do so.

Caution. Planners should use extreme care when considering appointing an investment advisor with the power to manage the trust assets. This is especially true when the trust does not give the trustee the power to remove the advisor.[8] In such cases, the CRT runs the risk of placing an impermissible restriction on the trustee's investment powers.

Third, the planner must ensure that the CRT's trust term satisfies the IRC's requirements. More specifically, the CRT's term must be for the life or lives of a named individual or individuals or for a term of years not exceeding 20 years.[9]

Fourth, planners must ensure that the CRT does not allow for any impermissible payments. More specifically, the annuity or unitrust amount must be payable to or for a named person or persons, at least one of whom is not a charitable organization. In other words, the CRT must not make any other kind of payment to a noncharitable recipient other than the annuity or unitrust payment.[10] For this purpose, payments made for full and adequate consideration are generally considered permissible.

Caution. If there is a possibility that any death taxes may be payable from the trust's assets at the client's death, the trust will not qualify. Therefore the trust should contain a provision that states that neither the trust assets nor the trustee will be liable for the payment of such taxes and that the client agrees to make other arrangements for their payment. CRTs may provide that a survivor's income interest is only effective if he or she provides the funds necessary to pay the death taxes attributable to the trust assets.[11]

---

[8] *See, e.g.,* Ltr. Rul. 8041100.
[9] Reg. § 1.664-2(a)(5)(i).
[10] Reg. §§ 1.664-2(a)(4)(i), 1.664-3(a)(4)(i).
[11] Rev. Rul. 72-395, 1972-2 C.B. 340, modified in Rev. Rul. 82-128, 1982-2 C.B. 7 1, and clarified in Rev. Rul. 82-165, 1982-2 C.B. 117.

Caution. Although planners may give the CRT trustee the power to sprinkle income payments among a designated group of permissible recipients, they must ensure that the CRT uses an independent trustee in such a case.[12]

Fifth, planners must ensure that the CRT instrument irrevocably assigns the CRT remainder interest to or for the use of one or more qualifying charitable organizations.

Planning Pointer. Before funding the trust, planners should check the named charitable beneficiary's qualification under the income, gift, and estate tax provisions of the IRC. The trust must designate alternative charities, or provide a method for the selection of alternative charities, if the named charities do not qualify.[13]

Planners should note that the grantor may designate multiple charities to receive the trust assets. Moreover, the grantor may reserve the right for his life, or the life of another income beneficiary, to change the charitable recipients.

Caution. If there is more than a remote probability that the CRT will exhaust the trust assets before the CRT terminates, the IRC will disqualify it.[14]

Sixth, planners must ensure that the CRT instrument includes provisions prohibiting it from taking actions that violate the private foundation excise tax provisions. Among other things, this rule requires the CRT to prohibit acts of self-dealing.[15]

Finally, CRTs must include special provisions concerning additional contributions after the CRT's formation. For an annuity trust, the CRT instrument must prohibit additional contributions.[16] For unitrusts, the CRT instrument must include a provision that specifies how the trustee must prorate income payments when additional contributions are made, after the CRT's formation.[17]

[B]   Trustee Selection

Planners must choose a trustee for the CRT. The grantor may serve as the trustee. Although this is allowable, planners must use great care when the

---

[12] Reg. §§ 1.664-2(a)(3)(ii), 1.664-3(a)(3)(ii); Rev. Rul. 77-285, 1977-2 C.B. 213.
[13] Reg. §§ 1.664-2(a)(6)(iv), 1.664-3(a)(6)(iv).
[14] Reg. §§ 20.2055-2(b)(1), 25.2522(c)-3(b).
[15] IRC §§ 4941, 4947(a)(2).
[16] Reg. § 1.664-(2)(b).
[17] Reg. § 1.664-3(b).

grantor serves as the trustee. More specifically, planners should consider the following risks associated with using the grantor as the CRT trustee:

1. The IRS may be more likely to challenge valuations of the trust assets, especially when the planner uses a unitrust, which must be revalued annually.
2. The IRS may be more likely to attempt to impute capital gain to the grantor on the sale of an appreciated asset when the grantor negotiated such sale before creating the trust. Alternatively, the IRS may argue that there was a prearranged sale, thereby imposing an impermissible investment restriction on the trustee and disqualifying the tax-exempt status of the trust.[18]
3. There is an increased risk that the grantor will not satisfy (a) the record keeping and reporting requirements, and (b) the self-dealing prohibitions imposed on CRTs.

Planning Pointer. When the grantor strongly wants to serve as trustee (for example, he may be contributing stock in a closely held corporation and desire to retain control over such stock), the planner should consider the following:

1. Using an independent co-trustee. The planner may use an independent co-trustee, which will decrease the risks associated with the grantor serving as the sole CRT trustee.
2. Using the charitable remainderman as trustee. The planner may use the charitable remainder beneficiary as the trustee in those states whose laws allow such organizations to serve as trustee. However, this structure creates a possible conflict of interest if the trustee is investing for the benefit of the remainder beneficiaries of the trust versus investing for the benefit of the income recipients. This arrangement is beneficial because the charitable organization (a) may do so without compensation, thus reducing the CRT's costs, and (b) is likely to be responsive to the grantor's wishes. On the other hand, this arrangement may not mitigate the increased risks of noncompliance with the CRT's record keeping or reporting requirements if the charitable beneficiary is unsophisticated.

The alternative to the grantor or the charitable beneficiary serving as trustee is for the planner to use a bank, trust company, or other independent trustee. This choice will generally be advantageous because (1) the IRS will be less likely to challenge actions taken by an independent trustee, and (2) banks or trust companies will be more likely to comply with record keeping and reporting requirements.

---

[18] Ltr. Rul. 7815017.

[C]   Annuity Trust or Unitrust

Planners must consider whether they should use an annuity trust or unitrust CRT. Generally, annuity trust CRTs are beneficial because their annual payments to noncharitable beneficiaries are fixed and will not vary despite the trustee's investment performance. Consequently, annuity trusts protect the income beneficiaries to a greater extent if there is a downturn in investment performance. Conversely, annuity trust CRTs are disadvantageous in that they do not provide any hedge against inflation.

When planners use unitrusts, such CRTs may pay either (1) a fixed percentage of the annually revalued trust assets, or (2) the lesser of a fixed percentage or the actual net income produced by the trust assets.

[D]   Selecting Payout Rate

Planners must consider what payout rate to use.

Caution. Regardless of what type of CRT the planner uses, the payout rate must be at least 5 percent per year.[19]

Caution. When planners use annuity trusts, they must ensure that the payout rate is not so high that the IRS may determine that it is likely that the CRT will exhaust the trust assets. If this occurs, the IRS will disqualify the CRT.

Planning Pointer. The most prudent payout rate for annuity trusts is the rate of return planners believe that the trustee can reasonably achieve.

Planning Pointer. When planners use unitrust CRTs, they should consider the effect of the recapitalization of excess earnings. More specifically, if the unitrust earns a greater income than it pays out each year, the corpus will grow and the payout amount will, in turn, grow each year. Additionally, planners should not choose a payout rate so low that the clients will have a larger charitable contribution than they can reasonably be expected to use.

[19] IRC § 664(d)(1)(A), (2)(A).

[E] Prearranged Sales

Another CRT consideration involves prearranged sales. Often, clients will have moved forward with sales on appreciated assets before either (1) they decide to use a CRT, or (2) they present the planner with facts that recommend use of a CRT. In such cases, planners must evaluate whether it is too late to use a CRT to avoid capital gains on the sale of the property in question.

> **Caution.** When taxpayers transfer property to CRTs that is subject to legally binding sales contracts, the IRS will impute any resulting capital gains tax on such sales of property to the transferring taxpayers. The IRS applies this rule even when the sale takes place after the client has transferred the property to the CRT.[20]

EXAMPLE 13-2

Winston and Emma own Blackacre, which they purchased for $100,000 several years ago. In 2005 Winston and Emma enter a contract with Albert Developer to sell Blackacre to Albert in 2007 for $1,000,000. After entering the contract, Winston and Emma visit Victoria Planner, who assists them in transferring Blackacre to a CRT. In turn, the CRT sells Blackacre to Albert, pursuant to the contract with Albert. Here, Winston and Emma must recognize capital gain although the CRT actually executes the sale of Blackacre to Albert.

> **Planning Pointer.** Planners should ensure that clients do not enter legally binding contracts to sell assets that they will transfer to a CRT before they actually transfer such assets to the CRT. Planners should note that their clients may market such assets. However, they must not accept any offers before the transfer of the asset in question to the CRT.

[F] Transferring S Corporation Interests into the CRT

Planners must be aware that transfers of S corporation interests to a CRT will terminate the S corporation status of the corporation on the CRT's funding.[21]

---

[20] *See* Rev. Rul. 78-197, 1978-1 C.B. 83; Palmer v. Commissioner, 62 T.C. 684 (1974), *aff'd*, 523 F.2d 1308 (8th Cir. 1975).

[21] *See, e.g.,* Ltr. Rul. 8922014.

[G] Retirement Planning

One planning technique planners should consider is using CRTs as a form of retirement plan. CRTs operate similarly to qualified retirement plans in certain respects. Specifically, clients may accumulate earnings within CRTs on a tax-deferred basis under both qualified retirement plans and CRTs. An income-only unitrust with a deficit makeup provision is particularly valuable for such a purpose. This results because the CRT may invest in property that appreciates, which does not generate any income that the CRT must distribute. Consequently, such income accumulates tax free inside the CRT until the grantor actually needs or wants such funds.

Planning Pointer. The trust should contain an accounting provision that provides that accruals on zero coupon bonds or growth in stocks or securities does not constitute distributable net income under IRC § 643(b).[22]

Planning Pointer. When planners use CRTs for retirement purposes, they should consider advising the CRT to invest in zero coupon bonds, growth stocks, or other assets that do not produce distributable net income. Therefore, these assets will continue to grow in value without being subject to income tax and without requiring distribution to the income beneficiary. When the client is ready to retire, the trustee can switch the investments into high-yield securities. The client will then receive both the CRT payout rate and, to the extent the CRT's income is sufficient, any deficit incurred in the years before retirement.

CRTs have the following advantages over qualified retirement plans:

1. Nondiscrimination rules, which apply to qualified retirement plans, do not apply to CRTs.
2. Client contributions are very flexible. For example, clients may contribute in some years, but not others.
3. By controlling the CRT's income, for income-only unitrusts, planners can vary the CRT's distributions. In contrast, qualified plans must begin distributions at certain specified times.

[H] Sample Inter Vivos One Life Charitable Remainder Unitrust, Rev. Proc. 2005-52, 2005-35 I.R.B. 326, § 4

Please see Form 13-9, Sample Inter Vivos One Life Charitable Remainer Unitrus, on the accompanying CD.

---

[22] Ltr. Rul. 8604027.

[I] Sample Inter Vivos One Life Charitable Remainder Annuity Trust, Rev. Proc. 89-21, 1989-2 C.B. 872, §4

Please see Form 13-10, Sample Inter Vivos One Life Charitable Remainder Annuity Trust, on the accompanying CD.

[J] Sample Inter Vivos Charitable Remainder Unitrust: Two Lives, Consecutive Interests, Rev. Proc. 2005-54, 2005-34 I.R.B. 353, §4

Please see Form 13-11, Sample Inter Vivos Charitable Remainder Unitrust: Two Lives, Consecutive Interests, on the accompanying CD.

[K] Sample Inter Vivos Charitable Remainder Unitrust: Two Lives, Concurrent and Consecutive Interests, Rev. Proc. 2005-55, 2005-34 I.R.B. 367, §4

Please see Form 13-12, Sample Inter Vivos Charitable Remainder Unitrust: Two Lives, Concurrent and Consecutive Interests, on the accompanying CD.

[L] Sample Testamentary Charitable Remainder Unitrust: One Life, Rev. Proc. 2005-56, 2005-34 I.R.B. 383, §4

Please see Form 13-13, Sample Testamentary Charitable Remainder Unitrust: One Life, on the accompanying CD.

[M] Sample Testamentary Charitable Remainder Unitrust: Two Lives, Consecutive Interests, Rev. Proc. 2005-58, 2005-34 I.R.B. 40, §4

Please see Form 13-14, Sample Testamentary Charitable Remainder Unitrust: Two Lives, Consecutive Interests, on the accompanying CD.

[N] Sample Testamentary Charitable Remainder Unitrust: Two Lives, Concurrent and Consecutive Interests, Rev. Proc. 2005-59, 2005-34 I.R.B. 412, §4

Please see Form 13-15, Sample Testamentary Charitable Remainder Unitrust: Two Lives, Concurrent and Consecutive Interests, on the accompanying CD.

[O]   Sample Inter Vivos Charitable Remainder Unitrust for a Term of Years, Rev. Proc. 2005-53, 2005-34 I.R.B. 339

Please see Form 13-16, Sample Inter Vivos Charitable Remainder Unitrust for a Term of Years, on the accompanying CD.

[P]   Sample Testamentary Charitable Remainder Unitrust Declaration for a Term of Years, Rev. Proc. 2005-57, 2005-34 I.R.B. 392

Please see Form 13-17, Sample Testamentary Charitable Remainder Unitrust Declaration for a Term of Years, on the accompanying CD.

[Q]   Sample Inter Vivos Charitable Remainder Annuity Trust: Two Lives, Consecutive Interests, Rev. Proc. 90-32, 1990-1 C.B. 539, § 4

Please see Form 13-18, Sample Inter Vivos Charitable Remainder Annuity Trust: Two Lives, Consecutive Interests, on the accompanying CD.

[R]   Sample Inter Vivos Charitable Remainder Annuity Trust: Two Lives, Concurrent and Consecutive Interests, Rev. Proc. 90-32, 1990-1 C.B. 539, § 5

Please see Form 13-19, Sample Inter Vivos Charitable Remainder Annuity Trust: Two Lives, Concurrent and Consecutive Interests, on the accompanying CD.

[S]   Sample Testamentary Charitable Remainder Annuity Trust: One Life, Rev. Proc. 90-32, 1990-1 C.B. 539, § 6

Please see Form 13-20, Sample Testamentary Charitable Remainder Annuity Trust: One Life, on the accompanying CD.

[T]   Sample Testamentary Charitable Remainder Annuity Trust: Two Lives, Consecutive Interests, Rev. Proc. 90-32, 1990-1 C.B. 539, § 7

Please see Form 13-21, Sample Testamentary Charitable Remainder Annuity Trust: Two Lives, on the accompanying CD.

[U] Sample Testamentary Charitable Remainder Annuity Trust: Two Lives, Concurrent and Consecutive Interests, Rev. Proc. 90-32, 1990-1 C.B. 539, § 8

Please see Form 13-22, Sample Testamentary Charitable Remainder Annuity Trust: Two Lives, Concurrent and Consecutive Interests, on the accompanying CD.

[V] Sample NIMCRUT Form

Please see Form 13-23, Sample NIMCRUT, on the accompanying CD.

§13.09 IRREVOCABLE LIFE INSURANCE TRUST

Life insurance constitutes an important component of asset protection plans.[1] This results because life insurance provides the following benefits, among others, for clients:

1. Risk-shifting benefits
2. Special income and transfer tax treatment
3. Exemption under federal and state debtor creditor and bankruptcy laws.

Generally, planners can obtain greater asset protection and estate planning benefits by using irrevocable life insurance trusts than by using an asset protection plan under which an individual owns life insurance outright.

Planning Pointer. The following consequences generally result from an asset protection plan that uses an irrevocable life insurance trust:

1. The life insurance policy, its cash value, and its proceeds may be protected from the reach of the client's creditors.
2. The transfer of the policy to the trust will constitute a taxable gift of a future interest, which will not qualify for the annual gift tax exclusion.
3. Future gifts of money to the trust, to enable the trust to make insurance

---

§ 13.09 [1] For a detailed discussion of life insurance and its use in the asset protection context, *see* § 8.03. For a detailed discussion of life insurance and irrevocable life insurance trusts as part of a general estate plan, see Georgiana J. Slade, Personal Life Insurance Trusts, Tax Mgmt. (BNA) No. 2104th, at A43-A44 (1991); Jonathan G. Blattmachr, The Master Living Trust, 23d Ann. U. of Miami Philip E. Heckerling Inst. on Est. Plan. Ch. 18 (1988); Lawrence Brody, The Use of Life Insurance (Including Survivorship Life Insurance) in Estate Planning, Focusing on Its Use in Irrevocable Insurance Trusts, in 21st Annual Estate Planning Institute September-November 1990, at 347 (PLI Handbook Series No. 197, 1990); Charles Severs III, Life Insurance Concepts, in 21st Annual Estate Planning Institute September-November 1990, at 215 (PLI Handbook Series No. 197, 1990).

premium payments, will not qualify for the annual gift tax exclusion
unless the trust includes *Crummey* powers.

4. The IRC will not include the life insurance policy in the insured's gross
   estate if the insured divests himself of all incidents of ownership in the
   policies transferred to the trust.
5. The trust will not recognize taxable income when the decedent dies
   and the insurance company pays the insurance proceeds to the trust
   because the IRC exempts the proceeds from income taxation.

Planning Pointer. When using life insurance in an irrevocable life insurance trust as part of an asset protection plan, planners should analyze the
following:

1. How the exemption statute applies to protect the insurance policy
   proceeds and cash value from the insured's creditors
2. How the exemption statute applies to protect the insurance policy
   proceeds and cash value from the beneficiary's creditors
3. What the gift tax consequences are of using the irrevocable life insurance trust
4. What the estate tax consequences are of using the irrevocable life insurance trust
5. What the income tax consequences are of using the irrevocable life
   insurance trust
6. Who should serve as the trustee of the irrevocable life insurance trust
7. What administrative powers the planner should give to the trustee of
   an irrevocable life insurance trust
8. Whether the planner should use a trust protector
9. Whether the planner should include a backup marital QTIP trust
   clause
10. What *Crummey* withdrawal powers should be given to beneficiaries
11. What practical matters the planner must consider regarding an irrev-
    ocable life insurance trust's administration.

[A]   Selection of Trustee

Planners must be very careful when using irrevocable life insurance trusts to
ensure that the choice of trustee does not inadvertently cause adverse tax consequences.

Caution. Planners should never use any of the following as trustees for
their irrevocable life insurance trusts:

1. Grantor

2. Grantor's spouse, or
3. Any trust beneficiary.

First, the planner should ensure that the insured grantor never serves as trustee of the irrevocable life insurance trust. If the insured grantor serves as the trustee, the IRC may treat him as possessing the incidents of ownership in the life insurance policies that the trust holds.[2] In such a case, the IRC will require the insured grantor to include the value of the life insurance policy proceeds in his gross estate.[3] This rule holds true even if the grantor is not a beneficiary of the irrevocable life insurance trust.

Planning Pointer. Planners should include language in their irrevocable life insurance trust instruments expressly prohibiting the insured grantor from serving as the trustee.

Second, the planner should ensure that the insured grantor's spouse does not serve as the trustee if the trust holds a second-to-die life insurance policy, under which the policy pays benefits on the death of the last to die of the spouses. Under such a policy, the IRC will consider both spouses to be insured individuals. Consequently, if either serves as trustee, he or she will possess incidents of ownership, which may trigger gross estate inclusion of the life insurance proceeds on the spouse's death.

Planning Pointer. Even when the planner originally does not intend to use second-to-die policies, because the possibility exists that the trust may acquire such policies in the future, planners should always ensure that their trust instruments expressly prohibit both the insured grantor and his or her spouse from serving as the trust's trustee.

Third, planners should also preclude any beneficiaries from serving as a trustee of the irrevocable life insurance trust. Planners should include language expressly precluding trust beneficiaries from serving as trustee of such trust.

Caution. Planners should also expressly preclude any individual who contributes property to the trust from serving as trustee. If such an individual serves as trustee, the IRC may cause inclusion of part or all of the trust in such person's gross estate under IRC §2035 and IRC §2036.

---

[2] IRC §2042(2); Reg. §20.2042-1(c)(4); Rev. Rul. 84-179, 1984-2 C.B. 195.
[3] IRC §2042(2).

[B] Trustee Administrative Powers

Planners should ensure that their irrevocable life insurance trust instruments convey appropriate powers on the trustee. More specifically, besides usual trust powers given to the trustee, the irrevocable life insurance trust instrument should give the trustee broad powers to specifically deal with any life insurance policies that the trust owns.

Planning Pointer. Planners should ensure that their irrevocable life insurance trust instruments convey the following powers upon their trustees.[4]

1. To buy life insurance policies payable to the trust on the life of any individual in which any beneficiary of the irrevocable life insurance trust has an insurable interest
2. To pay any premium on any life insurance policy
3. To exercise all options, rights, elections, and privileges allowable with respect to any life insurance policy held by the irrevocable life insurance trust
4. To dispose of the policies
5. To surrender or cancel any life insurance policy
6. To borrow upon or pledge any policy in connection with a loan
7. To direct the disposition of dividends or surplus on any policy
8. To convert any policy into a different form of insurance
9. To elect methods of settlement with respect to policies held by the trust
10. To enter into split-dollar arrangements
11. To terminate the trust and distribute the policies directly to the beneficiaries, if the funds in the trustee's hands are insufficient to pay the premiums and the grantor or other donor fails to supply additional funds necessary to make the premium payments
12. To execute and deliver any receipt or other voucher for the proceeds of any life insurance policy held by the trust
13. To institute any suit to enforce the payment of the proceeds of any life insurance policies held by the trust
14. To adjust, compromise, or otherwise settle any controversy concerning the life insurance policies.

[C] Trust Protector

Planners should consider using a trust protector. Trust protectors are persons who have the absolute power to remove any trustee and designate

---

[4] *See generally* Georgiana J. Slade, Personal Life Insurance Trusts, Tax Mgmt. (BNA) No. 210-4th, at A43-A44 (1991); Lawrence Brody, The Use of Life Insurance (Including Survivorship Life Insurance) in Estate Planning, Focusing on Its Use in Irrevocable Insurance Trusts, in 21st Annual Estate Planning Institute September-November 1990, at 347, 425-28 (PLI Handbook Series No. 197, 1990).

another.[5] By using trust protectors, planners can give the client indirect control over the trust. This results because if the grantor is unhappy with the trustee's management of the trust, the trust protector may be sympathetic to his point of view.

Caution. Planners should ensure that the office of trust protector is not filled by the grantor, any beneficiary, or any party who contributes or has contributed property to the trust.

Planning Pointer. Planners should include language in their irrevocable life insurance trust instruments expressly prohibiting any of the following from serving as trust protector:

1. Grantor
2. Any beneficiary of the irrevocable life insurance trust, or
3. Any party that contributes or has contributed property to the trust.

Planning Pointer. Planners should include language in their irrevocable life insurance trust instruments expressly prohibiting the trust protector from appointing any of the following as a trustee of the trust:

1. Trust protector
2. Grantor
3. Grantor's spouse, or
4. Any trust beneficiary.

[D] Backup QTIP Trust

When the grantor's spouse will be a beneficiary of the irrevocable life insurance trust, planners should consider including a backup QTIP trust provision in the trust instrument.[6] Such a provision would provide that if any of the assets contained within the irrevocable life insurance trust are included in the grantor's

---

[5] *See* Jonathan G. Blattmachr, The Master Living Trust, 23d Ann. 6. of Miami Philip E. Heckerling Inst. on Est. Plan. Ch. 18 (1988); Georgiana J. Slade, Personal Life Insurance Trusts, Tax Mgmt. (BNA) No. 210-4th, at A42 (1991).

[6] *See generally* Georgiana J. Slade, Personal Life Insurance Trusts, Tax Mgmt. (BNA) No. 210-4th, at A43-A44 (1991); Lawrence Brody, The Use of Life Insurance (Including Survivorship Life Insurance) in Estate Planning, Focusing on Its Use in Irrevocable Insurance Trusts, in 21st Annual Estate Planning Institute September-November 1990, at 347, 434-36 (PLI Handbook Series No. 197, 1990).

estate, without considering the backup QTIP provision itself, then the trustee must use those assets, which are includible in the grantor's estate, to fund a backup QTIP trust.

> **Planning Pointer.** When planners use a backup QTIP trust, they should review the tax clauses contained within the grantor's will and any revocable trust agreements. More specifically, planners should ensure that such tax clauses appropriately deal with the contingency of the insurance proceeds or the trust assets being included in the grantor's gross estate for federal estate tax purposes.

[E]   Crummey Powers

Gifts of life insurance policies to irrevocable life insurance trusts generally constitute gifts of future interests, which do not qualify for the annual gift tax exclusion.[7] Furthermore, gifts of or payments of premiums of life insurance policies held by trusts constitute gifts of future interests that do not qualify for the annual exclusion.[8]

> **Planning Pointer.** Planners should use *Crummey* powers in connection with irrevocable life insurance trusts. Such *Crummey* powers allow life insurance premium payments to qualify for the annual gift tax exclusion. *Crummey* powers are powers that the trust instrument gives to the trust's beneficiaries. They allow the beneficiaries to make effective outright demand for property held in trust, usually for a defined period following the gift of such property to the trust.[9] This right constitutes a present right to possession, which is deemed to be equal to actual present possession for annual gift tax exclusion purposes.

> **Caution.** Planners should be aware that holders of *Crummey* withdrawal powers may actually use such powers. Consequently, they should carefully select beneficiaries who hold such powers.

> **Planning Pointer.** Planners should consider including the following provisions in the *Crummey* clauses:

[7] Reg. § 25.2503-3(c), Ex. 2 (1983); Rev. Rul. 79-47, 1979-1 C.B. 312.
[8] Rev. Rul. 76-490, 1976-2 C.B. 300.
[9] Crummey v. Commissioner, 397 F.2d 82 (9th Cir. 1968); L.D. Solomon et al., Federal Taxation of Estates, Trusts and Gifts, 519-21 (1989).

1. Trust instrument should specifically provide that during the grantor's life each direct and indirect transfer to the trust, including the initial transfer of the life insurance policies and cash, will be subject to withdrawal by the beneficiaries of the trust.
2. The withdrawal right should be limited to $5,000 or 5 percent of principal, whichever is greater. Planners should note that if the withdrawal right exceeds this limitation, then if beneficiaries fail to exercise their withdrawal rights, this failure will cause the excess of the lapse of the withdrawal right over this amount to be treated as a gift to other trust beneficiaries.
3. The trust instrument should require the trustee to notify the donee or the donee's guardian of (a) the withdrawal right, and (b) contributions to the trust that are subject to such withdrawal right.[10]
4. The trust instrument should allow the beneficiaries a reasonable amount of time to exercise their withdrawal rights before such rights lapse. Generally, the trust instrument should require the trustee to notify beneficiaries of their withdrawal rights within 30 days of the commencement of the withdrawal period.[11] The trust instrument should also allow the beneficiary at least 60 days to exercise the withdrawal power.[12]
5. The trust instrument should provide that the withdrawal right is noncumulative, with nonwithdrawn contributions being added to principal.

Caution. If a beneficiary holds multiple, noncumulative withdrawal rights in one or several irrevocable life insurance trusts, then such withdrawal rights may be aggregated for purposes of determining whether that beneficiary has made a gift by failing to exercise its withdrawal power.[13]

Planning Pointer. If planners anticipate that their irrevocable life insurance trusts will have deductions that will exceed their income, then they should consider structuring the trust to qualify as a grantor trust. This would allow the grantor to deduct the deductions stemming from the trust.

[F] Irrevocable Life Insurance Trust Administration

Planners should be aware of certain steps that should be executed after the irrevocable life insurance trust's creation.[14] Planners should assign responsibility

---

[10] Rev. Rul. 73-405, 1973-2 C.B. 321. *See, e.g.,* Ltr. Rul. 8019038, Ltr. Rul. 8015133.

[11] Ltr. Rul. 8433024.

[12] Rev. Rul. 83-108, 1983-2 C.B. 167.

[13] Rev. Rul. 85-88, 19852 C.B. 201.

[14] *See generally* Georgiana J. Slade, Personal Life Insurance Trusts, Tax Mgmt. (BNA) No. 210-4th, at A43-A44 (1991).

for each step that they determine will need to be completed, in order to ensure that each such step actually is completed. More specifically, planners should consider the following administrative matters:

____1.   Open bank account. Generally, the trust will eventually need to open a trust bank account. However, if premiums are paid directly by the insured grantor or the insured's employer and the trust does not anticipate making any current disbursements, the trustee need not open a bank account until additional funds are added to the trust by the grantor or the proceeds of a life insurance policy become payable to the trust.

____2.   Obtain an employer identification number. Generally, the irrevocable life insurance trust will have to obtain an employer identification number.

____3.   Purchase or assign life insurance policy. After the irrevocable life insurance trust has been formed, the trustee must either buy a life insurance policy on the insured grantor's life or the insured must assign to the trust a preexisting life insurance policy. If trustees buy a life insurance policy, they must complete an application for the insurance with the life insurance company and arrange for the insured grantor to take the necessary medical examinations.

Caution. The planner must ensure that the life insurance application designates the trustee, rather than the insured, as both the owner and beneficiary of the life insurance policy.

If the insured wants to assign a preexisting life insurance policy to the irrevocable life insurance trust, the planner should review the policy to ensure that there are no restrictions on that policy's assignment. Also, the planner should determine what formalities must be completed to complete that assignment.

Caution. It is critical that the insured complete all steps necessary for an effective assignment of the policy. The failure to assign effectively a life insurance policy may have adverse federal and state estate and inheritance tax consequences as well as adverse state law consequences.

____4.   Designate the trustee as beneficiary of all life insurance policies. The planner must ensure that all life insurance policies contributed to the irrevocable life insurance trust designate the trustee as their beneficiary. Generally, such designation should not be irrevocable; otherwise, this may cause problems if the trust is terminated before the insured grantor dies.

____5.   Give notice to beneficiary or waiver of notice concerning *Crummey* withdrawal rights. After each contribution to the irrevocable life insurance trust, the trustee must notify all beneficiaries with *Crummey* withdrawal rights of such contribution and their right to make a *Crummey* withdrawal demand. The notice should:

- Describe the property transferred to the trust
- Describe the beneficiary's withdrawal rights resulting from the transfer
- Indicate the time in which the beneficiary may exercise his withdrawal power
- Be in writing, and
- Be given to the beneficiary's legal guardian, committee, or conservator if the beneficiary is a minor or under another legal disability.

____6. File Form 709: Federal Gift (and GST) Tax Return and Allocation of GST Exemption by Grantor. The grantor should consider filing a Form 709 under each of the following circumstances:
- When the grantor's contributions to the trust exceed the §2503(b) annual gift tax exclusion amount
- If the grantor wants to allocate any GST exemption to the transfer at the value of the transfer for gift tax purposes
- If the transfers to the trust are "direct skips" for GST tax purposes and the grantor does not want to have his or her GST exemption automatically allocated to the direct skip
- To "elect out" and not have his or her GST exemption allocated to the transfer.

____7. Pay life insurance premiums. It is critical that the trustee pay the life insurance premiums promptly when due. Failure to make such payments could cause the policy to lapse.

Planning Pointer. The planner should verify that the applicable life insurance company has the appropriate address and telephone numbers to contact concerning life insurance premium payments.

____8. File income tax returns for life insurance trust. The planner should determine the tax returns that the trust must complete and assign responsibility for such tax return preparation and filing.

____9. Collect life insurance proceeds. On the insured grantor's death, the trustee must collect the life insurance proceeds payable to the irrevocable life insurance trust. To accomplish this, the trustee may have to do one or more of the following:

- Submit proof of the insured's death to insurance company
- Execute and deliver a receipt or other documentation for the proceeds required by the insurance company
- Collect the proceeds.

[G]   Irrevocable Life Insurance Trust Instrument: One Life

Please see Form 13-24, Irrevocable Life Insurance Trust Instrument: One Life, on the accompanying CD.

[H]   Irrevocable Life Insurance Trust Instrument: Designed to Hold Joint Policy on Both Spouses' Lives

Please see Form 13-25, Irrevocable Life Insurance Trust Instrument: Designed to Hold Joint Policy on Both Spouses' Lives, on the accompanying CD.

§ 13.10   ALASKA ASSET PROTECTION TRUSTS[1]

Generally, when a person who creates and transfers assets to a spendthrift trust is also a beneficiary of that trust, the trust's spendthrift provision (a) will not prevent the settlor/beneficiary's creditors from reaching his interest in the trust, and (b) will not prevent the settlor/beneficiary from transferring his interest.[2] In contrast, the law of many foreign jurisdictions provides that when a person who creates and transfers assets to a foreign asset protection trust is also a beneficiary of that trust, he may include a provision that precludes his creditors from reaching his trust interest.

In 1997, Alaska statutorily modified its laws to reverse the general rule in the United States concerning self-settled spendthrift trusts, and shortly thereafter, Delaware similarly modified its laws.[3] Alaska and Delaware also repealed the rule against perpetuities. Subsequently, Nevada and Rhode Island enacted similar laws.[4] (For purposes of convenience, these types of trusts will be sometimes collectively referred to as Alaska type asset protection trusts). Because of these amendments, Alaska trusts provide asset protection planners with an extremely valuable tool for asset protection purposes. Moreover, even ignoring the asset protection benefits, these trusts provide outstanding estate planning opportunities. However, as with all asset protection tools, asset protection planners must evaluate the relevant risks presented by Alaska asset protection trusts.[5]

---

§ 13.10   [1] *See* § 5.14 of Volume 1 for a detailed discussion of Alaska asset protection trusts.

[2] Note that some courts have held that creditors of a settlor who is also a trust beneficiary cannot demand payment of any part of the trust assets where the settlor is merely eligible and not entitled to receive trust distributions. *See, e.g.,* Herzog v. Comm'r, 116 F.2d 591 (2d Cir. 1941); Uhl v. United States, 241 F.2d 867 (7th Cir. 1957); German v. United States, 85-1 U.S. Tax Cas. (CCH) ¶ 13,610 (Ct. Cl. 1985). *See also* Richard W. Hompesch II, et al., Does the New Alaska Trusts Act Provide an Alternative to the Foreign Trust, 2 J. Asset Protection 9 (July/August 1997).

[3] In Appendix G provides the full text of the Alaska trust legislation, and Appendix H provides the full text of the Delaware trust legislation.

[4] *See* Nev. Rev. Stat. § 166.040(1)(b) (1999); R.I. Gen. Laws §§ 18-9.2-1 to 18-9.2-5 (1999).

[5] *See generally* Leslie G. Giordani & Duncan E. Osborne, Will the Alaska Trusts Work? 3 J. Asset Protection 7 (Sept./Oct. 1997); Michael P. Franzmann & Alan R. Jahde, Onshore vs. Offshore Asset Protection Trusts: Which One Is Right for Your Client? 3 J. Asset Protection 9 (Nov./Dec. 1997); Jonathan G. Blattmachr et al., New Alaska Trust Act Provides Many Estate Planning Opportunities, 24 Est. Plan.

[A] Requirements for Alaska Trust Statute

If a trust that is governed by the Alaska trust statute contains a choice of law provision that provides that Alaska law governs that trust's validity, construction, and administration, and that provides that the trust is subject to the jurisdiction of Alaska, that provision will be valid, effective, and conclusive for the trust if it satisfies the following four requirements:[6]

[1] Some Assets Must Be Deposited in Alaska and Administered by a Qualified Person[7]

At least "some" assets must be "deposited" in Alaska, and a "qualified person" must administer such assets. For this purpose, the Alaska statute defines "deposited" in Alaska as including being held in a checking account, time deposit, certificate of deposit, brokerage account, trust company fiduciary account, or other similar account or deposit that is located in Alaska.[8]

The Alaska statute defines a "qualified person" as including the following:

- *Alaskan Individuals.* Individuals who, except for brief intervals, military service, attendance at an educational or training institution, or for absences for good cause shown, (a) reside in Alaska, (b) whose true and permanent home is in Alaska, and (c) who do not have a present intent of moving from Alaska, and who have the intention of returning to Alaska while they are away from Alaska[9]
- *Alaskan Trust Companies.* Trust Companies that are organized under Alaska Statute Section 06.25, and have their principal place of business in Alaska[10]
- *Alaskan Banks.* A bank that is organized under Alaska Statute Section 06.05, or a national banking association organized under 12 U.S.C. Sections 21-216d, if such bank or national banking association possesses and exercises trust powers and has its principal place of business in Alaska[11]

---

347 (Oct. 1997); David G. Shaftel, Newest Developments in Alaska Law Encourage Use of Alaska Trusts, 26 Est. Plan. 51 (Feb. 1999); Richard W. Nenno, Delaware Law Offers Asset Protection and Estate Planning Benefits, 26 Est. Plan. 3 (Jan. 1999); Stephen E. Greer & David G. Shaftel, Alaska Enacts Additional Estate Planning Legislation, 27 Est. Plan. 376 (2000); Robert L. Manley, Estate Planning with Self Settled Spendthrift Trusts: Steering Clear of Debts and Taxes, in Estate Planning Techniques (ALI-ABA 1999); Karen E. Boxx, Gray's Ghost—A Conversation about the Onshore Trust, 85 Iowa L. Rev. 1195 (May 2000); Thomas L. Flynn & Matthew T. Cronin, Self-Settled Spendthrift Trusts Move Close to Home, 2000 ABI Jnl. LEXIS 70 (Sept. 2000); John K. Eason, Home from the Islands: Domestic Asset Protection Trust Alternatives Impact Traditional Estate and Gift Tax Planning Considerations, 52 Florida L. Rev. 41 (Jan. 2000); Steward E. Sterk, Asset Protection Trusts: Trust Law's Race to the Bottom? 85 Cornell L. Rev. 1035 (May 2000).

[6] Alaska Stat. § 13.36.035(c) (2000).
[7] Alaska Stat. § 13.36.035(c)(1) (2000).
[8] *Id.*
[9] Alaska Stat. § 13.36.390(2)(A) (2000).
[10] Alaska Stat. § 13.36.390(2)(B) (2000).
[11] Alaska Stat. § 13.36.390(2)(c) (2000).

The Alaska statute does not define the term "some" for purposes of determining the amount of assets that must be deposited in Alaska. This results in some uncertainty as to what a trust must do to satisfy this requirement. Some commentators have stated that if a trust owns $10,000, which it holds in the form of a certificate of deposit or a brokerage account located in Alaska, this should satisfy this requirement.[12]

> **Planning Pointer.** One way to satisfy the requirement to deposit some assets in Alaska is to transfer the assets the client wishes to convey into the Alaska trust to an Alaska family limited partnership (FLP) or Alaska limited liability company (LLC), and then subsequently use the interests in such Alaskan limited partnership or Alaskan limited liability company to fund the Alaska trust.

[2] Trust Instrument or Court Must Designate a Qualified Person (i.e., Alaskan Person) as a Trustee[13]

Either the trust instrument or a court that has jurisdiction over the trust must designate a qualified person as a trustee of the trust.[14] The definition of "qualified person" for this purpose is the same as that discussed above. From a practical standpoint, this means that at least one trustee must be Alaskan to ensure that the trust qualifies as an Alaska trust.[15]

[3] Trust Provides Trustee with Required Powers[16]

The Alaska trust statute states that the powers given to the trustee who is a qualified person must include or be limited to the following:

- Maintaining records for the trust on an exclusive basis or a nonexclusive basis, and
- Preparing or arranging for the preparation of, on an exclusive basis or a nonexclusive basis, an income tax return that the trust must file.

[4] Alaska Administration[17]

At least part of the trust's administration must occur in Alaska, including maintaining trust records in Alaska. Some commentators have stated that holding trustee meetings in Alaska, holding meetings in Alaska with trust

---

[12] Jonathan G. Blattmachr & Douglas J. Blattmachr, An Overview of the Alaska Trust Act (1997).

[13] Alaska Stat. § 13.36.035(c)(2) (2000).

[14] Id.

[15] Jonathan G. Blattmachr & Douglas J. Blattmachr, An Overview of the Alaska Trust Act (1997).

[16] Alaska Stat. § 13.36.035(c)(3) (2000).

[17] Alaska Stat. § 13.36.035(c)(4) (2000).

beneficiaries, maintaining accounts in Alaska, or initiating "trades" in Alaska should satisfy this requirement.[18]

[B] Alaska Asset Protection Trust[19]

Please see Form 13-26, Alaska Asset Protection Trust, on the accompanying CD.

§13.11 GRANTOR RETAINED ANNUITY TRUSTS ("GRATS")

[A] What Is a GRAT?

A GRAT involves a transfer by a grantor to an irrevocable trust, which provides the grantor with an annuity for either a fixed period of time, or the life of an individual. More specifically, to establish a GRAT, the grantor would contribute money or other property to a GRAT in exchange for the right to receive a specified number of fixed annual annuity payments. After the final annuity payment has been made to the grantor, the trustees may either (a) pay the remaining funds that the GRAT holds at that time to the reminder beneficiaries, which are typically the Grantor's children, or (b) retain those funds and continue to administer the trust on behalf of the remainder beneficiaries, in either case, pursuant to the trust agreement.

[B] Wealth Preservation Benefits

For gift tax purposes, the grantor makes a taxable gift equal to the actuarial value of the remainder interest, determined when the GRAT is funded rather than when it terminates, and distributes its corpus to or for the benefit of the remainder beneficiaries. This has two consequences. First, even though the remainder beneficiary will receive the full value of the corpus, the gift tax will be computed on value of the remainder interest. The value of the remainder interest equals the full value of the property transferred to the GRAT, less the value of the annuity interest that the grantor retains.

EXAMPLE 13-3

George creates and funds a GRAT with $1 million. Under the GRAT's terms, George receives an annual annuity for ten years of $100,000 per year. At the

---

[18] Jonathan G. Blattmachr & Douglas J. Blattmachr, An Overview of the Alaska Trust Act (1997).

[19] The Alaska Protection Trust Agreement was graciously provided to the authors by the Alaska Trust Company.

end of ten years, the corpus passes to George's son, Bill. Assume the IRC § 7520 rate is 8 percent at this time. Here, the value of George's retained annuity interest equals $671,010, and the value of the remainder interest, which is subject to gift tax, equals $328,990. However, at the end of ten years, Bill receives $1 million, even though only $328,990 is subject to gift tax.

EXAMPLE 13-4

Assume the same facts as Example 1, except that the applicable IRC § 7520 rate is 6 percent. Here, the value of George's retained annuity interest equals $736,010, and the value of the remainder interest, which is subject to gift tax, equals $263,990.

If the GRAT generates a rate of return that exceeds the actuarial assumptions used to determine the value of the remainder interest, the excess passes outside the transfer tax system.

Because GRATs make annuity payments to their grantors for a fixed term, they provide a source of income to such grantors.

Some commentators believe that if the corpus of the GRAT increases substantially in value, grantors may effectively remove part of the GRAT corpus from their estates, even if they die during the annuity term. This results from Revenue Ruling 82-105,[1] which ruled that where a charitable remainder annuity trust grantor died during the annuity period, his estate only included the amount of trust corpus required to generate the promised annuity return. However, the IRS disagrees with this position.

Chapter 14 of the IRC does not apply to GRATs. Therefore, grantors may effect an estate "freeze" with respect to the GRAT property, without being subject to Chapter 14.

As long as the transfer to the GRAT does not constitute a fraudulent conveyance, a GRAT may provide some degree of asset protection for both the grantor and the remainder beneficiaries because the GRAT will (a) be an irrevocable trust, and (b) typically contain a spendthrift provision.

[C]   Structure and Implementation

A client would create a GRAT by transferring assets to an irrevocable trust, and retaining an annuity interest for a specified number of years. This involves the following steps or decisions:

1. **Trust agreement.** An attorney must prepare a Grantor Retained Annuity Trust Agreement.

§ 13.11   [1] 1982-1 C.B. 133.

2.   **Annuity payments.** The trust agreement must provide for annuity payments. These payments may be a fixed dollar amount, a percentage of the GRAT's initial value, or a fixed percentage of the annual value of the trust (*i.e.*, a GRUT or Grantor Retained Unitrust). Factors that grantors and their advisors must consider when determining the amount of the annuity payments and the length of the annuity term include the following:

   a.   **Annuity payments.** The larger the annuity payments, the lower the gift tax. However, to the extent the grantor does not consume or spend such annuity payments, the larger such payments are, the greater the amount retained in the grantor's taxable estate for estate tax purposes.

   b.   **Length of annuity term.** The longer the annuity term, the lower the gift tax and the longer that the GRAT provides the grantor with a stream of annuity payments. However, if the grantor dies during the annuity term, the GRAT's corpus will be included in his estate. Therefore, to obtain an estate tax planning benefit from a GRAT, the grantor must outlive the annuity term, and this must be considered in selecting the length of the annuity term.

3.   **Remainder interest and termination.** Upon the end of the annuity term, the GRAT stops the annuity payments, and either (a) pays the entire corpus to the remainder beneficiaries, or (b) continues to hold the corpus in trust for the remainder beneficiaries.

4.   **Appraisals.** The grantor must obtain appraisals of property transferred into the trust from their accountants or other appraisers.

[D]   *Zeroed Out GRATs*

A zeroed-out GRAT is a GRAT in which the value of the grantor's retained interest equals the value of the property transferred to the trust, resulting in a remainder, and a gift-tax value, of zero. Because of a recent case, involving the brother of Sam Walton, the founder of Walmart,

1.   Under Treas. Reg. § 25.2702-3(e), Example 5, the calculation of the taxable gift made when creating a GRAT always contained a mortality component. In such cases, the value of the GRAT remainder interest could never be "zeroed out," thereby eliminating a taxable gift on the creation of the GRAT. This was true even where the annuity was payable for a fixed term without a reversionary interest and was expected to exhaust the trust principal by the end of the term under IRS annuity valuation tables.

2.   A recent decision of the United States Tax Court, *Walton v. Commissioner,*[2] appears to have resolved the question of whether zeroed out GRATs are possible. Before *Walton,* Treasury Regulations provided that even if a grantor retained the right to receive an annuity over a fixed term in a GRAT, the value of the qualified annuity interest was determined as though the right to

[2] 115 T.C. 41 (2000).

the annuity was retained for the shorter of the fixed term or until the grantor's death, which is less than the right to receive an annuity for the entire fixed term. In other words, the IRS allowed the retained annuity interest to be valued only if the grantor would receive it during life, and any interest that passed to the grantor's estate if he or she died during the term of the GRAT would not be included in the value of the retained annuity interest. Therefore, the amount of the annuity was reduced by the probability of the individual's death before the end of the term and that amount is considered a remainder interest taxable as a gift to the remainder beneficiaries.

3. Under *Walton,* the value of an annuity payable over a term to the grantor and to the grantor's estate if the grantor dies during the GRAT term is not reduced by the value of the contingent interest that the grantor's estate if the grantor dies during the GRAT term because a fixed annuity payable to the grantor or the grantor's estate does constitute a "qualified interest" under section 2702. Therefore, a fixed GRAT period may be established in the trust document that will not terminate if the grantor dies during the GRAT term. A GRAT that pays the annuity amount to the grantor during his or her lifetime and to his or her estate if the grantor dies during the term of the GRAT will be included in the value of the retained annuity interest. This removes the decrease previously required to be made to the retained interest to account for the possibility of the grantor's death during the term and allows the GRAT to be zeroed out leaving a remainder of zero.

The benefit of a zeroed out GRAT is that a client may transfer an asset to a GRAT, at zero gift tax consequences, and any appreciation of the property will pass to the remainder beneficiaries at zero estate tax cost. In other words, the only downside or cost to such a wealth preservation technique is the costs of establishing the GRAT.

Impact of Low Interest Rates. GRATs are a more attractive when the interest rates are low, and specifically, when the IRC section 7520 rate is low. As the section 7520 rate decreases, the value of the retained interest in a GRAT increases. This occurs because a decrease in the assumed rate of return makes the right to receive fixed amounts in the future more valuable. Because the grantor may use a valuation formula, a GRAT allows the grantor to transfer a difficult to value asset without a significant risk of unexpected gift tax.

[E] *Situations Where a GRAT Should Be Considered*

[1] Leverage Unified Credit Gift with No Downside Risk

A GRAT allows a client to leverage transfers to children. As long as the asset appreciates more than the Code Section 7520 rate, the children win. If the asset does not outperform the Section 7520 rate, then the client receives back the asset with no tax consequences.

[2] Client Has Made Unified Credit Gift and Does Not Want to Pay Gift Tax

Some clients have made unified credit gifts and are reluctant to make additional gifts because of the aversion to paying gift tax. The client in this situation should consider a zeroed-out GRAT. A zeroed-out GRAT does not result in a taxable gift to the remainder beneficiaries and the client does not pay gift tax. If the trust assets outperform the Section 7520 rate, the client has made a transfer to children or other beneficiaries outside the transfer tax system.

[3] Asset with Significant Appreciation Potential in Short-Term

A GRAT may be an ideal vehicle for the transfer of significant appreciation on an asset. Assume the client owns an interest in a business that may go public in the near future. If the client transfers the business interest to a short-term zeroed-out GRAT, most of the appreciation will be transferred tax-free. If the client has more than one asset with this potential, it is wise to use a separate GRAT for each asset so as not to dilute the appreciation.

[4] Client Has Portfolio That Will Outperform the Code Section 7520 Rate and Wants to Minimize Transfer Taxes

The key to using a GRAT to leverage transfers is selecting assets that will outperform the Section 7520 rate.

[F] Grantor Retained Annuity Trust Instrument

Please see Form 13-27, Grantor Retained Annuity Trust Instrument, on the accompanying CD.

§13.11 CHECKLIST OF DOMESTIC TRUST FORMATION ISSUES

The planner should use the following checklist to ensure that no critical issue is overlooked in connection with the planner's preparation of domestic trusts.

[A] Revocable Trust

____ 1. Is the planner considering using a revocable trust as part of the asset protection plan?
If yes, the planner should note that although revocable trusts give the client more control over trust corpus, they provide less asset protection than irrevocable trusts. Also, they generally will be treated as grantor trusts

for income tax purposes, and the corpus must generally be included in the settlor's gross estate for federal transfer tax purposes.

____2. Is the asset protection client married, and is one spouse substantially more at risk, from an asset protection standpoint, than the other?
If yes, the planner should consider the following strategy:

    ____(a) Inventory all of the assets of each spouse.
    ____(b) Partition the property between the spouses.
    ____(c) Establish a revocable trust for each spouse where:

        ____ (i)   each spouse becomes the grantor, initial beneficiary, and trustee of his or her trust, and
        ____ (ii) the trust gives the other spouse a beneficial interest, but only if the grantor is the first spouse to die or disclaims his or her interest.

[B]   Irrevocable Trust

____3. Is the planner considering using an irrevocable trust as part of the asset protection plan?
If yes, the planner should note that, although irrevocable trusts give clients less control over trust corpus, they provide greater asset protection than revocable trusts. Additionally, the planner may choose (a) whether to make the trust a grantor trust or not for income tax purposes, and (b) whether to make the corpus includible in the settlor's gross estate for federal transfer tax purposes.
If yes, the planner should consider the following strategy:

    ____(a) Give the settlor an income interest in the irrevocable trust.
    ____(b) Give the settlor a special power of appointment over the trust corpus, only in favor of the objects of the settlor bounty (for example, the settlor's spouse or children).
    ____(c) Give the trustee the discretionary power to distribute trust corpus among the objects of the settlor's bounty, but prohibit the trustee from using this discretionary power to distribute to discharge any of the settlor's legal obligations to the objects of the settlor's bounty. This prevents the settlor from becoming a deemed beneficiary of the trust.
    ____(d) Include a spendthrift provision in the trust.

[C]   Charitable Remainder Trust (CRT)

____4. Is the planner considering using a CRT as part of the asset protection plan?
If yes, the planner should note that CRTs provide the greatest benefit to asset protection clients who (1) fall into a high income tax bracket, who (2)

desire both (a) asset protection, and (b) to sell highly appreciated property. In such cases, CRTs provide the client with the following benefits:

____(a) It generates a current charitable income tax deduction for the donation of a remainder interest in the trust in the year of the transfer to the trust.

____(b) It avoids capital gain tax on the sale of the appreciated property.

____(c) It increases the cash flow to the client or to individuals chosen by the client to receive an income interest in the trust.

____(d) It decreases the client's estate tax burden.

____(e) It may serve as a form of retirement plan for the client.

____5. When drafting the CRT instrument, the planner should ensure that the trust instrument guarantees that the trust satisfies the following:

____(a) The trust constitutes either an annuity trust or unitrust.

____(b) The trust does not include any provision that restricts the trustee from investing trust assets in a way that could result in the annual realization of a reasonable amount of income or gain from the sale or disposition of trust assets.

____(c) The trust's term lasts either for the life or lives of a named individual(s) or for a term of years that does not exceed 20 years.

____(d) The trust does not allow for any impermissible payments. Generally, the trust must not make any payments to a noncharitable recipient other than to the annuity or unitrust recipient or for full consideration.

____(e) The trust instrument must irrevocably assign the CRT remainder interest to or for the use of one or more qualifying charitable organizations.

____(f) The trust instrument must contain provisions that prohibit it from taking actions that violate the private foundation excise tax provisions.

____(g) Annuity trust instruments must prohibit additional contributions.

____(h) Unitrust instruments must specify how the trustee must prorate income payments when additional contributions are made after the CRT is formed.

____6. Does the grantor want to serve as the CRT's trustee?

If yes, the planner should consider the following risks associated with the grantor serving as the CRT's trustee:

____(a) The IRS may be more likely to challenge valuations of the trust assets, especially when the planner uses a unitrust, which must be revalued annually.

____(b) The IRS may be more likely to attempt to impute capital gain to the grantor on the sale of an appreciated asset when the grantor negotiated such sale before creating the trust. Alternatively, the IRS may argue that there was a prearranged sale, thereby imposing an

impermissible investment restriction on the trustee and disqualifying the tax-exempt status of the trust.

___(c)   There is an increased risk that the grantor will not satisfy (a) the
record-keeping and reporting requirements, and (b) the self-
dealing prohibitions imposed on CRTs.

___7.   Has the planner selected a payout rate for the CRT? The planner should
consider the following factors when determining the payout rate:

___(a)   The payout rate must be at least 5 percent per year.
___(b)   The payout rate must not be so high that the IRS may determine
that the CRT will likely exhaust its trust assets.
___(c)   For unitrust CRTs, planners should consider the impact of the
recapitalization of excess earnings.

___8.   Has the client entered a legally binding sales contract concerning property
that the planner wants the client to transfer to the CRT?
If yes, the planner should note that the IRS takes the position that in such
cases the transferring taxpayer must recognize any resulting capital gain
on the sale of such property.

___9.   Is the planner considering the transfer of any S corporation stock to the
CRT?
If yes, the planner should note that the transfer of such stock to the CRT will
terminate the corporation's S corporation election upon the transfer.

[D]   Life Insurance Trust

___10. Is the planner considering using a life insurance trust as part of the asset
protection plan?
If yes, the planner should resolve the following questions:

___(a)   How does the exemption statute apply to protect the insurance
policy proceeds and cash value from the insured's creditors?
___(b)   How does the exemption statute apply to protect the insurance
policy proceeds and cash value from the beneficiary's creditors?
___(c)   What are the gift tax consequences of using the irrevocable life
insurance trust?
___(d)   What are the estate tax consequences of using the irrevocable
life insurance trust?
___(e)   What are the income tax consequences of using the irrevocable
life insurance trust?
___(f)   Who should serve as the trustee of the irrevocable life insurance
trust?' Generally, planners should ensure that none of the following serve as trustee for the irrevocable life insurance trust:

___ (i)   grantor
___ (ii)   grantor's spouse, or
___(iii)   any trust beneficiary.

_____(g) What administrative powers should the planner give to the trustee of an irrevocable life insurance trust?

_____(h) Should the planner use a trust protector?

_____(i) Should the planner include a backup marital QTIP trust clause?

_____(j) What *Crummey* withdrawal powers should be given to beneficiaries?

_____(k) What practical matters must the planner consider regarding an irrevocable life insurance trust's administration?

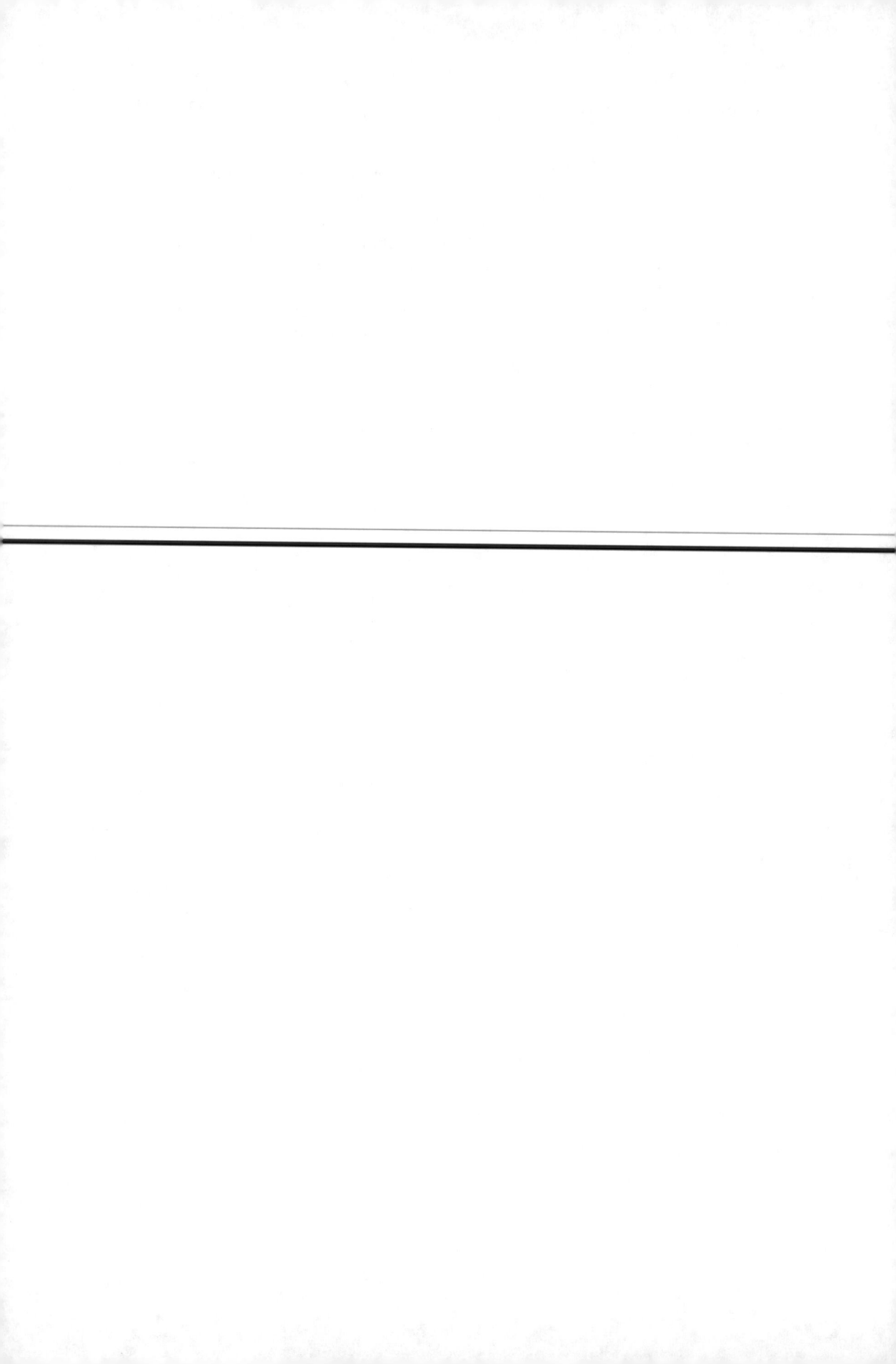

14

Foreign Trusts

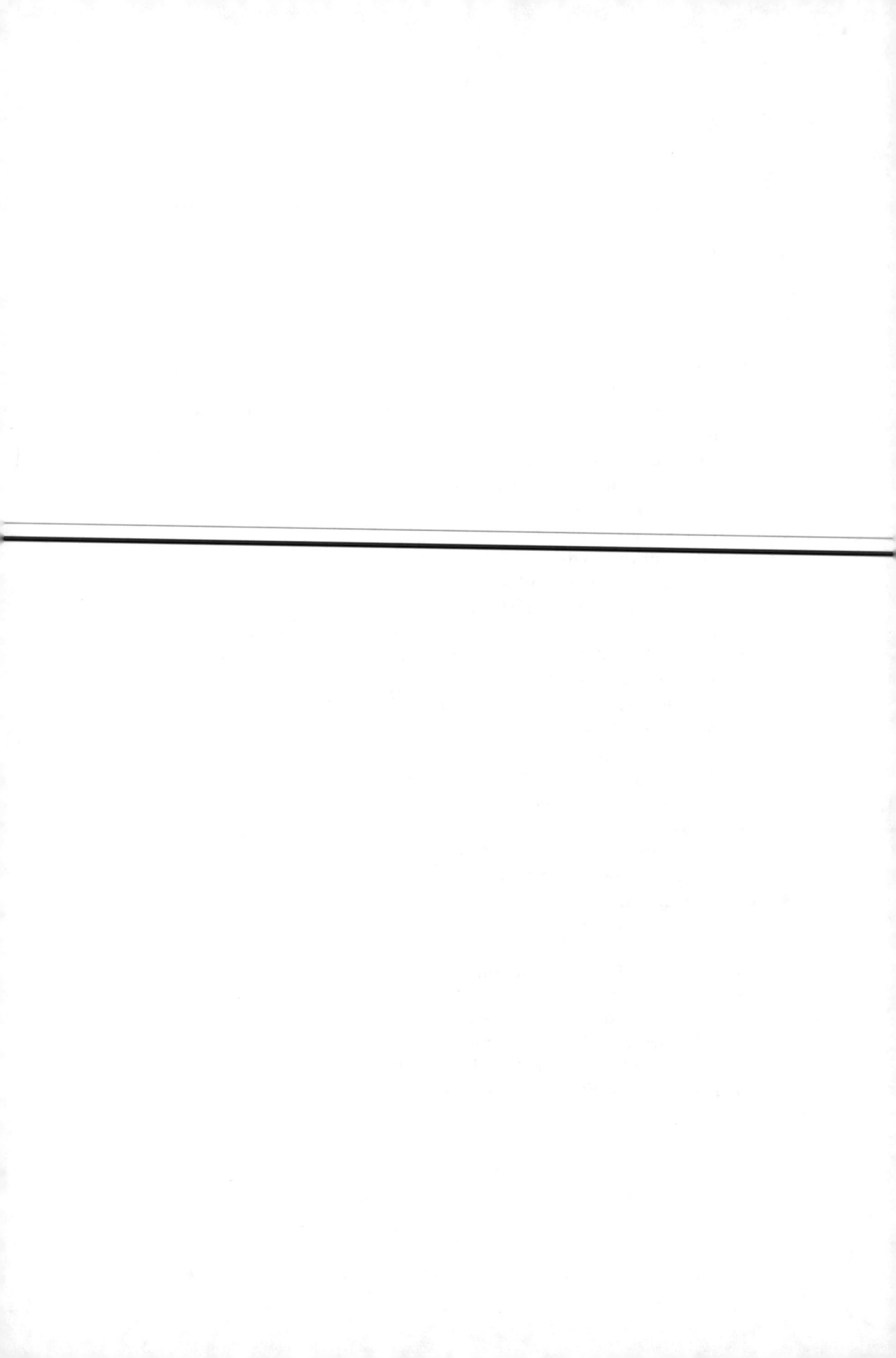

§ 14.01   IN GENERAL

Foreign asset protection trusts (FAPTs) are trusts that settlors establish in foreign jurisdictions that have enacted laws that protect trust assets to a greater extent than United States law does.[1] When properly used, an FAPT provides a greater amount of asset protection than any other type of trust. However, an FAPT is more expensive than other trusts and requires more competent advisors because of their increased complexity. Generally, when properly selected, the foreign jurisdiction provides such greater protection in the following ways:

1. The foreign jurisdiction does not recognize foreign (United States) judgments. This forces potential claimants to litigate their claims in the foreign jurisdiction, usually for a second time after having previously litigated the claim in the United States.
2. The foreign jurisdiction generally requires plaintiffs to use attorneys who are licensed in that jurisdiction, thus increasing the plaintiffs' costs and risks of prosecuting their cases.
3. The foreign jurisdiction generally prohibits contingency fee arrangements. This forces the plaintiff to finance the litigation himself instead of having a law firm finance the litigation through a contingency fee arrangement.
4. The foreign jurisdiction's substantive law is generally much more favorable to the defendant (that is, the asset protection client). For example, some foreign jurisdictions impose a higher standard of proof upon civil litigation plaintiffs, such as the "beyond a reasonable doubt" standard. This contrasts with the "preponderance of the evidence" standard for civil cases in the United States.

Caution. Before using an FAPT, planners must decide whether such vehicles are appropriate for the client involved. FAPTs are normally appropriate only for clients with substantial wealth. Also, clients must feel comfortable with transmitting a substantial amount of wealth to a foreign jurisdiction.

Planning Pointer. FAPTs may also serve purposes other than asset protection. Specifically, they may help clients achieve traditional estate planning goals, such as the orderly transfer of wealth between generations, and may serve a client's need for economic diversification. Also, clients may use them to manage foreign assets, foreign businesses, or foreign real estate. Finally, clients may use FAPTs as a unilateral method of premarital planning. In other words, they may be used as a surrogate for, or as a complement to, prenuptial agreements.

§ 14.01   [1] *See* Lewis D. Solomon & Lewis J. Saret, Asset Protection Strategies, Chapter. 6 (2006).

Planning Pointer. Planners should consider the following issues when analyzing an FAPT:

1. How should the FAPT plan be structured?[2]
2. What is the ability of United States creditors to reach the FAPT's assets?[3]
3. What are the tax consequences of the FAPT on the settlor?[4]
4. What reports must the planner ensure are properly filed?[5]
5. What factors should the planner consider when drafting an FAPT instrument?[6]

§ 14.02 DRAFTING FAPT INSTRUMENTS

The well-planned FAPT should contain certain features.[1] Specifically, the planner should make the FAPT irrevocable for a period of years. Generally, the settlor should not be a trust beneficiary, and the planner must choose the FAPT trustees with extreme caution. Further, the planner must ensure that the FAPT instrument contains anti-duress provisions. Also, the trust instrument should require the trustee to follow detailed guidelines regarding investments and distributions. The trust should allow the trustee to make discretionary payments from corpus or income to tax authorities to cover tax liabilities of the settlor that result from income attributed to him from the trust.

Caution. Planners must use extreme care when drafting foreign trusts. For example, they must be aware of the fact that foreign jurisdictions may attribute different meanings to language than the United States attributes to such language. Also, planners must deal with a body of substantive law that differs from domestic law.

Planning Pointer. Planners should have competent foreign counsel review foreign trust instruments that they have drafted. At a bare minimum, they

---

[2] *See* § 6.05.
[3] *See* § 6.02.
[4] *See* § 6.06.
[5] *See* Chapter 15.
[6] *See* § 14.02, *infra.*

§ 14.02 [1] *See generally* Jeffrey A. Schoenblum, Multistate and Multinational Estate Planning (1982 & Supp. 1990); International Trust Precedents (Nicola Bradbury et al. eds., 1989); Howard M. Zaritsky, Foreign Trusts, Estates, and Beneficiaries, Tax Mgmt. (BNA) No. 854 (2001); Charles M. Bruce & Stephen Gray, Offshore Protection of Assets Trusts, U.S. Tax'n of Int'l Operations (WGL) J.13,510 (1988); International Estate Planning: Principles and Strategies (Donald D. Kozusko & Jeffrey A. Schoenblum eds., 1991); Charles M. Bruce, United States Tax'n of Foreign Trusts (2000).

should have competent foreign counsel review the first foreign trust instrument that they draft for any particular jurisdiction.

Planning Pointer. Planners must consider the following types of provisional issues when drafting trust instruments:

1. Provision making FAPT irrevocable for a term of years
2. Beneficiary provisions
3. Rule against perpetuities
4. Governing law provisions
5. Trustees' powers
6. Settlor's powers
7. Notice provisions
8. Allocation of authority
9. Careful selection of trustees
10. Substitution of trustees
11. Branch office trustees
12. Duress Provisions
13. Provisions dealing with trust situs instability
14. Flight provisions
15. Protector
16. Protective provisions for property in third countries
17. Record keeping.

This chapter provides sample FAPT trust instruments for the Cook Islands,[2] the Bahamas,[3] and the Cayman Islands.[4]

[A] Provision Making FAPT Irrevocable for Term of Years

Planners must ensure that their FAPTs are irrevocable.[5] Many courts hold that the settlor's creditors may reach the trust corpus when the settlor retains the power to revoke the trust. Also, some jurisdictions have enacted statutes providing that when settlors retain an absolute or unqualified power to revoke the trust, they are deemed to be the absolute owners of the trust property for purposes of satisfying creditor claims. Where such statutes exist, the settlor's creditors can reach the trust corpus. Consequently, the planner must ensure that the FAPT is irrevocable.

Second, the trust should be for a period of years, which the client should select. The planner, however, must ensure that the trust period does not violate the rule against perpetuities, which is discussed below.

---

[2] *See* § 14.03, *infra.*
[3] *See* § 14.04, *infra.*
[4] *See* § 14.05, *infra.*
[5] *See* § 6.05[A].

Planning Pointer. The trust instrument should include an anti-duress provision that extends the trust term in cases of duress. This will protect the settlor from creditors who raise claims near the end of the trust's term. Alternatively, the planner may use an extensive trust term and give the trustees the ability to shorten this period, absent an event of duress.

EXAMPLE 14-1

Maggie Tulliver is an accountant with a large, multinational accounting firm, which operates in the form of a general partnership. She expects to become a partner within the next five years. She recently inherited a substantial amount of property from her father. Her inheritance includes $50 million of cash and marketable securities, and a rice mill that sits along a river, which is worth $10 million. Maggie becomes concerned about the liabilities that she will become exposed to when she becomes a partner. Consequently, she consults with her brother, Tom, an asset protection planner. Tom establishes the Tulliver FAPT to protect Maggie's assets. He establishes the Tulliver FAPT in a jurisdiction that does not recognize foreign judgments against assets transferred into a foreign trust that arise two years after such transfers are made. This jurisdiction also allows settlors to establish spendthrift trusts in favor of themselves.

Maggie contributes $10 million to the Tulliver FAPT. Tom designs the FAPT to include the following features:

- 100-year term, with the trustees possessing the power to shorten the trust term, absent a duress event, in their absolute and unfettered discretion.
- The FAPT instrument gives the trustees the right to distribute principal and income, in the trustees' sole and absolute discretion, to Maggie's two sons, George and Eliot.
- The FAPT instrument gives the trustees the right to distribute the trust corpus held by the trust at its termination to Maggie, her two sons, George and Eliot, or any of their issue, in whatever proportions they decide in their sole and unfettered discretion.

Five years after Maggie establishes the Tulliver FAPT, she becomes a partner in her accounting firm. Seven years later, a bank that another office of Maggie's firm previously audited goes bankrupt. After litigation, a court renders a judgment against Maggie's firm, and Maggie becomes jointly and severally liable for a $40 million debt. Here, the funds in the Tulliver FAPT are not subject to this obligation.

EXAMPLE 14-2

Same facts as example above, except that Tom structures the Tulliver FAPT instrument to obligate the trustees to distribute $100,000 to Maggie each calendar quarter. Here, even though the situs jurisdiction may allow settlors to establish spendthrift trusts in their own favor, Maggie's creditors may be able to reach her interest in the FAPT.

[B] Beneficiary Provisions

Generally, the FAPT should provide for either mandatory or discretionary distributions to a class of beneficiaries that does not include the settlor during the trust term, and for a final distribution of the trust principal and accumulated income to the settlor at the termination of the trust. Alternatively, the trust may provide for no income interests in the trust.

Planning Pointer. The planner should generally ensure that the settlor is not an income beneficiary of the trust. If the settlor retains an income interest, his creditors can reach that interest. Furthermore, the planner must ensure that all beneficial interests are protected by a spendthrift provision. When the client strongly desires to retain a beneficial income interest, the planner may allow this. However, the planner must advise the client that this interest will be at risk because creditors are generally able to reach beneficial interests retained by the client.

Planning Pointer. Under one optional structure, the planner may establish a corporation based in the United States to hold the assets that would otherwise be held directly by the trust. The settlor would then transfer all of the stock of the corporation to the FAPT. The settlor would serve as the sole director and officer of the corporation. When the requirements are satisfied, the corporation elects S corporation status. This structure allows the settlor to maintain direct control over the assets contained within the trust. The trust instrument would provide that during duress the trust would liquidate or encumber all the corporation's assets and send the cash proceeds to the offshore trustee, which would then invest those proceeds in financial institutions that would be located outside the United States. This also allows the corporation to pay a salary to the settlor, thus providing income to the settlor during the trust term. However, this structure is disadvantageous in that the settlor remains subject to U.S. court orders. Consequently, a U.S. court may prevent him from liquidating the corporate assets and transferring them to the FAPT trustee.

Alternatively, the settlor may establish a family limited partnership. This would work much like the corporation structure, except that the settlor would retain a one percent general partnership interest and would transfer a 99 percent limited partnership interest to the FAPT.

> **Planning Pointer.** The trust should be a discretionary trust for added asset protection.

[C]   Rule against Perpetuities

Planners must understand the applicable jurisdiction's law to ensure that their perpetuity provisions comply with such laws. For example, some jurisdictions impose no prohibitions at all. In others, attorneys typically use royal lives perpetuities clauses (that is, clauses that refer to the lives of the British royalty). Planners must consult local law.

> **Caution.** When using standby trusts, or there is any possibility that the trustees will move the trust in the future, planners must consider each applicable jurisdiction's rule against perpetuities.

[D]   Governing Law Provisions

Next, planners must include a governing law clause. Many offshore jurisdictions have enacted statutes giving effect to such clauses. When using jurisdictions that rely on English common law, planners should ensure that their trusts have some nexus to the jurisdiction whose law controls.[6]

> **Planning Pointer.** To ensure the FAPT possesses the necessary nexus to the jurisdiction whose law controls it, planners should consider creating their trusts in one jurisdiction whose law will control them, and then move their trusts to another jurisdiction where their trustees will administer them.[7] This strategy generally gives the first jurisdiction the required nexus. When using this strategy, planners must ensure that (1) the jurisdiction of creation permits transference of trusts, and (2) the second jurisdiction accepts trusts created elsewhere.

---

[6] Jeffrey A. Schoenblum, Multistate and Multinational Estate Planning §§ 18.16.3, 18.18.3 (1982 & Supp. 1990).

[7] Id.

EXAMPLE 14-3

Churchill, an asset protection planner, creates an FAPT for his client, Roosevelt. Churchill creates the FAPT in the Cayman Islands and them moves it to the Cook Islands to be administered. The FAPT instrument provides that Cayman Islands law will control it. Here, Cayman Islands law will govern the FAPT.[8]

[E] Trustees' Powers

Planners must pay close attention to clauses setting forth the trustees' powers, compensation, bonding requirements, exoneration from potential liability, and the necessity of accountings. This results because the foreign jurisdiction's law may contain unexpected restrictions on the trustee, and the FAPT will have a much wider selection of investments to choose from than most domestic trusts.[9] Examples of areas that planners should pay attention to include the following:

1. Timing and content of accounting reports to be provided
2. Rights of participants to demand information
3. Nature of geographic location of allowable investments, especially when the planner desires to exclude certain jurisdictions, such as the grantor's home jurisdiction.[10]

[F] Settlor's Powers

Planners must ensure that their trust instruments clearly set forth the settlor's retained powers. Planners should also draft the settlor powers provisions of their foreign trusts in detail. This will avoid uncertainty.

Caution. Planners should bear in mind that creditors generally may step into the settlor's shoes. Consequently, planners should restrict the powers given to the settlor.

[G] Notice Provisions

The geographic distance of the foreign jurisdictions of the FAPT's creation and administration requires planners to pay particular attention to notice provisions.

---

[8] Trust (Foreign Element) Law 1987 §4 (Cayman Islands).

[9] Howard M. Zaritsky, Foreign Trusts, Estates, and Beneficiaries, Tax Mgmt. (BNA) No. 854, at A-51 (1993).

[10] Jeffrey A. Schoenblum, Multistate and Multinational Estate Planning §§18.16.3, 18.18.3 (1982 & Supp. 1990).

For example, although mail may be acceptable notice for domestic trusts, the time delays for mail to or from an offshore jurisdiction will generally be unacceptable. Consequently, planners must consider including a provision specifying whether telephonic, facsimile, or specified forms of overnight mail directives will bind the trustee and release it from liability. Otherwise, the trustee may wait for days until receiving formal written instructions. Planners should also carefully set forth details regarding the manner in which notification of action taken by the trustee must be given and who is to receive such notification.

[H]   Allocation of Authority

Planners must also consider who to authorize to direct trustees under specified circumstances. More specifically, planners must delineate a clear chain of command so that trustees will know whether to honor a particular order. Planners must also clearly define the authority that each party associated with the trust possesses.

[I]   Careful Selection of Trustees

The planner must carefully select the FAPT's trustees. The planner should avoid using United States co-trustees. Such a co-trustee may cause severe problems both for the co-trustee and for the FAPT. For example, some reputable trust companies may not accept a United States co-trustee; some Statute of Elizabeth override statutes will not apply if there is a United States co-trustee; or the FAPT may not constitute a trust in some jurisdictions if there is a United States co-trustee. Finally, the foreign trustee should be an independent trust company or bank that has had experience managing FAPTs.

> **Planning Pointer.** In some jurisdictions the settlor may establish a corporation or company that will become the trustee of the trust. This allows the settlor to retain control over the trust.

The planner should also include a trust instrument provision that establishes a committee of trust protectors or advisors. The settlor would generally be the chairman of this committee, which may have the power to remove trustees and appoint a successor trustee. Also, the committee of protectors or advisors may provide nonbinding advice to the trustee concerning the investments that the trustee makes. Generally, the trust instrument suspends these powers during times of duress. This allows the settlor to retain control over the trust until a judgment creditor attempts to reach the settlor's assets.

> **Planning Pointer.** Beneficiaries of the FAPT or individuals with interests adverse to the settlor's interests should also sit on the committee of

protectors or advisors. This will minimize the risk that the settlor will be deemed to be a defacto trustee of the FAPT.

The trust should include a provision that provides for an emergency trustee. Such a provision provides that if an event of duress occurs in the trust situs jurisdiction, the trustee is deemed to transfer the trust fund and its income to the emergency trustee and to change the forum of management, control, and administration of the trust fund from its original location to the location where the emergency trustee resides. Generally, the emergency trustee resides in a second offshore location. For example, the original trustee may be located in the Cook Islands, and the emergency trustee may be located in the Cayman Islands. The trust also should provide for successor emergency trustees to protect the trust in the event that an event of duress occurs in the jurisdiction of the emergency trustee. The trust instrument must provide that the trustee must execute all necessary documents and do everything necessary to perfect the emergency trustee's tide. The trust instrument should include a schedule of emergency trustees that sets out the hierarchy of the emergency foreign trustees.

Planning Pointer. The safest strategy is for the settlor to transfer all control over liquid assets to the foreign trustee. Title to real property should not be transferred to the foreign trustee because U.S. courts would generally retain control over such property. Instead such property should either be (1) sold, or (2) encumbered, with the sale or loan proceeds sent to the foreign trustee for offshore investment.

[J] Substitution of Trustees and Relationship of Co-trustees

Planners must provide for the replacement of trustees if such an event becomes necessary. This is critical because if planners do not provide for trustee replacement, the applicable jurisdictions' laws may provide their own default succession rules. Such rules may implant in the office of the trustee a party who is not receptive to the needs of the settlor and the FAPT's beneficiaries.

Planning Pointer. Planners should either provide a mechanism for replacing trustees, or name several alternative trustees because the named successor trustee may either be unavailable when needed or not qualify in the applicable jurisdiction.

Planning Pointer. When planners use multiple trustees, they should clearly define the trustees' relative authority and the voting percentage needed to act. This becomes critical in jurisdictions that require a government agency to act as a co-trustee. When possible, such governmental entities should not be left with the balance of power in the trust. The planner should appoint several reliable co-trustees to ensure control of the FAPT. If the jurisdiction permits only local trustees to serve, planners should avoid that jurisdiction.

[K] Branch Office Trustees

Planners must use caution when using a branch or controlled trustee. Foreign governments that exercise authority over other branches may succeed in reaching the trust corpus or in compelling disclosure concerning the trust.[11] A secondary concern is that a court may hold that the situs is at the branch office's controlling office.[12]

> **Planning Pointer.** To eliminate doubts regarding situs when a planner uses a branch trustee, the FAPT instrument should provide for the designation of another trustee if uncertainty exists regarding the situs or if the trustee indicates that it intends to shift the situs of its operations.[13]

[L] Duress Provisions

Because the settlor or a close relative will often be a protector or advisor to the FAPT and because such settlor or relative will generally be a U.S. citizen subject to the personal jurisdiction of U.S. courts, the planner must include anti-duress provisions in the trust instrument. Specifically, the trust should provide that, in the event of duress, the following should occur. If the duress occurs in the trust's situs jurisdiction, the duress provision should provide that the trustee will be deemed to transfer the trust fund and income therefrom to an emergency trustee in a different jurisdiction and to have changed the forum of the management, control, and administration of the trust from the original jurisdiction (or prior jurisdiction in the event of a prior transfer) to the jurisdiction in which the emergency trustee resides. If the duress occurs in the United States, the duress provision should

1. Require the foreign trustee to discharge any United States co-trustees
2. Require the foreign trustee to ignore advice given by the committee of trust protectors or advisors when a U.S. court or trustee in bankruptcy compels such advice
3. Require the foreign trustee to ignore the decisions of the committee of trust protectors to discharge or replace trustees when such decisions result from court orders or other compulsion

---

[11] *See* § 9.05; Jeffrey A. Schoenblum, Multistate and Multinational Estate Planning § 18.18.9 (1982 & Supp. 1990).

[12] Jeffrey A. Schoenblum, Multistate and Multinational Estate Planning § 18.18.9 (1982 & Supp. 1990); D. Parker & A. Mellows, The Modern Law of Trusts 375-83 (3d ed. 1975).

[13] Jeffrey A. Schoenblum, Multistate and Multinational Estate Planning § 18.18.9 (1982 Supp. 1990).

4. When the planner structures the trust as the sole owner of a corporation of which the settlor is the sole director and officer, require the foreign trustee to liquidate the corporation immediately.

[M] Provisions Dealing with Trust Situs Instability

The primary issues regarding the stability of the FAPT jurisdiction encompass the following types of risks:

1. Changes in the situs jurisdiction's tax system
2. Changes in exchange controls and the free transferability of assets into and out of the situs jurisdiction
3. Changes in disclosure requirements
4. Imposition by the situs jurisdiction of excessive operating fees
5. Imposition by the situs jurisdiction of a requirement that its own representatives share control or exercise the trustee's duties
6. The expropriation of the trust property.

Under the act of state doctrine, the situs jurisdiction can probably sue in foreign courts and collect trust assets located in other countries around the world.[14]

Planning Pointer. To avoid situs jurisdiction instability problems, planners should (1) structure the asset protection plan so that the FAPT's assets will not be located at the trust situs, (2) diversify investments, and (3) place trust property in highly stable countries.

Caution. Planners should not place trust investments in jurisdictions where the grantor is at a high risk of being subjected to creditors' judgments. In such jurisdictions, creditors may try directly to attach trust assets without going through the trust situs jurisdiction.

Planning Pointer. In some jurisdictions FAPTs may enter prior agreements with the government. For example, the Cayman Islands will guarantee that it will not change the tax status of a trust for as much as 50 years. In such jurisdictions, planners should ensure that the FAPT enters such an agreement.

---

[14] Jeffrey A. Schoenblum, Multistate and Multinational Estate Planning §18.18.10 (1982 & Supp. 1990).

[N]   Flight Provisions

Generally, planners should always include flight provisions in FAPTs. Among other things, these provisions protect the FAPT from the following risks:

1. Expropriation or confiscation of FAPT property
2. Unwarranted interference with the FAPT's administration
3. Situs jurisdiction imposition of new and oppressive taxes on the FAPT's principal or income
4. Other restrictions on the FAPT trustees' discretion to deal with FAPT property.

Generally, flight provisions work by causing the FAPT to change jurisdictions automatically or at the discretion of a designated person upon the occurrence of a duress event. Duress events are events that cause the situs jurisdiction to no longer serve as a suitable situs jurisdiction for the FAPT.

Caution. Flight provisions may not protect FAPT assets that are physically located in the situs jurisdiction. Therefore, planners should separate the trust situs from the location of the trust assets.

Planning Pointer. When drafting flight provisions, planners should consider the following issues:

1. The flight provisions should provide for changes of the FAPT's governing law and the situs of the FAPT itself. This will protect the FAPT from legal changes in the situs jurisdiction that could harm the FAPT.
2. The planner must pay special attention when drafting which duress events will cause the FAPT to flee the situs jurisdiction. Overly expansive flight provisions will cause the FAPT to flee the situs jurisdiction under circumstances that do not justify such flight. Conversely, overly restrictive flight provisions will not allow the FAPT to flee the situs jurisdiction when the FAPT's assets are at risk. Planners may mitigate this problem by structuring the flight provisions to allow designated individuals to review duress events to decide whether they warrant a change in jurisdictions. Additionally, the FAPT may provide for retroactive flight from the jurisdiction.
3. The planner must consider the impact of flight provisions that provide for changes in the FAPT's governing law. First, planners must note that such provisions might not be effective [15] Second, planners must

[15] See L. Frank Chopin, Designing a Multifaceted Flight Structure Choice of Jurisdiction and Choice of Entity, in International Estate Planning: Principles and Strategies 471, 475 (Donald D. Kozusko & Jeffrey A. Schoenblum eds., 1991).

consider the impact that such a change in the FAPT's governing law will have on the FAPT itself. For example, if the planner includes a provision allowing the trust to satisfy the rule against perpetuities in the first jurisdiction, but does not consider the second jurisdiction's rule against perpetuities, that jurisdiction may deem the FAPT to be void because it violates its rule against perpetuities. To avoid such problems, planners should (1) draft FAPT instruments to comply with the most restrictive laws likely to govern such FAPTs, and (2) include savings provisions directing that such FAPT instruments be construed in a manner that causes the FAPT to be in conformity with the law of the jurisdiction then governing the trust and/or to authorize the new trustee or others to make conforming changes in the trust agreement effective at the time of the change in jurisdictions.[16]

4. Planners should consider using a standby trust. A standby trust is a secondary trust established in a second jurisdiction, which the planner generally leaves unfunded. The planner then gives the trustee of the primary FAPT the discretion to move trust assets into the standby trust at an appropriate time. Standby trusts avoid the drafting problems associated with one trust instrument serving under the laws of two or more jurisdictions. Such trusts also leave discretion in the hands of the trustee on the scene, the one able to act most expeditiously. On the other hand, the local trustee may prove highly susceptible to local pressure and ultimate takeover, and standby trusts also involve additional costs.

[O] *Protector*

Planners should consider using a protector in conjunction with the FAPT. A protector is a party in another jurisdiction, to whom the planner gives discretion over certain FAPT functions. Generally, planners give the protector the power to change the trust situs to another jurisdiction when duress events occur. Planners should give protectors the power to change the trustee or move the trustee to a new situs jurisdiction. Planners may use protectors with flight clauses or by themselves.

Using a protector provides added protection for the FAPT. However, planners must balance such added protection against the disadvantages of using such a device. These include, among others, the following:

1. Added cost
2. The protector's not being privy to the situs jurisdiction's local information or having an intimate sense of the situs' economic and political currents
3. The added burden of evaluating the protector's own reliability

---

[16] *Id.* at 476.

4.   A greater degree of complexity and ambiguity
5.   The lack of certainty that the trustee will follow the protector's directives.

[P]   Protective Provisions for Property in Third Country

When splitting the FAPT's administration from its assets, planners must consider using protective provisions that allow the trustees to shift investments quickly when they are threatened. Planners should consider appointing a local custodian. This provides a local party to manage the property on a daily basis who can also notify the trustees when any sudden developments occur that might threaten such assets' security.

[Q]   Record Keeping

Planners must ensure that the FAPT maintains duplicate files outside the trust situs jurisdiction.[17] If a local challenge to the trust is made, duplicate records elsewhere will enable identification and location of trust assets, proof of entitlement to principal and income, and authorization to assume administration. Such duplicate records will also ensure the continued operation and enforcement of the FAPT pursuant to the settlor's wishes. Simultaneously, such duplicate records will avoid the many uncertainties and disputes that the FAPT would inevitably encounter without such records. When the planner uses a standby trust, the foreign trustee can hold these duplicates.

§ 14.03   BAHAMAS

[A]   Bahamas Trust Indenture

Please see Form 14-1, Bahamas Trust Indenture, on the accompanying CD.

[B]   Bahamas First Schedule

Please see Form 14-2, Bahamas First Schedule, on the accompanying CD.

§ 14.04   CAYMAN ISLANDS

[A]   Cayman Islands Trust Indenture

Please see Form 14-3, Cayman Islands Trust Indenture, on the accompanying CD.

---

[17] Jeffrey A. Schoenblum, Multistate and Multinational Estate Planning § 18.18.23 (1982 & Supp.1990).

[B]   *Cayman Islands First Schedule*

Please see Form 14-4, Cayman Islands First Schedule, on the accompanying CD.

§ 14.05   COOK ISLANDS TRUST INDENTURE

Please see Form 14-5, Cook Islands Trust Indenture, on the accompanying CD.

§ 14.06   BERMUDA

[A]   *Bermuda Trust Indenture*

Please see Form 14-6, Bermuda Trust Indenture, on the accompanying CD.

[B]   *Bermuda First Schedule*

Please see Form 14-7, Bermuda First Schedule, on the accompanying CD.

§ 14.07   MULTIJURISDICTIONAL FOREIGN TRUST INSTRUMENT

Please see Form 14-8, Trust Instrument, on the accompanying CD.

§ 14.08   FOREIGN TRUST PREPARATION CHECKLIST

The planner should use the following checklist to ensure that no critical issue is overlooked in connection with the planner's preparation of foreign trusts.

Is the planner considering using a foreign trust? If yes, the planner must consider the following provisions and issues when drafting the FAPT instrument:

1. Irrevocable for a term of years
2. Beneficiary provisions
3. Rule against perpetuities
4. Governing law provisions
5. Trustees' powers
6. Settlor's powers
7. Notice provisions

8. Allocation of authority
9. Careful selection of trustees
10. Substitution of trustees
11. Branch office trustees
12. Duress provisions
13. Provisions dealing with trust situs instability
14. Flight provisions
15. Protector
16. Protective provisions for property in third countries
17. Record keeping.

15

Foreign Trusts: Forms Required for U.S. Tax Compliance

§15.01   IN GENERAL

When planners use foreign trusts, they should ensure that the appropriate parties file the following forms:[1]

- Form 1040, U.S. Individual Income Tax Return, and state income tax return
- Form 1040, U.S. Individual Tax Return, Schedule B–Interest and Dividend Income, Part III Foreign Accounts and Trusts
- Form SS-4, Application for Employer Identification Number
- Form 56, Notice Concerning Fiduciary Relationship
- Form 709, United States Gift (and Generation-Skipping Transfer) Tax Return
- Form 926, Return by a Transferor of Property to a Foreign Corporation, Foreign Estate or Trust, or Foreign Partnership
- Form 1040NR, Nonresident Alien Income Tax Return
- Form 1041NR, Nonresident Fiduciary Income Tax Return
- Form 1042S: Annual Withholding Tax Return For U.S. Source Income Of Foreign Persons
- Form 3520, Creation of or Transfers to Certain Foreign Trusts8
- Form 3520-A, Annual Return of Foreign Trust with U.S. Beneficiaries
- Form 4789, Report of International Transportation of Currency or Monetary Instruments
- Form 4970, Accumulation Distribution
- Form 8288, U.S. Withholding Tax Return for Dispositions by Foreign Persons of U.S. Real Property Interests
- Form 8288-A, Statement of Withholding on Disposition by Foreign Persons of U.S. Real Property Interests

§15.02   FORM SS-4, APPLICATION FOR EMPLOYER IDENTIFICATION NUMBER

Generally, the FAPT should file a Form SS-4 to obtain an employer identification number.

EXAMPLE 15-1

Dwight Churchill is a successful real estate developer who has been in business for more than 20 years. His net worth equals $800 million. He is concerned about asset protection and consults with Franklin Eisenhower, an asset protection planner. Eisenhower designs and helps Churchill execute an asset protection plan, which includes a trust in the Bahamas. The FAPT's name is the Dwight D. Churchill Trust. As part of this plan, Churchill transfers $5 million cash to the Dwight Churchill Trust on January 1, 2001. The

---

§15.01   [1] *See* Lewis D. Solomon & Lewis J. Saret, Asset Protection Strategies, Chapter 6 (2006).

trustee is Marshall G. Patton. Patton's address, which also becomes the trust's address, is 1 Charles Street, P.O. Box 100, Nassau, Bahamas. Patton's telephone number is 809-111-1111.

When Churchill executes the FAPT, Patton files a Form SS-4 for the FAPT. The form that Patton files is Form 15-1 (which can be found on the accompanying CD).

§ 15.03   FORM 56, NOTICE CONCERNING FIDUCIARY RELATIONSHIP

The FAPT's trustee may use Form 56 to notify the IRS of the creation of the fiduciary relationship. The trustee must submit evidence of authority, such as a copy of the trust instrument, along with Form 56. The trustee may file Form 56 when the fiduciary relationship is created or with the FAPT's first Form 1041. The planner should ensure that the Form 56 is filed because this will provide evidence of lack of concealment of the trust and transfers to it. This in turn will help the planner in rebutting fraudulent conveyance claims against the planner.

EXAMPLE 15-2

Same facts as Example 15-1, except that the Dwight Churchill Trust has received an employer identification number, which is #2-3456789. Patton also files a Form 56, Notice Concerning Fiduciary Relationship. The form that Patton files is Form 15-2 (which can be found on the accompanying CD).

§ 15.04   FORM 709, UNITED STATES GIFT (AND GENERATION-SKIPPING TRANSFER) TAX RETURN

Transferors will want to file a Form 709, if for no other reason to start the statue of limitations running with respect to gift tax on transfers to foreign trusts. The grantor must file Form 709 with the IRS Service Center where it files its federal income tax return on the April 15 immediately following the year of the transfer. If the grantor claims the transfer is incomplete and thus is not subject to federal gift tax, it should report the transaction and attach an explanation of relevant facts and a certified or verified copy of the trust instrument and instrument of transfer.

EXAMPLE 15-3

Same facts as Example 15-1, except that Churchill retains the power to appoint the trust corpus to any "relative" as defined in the trust instrument, and if Churchill fails to exercise his power of appointment, the corpus passes to his children or their issue, per stirpes. Churchill files the Form 709 that is located at Form 15-3 (which can be found on the accompanying CD).

§15.05 FORM 3520, ANNUAL RETURN TO REPORT TRANSACTIONS WITH FOREIGN TRUSTS AND RECEIPT OF CERTAIN FOREIGN GIFTS

The Treasury Department requires that U.S. persons file Form 3520, Annual Return to Report Transactions With Foreign Trusts and Receipt of Certain Foreign Gifts, for the purpose of reporting (a) transactions with foreign trusts, and (b) the receipt of certain large gifts or bequests from certain foreign persons.

Planning Pointer. Form 3520 must be filed if any of the following occur:

1. A person constitutes a "responsible party" for reporting a "reportable event," which occurs during the current tax year, or such person holds an outstanding obligation of a related foreign trust that such person treated as a "qualified obligation" during the tax year.
2. A U.S. person, during the current tax year, is treated as the owner of any part of the assets of a foreign trust under the grantor trust rules.
3. A U.S. person, during the current tax year, receives a distribution from a foreign trust, or a related foreign trust held an outstanding obligation issued by such person (or a person related to such person) that such person treated as a "qualified obligation" during the current tax year.
4. A U.S. person, during the current tax year, receives either:

    a. More than $100,000 from a nonresident alien individual or a foreign estate (including foreign persons related to that nonresident alien individual or foreign estate) that such individual treated as gifts or bequests or
    b. More than $10,931 from foreign corporations or foreign partnerships (including foreign persons related to such foreign corporations or foreign partnerships) that such person treated as gifts.

Form 3520 need not be filed to report the following transactions:

1. Certain transfers to foreign trusts described in IRC §§ 402(b), 404(a)(4), or 404A
2. Transfers for foreign market value to a foreign nongrantor trust

3. Fair market value (FMV) transfers by a U.S. person to a foreign non-grantor trust (or other transfers that are treated as FMV transfers by reason of the receipt of a qualified obligation)

4. Transfers to foreign trusts that have a current determination letter from the IRS recognizing their status as exempt from income taxation under section 501(c)(3)

5. Transfers to, distributions from, and ownership of Canadian Registered Retirement Savings Plans, if the trust would qualify for treaty benefits under the United States tax treaty with Canada

6. Distributions from foreign trusts that are taxable as compensation for services rendered (within the meaning of section 672(f)(2)(B) and its regulations), so long as the recipient reports the distribution as compensation income on its applicable Federal income tax return

7. Distributions from foreign trusts to domestic trusts that have a current determination letter from the IRS recognizing their status as exempt from income taxation under section 501(c)(3)

8. Domestic trusts that become foreign trusts to the extent the trust is treated as owned by a foreign person, after application of section 672(f).

EXAMPLE 15-4

Same facts as Example 15-3. Churchill files Form 3520, which is located at Form 15-4 (which can be found on the accompanying CD).

§ 15.06 FORM 3520-A, ANNUAL RETURN OF FOREIGN TRUST WITH U.S. BENEFICIARIES

Form 3520-A is the annual information return of a foreign trust with at least one U.S. owner. The form provides information about the foreign trust, its U.S. beneficiaries, and any U.S. person who is treated as an owner of any portion of the foreign trust.

A foreign trust must file Form 3520-A to satisfy its annual information reporting requirements. Each U.S. person treated as an owner of a foreign trust under Code Sections 671 through 679 is responsible for ensuring that the foreign trust files an annual return setting forth a full and complete accounting of all trust activities, trust operations, and other relevant information. In addition, the U.S. owner is responsible for ensuring that the trust annually furnishes such information as the IRS requires to U.S. owners and U.S. beneficiaries of the trust.

Form 3520-A does not have to be filed by the following foreign trusts:

1. A trust that is a Canadian Registered Retirement Savings Plan if the trust would qualify for treaty benefits under the Convention Between the United

States of America and Canada with Respect to Taxes on Income and on Capital. However, if for any taxable year the trust relies on the tax treaty with Canada to avoid information reporting, the U.S. owner is required to disclose this position pursuant to section 6114.

2. A foreign trust described in section 402(b), 404(a)(4), or 404A.

The FAPT must file a complete Form 3520-A (including pages 3 and 4) with the Internal Revenue Service Center, Philadelphia, PA 19255, by the 15th day of the third month after the end of the trust's tax year. It must also furnish copies of the Foreign Grantor Trust Owner Statement and the Foreign Grantor Trust Beneficiary Statement to the U.S. owners and U.S. beneficiaries by the 15th day of the third month after the end of the trust's tax year

---

EXAMPLE 15-5

Same facts as Example 15-4 except that the FAPT is a grantor trust, and the trust earns $500,000 of interest income during 2001 and incurs $15,000 of fiduciary fees and $15,000 of legal and accounting fees. The Form 3520-A that Churchill files is located at Form 15-5 (which can be found on the accompanying CD).

---

§15.07 FINCEN FORM 104, CURRENCY TRANSACTION REPORT

The Bank Secrecy Act requires financial institutions other than casinos to file a FINCEN Form 104, Currency Transaction Report for each deposit, withdrawal, exchange of currency, or other payment or transfer by, through, or to the financial institution that involves a transaction in currency of more than $10,000. Multiple transactions must be treated as a single transaction if the financial institution has knowledge that (1) such transactions are by or on behalf of any person, and (2) result in either cash into or cash out of the financial institution totaling more than $10,000 during any one business day. Individuals will not file such forms. However, they should be aware that when they engage in large currency transactions the financial institutions that they deal with will file such forms.

EXAMPLE 15-6

Same facts as Example 15-1 except that Churchill funds the Dwight D. Churchill Trust with a $5 million wire transfer from Big Bank to the Bahamas. The FINCEN Form 104 that Big Bank files is located at Form 15-6 (which can be found on the accompanying CD).

---

§ 15.08   FORM 8288, U.S. WITHHOLDING TAX RETURN FOR DISPOSITIONS BY FOREIGN PERSONS OF U.S. REAL PROPERTY INTERESTS, AND FORM 8288-A, STATEMENT OF WITHHOLDING ON DISPOSITIONS BY FOREIGN PERSONS OF U.S. REAL PROPERTY INTERESTS

If a foreign trust transfers U.S. real property, the IRC requires the transferee to file Forms 8288 and 8288-A within 20 days following the transfer and pay the required withholding tax. The forms require the transferor's and transferee's names, identification numbers, addresses, a description of the property transferred, the transfer date, the amount realized on the transfer, and the amount of any tax withheld.

EXAMPLE 15-7

Same facts as Example 15-1 except that Churchill transfers an office building in New York City to the trust on January 1, 2001. The trust sells the office building on August 1, 2001, to Bob Buyer for $100 million. Bob Buyer files the Form 8288 that is located at Form 15-7 and the Form 8288-A that is located at Form 15-8 (both of which can be found on the accompanying CD).

---

§ 15.09   FORM TD F 90-22.1, REPORT OF FOREIGN BANK AND FINANCIAL ACCOUNTS

[A]   Background

The requirement for filing this form arises from the Bank Secrecy Act (BSA), first enacted in 1970, amended, in order to add a number of anti-money-laundering provisions, in 1992, and amended most recently in October 2001 by the Patriot Act.[1] The BSA, in general, authorizes the Secretary of the Treasury to promulgate regulations requiring financial institutions and other persons to keep records and file reports that the Secretary determines will have a high degree of usefulness in criminal, tax, regulatory, intelligence, and counter-terrorism matters, and to implement counter-money-laundering programs and compliance procedures. Section 5314 of the BSA specifically authorizes the Secretary to require residents or citizens of the United States, or a person in and doing business in the United States, to keep records and/or file reports concerning transactions with a foreign financial agency. "This provision reflected

---

§ 15.09   [1] Titles 1 and II of Public Law 91-508, as amended, codified at 12 U.S.C. 1829b, 12 U.S.C. 1951-1959, and 31 U.S.C. 5311-5330.

congressional concern that foreign financial institutions located in jurisdictions with strict bank secrecy laws were being used to violate or evade domestic criminal, tax, and regulatory requirements"[2].

Pursuant to this provision, the Treasury Department promulgated regulations[3] stating:

> Each person subject to the jurisdiction of the United States (except a foreign subsidiary of a U.S. person) having a financial interest in, or signature or other authority over, a bank, securities or other financial account in a foreign country shall report such relationship to the Commissioner of the Internal Revenue for each year in which such relationship exists, and shall provide such information as shall be specified in a reporting form. . . .[4]

The form referenced is TD F 90-22.1 (Report of Foreign Bank and Financial Accounts, sometimes referred to as the Foreign Bank Accounts Report or FBAR). The most recent version of this form, dated July 2000, is available from the Internal Revenue Service (IRS) Web site.

The Secretary of the Treasury delegated the authority to administer this requirement to the Director of the Financial Crimes Enforcement Network (FinCEN). FinCEN is a bureau of the Treasury Department, alongside other bureaus and services, such as the IRS. FinCEN is responsible for the U.S. government's domestic and international anti-money-laundering efforts. Among other things, it engages in information collection, data analysis, dissemination of analytical products, and technological assistance. This bureau is overseen by the Undersecretary of Enforcement, who reports to the Secretary of the Treasury through the Deputy Secretary.

Both FinCEN and its sister organization, the IRS, have responsibilities and roles with respect to the FBAR. The FBAR is an information return or report that is filed with the IRS Detroit Computing Center and input into the BSA financial database, which is jointly administered by Detroit Computing Center and FinCEN. After FBARs are posted—presumably by hand—to the BSA financial database, the forms are available to FinCEN analysts, law enforcement, and appropriate regulatory authorities for use, among other things, in tracking flows of money.[5] For example, with proper authorization from supervisors, a revenue agent or international examiner can obtain access to this information.

Pursuant to Treasury Directive 15-41 (12/1/92), the Secretary of the Treasury delegated to the IRS the authority to investigate possible violations of 31 U.S.C. §5314 and 31 C.F.R. §103.24. The IRS examines for compliance with the FBAR requirements. The IRS/Criminal Investigation Division (CI) reviews failures to

---

[2] U.S. Treasury Department, REPORT TO CONGRESS IN ACCORDANCE WITH §361(b) OF THE USA PATRIOT ACT SUBMITTED BY THE SECRETARY OF THE TREASURY APRIL 26, 2002, p. 3 [hereinafter "TREASURY REPORT"]. This report is required to be made each year, but the one due April 26, 2003 had not been filed as of June 1, 2003.

[3] 31 C.F.R. Part 103 (2002).

[4] 31 C.F.R. 103.24 (2002).

[5] In the last several years it has become more common, it appears, for the IRS Detroit Computing Center to send requests for missing information to individuals who have filed an FBAR.

file identified by the IRS examination staff (revenue agents and international examiners, for example) for possible criminal investigation. CI forwards cases that it recommends for prosecution through the IRS Office of Chief Counsel (which conducts its own independent review) to the Department of Justice, which has the final say on whether to initiate a criminal prosecution.

More recently, FinCEN delegated its enforcement authority for the FBAR to the IRS, to increase enforcement with respect to FBARs. Such authority includes the authority to collect civil penalties, to investigate possible civil violations of these provisions, to employ the summons power of subpart F of part 103, and to take any other action reasonably necessary for the enforcement of such provisions, including the pursuit of injunctions.[6]

Note that the FBAR is not a tax return, as such, and is not attached to a taxpayer's Individual Federal Income Tax Return (Form 1040). It follows that the information appearing on an FBAR is not subject to the stringent disclosure restrictions of IRC Section 6103 (relating to confidentiality and disclosure of returns and return information). Thus, information contained in this form can be shared with other agencies of the federal government. In addition, "[t]he information collected may also be provided to appropriate state, local, and foreign law enforcement and regulatory personnel in the performance of their official duties."[7] What is not widely appreciated is that a private litigant may request and may well be given access to this information in a lawsuit. For example, a spouse might seek discovery of this information in the course of an action for divorce or separate maintenance. If the form has been filed, the information, one can anticipate, will be made available pursuant to a court order. If it has not been filed, but should have, the other spouse can be liable for all the very serious penalties described herein. If the other spouse says that he or she has not filed the form because there are no foreign bank accounts, and the requesting spouse doubts this is true, a court presumably could order the other spouse to request a copy of any and all filings with the IRS Detroit Computing Center.

Cases that CI declines to investigate as a criminal matter may be reviewed further by the IRS for possible civil enforcement action. If a taxpayer refuses to pay the penalty, the matter can be referred to the Department of Justice to institute a penalty action in which both liability and the amount of penalty must be litigated.

Complying with the statutory and regulatory requirement to report foreign financial accounts is a two-part process. Form 1040 Schedule B, Part III, instructs a taxpayer to indicate an interest in a financial account in a foreign country by checking "Yes" or "No" in the appropriate box. Form 1040 then refers the taxpayer to Form 90-22.1, which provides that it should be used to report a financial interest in or authority over bank accounts, securities accounts, or other financial accounts in a foreign country. The instructions for Form 1040, Schedule B, provide that the taxpayer must check "Yes" if he/she owns more that 50

---

[6] Financial Crimes Enforcement Network; Delegation of Enforcement Authority Regarding the Foreign Bank Account Report Requirements, 68 Fed. Reg. 26,489 (May 16, 2003) (to be codified at 31 C.F.R. § 103.56(g)).

[7] Privacy Act Notification on the face of Form TD F 90-22.1 (Rev. 7/00).

percent of the stock of any corporation (U.S. or foreign) that owns one or more foreign bank accounts or at any time during the year the taxpayer had any interest in or signature or other authority over a financial account in a foreign country (such as a bank account, securities account, or other financial account). Among the exceptions noted in these instructions, the only one of general application is the one stating that if the combined value of the accounts was $10,000 or less during the whole year, the "Yes" box need not be checked. If the account is denominated in a foreign currency, the value of the foreign currency is converted into U.S. dollars using the "official" exchange rate at the end of the year; "official" in the case of freely traded currencies probably means interbank or market rate of exchange.[8]

The deadline for filing an FBAR is June 30 of the year following the calendar year during which the threshold requirements are met (*see* discussion below).

While the number of FBAR filings has been steadily increasing—from 116,600 in 1991 to 177,151 in 2001—the Treasury Department believes that many persons that should file are failing to do so.

> It is difficult to determine with any accuracy how many taxpayers are failing to file required FBARs in any calendar year. Extrapolating from the limited information available concerning the number of foreign bank and credit card accounts held by United States citizens, the IRS estimates that there may be as many as one million U.S. taxpayers who have signature authority or control over a foreign bank account and may be required to file FBARs. Thus, the approximate rate of compliance with the FBAR filing requirements based on this information could be less than 20 percent.[9]

In the past, criminal and civil prosecutions under these provisions have been few and far between. Between 1996 and 1998, only nine indictments were filed charging failure to comply with section 5314. In the following two years, no one appears to have been charged. The Customs Service reports only three convictions since 1995.[10] This picture may be slightly distorted since it is the case that IRS agents will sometimes raise the issue with taxpayers and use a failure to file an FBAR as a means of obtaining a favorable settlement of the tax case. Also, the issue might be raised in a different form, for example, as a charge of willfully subscribing false tax returns in violation of IRC Section 7206(1) for failing to "check the box" on Schedule B of Form 1040.

[B] *Important Developments*

While in the past the FBAR has had a relatively low profile, it is receiving and undoubtedly will continue to receive much greater attention.

---

[8] With the precipitous rise in the value of the euro, many euro-denominated accounts, which were opened with an initial deposit of say $8,000 to $9,000 that were then converted into euros, will have drifted above the reporting threshold.

[9] TREASURY REPORT at p. 6.

[10] TREASURY REPORT at p. 8.

The government's focus on foreign bank accounts is clear. The following developments have occurred since October 2001:

- *Enactment of the Patriot Act,* which makes it easier for the Treasury Department to obtain foreign bank account information and puts the foreign bank somewhat at risk of losing its ability to maintain a correspondent account with a U.S. bank.[11] *See* discussion at § 5.08A[G], below.
- *The Treasury Department Report to Congress concerning FBAR reporting,* as mandated by the Patriot Act, which stated among other things that the only way to improve FBAR filing compliance among those individuals who are aware of the FBAR involves "a series of highly publicized criminal actions against intentional violators to raise the cost of being an FBAR scofflaw. Ideally, such cases would be brought not only as adjuncts to other types of criminal conduct such as tax evasion and bankruptcy fraud, but also as stand-alone cases."[12]
- *The implementation of the IRS Voluntary Compliance Initiative Program,* which offered taxpayers with unreported foreign bank accounts an opportunity to avoid many otherwise applicable penalties.[13]
- *The ongoing IRS John Doe summons investigations,* in which the IRS has issued a series of summonses to obtain information about U.S. citizens holding payment cards tied to foreign bank accounts. This investigation has produced numerous cases being referred to the Criminal Investigation Division of the IRS.[14]

On the other hand, the FBAR, which is a short, two-page form, is deceptively simple. Its concise format hides several latent issues. More critically, the FBAR filing requirements' broad applicability combined with the association in the minds of most practitioners and laypeople of the FBAR with so-called "tax cheats," who use unreported foreign bank accounts to commit tax fraud, causes many people to fail to understand that they must file an FBAR.

[C]   Who Must File an FBAR?

Each U.S. person with a financial interest in or signature or other authority over any financial account in a foreign country must file an FBAR if the aggregate value of all such accounts exceed $10,000 at any time during the calendar year. The FBAR must be filed on or before the June 30 after the calendar year in

---

[11] Almost all foreign banks that need to receive or make payments in dollars maintain a correspondent account with a U.S. bank, typically a large bank located in New York. Today, dollars are dealt with electronically through the DTC system, and access to this system is through the large banks that usually have one DTC account.

[12] TREASURY REPORT at p. 11.

[13] Rev. Proc. 2003-11, 2003-4 I.R.B. 311.

[14] *See Early Information Reveals Strong Response to Offshore Initiative, IRS Says,* 2003 TNT 85-17 (May 1, 2003).

which the relationship existed. The FBAR is required in addition to the reporting obligations with respect to foreign accounts on Form 1040, Schedule B.[15]

Certain people do not have to file an FBAR. These include officers or employees of certain banks and large publicly traded corporations with signature/other authority over foreign financial accounts maintained by that bank or large corporation, where they have no personal financial interest in the account, and they have been advised in writing by the corporation's chief financial officer that the corporation has filed a current FBAR, which includes such account. To illustrate, E, a General Motors executive based in London, with signature authority over a GM bank account in London in which E has no personal financial interest, and who otherwise satisfies the requirements of the exception, does not have to file an FBAR. In contrast, F, an executive in London under exactly the same circumstances but employed by a non-publicly traded company, must file an FBAR.

[D] Key Definitions

For FBAR purposes, a person has a "financial interest" in a foreign financial account if he is the owner of record or has legal title, regardless of whether that account is maintained for his own benefit or for the benefit of others, including non-U.S. persons. For joint accounts, each owner has a financial interest in that account. In addition, a U.S. person has a financial interest in a foreign financial account where the owner of record is any of the following:

- Another person who acts on such person's behalf (*e.g.*, agent, nominee, attorney).
- A corporation in which such person owns more than 50 percent of the value of the shares.
- A partnership in which such person owns an interest in more than 50 percent of the profits.
- A trust in which such person either has a present interest in more than 50 percent of the assets or from which such person receives more than 50 percent of the current income.[16]

A "financial account" includes any bank, securities, securities derivatives, or other financial instruments accounts. Such accounts generally also "encompass any accounts in which the assets are held in a commingled fund, and the account holder holds an equity interest in the fund." But there are many gray areas. To illustrate, if a U.S. person places $1 million cash into a safe deposit box in

---

[15] There is not a great deal of authority bearing on the "backfiling" of FBARs voluntarily or even after notice from the IRS or FinCEN. In the case of nonfilers who are "catching up" with their filing of income tax returns, the authors recommend that they also "backfile" FBARs. The recent Voluntary Compliance Initiative Program requires, among other things, the backfiling of FBARs.

[16] Tying reporting requirements to a percentage of profits or current income can cause difficulties, as the individual concerned may not know the total amount of profits or current income. In some cases another filing might help him/her, as is the case with beneficiaries of foreign trusts that may receive statements from the foreign trust showing the necessary figures.

Switzerland, does this constitute a financial interest in a foreign account, which triggers the FBAR filing requirements? As with many other FBAR issues, no authoritative guidance answers this issue. However, it appears that in the safe deposit box context, application of the FBAR requirements depends on the precise nature of the arrangement between the bank and the safe deposit box holder. For example, if the holder gives the bank the right to access more than $10,000 of cash in a safe deposit box in order to secure a credit card issued by that bank, then it appears that the holder may be required to file an FBAR. The rationale for this is that this arrangement is substantively no different than if the holder deposited such cash into a checking or other financial account with the bank, which would trigger the FBAR filing requirements. To illustrate a different situation, if a U.S. person creates a grantor trust, which in turn owns a foreign financial account valued at more than of $10,000, does the U.S. person need to file an FBAR? Here, it appears that the U.S. person must file an FBAR if he is treated as the grantor of the trust under the grantor trust rules.[17]

To determine whether the $10,000 filing threshold has been surpassed, "account valuation" is defined as "the largest amount of currency and nonmonetary assets that appear on any quarterly or more frequent account statements issued for the applicable year." If periodic account statements are not issued, the maximum account asset value is the largest amount of currency and non-monetary assets in the account at any time during the year. For this purpose, filers must convert foreign currency by using the year-end official exchange or conversion rate. The value of stock, securities, or other non-monetary assets is the fair market value at year-end, or at withdrawal from the account, if earlier. Each account must be valued separately in accordance with the foregoing rules. The $10,000 filing threshold is an aggregate threshold; that is, it applies if the aggregate value of all foreign financial accounts held by the person in question exceeds $10,000 at any time during the calendar year.

A person has "signature authority" over an account if he can control the disposition of money or other property in that account by delivery of a document containing his signature, or his signature along with that of one or more other persons, to the bank or other person with whom the account is maintained. A person has "other authority" if that person can exercise comparable power over an account by direct communication to the bank or other person with whom the account is maintained, either orally or by some other means. This definition occasionally has counterintuitive results. For example, it is clear that an individual who establishes a foreign bank account and receives a credit card secured by that account has the requisite signature authority to trigger the FBAR filing requirements. On the other hand, if a German entrepreneur gives his U.S. resident daughter a credit card issued to his German closely held company by a German bank, does the daughter now have to file an FBAR? If the credit card is secured by the German bank account the answer is yes. This results even though the daughter is certainly not the type of person the FBAR is directed at. On the other hand, if the credit card is unsecured, similar to most credit cards issued in the United States, then it appears the daughter need not file an FBAR.

---

[17] This point can be argued either way. The argument for the proposition that filing is required is based not on section 671 of the Internal Revenue Code but on the BSA provisions.

A U.S. person, for FBAR purposes, includes U.S. citizens and residents, domestic partnerships, domestic corporations, and domestic estates or trusts. This definition catches several types of people unaware. To illustrate, each of the following individuals must file an FBAR, even though they may not realize this:

- A U.S. citizen studying overseas who opens up a bank account at a foreign bank for convenience, which had over $10,000 at any time during the year.
- A child of a foreign entrepreneur who attends college in the U.S. and who has a foreign bank account from childhood on, worth more than $10,000, will become subject to the FBAR requirements if that child ultimately becomes a U.S. resident or if he/she obtains an immigrant visa permitting him/her to reside in the United States on a permanent basis (*i.e.*, a "green card").
- A U.S. citizen marries a Dutch citizen who is temporarily stationed in the United States. If the U.S. citizen, along with his or her new spouse, returns to Denmark, retains U.S. citizenship, and opens a financial account (e.g., a brokerage account) in Denmark, he or she must file an FBAR if the account value exceeds $10,000 at any time during the year.
- A U.S. citizen or resident is temporarily stationed in Mexico by his employer. The individual opens a bank account in Mexico, and maintains a nominal amount in that account throughout the year. At year-end, the employer gives the individual a $15,000 bonus, which he deposits in his bank account in Mexico.
- A so-called "accidental American" has an account outside the United States. An "accidental American" is someone who was born in the United States of foreign parents. For example, a couple give birth to a daughter while studying in the United States. The daughter is a U.S. citizen, even though she, together with her parents, lives in Switzerland, and she has never returned to the United States after leaving at a very early age. This individual should file an FBAR for all foreign accounts.

Each of the foregoing situations is common. In each situation, frequently, the individuals do not realize that they must file an FBAR, and that they are subject to both civil and criminal penalties for failing to do so. Moreover, often the accountants, attorneys, financial planners, and other professionals who advise such individuals do not think about the FBAR, thus exposing them to malpractice liability.

[E] *What Information Is Required?*

What about the FBAR itself? Is it difficult to complete? No, the FBAR itself is very easy to complete. It requires taxpayers to provide the following information:

- Filer's name, address, taxpayer identification number, date of birth, and country.

- Whether the accounts are jointly owned, and if so, the number of joint owners. If the filer owns the account jointly with only one other party, and all accounts listed are held jointly with that party, then the filer must provide the name of that party and its taxpayer identification number, if known.
- The number of foreign financial accounts in which the filer holds an interest.
- The type of account.
- The maximum value of the account during the year.
- The account number and the name of the financial institution with which the account is held.
- The name, address, and taxpayer identification number of the account holder.

If the filer has a "financial interest" in more than twenty-five foreign bank accounts, information for the accounts need not be provided but must be made available to the Treasury Department upon request. If the filer has an interest in fewer than twenty-five accounts, the information listed above must be provided for each account.

[F] Criminal and Civil Penalty Exposure

What happens if someone fails to file an FBAR? What is his or her liability exposure? Failure to file an FBAR or filing a false FBAR may trigger criminal penalties. The base penalty is a maximum fine of $250,000, a maximum term of imprisonment of five years, or both. The alternative penalty, which is a fine of not more than $500,000, or imprisonment of not more than ten years, or both, applies if the defendant violates any other U.S. law or if the violation was part of a pattern of any illegal activity involving more than $100,000 in a twelve-month period. In addition, the false-statement statute, 18 U.S.C. § 1001, may be violated if a false form is filed. For this purpose, a separate criminal violation will occur for each FBAR not filed or falsely filed. Because Form 1040, Schedule B outlines the FBAR reporting requirement, willfulness may not be exceptionally difficult for the government to prove.

In addition to criminal penalties, failure to file an FBAR or filing of a false FBAR may also trigger civil penalties. To illustrate, an individual who willfully violates the FBAR reporting requirement can be fined either $25,000 or an amount equal to the balance in the account at the time of violation (not to exceed $100,000), whichever is greater. Although not entirely clear, it appears that if multiple accounts exist, the fine would be a minimum of $25,000 per account, even if multiple accounts should have been reported on the same form.

[G] Caution—Danger Ahead

The requirement to file an FBAR falls within the anti-money-laundering programs instituted by the U.S. Government; section 5314, in fact, sits in the U.S. Code just a few sections away from a number of new provisions added by the

Patriot Act. Under section 5318 of Title 31 (Compliance, Exemptions, and Summons Authority) of Section II (Records and Reports on Monetary Instruments Transactions), of Chapter 53 (Monetary Transactions, which Chapter also deals with money laundering and related crimes), the Secretary of the Treasury or the Attorney General[18] may issue a summons or subpoena to any foreign bank that maintains a correspondent account in the United States and request records related to such correspondent account, including records maintained outside of the United States relating to the deposit of funds into the foreign bank. "Correspondent account" is defined in new section 5318A (Special Measures for Jurisdictions, Financial Institutions, or International Transactions of Primary Money Laundering Concern) as "an account established to receive deposits from, make payments on behalf of, a foreign financial institution, or handle other financial transactions related to such institution." Service and acceptance of service are streamlined by new provisions that, in effect, require the foreign bank to appoint an authorized agent for receipt of legal process for records regarding the correspondent account. (The U.S. bank that is operating the account will require this. The U.S. bank is referred to by the statute as a "covered financial institution.") If a foreign bank fails to comply with a summons or subpoena issued under these new provisions, the covered financial institution, upon notification by the Secretary of the Treasury or the Attorney General, can be forced to terminate (shut down) the correspondent account or itself face severe penalties.

While an FBAR is clearly not the only "predicate" to institution of these summons or subpoena procedures, it is one, and the requirement to file an accurate report is an easy one to point to. Foreign banks will want to take note of the connection between Patriot Act summonses and subpoenas and FBARs. They may wish to provide reminders to customers that the rules of countries, such as the United States, may require them, the customers, to report "foreign" accounts, and that information regarding the account may become the subject of a summons or subpoena directed at the bank. The bank may wish to notify its customers that it will comply with such formal requests and to obtain the customers' consent in advance. So far as summonses and subpoenas based on an FBAR or failure to file a correct and complete FBAR, these thoughts are, in general, only relevant to U.S. persons, that is, U.S. citizens, U.S. residents, U.S. partnerships, U.S. corporations, U.S. trusts, and U.S. estates.[19] Affected

---

[18] Apparently this authority does not run to a grand jury. This is a technical problem that may be fixed by legislation or otherwise.

[19] The regulations promulgated under 31 U.S.C. 5314 speak in terms of "[e]ach person subject to the jurisdiction of the United States (except a foreign subsidiary of a U.S. person) having a financial interest in, or signature or other authority over, a bank, securities or other financial account in a foreign country...." The instructions to the FBAR form, however, refer to "United States person" and define that term as a citizen or resident of the U.S., a domestic partnership, a domestic corporation, or a domestic estate or trust. The Internal Revenue Code contains a definition of "United States person" that is similar but not identical to the FBAR-related definitions, and clearly the FBAR rules are not simply cross-referencing the tax law definition. For example, a Delaware trust that "flunks" the test in IRC § 7701(a)(30)(E) is not a United States person for tax purposes but may be for FBAR reporting purposes. Also, there is no clarity as to the definition of a "domestic estate." Is the estate of a U.S. citizen who lived

individuals should know that these new mechanisms make it much easier for the U.S. government to look at foreign accounts.

The Patriot Act and newer generation mutual legal assistance treaties are obviously designed to make it easier for the U.S. government to obtain admissible evidence of undisclosed foreign accounts. Prosecutors, it is believed, will be urged to take a second look when deciding whether to charge an FBAR failure to file.

Also, it should be noted that the Senate version of the Jobs and Growth Tax Relief Reconciliation Act of 2003[20] would have added an additional $5,000 civil penalty that, if enacted, would have allowed the IRS to impose such penalty on any person who failed to properly file an FBAR, *without regard to willfulness*.[21] This change would make it considerably easier for a prosecutor to charge the violation. Although this provision did not make it into the final version of the Act, such proposals have a way of recurring until they are enacted.

The FBAR form almost certainly will be changed in many important respects in the very near future. In its Report to Congress dated April 26, 2002, the Treasury Department stated that FinCEN would take responsibility for updating this form and the accompanying instructions. The target date for doing so was set at December 31, 2002. One suspects that the delay is due in part to work on Patriot Act and other regulations, the contents of which will bear on this form.

The Foreign Bank Accounts Report Form has never been something to sneeze at, as it is a crime to violate the underlying rules. It is undoubtedly true, however, that individuals and their advisers have too often not given this form the attention it deserves. In light of the Treasury Department's and IRS's new focus on these provisions, born in large measure from the events of 9/11 and the drive to prevent money-laundering, and the Patriot Act provisions, TD F 90-22.1 must be treated with a great deal more respect. If in doubt, the answer should be to file the forms; there is no indication that the fact that one files triggers an audit. To do otherwise is dangerous.

§ 15.10 TAX RETURN COMPLIANCE CHECKLIST

____1. Form 1040
        Due Date: April 15 of year following income
        Party Responsible: _____

____2. Form 1040, Schedule B, Part III
        Due Date: April 15 of each year following ownership of useful interest in FAPT
        Party Responsible: _____

---

the last 40 years of his life in Europe, which estate is administered outside the U.S., a domestic estate? What if the decedent was not a U.S. citizen or resident but the estate owns commercial real estate in the U.S.? This last estate probably is a "foreign estate" under the income tax rules in IRC § 7701(a)(31). It is this type of confusion that needs to be dispelled.

[20] P.L. 108-27.

[21] *See* Ratzlaff v. United States, 510 U.S. 135 (1994), involving a different part of the BSA.

____3. Form 926
Due Date: On day of the transfer to FAPT
Party Responsible: _____

____4. Form 3520
Due Date: 90th day after FAPT's creation or transfer to FAPT
Party Responsible: _____

____5. Form 3520-A
Due Date: 15th day of 4th month following the end of transferor's or grantor's tax year
Party Responsible: _____

____6. Form 709
Due Date: April 15 of year following transfer
Party Responsible: _____

____7. Form 56
Due Date: When fiduciary relationship is created, or with FAPT's first Form 1041
Party Responsible: _____

____8. Form 1041
Due Date:
Party Responsible: _____

____9. Form SS-4
Due Date: At time of FAPT creation
Party Responsible: _____

____10. Form TD 90-22.1
Due Date: June 30 of each year following close of preceding year during which foreign account(s) existed and had a combined value of more than $10,000 at any time during the year
Party Responsible: _____

____11. Form 4790
Due Date: (a) Recipients: within 30 days after receipt, with the customs officer in charge at any port of entry or departure or by mail with the Commissioner of Customs, Attention: Currency Transportation Reports, Washington, D.C. 20229
(b) Shippers or mailers: if the currency or other monetary instrument does not accompany the person entering or departing the U.S., Form 4790 may be filed by mail on or before the date of entry, departure, mailing, or shipping with the Commissioner of Customs, Attention: Currency Transportation Reports, Washington, D.C. 20229
(c) Travelers: travelers carrying currency or other monetary instruments with them must file Form 4790 at time of entry into the United States or the time of departure from the United States with the customs officer in charge at any customs port of entry or departure
Party Responsible: _____

____12. Form 5471

Due Date: With income tax return for year of acquisition of 5%or greater interest in foreign corporation or partnership
Party Responsible: _____
____13. Forms 8288 & 8288-A
Due Date: Within 20 days following the transfer of U.S. real property
Party Responsible: _____

APPENDIX A

The International Trusts Act of 1984*

COOK ISLANDS

INTERNATIONAL TRUSTS ACT 1984 (AS AMENDED)

* The authors would like to acknowledge Asiaciti Trust Pacific Limited, Rarotonga, Cook Islands, for providing this latest version of the Act.

INTERNATIONAL TRUSTS ACT 1984
1994, NO. 14

An Act to provide for International Trusts

27 December 1984

BE IT ENACTED by the Parliament of the Cook Islands in Session assembled, and the authority of the same, as follows:

PART I

PRELIMINARY

1. **Short Title**—This Act may be cited as the International Trusts Act 1984.

2. **Interpretation**—(1) In this Act, unless the context otherwise requires:

"Commissioner" means the Commissioner for Off-Shore Financial Services appointed pursuant to the Off-Shore Financial Services Act 1998

["Court" means the High Court of the Cook Islands;]

["dispose and disposition" in relation to property includes—

(a) every form of conveyance transfer assignment sale gift lease license easement profit mortgage charge pledge encumbrance or other transaction absolute or limited by which any legal or equitable interest in property is created, transferred or extinguished;

(b) the disposal of an interest in or right over property by the exercise of a power of appointment, power of maintenance, power of advancement or other authority; and also includes the conferring or variation or surrender of such powers or authority;

(c) a contract to make any such disposition referred to in paragraph (a) or (b);]

"Foreign Company" means a foreign company under the International Companies Act 1981-82;

["formalities" in relation to a disposition of property means the documentary and other actions required generally by the laws of a relevant jurisdiction for all dispositions of like form concerning property of like nature, without regard to—

(a) the fact that the particular disposition is made in trust;

(b) the terms of the trust;

(c) the circumstances of the parties to the disposition;

(d) the rights interest or any claim in the property or against the person making the disposition held by a creditor; or

(e) any other particular circumstances, but includes any special formalities required by reason that the party effecting the disposition is not of full age, is subject to a mental or bodily infirmity or is a corporation;]

["governing law" has the same meaning as the expression "proper law";]

["heirship right" means any right, claim or interest in, against or to property of a person arising or accruing in consequences of that person's death, other than any such right, claim or interest created by will or other voluntary disposition by such person or resulting from an express limitation in the disposition of the property of such person;]

["Interested Party" means in relation to any trust, any settlor, donor, trustee, protector, beneficiary, and any person claiming through any one of such persons;]

"International Trust" means a trust which is registered under this Act and in respect of which:

(a) at least one of the trustees, [including a custodian trustee, or in the case of a disposition granting powers of appointment, maintenance or advancement, at least one of the] donors or holders of the power of appointment or power of maintenance or power of advancement is either:

(i) a registered foreign company; or

(ii) an international company; or

(iii) a trustee company; and

(b) the beneficiaries are at all times non-resident;

[and shall include, where the context so permits, a trust which is established or settled under the laws of another jurisdiction, but which, subject to paragraphs (a) and (b) of this definition, is registered as an International Trust under this Act;]

["Judgment" means a judgment or order given or made by a Court in any civil proceedings, or a judgment or order given or made by a Court in any criminal proceedings and includes an award in proceedings on an arbitration if the award has, in pursuance of the law in force in the place where it was made, become enforceable in the same manner as a judgment given by a Court in that place;]

"Minister" means the Minister of Finance;

"Monetary Board" means the Cook Islands Monetary Board established under the Cook Islands Monetary Board Act 1981;

"Non Resident" means:

(a) an individual not domiciled in the Cook Islands;

(b) an individual not ordinarily resident in the Cook Islands;

(c) an international company;

(d) a foreign company;

(e) a trustee company; or

(f) a subsidiary of a trustee company being either an international company or a foreign company;

Appendix A

["personal relationship" includes every form of relationship by blood or marriage, including former marriage, and in particular a personal relationship between two persons exists if:—

(a) one is the child of the other, natural or adopted (whether or not the adoption is recognized by law), legitimate or illegitimate; or

(b) one is married to the other (whether or not the marriage is recognized by law); or

(c) one cohabits with the other or so conducts himself or herself in relation to the other as to give rise in any jurisdiction to any rights, obligations or responsibilities analogous to those of parent and child or husband and wife; or

(d) personal relationships exist between each of them and a third person,

but no change in circumstances causes a personal relationship, once established, to terminate;]

"Power of Appointment"—includes a discretionary power to transfer, grant or create a beneficial interest in property; with or without the furnishing of valuable consideration by the beneficiary of the power, including a power, the exercise of which is subject to the consent of a third party;

"Prescribed" means prescribed by regulation or in the absence of such regulation as may be determined by the Registrar;

"Property" includes an estate or interest in real or personal property and includes any thing in action;

["protector" in relation to an international trust means a person who, by whatever name or title—

(a) has the power to appoint or remove a trustee, or

(b) directly or indirectly controls, whether by power of veto or otherwise, the trustees exercise of one or more of their powers, functions or discretion's under the trust, or

(c) holds the office of protector in accordance with subsection 20(1);

["publish" means to produce and issue, by whatever means, and whether for sale or not and includes to report as part of any law report or reports;]

"Registrar" means the Registrar of International Trusts and includes a Deputy Registrar;

"Registered Foreign Company" means a foreign company registered pursuant to Part X of the International Companies Act 1981-82;

["settlor" in relation to an international trust means and includes an assignor of property to an international trust and each and every person who, directly or indirectly, on behalf of himself or on behalf of any other or others, as owner or as the holder of a power in that behalf, disposes of property to be held in such trust or declares or otherwise creates such trust.]

"Trust" includes all trusts, settlements, dispositions of or in relation to property, [dispositions granting powers of appointment, maintenance or advancement,] powers in the nature of trusts or coupled with a trust and powers of appointment including a general power, whether testamentary or created intervivos and the expressions "trust" and "trustee" shall extend to resulting, implied and constructive trusts, and to cases where the trustee has a beneficial interest in the trust property and to the duties incident to the office of personal representative; and "trustee" where the context admits, includes that personal representative and the donor or holder of a power, including a general power of appointment;

["Trust Instrument", "instrument" or "registered instrument" means the deed, trust agreement, will, codicil, settlement or instrument establishing or creating a trust and includes any variation or amendment to such deed, trust agreement, will, codicil, settlement or instrument;]

"Trustee Company" means a company registered as a trustee company under the provisions of the Trustee Companies Act 1981-82 [and except in relation to section 15, includes a wholly owned subsidiary of a trustee company nominated pursuant to section 4A of the Trustee Companies Act 1981-82;]

[(2) Every reference to an instrument trust or disposition shall, unless the context otherwise requires include every variation or amendment thereto.]

In subs.(1):

"court": The definition of this term was inserted by s.2(a) of the International Trusts Amendment Act 1999

"dispose and disposition": The definition of this term was inserted by s.3(2) of the International Trusts Amendment Act 1989

"Disposition": A definition of this term was repealed by s.3(1) of the International Trusts Amendment Act 1989.

"formalities": The definition of this term was inserted by s.3(2) of the International Trusts Amendment Act 1989.

"governing law": The definition of this term was inserted by s.3(2) of the International Trusts Amendment Act 1989.

"heirship right": The definition of this term was inserted by s.3(2) of the International Trusts Amendment Act 1989.

"Instrument": The definition of this term was deleted by s.2(a) of the International Trusts Amendment Act 1995-96.

"interested party": The definition of this term was inserted by s.2(b) of the International Trusts Amendment Act 1995-96.

"International Trust": The definition of this term was amended by s.2(c) of the International Trusts Amendment Act 1995-96 and by s2(b) of the International Trusts Amendment Act 1999.

"Judgment": The definition of this term was inserted by s.3(2) of the International Trusts Amendment Act 1989.

"Personal Relationship": The definition of this term was inserted by s.3(2) of the International Trusts Amendment Act 1989.

"Protector": The definition of this term was inserted by s.2(d) of the International Trusts Amendment Act 1995-96

"publish": The definition of this term was inserted by s.2(c) of the International Trusts Amendment Act 1999.

"Settlor": The definition of this term was inserted by s.3(2) of the International Trusts Amendment Act 1989.

"Trust": The definition of this term was amended by s.2(e) of the International Trusts Amendment Act 1995-96.

"trust instrument", "instrument" or "registered instrument": The definition of this term was inserted by s.2(f) of the International Trusts Amendment Act 1995-96.

"Trustee company": The definition of this term was amended by s.2(g) of the International Trusts Amendment Act 1995-96.

Subs.(2) was added by s.3(3) of the International Trusts Amendment Act 1989.

3. **Saving of existing laws**—The laws applicable to trusts in force in the Cook Islands shall apply to international trusts except in so far as they are inconsistent with or have been modified by the provisions of this Act. This section was amended by s.3 of the International Trusts Amendment Act 1995-96

4. **Registrar and Deputy Registrar**—

(1) The Registrar of International and Foreign Companies appointed pursuant to Section 8 of the International Companies Act 1981-82 shall be the Registrar of International Trusts.

(2) A Deputy Registrar of International and Foreign Companies and any officer appointed pursuant to Section 8 of the International Companies Act 1981-82 shall be a Deputy Registrar of International Trusts, or officers as the case may be for the purposes of this Act.

(3) Anything authorized or required to be done by the Registrar under this Act may be authorized or done by a Deputy Registrar.

(4) All courts, judges and persons acting judicially shall take judicial notice of the seal and also the signature of the Registrar and any Deputy Registrar.

5. **Application of this Act**—

(1) Unless the context otherwise requires [and subject to section 15] the provisions of this Act shall apply to:

(a) international trusts [registered pursuant to section 15]; and

(b) all registered instruments whether they take effect on, before or after the commencement of this Act.

[(c) any disposition to or by an international trust.]

[(d) all questions and matters relating to or concerning an international trust;]

(2) A trust registered under this Act shall be a valid trust notwithstanding that it may be invalid according to the law of the settlor's domicile or residence or place of current incorporation.

(3) In determining the existence and validity of a trust registered under this Act the Court shall apply;

    (a) the provisions of this Act; and

    (b) any other law of the Cook Islands; and

    (c) any other law, which would be applied;

if to do so, would validate the trust.

> In subs.(1), para.(c) was added by s.4 of the International Trusts Amendment Act 1989.
> In subs.(1), para.(d) was added by s.4 of the International Trusts Amendment Act 1995-96

PART II

MODIFICATION OF THE LAWS APPLICABLE TO INTERNATIONAL TRUSTS

6. **Perpetuity period—**

(1) Notwithstanding any rule of law or equity to the contrary, the rule of law known as the rule against perpetuities or remoteness of vesting, and the rule of law known as the rule against perpetual trusts or against inalienability, shall each have no application to an international trust.

(2) Notwithstanding subsection (1), a trust instrument may make provision for vesting of all or any part of the property of the trust upon such terms as are prescribed by the trust instrument including, but not limited to, provision for—

    (a) a period within which the property of a trust shall vest in any beneficiary of the trust; or

    (b) the happening of an event upon which the property of the trust shall vest in any beneficiary of the trust; or

    (c) the property of the trust not to vest in any beneficiary of the trust or the trust not to terminate;

(3) Where a trust would, except for this subsection, be held by the Court to be void for uncertainty because of its terms relating to termination of the trust or vesting of the property of the trust, and such uncertainty would be removed by imposing a date for termination of that trust, then the trust shall terminate on the date 100 years from the date of creation of the trust, and the property of the trust shall vest in the beneficiaries on that date, unless termination or vesting occurs earlier in accordance with the trust instrument.

(4) Where a period or an event is specified within, or at the end of, or upon which the property of the trust then remaining shall vest in the beneficiary in accordance with the provision which specifies that period or event or in accordance with subsection (3), (as the case may be), and such vesting shall apply in relation to all property then remaining of that trust and every general or special power of appointment under that trust shall be exercised in a manner consistent therewith.

(5) Without limiting any other rights conferred on trustees to vary a trust instrument, the trustees of an international trust may with the prior consent of the interested parties, or if permitted by the trust instrument, vary the terms of the trust instrument to make provision—

(a) for a period being not less than the existing period provided for in the trust instrument within which the property of the trust shall vest in any beneficiary of the trust; or

(b) for the happening of an event being an event that will occur beyond the period within which the property of the trust would otherwise vest in the beneficiaries and upon the happening of which the property of the trust shall vest in any beneficiary of the trust; or

(c) to remove the period within which the property of the trust shall vest in any beneficiary.

(6) Except where there is express provision to the contrary contained in the trust instrument, where the proper law of an international trust is to be changed from that of the Cook Islands to that of another jurisdiction, the trustees may with the consent of the interested parties, or if permitted by the trust instrument, vary the terms of the trust instrument to provide for a lesser period in which the then remaining property of the trust shall vest in any beneficiary so as not to infringe the law of that other jurisdiction.]

This section was substituted for the original s.6 by s.5 of the International Trusts Amendment Act 1995-96

7. **Execution of a trust instrument**—
Notwithstanding any rule of law or equity to the contrary and except where there is express provision to the contrary contained in the trust instrument, a trust instrument and any counterpart thereof (whether an original or copy including a facsimile copy) may be executed by the settlor, trustee and any other parties thereto at different times and in different places whether within or outside the Cook Islands and a trust instrument so executed and a trust thereby created established or settled whether registered before or after the coming into force of this Act shall be deemed as valid as if the trust instrument were executed by the settlor and those parties simultaneously at the time the trust instrument was executed by the settlor, and at a place within the Cook Islands.]

This section was substituted for the original s.7 by s.6 of the International Trusts Amendment Act 1995-96

8. Abolition of the rule against double possibilities—

The rule of law prohibiting the limitation, after a life of an unborn person, of an interest in land to the unborn child or other issue or an unborn person is hereby abolished, but without prejudice to any other rule relating to perpetuities.

9. Abolition of the rule against accumulations—

(1) Where property is settled or disposed of in such manner that the income thereof may or shall be accumulated wholly or in part the power or direction to accumulate that income shall be valid if the disposition of the accumulated income is or may be valid but not otherwise.

(2) Nothing in this section shall affect the power of any person to terminate an accumulation that is for that person's benefit, or any jurisdiction or power of the Court to maintain or advance out of accumulations, or any powers of a trustee under any Act or law or under any instrument creating a trust or making a disposition.

(3) For the purpose of this Act the following enactment's are repealed:
  (a) Sections 41 and 42 of the Property Law Act 1952;
  (b) Section 2 of the Property Law Amendment Act 1963.

(4) The enactment's repealed by subsection (3) of this section and the corresponding provisions of any former enactment, shall be deemed in connection with the law applicable to international trusts, never to have applied to any power to accumulate.

10. Application of the rule in Saunders v Vautier—

[(1) Notwithstanding any rule of law or equity to the contrary, where a trust instrument empowers a trustee to accumulate income, or to refrain from making any distribution of capital or income until a specified date or event, or where any provision of the trust instrument otherwise prevents the making of any distribution of capital or income, notwithstanding that a beneficiary may, but for this section other wise be entitled to that accumulation oor distribution, the trustee may, in his absolute discretion, subject to any other express terms of the instrument, give effect to that direction as he thinks fit notwithstanding that a beneficiary shall requrest the trustee to immediately distribute the accumulation or distribution and will give a valid discharge to the trustee for such distribution; and]

(2) Notwithstanding anything contained in any Act to the contrary or any rule of law or equity, the power to vary the terms of a trust or disposition so as to vary or remove the direction to accumulate income [or

distribute capital] of the trust or to modify or remove the discretion of the trustee to accumulate income [or distribute capital] shall have no application where subsection (1) of this section applies.

This section was amended by s.7 of the International Trusts Amendment Act 1995-96 and s.4 of the International Trusts Amendment Act 1999.

11. Power of revocation—

(1) Unless an international trust contains an express power of revocation it shall be deemed to be irrevocable by the settlor and his legal personal representatives notwithstanding that it is voluntary.]

> This section was substituted for the original s.11 by s.5(1) of the International Trusts Amendment Act 1989.
> For saving provision refer to s.5(2) of the International Trusts Amendment Act 1989.

12. Charitable and Purpose Trusts—

(1) Notwithstanding any rule of law to the contrary an international trust shall be deemed to be charitable or for purposes which are charitable where it is a trust substantially for one or more of the following objects or purposes, namely:
    (a) for the relief of poverty;
    (b) for the advancement of education;
    (c) for the advancement of religion;
    (d) for other purposes beneficial to the community;
    notwithstanding that the object or purposes may not be of a public nature or for the benefit of the public, but may be for the benefit of a section of the public or members of the public, or that it may also benefit privately one or more persons or objects or persons within a class of persons or is liable to be defeated whether by the exercise of a power of appointment or disposition or that the trustee has the power to defer the enjoyment of any charity or other beneficiary of the trust for any period not exceeding the term of the trust, and notwithstanding further that the trust may be discretionary or contingent upon the happening of any event.
    (2) Notwithstanding any rule of law or equity to the contrary a trust settled or established by a non-resident of the Cook Islands shall not be void or voidable by virtue of the fact that the trust fund shall be held for a purpose or purposes, whether charitable or not, and any trust so created shall be enforceable on the terms set out in the trust instrument by the person or persons named in the instrument establishing the trust as the person or persons appointed to enforce the trust and the trust shall be enforceable

at the instance of the person or persons so named notwithstanding that such person or persons are not beneficiaries under the trust.

[(3) A person appointed to enforce the trust may resign or be removed or replaced in accordance with the trust instrument.]

[(4) If the person appointed to enforce the trust resigns, or is removed, or is unwilling, refusing, unfit or unable to act, and if no successor can be appointed in accordance with the trust instrument, the trustees shall forthwith apply to the Court for directions or for another person or persons to be appointed by the Court to enforce the trust, and the Court shall be empowered to make an order appointing a person or persons to enforce the trust on such terms as it sees fit, and pending appointment by the Court the Attorney-General shall be entitled, on such terms as he may require, to enforce the trust with the same rights and powers as the person appointed under the trust instrument to enforce the trust.]

Subsections (1) and (2) were amended and subsections (3) and (4) added by s.8 of the International Trusts Amendment Act 1995-96

13. Recording of title—

(1) For the purposes of identification and ease of administration, the trustees of an international trust may adopt a name for that trust.

(2) A trust instrument may authorize the trustees to cause the ownership or title of property of the trust to be recorded or registered in the name of that international trust rather than the name of the trustees.

(3) Where the trustees of a trust cause the ownership or title of property of that trust to be recorded or registered in the name of that trust, the trustees shall where permitted by the jurisdiction of the relevant registry lodge with the relevant registry or recording authority an affidavit, which affidavit shall contain the following particulars name,—

(a) the name of the international trust;

(b) the names and addresses of all the trustees;

(c) whether fewer than all the trustees are authorized to act on behalf of and in the name of the trust in any acquisition, conveyance, encumbrance, lease or other dealing with the property and if so—

(i) designate the trustees or the manner in which the trustees shall be designated;

(ii) specify the limitations (if any) upon the authority of such trustees;

(iii) be executed by all the trustees named pursuant to paragraph (b).

(d) where the affidavit does not provide for the matters contained in paragraph (c) then it shall be executed by at least one trustee named therein.

(4) Upon lodging an affidavit with the relevant registry or recording authority the affidavit shall constitute prima facie evidence of the facts recited therein, the authority of the deponent to execute and lodge the affidavit, and the authority of the trustees who are thereby empowered to convey or otherwise act on behalf of the trust insofar as the same affects title to any interest in the property.

(5) Subject to subsection (3), where an interest in property is recorded or registered in the name of an international trust, such interest shall only be conveyed, encumbered, leased or otherwise dealt with in the name of the trust by an instrument executed by all the trustees named in the affidavit.

(6) Where an interest in property is recorded or registered in the name of an international trust pursuant to the trust instrument, the legal title to that property shall be deemed to be held by the trustees.

(7) In the event of a change in any of the particulars contained in an affidavit under subsection (3) the trustees for the time being shall provide a further affidavit in accordance with that subsection.]

This section was substituted for the original s. 13 by s.9 of the International Trusts Amendment Act 1995-96

13A. **Bankruptcy**—

Notwithstanding any provision of the law of the settlor's domicile or place of ordinary residence or the settlor's current place of incorporation and notwithstanding further that an international trust is voluntary and without valuable consideration being given for the same, or is made on or for the benefit of the [settlor, settlor's spouse] or children of the settlor or any of them, an international trust and a disposition to an international trust shall not be void or voidable in the event of the settlor's bankruptcy insolvency or liquidation (other than in the case of an international company registered pursuant to the International Companies Act 1981-82 that is in liquidation) or in any action or proceedings at the suit of creditors of the settlor but shall, remain valid and subsisting and take effect according to its tenor subject to the provisions of section 13B.

This section amended by s.10 of the International Trusts Amendment Act 1995-96

13B. **Fraud**—

(1) Where it is proven beyond reasonable doubt by a creditor that an international trust settled or established or property disposed to an international trust—

(a) Was so settled established or disposed by or on behalf of the settlor with principal intent to defraud that creditor of the settlor; and

725

(b) did at the time such settlement establishment or disposition took place render the settlor, insolvent or without property by which that creditor's claim (if successful) could have been satisfied,

then such settlement establishment or disposition shall not be void or voidable and the international trust shall be liable to satisfy the creditor's claim out of the property which but for the settlement establishment or disposition would have been available to satisfy the creditor's claim and such liability shall only be to the extent of the interest that the settlor had in the property prior to settlement establishment or disposition and any accumulation to the property (if any) subsequent thereto.

(2) In determining whether an international trust, settled or established or a disposition, has rendered the settlor insolvent or without property by which a creditor's claim (if successful) may be satisfied, regard shall be had to the fair market value of the settlor's property, (not being property of or relating to the trust) at the time immediately after the settlement establishment or the disposition referred to in subsection (1) (b) and in the event that the fair market value of such property exceeded the value of the creditor's claim, at the time, after the settlement establishment or disposition, then the trust so settled or established or the disposition shall for all purposes be deemed not to have been so settled established or the property disposed of with intent to defraud the creditor.

(3) An international trust settled or established and a disposition to such trust shall for all purposes be deemed not to have been so settled or established, or the property disposed of with the intent to defraud a creditor:

(a) [[if]] settled established or the disposition takes place after the expiration of 2 years from the date that creditor's cause of action accrued; [[or]]

[(b) where settled, established or the disposition takes place before the expiration of 2 years from the date that the creditor's cause of action accrued, that creditor fails to commence in a court of competent jurisdiction proceedings in respect of that creditor's cause of action before the expiration of 1 year from the date such settlement establishment or disposition took place,]

[provided that this subsection shall not have effect if, and subject to subsection (5), at the time of settlement, establishment, or disposition, as the case may be, proceedings in respect of that creditor's cause of action against that settlor have already been commenced in a court of competent jurisdiction].

(4) An international trust settled or established and a disposition of property to such trust shall for all purposes be deemed not to have been so settled or established, or the property disposed of with intent to defraud a creditor, if the settlement or disposition of property took place before that creditor's cause of action accrued.

726

(5) A settlor shall not have imputed to him an intent to defraud a creditor, solely by reason that the settlor—

(a) has settled or established a trust or has disposed of property to such trust within two years from the date of that creditor's cause of action accruing;

(b) has retained, possesses or acquires any of the powers or benefits referred to in paragraphs (a) to (f) of section 13C.

(c) is a beneficiary, trustee or protector;

(d) has settled or established a trust, or has disposed of property to such trust, at a time when proceedings in respect of that creditor's cause of action against that settlor have already been commenced in a court of competent jurisdiction;

(6) Where an international trust is liable to satisfy a creditor's claim in the manner provided for in subsection (1)—

(a) the creditor's rights to recovery shall be limited to that property referred to in subsection (1), or to the proceeds of that property, to the exclusion of any rights against the trustees of the international trust or any of them, against any other property of the international trust, or against any other of the property or assets of the trustees of the international trust, or any of them;

(b) where the international trust is unable to satisfy the creditor's claim by reason of the fact that the property referred to in subsection (1) has been disposed of, other than to a bona fide purchaser for value, then any such disposition shall be void;

(7) For the purpose of this section the onus of proof of the settlor's intent to defraud the creditor lies on the creditor.

(8) For the purposes of this section and section 13K—

(a) the date of the cause of action accruing shall be, the date of that act or omission which shall be relied upon to either party or wholly establish the cause of action, and if there is more than one act or the omission shall be a continuing one, the date of the first act or the date that the omission shall have first occurred, as the case may be, shall be the date that the cause of action shall have accrued.

(b) the term "cause of action" means the earliest cause of action capable of assertion by a creditor against the settlor of an international trust or, as the case may be, against the settlor of property upon an international trust, by which that creditor has established (or may establish) an enforceable claim against that settlor;

(c) where a creditor has, or asserts, or could have asserted, multiple or successive causes of action against a settlor (whether by virtue of the nature of the relevant circumstances of the case, or by reason of having attained the status of a judgment creditor in respect of one or more of such causes of action, or by reason of asserting or being able to assert an allegedly fraudulent settlement of or disposition to an international trust, or otherwise) the entitlement of such a creditor to relief under this section shall be determined, and the periods referred to in this section shall be calculated with reference to one only of the creditor's causes of action, being that cause of action which accrued first in time in accordance with paragraph (b).

(d) nothing in paragraphs (b) or (c) shall apply so as to affect the right or requirement of a creditor to commence separate proceedings under this section in relation to a cause of action which is separate from and independent of another cause of action where the Court is satisfied, having regard to paragraph (c), that both the circumstances out of which the cause of action arose and the subject matter of that cause of action are wholly unrelated to those of the other cause of action.

(9) The provisions of this section shall apply to all civil actions and proceedings brought in the Court in which fraud, deceit, unconscionable conduct or any other inequitable conduct however described or any species of unjust enrichment is alleged, against any person (whether a party to the proceedings or not) with regard to the settlement or establishment of an international trust or the disposition of property to such a trust, or receipt of property by or for such a trust (or subsequent disposition of property from such a trust with the intention of prejudicing creditors of the settlor of such property or such trust), and the remedy conferred by subsection (1) shall be the sole remedy available in such an action or proceedings, to the exclusion of any other relief or remedy against any party to the relevant action or proceeding.

(10) The provisions of this section shall operate to the exclusion of any other remedy, principle or rule of law, whether provided for by statute, or founded in equity or in common law including, for the avoidance of doubt, the imposition of a constructive trust upon any interested party or the recognition and enforcement of any constructive trust imposed or recognized by the laws of any other jurisdiction.

(11) Subject to section 16(6), the provisions of this section shall apply to every international trust, and to every trust which having been registered as an international trust, is no longer so registered, and in respect of all dispositions to such a trust.

(12) For the purposes of this section the term "creditor" means a creditor of the settlor and includes any person who alleges a cause of action against a settlor.

(13) A creditor seeking to enforce a claim under this section in reliance on a foreign judgment may not enforce such claim until such time as it can demonstrate to the reasonable satisfaction of the court that,

(a) it has exhausted all remedies available to it against the settlor's remaining property, and

(b) all rights of appeal against that foreign judgment have been exhausted.

[(14) For the purposes of assessing the liability of an international trust to a creditor, where the amount of that creditor's claim against the settlor is, wholly or partly, in any way related to or evidenced by a foreign judgement, the court in making any award in facour of that creditor shall disregard and exclude any amount awarded in that foreign judgement to that creditor which comprise any form of exemplary, vindictive, retributory or punitive damages (by whatever name), or is an amount of damages arrived at by doubling, trebling or otherwise multiplying a sum assessed as compensation for the loss or damage (which types of damage are in this section together called "punitive damages").]

[(15) The burden of proof shall be on a creditor to establish that an amount awarded in a foreign judgement does not wholly or partly comprise punitive damages.]

[(16) Subsection (14) shall not have effect if at the time of settlement, establishment or disposition, as the case may be an award of punitive damages has already been made in a foreign judgement against a settlor;]

Subsections (2), (3), (4), (5), and (8) were amended, subsections (6), (9), and (10) were substituted for the original subs.(6), (9), and (10), and subs.(11), (12) and (13) were added by s. 11 of the International Trusts Amendment Act 1995-96.
Subsections (14), (15) and (16) were inserted by s.5 of the International Trusts Amendment Act 1999.

13C. <u>Retention of control and benefits by settlor—</u>

An international trust and a registered instrument shall not be declared invalid or a disposition declared void or be affected in any way by reason of the fact that the settlor, and if more than one, any of them, either—

(a) retains possesses or acquires a power to revoke the trust or instrument;

(b) retains possesses or acquires a power of disposition over property of the trust or the subject of the instrument;

(c) retains possesses or acquires a power to amend the trust or instrument;

(d) retains possesses or acquires any benefit interest or property from the trust or any disposition or pursuant to the instrument;

(e) retains possesses or acquires the power to remove or appoint a trustee or protector;

(f) retains possesses or acquires the power to direct a trustee or protector on any matter;

(g) is a beneficiary, [trustee or protector] of the trust or instrument either solely or together with others.

Subs.(g) amended by s.12 of the International Trusts Amendment Act 1995-96

13D. **Foreign judgments not enforceable—**

Notwithstanding the provisions of any treaty or statute, or any rule of law, or equity, to the contrary, no proceedings for or in relation to the enforcement or recognition of a judgment obtained in a jurisdiction other than the Cook Islands against any interested party shall be in any way entertained, recognized or enforced by any Court in the Cook Islands to the extent that the judgment—

(a) is based upon the application of any law inconsistent with the provisions of this Act or of the Trustee Companies Act 1981-2; or

(b) relates to a matter or particular aspect that is governed by the law of the Cook Islands.]

This section was substituted for the original s.13D by s.13 of the International Trusts Amendment Act 1995-96

13E. **Heirship rights—**

No international trust or any aspect of such trust governed by the laws of the Cook Islands and no disposition of property to be held upon the trusts thereof is void, voidable, liable to be set aside or defective in any fashion, nor is the capacity of any settlor to be questioned by reason that such trust or disposition may avoid or defeat the right, claim or interest of a person held by reason of a personal relationship to the settlor or by way of heirship rights.]

13F. **Spendthrift beneficiary—**

(1) For the purposes of this Act, and notwithstanding any rule of law or equity to the contrary, it shall be lawful for an instrument or disposition to provide that any estate or interest in any property given or to be given to any beneficiary shall not during the life of that beneficiary or such lesser period as may be specified in the instrument or disposition be alienated or pass by bankruptcy, insolvency or liquidation or be liable to be seized, sold, attached, or taken in execution by process of law and where so provided such provision shall take effect accordingly.

(2) Where property is given subject to any of the restrictions contained in subsection (1), the right to derive income from such property by a beneficiary and any income derived therefrom shall not pass by bankruptcy, insolvency or liquidation or be liable to be seized attached or taken in execution by process of law.

(3) Where property is given subject to a restriction against alienation then the right to derive income from that property shall not be alienated for as long as that restriction remains in force.

(4) A restriction imposed by this section or by an instrument or disposition that property or the right to derive income from such property shall not be alienated or that such property or the right to derive income or the income from such property shall not pass by bankruptcy insolvency or liquidation or be liable to be seized sold or attached or taken in execution by process of law may at any time after such property has been given be removed if provided for in the instrument or disposition and in the manner specified therein.]

Subs.(3) was substituted for the original subs.(3) by s.4 of the International Trusts Amendment (No. 2) Act 1989.

13G. **Governing Law**—

(1) In determining the governing law of an international trust regard shall first be had to the terms of that trust and to any evidence therein as to the intention of the parties; and the other circumstances of an international trust may be taken into account only if the terms of the trust fail to provide such evidence.

(2) A term of an international trust expressly selecting the laws of the Cook Islands to govern the trust is valid, effective and conclusive regardless of any other circumstances.

(3) Where a trust instrument so provides, or where in accordance with the powers contained in a trust instrument, the law of the Cook Islands is chosen to govern a particular aspect of an international trust, and law other than that of the Cook Islands is chosen to govern other aspects of that trust, then the choice of Cook Islands law and the choice of that other law as to their respective aspects shall be valid effective and conclusive regardless of any other circumstances.

(4) Where a trust instrument contains a power to change the governing law of that trust, that law may be changed to or from the law of the Cook Islands in accordance with that power, and that change shall be valid, effective and conclusive according to the terms of such power.

(5) A change in governing law shall, not affect the legality or validity of, or render any person liable for, any thing done before the change.

(6) A change in the governing law of a trust shall not of itself interrupt the continuity of the relationships whether in equity or law established by the trust and, without limitation, shall not constitute a resettlement of the trust.

(7) Subject to any other provision of this Act, the application of the governing law of a trust to that trust prior to a change in that governing law shall not be affected by that change.

(8) The disposition of any property to or from a trust in accordance with the governing law of that trust at the time of the disposition shall not be

avoided or otherwise invalidated by a subsequent change from that governing law to some other law.

(9) Where the donee of a power to change or cause to change the governing law of a trust exercises that power in accordance with the terms of the power so conferred, then the exercise of that power by the donee shall be deemed to have been properly exercised.

(10) The location of the interested parties, selection or imposition of jurisdiction, place of administration, or the situation of the property of the trust shall not in any way affect the validity or effect of a choice of the governing law of a trust made in accordance with the trust instrument.

(11) Where the governing law of a trust is changed to or from the law of the Cook Islands, the trustees shall be empowered to make all such consequential alterations or additions to the trust instrument as the trustees shall consider necessary or desirable to ensure the provisions, rights, liabilities, powers and obligations of and under the trust instrument shall be as valid and effective under the new governing law as they were under the previous governing law.

(12) Where a trust instrument contains provision for the governing law of a trust to change upon a determination being made in accordance with the trust deed as to either—

(a) the happening or non-happening of a specified event; or

(b) a state of affairs coming into existence

and that determination as to the happening or non-happening of the event or the existence of the state of affairs is so made then that provision shall take effect accordingly.

(13) Nothing in this section shall affect the application of section 13K(5) to an international trust.

Subs.(3) and (4) were substituted for the original subs.(3) and (4) by s.14(1) of the International Trusts Amendment Act 1995-96.

Subs. (6) to (13) were inserted by s.14(2) of the International Trusts Amendment Act 1995-96.

13H. **Matters determined by governing law—**

(1) All questions arising in regard to an international trust which is for the time being governed by the laws of the Cook Islands or in regard to any disposition of property upon the trusts thereof including, without prejudice to the generality of the foregoing, questions as to:—

(a) subject to subsection 2(c), the capacity of the settlor;

(b) any aspect of the validity of the trust or disposition or the interpretation or effect thereof;

(c) the administration of the trusts, whether the administration be conducted in the Cook Islands or elsewhere, including questions as to powers, obligations, liabilities and rights of trustees and their appointment and removal; or

(d) the existence and extent of powers, conferred or retained, including powers of variation or revocation of the trust and powers of appointment, and the validity of any exercise thereof,

are to be determined according to the laws of the Cook Islands, without reference to the laws of any other jurisdictions with which an international trust or disposition may be connected.

(2) Subject to the provisions of this Act subsection (1) shall—

(a) not validate any disposition of property which is neither owned by the settlor nor the subject of a power in that behalf vested in the settlor, nor does that subsection affect the recognition of foreign laws in determining whether the settlor is the owner of such property or the holder of such a power;

(b) take effect subject to any express contrary term of the trust or disposition;

(c) as regards the capacity of a corporation, not affect the recognition of the laws of its place of incorporation;

(d) not affect the recognition of foreign laws prescribing generally (without reference to the existence or terms of the trust) the formalities for the disposition of property;

(e) not validate any trust of real property or disposition [or transfer] of real property situate in a jurisdiction other than the Cook Islands which is void ab initio according to the laws of such jurisdiction;

(f) not validate any testamentary trust or testamentary disposition which is invalid according to the laws of the testator's domicile.

[[(3) A disposition of property located at a place beyond the Cook Islands to an international trust or a trust that shall subsequently become an international trust shall if made in accordance with the law of that place governing such disposition be deemed to be a valid disposition notwithstanding any law of the Cook Islands to the contrary.]].

Subs. (3) was added by s.3 of the International Trusts Amendment Act 1991.
Subs. (2)(e) was amended by s.15 of the International Trusts Amendment Act 1995-96.

13I. **Exclusion of foreign law—**

Without limiting the generality of section 13H it is expressly declared that no international trust governed by the laws of the Cook Islands and no disposition of property to be held upon the trusts thereof is void, voidable, liable to be set aside or defective in any fashion, [nor may relief be had under section 13B] nor is the capacity of any settlor to be questioned by reason that:—

(a) the laws of any foreign jurisdiction prohibit or do not recognize the concept of a trust either in part or in whole; or

(b) the international trust or disposition avoids or defeats rights, claims or interests conferred by the law of a foreign jurisdiction upon any person or, contravenes any rules of foreign law or any foreign judicial or administrative order or action intended to recognize, protect, enforce or give effect to any such rights, claims or interests; or

(c) the laws of the Cook Islands or the provisions of this Act or the principal Act are inconsistent with any foreign law.

Section 13I was amended by s.16 of the International Trusts Amendment Act 1995-96. Ss.13A-13I were added by s.6 of the International Trusts Amendment Act 1989.

13J. Community property—

(1) Where a husband and wife transfer property to an international trust or a trust that subsequently becomes an international trust and, immediately before being transferred, such property or any part or any accumulation thereof is, pursuant to the law of its location or the law of either of the transferor's domicile or residence, determined to be community property, then notwithstanding such transfer and except where the provisions of the trust deed may provide to the contrary, that property and any accumulation thereof shall, for the purposes of giving effect to that law, be deemed to be community property and be dealt with in a manner consistent with that law but in every other respect shall be dealt with in accordance with the trust deed and the governing law of that deed.

(2) Notwithstanding anything to the contrary herein contained, nothing herein shall be construed so as to cause the trust, the trust fund, the trustees or any of them, the protectors or any of them, to be liable or obligated for any debt or responsibility of the settlor merely by reason of this section.

This section was inserted by s.4 of the International Trusts Amendment Act 1989.

13K. Commencement of proceedings—

(1) No action or proceedings whether pursuant to this Act or at common law or in equity to,—

(a) set aside the settlement of an international trust; or

(b) set aside any disposition to any international trust, or

(bb) seek relief or remedy under section 13B;

shall be commenced, unless such action or proceedings is commenced,—

(c) in the High Court of the Cook Islands; and

(d) before the expiration of 2 years from the date of,—

(i) the settlement of the international trust; or

(ii) the disposition to the international trust,

as the case may be.

(2) No action or proceedings whether pursuant to this Act or at common law or in equity shall be commenced by any person,—

(a) claiming to have had an interest in property before that property was settled upon or disposed to an international trust; and

(b) seeking to derive a legal or equitable interest in that property, unless such action or proceedings is commenced,—

(c) in the High Court of the Cook Islands; and

(d) before the expiration of 2 years from the date that the property referred to in paragraphs (a) and (b) was settled upon or disposed to an international trust.

(3) No action or proceeding (whether substantive or interlocutory in nature) to which either this section or section 13B applies shall be heard, and no order shall be made or granted by the Court in respect of or relating to such action or proceeding (including any injunction or order that shall have the effect of preventing the exercise of, or the granting or restoring of, any right, duty, obligation or power, or of preserving, granting custody of, or detaining or inspecting any property, including for the avoidance of doubt any Anton Pillar order or any Mareva injunction) unless the Court having regard to the affidavit filed pursuant to subsection (4) shall first be satisfied, beyond reasonable doubt that—

(a) commencement of the action or proceedings is not precluded by the provisions of subsections (1) or (2); and

(b) the remedy or relief sought is not precluded by the provisions of subsection (6);

and in any action or proceedings to which section 13B applies that,

(c) the remedy or relief sought is not precluded by the provisions of section 13B; and

(d) the evidence as disclosed by the affidavit demonstrates the ability of the plaintiff to prove those matters necessary to establish a right to relief under section 13B(1);

(4) In every action or proceeding to which this section applies, or to which section 13B applies, the person or persons bringing the same (in this subsection referred to as "the plaintiff") shall, upon the commencement of such proceedings, file an affidavit which shall be made by the plaintiff or by any one of them (or in the case of a corporate plaintiff, by an officer thereof) who shall depose as to—

(a) the facts and circumstances giving rise to the action or proceedings;

(b) whether an action or proceedings have been commenced in any other jurisdiction between any of the parties in the action or proceedings or by any party against the settlor of any relevant trust or of property upon any relevant trust;

(c) such of the circumstances of the plaintiff as are or may be relevant to determine the quantum of security to be paid by the plaintiff or if there is more than one plaintiff, any one or more of them, either as non-residents, or in connection with the making of any interim order; and

(d) the date upon which the international trust or property, in respect of which the action or proceedings is brought, was settled or disposed of to the relevant international trust, as the case may be;

and in any case to which section 13B applies, the following further matters—

(e) the facts and circumstances of the creditor's cause of action and if the creditor shall have multiple or successive causes of action the facts and circumstances of the creditor's cause of action which accrued first in time (as defined by and determined in accordance with section 13B);

(f) the date upon which that creditor's cause of action accrued; and

(g) whether an action or proceedings have been commenced in any jurisdiction in respect of that creditor's cause of action and if so, the date upon which that action or those proceedings were commenced.

[(5) Notwithstanding any other provision of this Act, the provisions of this section and sections 13A to 13J inclusive of those sections shall apply to every international trust governed, or expressed to be wholly or partly governed, by the law of the Cook Islands, including a trust that formerly was not wholly or partly governed by the law of the Cook Islands but in respect of which the governing law of the trust has been changed (whether before or after registration) so that the trust, or any aspects of it, are governed, or expressed to be governed, by the law of the Cook Islands, and, without limiting the generality of the foregoing and notwithstanding any other law to the contrary, after the date of registration—

(a) the settlement or establishment of such trust; and

(b) every disposition to such trust, including any disposition occurring before the date of registration or change of law; and

(c) every proceeding commenced after the date of registration concerning such settlement, establishment or disposition,

shall be subject to the provisions of this section and of sections 13A to 13J inclusive of those sections as if upon the date that such settlement, establishment or disposition occurred, the trust was an international trust governed wholly and exclusively by the law of the Cook Islands.]

[(6) In any action or proceedings commenced, whether pursuant to this Act or at common law or in equity, wherein the usual or appropriate remedy (whether sought or not) would be either,—

(a) the setting aside of the settlement of, or disposition to, an international trust or

(b) the award of a legal or equitable interest in property settled upon or disposed of to an international trust,

but the grant of such a remedy is or would be precluded either by subsections (1) or (2), or by section 13B, then neither damages nor any other relief or remedy which has the effect of providing relief or remedy alternative to or consequential upon that precluded by the said provisions, shall be awarded in such action or proceedings.]

This section was inserted by s.5 of the International Trusts Amendment Act 1991.
Subs. (1) amended by s.17(1) of the International Trusts Amendment Act 1995-96.
Subs. (3) and (4) were substituted for the original subs. (3) and (4) by s.17(2) and (3) of the International Trusts Amendment Act 1995-96.
Subs. (5) amended by s.17(4) of the International Trusts Amendment Act 1995-96 and by s. 6 of the International Trusts Amendment Act 1999.
Subs. (6) was inserted by s.17(5) of the International Trusts Amendment Act 1995-96.

PART III

REGISTRATION OF TRUSTS

14. Application for registration—

(1) Application for registration of a trust as an international trust shall be made to the Registrar in the prescribed form, and accompanied by the prescribed fee, within 45 days of the date upon which a registered foreign company, international company or a trustee company, is appointed or declared a trustee of that trust.

(2) On application by a trustee of the trust, the Registrar may extend the period of 45 days referred to in subsection (1) subject to the Registrar being satisfied that the failure to register the trust as an international trust was as a consequence of inadvertence on the part of any interested party to the trust.

This section was substituted for the original section 14 by s.18 of the International Trusts Amendment Act 1995-96.

15. Registration—

(1) No trust shall be registered as an international trust until there has been filed with the Registrar:

(a) a certificate from a trustee company certifying that the trust upon registration will be an international trust; and

(b) a notice of the name and registered office of the trust.

(2) Upon receipt of a certificate and notice referred to in subsection (1) of this section the Registrar shall register that trust upon the Register of the

International Trusts kept for that purpose and issue a certificate of registration in the prescribed form.

(3) A certificate of registration under the hand and seal of the Registrar shall be conclusive evidence that all the requirements of this Act in respect of registration and other matters precedent and incidental thereto have been complied with and that the international trust referred to therein was duly registered under this Act.

[(4) Where upon settlement of a trust the trust instrument provides for the law of the Cook Islands to be the governing law of all or any aspects of that trust then that law and the provisions of this Act shall apply to those aspects of that trust governed by Cook islands law from the date of establishment creation or settlement of that trust if the trust is at any time thereafter, subject to section 14(1), registered as an international trust.]

[(5) Where a trust is established created or settled under a law other than that of the Cook Islands, but Cook Islands law is subsequently chosen to be, or becomes, the governing law of all or any aspects of that trust, then Cook Islands law and the provisions of this Act shall apply to those aspects of that trust governed by Cook Islands law from the date that trust became wholly or partly governed by Cook Islands law if the trust is at any time thereafter, subject to section 14(1), registered as an international trust.]

[(6) Nothing in this section shall affect the application of section 13K(5) to an international trust.]

Subs. (4), (5) and (6) were substituted for the original subs. (4) by s.19 of the International Trusts Amendment Act 1995-96.

16. Certificate of registration—

(1) A certificate of registration issued pursuant to section 15(2) shall be valid and effective for the period specified in that certificate, and registration of the international trust the subject of that certificate shall be valid and effective until that international trust is deregistered pursuant to subsection (6).

(2) Application for renewal of registration may be made upon—

(a) filing with the Registrar an application for renewal of registration in the prescribed form; and

(b) payment of the prescribed fee.

(3) Application for renewal of registration may be made within the period of 90 days of the date of expiry of the last certificate of registration and no application for renewal of registration pursuant to subsection (2) shall be granted where application is not made or the prescribed fee paid within that period [provided the Registrar may, in his sole discretion, if he is satisfied on application by a trustee of a trust that the failure to make the application for renewal and payment of the prescribed fee was as a

consequence of inadvertence on the part of any interested party to the trust, extend the time for registration accordingly].

(4) Every renewal of registration granted shall take effect from the date of expiry of the last certificate of registration.

(5) Every renewal of registration shall be for a period not exceeding five years as may be specified in the renewed certificate of registration.

(6) The Registrar may, on giving 7 days notice to the trustees at the registered office of the trust, deregister an international trust if—

(a) a completed application for the renewal of its registration is not filed within the period specified in subsection (3), or

(b) if he reasonably believes that trust no longer qualifies as an international trust in terms of the definition of "international trust" in section 2,

and on and from the date of de-registration the provisions of this Act shall cease to apply to that trust or, in respect of sections 13A and 13B, to any dispositions made to that trust prior to the date of deregistration, and if that trust is governed by the laws of the Cook Islands and, but for the provisions of this Act, would be held void by reason of breach of the rule against perpetuities or remoteness of vesting or the rule against perpetual trusts or against inalienability, such trust shall, unless otherwise provided in the trust instrument, be deemed varied immediately prior to de-registration such that the maximum duration of the trust shall be the period which ends on that day which is the 21st anniversary of the death or winding up of the settlor.

(7) A trust shall not be re-registered under this Act if it has been de-registered pursuant to this section.

(8) Except for the provisions of subsection (6), nothing in this section shall affect the application of section 13K(5) to an international trust.

Section 16 was substituted for the original section 16 by s.20 of the International Trusts Amendment Act 1995-96.
Subs. (3) was amended by s.7 of the International Trusts Amendment Act 1999.

17. **Registration of trust instrument—**

Any person who is a trustee may provide the Registrar with a copy of the trust instrument or any amendment thereto which shall be certified in the manner prescribed and the Registrar shall register that copy as a true copy and file the same.

18. **Registered office—**

(1) The registered office of an international trust shall be the registered office of the registered foreign company, international company or trustee company which is a trustee.

(2) The address for service of any documents upon an international trust shall be the registered office of that trust.

(3) Every trustee company shall keep and maintain at its principal place of business in the Cook Islands a register of the name of every international trust of which it is a trustee, which register shall be made available at all reasonable times for inspection by the Registrar.

> Subs. (3) was substituted for the original subsection (3) by s.21 of the International Trusts Amendment Act 1995-96.

19. Proceedings by or against an international trust—

Where any proceedings are instituted by or against an international trust it shall be sufficient to name the international company, registered foreign company or trustee company that is a trustee and it shall not be necessary to join in the action any other trustee.

~~PART IIIA~~

TRUSTEES

19A. Trustees duties to beneficiaries—

(1) Subject to subsections (2) and (3), a trustee in the performance of that trustee's duties to beneficiaries and in the exercise of any power, function or discretion shall exercise the care, diligence, and skill that a prudent person of business would exercise in managing the affairs of others.

(2) Subject to subsection (3), where a trustee's profession employment or business is or includes acting as a trustee on behalf of others, the trustee, in exercising any power, function or discretion shall exercise the care, diligence and skill that a prudent person engaged in that profession, employment or business would exercise in managing the affairs of others.

(3) All duties and obligations of a trustee shall apply to that trustee only to the extent that a contrary intention is not expressed in the trust instrument and shall have effect subject to the terms of the trust instrument.

19B. Delegation—

(1) Where a trust instrument authorizes a trustee to delegate any or all of that trustee's powers, duties, functions or discretion's then that trustee may delegate any or all of such powers, duties, functions and discretion's provided that a trustee may not delegate, other than to a co-trustee, any powers, duties, functions or discretion's involving the distribution or non-distribution of property of the trust to a beneficiary including, without limitation, distributions by way of payment, use, advancement, transfer or assignment.

(2) Except where the terms of a trust specifically provide to the contrary, a trustee may—

(a) delegate management of property of the trust (including the selection of investments) and employ professional or skilled persons as investment managers;

(b) employ professional or skilled persons to act in relation to any of the affairs of the trust or to hold any or all of the property of the trust.

(3) A trustee, who in good faith makes or continues such delegation or appointment, shall not be liable for any loss to the trust arising from or as a consequence of a delegation or appointment under subsections (1) or (2).

(4) A trustee may authorize a person referred to in subsection (2) to retain any commission or other payment usually payable in relation to any transaction.

(5) Where a trustee enters into an agreement for the employment of an investment manager under paragraph (a) of subsection (2), the trustee may agree on the same terms as are customarily found in an agreement between an investment manager and beneficial (as opposed to fiduciary) owner of property, including terms excluding or limiting the liability of the investment manager for negligent performance of duties, and, unless the trust instrument otherwise provides, the trustee shall not be liable for breach of trust by virtue of agreeing to such terms.

19C. **Investments**

(1) A trustee may invest any trust funds in any manner of investment or in any kind of property authorized for the investment of trust funds by and under the trust instrument or otherwise permitted by law.

(2) Where a trust instrument authorizes expressly, or by necessary implication, the investment of the property of the trust in any investments authorized by the law of the Cook Islands for the investment of trust funds, the instrument shall be deemed to authorize investment in such investments as may be expressed to be trustee investments by regulations made under this Act.

(3) Where a trust instrument expresses trustees' powers of investment in general terms including powers to undertake any manner of investment in any kind of property, or including powers equivalent to those of a natural person then, notwithstanding any rule of law or equity to the contrary, the trustee shall have such power and be authorized to invest trust funds and property accordingly, and every such authorization shall be given such fair large and liberal interpretation as to give full effect to its tenor and, except where the trust instrument so provides, any other provision in the trust instrument authorizing any specific manner of investment or investment in any specific property shall not derogate from or limit the generality of this section.

(4) Nothing in this section shall preclude a trust instrument from expressly excluding any manner of investment in any kind of property.

19D. **Trustee's majority decisions**

(1) Where a trust instrument provides for majority decisions of trustees such provision shall be valid and effective on the terms set out therein.

(2) Subject to any provisions contained in a trust instrument, every—

(a) decision made, resolution passed or power or discretion exercised by the trustees shall be valid if made passed or exercised by a majority of the trustees if there are more than 2 of them; and

(b) thing done and every deed or other instrument executed by the majority of trustees shall be valid and effective as if done or executed by all the trustees.

19E. **Trustees limitation of liability**

Where any provision of a trust instrument limits the liability of a trustee or provides relief or indemnity for a trustee, such provision shall be valid and effective according to its terms, and every such provision shall be given a fair, large and liberal interpretation so as to give full effect to its tenor, notwithstanding any rule of law or equity to the contrary.

19F. **Custodian trustees**

(1) Subject to the provisions of this section and to the trust instrument any person or group of persons may be appointed as custodian trustee under this section to be custodian trustee of any international trust in the same manner as a trustee may be appointed.

(2) Notwithstanding any other provision of this Act, but subject to the provisions of the trust instrument, where a custodian trustee is appointed of any international trust—

(a) all of the trust property shall be held by transferred to or vested in the custodian trustee as if the custodian trustee were sole trustee, and for that purpose vesting orders may, where necessary, be made by the Court on application by the custodian trustee or the managing trustee, but without prejudice to the managing trustee's control of that property.

(b) the management of the trust property and the exercise of all powers and discretion's exercisable by the trustee under the trust shall remain vested in the managing trustee as fully as effectually as if there were no custodian trustee;

(c) the sole function of the custodian trustee shall be to get in and hold the trust property, and invest its funds, and dispose of the assets, as the managing trustee in writing directs, for which purpose the custodian trustee shall execute all such documents and perform all such acts as the managing trustee may in writing direct;

(d) for the purposes of paragraph (c) a direction given by the majority of the managing trustees where there are more than one, shall be deemed to be given by all the managing trustees;

(e) the custodian trustee shall not be liable to any interested party or third party for acting on any direction of the managing trustee but if the custodian trustee is of opinion that any such direction conflicts with the trusts or the law, or exposes the custodian trustee to any liability, or is otherwise objectionable, the custodian trustee may apply to the Court for directions, but without being under any obligation to do so;

(f) The custodian trustee shall not be liable to any interested party or third party for any act or default on the part of the managing trustee or any of the managing trustees;

(g) all actions and proceedings touching or concerning the property of the trust shall be brought or defended in the name of the custodian trustee and the custodian trustee shall not be liable for the costs thereof apart from the property of the trust;

(h) no person dealing with the custodian trustee shall be concerned to inquire as to the existence of any direction, concurrence or otherwise of the managing trustee, or be affected by notice of the fact that the managing trustee has not issued any direction or concurred;

(i) the power of appointing a new trustee or trustees when exercisable by trustees, shall be exercisable by the managing trustee alone, but the custodian trustee shall have the same power as any other trustee of applying to the court for the appointment of a new trustee.

(3) Subject of the provisions of the trust instrument and subsection (8), on the application of the custodian trustee, or a managing trustee, and on satisfactory proof that it is in the best interest of the beneficiaries, or that on other grounds, having regard to the trust instrument, it is expedient to terminate the custodian trusteeship, the Court may make any order for that purpose, and may also make such vesting orders and give such directions as in the circumstances, seem to the Court to be necessary or expedient.

(4) Subject to the provisions of the trust instrument, in any case where remuneration or commission is payable to the trustee of any trust property, remuneration or commission may be paid to both the custodian trustee and the managing trustee, and subject as aforesaid the amount thereof shall be determined by the managing trustee if the managing trustee is entitled to fix its own remuneration.

(5) [Without limiting the provisions of this section, and except as varied by the trust instrument, the provisions of this Act and the Trustee Companies Act 1981-82 relating to a trustee's powers, liabilities, functions, duties and discretions, shall apply equally to a custodian trustee, and in

particular, without limiting the generality of the above, the Custodian Trustee—

(a) shall have the full powers of delegation conferred on trustees by section 13B;

(b) may permit assets to be held by or in the name of the managing trustee to facilitate the managing trustee's management and administration of the Trust assets or as otherwise directed by the managing trustee.]

(6) For the purposes of this section a reference to a managing trustee shall be a reference to a trustee other than the custodian trustee.

(7) Notwithstanding subsection (3)—

(a) a custodian or managing trustee may resign, be appointed, be removed or be replaced in the same manner as a trustee or as prescribed by the trust instrument.

(b) a trustee who accepts appointment as both managing and custodian trustee shall for all purposes be treated as, and be, an ordinary trustee, in which case the respective rights and obligations imposed on custodian and managing trustees under this section or the trust instrument shall have no further application to that trustee, and that trustee shall not be entitled to rely on the limited liability of a custodian trustee, nor charge remuneration as both a managing trustee and a custodian trustee.

(8) Subject to the trust instrument, upon termination of the appointment of the custodian trustee and unless there is a simultaneous appointment of a new custodian trustee, the following provisions shall apply—

(a) any restrictions upon the powers of the managing trustees by virtue of the appointment of the custodian trustee shall lapse, and the managing trustee shall thereafter be the only trustees; and

(b) the title to the property of the trust shall vest in the trustees.

(9) The powers, duties, functions, discretion's and office of the managing trustee, if vacant and not filled or replaced pursuant to subsections (2)(i) or (7)(a), may be assumed by or appointed to, a person or persons as prescribed in the trust instrument.

Subs (5) amended by s8 of the International Trusts Amendment Act 1999.

19G. Advisor to Trustees—

(1) Subject to the provisions of this section, a trust instrument may provide for any person or group of persons (in this section referred to as an "advisor") to be appointed as advisor under this section to advise the trustee of a trust in respect of all or some of the matters relating to the property of the trust.

(2) Where an advisor is appointed to an international trust the property and management of the trust and the exercise of all powers and discretion's

exercisable by the trustee under the trust shall remain vested in the trustee as fully as effectually as if no advisor was appointed except that;

(a) the trustee may consult the advisor, and the advisor may advise the trustee, on any matter relating to the property of the trust for which the advisor was appointed;

(b) the advisor shall not be liable as or considered a trustee of the trust in acting as an advisor;

(c) where any advice or direction is tendered or given by the advisor, or the majority of advisors if there are more than one, the trustee may follow the same and act accordingly, without being under any obligation to do so, and the trustee shall not be liable for anything done or omitted by them by reason of the trustee following that advice or direction;

(d) subject to the trust instrument, in any case where remuneration or commission is payable to the trustee of a trust, remuneration or commission may be paid to the advisor, at such rate as determined by the trust instrument, or by the trustee in the absence of any specific direction in the trust instrument.

(3) No person dealing with the trustee shall be concerned to inquire as to the concurrence or otherwise of the advisor, or be affected by notice of the fact that the advisor may not have concurred.

19H. **Holding of title to property**—

(1) Notwithstanding any rule of law or equity to the contrary a trust instrument may provide for the trustees of an international trust to delegate among themselves the function of holding title to trust property.

(2) Notwithstanding any rule of law or equity to the contrary a trust instrument may further provide that where property of an international trust is situated in a jurisdiction in which a trustee or trustees reside, any one or more of those trustees may hold title to that property in one or all of their names, and not in the name of all trustees of the international trust.

(3) where, whether before or after the coming into force of this Act, title to property is transferred to a trustee or trustees, other than to all of the trustees of an international trust, with the intention that it be held by that trustee or those trustees as trust property, then such transfer shall have the same effect as if the property had been transferred to all of the trustees to be held on the trusts set out in the trust instrument.

19I. **Protection of trust property**—

Without prejudice to any rights or remedies available to the creditors of a trustee qua trustee, that trustee's personal creditors shall have no right or claim against any property of any trust held by that trustee qua trustee.

19J. **Protection of third parties**—

(1) Where any property of a trust is disposed of by a trustee, including by way of sale, mortgage, charge, lien, or lease, to a third party for value, the

title of the third party to the property, and the enforceability of any contract related to that disposition—

(a) shall not be impeachable except on the ground of actual fraud by or with the knowledge of that third party, and

(b) shall not otherwise be affected on the ground that the transaction was unauthorized or not within the power of the trustee, or that the relevant power (if any) was otherwise improperly or irregularly exercised,

and that third party shall not be concerned to see to the application of the money or consideration paid by him, or be responsible for the misapplication thereof.

(2) Where any interested party has with the principal intent of defrauding a particular third party acted, or procured or permitted others to act, to dispose of or reduce the value of the property of the trust or the validity or enforceability of a trustee's indemnity, such action shall be voidable at the instance of the third party, provided that any disposition of property of the trust may not be avoided where that property has been disposed of to a bona fide recipient for value who at the time of the disposition did not have notice of the intention to defraud the third party.

(3) For the purposes of this section—

(a) "third party" means a person other than a person in a capacity as—

(i) a settlor, trustee, protector or beneficiary of the trust; or

(ii) any creditor of, or other person claiming through, a settlor, protector or beneficiary of the trust.

(b) the term "trustee's indemnity" shall mean that trustee's right of indemnity against the property of the relevant trust.

(4) Nothing in this section shall affect or limit the liability of a trustee to a beneficiary for a breach of trust.

Part IIIA was inserted by s.23 of the International Trusts Amendment Act 1995-96.

PART IV
PROTECTOR

20. Protector of a Trust

(1) The terms of a trust instrument may provide for the office of protector of that trust.

(2) A protector shall have the powers, delegations or functions as are conferred on the protector by the trust instrument or by this Act, or as may be prescribed.

(3) A protector of a trust may also be a settlor, a trustee or a beneficiary of that trust.

(4) Subject to the trust instrument, a protector of a trust shall not be liable or accountable as a trustee or other person having a fiduciary duty to any person in relation to any act or omission in performing the function of a protector under the trust instrument.

(5) Where there is more than one protector of a trust then, subject to the trust instrument, any power or function conferred on the protectors may be exercised if the majority of the protectors for the time being agree upon its exercise.

(6) A protector who dissents from a decision of the majority of protectors may require his dissent to be recorded in writing and filed at the registered office of the trust, and subject to the trust instrument, shall not be liable for the acts of the majority of protectors pursuant to such decision.

(7) Any powers or functions conferred by this Act on a protector, shall have effect subject to the terms of the trust instrument.

Section 20 amended by s.9 of the International Trusts Amendment Act 1999.

21. Consent of beneficiaries

(1) A trust instrument may provide for the protector or any other person or persons (in this section referred to as a "nominated person") to represent all or any beneficiaries who are minors, or beneficiaries yet to be ascertained, or beneficiaries not having legal capacity, or beneficiaries who, after the best reasonable endeavors of the trustees, are unable to be contacted (which beneficiaries are in this section referred to as a "represented beneficiary").

(2) A nominated person may, on behalf of a represented beneficiary, consent to or ratify any act or omission on the part of a trustee. Every consent or ratification provided shall be deemed to be the consent or ratification of the represented beneficiary and shall be construed by every Court as the consent or ratification of the represented beneficiary to that act or omission.

Part IV was substituted for the original Part IV by s.23 of the International Trusts Amendment Act 1995-96.

PART V
MISCELLANEOUS

22. Resident beneficiaries—

[(1)] The provisions of this Act shall not have any application to a beneficiary who is domiciled in the Cook Islands or who is ordinarily resident in the Cook Islands.

[(2)] For the purposes of this section an international company, a foreign company, an international partnership, and an international trust shall be deemed not to be resident in the Cook Islands.]

In subs.(1) the word in double square brackets was inserted by s.11(a) of the International Trusts Amendment Act 1989.
Subs.(2) was added by s.11(b) of the International Trusts Amendment Act 1989.

23. **Privacy**—

(1) Except where the provisions of this Act require and subject to this section, it shall be an offence under this Act for a person to divulge or communicate to any other person information relating to the establishment, constitution, business undertaking or affairs of an international trust.

(2) All judicial proceedings, other than criminal proceedings relating to an international trust shall, unless ordered otherwise be heard in camera and no details of the proceedings shall be published by any person except in accordance with subsection (3).

(3) Every decision of the Court in respect of any proceedings concerning the application or interpretation of this Act shall be published or reported for the purposes of affording a record of those proceedings, provided that in every case,

(a) the written decision of the Court shall be edited to such extent as shall be necessary to preserve secrecy in respect of the identity of the trust, of every interested party and of the subject matter of the proceedings, and

(b) no such decision shall be reported or published unless or until a judge of the Court shall have ascertained the views of the parties to the proceedings as to the adequacy of any editing undertaken, and certified in writing to the Registrar of the Court that the decision as edited may be released for publication or reporting.

(4) Unless excluded by the terms of a trust instrument, a trustee or an officer or employee of a trustee or trustee company may divulge or make available information relating to the establishment, constitution, business undertakings or affairs of an international trust,

(a) to any person or class of persons as that trustee, officer or employee considers necessary from time to time, in its complete discretion, for carrying out the management and administration of the trust assets in the ordinary course of business; or

(b) to a legal practitioner—

(i) for the purpose of obtaining legal advice relating to establishment, constitution, business undertakings or affairs of an international trust; or

(ii) for the purpose of prosecuting or defending any litigation relating to the establishment, constitution, business undertakings or affairs of an international trust.

Subs.(3) inserted by s.24 of the International Trusts Amendment Act 1995-96 and amended by s10 of the International Trusts Amendment Act 1999.
Subs.(4) inserted by s.10 of the International Trusts Amendment Act 1999.

24. Translations—

(1) Every document filed with the Registrar and not in the English language shall be accompanied by a certified translation.

(2) A document that is not in the English language and which is not accompanied by a certified translation at the time of filing shall not be accepted for registration by the Registrar.

(3) For the purpose of this section a certified translation is a translation into the English language, certified as a correct translation, by a translator to the satisfaction of the Registrar.

25. No action to lie against certain persons—

No action shall lie against the Government of the Cook Islands, any statutory body or authority, or a public or judicial officer in respect of any performance of its or his functions or duties under this Act.

26. Power of Exemption—

(1) The Minister may on his own motion or pursuant to an application in writing lodged with the Commissioner by an international trust or a trust, which if it were registered would be an international trust, exempt that international trust or trust from all or any of the provisions of this Act and any regulations made under this Act and may impose such terms and conditions as he thinks fit as a condition under which that exemption is granted. An exemption so granted may be revoked or varied by the Minister at any time.

(2) In dealing with an application under this section the Minister shall not be required to act judicially and his decision shall in all cases be final.

(3) Any exemption or condition imposed pursuant to subsection (1) of this section, shall take effect as from the date to be decided by the Minister in his discretion.

Subs.(1) amended by s.11 of the International Trusts Amendment Act 1999.

27. Prohibitions by Minister—

(1) The Minister shall have an absolute right of his own motion or otherwise and without assigning reasons to make an order:

(a) prohibiting the registration of any trust; or

(b) directing any international trust to cease carrying on its business or part of its business immediately or within such time as may be specified in the order.

(2) An order made under this section may be revoked or varied by the Minister.

(3) In making an order under this section the Minister shall not be required to act judicially and such order shall be final.

27A. **Guarantee by Crown—**

The Crown guarantees to all international trusts that there shall be no compulsory acquisition or expropriation of the property of such trusts, or their investors, situated in the Cook Islands except—

(a) in accordance with the due process of law;

(b) for a public purpose defined by law; and

(c) in payment of compensation as defined by law.

This section was inserted by s.12 of the International Trusts Amendment Act 1989.

27B. **Application of other enactment's**

(1) Subject to section 3 no enactment other than this Act and the enactment's set out in the Schedule to this Act shall—

(a) impose—

(i) any liability, duty, responsibility, obligation or restriction, or

(ii) any fee, impost, tax, levy, due, duty, or excise; or

(iii) any fine or penalty

on an international trust; or

(b) require—

(i) the deposit of any moneys in any public account; or

(ii) the filing of any accounts, returns, reports or records; or

(iii) the licensing or registration of any document act, matter or thing pertaining to an international trust by an international trust.

(2) Notwithstanding subsection (1), an international trust shall not be required to register as a foreign enterprise pursuant to the provisions of the Development Investment Act 1977 and shall not be subject to that Act by reason only that it

(a) carries on business with another international trust;

(b) carries on business with an international company registered under the provisions of the International Companies Act 1981-82;

(c) carries on business with a foreign company registered under the provisions of the International Companies Act 1981-82;

(d) carries on business with an international partnership registered under the International Partnership Act 1984;

(e) obtains legal advice or legal representation;

(f) obtains accounting advice or has its accounts prepared or audited;

(g) operates a bank account for the purpose of either depositing, receiving or transmitting money due or owing by such trust or undertakes a transaction with a bank for purposes principally associated with the objects of the trust;

(h) utilizes the services of a trustee company or any subsidiary of such company;

(i) undertakes any act matter or thing as may be prescribed by regulation.

(3) The Queen's Representative may by Order in Executive Council amend the Schedule to this Act by omitting therefrom or adding thereto any enactment (including any regulation) and may in like manner determine whether an enactment or regulation shall be omitted or added either in whole or in part.]

Section 27B inserted by s.25 of the International Trusts Amendment Act 1995-96.

27C. **Trust Records—**

(1) Any records, accounts or documents relating to a trust and held by either the Registrar or a trustee, including but not by way of limitation, the trust instrument, may be established, kept or recorded in written, magnetic, electronic or any other data storage form, provided that the records can be readily produced in written form.

(2) When an international trust has been terminated, or the Cook Islands trustee removed or has resigned, each trustee shall ensure that the records in the possession of that trustee are retained by that trustee for a period of three years from the said date of termination, removal or resignation as the case may be, but thereafter the said records may be destroyed.

(3) The Registrar may cause any records or registers in his possession to be destroyed after the expiration of three years from the date of de-registration, or from the date of expiry of the last certificate of registration of that trust under this Act."

Section 27C inserted by s.12 of the International Trusts Amendment Act 1999.

28. **Penalties—**

(1) Any person who:
(a) does anything which is forbidden by or under this Act; or

(b) omits to do something required or directed by or fails to comply with any provisions of this Act

shall be guilty of an offense against this Act and shall be liable on conviction to a fine not exceeding US$10,000 or to imprisonment for a term not exceeding 1 year or to both.

29. **Regulations—**

The Queens Representative may by order in Executive Council make regulations prescribing all matters and things required or authorized by this Act to be prescribed or which are necessary for carrying out or giving effect to this Act [and may in particular make regulations prescribing—

(a) the duties and liabilities of trustees;

(b) the powers of trustees;

(c) the protection of trustees against liability;

(d) the investment of trust funds;

(e) the manner in which an instrument or deed of trust may be executed;

(f) the appointment and discharge of trustees;

(g) the powers of the Court in respect of an application by a trustee for directions;

(h) the rules of procedure in respect of judicial proceedings;

(i) the distribution of trust property;

(j) the manner in which a trustee shall deal with property that is subject to any encumbrance or restriction whether such encumbrance or restriction is imposed or authorized by this Act or any other Act and the rights interests duties and liabilities of persons subsequent to such dealing;

(k) the manner by which property (whether of a particular class or otherwise) together with any accumulation thereto or any property in substitution therefore shall be identified as being subject to the provisions of section 13F;

(1) penalties for breach of such regulations.]

The words in square brackets were substituted for the original words "including the prescribing of penalties for breaches of such regulation" by s.13 of the International Trusts Amendment Act 1989.

SCHEDULE

International Companies Act 1981-82
International Partnership Act 1984
Off-Shore Banking Act 1981
Off-Shore Insurance Act 1981-82
Trustee Companies Act 1981-82

Monetary Board Act 1981
Development Investment Act 1977

This Schedule was added by s.10(1) of the International Trusts Amendment Act 1989.

THE INTERNATIONAL TRUSTS AMENDMENT ACT 1985

1985, No.7

An Act to amend the International Trusts Act 1984

26 July 1985

BE IT ENACTED by the Parliament of the Cook Islands in Session assembled and by the authority of the same, as follows:

1. Short Title—This Act may be cited as the International Trusts Amendment Act 1985, and shall be read together with and deemed part of the International Trusts Act 1984 (hereinafter referred to as "the principal Act").
2. *Repealed by s.9(1) of the International Trusts Amendment Act 1989.*

THE INTERNATIONAL TRUSTS AMENDMENT ACT 1989

1989, No. 23

An Act to amend the International Trusts Act 1984

(8 September 1989)

BE IT ENACTED by the Parliament of the Cook Islands in Session assembled, and by the authority of the same, as follows:

1. Short Title—This Act may be cited as the International Trusts Amendment Act 1989 and shall be read together with and deemed part of the International Trusts Act 1984 (herein referred to as "the principal Act").
2. Application of this Act—This Act shall apply to every international trust settled or established after the coming into force of this Act and every disposition of property to such trust made after the coming into force of this Act, whether such property is situated in the Cook Islands or elsewhere, unless, but without limiting the provisions of Section 13G, expressly provided in such trust or disposition that the governing law shall be other than that of the Cook Islands.

3.   (1)   *This subsection repealed a definition of "Disposition" in s.2 of the principal Act.*
    (2)   *This subsection inserted definitions of the terms "dispose and disposition", "formalities", "governing law", "heirship right", "Judgment", "personal relationship", "protector", and "settlor" in s.2 of the principal Act.*
    (3)   *This subsection added subs.(2) to s.2 of the principal Act.*
4.   *This section added para.(c) to s.5(1) of the principal Act.*
5.   (1)   *This subsection substitutes a new section for s.11 of the principal Act.*
    (2)   Notwithstanding the repeal of Section 11 of the Principal Act every matter, act or thing done pursuant to that section before the coming into force of this Act shall, if such matter, act or thing was validly done, remain so valid after the coming into force of this Act as if that section had not been repealed.
6.   *This section inserted ss.13A—I in the principal Act.*
7.   (1)   *This subsection added subs.(4) to s.15 of the principal Act.*
    (2)   A trust registered in accordance with section 15 of the principal Act before the coming into force of this Act shall, notwithstanding that it ~~was so registered after it was settled or established, be deemed to have been registered from the time that it was settled or established.~~
8.   (1)   *This subsection substituted new subs.(3) and (4) for subs.(3) of s.16 of the principal Act.*
    (2)   Every renewal of registration granted before the coming into force of this Act shall notwithstanding that such renewal may have been granted after the expiry of the certificate of registration be deemed to have been granted upon the expiry of that certificate of registration.
9.   (1)   *This subsection repealed s.20 of the principal Act.*
    (2)   Notwithstanding the repeal of Section 20 of the principal Act every matter act or thing done pursuant to that section before the coming into force of this Act shall if such matter act or thing was validly done remain so valid after the coming into force of this Act as if that section had not been repealed.
10.   (1)   *This subsection substituted a new section for s.21 of the principal Act.*
    (2)   The Queen's Representative may by Order in Executive Council amend the Schedule to this Act by omitting therefrom or adding thereto any enactment (including any regulation) and may in like manner determine whether an enactment or regulation shall be omitted or added either in whole or in part.
    (3)   Notwithstanding the repeal of section 21 of the principal Act, every matter, act or thing done pursuant to that section before the coming into force of this Act shall, if such matter, act or thing was validly done remain so valid after the coming into force of this Act as if that section had not been repealed.
11.   (a)   *This paragraph inserted the subsection number (1) to s.22 of the principal Act.*
    (b)   *This paragraph added subs. (2) to s.22 of the principal Act.*
12.   *This section inserted s.27A in the principal Act.*
13.   *This section amended s.29 in the principal Act.*

Appendix A

SCHEDULE

This Schedule has been incorporated in the principal Act, where it appears in this consolidation.

THE INTERNATIONAL TRUSTSAMENDMENT (NO.2) ACT 1989

1989, No. 31

An Act to amend the International Trusts Act 1984

(22 December 1989)

BE IT ENACTED by the Parliament of the Cook Islands in Session assembled, and by the authority of the same, as follows:

1. Short Title—This Act may be cited as the International Trusts Amendment (No.2) Act 1989 and shall be read together with and deemed part of the International Trusts Act 1984 (herein referred to as "the principal Act").
2. Application—This Act shall apply to every international trust settled or established on or after the 8th day of September 1989 and every disposition of property to such trust made on or after that date, whether such property is situated in the Cook Islands or elsewhere, unless, but without limiting the provisions of section 13G of the principal Act (as inserted by section 6 of the International Trusts Amendment Act 1989) expressly provided in such trust or disposition that the governing law of that trust or relating to that disposition shall be law other than that of the Cook Islands.
3. *This section amended s.13B(3) of the principal Act.*
4. *This section substituted a new subsection for subs. (3) of the principal Act.*

THE INTERNATIONAL TRUSTS AMENDMENT ACT 1991

1991, No. 32

An Act to amend the International Trusts Act 1984

(19 December 1991)

BE IT ENACTED by the Parliament of the Cook Islands in Session assembled, and by the authority of the same, as follows:

1. Short Title—This Act may be cited as the International Trusts Amendment Act 1991 and shall be read with and deemed part of the International Trusts Act 1984 (herein referred to as the "principal Act").

2. *This section added subs. (8) and (9) to s.13B of the principal Act.*
3. *This section added subs.(3) to s.13H of the principal Act.*
4. *This section inserted s.13J in the principal Act.*
5. *This section inserted s.13K in the principal Act.*
6. Repeals—The enactment titled, 13 Elizabeth I Ch 5 (1571) shall have no application to any settlement upon or disposition to an international trust.

The International Trusts Act is administered by the Cook Islands Monetary Board.

THE INTERNATIONAL TRUSTS AMENDMENT ACT 1995-96

1995-96, No.25

An Act to amend the International Trusts Act 1984 and to modify the law relating to international trust

(21 November 1995)

BE IT ENACTED by the Parliament of the Cook Islands in Session assembled and by the authority of the same, as follows:

1. Short Title—This Act may be cited as the International Trusts Amendment Act 1995-96, and shall be read together with and deemed part of the International Trusts Act 1984 (hereinafter referred to as "the principal Act").
2. Interpretation—*This section amended section of the principal Act as follows:*

    (a) *this subsection deleted the definition of "instrument";*
    (b) *this subsection inserted the definition of "interested party";*
    (c) *this subsection amended the definition of "International Trust";*
    (d) *this subsection substituted a new definition of "protector";*
    (e) *this subsection amended the definition of "Trust";*
    (f) *this subsection inserted the definition of "trust instrument", "instrument" or "registered instrument";*
    (g) *this subsection amended the definition of "trustee company".*

3. Saving of existing laws—*This section amended section 3 of the principal Act.*
4. Application of this Act—*This section amended section 5(1) of the principal Act.*
5. Power to specify perpetuity period—*This section substituted a new section for section 6 of the principal Act.*
6. Execution of a trust instrument—*This section substituted a new section for section 7 of the principal Act.*
7. Application of the rule in Saunders v Vautier—*This section amended section 10(1) of the principal Act.*
8. Charitable and Purpose Trusts—*This section amended section 12 of the principal Act.*

    (a) *this subsection amended subs.(1);*
    (b) *& (c) these subsections amended subs. (2);*
    (c) *this subsection inserted subsections (3) and (4);*

Appendix A

9. <u>Investments</u>—*This section repealed the previous section 13 of the principal Act and substituted the new section 13—<u>Recording of title</u> in the principal Act.*

10. <u>Bankruptcy</u>—*This section amended section 13A of the principal Act.*

11. <u>Fraud</u>—*This section amended section 13B of the principal Act.*

    (a)   *this subsection amended subs. (2);*
    (b)   *& (c) this subsection amended subs. (3) and (4);*
    (d)   *this subsection inserted the proviso to subs. (3);*
    (e)   *this subsection amended subs. (4);*
    (f)   *& (g) these subsections amended subs. (5);*
    (h)   *this subsection inserted para. (d) to subs. (5);*
    (i)   *this subsection substituted a new subsection for subs. (6);*
    (j)   *this subsection amended subs. (8);*
    (k)   *this subsection deleted para. (b) of subsection (8) and substituted paras. (b), (c), and (d) of subs. (8);*
    (l)   *this subsection substituted new subsections (9) and (10) for subs. (9) and (10);*

12. <u>Retention of control and benefits by settlor</u>—*This section amended section 13C (g) of the principal Act.*

13. <u>Foreign judgments not enforceable</u>—*This section substituted a new section 13D for section 13D of the principal Act.*

14. <u>Governing law</u>—*This section amended section 13G of the principal Act.*

    (1)   *this subsection substituted new subsections for subs. (3) and (4);*
    (2)   *this subsection inserted new subsections (6) to (13).*

15. <u>Matters determined by governing law</u>—*This section amended section 13H (2) (e) of the principal Act.*

16. <u>Exclusion of foreign law</u>—*This section amended section 13I of the principal Act.*

17. <u>Commencement of proceedings</u>—*This section amended section 17 of the principal Act.*

    (1)   *this subsection amended subs. (1);*
    (2)   *this subsection substituted a new subsection for subs. (3);*
    (3)   *this subsection substituted a new subsection for subs. (4);*
    (4)   *this subsection amended subs. (5);*
    (5)   *this subsection inserted subsection (6).*

18. <u>Application for registration</u>—*This section substituted a new section for section 14 of the principal Act.*

19. <u>Registration</u>—*This section repealed subsection (4) of section 15 the principal Act and substituted new subsections (4), (5) and (6).*

20. <u>Annual Certificate of Registration</u>—*This section substituted a new section for section 16 of the principal Act.*

21. <u>Registered office</u>—*This section substituted anew subsection for subsection (3) of the principal Act.*

22. <u>Part IIA—Trustees</u>—*This section inserted new Part IIIA into the principal Act.*

23. <u>Part IV—Protector</u>—*This section substituted a new Part for Part IV of the principal Act.*

24. <u>Secrecy</u>—*This section amended section 23 of the principal Act.*
25. <u>Application of other enactment's</u>—*This section inserted section 27B into the principal Act.*
26. <u>Transitional</u>—

   (1) Subject to the prior written consent of the interested parties being obtained, or if permitted by the trust instrument, a trustee of an international trust may within 2 years of the date of the coming into force of this Act or in the case of an international trust registered after the date of the coming into force of this Act within 2 years of the date of first registration and unless the trust instrument shall expressly exclude the application of this section or any other provision of this Act, vary the provisions of the trust instrument so as to facilitate the application of this Act to an international trust and include therein provisions consistent with the provisions of this Act and may make all such consequential alterations, amendments, or additions to the trust instrument as the trustees shall consider necessary or desirable to ensure the trust powers and provisions of the settlement shall be as valid and effective notwithstanding the variation and nothing in this subsection shall limit the liability of a trustee arising from the exercise of the power to vary a trust instrument.

   (2) Every variation pursuant to subsection (1) shall take effect from the date of the variation.

   (3) No variation made pursuant to this Act shall affect the liability of a trustee for any act or omission prior to the date of the variation taking affect.

27. <u>Application</u>

   (1) Except where expressly provided to the contrary in this Act the provisions of this Act shall apply to every international trust, whether registered before or after the commencement of this Act, and to all matters relating to or concerning every such international trust, or the interested parties to every such international trust.

   (2) The provisions of sections 10 to 17 (both inclusive) of this Act shall apply to every international trust settled or established on or after the 8th day of September 1989 and to every disposition of property to such trust made on or after that date, whether such property is situated in the Cook Islands or elsewhere, except that subsection 11(1)(d) of this Act shall not apply to any trust registered as an international trust on or before the coming into force of this Act.

   (3) The provisions of the principal Act as amended by sections 2 to 9 (inclusive) and sections 18 to 24 (inclusive) of this Act shall be deemed to have come into force on the same date as the principal Act provided always that—

      (a) the provisions of this subsection shall not apply to or in respect of matter act omission or thing inconsistent with any of those provisions if validly done or omitted prior to the coming into force of this Act.

    (b)   nothing in this subsection shall operate or be interpreted or construed to relieve any trustee from any liability arising prior to the passing of this Act or arising in respect of any matter act omission or thing occurring prior to the passing of this Act.

(4)   The provisions of sections 49 and 50 of the Trustee Act 1956 shall have no further application to an international trust provided however that every matter, act, omission, or thing done or omitted, pursuant to those provisions before the coming into force of this Act shall remain as valid after the coming into force of this Act as prior to its coming into force.

(5)   Nothing in this Act shall apply to or affect any proceedings commenced in the Court before the coming into force of this Act.

(6)   Where a trust instrument contains provisions consistent with the provisions of the principal Act as amended by this Act then those provisions of the trust instrument shall be as valid and effective as if the provision of the principal Act (as amended) with which it is consistent was in force as at the date that the provision of the trust instrument was incorporated therein.

28. Savings

(1)   Without limiting the provisions of the Acts Interpretation Act 1924 or any other provision of this Act, but subject to this Act, it is declared that no provision of this Act shall operate or be interpreted or construed to invalidate any matter, act, omission, or thing validly done or omitted, prior to the coming into force of this Act.

(2)   Without limiting the generality of section 3 of the principal Act, as amended, it is declared that the provisions of the Trustee Act 1956 (NZ) shall continue to apply to international trusts and in the event of any conflict or inconsistency between those provisions and those of the principal Act (as amended) the latter shall prevail over the former.

This Act is administered by the Cook Islands Monetary Board.

THE INTERNATIONAL TRUSTS AMENDMENT (NO.2)

1995-96, No.30

An Act to amend the International Trusts Act 1984 and to modify the law relating to international trust

(12 December 1996)

BE IT ENACTED by the Parliament of the Cook Islands in Session assembled and by the authority of the same, as follows:

1. Short Title—This Act may be cited as the International Trusts Amendment (No. 2) Act 1995-96 and shall be read together with and

deemed part of the International Trusts Act 1984 (hereinafter referred to as "the principal Act").

2. Fraud—Section 13B of the principal Act is amended by—

(a) omitting from subsection (3) the word "asserting" and substituting the words "in respect of";

(b) omitting from paragraph (5)(d) the words "asserting" and substituting the words "in respect of".

3. **Application**

(1) Except where expressly provided to the contrary in this Act the provisions of this Act shall apply to every international trust, whether registered before or after the commencement of this Act, and to all matters relating to or concerning every such international trust, or the interested parties to every such international trust.

(2) The provisions of section 2 of this Act shall apply to every international trust settled or established on or after the 8th day of September 1989 and to every disposition of property to such trust made on or after that date, whether such property is situated in the Cook Islands or elsewhere.

(3) The provisions of section 60 of the Property Law Act 1952 shall have no application to any settlement of an international trust or disposition to an international trust made on or at any time after the 19th day of December 1991.

(4) Nothing in this Act shall apply to or affect any proceedings commenced in the High Court before the coming into force of this Act.

This Act is administered by the Cook Islands Monetary Board.

THE INTERNATIONAL TRUSTS AMENDMENT (NO.3)

1999, No.30

An Act to amend the International Trusts Act 1984 and to modify the law relating to international trust

(3 March 1999)

BE IT ENACTED by the Parliament of the Cook Islands in Session assembled and by the authority of the same, as follows:

1. Short Title—This Act may be cited as the International Trusts Amendment Act 1999 and shall be read together with and deemed part of the International Trusts Act 1984 (hereinafter referred to as "the principal Act").

2. <u>Interpretation</u>—Section 2(1) of the principal Act is amended by—

(a) inserting immediately before the definition of "Court", the following new definition—

"Commissioner" means the Commissioner for Offshore Financial Services appointed pursuant to the Offshore Financial Services Act 1998;"

(b) deleting from the definition of "international trust" the word "subsequently";

(c) inserting after the definition of "protector" the following new definition—

"publish" means to produce and issue, by whatever means, and whether for sale or not and includes to report as part of any law report or reports,"—

3. <u>Abolition of the rule against accumulations</u>—Subsection (2) of section 9 of the principal Act is amended by deleting after the word "that" the word "if", and substituting the word "is".

4. <u>Application of the rule in Saunders v Vautier</u>—Section 10 of the principal Act is amended by—

(a) repealing subsection (1) and substituting the following—

"(1) Notwithstanding any rule of law or equity to the contrary, where a trust instrument empowers a trustee to accumulate income, or to refrain from making any distribution of capital or income until a specified date or event, or where any provision of the trust instrument otherwise prevents the making of any distribution of capital or income, notwithstanding that a beneficiary may, but for this section, otherwise be entitled to that accumulation or distribution, the trustee may, in his absolute discretion, subject to any other express terms of the instrument, give effect to that direction as he thinks fit notwithstanding that a beneficiary shall request the trustee to immediately distribute the accumulation or distribution and will give a valid discharge to the trustee for such distribution.";

(b) amending subsection (2) by inserting after the words "accumulate income" wherever they appear, the words "or distribute capital".

5. <u>Fraud</u>—Section 13B of the principal Act is amended by adding after subsection (13), the following new subsections—

"(14) For the purposes of assessing the liability of an international trust to a creditor under this section, where the amount of that creditor's claim against the settlor is, wholly or partly, in any way related to or evidenced by a foreign judgement, the Court in making any award in favour of that creditor shall disregard and exclude any amount awarded in that foreign judgement to that creditor which comprise any form of exemplary, vindictive, retributory or punitive damages (by whatever name), or is an amount of damages arrived at by doubling, trebling or otherwise multiplying a sum assessed as compensation for the loss or damage (which types of damage are in this section together called "punitive damages").

(15) The burden of proof shall be on a creditor to establish that an amount awarded in a foreign judgement does not wholly or partly comprise punitive damages.

(16) Subsection (14) shall not apply if, at the time of settlement, establishment, or disposition, as the case may be, an award of punitive damages has already been made in a foreign judgement against a settlor."

6. Commencement of proceedings—Section 13K of the principal Act is amended by repealing subsection (5) and substituting the following—

"(5) Notwithstanding any other provision of this Act, the provisions of this section and sections 13A to 13J inclusive of this sections, shall apply to every international trust governed, or expressed to be wholly or partly governed, by the law of the Cook Islands, including a trust that formerly was not wholly or partly governed by the law of the Cook Islands but in respect of which the governing law of the trust has been changed (whether before of after registration) so that the trust, or any aspects of it, are governed, or expressed to be governed, by the law of the Cook Islands, and, without limiting the generality of the foregoing and notwithstanding any other law to the contrary, after the date of registration—

(a) the settlement or establishment of such trust;

(b) every disposition to such trust, including any disposition occurring before the date of registration or the change of law;

(c) every proceeding commenced after the date of registration concerning such settlement, establishment or disposition—

shall be subject to the provisions of this section and of sections 13A to 13J inclusive of those sections as if upon the date that such settlement, establishment or disposition occurred, the trust was an international trust governed wholly and exclusively by the law of the Cook Islands."

7. Certificate of Registration—Section 16 of the principal Act is amended by—

(a) deleting from subsection (3) the words "subject to section 26"; and

(b) adding at the end of subsection (3) the words—

". . . . Provided the Registrar may, in his sole discretion, if he is satisfied on application by a trustee of a trust that the failure to make the application for renewal and payment of the prescribed fee was as a consequence of inadvertence on the part of any interested party to the trust, extend the time for registration accordingly."

8. Custodian trustees—Section 19F of the principal Act is amended by repealing subsection (5) and substituting the following—

"(5) Without limiting any provision of this section, and except as varied by the trust instrument, the provisions of this Act and the Trustee

Companies Act 1981-82 relating to a trustee's powers, liabilities, functions, duties and discretions, shall apply equally to a custodian trustee, and in particular, without limiting the generality of the above, the custodian trustee—

(a) shall have the full powers of delegation conferred on trustees by section 19B;

(b) may permit assets to be held by or in the name of the managing trustee to facilitate the managing trustee's management and administration of the Trust assets, or as otherwise directed by the managing trustee."

9. <u>Protector of a trust</u>—Section 20 of the principal Act is repealed and the following section substituted—

"(20) <u>Protector of a trust</u>—

(1) The terms of a trust instrument may provide for the office of protector of that trust.

(2) A protector shall have the powers, delegations or functions as are conferred on the protector by the trust instrument or by this Act, or as may be prescribed.

(3) A Protector of a trust may also be a settlor, a trustee or a beneficiary of that trust.

(4) Subject to the trust instrument, a protector of a trust shall not be liable or accountable as a trustee or other person having a fiduciary duty to any person in relation to any act or omission in performing the function of a protector under the trust instrument.

(5) Where there is more than on protector of a trust then, subject to the trust instrument, any power of function conferred on the protectors may be exercised if the majority of the protectors for the time being agree upon its exercise.

(6) A protector who dissents from a decision of the majority of protectors may require his dissent to be recorded in writing and filed at the registered office of the trust, and subject to the trust instrument, shall not be liable for the acts of the majority of protectors pursuant to such decision.

(7) Any powers or functions conferred by this Act on a protector shall have effect subject to the terms of the trust instrument."

10. <u>Secrecy</u>—Section 23 of the principal Act is hereby repealed and the following section substituted—

"23 <u>Privacy</u>—

(1) Except where the provisions of this Act require, and subject to this section, it shall be an offence under this Act for a person to divulge or communicate to any other person information relating to the establishment, constitution, business undertaking or affairs of an international trust.

(2) All judicial proceedings, other than criminal proceedings relating to an international trust shall, unless ordered otherwise be heard in camera and no details of the proceedings shall be published by any person except in accordance with subsection (3).

(3) Every decision of the Court in respect of any proceedings concerning the application or interpretation of this Act shall be published or reported for the purposes of affording a record of those proceedings, provided that in every case—

(a) the written decision of the Court shall be edited to such extent as shall be necessary to preserve secrecy in respect of the identity of the trust, of every interested party and of the subject matter of the proceedings; and

(b) no such decision shall be reported or published unless or until a judge of the Court shall have ascertained the views of the parties to the proceedings as to the adequacy of any editing undertaken, and certified in writing to the Registrar of the Court that the decision as edited may be released for publication or reporting.

(4) Unless excluded by the terms of a trust instrument, a trustee or an officer or employee of a trustee or trustee company may divulge or make available information relating to the establishment, constitution, business undertakings or affairs of an international trust—

(a) to any person or class of persons as that trustee, officer or employee considers necessary from time to time, in its complete discretion, for carrying out the management and administration of the trust assets in the ordinary course of business; or to a legal practitioner—

(i) for the purpose of obtaining legal advice relating to establishment, constitution, business undertakings or affairs of an international trust; or

(ii) for the purpose of prosecuting or defending any litigation relating to the establishment, constitution, business undertakings or affairs of an international trust."

11. Power of exemption—Section 26 is amended by deleting from subsection (1), the words "the Registrar" and substituting the words "the Commissioner".

12. Form of trust records—The principal Act is amended by adding after section 27B, the following new section—

'27C. Trust records—

(1) Any records, accounts or documents relating to a trust and held by either the Registrar or a trustee, including but not by way of limitation, the trust instrument, may be established, kept or recorded in written, magnetic, electronic or any other data storage form, provided that the records can be readily produced in written form.

(2) When an international trust has been terminated, or the Cook Islands trustee is removed or has resigned, each trustee shall ensure that the records in the possession of that trustee are retained by that trustee for a period of three years from the said date of termination, removal or resignation as the case may be, but thereafter the said records may be destroyed.

(3) The Registrar may cause any records or registers in his possession to be destroyed after the expiration of three years from the date of de-registration, or from the date of expiry of the last certificate of registration of that trust under this Act."

13. Application—

(1) Except where expressly provided to the contrary in this Act the provisions of this Act shall apply to every international trust, whether registered before or after the commencement of this Act, and to all matters relating to or concerning every such international trust, or the interested parties to every such international trust.

(2) Nothing in this Act shall apply to or affect any proceedings commenced in the Court before the coming into force of this Act.

(3) Section 50 of the Trustee Act 1956 (NZ) shall have no further application to an international trust, and any reference in a trust instrument to section 50 of the Trustee Act 1956 (NZ) shall be deemed a reference to section 19F of the principal Act.

This Act is administered by the Office of the Commissioner for Offshore Financial Services.

RAROTONGA, COOK ISLANDS: Printed under the authority of the Cook Islands Government—1999

INTERNATIONAL TRUSTS (FORMS AND FEES) REGULATIONS 1985

T.TANGAROA, Queen's Representative

ORDER IN EXECUTIVE COUNCIL

At Avarua, Rarotonga, this 18th day of April 1985.

PRESENT:
HIS EXCELLENCY THE QUEEN'S REPRESENTATIVE IN EXECUTIVE COUNCIL

PURSUANT to Section 6 of the International Trusts Act 1984 the Queen's Representative, acting by and with the advice and consent of the Executive Council, hereby makes the following regulations.

ANALYSIS

1. Title
2. Interpretation
3. Forms in Schedule to be used
4. Directions in forms
5. Particulars on accompanying documents
6. Application where no special form prescribed
7. General provisions relating to forms and other documents
8. Fees
9. Time for payment
10. Currency Schedule

REGULATIONS

1. **Title**—These Regulations may be cited as the International Trusts (Forms and Fees) Regulations 1985.

2. **Interpretation**—In these Regulations "the Act" means the International Trusts Act 1984.

3. **Forms in Schedule to be used**—The forms listed in the First Schedule and set out in the Second Schedule shall be the forms used for the purpose of the corresponding section of the Act as set out in the First Schedule.

4. **Directions in forms**—A form prescribed in these Regulations shall be completed in accordance with such directions as are specified thereon.

5. **Particulars on accompanying documents**—Where the Act requires prescribed particulars to be set out in a document to be lodged with the Registrar the particulars required to be included in the form set out in the Schedule for the purpose shall, unless express provision to the contrary is made by any other regulation made under the Act, be the prescribed particulars.

6. **Application where no special form prescribed**—Where application is made to the Registrar under any provision of the Act and no other form is provided, such application may be made on form, IPA/4 set out in the Second Schedule.

7. **General provisions relating to forms and other documents**—Every form lodged with the Registrar shall comply with the following requirements—

(a) the form shall be on paper of medium weight and good quality and of a size not less than 8 1/2 inches deep by 5 1/2 inches wide and not more than foolscap folio size;

(b) subject to the Act, the form shall be printed or handwritten and shall be clearly legible;

(c) except with the consent of the Registrar, the form shall have margin (sic) of not less than one inch on the left-hand side and a margin of not less than one-half inch on the right-hand side;

(d) where the form comprises two or more sheets—

(i) the sheets shall be bound together securely; and

(ii) each sheet shall have a margin of not less than one inch on the side on which it is bound in addition to any space required for binding;

(e) where the form comprises more than 20 sheets, it shall be bound securely inside a durable and flexible cover; and

(f) the form shall have endorsed on it—

(i) on the upper left-hand corner, the registered number allotted by the Registrar to the international partnership to which the form relates, and the name of the trustee company by whom the form is lodged; and

(ii) on the upper right-hand corner the identifying number of the form and the following words—

"Lodged on 19

Registrar"

8. **Fees**—Where the Act or any regulations made thereunder provides for the payment of a prescribed fee to be paid shall be the fee set out in the Third Schedule and shall be payable to the Registrar.(sic)

9. **Time for payment**—Where a prescribed fee is payable in respect of a form lodged with the Registrar, that fee shall be paid on the lodgment of that form.

10. **Currency**—The fees set out in the Third Schedule are in the currency of the United States of America.

———————

1985/07

International Trusts (Forms and Fees)

Regulations 1985

(Reg.3)

FIRST SCHEDULE

LIST OF FORMS

SECTION OF ACT FORMS	NUMBER OF FORM
13 CERTIFICATE BY TRUSTEE COMPANY	ITA/1
12 APPLICATION FOR REGISTRATION OF AN INTERNATIONAL TRUST	ITA/2

14 CERTIFICATE OF REGISTRATION OF AN INTERNATIONAL
     TRUST   ITA/3
     GENERAL FORM OF APPLICATION TO THE REGISTRAR   ITA/4

1985/07

International Trusts (Forms and Fees)

Regulations 1985

SECOND SCHEDULE

INTERNATIONAL TRUST (FORMS AND FEES)

REGULATIONS 1985

NO.OF TRUST: FORM NO: ITA/1
Lodged by: Lodged on: 19
Registrar

COOK ISLANDS

INTERNATIONAL TRUSTS ACT 1985

(Section 14)

CERTIFICATE BY TRUSTEE COMPANY

_____ a trustee company does hereby certify that the _____
, (the) constituted by Deed of Trust dated _____ 20 _____ is
an International Trust within the meaning of Section 2 of the International
Trusts Act 1984.

Dated the _____ day of _____ 19 ____

A duly authorized officer of the
above trustee company

1985/07

International Trusts (Forms and Fees)

Regulations 1985

INTERNATIONAL TRUST (FORMS AND FEES)

REGULATIONS 1985

NO.OF TRUST: FORM NO: ITA/2
Lodged by: Lodged on: 19 Registrar

Appendix A

COOK ISLANDS

INTERNATIONAL TRUSTS ACT 1984

(Section 13)

APPLICATION FOR REGISTRATION OF AN INTERNATIONAL TRUST

_____ hereby makes application for registration of the _____ as an international trust and states as follows:

1. The name of the trustee is _____.
2. The date of the trust deed is the _____ day of _____ 19____.
3. The address for service is _____.

The relevant certificate by a trustee company is attached herewith.

Dated the _____ day of _____ 19_____

_____

Authorized Signatory

1985/07

International Trusts (Forms and Fees)

Regulations 1985

INTERNATIONAL TRUST (FORMS AND FEES)

REGULATIONS 1985

NO.OF TRUST: FORM NO: ITA/1

Lodged by: Lodged on: 19

Registrar

COOK ISLANDS

INTERNATIONAL TRUSTS ACT 1984

(Section 15)

CERTIFICATE OF REGISTRATION OF AN INTERNATIONAL TRUST

THIS IS TO CERTIFY THAT THE _____ trust constituted by Deed of Trust dated _____ 19_____ is on and from the _____ day of _____ 19_____ registered under the International Trusts Act 199_____ as an International Trust and that this Certificate of Registration expires on _____ the _____ day of 19_____.

_____

Registrar of International Trusts

1985/07

International Trusts (Forms and Fees)
Regulations 1985
INTERNATIONAL TRUST (FORMS AND FEES)
REGULATIONS 1985

NO.OF TRUST: FORM NO: ITA/4
Lodged by: Lodged on:_____19_____
Registrar

COOK ISLANDS
INTERNATIONAL TRUSTS ACT 1984
(Section 15)
GENERAL FORM OF APPLICATION TO THE REGISTRAR

1. Application is made by

_____

_____

pursuant to section of the International Trusts Act 1984 for (insert the order, direction, approval or the like sought

_____

_____

2. The grounds upon which this application is made are as follows

_____

_____

_____

3. This application is lodged by
(insert name of agent)_____

to whom any requisitions or requirement for further information may be directed.

Dated the _____ day of _____ 19_____

_____
Authorized Signatory

International Trusts (Forms and Fees)
Regulations 1985

THIRD SCHEDULE

(Reg.9)

PRESCRIBED FEE

Fee No. _____ **Matter for which payable** Amount of fee (in United States dollars) $

1. On application to register trust   100:00
2. On application to renew registration   100:00

P.Tangata
Clerk of Executive Council

These Regulations are administered by the Cook Islands Monetary Board.

By Authority

T.KAPI, Government Printer, Rarotonga, Cook Island—1985

* The authors would like to acknowledge Asiaciti Trust Pacific Limited, Rarotonga, Cook Islands, for providing this latest version of the Act.

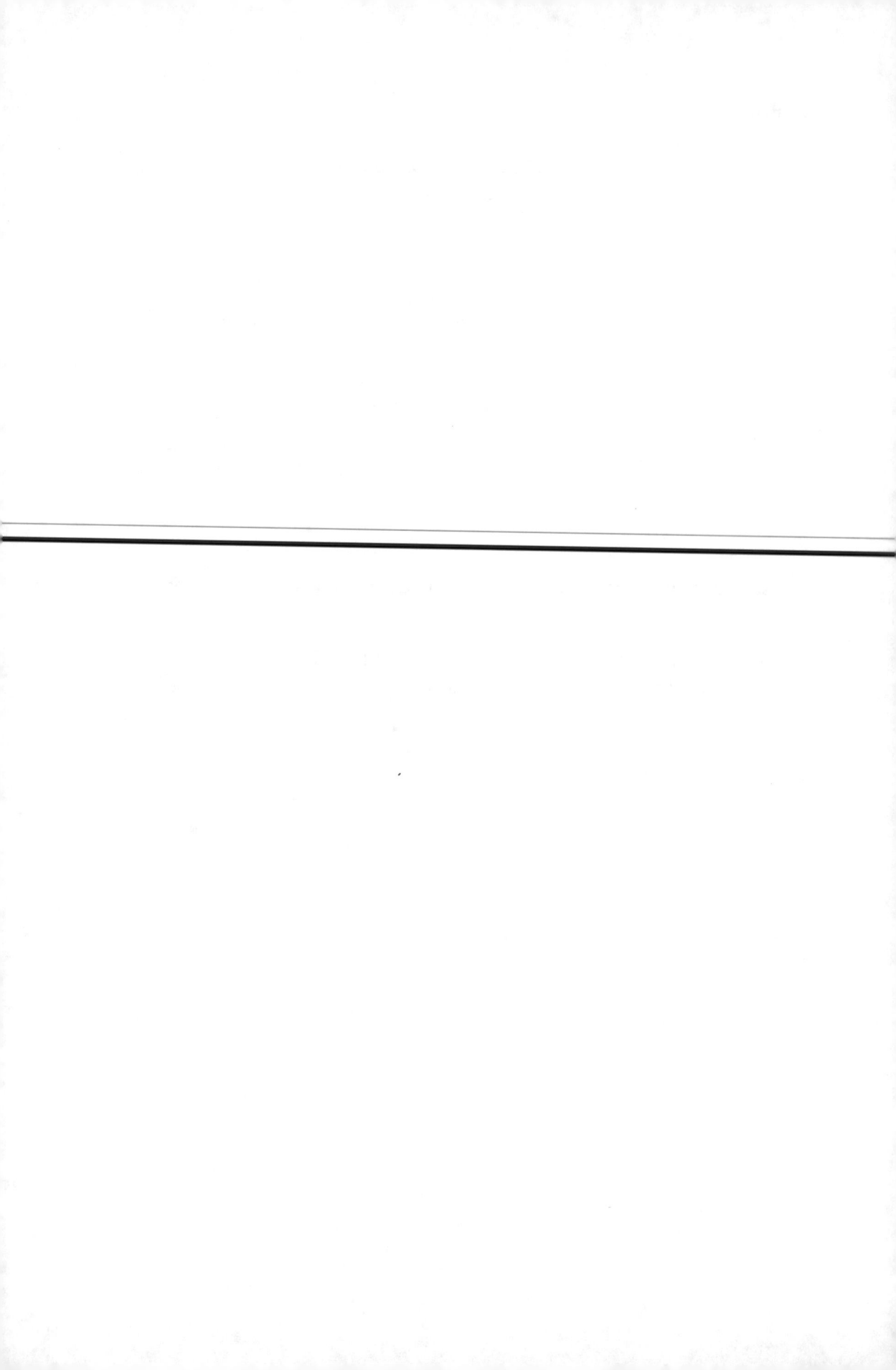

APPENDIX B

The Confidential Relationships (Preservation) Law (Law 16 of 1976)

A Law to give sanction to the day of non-divulgence of information imparted under conditions of professional confidence express or implied.

ENACTED by the Legislature of the Cayman Islands.

1. This Law may be cited as the Confidential Relationships (Preservation) Law.

2. In this Law, unless the context otherwise requires—

"bank" "licensee" and "trust company" have the meaning ascribed to them in the Banks and Trust Companies Regulation Law, 1966;

"business of a professional nature" includes the relationship between a professional person and a principal, however the latter may be described;

"confidential information" includes information concerning any property which recipient thereof is not, otherwise than in the normal course of business, authorized by the principal to divulge;

"criminal" in relation to an offence means an offence contrary to the criminal law of the Islands;

"entitled to possession of confidential information" means so entitled under the law of the Islands, in the normal course of business or by the specific consent of the relevant principal;

"Governor" means the Governor in Council;

"Inspector" means the Inspector of Banks and Trust Companies and to the extent of his authorization every person authorized by the Governor to perform his functions as such;

"normal course of business" means the ordinary and necessary routine involved in the efficient carrying out of the instructions of a principal including compliance with such laws and legal process as arises out of and in connection therewith and the routine exchange of information between licenses;

"principal" means a person who has imparted to another confidential information in the course of the transaction of business of a professional nature;

"professional person" includes a public or government official, a bank, trust company, an attorney-atlaw, an accountant, an estate agent, an insurer, a broker and every kind of commercial agent and adviser whether or not answering to the above descriptions and whether or not licensed or authorized to act in that capacity and every person subordinate to or in the employ or control of such person for the purpose of his professional activities;

"property" includes every present, contingent and future interest or claim, direct or indirect, legal or equitable, positive or negative, in any money, moneys worth, realty or personalty, movable or immovable, rights and securities thereover and all documents and things evidencing or relating thereto.

3. (1) This Law has application to all confidential information with respect to business of a professional nature which arises in or is brought into the Islands and to all persons coming into possession of such information at any time thereafter whether they be within the jurisdiction or thereout.

(2) This Law has no application, unless otherwise herein provided, to confidential information received or given—

> (a) to any professional person acting in the normal course of business or with consent, express or implied, of the relevant principal;
> (b) to constables investigating offenses committed or alleged to have been committed within the jurisdiction;
> (c) to constables, specifically authorized by the Governor in that behalf, investigating an offence committed or alleged to have been committed outside the jurisdiction which if committed in the Islands would be a criminal offence;
> (d) to the Financial Secretary or the Inspector.

4. (1) Subject to the provisions of sub-section (2) of section 3, whoever—

> (a) being in possession of confidential information however obtained;
> (i) divulges it; or
> (ii) attempts, offers or threatens to divulge it to any person not entitled to possession thereof;
> (b) wilfully obtains or attempts to obtain confidential information to which he is not entitled, is guilty of an offence and liable on summary conviction to a fine not exceeding $5,000 or to imprisonment for a term not exceeding 2 years or both.

(2) Whoever commits an offence under sub-section (1) and receives or solicits on behalf of himself or another any reward for so doing is liable to double the

penalty therein prescribed and to a further fine equal to the reward received and also to forfeiture of the reward.

(3) Whoever, being in possession of confidential information, clandestinely, or without the consent of the principal, makes use thereof for the benefit of himself or another is guilty of an offence and on summary conviction liable to the penalty prescribed in sub-section (2) and for that purpose any profit accruing to any person out of any relevant transaction shall be regarded as a reward.

(4) Whoever being a professional person, entrusted as such with confidential information, the subject of the offence, commits an offence under subsection (1), (2) or (3) is liable to double the penalty therein prescribed.

(5) For the removal of doubt it is declared that, subject to subsection (2) of section 3, a Bank which gives a credit reference in respect of a customer without first receiving the authorization of that customer is guilty of an offence under subsections (1) and (4).

5. Nothing in this Law shall by implication be deemed to derogate from the rule in Tournier v. National Provincial and Union Bank of England (1924) IKB, 461, (which deals with the civil duty of banks to preserve the confidentiality of the business of their customers) which rule is declared to have application to the Islands.

6. The Governor may make regulations for the administration of this Law.

7. No prosecution shall be instituted under this law without the consent of the Attorney General.

APPENDIX C

The Confidential Relationships (Preservation) (Amendment) Law, 1979 (Law 26 of 1979)

A LAW to amend the Confidential Relationships (Preservation) Law (Law 16 1976)

ENACTED by the Legislature of the Cayman Islands.

1. This Law may be cited as the Confidential Relationships (Preservation) (Amendment) Law, 1979.

2. Section 2 of the Confidential Relationships (Preservation) Law (hereinafter referred to as the principal Law) is hereby amended by deleting the definition "entitled to possession of confidential information."

3. Section 3 of the principal Law is hereby amended as follows—

(a) in subsection (1) thereof, by the substitution for the word "This" at the beginning thereof, of the words "Subject to subsection (2), this"; and
(b) by the repeal of subsection (2) and the substitution of the following new subsection therefore—

"(2) This Law has no application to the seeking, divulging, or obtaining, of confidential information—

(a) in compliance with the directions of the Grand Court pursuant to section 3A;
(b) by or to—
(i) any professional person acting in the normal course of business or with the consent, express or implied, of the relevant principal;
(ii) a constable of the rank of Inspector or above investigating an offence committed or alleged to have been committed within the jurisdiction;
(iii) a constable of the rank of Inspector or above, specifically authorised by the Governor in that behalf, investigating an offence

committed or alleged to have been committed outside the Islands which offence, if committed in the Islands, would be an offence against its laws; or

(iv) the Financial Secretary, the Inspector or, in relation to particular information specified by the Governor, such other person as the Governor may authorise;

(v) a bank in any proceedings, cause or matter when and to the extent to which it is reasonably necessary for the protection of the bank's interest, either as against its customers or as against third parties in respect of transactions of the bank for, or with, its customer;

(vi) the relevant professional person with the approval of the Financial Secretary when necessary for the protection of himself or any other person against crime; or

(c) in accordance with the provisions of this or any other Law."

4. The principal Law is hereby amended by the addition, immediately following section 3, of the following new section

3A. (1) Whenever a person intends or is required to give in evidence in, or in connection with, any proceeding being tried, inquired into or determined by any court, tribunal or other authority (whether within or without the Islands) and confidential information within the meaning of this Law, he shall before so doing apply for directions and any adjournment necessary for that purpose may be granted.

(2) Application for directions under subsection (1) shall be made to, and be heard and determined by, a Judge of the Grand Court sitting alone and *in camera*. At least seven days' notice of any such application shall be given to the Attorney General and, if the Judge so orders, to any person in the Islands who is a party to the proceedings in question. The Attorney General may appear as *amicus curiae* at the hearing of any such application and any party on whom notice has been served as aforesaid shall be entitled to be heard thereon, either personally or by counsel.

(3) Upon hearing an application under subsection (2) a Judge shall direct—

(a) that the evidence be given; or

(b) that the evidence shall not be given; or

(c) that the evidence be given subject to conditions which he may specify whereby the confidentiality of the information is safeguarded.

(4) In order to safeguard the confidentiality of a statement, answer or testimony ordered to be given under subsection (3)(c) a Judge may order

(i) divulgence of the statement, answer or testimony to be restricted to certain named persons;

(ii) evidence to be taken *in camera*; and

(iii) reference to the names, addresses and descriptions of any particular persons to be by alphabetical letters, numbers or symbols representing such persons the key to which shall be restricted to persons named by him.

(5) Every person receiving confidential information by operation of subsection (2) is as fully bound by the provisions of this Law as if such information had been entrusted to him in confidence by a principal.

(6) In considering what order to make under this section a Judge shall have regard to—

(a) whether such order would operate as a denial of the rights of any person in the enforcement of a just claim;

(b) any offer of compensation or indemnity made to any person desiring to enforce a claim by any person having an interest in the preservation of secrecy under this Law;

(c) in any criminal case, the requirements of the interests of justice.

(7) In this section, unless the context otherwise requires—

"court" bears the meaning ascribed to it in section 2 of the Evidence Law;

"given in evidence" and its cognates means make a statement, answer an interrogatory or testify during or for the purposes of any proceeding;

"proceeding" means any court proceeding, civil or criminal and includes a preliminary or interlocutory matter leading to or arising out of a proceeding."

5. Subsection (1) of section 4 of the principal Law is hereby amended as follows—

(i) in paragraph (a)(ii) thereof, by deleting the words "to any person not entitled to possession thereof.; and

(ii) in paragraph (b) thereof, by deleting the words "to which he is not entitled."

6. Section 5 of the principal Law is hereby repealed.

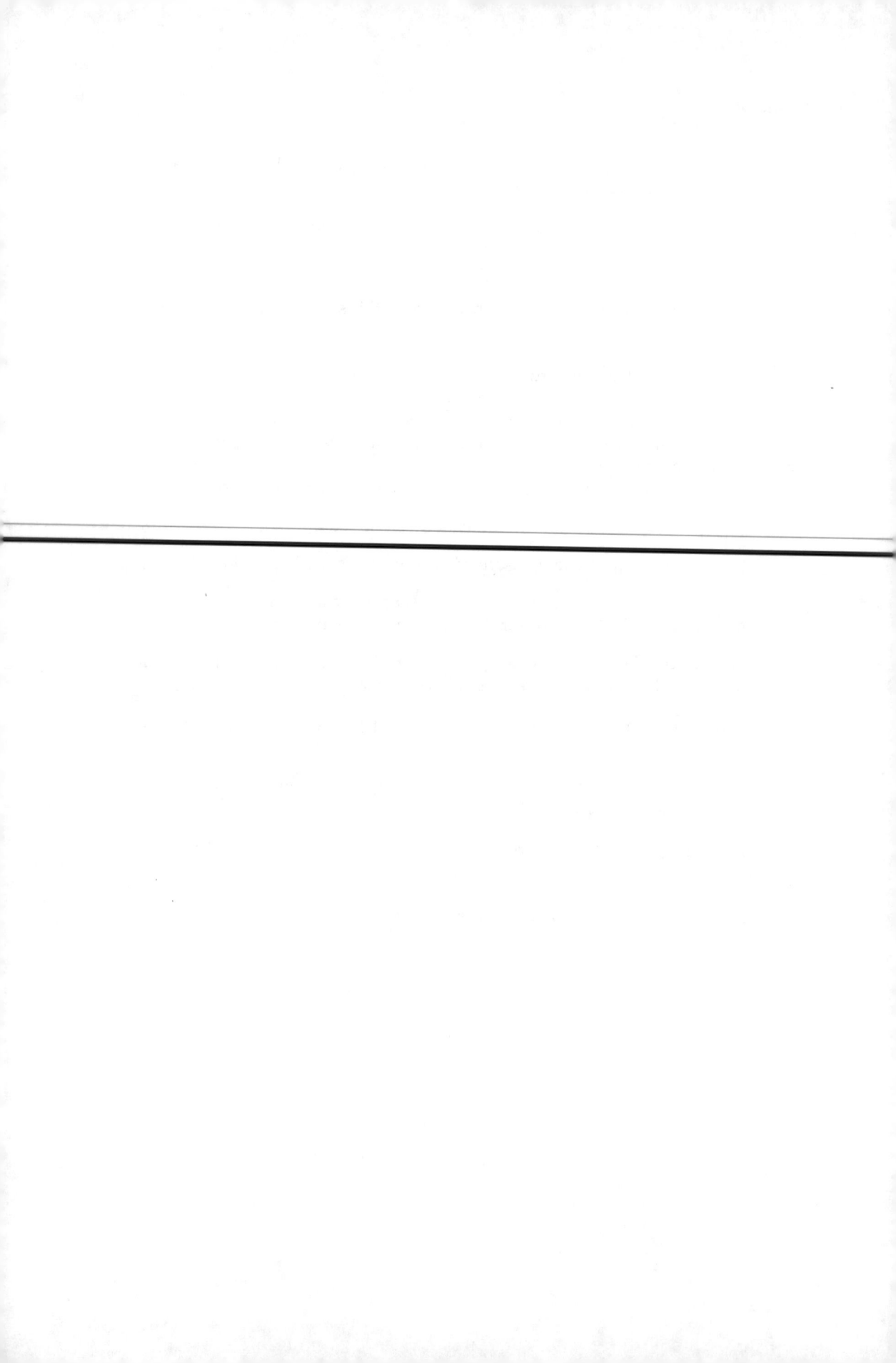

APPENDIX D

The Mutual Legal Assistance (United States of America) Law, 1986 (Law 16 of 1986)

A Law to make provision for giving effect to the terms of a Treaty made between the Government of the United States of America and the Government of the United Kingdom of Great Britain and Northern Ireland, including the Government of the Cayman Islands, for improving the effectiveness of the law enforcement authorities of the United States of America and the Cayman Islands in the prosecution and suppression of crime, through co-operation and mutual legal assistance in criminal matters, and for purposes connected therewith.

ENACTED by the Legislature of the Cayman Islands.

1. This Law may be cited as the Mutual Legal Assistance (United States of America) Law, 1986 and shall come into operation on a day to be appointed by the Governor by proclamation published in the Gazette.

2. (1) In this Law, unless the context otherwise requires

"Article" means an Article of the Treaty;

"authorised person" means a person authorised in accordance with section 8;

"Cayman Authority" means the Cayman Mutual Legal Assistance Authority;

"request" means a request made by one of the Parties to the other Party, in accordance with the terms of the Treaty;

"the Treaty" means the Treaty between the United States of America and the United Kingdom of Great Britain and Northern Ireland, including the Cayman Islands, dated the third day of July, 1986, relating to the mutual legal assistance in criminal matters, as more particularly set out in the Schedule;

"United States" means the United States of America; "United States Authority" means the Central Authority for the United States.

(2) In this Law, unless the context otherwise requires, any expression which is defined in the Treaty, shall have the same meaning as that given to it in the Treaty.

3. This Law shall apply for the purpose of giving effect to the terms of the Treaty, which has legal effect in the Cayman Islands, for the provision of mutual assistance between the authorities in the United States and in the Cayman Islands, for the suppression of criminal offences of the nature and in the circumstances provided in the Treaty, including any such ancillary civil or administrative proceedings by either of the Parties as are mentioned in paragraph (3) (c) of Article 19.

4. For the purpose of Article 2, the Cayman Mutual Legal Assistance Authority shall be the Chief Justice, who shall exercise his functions under the Treaty and this Law acting alone and in an administrative capacity, or another Judge of the Grand Court designated by the Chief Justice to act on his behalf.

5. Without prejudice to Article 5(4), the Cayman Authority shall notify the Attorney General immediately a request is received with particulars thereof, and copies of any documents relating thereto, and the Attorney General shall be entitled, in a manner analogous to *amicus curiae*, to appear

or to take part in any proceedings in the Cayman Islands, whether judicial or administrative, arising directly or indirectly from a request received by the Cayman Authority.

6. (1) Upon receipt of a request, the competent authorities in the Cayman Islands shall execute the request, in accordance with, but subject to, the provisions of the Treaty. Where the execution of a request requires the issue under the law of the Cayman Islands of a subpoena, search warrant, order for the seizure of any article or other necessary order by a magistrate, justice of the peace or officer of a court, a certificate given by the Cayman Authority that the issue of any such document or order is required for the purposes of a request to which the Law relates shall be sufficient authority for the issue or making of the same without further enquiry.

(2) Notwithstanding the provisions of any other Law, if the execution of any request requires the service of any document or order or the seizure of any article in pursuance of any instruction given by the Cayman Authority, any constable of the rank of Inspector of above, if so required by the Cayman Authority, shall assist in such service or seizure to the same extent as he would be required so to do in the case of the service of any document or order issued, or the seizure of any article, on the instructions of the Grand Court, and for that purpose he shall be deemed to have the same powers as if acting in pursuance of directions given by the Grand Court or any officer thereof.

7. (1) Where, in pursuance of the terms of a request, any person is required to testify or to produce in the Cayman Islands documentary information, which is in his possession or under his control, the Cayman Authority shall have the same powers as the Grand Court for compelling that person to comply with the request; and if that person wilfully fails or refuses so to do he shall be liable to be dealt with by the Grand Court as if he had failed to comply with an order for a similar purpose issued by the Grand Court.

(2) A person required to testify or to produce documentary information shall have the right to be represented by an attorney when he does so.

8. For the purpose of the authentication of any official documents or records of the Cayman Islands, as mentioned in Article 9, any person authorised in that behalf by the Attorney General of the Cayman Islands shall be deemed to be an authorised person.

9. Any person who enters the Cayman Islands in response to a request made by the Cayman Authority for the appearance of that person in accordance with Article 10, while in the Cayman Islands, shall not be subject to service of any process or subjected to any restriction of his personal liberty by reason of any act or conviction in the territory of either of the Parties or of the Contracting Parties prior to his departure from the territory of the United States in conformity with such request:

Provided that the immunity provided for by this section shall cease ten days after that person has been notified in writing by the Cayman Authority that his presence is no longer required in the Cayman Islands or, if he has earlier left the Cayman Islands, that he is not required by the Cayman Authority to return for the purposes of a request.

10. A person who divulges any confidential information or gives any testimony in conformity with a request shall be deemed not to commit any offence under the Confidential Relationships (Preservation) Law, or under any other Law for the time being in force in the Cayman Islands, by reason only of such disclosure or the giving of such testimony; and shall be deemed not to commit any offence under section 10 of the Banks and Trusts Companies Regulation Law (Revised) by reason only of such disclosure or the giving of such testimony; and such disclosure or testimony shall be deemed not to be a breach of any confidential relationship between that person and any other person, and no civil claim or action whatsoever shall lie against the person making such disclosure or giving such testimony or against such person's principal or employer by reason of such disclosure or testimony.

11. Section 3A of the Confidential Relationships Preservation Law shall be deemed not to apply to confidential information given by any person on the directions of the Cayman Authority given in pursuance of a request.

12. (1) A person who is in lawful custody in the Cayman Islands may be transferred to the United States in response to a request, for his presence as a witness, if, under Article 11, that person and the Cayman Authority consent to such transfer.

(2) A person transferred under the provisions of subsection (1) shall be deemed to be in lawful custody during such transfer and during the period in which he is in the United States, and such time shall count for all purposes under the laws of the Cayman Islands as if he had been in custody in the Cayman Islands.

(3) A person who is in lawful custody in the United States and who is transferred to the Cayman Islands under Article II shall be deemed to be in lawful custody during such transfer and during the period in which he is in the Cayman Islands.

(4) Any person who is transferred under the provisions of this section and Article I I may be released from custody upon such conditions as to bail or otherwise as may be agreed between the Parties, and shall in any event be released no later than the date on which he would have been released if he had not been so transferred.

13. (1) If so instructed by the Cayman Authority, the particulars of and all matters relating to a request shall be treated as confidential, and no person who is notified of a request, or is required to take any action, or produce any documents or supply any information in response to or in

relation to any matters to which a request relates, shall disclose the fact of the receipt of such request or any of the particulars required or documents produced to any other person except that person's attorney and such other persons as the Central Authority may authorise, for a period of ninety days from the date of the receipt of the request, or such further period as he may be notified by the Cayman Authority.

(2) This section shall be binding on the attorney of any person to whom subsection (1) applies as if he were that person.

14. (1) Any person in the Cayman Islands claiming to be entitled under Article 6 to be reimbursed by the United States Authority in respect of any expenses incurred shall submit his claim to the Cayman Authority for transmission to the United States Authority.

(2) The Cayman Authority shall have power to tax or make any enquiries to verify the details of any claim submitted under subsection (1) in similar manner to a claim for costs submitted to the Grand Court.

15. For the purposes of this Law and the Treaty, the service of any notice or document shall be sufficient if delivered by hand or posted by registered post to the registered or other office of the addressee. Affidavit testimony of delivery of the notice or document by hand or supporting the registration certificate shall be deemed sufficient proof of such service.

16. (1) Any person who, having been required by the Cayman Authority under the provisions of the Law to produce any documents which are in his possession or under his control, fails so to do, within such time, or any extension thereof, as may be specified by the Cayman Authority by notice, shall be guilty of an offence and liable on summary conviction to a fine not exceeding ten thousand dollars or to imprisonment for a term not exceeding two years, or to both such fine and imprisonment.

(2) Any person who, contrary to the provisions of section 13, informs any person, other than his attorney, of the fact of the issue of a request or of any communication relevant to the matter to which the request relates, shall be guilty of an offence and liable on summary conviction to a fine not exceeding one thousand dollars or to imprisonment for a term not exceeding six months, or to both such fine and imprisonment.

(3) Where any documents or other written information have not been produced in pursuance of a notice served under this Law by the Cayman Authority, any constable of the rank of Inspector or above, acting on the written instructions of the Cayman Authority may apply to any court, magistrate or justice of the peace for the issue of a search warrant to search for and seize any such documents or other written information, and thereupon the court, magistrate or justice of the peace shall issue a warrant to search for and seize the documents or information concerned. Such warrant, *mutatis mutandis*, shall be in

form similar to, and shall confer the same powers of entry, search and seizure as, any search warrant issued under section 24 of the Criminal Procedure Code.

(4) Any documents or other written information seized under a warrant issued under subsection (3) shall be brought immediately to the Cayman Authority to be dealt with according to law.

(5) Any person who, when required so to do in accordance with the instructions given by the Cayman Authority, or any subpoena served upon him, refuses to attend as required or to provide testimony in response to a request, shall be guilty of an offence and liable on summary conviction to a fine not exceeding five thousand dollars or to imprisonment for a term not exceeding one year, or to both such fine and imprisonment.

(6) The provisions of subsection (5) shall be without prejudice to the provisions of any other law with regard to the liability of any person to be dealt with for failure to comply with any subpoena or other order issued by any court, magistrate or justice of the peace and without prejudice to the provisions of any other law with regard to the liability of any person to be dealt with for any unlawful attempt to obtain from any person or body any confidential information:

Provided that no person shall be punished both under this section and any other law for an offence relating to the same failure to comply with the same order.

17. The Narcotic Drugs (Evidence) (United States of America) Law, 1984 shall be repealed on a day to be appointed by the Governor by Proclamation published in the Gazette.

SCHEDULE
(Section 3)

Treaty between the United States of America and the United Kingdom of Great Britain and Northern Ireland concerning the Cayman Islands relating to mutual legal assistance in criminal matters.

Arrangement of Articles

Article
1. Scope of Assistance.
2. Central Authorities.
3. Limitations on Assistance.
4. Form and Contents of Requests.
5. Execution of Requests.
6. Costs.
7. Limitations on Use.
8. Taking Testimony and Producing Evidence in the Territory of the Requested Party.

9. Providing Records of Government Agencies.
10. Appearance in the Territory of the Requesting Party.
11. Transferring Persons in Custody for Testimonial Purposes.
12. Location of Persons.
13. Service of Documents.
14. Search and Seizure.
15. Return of Documents and Articles.
16. Proceeds of Crime.
17. Exclusivity.
18. Consultations.
19. Definitions.
20. Ratification, Entry into Force, and Termination.

The Government of the United States of America

and

The Government of the United Kingdom of Great Britain and Northern Ireland, including the Government of the Cayman Islands

Desiring to improve the effectiveness of the law enforcement authorities of both the United States of America and the Cayman Islands in the investigation, prosecution, and suppression of crime through cooperation and mutual legal assistance in criminal matters,

Have agreed as follows:

Article 1
Scope of Assistance

1. The Parties shall provide mutual assistance, in accordance with the provisions of this Treaty for the investigation, prosecution, and suppression of criminal offences of the nature and in the circumstances set out in this Treaty, including the civil and administrative proceedings referred to in paragraph 3(c) of Article 19.

2. For the purposes of paragraph 1, assistance shall include:

(a) taking the testimony or statement of persons;

(b) providing documents, records, and articles of evidence;

(c) serving documents;

(d) locating persons;

(e) transferring persons in custody for testimony;

(f) executing requests for searches and seizures;

(g) immobilizing criminally obtained assets;

(h) assistance in proceedings related to forfeiture, restitution and collection of fines; and

(i) any other steps deemed appropriate by both Central Authorities.

3. This Treaty is intended solely for mutual legal assistance between the Parties. The provisions of this Treaty shall not create any right on the part of any private person to obtain, suppress, or exclude any evidence or to impede the execution of a request.

Article 2
Central Authorities

1. A Central Authority shall be established by each Party.

2. For the United States of America, the Central Authority shall be the Attorney General or a person designated by him. For the Cayman Islands, the Central Authority shall be the Cayman Mutual Legal Assistance Authority or a person designated by it.

3. Requests under this Treaty shall be made by the Central Authority of the Requesting Party to the Central Authority of the Requested Party.

Article 3
Limitations on Assistance

1. The assistance afforded by this Treaty shall not extend to:

(a) any matter which relates directly or indirectly to the regulation, including the imposition, calculation, and collection, of taxes, except for any matter falling within subparagraphs 3(d) and (e) of Article 19; or

(b) any conduct not punishable by imprisonment of more than one year.

2. The Central Authority of the Requested Party may deny assistance where:

(a) the request is not made in conformity with the provisions of this Treaty;

(b) the request relates to a political offence or to an offence under military law which would not be an offence under ordinary criminal law; or

(c) the request does not establish that there are reasonable grounds for believing:

(i) that the criminal offence specified in the request has been committed; and

(ii) that the information sought relates to the offence and is located in the territory of the Requested Party.

3. The Central Authority shall deny assistance where the Attorney General of the Requested Party has issued a certificate to the effect that the execution of the request is contrary to the public interest of the Requested Party.

4. Before denying assistance pursuant to this Article the Central Authority of the Requested Party shall consult with the Central Authority of

the Requesting Party to consider whether assistance can be given subject to such conditions as it deems necessary. If the Requesting Party accepts assistance subject to these conditions, it shall comply with the conditions.

Article 4
Form and Contents of Requests

1. Requests shall be submitted in writing by the Central Authority of the Requesting Party in such form as may from time to time be agreed between the Central Authorities.

2. The Request shall include the following:

(a) the name of the authority conducting the investigation or proceeding to which the request relates;

(b) the subject matter and nature of the investigation or proceeding for the purposes of which the request is made and in particular the criminal offence or offences for the investigation, prosecution or suppression of which the assistance is requested;

(c) information concerning the persons involved including, where available, their full names, dates of birth, and addresses;

(d) the information relied upon in support of the request;

(e) a description of the evidence, information or other assistance sought; such description shall specify where possible the time period to which any such evidence or information relates;

(f) the purpose for which the evidence or information or other assistance is sought; and

(g) the identity and presumed location, where known, of any person from whom evidence is sought.

3. To the extent necessary and possible, a request shall also include:

(a) the identity and location of a person to be served, that person's relationship to the proceedings, and the manner in which service is to be made;

(b) available information on the identity and whereabouts of a person to be located;

(c) a precise description of the place or person to be searched and of the articles to be seized,

(d) a description of the manner in which any testimony or statement is to be taken and recorded;

(e) a list of questions to be asked of a witness;

(f) a description of any particular procedure to be followed in executing the request;

(g) information as to the allowances and expenses to which a person asked to appear in the territory of the Requesting Party will be entitled; and

(h) any other information which may be brought to the attention of the Requested Party to facilitate its execution of the request.

Article 5
Execution of Requests

1. The Central Authority of the Requested Party shall promptly execute any request or, when appropriate, shall transmit it to the authority having jurisdiction to do so. The competent authorities of the Requested Party shall do everything in their power to execute the request. The Courts of the Requested Party shall have jurisdiction to issue subpoenas, search warrants, or other orders necessary to execute the request.

2. When execution of the request requires judicial or administrative action, the request shall be presented to the appropriate authority by the persons designated by the Central Authority of the Requested Party.

3. Requests shall be executed in accordance with the laws of the Requested Party except to the extent that this treaty provides otherwise. However, the method of execution specified in the request shall be followed except insofar as it is prohibited by the laws of the Requested Party.

4. If execution of the request would interfere with an ongoing criminal investigation or proceeding in the territory of the Requested Party, the Central Authority of that Party may postpone execution or make execution subject to conditions determined necessary after consultations with the Requesting Party. If the Requesting Party accepts the assistance subject to the conditions it shall comply with the conditions.

5. The Central Authority of the Requested Party shall promptly inform the Central Authority of the Requesting Party of the outcome of the execution of the request. If the request is denied, the Central Authority of the Requested Party shall inform the Central Authority of the Requesting Party of the reasons for the denial.

Article 6
Costs

1. The following expenses, and none other, incurred in executing a request shall be reimbursed by the Requesting Party upon application of the Central Authority of the Requested Party:

(a) travel expenses of a witness presenting testimony in the territory of the Requesting Party;

(b) fees of expert witnesses retained with the approval of the Central Authority of the Requesting Party;

(c) fees of counsel appointed or retained with the approval of the Central Authority of the Requesting Party for a witness giving testimony;

(d) reasonable costs of locating, reproducing, and transporting to the Central Authority of the Requesting Party documents or records specified in a request;

(e) costs of stenographic reports requested by the Central Authority of the Requesting Party, other than reports prepared by a salaried government employee; and

(f) reasonable costs of interpreters or translators.

2. A witness who appears in the territory of the Requesting Party pursuant to Article 10 shall be entitled to the same fees and allowances ordinarily accorded to a witness in the territory of the Requesting Party.

3. A witness who appears in the territory of the Requested Party pursuant to Article 8 shall be entitled to such fees and allowances as shall be agreed between the Central Authorities.

Article 7
Limitations on Use

1. The Requesting Party shall not use any information or evidence obtained under this Treaty for any purposes other than for the investigation, prosecution or suppression in the territory of the Requesting Party of those criminal offences stated in the request without the prior consent of the Requested Party.

2. Unless otherwise agreed by both Central Authorities, information or evidence furnished under this Treaty shall be kept confidential, except to the extent that the information or evidence is needed for investigations or proceedings forming part of the prosecution of a criminal offence described in the request.

3. The Central Authority of the Requesting Party may request that the application for assistance, its contents and related documents, and the granting of assistance be kept confidential. If the request cannot be executed without breaking confidentiality, the Central Authority of the Requested Party shall so inform the Central Authority of the Requesting Party which shall then determine whether the request should nevertheless be executed.

4. Except as may be permitted under paragraph 1, any information or evidence obtained under this Treaty which has been made public in the territory of the Requesting Party in a proceeding forming part of the prosecution of a criminal offence described in the request may be used only for the following additional purposes:

(a) where a trial results in a conviction for any criminal offence within the scope of this Treaty, for any purpose against the person(s) convicted;

(b) whether or not a trial results in the conviction of any person, in the prosecution of any person for any criminal offence within the scope of this Treaty; and

(c) in civil or administrative proceedings, only if and to the extent that such proceedings relate to—

(i) the recovery of the unlawful proceeds of a criminal offence within the scope of this Treaty from a person who has knowingly received them;

(ii) the collection of tax or enforcement of tax penalties resulting from the knowing receipt of the unlawful proceeds of a criminal offence within the scope of this Treaty; or

(iii) the recovery *in rem* of the unlawful proceeds or instrumentalities of a criminal offence within the scope of this Treaty.

Article 8
Taking Testimony and Producing Evidence in the Territory of the Requested Party

1. A person requested to testify or to produce documentary information or articles in the territory of the Requested Party may be compelled to do so in accordance with the requirements of the law of the Requested Party.

2. If the person referred to in paragraph I asserts a claim of immunity, incapacity, or privilege under the laws of the Requesting Party, the evidence shall nonetheless be taken and the claim made known to the Requesting Party for resolution by the authorities of that Party.

3. The Requesting Party shall furnish information in advance about the date and place of the taking of the evidence pursuant to this Article.

4. The Requested Party shall authorise the presence of such persons as are specified in the request during the taking of any evidence in the territory of the Requested Party and shall allow persons designated in the request to question the person whose testimony or evidence is being taken.

5. Documentary information other than official records produced in the territory of the Requested Party pursuant to this Article shall be authenticated by the attestation of a person competent to do so in the manner indicated in Form A appended to this Treaty.

Article 9
Providing Records of Government Agencies

1. The Requested Party shall provide the Requesting Party with copies of publicly available records of goverm-nent departments and agencies in the territory of the Requested Party.

2. The Requested Party may provide copies of any record or information in the possession of a government department or agency in the territory of that Party but not publicly available to the same extent and under the same conditions as it would be available to its own law enforcement or judicial authorities.

3. Official records produced pursuant to this Article shall be authenticated by the attestation of an authorised person in the manner indicated in Form B appended to this Treaty. The attestation shall be signed by, and state the official position of, the attesting person, and the seal of the authority executing the request shall be affixed thereto. Authentication of official records shall be carried out under the provisions of the Convention Abolishing the Requirement of Legalisation for Foreign Public Documents, dated 5 October 1961.

Article 10
Appearance in the Territory of the Requesting Party

1. When the appearance of a person who is in the territory of the Requested Party is needed in the territory of the Requesting Party for the purpose of the execution of a request under this Treaty, the Central Authority of the Requesting Party may request that the Central Authority of the other Party invite the person to appear before the appropriate authority in the territory of the Requesting Party. The response of the person shall be communicated promptly to the Central Authority of the Requesting Party. Such a person shall be under no compulsion to accept such an invitation.

2. A person appearing in the territory of the Requesting Party pursuant to this Article shall not be subject to service of process or be detained or subjected to any restriction of personal liberty by reason of any acts or convictions in either the territory of the Requesting or Requested Party which preceded his departure from the territory of the Requested Party.

3. The safe conduct provided for by this Article shall cease ten days after the person has been notified in writing by the appropriate authorities that his presence is no longer required, or if the person has left the territory of the Requesting Party and voluntarily returned to it.

Article 11
Transferring Person in Custody for Testimonial Purposes

1. A person in the custody of the Requested Party who is needed as a witness in connection with the execution of a request in the territory of the Requesting Party shall be transported to the territory of that Party if the person and the Requested Party consent.

2. A person in the custody of the Requesting Party whose presence in the territory of the Requested Party is needed in connection with the execution of a
request under this Treaty may be transported to the territory of the Requested Party if the person and both Parties consent.

3. For the purpose of this Article:

(a) the Receiving Party shall be responsible for the safety and health of the person transferred and have the authority and obligation to keep the person transferred in custody unless otherwise authorised by the Sending Party;

(b) the Receiving Party shall return the person transferred to the custody of the Sending Party as soon as circumstances permit or as otherwise agreed and in any event no later than the date upon which he would have been released from custody in the territory of the Sending Party; and

(c) the person transferred shall receive credit for service of the sentence imposed in the territory of the Sending Party for time served in the custody of the Receiving Party.

Article 12
Location of Persons

1. The Requested Party shall take all necessary measures to locate or identify persons who are believed to be in the territory of that Party and who are needed in connection with the investigation, prosecution or suppression of a criminal offence in the territory of the Requesting Party.

2. The Requested Party shall promptly communicate the results of its inquiries to the Requesting Party.

Article 13
Service of Documents

1. The Requested Party shall effect service of any document relating to or forming part of any request for assistance properly made under the provisions of this Treaty transmitted to it for this purpose by the Requesting Party; provided that the Requested Party shall not be obliged to serve any subpoena or other process requiring the attendance of any person before any authority or tribunal in the territory of the Requesting Party.

2. The Requesting Party shall transmit any such request for the service of a document inviting the appearance of a person before an authority in the territory of the Requesting Party to the Requested Party a reasonable time before the scheduled appearance.

3. The Requested Party shall return a proof of service in the manner specified in the request.

Article 14
Search and Seizure

1. A request for assistance pursuant to Article I involving the search, seizure and delivery of an article to the Requesting Party shall be executed if

it includes the information justifying such action under the laws of the Requested Party.

2. Every official who has custody of a seized article shall certify the continuity of custody, the identity, and the integrity of its condition. No further certification shall be required. The certificates shall be admissible in evidence in the territory of the Requesting Party as evidence of the truth of the matters set forth therein.

3. The Requested Party shall not be obliged to provide any item seized to the Requesting Party unless that Party has agreed to such terms and conditions as may be required by the Requested Party to protect third party interests in the item to be transferred.

Article 15
Return of Documents and Articles

The Requesting Party shall return any documents or articles furnished to it in the execution of a request under this Treaty as soon as possible unless the Requested Party waives the return of the documents or articles.

Article 16
Proceeds of Crime

1. The Central Authority of one Party may notify the Central Authority of the other Party when it has reason to believe that proceeds of a criminal offence are located in the territory of the other Party.

2. The Parties shall assist each other to the extent permitted by their respective laws in proceedings related to:

(a) the forfeiture of the proceeds of criminal offences;

(b) restitution of the victims of criminal offences; and (c) the collection of fines imposed as a sentence for a criminal offence.

Article 17
Exclusivity

1. Assistance and procedures set forth in this Treaty shall not prevent one Party from granting assistance to the other Party through the provisions of other international agreements or arrangements which may be applicable.

2. Subject to the terms of paragraph 1, a Party needing assistance as provided in Article I in the investigation, prosecution or suppression of a criminal offence as defined in Article 19 shall request assistance pursuant to this Treaty.

3. No Party shall enforce any compulsory measure, including a grand jury subpoena, for the production of documents located in the territory of

the other Party with respect to any criminal offence within the scope of this Treaty, unless its obligations under the Treaty have first been fulfilled pursuant to paragraph 4 of this Article with respect to a request concerning these documents.

4. Where denial of a request or unreasonable delay in its execution may be jeopardizing the successful completion of an investigation, prosecution or other proceeding, the Central Authority of the Requesting Party shall so inform the Central Authority of the Requested Party in writing. Thereafter, either Contracting Party may give at least 45 days notice in writing to the other Contracting Party that, unless otherwise agreed, the Parties' obligations under this Article shall be deemed to have been fulfilled; provided that in no case shall the obligations under this Article be deemed to have been fulfilled sooner than 90 days after the date of receipt of the request for assistance.

Article 18
Consultations

1. The Central Authorities will consult, at times mutually agreed by them, to enable the most effective use to be made of this Treaty. Such consultations shall include such information as may be lawfully disclosed concerning the status and disposition of proceedings utilising documentary information and other evidence secured pursuant to this Treaty.

2. In any case of difficulty either Central Authority may request the assistance of the Contracting Parties to resolve the difficulty by way of consultation.

Article 19
Definitions

For the purpose of this Treaty—

1. "The Contracting Parties" means the Government of the United States and the Government of the United Kingdom.

2. "The Parties" means the Government of the United States and the Government of the Cayman Islands.

3. "Criminal offence" which, except in the case of any matter falling within sub-paragraphs (d) and (e) of this definition, does not include any conduct or matter which relates directly or indirectly to the regulation, imposition, calculation or collection of taxes, subject always to those exclusions, means:

(a) Any conduct punishable by more than one year's imprisonment under the laws of both the Requesting and Requested Parties;

(b) "Racketeering" which means—

(i) the use or investment, directly or indirectly, knowingly by an person of any part of racketeering income, or the proceeds of such income, in the acquisition of any interest in, or the establishment or operation of, any enterprise which is engaged in, or the activities of which affect commerce, including interstate or foreign commerce;

(ii) the acquisition or maintenance knowingly by any person through a pattern of racketeering activity or through collection of an unlawful debt, directly or indirectly, of any interest in or control of any enterprise which is engaged in, or the activities of which affect commerce, including interstate or foreign commerce; or

(iii) where any person is employed by or associated with any enterprise engaged in, or the activities of which affect commerce, including interstate or foreign commerce, the conduct or participation in the conduct, directly or indirectly, knowingly by that person of the affairs of the enterprise through a pattern of racketeering activity or collection of unlawful debt;

and in respect of which—

(A) "Racketeering income" means any income of any person derived, directly or indirectly, from a pattern of racketeering activity or through collection of an unlawful debt in which such person has participated as a principal;

(B) "Racketeering activity" means unlawful gambling activity and the act or threat of any other criminal offence (which expression, for the avoidance of doubt, does not include any offence which relates directly or indirectly to the regulation including the imposition, calculation or collection of any tax) listed in this Article;

(C) "Pattern of racketeering activity" means at least two acts of racketeering activity, one of which occurred within ten years (excluding any period of imprisonment) after the commission of a prior act of racketeering activity;

(D) "Unlawful debt" means a debt—

(1) incurred or contracted in unlawful gambling activity or which is unenforceable in law in whole or in part as to principal or interest because of laws relating to usury, and

(2) which was incurred in connection with the business of gambling in violation of the law or the business of lending money or a thing of value at a rate usurious under law, where the usurious rate is at least twice the enforceable rate; and

(E) "Enterprise" includes any individual partnership, corporation, association, or other legal entity, and any union or group of individuals associated in fact although not a legal entity;

(c) "Narcotics trafficking" which means all offences or ancillary civil or administrative proceedings taken by either of the Parties or their agencies connected with, arising from, related to, or resulting from any narcotics activity covered by the Single Convention on Narcotic Drugs, 1961, or the Protocol Amending the Single Convention on Narcotic Drugs, 1961, or any other international agreements or arrangement binding upon both the Parties;

(d) Willfully or dishonestly obtaining money, property or valuable securities from other persons by means of false or fraudulent pretense or statements, whether oral or written, regarding or affecting benefits available in connection with the laws and regulations relating to income or other taxes;

(e) Wilfully or dishonestly making false statements, whether oral or written, to government tax authorities (e.g., wilfully or dishonestly submitting a false income tax return) with respect to any tax matter arising from the unlawful proceeds of any criminal offence covered by any other provision of this definition, except sub-paragraph (f), or wilfully or dishonestly failing to make a report to government tax authorities as required by law in respect of, or to pay the tax due on, any such unlawful proceeds;

(f) Wilfully or dishonestly failing to make to the Government a report which is required by law to be made to it in respect of an international transfer of currency or other financial transactions connected with, arising from or related to the unlawful proceeds of any criminal offence falling within any provision of this Article, except this sub-paragraph or subparagraph (e) above;

(g) "Insider trading" which means the offer, purchase, or sale of securities by any person while in possession of material non-public information directly or indirectly relating to the securities offered, purchased, or sold, in breach of a legally binding duty of trust or confidence;

(h) "Fraudulent securities practices," which means the use by any person wilfully or dishonestly of any means, directly or indirectly, in connection with the offer, purchase or sale of any security;

(i) to employ any device, scheme, or artifice to defraud;

(ii) dishonestly to make any untrue statement of a material fact or to omit to state a material fact necessary in order to make the statement made, in light of the circumstances under which it was made, not misleading; or

(iii) dishonestly to engage in any act, practice, or course of business which operates or would operate as a fraud or deceit upon any person;

(i) "Foreign corrupt practices" which means the corrupt offering, paying, or making of inducements by any person to any foreign official or foreign political party, official thereof or candidate for foreign official office in order to assist such person in obtaining or retaining business for himself or in directing business to any other person;

(j) Any of the abovedefined criminal offences, where United States federal jurisdiction is based upon interstate transport, use of the mails, telecommunications or other interstate facilities;

(k) Such further offences as may from time to time be agreed upon by exchange of diplomatic notes between the United States and the United Kingdom, including the Cayman Islands; and

(l) Any attempt or conspiracy to commit, or participation as accessory after the fact to, any of the above defined criminal offences.

Article 20
Ratification, Entry into Force, and Termination

1. This Treaty shall be ratified, and the instruments of ratification shall be exchanged at Washington as soon as possible.

2. This Treaty shall enter into force upon the exchange of instruments of ratification.

3. The Government of either the United States or the United Kingdom, including the Cayman Islands, may terminate this Treaty by giving three months notice in writing to the other Government at any time.

APPENDIX E

Conveyancing Amendment Act, 1993 (Bermuda)

WHEREAS it is expedient to amend the Conveyancing Act 1983 to make new provisions in respect of certain voidable dispositions:

Be it enacted by The Queen's Most Excellent Majesty, by and with the advice and consent of the Senate and the House of Assembly of Bermuda, and by the authority of the same, as follows:

Short title

1. This Act which amends the Conveyancing Act 1983 may be cited as the Conveyancing Amendment Act 1993.

Inserts new Part IV A

2. The Conveyancing Act 1983 is amended by inserting at the end of Part IV, immediately after section 36, the following new Part IV A—

PART IV A: PROVISIONS AGAINST DISPOSITIONS WITH REQUISITE INTENTION

Interpretation

36A. (1) In this Part—

"Appointed day" means the date on which this Part comes into operation;

"Disposition" means any disposition or series of dispositions of property of any nature whatsoever and however effected, and, without limiting the generality of the foregoing, includes any exercise of a power of appointment, any trust, gift, transfer, sale, exchange, demise, assignment, assurance, grant, lease, surrender, conveyance, reconveyance, release, reservation, any purchase or other acquisition, any covenant, contract or option and any compromise or other dealing or arrangement;

"Eligible creditor" means a person to whom—

(a) On, or within two years after, the material date the transferor owed an obligation and on the date of the action or proceeding to set aside the relevant disposition that obligation remains unsatisfied;

(b) On the material date the transferor owed a contingent liability and since that date the contingency giving rise to the obligation has occurred and on the date of the action or proceeding to set aside the relevant disposition that obligation remains unsatisfied; or

(c) On the date of the action or proceeding to set aside the relevant disposition, the transferor owes an obligation in consequence of a claim, made by that person against the transferor, arising from a cause of action which accrued prior to, or within two years after, the material date.

"Material date" means the date on which a relevant disposition is made;

"Obligation" means any obligation or liability, other than a contingent liability, to pay a sum of money or to transfer property;

"Property" includes money, goods, things in action, land and every description of property wherever situated and every description of interest, whether present or future or vested or contingent, arising out of, or incidental to, property;

"Relevant disposition" means a disposition to which section 36C applies;

"Requisite intention" means an intention of a transferor to make a disposition the dominant purpose of which is to put the property which is the subject of that disposition beyond the reach of a person or a class of persons who is making, or may at some time make, a claim against him;

"Transferor" means a person who directly or indirectly makes a relevant disposition or causes it to be made;

"Transferee" means the person to whom a relevant disposition is made and includes a successor in title of such person;

"Trust" includes a settlement;

"Undervalue", in relation to a disposition of property, means a disposition in respect of which—

(a) No consideration is given or

(b) The value of the consideration given is, in money or money's worth, significantly less than the value in money or money's worth, of the property.

Application

36B.

(1) Subject to subsections (2) and (3), with effect from the appointed day the provisions of this Part shall apply to every disposition of property made by any person whether that disposition was made before or after the appointed day and whether or not the property, the subject of the disposition, is situated in Bermuda or elsewhere.

(2) Notwithstanding subsection (1), where—

(a) Prior to, or within six months after, the appointed day; and

(b) Pursuant to a conveyance of property to which section 37 of the Conveyancing Act 1983 applies, any action or proceeding has been commenced, this Part shall have no application, and the provisions of the said section 37 shall have effect as if this Part had not been enacted.

(3) This Part shall not affect the operation of a disentailing assurance or the law of bankruptcy for the time being in force.

Avoidance of Dispositions Made With the Requisite Intention, Etc.

36C.

(1) Subject to subsection (2) and the provisions of this Part, every disposition of property made with the requisite intention and at an undervalue shall be voidable at the instance of an eligible creditor thereby prejudiced.

(2) Where a person seeking to set aside a relevant disposition was not, on the material date, a person—

(a) To whom an obligation was owed by the transferor;

or

(b) Who had made a claim against the transferor, the Court shall not set aside that disposition unless the Court is satisfied that that person was, on the material date, reasonably foreseeable by the transferor as [a person to whom an obligation might become owed by, or who might make a claim against, him].

(3) Subject to subsection (4), no action or proceeding to set aside a disposition shall be commenced pursuant to this Part unless such action or proceeding is commenced—

(a) In the case of an eligible creditor referred to in paragraph (a) of the definition of that expression, within six years after the material date or within six years after the date when the obligation became owed, whichever is the later date;

(b) In the case of an eligible creditor referred to in paragraph (b) of that definition, within six years after the material date;

(c) In the case of an eligible creditor referred to in paragraph (c) of that definition, within six years after the material date, or within six years after the date when the cause of action accrued, whichever is the later date.

(4) Except as provided in subsections (1) and (3) nothing contained in this section shall be construed as in any way affecting the operation of the Limitation Act 1984.

(5) For the avoidance of doubt it is hereby declared—

(a) That a disposition to which this Part applies shall not, by reason only that it was made at an undervalue, be set aside by the Court; and

(b) The Court shall, for the purpose of setting aside such a disposition determine, on a balance of probability, whether it was made with the requisite intention.

Savings of Certain Rights

36D.

(1) Where, pursuant to this Part, a relevant disposition is set aside and the Court is satisfied that the transferee has acted in good faith, then,—

(a) The transferee shall have a first and paramount charge over the property, the subject of the relevant disposition, for an amount equal to all costs (and not only such costs as the Court might otherwise allow) properly incurred by the transferee in the defence of the action or proceeding to set aside that disposition;

(b) The relevant disposition shall be set aside subject to all fees and costs properly incurred and subject also to any pre-existing rights, claims and interests of the transferee and of any person through whom the transferee claims and who has acted in good faith; and

(c) In the case of a trust, the relevant disposition shall only be set aside subject to the right of a beneficiary to retain any distribution made consequent upon the prior exercise of a trust, power or a discretion vested in the trustee of such trust or any other person, and otherwise properly exercised.

(2) The burden of proving that a transferee or any person through whom the transferee claims has not acted in good faith shall be upon the person making the allegation.

Extent of Avoidance of Relevant Disposition

36E. Subject to section 36D, a relevant disposition shall be set aside pursuant to this Part only to the extent necessary to satisfy the obligation owed to the eligible creditor at whose instance the disposition has been set aside.

Part Not to Validate Certain Dispositions

36F.

Nothing contained in this Part shall be construed as:

(a) Validating any disposition of property which is neither owned by, nor is the subject of a power of disposal with respect thereto vested in, the transferor; or

(b) Affecting the recognition of a foreign law in determining whether the transferor is the owner of such property or the holder of such power.

Relationship with Trusts (Special Provisions) Act 1989

36G.
Nothing in this Part shall be construed as creating or enabling any right, claim or interest on behalf of a creditor or person which right, claim or interest would be avoided or defeated by section 11 of the Trusts (Special Provisions) Act 1989, (which prohibits the variation or setting aside of trusts validly created under the Law of Bermuda).

Amends Real Estates Assets Act 1787

3. The Real Estates Assets Act 1787 is amended by repealing section 3.

Repeals Section 37

4. Section 37 of the Conveyancing Act 1983 is repealed.

Explanatory Memorandum

The purpose of this Bill is to repeal section 37 of the Conveyancing Act 1983 and to make new provision in respect of certain voidable dispositions.

Clause 1 of the Bill is self-explanatory.

Clause 2 of the Bill inserts, as a new Part IVA, sections 36A to 36G. The new clause 36A contains definitions of expressions used in the new Part.

The new clause 36B makes provisions in relation to the application of the new Part. The new Part applies to dispositions whether made before or after the Act comes into operation. It will not however affect voluntary conveyances in respect of which any action or proceeding had begun prior to, or within six months after the coming into operation of the new Part.

The new clause 36C, inter alia, makes voidable every disposition of property made with the requisite intention.

The new section 36D protects the right of persons affected by a disposition which has been set aside. If a transferee has acted in good faith the disposition can only be set aside subject to existing rights, claims and interests of the transferee and subject also to all costs and fees reasonably incurred by him. Similarly, in the case of a trust, if a beneficiary has acted in good faith the disposition can only be set aside subject to his right to retain any distribution made consequent upon the proper exercise by a trustee of a power.

The new section 36E ensures that a disposition can only be set aside to the extent necessary to satisfy the obligation owed to an eligible creditor and otherwise in accordance with the new Part.

The new section 36F avoids validation of dispositions made by a person who does not in fact own the property concerned.

The new section 36G ensures that the new provisions do not create any rights in conflict with section 11 of the Trusts (Special Provisions) Act 1989.

Clause 3 of the Bill repeals section 3 of the Real Estates Assets Act 1787. The purpose of this repeal of this section is to avoid duplicating provisions in respect of the same subject matter.

~~Clause 4 of the Bill repeals section 37 of the Conveyancing Act 1983.~~

APPENDIX F

The Trusts (Special Provisions) Act 1989 (Bermuda) as amended by The Trusts (Special Provisions) Amendment Act 1998[1]

ARRANGEMENT OF SECTIONS

[1] The authors thank Alex Anderson, with the law firm of Conyers Dill & Pearman, for providing them with this copy of The Trusts (Special Provisions) Act 1989, as amended by The Trusts (Special Provisions) Amendment Act 1998. Conyers Dill & Pearman is located at the following address: Conyers Dill & Pearman, Barristers & Attorneys, Clarendon House, 2 Church Street, P.O. Box HM 666, Hamilton, Bermuda HM CX, Telephone: (441) 295-1422, Facsimile: (441) 292-4720.

BERMUDA
1989: 62
THE TRUSTS (SPECIAL PROVISIONS) ACT 1989

[Date of Assent 28 December 1989]
[Operative Date 31 January 1990]
[Operative Date of Amendment Act 24 June 1998]

WHEREAS it is expedient to make provision on the law respecting trusts, to make provision respecting a trust for a purpose or purposes, to make provision for administrative powers in trusts and for matters connected therewith and incidental thereto:

Be it enacted by The Queen's Most Excellent Majesty, by and with the advice and consent of the Senate and the House of Assembly of Bermuda, and by the authority of the same as follows:

Short title and commencement

1. This Act may be cited as the Trusts (Special Provisions) Act 1989 and shall come into operation on 31 January 1990.

PART I
TRUSTS

Trust described

2. (1) For the purposes of this Part, the term "trust" refers to the legal relationship created, either inter vivos or on death, by a person, the settlor,

when assets have been placed under the control of a trustee for the benefit of a beneficiary or for a specified purpose.

(2) A trust has the following characteristics:

(a) The assets constitute a separate fund and are not a part of the trustee's own estate;

(b) Title to the trust assets stands in the name of the trustee or in the name of another person on behalf of the trustee;

(c) The trustee has the power and the duty in respect of which he is accountable, to manage, employ or dispose of the assets in accordance with the terms of the trust and the special duties imposed upon him by law.

(3) The reservation by the settlor of certain rights and powers, and the fact that the trustee may himself have rights as a beneficiary, are not necessarily inconsistent with the existence of a trust.

Application

3. This Part applies to trusts created voluntarily and evidenced in writing and also to any other trusts of property arising under the law of Bermuda or by virtue of a judicial decision whether in Bermuda or elsewhere.

Non-application

4. This Part does not apply to the extent that the law specified by section 5 or 6 does not provide for trusts or the category of trusts involved.

Governing law

5. (1) A trust shall be governed by the law chosen by the settlor whose choice shall be express or be implied in the terms of the instrument creating or the writing evidencing the trust, interpreted, if necessary, in the light of circumstances of the case.

(2) Where the law chosen under subsection (1) does not provide for trusts or the category of trusts involved, the choice shall not be effective and the law specified in section 6 applies.

No applicable law chosen

6. (1) Where no applicable law has been chosen, a trust shall be governed by the law with which it is most closely connected and in ascertaining the law with which a trust is most closely connected references shall be made in particular to

(a) The place of administration of the trust designated by the settlor;

(b) The situs of the assets of the trust;

(c) The place of residence or business of the trustee;

(d) The objects of the trust and the places where they are to be fulfilled.

(2) A trust that is governed by the law of Bermuda may provide terms to change the law governing the trust from the law of Bermuda to a new governing law but such change is valid and effective only if the new governing law recognises the validity of the trust and the respective interests of the beneficiaries.

(3) A change in the law governing a trust shall not affect the legality or validity of or render any person liable for anything done before the change.

Law governing validity and construction of trust

7. The law specified by section 5 or 6 shall govern the validity of the trust, its construction, its effects and the administration of the trust and in particular the law shall govern

(1) The appointment, resignation and removal of trustees, the capacity to act as a trustee, and the devolution of the office of trustee;

(2) The rights and duties of trustees among themselves;

(3) The right of trustees to delegate in whole or in part the discharge of their duties or the exercise of their powers;

(4) The power of trustees to administer or to dispose of trust assets, to create security interests in the trust assets, or to acquire new assets;

(5) The powers of investment of trustees;

(6) Restrictions upon the duration of the trust, and upon the power to accumulate the income of the trust;

(7) The relationships between the trustees and the beneficiaries including the personal liability of the trustees to the beneficiaries;

(8) The variation or termination of the trust;

(9) The distribution of the trust assets;

(10) The duty of trustees to account for their administration.

Choosing different laws

8. In applying this Part a severable aspect of the trust, particularly matters of administration, may be governed by a different law.

Jurisdiction of the Supreme Court

9. The Supreme Court has jurisdiction—

(1) Where a trustee is resident in Bermuda;

(2) Where any trust property is situated in Bermuda but only in respect of property so situated;

(3) Where the administration of any trust is carried on in Bermuda; or

(4) Where the Court thinks it appropriate.

Appendix F

Capacity to create trust

10. (1) Subject to subsection (2), a person has capacity to create a trust in the following cases:
  (a) Where the trust property is movable—
    (i) In the case of an inter vivos trust, if he has the capacity to create a trust of movable property by the law of Bermuda;
    (ii) In the case of a testamentary trust, if he has the capacity to create a trust of movable property by the law of his domicile;
  (b) Where the trust property is immovable, if he has the capacity to create a trust by the lex situs of the immovable.

  (2) All questions as to the capacity of any settlor arising in regard to a trust which is for the time being governed by the law of Bermuda or in regard to any disposition of property upon the trusts hereof are to be determined according to the law of Bermuda without reference to the law of any other jurisdiction with which the trust or disposition may be connected except that this subsection—
  (a) Does not validate any disposition of property which is neither owned by the settlor nor the subject of a power in that behalf vested in the settlor, nor does this subsection affect the recognition of foreign laws in determining whether the settlor is the owner of such property or the holder of such power;
  (b) Does take effect subject to any express contrary term of the trust or disposition;
  (c) Does not, as regards the capacity of a corporation, affect the recognition of the laws of its place of incorporation;
  (d) Does not affect the recognition of foreign laws prescribing generally (without reference to the existence or terms of the trust) the formalities for the disposition of property;
  (e) Does not validate any trust or disposition of immovable property situate in a jurisdiction other than Bermuda which is invalid according to the laws of such jurisdiction;
  (f) Does not validate any testamentary trust or disposition which is invalid according to the laws of testator's domicile.

Varying or setting aside trust

11. Where a trust is validly created under the law of Bermuda the Court shall not vary it or set it aside pursuant to the law of another jurisdiction in respect of—
  (1) The personal and proprietary effects of marriage;
  (2) Succession rights, testate and intestate, especially the indefeasible shares of spouses and relatives;
  (3) The protection of creditors in matters of insolvency,
  Unless the law of Bermuda has corresponding laws or public policy rules.

PART II
PURPOSE TRUSTS

12A. (1) A trust may be created for a non-charitable purpose or purposes provided that the conditions set out in subsection (2) are satisfied; and in this Part such a trust is referred to as a "purpose trust."

(2) The conditions are that the purpose or purposes are:
- (a) Sufficiently certain to allow the trust to be carried out,
- (b) Lawful, and
- (c) Not contrary to public policy.

(3) A purpose trust may only be created in writing.

(4) The rule of law (known as the rule against excessive duration or the rule against perpetual trusts) which limits the time during which the capital of a trust may remain unexpendable to the perpetuity period under the rule against perpetuities shall not apply to a purpose trust.

(5) The rule against perpetuities (also known as the rule against remoteness of vesting) as modified by the Perpetuities and Accumulations Act 1989 shall apply to a purpose trust.

Enforcement and variation of purpose trust by the court

12B. (1) The Supreme Court may make such order as it considers expedient for the enforcement of a purpose trust on the application of any of the following persons:
- (a) Any person appointed by or under the trust for the purposes of this subsection;
- (b) The settlor, unless the trust instrument provides otherwise;
- (c) A trustee of the trust;
- (d) Any other person whom the court considers has sufficient interest in the enforcement of the trust;

And where the Attorney-General satisfies the court that there is no such person who is able and willing to make an application under this subsection, the Attorney-General may make an application for enforcement of the trust.

(2) On an application in relation to a purpose trust by any of the following persons:
- (a) Any person appointed by or under the trust for the purposes of this subsection;
- (b) The settlor, unless the trust instrument provides otherwise;
- (c) A trustee of the trust,

The court may if it thinks fit approve a scheme to vary any of the purposes of the trust, or to enlarge or otherwise vary any of the powers of the trustees of the trust.

(3) Where any costs are incurred in connection with any application under this section, the Supreme Court may make such order as it considers just as to payment of those costs (including payment out of the property of the trust).

Effect of non-compliance

12C. Nothing in this Part affects the creation, termination or validity of any trust created under any other law, but, save as aforesaid, purpose trusts which do not comply with section 12A are invalid.

Land in Bermuda

12D. No interest in land in Bermuda shall be held, directly or indirectly, in a purpose trust.

PART III
INCORPORATION OF ADMINISTRATIVE POWERS BY REFERENCE

Incorporation by reference

17. Any instrument creating any trust may incorporate by reference any of the provisions set out in the Schedule, in which case the following expressions appearing in the provisions have, unless a contrary intention appears, the meanings respectively assigned to them:

(1) "The Settlor" includes a person who provides trust property or makes a testamentary disposition on trust or to a trust;

(2) "The Trustees" means the trustees for the time being of the trust;

(3) "The Trust Fund" means:

(a) The property in respect of which trusts are declared;

(b) All property paid or transferred to or otherwise vested in and accepted by the Trustees and in respect of which a memorandum signed by the Trustees is conclusive evidence;

(c) All income which, in accordance with the provisions of the trust, is accumulated by the Trustees and added to the capital thereof;

(d) All money, investments and other property from time to time representing all property and income mentioned in paragraphs (a), (b) and (c) and any part of the said property or income.

SCHEDULE

Trust for sale

1. (1) The Trustees shall stand possessed of any real property from time to time comprised in the Trust Fund Upon Trust to sell the same with power to postpone the sale thereof or of any part thereof for such period as they

shall in their absolute discretion think fit and shall stand possessed of all other investments comprised in the Trust Fund Upon Trust at such discretion either to retain the same in the existing state thereof for such period as they shall think fit or at any time or times to sell the same or any part thereof.

(2) The Trustees shall hold the net proceeds of any sale of investments comprised in the Trust Fund and all other monies held or received by them as capital monies Upon Trust to invest the same at their discretion in or upon any of the investments by this instrument authorised with power to vary or transpose such investments for or into any others of a like nature.

Powers of investment

2. TRUST moneys to be invested under the trusts of this instrument may be applied or invested in any currency and in any part of the world in the purchase of or upon the security of such common or preferred stocks shares mutual fund shares unit trust units or other securities or commodities (including precious metals) bonds notes debentures certificates of deposit or time deposits land or other investments or property of whatever nature (and whether or not income-producing or paying dividends or interest) and whether involving liabilities or not or upon such personal credit with or without security as the Trustees in their absolute discretion think fit without being restricted to trustee investments prescribed under the proper law governing this instrument and to the intent that the Trustees shall have the same powers in all respects as if they were absolute owners beneficially entitled And in addition (but without prejudice to the generality of the foregoing) the Trustees may invest the Trust Fund in the shares or debentures of any company whatsoever and wheresoever incorporated without the need for diversification and without being liable for any loss occasioned thereby.

Power with regard to mode of application of capital and income

3. ANY power by this instrument or by law conferred on the Trustees to pay transfer appropriate or apply the Trust Fund or any income thereof for the benefit of any beneficiary may at the discretion of the Trustees be validly exercised (without prejudice to the generality of such power or to any other mode of application)—

(1) By paying or transferring the same to the trustees of any settlement (whether or not such trustees are resident in Bermuda and whether or not the proper law of such settlement is the law of Bermuda) the provisions of which are in the opinion of the Trustees for the benefit of such beneficiary notwithstanding that such settlement may also contain trusts powers or provisions (discretionary or otherwise) in favour of other persons or objects Provided however that no such payment or

transfer shall be made so as to infringe the rule against perpetuities as applicable to the trusts created by this instrument; or

(2) (In the case of any such person who is a minor) by paying or transferring the same to such minor's parent or guardian or some other person for the time being having the care or custody of such minor upon the recipient undertaking to apply the same for the benefit of the minor;

And the Trustees shall not thereafter be under any obligation to see to the further application of the capital or income so paid or transferred and the receipt of such trustees parent guardian or other person shall be a full sufficient and complete discharge to the Trustees.

Additional Powers

4. THE Trustees shall have the following powers in addition to those conferred by law:

(1) Power to receive any property from any person as an addition to the Trust Fund either by gift inter vivos or by will or under the provisions of any other settlement or trust or otherwise;

(2) Power to borrow on the security of the Trust Fund and for such purpose to make any outlay out of the Trust Fund or the income thereof and to enter into such contracts mortgages charges or undertakings relating thereto as the Trustees may in their absolute discretion think fit;

(3) Power to lend any part of the Trust Fund to any person (whether or not a beneficiary) upon such terms (if any) as to security repayment rate of interest and otherwise as the Trustees in their absolute discretion may determine;

(4) With respect to any property comprised in the Trust Fund power to exercise all powers relating thereto as if beneficially entitled thereto and without being restricted in any way by the office of trustee including (without prejudice to the generality of the foregoing power)—

(a) Power to vote upon or in respect of any shares securities bonds notes or other evidence of interest in or obligations of any corporation trust association or concern whether or not the exercise of such power affects the security or the apparent security of the Trust Fund or the purchase or sale or lease of the assets of any such corporation trust association or concern;

(b) Power to deposit any such shares securities or property in any voting trust or with any depository designated thereby;

(c) Power to give proxies or powers of attorney with or without power of substitution for voting or acting on behalf of the Trustees as the owners of any such property; and

(d) Power to omit to register bonds or securities;

(5) Power (at the expense of the Trust Fund) to incorporate or register or to procure the incorporation or registration of any company (with

limited or unlimited liability) in any part of the world for any purpose including the acquisition of the Trust Fund or any part thereof and so that (if thought fit) the consideration on the sale of the Trust Fund to any such company may consist wholly or partly of fully paid shares debentures debenture stock or other securities of the company credited as fully paid which shall be allotted to or otherwise vested in the Trustees and be capital moneys in the Trustees' hands;

(6) Power at any time to apply any part of the Trust Fund of the income thereof in effecting or joining in effecting or otherwise acquiring any policy of assurance on the life of any beneficiary or of any other person or any endowment or other policy and to maintain surrender exchange exercise any option thereunder or otherwise deal with such policies as if the Trustees were absolutely entitled thereto;

(7) Power to pay out at any time any part of the Trust Fund in purchasing or acquiring or making improvements in or repairs to or on any land or building (whether freehold leasehold or of any other tenure or interest and of whatsoever description and situate in any part of the world) in the occupation of or intended for occupation by any beneficiary And power to permit any beneficiary to occupy until sale any land or building purchased or acquired as aforesaid or otherwise comprised in the Trust Fund upon such terms (as to payment or non-payment of rent outgoings repairs or otherwise) as the Trustees may think fit;

(8) Power at any time or times to lay out any part of the Trust Fund in the purchase or other acquisition of any yachts boats motor vehicles works of art household furniture plate linen china cutlery other articles of household use ornament or equipment and other chattels for the use of any beneficiary whether occupying a building purchased or acquired as aforesaid or otherwise And power to hand over to any such beneficiary for his use any property so purchased or acquired by the Trustees as aforesaid or otherwise forming part of the Trust Fund upon and subject to such terms and conditions (if any) as to insurance preservation maintaining inventories and otherwise as the trustees think fit;

(9) Power to grant options for such consideration and exercisable at such time or times or within such period as the Trustees think fit for the purchase of any property subject to the trusts of this instrument or the acquisition of any interest therein;

(10) Power to keep the Trust Fund either in or out of Bermuda and if the Trustees think fit to hold in any part of the world all or any securities or other property in bearer form or registered in the name of the Trustees or nominees without disclosing the fiduciary relationship;

(11) In the event of any duties fees or taxes whatsoever becoming payable in any part of the world in respect of the Trust Fund or any part

thereof in any circumstances whatsoever power to pay all such duties fees or taxes out of the Trust Fund or the income thereof with discretion as to the time and manner in which the said duties fees or taxes shall be paid and the Trustees may pay such duties fees or taxes notwithstanding that the same shall not be recoverable from the Trustees or from any persons interested under the trusts of this instrument or that the payment shall not be to the advantage of such persons;

(12) Power to make such reserves out of the Trust Fund or the income thereof as the Trustees deem proper for expenses taxes and other liabilities and to pay from capital or income or to apportion between capital and income any expenses of making or changing investments and selling exchanging or leasing (including brokers commissions and charges) and generally to determine what part of the expenses of administering the trusts of this instrument shall be charged to capital and what part to income;

(13) Power to make execute and deliver deeds assignments transfers leases mortgages instruments of pledge creating liens contracts and other instruments sealed and unsealed;

(14) Power to institute prosecute and defend any suits or actions or other proceedings affecting the Trustees or the Trust Fund and to compromise any matter of difference or to submit such matter to arbitration and to compromise or compound any debt owing to the Trustees or any other claims and to adjust any disputes in relation to debts or claims against them as trustees upon evidence that the Trustees shall deem sufficient and to make partition upon such terms (including if thought fit the payment or receipt of equality money) as the Trustees shall deem desirable with co-owners or joint tenants besides the Trustees having any interest in any property in which the Trustees are interested and to make partition either by sale or by set-off or by agreement or otherwise;

(15) Power to make any distribution of the Trust Fund pursuant to the trusts of this instrument in cash or in kind or partly in cash and partly in kind and in the case of a distribution to more than one person not strictly ratably but on the basis of equal or other proportionate value (as the case may require) according to the judgment of the Trustees which shall be binding on all persons interested under this instrument;

(16) Power to take at the expense of the Trust Fund or the income thereof the opinion of legal counsel concerning any question arising under this instrument or on any matter in any way relating to the Trust Fund or the duties of the Trustees in connection with this instrument And the Trustees shall not be liable for any action taken in good faith pursuant to or otherwise in accordance with the opinion or advice of such counsel;

(17) Power—

(a) To engage the services of such investment counsel adviser or manager ("the Investment Adviser") as the Trustees may from time to time think fit (including the Settlor or any trustee of this instrument or any corporate trustee or any parent subsidiary or affiliate of such corporate trustee) in order to obtain advice on the investment and reinvestment of the Trust Fund AND to delegate to the Investment Adviser without being liable for any consequential loss discretion to manage the portfolio or any part thereof within the limits and for the period stipulated by the Trustees and the Trustees

(i) Shall settle the terms and conditions for the remuneration of the Investment Adviser and the reimbursement of the Investment Adviser's expenses as in their uncontrolled discretion they deem proper and such remuneration and expenses may be paid by the Trustees from and out of the Trust Fund; and

(ii) Shall not be liable for any action taken in good faith pursuant to or otherwise in accordance with the advice of the Investment Adviser;

(b) To employ and pay at the expense of the capital or income of the Trust Fund any agent or agents in any part of the world whether solicitors bankers accountants stockbrokers managers or other persons (including the Settlor or any trustee of this instrument or any corporate trustee or any parent subsidiary or affiliate of such corporate trustee) to transact any business or to do any act requiring to be transacted or done in execution of the trusts of this instrument including the receipt and payment of money and the execution of documents and in any such event the trustee, the corporate trustee or the parent subsidiary or the affiliate of such corporate trustee is entitled to charge and be paid and to retain for his or its own account all usual professional and other fees and commissions normally paid for such services including fees and commissions shared with other agents;

Trustee may exercise powers despite personal interest

(18) Power for all or any of the Trustees

(a) To exercise or join or concur in exercising all or any of the powers and discretions by this instrument or by law given to the Trustees notwithstanding that such trustee may have a personal interest in the mode or result of exercising any such power or discretion or may be interested therein in some other fiduciary capacity but any trustee may abstain from acting except as a merely formal party in any matter in which he may be so interested as aforesaid and may allow his co-trustees to act alone in the exercise of such powers and discretions in relation to such matter; and

To effect transactions

(b) To purchase or sell any property notwithstanding that the vendor or purchaser is the same as or includes the Trustees or any of them PROVIDED that the price payable on any such purchase or sale is certified as fair and reasonable by an independent valuer employed for the purpose by the Trustees;

Residuary powers

(19) Power to effect any transaction concerning or affecting the Trust Fund or any other property whatsoever and to do all other acts and things which the Trustees may in their absolute discretion think expedient in the interests of the Trust Fund or any beneficiary And for the purpose of this sub-paragraph "transaction" includes any sale exchange assurance conveyance grant lease surrender reconveyance release reservation or other disposition and any purchase or other acquisition and any covenant contract licence option right of pre-emption and any compromise or partition and any company reconstruction or amalgamation and any other dealing or arrangement And "effect" has the meaning appropriate to the particular transaction And references to property include references to restrictions and burdens affecting the property;

Powers of sale, etc.

(20) All the powers of sale (by public auction or private contract) exchange mortgaging leasing or other disposition management repair building and improvement and all other powers of an absolute beneficial owner in respect of any property for the time being comprised in the Trust Fund including (without prejudice to the generality of the foregoing) the power of borrowing on the security of the Trust Fund and for such purpose to make any outlay out of the income or capital of the Trust Fund and to make such contracts and to enter into such undertakings relating thereto as the Trustees in their absolute discretion shall think fit;

Power to give guarantees

(21) Power at any time in the Trustees' discretion and on such terms as they deem fit to appropriate or to apply the capital or income of the Trust Fund or any part thereof in order to secure the payment of money owed by any beneficiary or the performance of any obligations of any beneficiary and to give any guarantee or to become surety for any beneficiary and for such purposes to mortgage or charge any investments or property for the time being forming part of the Trust Fund or to deposit or transfer any such investments or property with or to any person by way of security;

To release fiduciary power

(22) Power from time to time by deed revocable or irrevocable wholly or partially to release extinguish or restrict any power by this instrument or by law conferred on the Trustees notwithstanding the fiduciary nature of any such power (but not so as to invalidate any prior exercise thereof).

Exclusion of apportionments

5. UNLESS the Trustees in their absolute discretion shall otherwise determine all dividends and other income received shall be treated for all purposes as income accruing at the due date of payment whether or not such dividends or income may have been earned and accrued wholly or partially in respect of a period prior to such date.

Protection of third parties in dealings with trustees

6. (1) NO person or corporation dealing with the Trustees and no purchaser on any sale made by the Trustees shall be concerned to enquire into the propriety or validity of any act of the Trustees or to see to the application of any money paid or property transferred to or upon the order of the Trustees.

(2) NO firm association or corporation any of whose securities are comprised in the Trust Fund and no purchaser or person dealing with any trustee purporting to act under any delegation of authority from any other trustee shall be required to ascertain or enquire whether a case exists in which such delegation is permitted or whether such delegated authority is still subsisting.

(3) WHEN anything is dependent upon the value of any property or the existence of any fact a certificate of the Trustees as to such value or fact shall be conclusive in favour of anyone acting thereon in good faith.

Power in relation to underlying company/ies

7. ANY trustee of this instrument and any director officer or employee of a corporate trustee or of a parent subsidiary or affiliate of such corporate trustee may act as a director officer manager or employee of any company whose shares or debentures may be comprised in the Trust Fund or as a director officer manager or employee of any subsidiary or holding company of any such company and may retain for himself or itself any remuneration which he or it may receive as such director officer manager or employee notwithstanding that any votes or other rights attaching to such shares or debentures may have been instrumental either alone or in conjunction with other matters or by reason of their non-exercise in procuring or continuing for him or it his or its position as such director officer manager or employee

or that his or its qualifications for any such position may be constituted in part or in whole by any such position may be constituted in part or in whole by any such shares or debentures.

Trustee not bound to interfere with company management

8. THE Trustees shall not be bound or required to interfere in the management or conduct of the affairs or business of any company in which the Trust Fund may be invested (and whether or not the Trustees have the control of such company) And so long as no trustee of this instrument has notice of any wilful negligence wilful default or fraud or dishonesty on the part of the directors having the management of such company they may leave the same (including the payment or non-payment of dividends) wholly to such directors And no beneficiary is entitled as such beneficiary in any way to compel control or forbid the exercise (including in any particular manner) of any voting or other rights at any time vested in the Trustees with regard to such company including without prejudice to the generality of the foregoing any powers the Trustees may have (even if also directors of such company) of compelling such company to distribute any dividend.

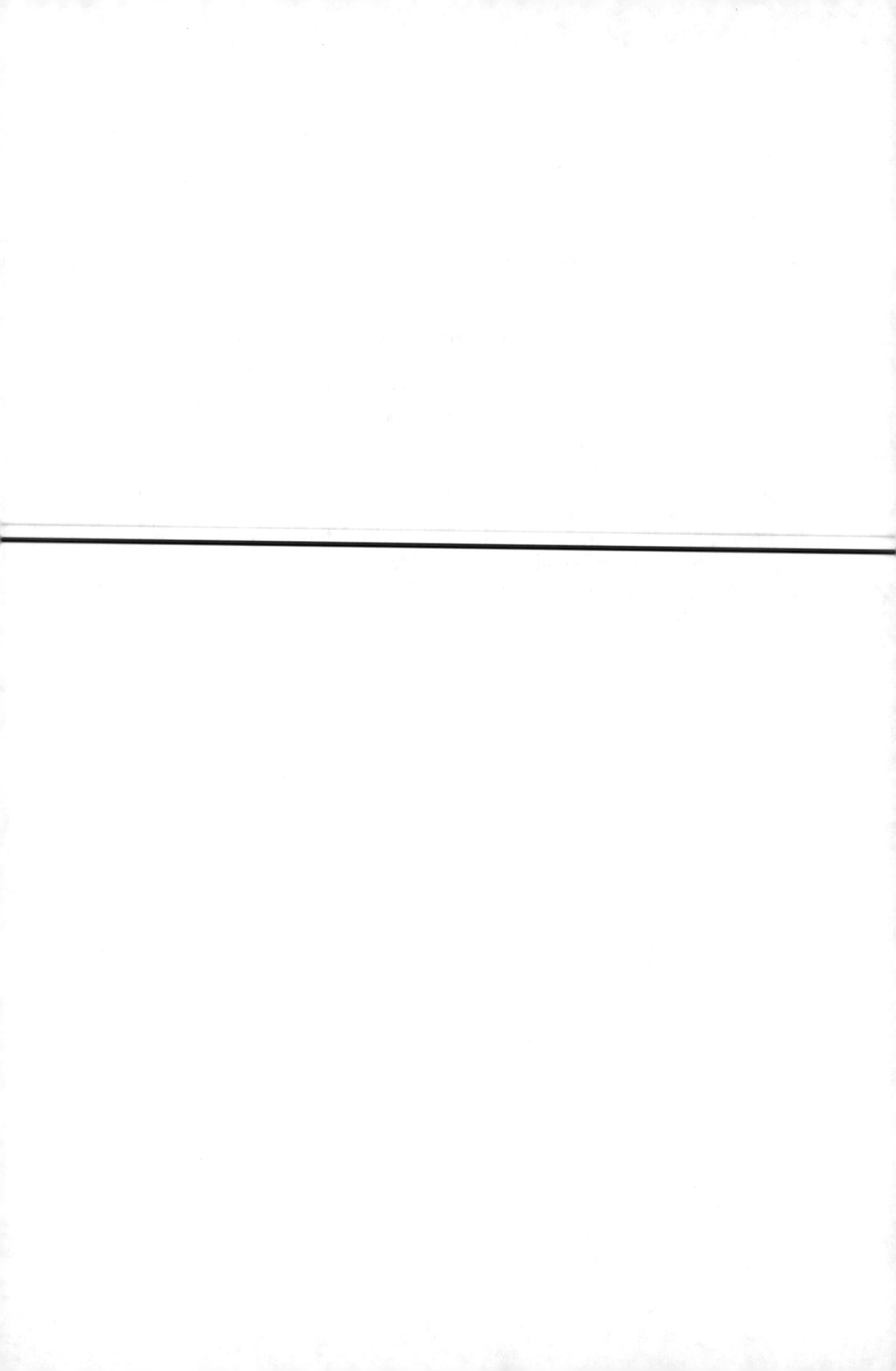

APPENDIX G

Alaska Trust Statute

AN ACT

Relating to certain irrevocable transfers in trust, to the jurisdiction governing a trust, to challenges to trusts or property transfers in trust, to the validity of trust interests, and to transfers of certain trust interests; and providing for an effective date.

BE IT ENACTED BY THE STATE OF ALASKA:

Section 1. AS 13.12.205 (2) is amended to read:

(2) Property transferred in any of the following forms by the decedent during marriage:

(A) An irrevocable transfer, *including an irrevocable transfer in trust with a transfer restriction under AS 34.40.110 (A)*, in which the decedent retained the right to the possession or enjoyment of, or to the income from, the property, if and to the extent the decedent's right terminated at or continued beyond the decedent's death; the amount included is the value of the fraction of the property to which the decedent's right related, to the extent the fraction of the property passed outside probate to or for the benefit of a person other than the decedent's estate or surviving spouse;

(B) A transfer in which the decedent created a power over the income or property, exercisable by the decedent alone or in conjunction with another person, or exercisable by a nonadverse party, to or for the benefit of the decedent, the decedent's creditors, the decedent's estate, or creditors of the decedent's estate; the amount included with respect to a power over property is the value of the property subject to the power, and the amount included with respect to a power over income is the value of the property that produces or produced the income, to the extent the power in either case was exercisable at the decedent's death to or for the benefit of a person other than the decedent's surviving spouse or to the extent the property passed at the decedent's death, by exercise, release, lapse, default, or otherwise, to or for the benefit of a person other than the decedent's estate or surviving spouse; if the power is a power over both income and property and the preceding provision defining the amount included produces different amounts, the amount included is the greater amount; and

Sec. 2. AS 13.36.035(a) is amended to read:

(a) The court has exclusive jurisdiction of proceedings initiated by interested parties concerning the internal affairs of trusts, *including trusts covered by (c) of this section, except as provided in (c) and (d) of this section, proceedings that* may be maintained under this section are those concerning the administration and distribution of trusts, the declaration of rights, and the determination of other matters involving trustees and beneficiaries of trusts. These include proceedings to

(1) Appoint or remove a trustee;

(2) Review trustees' fees and to review and settle interim or final accounts;

(3) Ascertain beneficiaries, determine any question arising in the administration or distribution of any trust including questions of construction of trust instruments, instruct trustees, and determine the existence or nonexistence of any immunity, power, privilege, duty or right; and

(4) Release registration of a trust.

Sec. 3. AS 13.36.035 is amended by adding new subsections to read:

(c) A provision that the laws of this state govern the validity, construction, and administration of the trust and that the trust is subject to the jurisdiction of this state is valid, effective, and conclusive for the trust if

(1) Some or all of the trust assets are deposited in this state and are being administered by a qualified person; in this paragraph, "deposited in this state" includes being held in a checking account, time deposit, certificate of deposit, brokerage account, trust company fiduciary account, or other similar account or deposit that is located in this state;

(2) A trustee is a qualified person who is designated as a trustee under the governing instrument or by a court having jurisdiction over the trust;

(3) The powers of the trustee identified under (2) of this subsection include or are limited to

(A) Maintaining records for the trust on an exclusive basis or a nonexclusive basis; and

(B) Preparing or arranging for the preparation of, on an exclusive basis or a nonexclusive basis, an income tax return that must be filed by the trust; and

(4) Part or all of the administration occurs in this state, including physically maintaining trust records in this state.

(d) The validity, construction, and administration of a trust with a state jurisdiction provision are determined by the laws of this state, including the

   (1) Capacity of the settlor;

   (2) Powers, obligations, liabilities, and rights of the trustees and the appointment and removal of the trustees; and

   (3) Existence and extent of powers, conferred or retained, including a trustee's discretionary powers, the powers retained by a beneficiary of the trust, and the validity of the exercise of a power.

   (e) In (d) of this section, "settlor" means a person who transfers property in trust; "settlor" includes a person who furnishes the property transferred to a trust even if the trust is created by another person.

Sec. 4. AS 13.36.045(a) is amended to read:

   (a) The court will not, over the objection of a party, entertain proceedings under AS 13.36.035 involving a trust registered or having its principal place of administration in another state, unless

   (1) All appropriate parties could not be bound by litigation in the courts of the state where the trust is registered or has its principal place of administration;

   (2) The interests of justice otherwise would seriously be impaired; or

   (3) *The trust satisfies AS 13.36.035(c).*

Sec. 5. AS 13.36 is amended by adding new sections to read:
Sec. 13.36.310. Challenges to trusts. Except as provided in AS 34.40.110, a trust that is covered by AS 13.36.035(c) or that is otherwise governed by the laws of this state, or a property transfer to a trust that is covered by AS 13.36.035(c) or that is otherwise governed by the laws of this state, is not void, voidable, liable to be set aside, defective in any fashion, or questionable as to the settlor's capacity, on the grounds that the trust or transfer avoids or defeats a right, claim, or interest conferred by law on a person by reason of a personal or business relationship with the settlor or by way of a marital or similar right. In this section, "settlor" means a person who transfers property in trust; "settlor" includes a person who furnishes the property transferred to a trust even if the trust is created by another person.
Sec. 13.36.390. Definitions. In AS 13.36,

   (1) "Qualified person" means

   (A) An individual who, except for brief intervals, military service, attendance at an educational or training institution, or for absences for good cause shown, resides in this state, whose true and permanent home is in this state, who does not have a present intention of moving from this state, and who has the intention of returning to this state when away;

(B) A trust company that is organized under AS 06.25 and that has its principal place of business in this state; or

(c) A bank that is organized under AS 06.05, or a national banking association that is organized under 12 U.S.C. 21-216d, if the bank or national banking association possesses and exercises trust powers and has its principal place of business in this state;

(2) "State jurisdiction provision" means a provision that the laws of this state govern the validity, construction, and administration of a trust and that the trust is subject to the jurisdiction of this state.

Sec. 6. AS 34.27.050(a) is amended to read:

(a) A nonvested property interest is invalid unless

(1) When the interest is created, it is certain to vest or terminate no later than 21 years after the death of an individual then alive;

(2) The interest either vests or terminates within 90 years after its creation; or

(3) The interest is in a trust and all or part of the income or principal of the trust may be distributed, in the discretion of the trustee, to a person who is living when the trust is created.

Sec. 7. AS 34.40.010 is amended to read:

Sec. 34.40.010. Invalidity generally, except as provided in AS 34.40.110, a conveyance or assignment, in writing or otherwise, of an estate or interest in land, or in goods, or in things in action, or of rents or profits issuing from them or a charge upon land, goods, or things in action, or upon the rents or profits from them, made with the intent to hinder, delay, or defraud creditors or other persons of their lawful suits, damages, forfeitures, debts, or demands, or a bond or other evidence of debt given, action commenced, decree or judgment suffered, with the like intent, as against the persons so hindered, delayed, or defrauded is void.

Sec. 8. AS 34.40.110 is repealed and reenacted to read:

Sec. 34.40.110. Restricting transfers of trust interests.

(a) A person who in writing transfers property in trust may provide that the interest of a beneficiary of the trust may not be either voluntarily or involuntarily transferred before payment or delivery of the interest to the beneficiary by the trustee. In this subsection,

(1) "Property" includes real property, personal property, and interests in real or personal property;

(2) "Transfer" means any form of transfer, including deed, conveyance, or assignment.

(b) If a trust contains a transfer restriction allowed under (a) of this section, the transfer restriction prevents a creditor existing when the trust is created, a person who subsequently becomes a creditor, or another person from satisfying a claim out of the beneficiary's interest in the trust, unless the

(1) Transfer was intended in whole or in part to hinder, delay, or defraud creditors or other persons under AS 34.40.0100;

(2) Trust provides that the settlor may revoke or terminate all or part of the trust without the consent of a person who has a substantial beneficial interest in the trust and the interest would be adversely affected by the exercise of the power held by the settlor to revoke or terminate all or part of the trust; in this paragraph, "revoke or terminate" does not include a power to veto a distribution from the trust, a testamentary special power of appointment or similar power, or the right to receive a distribution of income, corpus, or both in the discretion of a person, including a trustee, other than the settlor;

(3) Trust requires that all or a part of the trust's income or principal, or both, must be distributed to the settlor; or

(4) At the time of the transfer, the settlor is in default by 30 or more days of making a payment due under a child support judgment or order.

(c) The satisfaction of a claim under (b)(1)-(4) of this section is limited to that part of the trust to which (b)(1)-(4) of this section applies.

(d) A person may not bring an action with respect to a claim allowed under (b)(1) of this section if the person

(1) Is a creditor when the trust is created unless the action is brought within the later of

(A) Four years after the transfer is made; or

(B) One year after the transfer is or reasonably could have been discovered by the person; or

(2) Becomes a creditor subsequent to the transfer unless the action is brought within four years after the transfer is made.

(e) In this section, "settlor" means a person who transfers real property, personal property, or an interest in real or personal property, in trust.

Sec. 9. This Act does not apply to a trust unless the trust is created on or after the effective date of this Act.

Sec. 10. This Act takes effect immediately under AS 01.10.10.070(c).

APPENDIX H

Delaware Trust Statute

DELAWARE 139TH GENERAL ASSEMBLY

HOUSE BILL 356

HOUSE OF REPRESENTATIVES
139TH GENERAL ASSEMBLY
HOUSE SUBSTITUTE NO. 1
TO
HOUSE BILL NO. 356
1997 DE H.B. 356
AN ACT TO AMEND TITLE 12, DELAWARE CODE, RELATING TO
QUALIFIED DISPOSITIONS IN TRUST.

SYNOPSIS

The purpose of the Act is to facilitate the establishment in Delaware of
irrevocable trusts that will allow trust settlors to transfer assets from
their estates, in order to reduce the federal estate taxes that would
otherwise be due upon their death. In order to effectively remove such
assets from their estates, the settlors cannot retain any enforceable right
to the income or principal of the trusts, but may receive wholly discretionary distributions of income or principal if the trustee is not a related
or subordinate party. In addition, these trusts cannot be subject to the
claims of the settlors' creditors if they are to be excluded from the
settlors' estates. The Act renders these trusts fully subject to (1) obligations to children, spouses and former spouses under a domestic
agreement or court order, (2) obligations to any creditor who was
induced by a settlor to extend credit on the strength of the settlor's
financial statement or other written representation that the trust assets
were available to satisfy the debt; and (3) claims arising out of fraudulent transfers if such claims are brought within the time limits provided
for in this Act.

The Act is similar to legislation recently enacted in Alaska. It is intended to maintain Delaware's role as the most favored domestic jurisdiction for the establishment of trusts.

BE IT ENACTED BY THE GENERAL ASSEMBLY OF THE STATE OF DELAWARE:

Section 1. Amend Chapter 35, Title 12, by adding thereto a new subchapter, which subchapter shall read in its entirety as follows:

"Subchapter VI. Qualified Dispositions in Trust.

Section 3570. Definitions.

As used in this subchapter:

(1) 'Claim' means a right to payment, whether or not the right is reduced to judgment, liquidated, unliquidated, fixed, contingent, matured, unmatured, disputed, undisputed, legal, equitable, secured or unsecured.

(2) 'Creditor' means, with respect to a transferor, a person who has a claim.

(3) 'Debt' means liability on a claim.

(4) 'Disposition' means a transfer, conveyance or assignment of property, or the exercise of a power so as to cause a transfer of property, to a trustee.

(5) 'Property' includes real property, personal property, and interests in real or personal property.

(6) 'Qualified Disposition' means a disposition by or from a transferor to a trustee, with or without consideration, by means of a trust instrument.

(7) 'Transferor' means a person who, as an owner of property or as a holder of a general power of appointment, directly or indirectly makes a disposition or causes a disposition to be made.

(8) 'Trustee' means a person who:

a. In the case of natural person, is a resident of this State or, in all other cases, is authorized by the law of this State to act as a trustee and whose activities are subject to supervision by the Bank Commissioner of the State, the Federal Deposit Insurance Corporation, the Comptroller of the Currency, or the Office of Thrift Supervision or any successor thereto; and

b. Maintains or arranges for custody in this State of some or all of the property transferred to the trustee, maintains records for the trust on an exclusive or nonexclusive basis, prepares or arranges for the preparation of fiduciary income tax returns for the trust, or otherwise materially participates in the administration of the trust.

(9) 'Trust instrument' means an instrument appointing a trustee for the property that is the subject of a disposition, which instrument:

    a. Expressly incorporates the law of this State to govern the validity, construction and administration of the trust;

    b. Is irrevocable, but a trust instrument shall not be deemed revocable on account of its inclusion of one or more of the following: a transferor's power to veto a distribution from a trust, a testamentary special power of appointment or similar power vested in the transferor, or the transferor's potential or actual receipt of a distribution of income, principal, or both, in the sole discretion of a trustee who is neither the transferor nor a related or subordinate party of the transferor within the meaning of 26 U.S.C. Section 672(c); and

    c. Provides that the interest of a beneficiary in the trust property or the income therefrom may not be transferred or assigned, whether voluntarily or involuntarily, before the trustee distributes the property or income to the beneficiary.

Section 3571. No retained interest of transferor.

A qualified disposition that requires a trustee to distribute all or any part of the trust's income or principal, or both, to the transferor shall not be entitled to any rights or benefits arising under Section 3572, but a qualified disposition shall remain subject to Section 3572 notwithstanding that the trustee has the sole discretion, exercisable without regard to any ascertainable standard, to distribute trust income or principal, or both, to the transferor if such trustee is neither the transferor nor a related party or subordinate party of the transferor within the meaning of 26 U.S.C. Section 672(c).

Section 3572. Avoidance of qualified dispositions.

    (a) Notwithstanding any other provision of this Code, no action of any kind, including, without limitation, an action to enforce a judgment entered by a court or other body having adjudicative authority, shall be brought at law or in equity for an attachment or other provisional remedy against property that is the subject of a qualified disposition or for avoidance of a qualified disposition unless such action shall be brought pursuant to the provisions of Section 1304 or Section 1305 of Title 6.

    (b) Notwithstanding the provisions of section 1309 of Title 6, a creditor may not bring an action under subsection (a) hereof if:

    (1) The creditor's claim against the transferor arose before the qualified disposition was made unless the action is brought within 4 years after the qualified disposition is made or, if later, within 1 year after the qualified disposition was or could reasonably have been discovered by the creditor; or

(2) The creditor's claim against the transferor arose subsequent to the qualified disposition unless the action is brought within 4 years after the qualified disposition is made.

Section 3573. Persons not subject to qualified dispositions.

Notwithstanding the provisions of Section 3572, this subchapter shall not apply in any respect:

(a) To any person to whom the transferor is indebted on account of an agreement or order of court for the payment of support or alimony in favor of such transferor's spouse, former spouse or children, or for a division of distribution of property in favor of such transferor's spouse or former spouse, to the extent of such debt; or

(b) To any creditor who became a creditor of the transferor in reliance upon an express written statement of the transferor that any property that was the subject of the qualified disposition thereafter remained the property of the transferor and was available to satisfy any debt to such creditor incurred by the transferor; or

(c) To any person who suffers death, personal injury or property damage on or before the date of a qualified disposition by a transferor, which death, personal injury or property damage is at any time determined to have been caused in whole or in part by the act or omission of either such transferor or by another person for whom such transferor is or was vicariously liable.

Section 3574. Effect of avoidance of qualified dispositions.

(a) A qualified disposition shall be avoided only to the extent necessary to satisfy the transferor's debt to the creditor at whose instance the disposition had been avoided, together with such costs, including attorneys fees, as the court may allow.

(b) In the event any qualified disposition shall be avoided as provided in subsection (a) hereof then:

(1) If the court is satisfied that the trustee has not acted in bad faith in accepting or administering the property that is the subject of the qualified disposition,

a. The trustee shall have a first and paramount lien against the property that is the subject of the qualified disposition in an amount equal to the entire cost, including attorneys fees, properly incurred by the trustee in the defense of the action or proceedings to avoid the qualified disposition; and

b. The qualified disposition shall be avoided subject to the proper fees, costs, preexisting rights, claims and interests of the trustee (and of any predecessor trustee that has not acted in bad faith); and

c. For purposes of this subparagraph (1), it shall be presumed that the trustee did not act in bad faith merely by accepting such property; and

(2) If the court is satisfied that a beneficiary of a trust has not acted in bad faith, the avoidance of the qualified disposition shall be subject to the right of such beneficiary to retain any distribution made upon the exercise of a trust power or discretion vested in the trustee of such trust, which power or discretion was properly exercised prior to the creditor's commencement of an action to avoid the qualified disposition.

Section 3575. Application of subchapter.

This subchapter shall apply to qualified dispositions made on or after July 1, 1997.

Section 3576. Short title.

This subchapter may be cited as the "Qualified Dispositions in Trust Act."

Section 2. This Act shall become effective upon its enactment.

APPENDIX I

Trustee Act 1975 (as amended by the Trustee Amendment Act 1999, effective 10 July 1999) (Bermuda)[1]

ARRANGEMENT OF SECTIONS

[1] The authors thank Alex Anderson, with the law firm of Conyers Dill & Pearman, for providing them with this copy of the Trustee Act 1975 (as amended by the Trustee Amendment Act 1999, effective 10 July 1999). Conyers Dill & Pearman is located at the following address: Conyers Dill & Pearman, Barristers & Attorneys, Clarendon House, 2 Church Street, P.O.Box HM 666, Hamilton, Bermuda HM CX, Telephone: (441) 295-1422, Facsimile: (441) 292-4720.

Appendix I

PART VI—GENERAL PROVISIONS

FIRST SCHEDULE—AUTHORIZED INVESTMENTS

SECOND SCHEDULE—ENACTMENTS REPEALED (omitted)

BERMUDA
1975:2

TRUSTEE ACT 1975
(as amended by the Trustee Amendment Act 1999, effective 10 July 1999)

[31 January 1975]

[preamble and words of enactment omitted]

PART I
PRELIMINARY

Interpretation

1. In this Act, unless the context otherwise requires—

"authorized investments" means investments authorized by the instrument, if any, creating the trust for the investment of money subject to the trust, or by any provision of law;

"contingent right" as applied to land includes a contingent or executory interest, a possibility coupled with an interest, whether the object of the gift or limitation of the interest, or possibility is or is not ascertained, also a right of entry, whether immediate or future, and whether vested or contingent;

"convey" and "conveyance" as applied to any person include the execution by that person of every necessary or suitable assurance for conveying, assigning, appointing, surrendering, or otherwise transferring or disposing of land whereof he is seized or possessed, or wherein he is entitled to a contingent right, either for his whole estate or for any less estate, together with the performance of all formalities required by law for the validity of the conveyance;

"court" means the Supreme Court;

"estate representative" means the executor, original or by representation, or administrator for the time being of a deceased person;

"income" includes rents and profits;

"instrument" includes a statutory provision;

"mortgage" and "mortgagee" relate to every estate and interest regarded in equity as merely a security for money, and every person deriving title under the original mortgagee;

"pay" as applied in relation to stocks and securities in connection with the expression "into court" includes a deposit or transfer of the same in or into court;

"possession" includes receipt of rents and profits or the right to receive the same, if any; and "possessed" applies to receipt of income of and to any vested estate less than a life estate or interest in possession or in expectancy in any land;

"property" includes real and personal property, and any estate, share and interest in any property, real or personal, and any debt, and any thing in action, and any other right or interest, whether in possession or not;

"rights" include estates and interests;

"sale" includes an exchange;

"securities" include stocks, funds and shares and "securities payable to bearer" include securities transferable by delivery or by delivery and endorsement;

"stock" includes fully paid up shares, and so far as relates to vesting orders made by the court under this Act, includes any fund, annuity, or security transferable in books kept by any company or society, or by instrument of transfer either alone or accompanied by other formalities, and any share or interest therein;

"transfer" in relation to stock or securities, includes the performance and execution of every deed, power of attorney, act, and thing on the part of the transferor to effect and complete the title in the transferee;

"trust" does not include the duties incident to an estate or interest conveyed by way of mortgage, but with this exception the expressions "trust" and "trustee" extend to implied and constructive trusts, and to cases where the trustee has a beneficial interest in the trust property, and to the duties incident to the office of an estate representative, and "trustee" includes an estate representative, and "new trustee" includes an additional trustee;

"trust corporation" means—

(a) a corporation either appointed by the court in any particular case to be a trustee or licensed as a trust company under the Trust Companies Act 1991;[2] and

---

[2] Deemed to have come into force in accordance with Section 30 of the Trust Companies Act 1991 (i.e., 6 September 1991 or, in case of a company carrying on trust business immediately before that day, or 6 September 1992); any done during the validation period by a trust company purporting to act as a trust corporation shall be deemed to have been validly done when done. (Section 2(2) TAA.)

(b) the person for the time being holding office as public trustee in his capacity as corporation sole under the Public Trustee Act 1906 of the Parliament of the United Kingdom;

"trust for sale" in relation to land means an immediate trust for sale, whether or not exercisable at the request or with the consent of any person, and with or without power at discretion to postpone the sale;

"trust funds" include any funds in the hands of a trustee, whether at the time in a state of investment or not.

Application of Act

2. (1) This Act, except where otherwise expressly provided, applies to trusts including, so far as this Act applies thereto, executorships and administratorships constituted or created either before, on or after 1 March 1975.

(2) The powers conferred by this Act on trustees are in addition to the powers conferred by the instrument, if any, creating the trust, but those powers, unless otherwise stated, apply if and so far only as a contrary intention is not expressed in the instrument, if any, creating the trust, and have effect subject to the terms of that instrument.

(3) This Act does not affect the legality or validity of anything done before 1 March 1975, except as otherwise herein expressly provided.

PART II
GENERAL POWERS OF TRUSTEES AND ESTATE REPRESENTATIVES

General Powers

Power of trustees to sell by auction etc.

3. (1) Where a trust for sale or a power of sale of property is vested in a trustee, he may sell or concur with any other person in selling all or any part of the property, either subject to prior charges or not, and either together or in lots, by public auction or by private contract, subject to any such conditions respecting title or evidence of title or other matter as the trustee thinks fit, with power to vary any contract for sale, and to buy in at any auction, or to rescind any contract for sale and to re-sell, without being answerable for any loss.

(2) Where a trust for sale or a power of sale of land held on lease is vested in a trustee, he may make, on such terms and conditions as he may think proper, a sub-lease of the land or any part thereof with a nominal reversion, where such sub-lease amounts in substance to a sale and the trustees have satisfied themselves that it is the most appropriate method of disposing of the land.

(3) Where trustees lease any land pursuant to any power conferred on them by subsection (2) they may sell any rent reserved on any reversion expectant upon the determination of such lease.

(4) Where any sub-lease purports to have been made in exercise of a power conferred by this section, that power shall, until the contrary is proved, be assumed to have been properly exercised and—

(a) the sub-lessee shall not, either before or on the execution of the sub-lease, be concerned to see or enquire whether a case has arisen to authorise the execution of that sublease; and

(b) neither the sub-lessee nor any of his successors in title shall be concerned to see to the application of any moneys paid in consideration of the lease.

(5) A trust or power to sell or dispose of land includes a trust or power to see or dispose of part thereof whether the division is horizontal, vertical, or made in any other way.

(6) (a) A trust or power to sell or dispose of land includes a power, either with or without consideration, to grant by writing an option to purchase or take a lease of the land, or any part thereof, or any easement, right, or privilege over or in relation to the same, at a price or rent fixed at the time of granting the option;

(b) every such option shall be made exercisable within an agreed number of years not exceeding ten.

Power to sell subject to depreciatory conditions

4. (1) No sale made by a trustee shall be impeached by any beneficiary upon the ground that any of the conditions subject to which the sale was made may have been unnecessarily depreciatory, unless it also appears that the consideration for the sale was thereby rendered inadequate.

(2) No sale made by a trustee shall, after the execution of the conveyance, be impeached as against the purchaser upon the ground that any of the conditions subject to which the sale was made may have been unnecessarily depreciatory, unless it appears that the purchaser was acting in collusion with the trustee at the time when the contract for sale was made.

(3) No purchaser, upon any sale made by a trustee, shall be at liberty to make any objection against the title upon any of the grounds aforesaid.

(4) This section applies to sales and purchases made before, on or after 1 March 1975.

Power of trustee to give receipts

5. The receipt in writing of any trustee for any money, securities, or other personal property or effects payable, transferable, or deliverable to

him under any trust or power shall be a sufficient discharge for the same, and shall effectually exonerate the person paying, transferring, or delivering the same from seeing to the application or being answerable for any loss or misapplication thereof.

Power to compound liabilities

6. (1) Any one of several estate representatives, or a sole estate representative, or two or more trustees acting together, or a sole acting trustee where by the instrument, if any, creating the trust, or by any statutory provision, a sole trustee is authorised to execute the trusts and powers reposed in him, may, if and as he or they think fit—

(a) accept any property, real or personal, before the time at which it is made transferable or payable; or

(b) sever and apportion any blended trust funds or property; or

(c) pay or allow any debt or claim on any evidence that he or they may think sufficient; or

(d) accept any composition or any security, real or personal, for any debt or for any property, real or personal, claimed; or

(e) allow any time for payment of any debt; or

(f) compromise, compound, abandon, submit to arbitration, or otherwise settle any debt, account, claim, or thing whatever relating to the trust,

and for any of those purposes may enter into, give, execute, and do such agreements, instruments of composition or arrangement, releases, and other things as to him or them seem expedient, without being responsible for any loss occasioned by any act or thing so done by him or them in good faith.

Power to raise money by sale, mortgage, etc.

7. (1) Where trustees are authorised by the instrument, if any, creating the trust or by any provision of law to pay or apply capital money subject to the trust for any purpose or in any manner, they shall have and shall be deemed always to have had power to raise the money required by sale, conversion, calling in, or mortgage of all or any part of the trust property for the time being in possession.

(2) This section applies notwithstanding anything to the contrary contained in the instrument, if any, creating the trust.

Protection to purchasers and mortgages dealing with trustees

8. No purchaser or mortgagee, paying or advancing money on a sale or mortgage purporting to be made under any trust or power vested in the trustees, shall be concerned to see that such money is wanted, or that

no more than is wanted is raised, or otherwise as to the application thereof.

Devolution of powers or trusts

9. (1) Where a power or trust is given to or imposed on two or more trustees jointly, the same may be exercised or performed by the survivors or survivor of them for the time being.

(2) Until the appointment of new trustees, the estate representatives or representative for the time being of a sole trustee, or, where there were two or more trustees, of the last surviving or continuing trustee, shall be capable of exercising or performing any power or trust, which was given to, or capable of being exercised by, the sole or last surviving or continuing trustee, or other the trustees or trustee for the time being of the trust.

(3) In this section "estate representative" does not include an executor who has renounced or has not proved.

Power to insure

10. A trustee may insure against loss or damage from any cause any building or other insurable property to any amount, including the amount of any insurance already in force, not exceeding the full value of the building or property, and pay the premiums for such insurance out of the income thereof or out of the income of any other property subject to the same trusts without obtaining the consent of any person who may be entitled wholly or partly to such income.

Application of insurance money where policy kept up under any trust, power or obligation

11. (1) Money receivable by trustees or any beneficiary under a policy of insurance against the loss or damage of any property subject to a trust or settlement, from whatever cause, shall, where the policy has been kept up under any trust in that behalf or under any power statutory or otherwise, or in performance of any covenant or of any obligation statutory or otherwise, be capital money for the purposes of the trust or settlement, as the case may be.

(2) If any such money is receivable by any person, other than the trustees of the trust or settlement, that person shall use his best endeavours to recover and receive the money, and shall pay the net residue thereof, after discharging any costs of recovering and receiving it, to the trustees of the trust or settlement, or, if there are no trustees capable of giving a discharge therefor, into court.

(3) Any such money—

(a) if it was receivable in respect of property held upon trust for sale, shall be held upon the trusts and subject to the powers and provisions applicable to money arising by a sale under such trust;

(b) in any other case, it shall be held upon trusts corresponding as nearly as may be with the trusts affecting the property in respect of which it was payable.

(4) Such money, or any part thereof, may also be applied by the trustees, or, if in court, under the direction of the court, in rebuilding, reinstating, replacing, or repairing the property lost or damaged, but any such application by the trustees shall be subject to the consent of any person whose consent is required by the instrument, if any, creating the trust to the investment of money subject to the trust.

(5) Nothing contained in this section prejudices or affects the right of any person to require any such money or any part thereof to be applied in rebuilding, reinstating, or repairing the property lost or damaged, or the rights of any mortgagee, lessor, or lessee, whether under any statutory provision or otherwise.

(6) This section applies to policies effected either before, on or after 1 March 1975, but only to money received after such date.

Power of trustees of renewable leaseholds to renew and raise money for the purpose

12. (1) Subject to subsection (2), a trustee of any leaseholds for lives or years which are renewable from time to time either under any covenant or contract may, if he thinks fit, use his best endeavours to obtain from time to time a renewed lease of the same hereditaments on reasonable terms, and for that purpose may from time to time make or concur in making a surrender of the lease for the time being subsisting and do all such other acts as are requisite.

(2) Where by the terms of the instrument, if any, creating the trust the person in possession for his life or other limited interest is entitled to enjoy the same without any obligation to renew or to contribute to the expense of renewal, this section shall not apply unless the consent in writing of that person is obtained to the renewal on the part of the trustee.

Deposit of documents for safe custody

13. Trustees may deposit any documents held by them relating to the trust, or to the trust property, with any bank or trust company, and any sum payable in respect of such deposit shall be paid out of the income of the trust property.

Reversionary interests, valuations, and audit

14. (1) Where trust property includes any share, estate or interest in property not vested in the trustees, or the proceeds of the sale of any such

property, or any other thing in action, the trustees on the same falling into possession, or becoming payable or transferable may—

(a) agree or ascertain the amount or value thereof or any part thereof in such manner as they may think fit;

(b) accept in or towards satisfaction thereof, at the market or current value, or upon any valuation or estimate of value which they may think fit, any authorised investments;

(c) allow any deductions for duties, costs, charges and expenses which they may think proper or reasonable;

(d) execute any release in respect of the premises so as effectually to discharge all accountable parties from all liability in respect of any matters coming within the scope of such release,

without being responsible in any such case for any loss occasioned by any act or thing so done by them in good faith.

(2) The trustees shall not be under any obligation and shall not be chargeable with any breach of trust by reason of any omission—

(a) to apply for a writ of distringas or any stop or other like order upon any securities or other property out of or on which such share, estate or interest or other thing in action as aforesaid is derived, payable or charged; or

(b) to take any proceedings on account of any act, default, or neglect on the part of the persons in whom such securities or other property or any of them or any part thereof are for the time being, or had at any time been, vested;

unless and until required in writing so to do by some person, or the guardian of some person, beneficially interested under the trust, and unless also due provision is made to their satisfaction for payment of the costs of any proceedings required to be taken so, however, that nothing in this subsection shall relieve the trustees of the obligation to get in and obtain payment or transfer of such share, estate or interest or other thing in action on the same falling into possession.

(3) Trustees may, for the purpose of giving effect to the trust, or any of the provisions of the instrument, if any, creating the trust or of any Act, from time to time (by suitably qualified agents) ascertain and fix the value of any trust property in such manner as they think proper, and any valuation so made in good faith shall be binding upon all persons interested under the trust.

(4) Trustees may, in their absolute discretion, from time to time, but not more than once in every three years unless the nature of the trust or any special dealings with the trust property make a more frequent exercise of the right reasonable, cause the accounts of the trust property to be examined or audited by an independent accountant, and shall, for that purpose, produce such vouchers and give such information to him as he may require;

and the costs of such examination or audit, including the fee of the auditor, shall be paid out of the capital or income of the trust property, or partly in one way and partly in the other, as the trustees, in their absolute discretion, think fit, but, in default of any direction by the trustees to the contrary in any special case, costs attributable to capital shall be borne by capital and those attributable to income by income.

Power to delegate certain functions by estate representatives

15. (1) This section is subject to the terms of the will, if any.

(2) Estate representatives may delegate all or any of their functions as estate representative to—

(a) a delegate; or

(b) one of the estate representatives (a "co-estate representative"),

and may pay such delegate or co-estate representative out of the property of the estate, whether income or capital or partly each as they may think fit.

(3) Subsections 15A(3) and (4) apply, with the necessary changes, to the exercise of the power of delegation under subsection (2).

Power to delegate certain functions by trustees

15A. (1) This section and section 15B are subject to the terms of the trust, and without prejudice to any of the powers conferred by sections 17 and 24.

(2) Trustees of a trust may delegate any or all of their delegable functions to—

(a) a delegate, or

(b) one of the trustees (a "co-trustee"),

and may pay such delegate or co-trustee out of the trust property, whether income or capital or partly each as they may see fit.

(3) In exercising any power to delegate, and in supervising the delegate, the trustees shall exercise reasonable care, skill and caution.

(4) Delegation under this section to a delegate, but not to a co-trustee, may be made on terms which—

(a) limit the liability of the delegate;

(b) do not prohibit actual or potential conflicts of interest in dealing with the trust property; or

(c) permit sub-delegation, including on such terms as are mentioned in paragraphs (a) and (b);

and the trustees shall not, by reason of delegating on such terms, be responsible for the act or default of any delegate or sub-delegate, provided that the trustees honestly believed delegation to that delegate on those terms to be in the best interests of the trust as a whole.

(5) In this section "trustee" does not include an estate representative.

Meaning of "delegable functions"

15B. (1) For the purposes of section 15A, "delegable functions" shall be interpreted in accordance with this section.

(2) Functions of an administrative or managerial nature (including discretionary investment powers) are delegable functions.

(3) The following functions are not delegable—

(a) the formulation of policy criteria governing the investment or other application of trust property, and any decision as to the amount of money that may be raised on the security of trust property;

(b) the exercise of any discretionary duties or powers concerning distribution of income or capital to, or use of the trust property by, persons beneficially interested under the trust, or the appropriation of trust property in satisfaction of a beneficiary's entitlement to any capital;

(c) the exercise of any power to determine or to alter any interest of a person beneficially interested under the trust, including a power to deal with income or capital expenditure or receipts as if they were not of such income or capital nature and a power to bring, forward or postpone the closing date for the total or partial termination of the trust;

(d) the exercise of any power to add a person or class of persons to, or exclude a person or class of person from, those who are beneficially interested under the trust;

(e) the exercise of any power to add to, revoke or vary the administrative powers under the trust or to release or restrict any powers under the trust;

(f) the exercise of any power to appoint or remove trustees;

(g) the exercise of any power to change the proper law governing the validity, administration or any other severable aspect of the trust.

Power to concur with others

16. Where an undivided share in the proceeds of sale of land directed to be sold, or in any other property, is subject to a trust, or forms part of the estate of a testator or intestate, the trustees or estate representatives may (without prejudice to any trust for sale affecting the entirety of the land and the powers of the trustees for sale in reference thereto) execute or exercise any trust or power vested in them in relation to such share in conjunction with the persons entitled to or having power in that behalf over the other share or shares, and notwithstanding that any one or more of the trustees or estate representatives may be entitled to or interested in any such other share, either in his or their own right or in a fiduciary capacity.

Appendix I

Power to delegate trusts during absence abroad

17. (1) A trustee intending to remain out of Bermuda may, notwithstanding any rule of law or equity to the contrary, by power of attorney, delegate to any person (including a trust corporation) the execution or exercise during his absence from Bermuda of all or any trusts, powers and discretions vested in him as such trustee, either alone or jointly with any other person or persons so, however, that a person being the only other co-trustee and not being a trust corporation shall not be appointed to be an attorney under this subsection.

(2) The donor of a power of attorney given under this section shall be liable for the acts or defaults of the donee in the same manner as if they were the acts or defaults of the donor.

(3) The power of attorney shall not come into operation unless and until the donor is out of Bermuda, and shall be revoked by his return.

(4) In favour of any person dealing with the donee, any act done or instrument executed by the donee shall, notwithstanding that the power has never come into operation or has been revoked by the act of the donor or by his death or return to Bermuda or otherwise, be as valid and effectual as if the donor were alive and of full capacity, and had himself done such act or executed such instrument, unless such person had actual notice that the power had never come into operation or of the revocation of the power before such act was done or instrument executed.

(5) For the purpose of executing or exercising the trusts or powers delegated to him, the donee may exercise any of the powers conferred on the donor as trustee by any Act or by the instrument creating the trust, including power, for the purpose of the transfer of any securities, himself to delegate to an attorney power to transfer such securities but not including the power of delegation conferred by this section.

(6) The fact that it appears from any power of attorney given under this section, or from any evidence required for the purposes of any such power of attorney or otherwise, that in dealing with any securities the donee of the power is acting in the execution of a trust shall not be deemed for any purpose to affect any person in whose books the securities are registered with any notice of the trust.

Protection against liability in respect of rents and covenants

18. (1) Where an estate representative or trustee liable for—

(a) any rent, covenant, or agreement reserved by or contained in any lease; or

(b) any rent, covenant or agreement payable under or contained in any grant made in consideration of a rent charge; or

(c) any indemnity given in respect of any rent, covenant or agreement referred to in either of the foregoing paragraphs,

satisfies all liabilities under the lease or grant which may have accrued, and been claimed, up to the date of the conveyance hereinafter mentioned, and, where necessary, sets apart a sufficient fund to answer any future claim that may be made in respect of any fixed and ascertained sum which the lessee or grantee agreed to lay out on the property demised or granted, although the period for laying out the same may not have arrived, then and in any such case the estate representative or trustee may convey the property demised or granted to a purchaser, legatee, devisee, or other person entitled to call for a conveyance thereof and thereafter—

(a) he may distribute the residuary real and personal estate of the deceased testator or intestate, or, as the case may be, the trust estate (other than the fund, if any, set apart as aforesaid) to or amongst the persons entitled thereto, without appropriating any part, or any further part, as the case may be, of the estate of the deceased or of the trust estate to, meet any future liability under the said lease or grant;

(b) notwithstanding such distribution, he shall not be personally liable in respect of any subsequent claim under the said lease or grant.

(2) This section operates without prejudice to the right of the lessor or grantor, or the persons deriving title under the lessor or grantor, to follow the assets of the deceased or the trust property into the hands of the persons amongst whom the same may have been respectively distributed, and applies notwithstanding anything to the contrary in the will or other instrument, if any, creating the trust.

(3) In this section "lease" includes an underlease and an agreement for a lease or underlease and any instrument giving any such indemnity as aforesaid or varying the liabilities under the lease; "grant" applies to a grant whether the rent is created by limitation, grant, reservation, or otherwise, and includes an agreement for a grant and any instrument giving any such indemnity as aforesaid or varying the liabilities under the grant; "lessee" and "grantee" include persons respectively deriving title under them.

Protection by means of advertisements

19. (1)

With a view to the conveyance to, or distribution among, the persons entitled to any real or personal property, the trustees of a settlement or of a disposition on trust for sale may give notice by advertisement published three times at intervals of not less than one week in a newspaper for the time being approved as the Gazette, of their intention to make such conveyance or distribution as aforesaid, and requiring any person interested to send to the trustees within the time, not being less than one month from the publication of the last of the notices, fixed in the notice, particulars of his claim in respect of the property or any part thereof to which the notice relates.

(2) At the expiration of the time fixed by the notice the trustees may convey or distribute the property or any part thereof to which the notice relates, to or among the persons entitled thereto, having regard only to the claims, whether formal or not, of which the trustees then had notice and shall not, as respects the property so conveyed or distributed, be liable to any person whose claim the trustees have not had notice at the time of conveyance or distribution; but nothing in this section—

(a) prejudices the right of any person to follow the property, or any property representing the same, into the hands of any person, other than a purchaser, who may have received it; or

(b) frees the trustees from any obligation to make inquiries and searches or obtain official certificates of search similar to those which an intending purchaser would be advised to make or obtain.

(3) This section applies notwithstanding anything to the contrary in the will or other instrument, if any, creating the trust.

(4) This section does not apply to the protection of estate representatives by means of advertisements under section 53 of the Administration of Estates Act 1974 [title 26 item 12].

Protection in regard to notice

20. A trustee or estate representative acting for the purposes of more than one trust or estate shall not, in the absence of fraud, be affected by notice of any instrument, matter, fact or thing in relation to any particular trust or estate if he has obtained notice thereof merely by reason of his acting or having acted for the purposes of another trust or estate.

Power of trustees to pay to attorney appointed by beneficiary

21. A trustee acting or paying money in good faith under or in pursuance of any power of attorney shall not be liable for any such act or payment by reason of the fact that at the time of the act or payment the person who gave the power of attorney was subject to any disability or bankrupt or dead, or had done or suffered some act or thing to avoid the power, if this fact was not known to the trustee at the time of his so acting or paying so, however, that—

(a) nothing in this section shall affect the right of any person entitled to the money against the person to whom the payment is made;

(b) the person so entitled shall have the same remedy against the person to whom the payment is made as he would have had against the trustee.

Implied indemnity of trustees

22. (1) A trustee shall be chargeable only for money and securities actually received by him notwithstanding his signing any receipt for the sake of conformity, and shall be answerable and accountable only for his own acts, receipts, neglects, or defaults, and not for those of any other trustee, nor for those of any bank, broker, or other person with whom any trust money or securities may be deposited, nor for the insufficiency or deficiency of any securities, nor for any other loss, unless the same happens through his own deliberate, reckless or negligent breach of an equitable duty.

(2) A trustee may reimburse himself or pay or discharge out of the trust premises all expenses incurred in or about the execution of the trusts or powers.

Remuneration of trust corporations

22A. Subject to—

(a) any contrary intention in the terms of the trust, or

(b) any order of a court,

a trust corporation shall be entitled to reasonable remuneration for its services as trustee, in addition to reimbursement of its expenses under section 22(2).

Power to apply income for maintenance and to accumulate surplus income during a minority

23. (1) Where any property is held by trustees in trust for any person for any estate or interest whatsoever, whether vested or contingent, then, subject to any prior estates or interests or charges affecting that property—

(a) during the infancy of any such person, if his estate or interest so long continues, the trustees may, at their sole discretion, pay to his parent or guardian, if any, or otherwise apply for or towards his maintenance or education, or otherwise for his benefit, the whole or such part, if any, of the income of that property as may, in all the circumstances, be reasonable, whether or not there is—

(i) any other fund applicable to the same purpose; or

(ii) any person bound by law to provide for his maintenance or education; and

(b) if such person on attaining the age of twenty-one years has not a vested estate or interest in such income, the trustees shall thenceforth pay the income of that property and of any accretion thereto under subsection (3) to him, until he either attains a vested estate or interest therein or dies, or until failure of his estate or interest.

(2) In deciding whether the whole or any part of the income of the property is during a minority to be paid or applied for the purposes aforesaid, the trustees shall have regard to the age of the infant and his requirements and generally to the circumstances of the case, and in particular to what other income, if any, is applicable for the same purposes; and where trustees have notice that the income of more than one fund is applicable for those purposes, then, so far as practicable, unless the entire income of the funds is paid or applied as aforesaid or the court otherwise directs, a proportionate part only of the income of each fund shall be so paid or applied.

(3) During the infancy of any such person, if his estate or interest so long continues, the trustees shall accumulate all the residue of that income in the way of compound interest by investing the same and the resulting income thereof from time to time in authorised investments, and shall hold those accumulations as follows:—

(a) if any such person—

(i) attains the age of twenty-one years, or marries under that age, and his estate or interest in such income during his infancy or until his marriage is a vested estate or interest; or

(ii) on attaining the age of twenty-one years or on marriage under that age becomes entitled to the property from which such income arose in fee simple, or absolutely, or for an entailed estate or interest,

the trustees shall hold the accumulation in trust for such person absolutely, but without prejudice to any provision with respect thereto contained in any settlement by him made under any statutory powers during his infancy, and so that the receipt of such person after marriage, and though still an infant, shall be a good discharge; and

(b) in any other case the trustees shall, notwithstanding that such person had a vested estate or interest in such income, hold the accumulations as an accretion to the capital of the property from which such accumulations arose, and as one fund with such capital for all purposes, and so that, if such property is settled land, such accumulations shall be held upon the same trusts as if the same were capital money arising therefrom,

but the trustees may, at any time during the infancy of such person if his estate or interest so long continues, apply those accumulations, or any part thereof, as if they were income arising in the then current year.

(4) This section applies in the case of a contingent estate or interest only if the limitation or trust carries the intermediate income of the property, but it applies to a future or contingent legacy by the parent of, or a person standing in loco parentis to, the legatee, if and for such period as,

under any provision of law, the legacy carries interest for the maintenance of the legatee, and in any such case at last aforesaid the rate of interest shall (if the income available is sufficient, and subject to any rules of court to the contrary) be five per centum per annum.

(5) This section applies to a vested annuity in like manner as if the annuity were the income of property held by trustees in trust to pay the income thereof to the annuitant for the same period for which the annuity is payable, save that in any case accumulations made during the infancy of the annuitant shall be held in trust for the annuitant or his estate representatives absolutely.

(6) This section does not apply where the instrument, if any, under which the interest arises came into operation before 1 March 1975.

Power of advancement

24. (1) Trustees may at any time or times pay or apply any capital money subject to a trust, for the advancement or benefit, in such manner as they may, in their absolute discretion, think fit, of any person entitled to the capital of the trust property or of any share thereof, whether absolutely or contingently on his attaining any specified age or on the occurrence of any other event, or subject to a gift over on his death under any specified age or on the occurrence of any other event, and whether in possession or in remainder or reversion, and such payment or application may be made notwithstanding that the estate or interest of such person is liable to be defeated by the exercise of a power of appointment or revocation, or to be diminished by the increase of the class to which he belongs so, however, that—

(a) the money so paid or applied for the advancement or benefit of any person shall not exceed altogether the amount of the presumptive or vested share, estate or interest of that person in the trust property; and

(b) if that person is or becomes absolutely and indefeasibly entitled to a share in the trust property the money so paid or applied shall be brought into account as part of such share; and

(c) no such payment or application shall be made so as to prejudice any person entitled to any prior life or other estate or interest, whether vested or contingent, in the money paid or applied unless such person is in existence and of full age and consents in writing to such payment or application.

(2) This section applies only where the trust property consists of—

(a) money or securities which are not by any provision of law or in equity considered as land; or

(b) property held upon trust for sale, calling in and conversion and the proceeds of such sale, calling in and conversion are not in equity considered as land.

(3) This section does not apply to trusts constituted or created before 1 March 1975.

(4) For the avoidance of doubt, when exercising the power of advancement the trustees may—

(a) create any provisions, including—

(i) discretionary trusts and dispositive, administrative or managerial powers exercisable by any person, and

(ii) the delegation of discretion and duties to any person; and

(b) provide that the capital money may become subject to the terms of any other trust,

provided that the requirements of subsection (1) are satisfied.

Protective trusts

25. (1) Where any income, including an annuity or other periodical income payment, is directed to be held on protective trusts for the benefit of any person (in this section referred to as "the principal beneficiary") for the period of his life or any less period, then, during that period (in this section referred to as "the trust period") the said income shall, without prejudice to any prior estate or interest be held—

(a) upon trust for the principal beneficiary until whichever of the following events shall first occur—

(i) the trust period expires; or

(ii) the principal beneficiary (whether before or after the termination of any prior estate or interests) does or attempts to do or suffers any act or thing, or until any other event (not being an advance under any statutory or express power) happens whereby, if during the trust period the said income were payable to the principal beneficiary absolutely, he would be deprived of the right to receive the same or any part thereof; and

(b) upon trust, where any of the events referred to in subparagraph (ii) of paragraph (a) happens during the subsistence of the trust period, to apply the said income (as the trustees in their absolute discretion, without being liable to account for the exercise of their discretion, think fit) for the maintenance or support, or otherwise for the benefit, of all or any one or more exclusively of the other or others of the following persons—

(i) the principal beneficiary and his or her wife or husband, if any, and his or her children or more remote issue, if any; and

(ii) if as often as and while there is no living issue of the principal beneficiary, the principal beneficiary and his or her wife or husband, if any, and the persons who, if the principal beneficiary were actually dead without having married would for the time being be his next of kin, so that the trustees in the exercise of their discretion may apply any income accrued but unapplied in any previous year for the purposes of the trusts implied as aforesaid in any subsequent year.

(2) This section does not apply to trusts coming into operation before 1 March 1968, and has effect subject to any variation of the trusts implied as aforesaid contained in the instrument creating the trust.

(3) Nothing in this section operates to validate any trust which would, if contained in the instrument creating the trust, be liable to be set aside.

PART III
APPOINTMENT AND DISCHARGE OF TRUSTEES

Power of appointing new or additional trustees

26. (1) Where a trustee, whether original, substituted or additional, and whether appointed by a court or otherwise, is dead, or remains out of Bermuda for more than twelve months, or desires to be discharged from all or any of the trusts or powers reposed in or conferred on him, or refuses or is unfit to act therein, or is incapable of acting therein, then—

(a) the person or persons nominated for the purpose of appointing new trustees by the instrument, if any, creating the trust; or

(b) if there is no such person, or no such person able and willing to act, then the surviving or continuing trustees or trustee for the time being, or the estate representatives of the last surviving or continuing trustee,

may, by writing, appoint one or more other persons (whether or not being the persons exercising the power) to be a trustee or trustees in the place of the trustee so deceased, remaining out of Bermuda, desiring to be discharged, refusing, or being unfit or being incapable, as aforesaid.

(2) Where a trustee has been removed under a power contained in the instrument creating the trust, a new trustee or new trustees may be appointed in the place of the trustee who is removed, as if he were dead, or, in the case of a corporation, as if the corporation desired to be discharged from the trust, and this section shall apply accordingly.

(3) Where a corporation being a trustee is or has been dissolved, either before, on or after 1 March 1975, then, for the purposes of this section and of any statutory provision replaced thereby, the corporation shall be deemed to be and to have been from the date of the dissolution incapable of acting in the trusts or powers reposed in or conferred on the corporation.

(4) The power of appointment given by subsection (1) or any similar previous statutory provision to the estate representatives of a last

surviving or continuing trustee shall be and shall be deemed always to have been exercisable by the executors for the time being (whether original or by representation) of such surviving or continuing trustee who have proved the will of their testator or by the administrators for the time being of such trustee without the concurrence of any executor who has renounced or has not proved.

(5) But a sole or last surviving executor intending to renounce, or all the executors where they all intend to renounce, shall have and shall be deemed always to have had power, at any time before renouncing probate, to exercise the power of appointment given by this section, or by any similar previous enactment, if willing to act for that purpose and without thereby accepting the office of executor.

(6) Where a sole trustee, other than a trust corporation, is or has been originally appointed to act in a trust, or where, in the case of any trust, there are not more than three trustees (none of them being a trust corporation) whether original, substituted or additional and whether appointed by the court or otherwise, then and in any such case—

(a) the person or persons nominated for the purpose of appointing new trustees by the instrument, if any, creating the trust; or

(b) if there is no such person, or no such person able and willing to act, then the trustee or trustees for the time being,

may, by writing, appoint one or more other persons (whether or not being the persons exercising the power) to be an additional trustee or additional trustees, but it shall not be obligatory to appoint any additional trustee unless the instrument, if any, creating the trust, or any statutory provision provides to the contrary.

(7) Every new trustee appointed under this section as well before as after all the trust property becomes by law, or by assurance, or otherwise, vested in him shall have the same powers, authorities, and discretions, and may in all respects act as if he had been originally appointed a trustee by the instrument, if any, creating the trust.

(8) The provisions of this section relating to a trustee who is dead include the case of a person nominated trustee in a will but dying before the testator, and those relative to a continuing trustee include a refusing or retiring trustee, if willing to act in the execution of the provisions of this section.

(9) Where a trustee is incapable, by reason of mental disorder within the meaning of the Mental Health Act 1968 [title 11 item 36], of exercising his functions as trustee and is also entitled in possession to some beneficial interest in the trust property, no appointment of a new trustee in his place shall be made by virtue of subsection (1)(b) unless leave to make the appointment has been given by the judicial authority appointed to act for the purposes of Part IV of the Mental Health Act 1968.

Supplemental provisions as to appointment of trustees

27. On the appointment of a trustee for the whole or any part of trust property—

(a) the number of trustees may be increased; and

(b) a separate set of trustees may be appointed for any part of the trust property held on trusts distinct from those relating to any other part or parts of the trust property, notwithstanding that no new trustees or trustee are or is to be appointed for other parts of the trust property, and any existing trustee may be appointed or remain one of such separate set of trustees, or, if only one trustee was originally appointed, then, save as hereinafter provided, one separate trustee may be so appointed; and

(c) it shall not be obligatory, save as hereinafter provided, to appoint more than one new trustee where only one trustee was originally appointed, or to fill up the original number of trustees where more than two trustees were originally appointed but, except where only one trustee was originally appointed, a trustee shall not be discharged from his trust unless there will be a trust corporation, any other body corporate, wherever incorporated, with power to act as a trustee or at least two individuals to act as trustees to perform the trust; and

(d) any assurance or thing requisite for vesting the trust property, or any part thereof, in a sole trustee, or jointly in the persons who are the trustees, shall be executed or done.

Evidence as to a vacancy in a trust

28. (1) A statement, contained in any instrument coming into operation after 1 March 1975 by which a new trustee is appointed for any purpose connected with land, to the effect that a trustee has remained out of Bermuda for more than twelve months or refuses or is unfit to act, or is incapable of acting, or that he is not entitled to a beneficial interest in the trust property in possession, shall, in favour of a bona fide purchaser, be conclusive evidence of the matter stated.

(2) In favour of such purchaser any appointment of a new trustee depending on that statement, and any vesting declaration, express or implied, consequent on the appointment, shall be valid.

Retirement of trustee without a new appointment

29. (1) Where a trustee is desirous of being discharged from the trust or a severable part of the trust, and after his discharge there will be a trust corporation, any other body corporate, wherever incorporated, with power to act as a trustee or at least two individuals to act as trustees to perform the trust, then, if such trustee as aforesaid by deed declares that he is desirous of being discharged from the trust or the severable part thereof, and if his

co-trustees and such other person, if any, as is empowered to appoint trustees, by deed consent to the discharge of the trustee, and to the vesting in the co-trustees alone of the trust property, the trustee desirous of being discharged shall be deemed to have retired from the trust or a severable part thereof, and shall, by the deed, be discharged therefrom under this Act, without any new trustee being appointed in his place.

(2) Any assurance or thing requisite for vesting the trust property in the continuing trustees alone shall be executed or done.

Vesting of trust property in new or continuing trustees

30. (1) Where by a deed a new trustee is appointed to perform any trust, then—

(a) if the deed contains a declaration by the appointor to the effect that any estate or interest in any land subject to the trust, or in any chattel so subject, or the right to recover or receive any debt or other thing in action so subject, shall vest in the persons who by virtue of the deed become or are the trustees for performing the trust, the deed shall operate, without any conveyance or assignment, to vest in those persons as joint tenants and for the purposes of the trust the estate, interest or right to which the declaration relates; and

(b) if the deed is made after 1 March 1975 and does not contain such a declaration, the deed shall, subject to any express provision to the contrary therein contained, operate as if it had contained such a declaration by the appointor extending to all the estates, interests and rights with respect to which a declaration could have been made.

(2) Where by a deed a retiring trustee is discharged under the statutory power without a new trustee being appointed, then—

(a) if the deed contains such a declaration as aforesaid by the retiring and continuing trustees, and by the other person, if any, empowered to appoint trustees, the deed shall, without any conveyance or assignment, operate to vest in the continuing trustees alone, as joint tenants, and for the purposes of the trust, the estate, interest, or right to which the declaration relates; and

(b) if the deed is made after 1 March 1975 and does not contain such a declaration, the deed shall, subject to any express provision to the contrary therein contained, operate as if it had contained such a declaration by such persons as aforesaid extending to all the estates, interests and rights with respect to which a declaration could have been made.

(3) An express vesting declaration, whether made before, on or after 1 March 1975, shall, notwithstanding that the estate, interest or right to be vested is not expressly referred to, and provided that the other statutory requirements were or are complied with, operate and be deemed always

to have operated (but without prejudice to any express provision to the contrary contained in the deed of appointment or discharge) to vest in the persons respectively referred to in subsections (1) and (2), as the case may require, such estates, interests and rights as are capable of being and ought to be vested in those persons.

(4) This section does not extend—

(a) to land conveyed by way of mortgage for securing money subject to the trust, except land conveyed on trust for securing debentures or debenture stock;

(b) to land held under a lease which contains any covenant, condition or agreement against assignment or disposing of the land without license or consent, unless, prior to the execution of the deed containing expressly or impliedly the vesting declaration, the requisite license or consent has been obtained, or unless, by virtue of any rule of law, the vesting declaration, express or implied, would not operate as a breach of covenant or give rise to a forfeiture;

(c) to any share, stock, annuity or property which is only transferable in books kept by a company or other body, or in manner directed by or under any statutory provision.

In this subsection "lease" includes an underlease and an agreement for a lease or underlease.

PART III A
MANAGING TRUSTEES

Managing trustees

30A. A trust instrument may contain provisions by virtue of which the exercise of any of the trustees' powers may be reserved to a managing trustee, and no other trustee is liable for any of the decisions, acts or transactions of the managing trustee in so far as they amount to exercise of powers reserved by the trust instrument to the managing trustee.

PART IV
POWERS OF THE COURT

Appointment of New Trustees

Power of court to appoint new trustees

31. (1) The court may, whenever it is expedient to appoint a new trustee or new trustees, and it is found inexpedient, difficult or impracticable so to do without the assistance of the court, make an order appointing a new

trustee or new trustees either in substitution for or in addition to any existing trustee or trustees, or although there is no existing trustee.

(2) In particular and without prejudice to the generality of subsection (1), the court may make an order appointing a new trustee in substitution for a trustee who is incapable, by reason of mental disorder within the meaning of the Mental Health Act 1968 [title 11 item 36], of exercising his functions as trustee, or is a bankrupt, or is a corporation which is in liquidation or has been dissolved, or who for any other reason whatsoever appears to the court to be undesirable as a trustee.

(3) An order under this section, and any consequential vesting order or conveyance, shall not operate further or otherwise as a discharge to any former or continuing trustee than an appointment of new trustees under any power for that purpose contained in any instrument would have operated.

(4) Nothing in this section gives power to appoint an executor or administrator.

Power of court to authorise remuneration

32. The court may, in any case in which the circumstances appear to it so to justify, authorise any person to charge such remuneration for his services as trustee as the court may think fit.

Powers of new trustee appointed by the court

33. Every trustee appointed by a court of competent jurisdiction shall, as well before as after the trust property becomes by law, or by assurance, or otherwise, vested in him, have the same powers, authorities, and discretions, and may in all respects act as if he had been originally appointed a trustee by the instrument, if any, creating the trust.

Vesting Orders

Vesting orders of land

34. (1) Subject to subsection (2), where—

(a) the court appoints or has appointed a trustee, or where a trustee has been appointed out of court under any statutory or express power; or

(b) a trustee entitled to or possessed of any land or estate or interest therein, whether by way of mortgage or otherwise, or entitled to a contingent right therein, either solely or jointly with any other person—

(i) is an infant; or

(ii) is out of the jurisdiction of the court; or

(iii) cannot be found, or, being a corporation, has been dissolved; or

(c) it is uncertain who was the survivor of two or more trustees jointly entitled to or possessed of any estate or interest in land; or

(d) it is uncertain whether the last trustee known to have been entitled to or possessed of any estate or interest in land is living or dead; or

(e) there is no estate representative of a deceased trustee who was entitled to or possessed of any estate or interest in land, or where it is uncertain who is the estate representative of a deceased trustee who was entitled to or possessed of any estate or interest in land; or

(f) a trustee jointly or solely entitled to or possessed of any estate or interest in land, or entitled to a contingent right therein, has been required, by or on behalf of a person entitled to require a conveyance of the land or estate or interest or a release of the right, to convey the land or estate or interest or to release the right, and has wilfully refused or neglected to convey the land or estate or interest or release the right for twenty-eight days after the date of the requirement; or

(g) land or any estate or interest therein is vested in a trustee whether by way of mortgage or otherwise, and it appears to the court to be expedient;

the court may make an order (in this Act referred to as a "vesting order") vesting the land or estate or interest therein in any such person in any such manner and for any such estate or interest as the court may direct, or releasing or disposing of the contingent right to such person as the court may direct.

(2) Where an order made under subsection (1)—

(a) is consequential on the appointment of a trustee the land or estate or interest therein shall be vested for such estate or interest as the court may direct in the persons who on the appointment are the trustees; and

(b) relates to a trustee entitled or formerly entitled jointly with another person, and such trustee is an infant or out of the jurisdiction of the court or cannot be found, or being a corporation has been dissolved, the land estate interest or right shall be vested in such other person who remains entitled, either alone or with any other person the court may appoint.

Orders as to contingent rights of unborn persons

35. Where any estate or interest in land is subject to a contingent right in an unborn person or class of unborn persons who, on coming into existence

would, in respect thereof, become entitled to or possessed of that estate or interest on any trust, the court may make an order—

(a) releasing the land or estate or interest therein from the contingent right; or

(b) vesting in any person the estate or interest to or of which the unborn person or class of unborn persons would, on coming into existence, be entitled or possessed in the land.

Vesting order in place of conveyance by infant mortgagee

36. Where any person entitled to or possessed of any estate or interest in land, or entitled to a contingent right in land, by way of security for money, is an infant, the court may make an order vesting or releasing or disposing of the estate or interest in the land or the right in like manner as in the case of an infant trustee.

Vesting order in place of conveyance by estate representative of mortgagee

37. Where—

(a) a mortgagee of land has died without having entered into possession or into the receipt of the rents and profits thereof; and

(b) the money due in respect of the mortgage has been paid to a person entitled to receive the same, or that person consents to an order for the reconveyance of the land,

the court may make an order vesting the land in such person in such manner and for such estate or interest as the court may direct, where—

(i) an estate representative or devisee of the mortgagee is out of the jurisdiction of the court or cannot be found, or, being a corporation, has been dissolved; or

(ii) an estate representative or devisee of the mortgagee on demand made by or on behalf of a person entitled to require a conveyance of the land has stated in writing that he will not convey the same or does not convey the same for the space of twenty-eight days after a proper instrument for conveying the land has been tendered to him by or on behalf of the person so entitled; or

(iii) it is uncertain which of several devisees of the mortgagee was the survivor; or

(iv) it is uncertain whether the estate representative of the mortgagee or the survivor of several devisees of the mortgagee is living or dead; or

(v) there is no estate representative to a mortgagee who has died intestate as to the land, or where the mortgagee has died, and it is uncertain who is his estate representative or devisee.

Vesting order consequential on order for sale or mortgage of land

38. Where the court gives a judgment or makes an order directing the sale or mortgage of any land, every person who is entitled to or possessed of any estate or interest in the land, or entitled to a contingent right therein, and is a party to the action or proceeding in which the judgment or order is given or made or is otherwise bound by the judgment or order, shall be deemed to be so entitled or possessed, as the case may be, as a trustee for the purposes of this Act, and the court may, if it thinks expedient, make an order vesting the land or any part thereof for such estate or interest as the court thinks fit in the purchaser or mortgagee or in any other person.

Vesting order consequential on judgment for specific performance, etc.

39. Where a judgment is given for the specific performance of a contract concerning any estate or interest in land, or for the partition, or for sale or exchange of any estate or interest in land, or generally where any judgment is given for the conveyance of any estate or interest in land either in cases arising out of the doctrine of election or otherwise, the court may declare—

(a) that any of the parties to the action are trustees of any estate or interest in the land or any part thereof within the meaning of this Act; or

(b) that the estates or interests of unborn persons who might claim under any party to the action, or under the will or voluntary settlement of any deceased person who was during his lifetime a party to the contract or transaction concerning which the judgment is given, are the estates or interests of persons who, on coming into existence, would be trustees within the meaning of this Act;

and thereupon the court may make a vesting order relating to the rights of those persons, born and unborn, as if they had been trustees.

Effect of vesting order

40. A vesting order under any of the foregoing provisions shall in the case of a vesting order consequential on the appointment of a trustee, have the same effect—

(a) as if the persons who before the appointment were the trustees, if any, had duly executed all proper conveyances of the land for such estate or interest as the court directs; or

(b) if there is no such person, or no such person of full capacity, as if such person had existed and been of full capacity and had duly executed all proper conveyances of the land for such estate or interest as the court directs,

and shall in every other case have the same effect as if the trustee or other person or description or class of persons to whose rights or supposed rights the said provisions respectively relate had been an ascertained and existing person of full capacity, and had executed a conveyance or release to the effect intended by the order.

Power to appoint person to convey

41. Where a vesting order can be made under any of the foregoing provisions, the court may, if it is more convenient, appoint a person to convey the land or any interest therein or release the contingent right, and a conveyance or release by that person in conformity with the order shall have the same effect as an order under the appropriate provision.

Vesting orders as to stock and things in action

42. (1) Subject to subsection (2), where—

(a) the court appoints or has appointed a trustee, or where a trustee has been appointed out of court under any statutory or express power; or

(b) a trustee entitled, whether by way of mortgage or otherwise, alone or jointly with another person to stock or to a thing in action—

(i) is an infant; or

(ii) is out of the jurisdiction of the court; or

(iii) cannot be found, or, being a corporation, has been dissolved; or

(iv) neglects or refuses to transfer stock or receive the dividends or income thereof, or to sue for or recover a thing in action, according to the direction of the person absolutely entitled thereto for twenty-eight days next after a request in writing has been made to him by the person so entitled; or

(v) neglects or refuses to transfer stock or receive the dividends or income thereof, or to sue for or recover a thing in action for twenty-eight days next after an order of the court for that purpose has been served on him; or

(c) it is uncertain whether a trustee entitled alone or jointly with another person to stock or to a thing in action is alive or dead; or

(d) stock is standing in the name of a deceased person whose estate representative is under disability; or

(e) stock or a thing in action is vested in a trustee whether by way of mortgage or otherwise and it appears to the court to be expedient,

the court may make an order vesting the right to transfer or call for a transfer of stock, or to receive the dividends or income thereof, or to sue for or recover the thing in action, in any such person as the court may appoint.

(2) Where—

(a) an order made under subsection (1) is consequential on the appointment of a trustee, the right shall be vested in the persons who, on the appointment, are the trustees; and

(b) the person whose right is dealt with by an order made under subsection (1) was entitled jointly with another person, the right shall be vested in that last-mentioned person either alone or jointly with any other person whom the court may appoint.

(3) Where a vesting order can be made under this section, the court may, if it is more convenient, appoint some proper person to make or join in making the transfer so, however, that the person appointed to make or join in making a transfer of stock shall be some proper officer of the bank, or the company or society whose stock is to be transferred.

(4) The person in whom the right to transfer or call for the transfer of any stock is vested by an order of the court under this Act, may transfer the stock to himself or any other person, according to the order, and the bank and all other companies shall obey every order under this section according to its tenor.

(5) After notice in writing of an order under this section it shall not be lawful for the bank or any other company to transfer any stock to which the order relates or to pay any dividends thereon except in accordance with the order.

(6) The court may make declarations and give directions concerning the manner in which the right to transfer any stock or thing in action vested under this Act is to be exercised.

(7) The provisions of this Act as to vesting orders shall apply to shares in British ships registered in Bermuda as if they were stock.

Vesting orders of charity property

43. The powers conferred by this Act as to vesting orders may be exercised for vesting any estate or interest in land, stock, or thing in action in any trustee of a charity or society over which the court would have jurisdiction upon action duly instituted, whether the appointment of the trustee was made by instrument under a power or by the court under its general or statutory jurisdiction.

Vesting orders in relation to infant's beneficial interests

44. Where an infant is beneficially entitled to any property the court may, with a view to the application of the capital or income thereof for the maintenance, or education, or otherwise for the benefit of the infant, make an order—

(a) appointing a person to convey such property; or

(b) in the case of stock, or a thing in action, vesting in any person the right to transfer or call for a transfer of such stock, or to receive the dividends or income thereof, or to sue for and recover such thing in action, upon such terms as the court may think fit.

Orders made upon certain allegations to be conclusive evidence

45. Where a vesting order is made as to any land under this Act or under any Act relating to persons of unsound mind founded on an allegation—

(a) of the personal incapacity of a trustee or mortgagee; or

(b) that a trustee or mortgagee or the estate representative of or other person deriving title under a trustee or mortgagee is out of the jurisdiction of the court or cannot be found, or being a corporation has been dissolved; or

(c) that it is uncertain which of two or more trustees, or which of two or more persons interested in a mortgage, was the survivor; or

(d) that it is uncertain whether the last trustee or the estate representative of or other person deriving title under a trustee or mortgage, or the last surviving person interested in a mortgage is living or dead; or

(e) that any trustee or mortgagee has died intestate without leaving a person beneficially interested under the intestacy or has died and it is not known who is his estate representative or the person interested,

the fact that the order has been so made shall be conclusive evidence of the matter so alleged in any court upon any question as to the validity of the order; but this section does not prevent the court from directing a reconveyance or surrender or the payment of costs occasioned by any such order if improperly obtained.

Application of vesting order to property out of Bermuda

46. The powers of the court to make vesting orders under this Act shall extend to all property wherever situated.

Jurisdiction to make other Orders

Power of court to authorise transactions relating to trust property

47. (1) Where any transaction affecting or concerning any property vested in trustees, is in the opinion of the court expedient, but the same cannot be effected by reason of the absence of any power for that purpose vested in the trustees by the instrument, if any, creating the trust, or by any provision of law, the court may by order confer upon the trustees, either generally or in any particular instance, the necessary power for the purpose, on such terms and subject to such provisions and conditions, if any, as the

court may think fit and may direct in what manner any money authorised to be expended, and the costs of any transaction, are to be paid or borne as between capital and income.

(2) The court may, from time to time, rescind or vary any order made under this section or may make any new or further order.

(3) An application to the court under this section may be made by the trustees, or by any of them, or by any person beneficially interested under the trust.

(4) In this section, "transaction" includes any sale, exchange, assurance, grant, lease, partition, surrender, reconveyance, release, reservation, or other disposition, and any purchase or other acquisition, and any covenant, contract, or option, and any investment or application of capital, and any compromise or other dealing, or arrangement.

Jurisdiction of court to vary trusts

48. (1) Subject to subsection (2), where property is held on any trusts or settlements arising under any will, settlement or other disposition, the court may if it thinks fit by order approve on behalf of—

(a) any person having, directly or indirectly, an estate or interest, whether vested or contingent, under the trusts or settlements who by reason of infancy or other incapacity is incapable of assenting; or

(b) any person (whether ascertained or not) who may become entitled, directly or indirectly, to an estate or interest under the trusts or settlements as being at a future date or on the happening of a future event a person of any specified description or a member of any specified class of persons so, however, that this paragraph shall not include any person who would be of that description, or a member of that class, as the case may be, if the said date had fallen or the said event had happened at the date of the application to the court; or

(c) any person unborn; or

(d) any person in respect of any discretionary interest of his under protective trusts where the interest of the principal beneficiary has not failed or determined,

any arrangement (by whomsoever proposed, and whether or not there is any other person beneficially interested who is capable of assenting thereto) varying or revoking all or any of the trusts or settlements, or enlarging the powers of the trustees of managing or administering any of the property subject to the trusts or settlements.

(2) Except by virtue of subsection (1)(d) the court shall not approve an arrangement on behalf of any person unless the carrying out of the arrangement would be for the benefit of that person.

(3) In subsection (1), "protective trusts" means the trusts specified in section 25(1)(a) and (b) or any like trusts, "the principal beneficiary" has

the same meaning as in section 25(1) and "discretionary interest" means an interest arising under the trust specified in section 25(1)(b) or any like trust.

(4) Nothing in this section shall be taken to limit the powers conferred by section 47.

Persons entitled to apply for orders

49. (1) An order under this Act for the appointment of a new trustee or concerning any estate or interest in land, stock, or thing in action subject to a trust, may be made on the application of any person beneficially interested in the land, stock, or thing in action, whether under disability or not, or on the application of any person duly appointed trustee thereof.

(2) An order under this Act concerning any estate or interest in land, stock, or thing in action subject to a mortgage may be made on the application of any person beneficially interested in the equity of redemption, whether under disability or not, or of any person interested in the money secured by the mortgage.

Power to give judgment in absence of a trustee

50. Where in any action the court is satisfied that diligent search has been made for any person who, in the character of trustee, is made a defendant in any action, to serve him with a process of the court, and that he cannot be found, the court may hear and determine the action and give judgment therein against that person in his character of a trustee as if he had been duly served, or had entered an appearance in the action, and had also appeared by his counsel at the hearing, but without prejudice to any interest he may have in the matters in question in the action in any other character.

Power to charge costs on trust estate

51. The court may order the costs and expenses of and incidental to any application for an order under this Act or for any order or declaration in respect of any property subject to a trust, or of and incidental to any such order or declaration, or any document executed or act performed in pursuance thereof, to be raised and paid out of the property in respect whereof the same is made or performed, or out of the income thereof, or to be borne and paid in such manner and by such persons as to the court may seem just.

Power to relieve trustee from personal liability

52. (1) If it appears to the court that a trustee, whether appointed by the court or otherwise, is or may be personally liable for any breach of trust,

whether the transaction alleged to be a breach of trust occurred before, on or after 1 March 1975, but has acted honestly and reasonably, and ought fairly to be excused for the breach of trust and for omitting to obtain the directions of the court in the matter in which he committed such breach, then the court may relieve him either wholly or partly from personal liability for the same.

(2) In this section "trustee" includes a person who has ceased to be a trustee and the estate representative of a deceased trustee.

Power to make beneficiary indemnify for breach of trust

53. (1) Where a trustee commits a breach of trust at the instigation or request or with the consent in writing of a beneficiary, the court may, if it thinks fit, make such order as to the court seems just, for impounding all or any part of the estate or interest of the beneficiary in the trust estate by way of indemnity to the trustee or persons claiming through him.

(2) This section applies to breaches of trust committed as well before as on or after 1 March 1975.

Payment into court

Payment into court by trustees

54. (1) Trustees, or the majority of trustees, having in their hands or under their control money or securities belonging to a trust, may pay the same into court; and the same shall, subject to rules of court, be dealt with according to the orders of the court.

(2) The receipt or certificate of the proper officer shall be a sufficient discharge to trustees for the money or securities so paid into court.

(3) Where money or securities are vested in any persons as trustees, and the majority are desirous of paying the same into court, but the concurrence of the other or others cannot be obtained, the court may order the payment into court to be made by the majority without the concurrence of the other or others.

(4) Where any such money or securities are deposited with any bank, broker, or other depositary, the court may order payment or delivery of the money or securities to the majority of the trustees for the purpose of payment into court.

(5) Every transfer payment and delivery made in pursuance of any such order shall be valid and take effect as if the same had been made on the authority or by the act of all the persons entitled to the money and securities so transferred, paid, or delivered.

PART V
INVESTMENTS

Investment powers

55A. (1) A trustee's power of investment under this section shall be subject to any enlargement or restriction of his powers of investment set out in the instrument creating the trust.

(2) Nothing in this section shall restrict the powers of the court under section 47.

(3) A trustee may invest or otherwise apply trust property in the purchase or acquisition of property of any kind, whether or not situated in Bermuda, whether or not income-producing, with or without security, and whether for the purpose of—

(a) receiving an appropriate total return from income and capital appreciation;

(b) controlling or limiting risk; or

(c) benefiting persons interested in any way whatsoever in the income produced by trust property;

or for a mixture of such purposes.

(4) In so investing or otherwise applying trust property, a trustee shall act as a prudent investor would, by considering the purposes, terms, distribution requirements and other circumstances of the trust and by exercising reasonable care, skill and caution.

(5) In determining whether a trustee has acted In accordance with this section, any decision to invest or otherwise apply trust property shall be evaluated in the context of the trust property as a whole and as part of an overall investment strategy having risk and return objectives reasonably suited to the trust.

PART VI
GENERAL PROVISIONS

Indemnify to banks and others

64. This Act, and every order purporting to be made under this Act, shall be a complete indemnity to banks and to all persons for any acts done pursuant thereto, and it shall not be necessary for a bank or for any person to inquire concerning the property of the order, or whether the court by which the order was made had jurisdiction to make it.

Enactments repealed

65. [*omitted*]

Commencement

66. [*omitted*]

[*this Act was brought into operation on 1 March 1975*]

FIRST SCHEDULE
AUTHORIZED INVESTMENTS

1. Bonds, debentures, or other evidences of indebtedness—
(a) of or guaranteed by the Government of Bermuda;
(b) of or guaranteed by the government of an independent member country of the Commonwealth;
(c) of or guaranteed by the government of a member country of the European Economic Community;
(d) of or guaranteed by the government of the United States of America;
(e) of or guaranteed by the government of any province or state of any of the countries mentioned or referred to in (b), (c) or (d) above.

2. The bonds, debentures or other securities issued or guaranteed by the International Bank for Reconstruction and Development established by the Bank Agreement referred to in the Bretton Woods Agreements Act 1945, of the Parliament of the United Kingdom.

3. Deposit receipts, deposit notes, certificates of deposits, acceptances and other similar instruments issued or endorsed by any licensed bank to which the Banks Act 1969 [title 17 item 20] applies.

3A. Deposit receipts, deposit notes, certificates of deposit and other similar instruments—
(a) issued or endorsed by a deposit company licensed under the Deposit Companies Act 1974 [title 17 item 19]; and
(b) for discharging the obligations represented by which either—
(i) first mortgages on real property not exceeding 66 2/3% of the value of the property; or
(ii) other assets of a kind approved in writing by the Bermuda Monetary Authority,
have been earmarked and set aside in such manner as that Authority either generally or in relation to any particular deposit company or transaction have in writing approved.

4. Bonds, debentures or fully paid shares of a corporation whose issued and fully paid share capital is at least $3,000,000 or its equivalent in foreign currency at the time of investment if the price of such bonds, debentures or fully paid shares is quoted on a recognized stock exchange.

5. First mortgages of land in Bermuda conveyed to the trustee in fee simple subject to any proviso for redemption contained in the conveyance by way of mortgage.

Appendix I

6. First mortgages of land in Bermuda held for a term of years whereof the residue unexpired at the date of investment is at least sixty years.

7. Debentures issued under the authority of section 2 of the Hamilton Corporation Act 1910 and section 37 of the Municipalities Act 1923 [title 4 item 1].

8. Bonds, debentures or other evidences of indebtedness of Bermuda Electric Light Company Limited or Bermuda Telephone Company Limited.

SECOND SCHEDULE
ENACTMENTS REPEALED

[*omitted*]

TABLE OF CASES

References are to sections.

A

Abernathy v. LaBarge (In re Abernathy), 8.02[A][1]

Aboody, In re, 3.03[F]

Abruzzese v. Oestrich, 47 A.2d 883 (N.J. Ch. 1946), 5.02[B], 6.02[A]

Ackers v. First Nat'l Bank of Topeka, 387 P.2d 840 (Kan. 1963), *reh'g denied*, 389 P.2d 1 (Kan. 1964), 5.02[B][1]

Adams v. Coates, 626 A.2d 36 (1993), 5.02[A]

Adams v. Wilhite, 636 S.W.2d 851 (Tex. Ct. App. 1982), 2.03

Adwar, In re, 55 B.R. 111 (Bankr. E.D.N.Y. 1985), 2.04[A]

Adwar v. Capgro Leasing Corp. (In re Adwar), 55 B.R. 111 (Bankr. E.D.N.Y. 1985), 2.04[A]

Ainslie v. Inman, 577 S.E.2d 246 (Va. 2003), 3.05[D]

Albright, In re, 3.06[A]

Alexander, Estate of v. Commissioner, 81 T.C. 767 (1983), 5.05[C]

Allard v. Flamingo Hilton (In re Chomakos), 69 F.3d 769 (6th Cir. 1995), 2.04[A]

Alleco Inc. v. Harry & Jeanette Weinberg Found., Inc., 665 A.2d 1038 (1995), 5.02[A]

Allen, In re, 203 B.R. 928 (W.D. Va. 1997), 8.02[A][1]

Allen v. State Bar, 570 P.2d 1226 (Cal. 1977), 1.03[C]

Allied Prods. Corp. v. Arrow Freightways, Inc., 724 P.2d 752 (N.M. 1986), 2.04[C]

Allright Tex., Inc. v. Simons, 501 S.W.2d 145 (Tex. Civ. App. 1973), 3.03[B][6]

American Nat'l Bank of Jacksonville v. United States, 255 F.2d 504 (5th Cir.), *cert. denied*, 358 U.S. 835 (1958), 10.05[B][2]

American Trading & Prod. Corp. v. Fischback & Moore, Inc., 311 F. Supp. 412 (N.D. Ill 1970), 3.03[B][6]

Anderson v. Anderson, 123 P.2d 315 (Kan. 1942), 8.02[C][8]

Anderson v. Seaver (In re Anderson), 8.04[B]

Andrews v. Reynolds, 409 N.W.2d 128 (S.D. 1987), 2.03

Aquilino v. United States, 363 U.S. 509 (1960), 10.05[A]

Arbesman v. Winer, 468 A.2d 633 (Md. 1983), 7.02[A][2]

Arnold v. Phillips, 117 F.2d 497 (5th Cir.), *cert. denied*, 313 U.S. 583 (1941), 3.03[B][2]

Atkinson, In re, 63 B.R. 266 (Bankr. W.D. Wis. 1986), 2.04[C]

Ayers v. Ayers, 288 N.W. 679 (Iowa 1939), 8.02[C][8]

B

Backus v. Backus, 346 A.2d 790 (Pa. 1975), 7.02[D]

Baker, In re, 114 F.3d 636 (7th Cir. 1997), 8.04[C]

Baldwin, In re, 2006 Bankr. LEXIS 1700 (BA.P. 10th Cir. July 11, 2006), 3.05[E]

Baldwin, United States v., 391 A.2d 844 (Md. 1978), 5.08[A]

Ballard, In re, 65 F.3d 367 (4th Cir. 1995), 7.02[D], 10.05[B][2]

Bank of Nova Scotia, United States v., 691 F.2d 1384 (11th Cir. 1982), *cert. denied*, 462 U.S. 1119 (1983), 9.05[A]

Bank of Union v. Heath, 121 S.E. 24 (N.C. 1924), 5.10

C

Table of Cases

G

H

I

J

Table of Cases

M

Table of Cases

R

S

T

U

V

W

Table of Cases

Table of Internal Revenue Code Sections

Table of Treasury Regulations

Table of Treasury Regulations

Table of Internal Revenue Service Releases

References are to sections.

90-30, 1990-1 C.B. 534	5.12[A]
90-31, 1990-1 C.B. 539	5.12[B][4][b]
90-32, 1990-1 C.B. 536	5.12[A],
	5.12[B][4][b]
92-25, 1992-1 C.B. 741	8.03[G][3][d]
2003-11, 2003-4 I.R.B. 311	Vol. 1, 9.02[F]

IRS Notices

95-14, 1995-1 C.B. 297	4.04[A][1]

Technical Advice Memoranda

9550002	5.08[B][3]

9722001	5.05[C],
	5.07[B][2]
199943003	7.05

Others

FSA 200132003	3.03[I][2]
FSA 200026005	3.03[I][5]
Int'l Tech. Assistance Mem. 200024051	3.03[I][5]
Int'l Tech. Assistance Mem. 200238044	3.03[I][4]
Int'l Tech. Assistance Mem. 200247045	3.03[I][4]

INDEX

References are to sections.

Index

Index

Index

Index

Index

Index

SYSTEM REQUIREMENTS

- IBM PC or compatible computer with CD-ROM drive
- Windows 95 or higher
- Microsoft® Word 7.0 for Windows™ or compatible word processor
- 10 MB available on hard drive

The companion CD-ROM to the 2007 Edition of *Asset Protection Strategies* contains more than 30 forms that can be used in conjunction with this book.

Subject to the conditions in the license agreement and the limited warranty, which are reproduced at the end of this book, you may duplicate the files on this disc, modify them as necessary, and create your own customized versions. Using the disc in any way indicates that you accept the terms of the license agreement.

USING THE CD-ROM

The disc data is intended for use with your word processing software. Each document is provided in Rich Text Format or pdf. These files can be read by all compatible word processors, including Microsoft Word for Windows and WordPerfect 7 or above. Check your owner's manual for information on the conversion of the documents as required.

USING THE DOCUMENTS

The list of the Disc Contents is available on your disc in a file called _contents.rtf. The listing includes each individual form. You can open this file and view it on your screen and use it to link to the documents you're interested in, or print a hard copy to use for reference.

1. Open the file _contents.rtf in your word processor.
2. Locate the file you wish to access, and click on the hyperlinked file name. Your word processor will then open the file.
3. You may copy files from the CD-ROM to your hard disk. To edit files you have copied, remember to clear the read-only attribute from the file. To do this, select the name of the file in My Computer, right-click the filename, then choose Properties, and clear the Read-only checkbox.

SOFTWARE SUPPORT

If you experience any difficulties installing or running the electronic files and cannot resolve the problem using the information presented here, call our toll-free software support hotline at 800 835 0105 or visit our website at http://support.cch.com.

DISC CONTENTS

Form	Form Name	File Name	File Type
Form 13-14	Sample Testamentary Charitable Remainder Unitrust: Two Lives, Concurrent and Sconsecutive Interests, Rev. Proc. 2005-58, 2005-34 I.R.B. 40, § 4	Form1314	RTF
Form 13-15	Sample Testamentary Charitable Remainder Unitrust: Two Lives, Concurrent and Consecutive Interests, Rev. Proc. 2005-59, 2005-34 I.R.B. 412, § 4	Form1315	RTF
Form 13-16	Sample Inter Vivos Charitable Remainder Unitrust for Term of Years Rev. Proc. 2005-53, 2005-34 IRB 339	Form1316	RTF
Form 13-17	Sample Testamentary Charitable Remainder Unitrust Declaration for a Term of Years Rev. Proc. 2005-57, 2005-34 I.R.B. 392	Form1317	RTF
Form 13-18	Sample Intervivos Charitable Remainder Annuity Trust: Two Lives, Consecutive Interests, Rev. Proc. 90-32, 1990-1 C.B. 539, § 4	Form1318	RTF
Form 13-19	Sample Intervivos Charitable Remainder Annuity Trust: Two Lives, Concurrent and Consecutive Interests, Rev. Proc. 90-32, 1990-1 C.B. 539, § 5	Form1319	RTF
Form 13-20	Sample Testamentary Charitable Remainder Annuity Trust: One Life, Rev. Proc. 90-32, 1990-1 C.B. 539, § 6	Form1320	RTF
Form 13-21	Sample Testamentary Charitable Remainder Annuity Trust: Two Lives, Consecutive Interests, Rev. Proc. 90-32, 1990-1 C.B. 539, § 7	Form1321	RTF
Form 13-22	Sample Testamentary Charitable Remainder Annuity Trust: Two Lives, Concurrent and Consecutive Interests, Rev. Proc. 90-32, 1990-1 C.B. 539, § 8	Form1322	RTF
Form 13-23	The [full name of Grantor] Charitable Remainder Unitrust Agreement Of Trust	Form1323	RTF
Form 13-24	Irrevocable Life Insurance Trust Instrument for One Life	Form1324	RTF
Form 13-25	Irrevocable Life Insurance Trust Instrument for Both Spouses' Lives	Form1325	RTF
Form 13-26	[Insert Name] Alaska Asset Protection Trust	Form1326	RTF

Form	Form Name	File Name	File Type
Form 13-27	The [Full Name of Remainder Beneficiary of Trust] Remainder Trust Agreement of Trust	Form1327	RTF
Form 14-1	Bahamas Trust Indenture	Form1401	RTF
Form 14-2	First Schedule	Form1402	RTF
Form 14-3	Cayman Islands Trust Indenture	Form1403	RTF
Form 14-4	First Schedule	Form1404	RTF
Form 14-5	Cook Islands Trust Indenture	Form1405	RTF
Form 14-6	Bermuda Trust Indenture	Form1406	RTF
Form 14-7	First Schedule	Form1407	RTF
Form 14-8	Trust Instrument	Form1408	RTF
Form 15-1	Application for Employer Identification Number	Form1501	PDF
Form 15-2	Notice Concerning Fiduciary Relationship	Form1502	PDF
Form 15-3	United States Gift (and Generation-Skipping Transfer) Tax Return	Form1503	PDF
Form 15-4	Annual Return To Report Transactions With Foreign Trusts and Receipt of Certain Foreign Gifts	Form1504	PDF
Form 15-5	Annual Information Return of Foreign Trust With a U.S. Owner	Form1505	PDF
Form 15-6	Currency Transaction Report	Form1506	PDF
Form 15-7	U.S. Withholding Tax Return for Dispositions by Foreign Persons of U.S. Real Property Interests	Form1507	PDF
Form 15-8	Statement of Withholding on Dispositions by Foreign Persons of U.S. Real Property Interests	Form1508	PDF
Form 15-9	Report of Foreign Bank and Financial Accounts	Form1509	PDF
Form 15-9A	Draft Report of Foreign Bank and Financial Accounts	Form1509A	PDF

CCH, a Wolters Kluwer Business

SOFTWARE LICENSE AGREEMENT FOR ELECTRONIC FILES TO ACCOMPANY 2007 EDITION OF *ASSET PROTECTION STRATEGIES* (THE "BOOK").

PLEASE READ THE TERMS AND CONDITIONS OF THIS LICENSE AGREEMENT CAREFULLY BEFORE INSTALLING THE FILES FROM THE CD-ROM.

THE ELECTRONIC FILES ARE COPYRIGHTED AND LICENSED (NOT SOLD). BY INSTALLING THE ELECTRONIC FILES ("THE SOFTWARE"), YOU ARE ACCEPTING AND AGREEING TO THE TERMS OF THIS LICENSE AGREEMENT. IF YOU ARE NOT WILLING TO BE BOUND BY THE TERMS OF THIS LICENSE AGREEMENT, YOU SHOULD REMOVE THE SOFTWARE FROM YOUR COMPUTER AT THIS TIME AND PROMPTLY RETURN THE PACKAGE IN RESELLABLE CONDITION AND YOU WILL RECEIVE A REFUND OF YOUR MONEY. THIS LICENSE AGREEMENT REPRESENTS THE ENTIRE AGREEMENT CONCERNING THE SOFWARE BETWEEN YOU AND CCH, a Wolters Kluwer business (REFERRED TO AS "LICENSOR"), AND IT SUPERSEDES ANY PRIOR PROPOSAL, REPRESENTATION, OR UNDERSTANDING BETWEEN THE PARTIES.

1. License Grant. Licensor hereby grants to you, and you accept, a nonexclusive license to use the Software, and any computer programs contained therein in machine-readable, object code form only, and the accompanying User Documentation, only as authorized in this License Agreement. The Software may be used only on a single computer owned, leased, or otherwise controlled by you, or in the event of the inoperability of that computer, on a backup computer selected by you. Neither concurrent use on two or more computers nor use in a local area network or other network is permitted without separate authorization and the possible payment of other license fees. You agree that you will not assign, sublease, transfer, pledge, lease, rent, or share your rights under the License Agreement. You agree that you may not reverse engineer, decompile, disassemble, or otherwise adapt, modify, or translate the Software.

Upon loading the Software into your computer, you may retain the Software CD-ROM for backup purposes. In addition, you may make one copy of the Software on a set of diskettes (or other storage medium) for the purpose of backup in the event the Software files are damaged or destroyed. You may make one copy of any additional User Documentation (such as the README.TXT file or the "About the Computer Disc" section of the Book) for backup purposes. Any such copies of the Software or the User Documentation shall include the Licensor's copyright and other proprietary notices. Except as authorized under this paragraph, no copies of the Software or any portions thereof may be made by you or any person under your authority or control.

2. Licensor's Rights. You acknowledge and agree that the Software and the User Documentation are proprietary products of Licensor protected under U.S. copyright law. You further acknowledge and agree that all right, title, and interest in and to the Software, including associated intellectual property rights, are and shall remain with Licensor. This License Agreement does not convey to you an interest in or to the Software, including associated intellectual property rights,

which are and shall remain with Licensor. This License Agreement does not convey to you an interest in or to the Software, but only a limited right of use revocable in accordance with the terms of this License Agreement.

3. License Fees. The license fees paid by you are paid in consideration of the licenses granted under this License Agreement.

4. Term. This License Agreement is effective upon your installing this software and shall continue until terminated. You may terminate this License Agreement at any time by removing all copies of the Software and returning the CD-ROM to Licensor. Licensor may terminate this License Agreement upon the breach by you of any term hereof. Upon such termination by Licensor, you agree to return to Licensor the Software and all copies and portions thereof.

5. Limited Warranty. Licensor warrants, for our benefit alone, for a period of 90 days from the date of commencement of this License Agreement (referred to as the "Warranty Period") that the Program CD-ROM in which the software is contained is free from defects in material and workmanship. If during the Warranty Period, a defect appears in the Program CD-ROM, you may return the Program to Licensor for either replacement or, at Licensor's option, refund of amounts paid by you under this License Agreement. You agree that the foregoing constitutes your sole and exclusive remedy for breach by Licensor of any warranties made under this Agreement. EXCEPT FOR THE WARRANTIES SET FORTH ABOVE, THE PROGRAM CD-ROM, AND THE SOFTWARE CONTAINED THEREIN, ARE LICENSED "AS-IS," AND LICENSOR DISCLAIMS ANY AND ALL OTHER WARRANTIES, WHETHER EXPRESS OR IMPLIED, INCLUDING, WITHOUT LIMITATION, ANY IMPLIED WARRANTIES OF MERCHANTABILITY OR FITNESS FOR A PARTICULAR PURPOSE.

6. Limitation of Liability. Licensor's cumulative liability to you or any other party for any loss or damages resulting from any claims, demands, or actions arising out of or relating to this Agreement shall not exceed the license fee paid to Licensor for the use of the Software. IN NO EVENT SHALL LICENSOR BE LIABLE FOR ANY INDIRECT, INCIDENTAL, CONSEQUENTIAL, SPECIAL OR EXEMPLARY DAMAGES (INCLUDING, BUT NOT LIMITED TO, LOSS OF DATA, BUSINESS INTERRUPTION, OR LOST PROFITS) EVEN IF LICENSOR HAS BEEN ADVISED OF THE POSSIBILITY OF SUCH DAMAGES.

7. Miscellaneous. The License Agreement shall be construed and governed in accordance with the laws of the State of Delaware. Should any term of this License Agreement be declared void or unenforceable by any court of competent jurisdiction, such declaration shall have no effect on the remaining terms hereof. The failure of either party to enforce any rights granted hereunder or to take action against the other party in the event of any breach hereunder shall not be deemed a waiver by that party as to subsequent enforcement of rights or subsequent actions in the event of future breaches.